IJCAI-79

第6回人工知能国際会議

Proceedings of the Sixth International
Joint Conference on Artificial Intelligence
Tokyo, August 20-23, 1979
Volume Two

Sponsored by International Joint Conference on Artificial Intelligence, Inc., and Information Processing Society of Japan.

Distributed by
Morgan Kaufmann Publishers, Inc.
95 First Street
Los Altos, California 94022

These proceedings were printed with the partial assistance of a grant from "The Commemorative Association for the Japan World Exposition."

Cover design by J. Rindfleisch

ISBN 0-934613-47-8
Printed in the United States of America

TABLE OF CONTENTS

VOL I

VOL. II

STRUCTURAL ANALYSIS OF COMPLEX AERIAL PHOTOGRAPHS

Makoto Nagao
Department of
Electrical Engineering
Kyoto University
Sakyo, Kyoto, 606
JAPAN

Takashi Matsuyama
Department of
Electrical Engineering
Kyoto University
Sakyo, Kyoto, 606
JAPAN

Hisayuki Mori
Department of
Electrical Engineering
Kyoto University
Sakyo, Kyoto, 606
JAPAN

A new system for the structural analysis of complex aerial photographs is presented. This system has the ability of focussing its attention of the analysis on the limited local areas where objects are highly supposed to exist. Several kinds of strong and typical features are extracted, and these primary features of objects are combined to extract rough areas of the objects. This focussing mechanism saves the total processing time and facilitates the detailed analysis. The recognition process of the system is implemented according to the 'production system'. The knowledge sources in this system are object-detection subsystems which analyse their individually focussed local areas and recognize specific objects respectively. All the results of the analysis are written in the common blackboard, and the system finds out conflicts and recovers errors by backtracking to feature extractions and low level processings. This architecture enables us to organize smoothly the diverse knowledge required to describe the complex structure on the ground surface.

1. INTRODUCTION

Recently several systems for the analysis of aerial photographs have been developed to locate objects on the ground surface[1],[2],[3]. When we are going to get a description of the structure on the ground surface by analysing an aerial photograph, we find several difficulties which are not encountered in other image analysis areas:

(1) The size of a picture is very large.
(2) As it is impossible to control photographing conditions, the quality of a picture is apt to change.
(3) The sizes and the textural properties of objects vary quite widely.
(4) Variation of objects in a scene entails calculation of many different features and the diverse knowledge of the world.
(5) There are too many situations on the ground surface to build a general model which can represent all possible spatial arrangements of objects.

In order to overcome these difficulties and to realize an efficient and reliable analysis, we have developed a new system based on the 'production system'[4]. The system consists of a group of object-detection subsystems which individually search for specific objects by communicating with each other via a common 'blackboard'[5],[6].

The analysis process of this system is divided into the following steps.

(1) Segmentation: After noise removal, an aerial photograph is segmented into elementary regions according to the multispectral property.
(2) Global survey of the whole scene: Regions with characteristic properties are extracted. These are used to confine the spatial domains of objects where object-detection subsystems work.
(3) Detailed analysis of focussed local areas: Each object-detection subsystem focuses its attention on a specific local area and checks the existence of a specific object.
(4) Communication among object-detection subsystems: All the information about the properties of regions and recognized objects is stored in the blackboard. Object-detection subsystems interface with it in a uniform way. The system controls the overall flow of the analysis by managing the information in the blackboard. It solves conflict among object-detection subsystems, and corrects errors by backtracking.

This paper mainly describes the control structure of the system, and demonstrates its performance with experimental results. The detailed algorithms of picture processing routines are described in [7].

2. FOCUS OF ATTENTION IN THE ANALYSIS OF AERIAL PHOTOGRAPHS

Aerial photographs we want to analyse are 4 band multispectral images of complex suburban areas taken from the low altitude(Fig. 1).

As the size of a picture is very large, the analysis should be done as efficiently as possible. If each object-detection subsystem, which is very sophisticated and time-consuming, were applied to the whole picture area, it would take a prohibitive time to complete the analysis. In order to solve this problem, we adopted the focussing mechanism which human being seems to use when he interprets a complex scene. When he sees a scene, at first he globally surveys it to find the characteristic areas which attract his interest. Then, he goes into the detailed examination of some local area to find out objects using his knowledge of the world. The more intensively he focuses, the more specialized knowledge he comes to use.

In our system, several kinds of regions with prominent features(characteristic regions) are extracted by simple picture processing programs. Then, object-detection subsystems apply sophisticated programs only in the local areas where specific objects are supposed to exist. As the time-consuming processings are applied only in small local areas, the total processing time can be reduced very much. Fig.2 shows the schematic drawing of this focussing process.

In order to specify the spatial domains of objects as correctly as possible, we utilize such features as size, shape, brightness, multispectral properties, texture and spatial relations among regions. We extract seven types of characteristic regions, i.e. large homogeneous regions, elongated regions, shadow regions, shadow-making regions, vegetation regions, water regions and high contrast texture regions.

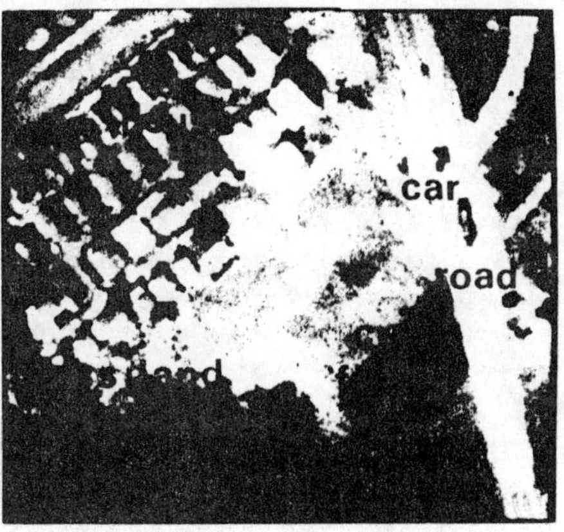

Fig.1 A picture of a complex suburban area

All the features used here are stable against the change of photographing conditions, and all parameters are automatically and adaptively determined from the picture data under analysis. Therefore extracted characteristic regions can be the reliable basis for the subsequent detailed analysis.

Fig.3 shows the characteristic regions extracted from the picture of Fig.1.

3. OBJECT-DETECTION SUBSYSTEM

An aerial photograph contains a variety of objects such as crop fields, forest areas, grass lands, roads, rivers, houses and so on. The diverse knowledge should be incorporated to describe the structure on the ground surface. In addition, these objects,especially in a small country as Japan, are intricately arranged without definite spatial relationships.

Taking these conditions into account, it seems to be natural to divide the system into a group of object-detection subsystems. Each of them is designed to find out specific objects using the knowledge of their intrinsic properties and the environments in which they are embedded. The diverse knowledge of the world is distributed in object-detection subsystems. This facilitates the implementation of the system.

The type of object-detection subsystems can be classified into two categories according to the information they use in selecting the candidate regions of objects.

(1) Picture data-driven subsystem

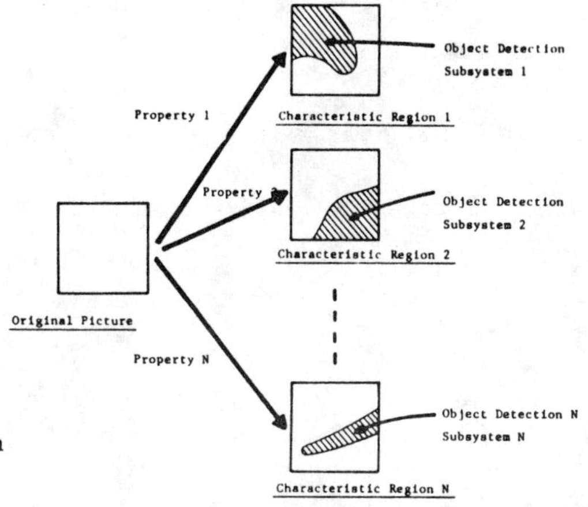

Fig.2 Focussing mechanism of the system

The subsystems of this type check the existence of the local areas with specified properties by combining characteristic regions. If there are such local areas, they examine them in detail by activating special purpose feature extraction programs.

(2) Model-driven subsystem
The subsystems of this type pick up the candidate regions by using the spectral and spatial relationships with already recognized objects. For example, it is very difficult to detect cars by a simple knowledge that they are rectangular unless we impose the condition that they are on the roads or the parking lots. Therefore the subsystem for the detection of cars entails the recognition of roads or parking lots.

The present system has thirteen object-detection subsystems for eight kinds of objects: crop field, bare soil(crop field without plantation), forest, grass land, road, river, car and house. Fig.4 shows intermediate results of detection of these objects.

4. THE STRUCTURE OF THE BLACKBOARD

Each object-detection subsystem interfaces with the common data base, the blackboard, in order to test conditions for activation and to write in the result of the analysis. All the communications among object-detection subsystems are made via this blackboard. Fig.5 shows the schematic drawing of the structure of the blackboard.

The blackboard contains global parameters as well as the properties of regions and objects. They denote the global properties of the picture data, that is, photographing conditions of an aerial photograph such as the direction of the sun, threshold values for checking the similarity of multispectral propreties and so on. From these global parameters, each object-detection subsystem gets the information of the quality of the picture data under analysis. Therefore, it can successfully find out objects in spite of unstable photographing conditions of aerial photographs.

In this system, elementary regions, which are segmented according to the multispectral property in segmentation, are considered as the basic units for all higher level processings. Their fundamental properties(the average gray level in each spectral band, size, location and some basic shape features) are stored in the property table in the blackboard(Fig.5).

We store LABEL PICTURE in the blackboard in order to denote the spatial relationships among elementary regions. It is the symbolic

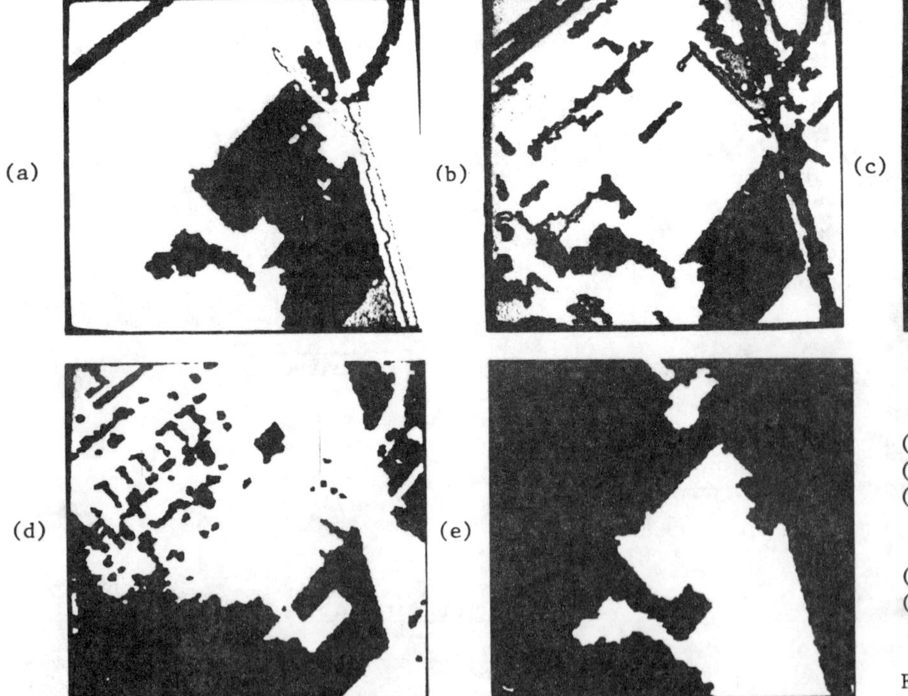

(a) large homogeneous region
(b) elongated region
(c) shadow region(enclosed by black lines) and shadow-making region(black regions)
(d) vegetation region
(e) high contrast texture region

Fig.3 Characteristic regions

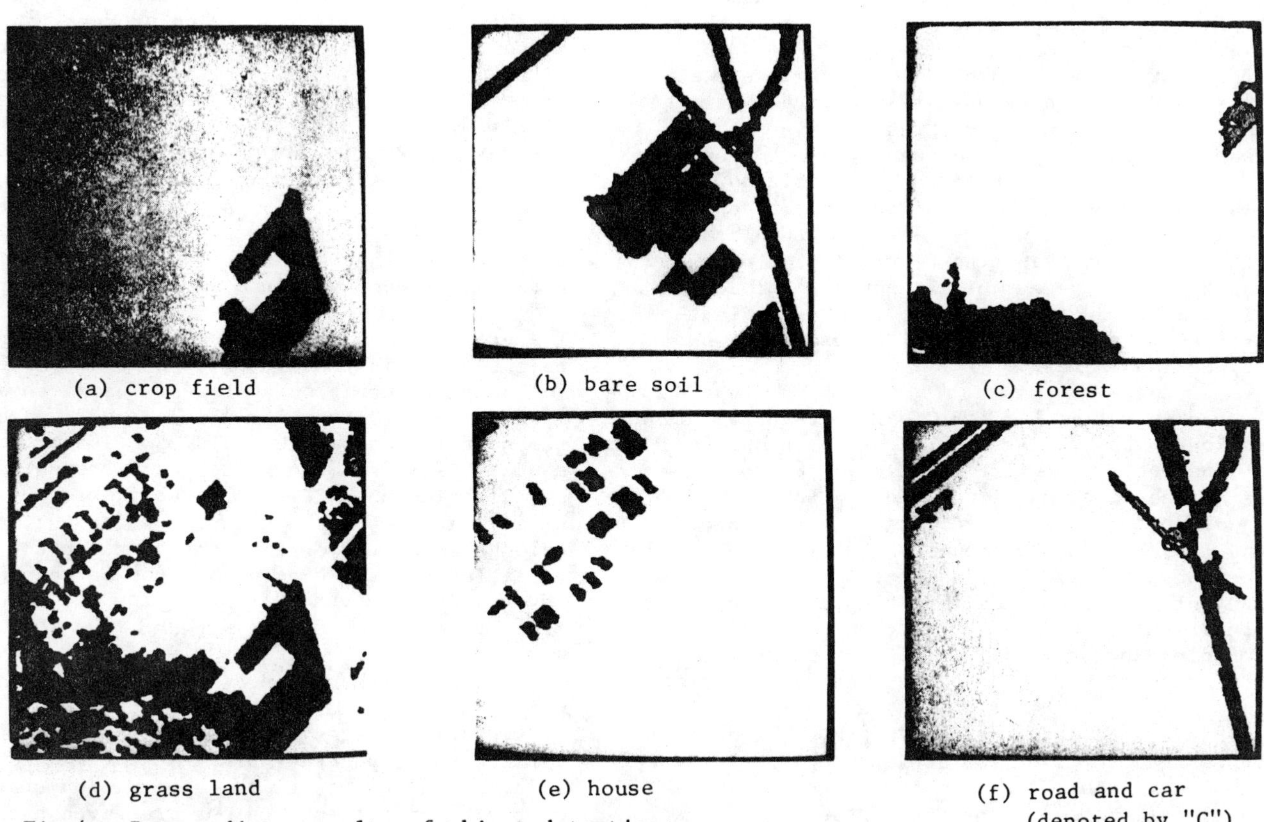

(a) crop field (b) bare soil (c) forest

(d) grass land (e) house (f) road and car (denoted by "C")

Fig.4 Intermediate results of object detection: Several regions are recognized as different objects. These conflicts are solved by the system(see Sec.5).

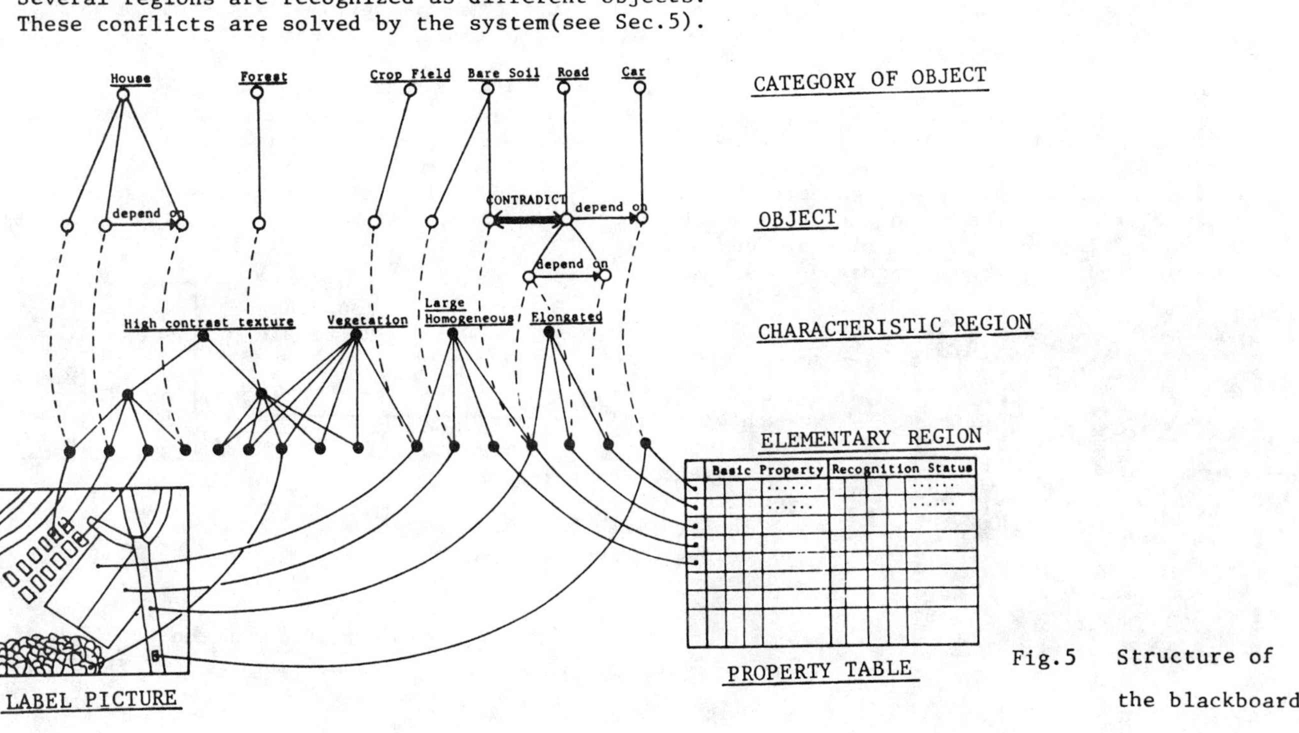

Fig.5 Structure of the blackboard

picture where each pixel in an elementary region is labeled with the same unique region number(Fig.6). The reason for this is:

The spatial relationships among regions used by object-detection subsystems are very different and depend on the properties of objects they want to find out. Therefore it is not economical, and is even sometimes impossible to calculate all spatial relationships in advance. For example, when we want to estimate the location of a house by using the regurality of the spatial arrangement of already recognized ones, it will take a long time to find a candidate region of a house if we do not use the two-dimendional image.

As each pixel in LABEL PICTURE contains an unique region number,we can easily get the properties of the region to which it belongs. On the other hand, the location of a region in LABEL PICTURE is denoted by the two coordinate pairs,(BX,BY) and (EX,EY), in the property table(Fig.7). When one wants to calculate a new feature of a region, one only has to scan within the rectangle area specified by these coordinate pairs(Minimum Bounding Rectangle). This is very useful to save the processing time of picture processing programs.

Each characteristic region in the blackboard is represented by a characteristic region node which denotes a group of elementary regions. Two-dimensional images of characteristic regions can also be constructed from LABEL PICTURE. These are very useful in locating clusters of elementary regions such as forest and residential areas.

When each object-detection subsystem recognizes an object, it generates an object node in the blackboard, and the object node and its constituent elementary regions are connected by part/whole relations. If the recognition of an object depends on the properties of already recognized ones, the node of a new recognized object is linked with those of old ones(Fig.5). By storing the history of the recognition process, the system can give back the state of the blackboard to the correct one when it finds out an error in it.

5. CONTROL MECHANISM OF THE SYSTEM

As each object-detection subsystem recognizes objects independently of the others, the system incorporates the mechanism to solve conflicts between these subsystems.

The property table has the field where each object-detection subsystem returns one of the following recognition statuses: "unanalysed", "recognized", "irregular shaped" and "rejected". the system checks this field, and if some elementary region is recognized as different objects by multiple subsystems, it evaluates the reliability value of each object to which that region belongs. Then the objects nodes except the most reliable one are deleted, and the corresponding recognition statuses of the region are changed from "recognized" to "rejected".

If there are other objects which have been recognized in connection with rejected objects, the system also deletes those object nodes by traversing the dependency links from rejected objects. In this case, the recognition statuses of their constituent regions are given back to "unanalysed", for they might be recognized by using the properties of the other objects of the same kind.

Errors in segmentation are also repaired by the system. Object-detection subsystems checks various properties of regions to recognize objects. They returns the recognition status, "irregular shaped", if the shape of a region is not suitable for an object while all the other properties

Fig.6 LABEL PICTURE: each pixel in an elementary region(enclosed by black lines) is labeled with an unique region number.

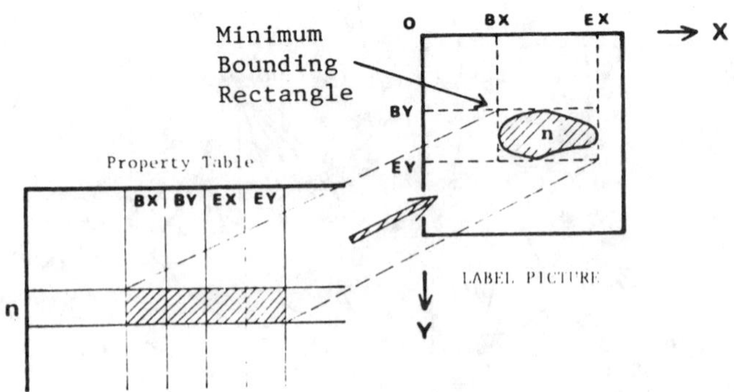

Fig.7 Specification of the location of an elementary region in LABEL PICTURE

are satisfactory. Then, the system re-analyses that region by applying the split/merge program. If the region has the bottle-neck as shown in Fig. 8, it is divided into small regions. If the boundary of the region is very rough and irregular (Fig. 9), neighboring small regions with the similar color are merged with it. These newly generated regions are added in the blackboard as temporary regions and analysed by object-detection subsystems. If a temporary region is successfully recognized, it is registered as a new elementary region in connection with its related object, and the original region is deleted from the blackboard. If the result of the recognition of the new region contradicts with that of the original one, the system deletes one of them depending on the reliability. When the temporary region is not recognized, it is removed from the blackboard, and the corresponding recognition status of the original region is changed to "rejected".

In the case of Fig. 8, the bottle-neck results from the error of mismerging two adjacent houses. When this region is splitted into two regions, the house detection subsystem comes to recognize them successfully. The region in Fig. 9 corresponds a crop field, but it is not recognized because of the irregularity of the boundary. After the merging process, it comes to take the smooth boundary, and is recognized as a crop field.

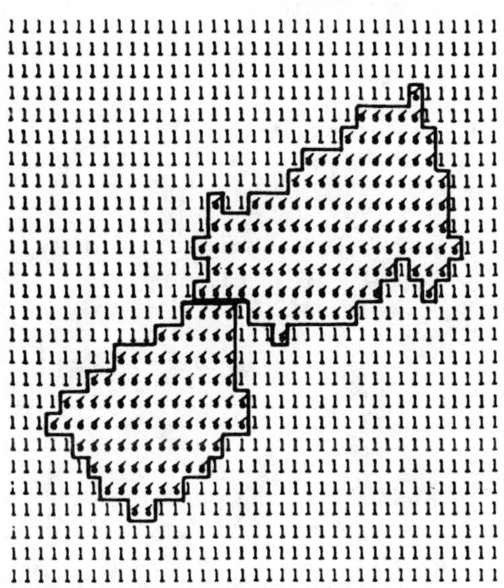

Fig.8 Splitting a region with a bottle-neck

By the benefits of the above-mentioned control mechanisms of the system, each object-detection subsystem can use the properties of already recognized objects without considering the results of recognition by the others. The system stops the analysis when no new objects are recognized.

Fig. 10 shows the final result of the analysis. Although white regions with no marks are left unanalysed, we can see that almost all objects which belong to clear semantic categories are successfully recognized. (As we do not have the ground truth data, the evaluation of the result is done by visual inspection.)

6. CONCLUSIONS

The system for the structural analysis of complex aerial photographs has been presented. The major conclusions on this system are the following:

(1) The focussing mechanism realizes the efficient analysis and successfully isolates objects. Table 1 shows the efficiency of this focussing mechanism.

(2) The production system architecture gives us the following benefits.

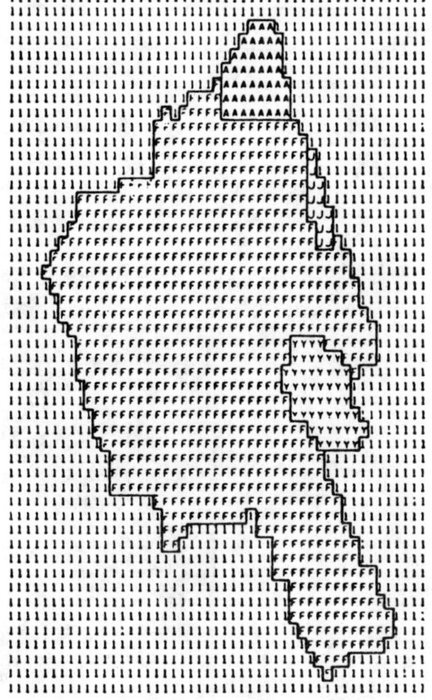

Fig.9 An irregular shaped region: the central large region is merged with neighboring samll regions.

A. Modularity : Diverse knowledge required to describe the structure of the ground surface can be individually implemented in object-detection subsystems.

B. Model-driven analysis: We can use the properties of already recognized objects in order to analyse unrecognized areas and to find out contextual-dependent objects.

C. General control mechanism: The system takes the full responsibility for the maintenance of the blackboard. It solves the conflicts among object-detection subsystems and corrects the errors in segmentation. If necessary, it undoes the content of the blackboard to remove the effects of errors. These mechanisms of the system integrate mutually independent object-detection subsystems.

This system is implemented on a large computer, FACOM M-190. The total CPU time was about 150 sec. in the picture of Fig.1. Experiments on several different aerial photographs have shown that this system works fairly well.

SCAN AREA	CANDIDATE REGION	TIME(sec.)
in MBR*	large homogeneous regions	0.14
whole area	large homogeneous regions	0.39
in MBR*	all regions	0.84
whole area	all regions	28.95

Table 1 Efficiency of the focussing mechanism: Time denotes the processing time for the crop field detection subsystem to calculate straightness of region boundaries. As we focus only on large homogeneous regions, we can save processing time very much.

* MBR denotes a minimun bounding rectangle(see Fig.7)

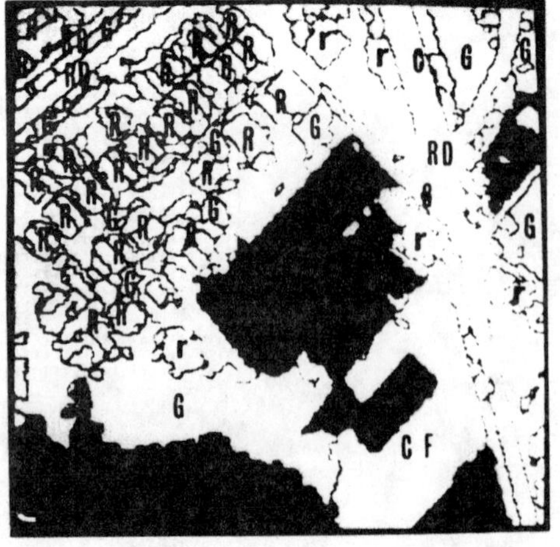

Fig.10 Final result of the analysis:
White regions without mark are unrecognized(20% of the whole picture area)
BS: bare soil (crop field without plantation)
CF: crop field
G : grass land
F : forest
RD: road
R : roof of a house
C : car
r : misrecognized roof (these regions have similar multispectral properties to that of true roof)

REFERENCES

[1] Barrow, H.G. et al "Interactive Aids for Cartography and Photo Interpretation: Progress Report, October 1977" In Proc. of the Workshop on Image Understanding, Oct., 1977, pp. 111-117

[2] Quam, L.H. "Road Tracking and Anomaly Detection in Aerial Imagery" In Proc. of the Workshop on Image Understanding, May, 1978, pp. 51-55

[3] Nevatia, R. and Price, K. "Locating Structures in Aerial Images" In Proc. IJCPR-78, Nov.,1978, pp. 686-690

[4] Davis, R. and King, J. "An Overview of Production Systems" AIM-271, Stanford A.I.Lab., 1975

[5] Erman, L.D. and Lesser,V.R. "A Multi-level Organization for Problem Solving Using Many Diverse Cooperating Sources of Knowledge" In Proc. IJCAI-75, 1975, pp.483-490

[6] Lesser, V.R. and Erman, L.D. "A Retrospective View of the HEARSAY-II Architecture" In Proc. IJCAI-77, 1977, pp. 790-800

[7] Nagao, M., Matsuyama, T. and Ikeda, Y. "Region Extraction and Shape Analysis of Aerial Photographs" In Proc. IJCPR-78, pp. 620-828

S-NET : A FOUNDATION FOR KNOWLEDGE REPRESENTATION LANGUAGES

Makoto Nagao
Department of Electrical Engineering
Faculty of Engineering
Kyoto University
Kyoto, JAPAN

Jun-ichi Tsujii
Department of Electrical Engineering
Faculty of Engineering
Kyoto University
Kyoto, JAPAN

A new knowledge representation scheme called S-Net is presented. The S-Net is a descendent of both semantic networks and recently developed AI languages. We are willing to introduce procedures into our network notations as FRL and KRL do. However, these languages have a serious disadvantage that the programmer should specify, explicitly by using indicators such as WHEN-FILLED, TO-FILL etc., when the attached procedures are invoked. This results in the restriction of system's abilities of solving problems. To avoid this, the programmer should always pay attention to the overal control issues during the coding of his procedures. In our new formalism, the explicit specification is not necessary. The problem solver based on the S-Net dynamically determines which procedure is invoked when, according to the problem solving situations, not to the pre-specified indicators. We also discuss the problems of property inheritance through hierarchy. The inheritance mechanism provided so far is so restrictive that the programmer should do all things in his procedures. In the S-Net, the property inheritance is further augmented by the 'explicit path specification'. The detailed construction of the problem solver, which performs both forward and backward reasonings appropriately, is also given.

1. INTRODUCTION

In this paper, we discuss a graphical notation called S-Net, which results in a foundation for recently developed AI languages. S-Net is a descendant of both semantic networks and recently developed AI languages. Semantic networks have been developed since the mid-sixties as a formalism for the representation of knowledge. Though the original idea of semantic networks is intuitively attractive, the recent formalisms of networks seem to lose the advantages which the researchers initially conceived. G. Hendrix [1975], L. Schubert[1976] and others have tried to formalize their networks based on predicate logic. As a result, their notations have become graphical analogues of logical formula. On the other hand, since the appearance of 'Frame' [Minsky 1975], great efforts have been made to develop programming languages and systems which realize the frame idea [Winograd 1977, Bobrow 1976, Goldstein 1977, Davis 1978]. They all have a certain data structure into which various sorts of knowledge, including both procedural and declarative ones, are integrated. However, their data structures are based only on the vague idea 'Frame', and, more seriously, lack rigidly defined semantics. Especially, the technique 'procedural attachment', though it is powerful tool for describing knowledge, makes the situation chaotic. There are no general mechanisms for managing the attached procedures appropriately. In most languages, the programmer must specify explicitly when an attached procedure should be invoked. Moreover, most aspects concerning the control of the interactions among the attached procedures are also left to the programmer. As a result, the programmer must always pay attention to the overall control issues during the coding of his procedures. We present in this paper a framework called S-Net on which descriptions and operations of these languages can be appropriately founded.

2. RELATED RESEARCH WORKS

Among others, FRL [Goldstein 1978] and KRL [Bobrow 1977] are the better known examples of recent AI languages. Because these two have both the advantages and disadvantages of recent attempts, we will consider them as typical examples and compare them with the S-Net notations throughout this paper.

As Goldstein said, FRL is a programming system rather than a language. It lacks the overall control mechanisms. It only provides a data structure and a programming package for manipulating it. The data structure, a frame system, consists of a set of mutually related knowledge units called 'frame'. A frame, in turn, is an aggregation of descriptive data and procedures. The core of a FRL frame is a property list. FRL generalizes the LISP property list in the following ways:

1. FRL supplies a mechanism for inheritance of properties through a generalization hierarchy.
2. The property value in a frame can be a procedure which knows how to get the actual value.
3. Procedures can be associated directly with frames. The programmer is required to specify explicitly, by using facet indicators such as $IF-ADDED, $IF-REMOVED, $IF-NEEDED etc., what sorts of operations on the frames will invoke the associated procedures.

In short, the essential features of FRL are

1. Inheritance of properties through a hierarchy.
2. Procedural attachment.

Though these two ideas are intuitively attractive, there remain a lot of difficult problems before they can be realized. We will consider these problems in this section. Note that because we restrict the discussion in this paper to the topic of problem solving mechanisms and their foundations, we will neglect many characteristic features of FRL or KRL which are very interesting in their own right.

2.1 Property Inheritance Through a Hierarchy

Fig. 1 shows an example in [Goldstein 1977]. The frame MINSKY inherits the properties STREET, CITY, STATE and ZIP from the frame MIT-AI. In FRL, 'the AKO (A Kind OF) link establishes a mapping by which properties of one frame may be distributed to related frames. Semantically, the mapping can represent a set/subset, part/whole, or other relationships[Goldstein 1977]'.

```
(FASSERT   MIT-AI
   (STREET   ($VALUE ( /545 Technology Square/ )))
   (CITY     ($VALUE ( /Cambridge/ )))
   (STATE    ($VALUE ( /MA/ )))
   (ZIP      ($VALUE ( /02139/)))      )

(FASSERT   MINSKY
   (AKO      ($VALUE ( MIT-AI )))
   (OFFICE   ($VALUE (  821   )))      )
```

Fig. 1 Description of an AKO Hierarchy in FRL.

This approach seems very promising and appropriate. However, some properties can be inherited through set/subset relations but not through part/whole relations and vice versa. From the view point of logic, property inheritance is a specific mode of inference associated with a predicate. In a extreme case, for example, children may inherit their second names from their parents but not any other properties. This inheritance rule is associated with a predicate, say, CHILD-OF. In FRL, there are no explicit provisions for representing such a kind of restricted property inheritance. The only possible solution is to embed such a rule in a procedure (Fig. 2). This solution is not a real solution of the problem. The programmer should do all things in his procedures. Because property inheritance through hierarchy provides only a very restricted inference mechanism, we need additional frameworks for supporting other kinds of inheritance mechanisms.

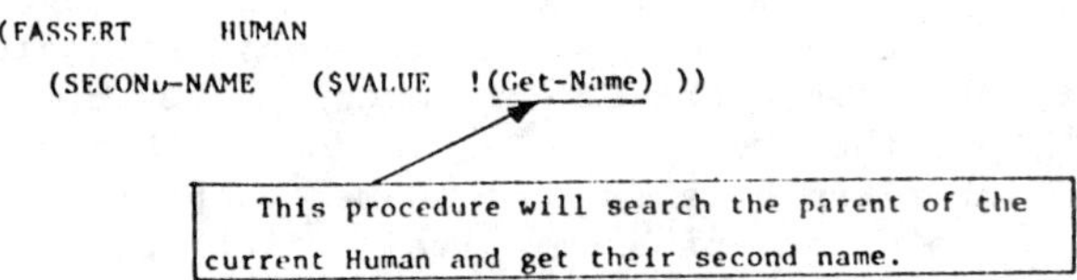

Fig. 2. Restricted Property Inheritance Embedded in a Procedure.

2.2 Procedural Attachment

One of the difficult problems in procedural attachment is how to decide when a procedure is evaluated. In most of the AI languages, the programmer should explicitly specify this.

```
DAY Frame
  Year
  Month
  Day-Number      WHEN-FILLED
                    (CHECK-RELATION  day-number, month)
  Day-of-Week     TO-FILL
                    (APPLY  calender-lookup
                           TO year, month, day-number)
                    (APPLY  anchor-date-method
                           TO year, month, day-number)
  ASCII-form*     WHEN-FILLED
                    (FILL  year, month, day-number)

        * ASCII-form for July 4, 1978 is 780704.
```

Fig. 3. Description for 'Day' in KRL.

$IF-ADDED in FRL and WHEN-FILLED in KRL indicators are used to indicate that the attached procedure should be invoked when a certain value is stored in the slot. However, this style of specification is often inadequate. Some procedures should be triggered when more than one slot is filled. Fig. 3 is an example by Winograd [1975]. The procedure Check-Relation, which checks the consistency between the Day-Number and the Month, will be triggered when the Day-Number slot is filled. If the Month slot has not been filled when the Day-Number is filled, the execution of the procedure should be suspended, and resumed again when the Month slot is filled. The control of such suspension and resuming of procedures may become very complicated, if it is implemented without any clear formalization. Moreover, the specification of TO-FILL and WHEN-FILLED indicators results in the restriction of the system's abilities. Consider a simple example in which we have two procedures which compute the slot-B's value from the slot-A's value, and the slot-C's value from slot-B's value respectively. There are four possibilities to embed such procedures by using TO-FILL and WHEN-FILLED indicators [Fig. 4]. In the first three, the slot-C's value can be obtained when the slot-A's value is given. However, it is not the case in the last representation.

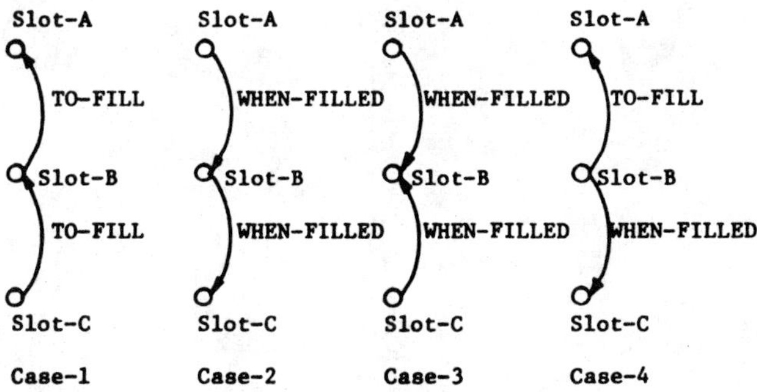

Fig.4 Explicit Pre-specifications of Invocation

To avoid this, we should carefully distinguish the two different kinds of knowledge: what logical or conceptual relationships the attached procedure embodies, and when the procedure will be invoked. It is often known beforehand that the evaluation of a certain procedure requires much more resources (time or space) than the others or that a certain direction of searching often leads us to success. These sorts of knowledge are called 'heuristics' and the programmers have been encouraged to embed them in their representation. However, it is our contention that such heuristics are only heuristics, i.e., they may be reflected on the problem solving process only to the extent that they will not restrict the system's abilities. TO-FILL (WHEN-FILLED) indicators not only recommend the backward (forward) usages of the attached procedures but also inhibit their forward (backward) usages.

In short, the pre-specification of the usages of attached procedures is too restrictive.

Our problem solver based on the S-Net alternately performs backward and forward reasonings. In that process, an attached procedure will be utilized either in forwards or backwards, according to the problem solving situations. In order to accomplish such mechanism, we introduce the concept of 'partially instantiated relationships' in the S-Net, which are dynamically created during the problem solving process [See 4.1 and 4.2].

3. S-NET REPRESENTATION

S-Net consists of several types of nodes and links. The node types which are used in the S-Net are shown in Fig. 5. The Disjoint node and the Condition node play the role of logical connectives. They are used for augmenting the generalization hierarchy (3.1). A property or a slot is represented in the S-Net by a node called Property node. All variable nodes in the S-Net are typed by certain data types. The definition of a type plays a central role in the S-Net.

A □ data type definition node for type A

◎ relation node

A ○ variable node typed as A

Ⓥ disjoint node

◇ condition node

▷ property node

● constant node or instance node

⦿ partially instantiated relation node

Fig. 5. Node Types in the S-Net.

A Type Definition node describes the basic behaviour of a data type. It corresponds to an atom in LISP. In LISP, an arbitrary character string identifies an atom, and all occurrences of the same character string in LISP programs and data are represented internally by a pointer which points to the atom. The behaviour of an atom is described by the property list attached to the atom. According to this convention, a data type in the S-Net is identified uniquely by its name, and there is one type definition node for each data type.

3.1 Augmentation of Generalization Hierarchy

Data types can be organized in a hierarchical structure. We use the term SORT, instead of

AKO or ISA, to refer to the link. In our problem solving procedure, the hierarchy of data types plays the central role for distributing properties, though explicit path specification (See 3.3) will further augment the inheritance mechanisms. When a problem description is given, the instance nodes of the corresponding data types are created. Because each instance in a problem description has its own data type name, the initial position of the instance in the hierarchy is determined by its name. However, the position should be determined not only by its type name but also its whole descriptions. For example, the instance

(OBJECT-1 NAME = ALCOHOL
(! TEMPARATURE) = 28°C))

is identified with the data type ALCOHOL by its type name. Moreover, because ALCOHOL is a subsort of MATERIAL and because an instance of MATERIAL whose temparature is between the boiling point and the congelation point is an instance of LIQUID, it should be identified as an instance of LIQUID. All properties of LIQUID should be distributed to this instance. In order to accomplish such an identification process, we need a framework in the S-Net for specifying when an instance is located lower in the hierarchy. For this purpose we introduce in the S-Net a new link SUBSORT and a new type of node Condition Node (See Fig. 6). A SUBSORT link is a link from a higher data type to a lower one. A Condition Node holds a condition when the transition from the higher to the lower data type is permitted. Moreover, because new information about an instance may be derived during the problem solving process or accumulated through the dialogue with the user, the position identification may be performed during the problem solving process.

We often find the following type of declarative sentences.

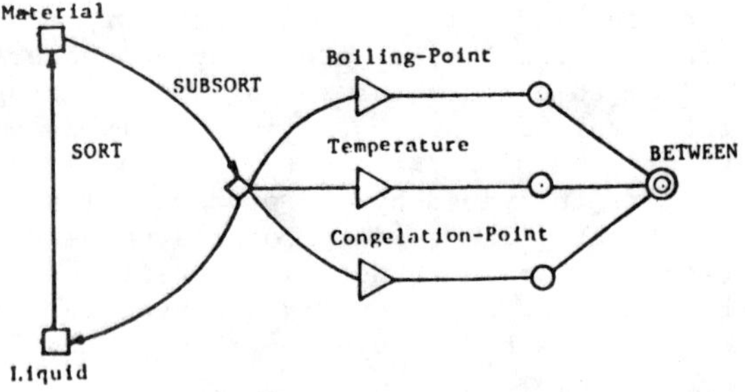

Fig. 6. SUBSORT Links with Condition Nodes.

Acid which dissolves copper is either Hydrochloric-Acid, Nitric-Acid or Sulphuric-Acid.

These statements describe mutually exclusive relationships among sets. A data type and a set do not necessarily correspond but they are closely related.

We call a set of data types 'Disjoint Set', if the data types in the set satisfy the following conditions:

1. If an instance is a certain data type in the set, it can never be other data types in the set.

2. We can determine the data type of an instance by determining which data type it is not equal to, i.e. by elimination.

In the S-Net, we represent a disjoint set by a node called Disjoint Node (Fig. 7). Disjoint nodes are often useful to inhibit semantically irrelevant information from entering into the search space. By combining the Condition nodes and Disjoint nodes, the generalization hierarchy in the S-Net becomes very powerful.

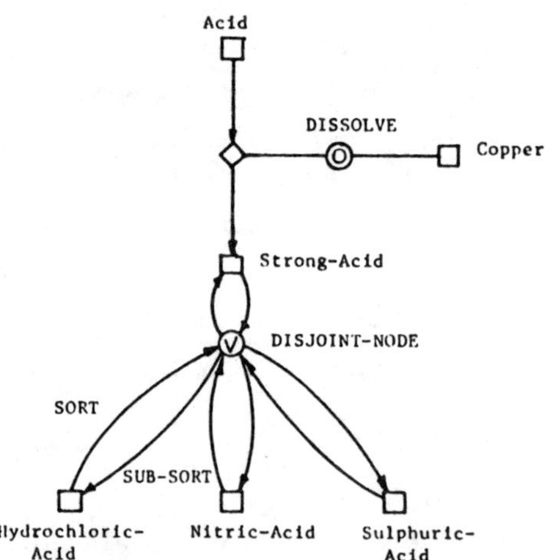

Fig. 7. DISJOINT-NODE.

3.2 Relation Nodes

A relation node in the S-Net expresses a certain dependency relationship among the slots, and also functions as entrance to some external procedures from the S-Net. Based on the dependency relationships, the S-Net problem solver determines how to solve a problem. For each relation node, a bunch of procedures is internally defined. The procedures embody how to utilize the relation in the problem solving. The problem solver decides which internal procedures is invoked, based on both the dependency relationships and the problem solving situations.

Logical predicates of certain kinds, arithmetic operators, external data bases and procedures in general are all equally represented in the S-Net by relation nodes. A relation node essentially corresponds to a logical predicate. A logical predicate extentionally specifies a set, possibly infinite, of tuples which satisfy the predicate. We assume that external data bases are constructed according to the relational data model. It consists of the tuples which satisfy a predicate or relationship, while a procecure in general expresses the mechanism for computing those tuples.

The description of a procedure in a relation node consists of two parts: Declaration part and Procedure body. The declaration part shows in which direction the procedure utilizes the relationship. This part, as demonstrated below, is fairly simple:

$$(arg_{i_1} \quad arg_{i_2} \quad \ldots \quad arg_{i_n}):(arg_{i_{n+1}} \quad \ldots \quad arg_{i_m})$$

This means that if $arg_{i_{n+1}}, \ldots, arg_{i_m}$ are known, $(arg_{i_1}, \ldots, arg_{i_n})$ can be computed by the procedure. The declaration part can be interpreted both forward and backward by the S-Net problem solver depending on the situation, i.e. if one of $arg_{i_1} \ldots, arg_{i_n}$ is required, then try to get the values of $arg_{i_{n+1}}, \ldots, arg_{i_m}$ (in the backward mode), or if $arg_{i_{n+1}}, \ldots, arg_{i_m}$ are all known, then try to compute the values of $arg_{i_1}, \ldots, arg_{i_n}$ by the procedure (in the forward mode). As for the backward and forward mode, see 4.2.

In a special case, the left hand side of the declaration part can be null. In this case, the procedure body will be invoked when the arguments of the right hand side are all filled, and check the consistency among them.

Some examples of relation nodes are shown in Fig. 8.

3.3 Nesting of Data Types — Explicit Path Specification

A data type or a frame can be recursively defined. A data type may arise in the definition of another type. The description

(DT NAME = Aqueous - Solution

(! Solvent) = (DT NAME = Water))

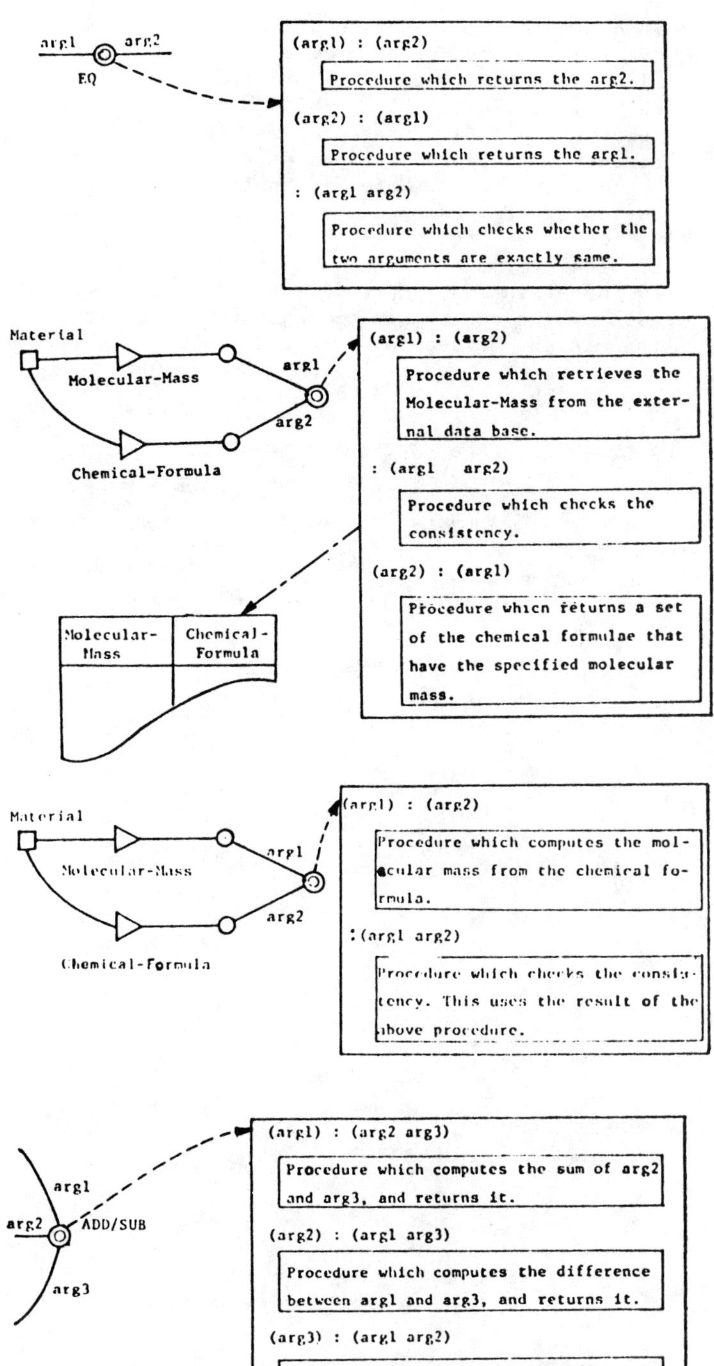

Fig.8 Examples of Relation Nodes and Their Internal Procedures

is a simple example of such descriptions. We treat an occurrance of a data type in the definition of another type as a variable typed by the data type. Thus, (DT NAME = Water) in the above example is represented as a typed variable. Since the variable is typed as Water, all information attached to Water is applicable to the variable. For example, we will have the value H20 when we retrieve the value of the property Chemical-Formula of the Solvent of a certain Aqueous-Solution. Moreover, a specific knowledge, which can be applied only to the water that is the solvent of a certain solution, but not to Water in general, is also attached to the variable.

```
(DT   NAME = Aqueous - Solution
      (!   Solvent) = (DT   NAME = Water)
      (ADD/SUB  (!  MASS) (!  Solvent MASS)
                          (!  Solute Mass)))
```

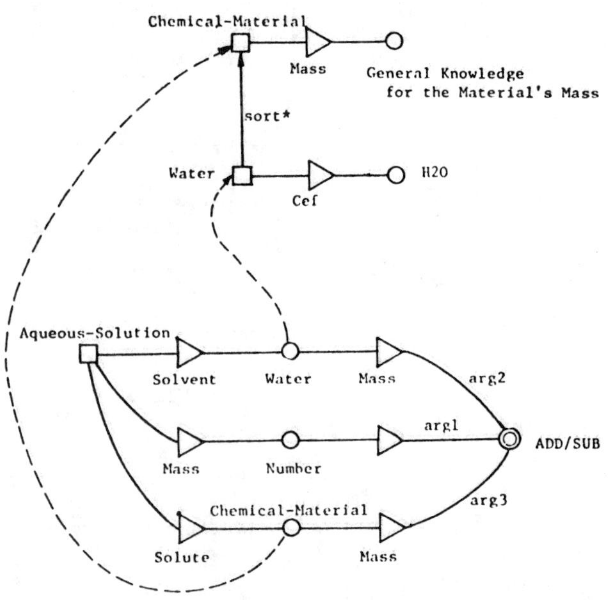

Fig. 9. Type Definition Node for 'Aqueous-Solutions'.

The S-Net for the above description is shown in Fig. 9. Retrieval of a value through a path description such as (FGET Aqueous - Solution Solvent Mass) will cause the evaluation of a procedure which is defined as the 'internal' procedure of the relation node ADD/SUB that computes the Solvent's mass from those of the Solution and the Solute. Moreover, if the procedure fails to compute it, more general procedures which are attached to the data type Water or more general data types than Water will be invoked. Thus, unlike in FRL, a path description in the S-Net is augmented automatically by the system.

Such a path description can be emplyed not only in the query expression but also in the S-Net descriptions as follows. The general statement

'If a researcher is a member of an organization, he inherits the address from the organization'

can be expressed by

```
(DT   NAME = Researcher
      (!  Organization) = (DT   NAME
                              = Organization)
      (EQ  (!  Address) (!  Organization
                            Address))).
```

In the above examples, all path descriptions begin with !'s which show that the paths start from the current data type. A path which starts from a data type that is different from the current one is also allowed in the S-Net. Thus, the statement 'A MIT-Researcher inherits his address from MIT-Al-Lab' can be expressed directly by

```
(DT  NAME = MIT - Researcher
     (EQ  (!  Address)  ((DT  NAME =
                    MIT-Al-Lab) Address)).
```

The S-Net for this is shown in Fig. 10. By using this mechanism, called 'explicit path specification', property inheritance or distribution among different data types can be obtained in a very intuitive way. Because EQ is represented as a relation node, the above expression can be used not only for retrieving the researcher's address but also for checking the consistency when the address of a certain MIT-Researcher is given.

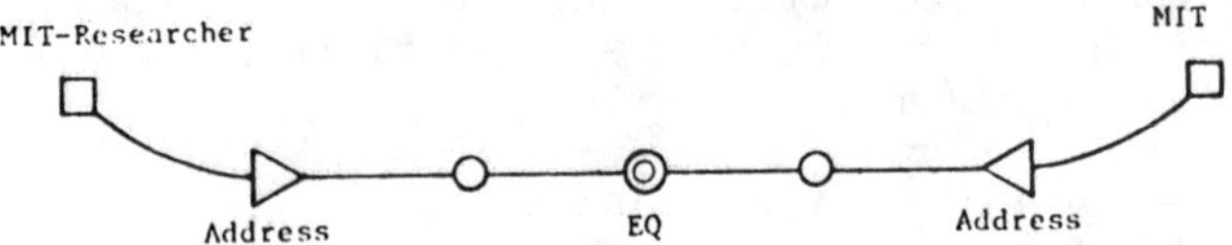

Fig. 10. Related Type Definition Nodes.

4. OPERATIONS ON THE S-NET

4.1 Creation of an Instance

A problem description may contain several instances. The description

```
(OBJECT-1   NAME = Solution
          (! Mass) = 100 gr
          (! Solvent) = (OBJECT-2  NAME = Water
                              (! Mass) = 98 gr)
          (! Solute) = (OBJECT-3
                              (! Cef) = Na-Cl))
```

contains three instances of different data types. They are instances of Solution(OBJECT-1), Water (OBJECT-2) and a data type without a name(OBJECT-3).

The type definition node for Solution contains various relationships among the properties. These relationships are also instantiated. For example, there may exist a relation node ADD/SUB that expresses the relationship among Solution's mass, Solvent's mass and Solute's mass. When the solution's mass is filled by 100 gr, the relationship is also partially instantiated, and the partially instantiated relation node is created (Fig. 11).

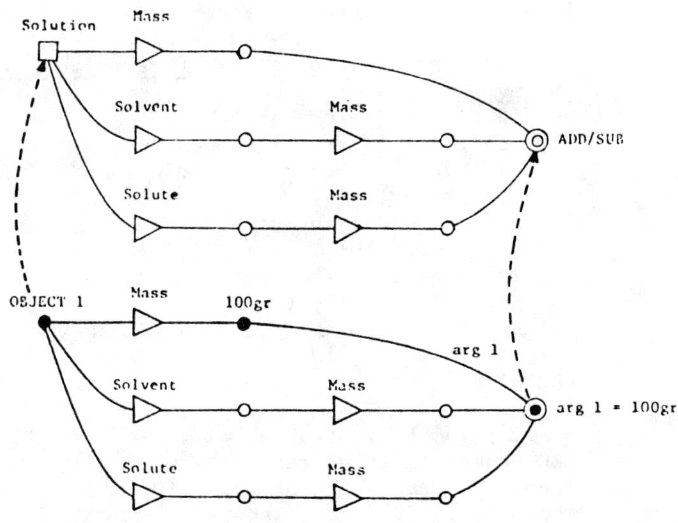

Fig. 11. Partially Instantiated Relation Node.

The instance OBJECT-2 is created as an instance of Water. Because the property Mass is filled by 98 gr, the relation nodes attached to Water's Mass are instantiated. Moreover, because OBJECT-2 is put in the property Solvent of OBJECT-1, the relation nodes attached to the Solvent's Mass are also instantiated. As a result, the instantiated relation node ADD/SUB is further instantiated, i.e., the arg-2 is bound to 98 gr. Since both arg-1 and arg-2 are known in this instantiated relation node, one of the procedures defined in this relation node which computes arg-3 becomes to be evaluable. The procedure is marked as evaluable and put into a list called EV-List (See 4.2). In the sequel, the final result will be such as shown in Fig. 12.

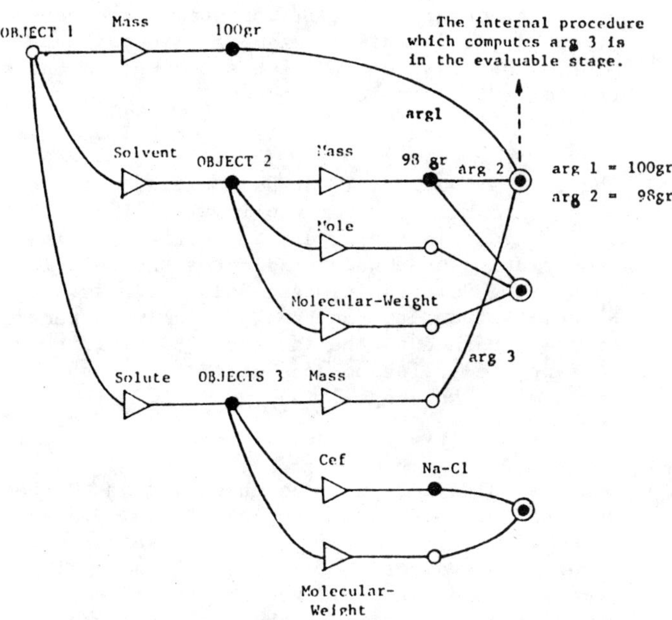

Fig. 12. Final Result of the Instantiation.

As described above, the instantiation of a data type recursively causes the instantiation of other data types. Some relation nodes are also instantiated during the process. The instantiation of relation nodes is propagated upward through the SORT-hierarchy: If a property of a certain data type is filled, the relation nodes attached to the same property of the higher data types in the hierarchy are all instantiated.

4.2 Backward and Forward Reasonings

As we described earlier, after the initial instantiation of variables, a certain set of procedures are only marked as immediately evaluable and put into the EV-list, because the immediate evaluation of these procedures will trigger the unlimited forward reasoning which may invoke many irrelevant procedures.

The next stage is performed backward. The initial goal, which is to solve the problem posed by the user, will be tried, and if not fulfilled, the goal will be further expanded into a set of subgoals. The expansion of a goal will be performed by utilizing the information attached to the instantiated data types, especially the declaration parts of internal procedures in the instantiated relation nodes. Because the instantiated relation nodes have already been partially instantiated during the preceding forward mode, it is reasonable to expect that these instantiated relationships are relevant to the current problem more than those which have not been instantiated. We illustrate this process by considering a simple example. Suppose the problem description in 4.1 has been given and that the following problem is posed.

'Retrieve the Density of OBJECT-1'

The initial goal will not be achieved, because the mass of OBJECT-3 is not explicitly given. The initial goal is expanded into subgoals. Since the relation node which indicates the relationship among Solution's Mass, Solute's Mass and Solution's Density has been partially instantiated and attached to the instance OBJECT-1, this instantiated relation node will be used to expand the goal. The subgoal is

'Retrieve the Mass of OBJECT-3'.

The reasoning mode will be changed from the backward mode to the forward mode. In this mode, the procedures in the EV-list will be evaluated in turn. The evaluation will further instantiate some variables in the S-Net so that some other procedures will enter in the evaluable stage. They are also marked accordingly, and put in the EV-list. They will be evaluated in the next forward mode.

In the above example, the internal procedure in the relation node ADD/SUB, which computes the Solute's(OBJECT-3's) Mass, is evaluated. The result of the evaluation fulfills the above subgoal. This will be checked in the next backward mode. The success of the subgoal will result in the success of the initial goal.

Thus, the whole process is performed forwards and backwards. If there are no procedures in the EV-list, only the backward mode will be continued until a certain procedure will be entered in the EV-list. Note that an internal procedure in a relation node will be used in both directions, forwards and backwards. Moreover, the two mode works cooperatively in the sense that the backward mode prefers to operating the partially instantiated relation nodes proposed by the preceding forward mode.

5. A SIMPLE EXAMPLE

In order to give the reader some idea about the operation of the problem solver, we will give an example in this section. Suppose the following problem is given.

```
(OBJECT-1      NAME = Solution
      (!   Solute) = ( OBJECT-2)
      (!   Volume) = 200 cc )         )
(OBJECT-2      NAME = Sodium
      (!     Mass) =  2 gr  )         )
 (RETRIEVE    OBJECT-1   Mol-Density) ?
```

In order to compute the Mol-Density, the problem solver should solve various subproblems such as computing the Solute's Mol-Number from the mass and the molecular-weight, retrieving the Molecular-Weight from the external data base, getting Sodium's Chemical-Formula for accessing the data base etc. The problem solver works fairly well and selects relevant knowledge appropriately even if there is much irrelevant knowledge in the S-Net.

6. CONCLUSION

In this paper, we have proposed a graphical notation called S-Net which provides a framework and a foundation for some of the operations of recent AI languages and systems. Especially,it is shown that the problems, 'when an attched procedure to be invoked' and 'how to represent restricted property inheritance in nonprocedural forms', can be solved in the S-Net representation. Moreover, various sorts of information about problem solving situations such as variable binding contexts etc. are distributively stored in the nodes(partially instantiated relation nodes etc.) so that the global controller, the problem solver, can be easily implemented. The current version is only one of possible constructions. We are now developing different problem solving strategies.

REFERENCES

[Bobrow 1976] D.G.Bobrow et.al., "An Overview of KRL, a Knowledge Representation Language," Technical Report, Xerox PARC, 1976

[Davis 1978] R.Davis, "Knowledge Acquisition in Rule-Based Systems," in Pattern Directed Inference Systems (eds. Waterman & Hayes-Roth), Academic Press, 1978

[Goldstein 1977] I.P.Goldstein et.al., "The FRL Primer," AI Memo 408, MIT, 1977

[Hendrix 1975] G.G.Hendrix, "Partitioned Network for the Mathematical Modeling of Natural Language Semantics," Ph.D Thesis, Univ. of Texas, 1975

[Minsky 1975] M.Minsky, "A Framework for Representing Knowledge," in the Psychology of Computer Vision (ed. Winston), McGraw Hill, 1975

[Schubert 1976] L.K.Schubert, "Extending the Expressive Power of Semantic Networks," Artificial Intelligence, Vol. 7, 1976

LISP MACHINE NK3 AND MEASUREMENT OF ITS PERFORMANCE

Makoto NAGAO   Jun-ichi TSUJII   Katsuto NAKAJIMA   Kei MITAMURA   Hachidai ITO

Department of Electrical Engineering
Faculty of Engineering
Kyoto University
Kyoto, Japan

A LISP machine NK3 is presented. The machine has various special hardwares not only for executing ordinary LISP programs very fast but also for implementing flexible control structures such as co-routines. Special care is taken in the architecture to realize rapid transfer of the pointer information in the system. Automatic management of the stack area and the guarantee of high speed and flexible stack operations are the other important design issues. NK3 is provided with a hardware stack which contains the top part of the stack and transfers data from/to the main memory independently with the CPU. Various instructions for manipulating the stack, such as 'exchange the stack content' etc., are prepared. The constructions of the hardware architecture, micro/macro instruction sets, and the software including the interpreter are described in this paper. Some results of performance evaluation are also shown.

1. INTRODUCTION

LISP is the most popular programming language in the research area of artificial intelligence. We have used LISP to develop natural language understanding systems and some problem solving systems. The most complicated systems among these is a programming language for natural language analysis called PLATON[NAGAO 1975], which is an extended version of Wood's ATN parser. It has the ability of pattern matching to check the applicabilities of the grammar rules. This makes the definition of a grammar very clear and easy to understand. However, because the pattern matching operation is very time consuming, it took a long time to analyze a sentence. The more poweful analysis we wish, the bigger the programs become, and require both a huge free cell area and high execution speed.

On the other hand, for natural language understanding systems the more flexible control structures are required than the recursive one the ordinary LISP systems provide. The idea of the 'society of experts'[HEWITT 1977] is also very important in natural language understanding systems. Implementing such a co-routine environment by an ordinary LISP may decrease the efficiency considerably. It is desirable that the hardware system supports such mechanisms.

From the above reasons, we decided, in 1975, to construct a special hardware system which can directly execute LISP codes. The LISP machine which we have developed is called NK3 and equipped with various hardwares such as a specially designed hardware stack. We have completed the hardware of NK3 and implemented the interpreter of LISP1.5 on it. We are now developping more sophisticated LISP interpreter, compiler, and micro coded instructions for the machine step by step in evolutional approaches. We have measured the performance of the machine from various view points: how often the data transfer between the hardware stack and the main memory occurs, how frequent each micro coded instruction is used etc. Based on these measurements, we are improving the constructions of the interpreter, compiler and micro coded instructions.

2. ARCHITECTURE OF LISP MACHINE NK3

Fig.1 shows the overall architecture of the LISP

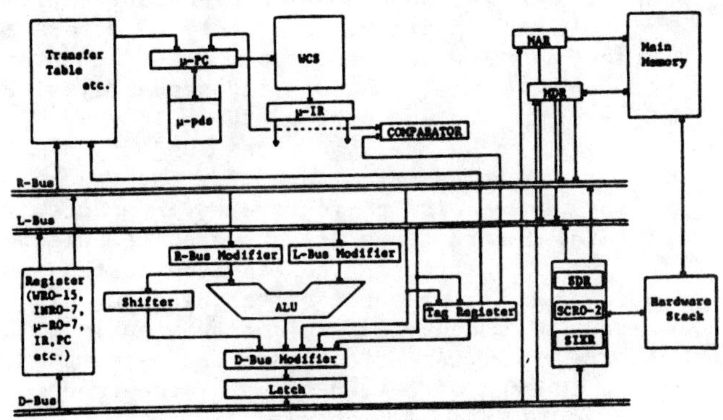

Fig.1 Architecture of NK3

machine NK3. NK3 is a micro-program machine. Micro-programs are stored in WCS(writable control store), and the macro-programs and LISP cells are stored in the main memory. The machine has three data buses, ordinary registers, ALU and some other functions. Special care is taken in the architecture to realize rapid transfer of the pointer information in the system. Automatic management of the stack areas and the guarantee of the high speed, flexible automatic pushing down and popping up operations are the other important design issues of the system. Some typical features of NK3 are the followings.

(i) Writable Control Store (4 kw, 42 bit/word)

This contains micro-programs of most built-in functions and most parts of the interpreter.

(ii) Main Memory (512kB, 800nsec)

The main memory is of the mini-computer INTERDATA 8/32 and is shared by NK3. Because of this memory sharing the access speed to the memory from NK3 takes about 2 μseconds, which is very slow. The input/output operations of NK3 are performed by INTERDATA 8/32. Since the OS is also shared, NK3 does not need to have any general facilities such as the file management.

(iii) Hardware Stack (16 words, 32 bits/word)

The top part of the stack is stored in these registers. The popping-up and pushing-down operations are generally performed in ordinary LISP programs alternately. Long consecutive popping (pushing) operations are rare. In such a situation, the usual double buffering technique is inadequate. It causes frequent data transfer. To avoid this, we have adopted quadruple buffering for the hardware stack. The hardware stack is divided into four blocks, each of which consists of four words. By transferring data from/to the main memory asynchronously with the CPU by the unit of four words, the hardware stack is guaranteed to contain always at least four words of the stack and four word spaces for the push-down information. Special circuits are provided to detect the errors such as stack overflow and underflow. The data transfer is done by burst DMA mode independently with the LISP program. Any part of the main memory can be assigned to be the stack area, and any number of areas can be reserved for different stacks in the memory to realize co-routine environments. Some special instructions are prepared to switch the active stack from the current one to the other etc. Because frequent switching among stacks is expected to occur, it is not reasonable to have a larger hardware stack than the present one. It will cause a data transfer of large amount, when the active stack is changed.

We have measured how often the consecutive popping and pushing operations occur in the usual execution, and how often the data transfer is performed between the hardware stack and the memory (See Table 1).

	push-down(=pop-up)	PUSH-DMA	POP-DMA	DMA-RATE
TPU-1	196,240	7,470	8,009	0.158

$$\text{DMA-RATE} = \frac{4*(\text{PUSH-DMA} + \text{POP-DMA})}{\text{push-down} + \text{pop-up}}$$

Table 1. Stack Operations and Data Transfer

The bench marck problem here is the theorem prover based on 'resolution principle' [Chang 1973]. From this table, one can see more than 84% of stack operations are effectively carried out without any data transfer.

(iv) Transfer Table (1 kw, 15 bit/word)

The interpreter frequently checks the data types of the cells and determines the jump position in the program. The data types of cells are expressed in the tag parts of the memory words(Fig. 2). The Transfer Table is used by micro-programs to determine the jump position directly from the description of the tag parts.

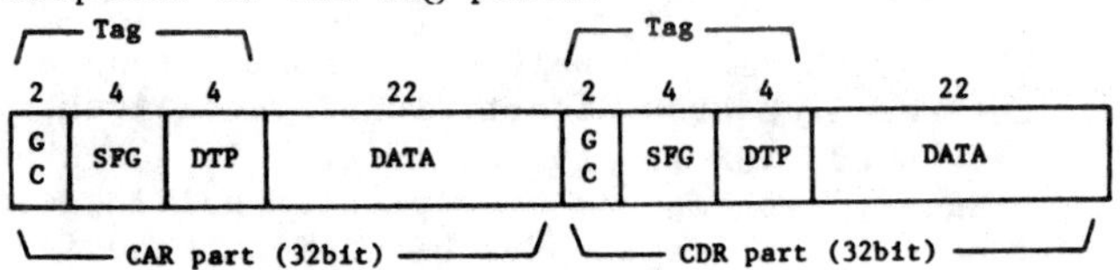

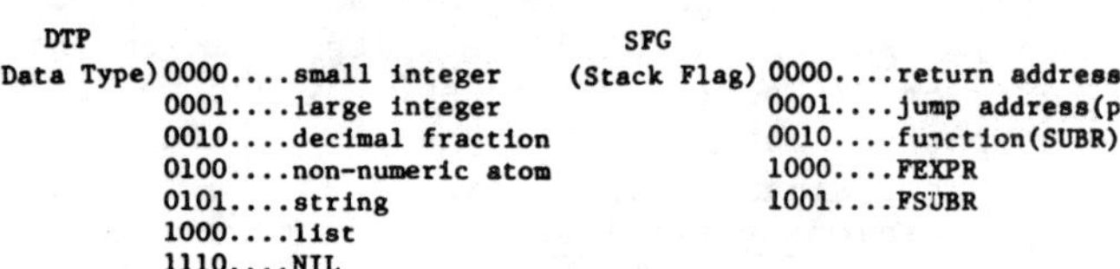

Fig. 2 Structure of LISP Cells

(v) Micro-Instructions

There are six types of micro-instructions. Those types are (1) Arithmetic and Logical operations, (2) Conditional Jumps, (3) Emit operations, (4) Transfer Table operations, (5) Patch operations, and (6) Shift operations. By Patch operations, we can patch arbitrary portions of L-Bus data and R-Bus data together. Combining this operation with the Shift operations enables us to manipulate the tag information efficiently. The format of the type 4 instruction is shown in Fig. 3.

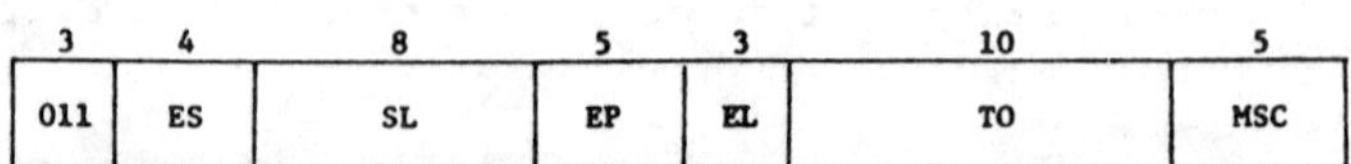

Fig. 3 Format of Type 4 Instruction

This instrution extracts the portion of the bus data (specified by ES - Extraction Source (R-Bus or L-Bus), EP - Extraction Position, and EL - Extraction Length), and adds it to TO (Table Offset). If the result is within SL (Search Length), it refers to the Transfer Table to determine the jump position. Otherwise, the instruction has no effect (See Fig. 4). This type of instruction is very useful for carrying out 'multi-way jump' in micro-programs, based on the tag information.

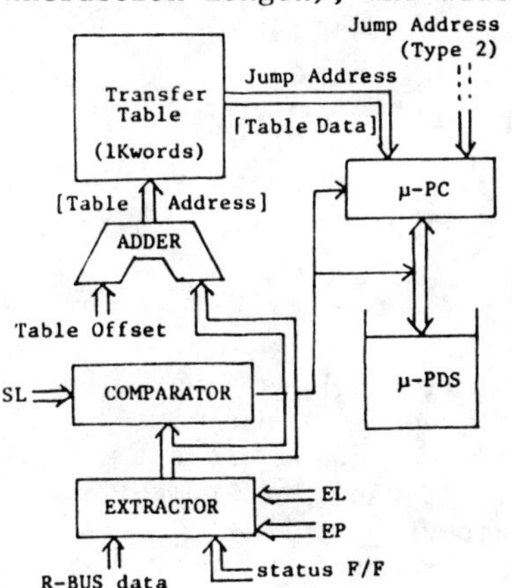

Fig. 4 Transfer Operation

3. HIGH LEVEL MACRO INSTRUCTIONS

NK3 is essentially a micro programmable computer which is equipped with various special hardwares. Therefore, in order to make the execution efficient, we should devise macro instructions which utilize these special hardwares well and are suitable for LISP operations. At present, most of built-in fuctions of LISP can be executed by single macro instructions. Moreover, some of them operates directly on the top of stack. Because of the hardware stack, these instructions are executed very fast.

A set of special macro instructions which facilitate the writing of LISP interpreters is provided. These are the parts of the interpreter which conceptually perform single tasks. For example, searching the value of a variable from the A-list, jumping to the appropriate locations in Eval or Apply according to the types of the arguments and so on are performed by single instructions. The instruction HASH is another example of high level macro instructions. The hashing operation on the atom's print-name is carried out by this instruction. It is very time consuming by the ordinary program to identify all the input character strings with the atoms already in the system. The HASH instruction performs this task very efficiently.

Some other special instructions have been devised to manipulate the hardware stack for implementing flexible control mechanisms directly. The instructions EXCHange and INITialize are the examples. The EXCH and INIT enables us to implement co-routine environments. Because NK3 is equipped with a single hardware stack, only one of the co-routines can be active at a time and the stack information for the routine is stored in the hardware stack. The EXCH is used to exchange the content of the hardware stack, in order to activate another co-routine in place of the current one. The older context will be appropriately saved. The instruction INIT is for invoking a new co-routine. It initializes a stack area and reserves a certain amount of memory area for that routine.

4. PERFORMANCE EVALUATION

We have written a LISP interpreter for LISP 1.5 by using the macro instructions described in 3, and have measured the performance and the effectiveness of these instructins. We are still seeking much more efficient set of macro instructions for LISP. Up to present we have experienced a drastic improvement of the execution times, for example two to three times, by setting up a good instruction set. On the other hand, another trial is in progress, which makes the macro instructions as big as possible in their functions. The limit in this direction is that the stack operations cannot be realized by micro programs. Because of this weak point, the interpreter as a whole cannot be realized by micro instructions only.

We also compared the execution speed of NK3 with some other LISP systems on big and small computers. The bench mark problems were a sorting program, a theorem prover, and some other typical LISP programs. The performance of NK3 might be judged as : it has a half of the power of very large machines (i.e. M190), and has several times of the power of small computer versions of LISP. If NK3 can use the main memory exclusively without sharing with INTERDATA 8/32, and if the stack mechanism can be utilized freely from micro-programs, the execution speed will improve drastically. These may be the main improvement to be taken soon.

REFERENCES

[CHANG 1973] C.Cang, R.Lee, "Symbolic Logic and Mechanical Theorem Proving," Academic Press, 1973

[HEWITT 1977] C.Hewitt, "Viewing Control Structures as Pattern of Passing Messages," Artificial Intelligence, vol. 8, No. 3, 1977

[MOSES 1975] J. Moses et.al., "Proposal for Personal Computer Capable for Executing Large LISP Programs," MIT, 1975

[NAGAO 1975] M.Nagao, J.Tsujii, "PLATON - A New Programming Language for Natural Language Analysis," Proc. of 2nd USA-Japan Computer Conference, Tokyo, 1975

A PARALLEL TREE SEARCH METHOD

Sei-ichi Nakagawa
Department of Information Science
Kyoto University
Kyoto, 606 Japan

Toshiyuki Sakai
Department of Information Science
Kyoto University
Kyoto, 606 Japan

We describe a new tree search method which searches best few paths with backtracking in parallel by the following algorithm (α-β-γ search). Expand the best α nodes at one time. If the number of new nodes which have been expanded by a selected node exceeds a pre-set threshold (β), only the best β nodes are kept and others are pruned. If the total number of newly generated node sequences and non-expanded node sequences exceeds a pre-set threshold (γ), only the best γ node sequences are kept, and others are removed. Repeat these consecutive processes until a complete sequence is generated. We evaluated this method by simulations and experiments, and obtained good performances both in the search efficiency and in the recognition rate.

1. INTRODUCTION

To recognize a perceptual input (ex. speech, image), all plausible candidates should be taken into consideration, because a system cannot know exactly what the input was, that is, the input is ambiguous. However, since the number of plausible candidate sequences becomes enormous in case of continuous speech recognition, image understanding and game, a system must select some best sequences and abandon the others. Therefore, the recognition of perceptual input contains the problems of tree search (pruning) and scoring mechanism.

In this paper, we describe a new tree search method employed in the LITHAN speech understanding system[1-4]. For convenience' sake, we would like to discuss the case of speech recognition as an example of recognition of perceptual input and the case of left to right parsing although various parsing strategies have been proposed[5,6].

2. SEARCHING STRATEGY OF ALTERNATIVE SEQUENCE

The aim of a speech recognition system is to determine, for an acoustic signal A and a task language L, a sequence of words W such that this sequence is consistent with the syntax, semantics and pragmatics of the task, and further that this sequence maximizes the a posteriori probability P(W/A,L). We assume an equal probability for the appearance of each sentence. Now $P(W/A,L) = P(W/L) \times P(A/W,L)/P(A/L)$. The term P(A/L) in the denominator is independent of W, and therefore does not have to be known. We assumed that P(W/L) was always constant for all correct sequences of words. Thus, P(W/L) does not also have to be known. Therefore, we can regard that P(W/A,L) is proportional to P(A/W,L). However, this algorithm consumes much computing time, because the approach is equivalent to searching all possible paths or words.

Seeing this difficulty, we coped with the problem by dividing the whole process into two stages: the acoustic signal-to-phoneme sequence and the phoneme sequence-to-word sequence. This division corresponds to approximating P(W/A,L) by $P(W/A,L) = \sum_{PH} P(PH/A,L) \times P(W/PH,L) \propto P(W/PH_0,L)$, where PH denotes a sequence of phonemes and PH_0 a recognized sequence of phonemes (that is, we assume the probability of recognized phoneme $\gg$ that of other phoneme). Furthermore, the maximum of $P(W/PH_0,L)$ is approximately obtained from tree search methods.

If an utterance is composed of s words, and t alternative words are identified for each of these, the number of sequences to be considered is s^t. Therefore the problem of continuous speech recognition can be seen as that of searching through a space of s^t word sequences to find the most acceptable sequence (that is, the sequence with the highest score), that does not contradict all the given knowledge; syntax, semantics, pragmatics, etc.

Fig.1 illustrates an example of a parsing tree. In this figure, the alphabetical symbol and numerical value on a branch denote an identified word and its likelihood, respectively. An encircled numeral on a node indicates the average likelihood for a word sequence corresponding to the path from the root node to that node. A double encircled numeral on a terminal node indicates the score of a complete sentence. The LITHAN system rejects words having a score below a pre-determined value, say, 80. It also rejects sentences below another value, say 85. Thus, in Fig.1, there are five complete sentences: BHM, BHN, CJO, CJP, and CK. If the best-first tree search is applied, the sentence BHN will be selected after the node selection sequence: B→BH→C→CJ→BHN. On the other hand, if we use the depth-first search, BHM will be selected (A→AE→AF→B→BG→BH→BHM). In the case of depth-first serach with ordering, BHN will be selected (B→BH→BHN). We would, however, like to select the sentence CJP. Now, the best-first search may guarantee the sequence with highest score, if the score of a word sequence has a true cost function for searching (namely the breadth-first search)[7]. However, such a method requires much computation time and many storage memories. Our searching scheme is not such a case. Although many techniques have been developed in artificial intelligence research[8,9], we will propose a new search technique and pruning method suitable for recognition of perceptual inputs.

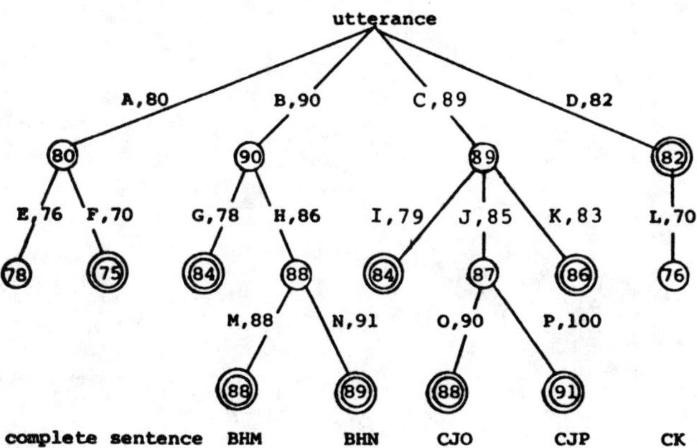

Fig. 1 An example of tree searching.

3. A PARALLEL SEARCH METHOD (α-β-γ METHOD)

We define the parameters which are used by this method.

α: number of nodes which are expanded in parallel at the same time.

β: number of nodes which are kept in all generated nodes at each branching point.

γ: total number of partial strings which are kept in a partial tree.

The score of a partial sentence is defined as the average of the score of words constituting this partial sentence.

Algorithm

step 1: Enter the root node into the set of OPEN NODE.

step 2: Expand α nodes in the set, each of which is the last node of one of partial strings with the highest α average scores. If the number of nodes in the set is less than α, these all nodes are expanded. If the expanded node is a terminal node, go to step 5.

step 3: Enter the β nodes with the highest β scores out of the generated nodes at each branching point into the set of OPEN NODE.

step 4: If the number of nodes in the set of OPEN NODE is more than γ, select the γ nodes, each of which is the last node of one of partial strings with the highest γ average scores, and the other nodes (or strings) are pruned. Go to step 2.

step 5: The string from root node to this terminal node is regarded as an input string. If the number of strings which are regarded as an input string is more than δ, stop. Otherwise, go to step 2.

We call the successive operations from the step 2 to the step 4 as one 'round'.

Although the method of Lowerre in the HARPY system (called beam search[10]) does not have the function of backtracking, our method has it implicitely in the case of α<γ. We call this method as α-β-γ tree search method (or best-α tree search) for convenience' sake.

For example, in Fig.1, let α, β, γ, and δ be 2, 3, 4 and 2, respectively. Here the following word sequences will be kept at each round (the two, α=2, underlined sequences are to be expanded at the next round).

Round 1: B, C, D
D may be a complete sentence in the case the score is less than 85, so it is rejected but may be reserved as a partial sentence.

Round 2: BH, CK, CJ, D
G and I are rejected. CK is a complete sentence.

Round 3: CK, BHM, BHN, CJO, CJP
These are all the complete sentences. In the end, CJP is selected as the recognized sentence.

Larger values of α, β and γ would bring a better recognition result, but such would also increase the tree search time. Therefore, we have to decide the optimum thresholds of α, β and γ.

4. COMPUTER SIMULATION

Our tree search method was evaluated by computer simulations. The evaluation of a tree search method depends on the depth of tree (DEPTH), branching factor (BRANCH), scoring mechanism and so on.

For each [DEPTH, BRANCH], 100 trees and the score of each node were generated by a random generator of a uniform distribution [from 0 to 100]. The score of a partial sentence was defined as the average score over all words in the partial sentence. We regarded the trees of [DEPTH=5, BRANCH=5] as the standard tree because a computer had the limitation of an amount of stored memories. The depth of all terminal nodes and the number of branches are same for a tree in this simulation. We define that the input sequence is the sequence with the highest average score. Thus, our problem is to find the sequence with the highest average score. Table 1 shows the kinds of trees which were generated by a random generator. LSSS shows the logarithm of the search space size of a tree. This value can be calculated from multiplying logarithm of DABF (dynamic average branching factor) by ASL (average sentence length)[4,11]. The table 2 shows the set of parameters for tree search which were evaluated. We can divide these parameter sets into the two types. Although the type 1 (α=γ) does not have the function of backtracking, the type 2 (α<γ) has it implicitely. The parameter δ was always set to 1.

Table 1 Kind of trees

type	number of branch	depth of a tree	LSSS	number of nodes
1	4	5	10.0	1364
2	5	4	9.3	780
3	5	5	11.6	3905
4	5	6	13.9	19530
5	6	5	12.9	9330

Table 2 Set of parameters

type	method	α	β	γ
1	1	1	1	1
	2	2	2	2
	3	3	3	3
	4	4	4	4
	5	5	5	5
2	6	1	5	10
	7	2	5	10
	8	3	5	12
	9	5	5	15

The simulation results are shown in Table 3 and Fig.2. The column '1' in the 'rank of recognit.·n result' corresponds to the number of trees which were recognized correctly. This number associates with "recognition rate". The column '2' indicates that the input was recognized as the second best candidate. As a logical conclusion, the larger LSSS becomes, the worser the recognition rate becomes. From Fig.2, we find when the tree is small, the type 2 is inferior to the type 1. On the other hand, when it is large, the type 2 is superior to the type 1. And also we can say that the best-first search which is simulated by [α=1, β=5, γ=10] is inferior to anyone of parallel search (α≧2).

Table 3 Simulation result (DEPTH=5, BRANCH=5)

α β γ	number of expanded nodes	rank of recognition result										
		1	2	3	4	5	6	7	8	9	10	11~
1 1 1	25	23	11	5	2	6	6	0	3	3	0	41
2 2 2	45	52	12	4	7	2	2	4	3	2	1	11
3 3 3	65	71	9	9	5	2	0	1	2	0	0	1
4 4 4	85	78	12	5	2	0	0	1	1	0	0	1
5 5 5	105	82	13	3	1	0	0	0	0	0	0	1
1 5 10	66	58	12	10	4	3	3	2	1	1	0	6
2 5 10	78	74	13	7	1	2	0	0	1	0	0	2
3 5 12	95	80	11	8	1	0	0	0	0	0	0	0
5 5 15	130	83	13	3	1	0	0	0	0	0	0	0

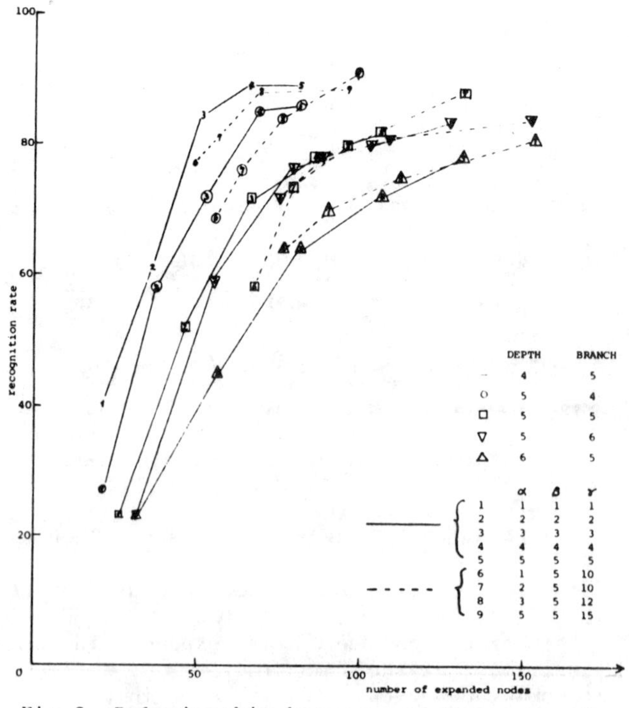

Fig.2 Relationship between recognition rate and number of expanded nodes.

This search method can control the search space size by taking the cost of search into consideration. That is, the scoring mechanism of a partial sentence is modified as follows. Let n be the number of words in a partial sentence and $S_1 \ldots S_n$ be the score of each word, respectively. The new score of this sequence is defined by average $[S_1 \ldots S_n] + W \times n$, where W is a weighting coefficient. If W is a negative value, the search space size becomes large and the recognition rate would be improved. In other wards, this leads that a string of short length is treated significantly than that of long length. If W is a positive value, the opposite results will be obtained.

Table 4 and Fig.3 show the results of this tree search method. Methods from 1 [α=1, β=1, γ=1] to 5 [α=5, β=5, γ=5], the type 1, are independent of this modification, because these methods always expand the partial sentences of same length in parallel. The simulation results are in approximate agreement with expected results. However, when W was smaller than -10, the recognition results became wrong. We found even if W is selected to an optimum value for the best first search, it is also inferior to any parallel search (refer to Fig.4).

Next, we investigated the effectiveness of parameters: β and γ. The simulation results for α=1, 2 are shown in Figs.4 and 5. In the case of these simulations [BRANCH=5], the best of β was 3~5. The larger the value of γ becomes, the better the recognition rate becomes and then it is saturated. On the other hand, the number of expanded nodes also becomes larger dramatically. Therefore, we must set the parameters α, β and γ according with the purpose of applications.

At least, we think that α should be larger than 2 in pattern understanding systems, although a best-first search has been often adopted in the first stage of speech understanding systems[12].

Table 4 Simulation result (DEPTH=5, BRANCH=5, WEIGHT=-4)

α	β	γ	number of expanded nodes	rank of recognition result										
				1	2	3	4	5	6	7	8	9	10	11~
1	1	1	25	23	11	5	2	6	6	0	3	3	0	41
2	2	2	45	52	12	4	7	2	2	4	3	2	1	11
3	3	3	65	71	9	9	5	2	0	1	2	0	0	1
4	4	4	85	78	12	5	2	0	0	1	1	0	0	1
5	5	5	105	82	13	3	1	0	0	0	0	0	0	1
1	5	10	86	70	14	7	2	2	1	1	0	0	0	3
2	5	10	93	76	16	5	2	1	0	0	0	0	0	0
3	5	12	113	83	12	4	1	0	0	0	0	0	0	0
5	5	15	145	85	12	3	0	0	0	0	0	0	0	0

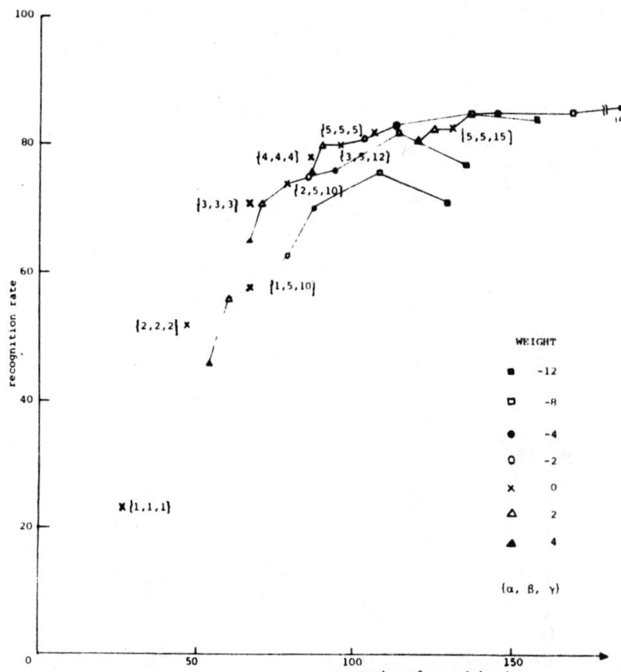

Fig.3 Relationship between recognition rate and number of expanded nodes. (DEPTH=5, BRANCH=5)

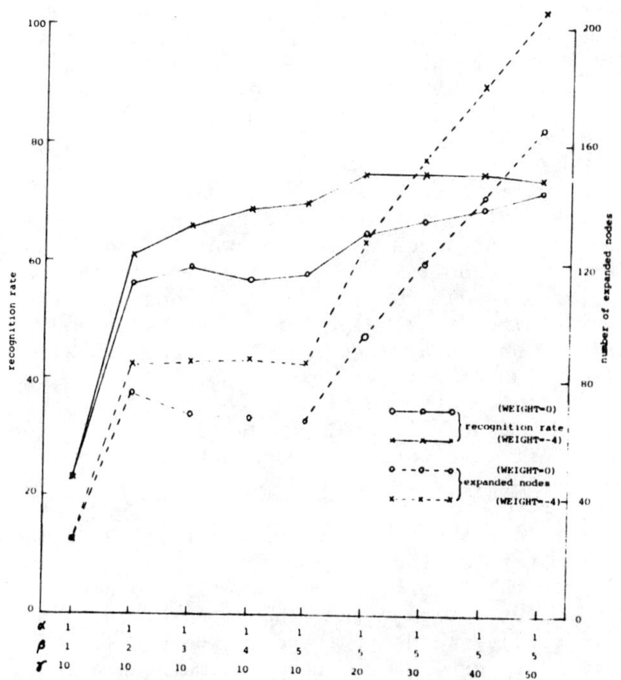

Fig.4 Relationship between recognition rate and number of expanded nodes. (α=1, DEPTH=5, BRANCH=5)

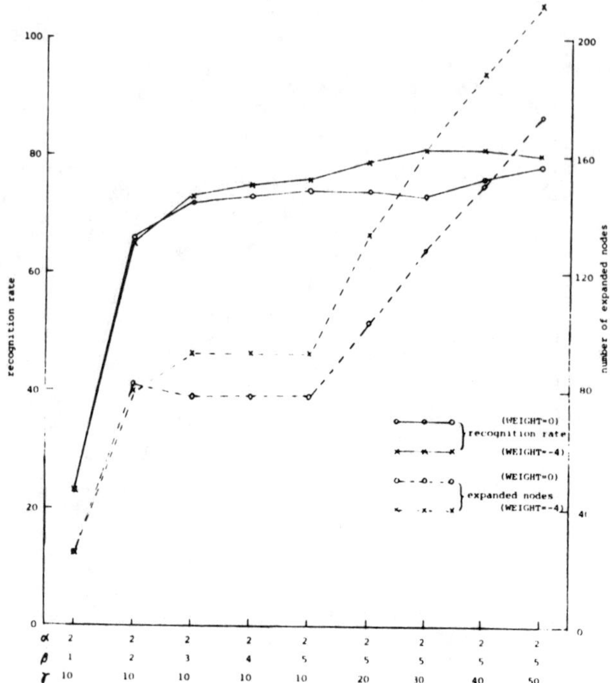

Fig.5 Relationship between recognition rate and number of expanded nodes. (α=2, DEPTH=5, BRANCH=5)

5. SPEECH RECOGNITION OF 'ARITHMETIC EXPRESSION'

We applied our tree search method to the speech recognition of 'Arithmetic Expression' as an example in a real world field[1,2]. In this task, the vocabulary size is 23, where each word has an average of 2.1 syllables. For example, this task accepts the sentence such as '1.2×(345 -6789.0)='.

The experiments of speech recognition of arithmetic expressions were tested on a total of 80 utterances containing 560 words, spoken by five male adults at a normal speed (these were uttered in Japanese). The reference patterns were common to all speakers. The DEPTH and BRANCH on the average were 7 and 10, respectively. The value of β is always pre-set at 5, because if a word really uttered belongs to one of predicted words probably it will be identified as one of the best five words (or candidates). The value of δ was set at 2.

The relationship between recognition rates and parameters of the tree search is shown in Table 5. In this table, the search time column indicates for each case the ratio of the number of verified words to the case where α=1, β=1 and γ=1. The results are in approximate agreement with simulation on the relative merits for nine search methods. However, the care is necessary to compare it with simulations, because the paths with highest scores in trees of these experiments are not always correct. From these results, we can also conclude that the best-few search (or parallel search) is superior to the best-first search.

Table 5 Recognition results of 'Arithmetic Expression'.

α	β	γ	search time	recognition rate word	recognition rate sentence	notes
1	1	1	1.0	80.1%	31.0%	no back tracking
2	2	2	2.0	88.4	47.0	〃
3	3	3	3.0	92.1	56.0	〃
4	4	4	4.0	93.1	58.0	〃
5	5	5	5.0	93.5	60.0	〃
6	5	6	6.0	93.8	61.0	〃
1	5	10	1.9	90.3	52.0	(nearly) best-first search
2	5	10	2.6	91.9	58.0	
3	5	12	3.3	93.2	60.0	
5	5	15	5.1	93.6	62.0	(rough) breadth-first search

6. CONCLUSION

We proposed a new tree search method which is suitable for the recognition of perceptual input. This is a parallel tree search method with backtracking implicitely. We evaluated this method by computer simulations and experiments of speech recognition. From these results, we found that the parallel search was superior to the best first search. By taking a weighting function into consideration, we would control the recognition rate and search space size. Further, we found that the larger the tree becomes, the more the performance of parallel search becomes effective.

ACKNOWLEDGEMENT

The authors would like to thank Mr. K. Goto for his co-operative help in computer simulations.

References

[1] T.Sakai and S.Nakagawa: Proceedings of the 3rd IJCPR, p.621 (1976).
[2] T.Sakai and S.Nakagawa: IECEJ Trans. Vol.E-60, No.1, p.13 (1977).
[3] S.Nakagawa and T.Sakai: Conference Record of 1978-ICASSP, p.726 (1978).
[4] S.Nakagawa and T.Sakai: Joint Meeting of ASA and ASJ,JASJ, Vol.64s, No.1 (1978).
[5] W.A.Woods: Proccedings of the 5-th IJCAI, p.18 (1977).
[6] F.Hayes-Roth and V.R.Lesser: Proceedings of the 5-th IJCAI, p.27 (1977).
[7] Y.Niimi and Y.Kobayashi: Conference Record of 1978-ICASSP, p.425 (1978).
[8] N.J.Nilsson: Problem-Solving Methods in Artifitial Intelligence (1971).
[9] P.H.Winston: Artifitial Intelligence (1977).
[10] B.T.Lowerre: Ph.D. Thesis, Carnegie Mellon University (1976).
[11] R.G.Goodman: Ph.D. Thesis, Stanford University (1976).
[12] W.H.Paxton: IEEE Trans. Vol.ASSP-23, No.5, p.426 (1975).

MUSIC INFORMATION PROCESSING SYSTEM AND ITS APPLICATIONS TO COMPARATIVE MUSICOLOGY

Yasuaki Nakamura and Seiji Inokuchi
Department of Control Engineering
Faculty of Engineering Science
Osaka University
Toyonaka, Osaka, Japan

In the application of digital data processing techniques to comparative musicology, it is an interesting subject to determine the type of scale in folk music and to compare the similarities in melody and rhythm between different musics. This paper describes two subjects: data entry technique for the realization of a music database and its application to comparative musicology. The former deals with dictation of melody sound. The latter concerns a method to find what scale is included in the melody, using knowledge in the modern ethno-musicology, and describes a certain measure of similarity of music.

1. INTRODUCTION

Digital data processing techniques gave the ethno-musicologists a large capacity of data processing ability never before obtainable [1]. This paper deals with data entry method for realization of a music database and its applications to comparative musicology.

It is difficult to compare the music information by listening to the melody or by watching the note. It is troublesome, still more, to search what scale is included in the melody and to detect the similarity between two different melodies.

Figure 1 shows the music information processing system which has been developed for this reseach. Musical information is expressed by two types of pattern: one is audible pattern -sound - and another is visible pattern -music note-. Though it has analogy with the language, which has speech pattern and character, it is difficult to dictate the sound of melody and to read the music note. This system has two data entry functions: dictation of melody and recognition of music note. A synthesizer and a display are used for monitoring the music.

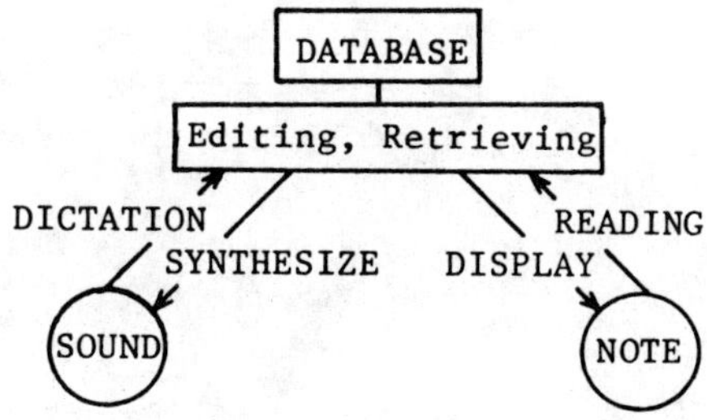

Fig.1 Music Information Processing System

2. DATA ENTRY AND DATABASE

2.1 Melody Analyser

In the early period, punched card or tape was used for comparative musicology [1]. In Japan there are a large number of folk musics which have never been collected before. So we have developed a melody analyser, which detects the pitch and the length of tone, for dictating folk music.

Pitch interval can be identified by detecting the fundamental frequency of sound. But the frequency difference ratio between the adjacent tones (semi-tone) is very small ($2^{1/12}$=0.059) and the duration of one tone may be very short, which requires that the measurement of the fundamental frequency should be done accurately during a short period [2].

As it is only fundamental frequency to be detected for pitch identification, a band-pass filter of Butterworth type ranging from 131 Hz (name of pitch: C_2) to 1047 Hz(C_5) is used. Sound signal is sampled with the relatively low sampling rate (6kHz).

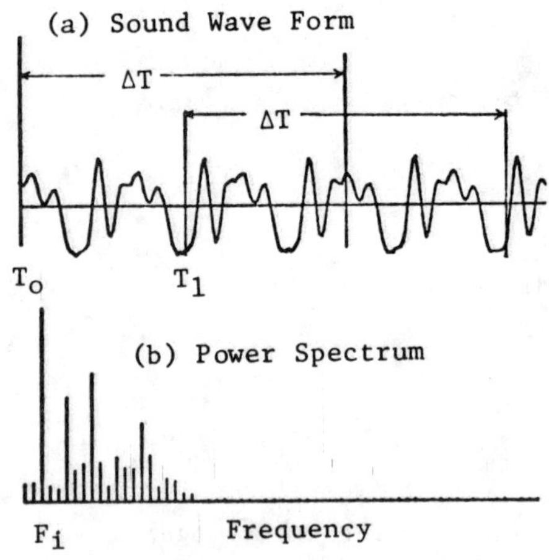

Fig.2 Frequency Analysis

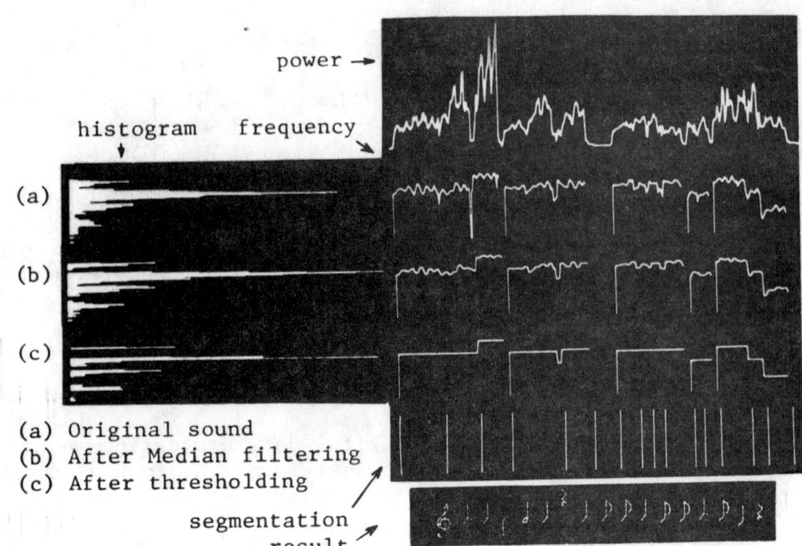

Fig.3 Dictation of Melody sound

For the identification of pitch, we transform the sound signal (a) in Fig.2 from T_o to $T_o+\Delta T$ into the power spectrum (b) using the FFT algorithm. In the discrete frequency analysis, the frequency difference ΔF between adjacent spectra, which is the inverse of data length ΔT, is too large. In order to obtain the accurate frequency F_p, we compensate spectral peak frequency F_i with the phase change as follows:

$$F_p = F_i + \left(\frac{\Theta_1-\Theta_o}{2\pi(T_1-T_o)}\right)$$

where Θ_1 and Θ_o are phases of F_i in the interval $[T_1,T_1+\Delta T]$ and $[T_o,T_o+\Delta T]$, respectively. Pitch P is expressed as follows:

$$P = 12\cdot\log_2(F_p/F_r)$$

where F_r is reference frequency.

The pitch obtained above has unstable frequency at the transition of tone. As the pitch of melody changes stepwise, a median filter gives good results rather than a moving averaging filter.

In case of vocal sound, F_p may vary over the range of semi-tone during the same tone because of the vibrato and the pitch scale may shift little by little for lack of absolute pitch. For the correction of them, the thresholding with hysteresis is carried out and the pitch is identified as the accumulation of the quantized pitch difference between the adjacent tones.

The segmentation is done at the time when one of the following conditions is satisfied: (1) Pitch changes stepwise, (2) Correlation of spectra between adjacent intervals becomes smaller than the predetermined value and (3) Power increases abruptly. Segmented length is quantized by using its histogram partition. Figure 3 shows an example of dictation of a Japanese nursery song.

2.2 Music Database

Music data are encoded into a three-number code as shown in Fig.4. The m, n and l represent pitch name in octave, octave position and note length, respectively. The m and n are obtained as:

$$m = \mathrm{Mod}_{12}[P] \quad \text{and} \quad n = [P/12]$$

Notation of the music note is not unique but the pitch code in database described above is unique [3].

Music data can be entered into the database not only by the melody analyser but also by an optical note reader or a data tablet.

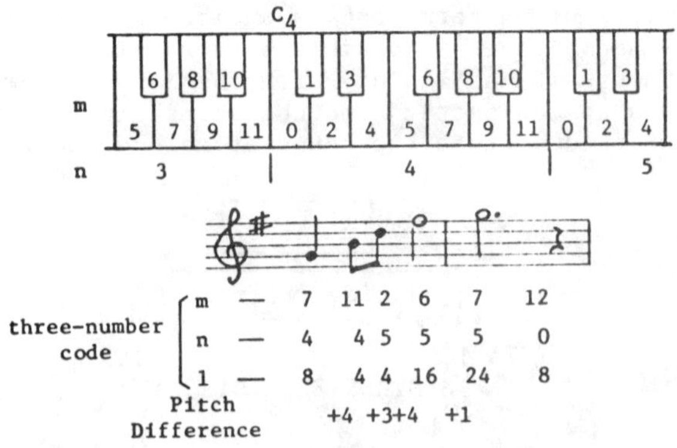

Fig.4 Data Format

3. APPLICATIONS TO COMPARATIVE MUSICOLOGY

3.1 Determination of Scale Type

In the past, the scale of Japanese folk music was classified into Ritsu, Ryo, Yo and In scales, as the European music is classified into major scale and minor one. These scales, named after their origin, were partially illogical. In the modern Japanese ethno-musicology, Koizumi[4] claims that Japanese folk music should be categorized into Minyo, Miyakobushi, Ritsu and Ryukyu scales as shown in Fig.5, where they are shown in the form of pitch difference sequence. And he also proposed that the type of scale should be determined by the type of tetrachord included in melody and the position of nuclear notes.

(1) Minyo scale	+3 +2 +2 +3 +2
(2) Miyakobushi scale	+1 +4 +2 +1 +4
(3) Ritsu scale	+2 +3 +2 +2 +3
(4) Ryukyu scale	+4 +1 +2 +4 +1

Fig.5 Scale Type of Japanese Folk Music (Underlines indicate Tetrachord)

Tetrachords are the fundamental units to compose a scale and a melody, as structured with two Tetrachords conjuncted.

Nuclear notes, which mean the important notes of melody, have the following features:
(i) Basic note of tetrachord, (ii) Median note of three adjacent notes, (iii) Very often final tone of melody and (iv) Upper note in two-tone melody.

This knowledge makes it possible to categorize the type of scale by [1] Finding tetrachord and making its histogram and [2] Finding nuclear note and scoring it.

3.2 Similarity of Melody

The melody may be considered as a finite Markov chain process, in which the state k_i is the pitch note in scale. The pitch transition probability p_{ij}, the conditional probability that the pitch k_i is followed by k_j, has the feature of the melody.

$$\mathbb{P} = \begin{array}{c} \\ k_1 \\ k_2 \\ \vdots \\ k_n \end{array} \begin{array}{c} \begin{array}{cccc} k_1 & k_2 & \cdots & k_n \end{array} \\ \begin{pmatrix} p_{11}, & p_{12}, & & p_{1n} \\ p_{21}, & p_{22}, & & p_{2n} \\ \vdots & & & \\ p_{n1}, & p_{n2}, & & p_{nn} \end{pmatrix} \end{array}$$

The weight of pitch note in scale can be expressed by its steady state probability $\mathbf{W}$, which can be solved by the following equations.

$$\mathbf{W} = \mathbf{W} \cdot \mathbb{P} \quad \text{and} \quad \sum_{i=1}^{n} w_i = 1$$

The weight of pitch is effective to express the similarity between different melodies belonging to the same scale class.

3.3 Complexity of Rhythm and Melody

Let's assume the rhythm ratio R_i as:

$$R_i = \log_2(l_i/l_{i+1}) = \log_2(l_i) - \log_2(l_{i+1})$$

Its standard deviation σ_R indicates the complexity of rhythm.

$$\sigma_R = (1/n-1) \sqrt{\sum_{i=1}^{n} R_i^2}$$

The root mean square of pitch difference in melody can indicate the complexity of melody:

$$d_m = \sqrt{(1/n) \sum_{i=1}^{n} (P_i - P_{i+1})^2}$$

where P_i is the pitch of note (m + nx12).

On (σ_R, d_m) plane, horizontal and vertical axes indicate the complexity of rhythm and melody, respectively.

4. CONCLUSION

A method for dictating music sound was proposed for the realization of a music database. Regarding the applications of a Japanese folk music database, this paper described an algorithm for determining the type of scale using the knowledge about the modern ethno-musicology. And some measures of similarity in melody and rhythm were proposed for the comparison of folk music.

REFERENCES

[1] W.H. Davidow Ed. "Music by Computer", from 1966-FJCC.

[2] H.B. Lincoln Ed. "The Computer and Music", Cornell University Press, 1970.

[3] H.C. Longuet Higgins, "On Interpreting Bach" Machine Intelligence 6, Edinburgh, 1971.

[4] F. Koizumi, "Research on Japanese Traditional Music", Ongaku-no-Tomo Sha,(in Japanese)

AN AUTOMATIC THEOREM PROVER
GENERATING A PROOF IN NATURAL LANGUAGE

Masakazu Nakanishi, Morio Nagata and Kenji Ueda
Faculty of Engineering, KEIO University
Hiyoshi, Yokohama, 223 JAPAN

An automatic theorem prover which displays a proof in natural language is described. This system proves properties of recursive programs, and constructs a proof tree corresponding to the proof. Then it translates the tree into the proof text in English by means of the tree traverse. The proof written by this system is easy to read, because the English text is placed instead of notations of logics, and some redundant and trivial statements are disappeared.

1. INTRODUCTION

Many automatic theorem provers have been implemented to verify programs or to prove properties of programs [2,5]. Some of them are based on a formal system in logics. However, users of such theorem provers are often confused by technical terms of logics appeared in the proof. And so it is desired that the system should display the proof in natural language without proper terms of logics. Chester [1] gives an algorithm which translates formal proofs into English. But we rarely find the systems which have such facilities. An algorithm to generate statements which are suitable to the context of a proof for a Gentzen-type formal system representing properties of functions is described.

TKP (Tsukuba-Keio Prover) is a family of theorem provers based on the formal system. As an ordinary prover, it combines a sequent calculus (decomposing a complicated theorem into parts which are easier to prove). The sequent is decomposed by applying the rules of inference. TKP displays a proof figure if the proof of a given theorem is completed. The proof figure consists of logical symbols and terms which are used properly in logics. Though these terms are important tools to prove theorems automatically, they are regarded as codes which only logicians or experts in artificial intelligence can read.

In this paper, we describe the method for displaying proofs in natural language without proper terms of logics.

2. OUTLINE OF TKP

The original version, TKP1 [4], proves properties of recursive programs and generates the <u>proof figures</u>. TKP2, described in this paper, generates effective proofs in <u>natural language</u> furthermore. The formal system of TKP includes the propositional calculus of Gentzen's LK and additional rules to prove properties of recursive programs. Its completeness is shown by T. Nishimura [3].

Our processor accepts a sequent to be proved and user supplied knowledge, then it generates a tree of the proof of the given problem.

<u>Def</u>: A sequent is called a <u>node</u>.

<u>Def</u>: If A is a sequent decomposed from B by applying a rule, the name of the rule is the <u>indicator</u> from B to A.

<u>Def</u>: A <u>proof tree</u> is defined as follows.

1. A node is a proof tree.
2. If m is a sequent, t1,t2,...,tn are proof trees and i1,i2,...,in are indicators from m to t1,t2,...,tn respectively, then

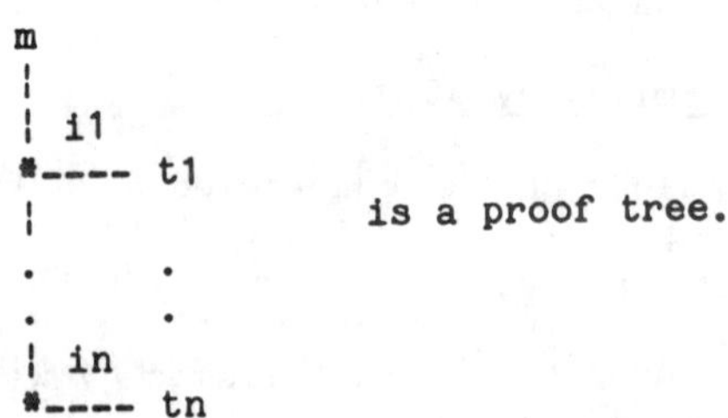

3. The only proof trees are those given by 1 and 2.

If TKP proves the given problem, the proof tree will be generated (see APPENDIX in [4]). The later passes (<u>analysis</u>, <u>reduction</u>, <u>generation</u>), converts it into an English text.

3. ANALYSIS AND REDUCTION

In analysis, each proposition, called a P-type formula, is valuated and formulas of each node are simplified, and an analyzed tree is generated.

Def: An environment is a list of pairs of a P-type formula and the truth value. The initial state of the environment is empty.

The algorithm of analysis is as follows:

Traverse the given proof tree from its root.
When a sequent S including the P-type formula p which does not occur in the environment, split the tree T whose root is S. Analyze T recursively in the new environment which is appended the pair of p and true to the environment E. Next, analyze T in the environment which is appended the pair of p and false to E. Construct a new tree T' whose root is S simplified in E and, whose subtrees are the above two analyzed trees (Fig. 1).

```
T  :  S                 T' :  S (simplified in E)
      |                       |
      | i                     | p.t
      *---- o                 *----  S (simplified in (p.true)+E)
            |                 |      |
            .      =>         |      | i
                              |      *---- o
                              |            |
                              |            .
                              | p,f
                              *----  S (simplified in (p.false)+E)
                                     |
                                     | i
                                     *---- o
                                           |
                                           .
```

Fig. 1 Analysis (1)

When a sequent S including P-type formulas which occur in the environment is encountered, simplify S (the rules of simplification is in Fig. 3). However, if S is transformed from S1 by the user supplied knowledge or the induction hypothesis, and P-type formulas occur in S by the replacement, simplify S except the formula replaced. The new node is named S'. Next, analyze the tree whose root is S, append the indicator VAL and the analyzed tree to S' (Fig. 2).

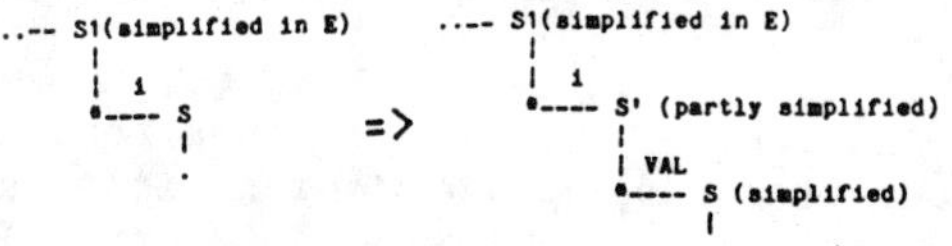

Fig. 2 Analysis (2)

In reduction, the analyzed tree is reduced and a final tree is recomposed by removing redundant nodes or subtrees from the analyzed tree.

The algorithm of reduction is as follows:

Traverse the analyzed tree.
If a node is identical to its son, remove the node together with the branch.
If a node satisfies either (I) or (II), remove the subtree connected with the node.
(I) The node becomes a logical axiom.
(II) $\Gamma \rightarrow \Delta$ is already proved and
The node is $\Gamma \rightarrow \Delta 1, \Delta, \Delta 2$

1: P-type formulas are replaced by their truth value, if exist in the environment.

2: Formulas and sequents

a) A&t, t&A, fvA, Avf ==> A
b) A&f , f&A , \t ==> f
c) Avt , tvA , \f ==> t
d) Γ1,t,Γ2 -> Δ ==> Γ1,Γ2 -> Δ
e) Γ -> Δ1,f,Δ2 ==> Γ -> Δ1,Δ2

Fig. 3 Rules of simplification

4. GENERATION OF A PROOF TEXT

Finally, the proof text in English is generated. A skeleton of the proof text is prepared for each type of tree. A skeleton is a rule of conversion of a tree to strings of characters. A typical skeleton is shown in Fig. 5. Traversing the reduced proof tree, a proof text is constructed by applying the skeletons.

In principle, a tree is traversed from root to leaf. A tree free from branch, however, is traversed from leaf to root (Fig. 4).

APPENDIX II is generated from the final proof tree in APPENDIX I which is the reduced proof tree of the proof shown in [4].

```
 s1
1|| 2
 v| -->
  *---- s2
 3|| 4
  v| -->
   *---- s3
     5|| 6
      v| -->
       *---- s4
       |  ^| 7
       || 8|| <--
      9||   *---- s5
       v| 10
       | -->
       *---- s6
          ^| 13
        14|| <--
           *---- s8
              ^| 11
            12|| <--
               *---- s7
```

Fig. 4 Tree traverse

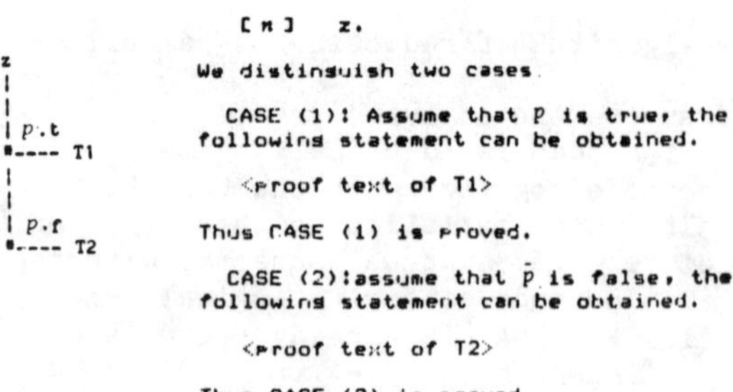

Fig. 5 An example of skeleton

5. CONCLUSION

Our system is implemented in about 1000 lines of Lisp program. In actual program, analysis, reduction and generation are executed at the same time. These are implemented in about 600 lines. Our algorithm, except for the last pass, is independent of languages, then TKP2 can write in other language by changing the skeletons of the statements.

The proof written by this prover is very easy to read, because the English sentences are placed instead of the logical symbols, and some redundant or trivial statements are disappeared. We believe that this system will be used as a training tool of program verification.

ACKNOWLEDGEMENT

We would like to thank Prof. Toshio Nishimura for several very helpful comments.

APPENDIX I

```
F<?>(K) -> G<?>(K,1)
 |L-v
 *--F<0>(K) -> G<?>(K,1)
 |L-v
 *--F<N+1>(K) -> G<?>(K,1)
     |R-v
     *--F<N+1>(K) -> G<N+1>(K,1)
         |D-1
         *--P(K)&1 v \P(K)&KxF<N>(K-1) -> G<N+1>(k,1)
             |P.t
             *--1 -> G<N+1>(K,1)
             |   |D-2
             |   *--1 -> P(K)&1 v \P(K)&G<N>(K-1,Kx1)
             |       |VAL
             |       *--1 -> 1
             |P.f
             *--KxF<N>(K-1) -> G<N+1>(K,1)
                 |HYP
                 *--KxG<N>(K-1,1) -> G<N+1>(K,1)
                     |D-2
                     *--KxG<N>(K-1,1) -> P(K)&1 v \P(K)&G<N>(K-1,Kx1)
                         |VAL
                         *--KxG<N>(K-1,1) -> G<N>(K-1,Kx1)
                             |T-1
                             *--G<N>(K-1,Kx1) -> G<N>(K-1,Kx1)
```

APPENDIX II

```
Prove that
        if  a = F<?>(K)  then  a = G<?>(K,1)
where
        1.  F<N+1>(X) = P(X)&1 v \P(X)&XxF<N>(X-1)
        2.  G<N+1>(X,Y) = P(X)&Y v \P(X)&G<N>(X-1,XxY)
using the theorem
        1.  if  a = XxG<N>(Y,Z)  then  a = G<N>(Y,XxZ)

PROOF
 [1]    if  a = F<?>(k)  then  a = G<?>(K,1)
will be proved by induction on N.
BASIS, for N = 0,
 [2]    if  a = F<0>(K)  then  a = G<?>(K,1).
This is valid, because F<0>(K) is undefined.
INDUCTION STEP.  Assume (as the indution-hypothesis)
that for every L < N+1,
        if  a = F<L>(K)  then  a = G<L>(K,1).
Now let's prove
 [3]    if  a = F<N+1>(K)  then  a = G<?>(K,1).
It is sufficient to prove that
 [4]    if  a = F<N+1>(K)  then  a = G<N+1>(K,1).
By definition 1, [4] is equivalent to
 [5]    if  a = P(K)&1 v \P(K)&KxF<N>(K-1)
                then  a = G<N+1>(K,1).
We distinguish two cases.
  CASE (1): Assume that P(K) is true.  The following
statement can be obtained.
 [6]    if  a = 1  then  a = G<N+1>(K,1).
Now, consider the following valid statement.
 [7]    if  a = 1  then  a = 1.
Since P(K) is true, [7] may be written as follows:
 [8]    if  a = 1  then  a = P(K)&1 v \P(K)&G<N>(K-1,Kx1).
By definition 2,
 [9]    if  a = 1  then  a = G<N+1>(K,1).
Thus CASE (1) is proved.
  CASE (2): Assume that P(K) is false.  The following
statement can be obtained.
 [10]    if  a = KxF<N>(K-1)  then  a = G<N+1>(K,1)
Now, consider the following valid statement.
 [11]    if  a = G<N>(K-1,Kx1)  then  a = G<N>(K-1,Kx1)
Since P(K) is false, [11] may be written as follows:
 [12]    if  a = G<N>(K-1,Kx1)
                then  a = P(K)&1 v \P(K)&G<N>(K-1,Kx1)
By definition 2,
 [13]    if  a = G<N>(K-1,Kx1)  then  a = G<N+1>(K,1)
By theorem 1,
 [14]    if  a = KxG<N>(K-1,1)  then  a = G<N+1>(K,1).
By the induction-hypothesis,
 [15]    if  a = KxF<N>(K-1)  then  a = G<N+1>(K,1).
Thus CASE (2) is proved.
This completes the proof.
```

REFERENCES

[1] Chester, D. "The translation of formal proofs into English." Artif. Intell. 7:3 (1976) 261-278.

[2] King, J.C. "A program verifier." PhD thesis, Carnegie-Mellon Univ., 1969.

[3] Nishimura, T. "Gentzen-type formal system representing properties of functions." Comment. Math. Univ. St. Pauli. 23:1 (1974) 37-44.

[4] Nishimura, T., Nakanishi, M., Nagata, M. and Iwamaru, Y. "Gentzen-type formal system representing properties of functions and its implementation." In Proc. IJCAI-75. Tbilisi, Sep., 1975, pp. 57-64.

[5] Suzuki, N. "Verifying programs by algebraic and logical reduction." In Proc. of Int. Conf. Reliable Software. 1975, pp. 473-481.

LINEAR FEATURE EXTRACTION AND DESCRIPTION

Ramakant Nevatia
Computer Science Department and
Image Processing Institute
University of Southern California
Los Angeles, California 90007

K. Ramesh Babu
Computer Science Department and
Image Processing Institute
University of Southern California
Los Angeles, California 90007

Abstract

A technique of edge detection and linking for linear feature extraction and its applications to detection of roads and runway like structures is described. Experimental results are included.

1. INTRODUCTION

The importance of effective early processing of visual input for a complete image understanding system is generally accepted. The early processing may consist of a description of image discontinuities, usually in the form of edges and lines, or segmentation into uniform regions. In this paper, we describe a technique for extracting linear features in an image by a process of edge detection and line linking and also of deriving higher level descriptions from the extracted lines. These techniques are aimed to be general. Applications to road detection and airport recognition tasks are described.

Edge detection and line finding techniques, of course, have been studied since the early days of this field. The literature is too numerous to list here; partial surveys may be found in [1-3]. In spite of the large amount of previous research in this area, no algorithms suitable for complex imagery are apparent. Here, we describe an edge detection and line finding technique with superior performance on a wide variety of images. Many of the steps in our process have been suggested by other researchers previously. However, due to limitations of space, we are unable to elaborate on these in this paper. More details may be found in [4].

2. EDGE DETECTION AND LINE FINDING

Convolution with Edge Masks

Edge detection starts by convolving a given image with masks corresponding to ideal step edges in a selected number of directions. The magnitude of the convolved output and the direction of the mask giving the highest output at each pixel are recorded as edge data. We have found 5 x 5 masks in six directions to be suitable for most images of interest.

This research was supported by the Defense Advanced Research Projects Agency of the Department of Defense under contract NO. F-33615-76-C-1203. Dr. Keith Price has been extremely helpful in many discussions and providing image manipulation software.

Thinning and Thresholding

The presence of an edge at a pixel is decided by comparing the edge data with some of the 8 neighboring pixels. An edge elements is said to be present at a pixel if:

1. the output edge magnitude at the pixel is larger than the edge magnitudes of its two neighbours in a direction normal to the direction of this edge. (The normal to a 30 degree edge is approximated by the diagonals on a 3 x 3 grid);
2. the edge directions of the two neighboring pixels are within one unit (30 degrees) of that of the central pixel; and
3. the edge magnitude of the central pixel exceeds a fixed threshold.

Further, if the conditions 1 and 2 above are satisfied, the two neighboring pixels are disqualified from being candidates for edges. This algorithm produces results independent of the order in which the pixels are examined.

Linking

The first step in boundary tracing is to determine the continuing neighbors on the boundary for each edge point. Typically each point has two neighbors, known as a predecessor and a successor, except for the end-points, isolated points and where two boundary segments join or intersect. This connectivity information is stored in two files, called p and s files, of the same size as the input image. Each element in these files contains an integer corresponding to the proceeding (or succeeding) edge among the 8 neighbors. Forks are indicated by an extra bit as explained later.

Our criteria for connecting two edge points is that they be neighbors, in the 8-neighbor sense, and that they have edge directions differing by not more than a certain value, set at 30 degrees for masks described previously. Due to the nature of thinning, only three locations are potential candidates for predecessor or successor elements as shown in Figs. 1(a) and (b) for edges of 0 and 30 degree directions respectively. The determination of successor (predecessor) pixels is elaborate due to the several cases that are possible at each pixel:

1. Only one element is an acceptable successor. In this case the successor (predecessor) is recorded in the s(p) file as an integer corresponding to its location.
2. Two candidates are acceptable successors. If they are not 4-neighbors, a fork is present as shown in Fig. 2(a). If they are 4-neighbors, a fork exists only if their directions differ by more than 2 units (60 degrees), as in Fig. 2(b). Otherwise no fork exists and the nearer of the two (using Euclidean distance), forms the successor (predecessor), as shown in Fig. 2(c). These rules are for smooth continuation of lines and were derived by complete enumeration of such configurations. In case of a fork, the stronger of the two candidates in edge magnitude forms the main stream. The fact that a fork exists is noted in the s(p) file by marking one bit. This information is sufficient to trace both streams of a fork by examining the p and s files simultaneously.
3. Three candidates are acceptable successors. Fig. 3 shows all possible such configurations for a vertical edge (no three successor configurations occur for 30 degree edges). In these cases, a fork exists. The main stream is formed by the nearer of the two edges having the same direction, and the other candidate with different direction froms the other branch.

The predecessor-successor representation of the linked edge elements is in contrast to explicit lists of elements forming a connected segment. For larger images, not entirely resident in core, it is more convenient to form predecessor and successor matrices first, as the processing requires only a sequential scan of the image file. Further, this representation is "iconic" and certain proximity computations can be made more easily.

Tracing Boundary Segments

Boundary segments containing ordered lists of edge elements are computed from the predecessor-successor (p-s) files. An edge point with no predecessors determines the starting point. A boundary segment is traced by following the successor elements until an element with no successors is reached. At a point with multiple successors, the "main" fork is chosen. The secondary branches of forks are picked up on a second pass that starts tracing at such points. A third pass is required to trace circular or closed segments. This pass begins arbitrarily at an edge point that has not been thus far visited, i.e. included in a segment. (A temporary binary file is used to store this information).

Linear Approximation

Each boundary segment is approximated by a series of piecewise linear segments. The algorithm used is a variation of the well known iterative end-point fit algorithm (see [5] pp. 338-339). Results of processing an airport image are shown in Figure 4.

3. OBJECT DESCRIPTION

A major goal of this research is to compute descriptions of objects useful for their recognition. Certain classes of objects, such as roads and airport runways, are characterized as being bounded by elongated parallel lines. These lines have opposite contrasts and we call them "anti-parallel" lines, abbreviated as "apars". These apars are conveniently described by a medial line and width of the pair. These descriptions were motivated as being two-dimensional special cases of Binford's "Generalized Cone" representation [6]. Finding apars in facilited by sorting line segments by their orientations.

Proper choice of apars that correspond to objects can be difficult and is like resolving figure-ground relationships However for many applications, such as for roads and runway detection, a choice of the closest pairs may suffice and be aided by knowledge of the desired objects being brighter or darker than the background.

Fig. 4(c) shows the axes of the apars computed from the segments in fig. 4(b). Only the closest pairs were retained. Work is in progress to recognize specific airports from the spatial relationships of the partial axes of the runways and taxiways as shown here.

REFERENCES

[1] A. Rosenfeld and A. Kak, Digital Picture Processing, Academic Press, 1976.
[2] W.K. Pratt, Digital Image Processing, John Wiley & Sons, 1978.
[3] L.S. Davis, "A Survey of Edge Detection

Techniques", Computer Graphics and Image Processing, Vol. 4, NO. 3, pp. 248-270, Sept. 1975.
[4] R.Nevatia and K.R. Babu, "Linear Feature Extraction," in USCIPI Report 840, Oct. 1978.
[5] R.O. Duda and P.E. Hart, Pattern Classification and Scene Analysis, Wiley, 1973.
[6] T.O. Binford, "Visual Perception by a Computer," IEEE Conf. on Systems and Controls, Miami, Dec. 1971.

a) 0° Edge b) 30° Edge

Fig. 1. Possible Successor Locations for Two Edges.

a) Non-neighboring Successors b) Successors Directions Differ by 60° c) Successors of Same Direction

Fig. 2. Three Instances of Two Successors.

a) b)

Fig. 3. All Instances of Three Successors.

a) Image b) Linear Segments c) Anti-Parallel Axes

Fig. 4. Processing of an Airport Image.

DESCRIBING NATURAL TEXTURES

Ram Nevatia, Keith Price, Felicia Vilnrotter
Image Processing Institute
University of Southern California
University Park
Los Angeles, California 90007

ABSTRACT

There have been many different approaches to texture description, primarily statistical techniques although there has been some work on structural texture analysis all along. We present here a technique which can be used to easily derive parts of the structural description - the regularity information in particular. Some limits on this method and its use in an overall texture description system are discussed.

1. INTRODUCTION

Areas of an image may be better characterized by their textures rather than by pure intensity information. Texture is the pattern of the spatial arrangement of different intensities. The different textures in an image are usually very apparent to a human observer, but automatic description of these patterns has been difficult. We wish to describe the texture in the same terms as a human observer, rather than by a purely statistical method.

Many statistical textural measures have been proposed and studied in the past [1-4], including analysis of the discrete Fourier transform [4], analysis of generalized gray-level co-occurence matrices [1], and analysis of the micro-edges in a subwindow [3]. We are not interested in finding one texture measure which will distinguish between all areas, but in finding a texture description to use in conjunction with many other features [9].

The work in structural texture description has been more limited. Maleson [5] used simple regions as the basic elements and used relations between regions and shape properties in his analysis. Tamura et al. [6] developed a set of operators to rate textures on several scales, comparable to their ratings by human subjects. The proposals of Marr [7] for texture analysis based on the primal sketch are similar to some of the analysis which we perform.

---

*This research was supported by the Defense Advanced Research Projects Agency and was monitored by the Wright Patterson Air Force Base under Contract F-33615-76-C-1203, ARPA Order No. 3119.

2. ANALYSIS OF TEXTURE

We have chosen to first explore the description of regular patterns (e.g. street patterns of certain cities shown in the top of Fig. 1). Other attempts to derive much of the structural information from the Fourier transform were only partially successful [4], so we felt other methods should be attempted. The individual textural elements could be located and analyzed [5], but the simple regions are unreliable when the textural elements are very small. Another option is to analyze an edge image to find the structure. The patterns in the original image will cause related patterns to appear in the edge image, which should be more consistent and easier to analyze than the original image data.

We are interested in the edges between adjacent textural elements and not so much in edges between adjacent textural patterns or extended regions. The edge operator has been applied to other types of analysis [8], and is applied over a 3 x 3 window to generate an edge magnitude and direction (1 of 8). Fig. 2 shows the edge output for the subwindows in Fig. 1.

The edge images retain the regularity of the initial image, but now the regularity is in the spacing of edges not texture elements. A Fourier transform applied to this binary edge image may indicate the repetitive nature of the edges, but is obscured by the degeneracies introduced by the binary nature of the input.

3. EDGE CO-OCCURRENCE ANALYSIS

Generalized gray level co-occurrence matrix analysis is a basis for much of the statistical texture analysis [1]. Basically a set of matrices are computed where the (I,J) entry of a matrix is the probability that a point with value J occurs at a given spacing and angle from a point with value I. Usually the image values are partitioned into a small set of values (8 rather than 256), so that it is even possible to compute the initial matrices. Also the computation is made for several spacings (1,2,3,8, etc.) and directions (0°, 45°, 90°, etc.). Because of the large number of matrices that are generated by this method, various measures are computed on the matrix values, and the classification is performed using these measures [1]. The common measures do not capture the important feature in the edge images: the regular spacing of edge elements. The measure we use is one that indicates the probability of edges occurring at two points at a certain distance and angle from each other, given that an edge occurs at one of the points.

There are several ways to determine if an edge occurs at two points, with different features indicated by the different comparison methods. Using all edges for every direction presents severe problems in the analysis of the output since long lines running in the same direction as the co-occurrence computation will be included along with lines running perpendicular to the direction. (Tamura et al. [6] used this feature to indicate linear patterns in their texture experiments.) The first limitation is to consider only those edge elements perpendicular to the direction of search, that is in the computation of co-occurrences in a horizontal direction, only vertical edges are considered. The variations on this basic restriction include: allow some freedom in the edge direction (45° either way), accept only perfect matches (up and up, down and down), and accept only opposites (up and down, not up and up).

4. DISCUSSION

None of this analysis would be worthwhile if it did not ease the task of describing regular textures. The highly regular patterns of the urban area (the top row of the image, and Fig. 3) and raffia (the bottom row and Fig. 4) produce strong periodic patterns in the plot of the co-occurrence measure. A high value in the graphed measure indicates that pairs of edges frequently occur at that particular spacing and angle.

The spacing of pairs of textural elements is given by the peak to peak spacing in the measure which matches edges only in the exact same direction (see Fig. 3). The size of individual elements is best given by the measure which allows edges in the opposite direction (see Fig. 4). The solid line in the graph indicates the size of dark objects and the dotted line the size bright objects. The size is from the first major peak, the succeeding peaks are caused by the repeated pattern. The patterns usually do not line up with one of the 4 directions, so there will be some response in 2 directions. When these directions are 45° apart the dominant direction is probably between them (urban, Fig. 3). But when they are 90° apart there should be a regular pattern in two directions (Raffia, Fig. 4). Thus, from the data we can say that the urban subwindow has a regular pattern of bright and dark regions oriented in one direction, near 45°, with the bright regions being larger (width about 10 pixels) than the dark ones (width about 4). Note that the size of the blocks in the other direction is near the size limit of the co-occurrence computation and also that few of the relevant edges are detected.

The irregular textural patterns (e.g.the suburban areas of the second row of Fig. 1, and the grass, sand, and wool of the third row,) do not produce the same clearly periodic patterns of raffia. But it is possible to derive certain useful features from the results, primarily that of the size of the textural elements.

This is not a complete description of the textures, but serves as a good initial description of the patterns. There are still other important features of the textures which are not derived by this method, but may be computed by other techniques. The simple edges are not intended to be the final elementary object in the texture description, others such as extended edges, lines and regions may be required for complete analysis. This procedure has been applied on many other less regular patterns with similar results [10].

5. CONCLUSIONS

General texture analysis is a very difficult problem, but this analysis of edge images appears to be an effective method to extract many important structural features from the textural patterns. One major unanswered question is whether or not all of the information derived by the human user can be reliably derived by a program. We are still working on the automatic extraction of this information from the data which is produced by this textural analysis method.

REFERENCES

[1] R.M. Haralick, K. Shanmugam, and I. Dinstein, "Textural Features for Image

Classification," IEEE Trans SMC-3, 1973, pp. 660-621.

[2] J. Weszka, A. Rosenfeld, "A Comparative Study of Texture Measures for Terrain Classification," IEEE Trans SMC-6, April 1970.

[3] A. Rosenfeld and Kak, Digital Picture Processing, Academic Press:New York, 1970.

[4] R. Bajcsy, "Computer Identification of Visual Surfaces," CGIP-2, Oct. 1973, pp. 118-130.

[5] J.T. Maleson, "Understanding Texture in Natural Images," University of Rochester, Ph.D. Thesis, to appear.

[6] H. Tamura, S. Mori, T. Yamawaki, "Textural Features Corresponding to Visual Perception," IEEE Trans SMC-8, June 1978, pp. 460-473.

[7] D. Marr, "Early Processing of Visual Information," AI-M-340, Artificial Intelligence Laboratory, MIT, Cambridge, MA, 1975.

[8] R. Nevatia, and K. R. Babu, "Linear Feature Extraction and Description," in proc. IJCAI-79, Tokyo, Japan, August 1979.

[9] R. Nevatia, and K. Price, "Locating Structures in Aerial Images," Proc. of 4th IJCPR, Kyoto, Japan, Nov. 1978, pp. 686-90.

[10] R. Nevatia, K. Price, and F. Vilnrotter, "Describing Natural Textures," USCIPI Report 860, USC, Los Angeles, CA, March 1979.

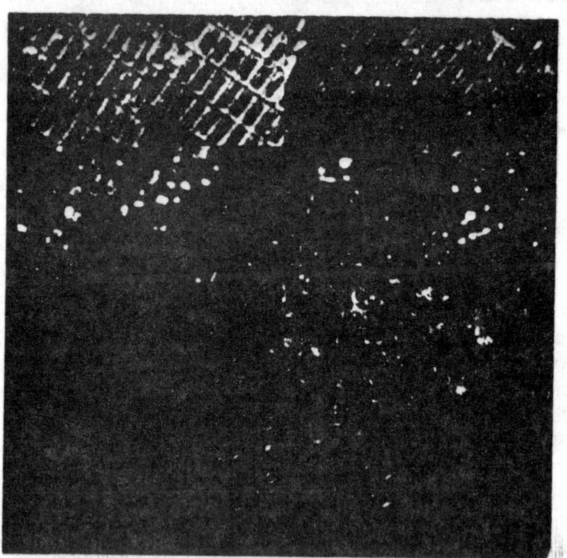

Fig. 1. 16 Subwindows for Texture Analysis.

Fig. 2. Edges from Fig. 4.

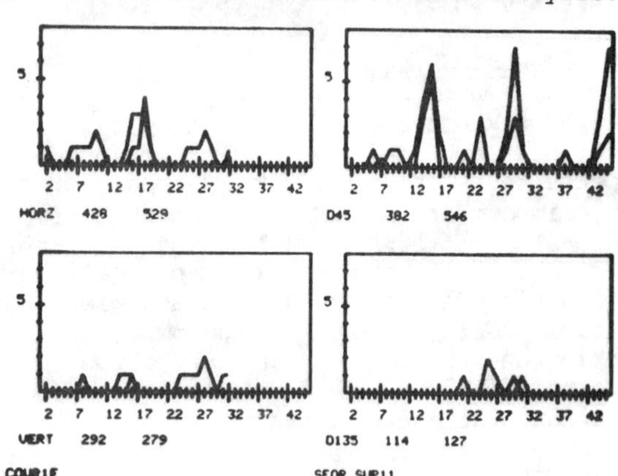

Fig. 3. Co-occurrence Results for San Francisco Exact Edge Direction Matches Only.

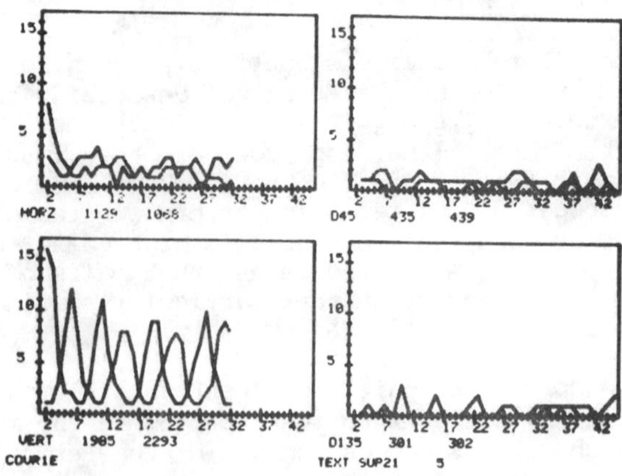

Fig. 4. Co-occurrence Results for Raffia Opposite Edge Direction Matches Only.

AGE (Attempt to Generalize): A Knowledge-Based Program for Building Knowledge-Based Programs

H. Penny Nii and Nelleke Aiello
Heuristic Programming Project, Computer Science Department
Stanford University, Stanford, Ca. 94305

The goal of the AGE project is to demystify and make explicit the *art of knowledge engineering*. It is an attempt to formulate the knowledge that knowledge engineers use in constructing knowledge-based programs and put it at the disposal of others in the form of a software laboratory. To achieve this goal, the task for AGE is divided into two main sub-tasks: (1) isolating techniques used in knowledge-based systems and programming those that are general and useful (2) building an intelligent agent to guide in the use of these techniques. Currently AGE has a facility to build programs using the Blackboard Model [8,13].

1. INTRODUCTION

This paper reports the goals and the current status of the AGE project.* Appendix I contains a protocol of a user solving a specific problem using AGE. The intent of the protocol is to show AGE from the user's point of view. The main body describes the motivations for and the description of the facilities in AGE.

1.1 Objectives

The general goal of the AGE project is to demystify and make explicit the art of knowledge engineering. It is an attempt to formulate the knowledge that we knowledge engineers use in constructing knowledge-based programs and put it at the disposal of others in the form of a software laboratory.

The design and implementation of the AGE program is based primarily on the experience gained in building knowledge-based programs at the Stanford Heuristic Programming Project in the last decade. The programs that have been, or are being, built are: DENDRAL, meta-DENDRAL, MYCIN, HASP, AM, MOLGEN, CRYSALIS [9], and SACON [2]. Initially, the AGE program will embody artificial intelligence (AI) methods used in these programs. However, the long-range aspiration is to integrate methods and techniques developed at other AI laboratories. The final product is to be a *collection of building-block programs* combined with an *intelligent front-end* that will assist the user in constructing knowledge-based programs. It is hoped that AGE will speed up the process of building knowledge-based programs and facilitate the dissemination of AI techniques by: (1) packaging common AI software tools so that they need not be reprogrammed for every problem; and (2) helping people who are not knowledge engineering specialists write knowledge-based programs.

The task of building such a software laboratory for knowledge engineers is divided into two main sub-tasks:

1. *The isolation of techniques used in knowledge-based systems.* It has always been difficult to determine if a particular problem solving method used in a knowledge-based program is "special" to a particular domain or whether it generalizes easily to other domains. In existing knowledge-based programs, the domain specific knowledge and the manipulation of such knowledge using AI techniques are often so closely coupled that it is difficult to make use of the programs for other domains.

2. *Guiding the user in the initial application of these techniques.* Once the various techniques are isolated and programmed for use, an intelligent agent is needed to guide the user in the application of these techniques.

1.2. User Profile

The design of the AGE system would depend, to a great extent, on the type of users we expect will benefit most from using AGE. *Initially,* AGE *is designed for AI scientists familiar with current problem solving techniques, and who can program in the* INTERLISP *language* [19] *(since* AGE *is implemented in* INTERLISP); *and are familiar with production-rule representations of knowledge* [5]. In other words, AGE is initially aimed at people who could conceivably write knowledge-based programs themselves.

For the person in this category, the advantages of using AGE are twofold:

1. The basic system components are already programmed (e.g., rule interpreters and other control mechanisms, traces, explanation modules, and other components basic to many systems).
2. AGE allows the user to experiment with different problem solving techniques without extensive reprogramming.

Eventually, AGE will be able to help the less knowledgeable or less experienced person.

1.3. Outline of the Paper

The term "knowledge engineering" is being used more frequently to refer to the process of writing application programs using primarily AI methods. The historical context in which knowledge engineering arose and the nature of the work are described by Feigenbaum [9]. Section 2 contains a brief description of the task for the AGE program within the context of knowledge engineers' work. It is followed by an overview of the facilities in the current version. Section 4 contains a short description of an organizational method by which frameworks are decomposed to form a basis for a software laboratory. It is followed by a summary section.

2. TASK FOR THE AGE SYSTEM

Currently there are several projects that aim to provide prepackaged tools for knowledge engineers (UNITS [18],

* This research was supported in parts by the Defense Advanced Research Projects Agency under ARPA Contract No. MDA 903-77-C-0322 and the National Institutes of Health Grant No. RR-00785.

EMYCIN [2]) or to provide programming languages (KRL [4], AIMDS [17]). In preprogrammed packages, all, or most, of the paradigm, system design, and implementation choices have been made by the package designers. In languages none, or very few, decisions have been made for the user. Neither approach guides the user in the design and the construction of knowledge-based programs. AGE has been conceived to bridge the gap between these two extremes--to provide some guidance in the *what, why*, and *how* of programming; plus some preprogrammed problem-solving frameworks.

Ideally then, AGE is an attempt to define and cumulate knowledge-engineering tools, with rules to guide in the use of these tools. It must itself be a knowledge-based system containing knowledge about building knowledge-based programs, combined with a facility that allow the user to explore and experiment with various concepts and techniques. It must provide the user with a variety of preprogrammed modules, allow her to modify them and to add her own. And above all, it must be able to produce running programs. How the AGE system itself is organized for modularity will be described in Section 4. In the next section we describe a framework currently available to the user to construct her knowledge-based program.

3. PROFILE OF THE CURRENT AGE SYSTEM

To correspond to the two general research goals described in the Introduction, the AGE program is being developed along two separate fronts. The first of these fronts is the development of tools to help the user build a variety of knowledge-based programs--the *generality* front. The second front is the development of *intelligence* in the interaction between the user and the AGE program; i.e., moving from dialogues on *how to use the tools* in AGE to *what tools to use*-- the *how-to-what* spectrum described by Feigenbaum [9].

3.1. Currently Implemented Tools

The building-block components currently available to the users have been carefully selected and modularly programmed to be useable in combinations. The current AGE system aims to provide the user with a framework useful for incremental hypothesis formation, known as the *Blackboard Model* [8, 13]. It can be described as follows:

1. There is a global data base (the blackboard) that is used as a means of communication and interaction among the KSs;
2. There are diverse knowledge sources (KSs) that are kept separate and independent; and
3. The KSs respond to changes in the blackboard.

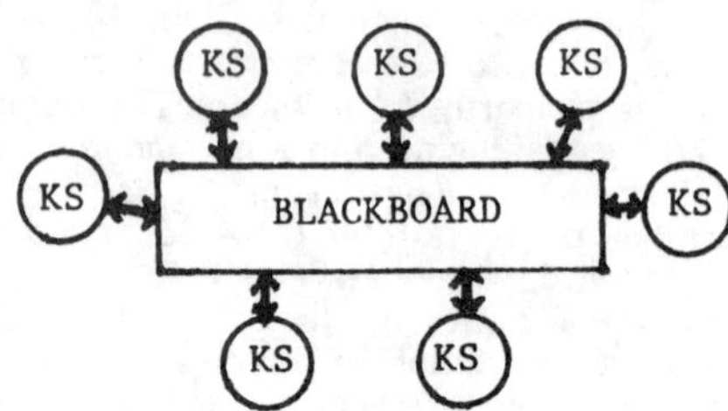

Figure 1. The Blackboard Model

The paradigm itself does not specify the structure of the data base, the representational form of the KSs, nor the response mechanisms. When a model is translated into a program, various architectural and implementation decisions are made by the designers, and programs that use the same paradigm may have different organization and behavior. For example, although HEARSAY-II [13] and CRYSALIS [7] use the Blackboard model, the basic architecture, knowledge representation, and knowledge utilization techniques differ. The differences can be attributed to many factors: the nature of the problem (understanding speech signals and interpreting x-ray crystallographic data); implementation language; real-time constraints; noise level of data; quality and amount of available knowledge; and, last but not least, the designers' tastes.

In AGE the Blackboard-based program design has been implemented to allow flexibility in representation and in the application of other problem solving methods within the framework. It consists of three major components:

1. **The Blackboard**: The blackboard contains hypotheses in a hierarchical data structure; it represents the task domain in terms of a hierarchy of analysis levels of the task.
2. **The KSs**: The KSs contain the knowledge of the task domain (which the user must provide) that can perform the analysis. The KSs are represented as sets of production rules.
3. **The Control**: The control component contains mechanisms that allow the user to (a) specify the conditions for the invocation of the KSs and (b) to select items on the blackboard for focus of attention [10].

In the remainder of this section these components will be described in more detail.

3.1.1. Blackboard

The combined process of KS selection and incremental changes to the blackboard is viewed as a general process of hypothesis formation consistent with the following definition:

An hypothesis can be generated [11]:
1. deductively, using *support from above*--this support can be
   a. *theoretical* support (or model-based support),
   b. support from more inclusive hypotheses that have independent evidential support; or
2. inductively, using evidential *support from below*.

This definition suggests that the most natural way to represent hypotheses is in some form of a hierarchy. The structure of the hierarchy may be strict; it may be flat consisting possibly of only two levels--input data and its translation; or, it may be complex, consisting of many related hierarchies (often referred to as blackboard planes [7]). Currently AGE can represent all of the above forms of hierarchy. An hypothesis is represented as hierarchically organized hypothesis elements integrated by links that represent support from above--called the *expectation-link*, or support from below--called the *reduction-link* (see example 1).

EXAMPLE 1: Hypothesis structure in CRYSALIS [7]

```
              Molecule                 Molecules, superatoms
            r/        \e               and atoms are hypothesis
                                       levels names.
  superatom-1        superatom-2
                                       "r" and "e" represent
   /r      \r            |e            reduction- and
atom-1   atom-2       atom-3           expectation-links.
```

An *hypothesis element* is a named node in the hypothesis structure that represents an aggregation (summary, interpretation, etc.) of lower level hypothesis elements. Each element contains information in the form of attribute-value pairs that are meaningful at that particular hypothesis level (see example 2). These information are inferences generated by the rules in the KSs and can, in turn, be used for further hypothesis formation.

EXAMPLE 2: A possible hypothesis element in CRYSALIS

```
Hypothesis level: ATOMS
Hypothesis element name: ATOMS-10
Inferred attribute-value pairs:
  Atom.name     Sulfur
  Location      (12.3 13.6 24.2 +- .02)
  Partof        (OR CYS14 CYS17)
  Bonded to     HEME-1
  Bondtype      Hydrogen
```

In some problems all the hypothesis elements needed to solve the problems are known *a priori*. In other problems the number of hypothesis elements in the solutions are not known in advance. For example, in PUFF (a program to diagnose pulmonary function disorder [12]) all the possible disease states which account for specific patient data are known in advance. On the other hand, in cryptogram problem (see Appendix I) the number of letters, words, parts of sentence, etc. are not known until a specific cryptogram is being solved. To accommodate both types of solution space, AGE allows the user to generate and name hypothesis elements in advance, generate and name them dynamically, or generate them in some combination.

The hypotheses are generated by inference rules in the KSs. What the KSs look like and how they work are described next.

3.1.2 Knowledge Representation

Knowledge representation in AGE is based on the premise that there are at least four broad categories of knowledge that are needed to solve problems:

1. knowledge of specifics,
2. knowledge of ways and means of dealing with the specifics,
3. knowledge of universals and abstractions in the task domain [3], and
4. knowledge of problem solving and knowledge utilization methods in the task domain.

Within the framework of incremental hypothesis formation using the Blackboard model, an attempt has been made to help the user identify, represent, and utilize these diverse types of knowledge.

Domain knowledge in AGE represents the knowledge necessary to accomplish the goals of the user's program. This knowledge reflects the *knowledge of specifics* and the *knowledge of ways and means of dealing with the specifics*. The knowledge is represented as production rules [5]. These rules are organized into sets called the Knowledge Sources (KSs).

Knowledge Sources

A *Knowledge Source* is a *mega-chunk of knowledge* consisting of a labeled set of rules that are *a priori* deemed to belong together. *How* the rules within a KS is organized and *what* rules are included in a KS depend on the intended role of the KS in the overall problem solving plan. For example, a KS may be organized to represent models--in which case all rules are grouped around some objects or concepts, much like schemata or frames. Or, a KS may be organized around events--in which case all rules which, for example, process input data, are grouped together. In order to solve problems within the framework of the Blackboard model, KSs must place their inferences on the Blackboard. In other words, KSs must generate hypotheses using rules that:

1. add or modify hypothesis element(s), or
2. add or modify relationships between elements by
   a. analyzing data (support from below),
   b. specializing or instantiating a more inclusive hypothesis element (support from above), or
   c. generating expectation(s) from
      1. models, or
      2. more inclusive hypothesis elements that must be verified by data.

Each KS has associated with it: (a) preconditions (a list of events) for its invocation; (b) a list of dotted pairs of hypothesis levels that it spans; (c) list of links generated by it; (d) "single" or "multiple" hit strategy to be used for the rules, and (e) a facility for variable bindings to set local context, to simplify expressions in the rules, to avoid multiple evaluations of the same expression, and to allow communication between the condition and the conclusion halves of a rule.

AGE allows the use of just one KS in the user's program if desired. Whether a single KS is sufficient to solve a problem or not, depends on the characteristics of the problem and on the formulation of the KS. MYCIN [16] is an example of a program that has an equivalent of one KS; all the rules are chained in a goal-directed fashion to represent a line of reasoning meaningful in that domain.

The set of domain-specific KSs may be manipulated in many ways by other higher level KSs [6, 14]. The higher level knowledge may reflect both the knowledge about *ways and means of dealing with the specifics*, *knowledge of problem-solving methods useful in the task domain*, and *knowledge about other knowledge* in the domain. These higher-level KSs are often integrated into the Control component described later.

Rules

A *rule* in AGE is a *chunk of knowledge* written in a syntax comprehensible to AGE. Each rule consists of a left-hand-side (LHS) and a right-hand-side (RHS). The LHS specifies a set of conditions or patterns for the applicability of the rule (i.e. premises). The RHS represents the implications or conclusions to be drawn under the situation specified in the LHS.

To be consistent with the various ways in which hypothesis elements can be generated, the current implementation of the RHS can:

1. add elements to the hypothesis; or add or modify the values of the attributes of elements or the relationship between elements;
2. generate expected elements or values of (or relationship between) elements in the hypothesis;
3. generate goals to establish some elements, or values or links, within hypothesis elements.

Rule Credibility

The domain rules that generate hypotheses are, more often than not, judgmental and uncertain. A *credibility value*, or *weight*, can be associated with the rules to reflect uncertainty. AGE provides means of associating weights (certainty values, probability, etc.) with inferences generated by the RHS of rules. It also provides some pre-programmed procedures for the manipulation of these weights, for example, an algorithm to compute Certainty Factors (CF) from MYCIN. For users who need different algorithms, AGE provides mechanisms for integrating user-provided algorithms.

EXAMPLE 3: Integrating weights

Note: The rules used in this example, and some others, are based on PUFF rules [12]. From pulmonary function test data, the PUFF program determines if a patient is normal, has obstructive airway disease (OAD), restrictive lung disease (RLD), or other pulmonary function-related diseases; and the severity of the diseases. It further determines if OAD is of type emphysema, asthma, or bronchitis. ("RV" in the example refers to a measurement--residual volume.)

```
Weight-adjuster: $ADJWT (MYCIN algorithm)
Rule to be evaluated:
  if (TYPE = OAD) & (RV > 220) then (PROPOSE
     (SEVERITY SEVERE .8))
Hypothesis element before rule evaluation:
     hypo-element name:  DISEASE-05
     type:  (OAD .8)
     severity:  (SEVERE .6)
Hypothesis element after rule evaluation:
     hypo-element name:   DISEASE-05
     type:  (OAD .8)
     severity:  (SEVERE .92)    <-----
```

Rule Evaluators

The applicability of a rule is determined by how the premises in the LHS are evaluated. The term "applicability" can have a different definition for different problems--it may mean that all or some of the premises in the LHS need be TRUE, or that the premises require more complex evaluation. The user can define this "applicability" in the form of a function to serve as the "LHS evaluator." Some pre-programmed LHS evaluators are available; for example, a type of threshold evaluator used in MYCIN.

EXAMPLE 4: LHS Evaluator: $ANDMIN (This function is similar to the one used in MYCIN where evidence with less than .2 value is ignored.)

```
Hypothesis element name:  DISEASE-03
     disease:  (OAD .8)
     subtype:  (EMPHYSEMA  .1)
     severity:  (SEVERE  .6)
Rule 1: if (isa disease OAD) and
              (isa subtype EMPHYSEMA) then...
Rule 2: if (isa disease OAD) and
              (grdeg severity MODERATE) then...
```

Using $ANDMIN, only *Rule* 2 is found applicable within the context of the given hypothesis state.

Example 5 shows how the features described thus far are represented within a KS. Note that some relevant features (e.g. credibility computation) reside outside the KS, because they are relevant to all the KSs in the user program.

Example 5: A KS Summary (AGE version of PUFF)

```
--Knowledge Source: OAD-SUBTYPERULES
Precondition:  (OAD-DEGREE)
Inference levels:  (from . to)
    (DISEASE . DISEASE)
Links between levels:  NONE
Hit strategy:  (MULTIPLE)
Local variable bindings:  NONE
[other relevant information
  LHS-evaluator:  $ANDMIN
  Wt-adjuster:  $ADJWT]
    --------------------------
if
  (GREQDEG ($VALUE OAD DEGREE) MILD)
  (GREQDEG ($VALUE PATIENT DIF-DEF) MILD)
  (GREQ    ($DATA TLC-BB:OBS/PRED) 110)
  (GREQ    ($DATA RV/TLC:OBS/PRED) 10)
then PROPOSE
  change.type  MODIFY
  hypo-element OAD
  attr-val/link  (SUBTYPE EMPHYSEMA .9)
   (FINDINGS "OAD, diffusion defect, elevated
    TLC and RV together indicate Emphysema")
  event.type  OAD-SUBTYPE
  comment  (Rule 31 of EMYCIN version)
```

3.1.3. Knowledge Utilization and Control Mechanisms

As mentioned earlier, the invoking of higher level knowledge about the appropriate use of problem solving methods and the invoking of other domain-specific knowledge appropriate to the situation, are both accomplished in the Control component. Until recently, very few attempts had been made to express *control* information explicitly. Davis [6] addressed the problem of expressing knowledge about other knowledge in production rule form and called it *meta-knowledge.* Nii [14] attempted to distinguish inference-generating KSs and knowledge-utilization KSs by organizing the KSs themselves into a hierarchy. In AGE, we have tried to provide concepts and mechanisms whereby users can express different types of higher level knowledge. The structure of the Control component is described below very briefly (see Appendix II for more detailed description). Whether the whole structure is sufficiently general to handle a variety of problems is still under study.

There are several system components grouped under the heading of *Control.* The various sub-components can be individually specified or programmed by the user. In order to simplify the designing process for the user, AGE provides pre-programmed components where appropriate. The control components that need to be specified are:

1. input data format,
2. initialization function,
3. processing method to be applied to each inference step,
4. rules or procedure to select the next step to be processed,
5. rules to select the relevant KS to process the selected step,
6. termination condition, and
7. post-processing function.

Components 1 and 2 deal with getting input data and performing setup operations in the user's program. The data can be brought in from a file or typed in from a terminal. The data elements are bound to names prespecified by the user. Within the initialization function the user may preprocess the data or perform other initialization activities--the only requirement for AGE is that the initialization function return a name of the first KS to be invoked.

Components 3-6, called the *control kernel* (Figure 2), constitute the core of the Blackboard control component. The primary functions of the control kernel are to select and invoke the appropriate KSs and to select the focus of attention within the blackboard. The control in the user's program is a simple loop:

1. *Rule evaluation*: In the invoked KS each rule is evaluated according to the user specified LHS-Evaluator (sec. 3.1.2). When the LHS meets the evaluation criteria, i.e. evaluates to True, the rule is *fired*.

2. *Inference generation*: Fired rules either (1) PROPOSE change in the hypothesis (this change is made in the hypothesis and is also placed on the Event-list), (2) indicate that some change in the hypothesis is EXPECTed to occur (this expectation is placed on the Expectation-list), or (3) indicate that the hypothesis needs to ACHIEVE a particular value or a state (this goal is placed on the Goal-list). Each of these actions is called a *Step*.

3. *Focus of attention*: Within the Step-selection module, select a step (an event, an expectation or a goal) and a hypothesis element or data to process next. Within the KS-selection module, choose a KS relevant to the selected step, and invoke that KS. (The KS may have associated with it a *processing method*; e.g., a KS may require a backward-chaining mechanism for the rules to achieve a goal.) [*go to 1*]

Components 5 and 6 deal with terminating the kernel control loop and processing the completed hypotheses. One characteristic of the Blackboard model is that there is no prescribed way that the incremental hypothesis formation process terminates short of running out of relevant KSs. Thus, the user needs to specify the conditions under which the processing is to terminate; AGE monitors for the occurrence of these conditions. In the postprocessing function, the user may perform any further processing she wishes, for example, print the current hypothesis.

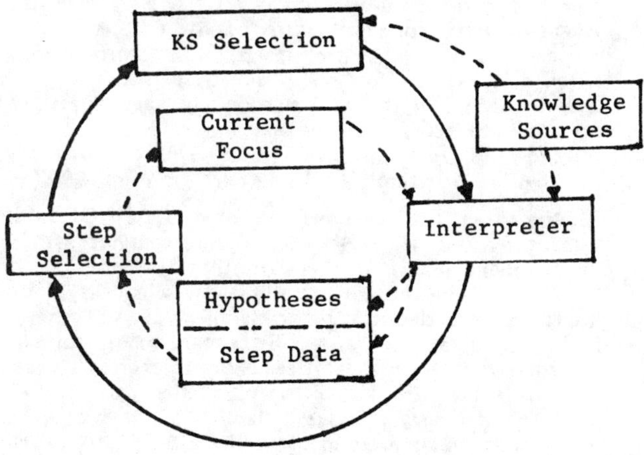

Figure 2. Control of Blackboard Model in AGE

Control Macros

Since the specifications required for the control kernel are quite complex, AGE provides control macros, currently one for *event-driven control* and one for *expectation-driven control*.

Event-Driven Macro: Event-driven hypothesis formation is characterized by incremental formation of hypothesis elements from evidence found in data or in lower level hypothesis elements. The elements can be processed by rules either on the basis of first-in-first-out, first-in-last-out, or best-first. These correspond roughly to breadth-, depth-, and best-first processing of the hypothesis space. When an element is chosen to be processed, it is called a *focused element*. The event-type associated with the focused element helps determine which KS is to be invoked in the future.

The control loop for the Event-driven macro is:

1. <rule> modifies the hypothesis and causes an event (with associated event-type).
2. If <event-type> = <KS-precondition> then invoke the KS. [Go back to 1]

Expectation-Driven Macro: Within an expectation-driven system, expectations in the hypotheses are generated by the rules. These rules are normally grouped around objects and their properties, similar to a schema (frame) organization. They usually form models of objects from which other properties can be inferred or can be expected to occur. For example, a rule of the form:

```
if (isa disease oad) & (isa severity severe)
   then (expect RV >200)
        (expect RV/TLC.RATIO >20)
             etc.
```

has a schema-like flavor and produces expectations that need to be verified.

In order to determine if an expectation has been met, or can be met, the user must provide an *expectation matching function*. AGE always checks to see if the expected situation has occurred either in data or in the hypothesis (i.e. performs a passive match of expectation).

The control loop for the Expectation-driven macro is:

1. <rule> generates an expectation.
2. If an expectation is met, then modify the hypothesis as specified. This action generates an event.
3. If <event type> = <KS precondition> then invoke the KS. [Go back to step 1]

For most problems, both the expectation-driven (or model based) and the event-driven (or data-driven) methods are needed in some combination. For the sake of completeness the control components from which the macros were created are described in Appendix II.

3.2. The Intelligent Front-end in AGE

AGE assumes that the user neither knows nor understands the concepts and implementations of the various program components described above. It is the task of the front-end to guide the user in constructing a program using the component parts. Currently the *intelligence* in the front-end is limited to: (a) a tutor subsystem that allows the user to browse through the textual knowledge base, and (b) a design subsystem that guides the user through each step of program specification. An "unfamiliar" user is always introduced to AGE by way of the tutor subsystem.

The textual knowledge base contains (a) a general description of the building-block components at the conceptual level, (b) a description of the implementation of these concepts within AGE, (c) a description of how these components are to be used within the user's program, (d) how they can be constructed by the user, and (e) various examples. The information is organized in a network to represent the conceptual hierarchy of the components and to represent the functional relationship among them.

The design subsystem guides the user in *design and*

construction. The knowledge necessary for AGE to accomplish this task is represented in a data structure in the form of an AND/OR tree that, on one hand, represents all the possible structures available in the current AGE system; and, on the other hand, represents the decisions the user must make in order to design her program. Using this schema, the design subsystem can guide the user (in the *guided* design mode) from one design decision point to another. At each decision point, the user has access to the textual knowledge base, to advice on the decisions to be made at that point, and to acquisition functions that aid the user in specifying the appropriate component. The user also has direct access (in the *unguided* design mode) to various acquisition and editing functions.

The reader is referred to Appendix I which contains extensive examples of the various interactions currently possible in AGE.

4. DECOMPOSITION OF FRAMEWORKS

Although the intention of this paper does not include discussion of the architecture of AGE itself, we briefly describe some of the motivation behind the decomposition of problem-solving frameworks into interchangeable parts.

Our concept of a software laboratory is a facility in which the users are provided with a variety of *preprogrammed problem-solving frameworks*--similar in spirit to designs of prefabricated houses. The user augments and modifies a framework to develop her own programs. In order to provide such a facility, a framework must be built with parts that can be "unplugged" and replaced. Each framework is decomposed into self-contained modules, creating a hierarchically organized set of component parts. These parts in turn are interpreted or evaluated by "various" managers. As an example, a part of the decomposed Blackboard framework is shown below:

EXAMPLE 6: Blackboard Model Decomposition

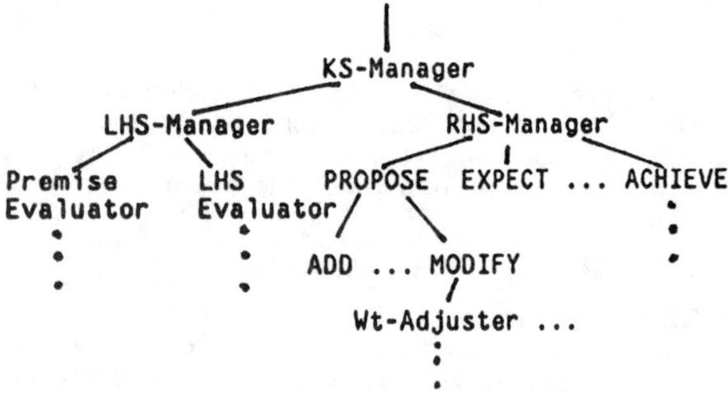

Theoretically, then, each module (with all of its subparts) is replaceable. For example, the whole RHS-Manager can be replaced if the user wants a definition of the RHS of rules different from the one we currently provide.

However, complete modularity is not achieved, because some of the modules are not independent. From a practical stand point the greatest barrier to replacing some of the modules is in their inaccessibility. Nevertheless, as in prefabricated houses, every module can be modified or replaced--some changes are more costly than others in terms of time and detailed knowledge of the implementation needed. In general, those parts nearer the bottom of the hierarchy are more accessible and easier to change. For example, the definition of ADD (add a new hypothesis element) can be changed by simply redefining the ADD function. Or, another function that makes changes to the hypotheses in a different way can be added. On the other hand, the LHS- and the RHS-Managers are not independent. For those components that are independent, and easily modified or replaced, AGE provides some aids for making changes--acquisition functions and descriptions in the textual knowledge base. For those more difficult to change, we provide less aid with the intention of discouraging novice users.

In order to have a useful software laboratory, we need to provide the user with diverse tools--some tools need to be flexible in their utility while others need to be fine-tuned for specific use; and some tools require substantial skill in their use while others do not. By organizing the program modules by their utility and providing easy access to those that are general and easy to use (but allowing skilled users access to all modules), we hope that the laboratory can be useful to a wide range of users.

5. SUMMARY AND CONCLUDING REMARKS

AGE is an experimental program currently running on PDP-10 at the SUMEX-AIM Computing Facility at Stanford University. The immediate goal of the project is to provide software tools with which a knowledge engineer can reduce the time it takes to build knowledge-based programs. The longer range goal is to aid people less knowledgeable in AI methods to build knowledge-based programs. We have taken a small step toward reaching these goals by exploring the various ways in which Blackboard-based programs can be built, and by implementing a set of parts from which such a program can be built.

In the process of building AGE, we have used it to write some programs: CRYPTO, a program that solves cryptogram problems; a portion of a bidding strategy problem in bridge games; two different versions of PUFF [9,12]--one using the Event-driven control macro and another using the Expectation-driven control macro [15]. Since the domain-specific knowledge for PUFF already existed and was being used in EMYCIN, the AGE version took about a week to bring up--time to reorganize the existing rules into KSs and to rewrite the rules in AGE rule syntax. Currently, the CRYSALIS program [7] is being rewritten using AGE.

To the extent that we have been able to use AGE to develop some programs, we feel encouraged to continue with further development. However, there are still many issues that need to be explored in the current work--the adequacy of the user interface and debugging facility; generality of the current functional breakdown of the Blackboard model; sufficiency of the current rule syntax and semantics to express a wide range of knowledge; adequacy of the production rule representation itself for a variety of tasks; reliability of the system; etc. We have made no progress in providing a facility for explanation within the object program; we need more basic research in this area before such a facility can be implemented.

APPENDIX I: Building Knowledge-Based Program with AGE

Introduction

This appendix shows the AGE system from an user's point of view. We have included an example program with parts of actual protocols to illustrate various facilities.

Cryptograms

The problem used as an example is translating cryptograms. The cryptogram solution consists of a four level hierarchical hypothesis structure. The rules to solve cryptograms were provided by a human "expert". The task for CRYPTO is to take a "newspaper" cryptogram (10 to 20 words long, about 100 letters) and using a set of heuristics, translate it into an English sentence. For example, the cryptogram "GSHSUO CI DXDV BSS CLESVBFGB BS HD NCGU HJB ISLD JGNCGU EDSEYD EVSXD BZFB BZDVD'I IBCVY F RDP SR JI PZS FVD BSS ILFYY." translates to "Nobody is ever too important to be kind but some unkind people prove that there's still a few of us who are too small." The word boundaries and punctuation are given. There is a one-to-one correspondence between the cryptletters and their translation, and no letter translates to itself.

Typical run

An AGE user typically builds a knowledge-based program over a period of time, conducting many *hands-on* sessions. In the first session the user gets acquainted with the system, learning the different components available and the system conventions, and discovering what information she must provide (i.e., what to think about before the next session). During the next few sessions the user designs and builds her program. Finally, the user iterates on checking out the program, running it, and modifying it.

TUTOR: *The TUTOR subsystem is described in Section 3.2.*

[*after the user logs on, AGE begins by determining if the user needs a tutorial*]
Are you already familiar with this system?: No
This and all subsequent sessions will be recorded.
The record will go on your directory as DRIB<name><date>.

Following is a list of AGE conventions which may be useful.
[*description of AGE user conventions*]

[*canned text on other topics*]
What follows is a tutorial session to acquaint you with AGE.
[*The following text describes the organization of the AGE on-line manual*]
Each topic in the AGE system has one or more modifiers attach to it. A modifier may be a descriptive word (e.g. Hypothesis.-element) or it may be one of the following:

ISA: Definition or definitional description.
FORMIS: Representation or structural description.
FORMEDBY: How <topic> is generated or created internally during the user program execution.
TOSPECIFY: Description of the acquisition function.
GEN: generally accepted description.
AGE: definition or description as interpreted for AGE.

[*canned text on further topics*]

[*The following interaction shows cross-referencing*]
---There are some pre-assembled control structures available for convenience. (See CONTROL.MACRO)

References are: Hypothesis.structure Control.macro
Do you want to see them now?: y
HYPOTHESIS.STRUCTURE Y/N:: y
The hypothesis structure in AGE is hierarchically organized. There may be more than one hierarchy in the hypothesis (generally known as blackboard planes). Each hierarchy consists of linked hypothesis elements, HYPOTHESIS.ELEMENT, grouped into levels of abstractions.

[*Tutorial session is eventually terminated.*]
This ends the AGE tutorial session. From this point on you will be given a menu of tasks to select from. To start, I suggest you begin with the DESIGN task.

DESIGN: *Refer to section 3.2 for a detailed description of the Design subsystem.*

What do you want to do next?
Tasks available are: [*These are top level tasks in AGE*]

```
name        description
----        -----------
Tutor       System explanation.
Browse      Browse thru the AGE manual.
Design      Create the user program.
SAve        Save the user program on a file.
Getsys      Get the user program from a file.
Check       Check syntax of the user program.
Run         Execute the user program.
SYsout      Save everything (ie. SYSOUT)
```

:: design
Create the user program.
What is the name of your system?:: CRYPTO
[*AGE determines if there already exists a program by that name*]

Do you want a Guided design session, or Unguided session?
:: g
[*Only a minimal number of consecutive letters that uniquely identifies the prompt is needed.*]

Beginning DESIGN and ACQUISITION: You will need to design and specify three major components of your program: the hypothesis structure, the domain-specific rules, and some control information.

You may begin working on : Hypothesis.Structure Knowledge.domain-rules Control

During this design session, in addition to specifying or editing components of the system, you may also ask for ADVICE, more INFORMATION from the manual, or to QUIT the session.

What do you want to do next?
Your options are: Hypothesis.structure Knowledge.domain-rules Control Advice Information Quit
Type H/K/C/U/A/I/Q : a [*asking for advice*]

Specify the hypothesis structure first; it will aid you in structuring your problem. Then enter some domain rules, followed by control information. Within the control specification, choose system-provided control methods to see how your rules work. More rules can be added or more sophisticated control can be specified later.

HYPOTHESIS: *See Section 3.1.1 for a general discussion of the Hypothesis.*

CRYPTO uses a four-level structure, as shown in Figure A1. At the highest level (SENTENCE) there is one named node CRYPTOGRAM, where information inferred about the whole cryptogram will be stored. At the WORD level, elements WORD1 to WORDn are created dynamically for each word of the cryptogram; and at the LETTER level, elements LETTER1 to

LETTER1 to LETTERm for each letter.

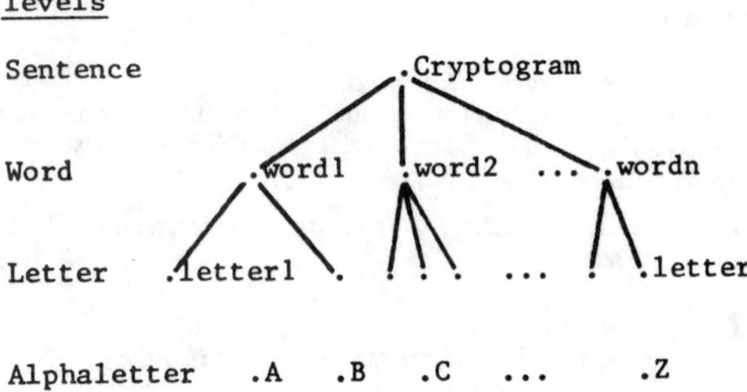

Figure A1. CRYPTO Hypothesis Structure

What follows is an example protocol of the acquisition of the hypothesis structure for CRYPTO.

What do you want to do next?
::Info [*ask for information*]
Select a topic.
::hypothesis.tospecify
Function: (HYPO)
The user is asked for the names of levels of hypothesis elements, and for the names of the attributes at each level. The level names must be unique; the attribute names need only be unique within a level. When AGE asks for attributes, only attributes should be given and not the names of the links between two levels. AGE will start from the highest level, LEVEL1.

Do you want to work on Hypothesis.structure?:: y
Aquiring HYPOTHESIS.STRUCTURE
Name of LEVEL1 ?
A level name can be any literal atom not already used for the name of another level. Type Done to quit.
:: sentence
Attribute?
Attributes must be unique within a level.
:: words
Attribute?
[*etc.*]
Name of LEVEL2 ?
:: wurd [*misspelled name--to be corrected later*]
Attributes?
:: letters
[*The remainder of hypothesis acquisition and editing deleted.*]
:: print [*print the hypothesis structure*]

```
LEVEL1 - SENTENCE
         WORDS - NIL
         ENGLISHWORDS - NIL
         LETTERS - NIL
LEVEL2 - WURD  [mispelled level name])
         LETTERS - NIL
         ENGLISHWORD - NIL
         ORDREINSENTENCE - NIL  [misspelled]
         POSSIBLEWORDS - NIL
LEVEL3 - LETTER
         CRYPTLETTER - NIL
         ORDERINWORD - NIL
         RELFREQ? - NIL
```

KSs: *Refer to Section 3.1.2 for a general description of the KSs as used in AGE. The protocol shows the partial acquisition of two KSs. The specification of each KS begins with some declarative information needed to evaluate the rules in the KS. Then the user is prompted for parts of the rules. The first KS is a set of rules that look at the whole cryptogram. It is called once after initialization and any time thereafter to find a new part of the cryptogram to focus on. This KS assumes that certain information already exists in the hypothesis structure as a result of initialization. The first rule looks for one-letter words which could either be A or I, with A more likely than I.*

You need to specify: Rule.evaluator Knowledge.sources Control
You may modify: Hypothesis.structure
[*AGE keeps track of what has and has not been specified*]
What do you want to do next?
:: kn
What is the name of the KS you want to create or add rules to?
:: wholesentencerules
[New knowledge source]
What events invoke this knowledge source?
:: always [*Always means any event can be a precondition to this knowledge source*]
Between which Hypothesis levels does this KS make inferences?
From?
:: letter
To?
:: alphaletter
From?
::none
Which links are used to record inferences made by this KS?
:: possiblevalue [*Possiblevalue links will connect elements from the letter level to possible values in the alphaletter level*]
Inverse link?
:: possiblevalue/of
Link?
:: assignedvalue [*Assignedvalue links will connect positively assigned values from the alphaletters to the cryptletters on the letter level*]
Inverse link?
[*etc.*]

Do you want to use multiple or single hit strategy for this KS?
You can specify Onceonly with Single or Multiple.
:: single onceonly [*Single to fire only one rule and Onceonly to mark that rule so that it won't be fired again*]

Local variables can be defined as (variable value) or (variable).
Define a local variable.
:: (wordnodes ($value 'cryptogram part))
[*Store the node names for the word nodes in WORDNODES. The function $VALUE retrieves those names by following the "part" link from the CRYPTOGRAM node*]
Define a local variable.
:: (word)
Define a local variable.
[*etc.*]

What is the first condition? Type None when done.
[*This problem involves searches which are awkward with the current rule syntax and requires extensive Lisp code. See Example 5 for the more usual use of rules.*]

```
::  (setq word (for wd in wordnodes thereis
       (and (eg (length ($VALUE wd letters)) 1)
```

```
            (null ($value wd englishword]
```
[*looking for a word of length 1, not already assigned a value*]
Next condition?
:: none

Next, you will be prompted for the RHS of the rule.
PROPOSE, EXPECT, GOAL, or LOOP?
::? propose [*ask about PROPOSE*]
PROPOSE is used to change the hypothesis structure.
:: prop [*specification of PROPOSE follows*]
ch.type:: supersede [*replace current value*]
hypo-element:: word [*of word element*]
attr-value:: (englishword 'a) [*with "a"*]
link-node:: none
event.type:: assignword [*name of the event it generates*]
comment:: (a one letter word is most likely 'a')

PROPOSE, EXPECT, GOAL, or LOOP?
:: propose [*more than one action allowed in the RHS*]
[*etc.*]
link-node:: (assignedvalue 'a) [*change the relational link*]
event.type:: assignletter
comment:: (assign the letter 'a' to the cryptletter)

PROPOSE, EXPECT, GOAL, or LOOP?
:: none
More rules?:: no
What is the name of the next KS you want?
:: fill-inrules
[New knowledge source]
[*some declarative infcrmation deleted*]
PROPOSE, EXPECT, GOAL, or LOOP?
::? loop [*ask about LOOP*]
LOOP is used to indicate an iterative action, either PROPOSE, EXPECT, or GOAL. If LOOP is used, you will be prompted for the name of an iteration variable and the name of a list of values on which to repeat the action.
:: loop
Iteration variable?
:: ol
Name of the list to be iterated on?
:: otherletters
PROPOSE, EXPECT, or GOAL?
:: propose
[*remainder of rule acquisition delete*]

CONTROL: *Refer to Section 4 and Appendix II for discussion of knowledge utilization and control mechanisms. The overall strategy for solving cryptograms is to focus on a particular word or a combination of letters that has "potential"; work on the focussed item and follow through on all the ramifications, which in turn may generate a new focus.*

:: control

Control specification: Currently there are three methods of specifying the control information. Two are macros which require minimal specification, EVENT-DRIVEN-MACRO and EXPECTATION-DRIVEN-MACRO. The third method, DETAILCONTROL, involves detailed specifications of several subcomponents.

New additions to design component: (Detailcontrol Control.macro. Event-driven Control.macro.expectation-driven)

[When a node is chosen, it opens other *nodes that require further specification*]

What do you want to do next?
:: detail
Detailed Control Specification: There are several components grouped under the heading of DETAILCONTROL. To simplify the designing process, AGE provides default specification where appropriate. The components that need to be specified are:

1. input data format: INPUTFORMAT,
2. initialization function: INITIALIZATION,
3. processing method to be applied to each step-type,
4. rules to select a step to be used as the current focus,
5. rules to select relevant KS (or procedure) to process the selected step: (3,4,5 part of KERNEL),
6. termination condition: TERMINATION, and
7. post processing function: POSTPROCESSING.

New addition to design component: (Inputformat Initialization Control.Kernel Termination Postprocessing)

What do you want to do next?
:: inputform
The input data you use in your system will be stored on an implicit level of the hypothesis structure called INPUTDATA. A function $DATA is available to access the data. At the beginning of each run you will be asked to input (from a file or TTY:) the actual data associated with each data name.
First name?
:: inputcryptogram
Next name?
:: done

What do you want to do next?
:: initial
You must provide a function that will return, as its value, the name of the first KS to be invoked. Within this function you may do any processing you whish.

[NEW FUNCTION]
What would you like to call your initialization function?
:: crypto-initialization
Your initialization function must return the name of a KS.
Please define CRYPTO-INITIALIZATION

```
(CRYPTO-INITIALIZATION (LAMBDA NIL
```
[*This line provided by AGE*]
```
  (prog (cg)
  (cg ← ($data inputcryptogram))
  (fill-inlevels)
  (computerelfreqs)
  (return 'wholesentencerules]
```
What do you want to do next?
:: terminate
You must provide a function which will determine when to terminate vour program.

What is the name of your termination function?
:: crypto-quit
[*define CRYPTO-QUIT function in the same manner at above*]

What do you want to do next?
:: post

you can provide functions for printing
the results, translating the results into a more readable form.

Take up this option or bypass it? [*optional component*]
:: take
What would you like to call your postprocessing function?
:: decodedprint
[*Define DECODEPRINT*]

What do you want to do next?
:: control.k
This function allows the user to specify various options which determine how events, expectations, and goals will be processed. First we will look at the event processing information.

Do you want to enter kernel information now?:: y
Which event selection method would you like to use? LIFO and FIFO are available or you can write your own function. Type LIFO, FIFO, or function name.
:: ?
The Event-selection is used to decide which event from the event list to process next. LIFO chooses the last event added. FIFO chooses the earliest event. You can provide your own function. For example, bestfirst might depend on the weights associated with each event.
:: lifo

Name an event type to be collected.
:: fill-in
:: done

The control rules are used to determine what step type to proces next. Each control rule consists of a condition and a step type.

STEPTYPE:: event
CONDITION:: expectationlist
STEPTYPE:: expectation
CONDITION:: none

USER FUNCTIONS: *The final information the user must provide is the names and definitions of the functions used in the rules or called from other user-defined functions. The user can name and define functions one at a time or load them from files.*

EDITING: *There are two ways to edit: (1) by calling the appropriate editing function from Unguided design session or (2) during the Check-out session. The Check subsystem described below.*

SYSTEM CHECKOUT: *The Check subsystem does a syntax check on the user created program. It finds errors in the designed structures and points out missing, but required, information. Check also allows the user to edit the errors as they are found by calling the appropriate editor.*

What do you want to do next? : check
Check syntax of the user program.
checking hypothesis levels - ALPHALETTER ...
checking knowledge sources -FILL-INRULES ...
Warning: 2 events not used as preconditions
ASSIGNWORD FILL-IN
[*they will be used by KSs to be defined later*]
1 syntax errors in the user program.
Do you want to edit the errors now?:: n

RUNNING: *Once all the information is specified, the user can run her program in two modes, debugging mode or normal mode. In debugging mode, AGE prints a trace of the control flow showing the rules evaluated, the actions taken, and the steps and focuses selected. In normal mode, AGE only prints the input data and the results.*

A complete run will begin with a request for input data. Next the user's initialization function which returns a KS name is evaluated. That KS is the first to be interpreted and starts the control loop, which will continue until the termination condition is met. Finally, the postprocessing function is called. The following is a sample run of the CRYPTO program. We have deleted a large section of the protocol to save space.

What do you want to do next?:: run [*top level prompt*]
Execute the user program.
Do you want to input data from a file or from a terminal?
(filename or TTY:):: crypto-data1 [*input from a file*]
((INPUTCRYPTOGRAM (GSHSUO CI DXDV BSS CLESVBFGB BS HD NCGU HJB ISLD JGNCGU EDSEYD EVSXD BZFB BZDVD'I IB RDP SR JI PZS FVD BSS ILFYY)))

Knowledge source invoked - WHOLESENTENCERULES
[*WHOLESENTENCERULES is the KS name returned by the initialization function.*]

Left hand side of applicable rule -
((SETQ WORD (for WD in WORDNODES thereis (AND ...
[*first rule to fire, word17, letter73, is probably "A". Two events result, ASSIGNLETTER and ASSIGNWORD*]

NAME OF NEW EVENT: ASSIGNWORD
NAME OF NEW EVENT: ASSIGNLETTER
****
NEXT STEP: EVENT [*choose the next step - EVENT*]

FOCUS EVENT-(ASSIGNLETTER(LETTER73)(ASSIGNEDVALUE A WHOLESENTENCERULES EV2 NIL)
[*Since the ASSIGNLETTER event was added to the EVENTLIST last, it is the next focus event under the depthfirst (LIFO) selection method. When there are no further ramifications of ASSIGNEDLETTER, ASSIGNWORD will become the focus event.*]

Knowledge source invoked - FILL-INRULES
Left hand side of applicable rule -
((SETQ OTHERLETTERS (for L in CRYPTLETTERNODES join
[*find other letters with same cryptvalue as letter73 FILL-IN those letters with value "A"*]

NAME OF NEW EVENT: FILL-IN
****
NEXT STEP: EVENT

FOCUS EVENT - (FILL-IN (LETTER92) (ASSIGNEDVALUE A) (ASSIGNEDVALUE A) EV13 NIL)
[*letter92 was assigned last, thus with a depthfirst selection method, it becomes the new focus.*]
[*etc.*]
[*The rest of the protocol continues in the same manner until terminated.*]

Summary

One common question asked about the CRYPTO system is, "When CRYPTO makes an incorrect assignment, can CRYPTO back up?" The answer is no. There is no back-up or alternative hypothesis capability. In CRYPTO we believe that with enough rules and with the POSSIBLEVALUE attributes and weights, the system will always make the correct assignments. This belief stems from the sessions recorded with the expert newspaper cryptographer, who never needed to "back up." The expert never guessed at a value or tried to confirm or contradict a guess by looking at its ramifications. However, we do recognize that the concept of alternative hypotheses is a powerful one, and we expect to add facilities to AGE to allow them in the future.

APPENDIX II: SUMMARY OF THE CONTROL KERNEL

The Control Kernel consists of several components (Figure B1) each of which must be specified by the user. The sequence of actions which are taken within the Kernel is described below.

1. Invoke rules (CONTROLRULES) to select the next step-type to process--EVENT, EXPECTation,or GOAL;

2. If the selected step-type is EVENT, then
   (a) Select an event, (SELECTIONMETHOD provided by the user);
   (b) Collapse the EVENTLIST by deleting/merging events referring to identical attributes and values of the events specified by the user (COLLECTIONRULES);
   (c) Select a KS (EVENTRULES generated by AGE from the KS preconditions).

3. If the selected step type is a goal (ACHIEVE), then
   (a) Select a goal (SELECTIONMETHOD);
   (b) Evaluate to determine if the goal has been met (MATCHER).
   (b) If not, apply a goal-seeking method (SEEKMETHOD).
   (d) If the goal has been met, execute the remainder of the RHS of the rule that generated the goal.

4. If the selected step-type is EXPECT, then
   (a) Select an expectation (SELECTIONMETHOD);
   (b) Evaluate to determine if the expectation has been met (MATCHER),
   (c) If so, process the expected event by executing the remainder of the RHS that generated the expectation.

Step-type	Event	Expectation	Goal
SELECTION METHOD	FIFO | LIFO | <fns name>	FIFO | LIFO | <fns name>	FIFO|LIFO | <fns name>
COLLECTION RULES	<KS name> | ()	---	---
MATCHER	[EVENTRULES]*	<fn name>| passivematch	<fn name>| nii
SEEKMETHOD	---	---	<fn name>

Figure B1. Summary of Control Kernel Components and Options

REFERENCES

[2] Bennett, J., Creary, L., Engelmore, R., Melosh, R., *SACON: A knowledge-based consultant for structural analysis*, Heuristic Programming Project Memo HPP-78-23, 1978.

[3] Bloom, B.S., Taxonomy of Educational Objectives, McKay, New York, 1956.

[4] Bobrow, D. G. and Winograd, T., *An Overview of KRL, a Knowledge Representation Language*, Cognitive Science, vol 1, no 1, pp3-46,1977.

[5] Davis, R. and King J., *An overview of production systems*, Machine Intelligence 8: Machine Representation of Knowledge, Elcock, E.W. and Michie, D. (eds.), John Wiley, 1977.

[6] Davis R. and Buchanan B.G., *Meta-level knowledge: overview and applications*, Proc. IJCAI 5, 1977, pp.920-927.

[7] Engelmore, R.S. and Nii, H.P., *A knowledge-based system for the interpretation of protein x-ray crystallographic data*, Heuristic Programming Project Memo HPP-77-2, January, 1977.

[8] Erman, L.D. and Lesser, V.R., *A multi-level organization for problem solving using many, diverse, cooperating sources of knowledge*, Proc. 4th IJCAI, 1975, pp.483-490.

[9] Feigenbaum, Edward A., *The art of artificial intelligence: I. Themes and case studies of knowledge engineering*, Proc. IJCAI 5, 1977, pp.1014-1029.

[10] Hayes-Roth, Frederick and Lesser, Victor R., *Focus of attention in a distributed-logic speech understanding system*, Proc. of IEEE Int. Conference on ASSP, Philadelphia, 1976.

[11] Hempel, Carl G., Philosophy of Natural Science, Foundations of Philosophy Series, Prentice-Hall, Inc., 1966.

[12] Kunz, J.C., Fallat, R.J., McClung, D.H., Osborn, J.J., Votteri, B.A., Nii, H.P., Aikins, J.S., Fagan, L.M., Feigenbaum, E.A., *A physiological rule based system for interpreting pulmonary function test results*, Heuristic Programming Project Memo HPP-78-20, (submitted to Computers and Biomedical Research), 1978.

[13] Lesser, V.R. and Erman, L.D., *A retrospective view of the HEARSAY-II architecture*, Proc. 5th IJCAI, 1977, pp. 790-800.

[14] Nii, H. P. and Feigenbaum, E.A., *Rule-based understanding of signals*, Pattern-Directed Inference Systems, D.A. Waterman and R. Hayes-Roth (eds.), Academic Press, 1978.

[15] Nii, H.P. and Aiello, N., AGE (Attempt to Generalize): Profile of the AGE-0 System, Stanford Heuristic Programming Project Memo HPP-78-5 (Working paper), June 1978.

[16] Shortliffe, Edward H., Computer-Based Medical Consultation: MYCIN, American Elsevier, New York, 1976.

[17] Sridharan, N.S., AIMDS User Manual, Report CBM-TR-89, Department of Computer Science, Rutgers University, June, 1978.

[18] Stefik, Mark, *An examination of a frame-structure representation system*, Stanford Heuristic Programming Project Memo HPP-78-13, September, 1978.

[19] Teitelman, W., et al, Interlisp Reference Manual, Xerox Palo Alto Research Center, October, 1978.

EXTRACTION OF ITEMS FROM ABSTRACTS

Fujio Nishida, Giichi Kishimoto and Shinobu Takamatsu
Department of Electrical Engineering,
Faculty of Engineering, University of Osaka Prefecture,
Sakai, Osaka, Japan 591

This paper presents a method of extracting prescribed items from a summary or an abstract of technical papers. An experimental system is now under development. The internal expression of an input sentence is transformed into a standard form which has the standard case-labels for extraction of items. The part of remaining sentences is combined with the adjacent sentence into an item section every main item. [1] And the prescribed items are extracted efficiently.

1. EXTRACTED ITEMS

This paper is primarily concerned with a textual analysis from the viewpoint of extraction of items in a specified form for filing. The kind of texts is chosen to a summary of some technical papers, the length of which is rather short. The first thing to be done will be the determination of the specification table of the extracted items rather than the construction of the rewriting rules. The main items to be extracted are generally chosen to the labels of main frames appearing in many summaries of technical papers which can be also considered to produce their respective detailes of the main frames of summaries by various transformation. For the whole of various kinds of technical papers, however, it is a difficult and significant problem to choose the main items and to construct a well organized tree or graph of these summaries. Hence, we confine the file of the main object to a specific one, for example, one of software systems such as language processing systems. In this scheme, a choice of main items is taken as shown in Table 1.

PRED-F: _ (PRED-F: $\underline{*}$, AG-S: $\underline{\underline{t_1 \cup t_2}}$, PAT: _##,
SO: _##, G: _##, M: _##)
AG-S: $\underline{t_1}$ (OBJ-S: $\underline{*}$, COMP-S: $\underline{\underline{t_2}}$)
INSTR-S: _ (PRED-F: _, AG-S: $\underline{*}$, PAT: _, SO: _,
G: _, M: _, INSTR-S: _#, USED-S: $\underline{\underline{t_1 \cup t_2}}$)
USED-S: _ (PRED-F: _, AG-S: $\underline{*}$, PAT: _, SO: _,
G: _, M: _, INSTR-S: $\underline{\underline{t_1 \cup t_2}}$, USED-S: _#)

Table 1. A Specification Table

In the above, two capital-letter sequents connected with a hyphen '-' are a case-label and a category of a term inserted to the case respectively. The specification of the category of a case is assumed optional. The abbreviated large symbols denote OBJect, COMPonent, PREDicate, AGent, PATient, SOurce, Goal, Modal or manner, INSTRument, USED system or location, PARTicipant, CHaracteristic, System, Function and Process. Each underline denotes a slot of a case and a small letter t denotes a term. Each term takes a form

C: t
or C: t (--, K: t, C_1: t_1, C_2: t_2, --),

which means a term t plays the role denoted by a case or a case-category label C in a specified upper case frame and it is sometimes modified by several terms in a case frame enclosed by parentheses.

In a modifying frame, the modified term and the case frame are described together with a predicative term when it is necessary to show the role of the modified term clearly. In the Table 1, the symbol * in a modifying frame denotes the modified term prefixed to the frame. The double underlined term specifies or defines the main case-label of the term prefixed to the modifying frame and are used for identification of the term. In a completed form for output, however, they are deleted for efficiency. The nested modification of a term is restricted to specified terms with the symbol '#' or '##' in order to avoid to store duplicated information and non-essential one. The term with the symbol '#' can be modified by a modifying frame which involves a term in the same case-label as the prefixed case-label recursively. The term with the symbol '##' can be modified by any modifying frame so long as it is not duplicated information.

A main item is defined as a pair of a case-label and the characterized term with a number instead of modifying frames appearing in the leftmost of the specification table. For a case-label, there are sometimes several terms in a union or serial form, where the union form is an unordered set of terms with a form ' C: $t_1 \cup t_2 \cup$ --- ' ,while the serial form is an ordered set of terms with a form ' C: $t_1 \wedge t_2 \wedge$ --- ', placed by a temporal or causal relation.

2. NORMALIZATION

Prior to extracting some specified items from summaries, it is preferable that each sentence of a summary is normalized to some extent. First, each input of a summary is transformed into the internal form by parsing. Each word of a pronoun or a common noun is characterized by attaching a number by means of the anaphoric analysis though the attached number is omitted except section 4 for simplicity. Then the internal form is transformed into the standard form which takes a concrete predicate word as a governor at every partial predicate or function expression and dose not involve any term of the same name as a case-label. Every transformation is done by refering to case-labels and categories of terms though the precise conversion procedures are omitted for simplicity. The outline of the conversions is described as follows.

2.1 Transform To Predicate-governor Forms

This is a form of a predicate expression every part of which generally takes a concrete predicative word as a governor if the part involves a concrete predicative word. For example, let us take an example of an internal form which involves a term of a function form that contains a predicative word p corresponding to a clause or a phrase.

$$(\text{PRED: } p_1, ---, K_0: t_1(K_1^{-1}: p_2(K_2: t_2, --))).$$

The predicate-governor form of the above is

$$(\text{PRED: } p_1, ---, K_0: t_1(\text{PRED: } p_2, K_1: *, K_2: t_2, --)).$$

If a function form lacks a predicative word, the term of the pseudo case of a predicative word is left empty.

[Example 1]
$K: t_1(\text{COMP: } t_2) \rightarrow K: t_1(\text{OBJ: } *, \text{COMP: } t_2),$

where the symbole '$\rightarrow$' shows the left side is to be replaced by the right side.

A term of the same name as a case label K is also transformed to an expression using the case-label K.

[Example 2]
$K(\text{OBJ: } t) \rightarrow \$(\text{OBJ: } t, K: \$),$

where the symbol '$' denotes a certain term to be replaced by a concrete term if it appears later.

2.2 Transform To Non-complementary Forms

A predicate part of a complement form is transformed to a non-complementary form by a case-transformation.

[Example 3]
$(\text{PRED: make, AG: } t_1, \text{PAT: } t_2(\text{PRED: } *, \mathbf{t}), \text{G: } t_3)$
$\rightarrow (\text{PRED: } t_2, \mathbf{t}, \text{INSTR: } t_1, \text{M: } t_3),$

where a bold letter $\mathbf{t}$ denotes a sequence of pairs of case-labels and terms.

2.3 Removal Of Formal Predicative Words

A formal predicative word such as 'be based on' or 'comprise' is removed, and the case-labels prefixed to the dependant terms are replaced by a more concrete case label implied by the removed predicative word.

[Example 4]
$(\text{PRED: use, AG: } t_1, \text{PAT: } t_2,$
$\text{PURPOSE: } t_3(\text{PRED: } *, \mathbf{t}))$
$\rightarrow (\text{PRED: } t_3, \mathbf{t}, \text{AG: } t_1, \text{INSTR: } t_2).$

The conversion rules in article 2.2 and 2.3 are implemented for each word in a word dictionary.

3. EXTRACTION OF ITEMS

From the normalized sentences of a summary the items in the specification table are extracted. First, the subject sentence is taken from a sentence of the summary which involves a predicative word of category 'process' and contains several terms involved in the main items of the specification table as well as in the title. The cases of these items are identified using the method described in section 1 and several case-transformation rules such as

$(\text{OBJ-S: } t_1, \text{COMPOSITE-S: } t_2)$
$\rightarrow (\text{OBJ-S: } t_2, \text{COMP-S: } t_1),$
$(\text{PRED-F: } t_1, \text{AG- S: } t_2, \text{INSTR-S: } t_3$
$(\text{PRED-F: } t_4, \text{AG-S: } *))$
$\rightarrow (\text{PRED-F: } t_4, \text{AG-S: } t_3, \text{USED-S: } t_2$

(PRED-F: t_1 , AG-S: *)).

Thereafter, the details of the main items are arranged as indicated in the specification table, combined with the main items and put into the edition area for output.

Subsequently, the remaining sentences are processed from the first sentence. First, the main item to which the current sentence belongs is identified. Second, the part to be extracted is arranged to the specified form. For example, if a sentence contains a serial relation, it is arranged as followes;

(PRED-F: t_1, AG-S: t_2, PAT: t_3,
MEANS-F: t_4(PRED-F: * , **t**) → (PRED-F: t_4,
t) ∧ (PRED-F: t_1, AG-S: t_2, PAT: t_3).

Then, the following sentence is taken and it is asked whether or not this sentence belongs to the same main item as the preceding one. If it does, the part to be extracted is arranged, combined with the preceding extracted part as an item section and rearranged using some temporal relations or combined rules such as

$$(K_0: t,\ K_1: t_1) \cup (K_0: t,\ K_2: t_2) \rightarrow (K_0: t,\ K_1: t_1,\ K_2: t_2).$$

If the following sentence dose not belong to the same item as the preceding one, the extracted part of the preceding item section are marked for later scanning, and its copy is combined and rearranged with the data in the edition area for output. Then the current sentence is processed as a new item sentence. At the end of the summary, the scanning restarts from the beginning of the summary for extracting the specified detail from the remaining parts of each sentence. Each term is stored from the output form into a tree-like file of categories together with several sequents of the prefixed case-labels and the document number.

4. EXAMPLE

4.1 An Example

(1) This paper describes TORUS, a natural language understanding system which serves as a front end to a data base management system in order to facilitate communication with a casual user. (2) TORUS uses a semantic network for understanding input statements and for deciding what information to output in response. (3) The semantic network stores general knowledge about the problem domain. (4) A number of functions of TORUS make it possible to integrate the meaning of an input statement to the semantic network, and to select a portion of the semantic network which stores information that must be output.

4.2 Standard Forms

(1) (PRED-P: describing, AG: paper'1,
PAT: TORUS
(PRED-F: understanding, AG: *,
PAT: natural-language'1)
(PRED-F: communicating, INSTR: *, M: easy,
COAGENT: casual-user'1)
(AG: *, USED: front-end'1 (AG: *,
USED: system'1 (PRED-F: managing,
AG: *, PAT: data-base'1)))),
(2) (PRED-F: understanding, AG: TORUS, INSTR:
semantic-network'1, PAT: input-statement'1)
∪ (PRED-F: deciding, AG: TORUS, INSTR: semantic-
network'1 PAT: information (DET: what)
(PRED-F: output, PAT: *,
ENVIRONMENT: response)),
(3) (PRED-F: storing, AG: semantic-network'1,
PAT: general-knowledge'1
(OBJ: *, PART: problem-domain'1)),
(4) (PRED-F: integrating, AG: TORUS, PAT:
meaning'1 (CH: *, OBJ: input-statement'2),
G: semantic-network'1, M: possible)
∪ (PRED-F: selecting, AG: TORUS, PAT: portion'1
(OBJ: *, COMPOSITE: semantic-network'1
(PRED-F: storing, AG: *, PAT: infcrmation'1
(PRED-F: output, PAT: *, M: must)))
M: possible).

4.3 Extracted Items

(PRED-F: understanding (PRED-F: *, AG: <u>TORUS</u>,
PAT: natural-language)
∪ integrating (PRED-F: *, AG: <u>TORUS</u>,
PAT: meaning (CH: *, OBJ: input-statement),
G: semantic-network, M: possible)
∪ slecting (PRED-F: *, AG: <u>TORUS</u>, PAT: portion
(OBJ: *, COMPOSITE: semantic-network))
∪ deciding (PRED-F: *, AG: <u>TORUS</u>, PAT: informa-
tion (DET: what) (PRED-F: output, PAT: *,
ENVIRONMENT: response)),
AG-S: TORUS,
INSTR-S: semantic-network (PRED-F: storing,
AG: *, PAT: general-knowledge, USED: <u>TORUS</u>)
(PRED-F: storing, AG: *, PAT: information),
USED-S: front-end (AG: *, USED-S: system
(PRED-F: managing, AG: *, PAT: data-base),
INSTR: <u>TORUS</u>)).

REFERENCE

[1] Hobbs,J.R. "Coherence and Interpretation in English Texts." In <u>Proc. IJCAI-77.</u> MIT, Cambridge, Mass., August, 1977, pp. 110-116.

PROBLEM SOLVING OF ELEMENTARY ALGEBRA BY HIERARCHICAL ABSTRACTION

Fujio Nishida, Yoneharu Fujita and Hiroji Kusaka
Department of Electrical Engineering,
Faculty of Engineering, University of Osaka Prefecture,
Sakai, Osaka, Japan 591

This paper presents a hierarchical problem-solving method which searches some applicable transformation rules to the precondition of the problem at various abstract levels using a tree-like address table and finds a global solving policy which reduces the difference between the current state and the goal. The frame of the problem is chosen from the field of elementary algebra.

1. INTRODUCTION

The abstraction of a problem and a relation which retains only their key characteristics will be indispensable for global solving of complicated problems. Many researches of mechanical problem solving using this concept have been actively done, but a lot of problems to be solved seem to remain for practical use.[1],[2]. This paper develops the method of EAPS(Elamentary algebraic Problem Solver) of the previous paper[3] by adding (i)a tree-like address table of theorems and global relations for the efficient access to them and (ii)a mixed abstract notation of problems for flexible representation.

2. ABSTRACT EXPRESSIONS

In mechanical problem solving, it is considered indispensable to introduce an abstraction or an abbreviation method of expressions at least in complicated quantitative relations. Along this idea, we introduce an abstract form for quantitative terms and relations as follows;

idname-k(C-name:value,···,C-name:value), (1)

where 'idname' takes a term 't', a literal 'rq' or a set of literals '$\overline{\text{rq}}$'. k is the identification number though it is omitted in Table 1 for simplicity. The C-names('C-' is the abbreviation of the word 'characteristic' in this paper) are a variable 'var', a function class 'fc', a form of a literal 'form' and a sign of terms 'sgn'. The value of 'var' is a set of variables in an expression. The values of 'sgn' are {p,z,n} and the combinations of them. The item 'form' takes the values 0,1,2 and 3 for a solution form q(x, t(var:φ)), a semi-solution form q(y,t(var:{x})), a transposed form q(t(var:{x}),0) and the general form q(t(var:{x}),t(var:{x})) respectively. An abstract form eq.(1) is obtained by parsing an objective expression by the aid of the rewriting rules shown in Table 1.

```
t(var:φ) ::= const
t(var:{x},fc:(x:{fs})) ::= fs(x)
t(var:{x,y},fc:(x:{fs1,fs3})(y:{fs2,fs3}))
 ::= fs3(t(var:{x},fc:(x:{fs1})),t(var:{y},fc:
     (y:{fs2})))
t̄(num:2,var:{x,y},fc:(x:{fs1})(y:{fs2}))
 ::= t(var:{x},fc:(x:{fs1})),t(var:{y},fc:(y:
     {fs2}))
q ::= =|>|<
rq(var:{x,y},fc:(x:{fs1})(y:{fs2}))
 ::= q(t(var:{x},fc:(x:{fs1})),t(var:{y},fc:(
     y:{fs2})))
r̄q̄(num:2,var:{x,y}) ::= rq(var:{x}),rq(var:{y})
L ::=∧|∨|∧∨
```

Table 1. A part of rewriting rules.

In Table 1, fs1, fs2 and fs3 are function symbols, $\overline{\text{t}}$ and $\overline{\text{rq}}$ denote sets of terms and literals respectively and num is the number of the elements of a set. The values of function classes about variables are polynomial 'poly', fractional 'fract' and so on. L is the abstraction of a compound logical operator.

The quantitative expressions in a given problem are reduced to three abstract forms; q(term,term), rq(C-name:value,···,C-name:value) and L(rq(C-name:value,···,C-name:value)). They are called the objective-based literal expression OBL, the characteristic-based literal expression CBL and the abstract compound-literals expression ACL. These three forms are consturucted at the general identification and are permitted to appear in an expression as a mixed form.

In addition to the general identificaiton, sevral special identification routines are implemented which identifies the C-value if the transformation rule to be applied contains a special kind of C-name such as the degree of a polynomial.

Problem descriptions take the following forms. Problems such as a proof-problem (Qx)(P(x)→R(x)) are expressed as ((Qx)P(x)|(Qx)R(x)) based on the state space representation, where Qx is a sequence of quantifiers and both P(x) and R(x) are predicates and called the precondition and the goal respectively. Value-finding problems are also expressed in a similar format to proof problems as follows;

$$((\exists ?x)P(x)\,\|\,(\exists ?x)\mathrm{Obj}(L(x=t(\mathrm{var}:\phi)))),$$

where '‖' stands for an equivalence relation, and the goal part denotes to require an objective form corresponding to the ACL expression L(x=t(var:ϕ)).

3. THEOREMS AND TRANSFORMATION RULES

Mathematical theorems are classified into several subsets by their characteristics and can be accessed by means of a tree-like address table shown in Fig.1.

Tree 1:d-p-pf-q-ℓ } (a) Classification items
Tree 2:{fc,npf}-d-p-q-ℓ

Ⓓ 'all domain of numbers' — Ⓟ '=' ···· Ⓛ '1'-address

(b) A part of Tree 1.

Fig.1 Address trees.

Tree 1 concerns primitive functions pf's such as addition, while Tree 2 concerns function classes fc's such as polynomials and also non-primitive functions npf's such as the absolute function. The C-item d means the domain where a theorem holds. p is the item that indicates an equality or inequality relation. p indicates the kind of quantifiers and ℓ is the number of literals included in a premise of a theorem.

In addition to theorems, some relations called transformation rules 'TR's are introduced in order to find a global solving policy. There are two kinds of TRs, one of them is C-TRs and the other is P-TRs(i.e. problem-TRs). The form of a C-TR takes an implication form (Qx)(r(x)→s(x)) (OP:S), where r(x) and s(x) are conjunctive normal forms of some abstract expressions of literals. The symbols '$\overset{P}{\rightleftarrows}$' and '$\overset{P}{\rightarrow}$' represent probable relations. The OP part indicates location areas of supporting theorems, TRs or procedures of the TR. Some of the TRs are shown in Table 2.

(1) Characteristic-TRs

① rq(var:{x},fc:poly)
  ⇄ L($\overline{\mathrm{rq}}$(var:{x},fc:poly(deg:{1,2})))(OP:TR ②)

② t(var:{x},fc:poly)
  $\overset{P}{=}$ Π(t(var:{x},fc:poly(deg:{1,2})))(OP:PROC factorization)

③ (∀x) (≥(t(var:$\bar{y}$∪{x},fc:poly(deg:(x:2))),0)
  $\overset{P}{\rightleftarrows}$(≥(Σ($\bar{t}$(sgn:pz,var:$\bar{y}$)),0))(OP:TH ①,TH ②)

④ Σ($\bar{t}$(sgn:pz)) = t(sgn:pz)

(2) Problem-TRs

① (T|Q)⇔(Q‖T) ② (Q_1|Q_2)⇔(Q_1→Q_2‖T)

Table 2. Transformation rules.

The universal quantifier of TRs are omitted for simplicity. The logical connective symbol L, the predicate symbol q and the variable symbols x and y in the TRs are variables for which any corresponding instance or variable can be substituted. The predicate symbol q denotes equality or inequality. TR ① means that a polynomial relation will be reducible to a combined logical form which consists of several linear or quadratic relations. TR ② suggests that a polynomial term will be factorized into several linear or quadratic terms by a procedure. TR ③ shows an absolute inequality which contains quadratic terms about a variable can be transformed to a sum of definite sign terms such as definite positive terms, where TH ① and TH ② are

a≠0→a*x**2+b*x+c=a*(x+b/(2*a))**2+c-b**2/(4*a)

and

a>0∧c-b**2/(4*a)≥0
  ⇄(∀x)a*(x+b/(2*a))**2+c-b**2/(4*a)≧0

respectively.
In P-TRs, the symbols Q,Q_1 and Q_2 are variables for which any logical formula can be substituted. The symbol T denotes a tautology such as t(sgn:p)>0.

The access to TRs is performed by the aid of a tree-like address table a part of which is shown in Fig.2.

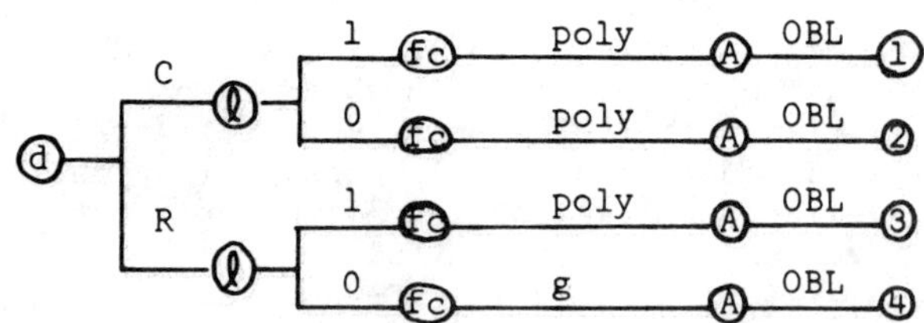

Fig.2. A part of address table of TRs.

In the address table, the items d,ℓ and fc have the same meanings as in Fig.1. The value C denotes the complex number domain, while R denotes the real number domain. ℓ0,ℓ1 and ℓ2 mean ℓ=0, ℓ=1 and ℓ≥2 respectively. A TR with ℓ=0 is a no-premise relation. The value g of the item fc denotes the general-function class. 'A' indicates the abstraction levels of premises of TRs. If a TR involves several literal expressions of different abstraction levels, its address is recorded at the respective abstraction levels.

The following describes the main part of application procedures of TRs to the conjunctive normal form of the precondition of a problem. At the first step of application procedures, if the abstraction level of a TR is lower than that of a problem, the abstraction level of the TR is raised to that of the problem by the identification of the TR, otherwise the usual unification algorithm is adopted. Let $P_1'\wedge\cdots\wedge P_n'\cdots$(a) and $P_{i1}\wedge\cdots\wedge P_{im}\rightarrow Q\cdots$(b) be a precondition of a problem and a TR respectively, where P' means an instantiation of P and {i1,···,im} is a subset of {1,···,n}, then the result of the application of (b) to (a) is $P_1'\wedge\cdots\wedge P_n'\wedge Q'$. If the implication symbol is replaced by the equivalence symbol in eq. (b), $P_{i1}',\cdots,P_{im}'$ are removed from the result.

4. SOLVING PROCEDURES

The solving procedures of EAPS are divided into three phases;(i)the identification of the current problem at the three abstract levels, ACL, CBL and OBL,(ii)the breadth-first search of a relevant global solving policies by the aid of the tree-like address table and (iii)the depth-first solving in a concrete form according to the suggestion of the obtained global solving policies. A part of a solving tree generated by EAPS is shown in Fig.3, where the forms of PB, PB_i and PB_i' are (P|G), (P|Q) and (Q|G) respectively. The global solving policies are placed in the ascending order of the difference between the precondition and the goal of PB_i' which is evaluated based on the assigned values to the fundamental C-items.

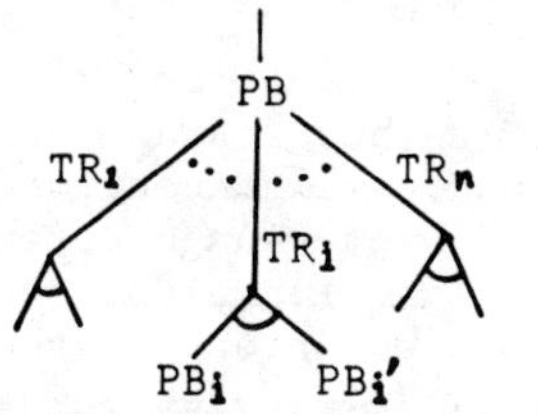

Fig.3 A part of a solving tree.

If no global solving policy is found, EAPS searches applicable theorems by the aid of the tree-like address table of theorems. If EAPS fails to find applicable theorems, it applies P-TRs to the current problem then retries to solve the problem.

[Example] 'Prove that if k is a real number, the equation x**2-2*k*x+2*k-2=0 of x has real roots'. The expression of the problem is

(k∈R|(∃x)root(var:x,rel:x**2-2*k*x+2*k-2=0) ⊂R) (1)

Since there is no applicable TR or TH to the precondition of eq.(1), the problem transformation is tried. The application of P-TR ① to eq.(1) yields

((∀k)(∃x)(~k∈R∨root(var:x,rel:x**2-2*k*x-2*k-2=0)⊂R‖T). (2)

After finding no applicable TRs, one candidate of applicable theorems

(∃x)(root(var:x,rel:a*x**2+b*x+c=0)⊂R) ⇄ b**2-4*a*c≥0

is found from the address area fc:poly-d:real-p:nq-q:∀-ℓ:1 involved in the address table of THs. The application of the above theorem to the precondition of eq.(2) results in

((∀k)~k∈R∨k**2-2*k+2≥0‖1≥0). (3)

The CBL form of eq.(3) is

((∀k)~k∈R∨rq-3·2(var:{k},fc:poly)‖ rq-3·3(var:φ,form:2)). (4)

The numbers 3·2 and 3·3 in eq.(4) denote the second and the third literals of eq.(3) respectively. The candidates of applicable TRs are ① and ③. The application of TR ① fails in the adoption of TR ② which is suggested by TR ①. The application of TR ③ to the OBL form of eq.(3) results in

((∀k)~k∈R∨≥(Σ(t̄(sgn:pz,var:{k})),0) ‖≥(t(sgn:pz),0)).

The application of the theorem TH ① suggested by TR ③ to eq.(3) leads to the result;

((∀k)~k∈R∨(k-1)**2+1≥0‖1≥0). (5)

The highest level of abstraction of applicable TRs to the precondition of eq.(5) is OBL, that is;

((∀k)~k∈R∨q-5·2(Σ(t̄(var:{k},fc:poly,sgn:pz)), 0)‖ ≥(t(sgn:pz),0)). (6)

The number 5·2 denotes the second literal of the precondition of eq.(5). The application of TR ④ to the precondition of eq.(6) yields

((∀k)~k∈R∨≥(t(sgn:pz),0)‖≥(t(sgn:pz),0))

which leads to the completion of the proof.

6. CONCLUSION

The first version of EAPS[3] implemented on a mini-computer in an assembly language solved problems such as those which involve a simultaneous linear equation symbolically in about ten seconds. The new EAPS with additional facilities presented in this paper is under development on a computer with a 768 kB memory in LISP 1.5.

ACKNOWLEDGMENTS

The authors wish to thank Mr. K.Imori for his help in the implementation of EAPS.

REFERENCES

[1] Sacerdoti, E.D. "Planning in a Hierarchy of Abstraction Spaces." Artif. Intell. 5:1 (1974) 115-135.

[2] Bledsoe, W.W. "Non-resolution Theorem Proving." Artif. Intell. 9:1 (1977) 1-35.

[3] Nishida, F. and Fujita, Y. "A Hierarchical and Heuristic Problem-solving in Elementary Algebra." In Proc. UJCC-78. UJCC Commitee, San Fransisco, California, October, 1978, pp. 99-103.

THE FRAMEWORK OF KNOWLEDGE REPRESENTATION AND ITS RETRIEVAL IN LGS -- THE LITERATURE GUIDE SYSTEM

Toyo-aki NISHIDA and Shuji DOSHITA
Department of Information Science
Kyoto University
Sakyo-ku, Kyoto 606, Japan

This paper describes the framework of knowledge representation and the techniques for information retrieval in a program called LGS (the Literature Guide System). LGS will answer questions about scientific literatures in natural language. Model theoretic approach is employed to represent the meanings of sentences in the abstracts of literatures. The knowledge base is a set of interpreted logical formulas, and is partitioned into possible worlds. User's own view to the knowledge base can be incorporated into objects called script frames. A script frame is defined in terms of logical formulas. A query to the knowledge base is presented as a pattern. A list containing all items which match the pattern will be returned as the result. A set of rules for pattern matching are defined in terms of logic, and are designed so as to cover the cases of paraphrases and categorical implications. LGS is composed of an accommodator, a retriever, and a natural language interface. It is under development on the personal LISP system.

1. INTRODUCTION

LGS [1] is an experimental system which integrates knowledge about scientific literatures and which will answer questions about them. LGS is toward a natural language data base system (NLDB system). In any NLDB system, the problems of knowledge representation and information retrieval are crucial.

We employ the model theoretic approach to a NLDB system. The model theory gives the formal semantics to the knowledge representation in a NLDB system. The meaning of a sentence is described as a logical formula of the intensional logic. Many aspects of natural language expressions such as modalities can be clearly explained by the concept of a possible world. Our approach to a NLDB system can be summarized in the following schema;

NATURAL LANGUAGE EXPRESSION
(STEP1) syntactic analysis
LAMBDA EXPRESSION
(STEP2) lambda calculus
LOGICAL FORMULA OF INTENSIONAL LOGIC
(STEP3) interpretation
DOMAIN DESCRIPTION BY META-LANGUAGE
(STEP4) accommodation
THE KNOWLEDGE BASE

The idea about STEP1 and STEP2 is formalized in MG (Montague Grammar) [2] which is implemented in the natural language interface. In this paper, we concentrate on STEP3 and STEP4. In STEP3, meta-language expressions are created from logical formulas, and in STEP4, they are accommodated into the knowledge base with some auxiliary data objects which are called frames.

Information retrieval plays an important part in question answering. Pattern matching among meta-expressions is a basic technique in information retrieval. Rules for pattern matching are defined in terms of logic. The concept hierarchy is defined as logical implications between concept predicates. The rules are presented to cope with the cases of paraphrases and categorical implications.

We are implementing those ideas as LGS. Currently, we have a limited version, LGS-0, where simple dialogs are available using Japanese or query commands.

2. KNOWLEDGE REPRESENTATION AND THE KNOWLEDGE BASE

2.1 Meta-language Expressions

In general, the interpretation of natural language, that is, the proper generation of domain description from a given natural language expression, is accompanied with much difficulty, especially when treating quantifiers. So, by employing some conventional expressions in meta-language to leave ambiguity in translation, we shall put aside those problems temporarily. Here we show some of those representations. (Representations in natural language are enclosed by "...".)

(E1) indef[x; program(x)] for "a program"
(E2) def[x; program(x)] for "the program"

Def and indef are a definite operator and an indefinite operator, respectively.

(E3) love("she","he") in a possible world P, for "he believes that she loves him."

Where the possible world P is the one which is "believed by him."

2.2 The Knowledge Base

Conceptually, the knowledge base is a set of meta-expressions which are partitioned into possible worlds. In the actual implementation, the knowledge base is constructed from data structures, called paragraphs, units, and frames. A paragraph is a possible world management block. A unit is a data structure for internal representation of a meta-expression. There are four types of a unit, I-, P-, F-, and O-unit. An I-unit (Individual-unit) is used for an object, which includes a set of references to the object. A P-unit (Predicate-unit) is for a predicate. Not only a set of references but also a list of 'case slot and filler' pairs for the predicate are included. A F-unit (Function-unit) is for a function. An O-unit (Operator-unit) is for an operator.

A frame is a data structure for representing more complicated but stereotyped knowledge. Two levels of a frame, a basic frame and a script frame are defined. A basic frame is a data structure defined for each predicate symbol and function symbol. It includes the definition of the symbol and the index of its occurences in the knowledge base. The concept hierarchy, which plays a key part in inference on the knowledge base, is embedded in the collection of basic frames as implication relationships among predicate symbols. A script frame is a data structure defined for more complicated situation. It includes case structure, frame definition, and knowledge base search strategies. Users can define script frames with their own case structure and knowledge base search strategies. Here we shall show an example of a script schema about a "natural language understanding system."

```
script-name:=
    NATURAL-LANGUAGE-UNDERSTANDING-SYSTEM;
    1) VARIABLE DECLARATIONS:
      DCL x,y,z,w objects;
      DCL P,Q,R,S,T,U predicates;
    2) INSTANTIATION CONDITIONS:
      P:understand(x,y) & Q:written-in(y,z) &
      R:natural-language(z) & S:system(x);
    3) CASE DEFINITIONS:
      name:=w such that name(x,w),
      theme:=y,
      method:=T such that method(P,T),
      performance:=U such that actor(U)=x;
```

Script frames will be created for all knowledge structures that fill the instantiation conditions.

2.3 Interpretation and Accommodation

In this section, we shall overview how the meta-expression is created from a given logical formula, and accommodated into the knowledge base. First, a paragraph is created for the actual world. Then the knowledge structure construction program reads logical formulas one by one. Let a given formula be f, then the construction process proceeds as follows;

1) set a pointer (WP) to the actual world.
2) seek a possible world which is related to the actual world by a modal operator or an intensional operator in the formula. If it is found, move WP to the possible world, and if not, create a new possible world corresponding to the operator and move WP to the new world. Remove the operator from f.
3) remove indef and def operators if possible. If f is a predicate P(...indef[x;q(x)]...), and P is an extensional predicate, create a new object c in the possible world pointed by WP, and generate internal structure corresponding to P(...c...) and q(c). If f is a predicate P(...def[x;q(x)]...), search the object that satisfies q(x), and if it is found, replace def[x;q(x)] by the object.
4) construct a network structure for the resulting formula and put it into the world pointed by WP.
5) add an index to the related basic frames.

Steps 2-5 may be called recursively when the given formula is nested. Script frames may be instantiated for the generated knowledge structure if the instantiation conditions are filled.

3. INFORMATION RETRIEVAL

An important type of an information retrieval request may be "for the given predicate P, find all objects (x's) such that P(x) is true in some possible world." Any object y should be retrieved if D(y)->P(y) holds in some possible world, where D(y) is the conjunction of all descriptions about y. In LGS, the pattern matching method is used to test the implication, since the direct proof of the implication by a resolution-based theorem prover is inefficient and inflexible. Each formula is regarded as a symbolic pattern. The predicate match[P*,y] is tested instead of D(y)->P(y), where P* is indef[x;P(x)].

The retriever consists of an index searcher, a matcher, and a modality generator. The index searcher examines the index structure of basic frames to produce a list of candidates. Then for each element y in the list of candidates, the matcher tests if the pattern matches y. Any candidates that do not match the pattern are removed from the list. Finally, the modality generator may add appropriate modal operators to the remaining candidates so that they may be the predicates in the actual world.

A set of rules are defined for pattern matching. Especially,

(RULE1) categorical implication rule:
a pattern P matches another pattern D if
$D \vdash P$.
(RULE2) paraphrasing rule:
a pattern P matches another pattern D if there exists a predicate Q such that
$P \vdash Q$ and $D \vdash Q$,
where natural deductions are used with the set of axioms for the concept hierarchy.

RULE1 covers the cases of categorical implications. For example, the pattern "animal" matches "human-being". RULE2 covers the cases of paraphrases. For example, a predicate
give(actor=A,object=B,direction=C)
can match the predicate
get(actor=C,object=B,source=A)
where the predicate Q is
transfer(object=B,source=A,direction=C).
The range of the applications of deductions in RULE2 should be limited for plausibility.

4. EXPERIMENTS

LGS is under development on the personal LISP system (LISP1.7) [3]. We currently have a limited version of LGS (LGS-0). LGS-0 can integrate the knowledge about the literatures and answer questions. The interactions can be done in natural language. LGS-0 consists of three program modules (the natural language interface, the accommodator, and the retriever) and the knowledge base. The natural language interface is used (1) to translate both sentences of literatures and queries into logical formulas of intensional logic, and (2) to generate natural language outputs as the replies to queries. The details are described in [1].

LGS-0 can perform simple dialogs like below in Japanese.

U: do you know any literature about a question answering system?
(Information retrieval is done.)
S: YES, I KNOW 20 SUCH SYSTEMS.
U: take one of them!
U: what is the name?
S: LGS
U: what kind of questions can it answer?
S: IT WILL ANSWER QUESTIONS ABOUT SCIENTIFIC LITERATURES.
(Question answering about the found object.)
U: which papers describe it?
S: THE PAPER THAT IS SUBMITTED TO THE 6TH IJCAI.
(A literature is guided.)
U: what aspects does it describe?
S: THE FRAMEWORK OF KNOWLEDGE REPRESENTATION AND INFORMATION RETRIEVAL IS DESCRIBED.
... (U: a user, S: the system)

5. CONCLUSION

In this paper, we have attempted to show our model theoretic approach to a NLDB system. We think LGS is a good example for such an approach. Of course, there are lots of problems to be solved in future. Especially, the problem of inferences in the possible world domain [4] is important.

REFERENCES

[1] T.Nishida "A Knowledge Based Question Answering system on Scientific Literatures." Master Thesis at Kyoto University, 1979, (Japanese)

[2] D.Dowty "A Guide to Montague's PTQ." Indiana University Linguistic Club, 1978

[3] S.Doshita, K.Hiramatsu, K.Kakui "Implementation of LISP System Using Direct Accessible Bulk Memory." Trans. of IECE Japan, vol.J61-D, no.5, 1978, (Japanese)

[4] R.Moore "Reasoning about Knowledge and Action." in Proc. IJCAI-77, pp.223-227, 1977

THE THEOREM PROVER USING A PARALLEL PROCESSING SYSTEM

Hitoshi Ogawa*, Tadahiro Kitahashi** and Kokichi Tanaka*

* Faculty of Engineering Science
Osaka University
Toyonaka, Osaka 560
JAPAN

** Toyohashi University of Technology
Toyohashi, Aichi 440
JAPAN

1. INTRODUCTION

An AND/OR graph is often used to solve problems. It abstractly expressed the concept of dividing one problem into several sub-problems which are independently solved. This makes it possible that the sub-problems are solved in a parallel process. In this paper, D-graph deduction is proposed, which is based on a reductio ad absurdum using D-graph (a kind of directed AND/OR graph). The D-graphs are corresponded to the predicate logic formulas which represent the axioms and the negation of the theorem proved.

If several sub-problems share the same variables in problem solving, then the way in which one problem is solved may affect the solution of the others. This prevents sub-problems from being solved independently. There is the same issue in the D-graph deduction. The use of micro -actors settles such an issue. The micro-actors are the modules which compose basic structure for the knowledge representation. They can be applied to search a D-graph, because the D-graph basically consists of OUT-AND arcs. It will be shown that the sub-problems are solved independently in a micro-actor system in which the micro -actors correspond to the nodes in the D-graph and the common variables.

2. D-GRAPH DEDUCTION

2.1 First Order Predicate Logic and D-graphs

The authors will propose a formal deduction method using a directed AND/OR graph, called D-graph deduction, which is based on a reductio ad absurdum argument for the first order logic using D-graphs. Nodes in the D-graph are corresponded to the predicate symbols, their negations, TN (which means true), and FN (which means false). A set of arcs indicates a clause (a predicate logical formula).

[Definition 1] A label (α,β) is attached to arc (A,B) corresponding to the formula $A(\alpha) \to B(\beta)$, as shown in Fig. 1. α and β are the arguments of the predicates A and B, respectively. Thus, a label to an arc is an ordered pair of variable vectors, whose components are the variables and Skolem functions of predicates corresponding to the start and the goal nodes.

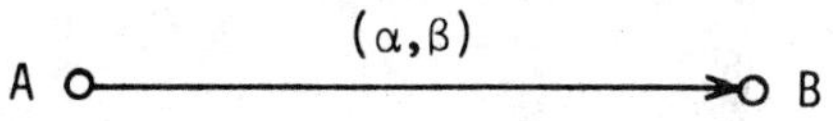

Fig. 1 D-graph representing $A(\alpha) \to B(\beta)$.

Let Greek lower-case letters express the tuple of constants, variables and Skolem functions.

[Definition 2] (Rules for translating clauses to a D-graph)

(1) Select a clause from a set of support, where the set of support is a non-empty subset K of the initial set S of clauses such that S - K is satisfiable. Let the clause be represented $L_1(\lambda_1)\vee\ldots\vee L_h(\lambda_h)$.

The clause may be modified as follows:

$$\text{True} \to L_1(\lambda_1)\vee\ldots\vee L_h(\lambda_h)$$
$$= (\text{True} \to L_1(\lambda_1))\vee\ldots\vee(\text{True} \to L_h(\lambda_h)).$$

Nodes $L_1, \ldots, L_h$ in the D-graph are regarded as OUT-AND nodes concerning TN, and arcs $(TN, L_1), \ldots, (TN, L_h)$ are grouped by a linking symbol. Attached to the arcs are the labels $(,\lambda_1), \ldots, (,\lambda_h)$ (See Fig. 2 (a)).

(2) Let $L_1(\lambda_1)\vee\ldots\vee L_m(\lambda_m)$ be a clause which has more than one literal, excluding the clause chosen at (1). This clause can be translated as follows:

$$\neg L_i(\lambda_i) \to L_1(\lambda_1)\vee\ldots\vee L_{i-1}(\lambda_{i-1})\vee L_{i+1}(\lambda_{i+1})\vee\ldots\vee L_m(\lambda_m)$$

$= (\neg L_i(\lambda_i) \rightarrow L_1(\lambda_1)) \vee \ldots$
$\vee(\neg L_i(\lambda_i) \rightarrow L_{i-1}(\lambda_{i-1})) \vee (\neg L_i(\lambda_i) \rightarrow L_{i+1}(\lambda_{i+1}))$
$\vee \ldots \vee (\neg L_i(\lambda_i) \rightarrow L_m(\lambda_m)).$

The D-graph representing this formula consists of OUT-AND arcs and nodes conserning $\neg L$ as shown in Fig. 2 (b). The above operation must be performed for all i (i = 1, ..., m).

(3) A unit clause $L(\lambda)$, which is not selected at (1), may be modified to $\neg L(\lambda) \rightarrow$ False. $L(\lambda)$ is therefore represented as the D-graph illustrated in Fig. 2 (c).

(4) $L(\lambda)$ and $\neg L(\lambda)$ are always inconsistent, so the clause set containing them is unsatisfiable. They are indicated by IN-AND arcs and nodes concerning FN, as shown in Fig. 2 (d).

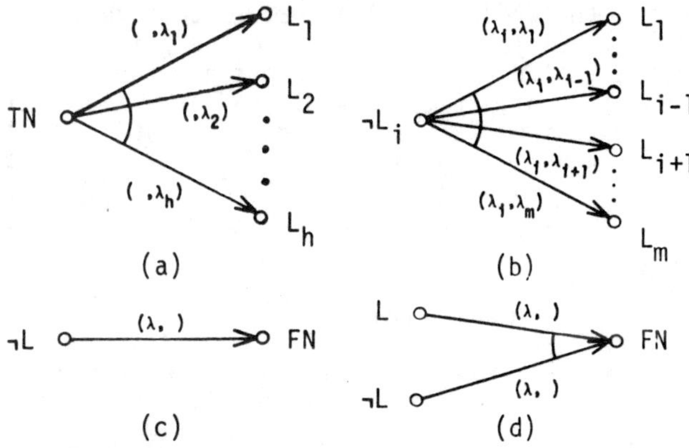

Fig. 2 D-graph
(a) $\text{True} \rightarrow L_1(\lambda_1) \vee \ldots \vee L_h(\lambda_h)$
(b) $\neg L_i(\lambda_i) \rightarrow L_1(\lambda_1) \vee \ldots \vee L_{i-1}(\lambda_{i-1})$ $L_{i+1}(\lambda_{i+1}) \vee \ldots \vee L_m(\lambda_m)$
(c) $L(\lambda)$
(d) $(L(\lambda), \neg L(\lambda))$.

2.2 Completeness of D-graph Deduction

D-graph deduction is carried out by communicating the state of a node to its successor and by referring to the labels. The following define the state of a node and its communication rule, and the relation between a node and FN in the D-graph.

[Definition 3] Suppose e, with lable (α, β), denotes the arc from node A to node B, and that γ represents the state of A. If there exists the most general unifier (m.g.u.) π of α and γ, the state γ of A is said to satisfy the label condition and e is said to be abailable. Then the state of B is $\beta\pi$. When the state γ of A does not satisfy the label condition of e, nothing is conveyed to B, i.e., this is equivalent to that saying arc e does not exist.

[Definition 4] (Achievability for a D-graph) Achievability is defined between any node and FN as follows:

(1) If a node A is connected to FN by an arc (A, FN) which is not an IN-AND arc and is available, then $A \xrightarrow{*} FN$.

(2) Suppose that the set of arcs $(A, N_1), \ldots, (A, N_m)$ forms an OUT-AND arcs concerning A. If each of the arcs is available and $N_j \xrightarrow{*} FN$ (i = 1, ..., m), then $A \xrightarrow{*} FN$.

(3) If there is a sequence of arcs $(\neg A, N_1), (N_1, N_2), \ldots, (N_n, A)$ (or $(A, N_1), (N_1, N_2), \ldots, (N_n, \neg A)$) and all arcs are available together with the most general unifier π for the states of A and $\neg A$, then $A \xrightarrow{*} FN$ ($\neg A \xrightarrow{*} FN$). If there are nodes $M_1, \ldots, M_m$ which have an OUT-AND relation with $\neg A$ (A), FN must be achievable from them and the state of M_i (i = 1, ..., m) applied must satisfy the label condition.

(4) $A \xrightarrow{*} FN$ is only generated by applying the above rules.

The D-graph deduction is carried out to determine whether FN is achievable from TN in D-graph which represents the axioms and the negation of the theorem. The states of nodes and the labels of arcs are employed to deal with the arguments of the predicates. The completeness of the D-graph deduction is guarenteed by Theorem 1.

[Theorem 1] Let G be the D-graph representing a set of S of clauses. S is unsatisfiable if and only if $TN \xrightarrow{*} FN$ in G.

3. PARALLEL PROCESSING SYSTEM

In this section, a parallel processing system is described to solve the problem using micro-actors. The micro-actors are the modules for the knowledge base. The micro-actor is composed of a script and an acquaintance. The script consists of the pairs of the message pattern and the action corresponding to the pattern. The micro-actor has the acquaintance as a memory space to hold the data and the names of the other micro-actors it directly knows about. Since only message passing is the interactive method between the micro-actors, the action of a micro-actor never affects the other micro-actors. This enable us to construct a parallel processing system.

3.1 Node Micro-Actors and Variable Micro-Actors

We will define two kinds of micro-actors. One is a node micro-actor (NMA), which corresponds to a node in a D-graph. Scripts of NMAs are the same. That is, they have a program which sends messages to the other NMAs according to their acquaintances. An NMA stores the relation between the node indicated by the NMA and the other nodes, in ELIST in its acquaintance. An example of ELIST is as shown in Fig. 4 (a).

Another is a variable micro-actor (VMA), which corresponds to a common variable and is made under searching a graph. Since a micro-actor is independent of the other micro-actors except for message sending, a VMA is independent of the other VMAs and NMAs. However, several NMAs must be able to refer to one VMA. There are two kinds of actions of a VMA:

(1) Add the sent data to the aquaintance.
(2) Reply the data which have flag sent.

The basic data of the acquaintance is in form of (F V), where F is a set of flags which are similar to sentence number, and V is a value. (When the value is not given, V is NIL.)

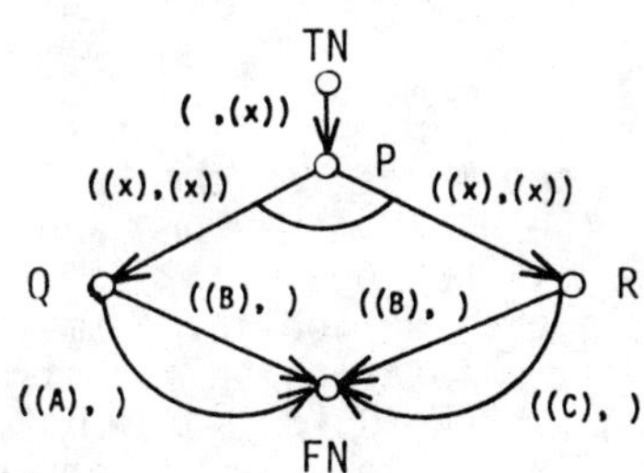

Fig. 3 A part of D-graph in Example 1.

TN-ELIST = ((NIL P (x)).
P-ELIST = (((?x) Q (x) R (x))).
Q-ELIST = (((A) FN NIL) ((B) FN NIL)).
R-ELIST = (((B) FN NIL) ((C) FN NIL)).

(a)

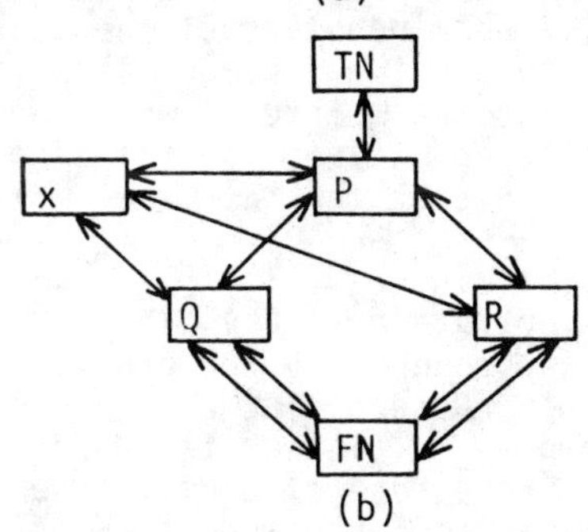

(b)

Fig. 4 ELISTs (a) and micro-actors (b) in Example 1.

[Example 1] The D-graph illustrated in Fig. 3 is a part of D-graph representing the following clauses:

axioms: $\neg P(x) \vee Q(x) \vee R(x)$, $\neg Q(A)$, $\neg Q(B)$, $\neg R(B)$, $\neg R(C)$.

negation of theorem: $P(x)$.

Where A, B and C are constants, and x is a variable. Fig. 4 (b) shows a micro-actor system corresponding to the D-graph in Fig. 3. Fig. 4 (a) shows ELISTs in the micro-actors. Graph searching begins when TN sends the messages and is carried out by sending message from NMAs to NMAs. NMAs perform one of three operations: expansion (sending the messages to successors), merging (merging several messages into one) and partial refutation (which is similar to ancestor resolution). FN replies to its ancestor. When a NMA receives a reply, the NMA checks the consistency of it. So the result of the system does not depend on the order of replies the messages which are sent concurrently. The system is stopped when a reply is sent to TN. Sending message from NMAs to NMAs makes the coroutine control, while sending message from NMAs to VMAs makes the subroutine control.

REFERENCES

[1] Hewitt, C. & Smith, B. "Towards a Programming Apprentice." IEEE Trans. on SE. SE-1:1 (1975) 26-45.

[2] Levi, G. & Sirovich, F. "Generalized AND/OR Graphs." Artif. Intell. 7:3 (1976) 243-259.

[3] Ogawa, H. & Tanaka, K. "A Structure for Representation of knowledge -- A Proposal for A Micro-Actor --." In Proc. IJCAI-77. (1977) 248-249.

[4] Ogawa, H., Nanba, H. and Tanaka, K. "An Active Frame for The Knowledge Representaion." In Proc. IJCAI-79. (1979).

[5] Robinson, J. A. "A Machine-Oriented Logic Based on The Resolution Principle." JACM 12 (1965) 23-41.

[6] Slagle, J. R. & Koniver, D. A. "Finding Resolution Proofs and Using Duplicate Goals in AND/OR Trees." Information Science, 3 (1971) 315-342.

AN ACTIVE FRAME FOR THE KNOWLEDGE REPRESENTAION

Hitoshi Ogawa*, Hideaki Nanba** and Kokichi Tanaka*

* Faculty of Engineering Science
Osaka University
Toyonaka, Osaka 560
JAPAN

** NIHON-DENSO
Kariya, Aichi 448
JAPAN

This paper describes micro-actors which construct the knowledge representation in which the modularity was established without sacrificing the interaction. The behavior of the micro-actor is defined in terms of only one kind of action: sending message to another micro-actor. The micro-actor is composed of a script and an acquaintance. The script consists of the pairs of the message pattern and the action corresponding to the pattern. The micro-actor has the acquaintance as a memory space to hold the data and the names of the other micro-actors it directly knows about. As a result of using the micro-actors, we can deal with knowledge about the actions as well as knowledge about the world states. The information about an action sent from a micro -actor is effective only in the micro-actor which received it. This guarantees the modularity of micro-actors.

An example shows that the continuation in a message make both the subroutine control and the coroutine control possible. The other indicates a dialogue in the question-answering system using the micro-actors.

1. INTRODUCTION

Artificial Intelligence is a branch of computer science which is mainly concerned with the problem solving, the cognition, and the comprehension of natural languages. Many approaches to the problem solving have been developed; for example, the algorithm A* (Hart) [4] for searching trees, the resolution principle (Robinson) [13], GPS [2] and its application: STRIPS (Fiks, Nilsson) and so on. The resent approach is the development of the programming language for artificial intelligence. The cognition is the intelligence process to acquire knowledge in the image understanding and the speech understanding. The comprehension of natural languages needs the integration of many approaches in artificial intelligence.

The common issues of the above mentioned themes are the knowledge representation and the mechanism of understanding and inference. In this discussion, "Knowledge" does not mean only the facts about a world state but also the techniques dealing with the facts. The artificial intelligence system obtains information from the scene and/or the statements in natural language. The system, then, acquires new knowledge by comparing the obtained information with the knowledge the system has. Therefore, the knowledge representation is necessary, in which it is easy to specify knowledge, modify it and refer to it. There have been two types for the representation of knowledge: the declarative one and the procedural one [17]. The modularity is emphasized in the former; e.g., the logical formulas. On the other hand, the interaction is stressed in the latter; e.g., PLANNER [5], QA4 [16], CONNEVER [9] and so on. The declarative representation has several benefits: The separation of knowledge into data and procedures brings the flexibility and economy of the declarative representation. The independence of the axioms or facts leads to the understandability and learnability of them. On the contrary, in the procedural representation, a frame axiom need not be specified. Furthermore, the heuristic knowledge can be treated in it. To utilize both benefits of the declarative representation and the procedural one, it is necessary to develop the method in which the modularity is established without sacrificing the possibilities for interaction.

KRL (Bobrow, D.G. & Winograd, T.) [1] and FRL (Roberts, R.B. & Goldstein, I.P.) [14, 15] are developed as the approaches to the problem mentioned above. Both KRL and FRL are based on frames, and attempt to integrate procedural knowledge with a broad base of declatative forms. By the way, there is some knowledge about the action; for example, the control of the reasoning mechanism, the data base processing and so on.

Such knowledge is preferable to be expressed by the procedures rather than the declarative forms. If declarative knowledge is integrated with the procedures which deal with it, and the procedures have the modularity, then we can freely use both declarative knowledge and procedural one.

This paper describes a micro-actor* as a method for knowledge representation. The script of a micro-actor contains procedural knowledge to deal with only the acquaintance of the micro -actor. The acquaintance has declarative knowledge in the form of frame.

2. REPRESENTATION OF WORLD-STATE

2.1 Frame Representation In Acquaintance

A micro-actor is composed of a script and an acquaintance. The script describes the behavior which the micro-actor should take when it receives a message. The acquaintance is the memory space for the micro-actor. The acquaintance stores the data that the micro-actor knows; for example, its native values, its attributes, the names of the other micro-actors it directly knows about, and the relation with them. The followings are the reason why the concept of Frame Theory [8, 10] is used for construction of an acquaintance:

(1) A frame is a data-structure representing a stereotyped situation.

(2) Several kinds of information can be attached to each frame, and some of this information is about how to use the frame.

(3) Frames enable us to represent knowledge in a hierarchical structure.

Fig. 1 shows a slot array representation to indicate a frame intuitively. A frame is, however, represented by the nested association lists as shown in Fig. 2 in its implementation. The respective substructures of a frame are named; Slot, Facet, Datum and Comment. A slot shows which property the data in it are connected with. A facet shows kinds of the data; e.g., values, constraints, procedures and so on. A datum is elementary information associated with the facet, and a comment is additional information

---

* The micro-actor was proposed as the implementation of some of abilities of actor (Hewitt, C.) [6, 7] in 1977 [11]. A new version of a micro-actor described in this paper has similar abilities of actor. Parallel process and coroutine control are possible in a micro -actor system. There is a slight difference between the micro-actor and the actor in point of notation.

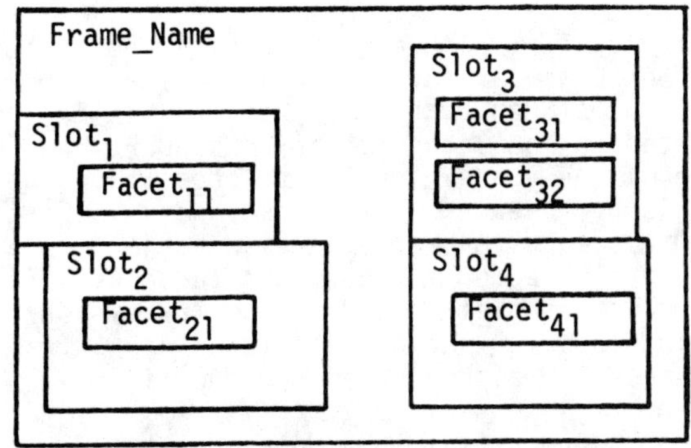

Fig. 1

Slot array representation of a frame.

(Frame_Name

$(S_1\ (F_{11}\ (D_{111}\ C_{111})\ \ldots\ (D_{11h}\ C_{11h})))$

$(S_2\ (F_{21}\ (D_{211}\ C_{211})\ \ldots\ (D_{21i}\ C_{21i})))$

$(S_3\ (F_{31}\ (D_{311}\ C_{311})\ \ldots\ (D_{31j}\ C_{31j}))$

$(F_{32}\ (D_{321}\ C_{321})\ \ldots\ (D_{32k}\ C_{32k})))$

......

......

$(S_s\ (F_{s1}\ (D_{s11}\ C_{s11})\ \ldots\ (D_{s1m}\ C_{s1m})))$

)

Fig. 2

Nested list representation of a frame.
S: slot, F: facet,
D: datum, C: comment.

for the datum.

2.2 Effect On Other Frames

An addition of procedures to a slot of a frame enables the frame to acquire information from other frames and to change the contents of the other frames. This may make it possible to combine the declarative knowledge and the procedural knowledge; that is, the modurality and the interaction. However, a question still remains to be solved.

A frame is freely dealt with using three basic functions; obtaining something from the frame, putting somthing to it, and removing from it. The use of only the three functions is, however, inconvenient and uneconomical when a frame is dealt with in several ways. New functions should be made either in advance or afterward. We will try to put box A on box B in a block world.

Assume that there are frames which correspond to box A and box B. To put box A on box B is executed by the following process; If both box A and box B are a kind of Block and Cleartop*, and box B is Supportable**, then let box A be supported on box B and let box B support box A. The knowledge concerning the process mentioned above is represented in three methods: (1) Function ON is made in order to put an object on another, and is added to the basic fuctions. (2) The process is distributed to the frames corresponding to box A and box B. (3) A new frame is created corresponding to the function ON.

In (1), there exists the chunk of procedures dealing with frames. A slight change of a procedure often affects the other procedures. As a result, (1) is not good to represent the knowledge about actions in A.I. system. General functions can be used in both (1) and (3). On the contrary, a procedure depends on a particular frame in (2). (2) is convenient to describe the procedure closely depending on the frame, and to establish the modularity among procedures. It is, however, wasteful when several frames have the similar function. (3) is equal to (1) in essence. So there remains the possibility of the unlimited and unrestricted interactions. However, the application of the idea of actor to (3) leads the module for representing knowledge with proper interaction method.

The actor model is suitable to control and describe the interaction between the modules. Namely, the action of an actor is defined in terms of only one kind of action; sending messages to the other actors, and any other side effect is not permitted. When the actor receives a message, it becomes active and tries to play its role. The authors think that the actor model is useful for parallel processing.

3. REPRESENTATION OF ACTION

The chapter 2 said that a frame is good for representing the knowledge about a world state, but not so good for representing the knowledge about an action. On the other hand, a micro-actor is very suitable for representing the action. The micro-actor, which is a procedure, is a basic module in order to construct the knowledge base. This chapter describes the form of script which represents the behavior, and illustrates how to deal with the knowledge about the world state using message passing.

---

* Cleartop means the state in which the box supports nothing.

** The box which is supportable can suppor another box.

3.1 Micro-Actor

The script of the micro-actor precisely represents the message passing, the parallel computation and the coroutine control. The form of the script is similar to Yonezawa's notation[19]. But the micro-actor is based on LISP whereas his notation is based upon PLASMA.

(i) Script

The script is specified with a set of pairs of message patterns and rules as follows:

$$
\begin{aligned}
&((\text{message\_pattern}_1 \;\; \text{rule}_{11} \cdots \text{rule}_{1m})\\
&\;(\text{message\_pattern}_2 \;\; \text{rule}_{21} \cdots \text{rule}_{2n})\\
&\qquad\vdots\\
&\;(\text{message\_pattern}_p \;\; \text{rule}_{p1} \cdots \text{rule}_{pq})).
\end{aligned}
$$

(ii) Message Pattern

There are two types for pattern:
(1) (MES: ?%N *content* TO: ?CONT).
(2) (RE: ?%N *content*).
?%N is only matched with the message number %n, where n is a positive integer. A message number is assigned to an input sentence or a message for distinguishing it from the others as a tag. The message number is also used to distinguish a datum from the others stored in the same micro -actor. The atoms prefixed by "?" (e.g., ?CONT) are the variables for pattern matching. The prefix "!" is used instead of the prefix "?" to refer to the pattern matching variables for their values; for example, !CONT. "MES:" means a message and "RE:" means a reply. "TO:" means that the continuation is !CONT. The continuation is the micro-actor which is sent a reply. Assign "NO-ONE" to !CONT in the case that the answer is not required. Assign "ME" to !CONT when the reply is demanded. This is equal to the subroutine control.

(iii) Rule

A rule is a set of programs, which carries out a job. The rule consists of three parts as follows:

$$
\begin{aligned}
&((\text{P-C:} \;\; \text{program}_{p1} \cdots \text{program}_{pq})\\
&\;(\text{N-C:} \;\; \text{program}_{n1} \cdots \text{program}_{nr})\\
&\;(\text{C-E:} \;\; \text{program}_{c1} \cdots \text{program}_{cs})).
\end{aligned}
$$

"P-C:" is an abbreviation for pre-condition. "N-C:" means next-condition which is an option. "C-E:" is an abbreviation for caused-events in which the messages are sent to the other micro -actors when both the pre-condition and the next-condition are satisfied. The form of the rule is given by Dr. Yonezawa, and it is suggested that the form of the rule is useful to deal with the parallel computation. The programs should be carried out in order of the appearance of them in the pre-condition and the next-condition. On the other hand, the programs in the caused-events can be executed concurrently.

(iv) Program

A program is written in the restricted LISP notation. The user can freely use the LISP functions which don't have influence upon the pointers to lists and atoms; e.g., MEMBER, ASSOC and so on. The variables are restricted to the form !m or !!n (Both m and n are positive integers.) for the LISP functions which have influence upon the pointers; e.g., SETQ and so on. This restriction prevents the behavior of a micro-actor from giving unitentional effect to other micro-actors. The variable !m is used as well as PROG variable, whicle !!n can be used in a special way as mentioned in the next section.

A specification for message passing is as follows:
(=> *the_name_ of_a_micro-actor a_message*).
The user uses the basic function (FGET, FPUT and FREMOVE) to deal with the acquaintance. These functions differ from those of FRL in point of the necessity of the frame name. The functions in this paper do not need the frame name because the micro-actor deals with only its acquaintance. Therefore, the execution of the basic function does not affect the other micro-actors.

(v) Behavior of Micro-actor

A micro-actor tries to find a message pattern which is matched with a messge M_1 when it receives M_1. If the message pattern P_1 is found, a rule R_1 is searched for, which is one of rules making a pair with the pattern P_1, and whose pre-condition should be satisfied. When there is the next-condition in R_1, all programs in the next-condition should be evaluated. If the next-condition is satisfied, the caused-events are executed. If there is no rule whose pre-condition is satisfied concerning the pattern P_1, the micro-actor tries to find another message pattern which is matched with M_1.

Since the system holds the COMMON-SCRIPT which is necessary for all micro-actor, the users may specify the micro-actor by the peculiar script. The COMMON-SCRIPT has the message pattern (MES: ?%N ?X TO: ?CONT) and acts as follows:
(a) If the variable !X (corresponding to ?X) indicates one of the basic functions (FGET, FPUT and FREMOVE), then it is put into practice.
(b) If !X shows one of the extension functions (i.e., there exists a micro-actor corresponding to it), the rules are obtained from the micro-actor corresponding to the extension function, and they are performed. The variables !!n (n = 1, ..., 5) are corresponded to the arguments; for example, !!1 means the first argument.
(c) If !X indicates a set of rules, then !X is accomplished.

3.2 Example

A block world gives us good examples to illustrate the representation of the script and the acquaintance of a micro-actor, and message passing. The following discussion concerns with the micro-actor PROPERTY. It is used in the implementation of putting an objict on another. The script of the micro-actor BOX1 is NIL, because it needs just only the COMMON-SCRIPT. The acquaintance is expressed by one slot as follows: ((AKO (:VALUE (BOX))). This means that box1 is a kind of box. The AKO slot has a higher level concept of box1 as the value marked by the :VALUE facet. Concerning the micro-actor BOX, the script is NIL as well as box1, and the acquaintance is as follows:

```
((AKO      (:VALUE (BLOCK)))
 (INSTANCE (:VALUE (BOX1 BOX2 BOX3)))
 (PROPERTY (:VALUE (SUPPORTABLE)))  ).
```

This shows the following facts: (1) Box is a kind of block. (2) The instances of box are box1, box2 and box3. (3) The native property is supportable which means that the box can support another box.

Fig. 3 gives the script and the acquaintance of the micro-actor PROPERTY which deals with the rules about the properties. In the rest of this paper, a variable prefixed by "!" indicates its value until it is quoted. The script has a rule to ask the micro-actor !B if it has the property !A. According to the rule, PROPERTY sends !B the rules in which !A is substituted for "!!1". The AKO slot means that PROPERTY is a kind of E-FUNCTION (which is an abbreviation of extension function). The CONTENT slot shows the rules which contain the following algorithm. If the micro-actor which executes the rules has the value SUPPORTABLE in its PROPERTY slot, then it sends the reply OK to !CONT. Otherwise, if it has the value A in the AKO slot, then A is sent the message to ask if A has the property SUPPORTABLE. If A has it, A sends the reply OK to !CONT; otherwise, A sends NIL to !CONT. Note that A need not answer the micro-actor which sent the message to A. This means the possibility of a coroutine control.

```
((MES: ?%N ?B PROPERTY ?A TO: ?CONT)
 ((P-C: (SETQ !1 (FGET CONTENT :VALUE)))
  (N-C: (SETQ !1 (*SUBS !1 (LIST (CONS
                        (QUOTE !!1) !A)) )))
 (C-E: (=> !B (MES: !1 TO: !CONT)))
))
```

(a)

```
(AKO     (:VALUE (E-FUNCTION)))
(CONTENT (:VALUE
  ((P-C: (SETQ !5 (FGET PROPERTY :VALUE))
         (ASSOC !!1 !5))
   (C-E: (=> !CONT (RE: !%N OK)))
  )
  ((P-C: (NOT (ASSOC !!1 (FGET PROPERTY :VALUE)))
         (SETQ !4 (FGET AKO :VALUE))
         (SETQ !4 (CAAR !4)))
   (C-E: (=> !4 (MES: !%N PROPERTY !!1
                              TO: !CONT)))
  )
  ((P-C: (NULL (FGET AKO :VALUE)) )
   (C-E: (=> !CONT (RE: !%N NIL)))
)))
```

(b)

Fig. 3

(a) The script of the micro-actor PROPERTY.
(b) The acquaintance of PROPERTY.

Fig. 4 shows the diagram of the message passing for the process to see if box1 is supportable. The user can communicate with the micro-actor system using the special micro-actor * as shown in Fig. 4. For example, when the user wants to know whether box1 is supportable or not, he may write as follows:

(* PROPERTY BOX1 PROPERTY SUPPORTABLE).

The first argument of * is the target of the message whose content follows the first argument. The micro-actor * composes the message and sends it to the micro-actor PROPERTY (See line1 and line 2 in Fig. 5).

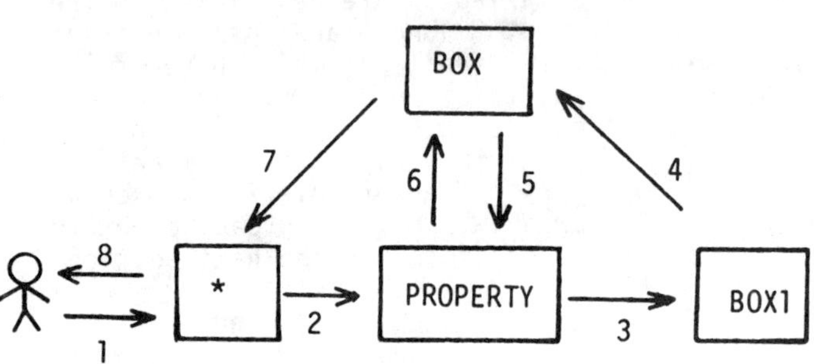

Fig. 4

The diagram of the message passing.

```
1 (* PROPERTY BOX1 PROPERTY SUPPORTABLE)
2 (* PROPERTY <= (MES: %2 BOX1 PROPERTY SUPPORTABLE TO: ME))
3 (*+ BOX1 <= (MES: %2 (((P-C: (SETQ !5 (FGET PROPERTY :VALUE))
                               (ASSOC SUPPORTABLE !5))
                        (C-E: (=> !CONT (RE: !%N OK)))  )
                       ((P-C: (NOT (ASSOC SUPPORTABLE (FGET PROPERTY :VALUE)))
                               (SETQ !4 (FGET AKO :VALUE))
                               (SETQ !4 (CAAR !4)) )
                        (C-E: (=> !4 (MES: !%N PROPERTY SUPPORTABLE TO: !CONT)))  )
                       ((P-C: (NULL (FGET AKO :VALUE)))
                        (C-E: (=> !CONT (RE: !%N NIL))) ) )
                 TO: ME))
4 (*++ BOX <= (MES: %2 PROPERTY SUPPORTABLE TO: ME))
5 (*+++* PROPERTY <= (MES: %2 FGET CONTENT :VALUE TO: ME))
6 (*+++* REPLY: (RE: %2 (((P-C: (SETQ !5 (FGET PROPERT :VALUE))
                                (ASSOC !!1 !5))
                         (C-E: (=> !CONT (RE: !%N OK)) ))
                        ((P-C: (NOT (ASSOC !!1 (FGET PROPERTY :VALUE)))
                                (SETQ !4 (FGET AKO :VALUE))
                                (SETQ !4 (CAAR !4)) )
                         (C-E: (=> !4 (MES: !%N PROPERTY !!1 TO: !CONT)) )  )
                        ((P-C: (NULL (FGET AKO :VALUE)) )
                         (C-E: (=> !CONT (RE: !%N NIL))) )
                 )))
7 (* REPLY: (RE: %2 OK))
8 (* RE: %2 OK)
```

Fig. 5

Messages and Targets shown in Fig. 4.

Fig. 5 gives us the messages and the targets illustrated in Fig. 4. Each line in Fig.5 shows the message passing which is represented by the arrow attached the same number that the line has. The front atom in each list (i.e., *, *+, etc.) illustrates the level of message passing. The symbol "*" means the subroutine control, and "+" means the coroutine control. Each line will be explained.

Line1: The user communicates to the system the messadge (* PROPERTY BOX1 PROPERTY SUPPORTABLE).

Line2: The micro-actor * composes and sends it to the micro-actor PROPERTY.

Line3: The micro-actor PROPERTY sends the BOX1 the message including the rules to see if the target has a datum SUPPORTABLE in its property slot. The continuation of the message on the line3 is the same one on the line2. In other words, "ME" means the micro-actor *.

Line4: BOX1 puts the rules into practice according to COMMON-SCRIPT. As BOX1 does not have a property slot, BOX1 sends the message to the BOX which is the higher level concept of box1. The continuation "ME" is BOX in this case, and this means the subroutine control.

Line6: PROPERTY returns the rules to BOX.

Line7: BOX carries out the rules. As BOX has the value SUPPORTABLE in the property slot, BOX sends OK to the micro-actor *.

Line8: * replies OK to the user.

This example shows about the method of the coroutine control and the subroutine control, and explains how the extension function defined as the micro-actor is used and is executed. Furthermore, it gives the preferred inference about the knowledge represented with frames.

4. QUESTION ANSWERING SYSTEM

In the question answering between a machine and a human, one of most important things is a topic of conversation and a context to understand what the partner said. We assume that the speaker and the listener have the common knowledge about the discourse. Consequently, the inference plays a great role to understand the partner's intention. The micro-actor can get a good policy from the acquaintance in which the facts of the world state are expressed by a frame.

4.1 Mapping From World

The authors consider that the knowledge about a world is a "snapshot (Bobrow, D.G.) of world state. The followings show the difficulty of mapping data from a world state to a knowledge state. What part of a house one directs his attention to when he sees it? Someone might direct his attention to the door. A gardener

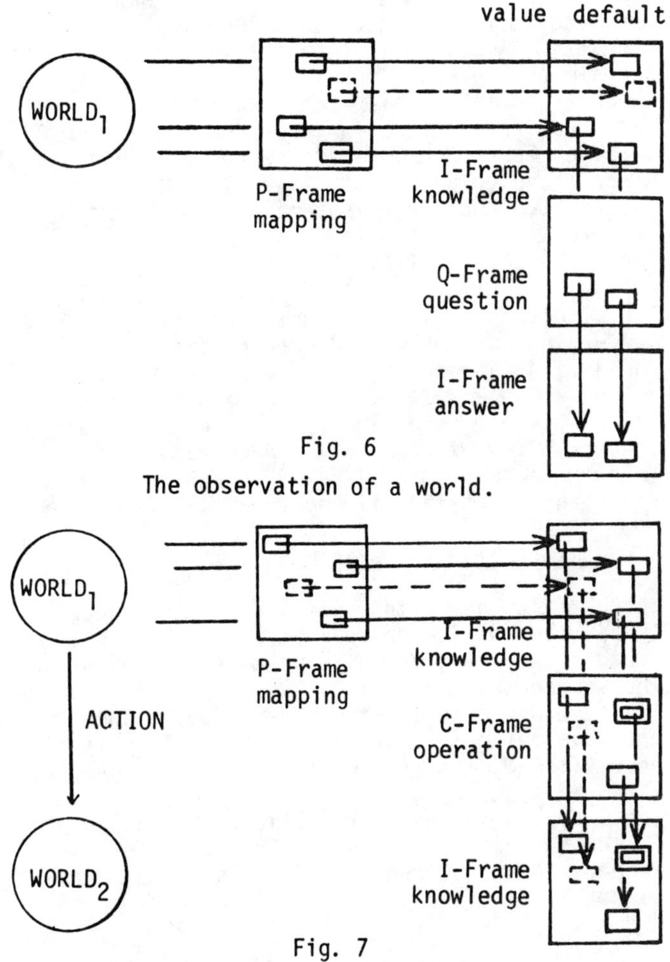

Fig. 6

The observation of a world.

Fig. 7

The change of a world.

might be interested in the trees and flowers in the garden. An architect might look the style of the house. Consider another example. When we hear "John is like a frog", what individuality do we assume about John? The answer depends on the context and the topic of the discourse. If one heard that Mike was a handsome boy just before, then he considers that John is ugly. If one heard that Mary was gentle then thinks that John is noisy.

The frame representation is suitable for extracting information from the world. The mapping method using the frame is to move a part of the world state to a slot of the frame. The data acquired by the mapping must satisfy the condition of the slots which depend on the topics and the context. So, we will use the frame called P-Frame (Prototype Frame), which has the slots to fill out. The P-Frame is used to compose an I-Frame (Instance Frame) which represents the knowledge state. The P-Frame has the default values which are communicated to the I-Frame if necessary. In the same way, using a Q-Frame (Quary Frame) whcih corresponds to "question", the I-Frame for the answer obtains the data from the I-Frame for the knowledge. A Q-Frame means such an action as human observes a world and gets the data (See Fig. 6). In Fig. 6, the knowledge is indicated by a frame for brevity. The knowledge is, however, represented by several frames in practice.

Fig. 7 gives two I-Frames which correspond to the world1 and the world2 changed from the world1. A C-Frame (Change Frame) represents the action which affects the world, or which changes the observer's situation (In the latter case, the world is not changed.). A C-Frame transfers the data from an I-Frame to another frame, and changes the data if necessary.

4.2 Conversation Examples

The question answering system about the geometrical figures is constructed with the micro-actors according to the consideration in 4.1. The user communicates with the system in the limitted Japanese for the present. The authors are developing a Japanese analyzer. After it is accomplished, the user will be able to converse with the system in Japanese. Fig. 8 presents the examples in the conversation. The sentences in the figure are written in English for the readers to understand. The user's sentences are marked by "*", and the replies are marked by "!".

The system has the geometrical world as the context in advance. The context, of course, is changed during the conversation. The system also has the knowledge about several kinds of triangles, the rectangle and square. The system tries to associate the input sentence with the knowledge. If it fails, the system asks the user about the sentence as shown in line2.

When the micro-actor <u>build</u> receives the sentence (line1), it tries to make the micro-actor <u>house</u>. As "house" is still undefined and the other parts of line1 are not associated with the knowledge, the system asks the user about a house (line2). The user defines the house as shown in line3, then <u>build</u> can create the micro-actor <u>house</u> (line4). The context plays a great role to decide kinds of slot in the acquaintance of <u>house</u> and to fill the slot with the data. In this case, <u>build</u> is regarded as P-Frame. As the world "roof" on line5 is not defined yet, the micro-actor <u>prefer</u> will associate an isosceles triangle with the knowledge as follows. Since

```
1.  * Build a house.
2.  ! What is a house.
3.  * It is the composition in which a triangle
      is on a rectangle.
4.  ! OK.
5.  * I prefer an isosceles triangle for the
      roof.
6.  ! Is the roof the triangle of the house?
7.  * Yes, it is.
8.  ! OK.
9.  * The house is like a tower.
10. ! OK.
11. * What a kind of house is it?
12. ! It is a tall house.
```

Fig. 8

Examples of the conversation.
*: user, !: computer.

the topic is about the house, <u>prefer</u> investigates the relation between the house and the isosceles triangle. The triangle is in the AKO slot of the micro-actor <u>isosceles triangle</u>. The house is in the PART-OF slot of <u>triangle</u>. Then <u>prefer</u> infers that the roof is a part of the house, and asks the user if the result of the inference is correct (line6). If the user answers yes (line7), <u>prefer</u> creates <u>roof</u> and adds the PREFER facet into the PART slot of <u>house</u> (line8). In this case, <u>prefer</u> acts as a C-Frame. The above process is smoothly performed using message passing between the micro-actors as mentioned in the chapter 3.

There have been several studies of metaphors using transfer frames [18]. Our system makes use of these studies (lines9,10,11 and 12). The <u>like</u> behaves like a P-Frame. That is, <u>like</u> receives the slot which has an extremal value from the <u>tower</u>, and communicates it to <u>house</u>.

5. CONCLUSION

This paper presented the micro-actors which construct the knowledge representation in which the modularity is established without sacrificing the interaction. The micro-actor is also suitable to represent the knowledge about the actions. The micro-actor mainly consists of the message patterns and the actions corresponding to them in the script. The micro-actor acts according to the script, refers to and modifies the acquaintance, and sends the messages to the other micro-actors if necessary. Since only message passing is the interactive method between the micro-actors, the modularity is established. The message can communicate enough information to the micro-actor. Furthermore, the continuation in a message makes both the subroutine control and the coroutine control possible. This is very useful for obtaining the data from another micro-actor, in particular, acquiring information from the higher level concept.

The acquaintance is a memory space whcih stores the data and the names of the other micro-actors. Since the frame is employed to represent the acquaintance, the data in the acquaintance is used smoothly. The acquaintance is treated by only the micro-actor which has it. This prevents the acquaintance from being affected by acother micro-actor.

The chapter 4 presented examples of the question answering system using the micro-actors. The dialogues show the following abilities: the creation of new micro-actors, the association using the higher level concetpt, the comprehension of metaphors, and the recognition of the constructed figures. These abilities greatly depend upon the frame representation. On the other hand, the form of the micro-actor is very useful to implement the system.

ACKNOWLEDGEMENTS

The authors appreciate many helpful conversations with several graduate students and members of Prof. Tanaka's Laboratory of Osaka University.

REFERENCES

[1] Bobrow, D.C. & Winograd, T. "An Overview of KRL, a Knowledge Representation Language", Cognitive Science, 1:1 (1977) 3-46.

[2] Ernst, G.W. & Newell, A. "GPS: A Case Study in Generality and Problem Solving", Academic Press, 1969.

[3] Fikes, R.E. & Nilsson, N.J. "STRIPS: A New Approach to The Application of Theorem Proving to Problem Solving", Artif. Intell. 2 (1971) 189-208.

[4] Hart, P.E., Nilsson, N.J. and Raphael, B. "A Formal Basis for The Heuristic Determination of Minimum Cost Paths", IEEE, Trans. on Sys. Sci. Cyb. SSC-4:2 (1968).

[5] Hewitt, C. "PLANNER: A Language for Proving Theorem in Robots", Proc. IJCAI-69 (1969) 295-301.

[6] Hewitt, C., Bishop, P. and Steiger, T. "A Universal Modular Actor Formalism for Artificial Intelligence", Proc. IJCAI-73 (1973) 248-249.

[7] Hewitt, C. & Baker, H. "Towards a Programming Apprentice", IEEE Trans. on Sof. Eng. (1975).

[8] Kuiper, B. "A Frame for Frames", Representation and Understanding, Academic Press (1975).

[9] McDermott, D.V. & Sussman, G.J, "The CONNIVER Reference Manual", MIT AI Lab, AI-MEMO No. 259 (1972).

[10] Minsdy, M. "A Framework For Representing Knowledge", The Psychology of Computer Vision, McGraw-Hill (1975).

[11] Ogawa, H. & Tanaka, K. "A Structure For the Representation of Knowledge --A Proposal for a Micro-Actor--", Proc. IJCAI-77 (1977) 248-249.

[12] Ogawa, H., Kitahashi, T. and Tanaka, K. "The Theorem Prover Using A Parallel Processing System", Proc. IJCAI-79 (1979).

[13] Robinson, J.A. "A Machine-Oriented Logic Based on the Resolution Principle", Jour. ACM 12 (1965) 23-41.

[14] Roberts, R. & Goldstein, I. "The FRL Manual", AI-MEMO 409 (1977).

[15] Roberts, R. & Goldstein, I. "The FRL Primer", AI-MEMO 408 (1977).

[16] Rulifson, J.F., Derksen, J.A. & Waldinger, R.J. "QA4: A Procedural Calculus for Intuitive Reasoning", SRI Tech. Note No. 73 (1972).

[17] Winograd, T. "Frame Representations and The Declaratve/Procedural Controversy", Representation and Understanding, Academic Press 1975.

[18] Winston, P.H. "Learning by Creatifying Transfer Frames", Artif. Intell. (1978) 147-172.

[19] Yonezawa, A. "A Specification Technique For Abstract Data Types With Parallelism", Res. Rep. C-17, Dept. of Information Science, Tokyo Institute of Technology (1978).

[20] Bobrow, D.G. "Dimension Of Representation", Representation and Understanding, Academic Press (1975).

THEORETICAL BASIS FOR A KNOWLEDGE REPRESENTATION SYSTEM

Setsuo Ohsuga
Institute of Space and Aeronautical Science
University of Tokyo
4-6-1 Komaba Meguro-ku Tokyo 153
Japan

Theoretical basis for a system named the SBDS (Structure Based Deduction System) including a formalism for representation of knowledge and an inferential algorithm is presented. This system is designed as a part of an intelligent interactive system to support man carrying out such the intelligent activities as engineering design, decision making, scientific research and so forth. The major emphases on the system are : (1) high processing efficiency, (2) high expressive power so that user can represent any knowledge he wishes and (3) easy access to databases.

1. INTRODUCTION

A system named the SBDS (Structure Based Deduction System) including a formalism for representing knowledge and an inference algorithm is presented. It is a subsystem of a total knowledge system named the KAU (Knowledge Acquisition and Utilization) system that is designed as an intelligent interactive system intended to support man's intelligent activities such as engineering design, decision making, scientific research and so forth. Thus the motivation for the research resides in what is called the intelligent agent view point by E. Feigenbaum [6].

SBDS adopts, as its basic framework for representation of knowledge, an extended form of the first order predicate logic, because it is, we think, suitable for converting to and/or being converted from any of three major forms of information used in computers today, i.e., (1) languages, (2) databases and (3) programs. In this paper, relations of (1) and (2) to SBDS are discussed. That of (3) to the first order logic has been discussed in [5] and [10].

As a matter of course, a knowledge system is required to have high expressive power in representation of knowledge. Though there have been some approaches adopting the first order logic in AI problems [5], [7], [10] and also in the more practical problem of databases [3],[9], the first order logic shows a shortage of expressive power for many real applications. The adoption of the higher order logic in its general form [8] as the main framework instead of the first order logic, however, is not good solution because it is too a general form for the practical purpose and therefore the inference is inefficient to be used in a real environment.

We therefore adopt a simpler form that is obtained by defining, first, a formalism to define the predicate and a deductive inference algorithm and, then, extending the first order logic towards higher order within the framework until the extended form can accommodate most of the language expressions that are almost sufficient to represent knowledge in many applications. The formalism for defining the predicate is combined with the hierarchical structure of entities defined in the universe. A fast deductive algorithm has been developed so as to use effectively the property of the structure.

On the other hand, for users working in the real applications, the use of databases is becoming inevitable. So far a number of databases and their management systems have been developed [4]. These DBMS's, however, are very inconvenient to be used for such the intelligent works as mentioned above. For an engineering designer, for example, the objective is to reach a final model through the repetitive processes of a model construction and its evaluation. He will require the data structure to be dynamically managed. But the conventional DBMSs can hardly do so because in these systems the structures of data are almost fixedly defined. Therefore it is desirable that the knowledge system takes over the dynamic restructuring of information and can accesses to databases only when the values of data are necessary. SBDS possesses such the capability. Thus the KAU of which the SBDS occupies the central part is intended to serve as an intelligent interface between users and DBMS's [12], [13].

A number of different approaches have been made and have also been developing for the problem of knowledge representation [1], [15]. The approach proposed in this paper is still different from them as seen from the system's point of view though it implies some concepts common to the others in part. Theoretical basis of our approach is on the first order predicate and the resolution principle [2],[14]. However as the SBDS also contains the concept of network, there are also some ideas in common between our method of deductive inference and methods developed for performing deductive inference on the knowledge represented in the network [15].

In this paper, we describe the SBDS with its mathematical foundation. A universe is defined as the collection of all concepts that can be referred through the language. Over this universe, the first order logic is defined and then extended toward higher order to the limited extent. A classical predicate logic is used rather than the resolution logic not only because it is intuitively understood by many people but, rather, because it is convenient to extend the first order logic and also to convert the predicates to the database operations.

An inference algorithm has been developed in which the information contained in user's query is effectively used for searching information and for deduction. The algorithm is also applicable to the extended form by slightly modifying its control mechanism.

2. INTERFACE TO LANGUAGE FOR EXPRESSING KNOWLEDGE

A problem world is described in many cases by means of language, and, therefore, we consider only the world that is describable by the language.

In reality, a vocabulary allowed to be used in the knowledge system is finite in which some words, -nouns- designate sets of entities or individual entities while the order words -verbs, adjectives, propositions, some nouns, etc.- represent the attributes of entities or the relations amongst entities. We call the former the entity words and the latter the relational words.

The syntax of the language defines sentences. There are a set of basic patterns of sentences or basic sentences in short such that all sentences can be analysed to the combination of some of them. If a system can understand the meaning of each basic sentence and also is given a parsing algorithm for analysing the compound / complex sentence to the logically connected set of basic sentences, then the system can understand the language. Here, by the term "understand" we mean that the system can process the information given in the form of language based on its meaning so that it responds correctly to users requests.

The set of basic patterns of sentences is finite in ordinary languages. In this paper, twenty-five patterns as shown in Table 1 are considered almost enough in case of English for expressing knowledge used in most of applications.

The vocaburaly, on the other hand, is different in every application. Though some common words can be defined independent of applications, some jargons are to be added in each application. Therefore the dictionary in the system must be an open set.

3. DATABASE

A relational model is considered exclusively in this paper [3],[4] though the system is not restricted to it. In this model a relation is defined as a set of n-tuple records, $(t_1, t_2, \cdots, t_n)$, where t_i is an occurence value in the domain T_i. A relation is represented in the form of a flat table with n colums and a relation name is given to it.

4. FIRST ORDER PREDICATE LOGIC IN A CLASSICAL FORM

In the classical predicate logic, an atomic formula or atom in short, is defined as $F(t_1, t_2, \cdots, t_n)$ where F is an n-place predicate symbol and $t_1, \cdots, t_{n-1}$ and t_n are terms. Then a well formed formula, or a formula in short is defined recursively as follows [2] :

a. An atom is a formula.

b. If F and G are formula, then $\sim F$, $F \cup G$, $F \cap G$, $F \Rightarrow G$ and $F \Leftrightarrow G$ are formulas where $\sim$, $\cup$, $\cap$, $\Rightarrow$ and $\Leftrightarrow$ are read as "negation", "disjunction", "conjunction", "imply" and "equivalent" respectively.

c. If F is a formula and x is a free variable in F_1 then $(\forall x)F$ and $(\exists x)F$ are formulas.

d. Formulas are generated only by a finite number of applications of a through c.

A formula can be written in the prenex normal form. In the following, it is written in a vector form as :

$$(\mathbf{Q}\,\mathbf{x})[S\{F_i(\mathbf{x}_i)\}], \qquad ---(1)$$

where $(\mathbf{Q}\,x) = (Q_1x_1)(Q_2x_2)\cdots(Q_nx_n)$ with each Q_i being either $\forall$ or $\exists$, S{ } stands for a logical structure composed of atoms, $F_i,(i=1\cdots m)$, by means of logical connectives shown in the above definition of the formula, and $(\mathbf{x}_i) = (x_i \cdots x_{ini})$.

In the resolution logic [2],[4], the formula is standardized by being converted to the conjunctive normal form and Skölemized. In this paper, instead of the standardization, the formula is modified in another way.

Firstly, no function symbol appears in the formula. In general, n-place function is a mapping from D^n to D where D denotes a domain of a variable. It is represénted in the SBDS by an n+1-place atom $*F_f(z;x_1 \cdots x_n)$ that is defined true iff $f(x_1 \cdots x_n)=z$ holds. Since to each of this kind of atoms corresponds a procedure that evaluates it procedurely, these atoms are called the procedural type atoms. The procedural type atom is identified by a symbol * on the left shoulder in the paper. An example is, *(ADD 5;2 3):"2 plus 3 is 5".

Secondly, in the resolution logic, Herbrand universe is defined as a set of which the elements are generated successively by means of the constants and function symbols appearing in the formula(s) while, in the SBDS, the universe $\mathbf{U}$ is first defined as the set of all objects that can be referred by the language.

Thirdly, the concept of sets is explicitly included in a formula. In the following, a variable free formula is called a ground formula. Any subset I of the set of all ground atoms, $F(t_1, \cdots, t_n)$, of which $t_1, \cdots, t_n$ are in the universe determines an interpretation where the meaning of an n-place predicate symbol F is a n-ary relation over the universe : $\{(t_1, \cdots, t_m):F(t_1, \cdots, t_n) \in I\}$. I is said to be a model of the formula if the truthhood of the formula is determined by the rules : F is true iff $F \in I$ and $\sim F$ is true iff $F \notin I$. When I is a model, the set of the tuple $\{(t_1, \cdots, t_n)|F(t_1, \cdots, t_n) \in I\}$ is denoted $\mathbf{D}_I$. Then $F(x_1, \cdots, x_n)$ is true iff $(x_1, \cdots, x_n) \in \mathbf{D}_I$. This fact is written as

$$(\forall\mathbf{x})[(\mathbf{D}_I \ni \mathbf{x}) \Rightarrow F(\mathbf{x})] \quad \text{where } \mathbf{x} = (x_1, \cdots, x_n) \quad --(2)$$

In many cases, $\mathbf{D}_I$ is a Cartesian product of X_i, (i=1, 2, $\cdots$, n), i.e., $\mathbf{D}_I = X_1 \times \cdots \times X_n$ where each X_i denotes a domain of the variable x_i. In this case, the formula (2) is rewritten as

$$(\forall x_1)\cdots(\forall x_n)[(X_1 \ni x_1)\cap\cdots\cap(X_n \ni x_n) \Rightarrow F(x_1, \cdots, x_n)] \quad ---(3)$$

or, equivalently,

$$(\forall x_1)\cdots(\forall x_n)[X_1{*}(x_1)\cap\cdots\cap X_n{*}(x_n) \Rightarrow F(x_1, \cdots, x_n)] \quad ---(4)$$

where $X_i{*}(x_i)$ is a predicate meaning "$X_i \ni x_i$". On the other hand, a fact that $F(x_1, \cdots, x_n)$ is true for some value $(t_1, \cdots, t_n)$ in $\mathbf{D}_I$ is written as

$$(\exists\mathbf{x})[(\mathbf{D}_I \ni x)\cap F(\mathbf{x})]. \quad ---(5)$$

If $\mathbf{D}_I$ is a product set, then

$$(\exists x_1)\cdots(\exists x_n)[X_1{*}(x_1)\cap\cdots\cap X_n{*}(x_n)\cap F(x_1, \cdots, x_n)]. \quad ---(6)$$

If both $\forall$ and $\exists$ appear in a formula, then a recursive relation is obtained:

$$(Q_1x_1)\cdots(Q_nx_n)[(X_1{*}(x_1)\overset{\circ}{_1}(X_2{*}(x_2)\overset{\circ}{_2}(\cdots X_{n-1}{*}(x_{n-1})\overset{\circ}{_{n-1}}(X_n{*}(x_n)\overset{\circ}{_n}F(x_1,\cdots,x_n))\cdots)] \quad ---(7)$$

where $\overset{\circ}{_i}$ represents either $\Rightarrow$ or $\cap$ depending on Q_i being $\forall$ or $\exists$. For example, if $\mathbf{D}_I = X \times Y \times Z$, $Q_x=\forall$, $Q_y=\exists$ and $Q_z=\forall$, then

$$(\forall x)(\exists y)(\forall z)[X{*}(x) \Rightarrow (Y{*}(y)\cap(Z{*}(z) \Rightarrow F(x,y,z)))] \quad ---(8)$$

In these representation of formulas, each variable is defined over $\mathbf{U}$ of which $X_i,(i=1,\cdots,n)$, is a subset. Then the formula can also be written in an abbreviated form as

$$(Q_1x_1/X_1)\cdots(Q_nx_n/X_n)F(x_1,\cdots,x_n) \quad ---(9)$$

meaning that the formula is true for assignment to each variable x_i of all or some values of X_i depending on the quantifier Q_i being $\forall$ or $\exists$, but otherwise it is not true. It is further simplified by abbreviating the variable symbols and moving F into the parenthesis as

$$(Q_1X_1)\cdots(Q_nX_n)(F,X_1,\cdots,X_n) \quad ---(10)$$

With this formalism, (2) and (5) are written as $(\forall\mathbf{D}_I)(F\,\mathbf{D}_I)$ and $(\exists\mathbf{D}_I)(F\,\mathbf{D}_I)$ respectively. A ground atom $(F,t_1,\cdots,t_n)$ is a reduced form of (9) in which every domain has only one element. It shoud be noted that the formula (10) can be transformed easily to a set-of-clauses form of the resolution logic.

Example:

$$(\forall X)(\exists Y)(\forall Z)(F\ X,Y,Z)=(\forall x)(\exists y)(\forall z)[(\sim X{*}(x)\cup(Y{*}(y)\cap(\sim Z{*}(z)\cup F(x,y,z))))]=(\sim X{*}(x)\cup Y{*}(f(x))\cap(\sim X{*}(x)\cup\sim Z{*}(z)\cup F(x,f(x),z)=\{C_1,C_2\}$$

$$C_1=\sim X{*}(x),Y{*}(f(x)),$$

$$C_2=\sim X{*}(x),\sim Z{*}(z),\ F(x,f(x),z) \quad ---(11)$$

where f(x) is the Skölem function.

The general form of the formula, then, is

$$(\mathbf{Q}\ \mathbf{X})[S'\ \{(F_i\ \mathbf{X})\}] \qquad ---(12)$$

5. THE UNIVERSE AS AXIOMATICALLY DEFINED SET

A predicate symbol of a formula corresponds to a relational word in a vocabulary set. Let the simple collection of all predicate symbols be $\mathbf{R}$. Then since the vocabulary is a finite set, $\mathbf{R}$ is also finite. Each F_i in $\mathbf{R}$ acts on $\mathbf{U}$ to define a basic pattern of atomic formula of which the predicate symbol is F_i. In other words, to each F_i, an ordered set $\{t_1,\cdots,t_{ni}\}$ is specified where each t_i is in $\mathbf{U}$ such that the ground atom $(F_i\ t_1,\cdots,t_{n_i})$ is in a model I.

The universe $\mathbf{U}$ is not so simple as $\mathbf{R}$. Many different types of elements must be included in $\mathbf{U}$. Consider, for example, two atomic formulas; (FATHER t_1,t_2):t_1 is father of t_2" and (CARD-NO t_3,t_4):"cardinal number of t_3 is t_4". Both t_1 and t_2 are of the same type in a sence that they can be the elements of a set, say, PERSON. On the other hand, t_3 is a set while t_4 must be an integer. In this case t_3 is said being of the different type and is one level higher than t_4. Each t_i in an atom can be of the different level as was seen in the case of CARD-NO.

These examples shows that any set of the elements in $\mathbf{U}$ must be an element of $\mathbf{U}$ too. Each predicate symbol specifies the level of each term to be an argument of the ground atom. Such a term is called a ground term for the atom and a symbol # is attached in the following.

On the other hand, in the atomic formula (10) defined as the collection of all ground atoms, X_i is a set of t_i's, and therefore is an element of $\mathbf{U}$ that is one level higher than t_i's. Thus an atom and its ground atom are defined over two levels of elements in $\mathbf{U}$ for each argument.

This definitions of formula requires the universe $\mathbf{U}$ being of multi-layers structure. For example, the concept of the power set is necessary to represent a formula such as : $(\forall T_3)(\exists$ INTEGER)(CARD-NO T_3 INTEGER)?:"For every set is there an integer which is the cardinal number?", where T_3 is a set of all sets. Fortunately such the set has been studied as an axiomatic set theory. We can use the Zermelo/Frankel axioms of set theory [11] as the universe though we don't touch on them here. We only point out that the set thus defined satisfies all conditions mentioned above $\mathbf{U}$ and, still further, such the set contains n-tuples, $(t_1,\cdots t_n)$ too, as it elements.

Based on this structure of the universe, a simple formalism for defining formula is obtained. That is, a formula is a pair $(F_i\ \mathbf{D}_I)$ attached by the information for quantification, $\mathbf{Q}$ where $F_i \in \mathbf{R}$ and $\mathbf{D}_I$ is a mapping of F_i into $\mathbf{U}$.

6. INFERENCE ALGORITHM

Inference algorithm is defined to the formula in the form of (12). This algorithm is logically equivalent to the resolution principle [2] but is designed to have high physical performance. It consists of the selection rule (SR), the test for implicative condition (TIC) and the replacement rule (RR). TIC corresponds to the unification algorithm and RR the resolution in the resolution logic respectively.

Suppose a formula P of the form

$$P:(\mathbf{Q}_p\mathbf{X})[(B_1,\ \mathbf{X}_1)\cap\cdots\cap(B_k,\ \mathbf{X}_k)\Rightarrow(A,\ \mathbf{X}_0)] \quad --(13)$$

exists in the knowledge base where $(\mathbf{Q}_pX)=(Q_{p1}X_1)\cdots(Q_{pm}X_m)$, $\mathbf{X}_i=\{X_{i1},\ \cdots,\ X_{i\alpha_i}\}$ and $\mathbf{X}=\{X_1,\ \cdots,\ X_m\}=\bigvee_{i=1}^{k}\mathbf{X}_i$, and a query Q of the form

$$Q:(\mathbf{Q}_q\mathbf{Y})[(C_1,\ \mathbf{Y}_1)\cap\cdots\cap(C_l,\ \mathbf{Y}_l)] \qquad ---(14)$$

is presented where $(\mathbf{Q}_p\mathbf{Y})=(Q_{q1}\ Y_1)\cdots(Q_{qn},Y_n)$, $\mathbf{Y}_j=\{Y_{j1},\ \cdots,\ Y_{j\beta j}\}$ and $\mathbf{Y}=\{Y_1,\ \cdots,\ Y_n\}=\bigvee_{j=1}^{l}\mathbf{Y}_j$.

Then a non-procedural type literal C_j is selected from Q by SR and the relation

$$(\mathbf{Q}'_p\ \mathbf{X}_0)(A,\ \mathbf{X}_0)\Rightarrow(Q'_q\ \mathbf{Y}_j)(C_j\ \mathbf{Y}_j) \qquad ---(15)$$

is tested by TIC where $(\mathbf{Q}'_p\ \mathbf{X}_0)$ and $(\mathbf{Q}'_q\ \mathbf{Y}_j)$ are the partial sequences of $(\mathbf{Q}_p\ \mathbf{X})$ and $(\mathbf{Q}_q\ \mathbf{Y})$ comprising only the variables included in $\mathbf{X}_0$ and $\mathbf{Y}_j$ respectively. Implicative condition (15) is tested by the following two steps:

(A) For each pair of corresponding variables, say X_{pi} and Y_{qi}, of left hand term and right hand term of (15), either of the set theoretical relations shown in Table 2 should hold depending on the combination of quantifiers of variables. This rule applies to all variables in the atoms of (15).

(B) There should not be such indices pair (i,j) that, in $(\mathbf{Q}'_p\ \mathbf{X}_0)(A,\ \mathbf{X}_0)$, i-th variable is universally quantified and is preceding to j-th existentially quantified variable while, in $(\mathbf{Q}'_q\ \mathbf{Y}_j)(C_j,\ \mathbf{Y}_j)$, corresponding i-th universally quantified variable is preceded by j-th existentially quantified variable.

If the implicative relation (15) is certified by TIC, then a new formula R of the form

$$R:(\mathbf{Q}_r\mathbf{Z})[(C_1,\ \mathbf{Z}_1)\cap\cdots\cap(C_{j-1},\ \mathbf{Z}_{j-1})\cap(B_1,\ \mathbf{W}_1)\cap\cdots\cap(B_k,\ \mathbf{W}_k)\cap(C_{j+1},\ \mathbf{Z}_{j+1})\cap\cdots\cap(C_l,\ Z_l)] \quad --(16)$$

is generated by RR where $(\mathbf{Q}_r\ \mathbf{Z})=(Q_{r1}Z_1)\cdots(Q_{ri}\ Z_n)$, $\mathbf{Z}_j=\{Z_j,\ \cdots,\ Z_{j r j}\}$, $\mathbf{W}_i=\{W_{i1},\cdots,W_{i\alpha i}\}$, and $\mathbf{Z}=\{Z_1,\ \cdots,\ Z_v\}=(\bigvee_{i\neq j}\mathbf{Z}_i)\vee(\bigvee_{i=1}^{k}\mathbf{W}_i)$. Each Z_i and its quantifier Q_i is decided by its corresponding variables, X_i and Y_i, in P and Q respectively, and their quantifiers as shown in Table 3.

Q_{pi}	$Q_{qi}(\overline{Q}_{qi})$	CONDITION
$\forall$	$\forall(\exists)$	$X_i \supset Y_i$
$\forall$	$\exists(\forall)$	$X_i \wedge Y_i \neq \phi$
$\exists$	$\exists(\forall)$	$X_i \subset Y_i$

Table 2 Implicative condition between single 1-atom formula

	Q_{pi}	Q_{qi}	Q_{ri}	Z_{ri}/W_{ri}
$X_i \in (\mathbf{X}_0 = \mathbf{Y}_j)$	$\forall$	$\forall$	$\forall$	Y_i
	$\forall$	$\exists$	$\exists$	$X_i \wedge Y_i$
	$\exists$	$\exists$	$\forall$	X_i
$Y_i \in (\mathbf{Y} - \mathbf{Y}_j)$	-	$\forall$	$\forall$	Y_i
	-	$\exists$	$\exists$	Y_i
$X_i \in (\mathbf{X} - \mathbf{X}_0)$	$\exists$	-	$\forall$	X_i
	$\forall$	-	$\exists$	X_i

Table 3 Replacement rule

It is not difficult to show that above rules of TIC are equivalent to the condition for the unification algorithm to terminate successfully in the resolution logic.

The set theoretical relations appearing in Table 2 can be represented in the logical form as

$(X \supset Y) \equiv (\forall x)[Y^*(x) \Rightarrow X^*(x)]$ - - -(17)

$(X \wedge Y \neq \phi) \equiv (\exists z)[X^*(z) \cap Y^*(z)]$ - - -(18)

The relation (15) is proved by showing that the negation of the relation, i.e.,

$\sim[(\mathbf{Q}'_p \mathbf{X}_0)(A\ \mathbf{X}_0) \Rightarrow (\mathbf{Q}'_q \mathbf{Y}_j)(C_j\ \mathbf{Y}_j)] \equiv (\mathbf{Q}'_p \mathbf{X}_0)(A, \mathbf{X}_0) \cap (\overline{\mathbf{Q}}'_q \mathbf{Y}) \sim (C_j, \mathbf{Y})$ - - -(19)

does not hold where $\overline{\mathbf{Q}}_q$ is obtained by exchanging $\forall$ and $\exists$ of each Q_{qi} in $\mathbf{Q}'_q$. (20) is transformed to the set-of-clauses form. Let it be denoted S. S is different to each assignment of quantifiers to variables. To avoid the notation becoming too complicated, let's pay an attention for a particular pair of variables (X_i, Y_i). The quantifiers of (X_i, Y_i) is denoted $(Q_{pi}, \overline{Q}_{qi})$. Then four different forms of S are derived according to the different specification for $(Q_{pi}, \overline{Q}_{qi})$. Then the validity of conditions listed in Table 2 is tested by applying a refutation process to these conditions combined with S. Here, only a case, $(Q_{pi}, \overline{Q}_{qi}) = (\forall, \exists)$, is shown.

In this case, $S = \{\cdots, \sim X^*_i(x_i), \cdots, A(\cdots x_i \cdots)\}, \{\cdots Y^*_i(f_{yi}(*))\cdots\}, \{\sim C_j(\cdots f_{yi}(*)\cdots)\cdots\}$ where $\cdots$ represent terms concerning to variables other then x_i and y_i. $f(*)$ is a Skölem function where $*$ represents a set of universally quantified variables preceding to y_i in the prefix $(\overline{\mathbf{Q}}_q\ \mathbf{Y}_j)$.

These set of clauses are put together with (17) in the standard form, $\{\sim Y^*(x), X^*(x)\}$. x_i can be substituted by $f_{yi}(*)$ because by the second law of TIC it is ensured that $*$ does not include x_i. Then $A(\cdots x_i \cdots)$ and $C(\cdots f_{yi}(*) \cdots)$ is unifiable if A and C is the same. Thus it is easy to show that the empty clause is deduced from the set of these clauses. The other cases are also proved by the similar procedures.

Example :

P: $(\forall X)(\forall Y)(\forall Z)$[(BROTHER X Y)$\cap$(PARENT Y Z) $\Rightarrow$ (UNCLE X Z)] "For every x, y, z, x who is brother of z's parent y is z's uncle"

Q: $(\exists U)$[(UNCLE U #Tom)$\cap$(ILL U)]? "Is there any uncle u of Tom, who is ill?"

where X, Y, Z and U represent the set PERSON and $x \in X$, $y \in Y$, $z \in Z$ and $u \in U$.

At the deduction SR selects $(\exists U)$(UNCLE U #Tom) from Q and TIC tests for

$(\forall X)(\forall Z)$(UNCLE X Z) $\Rightarrow (\exists U)$(UNCLE U #Tom) - -(20)

It holds because $X \wedge U \neq \phi$, $Z \supset \{\#Tom\}$. Then RR generate,

R: $(\exists U)(\exists Y)$[(BROTHER U Y)$\cap$(PARENT Y #Tom) $\cap$(ILL U)] - - -(21)

R is regarded as a new query.

The deductive procedure is repeated until either the formula of which the Boolean value can be obtained or the formula consisting only of the procedural type literals is reached. Further consideration is necessary to make the algorithm logically complete though it is abbreviated here. Refer [13] for the detail.

7. STRATEGY FOR SEARCHING THE CANDIDATE FORMULA

There may be a number of formulas stored in a knowledge system and, at a time only part of which participate to deducing the query. Therefore, quick selection of the relevant formula is very important.

The universe is represented by a hierarchical structure in which each node represents a set of objects. In the following a set is denoted by the upper case letter. A node is connected to another node by either of two types of arcs representing the set—theoretical inclusion and disjointness. The former is called the I-type arc and the latter the D-type arc. For instance, the set LIVING-THING(LIVTH in short), MAMMALIA, FISHES, BIRDS, MANKIND, DOGS,CATS etc. are in the set-theoretical relations such as LIVTH⊃MAMMALIA, FISH, BIRD, INSECT,··· MAMMAIL ⊃MANKIND, DOG, ··· and so on. We say "X is upper to Y" or "X is larger than Y" when X⊃Y and Y is connected to X by the I-type arc. On the other hand, the set MAN and WOMAN are disjoint to each other and are connected by the D-type arc. By applying the processes of linking by means of these arcs successively, a hierarchical structure of universe, called the semantic skeleton structure, or the skeleton in short, is formed. Some node is connected to more than two other upper nodes by the I-type arcs. Such a node represents a set defined as an intersection of the other sets. For instance, a set BOY is represented as the intersection of MAN and CHILD.

A formula that includes a set X_i as an argument is linked to the node X_i in the skeleton and is accessible from this node. Accordingly the formula (10) can be accessed from any of nodes X_1, X_2, ···, X_n.

Suppose a query (14) includes a constant or a variable, say Y_j, that is universally quantified. It is ordinary the case because a query of which every argument is existentially quantified variable is nothing else but a damp command. Then the formula P that satisfies the relation (15) to this query, if any, must be linked to some node X_j that is over Y_j in the skeleton from the rule (A) of TIC. Therefore, it is reachable by following the I-type arcs upward starting from Y_j. Since the skeleton expands downward, it reduces the search space considerably and formulas of which the predicate symbols are the same with the query but the variables are out of above condition are disregarded.

The formula thus found is called the candidate which satisfies the condition of TIC only with respect to the variable Y_j. It must be tested for the condition (Table 2) for the other variables too. The skeleton is used again. Since, this time, both left and right hand formulas of (15) are in hand and, therefore, both domains (sets) of corresponding arguments can be specified in the skeleton, the tests for the set theoretical relations of Table 2 are achieved by the test for the positional relations between nodes in the skeleton. Since its algorithm is very simple it can be implemented by the special but simple wired logic and therefore the test can be performed very fast. The SR selects a literal among all literals in the query that contains most constants / universally quantified variables.

The system further reduces the possibility of fruitless test being achieved. In case of conventional first order logic, the set of formulas such as

$$B_1 \Rightarrow A,\quad B_2 \Rightarrow A,\quad \cdots,\quad B_e \Rightarrow A \qquad ---(22)$$

often arises in the definition of the meaning of words. For instance, the relations between sets mentioned above are represented as

$$\left.\begin{array}{l}(\forall x)[\mathrm{MAMMALIA}^*(x) \Rightarrow \mathrm{LIVTH}^*(x)] \\ (\forall x)[\mathrm{FISH}^*(x) \Rightarrow \mathrm{LIVTH}^*(x)] \\ (\forall x)[\mathrm{BIRD}^*(x) \Rightarrow \mathrm{LIVTH}^*(x)]\end{array}\right\} \qquad ---(23)$$

Suppose $A \Rightarrow Q$ is satisfied to a query Q. Then the resolution logic will make an exhaustive test looking for a path leading to the empty clause. It is exhaustive because the refutation process proceeds in the direction from A to B_i in each formula (22) in a sense that A is unified with the query and B_i is remained for the next test.

In the SBDS every formula of the type(23) is represented by an arc in the skeleton. Searching the formula by following the I-type arcs upward in the skeleton corresponds to searching the refutation path proceeding in the reverse order of the resolution logic. Thus, as far as such the formulas as (23) are concerned, the exhaustive test is avoided.

8. ACCESS TO DATABASES

The formula (2) means that if a tuple $\mathbf{x}=(x_1, \cdots, x_m)$ is included in $\mathbf{D}$, a relation F holds among $x_1, \cdots, x_m$. Suppose then that a set of n-tuples, $\mathbf{D}$, is given as a data file in a table form. Then, the condition $(\mathbf{D} \ni \mathbf{t})$ for some n-tuple, $\mathbf{t}=(t_1, \cdots, t_m)$, is tested by a special procedure that searches $\mathbf{t}$ in the file. That is, the premise of (2) is represented by a kind of procedural type atom. Let it be denoted as $*(\mathrm{FGET}, D : x_1, \cdots, x_n)$ and be called the file type atom where D indicate the file name. Then the formula (2) is written as

$$(\forall X_1) \cdots (\forall X_n)[*(\mathrm{FGET}\ D : X_1, \cdots, X_n) \Rightarrow F(X_1, \cdots, X_n)] \qquad ---(24)$$

This formula gives a definition/description of a table type file D. A user input the system a set of data in the table form accompanied with a formula (24). After then, any user can use this file without any knowledge on it. The system determines itself how and when to access the file through the deductive operation and converts the formula to the relational algebra [4]. Only the outline of the conversion is shown without proof.

Suppose, a formula consisting only of the file type atoms.

$(\mathbf{Q}\ \mathbf{X})[S\{*(\text{FGET } D_i : \mathbf{X}_i)\}]$ - - -(25)

is obtained as the result of deductive operation$_k$where $\mathbf{X}_i=(X_{i1}, \cdots, X_{in_i})$ and $\mathbf{X}=(X_1, \cdots, X_n)=\bigvee_{i=1}\mathbf{X}_i$. Suppose each file D_i is the set of mi-tuples and each domain X_i is a finite set. Let $\mathbf{X}_i{*}=\mathbf{X}-X_i$. Then (25) is equivalent to

$(\mathbf{Q}\ \mathbf{X})[S\{*(\text{FGET } D_i{\times}\mathbf{X}_i{*} : \mathbf{X})\}]=(\mathbf{Q}\ \mathbf{X})[*(\text{FGET}, \hat{S}\{(D_i{\times}\mathbf{X}_i{*})\}, \mathbf{X})]$ - - -(26)

where $D_i{\times}\mathbf{X}_i{*}$ means a cylinder set in the n-dimensional space, $X_1 \times \cdots \times X_n$, $\hat{S}$ is a structure of the set theoretical operations that is obtained from S by replacing every $\cap$ and $\cup$ in S by $\wedge$ (intersection) and V (union) respectively, and $\hat{S}\{(D_i{\times}\mathbf{X}_i{*})\}$ means that the structure of the set operations $\hat{S}$ are applied to $(D_i{\times}\mathbf{X}_i{*})$. Since all the $(D_i{\times}\mathbf{X}_i{*})$'s, (i=1, 2, $\cdots$, k), are the set of n-tuples, $\hat{S}\{(D_i{\times}\mathbf{X}_i{*})\}$ is reduced to a set of n-tuples. Let it be denoted $\mathbf{D}*$. Then the formula (26) results in

$(\mathbf{Q}\ \mathbf{X})[*(\text{FGET } \mathbf{D}* : \mathbf{X})]$ - - -(27)

Here the following two file operations are introduced.

$\text{DIV}(\mathbf{D}*, X_i)=\{\mathbf{x}=(x_1, \cdots, x_{i-1}, x_{i+1}, \cdots, x_n) \mid \mathbf{x}{\times}X_i{\subset}\mathbf{D}*\}$ - - -(28)

$\text{PRJ}(\mathbf{D}*, X_i)=\{\mathbf{x}=(x_1, \cdots, x_{i-1}, x_{i+1}, \cdots, x_n) \mid (x_1, \cdots, x_{i-1}, x_i, x_{i+1}, \cdots, x_n){\subset}\mathbf{D}*\}$ - -(29)

These operations correspond to division and projection operations respectively of the relational algebra in the relational data base. Then the following relations between logical view and set-theoretical view hold.

$$\left.\begin{array}{l}(Q_1X_1) \cdots (Q_{n-1}X_{n-1})(\forall X_n)[*(\text{FGET } D* : X_1, \cdots, X_n)]=(Q_1X_1) \cdots (Q_{n-1}X_{n-1})[*(\text{FGET DIV}(D*, X_n):X_1, \cdots, X_{n-1})] \\ (Q_1X_1) \cdots (Q_{n-1}X_{n-1})(\exists X_n)[*(\text{FGET } D* : X_1, \cdots, X_n)]=(Q_1X_1) \cdots (Q_{n-1}X_{n-1})[*(\text{FGET PRJ}(D*, X_n):X_1, \cdots, X_{n-1})]\end{array}\right\} \quad (30)$$

These relations and operations are repeatedly applied to the formula (27) until finally $*(\text{FGET T} : \phi)$ is obtained where T is either 1 or 0 depending on if the operations can be continued to the end or these operations result in an empty file. If T=1, the original query formula proved true.

In practice, user must be able to designate some data to be output. Such the data must be saved during the above processes. When the other procedural type atoms besides the file type are included in a formula, a further consideration is necessary. For the details refer [13].

9. EXTENTION OF THE SYSTEM

9.1 Predicate Symbol as Variable

A hierarchical structure can be introduced in the set of predicate symbols. Consider, for example, two atoms, (BROTHER X Y) and (SIBLING X Y). When the same terms are substituted into the corresponding variables, then (Brother, t_1, t_2) $\Rightarrow$ (Sibling, t_1, t_2). In this case "Sibling" is said larger than "Brother". On the other hand, (Natural, X)$\cap$(Artificial, X) shows an inconsistancy. The predicate symbols being in such relations are said disjoint to each other. Based on these relations, the skeleton is formed for the predicate symbols and the predicate symbol can be dealt with as if it were a variable because it can be processed by the same algorithm as the other variables at the deduction. Then the atom can be rewritten as

$(\mathbf{Q}\ \mathbf{X})(\mathbf{X})$, $\mathbf{X}=(X_0, X_1, \cdots, X_n)$ - - -(31)

where the predicate symbol is denoted X_0. With this modification, the system can accept the query which asks the value in X_0, i.e., the predicate symbol. For example, a query Q:($\exists$ RELATION)(RELATION #Tom #Mary)?:"What is the relation holding between Tom and Mary?" can be answered by using P:(FATHER #Tom #Mary) if the relation FATHER$\subset$RELATION is given in advance as is the case of the other variables.

9.2 Recursive Form

Let the atom of the form (31) be called the n-atom when it comprises n terms including X_0. In ordinary predicate, n is larger than or equal to two. Suppose it can be extended to the case n=1. There are only two 1-atoms of the form, ($\forall$ X)(X) and ($\exists$ X)(X) with meanings "for all $x \in X$, $x \in X$" and "there is some x in X such that $x \in X$", respectively. Thus (X) shows the logical aspect of the set X. The applications of TIC rules to the 1-atoms reveala the rule (A) of TIC being just the implicative condition itself for two 1-atoms.

The SBDS has been described as including the concepts both of sets and of logic. It is for the purpose of taking advantage of the strength of each at the implementation. We can obtain the logical description of it by replacing X by (X) and the rule (A) of TIC by the implicative relation between 1-atoms. Then the universe is regarded as a collection of 1-atom'formulas and the formula (31) is rewritten as the relation among n 1-atom formulas to which the rule(A) of TIC, rephrased as the followings, is applied:

(A') To each pair of corresponding inner 1-atom formulas, the implicative condition should hold.

These concepts are extended. Assume that the universe can include not only 1-atoms but general formulas, by adding all possible formulas definable by **R** and **U** to **U** resulting in $\mathbf{U}_1$, then by adding all possible formulas definable by **R** and $\mathbf{U}_1$ to $\mathbf{U}_1$ resulting in $\mathbf{U}_2$ and so on. For many applications the extended universe $\mathbf{U}_k$ with finite K may be enough. The mechanism for defining the atom (ref. Sec.5) is unchanged. Then the SBDS has atoms in recursive form as

$$((FML)^{*}_{0}, (FML)_1 \cdots (FML)_n) \quad ---(34)$$

where $(FML)^{*}_{0}$ denotes a 1-atom corresponding to the predicate symbol and $(FML)_i, (i=1, \cdots, n)$, is a formula. The rule (A') is extended to :
(A") For each pair of corresponding inner formulas, the implicative condition should hold. The rule (A") is applied recursively to the formulas in form of (34) at the deduction.

As the result of this extention the SBDS acquires a large power of expression. But the extension is based on the assumption that any 1-atom formula can be replaced by a general formula. Further study on its validity is necessary.

Example: (VX)(VU)[(INTEND X (DO X U))∩(CAN X(DO X U)) ⇛ (DO X U)] :"Every one does thing if he intends to and can do it."
where X;PERSON, U;UNIVERSE,
(CAN X (DO X U)) : X can do U,
(INTEND X (DO X U)) : X intends to do U.

10. CONCLUSION

An outline for the SBDS, a central part of a knowledge system (KAU) designed as an intelligent support system, has been presented. Mathematical foundation for the formalism for representing knowledge, the deductive algorithm and the interface with databases has been mainly described. The major emphases on the SBDS design are : (1) high processing efficiency, (2) high power of expression so that user can represent any knowledge he wishes and (3) easy access to databases. The core of SBDS has been implemented and is being tested for its usefulness.

REFERENCES

[1] Bobrow, D.G.(chaired) "A Panel on Knowledge Representation." In Proc. 5th IJCAI,1977,pp.983-992.

[2] Chang,C.L.& Lee,R.C.T. "Symbol Logic and Mechanical Theorem Proving." Academic Press, 1973.

[3] Codd,E.F. "Recent Investigations in Relational Data Base Systems", Proc. IFIP Congress, Aug. 1974.

[4] Date C.J. "An Introduction to Database Systems", Addison-Wesley, 1975.

[5] Emden Van "Programming with Resolution Logic", Machine Intelligence 8, pp266-299.

[6] Feigenbaum E.A. "The Art of Artificial Intelligence, Themes and Case Studies of Knowledge Engineering", 5th IJCAI pp1014-1029.

[7] Green C. "The Use of Theorem Proving Techniques in Question Answering System", Proc. 23-rd Nat. Conf. ACM, 1968.

[8] Huet G.P. "A Mechanization of Type Theory" 3rd IJCAI 1973. pp.139-146.

[9] Kellog C.H. & Klahr P. "Adding a Deductive Capability to a Data Management System", Second VLDB Sept. 1976.

[10] Kowalski R.A. "Predicate Logic as Programming Language", Proc. IFIP-74. pp569-574.

[11] Krivine J. "Introduction to Axiomatic Set Theory", D.Reidel Pub. Co. 1971.

[12] Ohsuga S. "Semantic Information Processing in Man-Machine Systems", Proc. 1977 IEEE Conference on Decision & Control, pp1351-1358, Dec. 1977.

[13] Ohsuga S. "Towards Intelligent Interactive Systems", Proc. the IFIP W.G.5.2 Workshop Seillac II on Methodorogy of Interaction (to appear) North-Holland Pub. Co. 1979.

[14] Robinson J.A. "A Machine Oriented Logic Based on the Resolution Principle", JACM Vol.12 Jan. 1965.

[15] Shapiro S.C. "Path-Based and Node-Based Inference in Semantic Networks", TINLAP-2. Jan. 1978 pp219-225.

1) S-V-Direct Object 2) S-V-to-Infinitive 3) S-V-Noun-to-Infinitive 4) S-V-Noun-(to be)-Complement 5) S-V-Noun-Infinitive 6) S-V-Noun-Present Particle 7) S-V-Object-Adgective 8) S-V-Noun 9) S-V-Past Particle 10) S-V-Adjective 11) S-V-that clause 12) S-V-Noun-that clause 13) S-V-Conjunctive-to-Infinitive 14) S-V-Noun-Conjunctive-to-Infinitive 15) S-V-Conjunctive Clause 16) S-V-Noun-Conjunctive Clause 17) S-V-Gerund 18) S-V-Direct Object-Preposition-Prep.Object 19) S-V-Indirect Object-Direct Object 20) S-V-(for)-Complement 21) S-V 22) S-V-Predicative 23) S-V-Adverbial Adjunct 24) S-V-Preposition-Prepositional Object 25) S-V-to-Infinitive

Examples: 1) X likes Y :(LIKE X Y)
2) X intends to do·· :(INTEND X (DO X ··))
12) X tells Y that Z does ··· :(TELL X Y (DO Z ···))
17) X enjoys doing Y ·· :(ENJOY X (DO X Y ··))
19) X gives Y Z :(GIVE X Y Z)

Table 1 Basic patterns of sentences

A PRODUCTION SYSTEM FOR REGION ANALYSIS

Yu-ichi Ohta, Takeo Kanade, and Toshiyuki Sakai

Department of Information Science
Kyoto University
Kyoto, 606, JAPAN

Production system architectures are useful for knowledge representation. We have applied the architecture to image analysis in the framework of region growing and developed an outdoor-scene analyzer. In this paper, the following three problems are addressed to make production systems workable in scene analysis. 1) Appropriate size of knowledge represented in a production rule. 2) Reduction of computation. 3) Control of the analysis toward goal.

1. INTRODUCTION

A production system consists of a set of production rules and a database. A production rule is the unit of knowledge representation and the database records the facts about input image. The control structure of production systems is heterarchical. Each production rule is a pair of a condition and an action and is "watching" the database. Whenever the predicate in the condition part is satisfied, the system evaluates the action part and modifies the database. Because of this, it is easy to add or modify knowledge in production systems. This is a useful feature to organize an analysis system for complex scenes, such as outdoor scenes, which include various kinds of objects.

We have made an outdoor-scene analyzer in the framework of region growing using production system for knowledge representation and control structure[1]. In this paper, we describe the outline of our scene analyzer and discuss production systems from the view point of image analysis.

2. OUTLINE OF ANALYSIS MECHANISM

Figure 1 shows the schematic diagram of the analysis mechanism in our system. The system receives an input color image as digitized red-green-blue intensity arrays and constructs a semantic description of the scene.

Preliminary segmentation - The primary objective of the preliminary segmentation process is not the reduction but the structuring of raw image data into usable information; The input color image is segmented into a set of coherent "patches" and organized into a fully structured symbolic description. In the higher-level processes, all picture-processing operations are performed on this structured description rather than the raw image data. The "patch" is an important element to describe the input image and to build a production system in our region analyzer.

Plan generation - The plan generation process extracts the overall structure of the scene to obtain clues concerning which knowledge should be applied to what part of the scene. First, patches with large area are selected as key-patches from the segmented image. It is reasonable to assume that most of them correspond to large parts of objects in the scene. Labels of objects are assigned to each of the keypatches and the degree of correctness is computed using

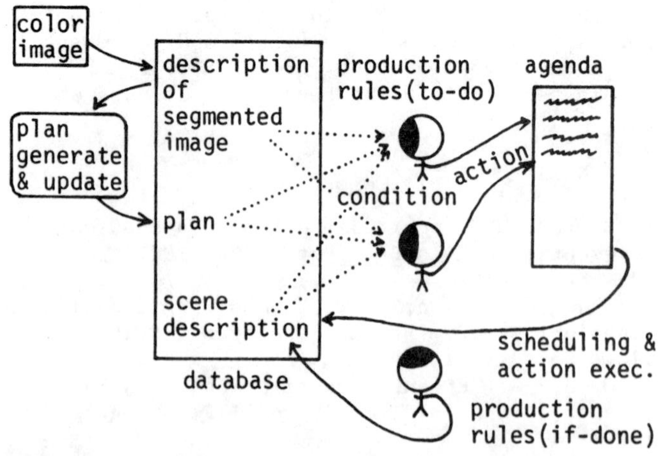

Fig. 1. Outline of the Analysis Mechanism

knowledge, which is represented as a collection of knowledge-blocks[2], about the properties of and the relations between objects. The result of the interpretation, called a plan, is a set of labels and their correctness values assigned to each keypatch, e.g. (sky=0.6, building=0.2, tree=0.1, road=0.1), etc. The plan is updated whenever significant fact, such as the position of scene horizon, is found by the production rules in the analysis process.

Database - The structured description of a segmented image, the plan, and the scene description so far obtained are all stored in the database. Figure 2 illustrates the structure of the scene description built as the result of analysis. Scene, object, region, sub-region, patch, and pixel are the important concepts which constitute the hierarchical structure of our description. The patch corresponds to the result of the preliminary segmentation. All the descriptive elements are organized into the hierarchical structure by "part-of" relation. Relations between parts of objects, such as "adjacent" or "occluded", are described between corresponding regions.

Production rules and agenda - There are two types of production rules in our system; to-do rules and if-done rules. They correspond to consequent and antecedent theorems of PLANNER[3],

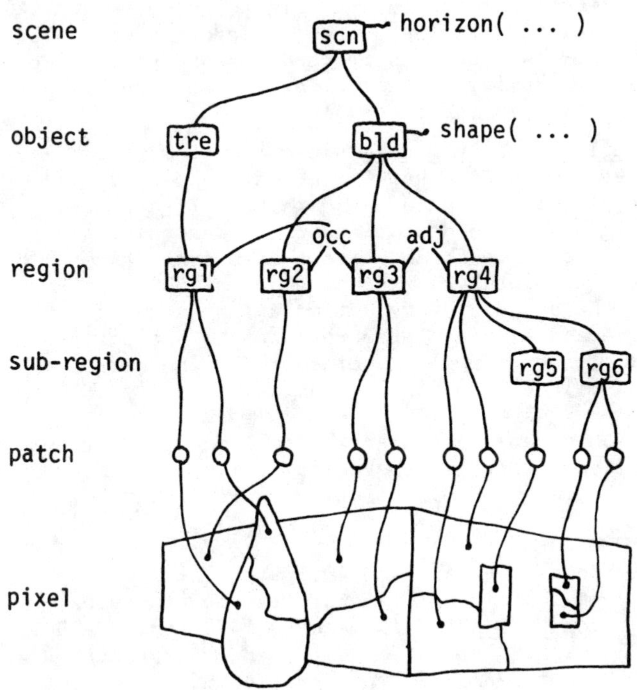

Fig. 2. Structure of the Scene Description.

respectively. A to-do rule performs basic operations in region growing process. It examines each patch which is not yet interpreted in the segmented image by the fuzzy predicate in its condition part and determines whether the action can be executed for it. The executable action is given a score to indicate its priority, and added into the agenda. The agenda manages those actions which are executable in the present context through their scores. The action with the highest score is executed and as the result the agenda is updated. An if-done rule is triggered by the execution of a certain action of the to-do rules. It performs an additional operation in making the scene description, such as extracting the position of scene horizon, etc.

3. DISCUSSIONS

We have to solve three problems to import the production system architecture to image analysis. The first is the problem of what "size" of production rule is appropriate for region analysis, the second is the problem of how to reduce the amount of computation, and the last is the problem of how to direct the analysis to goal.

° What "size" of production rule is appropriate?

What size of knowledge should be represented by one production rule? As an example of "large" knowledge size, it is possible that each production rule corresponds to one object to be extracted and has whole knowledge about the object. This scheme enables to perform skillful analysis according to the characteristics of each object. On the other hand, the rules become large and complex and it is difficult to manage them.

Small sized knowledge - In our system the size of knowledge represented by a rule is fairly small. Each rule is described as a combination of basic operations in region growing: selecting an un-interpreted patch from the segmented image, assigning a label to it, and assembling it into the scene description. This scheme has the following merits: each rule is simple and easy to modify, and the interaction among rules can be performed in a clear way because the access method to the database is simple.

Reinforcements - Because the analysis proceeds patch by patch in our scheme, it is difficult to deal with global constraints such as object shape or relation between objects. We took three steps to cope with this situation. First, a plan is generated as rough interpretation of the input scene. This enables the production rules to catch information about global structure of the scene. Secondly, patches can be dealt with as a set at a time, and it becomes possible to extract object which is defined as a combination of mutually constrained patches such as windows of a building or a car on road. Lastly, we have devised special rules which extract information from the segmented image without sticking to the patch-by-patch analysis. This kind of rules, for example, is used to extract the shape of a building.

° How to reduce the amount of computation?

In production systems the control program must grasp the state of executable actions at any moment in the analysis process. The agenda must be updated whenever the database is changed. Roughly speaking, the number of tests to be done each time is estimated as:

(the number of un-interpreted patches)
X (the number of production rules).

It becomes several thousand and it is too many. Furthermore, the predicate in the condition part of the production rules includes time-consuming picture-processing functions. It is necessary to reduce the number of the patches and production rules which must be actually examined at a time. For this, the structure of scenes must be taken into consideration.

"Globality" and "Locality" - A scene usually has two different properties from the view point of image analysis: "Globality" and "Locality". Analysis results such as determination of scene horizon or detection of objects may have significant influence on the analysis of overall structure of the scene. This property is called "Globality". On the other hand, the results of analysis in a small part of an object scarcely has influence on the analysis of other parts in the scene. This property is called "Locality". These two properties are utilized in the control structure of our scene analyzer.

Scene phase and object phase - In order to deal with such two properties of scenes, two phases are set up in the control program. They are scene phase and object phase. The task of the scene phase is to analyze overall structure of input scene without sticking to details. So, it is almost meaningless to examine small patches in the scene phase analysis and only the key-patches are examined. Whenever a keypatch is labeled, the scene phase is activated and all un-interpreted keypatches are re-examined. In the object phase, analysis of detailed structures are performed under the context of the results in the scene phase analysis. When a patch which belongs to a object is labeled, the object phase corresponding to the object is activated and the patches touching the patch just labeled are examined or re-examined.

Dividing rules into subsets - The set of production rules can be divided into subsets to be used in the scene phase and the object phases corresponding to each object. In each phase, only the subset corresponding to that phase is activated by the control program to examine the un-interpreted patches.

Consequently, the number of tests to be done at a time is reduced to several 10's.

° How to direct the analysis to goal?

It is an important feature of production systems that each production rule independently checks the database and modifies it whenever the condition is satisfied. However, two problems need to be considered to make this mechanism actually work; a method to direct the analysis to goal and a method to resolve the conflict among the executable actions which are inconsistent with each other.

Score - As was described, every executable action is registered in the agenda with its score and the action which has the highest score is executed to change the database. Then the score plays an important role to direct the analysis toward goal. The value of score associated to each executable action is calculated as the sum of a base value and a premium value. The base value is a constant given to each production rule, and it plays a role to specify the order of analysis. The premium value is given as the degree of satisfaction of the condition of production rule at the situation the rule was examined, and it plays a role to guide the analysis toward the correct interpretation. To sum up, the analysis proceeds toward goal guided by the premium values following the strategy specified by the base values.

Conflict resolution - In our system, the basic operation which changes the database is very simple: to assign an object label to a patch. This makes the detection of the inconsistent actions quite straightforward. Whenever a patch is interpreted by executing an action registered in the agenda, every action which is going to give a different interpretation to the patch just interpreted is decided to be inconsistent and deleted from the agenda.

In this paper, we described a production system which was applied to region analysis. Some problems and their solutions were discussed.

REFERENCES

[1] Ohta,Y. et al. "An Analysis System for Scenes Containing Objects with Substructures." In Proc. 4th IJCPR, November, 1978, pp.752-754.
[2] Sakai,T. et al."Model-based Interpretation of Outdoor Scene." Proc. 3rd IJCPR, Nov. 1976.
[3] Hewitt,C. "PLANNER" A.I.Memo No.168, MIT, October, 1968.

AN INFINITE-CONNECTED WORDS RECOGNITION SYSTEM FOR MALE SPEAKERS USING TIME-SPACE DYNAMIC PROGRAMMING

Ryu-ichi Oka
Pattern Processing Section
Information Sciences Division
Electrotechnical Laboratory
2-6-1 Nagata-cho, Chiyoda-ku
Tokyo 100, Japan

A new algorithm of pattern matching for time-space speech feature using Dynamic Programming is proposed for recognizing infinite-connected words spoken by male speakers without adaptation of speakers before the utterance. The new algorithm carries out frame-wisely two kinds of normalizations : the time normalization for removing speed variation of speech and the space normalization for removing speaker-dependence. This algorithm is realizable by a simple cellular automaton. The recognition rate 85.7% is obtained for 50 categories, 4 male speakers and 440 samples (connected words).

1. INTRODUCTION

The purpose of this paper is to propose a recognition system based on a new dynamic programming algorithm for recognizing continuous speech spoken by male speakers. This system is realizable as a simple cellular automaton.
Recently, recognition systems dealing with isolated words spoken by many speakers are proposed [1], [2]. Other systems dealing with several connected words spoken by a speaker are also proposed [3], [4]. The following abilities are desirable for a system; 1) dealing with infinite connected words in an utterence, 2) allowing for many speakers without speaker adaptation before the utterance, 3) working in real-time. We propose a system with these abilities.

2. RECOGNITION PRINCIPLE

The principle is based on a new pattern matching algorithm using dynamic programming called Time-Space Dynamic Programming (TSDP). With regard to speech feature with the time and space axes such as spectrum and vocal tract area function, TSDP is applicable for normalizing two kinds of variations occured in time-space axes of the feature. The one is time normalization for removing speed variation of speech and the other one is space normalization for removing speaker-dependence. Two normalization parts of TSDP are carried out frame-wisely without segmentation of a continuous speech. Segmentation problem of continuous speech is maintained to the final stage of recognition process. Two kinds of normalizations of TSDP are separable.

3. OUTLINE OF THE SYSTEM

The recognition of words is carried out frame by frame. We can divide this frame-wise recognition process into three stages as follows.

1) Extraction of a vocal tract area function.
2) Application of Time-Space Dynamic Programming.
3) Frame-wise decision of category.

4. VOCAL TRACT AREA FUNCTION EXTRACTION

We use a vocal tract area function as a parameter. The reason is that a vocal tract area function is more stable for different male speakers than other parameters such as spectrum. The pre-experimental results revealed this conclusion.
The extraction technics of a vocal tract area function from speech waveform have already developed by Wakita [6] and Nakajima et al [7] by using inverse filter technic to remove glottal wave. We used an improved technic of Nakajima's one that is a frame-wise inverse filtering method of second order critical damping with a positive or a negative pole. The used one is a frame-wise inverse filtering method with the only positive pole. This method is more suitable because it does not carry out over inverse filtering for the frames in the consonant part of speech waveform.
The analysis condition is as follows ; 10 kHZ

sampling, 20 msec window for analysis, 10 msec frame interval, 12 sections for a vocal tract area function and a vocal tract area function is normalized with regard to its volume.

5. TIME-SPACE DYNAMIC PROGRAMMING

5.1 Time Normalization Part

Let $\{ f(t,x) : 1 \le x \le L \}$ be a vocal tract area function of the time t, where x indicates the space axis, i.e. vocal tract, and L is the length of vocal tract. Let $\{ Z(\tau,x) : 1 \le \tau \le T, 1 \le x \le L \}$ be a standard pattern representing a word, where T indicates the length of the standard pattern and τ corresponds to the time axis of speech feature. We define a function A(t) representing the temporary minimum distance between a past input pattern with the optimum length and a standard pattern, i.e.,

$$A(t)=\frac{1}{J^*(t)} \min_{(\varsigma_j,\tau_j)\ j=1,2,..,T} \left\{ \sum_{j=1}^{T} K_j \left(\sum_{x=1}^{L} | f(t-\varsigma_j,x)-Z(\tau_j,x)| \right) \right\},$$

where $K_j=\varsigma_{j-1}-\varsigma_j+\tau_{j-1}-\tau_j$, $\varsigma_1 \ge \varsigma_2 \ge \cdots \ge \varsigma_j \ge \cdots \ge \varsigma_T \ge 0$, $\tau_1 \ge \tau_2 \ge \cdots \ge \tau_j \ge \cdots \ge \tau_T = 1$.

and $J^*(t)$ is the sum of K_j's determined from the optimum pairs (ς^*_j, τ^*_j) from j equals one to j equals T. We will propose an algorithm for calculating A(t) frame-wisely using Dynamic Programming. When we calculate A(t) by the following method, we call it the time normalization part of TSDP. This idea is suggested by so-called Max-Product Parallel Machine proposed by Y.Isomichi [5]. Three variables are necessary for describing the time normalization part of TSDP. The variable $Q(t,\tau)$ indicates the local distance, $P(t,\tau)$ indicates the optimum value obtained from integration of the values of $Q(\cdot,\cdot)$'s, and $C(t,\tau)$ indicates an integrated value of K_j's which are embedded in the value $P(t,\tau)$. The variable $C(t,\tau)$ is necessary for normalizing the length of the optimum pass.

$$P(0,\tau)=P(-1,\tau)=M \quad (1 \le \tau \le T)$$

$$P(t,1)=2Q(t,1)$$

$$P(t,2)=\min \begin{cases} P(t-2,1)+2Q(t-1,2)+Q(t,2) & (a) \\ P(t-1,1)+2Q(t,2) & (b) \\ P(t,1)+Q(t,2) & (c) \end{cases}$$

$$\underset{(3 \le \tau \le T)}{P(t,\tau)}=\min \begin{cases} P(t-2,\tau-1)+2Q(t-1,\tau)+Q(t,\tau) & (d) \\ P(t-1,\tau-1)+2Q(t,\tau) & (e) \\ P(t-1,\tau-2)+2Q(t,\tau-1)+Q(t,\tau) & (f) \end{cases}$$

$$C(0,\tau)=C(-1,\tau)=0 \quad (1 \le \tau \le T)$$

$$C(t,1)=2$$

$$C(t,2) = \begin{cases} C(t-2,1)+3 & \text{if } (a) \\ C(t-1,1)+2 & \text{if } (b) \\ C(t,1)+1 & \text{if } (c) \end{cases}$$

$$\underset{(3 \le \tau \le T)}{C(t,\tau)} = \begin{cases} C(t-2,\tau-1)+3 & \text{if } (d) \\ C(t-1,\tau-1)+2 & \text{if } (e) \\ C(t-1,\tau-2)+3 & \text{if } (f) \end{cases}$$

where $Q(t,\tau)=\sum_x | f(t,x)-Z(\tau,x)|$ and M is the fixed value. Then the following equations hold.

$$P(t,T)=\min_{(\varsigma_j,\tau_j)\ j=1,2,..,T} \left\{ \sum_j K_j \left(\sum_x | f(t-\varsigma_j,x)-Z(\tau_j,x)| \right) \right\}.$$

$$C(t,T)=J^*(t). \qquad P(t,T)/C(t,T)=A(t).$$

The detail discussion about these derivations is described in a paper [8].

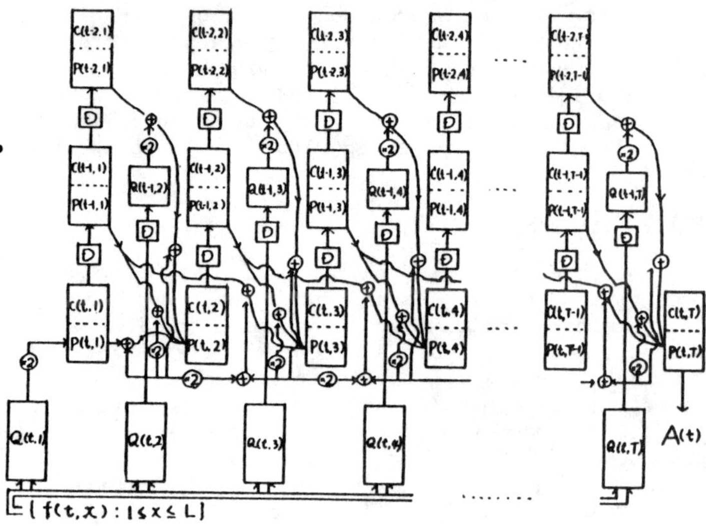

Fig. 1 Cellular Space Realization.

5.2 Space Normalization Part

The space normalization is applicable to the determination part of the value $Q(t,\tau)$ of the time normalization algorithm.
If we introduce a new variable $g(t,\tau,x,\xi)$ and suppose $1 \le \xi -1 \le x \le \xi +1 \le L$, then the space normalization algorithm is described as follows.

$$g(t,\tau,1,1)=2\ | f(x,1)-Z(\tau,1)|$$

$$g(t,\tau,x,\xi)=\min[g(t,\tau,x-1,\xi-2)+2|f(t,x)-Z(\tau,\xi-1)| + |f(t,x)-Z(\tau,\xi)|,\ g(t,\tau,x-1,\xi-1)+2|f(t,x)-Z(\tau,\xi)|,\ g(t,\tau,x-2,\xi-1)+2|f(t,x-1)-Z(\tau,\xi)|+|f(t,x)-Z(\tau,\xi)|].$$

If the time normalization part has $Q(t,\tau)$ defined by $Q(t,\tau)= g(t,\tau,L,L)/2L$, then the algorithm is called TSDP. The value $Q(t,\tau)$ indicates the local distance normalized with respect to the space x in f(t,x). The following equation holds about the output of TSDP A(t).

$$A(t)=\frac{1}{2L\,J^*(t)}\min_{(\varsigma_j,\tau_j)_{j=1,2,..,T}}\left\{\sum_j K_j\left(\min_i \sum_i W_i\left|f(t-\varsigma_j,x_i)-Z(\tau_j,\xi_i)\right|\right)\right\}$$

where $K_j = \varsigma_{j-1} - \varsigma_j + \tau_{j-1} - \tau_j$, $W_i = x_i - x_{i-1} + \xi_i - \xi_{i-1}$, $x_1=1$, $x_L=L$, $\xi_1=1$, $\xi_L=L$.

6. CATEGORY DECISION ALGORITHM

Let $\{A_i(t): i= 1,2,..,n\}$ be n values determined from TSDP, where i is the category number. Let t_F be the end time of a word in a continous speech. We never use t_F in the recognition system. Section 5. reveals that the value of $A_i(t_F)$ is the smallest among those of $A_j(t_F), j\neq i$, $A_i(t)$ $(t<t_F)$, and $A_i(t\ )$ $(t>t_F)$. We define $i1^*(t)$, $i2^*(t)$ so that $A_{i1^*(t)}(t)= \min A_i(t) \leq \lambda$, $A_{i2^*(t)}(t)= \min A_i(t) \leq A_{i1^*(t)}(t)+h \leq \lambda$ for $i\neq i1^*(t)$, where λ and h are the positive constants. Then we define the decision category number $i^*(t)$ by

$$i^*(t) = \begin{cases} i1^*(t) & \text{if } L_{i1^*(t)} \geq L_{i2^*(t)} \\ i1^*(t) & \text{if no } i2^*(t) \\ i2^*(t) & \text{if } L_{i1^*(t)} < L_{i2^*(t)} \end{cases}$$

where $L_{i1^*(t)}$, $L_{i2^*(t)}$ are the lengths of the standard pattern $i1^*(t)$, $i2^*(t)$. If $i1^*(t)$ does not exist, we set $i^*(t)=0$. The variable $i2^*(t)$ is the candidate category number of the second minimum distance. In general, further algorithm is necessary since there is a time sequence whose frames indicate the same nonzero recognition category number.

7. EXPERIMENTAL RESULTS

Recognition experiments were carried out for 50 words making weather forecast sentences (25 Japanese-city names and 25 Japanese words about weather forecast). The standard patterns are isolated utterances of the words spoken by a male speaker who is out of the tested 4 speakers. The uttered connected words take a form of a sentence with natural speed. Three types of error existed, i.e., confusion: the system decides an uncorrect category at the time when a word must be recognized, missing: the system decides no word at the time when a word must be recognized, ghost: the system decides a category at the time when no word must be recognized. Table 1 shows the two kinds recognition results of connected words (application of TSDP and the time normalization only of TSDP).

8. CONCLUSIONS

A new speech recognition system has been developed and evaluated from the viewpoint of continuous words recognition for male speakers without segmentation and speaker adaptation. The recognition system is realizable as a simple cellular automaton. We obtained 85.7 % as the recognition rate for 440 connected samples, 4 speakers and 50 categories using the standard patterns spoken by a male speaker who was out of the tested speakers.

ACKNOWLEGEMENTS

The auther would like to thank Dr.S.Mori and Dr.T.Nakajima and the menbers of the Speech Recognition Section for supporting this work.

SPEAKER NAME	STAND. NAME	CONNECT SAMPLES	CORRECT	ERROR C	ERROR M	ERROR G	RATE
I.M	R.O	109	93	13	2	6	85.3 %
S.Ishi.	R.O	113	101	7	4	2	89.4 %
S.Ita.	R.O	111	97	10	3	3	87.4 %
T.S	R.O	107	86	11	8	3	80.4 %
TOTAL	R.O	440	377	41	17	14	85.7 %
TIME-SPACE DYNAMIC PROGRAMMING							
R.O	R.O	500	466	15	19	28	93.2 %
9 males	R.O	48	30	5	12	7	62.5 %
ONLY TIME NORMALIZATION PART OF TSDP							

Table 1

REFERENCES

[1] Chiba,S., et al "A speaker-independent word recognition system." 4-th IJCPR, p.995, (1978).

[2] Kido,K., et al "Spoken word system for unlimited speakers using gross pattern of spectrum and linguistic information." 4-th IJCPR, p.980, (1978).

[3] Nakatsu,R., Kohda,M. "Speech recognition of connected words." 4-th IJCPR, p.1009, (1978).

[4] Sakoe,H. "Recognition of continuously spoken words based on two level DP-matching." Paper of Tech. Com. of Speech, A. S. J., S75-28 (1975-11).

[5] Isomichi,Y. "Segmentation-free recognition system for auditory pattern." Tech. Group of PRL, I.E.C.E.J., Paper PRL74-22 (1974).

[6] Wakita,H. "Direct estimation of the vocal tract shape by inverse filtering of acoustic waveforms." IEEE Trans. Vol.AU-21, No.5, pp.417-427, Oct. 1973.

[7] Nakajima,T., et al "Estimation of vocal tract area functions by adaptive inverse filtering methods." Bul. ETL, 34-4, p.50 (1973).

[8] Oka,R. "Continuous words recognition by use of Continuous Dynamic Programming for pattern matching." Paper of Tech. Com. of Speech, A. S. J., S78-20 (1978-6).

SUPP: UNDERSTANDING MOVING PICTURE PATTERNS BASED ON LINGUISTIC KNOWLEDGE

Naoyuki Okada
Department of Information Science
and Systems Engineering
Oita University
Oita 870-11, Japan

This paper presents a system for understanding moving picture patterns based on linguistic knowledge. In order to deal with the difference of knowledge level between picture pattern and natural language, a hierarchical structure is adopted for the representation of knowledge. At a certain level knowledge data is organized as frame centred around the concept of verb. The concepts of approximately five thousand Japanese verbs were systematically classified to construct such a knowledge system.
The program reads a picture pattern sequence. Pairing a picture pattern with the successive one in the sequence, it recognizes primitive pictures in the pair. Then, checking dynamic relations among primitive pictures, it organizes the relations into verb-centred events. It makes inferences about similarity between two concepts of verbs. Finally it describes each event in Japanese and English.

1. INTRODUCTION

It is a matter of course that image and natural language understanding are very important aspects of artificial intelligence researches. The research works in both areas have remarkably increased in number in recent years, but the results obtained in one area have not been sufficiently used for the research works in the other area. There is much difference of the present knowledge level between image, especially real world image, and natural language understanding: the knowledge level for the former is low while one for the latter is high.
In the last decade or more we have worked at constructing a system named SUPP(System for Understanding Picture Patterns) in order to raise the level of image understanding up to the linguistic knowledge level and to fill the gap between the works in the two areas. This paper is an overview of SUPP[1]-[7]. The theory developed there agrees with much of Minsky's frames idea[8]. SUPP can be viewed as a specialization of frames idea in the domain of linguistic understanding of image sequence. It has the following two characteristics:
a. A systematic and exhaustive investigation of the meaning of image is made from the linguistic viewpoint.
b. A theoretical basis is given for dealing with the structure and the meaning of change, be it motion, deformation or so forth, occuring in image sequences.

The research reported herein was supported in part by the Japanese Ministry of Education under Grant in Aid for Scientific Research, No. 320709.

2. CONCEPTUAL TAXONOMY OF JAPANESE VERBS

When an image or image sequence is given, infinite number of static or dynamic events can generally be observed in it. Suppose that the meaning of each event is described in natural language, the description sentences will amount to infinite number. An ordinary sentence is decomposed into simple sentences, each of which is governed syntactically and semantically by a verb. Since there are only finite number of verbs in each language, meanings of infinite number of events are roughly divided into meanings of those verbs and their interrelations.
An object in the real world which is identified by a verb is called "matter." It arises acompanying things, events and attributes, which are called "constituents," so its concept can be regarded as the concept of dynamic or static relation among constituents.
After due consideration about correspondence with the real world, the concepts of approximately 5,000 Japanese verbs were classified according to an algorithm. The concepts are divided into two large classes : "simple matter concept" and "non-simple matter concept." The former can not be decomposed into elementary matter concepts while the latter can be decomposed. They can further be classified according to their structural patterns and semantic contents. The results are described in [2] and [3].

3. THE KNOWLEDGE SYSTEM

The knowledge system contains a visual , a conceptual, a linguistic and a thesaurus component.

3.1 The Visual and the Conceptual Component

The visual component contains models of primitive pictures and syntactic rules among them . An example of model is shown in Fig. 4-(b). The rules are applied to picture pattern pairs , which Minsky called "before-after" frame-pairs. The conceptual component contains conceptual features, concepts and networks of concepts . A matter concept is expressed by [V : $c_1 c_2 \cdots c_l$ $d_1(E_1) d_2(E_2) \cdots d_m(E_m)$] where each c_i denotes a feature of matter itself and corresponds to a syntactic rule mentioned above . Each $d_j(\ )$ denotes the case or role of a constituent and must be filled by specific instance or concept of constituent. Features E_j ($= e_{j1} e_{j2} \cdots e_{jn}$) specify the conditions its assignment must meet . Networks are constructed among similar matter concepts.

3.2 The Linguistic and the Thesaurus Component

The linguistic component consists of dictionaries for the production of Japanese and English sentences. The thesaurus component contains all the classified concepts in Chap. 2 and supports to develop other components.

The knowledge system is discussed in detail in [1],[5],[6] and [7].

4. THE UNDERSTANDING PROCESS

The process of understanding a sequence of two-dimensional line drawings (handwriting is allowed) is described . The overall system is indicated in Fig. 1.

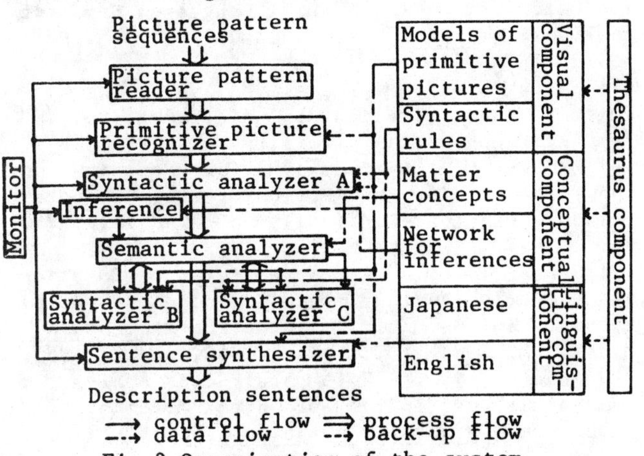

Fig.3 Organization of the system

4.1 Primitive Picture Recognition and Syntactic Analysis

The picture pattern reader is a curve follower that traces line segments by octagonal scanning. The recognizer is based on Evans's matching program[9] for graph-like line drawings but is improved to handle noisy ones.
The syntactic analyzer A decomposes the complex picture , in which two or more primitive pictures may intersect or touch each other , and recognizes them according to Gestalt criteria. The syntactic analyzer B performs Boolean operations on quantized primitive pictures to check such a relation as "MAN INSIDE HOUSE." The syntactic analyzer C performs numerical operations on the data such as coordinates and transformational coefficients of primitive pictures. The programs mentioned above are described in detail in [4] and [5].

4.2 Semantic Analyzer and Inference

The semantic analyzer detects the meaning of matter-centred change in picture pattern pairs by top-down analysis . Suppose that matter [$V(s,o_\alpha): c_1 c_2 \cdots c_l d_s(e_s) d_{o_\alpha}(e_{o_\alpha})$] is directed by the Inference. The analyzer assigns the role of s to one of the primitive pictures , say P_s , after checking whether P_s meets e_s. It assigns the role of o_α to another primitive picture $P_{o\alpha}$ in the same way. Then it analyzes each c_i by calling a correspondent sub-program in the syntactic analyzer B or C. If all the analyses end in success, the meaning of $V(s,o_\alpha)$ is detected. The present Inference makes inferences about all the similar concepts in the network in depth-first order , directing each matter concept at a node to the semantic analyzer.
Finally , the synthesizer produces Japanese and English simple sentences.

5. EXPERIMENTS

Almost all the programs were written in FORTRAN to run under the OSII/VS of the FACOM 230-38S medium scale computer at the Department of Information Science and Systems Engineering at Oita University. Experimental results [4]-[7] are shown in Fig. 2-5.

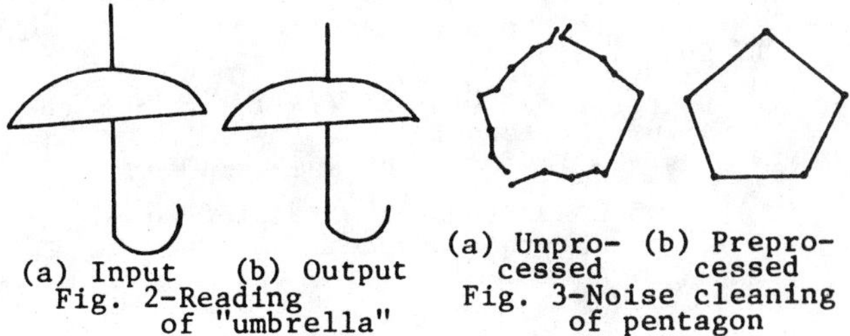
(a) Input (b) Output
Fig. 2-Reading of "umbrella"

(a) Unprocessed (b) Preprocessed
Fig. 3-Noise cleaning of pentagon

(a) Preprocessed input picture (b) The model of "bird[1]"

1. Pattern matching

$[p_7:q_5],[p_9:q_{14}],[p_{19}:q_6],[p_8: q_4],[p_6:q_{15}],$
$[p_{10}:q_{13}], [p_{18}: q_7], [p_5 : q_2] , [p_{11}:q_{12}],$
$[p_{17}:q_8],[p_{12}:q_9]$
$[p_{16}:q_{10}],[p_{12}:q_9],[p_{15}:q_{11}]$

2. Transformation and similarity

Translation : (524.4, 483.7), scaling : 2.173 times, rotation : 2.290 radian, reflection : in Y-axis. Similarity : 0.718($\leq$1)

Fig. 4-Recognition of "bird[1]"

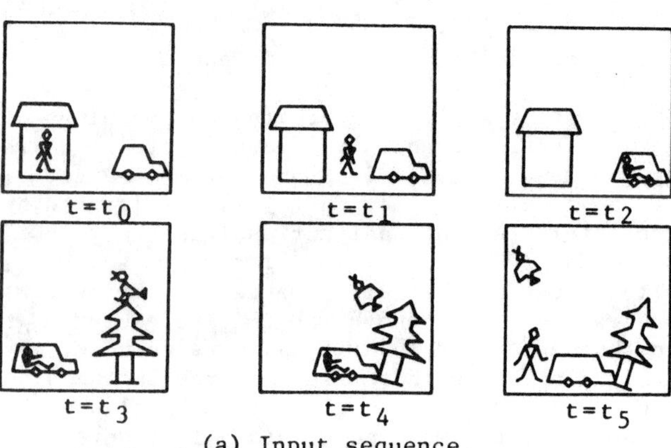

(a) Input sequence

$t=t_0$ * *OTOKO(4) GA IE NO UCHI NI ITA.*
* THE MAN[4] WAS IN THE HOUSE.

$t=t_1$ * *OTOKO(4) GA IE KARA DETA.*
* THE MAN[4] WENT OUT OF THE HOUSE.

$t=t_2$ * *OTOKO(4) GA KURUMA NI NOTTA.*
* THE MAN[4] RODE INTO THE CAR.

$t=t_3$ * *KURUMA GA HASHITTA.*
* THE CAR RAN.

$t=t_4$ * *KURUMA GA KI NI BUTSUKATTA.*
* THE CAR COLLIDED AGAINST THE TREE.

$t=t_5$ *TORI(1) GA KI KARA SATTA.*
THE BIRD[1] LEFT THE TREE.
* *OTOKO(3) GA KURUMA KARA ORITA.*
* THE MAN[3] ALIGHTED FROM THE CAR.

(b) Output sentences

1. Description of $t=t_0$ is for the picture pattern at $t=t_0$.
2. Description of $t=t_i$ ($i\geq1$) is for the picture pattern pair at $t=t_i$ and t_{i-1}.
3. The * marks were assigned by man.

Fig. 5-Understanding of a picture pattern sequence

6. CONCLUSIONS

A system has been surveyed that understands moving picture patterns linguistically. Badler's approach[10] basically agrees with ours in handling verb-centred events but differs in that SUPP is based on a systematic analysis of almost all the verbs used for everyday Japanese while he notes only motion verbs in English. By SUPP image understanding research has come closer to natural language understanding research.

ACKNOWLEDGEMENT

The author started to develop SUPP some ten years ago when he was at Kyushu University. The author wishes to express his gratitude to Prof. T.Tamati of Kyushu University for kind guidance and material support.

REFERENCES

[1] Okada, N. and Tamati, T. "Semantic Information of Natural Language and its Extraction and Classification." Trans. IECE Japan 52-C:10 (1969) 363-370.

[2] Okada, N. and Tamati, T. "An analysis and Classification of "Simple Matter concepts" for Natural Language and Picture Interpretation." Trans. IECE Japan 56-D:9 (1973) 523-530.

[3] Okada, N. and Tamati, T. "An Analysis and Classification of "Non-Simple Matter Concepts " for Natural Language and Picture Interpretation." Trans. IECE Japan 56-D:10 (1973) 591-598.

[4] Okada, N. and Tamati, T. "Automated Editing of Fuzzy Line Drawings for Picture Description." Trans. IECE Japan 57-A:3 (1974) 216-223.

[5] Okada, N. and Tamati, T. " Interpretation of the Meaning of Picture Patterns and its Description in Natural Language — Primitive Picture Recognition and Syntactic Analysis . " Trans. IECE Japan J59-D:5 (1976) 323-330.

[6] Okada, N. and Tamati, T. " Interpretation of the Meaning of Moving Picture Patterns and its Description in Natural Language—Semantic Analysis." Trans. IECE Japan J59-D : 5 (1976) 331-338.

[7] Okada, N. and Miura, A. "A System for Linguistic Interpretation of Picture Patterns." Rep. Fac. Engng. Oita University No. 5(1979) 61-70.

[8] Minsky, M. "A Framework for Representing Knowledge." In The Psychology of Computer Vision , Winston, P.H.(ed.), McGraw-Hill, 1975, pp. 211-277.

[9] Evans, T. G. " A Program for the Solution of Geometric Analogy Intelligence-Test Questions." In Semantic Information Processeing, Minsky, M. (ed.), MIT Press, 1968, pp. 271-353.

[10] Badler, N.I. " Temporal Scene Analysis : Conceptual Descriptions of Object Movements . " Tech. Rep. University of Toronto No. 80(1975) .

COMPUTER CONTROL OF MULTIJOINTED FINGER SYSTEM

Tokuji Okada
Automatic Control Division
Electrotechnical Laboratory
2-6-1 Nagata-cho, Chiyoda-ku
Tokyo 100, Japan

This paper treats computer control of multijointed fingers. First, we discuss optimum operational direction of multijointed fingers. The direction is determined from motional structure of the fingers and is important in the control stage of arm part. Second, general description about software system is presented with primitive programs to control hardware system. These have been implemented on the ETL object-handling system for manual industry. Third, experimental results of nut-turning task are presented which verify the feasibility of manual task by computer control.

1. INTRODUCTION

Multijointed fingers are useful not only for automation of manual industry but also for animal-like assistant robot from the standpoint of human welfares since they are suited to realize flexible motions that give us not fear but familiality. Further, the fingers provide a research tool for investigation of new modes of servoing, intelligent manipulation, interactive real-time real-world system and AI. Under this philosophy, we treat fingers with complicated structure in our research.

Most of multijointed fingers are not competent for manual task since they are not on a level of programmable manipulation. Hanafusa [1] performed flexible manipulation by using elastic fingers which have coil springs. The ETL object-handling system [3] of which the hardware is overviewed in a reference [2] realizes the flexible manipulation with multijointed fingers.

In this paper, an optimum operational direction of a finger part is discussed with generality. Then, Fundamental ideas for programming manual task are presented with primitive programs about the ETL finger system. Experimental results of nut-turning task by computer control are also shown.

2. OPERATIONAL DIRECTION OF A FINGER PART

Multijointed fingers have an adaptability to grasp an object and handle it from various direction in general. But it is reasonable to fix an operational direction for a finger part to have much flexibility in handling an object. We consider a volume in which the finger terminal can be located. We call the surface of it an envelope. Shape of the envelope depends on structure of the finger. In most cases, the shape is like an ellipsoid as shown in Fig.1 . It is mathematically expressed in the coordinate system (X_p, Y_p, Z_p) that has an origin at the center of the palm plate as

$$\frac{\{(X-x_j)\cos\psi_j-(Z-z_j)\sin\psi_j\}^2}{A_j^{\,2}}+\frac{Y^2}{A_j^{\,2}}+\frac{\{(X-x_j)\sin\psi_j+(Z-z_j)\cos\psi_j\}^2}{B_j^{\,2}}=1\ ,$$

where j is a subscript related to finger number, $(x_j, 0, z_j)$ denotes the coordinates of the finger root, A_j means effective finger length concerned with bend-in and bend-out joint, and B_j means that concerned with abduct and adduct joint. Mostly, the value of A_j is greater than that of B_j $(A=\ell_1+\ell_2+\ell_3+\ell_4,\ B=\ell_2+\ell_3+\ell_4)$.

We have determined an optimum operational direction of a finger part as the direction toward which a common point of multiple envelopes is viewed from the center of the palm plate (In Fig.1, W shows this direction). Even if the finger part is composed of a lot of fingers, the optimum operational direction of the finger part would be fixed on the finger system according to its structure. On the other hand, an object has

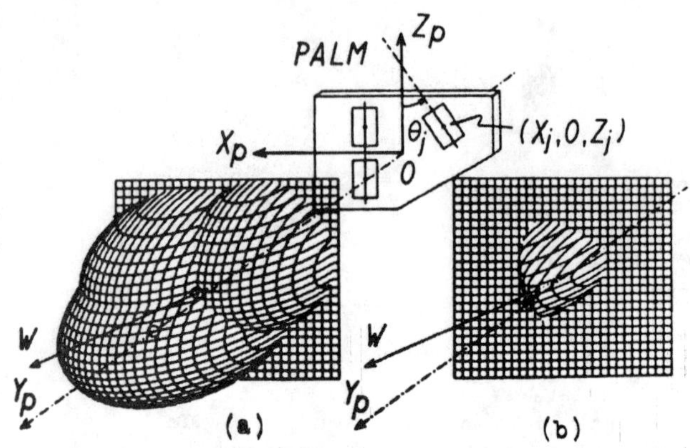

Fig.1 Total envelope related to three fingers

its own optimum operational direction as its property. It can be expressed by an axial line which is peculiar to the object. Therefore, adaptability of the fingers would be created by controlling the arm so that these operational directions might accord with each other.

3. SOFTWARE SYSTEM

3.1 General description

At present, the software system for manual task is on a low level since it is not described in the form like manipulator language or hand language. We consider the symboric notations [3] that are defined to fundamental motions of a finger are useful to develop the language. Finger operation for manual task would be programmed by applying these motions to a geometric model of an object. The use of sensors is important to make adaptable handling in real-world. As shown in Fig.2, our system has a short-range finding sensor (SRFS) [4] at the palm area for local inspection of the object. This sensor reduces complexity of programming since it augments the capabilities of the system so that it can find and acquire unindexed workpieces and cope with unexpected events in performing object handling and assembly operations. For example, in nut turning, it monitors the fixation between screw and nut, and provides the resulting displacement of a nut along a screw axis. Therefore, fingers' pushing or pulling operation is sensor-controlled according to the amount of its displacement.

3.2 Primitive Programs

Primitive programs control the hardware of the object-handling system. The next program is common to finger part and arm part.

TAFCON(IAF,IFMODE,XAF,YAF,ZAF)

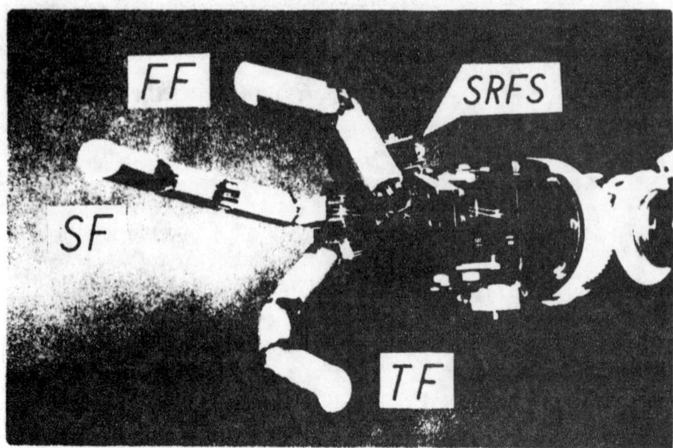

Fig.2 View of finger part

The argument IAF designates the part to be controlled. The meaning of it is

$$IAF = \begin{cases} 0 \ ; \ \text{Arm} \\ 1 \ ; \ \text{First Finger} \\ 2 \ ; \ \text{Second Finger} \\ 3 \ ; \ \text{Third Finger} \end{cases}$$

IFMODE is the argument concerned with the control mode about the finger terminal direction. This is effective when the value of IAF is not equal to zero. When IFMODE takes the value of 1, only the position of a finger terminal is controlled. But when the value of 2 or 3 is assigned to IFMODE, not only the position but also the direction of the finger terminal is controlled. Especially, when the value of 3 is assigned to IFMODE, the direction is controlled to be optimum. (XAF,YAF,ZAF) are the coordinates of the palm point for arm control or the terminal point for finger control in the coordinate system (X,Y,Z) that has an origin at the shoulder joint. When the value of IAF is equal to zero, the next program is used.

ARMSOL(XAF,YAF,ZAF,α,β,γ,IFLAG)

This program calculates an arm solution by using the parameters (α,β,γ) that are concerned with the optimum operational direction of the finger part. The argument IFLAG notifies whether the arm solution is obtained or not.

As far as the fingers are concerned, coordinates (XAF,YAF,ZAF) are the values expressed in the coordinate system (X,Y,Z). In order to obtain the coordinates (XF,YF,ZF) expressed in the coordinate system (X_f,Y_f,Z_f) that has an origin at the root of the finger, the next program for coordinates transformation is used;

TRANSF(J,XAF,YAF,ZAF,XF,YF,ZF)

The argument J takes the value equal to that of IAF and designates the finger to be controlled. Control values (P1,P2,P3,P4) for finger joints are obtained from programs FINSL1, FINSL2 and FINSL3 that are prepared according to the values of IFMODE. The command format to use these programs is written as follows:

FINSL*n*(J,XF,YF,ZF,P1,P2,P3,P4,IFLAG)

when the value of IFMODE is 2 or 3, the unit vector $\mathbf{V}_{jn}$ $(=u_{j1}X+u_{j2}Y+u_{j3}Z)$ which denotes the direction of the finger to be controlled is referred. Finger solution in FINSL2 and FINSL3 are obtained by hill-climbing method and exhausting method, respectively.

4. EXPERIMENTAL MANUAL TASK

Nut-turning task is performed in the experiment. In order to adapt the fingers to the task, arm part is controlled so that the optimum operational direction of the fingers accords with axial line of the screw. Then, each terminal point of the fingers is controlled to move along the contour which is assumed to be circular in mathematical model of the nut. Results of the task are shown in Fig.3. The values of IFMODE in (a) and (b) are equal to 1 and 2, respectively. In (b), both directions of the finger SF and TF are equal to screw axis, namely, $u_{21}=u_{23}=u_{31}=u_{33}=0$ and $u_{22}=u_{32}=1$. Time required to accomplish one cycle of turning for (b) is about 2.3 times long as compared with that for (a) under such condition that the resolution angle of the joint is 2 degrees. Incidentally, the time for the case of IFMODE=3 is about 3.5 times long. The fact shows that the more precisely the finger direction is controlled, the more time it takes. But the time required to obtain control values for the case of IFMODE=2 is not so long as we have supposed. We could hardly find the difference in the results between the cases of IFMODE=2 and IFMODE=3. This means the capability of real-time control of both the position and the orientation of multijointed fingers in IFMODE=2. In (a), finger supports the nut with a point. But in (b), it tends to support the nut with a line. The fingers would realize stable operation when the orientation of the fingers are controlled to fit to a surface of an object.

5. CONCLUSIONS

Nut-turning task has been carried out smoothly by computer control without influence of shape and size of the nut. This would show the feasibility of manual tasks by multijointed fingers with flexibility.

Each fingertip is assumed to be an ideal point. But in real, it is extended like a ball. Therefore, the extension of the nut should be considered in fine operation of an object. Further the fingers might be controlled not only in position but also in torque. We have just started to develop intelligent manipulation with cooperated control of these.

REFERENCES

[1] H.Hanafusa and H.Asada, "A Robot Hand with Elastic Fingers and its Application to Assembly Process." IFAC Symposium, Tokyo, 1977.

[2] T.Okada and S.Tsuchiya, "On a Versatile Finger System." Proc. 7th ISIR, 1977.

[3] T.Okada, "Object-Handling System for Manual Industry." IEEE Trans. Vol.SMC-9, No.2, 1979.

[4] T.Okada, "A Short-Range Finding Sensor for Manipulators." Bull. Electrotech. Lab. Vol.42, No.6, 1978.

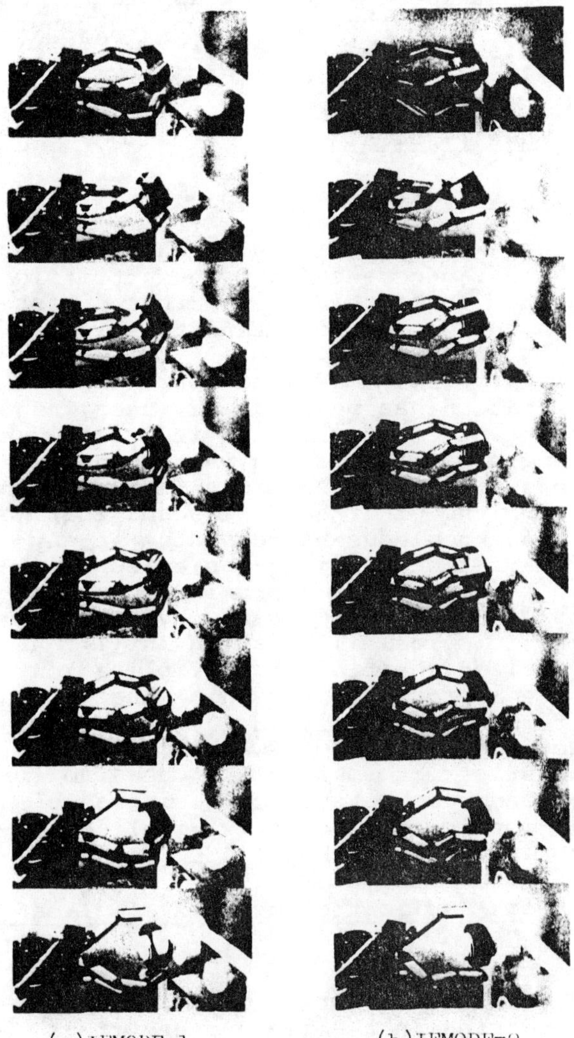

(a)IFMODE=1 (b)IFMODE=2

Fig.3 Nut-turning task

A MEASURE OF CLOSENESS OF WEAK IMPLICATION TO STRICT IMPLICATION

Masanori B. Okamoto
Faculty of Economics
Hiroshima University
Higashisenda-machi
Hiroshima City 730,Japan

The concept of weak implication introduced by R.Boudon is relevant to approximate reasoning which is a subject of the study in AI. The weak implication can be interpreted by the fuzzy material implication which is a binary fuzzy relation. A measure of closeness of weak implication to strict implication is defined as the maximum of distances within the given fuzzy relation,but constructed in the 2x2 contigency table. This measure agrees with the absolute value of Boudon's index f of closeness of weak implication to strict implication under some conditions.

1. WEAK IMPLICATION

1.1 Approximate Reasoning

In real-world domain in which reasoning is often judgemental and inexact,it is required to be able to say that " A suggests B" or "C and D tend to rule out E". As an application of AI to real-world problem a model of approximate implication has been already used,with a certainty factor which indicates the strength of implication,in the knowledge-based medical consultation system in [2]. On the other hand,it seems that we have no knowledge-based system in any field of social science as an application of AI. However approximate implication was discussed firstly by R.Boudon on sociological implication in [1]. He criticized the transitive implication on the approximate reasoning that H. Zetterberg have done in [7] and he proposed the concept of "weak implication" against strict implication. He also introduced some measure of closeness of weak implication to strict implication with a certain probabilistic measure.

1.2 Weak Implication as Fuzzy Implication.

R.Boudon's weak implication is fuzzy implication in a sense,because it is implication that has fuzzy truth value. Membership function which defines a fuzzy subset is different from probability as indicated in [3],thus it may be preferable to give another measure of closeness of weak implication to strict implication by the use of the fuzzy implication rather than probabilistic measure. This paper shows that weak implication can be well expressed with a binary fuzzy relation which gives the fuzzy material implication on the fuzzy linguistic variable given by L.A.Zadeh in [4],[5],[6] and another measure of closeness of weak implication to strict implication is newly defined by the maximum of some distances between of fuzzy binary relation which is fuzzy material implication.

2. FUZZY RELATION MATRIX OF WEAK IMPLICATION

2.1 Construction of Fuzzy Relation Matrix

We now construct a fuzzy relation matrix for a given 2x2 contigency table,in which the observed frequencies are shown under classification with the two attributes A and B. However it actually occurs that the classification is not proper because of ill-defined of A and

B or not-fitted in practice for that criterion of classification. Thus it is more natural to regard A,B (or $\bar{A}$,$\bar{B}$) as fuzzy subsets of possible universe of discourse X and Y,respectively. We assume that normalized frequencies in rows in the 2x2 contigency table (Table 1) are values of membership function of fuzzy subset A or $\bar{A}$;this table may

Table 1. Contigency table normalized in rows.

	B	$\bar{B}$	
A	$n_{11}/n_{1.}$	$n_{12}/n_{1.}$	1.0
$\bar{A}$	$n_{21}/n_{2.}$	$n_{22}/n_{2.}$	1.0

expess a fuzzy relation R in $A \times B \subset X \times Y$. This procedure intends to determine the grade of fuzzy subsets by empirical data.

2.2 Fuzzy Material Implication

The extension of the notion of material implication to fuzzy subsets is given by L.A.Zadeh in [6] as follows,

$$\text{IF A THEN B ELSE C} = A \times B + \neg A \times C$$

$$\text{IF A THEN B} = \text{IF A THEN B ELSE V} = A \times B + \neg A \times V$$

where U,V are two possible different universe of discourse;A,B and C are fuzzy subsets of U,V and V,respectively. The material implication is a binary fuzzy relation in UxV and here we simply denote them $A \Rightarrow B$. From the assumption that the normalized 2x2 contigency table is a fuzzy relation matrix,the fuzzy material implication is obtained for the given 2x2 contigency table. For example,we obtain fuzzy implication for a not strict but strong implication as follows;fuzzy subsets A=[1/1,0.2/2],B=[1/1,0/2],relation matrix

$$R=\begin{bmatrix}1 & 0\\ 0.2 & 0.8\end{bmatrix}, \text{ fuzzy implication } A \Rightarrow B$$

$$=A \times B + \neg A \times V=\begin{bmatrix}1 & 0\\ 0.2 & 0\end{bmatrix}+\begin{bmatrix}0 & 0\\ 0.8 & 0.8\end{bmatrix}=\begin{bmatrix}1 & 0\\ 0.8 & 0.8\end{bmatrix}$$

The several examples of fuzzy implication from strict to very weak implication are shown in Table 2.

Table 2. Examples of fuzzy implication.

STRICT IMPLICATION

A=[1/1,0/2],B=[1/1,0/2]

$$R=\begin{bmatrix}1 & 0\\ 0 & 1\end{bmatrix}, A \Rightarrow B = \begin{bmatrix}1 & 0\\ 1 & 1\end{bmatrix}$$

STRONG IMPLICATION

A=[1/1,0.2/2],B=[1/1,0/2]

$$R=\begin{bmatrix}1 & 0\\ 0.2 & 0.8\end{bmatrix}, A \Rightarrow B = \begin{bmatrix}1 & 0\\ 0.8 & 0.8\end{bmatrix}$$

WEAK IMPLICATION

A=[1/1,0.5/2],B=[1/1,0/2]

$$R=\begin{bmatrix}1 & 0\\ 0.5 & 0.5\end{bmatrix}, A \Rightarrow B = \begin{bmatrix}1 & 0\\ 0 & 0.5\end{bmatrix}$$

VERY WEAK IMPLICATION

A=[1/1,0.9/2],B=[1/1,0/2]

$$R=\begin{bmatrix}1 & 0\\ 0.9 & 0.1\end{bmatrix}, A \Rightarrow B = \begin{bmatrix}1 & 0\\ 0.9 & 0.1\end{bmatrix}$$

3. MEASURE OF CLOSENESS TO STRICT IMPLICATION

3.1 Definition of Measure of Closeness

We now give the definition of a measure of closeness of weak implication through fuzzy material implication.

The measure $d(A \Rightarrow B)$ of closeness of weak implication to strict implication is defined by

$$d(A \Rightarrow B) = \max(d_1(A \Rightarrow B), d_2(A \Rightarrow B)) \quad (1)$$

where

$$d_1(A \Rightarrow B) = |\mu_R(A,B) - \mu_R(\bar{A},B)|$$
$$d_2(A \Rightarrow B) = |\mu_R(A,\bar{B}) - \mu_R(\bar{A},\bar{B})| \quad (2)$$

are derived from the fuzzy material implication

$$A \Rightarrow B = \begin{bmatrix}\mu_R(A,B), & \mu_R(A,\bar{B})\\ \mu_R(\bar{A},B), & \mu_R(\bar{A},\bar{B})\end{bmatrix} \quad (3)$$

3.2 Examples of Measure of Closeness

The values of $d(A \Rightarrow B)$ are given for examples cited above in Table 3. Further we obtain values of $d(A \Rightarrow B)$ for several examples in sociology given by Boudon in [1];$d(A \Rightarrow B)=0.5$ for the conservation of religious tradition,$d(A \Rightarrow B)=0.31$ for the marriage system in ancient societies and the names called of mothers and mother's sisters,$d(A \Rightarrow B)=0.20$ for the effect of TV performance

Table 3. Values of $d(A \Rightarrow B)$

strict	strong	weak	very weak
1	0.8	0.5	0.1

of political candidate to audiences. The values of d in Boudon's counter example to Zetterberg's implication can be written as $d(A \Rightarrow B)=0.2$, $d(B \Rightarrow C)=0.3$, and $d(A \Rightarrow C)=0.1$ for fuzzy implication

$$A \Rightarrow B = \begin{bmatrix} 0.6 & 0.4 \\ 0.6 & 0.6 \end{bmatrix}, B \Rightarrow C = \begin{bmatrix} 0.7 & 0.3 \\ 0.6 & 0.6 \end{bmatrix}$$

and $A \Rightarrow C = \begin{bmatrix} 0.5 & 0.5 \\ 0.6 & 0.4 \end{bmatrix}$. However we have $d((A \Rightarrow B) \circ (B \Rightarrow C))=0.2 \neq d(A \Rightarrow C)=0.1$ for fuzzy compositional implication

$$(A \Rightarrow B) \circ (B \Rightarrow C) = \begin{bmatrix} 0.6 & 0.4 \\ 0.6 & 0.4 \end{bmatrix} \neq (A \Rightarrow C)$$

4. BOUDON'S INDEX AND CLSOSENESS MEASURE

4.1 Relation between Index f and Measure d(A⇒ B)

Boudon's index of closeness to strict implication is defined by

$$f=n_{11}/n_{1.}-n_{21}/n_{2.} \quad \text{or} \quad f=n_{11}/n_{.1}-n_{12}/n_{.2}$$

with the notation in Table 1, from which we obtain the following fuzzy subsets A and B when the maximum of components of relation matrix is $n_{11}/n_{1.}$;

$A=[(n_{11}/n_{1.})/1,(n_{21}/n_{2.})/2]$,

$B=[(n_{11}/n_{1.})/1,(n_{12}/n_{1.})/2]$ and

$$\mu_R(A, B)=(n_{11}/n_{1.}) \vee (n_{12}/n_{1.})$$

$$\mu_R(A, \bar{B})=(n_{11}/n_{1.} \wedge n_{12}/n_{1.}) \vee (n_{12}/n_{1.})$$

$$\mu_R(\bar{A}, B)=(n_{21}/n_{2.} \wedge n_{11}/n_{1.}) \vee (n_{22}/n_{2.})$$

$$\mu_R(\bar{A}, \bar{B})=(n_{21}/n_{2.} \wedge n_{12}/n_{1.}) \vee (n_{22}/n_{2.})$$

Noticing that $|(n_{11}/n_{1.})-(n_{22}/n_{2.})| = |(n_{12}/n_{1.})-(n_{21}/n_{2.})|$,

$$d(A \Rightarrow B)=\max(d_1(A \Rightarrow B), d_2(A \Rightarrow B))$$
$$=\max(|f|, |(n_{12}/n_{1.})-(n_{21}/n_{2.})|$$
$$=|f|$$

if $(1/2) > (n_{21}/n_{2.}) > (n_{22}/n_{2.})$ for $f>0$

$(n_{21}/n_{2.}) > (1/2) > (n_{22}/n_{2.})$ for $f<0$

$$d(A \Rightarrow B)=\max(|(n_{11}/n_{1.}) \cdot (n_{22}/n_{2.})|, |f|)$$
$$=|f|.$$

if $(n_{21}/n_{2.}) < (1/2) < (n_{22}/n_{2.})$ for $f>0$

$(1/2) < (n_{21}/n_{2.}) < (n_{22}/n_{2.})$ for $f<0$

It is, however, plausible to assume under meaningful weak implication that

$$(n_{21}/n_{2.}) < (1/2) < (n_{22}/n_{2.})$$

although another ill-conditioned case $(n_{21}/n_{2.}) > (1/2) > (n_{22}/n_{2.})$ occurs for a very weak condition. In fact, $d(A \Rightarrow B)$ have the same values as $|f|$ values for previous examples. Therefore we conclude that in the fuzzy relation matrix deduced by the 2x2 contigency table, the absolute value of Boudon's index $|f|$ is equal to our $d(A \Rightarrow B)$ under those conditions.

Similar procedure can be done for the pxq contigency table adding zero element to get square matrix. The grade of fuzzy subsets should be chosen to contain the maximum element of the matrix. The distances may be defined as follows;

$$d_j(A \Rightarrow B_j)= \max_{i,k} |\mu_R(A_i,B_j)-\mu_R(A_k,B_j)|$$

for a fixed j, thus we have

$$d(A \Rightarrow B) = \max_j d_j(A \Rightarrow B_j)$$

5. CONCLUSION

In the previous section we assumed that the 2x2 contigency table expresses a fuzzy relation after the normalization in rows. We must ask what kind of justification there are on this procedure, which gives actually frequency probabilities of A and B in Table 1. The question comes to the problem of the determination of the grade of fuzzy subset by empirical data. Some attempt to solve this problem has been done by S.Watanabe in [8] already. For generalized fuzzy set, a possible extension of the present idea could use his grade of implication θ instead of our $d_j(A \Rightarrow B_j)$.

REFERENCES

[1] Boudon, R. "Les Mathématiques en Sociologie. Press Univ. de France, Paris, 1971

[2] Davis, R., Buchanan, B. & Shortliffe, E. 'Production Rules as a Representation for a Knowledge-Based Consultation Program." Artif. Intell. 8:1 (1977) 15-45.

[3] Hirota, K. & Iijima, T. "Logical Basis in Probabilistic Set Theory." Trans. IECE. 62:D-2 (1979) 73-80.

[4] Zadeh, L.A. "The Concept of a Linguistic Variable and its Application to Approximate Resoning-I." Inform. Sci. 8:3 (1975) 199-249.

[5] Zadeh, L.A. "ibid-II" Inform. Sci. 8:4 (1975) 301-357.

[6] Zadeh, L.A. "ibid-III" Inform. Sci. 9:1 (1975) 43-80.

[7] Zetterberg, H. "On the Theory and Verification in Sociology." 3rd ed. Bedminster Press, New Jersey, 1966.

[8] Watanabe, S. "Fuzzification and Invariance." Proc. ICCS-78, 1. Japan, 947-951.

REGION SEGMENTATION OF IMAGES BY EXPANSION AND CONTRACTION OF EDGE POINTS

W. A. Perkins

Computer Science Department
General Motors Corporation

Research Laboratories
Warren, Michigan 48090

A new method for sègmenting images using edge points to separate regions of smoothly varying intensity is discussed. Region segmentation using edge points has not been very successful in the past because small gaps would allow merging of dissimilar regions. The present method uses an expansion-contraction technique in which the edge regions are expanded to close gaps and then contracted after the separate uniform regions have been identified. In order to perserve small uniform regions, the process is performed iteratively with increasing expansions, but no expansion for edge regions that already separate different regions. The final result is a set of uniform intensity regions (usually less than 100) and a set of edge boundary regions. The program has successfully segmented scenes with industrial parts, landscapes, and IC chips.

1. INTRODUCTION

It is generally agreed that it is necessary to organize the image data as the first step in image understanding. In organizing the image data two courses of action are generally employed: (1) Locating discontinuities in intensity (edge points) and connecting them [1,2], and (2) Trying to find regions of fairly uniform intensity by growing regions [3,4] or thresholding at a calculated level [5].

The goal of the latter approach is to segment the picture into a set of uniform intensity regions to increase the degree of organization. The early methods involved merging regions sharing the weakest boundary in an iterative process [3,4] until the weakest boundary was stronger than some threshold. To continue merging regions in complex pictures, it was necessary to use semantic information [4], limiting the general usefulness of the method. A thresholding technique developed by Ohlander [5] was found to be very effective on complex color pictures.

Because of the shortcomings of the region-growing method (without semantic information) and failure of the simple histogram thresholding approach to work on monochromatic pictures in general, we developed an entirely different method. It uses an expansion-contraction technique in which edge regions are expanded to close gaps and then contracted after the separate regions have been labeled. Expansion-contraction techniques have been very useful for the analysis of binary pictures [6], but their use on edge data has been limited [7,8].

2. SEGMENTATION METHOD

In transforming the gray-level picture into regions of uniform intensity, processes 2.1-2.8 are performed serially with processes 2.3-2.7 performed in three cycles of 0, 1, and 2 pixel expansion. The segmentation techniques will be illustrated using Fig. 1a. The resolution is 240 by 256 with 32 gray levels, and its intensity histogram is shown in Fig. 1b. Note that this picture is not thresholdable by Ohlander's criteria [5] of ratio of peak maximum to peak minimum ≥ 2.

2.1 Edge-Finding

Figure 1c was obtained by applying the Sobel edge operator [9] at every pixel of the gray-level picture (Fig. 1a).

2.2 Thinning

Eberlein's relaxation algorithm [10] was used to thin the edges. A threshold was calculated from the curvature of the thinned edge distribution [11]. Figure 1d shows the results of thinning and thresholding the edge picture.

2.3 Expanding Edge Points

Expansion of edge points is necessary to fill small gaps in the edge boundaries. The present method involves no expansion of pixels which touch two different regions [11]. The expansion was done in three stages: (1) no expansion (see Fig. 1d), (2) expansion of edge pixels to fill a 3 by 3 pixel square (see Fig. 2a), and (3) expansion of edge pixels to fill a 5 by 5 square (see Fig. 2b).

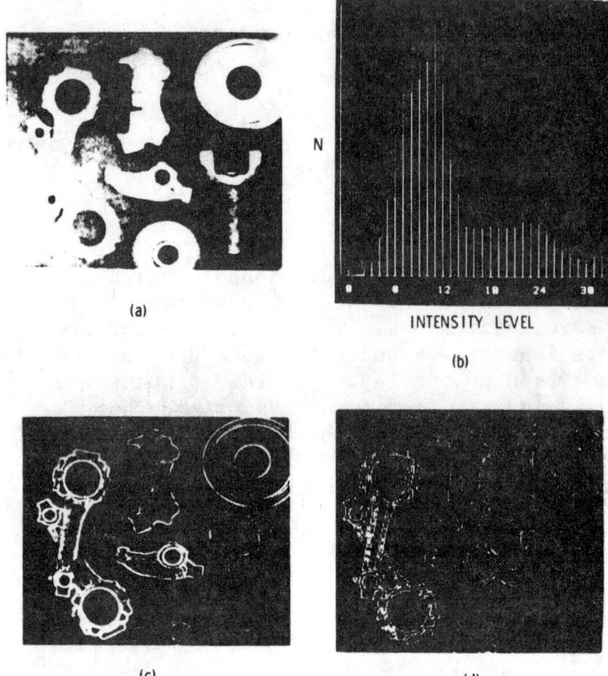

Fig. 1. (a) Digitized picture of some industrial parts. (b) Intensity histogram. (c) Edge magnitude. (d) Thresholded thinned edge array.

2.4 Labeling Uniform Intensity Regions with Connectivity Algorithm

Using the expanded edge boundary between uniform intensity regions, pixels in each uniform intensity region are connected by giving each pixel the same label with a four-connected algorithm [12]. Uniform intensity regions are taken to be four-connected and edge regions eight-connected [13].

2.5 Eliminating Small Uniform Intensity Regions

For simplicity, small uniform regions (less than 10 pixels) are eliminated by merging them into their surrounding edge region.

2.6 Shrinking Edge Regions

Edge regions are contracted by replacing "expansion" edge pixels with uniform intensity region numbers [11].

2.7 Placing Edge Boundaries Between Uniform Intensity Regions

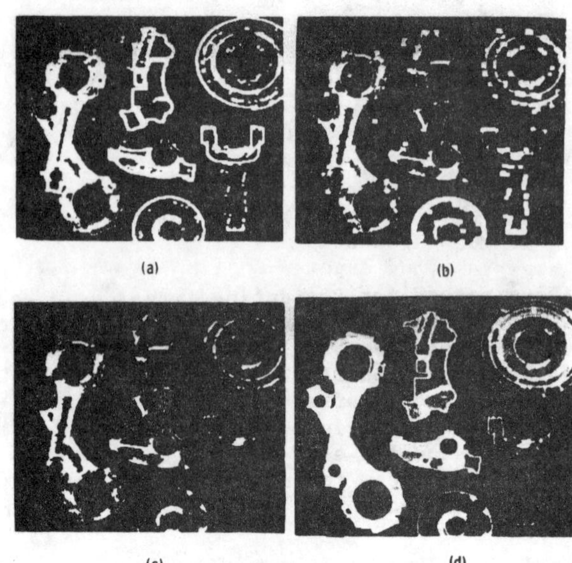

Fig. 2. (a) Expansion of edges to fill 3 by 3 square. (b) Expansion of edges to fill 5 by 5 square. (c) Edge regions after final contraction and elimination of small regions. (d) Reconstructed gray-level picture with bright edge regions. Total CPU time = 31 sec. on IBM 370/3033.

After removing artificial edges (process 2.6), some region pixels are replaced by edge pixels to separate different regions.

2.8 Eliminating Small Edge Regions

For simplicity, small isolated edge regions are eliminated after the segmentation into uniform intensity regions is finished. Figure 2c shows the final edge regions after shrinking and eliminating small regions. The thick edge regions are indicative of textured areas [11].

The gray-level picture of Fig. 2d was generated using the average-intensity region data. Edge regions are shown at the maximum brightness. A comparison of Fig. 2d and Fig. 1a shows that the initial data has been greatly simplified by the organizational process with a slight loss in detail. The final result is 72 uniform intensity regions and 10 edge regions.

3. RESULTS

This segmentation technique was tested on many scenes. Figure 3a (206 by 255 with 8 bit resolution) shows a landscape scene that was analyzed previously by a region growing technique (see Fig. C of [4]). The final result (Fig. 3d) has 38 uniform intensity regions and 5 edge regions which embody more of the meaningful information than the results of the non-semantic region grower (Fig. C2 of [4]).

When does this segmentation method fail? It fails if the gaps between the edge points are so large that the expansion cannot close them as illustrated in Figs. 1 and 2 for the universal yoke in the lower right-hand corner. Some possible methods of eliminating this type of failure (such as using boundary coincidence of edge points and intensity threshold [14]) are discussed in [11].

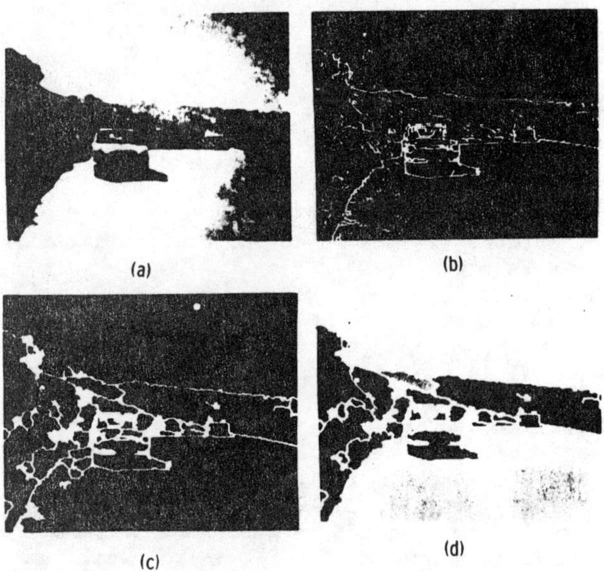

Fig. 3. (a) Digitized picture of landscape scene. (b) Thresholded thinned edge array. (c) Final edge regions. (d) Reconstructed gray-level picture with bright edge regions. Total CPU time = 27 sec. on IBM 370/3033.

4. CONCLUSIONS

The area segmentation method described here has some advantages over the region-growing and histogram-thresholding techniques. Without semantic information, it can segment an image better than the region growing technique. For many scenes (particularly monochromatic images) the intensity histograms do not have clearly separated peaks (see for example Fig. 1b) and often there is no optimum threshold, although clear edge boundaries exist [14].

ACKNOWLEDGEMENTS

The author wishes to thank L. Rossol and G. G. Dodd for their interest and encouragement throughout this project.

REFERENCES

[1] McKee, J. W., and Aggarwal, J. K., "Finding the Edges of the Surfaces of Three-Dimensional Curved Objects by Computer." Pattern Recognition. 7:1 (1975) 25-52.

[2] Perkins, W. A., "A Model-Based Vision System for Industrial Parts." IEEE Trans. Comput., C-27:2 (1978) 126-143.

[3] Brice, C. R., and Fennema, C. L., "Scene Analysis Using Regions." Artif. Intell. 1:3 (1970) 205-226.

[4] Yakamovsky, Y., and Feldman, J. A., "A Semantics-Based Decision Theory Region Analyzer." in Proc. IJCAI-73. Stanford, Stanford, Calif., 1973, pp. 580-588.

[5] Ohlander, R. B., "Analysis of Natural Scenes." PhD thesis, Carnegie-Mellon University, Pittsburgh, Pennsylvania, April, 1975.

[6] Rosenfeld, A., Park, C. M., and Strong, J. P., "Noise Cleaning in Digital Pictures." EASCON '69 Record, (1969) 264-273.

[7] Baird, M. L., "Image Segmentation Technique for Locating Automotive Parts on Belt Conveyors." in Proc. IJCAI-77. MIT, Cambridge, Mass., August, 1977, pp. 694-695.

[8] Jacobus, C., and Chien, R. T., "Variable Neighborhood Computations In Scene Analysis." University of Illinois CSL Report T-60 (1978).

[9] Duda, R. O., and Hart, P. E., Pattern Classification and Scene Analysis. Wiley and Sons (1973) pp. 271-272.

[10] Eberlein, R. B., "An Iterative Gradient Edge Detection Algorithm." Computer Graphics and Image Processing, 5: (1976) 245-253.

[11] Perkins, W. A., "Area Segmentation of Images Using Edge Points." IEEE Trans. Pattern Analysis and Machine Intelligence. To be published.

[12] Kelly, M. D., "Visual Identification of People by Computer." PhD thesis, Stanford Artif. Intell. Project Memo AIM-130, Stanford University, 1970, pp. 54-55.

[13] See [9] for example, pp. 284-285.

[14] Milgram, D. L., "Region Extraction Using Convergent Evidence." University of Maryland Report TR-674, June, 1978.

MOTION AND STRUCTURE FROM OPTICAL FLOW

K. Prazdny
Computer Science Department
University of Essex
Wivenhoe Park
Colchester Essex
England

We show that a moving observer can (in principle) compute the relative depth map of the environment given only the instantaneous positional velocity field on his "retina". The depth map (and surface normals) are computed by recovering the egomotion parameters which in turn determine the ratio of depth associated with any two neighbouring "retinal" points. The surface normal map may be computed to a degree of accuracy determined by the resolution of the "retina", and by the accuracy of approximation obtainable in the solution of three non-linear equations of the third degree in three unknowns.

1. THE PROBLEM

The problem addressed here is computing the surface layout of the environment, and the parameters of observer's motion (egomotion) from the information on the image plane. The problem is similar (though not equivalent) to the one tackled by the workers in computer stereo vision [1].

Consider a monocular observer with his "eye" and "head" fixed, with planar "retina", and moving along a smooth curvilinear path in a stationary 3D environment. Each discriminable optical element on his "retina" will possess a velocity; the whole comprising a positional velocity field. Such an observer can be viewed, instantaneously, as simultaneously rotating and translating for (again instantaneously) any 3D motion can be viewed as a rotation about some centre on some osculating plane. The instantaneous positional velocity field (IPVF) is then expressable as being due to the vector sum of two angular velocities due to the translational and the rotational components of the movement [2], [3].

Given a IPVF our task is to recover the egomotion parameters (i.e., the translational and rotational components of the egomotion). We do this with respect to an external, static reference frame instantaneously coincident with our egocentric reference frame (centered at O in Fig. 1).

The actual velocity of any point Q on the image plane is given by

$$\underline{V}'=(V1/S\ (\bar{V1} \times \bar{Q}) + \underline{A} \times \underline{Q} \qquad (1)$$

Here, V1 is the magnitude of the translational component (the speed of egomotion). $\bar{V1}$ is its direction vector. And S is the distance to the centre of polar projection of the environmental point P of which Q is the projection on the "retina" (see Fig. 1). $\underline{Q}$ is the position vector of the point Q in the egocentric reference frame centered at O. $\bar{Q}$ is the unit vector in this direction. $\underline{A}$ is the rotational angular velocity vector the components of which are to be recovered in the first place (for more detail see [4]).

Refer to Fig. 1. As can be seen, the "retinal" velocity vector of point Q, $\underline{V}''$ must necessarily lie in the plane spanned by $\bar{Q}$ and $\underline{V}'$. Given the IPVF, $\underline{V}'$ may be derived for each point Q, since

$$\underline{V}'=\underline{V}'' - (\bar{Q}.\underline{V}')\bar{Q} \qquad (2)$$

(This follows from the equivalence of angular velocities generated by $\underline{V}'$ and $\underline{V}''$.

Given that we know $\underline{V}'$, we can rewrite (1) to obtain

$$-(V1/S)Q\ ((\bar{V1} \times \bar{Q}) \times \bar{Q})=\underline{A} \times \underline{Q} - \underline{V}' \qquad (3)$$

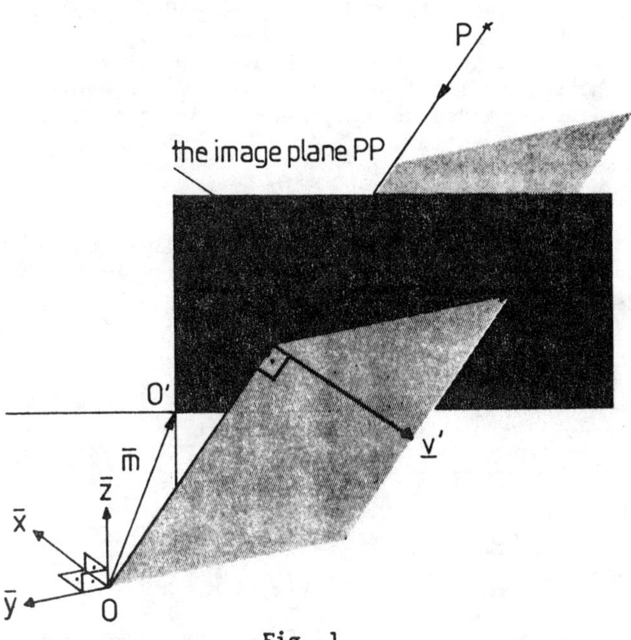

Fig. 1

An egocentric reference frame centered at the centre of polar projection, O, is defined, together with a planar projection surface PP. A "retinal" 2D rectangular coordinate frame centered at O is defined on PP.

V' and V" lie on the same plane, the unit normal of which is $(\bar{V}' \times \bar{Q})$.

Refer to Fig. 2. The vector $(\bar{V1} \times \bar{Q}) \times \bar{Q}$ lies in the plane of V1. Given the fact that V1 must lie in all such planes corresponding to different points Q, its direction will be determined as the intersection of these planes. The direction of the line of intersection of two planes specified by their normals NI, NJ is (NI x NJ). Referring back to (3) we see that

$$\underline{NI} = (\underline{A} \times \underline{QI} - \underline{VI}') \times \bar{QI} \tag{4}$$

lies in the direction of the vector normal to the plane PV1 (see Fig. 2). From this, using simple vector algebra, we see that for any three distinct "retinal" points QI, QJ, and QK the relation

$$[\underline{NI}, \underline{NJ}, \underline{NK}] = 0 \tag{5}$$

must hold. Here, the square brackets denote a scalar triple product of the three vectors. Equation (5), written out, is an equation of the third degree in 3 unknowns (the components of A). A set of 3 such equations (a minimum of 5 distinct "retinal" points is needed to define such a set) does not have an analytical solution: in general the solution can be obtained only using an iterative technique (a very fast and simple method reported in [5] is used in our computer implementation).

2. COMPUTER IMPLEMENTATION

The solution to a set of equations (5) can be computed locally, given some non-empty neighbourhood of a "retinal" point Q. In a 'real world' application one should not, however, use locally clustered points. To obtain accuracy in the presence of noise one should use points spread as widely as possible. Also, considering more points in the process of solving for A (perhaps by minimizing some suitable function of differences between the values of A computed at different regions locally) improves the accuracy with which A can be obtained.

A computer program incorporating the method has been written and experimented with using simulated input data (no distortions or noise). The program consists essentially of a local operator which computes A, V1, and the surface normal corresponding to a given image plane point. All three values are computed locally from a neighbourhood of a given "retinal" point. The size of the neighbourhood is presently (due to some computational limitations) about 1 degree of arc. The surface normal produced by the operator is essentially that of the best fit planar scale at a given point. The application of the operator to the whole image results in a surface-normal map.

The results are encouraging. Using the single precision arithmetic the accuracy of the surface normal map lies within the error of (approximately) 1 degree of arc.

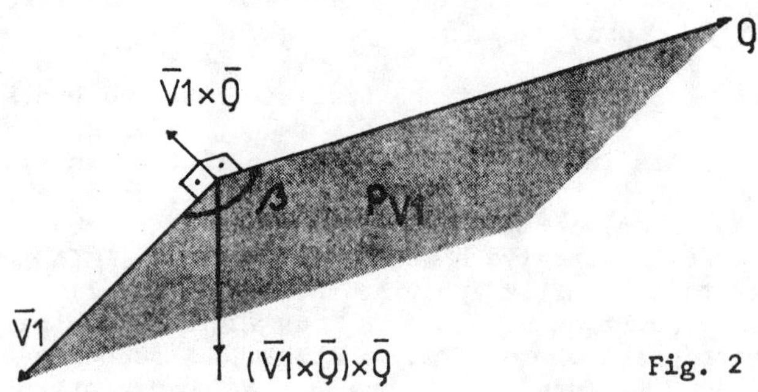

Fig. 2

$(\bar{V1} \times \bar{Q}) \times \bar{Q}$ and $\bar{V1}$ lie in the same plane, P_{V1}.

3. DISCUSSION

Using the preceeding analysis, it seems plausible that a relatively simple process may be used to recover the instantaneous egomotion parameters and surface normal map in a stationary world. The only assumptions made were the smoothness of the movement trajectory, rigidity of the objects, and the existence of the IPVF. This latter is taken for granted and constitutes the greatest weakness of this kind of approach. There is very little known about the behaviour of the correspondence computation-like methods suggested by Ullman [6] using real images, and these or similar mechanisms are, at present, the only way to generate the IPVF.

On the other hand, the above approach applies equally well to the case of a rigid 3D world of moving objects. To see this note the reciprocity between the motion of an object and the motion of the observer; for any objection motion there is an observer motion which, assuming the object to be stationary, generates the same IPVF in the region of the object. (This is the main reason that smoothness of path was the ONLY restriction put on the observer's motion.) Using a simple technique suggested by Nakayama and Loomis [3], we may compute the depth contours to perform a figure-ground separation. Applying the analysis above to each separated image region leads then directly to the surface normal map corresponding to the region. It is not possible, however, to recover the object motion since absolute distances (of which the optical flow is a function) are not recoverable from IPVF's.

4. CONCLUSION

A method is outlined which is capable (at least in principle) of delivering a surface normal map from an instantaneous positional velocity field (IPVF) generated by a curvilinearly moving observer. While the method is not as elegant and simple as the one developed in Clocksin [7] for the case of a rectilinearly moving observer, it is considerably more general.

It is possible that the analysis outlined above for the case of moving objects may offer some insights into the phenomena of position constancy ("How is it possible that when we move, and thus every optical element on the retina moves, we still perceive a stationary world?"). In that case, after applying the method locally, an "egomotion map" may be constructed which maps each point on the "retina" to this "egomotion space" (spanned by the orthogonal components of $\underline{A}$ and $\underline{V}1$). Some evaluation mechanism may be operating in this space, choosing, for example the point into which the 'majority' of image plane points maps as the stationary reference frame. All point mapping into this point (or perhaps some small neighbourhood of it) would then be regarded as projections of the stationary environment.

ACKNOWLEDGEMENTS

I'm in debt to Drs M. Brady and P. Hayes for many helpful suggestions, and to my wife Dasha who did the layout.

REFERENCES

[1] Gennery, D.B. "A stereo vision system for an autonomous vehicle", Fifth Int. Joint Conf. Artif. Intel., MIT, August, 1977.

[2] Wheatherburn, C.E. "Elementary vector analysis, Bell and Sons, London, 1965.

[3] Nakayama, K. and Loomis, J.M. "Optical velocity patterns, velocity sensitive neurons, and space perception", Perception, 3, (1974).

[4] Prazdny, K. "Egomotion and relative depth map from optical flow",(submitted for publication), 1978.

[5] Broyden, C.G. "Algorithm 214: solution of non-linear simultaneous equations", Computer Journal 12 (1969), pp.406-408.

[6] Ullman, S. "The interpretation of visual motion", Ph.D. thesis, MIT, 1977.

[7] Clocksin, W. "Perception of surface slant and edge labels from optical flow", DAI Working Paper, No. 33, University of Edinburgh, 1978.

A KNOWLEDGE-BASED SYSTEM FOR LOCATING MISSING HIGH CARDS IN BRIDGE

J.R. Quinlan
Basser Department of Computer Science
University of Sydney, Sydney, Australia 2006

A knowledge-driven system for locating missing Bridge honours in closed hands is described. The program is intended to follow the development given in an expert-level book. Although it is incomplete, being as yet confined largely to reasoning from the bidding and opening leads, its performance to date is promising; in roughly the first half of the book, it is able to replicate the conclusions about card location in more than eighty percent of the cases studied. The paper describes the three principal sections of the current program which deal with the analysis of the bidding, understanding the opening lead, and the 'inference engine' respectively.

1. INTRODUCTION

Recent years have seen the emergence of more and more high-performance systems whose power derives not so much from the merits of an underlying general algorithm, but rather from the richness of the knowledge structures they employ. So for instance, instead of having a system to do *X* that consists of a sophisticated quasi-decision process (such as a resolution theorem prover) together with a small number of axioms that are sufficient for *X* in the logical sense, a system of this new breed might be a simple generate-and-test type of data base interpreter together with a large collection of rules, advice, methodologies and distilled wisdom extracted in some more or less painful way from a human *X*-pert. A goodly sample of them appears in [8] while the much-cited survey [1] gives an excellent overview.

This paper describes the present status of such a knowledge-based system whose application area is one small corner of the game of Bridge. After the opening lead each player can see two hands—his own and that of the dummy—leaving two 'closed' hands. Any high card (ace, king, queen or jack) that does not appear in the open hands must be in one or the other of the closed hands, and often the ability to determine in which hand it lies holds the key to the development of a correct line of play. Expert players can usually do much better than guessing which closed hand holds a particular high card. Clues from the bidding and partial play of the hand may be sufficient to place any given high card with certainty or at worst with high probability. Several expert-level books, notably [2] and [3], are devoted to techniques for achieving this. Since Lawrence's book is particularly helpful, the goal of this system is to perform high-card location to the level of that found in [2] and using the techniques outlined therein.

There were two motivations for tackling this particular task. Unlike most games, Bridge is played with incomplete information; this characteristic has perhaps been responsible for the relative dearth of AI programs in this area (see [5,7]). Thus knowledge about card holdings can be unspecific (*East has either the ace or the king*) and uncertain (*he probably has the king*). Moreover information can come from different sources; what a player did or did not bid, what he led or did not lead, and so on. In short this problem is a microcosmic environment in which reasoning processes typical of 'real' problems can be brought into play. Secondly, it was used to investigate the utility and generality of some current rule-based models, their accessibility to a neophyte knowledge engineer, and their adequacy for this non-trivial problem.

As it stands, the system is only part-way towards its goal. The following sections give an illustration of the level of performance that it is currently able to achieve, and a comparison of results to date with the model (i.e. the book).

2. AN EXAMPLE

Imagine if you will that you are sitting in the South seat for the hand shown in figure 1. Your analysis as you attempt to locate the missing honours might run something like this:

> West led the ♥4. He would not underlead an ace, so he does not hold the ace in the suit lead. Neither the dummy nor I have it, so East must have the ♥A.
>
> West's lead is weak, suggesting that he was unable to make a stronger lead such as from the ace-king or king-queen of an unbid suit or from any sequence of honours in his own suit. In particular, then, he does not hold both the ♥Q and ♥J.
>
> It is unlikely that East would have played from the middle of a sequence. Since East holds both the ♥A and ♥K, he cannot also hold the ♥Q (otherwise he would not have played the king). Therefore West has it.
>
> Since West does not have both the ♥Q and ♥J, but does have the ♥Q, then East mus+ have the ♥J.
>
> There are 40 high-card points in all. Dummy and I together have 19, so East and West together hold 21. I already know that East has the ♥A, ♥K and ♥J for a total of 8 high-card points; if he held so much as another queen then West would have opened the bidding with at most 11 high-card points, which is unlikely. Therefore the ♦A and ♦Q and the ♣A are with West.

Reasoning along these lines, South is able to pinpoint each missing honour except the ♣J. In his analysis he has made

The work reported here was performed while the author was visiting the Computer Science Department, Stanford University, and using facilities made available there by the Heuristic Programming Project and the Artificial Intelligence Laboratory.

North
♠ K Q 5
♥ 6 2
♦ K 10 8 3
♣ Q 10 3 2

South
♠ A J 10 9 4
♥ 9 7
♦ J 7 5
♣ K 9 4

West	North	East	South
1♥	pass	2♥	2♠
pass	3♠	pass	pass
pass			

Opening lead: ♥4
First trick taken by East with ♥K

Figure 1: A sample hand for analysis.

use of several sources of information. Besides facts about this particular hand there are rules or guidelines that South believes his opponents will adhere to, such as

An opening bid indicates at least 12 high-card points.
Opening leaders avoid underleading an ace.
Third hand does not play from the middle of a sequence.

The guidelines are used in conjunction with facts to obtain new facts by 'everyday' reasoning processes. Knowing that West would not underlead an ace *(guideline)* and that he led the ♥4 *(fact)* give us that he does not have the ♥A *(fact)*. Having determined that he does not hold both the ♥Q and ♥J *(fact)* but that he has the ♥Q *(fact)* implies that he does not have the ♥J *(fact)*. The guidelines are also used negatively—patterns such as 'If he held *x* he would have done *y*; since he didn't, he does not hold *x*' are common in bridge books.

3. SUMMARY OF RESULTS

The first substantial chapter of the book basically restricts itself to analysis of who has what using information from the bidding and first trick. It contains fourteen case studies, in all of which the unknown hands belong to the defenders. For each study we are given the open hands, the bidding and opening lead, and sometimes further history of the play of the hand.

In its current state the system can handle these studies fairly comfortably. Its conclusions are identical to those of the book in twelve of the fourteen cases; the example of the previous section is one of them. Of the other two cases, one is almost correct—a single queen is mislocated. The remaining case is unusual in that the analysis in the book, which follows play down to the fifth trick, is concerned only with the more likely location of a single card, using both a rule for understanding play and a technique called *counting* that have yet to be incorporated in the program. On this example the system understandably flounders.

In the next chapter the focus is on the opening lead, with a battery of quizzes and eight more case studies. The system performs well on six of the eight, is slightly deficient in one case (missing out on one queen), and has substantial difficulty with the remaining case, which uses information from the first three tricks and once again requires counting. These chapters constitute about 40% of the material in the book. Of the twenty-two case studies they contain, the system locates the missing high cards with the same precision in eighteen cases, slightly lower precision in two cases, and with shortcomings attributable to the absence of crucial mechanisms in two cases.

As a further test, the program was run on some hands that had not been used in its development: those from the next chapter of [2] and from the bidding analysis chapter of [3]. For each of these 18 hands the program was given only the bidding, known hands and opening lead. It managed to locate a total of 14 honours with certainty (all correct), and made an additional 13 less specific asserions of the form 'x holds either y or z' (one error). It accurately established the high-card points of each closed hand (usually to within a range of two or three points) in all but one case when it was one point out.

4. DESCRIPTION OF THE PROGRAM

Like Gaul, the system is divided roughly into three parts concerned with bidding, opening leads and commonsense reasoning respectively. (There is in addition an embryonic play section which merely says that play from a sequence is either from the top or the bottom.) The system is written in INTERLISP [6] and takes a few seconds of DEC KA-10 time to complete the analysis of a hand.

4.1 Bidding

Bridge bidding is notoriously complex. The bidder must choose what incomplete information he wishes to convey about his hand and the most economical message for doing so unambiguously. However, our program does not have to *make* bids but instead *understand* them; it does not have the problems of choice of information or bid, but only the problem of decoding the message once the bid is made. The information extracted from a single bid is primarily the range of high-card points and suit holdings that it indicates, but more general distributional information for the opening lead module is also extracted from the bidding as a whole.

The method of determining the nature of a bid is simply to find a rule which it matches in context, so this part of the program is similar to a pure production system. The 2♥ bid in figure 1 matches a rule that may be stated as

if partner has just opened or overcalled in a suit, and
the intervening bidder has passed, and
this bid is a minimum raise of partner's suit
then this is a weak reply indicating 6–9 high-card points and three or more cards in the suit bid

To date only the more common bids have been included—the program understands passes; openings of one in a suit or strong no-trump; overcalls; second round openings; takeout doubles; free, weak and strong replies; and rebids. This entire body of bidding knowledge consists of 18 rules.

4.2 Opening Lead

The second principal source of facts is the opening lead. All twenty-two case studies reach a suit contract, so the program was restricted to analysis of opening leads against sub-slam suit contracts; sections for leads against no-trump and slam contracts should be quite similar.

Analysis of the lead requires mechanisms that are awkward to express in any conventional rule format. The underlying idea is that leads are ranked by their strength, and that a neutral or weak lead indicates an inability to make a stronger one. This ranking is most fluently represented as a strongly ordered sequence of rules of the form *If—then—else*, where no rule can fire unless all previous ones have failed to do so. For instance the first such rule developed tests for the lead of an ace in an unbid suit, while the second is

If the lead is a king of an unbid suit
then the leader also holds either the ace or queen of that suit, but not both
else the leader does not hold the ace-king or king-queen of any unbid suit

where the *else* clause uses the ordering of rules to establish that the lead was neither the ace nor king of any unbid suit.

The lead-understanding module in fact contains three components; a supplementary unordered set of productions, a procedural section to classify suits (e.g. as *unbid*), and 12 of these unorthodox *If—then—else* rules. Despite its simplicity it turns out to be surprisingly accurate, accounting exactly for all but three of the 80-odd such opening leads in the book. One error was the result of a strong lead of trumps, the other two were caused by perverse distributions. The procedural section attempts to identify suits in which the leader is likely to hold either a singleton or a doubleton, using information from the open hands and distributional clues from the defenders' bidding. If the real distribution of the suit led is very different from the predicted one then the lead can be misinterpreted. However the figures indicate that such situations are rare.

4.3 Commonsense Reasoning

The bidding and opening lead are sources of facts. The third component of the system is the embodiment of reasoning processes that inter-relate guidelines and facts to obtain new facts. This component was developed using AGE [4], a package that guides the novice in the design and testing of rule-based systems. The prototype AGE was limited to a 'blackboard' model in which rules are partitioned into 'experts' invoked by 'events', but this seemed quite appropriate for the reasoning task. The package did suffer from a real if temporary limitation, however, in that an event could invoke only a single expert. Rather than program around this and other very minor irritants, the structures developed were translated to INTERLISP pending a more advanced version of AGE.

The most interesting facts are naturally those ascribing particular high cards to particular hands. It is not always possible to discover facts of this form directly; instead, they must be derived from intermediate, less interesting facts. However the variety of facts that have bearing on the location of missing high cards is limited. A hand can be asserted to hold a particular card, one or more of a set of cards, or not all of a set of cards. It can also be described by the possible range of high-card points and suit holdings it contains. An event is taken as the discovery of any such fact, and can trigger one or more of eight experts containing a total of fifteen rules. Each expert encapsulates all knowledge of some facet of the reasoning task; for instance, one knows about the consequences of high-card point ceilings, another about the implications of locating a particular card. A sense of purpose is maintained by giving priority to experts capable of generating facts of the first (and most interesting) form.

5. CONCLUSION

The performance of the program to date is encouraging, especially in the light of the small number of rules with which it has been equipped. The next steps in its development are clear: the addition of a section for counting, the installation of a more powerful play-understanding component, and the filling in of the gaps in the system's knowledge of bidding and leading. None of these present any conceptual problem.

The program has one glaring weakness. While it can accomodate vagueness it cannot resolve conflict such as might arise if the opening lead indicates that one player does not have a particular ace, while arguments from high-card points indicate that he does. There is a need to be able to associate a degree of certainty with a fact or a guideline. Fortunately one of the most advanced features of AGE is its provision of mechanisms for specifying, propogating and updating such certainty factors. When the program is recoded in AGE this weakness should disappear.

The program in its present form represents about two man-months of effort and 13 pages of code. With the exception of the *If—then—else* rules, the concepts and techniques it uses are standard. This suggests that current ideas for rule-based systems, especially when incorporated in systems with a tutorial capability, have put knowledge engineering within reach of the masses.

ACKNOWLEDGEMENTS

The author is grateful to Penny Nii and Nelleke Aiello for access to the AGE system, and to Peter Friedland for helpful discussions on the Bridge content of the program.

REFERENCES

[1] Davis, R. and King, J. An Overview of Production Systems. In *Machine Intelligence* 8 (Elcock and Michie, Eds.), Wiley, NY, 1976.

[2] Lawrence, M. *How To Read Your Opponent's Cards: The Bridge Experts' Way to Locate Missing High Cards.* Prentice-Hall, NJ, 1973.

[3] Miles, M. *All Fifty-Two Cards: How to Read Bridge Hands the Way Experts Do.* Cornerstone Library, NY, 1968.

[4] Nii, H.P. and Aiello, N. AGE ('Attempt to Generalize'): Profile of the AGE-0 System. Working Paper HPP-78-5, Computer Science Department, Stanford University, 1978.

[5] Stanier, A. BRIBIP: a Bridge Bidding Program. In *Proc. 4th IJCAI*, Tbilisi, USSR, 1975.

[6] Teitelman, W. INTERLISP Reference Manual. XEROX Palo Alto Research Center, Palo Alto Cal, 1978.

[7] Wasserman, A. Realization of a Skillful Bridge Bidding Program. In *Proc. FJCC*, Houston Tex, 1970.

[8] Waterman, D. and Hayes-Roth, F. (Eds.) *Pattern Directed Inference Systems.* Academic Press, NY, 1978.

USE OF THEMATIC INFORMATION TO SPEED SEARCH OF SEMANTIC NETS

Lynne M. Reder
Department of Psychology
Carnegie-Mellon University
Pittsburgh, PA 15213

John R. Anderson
Department of Psychology
Carnegie-Mellon University
Pittsburgh, PA 15213

ABSTRACT

A model is proposed for the representation of thematically integratable information in semantic memory and a process for searching through this memory. We assume that related facts about an individual are not directly attached to the individual node, but rather, are indirectly attached via a thematic sub-node. Thematic sub-nodes allow much faster search of memory under certain conditions, but not others. We tested these predictions with human subjects and found support for these notions.

There is little doubt that the time to search a computer data base depends in part on the number of facts stored in it. Similarly, the time for humans to retrieve a specific fact from memory has been shown to depend on the number of other, related facts. A large number of reaction time studies (e.g., Anderson, 1974; Anderson & Bower, 1973; Hayes-Roth, 1977) have found that subjects are slower to recognize a fact the greater the number of facts learned to the same concept. For example, subjects are slower to recognize the fact "The psychologist wanted to go to Japan" if they have also studied "The psychologist thought the research was good" and "Everyone loves Japan" than if no other experimental facts share concepts with the probe. This particular result has been named the *fan effect* because latencies are found to be a function of the number of propositions *fanning* out of a given concept node in a propositional network representation (see Anderson, 1976). (Subjects are also slower to reject unstudied probes as a function of the fan of their concepts.)

There is a paradoxical aspect to the result that the more facts a person knows about a concept the slower he or she is to verify any one of them. It seems intuitive that experts (a) know lots of facts about certain topics, and (b) can answer more questions on those topics and answer them faster than anyone else. However, certain situations can be pointed out where experts seem to experience a type of interference that results from too much similar information. Learning a new text editor in many ways is much easier if one has used a similar editor before. However, the more editors a person uses, the harder it is to keep the commands straight.

Even though experts may sometimes suffer more interference than non-experts, it also seems that if their information can be *integrated* into various themes, then somehow the information should be less interfering. Consider the following knowledge representation for facts about an individual and process model for searching this knowledge: all facts studied about the individual are attached to that individual's concept node. However, propositions that can be considered to be thematically related are not attached directly to the person node; rather, they are attached to a theme node that is attached to the person node. Figure 1 gives a representation for the following four sentences: *Melvin crossed his skis. Melvin shussed down the slope. Melvin washed his car. Melvin got on the chair lift.* Facts that can be considered as having to do with Melvin-skiing form a sub-node attached to Melvin. Facts that are not so related are attached to Melvin directly. The *fan* out of the Melvin concept, then, is two rather than four.

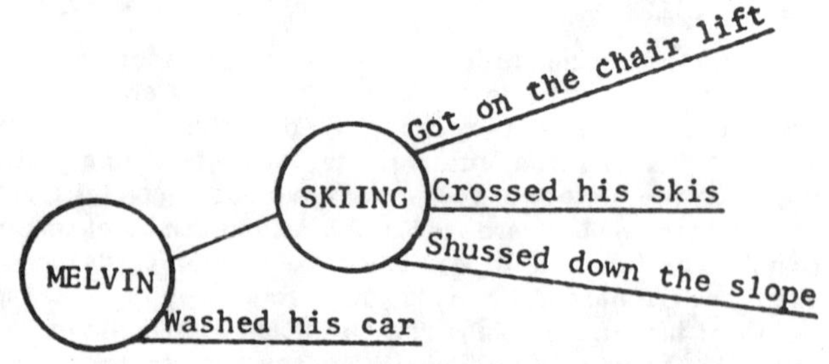

Figure 1: Portion of the Semantic Network encoding facts about Melvin.

This research was supported in part by NSF grants BNS76-00959 and BNS78-17463 to John R. Anderson and by an NIMH post-doctoral fellowship to Lynne M. Reder. We would like to thank T. Iwasawa for assistance in programming and in running subjects.

The search mechanism works as follows: The probe sentence is parsed. Each concept of the probe is activated in memory and activation spreads out along each arc attached to the concept. *Search energy* is assumed to be a constant for each activated concept. How much activation or search energy a particular arc receives is a function of the total number of arcs emanating from the concept (the amount of fan).

In earlier experiments on the fan effect, the facts associated to a person were unrelated. In those situations, the search mechanism predits a simple effect of number of facts on time to recognize a probe. However, our predictions are more complex for the representation in Figure 1. We would predict that the time to verify *Melvin washed his car* would be the same as if we had learned only two unrelated facts about Melvin. Our predictions about *Melvin crossed his skis* are somewhat more complex.

The fan out of the Melvin concept is two. The fan out of the Melvin-skiing sub-node is three. Whether there is an effect of sub-node fan when attempting to recognize one of several thematically related facts depends on the nature of the *foils* or false probes. If, for example, the probe to be rejected is *Melvin baked a cake*, search need not continue past the Melvin-skiing sub-node: it is clear to the subject that cake-baking is not part of the skiing theme. If, on the other hand, the probe to be rejected is *Melvin perfected his stem-christies*, search must proceed beyond the sub-node to inspect each proposition attached to it until the correct one is found or all stored propositions are exhausted.

EXPERIMENT

To verify this model* we conducted an experiment where subjects learned facts about various characters. These facts belonged to various themes, e.g., buying a car, jogging, going to a circus. A particular character could have one or two themes associated with him or her and one or three facts associated with a given theme. For example a character with six associated facts would have three facts about each of two themes. A character with four facts would have one fact from one theme and three facts from the other. Each condition in the experiment can be described by two digits, representing the number of facts in each theme associated with a given character. The conditions are (1,0),(1,1),(3,0),(3,1),(3,3). The *0*'s denote conditions where there was only one theme.

Subjects studied these character-predicate pairings until they knew the facts perfectly (could recall all the facts about each character several times in succession). After this phase was completed, subjects went into the critical phase in which reaction times were collected to answer questions about the material studied. One sentence was displayed on the screen at a time. The subject was told to press the yes or no response key depending upon whether the subject thought it had been studied during the acquisition phase. Test probes were presented in random order. The foils (sentences subjects had not studied) were of two types and were separated into different test blocks. One type was the *thematically related foil* (e.g., *Melvin enjoyed deep powder*), and the other type was the *unrelated foil* (e.g., *Melvin baked a cake*). Both types of foils have the property that their predicates (verb-phrase) were studied with another

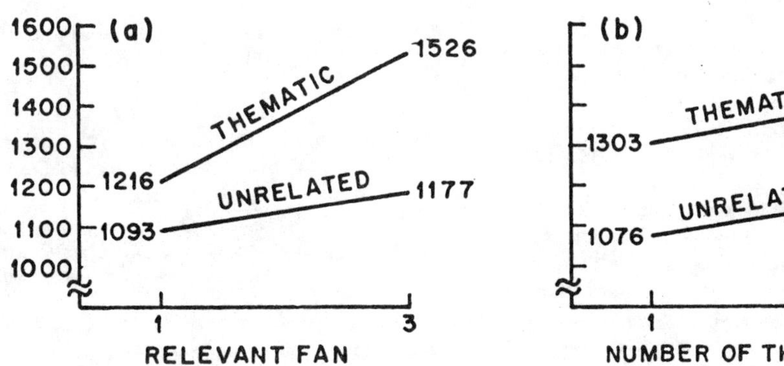

Figure 2: Mean reaction time to judge that a probe had been studied as a function of number of thematically related facts (graph a) and as a function of number of themes (graph b).

*We actually tested two alternative models in this experiment, but space constraints require this simplification.

character during the experiment. This ensured that subjects could not reject a probe simply on the basis of lexical familiarity.

We had two principal predictions for this experiment. First, when the foils are unrelated, there should be a much smaller effect of number of facts studied. This is because subjects should be able to make their judgments just by inspecting the theme subnodes.** They would not have to search the facts attached to these nodes. Our second prediction was that there should be an effect of themes (more themes means more arcs out of the person node), but that it should be small since subjects can quickly reject the wrong theme sub-node, and not be affected by type of foils since the extra sub-node is rejected in the same fashion regardless of foil-type.

RESULTS

Figure 2 displays the data (latencies in milliseconds to decide whether the probe had been studied or not) partitioned two ways: on the left, the data are analyzed as a function of the amount of fan relevant to the probe that is attached to the character in question. For example, the relevant fan for a Melvin skiing probe would be three because the subject studied three Melvin skiing facts. If the probe had concerned Melvin and his car, the relevant fan would have been one. On the right, the data are displayed as a function the number of themes associated with the character in the test probe, which can be one or two. Melvin has two themes, skiing and car washing. (There is no sub-node for car-washing because only one such fact was studied.)

Each graph plots two functions, one labelled unrelated and one labelled thematic. As explained above, the unrelated-thematic factor reflects the type of foils from which the subject had to discriminate the studied probes. The left panel plots the data as a function of the number of facts involving the same theme as the test probe. Subjects take longer to verify that a fact was studied the more other related facts were also studied. However, this fan effect is severely attenuated when the foils are not thematically related. Moreover, as predicted, subjects respond much faster in general when the foils are unrelated. We take this to mean that subjects have a less stringent criterion of saying "yes, this sentence is old" in these blocks. Subjects only search as far as the sub-node before responding when foils are not related to the sub-node. Smith, Adams, and Schnorr (1978) have also found that the fan effect is reduced with unrelated foils. (However, they did not have the other conditions of this experiment viz., testing with thematic foils, and manipulating the number of themes associated with a character.)

**If there is only one theme fact, we assume subjects do not bother to form a subnode. Inspecting one proposition is probably equivalent to inspecting a theme sub-node.

The data on the right shows the effect of number of themes. Here too there is an effect of fan for themes, however this effect is smaller and is not affected by the related/unrelated foil block distinction. The lack of interaction of theme-fan with foil-block type was predicted. Regardless of type of foil, the subject must at least find the relevant sub-node before responding "old". If there is only one theme associated with a character, the fan off the character node will be less. Therefore, search should be faster than with two sub-nodes or a fan of two off the character node.

CONCLUSION

The data support the view put forth in the introduction that facts are not necessarily attached directly to the concepts in their propositions, but rather can be organized into thematically consistent subnodes. It seems to us that, in general, sub-nodes in memory serve several functions. First, sub-nodes make plausibility judgments easy. Typically people are not asked to discriminate thematic foils from related statements; normally one would accept as plausible other related skiing facts about Melvin (see Reder, 1979, for a fuller discussion). Second, by having many sub-nodes in memory, the number of propositions that must be inspected is smaller. If a subject is searching for a fact about Melvin baking a cake, she or he need not search all of the skiing facts to find it--search stops on a wrong path as soon as the sub-node is reached.

References

Anderson, J.R. *Language, Memory, and Thought.* Hillsdale, N.J.: Lawrence Erlbaum Associates 1976.

Anderson, J.R. Retrieval of propositional information from long-term memory, *Cognitive Psychology,* 1974, 5, 451-474.

Anderson, J.R. and Bower, G.H. *Human Associative Memory.* Washington: Winston and Sons, 1973.

Hayes-Roth, B. Evolution of cognitive structures and processes. *Psychological Review,* 1977, *84,* 260-278.

Reder, L.M. The role of elaborations in memory for prose. *Cognitive Psychology,* 1979, *11,* 221-234.

Smith, E.E., Adams, N., and Schorr, D. Fact retrieval and the paradox of interference. *Cognitive Psychology,* 1978, *10,* 438-464.

THE STRUCTURE AND PERFORMANCE OF THE INTERIM.2 GO PROGRAM.

Walter Reitman and Bruce Wilcox
University of Michigan
205 Washtenaw Place
Ann Arbor, Michigan 48109

We describe interim variants of a Go program based on skilled human models. The program maintains a permanent, selectively-updated, multilevel network analogous to the skilled player's perceptual and cognitive representation of the game situation. Moves are chosen by a hierarchy of experts and critics operating on this network. Lookahead is a selective, goal-related process, one among many components of Go skill. After an overview of system organization, we illustrate the program's performance with three segments from actual games.

1. PROGRAM DESIGN CONSIDERATIONS

Berliner [1] suggests that though whole-board exhaustive search programs may one day play championship-level chess, "such an approach cannot possibly work for Go, and this game may have to replace chess as the task par excellence for AI." Go certainly has many features that recommend it for this purpose. Its primitive elements, black and white stones played on the 361 points of a 19 x 19 grid, generate complex patterns and problems that tax the highest levels of professional skill.

Go games typically run 200 moves or more, and each turn offers on average close to 250 legal plays. Brown and Dowsey [2] estimate the number of possible games of Go at about 10^{700}, compared with 10^{120} for chess, and they point out that exhaustive Go search only three moves deep would entail generating and evaluating about 8,000,000 whole-board positions. Yet videotaped game records [3] show that advanced amateur players can look 30 moves ahead, and the Go literature contains still deeper lookahead sequences. This means that lookahead in human Go play is a highly focussed, selective, goal-related process. The size of the possibility space appears to rule out a Go program organization analogous to the exhaustive whole-board lookahead and evaluation schemes used in most current chess programs.

The game also has a very strong visual or perceptual element. Local stone patterns and large-scale spatial relations among groups and territories both are crucial. Most of these patterns and relations continue unchanged from any one move to the next. This argues for a permanent, selectively-updated, multilevel network of data structures to represent the elements, patterns, and properties, as well as the interrelations within and across levels.

Finally, both positive and negative interactions are extremely significant at all levels. To play Go well, it is necessary not only to determine the most important objective at any given time, but also to advance it in ways that simultaneously achieve as many secondary benefits as possible. This motivates the use of hierarchies of experts and critics, each responsible for a class of options, properties, or functions associated with elements of a given type and level.

2. DATA STRUCTURES AND CONTROL FLOW

With these considerations in mind, turn now to Fig. 1**, which shows the flow of control in the INTERIM.2 program. At the top level, this consists of a two-part cycle. First, immediately following a play by either side,

---

* Support for this work under NSF grant MCS77-0880 is gratefully acknowledged.

** Fig. 1 is a simplified representation. Many function names have been changed for mnemonic reasons. Many other functions at the control levels depicted in the figure have been omitted altogether. To take an extreme example, DEVELOP.GROUP actually consists of about 20 distinct option specialists. Finally, PROBE is called at many points other than those shown, and is bracketed to indicate this.

```
MOVE
  UPDATE.POINT.TYPES
  UPDATE.STRINGS
  UPDATE.LENSES
  UPDATE.LINKS
  UPDATE.GROUPS
  UPDATE.WEBS
  UPDATE.SECTOR.LINES
  UPDATE.TERRITORIES
  UPDATE.TACTICAL.ANALYSES
    [PROBE]
  UPDATE.GROUP.STABILITY.ESTIMATES
REFLEX
  LOCAL.URGENT
    PLAY.JOSEKI
    STRING.ATTACK.AND.DEFEND
    LINK.ATTACK.AND.DEFEND
    RE.EDGE.LINK
      [PROBE]
    VITAL.SHAPE.POINT
    CONTACT.FIGHT
  DEVELOP.GROUP
    KILL.CUTTING.STRING
    EXTEND.AND.SQUEEZE
    COUNTERATTACK
    CROSS.SECTOR.LINE
    STABILIZE.POTENTIAL.TERRITORY
    RUN.TO
  ATTACK.GROUP
    WIPE.OUT
    SHAPE.POINTS
      [PROBE]
    SQUEEZE
    ENCLOSE
  RUN.TOWARD.DEAD.GROUP
  EXTEND.SECURE.INVADE
  DEVELOP.POTENTIAL.TERRITORY
  ENDGAME
```

Figure 1. Program Organization.

MOVE updates all those elements of GAMEMAP, the program's multilevel representation of the situation, that have been affected by the latest move. Next, if it is the program's turn to play, REFLEX chooses a move.

GAMEMAP is indexed through a set of interrelated GAMEBOARDS. Each board is an array that points to all data structures of a particular type. At the lowest level, the TYPEBOARD gives quick access to bit pattern information about specific points (empty, occupied by black, part of a white territory, etc.). Some boards, e.g., STRINGBOARD and LINKBOARD, index the basic game elements at the various levels (strings, linkages, groups, territories, and potential territories). Thus in Fig. 2, for example, looking up the board point B8 in the LINKBOARD array enables any program function to access the data structure

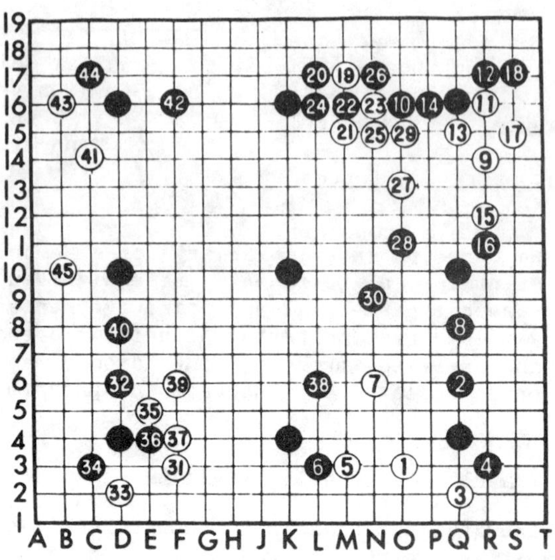

Figure 2. The First 45 Moves.

representing the linkage from the D8 string to the left edge of the board. Other boards, e.g., LENSBOARD, WEBBOARD, SECTORBOARD, and TACTICSBOARD, index elements analogous to those in a skilled Go player's perceptual and cognitive representation of the current situation. Lenses represent and monitor local stone patterns. Web data structures are surrogates for certain kinds of visual scanning. Webs follow the external configuration of groups, radiating out and indexing the surrounding board points. Thus they are useful in analyzing and detecting changes occurring around individual groups. Referring again to Fig. 2, looking up B8 in the WEBBOARD, for example, gives access to the webs around white B10 and around the black group on the lower left. Sector lines, e.g., the one between B10 and C14, correspond to those looser relations among stones that dynamically divide the board into tenuously defined regions. These sector barriers help define potential territories and strategic threats to groups. Finally, the TACTICSBOARD indexes tactical data structures associated with individual strings, linkages, and significant board points. These data structures record the results of analyses produced by calls to PROBE, the entry point to the subsystem responsible for all INTERIM.2 lookahead. This is selective, best-first lookahead. Each such analysis answers some specific tactical question about the associated element. The resulting tactical data structure is maintained as part of GAMEMAP unless invalidated by subsequent moves that affect strings or board points involved in the analysis, at which point PROBE is called to reanalyze the situation.

2.1 Updating the Representation after a Move

To fix ideas, consider the situation shown in Fig. 2. Ignore the order of play for the moment. As soon as white plays move 45 at B10, MOVE is called to update GAMEMAP. This updating is selective. Only structures directly or indirectly impacted by the move are affected. UPDATE.POINT.TYPES alters the TYPEBOARD entry for B10 from UNOCCUPIED to WHITE-OCCUPIED, and UPDATE.STRINGS sets up a string data structure representing B10. Now UPDATE.LENSES creates a lens that will monitor any future board changes around the pattern formed by white B10 and black D10. In addition, it sets up a shape lens which it associates with B10. This lens, when queried, will suggest locally good developmental plays for white, e.g., at B8 and B12. The existing shape lens associated with D10 is modified, since white B10 alters the shape development possibilities for D10. Finally, the existing lens monitoring the D8-D10 linkage also is altered, since white B10 changes the possibilities available for attacking and defending that linkage.

White 45 disrupts the linkage between black D10 and the edge of the board. Therefore, when UPDATE.LINKS is called, it deletes from GAMEMAP the data structure representing this linkage. Such changes in higher-order data structures may induce further changes in lower-order ones. This change, for example, results in UPDATE.-POINT.TYPES deleting from the TYPEBOARD the information that A10, B10, and C10 are involved in a black linkage to the edge of the board.

Some plays, e.g. white 43 and black 44 at the top left of Fig. 2, add stones to existing groups. Others, such as white 45 at B10, create new groups. UPDATE.GROUPS is responsible both for modifying existing group data structures and, as in the present case, creating new ones. GAMEMAP represents white B10 at both the string and group levels because the analyses and decisions at the two levels entail quite different kinds of considerations. Next, UPDATE.WEBS creates a web data structure indexing the board points surrounding B10. The web reaches out to the white group at B16 and C14, the open area around E12 and E13, and the black group beginning at D10 and running down toward the bottom of the board. Finally, as the B10 stone impinges on the existing webs radiating out from the white group on the upper left and the black group running down the left side, UPDATE.WEBS also modifies those webs, to reflect the presence of this white stone in their vicinities. These web data structures may be used by any REFLEX functions considering attacks on adjacent enemy groups, or defensive plays running a group toward friendly groups or out into unoccupied areas.

UPDATE.SECTOR.LINES now creates a data structure representing an imaginary line running from B10 to C14. This sector line is used by UPDATE.TERRITORIES when it creates a potential territory data structure corresponding to the area bounded by the two white groups on the left of the board. UPDATE.TERRITORIES also modifies the territory data structure running between the lower left edge of the board and the black group running down from D10. Before white 45, that territory was bounded at the top by the linkage from D10 to the left edge. Since UPDATE.LINKS has deleted that linkage, the territory must be redefined. This is done by designating the next nearest intact linkage, from D8 to the edge, as the new upper bound. This higher-level modification also induces changes in the TYPEBOARD, since points such as B9 and C9, which formerly were black territory points, now no longer are.

Now UPDATE.TACTICAL.ANALYSES calls PROBE to assess the tactical status of strings and linkages created or potentially affected by the most recent play. No actual lookahead is required for the B10 string, which is found to be tactically secure on the basis of context information from GAMEMAP. When contextual information is insufficient for a decision, PROBE may generate lookahead sequences running from a few hypothetical board positions to 50 or more. It is worth reemphasizing two points here. (1) All PROBE lookahead is intended to answer a specific question, e.g., about the tactical security of a string or linkage, posed by the function invoking PROBE. (2) PROBE records its results for each such element in a tactical data structure which is maintained as part of GAMEMAP until the analysis is called into question by some subsequent move. This tactical data structure can be accessed both from the data structure representing the string or linkage, and also through the TACTICSBOARD (see Section 5 for an example).

Finally, UPDATE.GROUP.STABILITY.ESTIMATES provides a stability rating for the B10 group. It also alters the stability rating for the black group running from D10 to C3. This is because white 45 has undercut the side territory associated with the group. This information will now be available to DEVELOP.GROUP when next it is invoked from REFLEX.

To summarize, MOVE and its subfunctions serve at least three vital purposes. They carry out, at progressively higher levels, the aggregation and analysis of the patterns and structures representing the game situation. Thus they provide the basic elements the REFLEX functions deal with. They maintain the data base that allows the REFLEX functions to deal with each element in context. This enables the program to locate interactions and find moves that do several jobs at once. Finally, MOVE updating corrects the representation after each play, deriving its immediate implications at every level it affects. This is how the program finds out the consequences of its own moves, and those of its opponent.

2.2 Choosing the Program's Next Move

Returning now to Fig.1, REFLEX is a temporary control structure that steps through an ordered list of functions and accepts the first move returned from them. LOCAL.URGENT and its subfunctions are responsible for dealing with any urgent problems that may have arisen as a consequence of the immediately preceding black-white move pair. Each subfunction uses information generated by MOVE, and each has a limited ability to assess the local significance of the class of problems it deals with. If STRING.ATTACK.AND.DEFEND finds that a significant friendly string is threatened with capture, it will attempt to generate a move to save it. If the threatened string serves no important function, however, control passes to the next subfunction. The situations dealt with by the LOCAL.URGENT subfunctions are illustrated in the examples that follow.

If there are no significant locally urgent situations resulting from the immediately preceding moves, control passes to DEVELOP.GROUP. This function, working both with the group stability data computed under MOVE, and with assessments of the values of each of the program's groups, selects the friendly group it considers to be most worth developing. It then invokes its subfunctions in the order shown in the figure. Each has information about a class of developmental options, the conditions under which these options are appropriate, and the means available for realizing them. KILL.CUTTING.-STRING, for example, determines whether there are any enemy strings separating the group to be developed from an adjacent friendly group. If so, it will try to kill one of them. Several other DEVELOP.GROUP subfunctions, e.g., CROSS.SECTOR.LINE and STABILIZE.POTENTIAL.-TERRITORY, also are described in the examples that follow.

If there are no valuable friendly groups in need of development, control passes to ATTACK.GROUP. This function considers the various enemy groups, again ordered by value and stability, and attempts through its subfunctions to generate suitable attacking moves against its target. Section 4 presents a detailed illustration of attacks generated by the SHAPE.POINTS subfunction.

If there are no attackable enemy groups, control passes to the remaining midgame and endgame functions, in the order indicated. Thus RUN.TOWARD.DEAD.GROUP is a midgame function that attempts to reduce the scale of capture of a friendly group. This function may be called for any of its groups the program considers to be strategically dead, i.e., incapable of development to the point of absolute stability.

To summarize, the move choice process proceeds from general problems and options to more specific ones. The system relies on the experts at each level to know a good deal about the options available there. This has two consequences. First, usually only the best few possibilities at any level are considered. Second, if higher level experts have chosen properly, then lower levels also need only consider the best more specific options. Thus, referring ahead to Section 4, if REFLEX is correct in concluding that at that point in the game its best option is to attack, and ATTACK.GROUP is correct in its choice of an appropriate target and a specific means of attack, then SHAPE.POINTS need only come up with the plays that best carry out this hierarchy of objectives in this situation. There may be other considerations at a lower level that might improve the final choice there, but that is the responsibility of the critics at that level. Since the functions at each level generally provide an ordered set of choices, the critics have alternatives to work with. And if the situation changes, so that the specific low-level objective no longer has priority, both the situational change and its immediate implications will be picked up on the next pass through the MOVE-REFLEX cycle.

2.3 Implementation

The INTERIM.2 programs are written in LISP/MTS and run on the AMDAHL/470. They compile into about 330k words, use about six cpu seconds per black-white pair of moves, and create about 86 hypothetical board positions per move pair. Real response time usually is a good bit faster than that of the program's human opponents. For additional information about lenses, webs, PROBE, and all aspects of the program code, see [4], [5], [6], and [7], respectively.

3. OPENING GAME PLAY

We begin our examples with Fig. 2, which showns the first 45 moves from a nine-stone handicap game against a 10 kyu* opponent. White's first two moves, and the program's responses, form a standard, mutually equitable, sequential pattern (joseki). The program plays out such sequences from information stored in a joseki lens. This is accessed under the control of the PLAY.JOSEKI subfunction of LOCAL.URGENT. We include in the program's knowledge base only a handful of the thousands of such patterns, because we are mainly concerned with developing the program's ability to analyze situations and generate appropriate responses on its own.

With black 6 at L3, the program leaves the joseki. Black 6 is generated by LOCAL.URGENT, because white 5 undercuts a black potential territory to the left of K4. Black 8 is motivated by white's jump at 7 to N6. Prior to white 7, the black group in the lower right is considered stable, in part because it is adjacent to an unthreatened potential territory (the area along the right side between Q6 and Q10). Edge potential territory is considered secure if neither of its side boundaries is (1) undercut, or (2) defined by a single stone flanked by an enemy stone (in which case an enemy invasion of the potential territory would, simultaneously, threaten the boundary stone), and if (3) there is no nearby enemy stone with access to the outer boundary. This third condition is assessed by determining whether there are any enemy webs that cross into the potential territory. After white 7 at N6, MOVE finds this third condition violated. The potential territory is therefore declared unstable, and this then causes UPDATE.GROUP.-STABILITY.ESTIMATES to declare the adjacent black group unstable.

When control passes from MOVE to REFLEX, since there are no significant LOCAL.URGENT situations, DEVELOP.GROUP is called to restabilize the lower right black group. Finding no good attack on an adjacent enemy group, DEVELOP.GROUP calls STABILIZE.POTENTIAL.TERRITORY in an attempt to restabilize the adjacent potential territory. This produces the play at Q8, which restabilizes the potential territory, unites the Q4 and Q10 groups, and lays claim to what is now a real territory along the side. After white 9 at R14 and black's joseki lens response at O16, white 11 at R16 branches off into a joseki not in the program's repertoire. Once MOVE has updated GAMEMAP, REFLEX calls LOCAL.URGENT, which finds three alerts. White 11 threatens black's claim to corner territory. It initiates a contact fight, because white's stone has been played in contact with one of black's [8]. And it creates a vital shape point at Q15. Reestablishing the territorial claim takes priority because the territory is large and contributes to the stability of the Q16 group. Therefore, RE.EDGE.LINK is called. Using lens pattern data for such a local configuration, RE.EDGE.LINK comes up with two move candidates, R17 and Q17. Of these, R17 is preferred because it gives white less room to maneuver. R17, however, would set up a linkage to Q16 that might, in some board configurations, be subject to a successful white cut. Thus RE.EDGE.LINK now invokes PROBE, to see whether the cut can be sustained in this context. PROBE finds it can not be, so REFLEX returns R17 for black 12.

White 13 at Q15 also triggers several LOCAL.-URGENT alerts. The first priority is to protect R17. Any move proposed is checked by PROBE lookahead to see if it also secures the threatened Q16-R17 linkage. The proposed move is further checked against two other sets of criteria, those applying to contact fights and those for plays around territorial boundaries. In this case, the move finally chosen satisfies both the priority objective and these others as well.

White 15 again threatens to undercut a territory, and so provokes black 16 at R11. This is appropriate since the opponent is stronger than the program, the territory is large, and protecting the territory helps keep the black side group stable. White 17 at S15 triggers a LOCAL.URGENT shape alert, since it threatens the followup at S17. The program

---

* Go ranking is explained in Section 6.

therefore plays 18 at S17, to deny white that point. The idea is to preempt and defuse such situations whenever it is locally advantageous for the program to do so.

With 19, white invades the program's top potential territory before it gets too large and secure. The program's response at L17, its first bad move, results from a bug. White 21 also is an error, however. And now through black 26 the program takes advantage of white's error to repair its own. MOVE updating discloses the threatened black linkage between L17 and O16, and this triggers a priority LOCAL.URGENT alert. When white 23 threatens to reconnect his stones and capture black M16, the program connects at L16. It does this under LOCAL.URGENT control, because the PROBE lookahead indicates that this starts a sequence that saves this stone, protects the L17-O16 linkage, and captures white M17. M17 is a cutting string, and capturing it unites the two black groups. Thus, when white 25 connects at N15, the program concludes the capture sequence with black 26 at N17. Note that the program plays 24, even though its shape critic complains about the inefficient shape it produces, because no other move achieves its priority objective.

White 27 and 29 put no LOCAL.URGENT pressure on black, so for the first time since black 8, control falls through to DEVELOP.GROUP. Now is black's chance to take the initiative. The program, however, believes that the whole black group on the lower right is unstable, so CROSS.SECTOR.LINE is called, and wastes 28 and 30 trying to restabilize it. Why does the program worry about this group? Because white Q2 undercuts the supporting territory. A human player can see the intervening corner, which mitigates this effect, but the program lacked the appropriate check. As this example suggests, making effective use of the information provided by the system's analogues for perception is a recurring problem.

Moves 31-34 in the lower left are joseki again. When MOVE updates after white 35, however, PROBE finds that although white E5 does not threaten any black strings or linkages, it does create a white linkage between F3 and E5 that can be cut. The program classifies this as an easy cut. The first move creates no new string and thus does not lead to complications. A LOCAL.URGENT alert is triggered, the program plays black 36 at E4, and white responds at F4. The idea here is to introduce defects in the opponent's position. These defects may or may not be utilized subsequently, depending upon the opponent's response and the surrounding conditions. In this case, after white 37 the program does not cut at F5 because such a play would not be supported by any existing black group. Here we see a real limitation of the INTERIM.2 program, the lack of strategic analysis. A strong Go player would have made a strategic analysis before playing 36, found he could make no immediate use of the cut at F5, and deferred the preparatory move at E4 until he could see some strategic purpose to the sequence.

White 37 does not produce any LOCAL.URGENT alerts, but since white 35 created a sector line between E5 and N6, DEVELOP.GROUP calls CROSS.SECTOR.LINE, which proposes black 38 at L6. This takes the unstable black bottom center group out across the line. White 39, played to protect the cut point at F5, destabilizes the lower left black potential territory and group, and induces black 40 at D8. The motivations and operations are the same as those described for white 7, black 8 on the right side. The next four moves are joseki again, followed by a white slide to B10, at which point the opening terminates and the game moves into a protracted midgame fight.

Summarizing the results of the play to this point, although the program has made several errors, mostly owing to minor bugs, it nonetheless has secured all of its groups, and it has center influence, 60-70 points of reasonably secure territory, and prospects for more. White still has insecure groups, only about 15 points of secure territory, and no immediate prospects of gaining much more. This is a high handicap game, so we should expect black still to be ahead. But white can hardly be satisfied with his progress.

4. <u>MIDGAME SHAPE ATTACKS</u>

The second sequence we consider starts from the situation shown in Fig. 3. The sequence itself is presented in Fig. 4. (Move 111 is shown in the figure as 11, etc.). White 111 at M4 triggers no LOCAL.URGENT or DEVELOP.GROUP alerts, so control falls through to ATTACK.GROUP. There is only one attackable candidate, the white group at the upper right. The program has been making preparatory moves against this white group for some time, and now at move 112 the program tries for the kill. The white group has one internal liberty (eye) at P15, but to live it needs either to get one more, or else to connect to some other secure white group. With white already bounded and enclosed, the attempt to kill is largely a

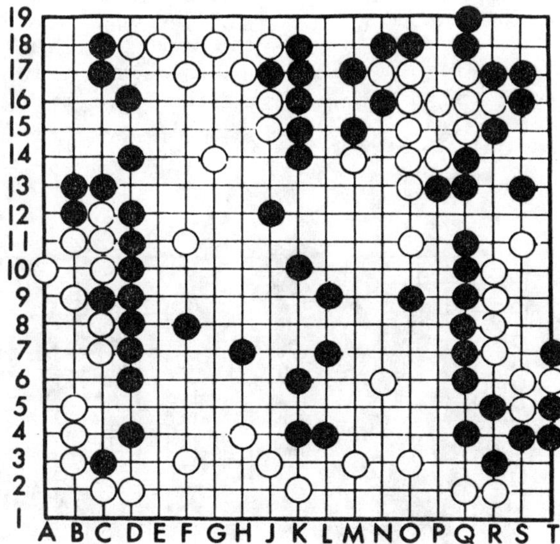

Figure 3. Board Prior To Attack.

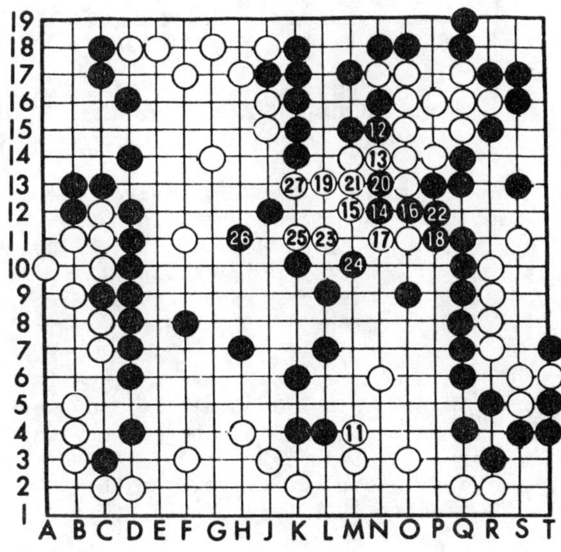

Figure 4. The Shape Attack Sequence.

matter of shape attacks to keep white from forming eyes.

The attack is under the immediate control of SHAPE.POINTS. To understand how shape attacks are made, recall from Section 2.1 that whenever any stone is played, a shape lens is set up to monitor its shape-development possibilities. The prototype fields for the lens will check for significant proximal stones. Take the white stone at M14 in Fig. 3. When this stone was added at move 99 to the existing white group, one of the prototype shape fields checked for a two-stone pattern at a one-point jump from the focal M14 stone, and found white O14 and O13. A field covering this base shape of three stones (M14, O14, and O13) was then instantiated as part of the lens monitoring the local area around M14. Every completed lens includes fields monitoring each of the recognized base shapes involving the focal stone. Each field is maintained until its occupancy preconditions are violated by a subsequent move. Every completed lens also lists good moves for developing, and spoiling, the eye potential of the board area monitored by the lens. Thus in our example SHAPE.POINTS can now read off white's shape development moves, e.g., M12 and M13, as well as the local black shape attack points. In general, the more stones in the base shape of a field, the faster the empty points in the field can be used to create a good eye, using the eye potential of all the base stones working together. The final shape attack move is chosen on the same principle, i.e., it is the move that deprives the largest possible subset of enemy stones of their eye-forming potential. There presently is one severe restriction on permissible shape attack moves. The play finally chosen must form a connection with an existing friendly group. This is a temporary restriction, to reduce the possibilities for complications, and does not apply to eye-destroying moves, e.g., throw-ins, played inside real territory.

After black N15 and white N14, the dominant white lens field is the one defined by the triple of M14, N14, and O13. This suggests attacking moves at M12 and N12. Both form connections with black groups, but the lens information designates N12 the more severe. It destroys white's shape in this area completely. In addition, N12 also threatens the white O11-O13 linkage. Black 114 induces 115 at M12. This is the only reasonable move for white. Black 116 is played from a LOCAL.URGENT alert, to save N12. N11 would have been better, to further reduce white's shape possibilities, but the early INTERIM.2 versions cannot exploit interactions across the top level REFLEX functions, in this case across LOCAL.URGENT and ATTACK.GROUP. After white 117 at N11,

LOCAL.URGENT proposes P11, to save the black string. P12 would have been better, but this again would require multiplexing across top-level functions. White 119 at L13 both continues trying to make shape, and also threatens one of the enclosing black linkages. Black 120 directly blocks an eye, but L11, aiming at falsifying the eye and also denying white some additional shape possibilities, would have been better. Finding this move takes lookahead, however, and the shape attack system presently uses PROBE only for determining safety and connection. After the M13, P12 exchange, white continues to try to make shape with 123 at L11. At this point, black has two possibilities, at M10 and K12. The program, again not able to call PROBE, plays 124 at M10, the wrong choice. White 125 at K11 contributes both to his shape and his breakout possibilities. Not being capable of strategic analysis, the program is compelled to abort the shape attack at this point in order to reenclose white with 126 at H11. As white 127 at K13 threatens both to break out and also to form an eye, the white group is now secure, and the program abandons the attack.

5. PROBE LOOKAHEAD PRODUCES A KILL

We conclude with an example of the INTERIM.2 system at its best. Fig. 5 shows a midgame situation from a game against a 3 kyu opponent.

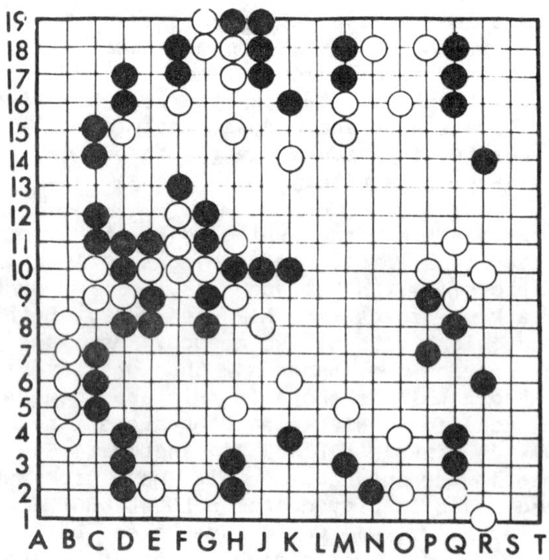

Figure 5. Board Prior To PROBE Reanalysis.

Although white has lost a small group around F10, he is otherwise in fine shape. In particular, white has enclosed the program's top and bottom groups tightly enough that both black and white are treating them as strategically dead, incapable of achieving absolute stability. Per Fig. 6 (move 101 shown as 1, etc.), the program plays its next move, black 86, at H13. White evidently

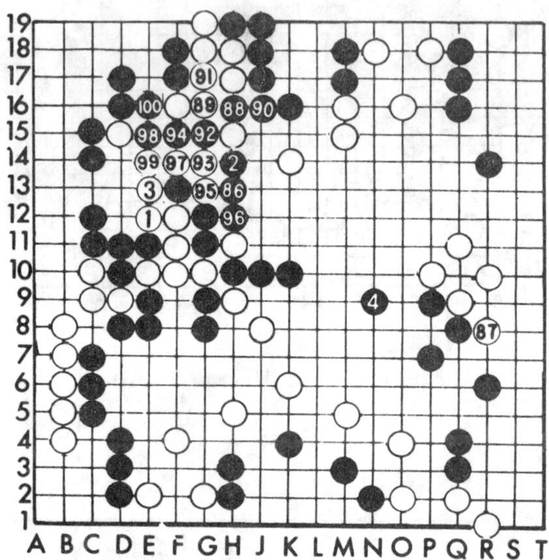

Figure 6. PROBE Lookahead Produces A Kill.

regards this move as locally insignificant, and he plays 87 on the right side. The program then plays black 88 at H16, and in the 16 moves that follow, not only kills the white G19-G18-H18-H17 string, but thereby also saves his entire top group.

How did this come about? Ever since white's efforts to save his F10 stones led to black and white plays around G12, the program has been reanalyzing the tactical status of the white H17 string after every move in the G12 area. This is because PROBE previously had determined that any change in the status of the empty points around G12 might invalidate its conclusions about the tactical security of the H17 string. Therefore it put those points in the relevant points list of the tactical data structure associated with the H17 string, and also stored a pointer to this tactical data structure with each cell in the TACTICSBOARD corresponding to one of these relevant points. Thus, once black has played 86 at H13, on the next entry to the MOVE-REFLEX cycle, MOVE updating accesses this tactical data structure through the TACTICSBOARD cell for H13 and passes it to UPDATE.TACTICAL.ANALYSES. This time, when PROBE reanalyzes the tactical status of the white H17 string, it comes up with a killing sequence. When REFLEX takes control, LOCAL.URGENT discovers that an important enemy string has just been flagged as killable, and it returns H16, the initial move proposed by PROBE, as the program's next play. The program's performance here is at the intermediate amateur level or better, both in detecting the opportunity, and in following through.

6. OVERALL PROGRAM PERFORMANCE LEVEL

Human Go players are ranked on a scale consisting of about 44 unit-interval steps, labelled as follows. A total novice is ranked 35 kyu. As a player's skill improves, the numerical value of his kyu ranking decreases. Thus intermediate amateurs conventionally rank from about 5 kyu to 1 kyu. The next rank after 1 kyu is 1 dan. Advanced amateur ranks run from 1 dan to an upper limit approaching 9 dan. Professional players roughly overlap the region from 6 to 9 dan on the amateur scale.

The groundbreaking programs of Ryder [9] and Zobrist [10] rank close to the total novice level. The one game Ryder reports was played against such a novice. The program's play was quite interesting at many points, but it eventually lost by a substantial margin. The stronger of Zobrist's two versions achieved a rank of about 31 kyu. The first of our programs, INTERIM.1 [4], ranked about 27 kyu. The initial INTERIM.2 versions, from which the examples presented above were taken, rank about 20 kyu. For an evaluation of an entire INTERIM.2.0 game, see Mann [11]. Introduction of the PROBE system is responsible for most of the difference in playing strength between the INTERIM.1 and INTERIM.2 systems. Our current version, INTERIM.2.3, which allows multiplexing at top REFLEX levels, ranks around 15 kyu.

7. CONCLUSION

We have described the operations that create, update, and use the INTERIM.2 program's multilevel representation to play Go. We also have illustrated the system's performance with three examples from actual play. As these indicate, the interim versions of the projected system produce sustained play, serving reasonable goals, at approximately the level of a knowledgeable beginner. The system has a good way to go, however, before it can claim to be an adequate solution to Berliner's AI task par excellence.

ACKNOWLEDGEMENTS

We are much indebted to D. B. Benson, H. J. Berliner, D. J. H. Brown, B. Hilditch, D. McArthur, R. Nado, and J. Reitman for their very helpful comments and suggestions.

REFERENCES

[1] Berliner, H.J. A chronology of computer chess and its literature. Artif. Intell., 1978, 10, 201-214.

[2] Brown, D.J.H., and Dowsey, S. The challenge of Go. New Sci., 1979, 81, 303-305.

[3] Kerwin, J. and Reitman, W. A Go protocol with comments. IP-20, unpublished, Univ. Michigan, 1973.

[4] Reitman, W. and Wilcox, B. Pattern recognition and pattern-directed inference in a program for playing Go. In D. Waterman and R. Hayes-Roth (Eds.), Pattern-directed inference systems. New York: Academic Press, 1978. Pp. 503-523.

[5] Reitman, W., Nado, R., and Wilcox, B. Machine perception: what makes it so hard for computers to see? In C.W. Savage (Ed.), Perception and cognition. Minneapolis: Univ. of Minnesota Press, 1978. Pp. 65-87.

[6] Reitman, W. and Wilcox, B. Modeling tactical analysis and problem solving in Go. Proc. Tenth Annual Pittsburgh Conf. on Modeling and Simulation. In press.

[7] Wilcox, B., Reitman, D., and Reitman, W. Tutorial documentation for the INTERIM.2 Go program. IP-35, unpublished, Univ. Michigan, 1978.

[8] Wilcox, B. Instant Go: contact fights. Am. Go J., 1978, 13 (1), 4-21.

[9] Ryder, J.L. Heuristic analysis of large trees as generated in the game of Go. Ph.D. Dissertation, Stanford Univ., 1971.

[10] Zobrist, A.L. Feature extraction and representation for pattern recognition and the game of Go. Ph.D. Dissertation, Univ. Wisconsin, 1970.

[11] Mann, B. [Untitled]. Personal Comput., 1979, 3 (6), 83-86.

Building and Exploiting User Models

Elaine Rich
Computer Science Department
Carnegie-Mellon University
Pittsburgh, Pa. 15213

This paper describes the issues involved in building and exploiting individual user models in order to guide the performance of an interactive system. A system called Grundy, that recommends novels to people, is described and analyzed as a forum in which to explore those issues. One of the major techniques exploited in Grundy is the use of stereotypes as a mechanism for quickly producing an initial approximation to a model of the user. Experiments with the system show that despite the fact that stereotypes are inherently imperfect, their use does contibute significantly to the system's ability to build useful models of its users.

1. Introduction

As computers come to be used by a larger number of people to help perform a great variety of tasks, it is becomming more and more important for them to be easy for people to use. There are many factors that can contribute to the ease of use of a computer system, ranging from the good design of terminals to the speed of the system's response, the appropriateness of its response, and the naturalness of its input and output languages. Yet another factor that can significantly affect the ease with which people can use a system is the ability of the system to tailor its behavior to the specific needs of an individual user. It is this aspect of the habitability problem than will be discussed in this paper.

In order for a system to be able to respond to the individual needs of its users, it must have access to some kind of model of each user. Because the term "user model" can be used to mean several different things, it is important to specify what we mean by it. The three major dimensions along which user models can be classified are:

- Are they models of a canonical user or are they models of individual users?

- Are they constructed explicitly by the user himself or are they abstracted by the system on the basis of the user's behavior?

- Do they contain short-term, highly specific information or longer-term, more general information?

The work described here has concentrated on user models in one corner of this space. Models of individual users were built because of the facility for personalization they provide that is lacking in a canonical user model. Implicitly constructed models were used because of the inherent inaccuracy and the annoyance of requiring users to construct their own models of themselves. The choice of position along the third dimension was much less clear cut. Both short-term knowledge (such as the topic currently being discussed or the goal now being pursued) and long-term knowledge (such as the level of the user's knowledge about the problem domain or goals that are likely to be pursued) can be important to the performance of an interactive system. But it appeared likely that different techniques would be appropriate for dealing with the two types of knowledge. Models of long-term user characteristics were chosen because very little work has been done with them, while short-term user models were already being explored, particularly in the context of natural language understanding. So the rest of this work will deal explicitly with the issues involved in individual user, implicit, long-term user modeling.

2. Some Requirements for an Individual-User, Implicit, Long-Term User Modeling System

<u>The model must be built dynamically, as the system is interacting with the user and performing its task.</u> Because the model is to be built implicitly and because users do not want to be forced to answer a long list of questions before they can begin to use the system, it is necessary that the system be able to exploit a partially constructed user model and that it be able to tell, as it is performing its major task, when it is appropriate to update the user model and how to do so.

<u>The system should be able to infer as much knowledge about the user from as little information as possible.</u> This is important if the user is not to be required to answer a large number of questions about himself. The major technique that can be exploited to do this is the use of stereotypes. A stereotype can be activated on the basis of a single action and can suggest a large

*This research was sponsored in part by the Defense Advanced Research Projects Agency (DOD), ARPA Order No. 3597, monitored by the Air Force Avionics Laboratory Under Contract F33615-78-C-1551. The author was supported by a grant from the Xerox Corporation.

The views and conclusions contained in this document are those of the author and should not be interpreted as representing the official policies, either expressed or implied, of the Defense Advanced Research Projects Agency or the US Government.

array of likely characteristics of the user. Stereotypes serve a function very similar to that of scripts [2]; they group together frequently co-occurring events to provide useful predictions than can guide the system.

The user modeling system must be able to cope with the uncertainty that will arise from the fact that most of what it believes about the user is really just a good guess. Because most of the knowledge about the user will be based only on likely inferences drawn from his behavior, the system must associate with those inferences some measure of how confident it is of them. It must also remember the basis for each inference so that when conflicts arise (as they are sure to do), it will be able to resolve them in some reasonable way. Of course, to do this, it must also possess some conflict resolution rules. In this respect, user modeling systems are similar to other probabilistic reasoning systems, such as MYCIN [3].

It must be possible to modify the data base of stereotypes so that they will eventually characterize the system's users as accurately as possible. Since it will almost never be possible to construct stereotypes that are completely accurate and since the stereotypes are so important to the function of the system, it is important that the system monitor their accuracy and change both them and their triggers as warrented by the actions of the users.

3. A Brief Description of Grundy

In order to have a forum in which to explore these issues and to be able to make a convincing case that some solutions had been found, it was deemed necessary to tackle the issues in the context of a specific task domain and actually to build a system into which the solutions to the issues could be incorporated. The task that was chosen for this experiment is to suggest to users novels that they might like to read. This is an appropriate domain since a wide variety of people read novels, but they do not all like the same ones; and there is enough flexibility in the task that knowledge about the individual user can be exploited.

The novel recommending program, called Grundy, first asks one or two questions, on the basis of which it begins to build its model of the user, usually by evoking one or more stereotypes. Then it begins the process of recommending novels. Each time it selects a book, it asks the user whether or not he has read it. If he has, he is then asked whether he liked it. If he did, Grundy can update its model of him on the basis of the known characteristics of the book. If he did not like the book, Grundy attempts to find out why not and then to update its model of the user appropriately. If, on the other hand, the user has not read the book, then he is given a description of it and then asked whether he thinks he would like it. If he thinks he would, Grundy need do nothing -- it appears to be on the right track. But if he thinks he would not like it, Grundy must try to discover why not and then to update its model of him. Thus, as Grundy interacts with the user, its model of him will evolve and begin to contain specific knowledge about him, infered on the basis of his responses, in addition to its early beliefs, which were principally based on the predictions of stereotypes.

4. The Performance of Grundy

In order to collect evidence that Grundy is successfully exploiting user models, twenty-three people were observed using the system. Several aspects of Grundy's performance were investigated.

4.1. Grundy's Success at Recommending Novels

Although building the ideal novel recommending program was not the primary goal of this research, it is important to establish that Grundy exhibits some form of intelligent action in order to show that the user modeling techniques are effective. In order to measure the system's success, a small experiment was conducted at the end of each conversation Grundy had with a user. Some books were selected randomly from the data base and then suggested to the user. It was then possible to compare Grundy's rate of success at recommending books that looked good to the users both when it was exploiting the user model and when it was not. Figure 1 shows the results of the comparison. It shows the number of good suggestions (i.e. the user said he might like) and the number of bad ones (i.e. the user said he would not like) in both the controlled and random modes. The data clearly demonstrate that the user models do contribute significantly to Grundy's performance as a novel recommender.

	CONTROLLED	RANDOM
GOOD	102	54
BAD	39	60

Figure 1: GRUNDY's Success Rate

4.2. Grundy's Success at Building Models of Its Users

Several attempts were made to test more directly Grundy's success at building models of its users, by comparing the models built by Grundy to self-descriptions provided by the users. This is not a perfect measure of Grundy's success, however, because people's descriptions of themselves do not tend to be very accurate (or even consistent). Despite this, the data indicate that Grundy is doing quite a good job at building models of its users. This conclusion is not, of course, surprising in light of the data on Grundy's success at recommending books.

4.3. Learning in Grundy

As has already been discussed, it is important that the stereotypes and triggers that form the bulk of the database of a user modeling system be able to change to reflect the actual body of users of the overall system. On the other hand, it is important that no single user be allowed to have a momentous effect on a system's global view of the class of all users. So in running Grundy with about twenty users, only the most commonly invoked stereotypes could be expected to change significantly. The most frequently activated stereotype was the MAN stereotype, and it did show interesting and significant change over the period Grundy was run. For example, the stereotype initially predicted that men would like books that are very fast-moving and full of suspense. The values of both of those characteristics decreased considerably on the basis of Grundy's experience with its users. Both of these changes can easily be explained by the difference between the group the stereotype was originally intended to characterize (all adult male Americans) and the group it was actually applied to in practice (some adult male intellectuals). The people who used the system, although they were men and did seem to like fast-moving, exciting books, also tended to like philosophical novels and literary classics, which tend to be much calmer. Thus by the end of the experiment, Grundy had a more accurate picture of the men it was encountering than it had had at the outset. This suggests that the learning mechanisms are capable of causing at least some sorts of improvement in the stereotype data base of a user modeling system.

4.4. The Effectiveness of Stereotypes

In looking at the results of GRUNDY's attempts to use stereotypes to build useful models of people, one is reminded of one important characteristic of stereotypes and thus of systems that use them. Although a stereotype may often provide highly appropriate and useful information about a person, it is, at best, an expression of a tendency and not an absolute truth. One example will serve to illustrate this point clearly.

Several stereotypes in GRUNDY predict that people who fit them will be interested in the conflict "art-vs-science". Those predictions caused GRUNDY to believe, correctly, that several users were interested in that conflict and thus to recommend books involving it. But one person, who fit three stereotypes that predict an interest in that conflict said, on the second questionnaire, that he was definitely not interested in it. Figure 2 shows all the situations in which GRUNDY believed the user was interested in art-vs-science.

User	Stereotypes Predicting Interest	Interested?
4	Intellectual, Contemplative, Scientist	yes
6	Intellectual	yes
7	Intellectual, Contemplative	yes
8	Intellectual	yes
9	Contemplative	yes
10	Intellectual, Artist	yes
11	Intellectual	yes
13	Intellectual	yes
20	Intellectual	yes
22	Scientist, Artist, Contemplative	NO

Figure 2: An Illustration of the Fallibility of Stereotypes

5. Conclusion

If one were to distill this thesis into its most essential points, there would, I think, be three.

The first is the awareness of the potential usefulness of user models of this sort. This awareness is just now becoming more important as the use of computers spreads further and further into the daily lives of more and more people. If this thesis does nothing except make people think about building these computer systems so that they can better serve their users, this effort will not have been wasted.

But realizing a need and satisfying it are not the same thing. The second significant point of this thesis is that, for at least one such system, in at least one domain, an individual user model was made to work and to guide a performance system successfully.

And yet the third contribution, after arguing for necessity, and demonstrating feasibility, is suggesting technique. Not only are user models useful and doable, specific techniques for building them have been developed. Although no claim is being made that these techniques are the perfect ones, they have been shown to be workable in one domain and extensible to others.

These three points, the usefulness, the feasibility, and the techniques of user modeling, constitute the major contribution of this thesis.

A more detailed discussion of all of the issues that were mentioned in this paper, as well as several that were not, including a description of the actual mechanisms employed, and a discussion of how to extend the ideas to other domains, can be found in [1].

References

[1] Rich, E. A.
Building and Exploiting User Models.
PhD thesis, CMU, 1979.

[2] Schank, R. C. and R. P. Ableson.
Goals, Plans, Scripts and Understanding: An Enquiry into Human Knowledge Structures.
Erlbaum Press, 1977.

[3] Shortliffe, E. H.
MYCIN: Computer-based Consultations in Medical Consultations.
American Elsevier, 1976.

WORD EXPERT PARSING*

Chuck Rieger and Steve Small

Department of Computer Science
University of Maryland
College Park, Maryland 20742

An approach to natural language meaning-based parsing in which the unit of linguistic knowledge is the word rather than the rewrite rule is described. In the Word Expert Parser, knowledge about language is distributed across a population of procedural experts, each representing a word of the language, and each an expert at diagnosing that word's intended usage in context. The parser is structured around a coroutine control environment in which the generator-like word experts ask questions and exchange information in coming to collective agreement on sentence meaning. The Word Expert theory is advanced as a better cognitive model of human language expertise than the traditional rule-based approach. The technical discussion is organized around examples taken from the prototype LISP system which implements parts of the theory.

1. Background

In building a natural language understanding system, one of the first major decisions to be made is that of how to express and organize linguistic and conceptual knowledge for the parser. Depending upon the level of analysis desired (e.g., from simple keyword and key phrase recognition to "full" conceptual understanding in context), different methods suggest themselves. For the most part, models of parsing to this point have made the assumption that systems of rewrite rules are good media for expressing knowledge about sentence-level parsing. Examples of relatively successful systems and theories based on this assumption can be taken from every nearly every level of analysis, from the simple keyword analysis of PARRY [1], the syntactic analysis of LUNAR, up to more semantic and conceptual parsers such as those by Riesbeck [2], [3], and Wilks [4], [5]. Although the implementation styles of these models differ markedly, they share the view that rules of language understanding are best captured by rules which span relatively large sentence constituents (e.g., a phrase, a "picture producing" clause, a verb case framework). This assumption preordains a certain view of language comprehension by imposing structure at the sentence level and treating the words of the language as tokens which simply participate in comprehension by virture of their inclusion in sentence and concept level rules.

While it is highly likely that any knowledge whatsoever about language can be expressed in the form of a system of rewrite rules, this form of representation defines a particular point of view in which individual words of the language mean nothing outside the system of rules which make reference to them. This seems peculiar, since we intuitively know that each word of our language is an object with an often very rich knowledge structure attached to it. We know many contextual uses of each word (sense), we know its morphology, perhaps its history in some usage, perhaps when we first learned it, its idiosyncratic uses, perhaps even idiosyncratic uses of it with respect to some particular speaker we know. Intuitively, there is a considerable amount of knowledge associated with each word.

One can easily argue that all such knowledge can be captured in a system of rules which make reference to the word; indeed, each rule we add to the system will incrementally extend our knowledge about the words to which it makes reference. To extend the system, one adds new rules and revises or deletes old ones. If asked what it knows about any given word, the system can report all patterns in which the word participates. During comprehension, if the patterns of the system have been written to include enough sentential and conceptual context, exactly the right rules will filter to the forefront to drive the parser in its extraction of meaning and/or syntax. Such a system is clearly theoretically adequate.

We believe, however, that the underlying assumptions of this traditional approach are not correct. Out of curiosity a while back, we posed the following question: What would the knowledge in a language comprehension model look like if organized around words rather than systems of rewrite rules? Superficially, this seems like an engineering matter; one symbol's forward pointer is another symbol's backward pointer! But, as we have found, a remarkably different set of issues arises, and a considerably different approach to parsing suggests itself when the model defines the unit of knowledge to be the word rather than the rewrite rule.

This paper describes our "word expert" view of natural language comprehension. In the following sections, we describe why the theory seems more attractive than rule-based system, and we describe the architecture and operation of the Word Expert Parser, a LISP implementation of the ideas.

2. Word Experts

Our thinking on these matters was first stimulated by a simple observation about existing models. This observation was that no model (except for Wilks' model of preference semantics) seems ever to have made more than a token attempt at handling multiple senses of any given word in its vocabulary. Riesbeck's impressive parser, for example, while pioneering in many of its ideas about control via conceptual dependency schemata, was designed in a way that made it awkward to deal with highly ambiguous words; although the system did (and does) clever rule and expectancy switching on a limited set of examples of conceptual ambiguity, the system does not deal with the problem in generality. Wilks' system, on the other hand, is designed to deal with exactly this problem of word ambiguity, but at a more semantic (e.g., "things which are human eat things which are food"), rather than fully conceptual level where arbitrary world knowledge might be required for understanding. It is a mixture of Riesbeck's and Wilks' goals that most closely defines our goals, since we feel that word sense disambiguation in the context of open-ended world knowledge is of ultimate importance in a natural language system.

We therefore took the point of view that mechanisms for dealing with word ambiguity should be deeply built in to the model, perhaps even the most central mechanisms of the comprehension process. To gain some empathy for this point of view, consider almost any common English noun, verb or adjective. With twenty minute's thought, and perhaps a few reminders from Webster's, it is usually possible to identify dozens of different usages of that word. (We have looked at words like "take", "make" and "give" in some detail; each has dozens of distinct usages.)

How do we approach the problem of representing all the contextual usages of such highly ambiguous words? The traditional approach would be to write one rule for each usage. Each such rule would contain enough contextual probes so that it would fire at exactly the appropriate moments. But there are several negative features of this approach. First, each rule must be self-contained, and have enough information to fire only when the appropriate sentential and conceptual context pertained. This quickly leads to large, often highly redundant context descriptions in each rule. Second, some uniform interpreter capable of rule arbitration must exist to select the "most appropriate" competitor from among the several rules which will typically fire as potential interpretations. Third, being separate from all the other competitors, each rule must be able to place an absolute judgement on its relevance to the context at hand; there is no convenient way to have a rule decide on its <u>relative</u> appropriateness, with respect to its competitors.

These observations pointed away from rule systems, and toward the idea of writing more unified word experts. This led us to the notion of <u>word (sense) experts</u>. In our present model, each word expert is <u>a procedural entity</u> cognizant of all the possible contextual interpretations of the word it represents. When placed in a run-time context (i.e., informed of its position in the sentence, and given access to the neighboring experts and to a database of world knowledge context at that point in the comprehension of the larger fragment of which the sentence is a part), a word expert should be capable of issuing an orderly progression of inquiries about its context, and making a set of decisions based on the responses (or lack thereof) to its queries which lead to a selection of the best <u>relative</u> interpretation of its word in that context. Each <u>word expert</u> is, in effect, a unified compilation of what otherwise would be

*The research described in this report is funded by the National Aeronautics and Space Administration under grant number NSG-7253. Their support is gratefully acknowledged.

a collection of rules describing the contextual variants of the word. By unifying them, we create a central knowledge structure which can pose more concise questions to differentiate contextual usages, and which superimposes a unifying framework on all possible interpretations of a word.

In further pondering the nature of word experts, it occurred to us that what we are really talking about is not so much words, but rather lexical units that are capable of contributing meaning or structure to a sentence. From this idea, it becomes clear that we want experts not only for words, but also for common morphemes ("-ing", "-ed", etc.), and possibly even for punctuation. The sentence (and a host of others like it, studied heavily in linguistics circles) "The man eating spaghetti growled." illustrates very clearly the desirability of an "-ing" expert. Looking to its left and right experts (or the concepts they may already have constructed), "-ing" should be able to decide how the concepts referenced by "man" and "eat" in this sentence best fit together. Because of observations like this one, we have come to take a broad view of sense experts that will allow meaning-contributing units other than words.

<u>Parser Overview.</u> Naturally, adopting the word and morpheme rather than the rule as the base unit expressing knowledge leads to differences in the organization and control of the parser. Rather than a uniform rule interpreter/applier, the Word Expert Parser is more a model of coroutine control and intercommunication. As we are about to describe, in the Word Expert Parser, the parse of each sentence involves the paging in of all required experts, the initialization of community and private workspaces, then the control of the numerous experts as they execute, suspend themselves, ask questions of one-another, and contribute fragments of meaning to the final interpretation of the sentence. Because of its organization, the Word Expert Parser must define not only the structure and contents of each expert, but also a cognitively plausible control paradigm for coordinating the experts.

The body of the paper is a description of our present model of word experts and their control. Briefly, each word expert is a generator-like coroutine whose decision logic is organized as a discrimination net. Terminals of the net are the distinct usages of the word (its senses), while non-terminals are multiple-choice questions which probe the run-time environment. Also at each non-terminal node is control information describing what to do in case the question is not yet answerable (e.g., make an assumption, forward a suggestion to another expert, suspend temporarily). Meaning representation of the final interpretations (i.e., the meaning patterns stored at the terminal nodes of the experts) has not been an issue in the development of the parser to this point. We presently use predicates that are descriptive of each of the different senses of the word, and have not made attempts to develop a consistent representation. Although the nature of the parser may well be affected by eventual commitments to one particular representation, we have so far been able to develop the ideas about word expert structure and content, and about parser control without regard for the form of the final representation.

We hope to convey our intuitive feeling that word level organization of knowledge about language is both natural and powerful. In addition to dictating an interesting style of parser control, solving some important problems about word sense ambiguity, and addressing the issue of relative (rather than absolute) selection of the most appropriate interpretation of each word, the word expert organization leads to some other interesting ideas about language, particularly about language learning. We discuss several of these ideas in the final section. Additional discussion of the Word Expert topic can be found in [6], [7], [8], and [9].

3. <u>The Word Expert Parser</u>

The Word Expert Parser is a model of the human interface between an external language of inter-human communication, and an internal representation language of concepts and ideas. As a human reader processes a sentence, various conceptual conglomerates are created that provide the key to his understanding [10]. The process of creating these structures is as important as the structures themselves -- not only do stages in the processing of a sentence often depend on aspects of earlier processing, but sometimes the meaning of a sentence is explicitly influenced by how it is processed [11]. This should be quite clear for spoken language, but is so for written text as well if any degree of ungrammaticality or fragmentation is to be tolerated. The Word Expert Parser is a model of conceptual language analysis that strives for theoretical perspicuity of process.

3.1. <u>Model Overview — A Simple Example</u>

We will first describe the execution of the Word Expert Parser on the phrase "the heavy rain" to illustrate the model's procedural framework on a simple example. Initialization of the parser commences with the creation of a <u>sentence level workspace</u> for this particular input. This workspace consists of a collection of <u>word bins</u> and their associated <u>word sense discrimination experts</u> (<u>word experts</u> or <u>sense experts</u>). A word bin is a repository for information about a single word (or sub-lexical morpheme) of the input, and its corresponding word expert contains the word-specific (and procedural) linguistic knowledge that directs this particular execution of the parser. Each word expert is capable of disambiguating its word in any context, and interactions among word experts deterministically disambiguate the meaning of the sentence.

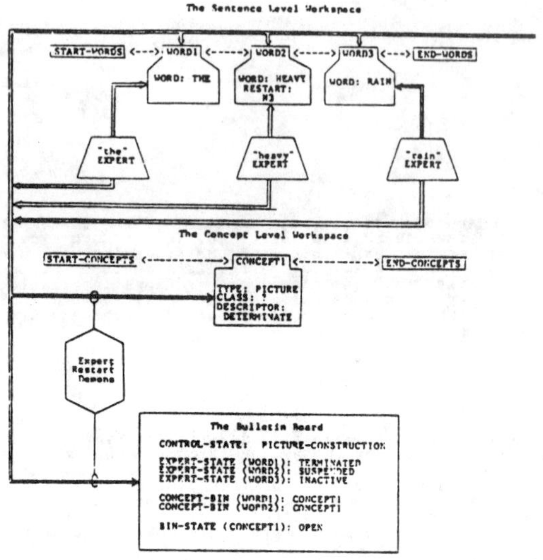

<u>Figure 1: Parser Workspace</u>

<u>The "the" expert runs.</u> The parser begins execution with the word expert for "the", which is the first on the RUN-ME queue (initialized to the input sentence). The flow of control now becomes unpredictable (in theory), as the word experts themselves completely determine control state changes and conceptual actions of the model. The "the" expert tries to determine its role in the sentence, knowing only that it is the first expert to run. Since the role of "the" is usually obvious (as it is here), its expert immediately changes the control state description of the parser from "new sentence" to "picture construction". This state involves the creation of a new conceptual object (called a <u>concept bin</u>) and associating with it a (partial) description. The "the" expert proceeds to create this concept, mark it "determinate", and terminate.

<u>The "heavy" expert runs.</u> The RUN-ME queue now consists of "heavy" and "rain", and the expert for "heavy" is removed and started executing. Since a concept bin is currently active, "heavy" knows to contribute its conceptual descriptions to that bin. If no appropriate concept bin is active when an expert runs, it creates one (as "the" almost always does). If the word describes the same concept as the one preceding it in the sentence, on the other hand, its expert performs as the "heavy" expert does here. This first step completed, the word expert must now discriminate among the many senses of "heavy" and resolve on a single contextually accurate word sense. Since it has not yet seen the word to its right (as we have!), it cannot discriminate among the senses meaning "having large mass", "being in large quantity", or "being serious or emotional".

This ambiguity causes the expert to suspend its execution temporarily until it has seen the word to its right. For an expert to suspend, it must specify the conditions upon which it is to be reawakened and the location in the RUN-ME queue at which it should be placed. The "heavy" expert specifies resumption when the word expert to its right terminates, the end of the sentence reached, or a new concept created. Before suspending, however, this expert also posts a memo to the experts on its right, telling them to expect one of the conceptual object types that "heavy" could describe (e.g., "abstract object"). Expectations in the model are treated differently from constraints -- they provide guidance but are not binding. The "heavy" expert is now suspended, and the execution state of the model corresponds to Figure 1.

The resumption of suspended word expert processes is through spontaneous mechanisms which respond to both conceptual information and changes in the control states of model processes. The restart conditions may be quite complex in general, and have been modeled after the <u>spontaneous</u>

computations of Rieger [12]. When a restart condition involves process control states, it is called a control state demon. For control state demons to be practicable, a central tableau of information about the control structures of the model must be maintained. In the Word Expert Parser, the bulletin board is the center of this control knowledge. Control state descriptions of word experts, the parser itself, and the concept bins are delineated on the bulletin board. In addition, the model's expectations, such as those contributed by the "heavy" expert above, are posted on this board. By making this knowledge of process available to the word experts, control states and expectations of various model components can affect the execution of the others.

The "rain" expert runs. Processing now continues with the expert for "rain" which has become the first on RUN-ME. This expert process contributes its conceptual information to the existing concept bin, and as a consequence of "heavy"'s expectations and "rain"'s simple usage, immediately determines its sense and terminates. Termination of "rain" causes the spontaneous resumption of the "heavy" expert, which continues processing where it left off. Since two of "heavy"'s three senses become meaningless in describing rain, the "heavy" expert resolves upon "being in large quantity" and terminates. This causes the model's single concept bin to close, completing the parse.

The control possibilities are clearly quite complex, and the processing is not always going to give as clear and successful parse as it did on "the heavy rain". However, the Word Expert Parser is a model of cognitive processing, and as such, the state of the parser after incomplete processing must be of psychological appeal. The parser's actions on ambiguous input (extremely rare when considered contextually) demonstrates its cogency -- the end result would be a collection of partially completed suspended processes, coupled with a set of reawakening conditions specifying the reasons for the ambiguity (actually, the requirements for its resolution).

3.2. Workspace Representation

The sentence level and concept level workspaces of the model are represented as partitions of a PLANNER-like associative database. The data in a bin of either workspace is therefore accessible by any of its contents, and in fact, declarative representations can be retrieved associatively from any bin. Descriptors of a particular conceptual object can be accessed by the internal name of the concept (its bin), and more significantly, the objects in the concept-level are retrievable by their descriptions. In this way, a word expert determines the nature of any concepts in the workspace that could influence its actions.

The Sentence Level Workspace. In the initial state of the parser, the word bins contain two pieces of information -- the literal word corresponding to the name given it by the parser (e.g., "the" for WORD1) and the left and right neighbors of the word in the input sentence. These word bins acquire a more subtle and interesting role, however, as the word expert processes are initialized. At this point, each word bin contains the restart information (stack frame [13]) for the process, including its local variables and bindings, and instruction pointer. By representing this information in the word bins, a word expert can easily constrain another by simply altering its local variables or the place that it starts (or resumes) execution.*

The Concept Level Workspace. Each concept in the parser has a type which determines the kind of information found in its concept bin. The parser counts three such conceptual object types, pictures, settings, and events. A picture concept [14] involves physical and abstract objects and their descriptions. A setting is a time, location, or situation. The creation of a setting is frequently introduced by a preposition in the sentence. For example, "in the morning", "in the house", and "in trouble" are examples of time, location, and situation examples (respectively) of setting concepts. Event concepts consist of conceptual case schemata.

The Bulletin Board. Posted on the bulletin board is a collection of control state information about the processing by the model. The process state of each word expert in the model, the status of each conceptual object, and a description of the state of the entire parser are found on this board. Any spontaneous computation triggered by some indication of control state is attached to a memo posting function (or server [15]) on the data channel to the bulletin board.

The Word Expert Parser can be in one of the following global states: NEW-SENTENCE, PICTURE-CONSTRUCTION, SETTING-CONSTRUCTION, EVENT-CONSTRUCTION, or UNKNOWN. These designations describe the actions of the parser as a whole and are based on lower-level descriptions of expert states and concept states. A concept can be UNOPEN, OPEN, or CLOSED, depending on its state of completion. Word experts are processes and are therefore described by the states INACTIVE, SUSPENDED, and TERMINATED. As work on the Word Expert Parser continues [16], refinements of these state descriptions will emerge, clarifying the strength of our work as a process model of human cognitive behavior.

*The modularity of the experts requires that external manipulation of restart pointers be carefully controlled. Each word expert contains a descriptive header that explicitly states how the expert may be constrained.

3.3. Word Sense Discrimination Experts

The principal knowledge structure in the Word Expert Parser is the word sense discrimination expert. A word expert is a representation of the linguistic knowledge (procedural) needed to disambiguate the meaning of a single word in any context. A word's context includes both sentential and conceptual information -- not only are the immediate lexical neighbors of a word important, but conceptual knowledge of the entire text and even the physical world are frequently crucial in understanding it. A word expert performs its discrimination processing by asking context-related questions of the various components of the parser or the story comprehension model in which it is embedded (see [7] and [8] about the GRIND story understanding model).

The important aspects of a word expert are the questions that it asks (and of whom it asks them) and the actions that it performs upon receiving the answers. Sometimes an action is taken because no answers were forthcoming, namely, suspending execution until the information is available or until control states are reached at which point the availability is likely (or non-availability is significant). Other word expert actions include creating and building up concepts, constraining other experts, posting expectations on the bulletin board, and changing the control state of the parser.

3.3.1. Word Expert Structure

Each word expert exists in two forms in the model -- a declarative representation which is a directed acyclic graph and called a word sense discrimination network (or sense net), and a procedural representation like a CONNIVER generator (or stack group [17]) which is called a word expert process. Both representations are briefly discussed here, and their raisons d'etre explained.

Network Representation. A word sense discrimination network is a graphic representation of the contextual disambiguation of a single word. This structure was motivated by the central theoretical notion of the sense net theory of language, that each word of English carries with it the information necesssary to determine its contextual meaning. Each node in a sense net represents an ordered set of decisions that converge on a single appropriate sense of a word.

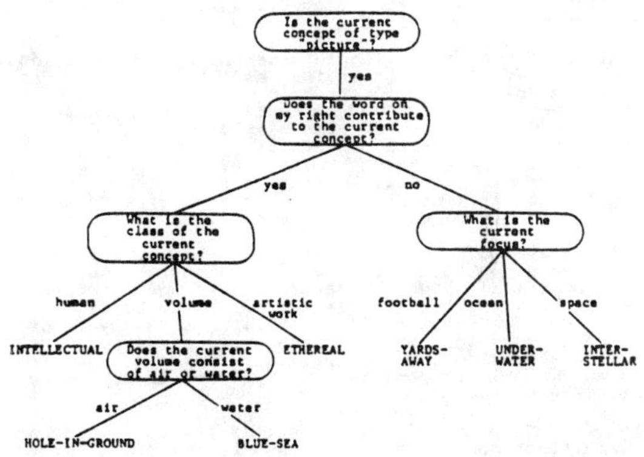

Figure 2: Sense network for "deep"

An example network for "deep" is shown in Figure 2, and shows several of its senses. The first two questions of the network are aimed at determining if "deep" denotes an object ("the deep") or a description (e.g., "the deep thought"). As a question is answered, one branch of the graph is favored over others, and the number of possible senses of a word is reduced. Finally, a terminal node is reached, and a single word sense chosen.

The possibility arises that a question cannot be answered because it depends on information from other networks that is not yet available. In such a case, a sense net must remember its location in the graph and wait for the information it needs to continue. Another aspect of inter-network activity is when a sense net determines constraints on another -- a network waiting for certain data is told to restart at its root node, or told to resume at a different node than it expects. The influence of one sense net on another reflects the crucial contextual nature of their word sense disambiguation tasks.

Process Representation. The Word Expert Parser compiles each sense discrimination network into an executable process when it is first called to perform its task. Although every word expert has a representation as a sense network, this graphic representation lacks important aspects of a true executable expert process. In particular, whereas the details of an expert's suspension and resumption, or interactions with other experts, may seem irrelevant at certain levels of explanation, they are in reality quite significant to the view of the parser as a process model of human language analysis. The network representation also fails to capture the important side-effect actions performed by an expert. The structure and execution of word experts therefore will be outlined through the process representation. Use of an expert's implicit graph structure as a metaphor, however, will certainly be useful.

The compilation of a word expert is significant in that certain nodes of a sense network may be pruned away before it becomes an expert process. In this way, contextual information about the plot of a story, its characters, the current focus (see [18]), and so forth, can be used to eliminate a word's irrelevant senses. In reading "the ship cruised" in a nineteenth century story, for example, a sense of "ship" denoting something which travels between planets can be pruned away immediately. Certain constraints cannot be made a priori, however, and in such cases, an already compiled process must be manipulated.

Word expert processes are implemented in the model in a manner resembling CONNIVER generators. They can be suspended in the middle of execution and resumed spontaneously according to a variety of trigger patterns. These include not only the standard patterns of conceptual data, but data about the control states of other processes as well. Processes can commmunicate by affecting the local variables of another, including those which tell the process where to start (or resume) execution. This effectively prunes the implicit graph structure of the expert. Word expert processes also provide information to other experts by posting control data and expectations on the central bulletin board.

3.3.2. What Word Experts Can Do

The role and significance of word experts in the model are most easily understood through an examination of both their internal actions like the questions they ask, and their side effects, actions that affect the rest of the model. A word expert can ask questions about the other words of the sentence, concepts introduced, expectations, the control state of the parser, or the control states of other experts. An expert can affect the data found in word bins, concept bins, the bulletin board, and the process restart queue of spontaneous computations.

Internal Process Actions. The fundamental internal actions of a word expert are question-asking and branching. One of the important contributions expected in development of the Word Expert Parser is the taxonomy of context-probing questions asked by experts. The nature of some of these questions is emerging and is of several varieties -- lexical, conceptual, global, and control. This last category consists of questions about the state of the cognitive processing task thus far, representationally encompassing the states of word experts, the parser state, and the states of the bins.

The existence of a particular word to the immediate left or right of a given word can often discriminate among its senses. A word expert asks about the nature of the words arbitrarily far to its left and right in the sentence. Furthermore, it can ask about a word's senses (in totality or only those still remaining) through the word's conceptual categories, subclasses of these categories, or the explicit names given to its senses. When a word expert is constrained, the pruning may be done along any of these same dimensions.

Conceptual information is usually very important in discriminating among word senses, as are the posted expectations about this information. The concept bin to which the executing process contributes also contains conceptual data from other experts which is often crucial to understanding the current word. A simple example was given in the model overview, when the "heavy" expert needed information from its own concept bin (i.e., data regarding "rain") before it could determine the correct sense. The concepts to the left and right of the active concept are useful in the same way. It is likely, however, that in the initial left to right scan of the sentence, concept bins to the right of a given one may not yet exist. This fact indicates that a strict ordered scan of a sentence is sufficient to parse it only if no expert needs information from concepts to its right. The organization of the Word Expert Parser therefore supports our common sense intuition about conceptual parsing by humans.

The Word Expert Parser is embedded within the GRIND story comprehension model, and as such, has access to the global world of a children's story. Relevant aspects include the personalities of the characters, interactions among characters, the plot line, anaphoric references, and current foci of interest. The plot of a medieval story, for example, might tell the reader that "knights", "lords", "maids", and "workers" take certain strict interpretations in local contexts. Or the focus of understanding in a story might be the Algonquin Round Table, in which case "the deep" ought to be interpreted as referring to those intelligent persons who regularly ate lunch together at that hotel. Global context significantly influences the understanding of certain sentences of texts.

Control State Descriptions. A new and important aspect of the Word Expert Parser is that control information is accessible to (and often used by) the discrimination processes. The fact that the expert to the immediate left of the executing expert is suspended, or that the expert to its right has not yet executed, is often the central datum enabling its successful termination. The state of a concept bin is also useful information, particularly in deciding where one concept ends and the next begins. A concept bin is closed only when the conceptual notion it represents is complete; that is, when a change in its data requires the kind of severe backtracking that humans perform extremely rarely (on so-called "garden paths"). In the example parse of "the heavy rain", the control state of the parser aided the executions of the "heavy" and "rain" experts. Control state knowledge is fundamental to the successful conceptual analysis of most sentences. In both the internal nature of the expert processes and their relationship to the entire model (suspension and resumption), the self-examining knowledge of control flow and processing states is fundamental.

Process Side Effects. Conceptual analysis is an inherent part of natural language understanding but not the whole part. As such, word sense discimination by the Word Expert Parser must provide the information it acquires to other components of a large understanding model to complete the task. Assimilation of new data into a picture of the world (see [19] for a discussion of modeling belief systems) by making the necessary inferences, disambiguating references, and so forth (see [8]), constitute the other facets of understanding a text. The side effects of the processing by a word expert provide the information required for further stages in the conceptual analysis phase of understanding, as well as conceptual data for the subsequent phases.

Conceptual knowledge is augmented by creating new concepts and storing new facts about old concepts. A word expert's first task is to determine the conceptual notion to which it contributes. If a concept bin is active at the time, the expert could choose to contribute to it. This would mean that the word it is trying to disambiguate participates in the same concept as the word to its left in the sentence. If no concept bin is active, or if the expert determines that its word starts a new concept anyway, the word expert would open an new one. It is possible (in certain circumstances likely) that an expert would not know which bin to contribute to -- in this case it would suspend its execution until the expert to its right has executed (this is usually enough).

When a word expert has determined its concept, it may store facts there. If it opens the bin itself, it must provide a type (picture, setting, or event) to the bin. Otherwise, it may provide the concept's class, or augment its descriptor. An expert that completes a concept may close its concept bin, indicating that its word is the last (rightmost) one contributing to that concept. If all experts participating in the concept have not yet terminated when one of them attempts to close it, however, the model will plant a demon to close the bin when the last of the relevant experts terminates.

A word expert also affects certain internal data structures, useful solely by the parser. These are extremely important and include suspending itself and constraining other experts. The example execution of "the deep pit" (see below) demonstrates this constraining action -- since neither "deep" nor "pit" can determine its correct sense on the first try, "deep" finally tells "pit" to be one of the things that "deep" can describe, namely, a hole in the ground or a person. It does this by changing the place in "pit"'s network where it begins execution, thus making it believe that it had successfully discriminated farther than it really had. After constraining it in this way, the parse can complete. If "pit" had not yet been compiled, the sense net itself could have been pruned before compilation.

An expert suspends its execution if the model's lack of certain information keeps it from proceeding. When this occurs, the expert stops execution and plants a demon to wake it up when the fact it needs becomes available. These facts can be of any variety, including data regarding the states of other processes. A typical suspension consists of an expert process needing something from a not-yet-executed process to its right, and waiting until it has executed (SUSPENDED or TERMINATED) to resume. Another example in "in the morning" involves a setting, where the "in" network waits until a picture bin is closed before it resumes. At that time, it can complete its own setting concept, knowing the class and description of the picture to its right. As a result of these suspensions and spontaneous resumptions, the range of control flows in the conceptual analysis model is wide and complex -- our confidence in the model's cogency is only strengthened by this variety.

3.4. Example: "the deep pit"

The Word Expert Parser is illustrated below through the example phrase "the deep pit". An actual trace of the parser's execution is presented, accompanied in the righthand column by some explanatory annotations. The example phrase causes the creation of a single concept of type "picture". The word sense ambiguity of the component words causes a number of expert suspensions and resumptions, demonstrating the strength of the system.*

Execution of "the deep pit" is an interesting example of the complexity of control flow in the Word Expert Parser. Since both "deep" and "pit" have more than a single sense, they must exchange pieces of information about themselves before either can succeed at determining its sense.

```
EVAL: (%PARSE: THE DEEP PIT)
CONTROL-STATE: NEW-SENTENCE
VALUE:    T
```

The %PARSE function initializes the parser workspace by retrieving (from a disk file) the word experts for the input phrase, and creating for each one an associated data repository called a "word bin". Each word expert is placed on the RUN-ME queue, and then executed in turn, with the experts themselves eventually determining the flow of control in the model.

```
EXECUTING 'THE' EXPERT: WORD1
*****TRANSLATING SENSE EXPERT FOR WORD1
**EXPERT COMPILE TIME: 56
**OPTIMIZATION TIME: 1237
*****EXPERT FOR WORD1 TRANSLATED
====> AT NODE: N1
NEW CONCEPT: CONCEPT1   TYPE: PICTURE
CONTROL STATE: PICTURE-CONSTRUCTION
EXPERT TERMINATED: WORD1
```

The word expert for "the" is translated from a network representation into a coroutine, which is then executed. It creates a new concept of type PICTURE, changes the parser state to PICTURE-CONSTRUCTION, and terminates.

```
EXECUTING 'DEEP' EXPERT: WORD2
*****TRANSLATING SENSE EXPERT FOR WORD2
**EXPERT COMPILE TIME: 281
**OPTIMIZATION TIME: 5808
*****EXPERT FOR WORD2 TRANSLATED
====> AT NODE: N0
====> AT NODE: N1
EXPERT SUSPENDED: WORD2
```

The "deep" expert is translated and started executing. After a short time, however, it needs information from the word expert to its right. Since the "pit" expert has not yet run at all, "deep" temporarily suspends execution until "pit"'s word expert has SUSPENDED or TERMINATED. Although permitted to do so, "deep" posts no expectations and makes no constraints, thereby insuring that the expert for "pit" has full freedom.

```
EXECUTING 'PIT' EXPERT: WORD3
*****TRANSLATING SENSE EXPERT FOR WORD3
**EXPERT COMPILE TIME: 307
**OPTIMIZATION TIME: 5852
*****EXPERT FOR WORD3 TRANSLATED
====> AT NODE: N0
====> AT NODE: N1
====> AT NODE: N2
   **RESTART DEMON FOR WORD2 TRIGGERED:
   *     (*EXPERT-STATE* WORD3 SUSPENDED)
   **EXPERT FOR WORD2 QUEUED FIRST
EXPERT SUSPENDED: WORD3
```

"Pit" now runs, but cannot discriminate between its two noun senses of "fruit pit" and "hole in the ground". It suspends its execution until something happens to help resolve its word sense deadlock. Since "pit" has now executed, "deep" is spontaneously reawakened.

```
EXECUTING 'DEEP' EXPERT: WORD2
====> AT NODE: N1
====> AT NODE: N4
   **RESTART DEMON FOR WORD3 TRIGGERED:
   *     (*EXPERT-STATE* WORD2 SUSPENDED)
   **EXPERT FOR WORD3 QUEUED LAST
EXPERT SUSPENDED: WORD2
```

Resumed by the suspension of the "pit" expert, the "deep" expert now says: "I gave the word to my right a chance to be what it wanted and it had no idea. Now I'll constrain it to be something that I can describe -- a hole in the ground or a person." At his point, therefore, "deep" constrains "pit" and suspends itself until "pit" terminates. Since "pit" was waiting for exactly this sort of activity, one of its restart demons fires, and the word expert for "pit" is queued up.

```
EXECUTING 'PIT' EXPERT: WORD3
====> AT NODE: N2
====> AT NODE: N3
CONTROL STATE: UNKNOWN
   **RESTART DEMON FOR WORD2 TRIGGERED:
   *     (*EXPERT-STATE* WORD3 TERMINATED)
   **EXPERT FOR WORD2 QUEUED FIRST
EXPERT TERMINATED: WORD3
```

"Pit" now runs for the last time, its constraints focusing the discrimination. Since "pit" terminates, the restart demon for "deep" is triggered, and "deep" is queued.

```
EXECUTING 'DEEP' EXPERT: WORD2
====> AT NODE: N1
====> AT NODE: N3
====> AT NODE: N2
EXPERT TERMINATED: WORD2
CONCEPT CLOSED: CONCEPT1

VALUE:    T
```

Finally, "deep" runs for the last time, terminating with the sense of "large volume". Although "pit" tried to close its concept bin, "deep" still had not terminated, and so a demon was planted to close the concept when "deep" finished. Thus, the picture concept is now closed and the parse complete.

```
EVAL: (%SCAN 'CONCEPT1)

(*DESCRIP* (SIZE-DIMENSION DEPTH) WORD2)
(*DESCRIP* (SIZE LARGE) WORD2)
(*DESCRIP* (VOLUME-TYPE HOLE-IN-GROUND) WORD3)
(*DESCRIP* (CLASS VOLUME) WORD3)
(*DESCRIP* DETERMINATE WORD1)
(*CONCEPT-CLASS* VOLUME)
(*CONCEPT-TYPE* PICTURE)

VALUE:    CONCEPT1
```

As the Word Expert Parser analyzed the input phrase, it created and augmented a data repository of conceptual information. This "concept bin" contains description of the meaning content of the phrase as well as various pieces of control state data. The concept bin for "the deep pit" is called CONCEPT1 and contains several descriptors which together describe a large volume of air in the ground.

---

*Execution traces of the Word Expert Parser are available from the authors. All examples referred to in this paper as well as later examples of full sentence parses are obtainable on request.

4. Summary and Conclusions

We have mapped out a theory of organization and control for a meaning-based language understanding system. In this theory words, rather than rules, are the units of knowledge, and assume the form of procedural entities which execute as generator-like coroutines. Parsing a sentence in context demands a control environment in which these experts can ask questions of each other, forward hints and suggestions to each other, and suspend. Our theory is a cognitive theory of both language representation and parser control. It has stemmed from feelings about the fundamental inadequacies of rule-based theories.

In addition to the advantages already discussed, the word expert approach enjoys a number of other pragmatic and theoretical advantages. By way of conclusion, we enumerate what we feel are the important theoretical and practical characteristics of the theory.

1. It allows for the modular growth of language knowledge in the implemented model. Unlike a rule-based system (where obscure interactions and dependencies among seemingly unrelated rules can occur), each word expert is a relatively perspicuous, central aggregate of knowledge about one easily identified unit of language knowledge, i.e., the word. One can look at that structure and more easily say whether or not it takes any given usage into account. If it does not, it is clearer where knowledge about that new usage should be grafted in.
2. It encourages a healthy type of redundancy in the codification of language knowledge. When writing a word expert, one's goal is to create a stand-alone agent able to function in a wide variety of run-time contexts. We have noticed that this nearly always leads to bi-directional handshaking when two experts interact; they come to some mutual agreement because they find common ground. This type of redundancy is healthy, since it is then less likely that the shortcomings of one expert will block the comprehension of the sentence or concept in which that expert occurs.
3. It suggests some approaches to language acquisition. Since each word expert reflects the state of knowledge about a given word, when new usages of the word are perceived, rather than writing absolute rules to describe the new context, it is possible to grow a new branch within the word expert. This branch need only capture one relative difference between the existing usages and the new usage, an intuitively simpler and safer operation than generating an entirely new rule. Since the scope of the change is intuitively smaller, it is less likely to interfere with other experts in the system.
4. It encourages the codification of idiosyncratic uses of language by providing uniform data structures as focal points for that diverse knowledge. If, for example, there is an esoteric sense of the word "take", one need only sprout a branch of the "take" expert's decision logic to include it. Because of the branching logic organization of the experts, little overhead is incurred by adding special cases. We have felt all along that an organization which encourages knowledge about individual words to grow to large proportions without degrading the efficiency of the system at large is highly desirable.
5. It adapts well to largeness. Even if there are 100,000 word experts, each of which on the average requires 1000 words of computer memory, actual memory space required to parse any given sentence will be small. This is because the parser requires only the experts involved in the sentence at hand to be in core. This is a modest requirement when compared to large rule systems where all the rules must be kept in core at once (for efficiency), or where potentially complex paging systems must be devised to interact with a rule system on mass storage. While this is strictly an engineering issue, it has immediate consequences on today's computers!
6. It forces the parallel development of cognitively plausible theories of sequential, coroutine-like process models of humans. If the assumption about word (rather than rule) primacy in humans is correct, we stand a chance of making reasonable conjectures about flow of control in a human language understander. That is, some fairly crisp pictures of word expert control follow directly from the structure of the word experts themselves. As we discover how to control the experts in a LISP model, we may also be discovering how humans think when comprehending language.

Although much remains to be worked out, we find ourselves increasingly convinced of the appropriateness of the word expert approach. In the near future, we hope to be able to demonstrate the system at work on complete sentences, and hope to provide convincing evidence that large experts with many word usage alternatives are practical to develop and coordinate.

ACKNOWLEDGEMENTS

The authors would like to thank the following people for interesting discussions that helped refine the ideas presented in this paper: Phil Agre, Milt Grinberg, Phil London, Jim Reggia, and Rich Wood. In addition, Steve Small wishes to thank Professor James Meehan of the University of California at Irvine and Professor Robert Simmons of the University of Texas at Austin for comments on the research proposal which led to the parser implementation discussed here.

REFERENCES

[1] Colby, K., Artificial Paranoia, Pergamon Press, 1975.

[2] Riesbeck, C., Computational Understanding: Analysis of Sentences and Context, AI-Memo 238, Stanford University, 1974.

[3] Riesbeck, C. and R. Schank, Comprehension by Computer: Expectation-based Analysis of Sentences in Context, Research Report 78, Yale University, 1976.

[4] Wilks, Y., Preference Semantics, AI-Memo 206, Stanford University, 1973.

[5] Wilks, Y., Making Preferences More Active, AI-Report 32, University of Edinburgh, 1977.

[6] Small, S., Conceptual Language Analysis for Story Comprehension, Technical Report 663, University of Maryland, 1978.

[7] Rieger, C., GRIND-1: First Report on the Magic Grinder Story Comprehension Project, Discourse Processes, vol. 1, no. 3, 1978.

[8] Rieger, C., Five Aspects of a Full Scale Story Comprehension Model, Associative Networks -- The Representation and Use of Knowledge in Computers, Findler (ed.), Academic Press, 1979.

[9] Rieger, C., Viewing Parsing as Word Sense Discrimination, A Survey of Linguistic Science, Dingwall (ed.), Greylock Pub., 1977.

[10] Adams, M. and A. Collins, A Schema-Theoretic View of Reading, Technical Report 32, Center for the Study of Reading, 1977.

[11] Lakoff, G., Some Remarks on AI and Linguistics, Cognitive Science, vol. 2, no. 3, 1978.

[12] Rieger, C., Spontaneous Computation in Cognitive Models, Cognitive Science, vol. 1, no. 3, 1977.

[13] McDermott, D. and G. Sussman, The Conniver Reference Manual, AI-Memo 259a, Massachusetts Institute of Technology, 1974.

[14] Schank, R., Conceptual Dependency: A Theory of Natural Language Understanding, Cognitive Psychology, vol. 3, no. 4, 1972.

[15] Bobrow, D. and T. Winograd, An Overview of KRL, A Knowledge Representation Language, Cognitive Science, vol. 1, no. 1, 1977.

[16] Small, S., Word Expert Parsing, Proceedings of the 17th Annual Meeting of the Association for Computational Linguistics, 1979.

[17] Lisp Machine Group, LISP Machine Progress Report, AI-Memo 444, Massachusetts Institute of Technology, 1977.

[18] Grosz, B., The Representation and Use of Focus in Dialog Understanding, University of California at Berkeley, 1977.

[19] London, P., Dependency Networks as a Representation for Modeling in General Problem Solvers, Technical Report 698, University of Maryland, 1978.

COREFERENCE IN A FRAME DATABASE*

Steve Rosenberg
Lawrence Berkeley Laboratory
University of California
Berkeley, CA 94707

Bruce Roberts
Artificial Intelligence Laboratory
Massachusetts Institute of Technology
545 Technology Square
Cambridge, MA 02139

This paper analyzes coreference within a frame-based semantic system. We discuss mechanisms for determining whether a new piece of knowledge (expressed as a frame) is actually a previously known referent. We propose frame database heuristics that allow new knowledge to be uniquely disambiguated for coreference so that concepts initially represented in many forms can be assimilated to those parts of the database that express the same knowledge, though perhaps in a different form. We hypothesize that these coreference mechanisms can be used by a text processing module whose control structure makes use of the organization of the text to reduce the combinatorial explosion of coreference searches in a database.

1. Introduction

We will present in this paper a computational model of coreference. We hypothesize that reference in text makes use of an underlying, modality-independent coreference module. When we understand a piece of text, we translate the individual sentences into some formal linguistic representation such as an annotated surface structure [2] with associated case information. This linguistic representation can in turn be translated into a "deep structure" consisting of (a set of) partially instantiated frames. These candidate frames will be the formal input to our reference mechanisms, whose output will consist of target frames located in the database, which are coreferential with the candidate frame. Thus frames represent the formal semantic objects on which our reference mechanisms operate. An example of transforming text into an internal frame representation is the PAL system [6,8]. PAL takes English input from the domain of office scheduling and maps this first into an annotated surface structure and from this into FRL. FRL will be briefly described in Section 2. It serves as our formalism for representing meaning as frames.

The translation from English language text into a formal semantic structure is independent of the coreference module, which operates on the frames and not on the the text input. By viewing text processing in this light, we transform the problem of intersentence reference into the more tractable problem of how, given (a) some semantic representation, which we will formally specify in FRL, and (b) some new piece of knowledge, which can also be represented in FRL, we can determine if any frames in (a) are coreferential with those in (b). Thus reference in text processing is a special case of the general problem of determining coreference in memory. FRL in fact provides a general formalism for representing knowledge gained from several sources, not just linguistic. Each mode of input may be structured so as to support reference mechanisms that are peculiar to the mode. Language, for example, contains a number of special reference mechanisms that make use of such particularly linguistic evidence as pronominal reference. However, since information once translated into FRL is modality independent, we propose that a modality independent coreference module supports these more specific reference mechanisms.

A coreference module is necessary in large databases where knowledge is constantly being accessed, added and removed. There is a danger that new knowledge will actually be identical to, or closely related to, what is already known, but that this relation will not be perceived. In fact, the size of the database is less critical than the range of allowable descriptions of the data. If Fahlman [3] is right, then implementing search mechanisms in a hierarchically organized database will be efficient regardless of its size. But even in a database containing only a few facts, one would like to be able to refer to them in a variety of ways.

2. Knowledge Representation

Roberts and Goldstein [7] have developed a working frame system that forms the basis for our knowledge representation. Their Frame Representation Language has been used successfully to represent knowledge from a variety of domains: office scheduling [4], the wheat commodities market [9], places and travel [5]. FRL extends the traditional characterization of properties as attribute/value pairs to allow comments (meta-knowledge), abstractions, defaults, constraints and attached procedures. A frame is a named collection of slots and forms the semantic definition of a concept. A slot has an arbitrary number of user- and system-defined facets. In addition to the Value facet, useful system defined facets are: Default, which specifies a default value;

*This report describes research done by both authors at the Artificial Intelligence Laboratory of the Massachusetts Institute of Technology. It was supported in part by the Advanced Research Projects Agency of the Department of Defense under Office of Naval Research contract N00014-75-C-0643.

Require, which specifies procedural constraints on the values for that slot; If-Needed, which specifies procedures that compute a value for the slot; and If-Added and If-Removed, which specify actions to be taken when a value is modified.

FRL allows concepts (represented as frames) to be arranged in an inheritance hierarchy. The value of the AKO slot (meaning "is a kind of") is a generic frame of which the current frame is a specialized INSTANCE. Thus the frame system forms a tree structure. Generic knowledge is stored higher up in the hierarchy and shared by frames lower down; specialized frames specify new distinguishing characteristics. Generic knowledge, including all attached procedures, is inherited automatically. For instance, in Fig. 1, the frame Appointment-72 is AKO Appointment. This means that the requirement on the Participants slot of the Appointment frame applies to the Appointment-72 frame, although it is not specified explicitly in the description of that frame. The requirement states that Appointment can have (by definition) only two Participants. It is a procedure that evaluates whether or not the restriction is satisfied. Appointment-72 also has values for the various slots that form the definition of an appointment.

```
MEETING
  AKO            -VALUE- MEETING
  CLASSIFICATION -VALUE- GENERIC
  INSTANCE       -VALUE- APPOINTMENT, PARTY, CLASS
  PARTICIPANTS   -REQUIRE- (?? (AKO -VALUE- PERSON))
  PLACE          -REQUIRE- (?? (AKO -VALUE- PLACE))
  TIME           -REQUIRE- (?? (AKO -VALUE- TIME))
  SELF           -MATCH- (MATCHSLOTS PARTICIPANTS PLACE TIME)

APPOINTMENT
  AKO            -VALUE- MEETING
  CLASSIFICATION -VALUE- GENERIC
  INSTANCE       -VALUE- APPOINTMENT-66, APPOINTMENT-72
  PARTICIPANTS   -REQUIRE- (= (NUMBER !PARTICIPANTS) 2)

APPOINTMENT-66
  AKO            -VALUE- APPOINTMENT
  CLASSIFICATION -VALUE- INDIVIDUAL
  PARTICIPANTS   -VALUE- MARY, JOHN
  PLACE          -VALUE- OFFICE-75        ;John's office
  TIME           -VALUE- 11:45AM

APPOINTMENT-72
  AKO            -VALUE- APPOINTMENT
  CLASSIFICATION -VALUE- INDIVIDUAL
  PARTICIPANTS   -VALUE- BILL, JOHN
  PLACE          -VALUE- OFFICE-75        ;John's office
  TIME           -VALUE- 1:30PM
```

Fig. 1 -- Examples from the Frame Database.

3. An example of reference

The following scenario depicts a hypothetical dialogue between a person and a scheduling program. *Italics* indicate the person's requests, the normal font indicates the scheduler's response.

(S1) *What is the schedule for this afternoon?*
(S2) There is a meeting at 3 in Fred's office.

(S3) *Who will be there?*
(S4) You, Bill, and the Marketing people.

(S5) *When is my first meeting today?*
(S6) An appointment at 11:45, with Mary.

(S7) *Change the place of that sales meeting to be my office.*
(S8) OK.

(S9) *What will be discussed?*
(S10) The report on the recent advertising error.

(S11) *What was the report's conclusion?*
(S12) The incident was not considered harmful.

We will ignore the sophisticated language processing this scenario implies, and focus on the forms of reference visible in this passage.

3.1 Name Reference

A concept can be directly referenced through its names. Some names used in this scenario were: Fred, Bill, office, and Marketing people. Names in text reference the frame if it already exists in the active data base, or else cause retrieval of the generic frame and the addition of an instance of it to the database for the scenario. Suppose, after reading a sentence with "Bill" as its topic, we then are given a sentence containing "Marketing V.P.". Presumably this also is another name for the same frame (if this is Bill's job title). There are other names that can be used as unique designants of the frame, whose use results in a reference to the "Bill" frame if a previous use of a name has added it to the database. Each frame must have an associated list of allowable names which directly access it.

Names often serve as a shorthand for other forms of reference. They summarize the results of more complex reference processes, eliminating needless duplication of effort when the same reference reoccurs. Many of these names are widely used in general discourse ("O.P.E.C.", for example). Other names, however, are unique only within a specified context. The name therefore must be contextually bound. For instance, there are other vice presidents of marketing. Ambiguities among global names can only be resolved by recourse to contextual information. Names sometimes contain descriptors that can be used to distinguish among several possible frames (e.g., "this month's report" distinguishes a particular Report frame). These modifiers often require linguistic solutions (e.g., "this" versus "that").

3.2 Contextual Reference

Contextual reference is the use of a descriptive term in a context where it functions as a reference. In the scenario, the use of the phrase "The incident" in (S12) is an unambiguous reference to the "advertising error" of (S10). In the context of the discourse, only the "advertising error" is an incident. Other contexts might result in the phrase having a different referent. Contextual reference involves the use of a general term in a context where its referent can be uniquely disambiguated. Repeated use of a particular contextual referent in a text causes it to become a local name. After its initial introduction, "incident" would refer to the "advertising error" throughout the scenario. If "incident" itself had names, these would also function as local referents to "advertising error".

Contextual reference is reference by description, where the description is contextually bound. Consequently, in determining these referents we will need two things: a search space that defines the local context, and a description. We shall see that using a hierarchical semantic system allows us to generate both of these from the referent. In contextual reference, the search space can grow very large, since such referents may not lie in the direct heritage branch of their referents. In a descriptively rich system it is possible to describe a complicated concept, object, or event in many ways. For instance, fighting in the Middle East could be described as "an international incident", "a border clash", "a skirmish", and so on. Or, consider a "forecast". Almost anything can be a forecast, since all that is required is that it not yet have occurred. However, we do not wish to make everything inherit from the Forecast frame. There may be no unique semantic arrangement in terms of a tree hierarchy, such that all terms are exactly superior to just those terms they dominate. Achieving this would require a tangled hierarchy; one in which a frame could be AKO several other frames.

3.3 Generic Reference

Generic reference is the use of names that have a direct relation to the referent in the heritage structure. Two frames may be coreferential if the heritage path of one entirely contains the heritage path of the other. If one frame matches another frame's heritage path, but descends deeper into the frame tree, we have a possible generic reference. There exists along the AKO link a direct path in the frame tree between these two terms. A reference to a frame is also a potential reference to any frames which inherit from it. The reverse is equally true. A daughter frame can be a reference to superior frames in its heritage path. This follows from the fact that on the one hand, the more generic concept subsumes the more specific one, while on the other hand, the more specific concept contains all the semantic properties of the more generic concept. In (S6) of the scenario, appointment functions as a generic reference to the meeting of (S5). Fig. 2 shows the hierarchical organization of meetings, appointments and other activities in our scenario. Generic links can be found by determining if the heritage path for a new frame contains any other new instances, and then matching the reference to the candidate frames.

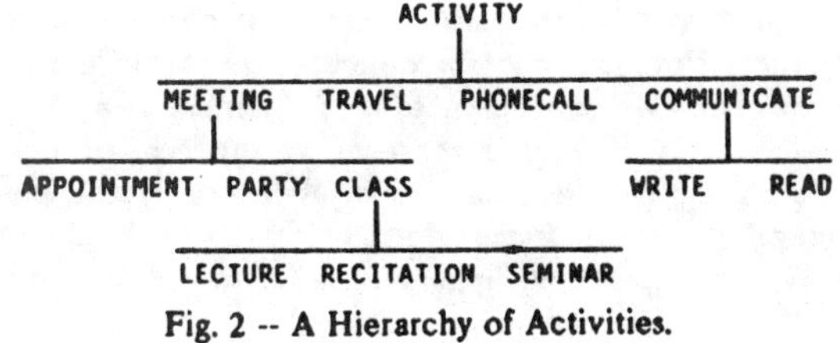

Fig. 2 -- A Hierarchy of Activities.

3.4 Frame Reference

Frame reference is a function of the empty slots of a frame. The sentences (S2) and (S3) can be linked through the realization that the meeting in (S2) has an unspecified slot for participants. (S3) specifies this slot in its request for information, eliciting the value of this slot in the reply (S4). Frame reference inherently involves forward expectations. Any new item in the database might potentially be a part of any empty slot in an existing frame. In a database of any size, checking all these empty slots for each new item is prohibitively expensive. Instead we think of empty slots generating expectations which search for an instantiation among new items. Thus frame reference involves the issue of control, as well as a matching problem. Later on in Section 5 we will discuss one mechanism, Sentinels, for controlling matching in FRL. Sentinals require a description of the referent, and this will involve the same matching processes as the other reference processes. They differ only in when the match is carried out.

4. Reference mechanisms in FRL

We will now refine our discussion of reference by developing a formalism within which we can extract the common elements and underlying mechanisms involved in these reference processes. Consider a general model for matching two frames. Matching a reference (candidate frame) to a referent (target frame) requires three things: (a) a search space; (b) a matcher that is capable of using (c) a candidate frame description that can be matched against frames in the search space to produce a a set of target frames.

4.1 Specifying a search space

Consider first how two frames can be related within FRL. Any two frames will share a common heritage path in the frame tree descending from the topmost frame, the THING frame, which will branch at some daughter frame. For instance, in Fig. 2, both Appointment and Party inherit from Meeting. This branching node, together with the semantic features inherited from its father frames (such as Activity), defines the minimum semantic concept which includes both frames. It contains the intersection of semantic features common to any frame in one branch with any frame in the other branch of the heritage tree. Frames in the branching portions define semantic characteristics of the heritage path which are not common to both frames through additional slots on the frames themselves.

A search space for reference in FRL consists of a piece of the heritage tree which contains both referent and reference. We can specify this space by giving a node in this heritage tree which we know dominates both the referent and the reference. Call it a Location. Only frames below this node need be considered by the matcher.

The minimum search space is defined by the lowest node on the frame tree from which both frames inherit. If the reference and referent are on different branches, then the frame at which these two branches diverge defines the minimum search space. Any frame lower down in the tree will exclude one or the other frame, while frames higher up will include more irrelevent frames. If the reference and referent are on the same branch, the superior frame defines the minimum search space. As we go up the heritage tree from the minimum search space, each new superior node will dominate more branches, until we arrive at the topmost node, the Thing frame. This defines the maximum search space; namely, the entire frame system.

We continue now with the overview of our model. Each reference is turned into a pattern to be used by the matcher. The pattern contains two kinds of information: a Location, specified as a frame name, that the matcher uses to define a search space; and a Description, specified as a pattern frame, that the matcher compares to frames in the search space.

4.2 Constructing the description

A matching process comprises two parts: search and compare. The search space is defined by the Location, and searching is restricted to the branches descending from this node. A pattern is a frame-like description that can be compared against frames in the search space. It is a prototype of what the target frame looks like, containing information to delimit the search space as well as information about how to compare the frame with possible candidates. The pattern construction process differs slightly from one type of reference to another, but the pattern itself, once complete, is a unifying thread. It makes possible the use of a single general purpose matcher. The following two operations, common to all forms of reference, must be done to construct an initial partial pattern.

4.2.1 Collect requirements

Each of the slots in the reference frame has a counterpart in the partial pattern. Defining characteristics for each slot of the pattern are gathered by inheriting the information in the slot's REQUIRE facet from each frame along the AKO branch of the reference frame. In addition, since FRL allows slot description frames that describe the role played by a particular slot in a frame, further requirements for individual slots of the pattern may be discovered by inspecting any slot description frame for that slot. Global requirements, applicable to the frame as a whole, reside on a special SELF slot of the pattern and are gathered from the reference frame just like the requirement on any other slot.

Requirements are either procedures to be applied to the value in the target frame or, in the case that the value itself is another frame, sub-patterns to be matched against the slots of the value. A typical requirement might check that the value is one of a set of permissible types, for example. Not all requirements are relevant to a particular match. Furthermore it is possible for specialized matching constraints to coexist in the same frame with requirements used for other purposes. Appropriate requirements are selected using identifying comments attached to each one.

4.2.2 Assign slot and frame matching procedures

A corresponding process of collection and selection assigns a matching procedure to the frame pattern and its slots. These procedures occupy the MATCH facet of the reference frame, and will bear the local responsibility for determining whether the pattern matches a target frame. Again, the SELF slot supplies global knowledge; in this case, the procedure that controls the actual comparison between the pattern and a target frame. Explicit matching procedures for the frame provide the flexibility to vary the "weight" given to various slots and conditionally alter the course of the match. Matching knowledge is thus distributed throughout the frame hierarchy like other forms of procedural attachment in FRL.

Local matching procedures allow a pattern to specify for a particular match the actual criteria under which the match will succeed. Not all slots are relevant in effecting a match. Some non-essential slots may be safely ignored. The slot description frames already mentioned can supply other information useful to the matching process, since they include knowledge about the relation represented by the slot; for example, that it is transitive, or that it has an inverse? The kinds of matches that occur in practice will be discussed in a later section.

The details of the pattern construction process differ with the type of reference.

Generic Reference: Either a GENERIC or a INDIVIDUAL frame is specified, and this frame becomes the pattern with the addition of matching information to specify the direction of the match, from value to requirement (INDIVIDUAL), or from requirement to value (GENERIC).

Frame Reference: The matching procedures specify that the local and global requirements from only the unfilled slots are compared against the pattern.

Contextual Reference: The input is a prototype from the database. It has all the characteristics of a regular frame except that it is not a part of the AKO hierarchy.

Name Reference: The pattern is trivial -- a frame with the name used, or one looked up in the paraphrase list.

Since all referents are turned into a pattern, only one matcher is needed to handle all forms of reference. The different behavioral types of reference, which can be specified in FRL, can now be seen to really be underlying variations on a pattern containing two parts: a Location, specified in terms of a node on the frame tree; and a Description, specified as a frame pattern.

4.3 Matching frames

Two frames may share all semantic features in common, expressed by identical slots, but contain different values for those slots. They are then different instances of a generic frame. We shall call this potential difference between two instances of a generic frame a pragmatic difference. Since procedural attachments are defined on the generic frame's slots, these will be held in common also. For example, the Appointment-72 and Appointment-66 frames are both instances of the generic Appointment frame. Both the Appointment-66 and Appointment-72 frames have a slot for participants, and inherit the same REQUIRE facet of this slot. However the value for this semantic feature will differ in the two instances; the two participants in the Appointment-66 frame are Mary and John, while the participants in the Appointment-72 frame are Bill and John. This pragmatic difference allows two instances to not be coreferential.

Matches between a reference and target frames in the search space will always have a semantic and pragmatic component. The semantic constraints can conflict. The two frames might not have identical semantic features (i.e. slots). It is not necessary for a successful match for both frames to have identical slots. In Generic Reference one set of slots subsumes the other. The inherent semantic relationship between generic referents means that we need only compare the common slots. We can assume the extra slots on one frame do not cause any semantic conflicts.

Contextual reference involves two frames that share some slots, but can each contain slots not on the other frame. It is possible that these differences exclude coreference. For instance, a Tree and a Dog each have unique slots when compared to each other, and are not coreferential. If a Dog has a slot for ambulation, whereas a Tree is explicitly marked as stationary, these two slots are mutually exclusive. (We exclude the case of conflicting slot values, as in a breathing slot marked "yes" for Dog, but "photosynthesis" for Tree.) By comparing the non-equivalent slots on different branches for mutual exclusion, the matcher can determine if frames on one branch are able in principle to function as contextual referents. However, it is also true that two frames whose slots form a partial set intersection can be coreferential. Take the case of a Father frame, which is AKO Person, and a Marketing V.P. frame which also is AKO Person. Clearly Fathers and Marketing V.P.s can each have properties that the other doesn't. Yet Fathers and Marketing V.P.s can be coreferential. Even a partial match requires that we are able to determine none of the slots on the Marketing V.P. frame conflict with those on the Father frame. In this case, the reference provides a best match, though not necessarily a complete match.

If there is no semantic conflict, the two frames are potentially coreferential. A match of the pragmatic features will determine this. (Note that by using the notion of a search space, very few inappropriate semantic matches need be entertained. We should seldom get in the position of considering whether dogs are references to trees, for example, since they do not bear a close relation in the frame tree.) This pragmatic match will compare values for the slots which are held in common. These values may be identical; they may differ, but be in slots which take a set of values; or they may conflict. If the slot accepts a set of values, and the values don't match, but meet the requirements of the slot, we may still be willing to consider it a match. Similarly, if the values conflict, but are ephemeral, like hair color, we may not require them to be identical unless there are multiple candidates to be discriminated among. One frame might have a slot value, while the other has none, but does have requirements; one value may be a subset of the other value. If a slot on one frame has a value, but doesn't on the other, this value must be consistent with those that the value-less slot can take. New values for uninstantiated slots may trigger associated procedures that evaluate the potential new value.

The matcher makes use of procedural knowledge associated with frames since it does not itself contain the knowledge. Thus, (a) the matcher must know how to use this knowledge, which is not explicitly put in for matching (it is there for semantic definition), and (b) the matcher must make use of the fact that knowledge is distributed in the frame hierarchy and can be collected appropriately in the pattern. Not every slot needs its matching requirements explicitly stated if it can be inherited efficiently. The requirements for the particular slots will determine the outcome, and will also contain knowledge about how they can be relaxed, as in the case of values which change over time. Consequently there will be a degree of matching determined by the assigned value matching procedures. This allows us to formalize the notion of a good match as being a continuum.

5. Controlling the Matcher

The system we have been proposing is an "ideal" system in that it ignores the time dimension. Both reference and referent exist at the same time. However, information, as in the scenario, is understood over time. Reference may be forward or backward. A reference may be added at some future time, as well as already existing in the database. Indeed, there is no guarantee that the reference will ever occur! If for each new item in the database we always check to see if it is a reference, we will be making many useless searches. Therefore deciding when to compute reference is an important process. There is one class of reference where this choice can be reasonably determined. Frames will often have empty slots, and many of these slots are filled in by subsequent information.

To implement Frame Reference, we have chosen an approach that treats the empty slots of a frame as expectations. In practice, the decision to use forward expectations must take into account the extra computational burden this would place on the system. Maintaining forward expectations is useful to the extent that new information can be uniquely recognized by a set of special demons [1] called Sentinels created for the purpose. Sentinels were developed with James Stansfield by one of the authors (Steve Rosenberg). If all new frames are matched against all empty slots, a goal driven strategy of using expectations is equivalent to a data driven one of matching each new input against empty slots. However, by using the information available in the frame tree, we can reduce the number of matches each expectation requires, combining the best aspects of a goal driven and data driven approach in the notion of Sentinels.

Many demons in a database can slow processing, since the traditional notion of demons does not make use of the semantic organization inherent in frame based hierarchical system. Thus we introduce the concept of instance-driven demons. Consider a demon attached to the instance slot of a particular frame; e.g., the Instance slot of Meeting. Whenever a new instance occurs that inherits from Meeting, the demon matches its pattern against that new frame. Thus, if the following sentence occurs:

(S13) *There is another meeting.*

another instance of Meeting is created, triggering this demon. Other new frames that do not inherit from Meeting (e.g., a new instance of Travel) do not trigger the demon. Such a demon will match against only a selected subset of new input. By choosing the appropriate frame to attach such demons to we insure that they match against only likely candidates with precise semantic relations to the frame.

Sentinels are initially goal-driven, in that they are created as active expectations. However, they draw on the information available about frames that car satisfy the expectation to place data driven triggers, called sensors, in appropriate places in the frame tree. These sensors are activated by only a small subset of the input, that subset with the highest likelihood of fulfilling the expectation. Whenever a sentinel is triggered, through the addition of a new instance that meets the sensor's requirements, it evaluates this triggering value, and determines if it fits the expectation. If so it adds the new instance as the value of the appropriate slot and frame. Once this is done the sentinel will erase itself and its sensors. Thus the system will not be cluttered with unneeded procedures that fire inappropriately. Sentinels are a way to create and manage demons in an organized semantic system. Two of their features are a limited life span, and the ability to move sensors around in response to a condition that is computationally determined as it develops. A sentinel can have several sensors which report to it. The sentinel is satisfied when some arbitrary logical or temporal conjunction of its sensors succeed. A sentinel has the capacity to evaluate conditional relations among its sensors, and even to remove current sensors and place new ones as a response to these conditional constraints.

In order for sentinels to efficiently encode expectations, they must be given a Location. New instance values inherit procedural attachments from up the tree. Thus a sensor on the Instance slot of the Thing frame would be triggered by any new instance added to the system. This is equivalent to testing every new instance against every expectation, exactly the case we wished to avoid by making use of the organization of the semantic network! On the other hand, if we do not know the precise form of the expectation, we would like to place the sensor at a location in the hierarchy where it is sure to be triggered by the right value, although there may be some false alarms. Thus the use of the frame hierarchy lets us place sensors where they will be triggered by semantic classes of items that are sure to contain the target items. If the description of the expectation is vague, we will need to accept more false alarms, but in any case we can use the organized hierarchy to make use of descriptions so that the expectations are optimally placed. In sparse databases such sentinels act as more efficient demon implementations. In rich databases, with much inferencing, they allow us to suspend processing at many places, since such processing will only be reactivated in highly appropriate circumstances.

Frame Reference uses the slot name and requirements to generate a pattern which defines a lowest possible node in the frame tree from which an instantiating value must inherit. For example, the Participants slot of a Sales-Meeting frame might inherit a requirement, in the form of a sub-pattern specification, from Meeting that says "AKO employee"; the slot itself has the additional requirement "includes Marketing-people". The sentinel on the instance slot of this indicated frame will examine each new token inheriting from this employee frame, and finally fulfill the expectation when at least two proper instances of employees have occured, one of which also has a job slot value which is AKO Marketing-people.

6. Conclusions

We propose a model of coreference for frame databases. We discuss coreference from the behavioral standpoint in terms of the FRL formalism, and present a single elegant mechanism for handling all the coreference forms discussed. This mechanism consists of a pattern and a search space, both generated from the reference. The pattern is matched to items in the search space to generate target references. We briefly explore the issues involved in controlling such a reference module, principally through the use of Sentinels.

Once input has been translated into a frame representation, the coreference problem becomes independent of the medium in which the information was originally expressed. An intimate connection does exist between the form of the memory and the operation of the reference mechanism. We view text or discourse structure as providing a control mechanism which drives the underlying processes of memory. Thus the use of themes and topics, as well as more specifically linguistic clues, restricts the context for reference so that it works efficiently.

References

[1] Charniak, Eugene "Toward a model of Children's Story Comprehension". MIT AI-TR-266, December 1972.

[2] Chomsky, Noam "Conditions on Rules of Grammar", Linguistic Analysis, 2:303.

[3] Fahlman, Scott E. NETL: A System for Representing and Using Real-world Knowledge. MIT Press, Cambridge, MA, 1979.

[4] Goldstein, Ira and Bruce Roberts "NUDGE, a Knowledge-based Scheduling Program". In Proc. IJCAI-77, Cambridge, MA, August 1977, pp. 257-263.

[5] Jeffery, Mark J. "Representing 'Place' in a Frame System", M.S. Thesis, MIT, 1978.

[6] Marcus, Mitch A Theory of Syntax Recognition in Natural Language. MIT Press, Cambridge, MA, 1979.

[7] Roberts, Bruce and Ira Goldstein "The FRL Manual", MIT AI Memo 409, 1977.

[8] Sidner, Candace "A Progress Report on the Discourse and Reference Components of PAL", MIT AI Memo 468, 1978.

[9] Stanfield, James L. "COMEX: A Support System for a Commodities Expert", MIT AI Memo 423, 1977.

REASONING IN INCOMPLETE DOMAINS

Steven Rosenberg
Information Methodology Research Project
Lawrence Berkeley Laboratory
University of California
Berkeley, California 94720

Most real world domains differ from the micro-worlds traditionally used in A.I. in that they have an incomplete factual database which changes over time. A traditional rule interpreter such as Planner can be extended to construct plausible inferences in these domains by (A) allowing assumptions to be made in applying rules, resulting in simplifications of rules which can be used in an incomplete database; (B) monitoring the antecedents and consequents of a rule so that inferences can be maintained over a changing database.

Many real world databases are:

a. Incomplete, because not all the information needed for an inference is available at a particular time.

b. Unstable, since the particular subset of information available can change fairly rapidly in the real world.

For example, a farmer, in deciding how large a wheat crop to plant, has incomplete information about ultimate wheat price and demand, based on rapidly changing information, such as daily weather reports, weekly crop surveys, and so on.

1. INCOMPLETE DOMAINS

A traditional reasoning program, such as Planner [6], has difficulty dealing with incomplete information. Consider how such a program might make inferences about the price of wheat. We, formulate the problem as follows:

This report describes research done at the Artificial Intelligence Laboratory of the Massachusetts Institute of Technology. Support for the Laboratory's artificial intelligence research is provided in part by the Advanced Research Projects Agency of the Department of Defense under Office of Naval Research contract No. 14-75-C-0643. The author is now with the Information Methodology Research Project, Lawrence Berkeley Laboratory, Berkeley, CA 94720.

(Thgoal (price-increase wheat))

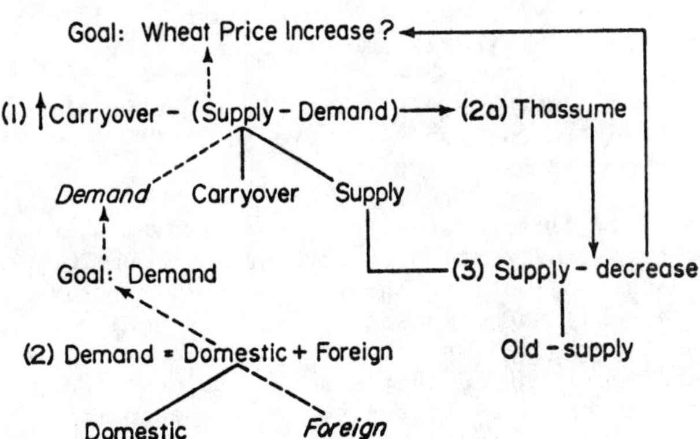

(In the diagrams, italics and a dashed line indicate antecedents which are missing; a solid line indicates an existing antecedent; a solid line and arrow indicate deduced links between rules and assertions; a dashed line and arrow indicate inferences which have failed.)

Thm1 states that to show a price increase for wheat, show that the difference between supply and demand is less this year than last. Suppose that no assertions for wheat demand exist in the database. In this case, Thm1 would fail, since one of its antecedents is missing. For such cases, Planner provides a strategy. If an assertion is not in the database, Planner will try and prove it. Thm2 states that to deduce demand for a commodity, find the foreign and domestic demand for this commodity, and add these together. We will assume no assertion for foreign demand exists. Thus Thm2 will fail. If there are no other methods for proving the missing assertion, the inference process will fail.

The inference attempt failed not necessarily because it was wrong, but because not enough information exists to make correct inferences. By making assumptions about missing information in such cases we can often succeed by using a simpler rule. For example, a farmer might reason that as long as the supply of wheat is decreasing, it will be worthwhile to plant more regardless of demand. Thus, if the full set of assertions concerning supply, demand and carry-over are unavailable, we might try to prove that supply has decreased. By substituting goals that require only a subset of the assertions that the original theorem required, we develop a notion of rule simplification.

The knowledge of which other rules can be used as simplifications, and under what circumstances, must be represented. A rule interpreter can make use of this metaknowledge [1] to substitute simpler theorems for a rule which fails. The appropriate place to specify this metaknowledge is in a separate class of theorems. e.g.

```
(Thassume Thm2A (X) (Supply-&-demand ?X)
    (Thgoal (supply-decrease ?X))
    (Thcaveat (Default)))
```

This new class of theorems, such as Thm2A, contains information concerning simplifications and assumptions. A Thassumption will specify A) a goal; theorems satisfying this goal can function as a simplification; B) the assumptions involved in using that simplification. These are expressed as a caveat. If the assumption being made is that the missing antecedents can be ignored, the caveat will contain a Default.

Using a simplification always reduces the plausibility of the reasoning. By ignoring the demand for wheat, a farmer is willing to assume that if demand changes, it will not change in a direction or quantity which would invalidate his reasoning. By making explicit this notion of assumptions, we can extend the list of options available. For example, we can encode constraints on our use of assumptions through the caveats.

Returning to our example, after Thm2 fails, simplifications will be considered, and Thm2A (proving a decrease in wheat supply) found. Thm2A first tries to satisfy the goal (Thgoal (Supply-decrease ?X)). Thm3 can be used to prove this. Thm3 states that to show a decrease in supply, show that last year's supply is greater than current supply. If current supply and old-supply are known, Thm3 will succeed, and support the hypothesis of higher wheat prices.

2. UNSTABLE DOMAINS

As the database changes, our goals may remain relatively stable. Support for an hypothesis is conditional on the assertions available at the time it was first considered (i.e., the inferences which were possible at that time). However in many deductive systems, once deductions are made from a set of assertions, no effort is made to insure that while the results of those deductions are used, the assertions still hold true. Generally, the user does not expect the database to change so as to invalidate prior inferences.

We can extend our concept of rule interpretation by making the maintenance of rule instances a function of their interpretation. We implement this by giving each active rule the autonomy to respond to changes in its environment. As each rule is applied, an associated Sentinel is created. The Sentinel knows how to respond to changes in that rule's antecedents or consequents. The result is the maintenance of hypotheses through a method of local autonomy. A rule instance must be continuously enabled while it is used in support of some hypothesis.

A Sentinel associated with a rule instance will place sensors in the database. A sensor is a demon which responds to changes in the pattern that triggers it, and evaluates whether these changes violate some criterion. If so, the sensor reports to the Sentinel. The Sentinel is satisfied when some arbitrary logical conjunction of its sensors succeed. The Sentinel can then take a variety of actions. The standard ones are to A) erase itself; B) erase the rule instance; C) reinvoke the goal.

Individual rules will succeed or fail as a function of their antecedents. When a successful rule's antecedents change, its sentinel will be triggered. When this happens the sentinel causes the goal the rule was supporting to be re-evaluated. At this point the sentinel can erase itself. (Note: A sentinel causes a goal to be re-evaluated. There is no constraint that the same rule be used again. Another rule may now be the best choice. However, in this example it is assumed that there have been no other changes in the state of the system that would cause another rule to be selected first.)

If a rule's goal is removed, its sentinel will also be triggered. In this case we do not wish to re-evaluate the goal. The sentinel will remove itself and erase the associated rule instance.

Consider how this local association of rule instances with sentinels can give rise to the right global behavior. Suppose that a failed rule now is capable of succeeding, through its missing antecedent being asserted. For instance, the missing foreign demand for wheat can be asserted.

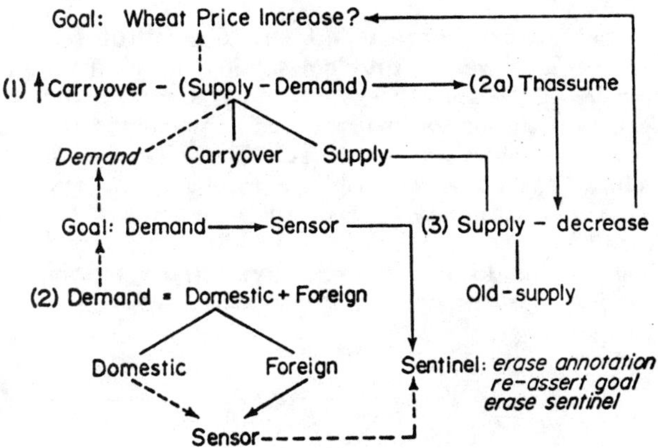

This will trigger the associated sentinel to erase the annotation for this rule instance, reassert the goal as something to be proved, and then to erase itself. This time Thm2 succeeds, resulting in a proof of the missing demand for wheat. This will in turn trigger the sentinel associated with the rule instance of Thm1 for which the missing demand is an antecedent.

This sentinel repeats the actions of the prior sentinel. However, in erasing the annotation, it erases the record of the assumption made. This will trigger the sentinel on Thm3, the simplification. Since the use of a simplification is conditional on another rule failing, the sentinels associated with theorems used as simplifications monitor the annotation recording that failure, so that they will know when the simplification is no longer required. They will then respond to the erasure of this annotation by erasing the annotation for the simplification. Since the formerly missing antecedent for demand has now been inferred, Thm2 succeeds, as does our inference attempt.

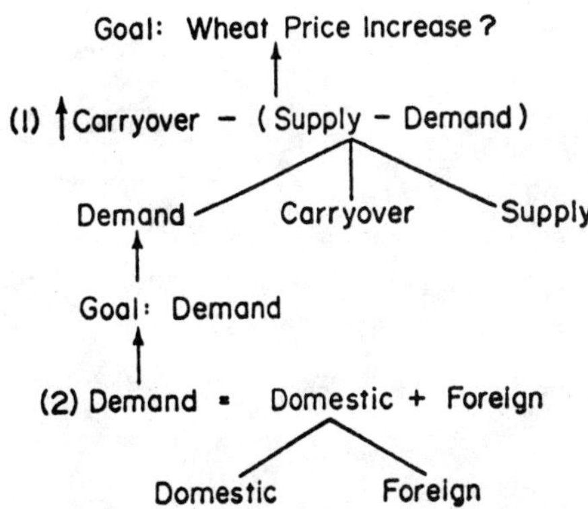

Thus, unneeded rule instances will know when to remove themselves. Through local propagation, the representation responds to changes in the available database. Changes in the database can reinvoke the goal of inferencing, which can then proceed. Doyle [2] has developed a scheme for recording deductive dependencies so that when facts turn out to be incorrect, the entire "context" of dependent facts can be removed from the database. The current approach does not allow explicit manipulation of deductive dependencies, since the changes it is designed to respond to are those imposed on the domain by "outside" changes in the data, and not ones due to deduced inconsistencies. McDonald [3] has contrasted this approach to other methods.

The rule interpretation features of sentinels and simplifications were programmed in FRL (Frame Representation Language) [4].

REFERENCES

[1] Davis, R. and Buchanan, B.G., "Meta-Level Knowledge: Overview and Applications." Proceedings of the 5th International Joint Conference on Artificial Intelligence, Cambridge, Mass., 1977.

[2] Doyle, J., "Truth Maintenance Systems for Problem Solving." MIT Artificial Intelligence Laboratory Technical Report 419, 1977.

[3] McDonald, D., "Story Understanding: the Beginning of a Concensus." MIT-AI Working Paper 168, 1978.

[4] Roberts, B.R. and Goldstein, I.P., "The FRL Manual." MIT-AI Memo 409, 1977.

[5] Sussman, G.J., Winograd, T. and Charniak, E., "Micro-Planner Reference Manual." MIT-AI Memo 203A, 1971.

A SEMANTIC NETWORK OF PRODUCTION RULES

IN A SYSTEM FOR DESCRIBING COMPUTER STRUCTURES

Michael D. Rychener
Carnegie-Mellon University
Department of Computer Science
Schenley Park
Pittsburgh, PA 15213

A novel implementation of the basic mechanisms of a semantic network is presented. This constitutes a merging, in terms of the underlying language architecture, of a powerful problem-solving mechanism, production-rule systems, with a proven representation formalism. Details are presented on the most basic aspects of the network, namely on representing nodes and on mechanisms for their access. Commands for definition, modification, and search-based displays of network information are discussed. The relations of the network are divided into six groups: taxonomic, structural, functional, descriptive, means-ends, and spatial. The importance of uniformly representing methods and network, and the importance of distinguishing temporary from permanent states are discussed. There is sketched a production system position on a number of relevant issues for advanced capabilities. The domain of application is the symbolic description and manipulation of computer structures at the PMS (processor-memory-switch) level. The system will ultimately be used for computer-aided design activities.

1. SYMBOLIC DESCRIPTION AND MANIPULATION AS A TASK FOR AI

1.1. Motivation and research context

One aspect of computer-aided design is the manipulation of symbolic descriptions of physical systems. Problems in this area have been discussed by Eastman [3] and by Sussman [12]. Other AI research has discussed mechanisms that may be applicable to design systems while maintaining a general viewpoint and vocabulary, eg, Rieger's Commonsense Algorithms [9] and Moore's MERLIN [8]. The present research* aims to deal with the following problem areas:

1. Describing the basic system components.
2. Organizing those components into structures.
3. Establishing hierarchies of components and structures ranging from abstract ones to various concrete realizations.
4. Comparing structures and putting them into correspondence with each other (mapping).
5. Analyzing structures and determining effects of changes.
6. Synthesizing structures from elementary components, trying to fulfill functional specifications.
7. Coordinating multiple viewpoints of the same system.
8. Searching the design space.
9. Simulating system behavior symbolically, to ascertain dynamic properties.

An approach to these problem areas would be applicable to a wide range of systems: buildings, software systems, chemical processes, cities, etc. In addition, it could provide a central mechanism for diagnostic, tutorial, explanatory, and theory explication systems.

Computer structures at the processor-memory-switch (PMS) level are the domain of the IPMSL (Instructable PMS Language) system. The basis is that of Bell and Newell [2]. In particular, the following abstract components are considered:

*This research was sponsored by the Defense Advanced Research Projects Agency (DOD), ARPA Order No. 3597, monitored by the Air Force Avionics Laboratory Under Contract F33615-78-C-1551. The views and conclusions contained in this document are those of the authors and should not be interpreted as representing the official policies, either expressed or implied, of the Defense Advanced Research Projects Agency or the US Government.

C	Computer	L	Link
P	Processor	D	Data-operation
M	Memory	N	Network
S	Switch	X	External (non-digital)
K	Controller	T	Transducer
H	Port		

Knudsen's [7] work in the PMS area is a direct predecessor to the present effort, with strong influences from Barbacci and Siewiorek [1].

2. THE IPMSL SYSTEM: BASIC SEMANTIC NET REPRESENTATIONS

IPMSL (Instructable PMS Language) is a set of production rules for building semantic net structures in response to user commands.* IPMSL starts out as a set of "procedural" productions that perform the basic net-building operations. The net itself is composed of "declarative" productions whose contents are the net's facts. There are a few "procedural" productions devoted to constructing the "declarative" ones, on command and also as a result of other processing. Both kinds of productions are interpreted according to the same basic recognize-act cycle. The user sees the information he enters being structured into a semantic network, while underneath, that information is stored as, and manipulated by, rules.

2.1. Underlying problem-solving architecture

The implementation language for IPMSL is the OPS2 [4, 10] architecture, extended for this task by changing its external appearance. The extension is named OPS3RX. The primary capability afforded by OPS3RX is the ability to represent data elements as sets of attribute-value pairs. OPS3RX makes things look much more like "schemas" or "frames", and development of the language will continue in this direction. (In fact, production rules seem to be an ideal way of expressing procedures in a frame-based system.) There are usually about 100 attribute-value sets in Working Memory (WM), each containing about five attribute-value pairs.

Rules are used to implement both the interpreter of the network and the network itself. WM serves both to hold onto various processing goals and to accumulate temporary network structures. A network rule stores the facts of only one node in the network plus pointers to other nodes. When some goal requires the expansion of the net in WM along some direction (eg, in order to search for some piece of information), a subgoal appropriate to going in that direction is formed, resulting in a rule being executed. This causes appropriate structures to be hooked into existing WM structures, both by creating new WM nodes and by using pattern matching to detect appropriate linking locations.

2.2. Basic network design

IPMSL divides its knowledge about computer structures, and about itself, into six subnets, each containing a particular sort of knowledge:

- Structural. Parts, Partof, and Coparts relations. A component of a computer can be considered as a black box, or as an assemblage of known parts. Components are related to each other at the same structural-hierarchy level with the Coparts relation.

- Taxonomic. FSs and FSof relations. "FS" stands for "further specification", as used in the Merlin system [8]. An object is an FS of another if it can be viewed as the other with some additional characteristics (cf "ISA"). More precisely, the set of attributes in the description of the FS is a superset of those that describe the parent, and the values of those attributes may be modifications of the corresponding ones in the parent.

- Descriptive. This category includes various attributes that don't fit elsewhere, eg, cycle time, memory size, and bandwidth. Further classification may occur later.

- Physical. This includes: cabinet size, power supply requirements, cooling requirements, and noise, to name a few.

- Functional. Here are collected properties having to do with how a component functions or behaves within an assembly of other components. Specifications of inputs and outputs are examples (see [6]).

- Means-ends. Relations in this subnet directly correspond to the language for expressing methods (discussed below).

Figure 1 depicts a fragment of a network including three of the subnets (the structural subnet is represented graphically; this picture is manually generated).

The figure suppresses some details about the actual node and link structure; it is intended primarily to be an example of the kinds of information dealt with, and how the six subnets partition them. Note that the division into subnets essentially assigns one set of nodes and interconnects them using six different sets of relations. As will become evident from details below, the implementation actually attaches six subnet nodes to each main node, one for each subnet, and then attaches relations emanating from that node to the appropriate subnet nodes. Relations coming into a node from others in the net all point at the one main node, however (ie, they use only the name of the node).

*An expanded version of this paper is available from the author, under the same title.

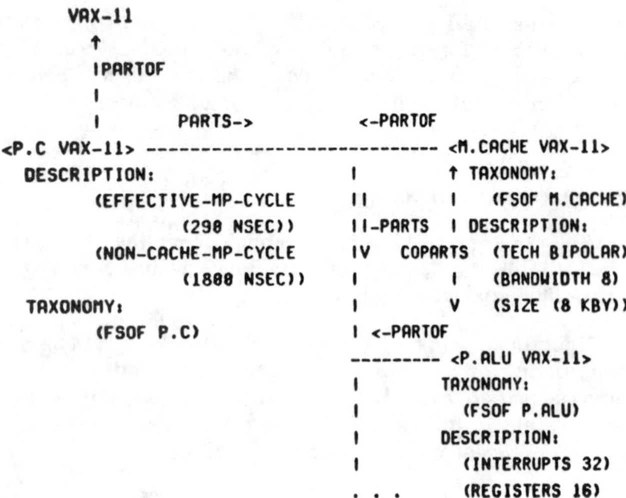

Figure 1: A fragment of a PMS network

Nodes in WM are temporary and consist of temporary symbols with attribute-value pairs attached. There is a main node for each object in the network, and a subnet node for each subnet that is defined and evoked. Figure 2 shows the WM elements for a typical component, with Lisp internal formats translated to a more readable graphic arrangement.

```
S0123                          S0136
  KNOWLEDGE-ABOUT P.C            KNOWLEDGE-ABOUT P.C
  ROLE      MAIN                 NET     S0123
  STRUCTURE S0136                SUBNET STRUCTURE
  TAXONOMY  S0138                PARTS   (D.ALU M.REG)
                                 PARTOF C
                                 STRUCTURE P109
S0138
  KNOWLEDGE-ABOUT P.C
  NET     S0123
  SUBNET TAXONOMY
  FSOF    P
  FSS     (<P.C LSI-11> <P.C VAX-11>)
  TAXONOMY P202
```

Figure 2: WM elements for a typical component

Figure 2 includes a main node and two subnet nodes for the P.c (central processor) component: S0123 is the temporary name for the main node, S0136, for the structure subnet node, and S0138, for the taxonomy subnet node. Each node is identified by the "knowledge-about" attribute - this serves to tie together the three nodes, in such a way that pattern- matching in rules can easily collect together the separate nodes. The main node has two pointers to its subnet nodes, and each subnet node has a pointer back to the main node. The two subnet nodes include, as values of "structure" and "taxonomy" attributes, the names of the productions that built them, so that modifications can be done. (The main node is built by a general production, so it doesn't need such a pointer.)

The production that builds the subnet node for the structure of P.c is the following:

```
P190: IF THE GOAL IS KNOWLEDGE-ABOUT THE STRUCTURE SUBNET OF
        P.C
   AND THERE IS KNOWLEDGE-ABOUT THE NODE OF P.C WITH THE MAIN
        ROLE,
THEN BUILD A KNOWLEDGE-ABOUT P.C NODE WITH SUBNET STRUCTURE,
      WITH NET THE NODE OF P.C WITH THE MAIN ROLE, WITH PARTS
        (D.ALU M.REG), AND WITH PARTOF C,
   AND MARK THE GOAL SATISFIED
   AND ADD TO THE NODE OF P.C WITH THE MAIN ROLE THAT ITS
        STRUCTURE IS THE NEW NODE.
```

The syntax used here is a hand translation from the list-structure version, for readability. Some clumsiness remains, due to the effort to retain as much of the attribute-value flavor of the representation as possible. "Of" and "with" denote a relation between a pair and the object name to which the attributes apply.

All such network-information rules have a similar structure: a simple "if" part that detects the goal to access the knowledge and gets from WM existing information about the main node for the component desired; and a "then" part that constructs the appropriate dynamic node for the particular subnet, along with updating pointers back and forth.

Two general productions are involved in accessing network knowledge, one to build the "main role" node when it is absent from WM, and the other to notice that the knowledge desired is already in WM, and thus to mark the "knowledge-about" goal to be satisfied. These are P98 and P99, respectively, and are displayed below:

```
P98: IF THE GOAL IS KNOWLEDGE-ABOUT SOME SUBNET OF SOME
        OBJECT
   AND THERE IS NO KNOWLEDGE-ABOUT THE NODE OF THAT OBJECT
        WITH THE MAIN ROLE,
THEN BUILD A KNOWLEDGE-ABOUT NODE FOR THAT OBJECT WITH ROLE
        MAIN.

P99: IF THE GOAL IS KNOWLEDGE-ABOUT SOME SUBNET OF SOME
        OBJECT
   AND THERE IS KNOWLEDGE-ABOUT THE NODE OF THAT OBJECT WITH
        THE MAIN ROLE WITH THAT SUBNET BEING SOME NODE
   AND THERE IS KNOWLEDGE-ABOUT THAT NODE,
THEN MARK THE GOAL SATISFIED.
```

Note that "some" and "that" refer to unrestricted pattern variables in the actual productions; the word following them is not a semantic restriction on values assumed by the variables, but enhances human readability only. The way that these three types of knowledge-access productions work together is dependent on the conflict resolution strategy of OPS2, particularly the special-case criterion, by which the rule that matches more data is preferred. P98 is the least special-case of the three, and its condition is explicit enough that it will be true only when the others cannot be, so special-case is not so critical for it. But neither P190 (and all others of its type) nor P99 has any negative conditions, so P190 can be true at the same time as P99, and here the special-case criterion makes the difference.

One other form of access is used: access to a particular attribute of an object, where the particular subnet is not known, an example of which is P145:

```
P145: IF THE GOAL IS KNOWLEDGE-ABOUT THE PARTS ATTRIBUTE OF
        SOME OBJECT,
   THEN ADD TO THE GOAL THAT THE SUBNET IS STRUCTURE.
```

There is a production like P145 for each attribute that is known to the system. Note that P145 remains true even after it fires, but that conflict resolution prevents it from repeating in a couple of ways (one is sufficient, of course): the refraction principle inhibits such repetition explicitly; the lexicographic recency will give preference to other rules whose conditions include the subnet information that P145 adds - the productions displayed above are all good candidates so that those others will fire next.

The kind of action done by P145 is typical of the production system style used here: a goal is a symbol structure to which a variety of rules can contribute small pieces, until enough is accumulated to make the goal satisfied.

2.3. Basic IPMSL methods

The above has sketched the mechanisms of basic access of information in IPMSL. Now we turn to three central IPMSL commands, which build on the basic access to form actions with wider effects.

A user causes the construction of new network nodes with the *DEFINE* command. The method for doing this involves taking the information from the user and embedding it in the fixed structure common to all knowledge-access productions, of which P190 above is an example.

Modification of existing net structures is done with the *LET* command, which includes the attribute and the new value of the symbol to be modified. WM structures are modified directly. PM (Production Memory) structures are accessed via the appropriate pointers in WM (ie, rule names that are kept with each node) and then their actions are edited so that future executions will result in the modified structures being built in WM. Usually the Let command has the proper subnet filled in by rules that know which attributes are part of which subnets, eg, P145 above. This subnet inferral is done in the process of accessing the knowledge, as part of Let. The purpose of this access is to check that the Let command is actually specifying a change to existing information.

The user can evoke a region of the network and have it displayed in a tree format by using the *SHOW* command. This command sets up goals to search from a starting node through all nodes related to it in specified ways. At each node visited, information is collected into a tree structure, and after the search is completed, this tree is printed. The Show command has a number of options, which specify what kind of additional information is to be collected at each node.

To summarize, the basic IPMSL commands provide access (query), definition, modification, and search-and-display capabilities. Generality has been maintained: there is very little in IPMSL that is specific to the division into six types of subnets, or to the PMS domain. Also, the methods, expressed as rules, have proved to be easily modifiable. Two other design issues can be mentioned:

- The net is divided into six subnets for several reasons: to make rules a reasonable size, to avoid extra information being added to WM, to impose some structure on knowledge as it comes into the system from the user, and to modularize the methods that work with the net.

- Efficiency is a concern, since IPMSL is intended to be worked with interactively. Response times for network definition commands are in the range of one to two minutes on our time-shared DEC KL-10. This is usually significantly exceeded the time it takes a user to decide how to formulate the next piece of network to be added, and is therefore a tolerable response delay.

3. THE IPMSL APPROACH TO INSTRUCTION AND AUGMENTATION

IPMSL started out as a small set of productions (less than 50) called Kernl2 (Kernel, version 2). Kernl2 allows simple kinds of interaction to take place, including interaction that leads to adding new rules. The first interactions with Kernl2 involved adding to and improving Kernl2's capabilities, while later ones were more and more devoted to adding the basic IPMSL commands. Kernl2's essence is a set of methods for interpreting and executing user inputs that are expressions in a simple method language. This method language allows the user to designate elementary components of a method. After a number of such designations, the user gives a command essentially saying that the method is ready to be formed into productions, and Kernl2 does the rest of the work: keeping track of what is designated and finally putting it together into rules. Kernl2 also includes rules that describe itself in a declarative way. Thus, a user can both construct methods of his own for new goals and access the Kernl2 network to understand and augment Kernl2 itself. Both of these operations have in fact taken place as IPMSL has grown.

The Kernl2 approach to growing a system, ie to instruction, builds on two previous independent approaches: that of the Instructable Production System project [11] and that of Waterman's Exemplary Programming [13].* The idea behind having Kernl2 be a part of what is basically a semantic network system has three aspects. First, the method language of Kernl2 allows a user to easily build up new system behavior, ie, it is a means to making the system fully extensible. Second, method construction takes place within a dynamic WM context that is similar to that in which the method will work after it is finished. Third, all of the above-mentioned method language facilities are available both to the user and to internal methods built from rules.

The basic IPMSL system is composed of 316 rules, of which about a third are network rules, another third are Kernl2 rules, and the remainder are IPMSL methods.

Some auxiliary software has been added to aid the direct coding of rules, bypassing the method language approach to growing the system whenever this seems expedient. This includes a facility for abstracting and displaying all or a select part of the rules in a particular method in a relatively small screen space; more flexible rule entry and editing, including the ability to copy information from one rule into another (thus one can make a new rule "like" another, and then edit in the discriminating elements); and the ability to make listings of the rules organized according to method. With these aids, it is possible to grow and debug the system at a rate of about two to five rules per on-line hour.

4. ADVANTAGES AND DISADVANTAGES OF USING RULES FOR A NETWORK

My evaluation of production rules as a basis for a semantic network system consists so far of a set of subjective impressions and design characteristics. The existing implementation of a net is an unusual mix of procedural and declarative components. The net is active in a real sense, though controlled by particular activation goals. Control in general for the net can be distributed around, as rules, but since WM is global and inspectable at all cycles by all rules, there can be global (centralized) control to a large extent. As yet, there has been no problem of searches in the net getting out of control, and in particular, unexpected rule firings have not interfered with processing.

The following lists a number of specific advantages that production-rule systems seem to have for network systems.

- WM serves as a large dynamic context. It records uniformly both the state of methods that are being executed and the state of the network as it is searched.

- The single shared dynamic state allows flexible control of searches. That is, ordinary searches can be monitored by global, general rules, by specific search heuristics, and by control knowledge that is distributed throughout the net - all expressed as rules.

- WM is useful for growing large, hybrid, temporary structures and mappings - things that one would not necessarily want to become a permanent part of the net.

- Rules can bring together (by recognition) complex patterns of diverse knowledge, thus making it possible to integrate information in new ways.

- The rules are readily organized into an instructable structure.

- Searching methods and others can themselves be described using the same network conventions as the subject domain.

- Goals are interrelated in ways that can be much more open (heterarchical) than conventional recursive (hierarchical) forms: the goals are global structures in WM that can be processed in varied orders, can be satisfied in accidental ways, and can be examined and re-ordered flexibly.

- Existing efficiency techniques for production-rule systems can be immediately carried over to network searches. In fact, the rules in OPS2 are compiled by converting their patterns into a very efficient network structure, developed by Forgy [5].

- The recognition part of the execution cycle is amenable to simple parallel implementation.

- The net need not be uniformly encoded: one could do various arbitrary things to evoke information (or to respond to it) in special cases.

The above positive features can be balanced with the following disadvantages.

- Space usage seems high: a few attribute-value pairs require a good bit of surrounding rule structure. But any such network requires some space overhead.

- Search is serial: nodes are developed one at a time. But as mentioned above, given a parallel processing architecture, production systems are favorable for exploiting it.

---

*The interested reader should consult those references and the detailed version of this paper, available from the author.

5. CONCLUSIONS

In concluding, a few major points can be re-emphasized. Implementing the network as production rules has allowed the fruitful merging of two hitherto separate technologies: a problem-solving procedure formalism and a semantic net representation formalism. The network organizes both domain information and information about the methods of the system itself. Using production rules allows the system to take advantage of recent progress in techniques for growing such systems.

The production system architecture provides a number of useful features. Methods and network share the same working space (WM), so that rules are readily applicable both to control the evocation of network information and to provide useful information for methods to use.

Advantages of using a semantic net implemented as production rules appear to outweigh the disadvantages, and examination of problems that can be expected when more demands are made of the system supports the continuation of this line of work. IPMSL has so far proven effective for defining, updating, and displaying a network for the DEC VAX-11 computer. Research is currently proceeding on using the basic ingredients presented here to provide IPMSL with higher-level capabilities, approaching operations that will prove useful to its intended domain of computer-aided design. The work so far has advanced knowledge on at least two fronts: In formulating knowledge precisely so that a system such as IPMSL can encode it, one inevitably improves the basic knowledge of the domain, in organization, precision of detail, and explicitness of assumptions. In addition, we continue to improve our knowledge about the requirements that demanding intellectual tasks place on the production system architecture and on the whole body of AI concepts and techniques.

ACKNOWLEDGMENTS

The idea of representing a network as rules was first discussed with Allen Newell and Don Waterman. I am also indebted to Newell for suggesting and helping to formulate the task domain. Valuable comments ,were made on this paper by Lanny Forgy, John McDermott, Allen Newell, and the IJCAI reviewers.

ADDENDUM

As of the time of final revision of this paper, IPMSL has grown to a size of 610 rules with no degradation in its overall manageability, and with very little decrease in efficiency of interpretation. The total system size relative to the PDP-10 is becoming much more of a problem. Of the new rules, about 23% are network, as compared with 30% in the system detailed above, with the remainder being new methods for display of information, better handling of descriptive attributes of computers, and better network access and editing capabilities.

REFERENCES

1. Barbacci, M. and Siewiorek, D. The CMU RT-CAD system: an innovative approach to computer aided design. *CMU Computer Science Research Review 1974-1975* (1974-1975), 39-53.

2. Bell, C. G. and Newell, A. *Computer Structures: Readings and Examples.* McGraw-Hill, New York, NY, 1971.

3. Eastman, C. The representation of design problems and maintenance of their structure. IFIPS Working Conference on Application of AI and PR to CAD, North Holland, 1978.

4. Forgy, C. L. and McDermott, J. OPS, a domain-independent production system language. Proc. Fifth International Joint Conference on Artificial Intelligence, IJCAI, 1977, pp. 933-939.

5. Forgy, C. L. *On the Efficient Implementation of Production Systems.* Ph.D. Th., Carnegie-Mellon University, Department of Computer Science, Pittsburgh, PA, February 1979.

6. Freeman, P. and Newell, A. A model for functional reasoning in design. *Proc. Second International Joint Conference on Artificial Intelligence London* (1971), 621-640.

7. Knudsen, M. J. *PMSL, an Interactive Language for System-Level Description and Analysis of Computer* Structures. Ph.D. Th., Carnegie-Mellon University, Department of Computer Science, Pittsburgh, PA, 1973.

8. Moore, J. A. and Newell, A. How can MERLIN understand?. In Gregg, L., Ed., *Knowledge and Cognition*, Lawrence Erlbaum Associates, Potomac, MD, 1973.

9. Rieger, C. and Grinberg, M. The declarative representation and procedural simulation of causality in physical mechanisms. Proc. Fifth International Joint Conference on Artificial Intelligence, IJCAI, 1977, pp. 250-256.

10. Rychener, M. D. Control requirements for the design of production system architectures. *SIGART Newsletter* , 64 (August 1977), 37-44. ACM

11. Rychener, M. D. and Newell, A. An instructable production system: Basic design issues. In Waterman, D. A. and Hayes-Roth, F., Ed., *Pattern-Directed Inference* Systems, Academic Press, New York, NY, 1978.

12. Sussman, G. J. Electrical design: A problem for artificial intelligence research. Proc. Fifth International Joint Conference on Artificial Intelligence, IJCAI, 1977, pp. 894-900.

13. Waterman, D. A. Rule-directed interactive transaction agents: An approach to knowledge acquisition. R-2171-ARPA, The RAND Corporation, February, 1978.

BIOLOGICAL SOFTWARE

Erik Sandewall
Informatics Laboratory
Linköping University
Linköping, Sweden

Abstract and introduction: The robot in the common science fiction novel appears as a man on the surface, but is built mechanically from wheels and levers inside. In A.I., we usually visualize an A.I. system as having a similar structure: it communicates in man's language (English), or performs other tasks which make it appear man-like, but it is in fact a large program, written in a programming language, and executed under a common time-sharing system.

The present paper argues on the contrary that A.I. systems *should not* need to appear man-like, *and* that it is necessary, both from the A.I. point of view and from the software engineering point of view, that the next level down in the A.I. system has quasi-biological properties, such as the ability to reproduce.

Remark: due to space limitations, this paper has been written in a condensed style.

1. *Reproduction is a mechanism for a species to adapt.* It is natural to make analogies between the biological system that forms the substrate of natural intelligence, and the computer hardware/software system that forms the substrate of A.I. Among characteristic properties of organisms we find homeostasis and the ability to reproduce. Do they have counterparts in software?

The common game of writing programs that create many identical copies of themselves, misses an important reason for biological reproduction: it is *a mechanism for adaptation*, from the point of view of the species. Human reproduction involves not only copulation and child-birth, but also two decades of work for training the new individual (sometimes called "social reproduction" by sociologists). In the training process, the new person inherits some knowledge, but also selects, reviews and reorganizes his or her intellectual heritage. Imagine how much progress there would be if humans lived forever and never reproduced!

2. *Software also needs to adapt, in response to changing user needs.* Conventional software does not *adapt autonomously to any significant extent: it is adapted* by a programmer who changes the program (*"maintenance"*) or throws it away and writes a new one.

Future software systems with a more complex behavior will have much bigger needs to adapt, and will be harder to change from the outside. They should therefore be enabled to change without programmer intervention, in response to requests from the end user. They can do so either by modifying their internal state, or by creating a modified copy of themselves. *Both of these methods are viable if the programming technique of* conceptual programming *is used.*

Remember that adaptation was a topic of interest in earlier A.I. work, but it has gone out of fashion because it seemed one could only do trivial things with it, such as adjusting numerical parameters. What one would really like to do was to adapt programs, but that seemed too hard, and had to wait for automatic programming to happen first.

But there is a trend in several areas of software to use specialized application languages (implemented either as interpreters i.e. general, highly parametrized programs, or as program generators) to develop applications. Examples of this trend are:

- commercial program generators for reports, screen layouts, data base queries, etc.
- the system for information-flow applications, developed in our group (ref. 1).
- special-purpose languages in A.I. research e.g. grammar languages.

These are signs of an emerging software technology where computer applications are implemented by selecting a small number of general-purpose tools, combining them in appropriate ways, and providing them with a description of the application in (several) specialized application languages. This style of programming has been called *conceptual programming* in ref. 2,3,4.

Self-modification in a system should clearly be relatively easy if it can be performed by modification of parameters or application-language expressions, as compared to direct self-modification of a conventional program. This is both because easier "maintenance" is one of the reasons for specialized languages, and because end-user requests for modification are naturally expressed in application-language terms.

3. *Should an A.I. system 'live' forever?* In other words, is internal self-modification sufficient as an adaptation mechanism, and is reproduction unnecessary? The answer is that perhaps it is not practical for software to adapt forever. For adaptation, new knowledge has to be added to a system, which means that other knowledge has to give way, otherwise the system will grow indefinitely. But whenever knowledge is removed, one encounters a well-known but yet un-named problem which I propose to call *the delete problem,* for example in the following simple form: suppose A has been asserted in a data base, and B has also been asserted by forward inference using "A implies B", and later A is to be deleted. Should B be deleted as well? There might be other, independent support for B, so that it should not be deleted. The problem is well-known on many software levels, from conventional garbage collectors to semantic networks.

The conclusion is that for a system to be indefinitely adaptible, it must contain a considerable overhead of information about the details of its own insides, such as back pointers from B to all its independent supports, in the example. Reproduction offers an alternative, with copying garbage collection as an example on the low software level, and training of off-spring as examples among animals and (I conjecture) for A.I. systems.

4. *Reproduction takes many forms; ours is a biological exception.* Reproduction in mammals has a simple structure: two individuals together generate an offspring which grows up continously. But butterflies, ants, fish, jellyfish, frogs, and funghi offer a rich reportoire of more complicated schemes, where the organism exists in more than one physical form during the reproductive cycle.

In several projects in our research group, I have seen needs for similar, non-trivial schemes for reproduction in software.

- *Background: some of the group's work assumes that the programming techniques that have been developed in A.I. research, are a significant spinoff result of that research, and should be used for other purposes as well.*

Two specific cases are of interest:

A) Use of the Interlisp system for development of pilot versions of application programs. (A pilot version is one which can easily be changed until the end users are happy). Development of the initial program went smoothly, but the subsequent user-initiated modifications were clumsy to make. Analysis: when conventional languages are used, one does debugging in the production environment (i.e. using the regular compiler). The Interlisp system provides a "dry-dock" environment for program development, which implies that a non-trivial effort is required to take the program into and out of the "dry dock". This is worthwhile if a lot of work has to be done there, and in particular if the program never really leaves the development environment, as is often the case in A.I. research. But the same programmer support did not seem worthwhile as the programmer's effort for transfer from development environment to production environment was much bigger than the effort of the update itself.

The problem was solved by allowing each application to exist in two forms: a development system and a production system. The development system was the one that really 'adapted', and it had the ability to create corresponding production versions.

This solution embodies the following basic attitude: a programming system should not be like a street-front clinic, where a program walks in to be operated on (for example, for being compiled, or debugged during a debugging session), and then leaves again. It should instead be a permanent dwelling for the program. The programming system plus the program it accomodates, should be viewed as an organism, which contains a fair amount of knowledge about itself, and in particular has the ability to generate systems which are similar to itself although tuned for production use - like a queen bee does.

B) Modelling information-flow systems. Many data processing applications can be characterized as information-flow systems: there are specialized work-stations for different people or roles in the organization; information packets ("transactions") are generated in such stations, sent in channels from one station to the next, accumulated in files that are local to each station, and the task of the person at a station is to review the information that flows by, take actions, add more information to the transactions, and pass them on.

Recent work in our group has resulted in a prototype software tool which allows the various aspects of the information-flow application to be described in specialized languages, and which allows one to do pilot execution of the system. work on a generator of production systems is in progress. The system is designed with the programming techniques that are usual in A.I. programing, such as strongly parametrized programs, handles, and data-driven procedure calls.

In the terms of the previous sections, this system is "organism-like" in that it can create modified copies of itself, namely copies for each of the work-stations. These specialized production-phase copies have been obtained by selecting subsets of the parameter structure, and by specializing programs through "smart" compiler macros.

These and other applications in our group are using a general-purpose tool for accomplishing system reproduction, called ACTEMAN (ref. 5).

5. *Knowledge acquisition.* The reproduction in these two examples as presently implemented, does not involve any selective acquisition of knowledge by the off-spring. (There is however a rea' need already to have that). The major reason for the examples is to illustrate that multiple 'life-forms' and unusual (for us) reproduction structures may be useful for software systems.

With a system which is organized along the lines of conceptual programming, as mentioned above, knowledge acquisition by the young off-spring could be organized as follows:

- let the ancestor generate a basic system (for example a fresh instance of the Lisp system), and load the appropriate general programs into it. Also let the ancestor transfer the appropriate parameters and datadriven procedures to the descendant, but usually only a subset of what the ancestor "knows"
- let the descendant engage in work, usually by serving a human user, where in doing so one identifies missing parts in its structure and obtains the information by communication with senior computer systems, (in particular, systems similar to the "deveopment phase" system described above, which contain extra knowledge and which specialize in training new systems), and only in hard cases, communication with a human programmer.

In such an architecture, it is possible but not natural to let the computer systems communicate between themselves in human natural language. It is much more natural to exploit the properties of the computer medium, and let them communicate in terms of program segments, data structures, and so forth. (This does not preclude that some of the characteristics of naturallanguage communication will still be needed)

6. We can now proceed to the other issue mentioned in the introduction to this paper: *The emphasis in current A.I. research on systems with humanoid behavior.* Its main historical reasons are:

A) The training issue: it has been argued that intelligence presumes knowledge, and that the computer can only gain knowledge by talking to people and/or being among people, as a robot.

B) The usefulness issue: it has been argued that an intelligent computer system can only be useful to us people, if it can talk to us in our language (which is assumed to be natural language).

The training argument addresses the wrong bottleneck. It is true that a lot of work will have to be spent by people for transferring knowledge to computer systems, and it is conceivable that it will be facilitated if natural language may be used. But already scores of programmers have as their profession to transfer knowledge and ability to computers. The significant problem is instead that computer systems can not transfer knowledge to each other. If one computer system could train others, then it would not matter if the initial knowledge transfer to one computer system had to be done in a formal language

The reproduction chain can start when we have built systems which have the necessary properties for being useful, and for generating useful offspring, recursively. In order to start it, we ourselves will have to understand the reproduction process fairly much in detail. It then seems more convenient to create the first generation by performing manually the operations that will later be done by the ancestor, rather than create a natural-language understanding capability only for the purpose of the first system generation.

The usefulness argument (B) is valid if we consider current research results as given, and search for possible applications. But suppose instead that we would focus on *current* data processing (D.P.) applications, and ask what role programmed intelligence could play in them. The role might not be dominant: the resulting thought product is not necessarily a computer intelligence incarnated into an application. A car with a micro computer in it is well described as a car and not well described as a computer, and intelligence might be very useful in a similar, subordinate role in the D.P. system.

7. *There is a significant area of common interest for A.I. and software engineering.* In A.I., conventional programming has traditionally been considered

- as an intelligence-requiring activity that is observed to occur in real life, and which therefore is a candidate A.I. application, and
- as a part of the support work for an A.I. lab and a temptation for the graduate student to waste his time on

It is then assumed that software engineering and A.I. are disjoint areas. The arguments of the present paper imply on the contrary that

- systems which adapt, internally and by reproduction, are necessary both for A.I. and for future software engineering
- conceptual programming techniques may facilitate design of large and complex systems (which is a topic of common interest for A.I. and S.E.) as well as adaptation and reproduction.
- such systems, performing conventional D.P. tasks, are a likely early application area for A.I. research. But intelligence can not then be obtained as an add-on: the system has to be built from the start using some of the programming techniques which are common in A.I.

8. *How does this fit in with other work in A.I.* Hewitt's actor concept is clearly related in the abstract sense that he also talks of structures formed by individuals with a local autonomy and initiative. However, he has mostly worked with actors of very simple structure, in particular as an elementary object in a theory of computation. We emphasize systems which are complex enough to contain intelligence; systems which are pseudo-individuals. Marr's work in computer vision has already started a trend to take the biological foundations of intelligent systems seriously again

Acknowledgements

Jim Goodwin and Sture Hägglund have contributed strongly to the ideas expressed in this paper.

References

1. Erik Sandewall: *A description language and pilot-execution executive for information-transport systems.* Proc. Very Large Data Bases conference, 1979.

2. Terry Winograd: *Five lectures on artificial intelligence.* Stanford A.I. Memo, 1974

3. Erik Sandewall: *Some observations on conceptual programming.* Machine Intelligence 8, 1977

4. Bob Wielinga: *A I Programming Methodology.* Proceedings of the AISB/GI Conference on Artificial Intelligence, Hamburg, 1978

5. Erik Sandewall: *Self-organizing Information and Operations for Reproduction in Distributed Programming Systems.* Internal report, Informatics Laboratory, Linköping University, 1979.

AN OVERVIEW OF
AN AUTOMATICALLY COMPILABLE HIERARCHICAL DEFINITION MATCHER

Barbara C. Sangster*
Laboratory for Computer Science Research
Rutgers University
New Brunswick, N.J. 08903

The problem addressed in this paper is that of determining whether the conditions expressed in the definition of a concept are satisfied by a set of assertions (a task of attempting to match the assertions to the definition). The approach presented here is to precede the matching activity proper with a one-time preprocessing phase, during which the definition is automatically transformed from a rather complex form in which it is originally expressed into a simpler form which appears to be more suitable to the matching task at hand. Use of this transformation process permits the functions of recognition and interpretation to be separated, thereby improving the efficiency of the matching process. This separation is performed by distinguishing those components of the definition which must be found to be true from those whose truth may subsequently be inferred and those whose truth is irrelevant to the matching process. The transformation is performed by means of a process of symbolic instantiation of the definition -- the translation of the definition from a set of criteria for satisfying the definition into an exemplary instance of the concept itself. The algorithm for the transformation and the subsequent matching process are outlined and illustrated in the text.

1. FORMULATION OF THE TASK

This paper describes an approach to a problem that has arisen within the TAXMAN II project on Legal Reasoning [4], [5], [6], [7], [9] -- the design and implementation of a MATCHER that will correctly identify exactly those subcases within a case description (i.e., that will identify those subsets of the facts of a legal case) that satisfy the conditions expressed in the definition of some legal concept. As the purpose of the TAXMAN II project is to investigate the structure of legal concepts, and of decisions based on those concepts, through the representation of those concepts and decisions in AIMDS, it is evident that a MATCHER will be required to play a central role in the envisioned system. The MATCHER described in this paper was designed to meet that need.

Work in the first few months of the TAXMAN II project has centered on a single concept in the domain of corporate tax law -- a kind of corporate reorganization called a BREORGANIZATION. A BREORGANIZATION is a complex concept, involving the exchange between two corporations (related in certain ways) of property bearing a particular, rather intricate, relationship to those two corporations. The initial task posed for the MATCHER (the task with which we shall be concerned in this paper) was, therefore, to take a case description consisting of a possibly very large set of possibly very intricately related facts, and to identify every subcase (i.e., every subset of those facts) that indicated the existence of some instance of a BREORGANIZATION.

A later version of the MATCHER is expected to be able to take a set of legal concepts

---

*The research reported in this paper was partially supported by the National Science Foundation under Grant #SOC-7811408 and by the Research Foundation of the State University of New York under Grant #150-2197-A.

The views and conclusions contained herein are those of the author and should not be interpreted as necessarily representing the official policies, either expressed or implied, of the National Science Foundation or the Foundation of the State University of New York.

(AREORGANIZATION, BREORGANIZATION, CREORGANIZATION, and so forth), and, in a single pass, identify for each concept all those subcases satisfying its definitional conditions. Another extension to the MATCHER that we contemplate is of a different kind: the current MATCHER identifies a subcase S as a match to the definition if and only if S exactly meets the definitional conditions; a future version of the MATCHER will permit, in the absence of an exact match, a sequence of gradual deformations until a match to S has been found.

Let us return to the version of the MATCHER currently under development. Careful examination of the definition given for BREORGANIZATION and of representative case descriptions disclosed

1) that some of the assertions comprising the definition were irrelevant to the determination of whether the definitional conditions had been met -- that is, they did not need to be true; these clauses seemed somewhat better suited to a _description_ than to a _definition_;

2) that some other assertions comprising the definition, while they did have to be true, could be inferred to be true on the basis of certain other knowledge; the issue of mutual inferrability was not directly addressed, as mutually inferrable sets of assertions in this domain appeared to be expressible in terms of a canonical set of clauses whose truth had to be observed -- that is, clauses of neither type 1 nor type 2.

For example, consider that the following is part of a definition of a ZOPPLE

Every creature with a beak and feathers is a ZOPPLE.

Every ZOPPLE has wings.

A ZOPPLE may have orange feathers.

If we encounter a creature with a beak and feathers, then we know it is a ZOPPLE without concerning ourselves further. The color of the feathers (type 1 above) is irrelevant to our classification of the creature; the presence of wings may be inferred (type 2), once the creature has been identified.

From the characterization of the problem given above, we may readily admit the desirability of

SPEC1) reducing combinatoric problems wherever possible,

SPEC2) identifying as a valid BREORGANIZATION every subcase for which all of the conditions included within the definition -- aside from assertions of the types described in 1 and 2 above -- were true, and subsequently devising some means of filling in whatever additional information could then be filled in.

In terms of the example presented earlier, we might identify as a ZOPPLE any creature with a beak and feathers, subsequently inferring the presence of wings, and adding the fact the feathers are orange, wherever this is true of the ZOPPLE in question.

In view of our plans for later phases of the work, we should also like our design to permit the easy representation of the process of partial matching.

SPEC2 permits us to characterize our task in terms of the paradigms of _recognition_ and _interpretation_. _Recognition_ is the process of determining whether or not a particular object satisfies any of a set of conditions -- i.e., given an object and a set of sets C of conditions, it returns a _yes_ or a _no_ for each C. _Interpretation_ associates with an object not only a classification -- or a set of classifications (recognition), but (for at least one of the classes) additional material as well, such as a structural description. For example, a structural matcher, by distinguishing between the presence and absence of an isomorphism between two networks, performs recognition; a parser, by distinguishing between the grammatically valid and invalid strings presented to it (recognition), and associating at least one parse tree with every grammatically valid string, performs interpretation. Note that a parser may be viewed as performing recognition by means of interpretation.

As we can see, our task may be decomposed into two modules -- one in which the _recognition_ of valid BREORGANIZATIONs is performed, and one in which an _interpretation_ is produced for every valid BREORGANIZATION. Note that, by this method, the classification of a case as a valid or invalid instance of a BREORGANIZATION would be completed by the recognition module, and that, unlike the parsing analogue, our interpretation module would be required only for the creation of the appropriate structural descriptions.

This design strategy

1) would successfully avoid certain combinatoric problems often encountered by parsers

a) by eliminating the requirement that the conditions for recognition failure (i.e., the conditions requiring a no to be produced by the recognition module) must be identified through the failure of interpretation (i.e., through the inability of the interpretation module to create an interpretation), and

b) by removing the necessity of generating interpretations for matching subcases when only recognition was desired,

2) would successfully avoid a problem encountered by many structural matchers, by eliminating the possibility of recognition failure caused solely by the absence in the case description of non-essential information which was present in the original definition, and

3) would permit the computation of missing but inferrable information to be performed by the interpretation module.

Before we proceed to a discussion of the means selected to meet the two specifications given above, let us look more closely at the way in which the definitions and the case descriptions are represented. The representation is in AIMDS, a frame-based language [8]. AIMDS allows the representation of a set of types, a set of instances of the types, a set of typed relations that may be asserted to hold between pairs of instances of the appropriate types, and a set of pattern-directed inference rules called consistency conditions (CCs) which specify the allowable combinations of assertions about relations between instances.

One of the attractions of representing sets of assertions in AIMDS is that those representations have an analogue in network form. Several powerful methods have been devised for manipulating structures which permit a network representation. Two such methods involve the use of recognition networks and structural matchers for networks.

A recognition network performs much like a parser for pieces of subnet, performing recognition by assigning a full semantic net to the input subnets (interpretation). An automatically compilable recognition network (ACORN), developed by F. Hayes-Roth and D. J. Mostow [3], has been used in the understanding of connected speech. A structural matcher, on the other hand, performs recognition by determining whether every component of a criterial network has a unique counterpart in the network whose recognition is being attempted. A program with the capability of structural matching, called DMATCH, was developed by D. Touretzky [12] for use with AIMDS.

In order to see to what extent either or both of these methods might be applicable to our own task, let us look more closely at the degree to which the representations in AIMDS of definitions and case descriptions have analogues as networks.

A case description is a set of assertions about relations between instances. For example, an assertion in a legal case description represented in AIMDS might say that the instance TRANS-1 of the type TRANS has in AGENT relation the instance ACTOR-1 of the type ACTOR. A case description may be represented as a network in which the nodes correspond to the instances, and the links correspond to the relations between them.

A definition, which specifies all structures meeting a set of conditions, consists of 1) a set of propositions specifying the allowable relations between instances, and 2) a set of consistency conditions (CCs) expressing constraints on how the propositions in the first set may be instantiated. For example, in the domain of corporate tax law, propositions of the first set might state that an instance of the type TRANS (a transfer of property) may have an instance of ACTOR in AGENT relation, and may have an instance of ACTOR in OLDOWNER relation. A CC in this domain might state that an instance of TRANS may have an instance of ACTOR in AGENT relation if and only if that instance of ACTOR is also in OLDOWNER relation to that instance of TRANS. The propositions of the first set may be represented as a network in which the links correspond to relations, and the nodes stand, not for instances, but for the types of instances. No obvious analogous way of also representing CCs in network form presents itself. (Possible graphical representations of CCs, such as those based on Petri nets, would not appear to have useful analogues in case descriptions.)

These observation have failed to show us how we might formulate an analogue to a definition in solely network form (as we have said that an analogue to a case description may be formulated). They do permit us, however, to see more clearly how a solution to our problem might be devised, or, at least, what problems stand in the way of our working out a solution. Let us summarize the crucial observations.

1) We have seen that only a subset of the assertions in the definition need be found to be true in a subcase S for S to match the definition.

2) We have seen that, given two networks (N1 and N2), it is possible to use a structural matcher to recognize that every component of N1 has a unique counterpart in N2.

3) We have seen that methods have been devised for generating a full semantic net (an interpretation) from a set of subnets.

If we can identify that subset of the assertions in the definition that have to be found to be true, and represent them, together with the CCs, in network form, then, by performing a structural match, with this network as N1 and a case description as N2, we can determine whether or not N2 satisfies the definitional conditions (recognition). If it does so, then we may try to utilize methods analogous to those used in the original ACORN to fill in whatever missing assertions we can (interpretation).

Such a strategy, if it could be implemented, would have clear advantages. By permitting the representation of the definitional conditions in a single mode, it would be conducive to easy understanding and, most probably, economy of storage. By permitting recognition to take place through a single kind of process, it would be likely to further enhance comprehensibility and storage economy, as well as efficiency of operation. For example, elimination of the need during recognition for pattern-directed inference processes (which very likely would have been used if interpretation were also being done at this time) would permit recognition to be performed in LISP directly on the data structures without the overhead required for running AIMDS (which is written in the language FUZZY, which is itself written in LISP). Furthermore, since the single representational mode (that of a network) and the single recognition process (that of structural matching) have been the objects of both theoretical and empirical study by many researchers, the strategy outlined above would most probably enable us to draw on the results of others in improving our own design and implementation.

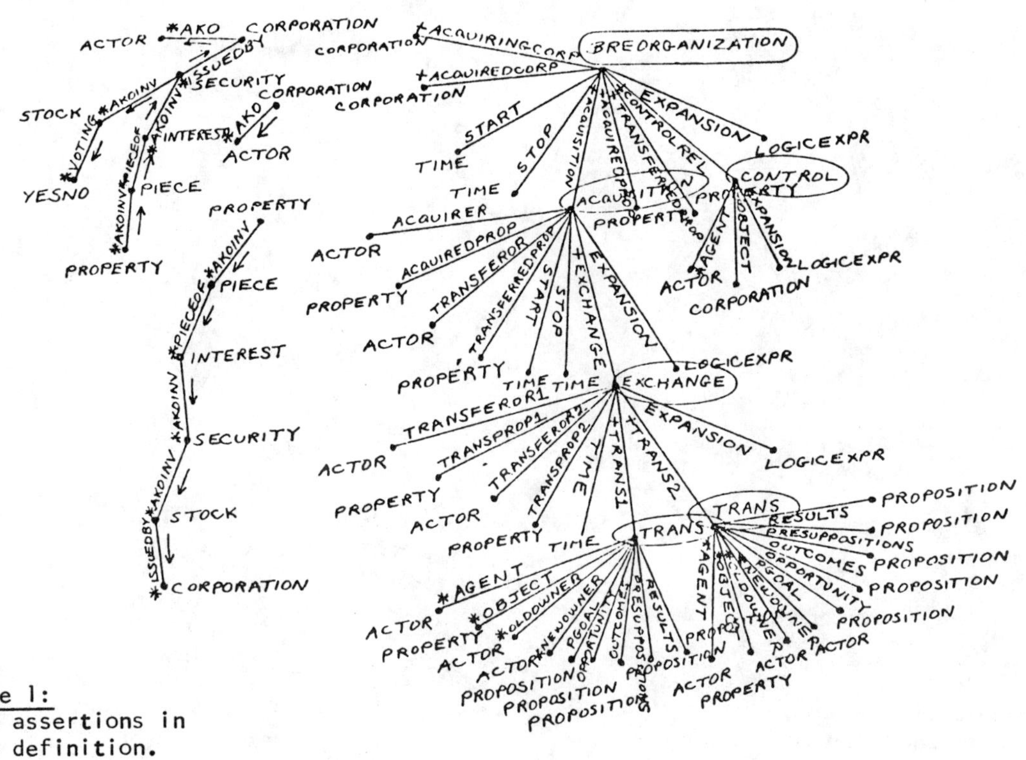

Figure 1:
The assertions in the definition.

If we decide to attempt such a strategy, the following two questions arise:

Given a definition of a legal concept expressed in AIMDS,

QUESTION1) can we generate the network to serve as N1 in our structural matcher, and if so, how?

QUESTION2) can we generate an ACORN module to fill in all the information that is missing in the case description but can be inferred from other knowledge, and if so, how?

2. SKETCH OF A SOLUTION

An answer to the questions posed above was devised, and is outlined below.

to take all the assertions (in the form of relations between typed variables) present in the definition, and, for all the variables contained in the assertions, to perform, using the consistency conditions (CCs), a process of <u>symbolic instantiation</u> of the variables, in such a manner that two variables are bound to the same instance if and only if they are required to have the same binding in all case descriptions satisfying the definition. (The use of a single symbolically instantiated form is sufficient for the syntactic class of definitions under discussion here. These definitions contain conjunction, but neither disjunction nor negation, either of which would require a more complex symbolically instantiated structure. For further discussion, see [6] and [7].) The assertions in the definition for a BREORGANIZATION (before symbolic instantiation) are illustrated in Fig. 1.

We can then divide the assertions (now in the form of relations between instances) into four sets:

A) those whose truth must be observed in the case description -- these will provide us with all the bindings we are required to identify in S (The assertions of set A for a BREORGANIZATION are illustrated in Fig. 2.);

B) those which can be used to pass these bindings on as the structural description is built up during interpretation;

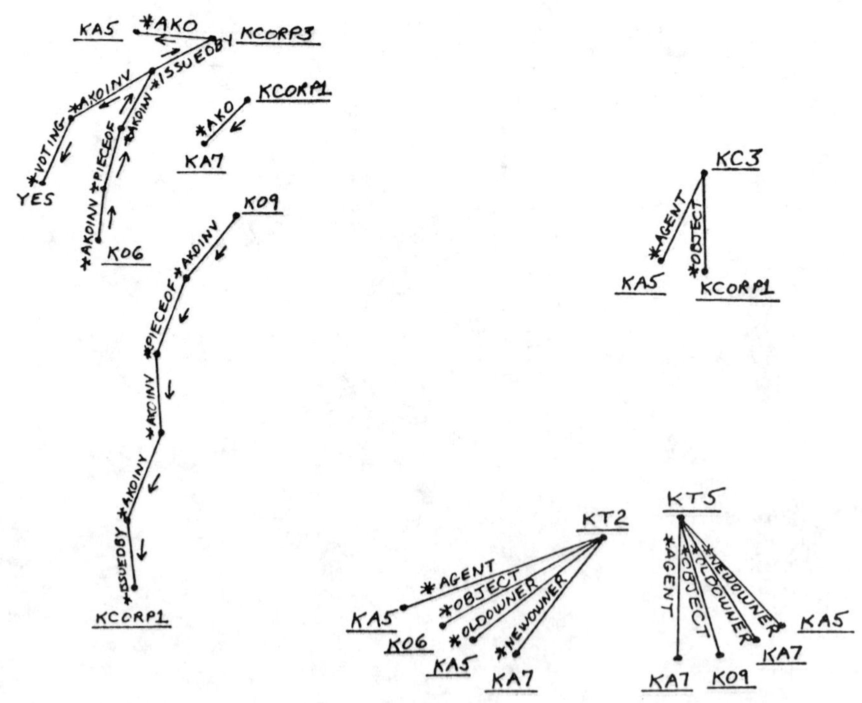

Figure 2:
The assertions of set A.

C) those whose truth can be inferred, on the basis of the CCs, from that of the assertions in sets A and B;

D) those whose truth is not relevant to a determination of whether the definition has been satisfied.

Sets A, B, and D, each of which now consists of sets of instantiated assertions, can then be used to produce the recognition and interpretation modules characterized above. Set A is used to create the network to which a structural match of a subcase can be attempted by the recognition module (N1 in the preceding section). We call this the KERNEL structure for the definition (or, more simply, the KERNEL structure). The assertions of set B are transformed into a set of commands to make additional assertions -- that is, to add new assertions to those already present -- this plays part of the role of the ACORN module mentioned in the preceding section, and creates the first part of the desired interpretation. We call this set of commands the INNER ACORN generator. The assertions of set C are discarded. After the first part of the interpretation of a recognized subcase S has been completed, those assertions of set D that are true for S are used to add (with additional commands) to the structural description of S, thereby completing the role of the ACORN module, and concluding the interpretation process. This additional set of commands, which we call the AUGMENTED ACORN generator, augments the interpretation of the recognized subcase with clauses of a descriptive, rather than a definitional, character. We call the combination of the INNER ACORN generator and the AUGMENTED ACORN generator simply the ACORN generator.

The compilation process sketched above thus results in a KERNEL structure and an ACORN generator, which can then be used for recognition and interpretation whenever a case description is presented for comparison with the definition. The compilation and execution processes are illustrated in Figures 3, 4, and 5.

The way in which the compilation algorithm has been formulated makes it possible to construct an informal proof that the algorithm correctly transforms any well-formed definition with the purely conjunctive structure sketched above. The algorithm and the proof are presented in detail in [6]. Details on representational issues involved in our method for manipulating definitions may be found in [7].

3. EXECUTION

In the preceding section, we saw how the compilation of the KERNEL and ACORN for a definition with a conjunctive structure

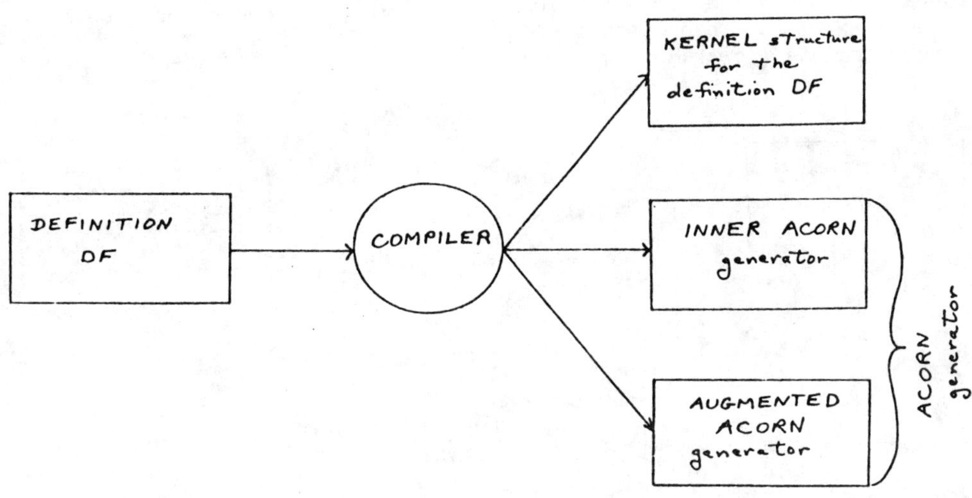

Figure 3:
Compilation of KERNEL structure and ACORN generator.

proceeds. Once this compilation has been completed, it need never be repeated (unless the definition itself should change), and the compiled KERNEL structure and ACORN generator may be used directly for comparison with the definition whenever a case description is presented.

The matching of subcases against the KERNEL structure takes place first; at the option of the user, this process may terminate with the identification either of a single matching subcase, or of a larger set of matches (including the set of all matching subcases). When the desired number of matching subcases have been recognized (or when all cases in the case description have been examined), control returns to the user's program. At this point, any procedures of the user's choice may be executed, including (whenever desired) execution of the ACORN generator to produce interpretations for any or all of the matching subcases identified by the recognition routine.

In order to control possible combinatoric difficulties, the KERNEL is decomposed into a set of small networks, against each of which all substructures of the same type in the case description are tested for an exact DMATCH (STAGE1). (We hope to be able to select "small networks" from the KERNEL in such a way that matching to any single small network will involve a minimal degree of combinatoric complexity.) The substructures that survive STAGE1 (and no others) are then combined in all possible valid ways into larger networks of some degree of increase in complexity. A DMATCH of each of these structures with the corresponding substructure of the KERNEL is then attempted, and bindings constraints between formerly separate components of the new network are thereby tested. This process is repeated with surviving substructures until the DMATCH is conducted against the KERNEL structure itself. This final stage of DMATCHing will be terminated as soon as the desired number of matching subcases have been recognized. If this stage is permitted to run to completion, the survivors represent all and only the subcases in the case description that meet the conditions expressed in the definition.

The execution of the recognition component is illustrated in Fig. 6. For this example, 5 instances of TRANS (T1, T2, T3, T4, T5), 2 instances of CONTROL (C1, C2), and 2 instances of OBJECT (O6, O9) were used. The value of MAKEFULLLIST shows the survivors of STAGE1. The value of BGO shows the single valid instance of a BREORGANIZATION that can be created from these components.

If interpretations of any of the identified matches are desired, the ACORN generator may then be used to produce them.

4. IMPLEMENTATION

Implementation activity on the matcher has taken two directions. First we constructed and ran an automated demonstration of the execution of a hand-compiled KERNEL and ACORN. Having demonstrated the feasibility of the design for our application, we began work on the compiler for the KERNEL and ACORN, concurrently refining the algorithm outlined in this paper, and presented in detail in [6]. This effort has so far yielded encouraging results.

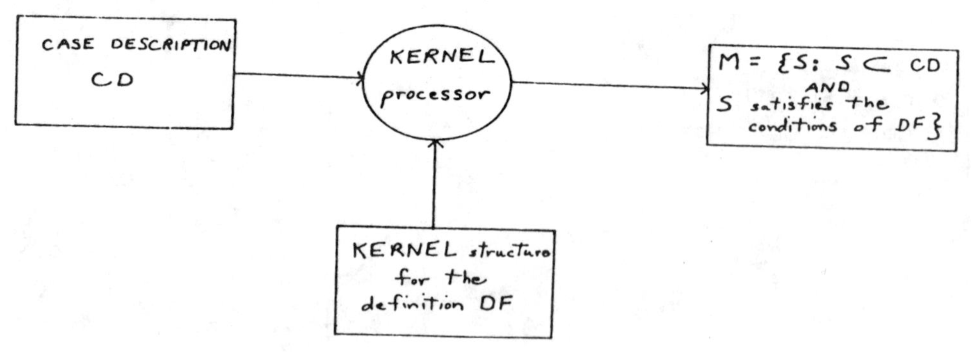

Figure 4:
Execution of recognition component, using the compiled KERNEL structure.

5. IMPLICATIONS

The primary attractions of the definition matcher appear to stem from the separation of recognition and interpretation, and from the reduction of the recognition process to the structural matching of networks. This design strategy significantly enhances matching efficiency by eliminating the requirement that the absence of a match must be recognized through the failure of interpretation, by removing the necessity of generating interpretations for matching subcases when only recognition is desired, and by permitting the recognition process to be performed without the overhead associated with the use of pattern-directed inference rules. In addition, this strategy eliminates the possibility of match failure caused solely by the absence of non-essential information, and permits the computation of missing but inferrable information to take place during the interpretation phase.

In addition to its immediate practical advantages, the use of the KERNEL+ACORN paradigm seems not only to induce a more accurate representation of definitions, but also to provide a sound basis for the expected development within the Legal Reasoning Project of a deformation-oriented definition matcher.

ACKNOWLEDGEMENTS

The author thanks S. Amarel, V. Ciesielski, L. T. McCarty, T. Mitchell, N. S. Sridharan, D. Touretzky, and an anonymous referee for providing some very helpful suggestions and comments on an earlier draft of the paper, and especially for identifying areas of particular obscurity. The author is also very grateful to N. S. Sridharan and D. Touretzky for speedy assistance in adding a new capability to AIMDS required in an early phase of the implementation effort. It should, however, not be inferred that any of the above necessarily endorses all the conclusions reached in this paper -- with the sole exception of the author, who takes full responsibility for its contents.

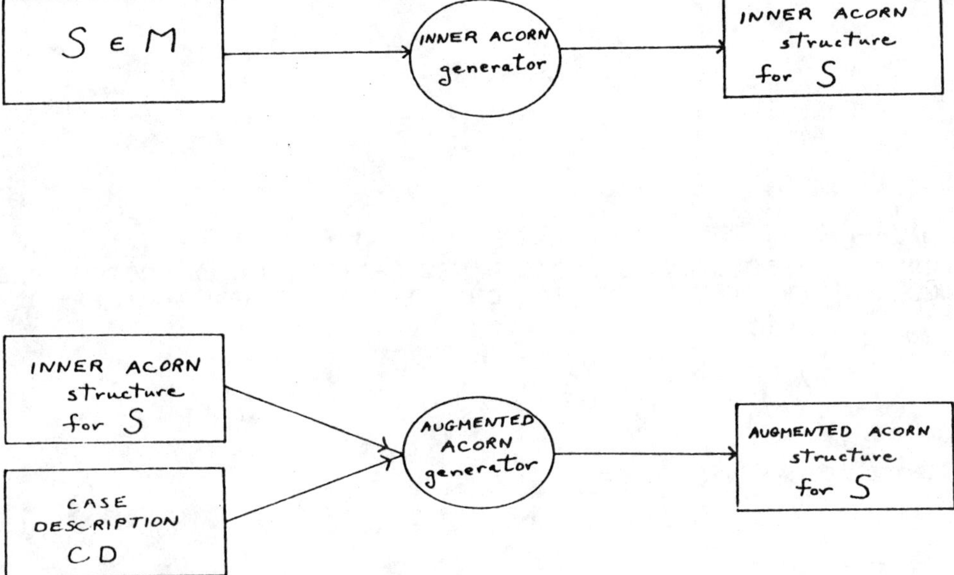

Figure 5:
Execution of the interpretation component, using the compiled INNER ACORN generator and AUGMENTED ACORN generator.

REFERENCES

[1] Freuder, E. C. 1978. "Synthesizing Constraint Expressions". CACM, vol. 21, pp. 958-966.

[2] Haralick, R. M. and L. G. Shapiro. 1979. "The Consistent Labelling Problem: Part I". IEEE Transactions on PAMI, vol. 1, pp. 173-184.

[3] Hayes-Roth, F. and D. J. Mostow. 1975. "An Automatically Compilable Recognition Network for Structured Patterns". Proceedings of IJCAI-75, vol. 1, pp. 246-251.

[4] McCarty, L. T. 1977. "Reflections on TAXMAN: An Experiment in Artificial Intelligence and Legal Reasoning". Harvard Law Review, vol. 90, pp. 837-893.

[5] McCarty, L. T., N. S. Sridharan, and B. C. Sangster. 1979. "The Implementation of TAXMAN II: An Experiment in Artificial Intelligence and Legal Reasoning". Rutgers University Report #LCSR-TR-3.

[6] Sangster, B. C. 1979a. "An Automatically Compilable Hierarchical Definition Matcher". Rutgers University Report #LRP-TR-3.

[7] Sangster, B. C. 1979b. "On the Automatic Transformation of Class Membership Criteria". Proceedings of the 17th Annual Meeting of the Association for Computational Linguistics. Univ. of California at San Diego, La Jolla, CA.

[8] Sridharan, N. S. (ed.) 1978a. "AIMDS User Manual, Version 2." Rutgers University Report #CBM-TR-89.

[9] Sridharan, N. S. 1978b. "Some Relationships between BELIEVER and TAXMAN". Rutgers University Report #LCSR-TR-2.

[10] Sridharan, N. S. and C. F. Schmidt. 1978. "Knowledge-Directed Inference in Believer". In Pattern-Directed Inference Systems, ed. by D. Waterman and F. Hayes-Roth.

[11] Srinivasan, C. V. 1976. "The Architecture of Coherent Information System: A General Problem Solving System". IEEE Transactions on Computers, vol. 25, pp. 390-402.

[12] Touretzky, D. 1978. "Learning from Examples in a Frame-Based System". Rutgers University Report #CBM-TR-87.

[13] Woods, W. A. 1975. "What's in a Link: Foundations for Semantic Networks". In Representation and Understanding, ed. by D. G. Bobrow and A. Collins. Academic Press.


```
SECOND-CONTEXT >>        (BGO)

Enter MAKEFULLLIST:
!      PROTS = (PROTOTRANS1 PROTOTRANS2 PROTOCONTROL1 PROTO09 PROTO06)
MAKEFULLLIST = ((O6) (O6 O9) (C1 C2) (T2 T4 T5) (T2 T4 T5))



((T2 T5 C2 O9 O6) NIL)
```

Figure 6:
Sample execution of the recognition component.

TOWARDS A MATHEMATICAL THEORY OF PROGRAM SYNTHESIS

Masahiko Sato*

Department of Information Science
Faculty of Science, University of Tokyo
Hongo, Tokyo 113, Japan

This paper attempts to set a theoretical foundation for Program Synthesis. A programming language Prog is introduced together with its interpretation in the semantic domain D. A formal system QFT, which is an extension of the Heyting arithmetic, is then introduced in order to express specifications formally. Roughly stated, the main result is: Given a QFT-proof of the specification ∀x∃zA[x,z], it is possible to construct a program p such that A[x,p[x]] is true in D for any input x. Moreover, a formal proof of ∀xA[x,p[x]] can also be obtained. Since any program p in Prog always terminates, the above result establishes the total correctness of the synthesized program at the same time. Finally, it is shown that any program p in Prog can be faithfully simulated by means of LISP.

0. INTRODUCTION

Before we start talking about *program synthesis*, we wish to clarify our standpoint as to what we mean by the terms such as *program*, *specification* and *verification*. A *program* is a well-formed expression in some formal language (i.e., a *programming language*). We write a program in order to solve a certain problem. We need a theory to specify the problem precisely. (See [Burstall and Goguen 1977]. They give an example of matrix inversion. I.e., we need a theory of matrices to state the problem of matrix inversion.) As far as program synthesis is concerned, we must further have a formal language (i.e., a *specification language*) in which the above theory can be formalized. Then, in the specification language, we can *specify* the problem formally by a formula A[x,z] which describes an input-output relation between the input variable x and the output variable z. We say that a program P *realizes* the specification A[x,z] if, under a certain interpretation, A[x,P[x]] is true for any input x, where P[x] denotes the result of executing P for the input x. Here we remark that we are implicitly assuming that our specification language essentially contains the programming language in which the program P is written. If we furthermore wish to formally *verify* that P realizes the specification A[x,z], we need a formal theory such that the formula ∀xA[x,P[x]] is provable in it. Thus this theory must contain the theory which we required for the specification of the problem. We call the former theory *verification theory* and the latter theory *specification theory*. Now we can formulate the problem of program synthesis as follows.

Program Synthesis Problem (PSP): *Find a procedure which produces, from a given specification* A[x,z], *a program* P *which realizes the specification.*

Even though at a rather meta-level, we need a theory to specify PSP. As the specification theory of PSP, we adopt the theory QFT which is a quantificational extension of the theory FT of primitive recursive functionals of finite type. (Theory of primitive recursive functionals of finite type was initiated by [Gödel 1958], as a device to prove the consistency of the Peano arithmetic. Our systems QFT and FT are very similar to the corresponding systems due to [Schütte 1977].)

The reasons of our adoption of QFT and FT are as follows.

(1) Every provably recursive function (in the sense of [Takeuti 1975] p.123) is expressible in FT, so that a large class of interesting algorithms can be dealt with.

(2) QFT contains the Heyting arithmetic HA as a subsystem, so that we can discuss the synthesis of programs which compute number theoretic functions.

(3) Every functional of type $\sigma \to \tau$ in FT may be regarded as a program which computes a functional of type τ from a given functional of type σ. Thus we can discuss the synthesis of a program which yields another program from a given program, in case both σ and τ are not of type 0.

(4) Important proof-theoretic results concerning FT and QFT can be used as theoretical foundations for program synthesis.

(5) The computation in FT can be easily simulated by LISP.

We will solve PSP under the following framework:

(a) A program is a (closed) term in FT.
(b) The specification theory is QFT.
(c) The verification theory is QFT.

Suppose that the specification A[x,z] of a problem is given. Then either by a theorem prover

----

* This work was supported in part by the Sakkokai Foundation.

or by a man-machine interactive proof checker, we try to construct a QFT-proof π of the formula $\forall x\exists zA[x,z]$. (This is the most challenging part of our procedure, since no decision procedure exists for the provability of a QFT-formula. Other parts of our procedure are completely mechanical.) If we succeed in constructing such a π, then from π we can construct, primitive recursively, a program P such that A[x,P[x]] is provable in QFT (Theorem 9). Furthermore we can formally verify that P realizes the specification, since $\forall xA[x,P[x]]$ is provable in QFT. We note that, according to Theorem 1, the program P always terminates for any input x. Hence, the total correctness of the program will be established at the same time.

We think that it is fundamental for any program synthesis approach, which may be called mathematically well-founded, to satisfy the following conditions.

1. The semantics of the programming language is precisely specified.
2. The specification theory is precisely specified.
3. The verification theory is precisely specified.

However, it seems to us that many of the existing approaches to program synthesis are too naive to satisfy any one of the above criteria. In contrast, our approach to be described below satisfy all of the above criteria, and hence is mathematically well-founded.

1. FUNCTIONALS OF FINITE TYPE

1.1 Types

Definition of *types*:

1. The symbol 0 is a type.
2. If σ and τ are types then $[\sigma\to\tau]$ is a type.

For brevity we write $\sigma_1\to\sigma_2\to\ldots\to\sigma_n\to\tau$ instead of $[\sigma_1\to[\sigma_2\to\ldots\to[\sigma_n\to\tau]\ldots]]$. The set of all the types will be denoted by Type.

1.2 Terms and programs

The terms of FT will be constructed from the following language LFT:

1. Denumerably infinite set FV^σ of *free variables* for each type σ: $FV^\sigma=\{a1^\sigma,a2^\sigma,a3^\sigma,\ldots\}$. We put $FV=\cup\{FV^\sigma|\sigma\in Type\}$.
2. Denumerably infinite set BV^σ of *bound variables* for each type σ: $BV^\sigma=\{x1^\sigma,x2^\sigma,x3^\sigma,\ldots\}$. We put $BV=\cup\{BV^\sigma|\sigma\in Type\}$.
3. Constants: 0(zero), S(successor) and J_σ(iterator) for each type σ.
4. Lambda abstraction symbol: λ.
5. Parentheses: (and).

As auxiliary symbols, we have denumerably infinitely many *nominal symbols*: *1,*2,*3,... . By an *n-place* (LFT) *nominal form* we mean a finite string of symbols which contains, in addition to the symbols of LFT, at most the nominal symbols *1,*2, ...,*$\bar{n}$, where $\bar{n}$ is the decimal numeral which represents the natural number n. If *A* is an n-place nominal form and $r_1,\ldots,r_n$ are strings of symbols, then $A[r_1,\ldots,r_n]$ denotes the result of replacing every occurrence of *$\bar{i}$ in *A* by r_i $(1\le i\le n)$. We will use *italic* letters to denote nominal forms.

Definition of the set Tm of *terms*, type: Tm$\to$Type and bvar: $Tm\to 2^{BV}$:

1. $a\in FV \Rightarrow a\in Tm$, type[a]=$\sigma$, bvar[a]=$\emptyset$.
2. $0\in Tm$, type[0]=0, bvar[0]=$\emptyset$.
3. $S\in Tm$, type[S]=$0\to0$, bvar[S]=$\emptyset$.
4. $J_\sigma\in Tm$, type[J_σ]=$0\to[\sigma\to\sigma]\to\sigma\to\sigma$, bvar[$J_\sigma$]=$\emptyset$.
5. r, $s\in Tm$, type[r]=$\sigma\to\tau$, type[s]=σ, bvar[r]$\cap$bvar[s]=$\emptyset$ => (r s)$\in$Tm, type[(r s)]=τ, bvar[(r s)]=bvar[r]$\cup$bvar[s].
6. r[a]$\in$Tm, type[r[a]]=τ, $a\in FV^\sigma$, $x\in BV^\sigma$-bvar[r[a]] => $\lambda x r$[x]$\in$Tm, type[$\lambda x r$[x]]=$\sigma\to\tau$, bvar[$\lambda x r$[x]]=bvar[r[a]]$\cup\{x\}$.

Tm is the least set which satisfies the above conditions. We put $Tm^\sigma=\{t\in Tm|type[t]=\sigma\}$. An element in Tm^σ is called a *term of type* σ. Two terms r and s are *congruent* if they are constructed exactly in the same manner, except that possibly different bound variables are selected in the applications of 6 above. We will henceforth identify congruent terms. This identification has the effect of making bound variables really dummy. A *program* is a term containing no free variables. We write Prog for the set of programs, and we put $Prog^\sigma=\{t\in Prog|type[t]=\sigma\}$. We use r, s, t etc. as syntactic symbols denoting terms or programs. For brevity we write $r_1r_2r_3\ldots r_n$ instead of $((\ldots(r_1\ r_2)\ r_3)\ldots)\ r_n)$.

Definition of a binary relation red on Prog:

1. ($\lambda x r$[x] s) red r[s].
2. J_σ0st red t.
3. J_σ(Sr)st red s($J_\sigma$rst).
4. r red r' => (r s) red (r' s).
5. s red s' => (r s) red (r s').

We let red* be the reflexive and transitive closure of red. A program p is *normal* if p red q for no q.

Definition of the *numerals* N_n(n: a natural number):

1. N_0=0.
2. N_{n+1}=(S N_n).

The following three lemmas can be proved by a standard technique. (See, e.g., [Schütte 1977], [Troelstra 1973], [Howard 1970].)

Lemma 1. *A program* p *of type* 0 *is normal if and only if* p=N_n *for some natural number* n.

Lemma 2. *If* p red* q, p red* q', *and both* q *and* q' *are normal, then* q=p'.

Lemma 3. *For any program* p *there exists an normal program* q *such that* p red* q.

Putting Lemma 2 and Lemma 3 together, we have:

Theorem 1. *For any program* p *there uniquely exists an normal program* q *such that* p red* q.

The program q in the above theorem is called the *normal form* of p, and is denoted by **[p]**. We write D for the set of programs in normal form, and we put $D^\sigma=\{p\in D|\text{type}[p]=\sigma\}$.

1.3 Interpretation of terms

We can use the function $[\![\ ]\!]$: Prog→D which sends a program p to its normal form $[\![p]\!]$, as a semantic function. For instance, a program p of type $\sigma\to\tau$ may be considered as denoting a functional $\mathfrak{p}$: $D^\sigma\to D^\tau$ such that $\mathfrak{p}[s]=[\![(p\ s)]\!]$ for any $s\in D^\sigma$. Furthermore, we remark that, by Lemma 1, D^0 is isomorphic with the set $\mathbb{N}$ of natural numbers. With this interpretation in mind, we define the formal system FT of primitive recursive functionals of finite type as follows.

2. THE FORMAL SYSTEM FT

2.1 Definition of the system FT

Definition of the set Form of FT-*formulas*:

1. $s, t\in Tm^\sigma \Rightarrow s=t\in$Form.
2. A, B∈Form => (A⊃B), (A∧B), (A∨B)∈Form.

We use Γ, Δ etc. to denote finite (possibly empty) sequences of formulas. If Γ is the sequence '$A_1,\ldots,A_n$' then Γ⊃B is the abbreviation of $A_1\supset\ldots\supset A_n\supset B$ which, in turn, is the abbreviation of $(A_1\supset(\ldots\supset(A_n\supset B)\ldots))$. If Γ='$A_1,\ldots,A_n$' and Δ='$B_1,\ldots,B_m$' then Γ⊆Δ means that the set $\{A_1,\ldots,A_n\}$ is included in the set $\{B_1,\ldots,B_m\}$. We define the connective ¬ by: $\neg A=A\supset S0=0$. A formula containing no free variable is called a *closed* formula. A formula which only contains equations between terms of type 0 is said to be a *basic formula*.

Definition of the provability relation ⊢ in FT:

Axioms:

(λ) ⊢ $(\lambda x r[x]\ s)=r[s]$.
($J_\sigma 0$) ⊢ $J_\sigma 0st=t$.
($J_\sigma^\sigma S$) ⊢ $J_\sigma^\sigma(Sr)st=s(J_\sigma rst)$.
(=) ⊢ $s=t\supset F[s]\supset F[t]$.

Inference rules:

(Str) ⊢ Γ⊃B, Γ⊆Δ => ⊢ Δ⊃B.
(Cut) ⊢ Γ⊃A, ⊢ A⊃B => ⊢ Γ⊃B.
(CI) ⊢ $F[0]$, ⊢ $F[a]\supset F[Sa]$, $a\in FV^0$, $a\notin F$, $t\in Tm^0$ => ⊢ $F[t]$.
(∧l) ⊢ A⊃B⊃C => ⊢ (A∧B)⊃C.
(∧r) ⊢ Γ⊃A, ⊢ Γ⊃B => ⊢ Γ⊃(A∧B).
(∨l) ⊢ A⊃C, ⊢ B⊃C => ⊢ (A∨B)⊃C.
(∨r) ⊢ $\Gamma\supset A_i$ => ⊢ $\Gamma\supset(A_1\vee A_2)$ (i=1,2).

In the above definition, $a\notin F$ means that the free variable a does not occur in the nominal form F. A formula A is said to be *provable* (in FT) if ⊢A.

2.2 Consistency and weak completeness

Definition of *truth* and *falsity* for a closed formura:

1. A closed formula s=t is *true* iff $[\![s]\!]=[\![t]\!]$.
2. A closed formula A⊃B is *true* iff A is *false* or B is *true*.
3. A closed formula A∧B is *true* iff A is *true* and B is *true*.
4. A closed formula A∨B is *true* iff A is *true* or B is *true*.
5. A closed formula A is *false* iff A is not *true*.

We write ⊨A if A is true. We then have the following consistency theorem. (See [Schütte 1977], Theorem 17.2.)

Theorem 2. ⊢A, A: *closed* => ⊨A.

Although not all true closed formulas are provable in FT (example: $\neg J_0(S0)S=S$), we have the following weak completeness theorem.

Theorem 3. ⊨A, A: *basic* => ⊢ A.

Putting Theorem 2 and Theorem 3 together, we have:

Theorem 4. *A closed basic formula is provable in* FT *if and only if it is true.*

3. THE FORMAL SYSTEM QFT

3.1 Definition of QFT

Definition of the set Form of QFT-*formulas* and bvar:Form→2^{BV}_0:

1. $s, t\in Tm^0$ => s=t∈Form, bvar[s=t]=bvar[s]∪bvar[t].
2. A, B∈Form => (A⊃B), (A∧B), (A∧B)∈Form, bvar[(A⊃B)]=bvar[(A∧B)]=bvar[(A∨B)]=bvar[A]∪bvar[B].
3. $A[a]\in$Form, $a\in FV^\sigma$, $x\in BV^\sigma$−bvar$[A[a]]$ => $\forall xA[x]$, $\exists xA[x]\in$Form, bvar$[\forall xA[x]]$=bvar$[\exists xA[x]]$=bvar$[A[a]]$∪{x}.

Two formulas are *congruent* if they are constructed exactly in the same manner, except that possibly different bound variables are selected in the applications of 3 above. We will henceforth identify congruent formulas. A formula is *quantifier free* if it contains no occurrence of ∀ or ∃. A quantifier free QFT-formula is just a basic FT-formula. We define the negation ¬A of a formula A by ¬A=A⊃S0=0.

Notational conventions: Let s='$s_1,\ldots,s_n$' be a sequence of terms $s_1,\ldots s_n$ and let t='$t_1,\ldots,t_m$' be a sequence of terms $t_1,\ldots,t_m$, where m,n≥0. Suppose that type$[s_i]=\sigma_1\to\ldots\to\sigma_m\to\tau_i$ (1≤i≤n) and type$[t_j]=\tau_j$ (1≤j≤m). Then we let (s t) denote the sequence '$s_1t_1\ldots t_m,\ldots,s_nt_1\ldots t_m$'. We use r, s, t etc. to denote sequence of terms. Similarly, we use a, b, c etc. to denote sequences of free variables, and x, y, z etc. to denote sequences of bound variables. If x='$x_1,\ldots,x_n$', t='$t_1,\ldots,t_n$' and A is an n-place nominal form, then $\forall xA[x]$, $\exists xA[x]$ and $A[t]$ are the abbreviations of $\forall x_1\ldots\forall x_nA[x_1,\ldots,x_n]$, $\exists x_1\ldots\exists x_nA[x_1,\ldots,x_n]$ and $A[t_1,\ldots,t_n]$, respectively.

Definition of the provability relation ⊢ in QFT:

Axioms:

(FT) ⊢ A (in FT), A: basic => - A.
(∀l) ⊢ $\forall xA[x]\supset A[t]$.
(∃r) ⊢ $A[t]\supset\exists xA[x]$.
(IP_0') A:quantifier free => ⊢ $(\forall xA[x]\supset\exists yB[y])\supset\exists y(\forall xA[x]\supset B[y])$.
(M') A:quantifier free => ⊢ $\neg\neg\exists xA[x]\supset\exists xA[x]$.
(AC) ⊢ $\forall x\exists yA[x,y]\supset\exists z\forall xA[x,zx]$.

Inference rules

(Str), (Cut), (CI), (∧l), (∧r), (∨l) (∨r): same

as in FT for QFT-formulas.

(∀r) $\vdash \Gamma \supset A[a]$, $a \notin A$ => $\vdash \Gamma \supset \forall x A[x]$.

(∃l) $\vdash A[a] \supset B$, $a \notin A$ => $\vdash \exists x A[x] \supset B$.

In the above definition, $a \notin A$ means that none of the free variables in the sequence a occurrs in the nominal form A. Also in the above definition, IP, M and AC stand for 'independence of premiss', 'Markov's principle' and 'axiom of choice', respectively. Two formulas A and B are *equivalent* in QFT if both $A \supset B$ and $B \supset A$ are provable in QFT.

3.2 Interpreting formulas

A QFT-formula F is an *interpreting formula* if it is of the form $\exists x \forall y F_0[x,y]$, and F_0 is quantifier free. (We use the subscript 0 to denote a quantifier-free nominal form.)

Definition of Gödel translation: With each QFT-formula F, we associate an interpreting formula F* (*Gödel translation* of F) as follows.

1. F: quantifier free => F*=F.

Let $A^* = \exists x_1 \forall y_1 A_0[x_1, y_1]$ and $B^* = \exists x_2 \forall y_2 B_0[x_2, y_2]$.

2. $F = A \supset B$ => $F^* = \exists \tilde{x}_2 \exists \tilde{y}_1 \forall x_1 \forall y_2 (A_0[x_1, \tilde{y}_1 x_1, y_2] \supset B_0[\tilde{x}_2 x_1, y_2])$.
3. $F = A \wedge B$ => $F^* = \exists x_1 \exists x_2 \forall y_1 \forall y_2 (A_0[x_1, y_1] \wedge B_0[x_2, y_2])$.
4. $F = A \vee B$ => $F^* = \exists z \exists x_1 \exists x_2 \forall y_1 \forall y_2 (z=0 \supset A_0[x_1, y_1] \wedge \neg z=0 \supset B_0[x_2, y_2])$.

Let $(A[a])^* = \exists x_1 \forall y_1 A_0[x_1, y_1, a]$

5. $F = \forall x A[x]$ = $F^* = \exists \tilde{x}_1 \forall x \forall y_1 A_0[\tilde{x}_1 x, y_1 x]$.
6. $F = \exists x A[x]$ = $F^* = \exists x \exists x_1 \forall y_1 A_0[x_1, y_1, x]$.

The following theorem can be verified without difficulty. (AC) plays a role in the proof.

Theorem 5. *For any* QFT-*formula* F, F and F* *are equivalent in* QFT.

3.3 Reduction of QFT to FT

Let $F = \exists x \forall y F_0[x,y]$ be an interpreting formula. A quantifier free formula $F_0[t,a]$ is called a *reduction* of F, if a is a sequence of free variables such that $a \notin F_0$, and if t is a sequence of terms whose free variables, if any, always occur in F_0. Note that $F_0[t,a]$ is a basic FT-formula. Also, note that t is closed if F_0 contains no free variable. We then have the following important theorem due originally to [Gödel 1958]. (Gödel gives the reduction of the Heyting arithmetic HA to FT. Reduction of a system which admits quantifications over functionals of any type to FT was first carried out by [Yasugi 1963]. For a correction to [Yasugi 1963], see [Troelstra 1972].

Theorem 6. *If a* QFT-*proof of an interpreting formula* $F = \exists x \forall y F_0[x,y]$ *is given, then we can construct, primitive recursively, a reduction* $F_G = F_0[t,a]$ *of* F *and its proof in* FT.

We call above F_G the *Gödel reduction* of F. By Theorem 2 and Theorem 6, we have the following consistency theorem for QFT.

Theorem 7. *The system* QFT *is syntactically consistent, i.e., there exists a* QFT-*formula* A *which is not provable in* QFT.

3.4 Truth definition for QFT-formulas

Definition of *truth* and *falsity* for a closed QFT-formula:

1. A=s=t => A is *true* iff [s]=[t].
2. $A = B \supset C$ => A is *true* iff B is *false* or C is *true*.
3. $A = B \wedge C$ => A is *true* iff B is *true* and C is *true*.
4. $A = B \vee C$ => A is *true* iff B is *true* or C is *true*.
5. $A = \forall x B[x]$, $x \in BV^\sigma$ => A is *true* iff $B[t]$ is *true* for all $t \in D^\sigma$.
6. $A = \exists x B[x]$, $x \in BV^\sigma$ => A is *true* iff $B[t]$ is *true* for some $t \in D^\sigma$.
7. A is *false* iff A is *true*.

In contrast to the constructive definition of truth for FT-formulas, the above truth definition is nonconstructive because of 5 and 6 above. A true QFT-formulas will be referred to as *classically true* when we wish to emphasize this nonconstructive character of truth definition. Anyway, we remark that the above definition gives a (at least classically) natural interpretation of QFT-formulas in the domain D.

We now extend the truth definition to any QFT-formulas as follows. An *assignment* is a type preserving function ϕ: FV→D. Let ϕ be an assignment, and A be any QFT-formula. Let a='$a_1, \ldots, a_n$' be the stock of all free variables occurring in A (a is empty if A is closed). Then A is of the form $A[a_1, \ldots, a_n]$. Now, A is *true under* ϕ (notation: $\phi \models A$) if the closed formula $A[\phi[a_1], \ldots, \phi[a_n]]$ is true. A is *valid* ($\models A$) if $\phi \models A$ for any assignment ϕ. A closed formula is valid iff it is true.

A tricky point about the system QFT is that the axiom schema (AC) is not always valid. For by Problem 9-(b) in Chapter 8 of [Shoenfield 1967], there is a recursive function $f: D^0 \to D^0$ such that (i): $f \neq \hat{r}$ for all $r \in D^{0 \to 0}$, (See §1.3 for the definition of $\hat{r}$. $f \neq \hat{r}$ means that two functions are extensionally distinct, i.e., there exists some $s \in D^0$ such that $f[s] \neq \hat{r}[s]$.) and (ii): there is a QFT-formula $A[a,b]$ such that $\phi \models A[a,b]$ iff $\phi[b] = f[\phi[a]]$. Hence the following instance of (AC) is not valid: $\forall x \exists y A[x,y] \supset \exists z \forall x A[x, zx]$. (See also II-§5-2.5.3-(iv) of [Troelstra 1973].) Then, by Theorem 8 below, we see that the Gödel translation F→F* does not always preserve the classical truth value.

The above observation suggests us to define the following variants of QFT: We define the system QFT_0 as the system which results from QFT by deleting the axiom(AC). We obtain the classical system $CQFT_0$ by adding the following axiom (¬¬) to QFT_0:

(¬¬) $\neg\neg A \supset A$.

We have the following semantical consistency theorem.

Theorem 8. 1) $QFT_0 \vdash A$ => $CQFT_0 \vdash A$ => $\models A$.
2) $QFT \vdash A$ => $\models A^*$.

4. PROGRAM SYNTHESIS

4.1. The problem of program synthesis

Definition of a specification: A *specification* is a triple Σ=<A; '$b_1,\ldots,b_n$'; '$a_1,\ldots,a_n$'> where A is an m+n-place nominal form such that $A[b,a]=A[b_1,\ldots,b_n,a_1,\ldots,a_m]$ is a formula containing at most b and a free. We put

$D_I(\Sigma)=D_{\sigma_1}\times\ldots\times D_{\sigma_m}$, where σ_i=type$[a_i]$,

$D_0(\Sigma)=D_{\tau_1}\times\ldots\times D_{\tau_n}$, where τ_j=type$[b_j]$ and

$R(\Sigma)=\{(s,t)\in D_I(\Sigma)\times D_0(\Sigma)\mid \models A[t,s]\}$.

We call $D_I(\Sigma)$ the *input domain* of Σ, $D_0(\Sigma)$ the *output domain* of Σ and $R(\Sigma)$ the *input-output relation* of Σ. An element s in $D_I(\Sigma)$ is called an *input*. We identify $s=(s_1,\ldots,s_m)\in D_I(\Sigma)$ with the sequence '$s_1,\ldots,s_m$'. Two specifications Σ and Σ' are *equivalent* if $R(\Sigma)=R(\Sigma')$. A sequence of programs will simply be called a program.

Definition of realization: A program p *realizes* the specification Σ if A[ps,s] is *true* for any input $s\in D_I(\Sigma)$.

A specification Σ then determines the following. *Program synthesis Problem* PSP(Σ): "*Construct a program* p *which realizes the specification* Σ."

In order that PSP(Σ) may have a solution, it is necessary that the formula $B=\exists y\forall xA[yx,x]$ is true. (Because if a program p realizes Σ, then $\models$B.) We note that B is true iff there exists a program p='$p_1,\ldots,p_n$' such that $\{(s,\mathfrak{p}[s])\in D_I\times D_0 \mid s\in D_I\}\subseteq R(\Sigma)$, where $\mathfrak{p}[s]=(\mathfrak{p}_1[s],\ldots,\mathfrak{p}_n[s])$ and $\mathfrak{p}_i[s]=[\![(p_i\ s)]\!]$. Roughly speaking, B is true iff R(Σ) contains the graph of a program. We also remark that the formula B semantically entails the formula $C=\forall x\exists zA[z,x]$. The formulas B and C are equivalent in QFT, but, as we have seen in §3.4, they are not necessarily semantically equivalent.

By a *prenex formula* we mean a formula of the form $Q_1x_1\ldots Q_nx_nA_0[x_1,\ldots,x_n]$, where Q_ix_i is either $\forall x_i$ or $\exists x_i$. Since $CQFT_0$ is a classical system, any formula A can be transformed into a prenex formula B, which we call the *prenex normal form* of A, such that A and B are equivalent in $CQFT_0$. We have the following easily verifiable lemma.

Lemma 4. *If* A *is a prenex formula, then* $QFT_0\vdash A^*\supset A$.

We are now in a position to prove the following Main Theorem:

Theorem 9. *Let* Σ=<A;b;a> *be a specification, and let* B[b,a] *be the prenex normal form of* A[b,a]. *Then if a* QFT-*proof of the formula* $\forall x\exists yB[y,x]$ *is given, we can construct, primitive recursively, a program* p *which realizes the specification* Σ. *Moreover, we can formally verify that* p *realizes* Σ, *i.e., the formula* $\forall xA[px,x]$ *is provable in* $CQFT_0$.

Proof. Define a nominal form B^* by $B^*[b,a]=(B[b,a])^*$. Then $B^*[b,a]$ is of the form $\exists u\forall vB_0[b,a,u,v]$. Let $C=\forall x\exists yB[y,x]$. Then $C^*=(\forall x\exists yB^*[y,x])^*=\exists z\exists w\forall x\forall vB_0[zx,x,wx,v]$. Then by Theorem 6, we have FT $\vdash (C^*)_G$, where $(C^*)_G$ is of the form B_0[pa,a,qa,c] (p and q are sequences of closed terms, i.e., programs, since C* is closed, and a,c are sequences of free variables). Then we have:

FT $\vdash B_0$[pa,a,qa,c]

=>	$QFT_0\vdash\exists w\forall x\forall vB_0$[px,x,wx,v]	(by ($\forall$r),($\exists$r),(MP))
=>	$QFT_0\vdash\forall x\exists u\forall vB_0$[px,x,u,v]	(by Lemma 4)
=>	$QFT_0\vdash\exists u\forall vB_0$[pa,a,u,v]	(by ($\forall$l),(MP))
=>	$QFT_0\vdash B$[pa,a]	(by Lemma 4)
=>	$CQFT_0\vdash A$[pa,a]	(by assumption)
=>	$CQFT_0\vdash\forall xA$[px,x]	(by ($\forall$r)).

We have thus established the second part of the theorem. That p realizes Σ now follows by Theorem 8-(1).

Remark. 1. If A is quantifier free, then B is identical with A. We note that this category already contains many working examples such as quotient-remainder, GCD etc. For more examples see [Takahashi 1977].

2. Note that we have solved the problem by changing the given specification Σ to its equivalent variant Σ'=<B;b;a>, providing the problem does not fall in the category mentioned above. (A and B are equivalent in $CQFT_0$!) That this modification is necessary can be seen as follows. Let $Ac=\forall x\exists yF[x,y]\supset\exists z\forall xF[x,zx]$ be a *false* instance of (AC). (See §3.4.) Let Σ be the specification <A;'b';'a'> where A=Ac$\wedge$*1=0 and type[a]=type[b]=0 so that A[b,a]=Ac$\wedge$b=0. Then Σ'=<B;'b';'a'>, where B[b,a] is the prenex normal form of A[b,a]. Now, if we feed the formula $\forall x\exists yA[y,x]$ to a QFT-therem-prover, then since it is provable in QFT, we will have a program p=λx0 whose graph is $D_0\times\{0\}$. But R(Σ) is empty since Ac$\wedge$b=0 is *false* under any assignment $\emptyset$. Thus our program p does not realize the specification Σ. (Caution: That a false formula is provable in QFT does not imply its inconsistency. See Theorem 8-(2).) We have avoided such awkwardness by shifting from Σ to its equivalent variant Σ'. In this case the formula $\forall x\exists yB[y,x]$ is simply unprovable in QFT.

3. There are several interesting relations between the inference rules employed in the proof of B[b,a] and the structure of the synthesized programs, of which we cannot go into details because of the limitation of space. Roughly speaking, (MP), [($\vee\to$), ($\to\wedge$), (Str)] and (CI) correspond to composition of programs, conditional (*if_then_else*) and primitive recursion, respectively. In particular, a *structured proof* yields a *structured program*.

4.2 Simulation by LISP

We have seen that the semantic function $[\![\ ]\!]$:Prog $\to$D is recursive (Theorem 1). In order to simulate this function by a LISP S-function, we proceed as follows. Let Sexp denote the set of LISP S-expressions.

Definition of ψ:Prog Sexp:

$\psi[0]=0$, $\psi[S]=S$, $\psi[J_\sigma]=J$, $\psi[x\bar{i}^\sigma]=X\bar{i}$

$\psi[(r\ s)]=(\psi[r]\ \psi[s])$, $\psi[\lambda x r[x]]=(L\ \psi[x]\ \psi[r[x]])$.
Definition of the S-function reduce:

```
reduce[x]=
[normal[x]→x;
 atom[caar[x]]→[eq[caar[x];L]→reduce[lconv[x];
                T→subreduce[x] ];
 atom[caaar[x]]→
  [eq[caaar[x];J]→[atom[cadaar[x]→reduce[cadr[x]];
                   atom[caadaaar[x]]→[eq[caadaar[x];S]→
reduce[list[cadar[x];list[list[list[J;cadadaar[x]];cadar[x]];
                      cadr[x] ]]];
                                  T→subreduce[x] ];
                   T→subreduce[x] ];
   T→subreduce[x] ];
 T→subreduce[x] ]

subreduce[x]=reduce[list[reduce[car[x]];reduce[cadr[x]]]]

normal[x]=
[atom[x]→T;
 atom[car[x]]→subnormal[x];
 atom[caar[x]]→[eq[caar[x];L]→NIL;T→subnormal[x]];
 atom[caaar[x]]→[eq[caaar[x]];J]→
  [atom[cadaar[x]]→[eq[cadaar[x];0]→NIL;
                   T→subnormal[x] ];
   atom[caadaar[x]]→[eq[caadaar[x];S]→NIL;
                    T→subnormal[x] ];
   T→subnormal[x] ];
 T→subnormal[x] ]

subnormal[x]=[normal[car[x]]→normal[cadr[x]];T→NIL]

lconv[x]=lconvl[caddar[x];cadar[x];cadr[x]]]

lconvl[x;v;y]=lcnv[x;NIL;v;y]

lcnv[x;bv;v;y]=
[atom[x]→[eq[x;v]→[memq[v;bv]→x;T→y];T→x];
 atom[car[x]]→[eq[car[x];L]→list[L;cadr[x];lcnv[caddr[x];
append[cons[cadr[x];NIL];bv];v;y ]];
                 T→list[lcnv[car[x];bv;v;y];
                          lcnv[cadr[x];bv;v;y] ] ];
 T→list[lcnv[car[x];bv;v;y];lcnv[cadr[x];bv;v;y]] ]
```

Theorem 10. *The diagram below commutes*:

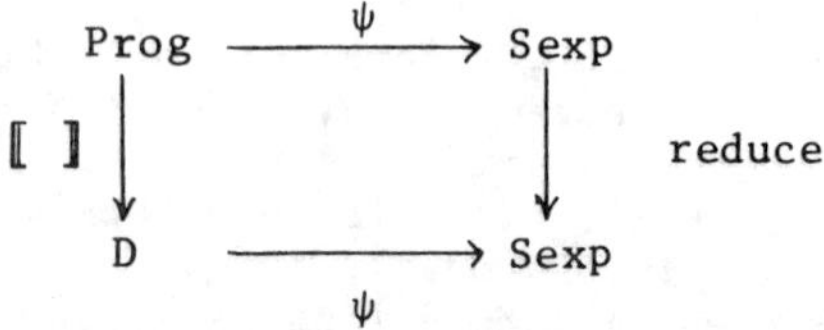

Thus we have seen that the function reduce simulates the semantic function $[\![\ ]\!]$. If ψ were a one-to-one function, then we could compute $[\![\ ]\!]$ by the equation $[\![p]\!]=(\psi^{-1}\cdot\text{reduce}\cdot\psi)[p]$. But ψ is not one-to-one since $\psi[J_\sigma]=J$ for any σ Type. However, we note that $\psi\times\text{type}:\text{Prog}\to\text{Sexp}\times\text{Type}$ such that $(\psi\times\text{type})[p]=(\psi[p],\ \text{type}[p])$ is one-to-one. Hence we can compute $[\![\ ]\!]$ by the scheme $[\![p]\!]=(\psi\times\text{type})^{-1}[\text{reduce}[\psi[p]],\ \text{type}[p]]$. (Note that $[\![\ ]\!]$ preserves type.)

4.3 Concluding Remarks

We believe that we have successfully set a theoretical foundation for program synthesis. It is not difficult to implement our procedure, and we wish to encourage the interested readers to actually implement it. In fact, at a suggestion of the author, [Goto 1978] has implemented a system of program synthesis. However, his system differs at an essential point from the one described above, and, at present, no proof exists which guarantees the correctness of the program synthesized by Goto's system. The possibility of using Gödel interpretation as a tool for program synthesis has also been suggested by [Kreisel 1977]. [Takasu 1978] also studies the application of Gödel interpretation to program synthesis using the formalism of Gentzen's sequential calculus.
Since the basic data type of Prog is natural number, it may appear that such data types as list, stack etc. cannot be dealt with in our formalism. However it is not the case, and we can treat these data types as well by treating them as abstract data types. We wish to discuss this point further in a paper to be published later.

ACKNOWLEDGMENTS.
The author wishes to thank Professor Satoru Takasu of Kyoto University for many stimulating discussions with the author. The author wishes to thank Mr. Hayao Nakahara for correcting errors in the original definition of the function reduce.

REFERENCES

[Burstall, R.M. and Goguen, J.A. 1977] *Putting thories together to make specifications*, Proc. IJCAI-77. MIT, Cambridge, Mass., 1045-1058.
[Gödel, K. 1958] *Über eine bisher noch nicht benützte erwriterung des finiten Standpunktes*, Dialectica, 12, 280-287.
[Goto, S. 1978] *Program synthesis through Gödel's interpretation*, Proc. International Conference on Mathematical Studies of Information Processing, 287-306, Kyoto.
[Howard, W.A. 1970] *Assignment of ordinals to terms of primitive recursive functionals of finite type*, Intuitionism and Proof Theory, 443-458, North-Holland.
[Kreisel, G. 1977] *Some uses of proof theory for finding computer programs*, *Colloque* International des Logique, 123-134, Paris.
[Shoenfield, J.R. 1967] Mathematical Logic, Addison Wesley.
[Shütte, K. 1977] Proof Theory, Springer.
[Takahashi, M. 1977] *A foundation of finite mathematics*, Publ. RIMS, Kyoto Univ., 12, 577-708.
[Takasu, S. 1978] *Proofs and programs*, Proc. 3rd IBM symposium on Mathematical Foundations of Computer Science, IBM Japan.
[Takeuti, G. 1975] Proof Theory, North-Holland.
[Troelstra, A.S. 1972] *Review of* [Yasugi 1963], J. of Symbolic Logic, 37, 404.
[Troelstra, A.S. 1973] Mathematical Investigations of intuitionistic arithmetic and analysis, Lecture Notes in Mathematics 344, Springer.
[Yasugi, M. 1963] *Intuitionistic analysis and Gödel's interpretation*, J. Math. Soc. Japan, 15, 101-112.

Automotive Stereo Vision using Deconvolution Technique

Tomomasa Sato

Automatic Control Division
Electrotechnical Laboratory
Tokyo, Japan

A new stereo vision system using deconvolution technique is proposed. This system is composed of the upper and the lower camera. By deconvoluting the upper image with the lower one, the system constructs a horizontal section image. After the automobiles are separated from the other things in this horizontal section image, the distances and relative velocity are measured. This segmentation is realized by the thresholding procedure which utilizes the relation between the distance and the breadth of the automobile. The experimental results are presented. It is also shown that the deconvolution technique is able to construct a finer and higher resolutional horizontal section image compared with a correlation technique. Although the SN ratio of the horizontal section image is inconsistent with range resolution, the possibility of the adjustment between the SN ratio and the resolution is presented.

1. Introduction

In order to avoid the motorcar accidents, it would be the effective method that the driver is assisted with the warnings by a computer system for safety. This system needs the sensors which detect traffic conditions. Measuring the distances and relative velocity between the driver and the automobiles around him is the most basic function of these sensors. Because of the difficulties to identify the automobiles from other things, this problem has not complitely solved yet. The most important kye to solve this problem is a fast processing of the horizontal section images around the driver. This horizontal section image can be obtained by a stereo vision (trianguration system) via measuring the value of the shift between two images. In order to measure the value of this shift, many techniques have been utilized (i.e. the correlation technique [1], the technique which utilizes the phase shift of the narrow bandwidth of the target Fourier spectrum [2], etc.). This paper describes an alternative technique using deconvolution.

2. Stereo Vision using Deconvolution Technique

2-1 Obtaining the Horizontal Section Image

With the stereo vision system shown by Fig.1 , it is possible to approximate the upper image $f_2(x)$ is the shifted image of the lower one $f_1(x)$.

$$f_2(x) \doteq f_1(x-\tau) \quad \left[= \int f_1(x') * (x' - (x-\tau)) dx' \right] \tag{1}$$

In other word, it can be said that $f_2(x)$ is a convoluted image of $f_1(x)$ and $\delta(x-\tau)$. By measuring the value of the shift τ ,we can obtain the distance between the target ahead and the system. Therefore, one line of the horizontal section image can be obtained by plotting with light and shade the correlation curve, which is obtained by calculating the degree of matching between two images when the upper image is shifted relative to the lower one. Scince the lower camera of this system always gives the front view of the targets on the road as a reference image, this camera arrangement is suited for detecting the traffic obstacles.

The algorithm to obtain horizontal section image is as follows. [see Fig.2]

[1] Two windowed images are obtained by the upper and the lower cameras. [Fig.4(b)and(c)]

[2] The Fourier transformations of the obtained images are carried out by FFT.

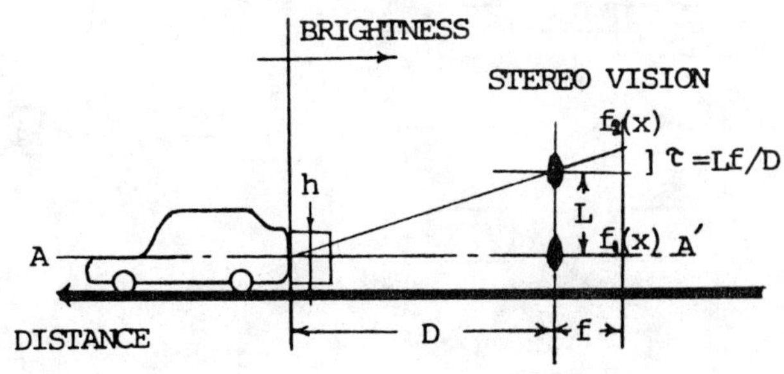

Fig.1 The principle of stereo vision

$$Fi(\omega)=\int_{-\frac{X}{2}}^{\frac{X}{2}} fi(x)*e^{-j\omega x}dx \quad (i=1,2) \tag{2}$$

where X refers to the length of the image.

[3] By deconvoluting the upper image with the lower one, we calculate the correlation curve in the frequency domain ; $G(\omega)$.

$$G(\omega)=F_2(\omega)*D(\omega)$$

$$D(\omega)=\begin{cases} 1/F_1(\omega) & ; F_1(\omega)\geq F_1 max(\omega)/a \\ 0 & ; \text{otherwise} \end{cases} \tag{3}$$

where "a" [=30 for the following examples] is a constant.

[4] By the inverse Fourier transformation of $G(\omega)$, the correlation curve $g_d(z)$ is obtained. [Fig.3(a)]

$$g_d(z)=\int_{\omega_1}^{\omega_2} G(\omega)*e^{j\omega z}df \tag{4}$$

where $\omega_1(\omega_2)$ is the lowest (highest) angular-frequency of the target Fourier spectrum.

Repeating these procedures ([1]~[4]) along the horizontal right/left direction, the horizontal section image is obtained. [Fig.4(d)]

2-2 Automobiles Identification and Velocity Measurement

Once the horizontal section image is constructed , the automobiles are separated from the other things by thresholding procedure which utilizes the relation between the distance and the breadth of the automobile. The result of this segmentation is presented by Fig.4(f). Finally, relative velocity is measured by processing two sequential horizontal section images.

3. Deconvolution and Correlation Technique

The horizontal section image can also be constructed using correlation technique. Assuming that the brightness distribution of the vehicle image has a square shape as shown on Fig.1, the comparizon of these methods are derived.

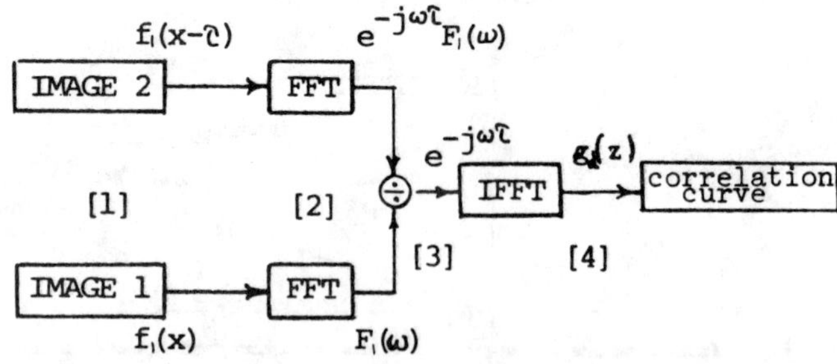

Fig.2 The algorithm of calculating the correlation curve.

3-1 Quality of Horizontal Section Image

(a) Deconvolution Technique : Substituting Eqs.(1),(2) into Eq.(4) , the correlation curve $g_d(z)$ is given by Eq.(5).

$$g_d(z)=\int_{\omega_1}^{\omega_2}\frac{e^{-j\omega\tau}F_1(\omega)}{F_1(\omega)}e^{j\omega z}df=\int_{\omega_1}^{\omega_2}e^{j\omega(z-\tau)}df$$
$$=\frac{\Omega}{2}e^{j\Omega m(z-\tau)}*SINC[\frac{\Omega}{2}(z-\tau)] \tag{5}$$

where $\Omega=\omega_2-\omega_1$, $\Omega m=(\omega_1+\omega_2)/2$.

The range resolution δ_d [$=2\pi/\Omega$ =h/2a; Fig.3(a)] is generally small and adjustable by varying the value of "a".

(b) Correlation Technique : The correlation curve $g_c(z)$ is derived as follows.

$$g_c(z)=\int_{\omega_1}^{\omega_2}F_1(\omega)*F_1^*(\omega)e^{j\omega(z-\tau)}df \tag{6}$$

The range resolution δ_c[=h ; Fig.3 and Fig.4(d),(e)] is generally large.

Comparing these techniques, the correlation curve using deconvolution has a constant shape of SINC function, and its shape depends only upon the target Fourier spectrum. On the other hand the correlation curve using correlation depends upon the target Fourier spectrum itself. Therefore, a finer (easy to process) horizontal section image is obtainable using deconvolution technique.

3-2 Effects of White Noise

When the white noise (its power spectrum is N_0) is added to the square shaped image, the SN ratio [the ratio of peak (matching point) power to the mean noise power] of the horizontal section image is analized as follows [3].

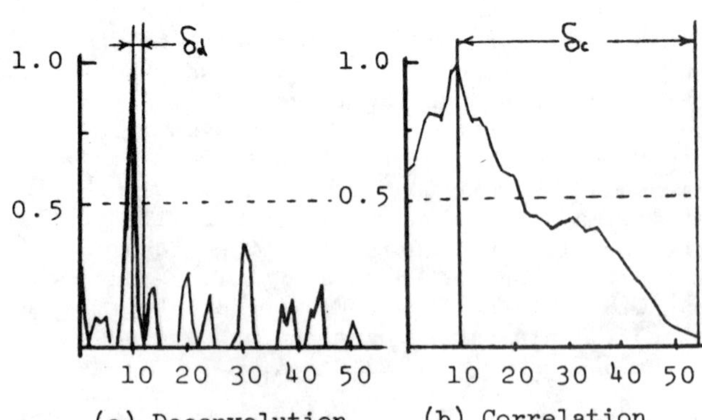

The ordinate represents the degree of matching. The abscissa represents the length of shift between two images. The two images are matched when the length of shift is equal to 10.

Fig.3 The shape of correlation curves.

(a) Deconvolution Technique: $SN_d = 3h/\pi N_0 a$ (7)
(b) Correlation Technique: $SN_c = 2h/N_0$ (8)

Considering δ_d and Eq.(7), the deconvolution technique enable us to adjust the range resolution and the SN ratio by varying "a". It is also possible to prove that the additive white noise causes no peak position error of correlation curve by any these two techniques. In the analysis stated above, the input data is assumed to be continuous. Scince real data is not continuous, the discrete calculation (FFT) brings the data a cyclic property. However, this effect can be reduced by windowing and filling zeroes around the input data.

4. Conclusions

1] A stereo vision using deconvolution technique is proposed.
2] This vision system is able to construct a finer and higher resolutional horizontal section image compared with a system using correlation technique.
3] It is also shown that the adjustment between range resolution and the SN ratio of the horizontal section image is easily realized by this technique.
4] The identification of the automobiles from the other things and the measurement of the distances and relative velocity between the driver and the automobiles ahead of him are presented by processing these horizontal section image sequentially.

References

[1] Yakimovsky, Y. and Cunningham, R. "A System for Extracting Three-Dimensional Measurements from a Stereo Pair of TV Cameras" Computer Graphics and Image Processing 7 , pp 195-210 (1978)
[2] Arking, A. A.,Lo, R. C. and Rosenfelt, A. "An Evaluation of Fourier Transform Techniques for Cloud Motion Estimation" Computer Science Technical Report TR-351, University of Maryland (1975)
[3] Urkowitz. H "Filters for Detection of Small Signals in Clutter" J. Appl. Phys., Vol.24, No.8, pp 1024-1031 (1953)

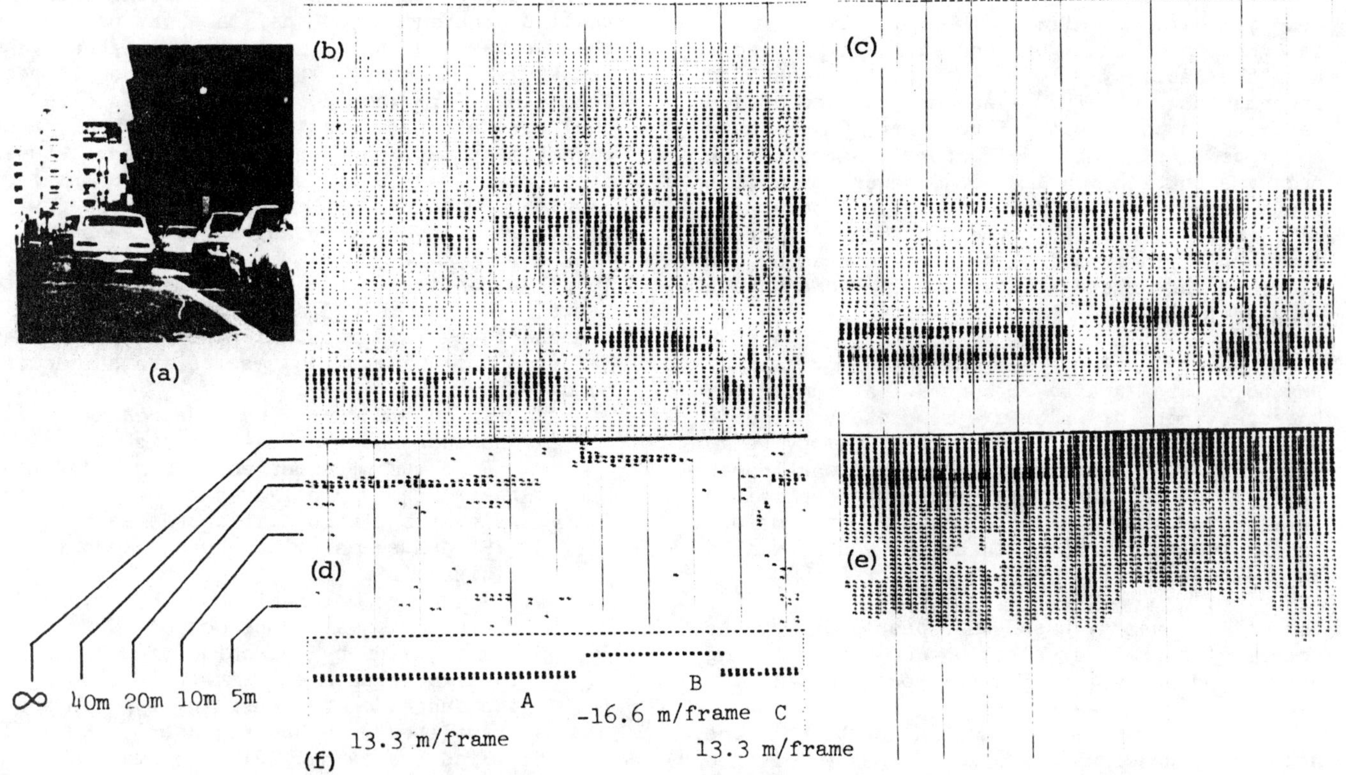

(a) The photograph used for experiments. (b) Upper image. (c) Lower image
(d) The horizontal section image via deconvolution technique.
(e) The horizontal section image via correlation technique.
(f) The result of the segmentation of the automobiles and measurement of velocity.

Fig.4 The experimental results

RETRIEVING INFORMATION FROM AN EPISODIC MEMORY
OR
WHY COMPUTERS' MEMORIES SHOULD BE MORE LIKE PEOPLE'S *

Roger C. Schank and Janet L. Kolodner
Computer Science Department
Yale University
Box 2158 Yale Station
New Haven, CT 06520

A computer memory organization modeled after human memory is proposed, along with strategies for accessing that memory. CYRUS, a program which implements the theory, is described.

Do A.I. programs understand what they read? Much debate has taken place on this issue (e.g., [6]) with little agreement. One thing seems clear, however. No computer program can seriously be said to have understood anything unless it can pass a simple test of remembering what it has supposedly understood. This problem seems obvious and easily solved. We can point to programs that paraphrase or summarize. Clearly, they remember. Or do they?

Memory, after all, also involves the integration of new knowledge with old knowledge and the ability to use newly obtained information for future and as yet unspecified tasks. In our own laboratory, we have developed a number of story understanding programs that summarize or answer questions about the stories they have understood (e.g. SAM, PAM, FRUMP). But none of those programs can apply information gained in reading one story to understand a later story. None have a long-term memory.

What would a long-term memory look like? Psychologists have proposed a number of theories, none of which are completely adequate for describing the structure of memory (e.g. [3], [7], [1]). One way to discover what human memory looks like, and what computer memory should look like, is to look at the memory tasks humans perform that we would want a computer to do.

Some of the memory tasks that people do in the course of normal conversation and understanding are listed below (see [5] for more detail):

1. Reminding
2. Relating events by time.
3. Recognizing when statements or questions are non-sensical.
4. Recognizing when something has not happened.
5. Making inferences.
6. Using time and place specifications.
7. Using maps and other aids.
8. Extensive memory search.

If we want to build an understanding machine that understands in the same way people do, then we have to take into account the vast number of memory tasks that people do. Reminding, for example, is a prerequisite to the process of creativity. Machines that cannot make new, undirected connections between items in memory will never be able to dream or imagine. Machines that cannot be reminded will not be able to think in any serious sense.

To get a handle on the way humans do these tasks, we examined people's responses to a request to tell us about all the museums they had been to ([5]). The results are summarized below:

1. Find museums by searching for instances of the museum script.
2. Find museum experiences (instances of the museum script) by searching for them as events within trip instances.
3. Find museums by searching memory for cities visited.
4. Find museum experiences by searching for experiences in places of residence.
5. Find trips by searching for trips to foreign countries or within country of residence, or by searching for episodes associated with those places.
6. Find places by using a map of the general area.

Rules such as these can be stored in the

----

*This work was supported in part by the Advanced Research Projects Agency of the Department of Defense and monitored under the Office of Naval Research under contract N00014-75-C-1111.

computer as features of the scripts and other stereotypes that they refer to. A memory set up this way would have its scripts and other stereotypes pointing to information about where in memory their instances could be found. In this way, _each stereotype would specify a set of strategies for searching memory to find its instances_. Each script and stereotype would include information about what other scripts or macro-scripts it could be a part of (e.g.,the museum script can be an event in a trip macro-script); which of its parts are important cues for finding its instances (e.g.,look for places different than home to find trips); and what other memory structures can be used to find its instances (e.g., go through a mental map of an area to find places). Using this organization, the following general rules for searching memory can be used:

7. To find instances of a script, search for other scripts and macro-scripts it can be part of.
8. To find objects, search for stereotypical events (such a scripts) associated with that object.
9. To find an instance of a stereotype in memory, find instances of the parts of it that are specified as important.
10. To find places, use a map.

In order to apply these strategies to a memory search, memory must be well-organized. It should be able to answer "Where did John go to law school?" without having to go through John's experiences in elementary school. it seems that experiences that happen to a person are grouped in terms of the larger contexts in which they were embedded. Knowing when an event might have occured, or what events might have occurred before or after it, can help us know where in memory to look for it.

Thus, one good way of organizing experiences is temporally, but with the time line broken into workable parts, each with some unique characteristic. These pieces are called _eras_ ([2]). The three years of going to law school, for example, make up a professional school era. Some standard ways of breaking up a personal time line are: places lived, jobs held, schools attended, and family situation. An event in a person's life would be organized on the event list of its corresponding era or eras.

Strategies for searching memory can take advantage of this memory organization. When searching for any particular event, only eras relevant to it must be searched. To find an event having to do with someone's job, only relevant occupational eras will have to be searched. To implement this on a computer, each script and other stereotype needs to have information about which times in someone's life he might be involved in that type of activity, and which types of eras and era sequences it can be found in.

The following additional rules can be used for searching a memory organized as described above:

11. To find an instance of a stereotype in memory, search the types of eras and era sequences it could be found in.
12. To find an instance of a stereotype in memory, search the appropriate eras going on at the time when this event is most likely to have taken place.
13. To find an era, search in the appropriate era sequence at the time specified relative to other eras in that sequence and in other sequences.

The CYRUS system ([2]) is a memory model that organizes biographical information about people and uses knowledge about its organization for retrieval and automatic updating. An important aspect of the CYRUS system is that the organization of its memory represents an attempt to model memory in people, and its retrieval and updating procedures mirror the way we believe people access their memories. CYRUS is an implementation of the ideas about memory organization and retrieval described above. A sample dialogue with CYRUS, showing input and output, follows:

Q1: Who is Cyrus Vance?
A1: United States Secretary of State.
Q2: How did he become Secretary of State?
A2: He was appointed by President Carter.
Q3: Where is he today?
A3: Egypt.
Q4: Why did he go there?
A4: He went to negotiate a compromise agreement to Egypt.
Q5: Has he met with the Israelis recently?
A5: Yes, in Washington right before he left for Egypt.
Q6: Who was at the meeting?
A6: Moshe Dayan and Israeli legal experts.
Q7: Will he meet with them in Israel?
A7: Yes, to discuss the compromise.

Each of the memory structures and strategies mentioned above is implemented in CYRUS. The CYRUS episodic memory contains events in the lives of the people represented. CYRUS' stereotype memory holds all the stereotypes that can be used for representation along with information relevant to each of them.

Eras in CYRUS are characterized by the major role themes a person is involved in at each point in his life ([4]). In CYRUS, each person represented has an occupational sequence of eras (including school), a family sequence of eras, a social sequence of eras, and a residential sequence of eras (where each era corresponds to a place the person has lives). Eras contain all the events in a person's life occurring during that time span and pertaining to that role theme or place of residence. Thus, Cyrus Vance's current occupational era is characterized by his being Secretary of State; his current family era is characterized by his being a husband and father.

CYRUS makes use of information attached to its scripts and other stereotypes to apply the strategy rules described above (rules 7-13). In answering the question, "When was the last time Vance met with Begin?", CYRUS uses information from the attend-meeting script to guide its memory search. CYRUS searches for the meeting by looking in eras and macro-scripts specified by the meeting script as appropriate to meetings. CYRUS' general knowledge tells it that the place for a meeting is usually the country of residence of one of the participants; and that a person must take a trip to get to a place other than his residence. A trip's type and location in memory are determined by the events which happen during the trip, so CYRUS searches for the trip by searching in an era appropriate to the original event being searched for. Input and output from CYRUS follow:

```
>When was Vance's last meeting with Sadat?
  Searching Vance's occupational eras for
  meetings with Sadat
  Searching Vance's occupational eras for
  trips to Egypt
  Found CON562
  Searching CON562 for meetings with Sadat
  Found CON547
  Searching CON547 for meetings with Sadat
  Found one
December 15, in Egypt.
```

CYRUS uses the strategy of searching for meetings to answer this question. Alternative strategies could have also been used to answer this question. Experiences associated with Sadat could have been searched, and a recent meeting with Sadat might have been found that way. Alternatively, Vance's experiences associated with the Arab-Israeli conflict or the Egyptian-Israeli peace talks could have been searched (after inferring that a meeting between Vance and Sadat probably had to do with one of those issues).

Eras and era sequences in Cyrus can also be used to relate events through time. If asked "When did Vance get married?", CYRUS would answer "Soon after he began to work as a lawyer." If asked, "When was he last in Paris?", it would answer "During the Vietnam peace talks, when he was an advisor to President Johnson."

CYRUS infers things not explicitly in memory by making use of expectations derived from the scripts, macro-scripts, and role themes it knows about. It can use its knowledge about enablement conditions for role themes to answer questions such as "How did Vance become Secretary of State?" It uses its knowledge about trips to answer questions such as "How did Vance get to Russia?" by inferring that he took an airplane, even if that information is not explicitly in memory.

References

[1] Bobrow, D. G. and Norman, D. A. (1975). Some principles of memory schemata. In Bobrow, D. G. and Collins, A., ed. Representation and Understanding. Academic Press, Inc., New York.

[2] Kolodner, J. L. (1978). Memory organization for natural language database inquiry. Research Report #142. Department of Computer Science. Yale University, New Haven, CT.

[3] Quillian, M. R. (1968). Semantic Memory. In M. Minsky (ed.), Semantic Information Processing.MIT Press, Cambridge, MA.

[4] Schank, R. C. and Abelson, R. P. (1977). Scripts, Plans, Goals, and Understanding. Lawrence Erlbaum Press, Hillsdale, N.J.

[5] Schank, R. C. and Kolodner, J. L. (1979). Retrieving information from an episodic memory (long version). Research Report #157. Department of Computer Science. Yale University, New Haven, CT.

[6] Weizenbaum, J. (1977). Computer Power and Human Reason: From Judgement to Calculation. Freeman, San Francisco.

[7] Williams, M. D. (1978). The process of retrieval from very long term memory. Center for Human Information Processing Memo CHIP-75. University of California at San Diego.

THE CONCEPTUAL CONTENT OF CONVERSATION

Roger C. Schank and Wendy Lehnert
Department of Computer Science
Yale University
Box 2158 Yale Station
New Haven, CT 06520

This paper outlines a strategy for conversational analysis that utilizes multiple levels of information flow in order to characterize the conceptual content of a conversation. The role of predictive knowledge structures and contextual information is illustrated in an analysis of a sample conversation, along with a partial outline of conversational rules specific to particular levels of conversational analysis.

1. Introduction

A large portion of the conversational process takes place beneath the surface of the actual conversation. In trying to spell out the rules that people use in conversation, it is necessary to account for all this "hidden" communication; explanations that are limited to the surface interaction will not provide a sufficient perspective.

Consider the following conversation:

A1: Why were you out so late last night?
B1: I went bowling with the boys.

A2: I thought you hated bowling.
B2: It's ok when I have some company.

A3: Aren't I company?
B3: It's not the same.

A4: Sure, you can't pick up women at home.
B4: I don't pick up women at the bowling alley.

We can analyze any given conversation in terms of [1] the implicit information that is present underneath the surface of the conversation, or [2] the rules of conversation that are operating at various levels of interaction.

2. Contextual Knowledge

We will now consider the various types of knowledge that must be accessed in order to understand our husband/wife conversation.

This work was supported by the Office of Naval Research under contract N00014-75-c-1111.

A1: Why were you out so late last night?

Because we know a woman is directing this question to her husband, we understand that she had an expectation about his arrival time which was violated. "So late" can only be interpreted in terms of her expectations. Married people expect to be with each other at night, and any deviation from this normative pattern deserves explanation. The same question would make far less sense in the context of a night clerk at a hotel confronting a registered guest.

Knowledge of goals and plans is needed to understand that

A4: Sure, you can't pick up women at home.

is in fact an accusation. Had she countered with, "Sure, you can't burn envelopes at home," it would be difficult to understand her rejoinder. (Why would anyone <u>want</u> to burn envelopes?) Picking up women on the other hand, is easily understood as a plan designed to satisfy the cyclic satisfaction goal of S-sex [1] But the fact that picking up women makes sense is not sufficient for this to be an accusation. It is an accusation only because we know that the marriage role theme assumes a goal subsumption strategy for S-sex which furthermore precludes all other behavior directed towards the satisfaction of that goal. An admission of such behavior is a rejection of his marital agreement. With such a major role theme at stake, we are not surprised to hear his denial.

3. Levels of Conversation

We have thus far detected twelve distinct levels of conversational interaction:

TWELVE LEVELS OF CONVERSATION

1. Direct Q-A: This is the explicit surface level of communication where "literal" content is processed.

2. Knowledge State: Statements here address the knowledge state of the hearer.

3. Dominance Games: At this level a speaker tries to get the upper hand in an adversary type conversation.

4. Emotions of A: Many statements can be interpreted as expressions of how the speaker is feeling at the moment.

5. Emotions of B: This is the same as the one above it, except that it refers to the emotions of the other speaker.

6. Relationship of A and B: This is the level at which implicit or explicit statements are made about the relationship between the participants.

7. Argument strategy: This level describes strategic exchanges when the conversation seeks to resolve some disagreement.

8. Import: This level of analysis identifies and tracks the most significant or compelling aspect of conversational interactions.

9. Implicit Beliefs: Personal beliefs are most often present as presuppositions.

10. Points: The ultimate goal of a conversation can often be about something other than what it seems to be about.

11. Topic Shifts: Statements such as 'Don't change the topic' are surface realizations of this level. Topics themselves are tracked and can be discussed.

12. Truth and trust: The truth, believability, or trust of the other participant are constantly monitored.

The twelve levels of conversation each carries a set of rules which control responses at that level. We shall now consider what the rules are like for a few of the levels. We will examine our example sentence A1: "Why were you out so late last night?" and we will consider the conceptual content of this question at various levels of conversational analysis. To begin we will look at level 3:

CATEGORY: level 3: Dominance Games
INPUT ANALYSIS: "You are going to be on the defensive now!"
HOW WE KNOW: 'Why questions' are candidates for level 3 analysis. If the reason being asked for addresses a role theme violation (or other potential inadequacy on the part of the hearer), then the above analysis applies.
WHY WE LOOKED THERE: A sufficient condition for a level 3 analysis is an inadequacy or failure to conform to expectations.
RESPONSE REQUIREMENTS: Level 3 responses are almost always under the surface. When one is put on the defensive, one has the choice of either returning the fire or accepting the defensive. The decision is based on the emotional relationship and power relationship of the participants. Once the choice has been made it affects the form and content of the response.
HOW WE KNOW WHAT TO SELECT: A consistency check on any presuppositions is needed to determine whether the attack is valid. Thus, we need to check facts that exist in memory.

Our sample conversation can be viewed many ways, one of which is as a kind of battle. In this conversation A is attacking B. B is on the defensive initially, but B fires back in B2 by saying "It's (bowling) okay when I have company". Now this statement says many things, but on the level of dominance games, it is a covert attack on A's value as company. A responds explicitly to the attack but not to the dominance game. An explicit response to the dominance game might have been, "Don't attack me just when I've got you!".

A retakes the offensive in A4 by averring that B is picking up women at the bowling alley, which is presumably an agreed upon bad thing. This puts B back on the defensive again in B4.

Another conversational level is level 4:

CATEGORY: level 4: emotions of A
INPUT ANALYSIS: "You don't love me anymore"
HOW WE KNOW: Violations of themes are always checked. A violation implies that thematic preconditions are no longer valid.
RESPONSE REQUIREMENTS: Assure, sympathize, ignore, etc.
WHERE FROM: What to do is determined by the hearer's emotional responses.
HOW WE KNOW WHAT TO SELECT: The appropriateness of an explicit response on this level is dependent on the current emotional relationship and the desires of the speaker.

In our sample conversation A3 ("Aren't I company?") can be considered to be a statement at level 4 meaning 'You don't love me, do you?' B's response to that, ("It's not the same"), can be understood as explicitly ignoring the issue which in a sense, is a qualified assent. This analysis can be seen as part of the reason for the escalation of matters by A in A4. At this point she goes directly on the attack, stating her suspicions overtly. This is consistent with B's previous refusal to discuss the level 4 aspect of the conversation. That is, B has rejected A by not reassuring her. To see how level 4 can actually appear on the surface, we need only change response B3 to "I still love you." Such a response would make no sense at any other level of conversational analysis or with any other rules of continuity. Yet is is nevertheless an appropriate response here because level 4 has been implicitly brought up by A and can therefore be explicitly addressed by B if he so chooses.

At level 9 rules about beliefs drive the interaction. When beliefs are presented by a speaker the hearer either (1) implicitly acknowledges their validity by responding on other levels or (2) contradicts them by an explicit rejection.

CATEGORY: level 9: beliefs
INPUT ANALYSIS: "Husbands are supposed to be home with their wives at night"
"Husbands should tell wives what they do"
HOW WE KNOW: Checking the husband role theme. Statements that implicitly refer to a role theme violation covertly assert one's belief in that role theme.
WHY WE LOOKED THERE: Beliefs about husbands' behavior are relevant when a wife is talking to a husband. The husband role theme thus constitutes a background against which inputs are checked.
RESPONSE REQUIREMENTS: To ignore this level is to accept covert beliefs. A belief must be countered if it is not shared.
WHERE FROM: To do this, one must consult one's own beliefs.
HOW WE KNOW WHAT TO SELECT: Contradictory beliefs are selected to be explicitly output if they exist. Thus if B does not share A's belief he can tell her "Being married shouldn't be a jail sentence."

4. Conclusions

Our final example is intended to illustrate the complexity of this problem by examining possible responses to an admission by B later on in the conversation.

> All right. I was at Joe's house. We had a few beers and smoked some dope. I didn't want to tell you because I know you can't stand Joe.

This can be responded to on each level as follows:

1. Direct Q-A: How can you stand Joe?
2. Knowledge State: Why didn't you tell me that in the first place? I really like Joe, I just never told you about my change of heart about him.
3. Dominance Games: Well I've got news for you. I've been seeing Joe when you actually do go bowling.
4. Emotions of A: I can't love a person who lies to me like that.
5. Emotions of B: You couldn't love me and be friends with him.
6. Relationship of A and B: I want a divorce.
7. Argument strategy: You mean you created this giant argument out of just that little thing?
8. Import: That's what you were worried about? I don't care about that.
9. Implicit Beliefs: You were smoking dope? That's immoral. I won't stand for it.
10. Points: That's my point exactly. You are a liar.
11. Topic Shifts: (The topic has not been shifted so this is also inappropriate.)
12. Truth and trust: How can I trust you after you lied to me like that?

In addition to what we have listed above, it is also possible to combine many of the levels in one response. (Indeed it is quite difficult to avoid such consolodations.)

To effectively model conversation then, it is necessary to find the levels at which people communicate, the rules people use to relate inputs to these levels, the methods of response generation at each of these levels, and the rules people use to select from alternative responses. When we have understood how to do all this, we will have made a start at analyzing the process of conversation and will then be ready to attempt the construction of an automated conversationalist.

References

[1] Schank, R.C. and Abelson, R.P. (1977). Scripts, Plans, Goals and Understanding: An Inquiry Into Human Knowledge Structures, Lawrence Erlbaum Associates, Hillsdale, New Jersey. New Haven, Conn.

PARSING DIRECTLY INTO KNOWLEDGE STRUCTURES

Roger C. Schank, Michael Lebowitz, and Lawrence Birnbaum
Department of Computer Science
Yale University
Box 2158 Yale Station
New Haven, CT 06520

A new type of natural language parser is presented. The idea behind this parser is to map input sentences into the deepest form of the representation of their meaning and make appropriate inferences during the parsing process, using interest to guide the processing.

1. Introduction

Over the course of the last ten years, researchers in our project have designed and programmed a large number of parsers - programs that mapped English sentences into the Conceptual Dependency (CD) representation of their meaning. They have all had one methodological assumption in common: the parsing algorithm that they employed was to be as psychologically correct as possible. This assumption brought with it an operating principle which was (with one exception to be discussed later) always followed, namely that the parsing algorithm was a strict left-to-right, one-pass operation, without backup.

One of the major problems with most of our story understanding programs, including their parsers, was their inability to handle genuinely new texts for which they were unprepared. A new vocabulary item, domain of discourse, or previously unencountered syntactic construction would often throw things into disarray. It seemed to us that we could produce one of the desired end-products of a story understanding system, a summary, with a much more robust and much faster program. This was the reason behind the design of FRUMP [1]. FRUMP skims for what it is interested in, looking for precisely the items of information it wishes to include in its summary for any particular domain that it has knowledge about. However, since FRUMP is very top down it cannot respond to things it is unprepared for. Therefore it is not a complete understanding system.

This work was supported in part by the Advanced Research Projects Agency of the Department of Defense and monitored by the Office of Naval Research under contract N00014-75-C-1111.

Ideally what we would like is a program with the robustness of FRUMP but with the ability to understand what it does not expect to see. Perhaps a human understander is top-down when appropriate, but bottom-up at other times. What is needed is an understanding system that can do both and be robust at the same time.

Many other researchers have investigated the problem of parsing natural language input into an internal representation. Virtually all of their methods concentrate on syntactic analysis. One very popular technique has been the Augmented Transition Network (ATN). Parsers of this sort have been discussed by Woods [10], Kaplan [2], and others. ATN's have tended to deal almost exclusively with syntax, perhaps with an occasional check of a few simple semantic properties of words. A more recent parser which views syntax parsing as an isolable sub-part of language understanding is by Marcus [3]. All of these programs view syntactic parsing as a process largely isolable from the rest of understanding. Our view, as described by Riesbeck [5] and Riesbeck and Schank [6] has always stressed the integration of semantics and syntax in parsing. A similar view was expressed by Wilks [9]. In this paper we will further contend that parsing should be integrated with the overall understanding process.

2. Processing Limitations

Now let us consider the design of a human-like parser. One important feature in such a parser is the speed with which humans can read text. Considering all the inferences, access of background knowledge, and other problems that an understander must deal with in the course of reading or listening to a sentence, people are very fast at the job. This is especially true when we recognize that understanding is basically finished as soon as a sentence ends. This implies that high level processes cannot wait until the end, after parsing is finished, and also that human processing is integrated. People must be making inferences as soon as they begin to process a sentence. From this it follows that people will actively use whatever they discover, using high level conclusions to guide low level processing. Thus, as models of human processing, systems that first do a complete parse and then begin to make inferences are not sensible. It seems plausible that the processing requirements for complete understanding frequently overwhelm the total available processing capability (see [4]). This means some words must be processed very superficially in order to gain time to extensively process words of semantic, syntactic or inferential importance.

It is likely that people are deciding as they go what words to pay serious attention to and what to glide over. Such decisions can be explained on the basis of many factors. One obvious one is interest. That is, people are liable to pay attention to (that is, devote their processing time to) what interests them. We have discussed the concept of interest and its ramifications for the inference problem in [7]. The main conclusion there was that inference is controlled by interest. This is also likely to be true at the parsing level since we are now viewing the entire understanding process as an integrated phenomenon.

Taking advantage of interest to reduce the time spent on many words has certain implications on processing. One is that the understanding process may not be strictly left to right. Since the most important words often come at the end of a phrase, the preceding words may be skimmed over until they are known to be important and then 'gathered up.' To do this the understanding process must be top down in order to allow the understander to know what to ignore. Uninteresting words are simply stored in a buffer in short term memory until a word that requires them to be processed is found. When (and if) such a word is found, the words in the buffer are gathered up and analyzed more fully. Under this theory there is little wonder at the fact that understanders frequently cannot remember the actual words that they read. They may never have actually read them at all!

3. A Detailed Example

A front page story in the New York Times began, "An Arabic speaking gunman shot his way into the Iraqi Embassy here [Paris] yesterday morning, held hostages through most of the day before surrendering to French policeman and then was shot by Iraqi security officials as he was led away by the French officers."

We will examine this sentence word by word and consider the kind of processing that would be desirable in an integrated understanding scheme. Our model will use interest to enable it to be psychologically plausible, a requirement forcing it to be completely finished with each sub-part of the sentence as it is processed.

Since language is received as a stream of words, we can assume words become available in chunks, both visually (clauses) and aurally (delineated by pauses). Thus in our processing we can always assume that the next word of a sentence is available, often simplifying the problem of disambiguation.

****
An Arabic speaking gunman...
****

AN is a word that can be skipped initially. This means that it is looked up in the dictionary, and what is found there are instructions to go to the next word and place AN in short term memory (STM).

ARABIC is listed in the dictionary as a word that is skippable, so it is skipped and saved in STM. (The information that ARABIC, like many uninteresting adjectives, is skippable has already been compiled and it is simply looked up here. The procedure for determining what can be skipped is obviously one of the interesting problems in the issue of the development of language ability. Schank and Selfridge [8] discuss these issues.)

SPEAKING is also skippable as long as no potential actors have been encountered. A search for actors in STM finds none, so this word is also skipped.

GUNMAN is marked as a HIGH INTEREST ACTOR, demanding immediate processing. It causes us to create top down requests to find certain information, such as the answers to the following questions:

WHO is he? -- causes us to gather up saved
adjectives and add them to
the memory token for this GUNMAN

WHAT did he do? --
in GUNMAN's permanent memory we find
he SHOT someone. An inference that
he shot or will shoot is made and
we predict we will hear more about it.

WHO did he shoot? -- creates interest in the
verb's syntactic object.

WHY did he shoot? -- makes us look for a reason

WHERE did this happen? -- makes us look for
a location

WHAT SCRIPTS might this instantiate? --
GUNMAN can indicate a script may be
instantiated. Candidates are $ROBBERY,
$TERRORISM, $KIDNAP. We try to confirm.

The formulation of the above questions (as requests, see the next section) now guides the process of understanding this story. These requests relate to matters of parsing, inference, script application and goal pursuit - all levels of the understanding process.

****
shot his way into the Iraqi Embassy...
****

SHOT is encountered and found to satisfy an expectation created by GUNMAN so we now build the first conceptual structure, a SHOOT event with the gunman token as actor, and an unfilled slot for the victim. The parser is now interested in finding the victim, which can be done by looking for the next main noun.

HIS is skipped and saved in STM.

WAY does not satisfy the expectation to fill the empty slot. WAY is listed as both skippable and pointing to a direction or location. A request is set up for the location and we attempt to find it.

INTO is skipped.

THE and IRAQI are skipped and saved in STM.

EMBASSY is found and set up as the location of the SHOOT event. Furthermore, EMBASSY is marked as a place of political significance. This piece of information causes us to instantiate the $TERRORISM script that had (among others) been predicted from GUNMAN. Since EMBASSY is interesting, its requests are activated. One of these is for the nationality of the EMBASSY. IRAQI is found in STM as satisfying this request and is picked up.

Setting up $TERRORISM causes us to lose interest in the representation of the isolated sentence and focuses us on setting up that script as the representation for the entire story. Thus, we now expect answers to the following questions:

Were HOSTAGES taken?
Were demands made? (money?) (free prisoners?)
Was any damage done?
Were measures to counteract the terrorist
taken? (return fire; arrest; free hostages)

****
here yesterday morning...
****

HERE, in a news story, means to add the dateline to the location.

YESTERDAY is found to be a time word and is added to the time slot of the event.

MORNING is also handled in this manner.

****
held hostages through most of the day....
****

HELD is skipped and saved since it matches none of the requests. The dictionary entry for HELD says only that it is a verb. No verbs were needed so we skip it. Only had it been inherently interesting would we have done detailed processing. The advantages of this system of parsing are clearly shown here. HELD is a highly ambiguous word that previously might have demanded great effort to disambiguate. An integrated understanding system simply goes on and waits for something interesting.

HOSTAGES satisfies an extant request. The TAKE HOSTAGES scene of $TERRORISM is instantiated. At this point a check is made on the saved verb, HELD, to see if doing this is okay. HELD is found to be precisely the kind of word desired. The important point is that HELD never had to be disambiguated, which is nice because words like HELD really do not have any particular meaning. Its meaning is derived from its connection to HOSTAGES and HOSTAGES is understandable only through $TERRORISM.

THROUGHOUT is found to point to either a time or place so a request is made for a time or place word. However, at this point our understanding system knows that this information is not as interesting as the outstanding expectations, because there are death-related requests active (see [7]). Thus the rest of this phrase is virtually ignored due to lack of interest.

MOST, OF and THE are skipped and saved in STM.

DAY is saved and ignored. It satisfies the low level request for a time word.

****
before surrendering to French policemen...
****

BEFORE is a time ordering word that predicts a new event and marks its time relative to the preceding event.

SURRENDERING is a word that is marked as an important part of a number of scripts, including $TERRORISM. The surrender scene of $TERRORISM is instantiated and requests are fired off looking for reasons for this action, the captors, etc. Predictions are made about certain words that might follow. 'To' would mark off captors, for instance.

TO tells us that the captors are coming (from the prediction).

FRENCH is skipped and saved in STM.

POLICEMEN is marked as an ACTOR so STM is consulted to gather up any modifiers. POLICEMAN is a possible captor, so it fulfills an expectation.

****
and then was shot by Iraqi security officials..
****

AND says a new event is coming.

THEN orders the event.

WAS specifies that the actor stored in STM is the conceptual object of the new event. This sets up requests for the actor, indicated by 'by', and the action.

SHOT is found to be interesting and is treated similarly to the way that GUNMAN was except that we expect only the things that were particular to the SHOOT action. Thus we have:

WHO was shot? -- GUNMAN
WHO shot him? -- not answered
WHY was there a shooting? -- not answered
WHERE did this happen? -- already known
WHAT SCRIPTS does this instantiate? --
SHOOT can also instantiate a script. Candidates are $ROBBERY, $TERRORISM, $KIDNAP, ordinarily. But in a context set up by $TERRORISM, none of the above fit easily. We look for plans and goals.
WHAT were the RESULTS of this action?--
A request is set up to find the results. If not satisfied the usual results are inferred - the victim's death.

BY tells us the actor of the SHOOT will follow.

IRAQI and SECURITY are skipped and saved in STM.

OFFICIALS ends the processing of the noun group. It satisfies the requests for WHO did the shooting and, as we now have an actor we ask about why he would kill a TERRORIST. There is no obvious reason, so we are surprised by this event. We seek to explain it by postulating a REVENGE or SHUT HIM UP type theme, but this is a guess.

****
as he was led away by French officers.
****

We are basically done now as no further requests need to be satisfied immediately. We are still interested in the goals of each of the actors, however, so WHY requests are still alive.

AS is known to be a time co-occurrence word. Since we are only interested in anything that occured at the same time if it is itself interesting, we can now skip ahead looking for something interesting.

HE and WAS are skipped.

LED is uninteresting and is both noticed and then skipped.

AWAY, BY, THE, and FRENCH are all skipped.

OFFICERS is skipped because there are no requests asking for it.

The period tells us we are done.

The final representation for this sentence:

```
$TERRORISM                        UNEXPECTED RESULT
ACTOR Arab gunman                 ---------- ------
PLACE Iraqi Embassy               $SHOOT
SCENES                            ACTOR Iraqi officers
 $HOSTAGES some                   OBJECT - Arab gunman
 $CAPTURE                         RESULT
 ACTOR French policemen           STATE dead
 OBJECT Arab gunman               ACTOR Arab Gunman
 PLACE  Iraqi Embassy
```

4. An Integrated Partial Parser

We will now look briefly at the integrated partial parser (hereafter IPP) we have written to implement the theories we have been describing here. This program was written to handle a limited class of stories, namely newspaper stories about terrorism and related areas. We have not tried to address all the issues involved in parsing, instead concentrating on the areas crucial to integrated partial processing. The parser, written in LISP on a DEC System 20/50, currently handles over 50 stories taken directly from newspapers. We are in the process of increasing its vocabulary and its domain of interest.

IPP is structured about a classification of words, which determines on how each word type should be processed by an understander, independent of strict syntactic classification. The immediate fate of a word upon being read determines its primary classification. There are three classes. The first consists of words requiring immediate action. These are interesting words which add crucial information to our story representation and generate expectations which guide further processing. The class is subdivided into words which build event structures (Event Builders, or EBs) and words which fill in slots in event structures (Token Makers, TMs).

EBs build the event structures which provide the framework for a final representation. Events structures which are predicted or interesting by themselves are instantiated and their expectations activated. Events which are not predicted, and not interesting are virtually ignored.

The discovery of a TM causes a token to be created. If the token satisfies an expectation, is interesting, or an interesting modifier is in STM, then the modifiers in STM are applied to the token. If the token is interesting the expectations included in the TM's dictionary entry, are activated. These expectations may, for example, look for plausible scripts.

The second class of words do not require immediate attention, but may be needed later. These words are processed by a skip and save strategy, keeping them in one of several short erm memory locations until, and unless, they are needed. This typically occurs when an interesting EB or TM is found. Frequently these words will never be used again, making the total effort needed to process them negligible.

The final class of words are those we skip entirely. The only processing effort is in identifying them. While few words are skippable in all domains, in any particular domain, a surprisingly large number of words can be totally skipped without degrading understanding. Clearly it is advantageous for an understander if this class is as large as possible, since processing time for skippable words is negligible.

Much of IPP's processing knowledge is implemented in the form of requests [5]. A request is a form of production, or test-action pair. If the test of an active request is found to be true, then the corresponding action is performed.

The tests and actions performed by IPP requests perform only a limited set of functions. As actions, requests may build new conceptual structures, fill slots in conceptual structures with other conceptual structures, activate new requests, and de-activate requests no longer appropriate. The tests may check for concepts (tokens or events) of a specified type, specific lexical items, or lexical items satisfying some property.

5. Computer Runs

What follows are computer runs of IPP on stories from the New York *Times*.

```
*(IPP S1)

Input:

(AN ARABIC SPEAKING GUNMAN SHOT HIS WAY INTO
THE IRAQI EMBASSY HERE THIS MORNING HELD
HOSTAGES THROUGHOUT MOST OF THE DAY BEFORE
SURRENDERING TO FRENCH POLICEMEN AND THEN WAS
SHOT BY IRAQI SECURITY OFFICIALS AS HE WAS LED
AWAY BY FRENCH OFFICERS)

Output:

** MAIN EVENT **
SCRIPT  $TERRORISM
ACTOR   ARAB GUNMAN       PLACE   IRAQI EMBASSY
CITY    PARIS
SCENES
 SCENE   $HOSTAGES        SCENE   $CAPTURE
 PLACE   IRAQI EMBASSY    PLACE   IRAQI EMBASSY
 ACTOR   ARAB GUNMAN      OBJECT  ARAB GUNMAN
                          ACTOR   POLICEMEN

** UNEXPECTED EVENTS **
ACTION  $SHOOT
ACTOR   IRAQI OFFICIALS   OBJECT  ARAB GUNMAN
AFTER   SCENE $CAPTURE
RESULT
 STATE  DEAD      ACTOR  ARAB GUNMAN

673. msec CPU (0. msec GC)

*(IPP S2)

Input:

(A GUNMAN WHO DIVERTED A VERMONT BOUND BUS
WITH MORE THAN TWENTYFIVE PASSENGERS FROM
THE BRONX TO KENNEDY INTERNATIONAL AIRPORT
AND KILLED TWO HOSTAGES SURRENDERED ON A
RUNWAY LATE LAST NIGHT ENDING A DAYLONG
SIEGE OF TERROR AND GUNFIRE)

Output:

** MAIN EVENT **
SCRIPT    $HIJACK
ACTOR     GUNMAN   CARRYING (GREATERTHAN 25)
VEHICLE   BUS               PASSENGERS
RELATED
 ACTION    DO      RESULT
 ACTOR     GUNMAN   STATE     DEAD
                    ACTOR     TWO HOSTAGES
SCENES
 SCENE     $CAPTURE
 OBJECT    GUNMAN
 ACTOR     POLICE

718. msec CPU (0. msec GC)
```

References

[1] DeJong, G. F. (1977) Skimming newspaper stories by computer. Research Report 104, Department of Computer Science, Yale University.

[2] Kaplan, R. M. (1975) On process models for sentence analysis. In D. A. Norman and D. E. Rumelhart, eds., Explorations in Cognition. W. H. Freeman and Company, San Francisco.

[3] Marcus, M. (1977) A theory of syntactic recognition for natural language. Unpublished Ph.D. thesis, MIT.

[4] Norman, D. A. and Bobrow, D. G. (1975) On data-limited and resource-limited processes. Cognitive Psychology, Vol. 7, pps. 44-64.

[5] Riesbeck, C. K. (1975) Conceptual analysis. In R. C. Schank (ed.), Conceptual Information Processing. North Holland, Amsterdam.

[6] Riesbeck, C. K. and Schank, R. C. (1976) Comprehension by computer: Expectation-based analysis of sentences in context. Research Report 78, Department of Computer Science, Yale University.

[7] Schank, R. C. (1978) Interestingness: Controlling inferences. Research Report 145, Department of Computer Science, Yale University.

[8] Schank, R. C. and Selfridge, M. (1977) How to learn / what to learn. Fifth International Joint Conference on Artificial Intelligence, August 1977, Cambridge, Massachusetts.

[9] Wilks, Y. (1973) An artificial intelligence approach to machine translation. In R. C. Schank and K. Colby, eds., Computer Models of Thought and Language. W. H. Freeman and Co., San Francisco.

[10] Woods, W. A. (1970) Transition network grammars for natural language analysis. Communications of the ACM. Vol. 13, p 591.

PROBLEMS WITH PARTS

Lenhart K. Schubert
Department of Computing Science
University of Alberta
Edmonton, Alberta T6G 2H1*

Abstract. Two problems in representing and using relationships among parts of objects are analysed, and partial solutions are proposed. The first is the problem of extracting information from overlapping partitioning hierarchies. Contrary to a common assumption, "part -of" relationships cannot be extracted from arbitrary sets of partitioning assertions by simple label-propagation methods: the problem is in general $\overline{NP}$-complete. However, if the lowest-level parts of all entities under consideration are drawn from a common pool of pairwise disjoint "ultimate" parts, then relatively simple, complete inference methods for deriving "part -of" and other relationships can be supplied. The second problem is that of property inheritance, i.e., the transfer of relationships among parts of a generic object to corresponding parts of a successor of that object in the type hierarchy. Earlier solutions are criticized and a new solution based on function tables attached to concepts is proposed.

1. Introduction

Much of our knowledge of enduring relationships (as opposed to events) concerns relationships among parts of physical and abstract objects. Yet part-whole relationships have until recently received scant attention in the AI literature, compared for example to generalization (IS-A) relationships. Interest in parts structure has been confined almost exclusively to its role in relational models for computer vision (e.g., [1-5]). However, the ability to reason about parts was an important feature of Raphael's program SIR[6]. It was able to chain together both particular and generic subpart relationships, and to combine parts inference with subset inference to answer questions about (sets of) parts of (sets of) individuals. The "slots" of Minsky's frames [7] may facilitate the representation of part-whole relationships, among others, but do not presuppose any particular theory of such relationships. To date, the most elaborate proposals for representing and reasoning about parts structure appear to be those of Philip Hayes [8,9].

The present paper addresses two problems in the use of parts knowledge which people find trivially easy but which have not been adequately mechanized: the extraction of "part-of" relationships (and disjointness relationships, etc.) from overlapping parts hierarchies, and relationship inheritance for parts of objects in a type hierarchy.

Sec. 2 introduces a convenient representation for sets of partitioning assertions, called "parts graphs". Although based on partitionings, parts graphs can represent non-exhaustive and overlapping decompositions of parts structure.

Sec. 3 notes that label-propagation methods for extracting "part-of" (and other) relationships from simple partitioning hierarchies do not generalize to arbitrary parts graphs; the problem is in general $\overline{NP}$-complete. A restricted type of parts graph, called "closed", is defined, which reduces all parts of the top-level object to a common set of pairwise disjoint ultimate (lowest-level) parts. For closed parts graphs, efficient complete inference methods can be supplied.

In Sec. 4 a relationship inheritance scheme is proposed in which corresponding parts of concepts in a type hierarchy are identifiable by the names of their Skolem functions. This overcomes a difficulty with Hayes' [8,9] property inheritance scheme, without sacrificing any of its advantages.

---

* The work reported was done while the author was on leave at Universität Karlsruhe, Institut für Informatik I, W. Germany

2. Parts graphs

The following takes for granted a notion of "part-of" which is at least a partial ordering with the extension property (if all parts of x are part of y, then x is part of y), and for which there exists a unique empty part θ, a dyadic "overlap" function $\sqcap$ (the largest entity which is part of both arguments), an n-adic "merge" function $\sqcup$, n=2,3,... (the smallest entity which has all of its arguments as parts), and a dyadic "remainder" function $\setminus$ (the part of the first argument which is not part of the second). These properties are stated formally in [10]. Bunt's [11] axiomatization of "part-of" satisfies these constraints and leads to a logically consistent generalization of Zermelo-Fraenkel set theory. Thus the theories of "part-of" and "subset-of" are closely related, and much of what is said here about the representation and use of parts knowledge also applies to the representation and use of knowledge about set inclusion relationships.

People tend to conceptualize objects in terms of pairwise disjoint, jointly exhaustive parts, i.e., in terms of partitionings. For example, the top level of a human parts hierarchy might reasonably divide the human body x into a head h, neck n, torso t, arms a&a', and legs l&l'. Thus it is natural to base computer representations of parts structure on a partioning relation P,[1] where [x P $x_1 \ldots x_m$] iff

$$\bigwedge_{1 \le i < j \le m} [(\sqcap\ x_i\ x_j) = \theta] \quad \& \quad [(\sqcup\ x_1 \ldots x_m) = x].^{2}$$

Thus (∀x)(∃hntaa'll')[[x human]→ [[x P h n...l']&[h head]&[n neck]&...&[l' leg].

It is important to notice that "part-of" is expressible in terms of P. For example, [b part-of a] can be rewritten as [a P b c], where c is a previously unused constant denoting ($\setminus$ a b), i.e., the (possibly empty) remainder of a with respect to b. In general, arbitrary sets of "part-of" assertions and disjointness assertions can be converted to sets of partitioning assertions. However, the conversion may introduce parts wich are possibly empty, even if all of the original parts are known to be nonempty.

----

[1]cf. the partitionings of Grossman [12] and "complete splits" of Fahlman [13] for concept taxonomies.

[2]In the form of predicate calculus used here sentential formulas are in infix form and delimited by square brackets (so that the second list element is the predicator or operator) and functional expressions are in prefix form and delimited by round brackets; e.g., (∀xy)[[x =(mother-of y)] → [x female]].

Sets of partitioning assertions can be represemted as "parts graphs" as illustrated in Fig.1.

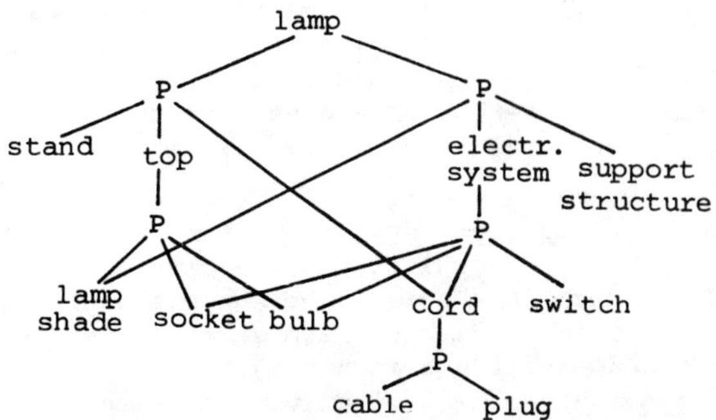

Fig.1. Parts graph for a desk lamp. The nodes marked "P" represent partitioning assertions while the named nodes represent parts.

This shows two overlapping parts hierarchies for a particular (as opposed to generic) lamp, with a "structural view" on the left and a "functional view" on the right.

In the graphical representation, partitioning assertions and particular parts are represented as assertion nodes and constant nodes respectively. Assertion nodes are marked "P" and have an incoming edge from the first argument of the assertion and outgoing edges to the remaining arguments. Such parts graphs are readily represented as semantic nets in the network formalism of [14].

Hierarchies are distinguished from unrestricted parts graphs by having exactly one downward edge from each nonleaf parts node and a unique path from the root to each parts node. As Fig.1 shows, the available knowledge about an object need not form a single hierarchy."Tangled" hierarchies result when there are multiple views of the same object, known overlap regions such as shoulders, waist, or knees, or parts with unknown mutual overlap.

3. Extracting information from parts graphs

A partitioning hierarchy has the important advantage of allowing efficient inference of part-of and disjointness relationships. In fact, if a and b are any two nonempty parts appearing in a hierarchy, then b is part of a iff a is an ancestor of b, and a and b are disjoint iff neither is an ancestor of the other.[3]

For parts within a common subhierarchy of a

----

[3]Incidentally, these conditions can be checked in constant time using a method based on left-to-right numbering of the leaves, whereas the worst-case complexity of label-propagation methods is inear in the number of edges.

non-hierarchic parts graph the same methods can be used. For example, in Fig.1 the plug must be part of the electrical system since the latter is an ancestor of the former in the "functional view" of the lamp; the cord is disjoint from the bulb since neither is an ancestor of the other in the "structural view".

However, not all implicit part-of and disjointness relationships can be extracted in this way. In Fig.1, the switch must be part of the stand; in fact, the switch and support structure must partition the stand, because the stand on the one hand and the switch plus support structure on the other are the only nonoverlapping parts of the two lamp hierarchies. Another point worth noting is that even without the assertion [lamp P stand top cord], it follows from the graph that "top" is part of the lamp, because all of its parts are.

One can devise additional inference methods to handle these particular cases, but such stop-gap measures are almost surely futile because of the following result.

Theorem 1. The problem of confirming [b part-of a], where a and b are nodes of a parts graph, is $\overline{\mathrm{NP}}$-complete.

This is proved in [10] by mapping the unsatisfiability problem of the propositional calculus into a "part-of" problem for a parts graph, and vice versa.

This suggests that additional constraints should be imposed on parts graphs so as to permit efficient information extraction, while still allowing for overlap parts and multiple views of the same part. Such constraints are obtained by requiring parts graphs to be closed: G is closed iff any two of its parts nodes are projectible into a common subhierarchy. A node a is projectible into a subhierarchy H if G contains a subhierarchy rooted at a whose leaves lie in H. (Since a single parts node is a subhierarchy, any parts node is trivially projectible into any subhierarchy to which it belongs. Hence any two nodes of a subhierarchy H are projectible into a common subhierarchy, viz.,H).

For example, if the left and right views of the lamp in Fig.1 are called H_L and H_R, then "top" and "bulb" are projectible into H_L (because they belong to H_L), and "top" and "electrical system" are projectible into H_R (because the leaves {lamp shade, socket, bulb} of a subhierarchy rooted at "top", as well as "electrical system", belong to H_R). However, neither "stand" and "switch", nor "stand" and "support structure" are projectible into any common subhierarchy. Thus the graph is open, but could easily be closed by addition of the assertion [stand P switch support-structure].

The notion of a closed graph becomes clearer if parts graphs are required to be "fully consistent" in the sense that none of the parts they represent are necessarily empty. This rules out graphs, for example, in which two disjoint parts (distinct leaves of a single subhierarchy) have a common descendant, or in which one "view" of a part terminates in a proper subset of the leaves of another "view" of that part.

It is proved in [10] that all leaf nodes of a fully consistent, closed graph belong to a single (not necessarily unique) main hierarchy whose root represents the whole entity. All nodes of the graph are projectible into this main hierarchy. In such a graph, therefore, all leaves are pairwise disjoint and each parts node corresponds to a subset of the leaves. The graph of Fig.1 is now easily seen to be open, since the leaf nodes "stand" and "switch", for example, do not belong to any common subhierarchy.

Fig.2 shows a closed graph with a main hierarchy rooted at a, an overlap part b made up of two parts occurring in the main hierarchy, and two "views" of a part c.

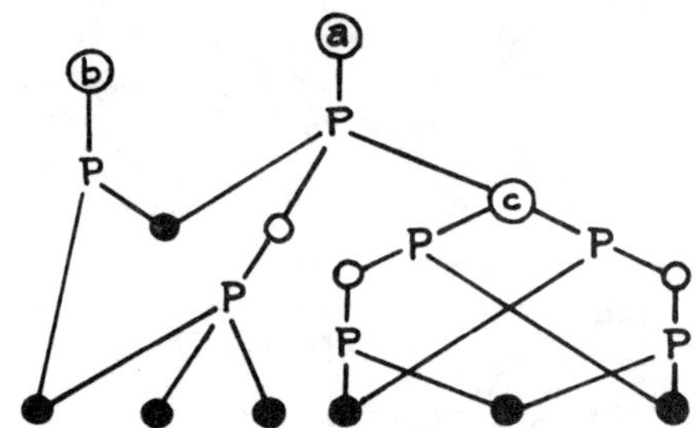

Fig. 2. A closed parts graph with an "overlap part" b and two "views" of a part c. The darkened nodes represent the ultimate parts of a.

Surprisingly, the syntactical restrictions of closed graphs do not lead to any logical restrictions:

Theorem 2. For every parts graph there is a logically equivalent closed graph.

The proof and a procedure for constructing a closed graph from a set of partitioning assertions are given in [10]. The sort of idea involved is illustrated in Fig.3. Admittedly, the size of the equivalent closed graph may be exponential in the size of a given open graph. However, this exponential growth is associated with unknown and unrestricted overlap between sets of parts, a situation which rarely, if

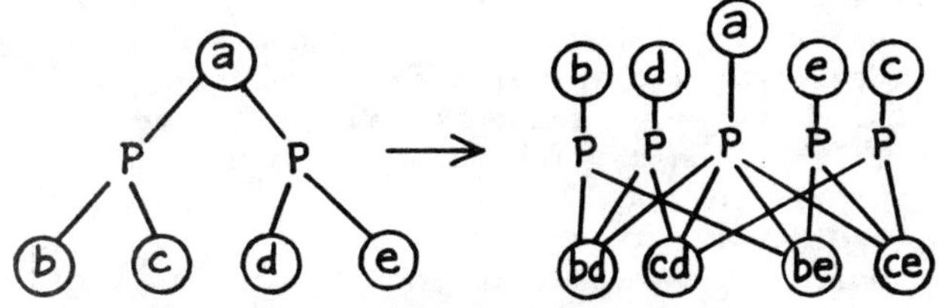

Fig. 3. An open graph and a logically equivalent closed graph.

ever, occurs in our conception of real objects.

The following methods are complete for answering questions of the form ?[b part-of a] and ?[a disjoint-from b] in fully consistent, closed graphs. Projecting a node a into a hierarchy H means determining a set of nodes $A = \{a_1,\ldots,a_m\}$ which lie in H and are the leaves of a subhierarchy with root a (if a already lies in H then $A = \{a\}$).

Preliminary step: Project a and b into a common subhierarchy H, obtaining respective projections $A = \{a_1,\ldots,a_m\}$ and $B = \{b_1,\ldots b_n\}$.

To answer ?[b part-of a]: If every node with an ancestor in B has an ancestor or descendant in A, return "yes"; if some nodes with ancestors in B have no ancestors and no descendants in A, and the merge of these nodes is known to be nonempty, return "no"; else return "unknown" (see Fig.4)

To answer ?[a disjoint-from b]: If no $a_i \in A$ has an ancestor in B and no $b_j \in B$ has an ancestor in A, return "yes"; if some nodes in A have an ancestor in B and/or some nodes in B have an ancestor in A, and the merge of these nodes is known to be nonempty, return "no"; else return "unknown" (see Fig.5).

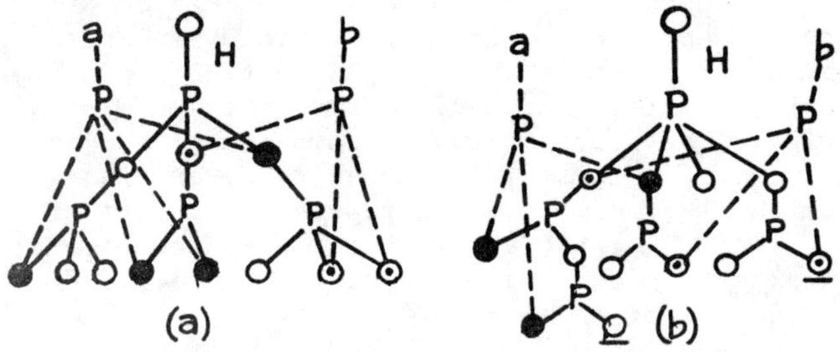

Fig. 4. Answering ?[b part-of a] in a closed graph. In (a) the answer is "yes" (Note that one part of b has no ancestor in A, but is partitioned into parts belonging to a). In (b) the answer is "no" if the merge of the underlined nodes is known to be nonempty, and "unknown" otherwise.

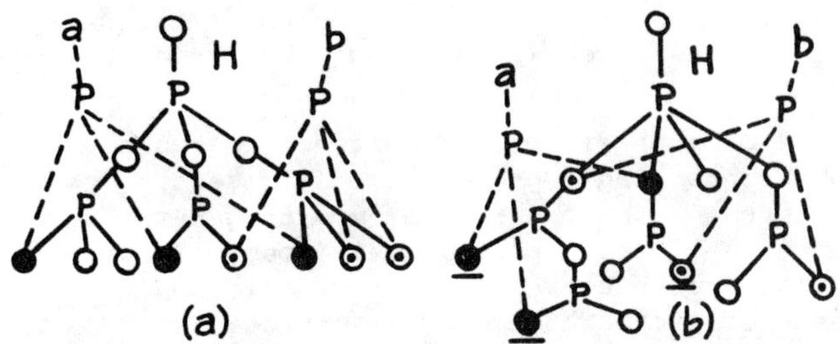

Fig. 5. Answering ?[a disjoint-from b] in a closed graph. In (a) the answer is "yes". In (b) the answer is "no" if the merge of the underlined nodes is known to be nonempty, and "unknown" otherwise.

In [10] the completeness claim is made precise and proved. It is assumed that the merge of a set of nodes $A = \{a_1,\ldots,a_m\}$ is known to be nonempty iff$[(\sqcup a_1 \ldots a_m) \neq \Theta]$ is a logical consequence of the graph, the assumed properties of "part-of", and a set of "nonemptiness assertions" of the form $[a = \Theta]$ about some of the nodes of the graph. It is shown that the predicate "known to be nonempty" is efficiently decidable when so defined. The given question-answering methods are then shown to be implementable in linear space-time relative to the number of edges of the closed graph. Heuristic methods are discussed which can often give nearly constant question-answering times for closed graphs.

Similar methods can be used to compute the "disjoint merge" of two parts, i.e., a set of disjoint parts whose merge equals the merge of the given parts (retain elements of A∪B which do not have ancestors in B), the overlap of two parts (retain elements of A with ancestors in B and vice versa), and other functions over tuples of parts. Thus questions involving such functions could also be answered.

Needless to say, reasoning about parts cannot in general go very far on the basis of "part-of" predications or partitionings alone. In the case of physical objects, for example, knowledge about the mode of connection and relative position of parts is indispensable. But the fact remains that people can answer questions such as "Is a toe part of a leg?" or "Is a spark plug part of an automobile engine?" with consummate ease. The proposed methods may help to equip machines with comparable abilities.

One serious limitation of the proposals is that they do not allow for disjunctive parts relationships (even "alternative viewpoints" are logically conjoined). A second is that only the structure of particular objects has been considered, whereas much human parts knowledge is generic. A third is that no provision has been made for avoiding individual mention of multiple parts of the same type, such as a centipede's legs or a human being's neurons.

In [10] some extensions to generic graphs and graphs containing representations of sets of parts are sketched. The chief problem with generic graphs is that they are dispersed over (possibly overlapping) type hierarchies. For example, only elephant-specific partitioning assertions, such as those subdividing the proboscis, would be associated directly with the concept of an elephant. Most of the remaining partitioning assertions, such as that dividing the body into head, neck, torso, tail, and limbs would be associated with higher-level concepts, such as that of a legged animal. Assuming that the fragments form a closed graph when brought together at corresponding nodes, the question-answering methods of this section can be adapted to generic graphs. The main requirement is the availability of methods for identifying corresponding nodes. This problem is discussed in a more general context in the next section.

The introduction of nodes representing sets of parts into parts graphs complicates both their syntax and use. Additional partitioning relations are needed (e.g., for partitioning an object into a set of parts, and for partitioning the sets themselves), and methods must be provided to deal with more complicated questions, such as "Is every leg part of some body segment?" Nevertheless, the definition of a closed graph can be modified to allow for sets of parts, and linear or sublinear methods can be provided for answering several types of questions for such graphs.

4. Property inheritance

When one describes a type of object, such as a robin, in some representation system, one would like many of its anatomical characteristics to be "inherited" from the description of a superordinate concept; for example, the position of the beak on the head or of the wings on the body should transfer smoothly from "bird" to "robin".

Hayes [8,9] has discussed two alternative network methods for facilitating property and relationships inheritance from parts of more general to parts of less general kinds of objects. The first method involves connecting corresponding parts with "binders" which then serve as inheritance paths. The second method actually uses the same nodes for corresponding parts of the two kinds of objects; however, the "depictions"[4] for the two kind of objects provide access to different sets of propositions about the parts. The latter proposal was adopted and given a logical interpretation in terms of shared variables in [15]. However, a serious flaw has become apparent in this scheme. The telescoping of nodes, carried all the way down to the level of instances, assigns all instances of a concept to a single node, and similarly for corresponding parts of those instances. As a result, relationships between distinct instances or parts of distinct instances, such as "Polly's beak is larger than Tweety's" cannot be stated. Even above the level of instances, the sharing of nodes prevents expression of relational propositions such as "The African elephant has larger ears than the Indian elephant", "Seagulls recognize each other by the colouration of their eyelids", "Dogs hate cats" (assuming "dog" and "cat" have a common superordinate concept), "No two dollar bills have the same serial number", etc.

The key to a logically respectable alternative which avoids these difficulties lies in the use of functions. For example, suppose that h is the Skolem function determined by the statement "Every higher animal has a head". Suppose further that the head of the universally quantified robin y has been identified with the value (h y) and similarly, that the head of the universally quantified bird x has been identified with the value (h x). If other corresponding parts have been similarly linked via their functional names, it is clear that parts relationships can be trasferred from parts of the bird to parts of the robin as easily as the corresponding universally quantified variables can be matched and the function values dependent on those variables located.

Locating values of functions can be made efficient by attaching a "function table" to each node, in which known values (nodes) of functions applicable to that node are indexed by function name. This scheme resembles Hayes' "binder" scheme, but the correspondence between a part of a subordinate concept and a part of a superordinate concept several levels above it are established **in a** single, trivial matching operation, instead of a series of binder traversals. Some complications are described in [10], including those arising from the presence of nodes representing sets of parts, and from the application of a function at different levels of a parts hierarchy (e.g., application of a "heart-of" function at the level of the whole animal and at the level of the animal's chest).

Any system for representing parts correspondences explicitly, whether it is based on shared nodes, binders, or functional indexing, presupposes a method of establishing these correspondences in the first place. Hand-coding such correspondin-

---

[4] Essentially, a "depiction" is a list of assertions which are specific to a particular (kind of) object, accessible via the name of that object.

ces ought to be a temporary expedient, to be replaced eventually by a method of inferring and representing them on the basis of arbitrary sets of parts relationships such as might be obtained from natural language input. To see the problem and an approach to a solution, suppose that a natural language system is told for the first time that "A bird has a tail". The system cannot assume that "tail" is translatable as a logical function; for this would lead to the unwarranted (and false) conclusion that "a bird with two tails" is a contradiction in terms. A plausible translation is

$(\forall x)(\exists y)[[x \text{ bird}] \rightarrow [[y \text{ tail}] \& [y \text{ part-of } x]]]$.

At the same time, a conjecture that y is normally the only tail should be stored, since the wording would more likely have been "at least one tail", "one or more tails", or something to that effect, had that been the interpretation intended by the informant. Skolemization of y gives

$(\forall x)[[x \text{ bird}] \rightarrow [[(t\ x) \text{ tail}] \& [(t\ x) \text{ part-of } x]]]$.

If told subsequently that "A magpie has a long tail", how could the system identify "a...tail" with t applied to the universal "magpie" variable instead of creating a new Skolem function? It would at least have to check for a possible referent of "a...tail" among the parts of concepts superordinate to "magpie". After finding such a part at "bird", and verifying that this is probably the only part of a bird satisfying the predicate "tail", it could transfer the name of the Skolem function into the new context, at least tentatively.

In general, a wider search of prior instantiations of "tail" would be required since the first occurrence need not have been at the superconcept level, but might instead have been at the subconcept level, or in connection with a concept which is neither a superconcept nor a subconcept of "magpie" (e.g., "dog"). If an occurrence of "tail" is found for a subconcept of "magpie", then the name of the corresponding Skolem function can be transferred to the "magpie" context, provided that the newly mentioned "tail" is likely to be the magpie's only "tail" (in which case it is also the subconcept's only "tail"). If an occurrence of "tail" is found for a concept such as "dog", then again the Skolem function can be transferred to the "magpie" context provided that both the magpie's tail and the dog's tail are likely to be unique (this policy prevents later naming conflicts at the level of common superconcepts of "magpie" and "dog").

This approach is also workable for compound identifying descriptions. For example, the information that a perch has a spiny fin on its back might be rendered as

$(\forall x)(\exists y)[[x \text{ perch}] \rightarrow [[y \text{ fin}] \& [y \text{ part-of } x] \& [y \text{ joins}(\text{back-of } x)] \& [y \text{ spiny}]]]$.

If a part can be found for the superconcept "fish" which uniquely satisfies "is a fin, is part of the fish, and joins the back of the fish", then its Skolem function name can be used in the Skolemization of the perch's fin y. Much the same as before can be said about occurrences of parts satisfying the description in question but belonging to subconcepts or unrelated concepts.

All this presupposes a method for locating parts satisfying given descriptions, i.e. associative accessing. This topic cannot be covered here; Hayes' associative accessing methods are easily modified for use with semantic nets in which corresponding nodes are linked via their Skolem function names, rather than being telescoped or connected with binders.

5. Concluding discussion

The seemingly trivial problem of extracting parts relationships from sets of partitioning assertions was seen to be quite difficult. The suggested methods for "closed graphs" provide a partial solution.

Effective property inheritance requires effective ways of establishing node correspondences. A method of establishing correspondences through names of Skolem functions was suggested which overcomes a difficulty with Hayes' node-sharing method.

Many problems in generalizing the proposed methods remain to be solved, such as that of providing detailed inference algorithms for extracting "part-of" relationships from fragmented generic parts graphs, or for establishing node correspondences on the basis of composed functions such as (f (h x))). Moreover, several important problems with parts have not been touched on here, such as the problem of inferring the mode of connection and relative position of parts of physical objects, the problem of determining the number of parts of a given type of a given object (counting the known instances only provides a lower bound on that number), and the problem of accessing parts associatively on the basis of compound descriptions (Hayes considered unitary descriptions only).

In view ot the centrality of parts relationships in human thought, these are important areas for future research.

Acknowledgements

Alan Covington and Randy Rawson contributed to this paper through discussions and their work on a semantic net system. Pat Hayes' careful refereeing provided much useful guidance. The research was supported by an Alexander von Humboldt Fellowship and by Operating Grant No. A8818 of the National Research Council of Canada.

References

[1] Clowes, M.B. (1969). "Transformational grammars and the organization of pictures", in Grasselli, A., Automatic Interpretation and Classification of Images, Acad. Press, New York, pp. 43-77.

[2] Winston, P. (1970). "Learning structural descriptions from examples", Ph.D. Thesis, MIT, TR-76, Cambridge, MA.

[3] Guzman, A. (1971). "Analysis of curved line drawings using context and global information", Mach. Intell. 6, Meltzer, B. & Michie, D. (eds.), American Elsevier, New York, 325-375.

[4] Barrow, H.G., Ambler, A.P., & Burstall, R.M. (1972). "Some techniques for recognizing structures in pictures", in Watanabe, S. (ed.), Frontiers of Pattern Recognition, Academic Press, New York, pp. 1-29.

[5] Kaneff, S. (1972). "Pattern cognition and the organization of information", in Watanabe, S. (ed.), Frontiers of Pattern Recognition, Academic Press, New York, pp. 193-222.

[6] Raphael, B. (1968). "SIR: A computer program for semantic information retrieval", in Minsky, M.L. (ed.), Semantic Information Processing, MIT Press, Cambridge, MA, pp. 33-134.

[7] Minsky, M. (1975). "A framework for representing knowledge", in Winston, P. (ed.), The Psychology of Computer Vision, McGraw-Hill, New York.

[8] Hayes, Philip J. (1977a). "On semantic nets, frames and associations", Proc. 5th Int. Joint Conf. on Artificial Intelligence, MIT, Cambridge, MA, Aug. 22-25, pp. 99-107.

[9] Hayes, Philip J. (1977b). "Some association - based techniques for lexical disambiguation by machine", TR25, Comp. Sci. Dept., University of Rochester, Rochester, N. Y.

[10] Schubert, L.K. (1979). "Representing and using knowledge about parts", in preparation as Computing Science Tech. Note, University of Alberta, Edmonton, Alberta.

[11] Bunt, H.C. (1978). "A formal semantic analysis of mass terms and amount terms", Amsterdam Papers on Formal Grammar, Vol. 2 (Proc. 2nd Amsterdam Symp. on Motague Grammar & Related Topics, Amsterdam, Jan. 9-13, 1978).

[12] Grossman, R.W. (1976). "Some data-base applications of constraint expressions, LCS TR-158, MIT Lab. for Computer Science, MIT, Cambridge, MA.

[13] Fahlman, S.E. (1977). "A system for representing and using real-world knowledge", AI-TR-450, AI Lab., MIT, Cambridge, MA.

[14] Schubert, L.K. (1976). "Extending the expressive power of semantic networks", AI Journal 7, pp. 163-198.

[15] Schubert, L.K., Goebel, R. & Cercone, N. (1979). "The representation and organization of a semantic net for comprehension and inference" in Findler, N.V. (ed.), Associative Nets - The Representation and Use of Knowledge by Computers, Academic Press; Preliminary version: Techn. Rep. TR78-1, Dept. of Computer Science, University of Alberta, Edmonton, Alberta.

A LEARNING SYSTEM ABLE TO SYNTHESIZE ARITHMETICAL FUNCTIONS

François SCHYN

Laboratoire de Recherche en Informatique
Equipe de Recherche Associée au CNRS "AL KHOWARIZMI"
Université de Paris Sud
91405 - ORSAY (France)

Gérard GUIHO

Laboratoire de Recherche en Informatique
Equipe de Recherche Associée au CNRS "AL KHOWARIZMI"
Université de Paris Sud
91405 - ORSAY (France)

This paper describes a system able to synthesize functions and predicates from examples taken in an arithmetical domain. Numbers are represented as characters strings. They are not represented as bags as in Lenat or Knapman's works. The representations of functions and predicates are sets of Horn clauses and the synthesis lies in the construction of new clauses or in the debugging of the existant ones. The paper describes the concepts which are used in the system and the synthesis process.

Keys Words : Learning, Horn clauses, Program synthesis

I. INTRODUCTION

Program synthesis from examples have been studied quite recently. They can be classified according to the following categories :

- Systems which construct function from non-ambiguous and self-contained examples. That means that all the information which is necessary for the synthesis is contained in the example and that there is no ambiguity in the construction of elementaries functions [see [10], [1], [4],[5]

- Systems which are considered as the growing of a knowledge base. The examples do not need to be self-contained or non-ambiguous. That is the case with [17][11], in some sense [8], and more recently [6]

Our system belongs to the second category. It is able to construct some recursive concepts (predicates or functions) as in [8] but uses a more significance and effective representation of numbers than [8] or [6] representation. The representation of numbers which is discovered by the system consists in strings of digits rather than bags as a PEANO representation. The concepts of arithmetical operators (Like successor) are then more effective but they are less obvious to infer.

II. TECHNICAL TOOLS OF THE SYSTEM

II.1 Functions and predicates representation

Functions and predicates are represented as sets of Horn clauses as in First Order Logic. In fact we use an equivalent representation which more accuratly represents a procedural form of clauses.

For instance, if Eq is the Equal predicate, the classical clause

$$Eq(z,A(x,y)) \subset Eq(F(z),B(H(x),V(y))) \wedge P(H(x),y) \wedge Eq(z,V(y))$$

will be represented by

$$z \leftarrow A(x,y) \subset a \leftarrow F(z),\ b \leftarrow H(x),\ z \leftarrow V(y),\ a \leftarrow B(b,z),\ P(b,y)$$

II.2 Examples

An expert can interact with the system in two different ways.

- Examples of inputs and of the corresponding output are given to the system as in
  2258 ← SUC(2257)
  NUMBER (12329)
- An input is given to the system with an interrogation on the output
  ? ← SUC(159)

The system tries to answer correctly. After having been told by the expert if it has succeded, a positive example is generated. If the system gives a wrong output, a negative example is then generated and the expert gives the correct output. For instance let us suppose that the current answer to the question ? ← SUC(159) is 1510. The expert indicates the correct answer -160- and then both a negative example [x=159,y≠1510] and a positive example [x=159,y=160] are generated.

As [17] and in opposition to [6] , we think that negative examples (which are near-miss in our system) are fundamental for a complete function synthesis and, above all, for predicate synthesis.

II.3 Memory

There are in fact three memories.

- A long term memory which contains every clause of the system. They are referred to names

- An active memory which is a short term memory. This memory will contain the names of functions or predicates which have been recently learnt or used.

- A predicate hierarchy which is a concept hierarchy as in [6]. For each new predicate, we try to find a correct position in the hierarchy and in fact we find more than one possibility. The candidate positions are organized in subhierarchies which are also attached to the name of the predicate.

II.4 Evaluator

Our evaluator is a Prolog like evaluator which includes a sophisticated tool used when the prolog evaluator fails. For instance, during the learning of the successor function, when this learning is incomplete, a Prolog evaluator will answer "False" with the input 2750←SUC(2749) (carry on successor of 9 has not been encountered yet).

A simple answer "False" is not sufficient for us. since we specially want to know the point where the failure is the most relevant. Such a failure point is unique in a Prolog evaluator but it is not so if we change the order of clauses or terms. We need an evaluator which gives the "best" failure point on all these orders (or one point which is reasonably close to the best one). The evaluator we use in the system is described in [12].

II.5 Locking

A clause is locked if paths exist from the inputs (here x and y) to the output (here z) which allow to calculate the output. (see [4]).

Often during the learning process, the generated clauses are not locked and a significant part of the system deals with locking of clauses.

Locking of predicates is more frequently used to place the predicate in the hierarchy than to actually construct the predicate.

II.6 Learning heuristics

This paragraph describes the main heuristics which are used in the learning process. Some of them are expanding heuristics, some others deal with reduction or simplification.

II.6.1 Catching

When the evaluator fails on an example, it gives a clause which represents the most relevant failure. Catching is then a partial copy of that clause. Predicates or functions which are compatible with the example are copied. Predicates which are false in the example become negative in the catching clause. Multiple values are separated, when a value is out the input domain of a function, a new function is created.

This last action could be considered as an unavoidable combinatorial explosion but subsumption will reduce it.

II.6.2 Remarks

The "remark" heuristic is used with three elements a clause, an example on this clause and the active memory. It is a combinatorial testing of all concepts which are in the active memory, these concepts being tested on all the values induced by the example.

II.6.3 Unfolding

Our unfolding is the classical one [3]. To unfold a function F (or a predicate) which appears on the right part of a clause is to add to this clause the right part of a clause in which F constitutes the left part.

Unfolding is controlled by an example and then the right part of F which is added must be compatible with the example.

II.6.4 Locking by constant

When the three preceding heuristics (catching, remarks, unfolding) have failed to lock the clause. A localization process delivers a set of variables which can be replaced by constants.

II.6.5 Simplification

Near the end of the learning process, many terms become useless, particularly in a recently created clause. The objective of the simplification process is to detect these terms and to get rid of them.

II.6.6 Subsumption [9]

A clause C is said to subsume a clause D if all the positive examples of D are accepted by C. D can be cancelled and all its positive examples become positive examples of C.

II.7 Learning process

As the heuristics can be greatly changed, many different learning processes are possible. The objective of the newly designed system is to study experimentally these different kinds of heuristics or learning processes. For this reason we are presently designing a new version of the system which will allow a more flexible change of heuristics or the learning process. The one which is now described here is very close to the first version of the system. [13].

After the expert introduces an example, the system works in this manner :

- for a function

1. EVALUATION
2. If the example is compatible, it is added as a positive example to the clause which accepted it and the process stops
3. If not the CATCHING heuristic is used
4. If the new clause is not LOCKED try REMARKS
5. If the clause if locked now do SUBSUMPTION, if possible, then SIMPLIFICATION and stop.
6. Try UNFOLDING
7. If the clause is not LOCKED try REMARKS again
8. If the clause is still unlocked, LOCK it by CONSTANT function
9. Try SUBSUMPTION, then do SIMPLIFICATION and stop

- for a predicate

1. EVALUATION
2. If the example is compatible add it to the clause. If there is no subhierarchy, then stop
3. If not, do CATCHING
4. Then do REMARKS
5. If the clause is LOCKED, do an EVALUATION on negative examples. If there is no problem try SUBSUMPTION, SIMPLIFICATION and STOP, else refine the subhierarchy
6. Try UNFOLDING
7. If the clause is not locked, LOCK it by CONSTANT function, try SUBSUMPTION, SIMPLIFICATION and stop
8. Else do an EVALUATION on negative examples, refine the SUBHIEARCHY, try SUBSUMPTION, SIMPLIFICATION and stop

III. Some of the experiments :

The initial knowledge of the system is composed as characer strings and some basic functions or predicates.
LAST which gives the last character of a string
PREF which gives the whole string except the last character
CONC which gives the concatenation of two strings
NUL which is true is a string is empty
K which is true if the string is a one character string
ST which is always true on strings

Once NB (number) and D (digit) predicates have been learned : the following inputs :
1←SUC(0), 2←SUC(1)...9←SUC(8)
123←SUC(124), 360←SUC(359), 100←SUC(99)
will give as output :

```
y←SUC(x)⊂x←0,y←1,D(x),D(y)
        ⊂x←8,y 9,D(x),D(y)
        ⊂a←PREF(x,),b←LAST(x),c←SUC(b)
         y←CONC(a,c),x←CONC(a,b),a←PREF(y)
         c←LAST(y),NB(a),D(b),D(c),¬D(x),¬D(y)
         [x= 123, y=124]
        ⊂a←PREF(x),b←LAST(x),c←F(b),d←SUC(a),
         y←CONC(d,c),x←CONC(a,b),d←PREF(y),
         c←LAST(y),NB(a),NB(d),D(b),D(c),¬D(x)
         ¬D(y),  [x=99,y=100]   [x=359,y=360]
        ⊂a←PREF(x),d←G(a),c←F(x),y←CONC(d,c)
         d←PREF(y),c←LAST(y),NB(d),D(c),D(x),¬D(y)
         [x=9,y=10]
y←F(x)⊂x←9,y←0,D(x),D(y)             [x=9,y=0]
y←G(x)⊂x←∅,y←1,NUL(x),D(y)           [x=∅,y=1]
```

A complete description of the example can be found in [14].

IV. Conclusion

The system which has been described here presents some particularities
- The learning capacity is greatly related to the expert pedagogy. One of our further interests is to study how the modifications or introductions of heuristics can more or less allow a sophisticated pedagogy.
- The concepts which have been synthetized here are relatively complex. In Lenat's work, the concept of addition is simple because addition is a particularisation of union on bags. Our representation of numbers is more realistic. The synthesis of the successor function is constructive and is not a restriction of a previously known concept. However the system is able to infer simple concepts and can be used as a powerfull learning-knowledge-base.

References

1 BIERMAN & SMITH : "A production rule mechanism for generating LIPS CODE", Duke University, 1977

2 COLMERAUER & AL : "Un système de communication homme-machine en français", Rapport prélimaire, Groupe de Recherche en I.A. Aix Marseille Luminy, 1972

3 DARLINGTON : "A system which automatically improves programs" IJCAI 3th, 1973

4 GUIHO & JOUANNAUD : "Inference of function with an interactive system", Machine Intelligence n° 9, 1977.

5 KODRATOFF : "Choix d'un programme LISP correspondant à un exemple" AFCET, reconnaissance des formes, 1977.

6 KNAPMANN : "Artificial learning", Ph.D. Thesis Edinburgh, 1977.

7 KNOBE & KNOBE : "A method for infering context free grammars", Information and control 31, pp 123-146 (1976).

8 LENAT : "AM : an artificial intelligence approach to discovery in mathematics or heuristics search", SAIL AIM-286, AI Lab., Stanford University, 1976.

9 NILSON : "Problem solving methods in artificial intelligence", Mc Graw Hill, 1971.

10 SUMMERS : "A methodology for LISP program construction from example", Journal of ACM, 24-1, 1977.

11 SUSSMAN : "A computational model for skill acquisition", Ph.D. MIT, Massachussetts University.

12 MELESE & TREUIL : "Failure analysis in sequence of linear resolutions", Memo LRI n° 30

13 TREUIL & SCHYN : "The system LQAS", LRI, Orsay France, 1978.

14 SCHYN & GUIHO : "A learning system able to synthesize arithmetical functions", Memo LRI n° 29.

15 VERE : "Induction of concepts in the predicates calculus ", Proc 7th IJCAI Tbilissi USSR 1975 pp 281-287.

16 WEGBREIT : "Goal directed program transformation", IEEE trans. on software eng. Vol 2 n° 2, 1976.

17 WINSTON : "Learning structural description from example", Ph. D. Mc Graw Hill, N. Y. 1975.

PLAS, A Paradigmatic Language Acquisition System: An Overview

V. Sembugamoorthy
Computer Centre
Indian Institute of Technology, Powai
Bombay 400 076, India

This paper informally describes the capabilities of a teachable analogy-based language - independent natural language acquisition system known as PLAS. Its language comprehension is intended to resemble that of pre-school children in certain significant aspects. It can be taught, through examples, to understand and acquire the situational aspects (i.e., physical objects, agents, their sensori-motor properties and spatial relations) described in a text. It has no built-in knowledge of English or the domain of discourse. Neither it infers any formal grammar of English.

1. INTRODUCTION

This paper informally describes the capabilities of a primitive natural language acquisition system known as PLAS. The version reported here has been implemented using UCI-LISP on the DEC-10 system at the NCSDCT, TIFR, Bombay. Its linguistic comprehension is intended to resemble that of a pre-school child in certain significant aspects. PLAS can be taught, through examples, to understand and acquire language utterances representing physical objects, agents, their sensori-motor properties (e.g: colour, height, etc.) and spatial relations (e.g: on the chair, to the left of, etc.). To this end, PLAS has to acquire and use the knowledge to analyse and interpret linguistic utterances, understand proforms, obtain the subject of a sentence,and identify and associate the sensori-motor properties and relations with the subject.

PLAS differs significantly from the reported language acquisition systems [3, 4, 5, 6] in one or more of the following aspects: PLAS is neither based on any built-in knowledge of English nor designed to acquire any formal grammar of English. The language understanding and generation procedures are analogy-based. The primitives of the internal representation of language behaviour and world knowledge are either acquired through natural language interaction, or built-in and independent of any language, task or domain.

Within its scope, PLAS provides a solution to the issue of assimilation and accommodation raised in [7].

The machinery of PLAS has been motivated primarily by our long-term goal to model child language behaviour. Nevertheless,the computational machinery should be useful towards constructing practical expansible natural language interaction systems. Refer to [1, 2] for the psychological aspects of PLAS, the explicit substantiation of its features mentioned above and the detailed discussion of its computational machinery.

2. AN EXAMPLE OF INTERACTION

Initially PLAS does not possess any knowledge of English or the domain of discourse. Using a simulated teaching environment called 'Teach-names', the teacher first associates a set of names with the physical objects and agents that he proposes to deal with in his interaction. Note that neither all names of an object/agent nor all objects that a word or a phrase can name need be associated using 'Teach-names'. A typical input to 'Teach-names' is:

1. CHAIR 1, CHAIR2; CHAIR; (OBJECT MADE-OF-WOOD).

This means that the language expression 'CHAIR' is a name of the physical objects 'CHAIR1' and 'CHAIR2'; '(OBJECT MADE-OF-WOOD)' is called a taglist. It is intended to simulate the structured complex of sensori-motor mechanisms which is responsible for the perception/manipulation of 'CHAIR1' and 'CHAIR2'. However, since articulating this structure is itself a challenging open problem, a taglist is presently assumed to be an unstructured set of tags where each tag relates to a sensori-motor mechanism. As we shall see in section 3, the taglist plays an important role in understanding linguistic utterances. Moreover, it is significant to note that the language expressions used to name tags (e.g: MADE-OF-WOOD) do not function as language expressions as far as PLAS is concerned. Let us assume that using 'Teach-names', the teacher has taught PLAS the following words and phrases:

2. TABLE, THE TABLE; 3. WINDOW; 4. DESK; 5. ROOM, THE ROOM; 6. FOUNTAIN, THE FOUNTAIN; 7. BOX; 8. SHELF.

Next, the teacher teaches, using another teaching device called 'Teach-aspects', a set of words and phrases known as aspect tokens as shown below (Aspect tokens are language expressions that denote properties of, and relations between, objects and/or agents):

9. NAC (BROWN; (COLOUR)).
This means that 'BROWN' is an aspect token of a New Aspect Category (NAC for short). '(COLOUR)' is the taglist associated with 'BROWN' at the sensori-motor level.

10. (GREEN; (COLOUR)) SAC (BROWN; (COLOUR)).
The aspect tokens 'GREEN' and 'BROWN' belong to the Same Aspect Category (SAC).

11. (RED; (COLOUR)) SAC (GREEN; (COLOUR)).
12. (RED IN COLOUR; (COLOUR)) SAS (RED; (COLOUR)).
'RED IN COLOUR' and 'RED' represent the Same Aspect (SAS). Let us assume that using 'Teach-aspects', the teacher has taught the following aspect tokens:

13. PLASTIC; 14. WOOD; 15. NEAR THE FOUNTAIN; 16. IN THE MIDDLE OF THE FOUNTAIN; 17. INSIDE THE DESK; 18. ON THE BOX; 19. MADE OF PLASTIC; 20. HEAVY 21. LIGHT.

Next, the teacher uses a teaching device called 'Teach-Proforms' to teach proform tokens as shown below:

22. (THE CHAIR NEAR THE TABLE) ASS (THE ONE NEAR THE TABLE).
This means that 'THE CHAIR NEAR THE TABLE' is an ASSignment (ASS for short) of the proform 'THE ONE NEAR THE TABLE'.

23. (THE CHAIR) ASS (IT).
Before we proceed further, it is worthwhile to point out that (i) in principle, 'Teach-names', 'Teach-aspects' and 'Teach-proforms' can be employed in any order and any number of times; (ii) the teaching devices 'Teach-aspects' and 'Teach-proforms' are unrealistic from the viewpoint of modelling the learning environment of pre-school children and can be eliminated, as shown in [1], by incorporating, in PLAS, a question-answering environment.

Next, the teacher teaches a text (call Text1) as shown below:

24. ((A CHAIR) REF 'CHAIR1' AND (A TABLE) REF 'TABLE1') REF (COLLECTION1 AGG CHAIR1, TABLE1) ARE NEAR THE WINDOW.
This means that the tokens ' A CHAIR','A TABLE' and 'A TABLE AND A CHAIR' refer to 'CHAIR1', 'TABLE1' and 'COLLECTION1' respectively; 'COLLECTION1' consists of 'CHAIR1' and'TABLE1'. The sentence taught is 'A CHAIR AND A TABLE ARE NEAR THE WINDOW'. REF and AGG, which stand for 'reference-of' and 'aggregate-of', simulate the extra-linguistic means employed by the language community to associate a language expression with its referent, and to specify the members of an aggregate of objects/agents respectively. Besides interpreting these extra-linguistic markers, PLAS has to analyse and interpret 'NEAR THE WINDOW' using 15 i.e, step 15; identify 'A CHAIR AND A TABLE' as the subject token; associate the aspect token 'NEAR THE WINDOW' with 'COLLECTION1' and thereby with 'CHAIR1' and 'TABLE1'.

25. THE CHAIR IS BROWN IN COLOUR.
Using 1 and 2 i.e., using the knowledge acquired in 1 and 2, PLAS interprets 'THE CHAIR' as 'CHAIR1'; acquires 'BROWN IN COLOUR' using 12; identifies the subject token 'THE CHAIR'; associates 'BROWN IN COLOUR' with 'CHAIR1'.

26. THE TABLE IS RED IN COLOUR.
PLAS uses 25 to understand this sentence since it is similar to the one in 25.

27. A DESK AND A CHAIR ARE IN THE MIDDLE OF THE ROOM.
'A CHAIR' is interpreted as 'CHAIR2' because 'CHAIR1' has been associated with 'NEAR THE WINDOW' in 24. 'IN THE MIDDLE OF THE ROOM' is understood using 16.

28. THE BROWN CHAIR IS MADE OF WOOD.
PLAS interprets 'THE BROWN CHAIR' as 'CHAIR1' and not as 'CHAIR2'. Note that 'CHAIR1' has been associated in 25 with 'BROWN IN COLOUR'. PLAS uses 12 to equate 'BROWN IN COLOUR' and 'BROWN', and to correctly interpret 'THE BROWN CHAIR' as 'CHAIR1'.

29. THE ONE IN THE MIDDLE OF THE ROOM IS MADE OF PLASTIC.
PLAS assigns 'THE CHAIR IN THE MIDDLE OF THE

ROOM' to the proform 'THE ONE IN THE MIDDLE OF THE ROOM'. Note that the teacher has taught, in 22, only the assignment 'THE CHAIR NEAR THE TABLE'. Moreover, PLAS has to use 27 to interpret 'THE CHAIR IN THE MIDDLE OF THE ROOM' as 'CHAIR2' and not as 'CHAIR1'.

The teacher next tests PLAS by asking it to understand a similar new text. For example,
Text 2
THIS IS A CHAIR. THERE IS A BOX ON THE CHAIR. IT IS HEAVY. THE BOX INSIDE THE SHELF IS LIGHT. THE HEAVY BOX IS GREEN IN COLOUR.
Note that PLAS can understand Text2 even though the underlying sentential forms and the described situational aspects vary significantly from those of Text1. Moreover, PLAS should interpret 'IT' in the third sentence as the box referred to in the second sentence even though the teacher has associated only 'THE CHAIR' with 'IT' in 23. Now, as requested by the teacher, PLAS generates the following sentences using 'CHAIR' and 'RED':
THE HEAVY CHAIR IS RED IN COLOUR. THE LIGHT CHAIR IS RED IN COLOUR. THE RED CHAIR IS MADE OF WOOD. THE RED CHAIR IS MADE OF PLASTIC. THE CHAIR IS RED IN COLOUR.
Note that none of these sentences appears in Text1 or Text2. Moreover, PLAS has not generated any semantically anemolous sentence like 'THE RED CHAIR IS GREEN IN COLOUR'.

3. THE COMPUTATIONAL MACHINERY

Interaction procedures simulate the teaching and testing environments discussed in section2. They invoke sensori-motor procedures and language behaviour procedures to process the sensori-motor level information (i.e,physical objects, taglists, extra-linguistic markers) and the linguistic expressions respectively. In what follows we shall sketch only the language understanding procedure. To understand a language expression, say 'ON THE TABLE', PLAS first invokes the segmentation procedure to analyse it into a known language schema, say 'on -' (' - ' stands for a variable) and the filler 'THE TABLE'; 'THE TABLE' itself has to be understood before it is accepted as a filler. The segmented language expression is then validated. For instance, if 'NEAR THE CHAIR' is an already known valid filler for the second variable of the schema '- IS -', then 'ON THE TABLE' is accepted as a valid filler for the same variable provided the taglists associated with the two aspect tokens match (presently two taglists match iff they contain identical tags). The interpretation procedure then interprets the validated token. For example, using the knowledge that the referent of 'JOHN'S BOOK' is say 'BOOK10', 'JILL'S TABLE' will be interpreted as, say 'TABLE5'. A successfully segmented, validated and interpreted language expression is said to be understood. If the schema 'On -' is not known already, it will be abstracted out of it by the schematization procedure by replacing understandable or already known language expressions in it. In this case also, before 'ON THE TABLE' is declared understood, it has to be validated and interpreted. Note that what underlies the language understanding procedure is not any language-specific information but are the capabilities to assimilate the unknown in terms of the known, and to accommodate the unknown if assimilation fails. These capabilities are analogy-based. To enable these capabilities is the main function of the data spaces of PLAS.

ACKNOWLEDGEMENTS

The valuable guidance of Prof.R.Narasimhan is gratefully acknowledged.

REFERENCES

[1] Sembugamoorthy,V. 'A Paradigmatic Language Acquisition System', Ph.D.Thesis, Indian Institute of Tech., Bombay, India, May, 1978.

[2] Narasimhan, R. 'Modelling Language Behaviour', Tech.Report, Computer group, TIFR, April,1973.

[3] Jordan, R.S. 'A Natural Language Understander Based on a Freely Associated Learned Memory Net', Int.J.Comput.Inf.Sci.6:1 (1977) 10-25.

[4] Reeker,L.H. 'The Computational Study of Language Acquisition' in Advances in Computers, Rubinoff, M., and Yovits, M.C., (Eds) Academic Press, 1976, pp.181-235.

[5] Siklossy,L. 'Natural Language Learning by Computer' in Representation and Meaning: Experiments with Information Processing Systems, Prentice-Hall, NJ, 1972, pp.288-328.

[6] Harris, L.R. 'A System for Primitive Natural Language Acquisition', Int. J.Man-Mach. Stud.9 (1977) 153-206.

[7] Moore, J. and Newell,A. 'How can Merlin Understand?' in Knowledge and Cognition, Gregg, L. (Ed), Lawrence Erlbaum Assoc. Potomoc, Md., 1973.

NUMERICAL QUANTIFIERS AND THEIR USE IN REASONING WITH NEGATIVE INFORMATION

Stuart C. Shapiro
Department of Computer Science
State University of New York at Buffalo
4226 Ridge Lea Road
Amherst, New York 14226

Numerical quantifiers provide simple means of formalizing such statements as, "at least three people are in that room", "at most fifteen people are in the elevator", and "everybody has exactly two parents". Although numerical quantifiers generalize the existential quantifier, they have different uses in reasoning. The existential quantifier is most useful for supplying referents for designating phrases with no previously explicitly mentioned referent. Numerical quantifiers are most useful for reasoning by the process of elimination. Numerical quantifiers would, therefore, be a useful addition to the operators of a reasoning program or deductive question-answering system. They have been added to SNePS, the Semantic Network Processing System, to further enhance its inference capabilities.

1. INTRODUCTION

Logic based reasoning programs, that is reasoning programs based on operators (connectives, quantifiers, modals) which have been studied as part of formal logical systems benefit from the fact that the inferential properties of their operators are clear and well known. They need not be restricted, however, to a minimal set of operators. Minimal sets of operators are useful for proving properties of logical systems such as consistency and completeness, but using a logical system for carrying out inferences is simplified (for people) by enlarging the set of basic operators. This is one reason that natural deduction systems like those of [1], [4] and [11], with reasonable sets of connectives and two rules of inference for each one, are easier to use than axiomatic systems with minimal sets of connectives, rules and axioms.

This paper is motivated by an interest in programs that represent knowledge, including the knowledge of rules of reasoning, and that use those rules to perform reasoning. I believe that such programs are enhanced by the availability of a large set of operators that typify and formally model as many of the modes of human reasoning as possible. This paper discusses a set of operators, the numerical quantifiers, which can be implemented in reasoning programs as a single parameterized operator, and which model an important mode of human reasoning.

Numerical quantifiers, discussed briefly in [10, pp. 63-64], are generalizations of the existential quantifier. They can be used to formalize such statements as:

There are at least two numbers z, such that $z+2<6$.
There are exactly two numbers x, such that $x^2+4=4x$.
There are at most two numbers y, such that $y+5<11-2y$.
(all from [10, pp. 64, 67].)

One numerical quantifier is the more commonly encountered unique existential, expressed as $\exists! xA(x)$ in the notation of [2, p. 199]. We will use the notation $\exists_i^j xA(x)$ for "there exists at least i and at most j x such that A(x)". The usual existential quantifier, $\exists xA(x)$, can then be considered an abbreviation of $\exists_1^\infty xA(x)$ (although later we will make a distinction), and the unique existential becomes $\exists_1^1 xA(x)$. In general, $\exists_n^n xA(x)$ are the "numerically definite quantifiers" mentioned in [3, pp. 165, 6].

We have found the numerical quantifiers particularly useful for the mode of reasoning by the process of elimination: if the maximal number of positive cases are found, the rest must be negative; if the maximal number of negative cases are found, the rest must be positive. Numerical quantifiers thus can introduce explicit negative information into a data base, and can make use of negative information to

----

*This material is based on work supported in part by a Faculty Research Fellowship from the Research Foundation of State University of New York, and in part by the National Science Foundation under Grant No. MCS78-02274.

derive positive information. To set the stage for this discussion, we will first discuss the role of the simple existential quantifier in deductive question-answering.

2. THE EXISTENTIAL QUANTIFIER

Let us consider statements which:
1) include an existential quantifier;
2) are to be stored in the data base of a deductive question-answering system (QAS);
3) are to be used by the system to answer questions.

We will consider what contribution such statements (we call these, as well as other general statements, deduction rules) can make to the question-answering process.

Existential quantifiers can either be outside or inside the scope of universal quantifiers. If outside the scope of any universal quantifier, for example "There is a man who owns a dog" or $\exists x(Man(x)\&\exists y(Dog(y)\&Owns(x,y)))$, there is no need to retain the quantifier in the data base, one can simply create new individual constants (Skolem constants) and substitute them for the quantified variables, storing, in this example, the three facts Man(ml), Dog(dl), and Owns(ml,dl).

Existential quantifiers within the scope of universal quantifiers can be eliminated by replacing them with Skolem functions. So,
(1) Every person has a mother
can be represented by $\forall x(Person(x)\rightarrow\exists y(Person(y)\&Mother(y,x)))$ or by $\forall x(Person(x)\rightarrow(Person(f(x))\&Mother(f(x),x)))$, where f is a new function. This rule could be used to answer the question, "Does John have a mother?", but the point of the Skolem function is that for each person a new person must be postulated to be his or her mother. So, knowing just (1), and that John is a person, if we asked "Who is John's mother?", the answer would be some individual about whom we know nothing except that she is a person and is John's mother.

It may seem strange that asking a question can cause the creation of a new individual, but consider definite descriptions that refer to individuals which have not been explicitly introduced, as in the statement "John's mother owns a dog". Normally, we would look in the data base for John's mother and assert that she owns a dog, but in this case there is no record of John's mother in the data base. However, rule (1) justifies creating a new individual to be John's mother. "John's mother owns a dog" presupposes that John has a mother. With neither an explicit mother, nor the rule, the sentence has a failed presupposition and should not be accepted.

If the data base contained both rule (1) and "Jane is John's mother", and we input, "John's mother owns a dog," rule (1) is at best useless, and at worst, harmful. If the rule were activated, it would have to produce a new mother, and the phrase "John's mother" would be ambiguous. If rule (1) were not activated, "Jane owns a dog" would be stored. This is technically wrong (consider replacing "mother" with "parent"), but probably what the speaker intended.

In summary, existential quantifiers need be stored in the data base of a QAS only when within the scope of a universal quantifier, and they are most useful for supplying referents for designating phrases with no previously explicitly mentioned referent.

3. MAXIMAL NUMERICAL QUANTIFIERS

Consider the data base containing "Jane is John's mother" and the question, "Is Mary John's mother?" In order to get the correct answer, "No", we need the rule
(2) Every person has at most one mother.
(We will ignore, in this paper, the problem of identity or extensional equivalence. That is, the even more correct answer, "Only if Mary is the same person as Jane". See [7] for a solution to this problem using a combination of path tracing and deduction rules.) Let us call quantifiers of the form $\exists^j xA(x)$, read "there exists at most j x such that A of x", maximal numerical quantifiers. In this notation, (2) becomes
(2') $\forall x(Person(x)\rightarrow\exists^1 y(Person(y)\&Mother(y,x)))$

Unlike the simple existential quantifier, the maximal numerical quantifiers do not justify the introduction of new individuals. However, we can derive negative statements from them once the maximal number of individuals satisfying the quantified statement are known. In our example, rule (2) justifies the answer, "No, Mary is not John's mother".

If a data base consisted of rules (1) and (2) only, and we asked, "Is Jane John's mother?", it might seem that rule (1) would create a new Skolem constant to be John's mother, and then by rule (2) the answer would be "No". However, rule (1) must not be invoked in this case, because it is illegal to instantiate an existentially quantified variable to a constant we already know something about. Since John's mother is not known explicitly, Jane is not ruled out and the correct answer in this case is "I don't know".

The formula $\exists^j xA(x)$ is therefore useful when we already know j different individuals satisfying A and are asked if a (j+1)st individual, t, also satisfies A. The formula $\sim A(t)$ is then derivable.

4. MINIMAL NUMERICAL QUANTIFIERS

Now consider formulas of the form, $\exists_i xA(x)$, read "There exists at least i x such that A of of x". We will call quantifiers of this form, minimal numerical quantifiers. What useful information does this provide that is not provided by $\exists xA(x)$? If the universe under discussion contains n individuals, and we already know of n-i individuals y such that $\sim A(y)$, we can deduce about any (n-i+1)st individual, t, that A(t). Consider five professors, three of whom are in a meeting. If I know who the five people are, and I've seen two in the hall, I can deduce who is in the meeting.

Since the usefulness of minimal numerical quantifiers depends on some universe of objects, it is convenient to introduce domain restricted minimal numerical quantifiers. We will use the notation $\exists_i x(P(x):Q(x))$, where P(x) and Q(x) are arbitrary formulas with x free, to mean, "of all objects x such that P(x), at least i of them satisfy Q". In a data base without the closed world assumption [5], we can seldom be sure that the objects known to satisfy P are the only ones that actually do. For example, the following corpus, representing the example above, is insufficient for deducing who is in the meeting.

(3) $\exists_3 x$(Professor(x):In(x,meeting))
(4) $\forall x$(In(x,hall)$\rightarrow\sim$In(x,meeting))
(5) Professor(Pat)
(6) Professor(Gabor)
(7) Professor(Nick)
(8) Professor(John)
(9) Professor(Stu)
(10) In(Pat,hall)
(11) In(Nick,hall)

However, it may be that whoever provided rule (3) knows that there are only five professors. To record such information, we will add another parameter to the minimal numerical quantifiers giving the schema, ${}_n\exists_i x(P(x):Q(x))$, where n is the number of objects which satisfy P. Notice that this amounts to a closed sub-world assumption. If we replace (3) in the above corpus by

(3') ${}_5\exists_3 x$(Professor(x):In(x,meeting))

stating that "Of the five professors, at least three are in the meeting", then we can derive In(Gabor,meeting),In(John,meeting) and In(Stu, meeting).

With minimal numerical quantifiers, negative information can be used to deduce positive information. Given the rule ${}_n\exists_i x(P(x):Q(x))$, and n-i individuals y such that P(y)&$\sim$Q(y), we can deduce for any other individual t such that P(t) holds that Q(t) also holds.

5. NUMERICAL QUANTIFIERS

The minimal and maximal numerical quantifiers can be combined into what we shall simply call the numerical quantifiers, ${}_n\exists_i^j x(P(x):Q(x))$, which are read, "Of the n individuals x such that P(x), at least i and at most j are such that Q(x)", or simply, "Between i and j of the n Ps are Qs". The other quantifiers we have discussed may be obtained by leaving out appropriate parts of this schema.

If a data base contains a rule of the form ${}_n\exists_i^j x(P(x):Q(x))$ and j individuals are found satisfying P(x)&Q(x), it may be deduced that the remaining n-j individuals satisfying P(x) satisfy $\sim$Q(x). However, if n-i individuals are found to satisfy P(x)&$\sim$Q(x), it may be deduced that the remaining i individuals satisfying P(x) also satisfy Q(x).

The regular existential quantifier, $\exists xA(x)$, is the same as the numerical quantifier $\exists_1^\infty xA(x)$. It is now clear why it seldom helps us determine whether A(t) holds for a fixed individual, t. $\exists_1^\infty xA(x)$ cannot derive $\sim$A(t), since there is no maximum -- all individuals might satisfy A. It can seldom produce A(t), since that would require knowing that all other individuals satisfy $\sim$A, and we rarely have a finite list of all the individuals in the domain. Because of this, the implementor of a deductive QAS may wish to distinguish the existential quantifier from the numerical quantifiers, and continue to prohibit invocation of a rule that would bind an existentially quantified variable to a constant.

6. NUMERICAL QUANTIFIERS IN SNePS

Numerical quantifiers have recently been added to SNePS, the Semantic Network Processing System [6; 8], which already included universal and existential quantifiers as well as a set of non-standard connectives. SNePS accepts numerically quantified formulas of the form

(12) ${}_n\exists_i^j\bar{x}(P_1(\bar{x}),\ldots,P_k(\bar{x}):Q(\bar{x}))$
(13) ${}_n\exists_i\bar{x}(P_1(\bar{x}),\ldots,P_k(\bar{x}):Q(\bar{x}))$
(14) $\exists^j\bar{x}(P_1(\bar{x}),\ldots,P_k(\bar{x}):Q(\bar{x}))$

where $k\geq 0$ and $\bar{x}$ represents a sequence of variables $\langle x_1,\ldots,x_m\rangle$ each of which is free in at least one of $P_1(\bar{x}),\ldots,P_k(\bar{x}),Q(\bar{x})$. The meaning of (12) is that there are n sequences of individuals, $\langle t_1,\ldots,t_m\rangle$ such that $(P_1(\bar{x})\&\ldots\&P_k(\bar{x}))[t_1/x_1,\ldots,t_m/x_m]$ is true and that at least i and at most j of these n sequences also satisfy $Q(\bar{x})$. The meanings of (13) and (14) are the appropriate simplifications of this.

As an example of (12), consider the many-many relationship of dog ownership. Several people may jointly own one dog, and several dogs may be owned by the same person. The formula $_5\exists_2^4 x,y(\mathrm{Person}(x),\mathrm{Dog}(y),\mathrm{Owns}(x,y):\mathrm{Spoils}(x,y))$ says that of the five dog ownership relations (e.g. <John,Rover>, <John,Spot>, <Jane,Spot>, <Mary, Lassie>, and <Jim,Lassie>), between two and four involve spoiling the dog.

Rules of the form of (12) are represented in the SNePS network by a node with: an auxiliary arc labeled EMIN to i; an auxiliary arc labeled EMAX to j; an auxiliary arc labeled ETOT to n; descending arcs labeled PEVB to the nodes representing the variables in $\overline{x}$; descending arcs labeled &ANT to the nodes representing the formulas $P_1(\overline{x}),\ldots,P_k(\overline{x})$; a descending arc labeled CQ to the node representing $Q(\overline{x})$. In SNePS, auxiliary arcs may connect semantic network nodes to arbitrary data structures, including numbers. A descending arc goes from a network node to another network node and has a paired ascending arc in the reverse direction.

7. EXAMPLES

In this section, we will show SNePS runs of the three major numerical quantifier examples from above. Lines beginning with "**" or "*" were typed by the user. The character ";" indicates that the rest of the line is a comment. Input is in SNePSUL, the SNePS User Language, [8]. Each input and each deduced fact is commented by its English translation. Each rule is also commented by its translation into the logical syntax used previously in this paper. The runs were transcribed to make them easier to read, and edited only to add the comments and to remove some trace printing. SNePS is written in Lisp and runs interactively on a CYBER 173. A compiled version was used for these examples.

7.1 Example 1

We assert that Jane is John's mother and that everyone has at most one mother. Then we ask if Mary is John's mother, and SNePS responds that she is not.

```
**;Jane is a person.
*(BUILD MEM JANE CLASS PERSON)
(M13) ;The SNePS node representing the assertion.
8 MSECS
**;John is a person.
*(BUILD MEM JOHN CLASS PERSON)
(M14)
8 MSECS
**;Jane is John's mother.
*(BUILD A JANE R MOTHER O JOHN)
(M15)
12 MSECS
**;Every person has at most one mother.
*;∀x[Person(x)→ ∃¹y(Person(y) : Mother(y,x))]
*(BUILD AVB $X
* ANT (BUILD MEM *X CLASS PERSON)
*  CQ (BUILD EMAX 1 PEVB $Y
*       &ANT (BUILD MEM *Y CLASS PERSON)
*         CQ (BUILD A *Y R MOTHER O *X)))
(M21)
65 MSECS
**;Mary is a person.
*(BUILD MEM MARY CLASS PERSON)
(M22)
7 MSECS
**;Is Mary John's mother?
* (DESCRIBE (DEDUCE A MARY R MOTHER O JOHN))
(M24 (MIN(0)) (MAX(0)) (ARG(M23)))
     ; It is not the case that
(M23 (A(MARY)) (R(MOTHER)) (O(JOHN)))
     ; Mary is the mother of John.
(DUMPED)
1120 MSECS
```

7.2 Example 2

At least three of the five professors are in the meeting. We see Pat and Nick in the hall. When we ask who is in the meeting, SNePS deduces that Pat and Nick are not, but Gabor, John, and Stu are.

```
**;At least 3 of 5 professors are in a meeting.
*;₅∃₃x[Professor(x)→In(x,meeting)]
*(BUILD ETOT 5 EMIN 3 PEVB $X
* &ANT (BUILD MEM *X CLASS PROFESSOR)
*   CQ (BUILD A *X R IN O MEETING))
(M4)
44 MSECS
**;Whoever is in the hall is not in the meeting.
*;∀x[In(x,hall)→~In(x,meeting)]
*(BUILD AVB $X
* ANT (BUILD A *X R IN O HALL)
*  CQ (BUILD MIN 0 MAX 0
*       ARG (BUILD A *X R IN O MEETING)))
(M8)
50 MSECS
**;Pat is a professor.
*(BUILD MEM PAT CLASS PROFESSOR)
(M9)
10 MSECS
**;Gabor is a professor.
*(BUILD MEM GABOR CLASS PROFESSOR)
(M10)
8 MSECS
**;Nick is a professor.
*(BUILD MEM NICK CLASS PROFESSOR)
(M11)
8 MSECS
**;John is a professor.
*(BUILD MEM JOHN CLASS PROFESSOR)
(M12)
8 MSECS
**;Stu is a professor.
*(BUILD MEM STU CLASS PROFESSOR)
```

```
(M13)
9 MSECS
**;Pat is in the hall.
*(BUILD A PAT R IN O HALL)
(M14)
11 MSECS
**;Nick is in the hall.
*(BUILD A NICK R IN O HALL)
(M15)
10 MSECS
**;Who is in the meeting?
*(DESCRIBE (DEDUCE A %X R IN O MEETING))
(M17 (MIN(0)) (MAX(0)) (ARG(M16)))
(M16 (A(PAT)) (R(IN)) (O(MEETING)))
     ; Pat is not in the meeting.
(M19 (MIN(0)) (MAX(0)) (ARG(M18)))
(M18 (A(NICK)) (R(IN)) (O(MEETING)))
     ; Nick is not in the meeting.
(M20 (A(GABOR)) (R(IN)) (O(MEETING)))
     ; Gabor is in the meeting.
(M21 (A(JOHN)) (R(IN)) (O(MEETING)))
     ; John is in the meeting.
(M22 (A(STU)) (R(IN)) (O(MEETING)))
     ; Stu is in the meeting.
(DUMPED)
1427 MSECS
```

7.3 Example 3

We assert that between two and four dog ownership relations involve spoiling, and assert four such spoiling relations. SNePS deduces that Jim does not spoil Lassie.

```
**;Of 5 dog ownership relations,
* ;between 2 and 4 involve spoiling.
*;5∃2^4 x,y [Member(x,person),Member(y,dog),
*;        Owns(x,y) : Spoils(x,y)]
*(BUILD ETOT 5 EMIN 2 EMAX 4 PEVB($X $Y)
* &ANT ((BUILD MEM *X CLASS PERSON)
*       (BUILD MEM *Y CLASS DOG)
*       (BUILD A *X R OWNS O *Y))
*   CQ (BUILD A *X R SPOILS O *Y))
(M5)
81 MSECS
**;John is a person.
*(BUILD MEM JOHN CLASS PERSON)
(M6)
10 MSECS
**;Jane is a person.
*(BUILD MEM JANE CLASS PERSON)
(M7)
10 MSECS
**;Mary is a person.
*(BUILD MEM MARY CLASS PERSON)
(M8)
9 MSECS
**;Jim is a person.
*(BUILD MEM JIM CLASS PERSON)
(M9)
9 MSECS
**;Rover is a dog.
*(BUILD MEM ROVER CLASS DOG)
(M10)
9 MSECS
**;Spot is a dog.
*(BUILD MEM SPOT CLASS DOG)
(M11)
12 MSECS
**;Lassie is a dog.
*(BUILD MEM LASSIE CLASS DOG)
(M12)
10 MSECS
**;John owns Rover.
*(BUILD A JOHN R OWNS O ROVER)
(M13)
11 MSECS
**;John owns Spot.
*(BUILD A JOHN R OWNS O SPOT)
(M14)
11 MSECS
**;Mary owns Lassie.
*(BUILD A MARY R OWNS O LASSIE)
(M15)
13 MSECS
**;Jane owns Spot.
*(BUILD A JANE R OWNS O SPOT)
(M16)
11 MSECS
**;Jim owns Lassie.
*(BUILD A JIM R OWNS O LASSIE)
(M17)
12 MSECS
**;John spoils Rover.
*(BUILD A JOHN R SPOILS O ROVER)
(M18)
10 MSECS
**;John spoils Spot.
*(BUILD A JOHN R SPOILS O SPOT)
(M19)
12 MSECS
**;Jane spoils Spot.
*(BUILD A JANE R SPOILS O SPOT)
(M20)
12 MSECS
**;Mary spoils Lassie.
*(BUILD A MARY R SPOILS O LASSIE)
(M21)
11 MSECS
**;Who spoils whom?
*(DESCRIBE (DEDUCE A %X R SPOILS O %Y))
(M18 (A(JOHN)) (R(SPOILS)) (O(ROVER)))
     ;John spoils Rover.
(M19 (A(JOHN)) (R(SPOILS)) (O(SPOT)))
     ;John spoils Spot.
(M20 (A(JANE)) (R(SPOILS)) (O(SPOT)))
     ;Jane spoils Spot.
(M21 (A(MARY)) (R(SPOILS)) (O(LASSIE)))
     ;Mary spoils Lassie.
(M23 (MIN(0)) (MAX(0)) (ARG(M22)))
(M22 (A(JIM)) (R(SPOILS)) (O(LASSIE)))
     ;Jim does not spoil Lassie.
(DUMPED)
1341 MSECS
```

8. SUMMARY

We have discussed the roles of existential and numerical quantifiers in reasoning programs. The roles are different and both are important. The existential quantifier is most useful for supplying referents for designating phrases with no previously explicitly mentioned referent. Numerically quantified rules are concise representations of rules that govern reasoning by the process of elimination and can introduce explicit negatives into a data base or can use negative statements for deriving positive statements. The most general schema for numerical quantifiers that we have discussed is ${}_{n}\exists_{i}^{j}\bar{x}(P_1(\bar{x}),\ldots,P_k(\bar{x}):Q(\bar{x}))$, which says that at least i and at most j of the n sequences of individuals that satisfy $P_1(\bar{x})\&\ldots\&P_k(\bar{x})$ also satisfy $Q(\bar{x})$. We showed how rules of this form can be represented in SNePS, the Semantic Network Processing System, and gave examples of SNePS runs that used such rules for carrying out inferences.

Two aspects of numerical quantifiers might limit their immediate usefulness. One is the n parameter, required whenever the minimal parameter is present. In formulating numerically quantified statements, we have found specifying n to be bothersome. The parameter could be eliminated if the inference system had another means of determining how many individuals satisfy the restriction, for example if the closed world assumption held. The other problem is that inherent in any counting argument is the assumption that any two individuals are, in fact, distinct. If this assumption does not hold, the use of numerical quantifiers depends on a solution to the identity problem mentioned in Sec. 3. Except for these two problems, numerical quantifiers seem to be useful additions to the tool kit of representation and inference.

ACKNOWLEDGEMENTS

The author is grateful to Don McKay for help in SNePS development and to him and Rich Fritzson for SNePS and Lisp system support. He is also grateful to Brian Funt and Don McKay for comments on an earlier draft.

REFERENCES

[1] Fitch, F.B. Symbolic Logic:An Introduction. Ronald Press Co., New York, 1952.

[2] Kleene, S.C. Introduction to Metamathematics. D. Van Nostrand, Princeton, New Jersey, 1950.

[3] Lemmon, E.J. Beginning Logic. Hackett, Indianapolis, 1978.

[4] Prawitz, D. Natural Deduction - A Proof-Theoretical Study. Almqvist and Wiksell, Stockholm, 1965.

[5] Reiter, R. On closed world data bases. In H. Gallaire and J. Minker, eds. Logic and Data Bases, Plenum Press, New York, 1978.

[6] Shapiro, S.C. Representing and locating deduction rules in a semantic network. Proc. Workshop on Pattern-Directed Inference Systems. SIGART Newsletter, 63 (June, 1977), 14-18.

[7] Shapiro, S.C. Path-based and node-based inference in semantic networks. In D. Waltz, ed. TINLAP-2: Theoretical Issues in Natural Language Processing-2. ACM, New York, 1978, 219-225.

[8] Shapiro, S.C. The SNePS semantic network processing system. In N. Findler, ed. Associative Networks - The Representation and Use of Knowledge by Computers, Academic Press, New York, 1979, 179-203.

[9] Shapiro, S.C. and McKay, D.P. The representation and use of deduction rules in a semantic network. Department of Computer Science, SUNY/Buffalo, Amherst, New York, forthcoming.

[10] Tarski, A. Introduction to Logic and to the Methodology of Deductive Sciences. Oxford University Press, New York, 1965.

[11] Weyhrauch, R.W. A users manual for FOL, Memo AIM-235.1, Stanford Artificial Intelligence Laboratory, Stanford, California, 1977.

A SCRABBLE CROSSWORD GAME PLAYING PROGRAM

Stuart C. Shapiro
Department of Computer Science
State University of New York at Buffalo
Amherst, New York 14226

A program that plays the SCRABBLE Crossword Game has been designed and implemented in SIMULA 67 on a DECSystem-10 and in Pascal on a CYBER 173. The heart of the design is the data structure for the lexicon and the algorithm for searching it. The lexicon is represented as a letter table, or trie using a canonical ordering of the letters in the words rather than the original spelling. The algorithm takes the trie and a collection of letters, including blanks, and finds all words that can be formed from any combination and permutation of the letters. Words are found in approximately the order of their value in the game.

1. INTRODUCTION

The SCRABBLE Crossword Game is a well known game considered to require a fair amount of intelligence, strategic and tactical skill, facility with words, and luck. Unlike most games in the artificial intelligence literature, it can be played by two or more players and is neither a zero sum game nor a game of perfect information. For these reasons, minimax searching procedures do not seem applicable. When humans play the game, a large easily accessible vocabulary seems to be the most important determiner of victory. One might, therefore, think that it would be easy to write a program that plays the SCRABBLE Crossword Game at the championship level. We are examining this question by concentrating our efforts on the design of the lexicon and the algorithm for searching it and paying much less attention to the strategies and tactics of actual play.

Our lexicon differs from those usually used in natural language processing programs because of the use to which it is to be put. Usually one is confronted with a possible word. One must determine if it is a word, and, if so, segment it into affixes and stem, and retrieve lexical information associated with the stem. The problem for the SCRABBLE Crossword Game lexicon is, given a set of letters, find all the words that can be made from any combination and permutation of them. This is a very different problem.

We have designed a program that plays the SCRABBLE Crossword Game and implemented two versions. At Indiana University, Howard Smith implemented a program in SIMULA 67 [2, 3] on a DECSystem-10. At SUNY/Buffalo, Michael Morris and Karl Schimpf implemented a version in Pascal [6] on a CDC CYBER 173 that manages a game between any number of players, and each wrote a program player.

In the sections that follow, we will briefly describe the game manager, basing the description on the Pascal version, which is more general than the SIMULA version. We will then describe the lexicon data structure and search algorithm in more detail. Finally, we will briefly describe the three program players that have been written.

2. THE GAME MANAGER

Figure 1 shows the overall organization of the system, assuming one human player and one program player. In reality, there may be any number of human players and any number of program players as long as there are at least two players.

The game manager module handles all interaction with human players and either deals tiles or accepts tiles picked by human assistants. After

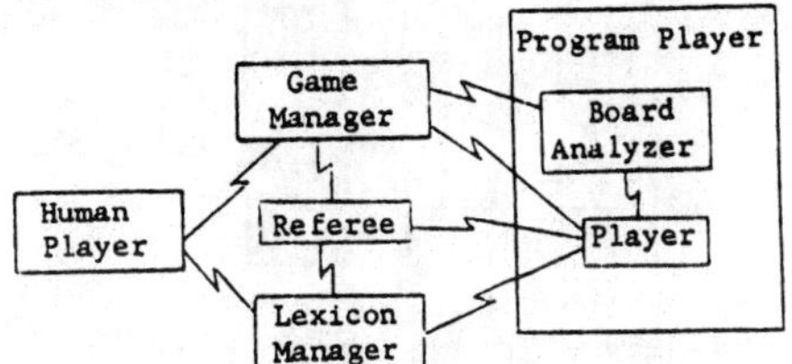

Figure 1: Overall system organization

each move, it reports the move to the board analyzer modules of all program players in the game, so they may "start to think about their next plays" while the humans are playing.

2.1 The Referee

The referee checks proposed plays for legality

and computes the score of legal plays. If a human proposes a word not in the lexicon, the referee asks if it is really a word. If the human says it is, it is added to the lexicon. Otherwise the play is considered illegal.

Program players may use the referee to find legal plays and to choose the best among several legal plays.

2.2 The Human Opponent

A human player interacts with the game manager in a notation close to the official notation of the SCRABBLE Crossword Game Players, Inc. [1]. The word is typed with each letter already on the board preceeded by a "$". When a blank tile is played, a "@" is typed followed by the letter it is being used as. The location of the word is indicated either by a row and the beginning and ending columns (e.g. 8K-N), or by a column and the beginning and ending rows (e.g. C2-7).

2.3 The Lexicon Manager

The lexicon manager is used by the referee to check whether words and crosswords are contained in the lexicon, and to add words which a human player claimed are words, but were not already in the lexicon. The program players use the lexicon manager to find words to play. A human player may use the lexicon manager to interact with the lexicon without ending the game.

3. THE LEXICON

3.1 The Data Structure

The lexicon was designed for the particular problem, "given a collection of letters, find all words that can be formed from any combination and permutation of the letters, and find these words in approximately the order of their value in the SCRABBLE Crossword Game". Two key ideas were combined in the design of the data structure - letter tables [4, 5, 8], or tries [7], and canonical ordering.

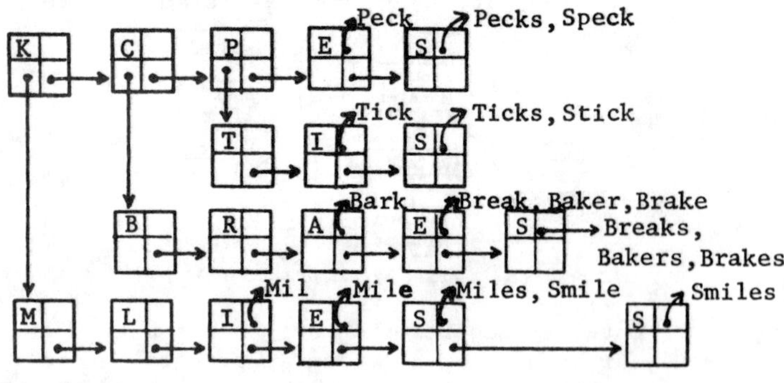

Figure 2: An example lexicon trie

Key:

letter	words
fail	success

Each node in the lexicon trie contains a letter, a list of words, a success pointer and a fail pointer. If $\underline{L}$ is the sequence of letters contained in all nodes on the success path from the root to some node, $\underline{n}$, excluding the letter in $\underline{n}$, and $\underline{\ell}$ is the letter in $\underline{n}$, then the list of words in $\underline{n}$ is all words that are permutations of the letters in $\underline{L}$ plus $\underline{\ell}$, the success pointer points to a subtrie containing words formed from $\underline{L}$, $\underline{\ell}$, plus other letters, and the fail pointer points to a subtrie containing words formed from $\underline{L}$, other letters, but not $\underline{\ell}$. The order of letters on both success and fail paths is the canonical order discussed below. Figure 2 shows a small lexicon trie.

3.2 The Search Algorithm

Briefly, the algorithm for searching the lexicon is to take a set of tiles, order them according to the canonical ordering, search the fail path of the root until the letter of the first tile matches the letter in a node, then search the success subtrie with the remaining tiles of the set. Then, to get words formed from subsets of the original set, ignore the letter that matched the node and also search the fail subtrie. So, if the lexicon of Figure 2 is searched with the letters KCPTIE, "peck" will be found, and then, ignoring "p", "tick" will be found.

So that words can be found in approximately the order of their values in the SCRABBLE Crossword Game, the major sort used in the canonical ordering is the value of the letters in that game. Since when a letter of a lexicon node is in the search set both its success and fail subtries are searched, but if it is not only its fail subtrie is searched, the secondary order is frequency of the letter in the game set, least frequent first. The tertiary sort is frequency in English, most frequent first, to help minimize the size of the lexicon trie. Contrary to this ordering, "S" was placed last, because of the large number of words that can have "S" added and remain words. For example, Figure 2 has 21 nodes, but if "S" were placed before "L", where it belongs, the same lexicon would have 32 nodes. The final ordering used was "QZXJKHFYWVCMPBGDLUTNRIOAES".

Four details were ignored in the above brief description of the search algorithm. First, longer words, like "smiles" are more valuable than shorter words using the same letters, like "mil", so words on the same success branch are collected in the order of leaf toward root, rather than root toward leaf. Second, the search set of tiles may contain blanks, which can match any letter. Blanks are initially placed first in the search set so they can match nodes high in the lexicon trie, and later shuffled down in the search set to match lower nodes. Third, the search set can contain letters that are required to be in found words, so are never ignored by the search algorithm. Fourth, the search terminates after each word is found in case that word is acceptable to the player and no further search is required. If this is not the case, the search can be resumed from where it left off. The SIMULA 67 version uses the detach facility for this purpose. Space precludes presenting the complete algorithm here. It can be found as procedure findwords2 in [9].

3.3 Use of Secondary Storage

We have used two different schemes for maintaining the lexicon on disk. The SIMULA 67 version uses a sequential file of characters and digits. The letter of each node is followed by the list of words, if any, and then by one of the digits 0-3 indicating which kinds of subtries the node has. If both are present, the success subtrie preceeds the fail subtrie. This organization allows the lexicon to be searched while the file is read in the forward direction only. However, a node's entire success subtrie must be read to find its fail subtrie. The SIMULA version, with a lexicon of about 1500 words, averaged about 42 CPU seconds per pair of moves (program and human).

The Pascal version uses a segmented file of records, where each record is a lexicon node containing at most one word. If necessary, successive records with dummy letters contain additional words. Except for this, the root of the success subtrie of a node immediately follows the node. A node with no success subtrie is followed by an end-of-segment mark. The root of the fail subtrie of a node is the first node of some segment later in the file, so that to find a node's fail subtrie, the entire success subtrie needn't be read, just the first node of each intervening segment. Currently, this lexicon contains 2126 words, in 4262 node records and 1666 segments. The Pascal program averages about 29 CPU seconds per pair of program vs. program moves when run in batch, but has been too slow to run interactively due to system overhead.

4. PROGRAM PLAYERS

Three program players have been written, SIMSCRB, written by Howard Smith in SIMULA 67, and two Pascal programs -- Gerry, by Michael Morris, and Joanne, by Karl Schimpf. SIMSCRB only plays across existing words, never extending a word or playing parallel to a word. Joanne also considers parallel plays, but not extending words. Gerry considers all types of plays. Each board analyzer maintains a list of playable positions ordered by expected value of a play there. The programs consider the best p positions and the first w words found in the lexicon for each position. The chosen play is the first that is worth at least m points, or the best of the pw plays, or, if these are all illegal, they exchange their racks. Joanne first tries playing parallel to existing words, considering upto w2 words formed entirely from the rack.

Table 1 shows the results of interactive games of SIMSCRB against humans DRF and SJ, and batch games of Gerry against itself and Joanne against itself. The programs play approximately at human

TABLE 1

Summary of Four Games

Player	Number of Moves	Number of words played	Score Before Reduction	Avg. Score per word played	Final Score
DPF	26	25	347	13.88	339
SIMSCRB	25	16	210	13.13	208
SJ	20	18	216	12	212
SIMSCRB	19	15	211	14.07	198
Gerry 1	12	6	71	11.83	61
Gerry 2	11	6	76	12.67	63
Joanne 1	30	13	135	10.38	119
Joanne 2	30	20	208	10.4	204

level. The major difference is the number of times the programs exchange tiles. This is partly due to small vocabularies, and partly to wasting many of the limited pw tries on positions for which legal moves could not be found.

ACKNOWLEDGEMENTS

Ben Shneiderman, Margaret Ambrose and Barbara Rasche cooperated on an early version of the program. Howard R. Smith implemented the SIMULA 67 version, and was partially responsible for the lexicon search algorithm. Michael Morris Jr. and Karl Schimpf implemented the Pascal version.

REFERENCES

[1]. Conklin, D.K.(Ed.) The Official SCRABBLE Players Handbook. Harmony Books Division, Crown Publishers, Inc., NY, 1976.

[2]. Dahl, O.-J., Myhrhang, B.; Hygaard, K. The Simula 67 Common Base Language. Norwegian Computing Centre, Forskningsveien 1B, Oslo 3, 1968.

[3]. Dahl, O.-J., and Nygaard, K. Simula-an Algol-based simulation language. Comm. ACM 9, (Sept., 1966), 671-678.

[4]. De La Briandais, R. File searching using variable length keys. Proc. WJCC, AFIPS Press, Montvale, NJ, 1959, 295-298.

[5]. Hays, D.G. Introduction to Computational Linguistics. American Elsevier, NY, 1967, 92-94.

[6]. Jensen, K. and Wirth, N. PASCAL User Manual and Report. Springer-Verlag, NY, 1976.

[7]. Knuth, D.E. The Art of Computer Programming Vol. 3/Sorting and Searching. Addison-Wesley, Reading, MA, 1973, 481-487.

[8]. Lamb, S.M and Jacobsen, W.H., Jr., A high-speed large-capacity dictionary system. Mechanical Translation, 6 (Nov., 1961), 76-107.

[9]. Shapiro, S.C. and Smith, H.R., A SCRABBLE Crossword Game Playing Program. Tech Rpt. No. 119, Dept. of Computer Science, SUNY/Buffalo, NY, 1977.

SPEECH TRAINING SYSTEMS USING LATERAL SHAPES OF VOCAL TRACT AND F1-F2 DIAGRAM FOR HEARING-IMPAIRED CHILDREN

Minoru Shigenaga
Department of Computer Science
Faculty of Engineering
Yamanashi University
Takeda-4, Kofu 400
Japan

Yoshihiro Sekiguchi
Department of Computer Science
Faculty of Engineering
Yamanashi University
Takeda-4, Kofu 400
Japan

Three speech training systems for hearing-impaired children were designed and constructed using a minicomputer and a microprocessor. The first system displays the lateral shape of the vocal tract for each vowel estimated from the speech sound. In this system, three storages are prepared. One of them can be used to store a reference shape which may be estimated from a teacher's voice or a prepared standard shape. A child can articulate seeing the reference shape and re-articulate comparing his own first articulation with the reference shape. The system can also compare the estimated shape with the reference one and produce instructions with animated cartoons which show where any articulatory defects exist. The second system displays successively the lateral shapes for articulation of any phoneme sequences containing consonants. The third system displays the first two formant frequencies extracted from speech as a spot on the F1-F2 plane, where the regions of vowels are shown in color. Preliminary use of these devices has shown that they complement each other to form a more effective system of speech training.

1. INTRODUCTION

If hearing-impaired children can see their articulation and compare it with a reference articulation in order to bring their articulation closer to the reference, or if they can see the formant frequency locus for their utterance on a F1-F2 plane, where the regions of the vowels are shown, they might be able to understand how they articulated or how they should articulate. In addition, teachers might be more able to teach them how to articulate or know where their articulatory defects exist. Therefore, we have constructed three speech training systems using a minicomputer and a microprocessor. For vowel articulation the first system estimates a lateral shape of the vocal tract from the speech sound and displays it on a storage CR-tube. And it can compare the estimated shape with the reference one and produce instructions with animated cartoons which show where any articulatory defects exist. For consonant articulation we cannot yet estimate a vocal tract shape from the speech sound, but our second system can display successively the lateral shapes of the vocal tract for the articulation of any phoneme sequence containing consonants. Our third system displays the first two formant frequencies extracted from a speech sound as a spot on the F1-F2 plane, where the regions of the vowels are also shown in color. It can also display pitch frequencies.

2. SYSTEM 1

This system estimates shapes of the vocal tract for vowels by evaluating PARCOR coefficients and instructs where any articulatory defects exist and also indicates how a child should correct his articulation. Fig. 1 shows the main flow of our procedures. The operation of this system is simple, and one has only to type a number or YES/NO in reply to the system inquiry " = " or " ? " shown in the state ▭ of this diagram. Then the system proceeds to the next state executing the action described along the line, types the characters shown in the new state and waits for the next reply. Referring to the marks in the diagram we will explain what this system can do chiefly.

(a) In order to avoid disturbance from the room noise, you can specify a threshold value in reply to the inquiry "Cut level=" at which the system begins to store the input speech wave for 3.2 sec.

(b) The system displays the reduced input speech wave on a storage CR-tube as shown in Fig. 2 by typing "N" at the state (ii) [Again?]. Therefore you can examine the speech wave envelope and select the places where you want to obtain the vocal tract shape.

(c) At the state (iii) you can enlarge the wave form at any specified place and find its pitch period as shown in Fig. 3.

Fig. 2 Display of the uttered speech wave.

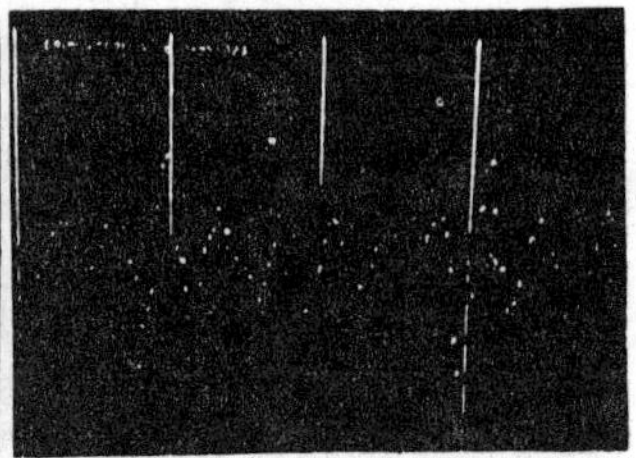

Fig. 3 An enlarged speech wave.

(d) Two storages labelled "1,2" for storing the estimated shapes are prepared and you can respond with one of them to the inquiry "Pattern=" at (v). While, in the third storage labelled "0" you should store the shape which you want to use as a reference.

(e) For the inquiry "Display shape=" at (vi) you can specify any storage containing the shape. Then the specified shape is displayed.

(f) At the state (viii) [Reference = 0,..?], if you input "0" then the estimated shape is compared with the content in the storage "0", and if you input "1" or "2" then the estimated shape is compared with the standard reference shape which was specified at the state (vii) [Present vowel=]. Comparison between the estimated shape and the reference one is done for the two features: the place of articulation and the lip-opening. If the difference between the places of articulation of both shapes is over a certain threshold value, an instruction such as "Draw back your tongue" is shown and the estimated lateral shape moves gradually toward the reference shape as shown in Fig. 4. And if the difference between lip-openings of both shapes is large, an instruction such as "Open your lips" is written and the lips represented by an ellipse move gradually toward the reference opening (Fig.4). If the difference is a little, the instruction "OK" is written as shown in Fig. 5. The reference shape stored in the storage "0" can be the prepared standard shape or the estimated shape which has been estimated from the teacher's voice through the above-described routine.

(g) Going along the route 3 by inputting "3" at the state (i) [Link order=], we can estimate and display successively the vocal tract shapes of the vowels at the pre-specified places.

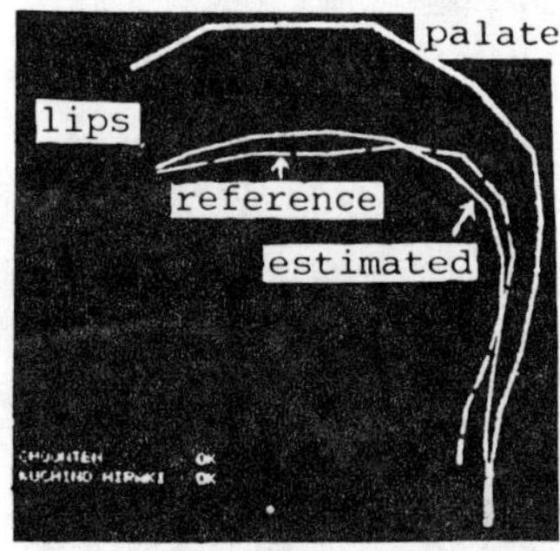

Fig. 5 An example of practice. One can articulate seeing the reference shape shown by broken line. In this case both instructions for articulation of /a/ are "OK".

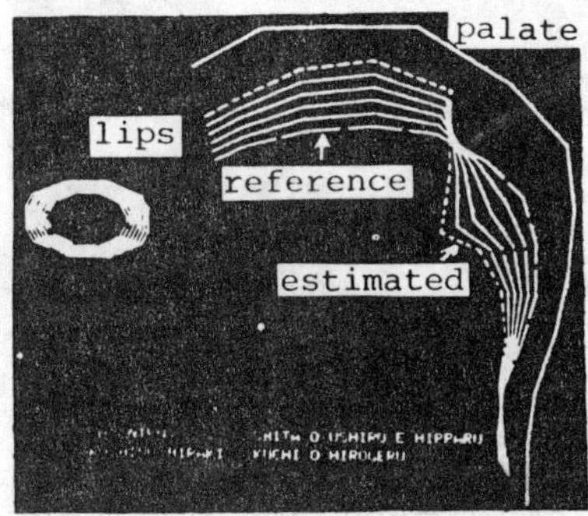

Fig. 4 An example of instructions for articulation. In this case /i/ was uttered and the estimated shape shown by dotted line was moved toward the prepared reference shape /a/ shown by broken line. The lip-opening was also moved. The instructions mean that place of articulation: Draw back your tongue, lip-opening: Open your lips.

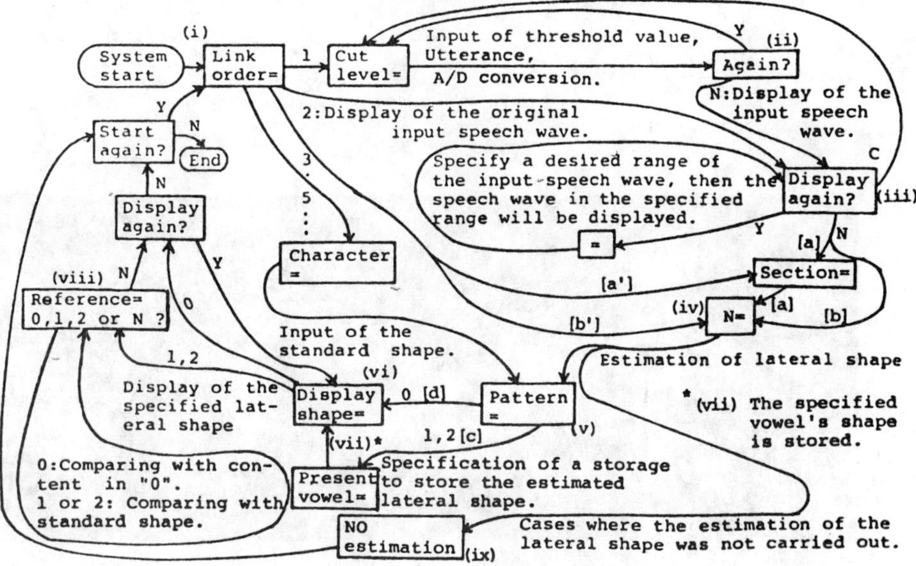

Fig. 1 Flow diagram of the speech training system which estimates the lateral shape of the vocal tract from the speech wave and instructs how one should articulate.

For practice, at first you should display a standard shape prepared previously or a shape estimated from your own utterance. Then a child can articulate seeing the reference shape, and re-articulate comparing his own articulation with the reference shape (Fig. 5). The practice shapes of the child should be stored in either storage "1" or "2", then he can successively compare his articulation with the previous articulation or the reference shape, if he wants, looking at instructions.

3. SYSTEM 2

We have prepared a system which displays synthetic articulatory movements for monosyllable utterances or words containing consonants, because it is very difficult to estimate a vocal tract shape from a speech wave for any of the consonants. The lateral shape of the vocal tract for Japanese phoneme sequences are produced by our speech synthesizer using an articulatory model [1]. The synthesized lateral shapes are stored on a drum storage and displayed with arbitrary speed. A child can easily look at the articulatory movements containing stop or fricative consonants. Fig. 6 shows the synthesized shapes in the sequence /ika/.

4. SYSTEM 3

This system displays the first two formant frequencies extracted from speech as a spot on the F1-F2 plane, where the regions of the vowels are shown in color as shown in Fig. 7. It can also display pitch frequencies. This system uses a microprocessor and a color TV set.

This system is useful by itself, and also helpful in order to know the quantative vowel quality.

5. DISCUSSION AND CONCLUSION

Our estimated shapes of the vocal tract are not accurate, but we can approximate the place of articulation for vowels and point out the defect of articulation and, of course, the systems function properly for hearing-impaired children. But an infant is unable to understand instructions such as "Draw back your tongue body", so these systems should be used to offer information to a teacher.

We also hope that these systems are used by older persons for self-teaching.

Though we have not yet evaluated the effectiveness of these systems, preliminary use of these devices has shown that they complement each other to form a more effective system of speech training. Especially it is instructive to use the systems 1 and 3 simultaneously, because we can get articulatory information in both articulatory and frequency domains.

Authors would like to express their gratitude to O. Tanaka, T. Nishide, Y. Furuya and other students in our laboratory for their help.

REFERENCE

[1] Shigenaga, M. and Ariizumi, H. "Articulatory Movements by Rule" in Modeles Articulatoires et Phonetique edited by Carre, R. et al. (G.A.L.F. Groupe de la Communication Parlée), 1977, pp. 193-202.

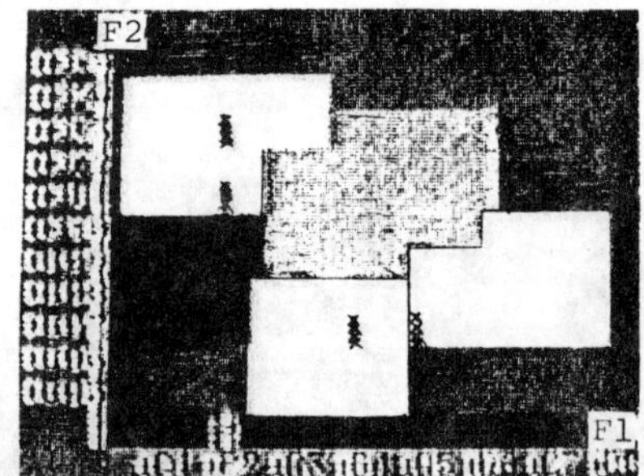

Fig. 7 An output in the system 3 for /aoi/.

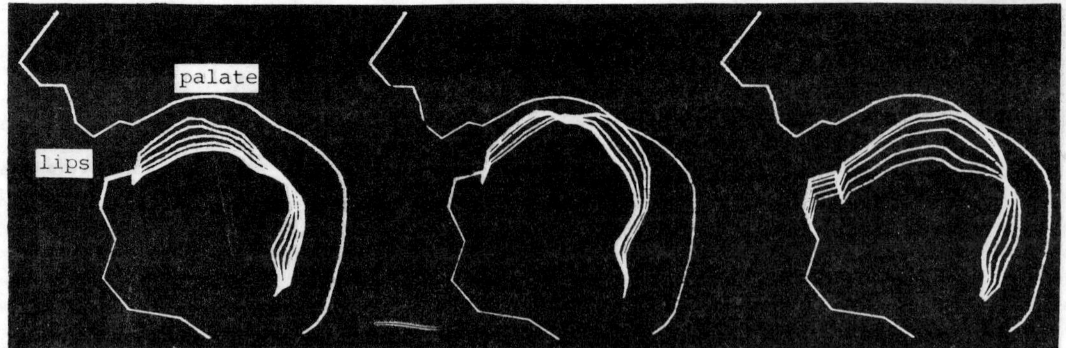

(a) from uniform tube to /i/ (b) from /i/ to /k/ (c) from /k/ to /a/

Fig. 6 Synthesized lateral shapes of the vocal tract for /ika/. In our synthesizer the shape of the vocal tract begins to move from a uniform tube, therefore in (a) it starts from the shape parallel to the upper wall and moves toward the reference shape of /i/.

EXPERIMENTAL JAPANESE LANGUAGE QUESTION ANSWERING SYSTEM MSSS78
- Use of Case Patterns with Procedures -

Akira SHIMAZU and Hitoshi IIDA

Musashino Electrical Communication Laboratory
Nippon Telegraph and Telephone Public Corporation
Musashino-shi, Tokyo, 180, Japan

MSSS78 is an experimental computer system made in a series of research efforts to construct a natural language man-machine interface. The system accepts sentences about arithmetic or geography, and then responds to the queries on the basis of its own knowledge and dialogue context.
The system analyzes sentences, using Case Patterns, in which procedures are embedded. Case Patterns are linguistic knowledge associated with main words. The system uses Case Patterns for syntactic and semantic analysis. Additionally, Parsing is controlled by the utilization of a pushdown stack and a list.
The system generates somewhat intelligent responses, considering results of the database reference or lack of input information.

1 INTRODUCTION

Various natural language understanding systems or sentence analysis programs, including those for Japanese language, uses case frames[1] [2]. The method using case frames seems to benefit problems such as modularity and extendability to many components, which construct an intelligent understanding system.

Mainly from such the case frame viewpoints, an experimental Japanese language question answering system, MSSS78, was made in a series of research efforts intended to construct a natural language man-machine interface. The system uses Case Patterns, which are linguistic knowledge associated with main words. Case Patterns can be regarded as a new style of case frames. There are three features concerning the parsing mechanism.

(1) Case Patterns are used for both syntactic and semantic analysis.
(2) Procedures are usually embedded in Case Patterns to accomplish fine analysis and construct semantic structure.
(3) A list, called RLIST, is introduced to effectively control parsing as to reanalysis.

As another feature, the system generates somewhat intelligent responses, considering results of the database reference, or lack of input information. A deduction program based on a PLANNER-like pattern matching method uses three logical values, true, false and unknown to make sensible responses.

MSSS78 accepts sentences about arithmetic or geography, and responds to the sentences from its own knowledge and context of dialogue (Fig.1). Input sentences are typed in KATAKANA, a square form of KANA (the Japanese vowel and consonant combination syllable symbols), or ROMAJI (a method of writing Japanese language using the Western alphabet). The system responds by output sentences spelled in KATAKANA. Additionally, the system displays KANJI-KANA-MAJIRI-BUN (Japanese ordinary style of writing, spelled in KANJI (Chinese ideographs) and KANA) for both input and output sentences.

2 SENTENCE ANALYSIS OUTLINE

The MSSS78 analyzes a sentence by Case Patterns, carrying out syntactic and semantic analysis, and then solve a problem, which the system has to deal with.

The analysis process, roughly speaking, consists of two phases. First, the system analyzes all the possible sentence structures. Second, the system performs processing, such as composition and execution of a command to search database, composition of equations, etc. In the first analysis, the system fills case slots with return values of procedures embedded in Case Patterns. In the second analysis, another procedure, embedded in the Case Patterns, interprets the filled case slots for the system purpose from its own knowledge and dialogue context.

3 BUNSETSU ANALYSIS (MORPHOLOGICAL ANALYSIS)

A Japanese sentence can be divided into a sequence of BUNSETSUs, a kind of syntactic unit. A BUNSETSU consists of two parts, a main part and an auxiliary part. The main part is a MEISHI (Japanese noun), a root of a DOUSHI (verb) or KEIYOUSHI (adjective), a FUKUSHI (adverb), or a RENTAISHI etc. The auxiliary part is a JOSHI (postpositioned word), KATSUYOU-GOBI (inflectional ending of a verb or an adjective), or JODOUSHI (auxiliary verb). They convey miscellaneous information, such as case information, tense information, or modal information. In addition, they show how a focused BUNSETSU modifies a succeeding BUNSETSU.

ｶﾞﾎﾞﾝﾊ ﾄﾞｺﾆ ｱﾘﾏｽｶ. is a sentence written in KATAKANA, which means "where is Gabon", where ｶﾞﾎﾞﾝﾊ, ﾄﾞｺﾆ and ｱﾘﾏｽｶ。 are BUNSETSUs. Each BUNSETSU is internally transformed to a BUNSETSU spelled in ROMAJI, GABONWA, DOKONI and ARIMASUKA. BUNSETSU analyzer separates a BUNSETSU into main and auxiliary parts, that is, GABON-WA, DOKO-NI and AR-I-MAS-U-KA-. where GABON, DOKO, and AR are main parts, and WA, NI, and I-MAS-U-KA-. are auxiliary parts. In detail, GABON (noun) is a place name, DOKO (pronoun) means "where". AR is a root of a verb ARU which means "be" or "lie". WA and NI, usually connected to a noun, are JOSHI. I-MAS-U-KA-. is a composition of I (KATSUYOU-GOBI of ARU), MAS (root of an auxiliary verb MASU which indicates politeness), U (KATSUYOU-GOBI of MASU), KA (JOSHI which represents a question) and . (period). We can expresses such relations between main parts and auxiliary parts, or between auxiliary parts, by a transition network dictionary.

In Japanese written language, it is not a recognized custom to leave a space between BUNSETSUs. In MSSS78, Input sentences can be typed while not leaving a space between BUNSETSUs. The network dictionary has special symbols, which designate an ending of a BUNSETSU element. BUNSETSU analyzer can identify a BUNSETSU by the special symbols.

4 CASE PATTERNS WITH PROCEDURES

Case frames of many case systems can be viewed more or less as frame-like linguistic knowledge. Case Patterns in this paper can be regarded basically as a new member of case frames. Case Patterns accomplish various kinds of processing, including syntactic and semantic analysis. Especially, elaborate analysis is

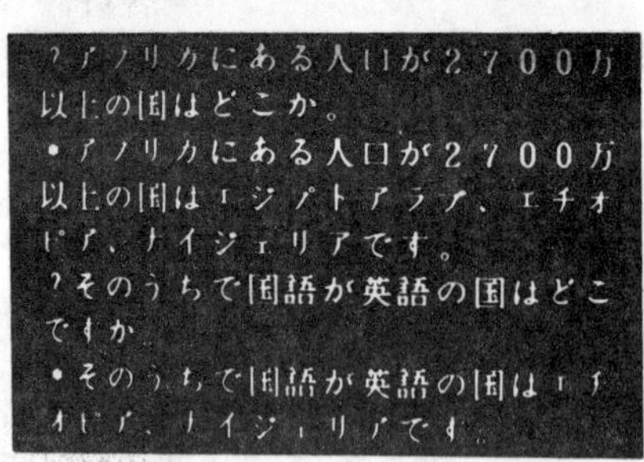

#Quadruple X plus thrice Y is 20. What is X?

The number of equations is insufficient.

#6Y minus 7X equals 8.

X is 32 over 15.

#What are African countries whose population is 27 million or more?

African countries whose population is 27 million or more are Egypt, Ethiopia, Nigeria.

#What are the countries among them whose language is English?

The countries among them whose language is English are Ethiopia, Nigeria.

Fig.1 An actual dialogue with MSSS78. Left is the displays of the KANJI-KANA-MAJIRI-BUN for input and output sentences. Right is the translated English, where # is a prompt for input sentences.

possible by procedures embedded in Case Patterns. Case patterns are given in advance to main words, such as noun, verb and adjective. Case Patterns are constructed as follows.

```
Case-Patterns = (Case-Pattern
                 ...
                 Case-Pattern )
Case-Pattern = (slots  [procedure-1])
slots = (slot  ...  slot)
slot = (slot-name
        syntactic-conditions
        semantic-conditions
        procedure-2
        [procedure-3] )
```

The parser locates dependent BUNSETSUs or phrases by matching BUNSETSU sequence with slots. The evaluation of slot constituents; syntactic conditions, semantic conditions and procedures, carries out the matching. Each slot may be regarded as a surface case.

The following is an explanation of Case Pattern constituents.

(1) Slot name provides a tag, by which the slot is associated in the succeeding analysis.

(2) Syntactic conditions provide conditions as to whether or not a BUNSETSU modifies a focused BUNSETSU. The focused BUNSETSU invokes the Case Patterns used. The modifier BUNSETSU is the right most BUNSETSU of a phrase, and the right most BUNSETSU represents the phrase. Syntactic conditions are generally JOSHI, or BUNSETSUs connection information in case a main part of BUNSETSUs is a verb or an adjective. Conjugation form of a verb or an adjective, or auxiliary parts of the BUNSETSU determins connection information. A special tag in syntactic conditions shows an obligatory or optional category for a slot.

(3) Semantic conditions provide semantic or conceptual conditions which a main part of a modifier BUNSETSU has to satisfy. These conditions make more detailed analysis, and exclude syntactically correct but semantically meaningless sentences. BUNSETSU main parts normally show semantic information to be examined. Semantic information is given in advance by the dictionary. In some cases, procedure-2 changes the information later on.

(4) Procedure-2 carries out miscellaneous processing: the examination of other conditions, which the above syntactic conditions or semantic conditions cannot cover; the utilization of context information; or the extraction of semantic structure, etc. Syntactic conditions and semantic conditions provide conditions of a modifier BUNSETSU itself, rather than a phrase, although the BUNSETSU represents the phrase implicitly. Procedure-2 can examine the phrase structure explicitly, if necessary.

If a procedure-2(3) returns a non NIL value, the parser judges that the examined BUNSETSU (phrase) satisfies the slot, that is, the BUNSETSU modifies the focused BUNSETSU. In addition, if the value is non NIL value other than T, the value fills the slot. This slot is kept with the focused BUNSETSU, and is used by the succeeding analysis.

(5) Procedure-3 is a kind of procedure-2 for use when a connective form of a BUNSETSU to a focused BUNSETSU is RENTAI modification, a kind of a participial modification.

(6) Procedure-1 is invoked for a phrase (in MSSS78, a sentence) interpretation, when there aren't any more BUNSETSUs which modify the phrase. The procedure-1 interprets slots filled by evaluation of Case Patterns slots, and accomplishes processing, which the system has to deal with. The processing by procedure-1 may be considered as problem solving processes, or as a sort of deep structure analysis.

5 PARSING MECHANISM

5.1 Matching by PSTACK

The parser analyzes a sentence from left to right and from bottom to top, matching Case Patterns to a sequence of BUNSETSUs, or phrases put in a pushdown stack called PSTACK[3].

5.2 Reanalysis by RLIST

Parsing by case patterns doesn't necessarily succeed in a forward direction. In some cases, the parser must examine the rest part of a sentence to determine whether or not a BUNSETSU modifies a focused BUNSETSU. Augmented Transition Network grammar shows a similarity in the selection of several paths from a state[4]. In MSSS78, the parser uses a list, called RLIST, to reanalyze an input sentence.

If a sentence can be segmented into different BUNSETSU sequences, or some word has a homonym, the parser can reanalyze the sentence on the same framework.

6 ANALYSIS EXAMPLES BY CASE PATTERNS

(1) Syntactic conditions: In the following sentences,

820WO 79DE WARUTO IKURAKA.
(Divide 820 by 79, what do you get?)

WO and DE (auxiliary parts of BUNSETSUs) make a difference between a dividend and divisor. The next Case Pattern to WARU (divide) provides the syntactic conditions.

```
(((TSY1 (WO ZERO) (KAZU HENSUU) (F-S-SISOKU2))
  (TSY2 (DE RNT)
        (KAZU HENSUU)
        (COND
         ((AND
           (EQ GVN-SYNTYP 'DRENTAI)
           (CDDR TREE)
           (EQ (SYNTYPE (CAAAR (CDDR TREE)))
            'ZERO ))
          NIL )
         ((F-S-SISOKU2)) )
        (S-ASSOC 'ATAI (CDDR SS)) ))
 (SISOKU) )
```

(2) Semantic conditions: In the next two phrases, which have the same meaning,

KOKUGOGA HURANSUGONO KUNI
(the country whose language is French)
HURANSUGOGA KOKUGONO KUNI
(the country where French is its language)

the concepts expressed by the underlined phrases are both language, but one, HURANSUGO (French), which is a compound of HURANSU (France) and GO (language), is an instance of languages, and the other, KOKUGO (language), is a generic concept. Procedure-2 of a Case Pattern to GO or KOKUGO determines a modifier of the underlined phrase by the next inner representations of modifiers.

```
(GNN KOKUGO)              ;KOKUGO
(TSB KOKUGO (IDN 2))      ;HURANSUGO
```

(3) Context: The following dialogue in MSSS78 shows an example concerning context processing.

#YO-ROPPADE MOTTOMO ZINKOUNO OOI KUNIWA DOKO DESUKA.
(What is the most heavily populated country in Europe?)
YO-ROPPADE MOTTOMO ZINKOUNO OOI KUNIWA NISHIDOITSU DESU.
(The most heavily populated country in Europe is West Germany.)
#[SONO] ZINKOUWA DOREKURAI DESUKA.
(About how large is the population?)
ZINKOUWA 61830000 NIN DESU.
(It is 61830000.)

where # is a prompt symbol to accept input sentences, and words surrounded by [and] can be omitted. ZINKOUWA (the population) in the underlined sentences implicitly indicates the population of West Germany. If there is SONO (its) before ZINKOUWA, SONO explicitly indicates West Germany. Procedure-2 to SONO recognizes this indication from the context information in STM (short-term memory). The Japanese language contains no articles, but it seems that the function, which corresponds to the work done by an article, covers many different modes of expression. In this example, WA in ZINKOUWA functions as a definite article to indicate the context.

In the next sentence,

1WO 2NI TASHI 3WO KAKERUTO IKURA DESUKA.
(Add 1 to 2 and multiply the result by 3, then what do you get?)

the result of "1WO 2NI TASHI" (add 1 to 2) implicitly indicates the multiplicand of KAKERU (multiply). Procedure-2 to KAKERU references the result through a slot attached to the phrase.

(4) Compound nouns: The parser analyzes the phrase,

100 MAN NIN IZYOU
(one million persons or more)

as a compound of 100 (one hundred), MAN (ten thousand), NIN (person), and IZYOU (or more). In Japanese language, we normally consider IZYOU as a word like a suffix, but here the system treats IZYOU as a noun whose concept is a suffixal number. Procedure-2 to IZYOU changes the concept of the right most BUNSETSU, IZYOU, which represents the phrase, to a number. In the suceesing analysis, the BUNSETSU, IZYOU, is treated as a number.

(5) Reanalysis: In the next two sentences,

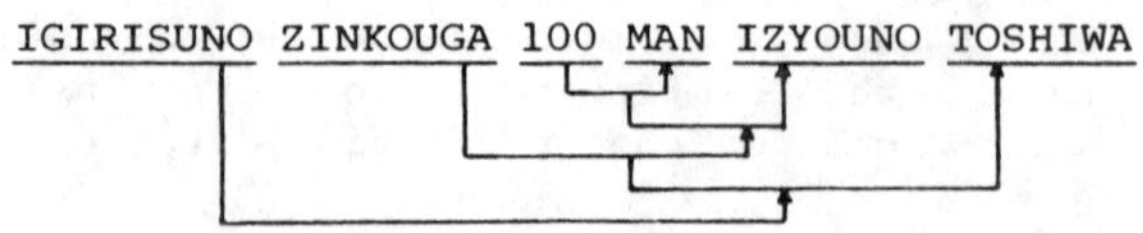

(British cities of a million or more population)

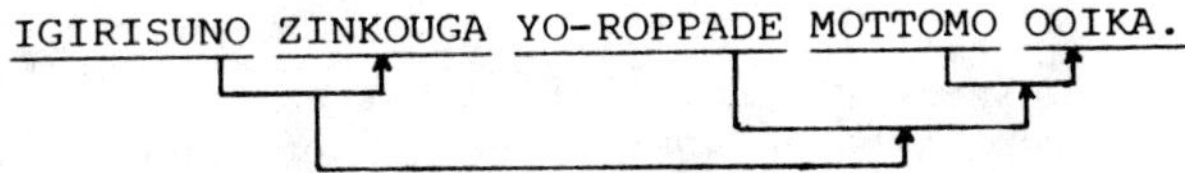

IGIRISUNO ZINKOUGA YO-ROPPADE MOTTOMO OOIKA.

(Is British population the largest in Europe?)

when the parser focuses on ZINKOUGA (population), there is a possibility that IGIRISUNO (British) either modifies ZINKOU, or not. Procedure-2 to ZINKOU reports the alternative possibilities to the parser by the flag setting. At this stage, the parser takes the relation, wherein IGIRISUNO modifies ZINKOU, as the first selection, and holds the information about the other relation, wherein IGIRISUNO does not modify ZINKOU, in RLIST with the environment information. Later on, the parser picks out the element from the RLIST, and reanalyzes the sentence from the state reset by the element.

(6) Ambiguity: Ambiguity is an interesting problem for an understanding system to deal with, from various viewpoints, such as syntax, semantics and pragmatics. In MSSS78, the system parses the underlined phrase in

1 TASU 2NO 3BAIWA IKURA DESUKA.

into two phrases,

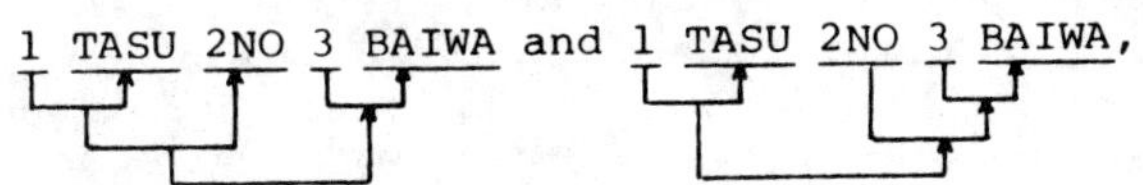

1 TASU 2NO 3 BAIWA and 1 TASU 2NO 3 BAIWA,

where each phrase has either meaning of (1 + 2) x 3, and 1 + 2 x 3. At present, the system responds to the sentence as an ambiguity sentence, and asks for reinput.

As an ambiguitiy dependent upon the knowledge of the problem domain, the system interprets the underlined phrase in

1 TASU 2 KAKERU 3WA IKURA DESUKA.

as either meaning (1 + 2) x 3, or 1 + 2 x 3, from arithmetic knowledge. Procedure-2 in a Case Pattern to a number detects this ambiguity at the stage of the underlined phrase analysis.

(7) A variety of expressions: The following are among those which can be analyzed by Case Patterns to words whose concept is an equality, a number or a variable.

4WA X KAKERU 2NI HITOSHII.
4TO XNO 2BAIWA HITOSHII.
(4 is equal to twice X.)

3X TASU 2YWA 1NI HITOSHII.
3XTO 2YNO WAWA 1NI HITOSHIIDESU.
(3X plus 2Y is equal to 1.)
1NI 2WO TASUTO 3NI HITOSHII.
1NI 2WO TASUTO SONO KEKKAWA 3NI HITOSHII.
(1 plus 2 is equal to 3.)

7 SEMANTIC INTERPRETATION

7.1 Interpretation by Procedure-1

The parser analyzes a sentence by evaluation of Case patterns slots towards the solution of the problem, which the system has to deal with. Procedure-1 of a Case Pattern to a BUNSETSU, which represents a phrase(in MSSS78, a sentence), interprets the resulting filled case slots to set up an equation, or construct and execute command to query database, etc.

From the underlined part in the next sentence,

AHURIKANI ARU ZINKOUGA 1000 MAN NIN IZYOUNO KOKUGOGA EIGONO KUNIWA DOKO DESUKA.
(What are countries in Africa, whose population is ten million or more, and whose language is English?),

the parser recognizes three phrases, such as the country in Africa, the country whose population is ten million or more, and the country whose language is English. The inner representation including filled slots to the phrases is as follows.

```
(GNN KUNI
  (RNT ARU (TSY1 (TSB TAIRIKU (IDN 2)))
  (ZMK (TSB KAZU
         (ATAI "G10000000")
         (GNN ZINKOU) ))
  (ZMK (TSB KOKUGO (IDN 212))) )
```

Procedure-1 to DESU constructs the next command by interpretation of the filled slots, and executes the command.

```
(TEST ((KUNI 2 (V KUNI))
       (WAWA (V KUNI) KUNI)
       (ZINKOU (V KUNI) "G1000000")
       (WAWA (V KUNI) KUNI)
       (KOKUGO (V KUNI) -3) ))
```

The TEST commmand searches into database by means of PLANNER-like procedural deduction mechanism (no backtracking unlike PLANNER). According to the return value of the command, a sentence generator constructs response sentences. (The sentence generator reconstructs an output sentence from a parsed tree of an input sentence, supplementing or replacing necessary words according to the input sentence pattern or the result of a problem solving.)

7.2 Interpretation by World Knowledge

Complete set of objects and relations in the geography world is unknown[5]. In MSSS78, the answer to the question

KANADANO SYUTOWA MONTORIO-RU KA.
(Is the capital of Canada Montreal?),

turns out to be

IIE, KANADANO SYUTOWA MONTORIO-RU DEWAARIMASEN. KANADANO SYUTOWA OTAWA DESU.
(No, the capital of Canada isn't Montreal. The capital of Canada is Ottawa.),

or

KANADANO SYUTOWA MONTORIO-RU KA WAKARIMASEN.
(I don't know that the capital of Canada is Montreal.)

according to whether or not the fact that the capital of Canada is Ottawa is in the database. For the above responses, the deduction program uses three logical values, true, false and unknown. Procedural type knowledge prepares logical value and additional information.

8 CONCLUSION

The experimental Japanese language question answering system, MSSS78, was made in a series of research efforts intended to construct a natural language man-machine interface. The system uses Case Patterns for syntactic and semantic analysis. The Case Pattern method seems to produce modularity and extendability of syntactic and semantic programs, and the readiness of system making.

Procedures in Case Patterns are a good tool for testing various processings. However, from a viewpoint of easy descriptiveness and system stability, it would be better to describe various functions absorbed in the procedures, using the so-called declarative style.

MSSS78 generates a response based on three logical values as well as additional information as to the result of the reference to the database. Such responses can be thought to place reliance on database. For the reference to a database, it seems convenient to be able to utilize the previous reference result in accordance with the context indication.

For written Japanese, it is better to display KANJI-KANA-MAJIRI-BUN for input and output sentences. In KANJI-KANA-MAJIRI-BUN display, output sentences are redundant at present.

MSSS78 was implemented on PDP11/55 with extensive utilization of disk memory capacity. The language used for the implementation is mainly LIPX, an extended version LIPQ[6], plus a little bit of assembler. The dictionary contains more than 600 words at the time. To analyze and respond to each sentence, takes from a few seconds to a few minutes, where most of the latter is search time for data in the database.

ACKNOWLEDGEMENTS

The authors gratefully thank Dr. N. Ikeno for his guidance and encouragement, and also thank Dr. H. Nomura and N. Osato for their cooperation in the implementation. They express their gratitude to the members of the Visual Communication Applications Section in ECL for their offer of KANJI and KANA pattern data.

REFERENCES

[1] Bruce, B., "Case Systems for Natural Language", Artificial Intelligence 6, 1975.
[2] Tanaka, H., Sato, T., and Motoyoshi, F., "EXPLUS, A Semantic Parsing System for Japanese Sentences", In Proc. of 3rd UJCC, 1978.
[3]Amamiya, M., Shimazu, A. and Wakana, T., "Japanese Question Answering System on the Topic of Figure Manipulation", Review of the ECL, NTT, Vol.26, Nos.7-8, 1978.
[4]Kaplan, R. M., "On process models for sentence analysis", In Norman, D. A., Rumelhart, D. E. and the LNR reseach Group, Explorations in Cognition, San Francisco, Freeman, 1975.
[5] Collins, A., Warnock, E., Aiello, N. and Miller, M. "Reasoning from incomplet knowledge", In Representation and Understanding, edited by Bobrow, D. G. nad Collins, A., Academic Press, 1975.
[6] Takeuchi, I. and Okuno, H., "A List Processor LIPQ", Review of the ECL, NTT, Vol.26, Nos.5-6, 1978.
[7] Minsky, M. A., "Framework for Representing Knowledge", In The Psychology of Computer Vision, edited by Winston, P. H., McGraw-Hill, NY, 1975.
[8] Bobrow, D. G. and Winograd, T., "An Overview of KRL, a Knowledge Representation Language", Cognitive Science, 1, 1, 1977.

RESOLUTION IN A NEW MODAL LOGIC

Masamichi SHIMURA
Department of Computer Science
Faculty of Engineering
Tokyo Institute of Technology
Oh-okayama, Meguro, Tokyo, 152

This paper proposes a new logic called manner logic(ML) and considers resolution techniques for mechanical theorem proving in the ML. The ML deals with statements which contain adverbs or verbs representing manner such as possibility, uncertainty and causality. Manner is expressed by a manner operator "*", which is a monadic operator. By using manner operators, a postulate can be four-valued; true(T), true in the sense of "*" (T*), false in the sense of "*" (F*), or false(F). In the ML, an atomic formula is assigned a value T or F, but a well-formed formula is assigned a value T, T*, F*, or F. Therefore, the ML can represent more complicated statements than the ordinal predicate logic. Its logical manipulation is quite simple, since it can be considered an extension of the oridinal binary logic. This paper also discusses resolution techniques in a refutation process. In our method, an additional valid clause is used in a refutation process to resolve clauses with manner operators which cannot be resolved directly.

1. INTRODUCTION

In the real world, the situation is often encountered where a postulate can be many-valued rather than two-valued. However, the many-valued logic is too complex to be applied to predicate calculus in artificial intelligence.

There are some other interesting logics such as a modal logic, tense logic or fuzzy logic. The modal logic [2], [3] had its effective beginning with work of C.L. Lewis[3] some sixty years ago, and is known as the logic of necessity and possibility. The tense logic [4], [6] deals with statements containing tensed verbs or explicit temporal references, and is logically similar to the modal logic. In these logics, the mode and tense are represented by two monadic symbols, and a postulate can be two-valued; true or false.

The present paper proposes a new logic which falls under the heading of the ordinal modal logic in a wide sense. The proposed logic deals with statements which contain adverbs or verbs representing manner such as possibility, uncertainty and causality. Monadic operators called manner operators are introduced to express such manner. A postulate in the logic can be four-valued; for example, true, possibly true, possibly false, or false. That is, a value T or F is assigned to each atomic formula in a well-formed formula(wff), but a value T, T*, F*, or F is assigned to the wff as described in the following sections. Consequently, we call the new logic the multi-binary logic or manner logic(ML). The manner logic can represent more complicated statements than the ordinal predicate logic, since it is essentially a four-valued logic.

Thus we are interested in the application of the ML to solve intellectual difficult problems. As is well known, the resolution principle due to Robinson[7], [8], [9] is a simple but extremely useful technique for mechanical theorem proving. It is difficult, however, to apply the Robinson's resolution principle to the ML, because clauses contain manner operators. To circumvent this difficulty, additional clauses which are valid are used in a refutation process. The present paper considers some fundamental properties of the ML, and gives a new rule of inference for mechanical theorem proving.

2. FUNDAMENTAL PROPERTIES

This section is devoted to consideration of fundamental properties of the ML. We shall introduce the symbol "*" with intention of interpreting it as a manner operator, which is placed on the shoulder of well-formed formulas. Suppose a proposition P is interpreted as "She is beautiful". Then P* is "She is possibly beautiful", "She will be beautiful", or "She seems to be beautiful" or "She is very beautiful", in the sense of the modal, tense or fuzzy logic, respectively.

The symbols such as P, Q and R, that are used to denote propositions are called atoms.

Definition 1 Well-formed formulas (wff) or formulas for short in the ML are defined recursively as follows:

1. An atom is a formula.
2. If G is a formula, then so are $\sim G$ and G^*.
3. If G and H are formulas, then so are $G \vee H$, $G \wedge H$, $G \rightarrow H$.
4. All formulas are generated by applying the above rules.

In the ordinal logic, a well-formed formula can be either true or false. Here we represent "true" by T and "false" by F. Therefore, $\sim G$ is T when G is F, and is F when G is T. In the similar manner, G* is T* when G is T, and is F* when G is F. Consequently, a well-formed formula G can be T, T*, F* or F; that is, true, true in the sense of "*", false in the sense of "*", or false. For example, G is true, G is probably true, G is probably false, or G is false.

We begin by defining some logical symbols used here by means of Table 1. They are $\sim$ (negation), *(manner), $\vee$(disjunction), $\wedge$ (conjunction), and $\rightarrow$(implication). This table expresses the truth value of the statements. It is seen from Table 1 that the implication can be represented by a negation and disjunction as follows:

$$X \rightarrow Y = \sim X \vee Y$$

where X and Y are wffs.

Some examples of statements containing manner operators are shown below. Let P and Q be propositional symbols interpreted as

P : She is young.
Q : She is beautiful.

Then the expression $X \rightarrow Y$ asserts as follows:

$P \rightarrow Q$: If she is young, then she is beautiful.

P	F	F	T	T
Q	F	T	F	T
$\sim P$	T	T	F	F
P^*	F*	F*	T*	T*
$(P^*)^*$	F*	F*	T*	T*
$\sim(P)^*$	T*	T*	F*	F*
$(\sim P)^*$	T*	T*	F*	F*
$P \vee Q$	F	T	T	T
$P \vee Q^*$	F*	T*	T*	T*
$P^* \vee Q$	F*	T	T*	T
$P^* \vee Q^*$	F*	T	T	T*
$P \wedge Q$	F	F	F	T
$P \wedge Q^*$	F	F	F*	T*
$P^* \wedge Q$	F	F*	F	T*
$P^* \wedge Q^*$	F*	F	F	T*
$P \rightarrow Q$	T	T	F	T
$P \rightarrow Q^*$	T	T	F*	T
$P^* \rightarrow Q$	T*	T	F*	T
$P^* \rightarrow Q^*$	T	T*	F	F

Table 1 Truth table

$P \rightarrow Q^*$: If she is young, then she seems to be beautiful.

$P^* \rightarrow Q$: If she seems to be young, then she is beautiful.

$P^* \rightarrow Q^*$: If she seems to be young, then she seems to be beautiful.

$(P \rightarrow Q)^*$: It seems that if she is young she is beautiful.

As shown in the above examples, more complex statements can be represented if manner operators are employed.

Now, we consider the fundamental properties of the ML. Let P, Q, and R be atoms, and X, Y, and Z be well-formed formulas. From the truth table, Table 1, we have the following laws:

Idempotent laws

$$X \vee X = X, \quad X \wedge X = X \tag{1}$$

Absorption laws

$$X \vee (X \wedge Y) = X, \quad X \wedge (X \vee Y) = X \tag{2}$$

Commutative laws

$$X \vee Y = Y \vee X, \quad X \wedge Y = Y \wedge X \tag{3}$$

Associative laws

$$X \vee (Y \vee Z) = (X \vee Y) \vee Z, \quad X \wedge (Y \wedge Z) = (X \wedge Y) \wedge Z \tag{4}$$

Distributed laws

$$X \vee (Y \wedge Z) = (X \vee Y) \wedge (X \vee Z), \quad X \wedge (Y \vee Z) = (X \wedge Y) \vee (X \wedge Z) \tag{5}$$

Involution laws

$$\sim(\sim X) = X. \tag{6}$$

De Morgan's laws

$$\sim(X \vee Y) = \sim X \wedge \sim Y, \quad \sim(X \wedge Y) = \sim X \vee \sim Y. \tag{7}$$

Contradiction laws

$$X \vee \sim X = T, \quad X \wedge \sim X = F. \tag{8}$$

Complement laws

$$X \vee F = X, \quad X \wedge T = X \tag{9}$$

$$X \wedge F = F, \quad X \vee T = T. \tag{10}$$

These laws are the same as those in the ordinal logic, but the following laws are peculiar to the ML.

o $(P^*)^* = P^*$. (11)

o $\sim(P^*) = (\sim P)^*$. (12)

o $P^* = (P \wedge T^*) \vee (\sim P \wedge F^*)$, $(\sim P)^* = (P \vee T^*) \wedge (\sim P \vee F^*)$. (13)

o $(X \vee Y)^* = (X^* \vee Y^*) \wedge T^* \vee (X^* \wedge Y^* \wedge F^*)$. (14)

o $(X \wedge Y)^* = (X^* \wedge Y^* \vee F^*) \wedge (X^* \vee Y^* \vee T^*)$. (15)

Using the laws (1) - (15), we have the logical equivalences as follows:

o $P \wedge P^* = P \wedge T^*$, $\sim P \wedge \sim P^* = \sim P \wedge T^*$,

o $P \wedge \sim P^* = P \wedge F^*$, $\sim P \wedge P^* = \sim P \wedge F^*$. (16)

[Proof] The proof is obtained from Eq. (13).

o $P \vee P^* = P^* \vee F^*$, $\sim P \vee \sim P^* = \sim P^* \vee F^*$,

o $P \vee \sim P^* = P \vee T^*$, $\sim P \vee P^* = \sim P \vee T^*$. (17)

[Proof] The proof is obtained from Eq. (13).

o $(\sim P \vee P^*) \wedge (P \vee \sim P^*) = T^*$,

o $\sim P \wedge P^* \vee P \wedge \sim P^* = F^*$. (18)

[Proof] The proof is obtained from Eqs. (16) and (17).

o $(P \wedge P^*) \vee (\sim P \wedge \sim P^*) = T^*$,

o $(P \vee P^*) \wedge (\sim P \vee \sim P^*) = F^*$. (19)

[Proof] The proof is obtained from Eqs. (16) and (17).

o $(P \vee Q)^* \wedge (\sim P \vee \sim Q)^* = (P \wedge \sim Q \vee \sim P \wedge Q) \wedge T^*$,

o $(P \vee \sim Q)^* \wedge (\sim P \vee Q)^* = (P \wedge Q \vee \sim P \wedge \sim Q) \wedge T^*$. (20)

[Proof] The proof is obtained from Eqs. (14) and (15).

o $(P^* \wedge \sim Q^*) \vee (\sim P^* \wedge Q^*) = (P \wedge \sim Q) \vee (\sim P \wedge Q)$,

o $(P^* \wedge Q^*) \vee (\sim P^* \wedge \sim Q^*) = (P \wedge Q) \vee (\sim P \wedge \sim Q)$. (21)

[Proof] The proof is obtained from Eqs. (14) and (15).

o $(P^* \vee Q)^* = (P^* \vee Q^*)^* = (P \vee Q)^*$,

o $(P^* \wedge Q)^* = (P^* \wedge Q^*)^* = (P \wedge Q)^*$. (22)

[Proof] The proof is obtained from Eqs. (14) and (15).

o $P \wedge Q \wedge (P \wedge Q)^* = P \wedge Q \wedge P^* \wedge Q^* = P \wedge Q \wedge T^*$,

o $P \vee Q \vee (P \vee Q)^* = P \vee Q \vee P^* \vee Q^* = P \vee Q \vee F^*$. (23)

[Proof] The proof is obtained from Eqs. (14) and (15).

o $P^* = P^* \wedge (P \vee F^*) = P^* \wedge (\sim P \vee T^*)$

$= P^* \vee P \wedge T^* = P^* \vee \sim P \wedge F^*$,

o $\sim P^* = \sim P^* \vee \sim P \wedge T^* = \sim P^* \vee P \wedge F^*$

$= \sim P^* \wedge (\sim P \vee F^*) = \sim P^* \wedge (P \vee T^*)$. (24)

[Proof] The proof is obtained from Eqs. (18) and (19).

o $(P \rightarrow Q)^* = (P^* \rightarrow Q^*) \wedge (P \rightarrow Q^*) \wedge (P^* \rightarrow Q)$. (25)

[Proof] The proof is obtained from Eqs. (14) and (15).

Now, we will show that a formula Y can be represented in the conjunctive and/or disjunctive normal form.

Definition 2. A formula Y is said to be in a conjunctive or disjunctive normal form if and only if Y has the form

$$Y = Y_1 \wedge \dots \wedge Y_n$$

or

$$Y = Y_1 \vee \dots \vee Y_n,$$

where each of $Y_1, \dots, Y_n$ is a disjunction or conjunction of literals with and without manner operators, respectively.

Let $P_1, P_2, \dots, P_m, Q_1, Q_2, \dots, Q_n$ be atoms, and $Y(P_1, P_2, \dots, P_m, Q_1^*, Q_2^*, \dots, Q_n^*)$ be an $(m + n)$adic formula.
Then we have

$$\begin{aligned} &Y(P_1, P_2, \dots, P_m, Q_1^*, Q_2^*, \dots, Q_n^*) \\ &= P_1 \wedge Y(1, P_2, \dots, P_m, Q_1^*, Q_2^*, \dots, Q_n^*) \\ &\quad \vee \sim P_1 \wedge Y(0, P_2, \dots, P_m, Q_1^*, Q_2^*, \dots, Q_n^*) \\ &\quad \vee \dots\dots\dots \\ &= (P_1 \wedge P_2 \wedge \dots \wedge P_m \wedge Q_1 \wedge Q_2 \wedge \dots \wedge Q_n \\ &\qquad \wedge Y(1, \dots, 1, 1^*, \dots, 1^*)) \\ &\quad \vee \dots\dots\dots \\ &\quad \vee (\sim P_1 \wedge \sim P_2 \wedge \dots \wedge \sim P_m \wedge \sim Q_1 \wedge \sim Q_2 \wedge \dots \wedge \sim Q_n \\ &\qquad \wedge Y(0, \dots, 0, 0^*, \dots, 0^*)). \end{aligned} \tag{26}$$

$$Y(P_1, P_2, \ldots, P_m, Q_1^*, Q_2^*, \ldots, Q_n^*)$$
$$= (P_1 \vee Y(0, P_2, \ldots, P_m, Q_1^*, Q_2^*, \ldots, Q_n^*)$$
$$\wedge(\sim P_1 \vee Y(1, P_2, \ldots, P_m, Q_1^*, Q_2^*, \ldots, Q_n^*))$$
$$= (P_1 \vee \ldots \vee P_m \vee Q_1 \vee \ldots \vee Q_n$$
$$\vee Y(0, \ldots, 0, 0^*, \ldots, 0^*))$$
$$\wedge \ldots\ldots\ldots$$
$$\wedge(\sim P_1 \vee \ldots \vee \sim P_m \vee \sim Q_1 \vee \ldots \vee \sim Q_n$$
$$Y(1, \ldots, 1, 1^*, \ldots, 1^*)). \quad (27)$$

The former is the disjunctive normal form and the latter is the conjunctive normal form. As mentioned before, Y(........) can be T, T*, F* or F, and then T* and F* appear in Eqs. (26) and (27). Using Eqs.(18) and (19), however, we can eliminate T* and F*. Therefore, any formula can be represented by using

$\sim$, $*$, $\vee$, and $\wedge$.

3. RESOLUTION TECHNIQUES

As is well known, the resolution principle is a useful technique for making deduction in the system of the first-order predicate calculus. Here we consider techniques based on the resolution principle for the ML system. Some important definitions of terminology are given as follows:

Definition 3 A formula G is said to be satisfiable or semi-satisfiable if and only if there exists an interpretation I such that Y is evaluated to T or T*, respectively. In this case, we say I satisfies or semi-satisfies Y.

Definition 4 A formula is said to be unsatisfiable or semi-unsatisfiable, if and only if it is F or F* under all its interpretation. A formula is said to be satisfiable or semi-satisfiable if and only if it is not unsatisfiable or not semi-unsatisfiable, respectively.

Definition 5 A formula G is said to be a logical consequence or semi-consequence of a given set of formulas S, if and only if every interpretation satisfying or semi-satisfying S also satisfies or semi-satisfies G, respectively.

Definition 6 Given a formula G, a formula $\bar{G}$ obtained by removing all manner operators in G is said to be a reduced formula of G.

Definition 7 Given a clause C, a clause $\bar{C}$ obtained by removing all manner operators in C is said to be a reduced clause of C.

Definition 8 A clause which takes F or F* is said to be an empty or semi-empty clause, respectively.

Processes for showing the unsatisfiability or semi-unsatisfiability are called refutation processes. The following theorems give basic properties used for refutation processes.

Theorem 1

The following clauses C_1 and C_2 are valid.

C_1 : $(\sim P \wedge P^*) \rightarrow F^*$

C_2 : $(P \wedge \sim P^*) \rightarrow F^*$.

[Proof]

From Eq. (17), we have

$$(\sim P \wedge P^*) \rightarrow F^* = P \vee \sim P^* \vee F^*$$
$$= T,$$

which gives the proof. q.e.d.

Theorem 2

Given formulas $Y_1, \ldots, Y_n$ and a formula G, G is a logical consequence or semi-consequence of $Y_1, \ldots, Y_n$ if and only if the formula $(Y_1 \wedge \ldots \wedge Y_n \wedge \sim G)$ is unsatisfiable or semi-unsatisfiable, respectively.

[Proof]

($\Rightarrow$) Suppose G is a logical consequence or semi-consequence. In an interpretation I satisfying or semi-satisfying $Y_1, \ldots, Y_n$, G is T or T* and then $Y_1 \wedge \ldots \wedge Y_n \wedge \sim G$ is F or F*, respectively.

($\Leftarrow$) Suppose $Y_1 \wedge \ldots \wedge Y_n \wedge \sim G$ is unsatisfiable or semi-unsatisfiable. For any interpretation I, if $Y_1 \wedge \ldots \wedge Y_n$ is T or T*, then G must be T or T* in I. Therefore, G is a logical consequence or semi-consequence of $Y_1, \ldots, Y_n$.

Now, we consider the application of the resolution principle due to Robinson to the theorem proving in the ML.

The resolution principle is essentially an elegant technique to check whether a given set of clauses is unsatisfiable or semi-unsatisfiable.

Consider the following set of clauses

$S_1 = \{C_1, C_2, C_3\}$

C_1 : P

C_2 : $P \rightarrow Q^*$ or $\sim P \vee Q^*$

C_3 : $\sim Q$.

The resolution technique is very similar to that of Robinson except that clauses may contain manner operators. In this case, the resolvent Q* (clause C_4) is obtained by deleting the pair of literals P and $\sim$P from clauses C_1 and C_2:

C_4 : Q* from C_1 and C_2.

However, we have no way to get the resolvent from clauses C_3 and C_4. Thus, a new set of clauses S_2 is introduced such that

$$S_2 = S_1 \cup C_5$$
$$= \{C_1, C_2, C_3, C_5\}$$

$$C_5 : Q \vee \sim Q^* \vee F^*.$$

Since C_5 is a tautology from Theorem 1, S_2 is equivalent to S_1 from the point of view of refutation processes. Thus we have

$C_6 : \sim Q^* \vee F^*$ from C_3 and C_5

$C_7 : F^*$ from C_4 and C_6.

Therefore, S_2 is semi-unsatisfiable and so is S_1.

In the above example, however, if $C_3' = \sim Q^*$ is used instead of C_3, then we have the empty clause as the resolvent of C_3' and C_4.

Here a question arises : In what case a set of clauses is semi-unsatisfiable ? As described before, a formula G is a logical semi-consequence of $Y_1, \ldots, Y_n$ if a semi-empty clause is obtained as a resolvent in a refutation process. This means, therefore, that G is true in a sense of "*". For example, consider the case where "G*" asserts "It possibly rains". If a semi-empty clause is obtained, the proof is possibly true or the inference is possibly correct. That is, it is possibly true to conclude that it rains. On the other hand, the proof is true if an empty clause is obtained. The following sets of clauses are also semi-unsatisfiable and give the same results as above.

$\{P, \sim P \vee Q, \sim Q^*\}$

$\{P^*, \sim P \vee Q, \sim Q\}$

$\{P, (\sim P \vee Q)^*, \sim Q\}$.

Now we will show some important properties of a resolvent in the following theorems.

Theorem 3

A resolvent of given two clauses C_1 and C_2 is a logical consequence or semi-consequence of C_1 and C_2.

[Proof]

Let C_1, C_2 and C_3 be denoted as follows: $C_1 = X \vee C_1'$, $C_2 = \sim X \vee C_2'$, $C_3 = C_1' \vee C_2'$. The proof will be made in the case (i) X = F, (ii) F*, (iii) T*, and (iv) T. Suppose there exists an interpretation I for which C_1 and C_2 are T or T*. In cases (i) and (ii), C_1' must be T or T*, and thus C_3 = Γ or T*. In cases (iii) and (iv), C_2' must be T or T*, and thus C_3 = T or T*. This gives the proof. q.e.d.

Theorem 4

Let S be an unsatisfiable or semi-unsatisfiable set of clauses and $\bar{S}$ be a reduced set of S. If an empty clause is obtained from $\bar{S}$ by applying the resolution principle, then either an empty or semi-empty clause is obtained from S.

[Proof]

Let $\bar{C}_3$ be a resolvent of reduced clauses $\bar{C}_1$ and $\bar{C}_2$. If $\bar{C}_1$ and $\bar{C}_2$ can be resolved, then they must be indicated as follows: $\bar{C}_1 = L \vee C_1'$, and $\bar{C}_2 = \sim L \vee \bar{C}_2'$, where L is a literal. Therefore, we have (i) $C_1 = X \vee C_1'$, $C_2 = \sim X \vee C_2'$, or (ii) $C_1 = P \vee C_1'$, $C_2 = \sim P^* \vee C_2'$. It is clear that an empty clause is obtained as the resolvent in the case (ii) and that an empty or semi-empty clause is obtained in the case (i).

Fig. 1 illustrates an example of refutation graphs for a set of clauses as follows:

$$S = \{P(a), \quad (P(x) \rightarrow Q(y))^*, \quad \sim Q(b)\}$$
$$= \{P(a), \ (\sim P(x) \vee Q(y))^*, \ \sim Q(b)\}$$
$$= \{P(a), \ \sim P(x) \vee Q^*(y), \ \sim P^*(x) \vee Q(y), \ \sim P^*(x) \vee Q^*(y), \ Q(b)\}.$$

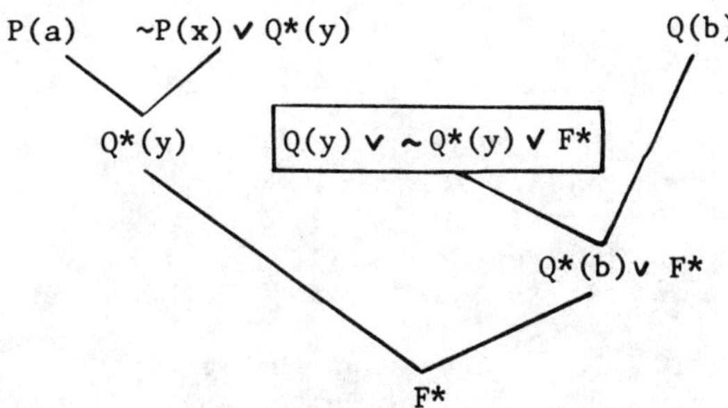

$\sim P^*(x) \vee Q(y)$ $\sim P^*(x) \vee Q^*(y)$: unused clauses

$Q(y) \vee \sim Q^*(y) \vee F^*$: tautology

Fig. 1 A refutation graph for S = {P(a), (P(x) → Q(y))*, ~Q(b)}

4. CONCLUDING REMARKS

We have considered a new logic called the ML and derived its mathematical properties. Due to manner operators introduced here, the ML can express more complex statements than the ordinal logic. Since the ML can be considered an extension of the ordinal binary logic, its logical manipulation is quite simple, although it is a four-valued logic. Four values are true(T), true in the sense of "*" (T*), false in the sense of "*"(F*) and false (F). Furthermore, we have developed some interesting applications of the ML to mechanical theorem proving in artificial intelligence. A refutation process for the ML system is similar to that of the ordinal propositional or predicate logic. The idea of semi-unsatisfiability is introduced in the refutation process. That is, a semi-empty clause is obtained as a resolvent if a set of clauses is semi-unsatisfiable. In the refutation process for mechanical theorem proving, therefore, the appearance of a semi-empty clause means that the inference is not completely true but true in the sense of "*". This is one of the advantages of our system.

Several directions seem to be interesting for furthering investigations of the ML from both a mathematical and applicational point of view. The author believes that the ML system is quite useful for solving complex problems.

REFERENCES

[1] Chang, C.L. and Lee, R.C.: "Symbolic Logic and Mathematical Theorem Proving," Academic Press, New York (1973).

[2] Hughes, C.E. and Cresswell, M.J. : "An Introduction to Modal Logic," Methuen and Co Ltd., London (1968).

[3] Lewis C.I. : "Interesting theorems in symbolic logic," J. of Philosophy, vol. 10, pp. 239-242 (1913).

[4] McArthur, R.P.: "Tense Logic," D. Reidel Publishing Co., Boston U.S.A., (1976).

[5] Nilson, N.J.: "Problem Solving Methods in Artificial Intelligence," McGraw-Hill, New York (1971).

[6] Prior, A.: "Past, Present and Future," Oxford University Press (1967).

[7] Robinson, J.A.: "A machine-oriented logic based on the resolution principle," J. ACM, vol. 12, no. 1, pp. 23-41 (1965).

[8] _______ : "The generalized resolution principle," in D. Michie(ed.), "Machine Intelligence 3," pp. 77-93, American Elsevier, New York (1968).

[9] Robinson, J.A.: "Mechanizing higher order logic," in B. Melzer and D. Michie(eds.), "Machine Intelligence 4," American Elsevier, New York (1969).

TOWARDS MINIMAL DATA STRUCTURES
FOR DETERMINISTIC PARSING

David W. Shipman
Bell Laboratories
Room 2D-443
Murray Hill, New Jersey 07974

Mitchell P. Marcus
Artificial Intelligence Laboratory
Massachusetts Institute of Technology
545 Technology Square
Cambridge, Massachusetts 02143

The determinism hypothesis suggests that natural language may be parsed in a single pass without resort to backtracking techniques. The PARSIFAL system, developed by Marcus, incorporates this philosophy in an English language parser. Here, we show that the data structures used by this parser may be considerably simplified resulting in more elegant grammatical specifications.

Keywords: artificial intelligence, natural language processing, deterministic parsing

1. THE DETERMINISM HYPOTHESIS

Marcus [1][2] proposes that natural language may be parsed in a fully deterministic manner. Under this determinism hypothesis portions of the parse-tree, once constructed, necessarily become part of the final parse-tree output. This is in contrast to the traditional backtracking paradigm in which "guesses" are made about the syntactic structure of the input sentence; and, when the guess proves later to be incorrect, any parse-tree structures resulting from that guess must be erased prior to testing alternate hypotheses.

An important discovery was that English could be parsed deterministically by using an, at most, three-constituent look-ahead strategy. This differs from the k-token look-ahead strategy used by an LR(k) parser in that the bounded look-ahead is with reference to parsed constituents rather than to individual words of the sentence. For example, the sequence <auxverb> <noun phrase> appearing at the beginning of the sentence would indicate that a yes-no question was being parsed. Note that in order for this sequence to appear in the look-ahead buffer, it would have been necessary to first parse the noun phrase in the second position. This is accomplished by means of an attention shifting rule in the grammar. In the example above, the attention shifting rule would detect the beginning of a noun phrase starting in the second position of the look-ahead buffer. It would then shift the look-ahead window one position to the right, just past the <auxverb>, and activate grammar rules suitable for parsing noun phrases. The noun phrase parse then operates only with respect to words in the input sentence to the right of the <auxverb>. When the noun phrase parse is complete, attention shifts back to the original look-ahead window position with the <auxverb> in first position and the new <noun phrase> in the second position.

By using such an approach it is possible to parse natural language in a time on the order of the length of the input sentence. A more detailed discussion, including arguments for the psychological reality of the determinism hypothesis can be found in [1][2].

This deterministic mechanism has been incorporated as part of the PARSIFAL system developed by Marcus. In this paper we propose a simplification of the data structures employed by PARSIFAL. The change significantly lessens the amount of detail which must be explicitly specified in the rules of the grammar. This results from the fact that this detail can now be implicitly embedded in the control structure of the parser.

The new approach will be presented after a cursory overview of the current PARSIFAL mechanisms.

"Is the boy John saw yesterday going to the party?"

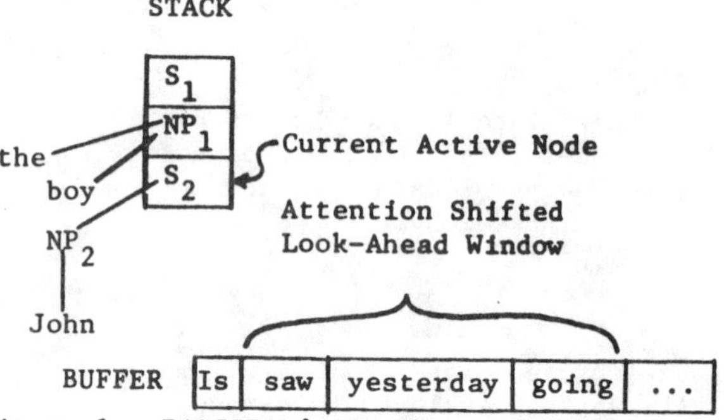

Figure 1. PARSIFAL's STACK and BUFFER

2. THE PARSIFAL APPROACH

2.1 Data Structures

PARSIFAL uses two data structures to record parsing progress (Fig. 1). These are the Stack and the Buffer. The Buffer is the look-ahead buffer discussed in the previous section. The Stack is used to hold partial structures which have already been parsed by the system. The Buffer contains only terminals and complete sub-trees, while the Stack contains sub-trees under construction. (Note that the Stack differs from the pushdown stack used by backtracking parsers in that structures once parsed and placed on the Stack are always used later as subordinates of larger structures.) Instructions to move nodes between the Buffer and the Stack must be explicitly stated in the system's grammar rules. Grammar rules build the structures on the stack by removing elements from the Buffer and attaching them to the most recent node on the Stack, this may be a newly created non-terminal node or a previously created non-terminal which already has some subordinate structures attached to it. When a complete sub-tree has been built on the stack, the parent node is dropped from the stack back into the buffer to be used there in the construction of higher-level constituent structures.

2.2 Attention Shifting Rules

Attention shifting rules are responsible for adjusting the look-ahead window of the Buffer to the proper position for parsing a new sub-constituent. They must be treated as a special case since they need to be able to scan the buffer to locate the beginning of the sub-constituent. Once this has happened, the new node is created, pushed on the stack and the look-ahead window is explicitly advanced. Special attention must also be given to the problem of restoring the look-ahead window after the sub-constituent parse is complete.

2.3 Node Reactivation Rules

An additional type of grammar rule is the node reactivation rule. Its function can perhaps best be explained through an example. Consider the case of a noun phrase which includes an attached relative clause. During the processing of the relative clause it is sometimes necessary to access the attributes of parent nodes of the noun phrase under construction. However, since the noun phrase sub-tree has not yet been completed at the time the relative clause is being parsed, the noun phrase is not attached to a parent. Thus, access to parent attributes from the relative clause would be impossible. To remedy this situation, the noun phrase parse tree is prematurely taken to be complete just prior to parsing the relative clause. The noun phrase can then be attached by its parent node. A node reactivation rule is then called into play. It "reactivates" the noun phrase processing in order to parse the relative clause. Now, the grammar rules for processing the relative clause are able to reference the parents of the noun phrase.

Thus, in figure 1, if it were desirable to attach the NP_1 to S_1 as its subject, NP_1 would have to be prematurely marked complete and later reactivated to continue parsing the phrase.

Node reactivation rules were intended to be only a temporary solution to certain parsing problems. The data structuring approach described in the next section eliminates the need for such a reactivation mechanism.

3. THE UNIFIED APPROACH

3.1 A Unified Data Structure

Under the proposed strategy, the former Stack and Buffer are combined into a single Buffer.

"Is the boy John saw yesterday going to the party?"

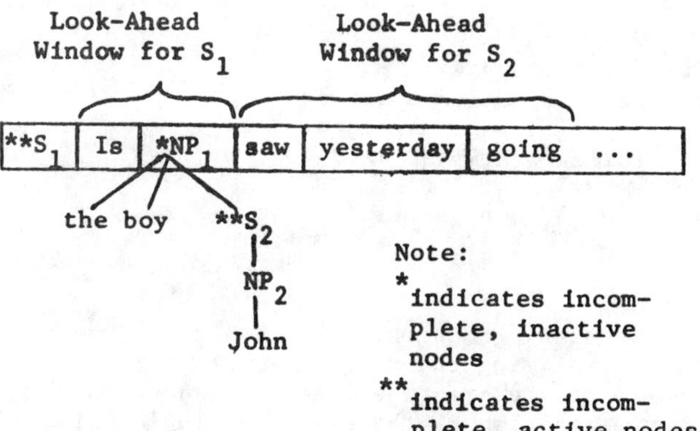

Figure 2. Unified BUFFER Organization

This buffer holds both complete and incomplete sub-trees (see Fig. 2). For each incomplete sub-tree, the most subordinate incomplete node is considered to be the active node for that subtree. A parsing process is associated with each active node. This parsing process operates over a look-ahead window consisting of the three Buffer cells following that Buffer cell which contains the active node.

Because the new Buffer structure now contains all the information previously contained in the Stack as well, the explicit instructions which transfered data between the two structures are no longer necessary.

"Is the boy John saw yesterday going to the party?"

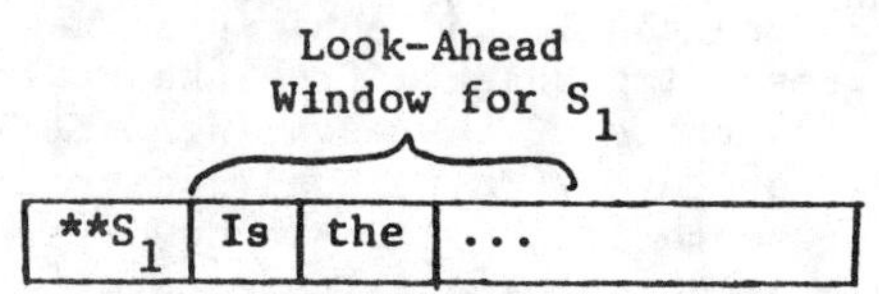

(a) Before attention shift rule for NP

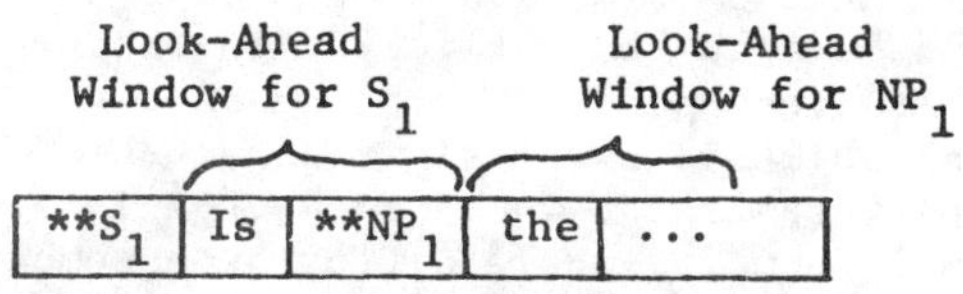

(b) After attention shift rule for NP

Figure 3. Automatic Attention Shifting

3.2 Automatic Attention Shifting

Under this scheme, the attention shifting rules simply insert a newly created node into the Buffer (see Fig. 3). Since a newly created node is necessarily an incomplete node, it is automatically active. The look-ahead window for the new node, as for any active node, is defined to be the next three cells in the Buffer. No explicit mechanism for shifting attention is needed.

3.3 Automatic Node Reactivation

All active nodes are considered to be parsing their look-ahead windows in parallel. Note however that the look-ahead may not extend beyond an incomplete node. This is because this portion of the buffer is actively being considered for attachment by the incomplete node.

Thus, in figure 3b, it would be possible for S_1 to attach NP_1 as its subject without a deactivation and subsequent reactivation of NP_1.

The mechanism can be thought of as a kind of linear cellular automaton where each cell has access to the contents of up to three cells to its right. Because multiple cells can be active at the same time, there is no need for an explicit reactivation mechanism.

REFERENCES

[1] Marcus, M. P. A Theory of Syntactic Recognition for Natural Language Ph.D Thesis, Department of Electrical Engineering, Massachusetts Institute of Technology, Cambridge, Massachusetts 1978

[2] Marcus, M. P. "A Computational Account of the Syntactic Recognition of Natural Language" Proceedings of the Workshop on Computational Aspects of Linguistic Structure and Discourse Setting Cambridge University Press [to appear]

A COMPACT RELATIONAL STRUCTURE REPRESENTATION

M. Shneier
Department of Artificial Intelligence
University of Edinburgh
Edinburgh, Scotland

Current Address:
Computer Science Center
University of Maryland
College Park, MD 20742

This paper is concerned with the representation of objects by computer. It presents a compact relational structure representation derived by generalizing the properties of objects. Objects are described by means of surface primitives (basic descriptive elements) and relations between the primitives. The essence of the representation is the use of a single primitive to describe all identical parts. The representation involves abstracting properties of individual scene elements. Similarly, relations between parts of objects that hold for particular instances of the objects are generalized to ensure that they will be valid for all instances. Common primitives and relations are shared both within and across models. This leads to a compact representation that has many desirable properties. A computer implementation of a version of the representation has been developed. It is used to illustrate the descriptive power of the representation. A recognition system has been developed that takes advantage of the representation in its operation. It is described elsewhere (Shneier (1977), Shneier (1978)).

1. INTRODUCTION

The way in which information is represented is critically important to the effectiveness of any system in Artificial Intelligence. Using a good representation, tasks that would otherwise be intractable become amenable to solution. In machine vision, representations have usually been tailored to specific, small domains. Recognition algorithms have been developed that depend for their effectiveness on specific knowledge about the objects in the domain. This paper presents a new representation for describing objects. The system is intended to be generally applicable, but was developed primarily for the domain of three-dimensional machine vision. It has also been applied to a second domain, that of spelling correction. The presentation of the system will be in terms of machine vision.

The representation takes advantage of similarities in the descriptions, or models, of objects. If two parts of an object, or two parts of different objects, have the same description, then these parts are represented by a single description in the representation. The basic idea is to share descriptions that are common within models and across models. When this sharing is accompanied by a comprehensive indexing scheme, it leads to a representation that has many advantages over previous representations (e.g. Barrow and Popplestone (1971), Falk (1972), Ambler et al. (1975)) and suffers few disadvantages.

Some constraints were placed on the implementation of the system. The first constraint was that the descriptions of objects should be acquired automatically from visual data. This is a sensible constraint because it allows the domain to be changed easily and confronts the problems of representing objects from the real world, rather than those of representing artificially-created objects. The second constraint was thatthe representation should not be domain-dependent. It should be possible to change or expand the domain with as little effort as possible, and the information known about objects should be acquired entirely from the objects themselves rather than being partly dependent on built-in assumptions about the domain. This constraint would be useful in a robot assembly domain, where different assembly tasks might use widely different parts. Instead of having to re-program the system for each new task, it would be preferable for it to acquire descriptions of the parts visually.

Some of the problems to be confronted when a

representation and a recognition system are being designed become amenable to solution in a more natural way using the new representation than using earlier representations. It becomes easier to compare descriptions of objects, the domain of objects may be changed or expanded with very little effort, and the problems of matching symmetrical objects disappear. There is a great deal of flexibility in the choice of how to describe objects, and the form of the representation makes recognition of objects easier.

A recognition algorithm based on the representation has been developed and implemented. It makes use of the form of the representation to enable it to recognize objects in a robust and efficient manner. An earlier version of the algorithm appears in Shneier (1977). It is discussed in more detail in Shneier (1978), and examples are presented of its use in three-dimensional vision and in spelling correction.

2. COMPACT MODELS

The approach taken here differs from earlier work in two major respects. The first difference concerns the nature of models. Those authors who have previously made use of models of objects (e.g. Falk (1972), Barrow and Popplestone (1971), but not Waltz (1975)) have given the term "model" certain implicit characteristics. A model has been defined as a description of an object with a one-to-one relationship between parts of the object (e.g. edges, surfaces, volumes) and parts of the model. For example, the model for a cube consists of a separate description of each of the six sides of the cube, and of relationships between the sides.

There are a number of reasons why this concept of model, while natural, is not the best for machine vision. It means that each model has to be treated as a separate entity because there is no sharing of structure between models or parts of models. Most systems have performed matching separately on each model in turn, with models being rejected one by one until a match was found. It was desired to be able to match with all possible models in parallel, finding the best match in the most efficient manner possible. Grape (1973) attempted to match in this way by compiling a central list of features against which to match. He was not entirely successful, however, because he had to match against each element of the feature list in turn.

Another reason for re-examining the notion of model concerns the analysis of models of symmetric objects. Underwood and Coates (1972) were unable to deal with symmetric objects because of problems of finding the correct correspondence between parts of the scene and parts of the model. Other authors have had to content themselves with finding all possible correspondences between the scene and a model, and then choosing one of these arbitrarily (e.g. Barrow and Popplestone (1971), Ambler et al. (1975)). The problem arises because the model of a symmetrical object contains several parts that are described in a very similar fashion. When an object model is being constructed from several views, it is not clear when to construct a new part in the model and when to assume that all parts have already been seen. Similarly, when trying to recognize an object, it is not clear which of a number of parts of a model should be matched against a scene fragment. If the system is to work in a world of man-made objects, it seems advisable to be able to handle symmetry in a more acceptable manner.

Our solution to these problems with models is to broaden the concept of a model. A model is defined as a collection of descriptions of the kind of parts that make up an object and the set of the relations between them. There is no requirement of a one-to-one correspondence between object parts and model parts. Rather, there is one model part for each _distinguishably different_ object part. This is similar to systems of mathematical logic, where a model is a collection of axioms describing a world, and where no axioms are repeated.

So, for example, a model of a cube consists of only one part description--that of a square plane. Relations are defined between _instances_ of the part, so that a form of relational structure is the basis of the representation.

Figure 1 depicts the difference between the conventional relational structure model of a cube and the model described in this paper. The conventional model has one node for each surface in the cube, whereas the new model has a single node describing all the surfaces. Similarly, while there are many relations defined between the surfaces in the conventional model, the new model needs only a single relation to represent them all. There is a great saving in the size of the model.

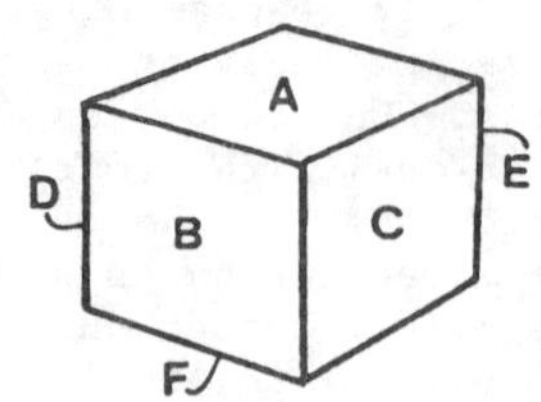

"cube"

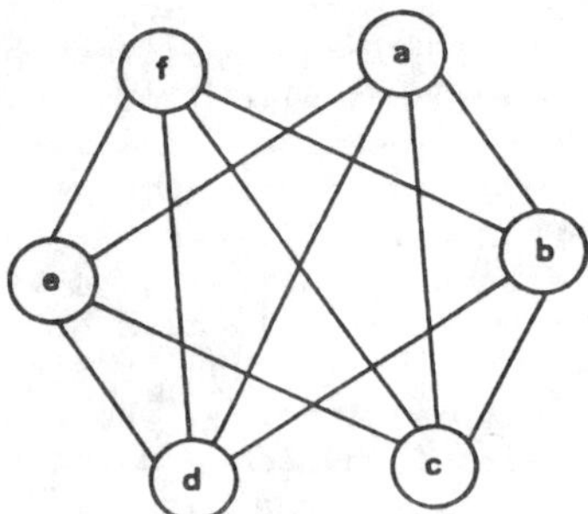

Conventional Model

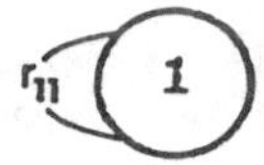

New Model

Figure 1

In fact, the models are even more like those of the logician than has been described so far. A logician describes a whole world with one set of axioms. Similarly, the models in this representation all share one structure, instead of the usual separation of models of different objects. The advantages of such a system are manifold. Matching is enormously simplified and matches occur with all possible models at once. Models are compact and are easily compared. Similarities are evident in shared structure, and differences are reflected by structure that is not shared.

The second difference between the new system and earlier work is more specific, and arises as a result of the formulation of the models as relational structures. A relational structure is defined as a set E of elements, together with a set of properties P and a set of relations R over E (Ambler et al, 1975)). Scene analysis based on relational structures has been concerned with the following kind of matching: Given two relational structures $\langle E_1,P,R\rangle$ and $\langle E_2,P,R\rangle$ define a match between them as a set $T_1 \subseteq E_1$, a set $T_2 \subseteq E_2$, and an isomorphism between T_1 and T_2 preserving properties and relations. That is, $e_1 \simeq e_2$ implies $p(e_1)$ iff $p(e_2)$ for each $p \in P$. Also, $e_1 \approx e_1'$ and $e_2 \approx e_2'$ implies $r(e_1,e_1')$ iff $r(e_2,e_2')$ for each $r \in R$. A match represents a common substructure in the relational structures.

This definition will be changed to allow the two relational structures to have a different relationship. For recognition, the structure of models and the structure obtained from the scene being recognized are described in terms of different basic elements. That is, the structure obtained from the scene (called the <u>scene graph</u>) represents the parts of the scene as they actually appear, whereas the structure of models (the <u>graph of models</u>) represents a meta-description of the objects possibly in the scene. Several parts of the scene graph may map into a single node of the graph of models. There is an isomorphism from the scene graph to a structure derived from the graph of models, but not to the graph of models itself. The structure derived from the graph of models is a conventional relational structure with each part of the object described individually, even if the parts have similar descriptions. Relations between the parts are also made explicit.

Thus it is necessary to distinguish three levels in the representation. There is the representation of the actual sense data in the scene graph, there is the structure representing the models of the objects known to the system, and in between there is a structure instantiated from the graph of models to aid in the analysis of the particular scene being studied. The relationship described above for matching relational structures holds between the scene graph and the intermediate structure, but this intermediate structure is only one of many possible such structures that can be instantiated from the graph of models.

Winston (1975), with his TYPICAL-MEMBER labels, went some way towards this position. He did not explore the potential of such a representation, but relied on the conventional structure representation.

3. REPRESENTATION

A representation has been implemented that is simple to construct and is powerful enough to describe a large class of objects. The representation is based on primitives and relations. Ideally, primitives could be descriptions of any scene elements that are easy to extract, have a canonical description, and have sufficient variation to allow the representation of an interesting class of objects. A small set of easily calculated relations is desired that succinctly describe the relationships between instances of the primitives in an object.

Relations are stored as schemata; their arguments are abbreviated surface descriptions instead of full surface descriptions. The form of the representation is a network whose nodes are primitives, and in which an arc is drawn between nodes if a relation is defined between the primitives at those nodes. Arcs are labelled with the set of relation schemata that justifies them. An object will be described by some set of these nodes and arcs, but many nodes and arcs in the network may be common to several object models. A primitive is represented by a single node, so should an instance of a primitive occur in several objects, the models produced from these objects would share that node. In addition, models may share relations, should common primitives occur in similar relationships in both models. The only thing that two models may not share is a name.

The network for the two objects of Figure 2 is given in Figure 3. The objects are a cube (called "cube"), and a rectangular parallelepiped ("rect") whose model shares a side with the cube.

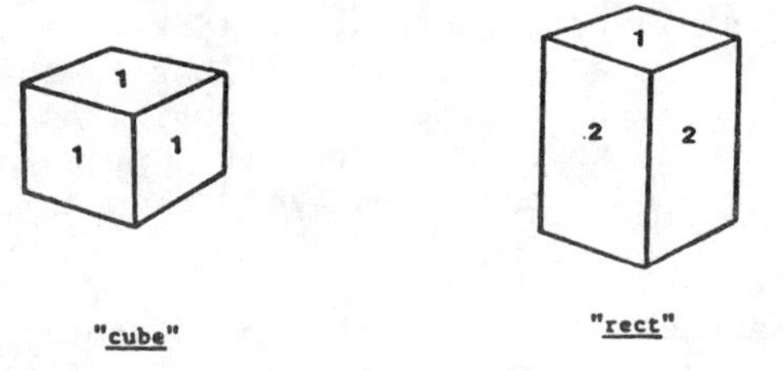

Figure 2

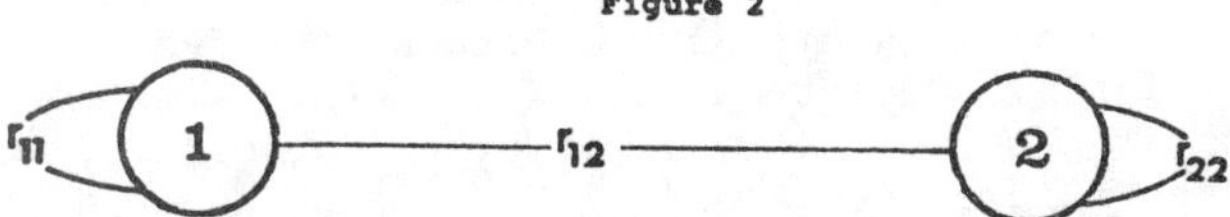

r_{11} = {<RELANGLE P1 P1 90°>, <RELANGLE P1 P1 180°>}

r_{12} = {<RELANGLE P1 P2 90°>}

r_{22} = {<RELANGLE P2 P2 90°>, <RELANGLE P2 P2 180°>}

Figure 3

Definitions

The definitions are of the terms used to describe the representation. They are in terms of labelled graphs.

1. Let $P = \{p_1, p_2, \ldots, p_n\}$ be a set of primitives. Each p_1 forms one (and only one) node of the graph.

2. Let $R = \{r_1, r_2, \ldots, r_m\}$ be a set of relation schemata. Each r_1 is of the form: <function name, $arg_1, arg_2, \ldots, arg_n$, value>. The arguments $arg_1, arg_2, \ldots, arg_n$ are typed variables which may take as values instances of individual elements of P (possibly repeated). The value FALSE (0) is not considered legal for a relational schema. The labels on the arcs of the graph are sets of relation schemata, subsets of R, called label sets.

3. Let $M = \{n_1, n_2, \ldots, n_k\}$ be a set of names of models.

4. The graph obtained from modelling objects is called the graph of models.

5. A model in the system is represented by a subgraph of the graph of models. The nodes in the subgraph are those primitives that occur in the model. The arcs in the subgraph are those that have relation schemata in their label sets that occur in the model. The label set of an arc in the subgraph consists of the subset of relations that occur in the model.

A rich indexing structure is maintained by the representation. Each primitive indexes the models in which it occurs. If a primitive forms part of the description of an object, it must index the model for that object.

Relation schemata index the models in which they occur and the primitives that form their arguments. To test whether or not a relation is satisfied requires finding instances of its arguments, while to derive any benefit from such a test requires that the information obtained be available to the models that can use it.

The models index both the primitives that form their parts and the relation schemata that describe how the parts are related.

4. THE MODELLING PROCESS

4.1 Extraction of surfaces

The implementation discussed here makes use of range data obtained from a triangulation ranging system (Popplestone et al. (1975)). An object to be modelled is placed on a turntable (Figure 4). The object is passed under a plane of light, and scanned at fixed intervals. When the scan is complete, the object is rotated by a known amount, and scanned again. This process is repeated until all desired views of the object have been scanned (Figure 5).

Figure 4

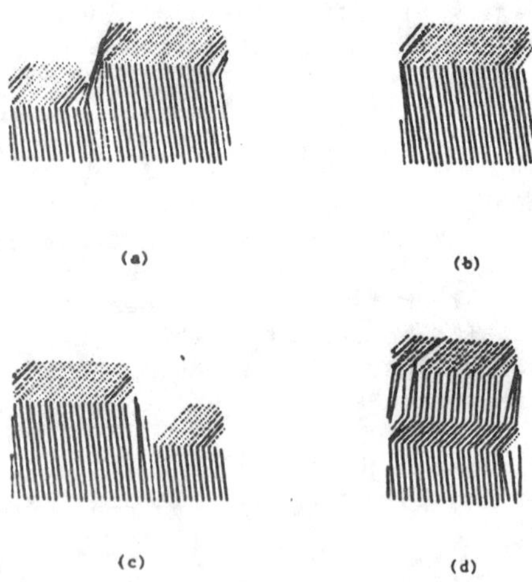

Figure 5

The result of processing the data obtained in this way is a set S of surfaces, each described by:

1. The surface type (plane or cylinder).

2. The equation of the surface.

3. The three-dimensional coordinates of the centroid of the surface.

4. The radius of a cylindrical surface.

5. The segments of lines that make up the surface.

Some further processing is done on this information before a model is produced. The aim of this processing is to derive simple, non-coordinate-specific information about the surface, which can be used to form primitives. The information chosen is a measure of the dimensions of the surface.

4.2 Primitives and relations

From the set S of surfaces, a list P' of surface descriptions is constructed, one for each surface. Elements of P' may be repeated. The elements of P' will be used to construct the set P of nodes in the graph of models. The descriptions are constructed from the surfaces by extracting the type of surface and its dimensions. All coordinate-specific information is discarded when forming the descriptions. This information is, however, still available to the rest of the system, and will be used to construct the relation schemata. At the same time, the set

$$SP = \{\langle s,p \rangle \; s \in S, p \in P\}$$

of pairs of surfaces and their associated descriptions is constructed. SP links the surfaces in the image with the descriptions in the model world. The three-dimensional positions of the surfaces and their relationships with other surfaces will be used in building the model.

The next step is to determine the relationships between the surfaces in the object being modelled. In the implementation, relations have been restricted to having at most two arguments, for ease of acquisition and because the number of relation schemata produced for n-ary relations can be very large. In practice, binary relations are adequate for the domains under consideration, although Shneier (1978) presents an argument to show that this is not true in general.

The choice of the relations with which to model an object is left to the user, who lists the names of the functions to be applied at the time the model is constructed. The use of a relation requires that an executable function exist which can calculate values for instances of its arguments. A number of different functions have been used in experiments. Some of these are:

ADJACENT: If the light plane in some subscan passed over both surfaces at the same time, and the line segments produced by the light plane were touching, then the surfaces are adjacent.

RELDIST: The distance from the centroid of one surface to that of another.

RELANGLE: The angle between two surfaces, from the viewpoint of the first.

Whereas ADJACENT is a true relation, in that it has values "true" or "false," RELDIST and RELANGLE can have a large number of values, each of which will give rise to a new schema when it is encountered in an object being modelled. (There will not, however, be an infinite number of such values, since a range of values which are sufficiently similar will be grouped into an equivalence class.)

The schemata are constructed as follows. For each pair of surfaces in S, the chosen set of functions is applied. The result of the application is used as the expected value slot in the schema. The name of the function that was applied is the value of the function name slot, while the argument slots are filled by the descriptions that correspond to the surfaces used in the evaluation. The correspondence is obtained from the set SP of pairs of surfaces and their descriptions. Using abbreviated descriptions, rather than full surface descriptions, generalizes the relations to make them valid for all surfaces that match the abbreviated descriptions. If the value of the function is FALSE (0), a schema is not constructed.

4.3 Producing the graph of models

At this stage there is

1. A list P' of surface descriptions.
2. A set of relation schemata.
3. A model name.

This information must be integrated into the graph of models. Any new information should be retained, but duplication or spurious arcs should not be introduced.

Each of the descriptions in P' is matched against the primitives in P, the set of nodes of the graph of models. Only if there is no match (i.e. if a description is sufficiently different) is a new primitive node created for the description and added to P. Primitives are described in exactly the same way as surface descriptions, but there is only one primitive with a particular description. The result is a set $P \cup P'$ of primitives. Matching requires that the surface types be the same in the primitives and the surface descriptions, and that the dimensions be within some fixed tolerance of each other (currently, dimensions are allowed to vary by about 20% before the match fails).

When a surface description matches with a primitive already in the graph, the values of the primitive in the graph are updated. The mean of each description in the surface and the primitive becomes the dimension for the primitive in the graph.

The name of the model is added to the set of names if it is not already a member. The new set of relation schemata is added to the set R of schemata that already exist as follows. If a new schema is not already a member of R, it is added to R, and indexes only the new model. If a relation scheme already exists in R, it is not duplicated. Instead, the schema is altered so that it indexes the new model in addition to any others it might already index. The model indexes the primitives and relation schemata that occur in it, and the primitives index the new model.

4.4 Example

Figure 4 shows a picture of a toy car resting on the turntable. The car was scanned by the ranger, rotated through 90 degrees, and scanned again. This process was repeated four times, giving four views, each perpendicular to its predecessor. The four views cover all surfaces of the car except its base (Figure 5).

After scanning the car, the range map produced from the scans is processed to find the surfaces of the car. There are seven of these, corresponding to the roof, two sides, back, front, windshield, and bonnet of the car. Some of these surfaces were visible in more than one view of the car. The roof appeared in all four scans, and the bonnet in three (Figure 5). Notice that the sides of the car appear smooth because the axle holes were not large enough to be perceived by the ranger.

From the set of surfaces, the program must produce a description of the car. To be able to do this, three pieces of information are necessary. The first is a name for the object--it will be called "CAR". The second requirement is a file containing the surface data, and the third requirement is a list of functions to be applied to pairs of surfaces to produce the relation schemata. In this example, a single function that finds ADJACENT relationships between surfaces will be used.

The first thing that the program does is to work out descriptions for each surface. It finds the type of the surface (in this example, all surfaces are planes) and two numbers that describe the dimensions of the surface.

When the program tries to find the dimensions of the roof of the car, it discovers that there are several views of the surface, that is, the roof was scanned more than once by the ranger. Each of these views is processed separately, and the results are merged. The bonnet of the car is treated similarly.

Having described the surfaces, the next stage is to construct the relational structure to describe the object. First, the program examines the surface description. If two descriptions are similar, they are represented by a single primitive node (PRIMITIVE) in the graph of models. In the example, three primitives are found to be sufficient to describe the seven surfaces. This is less than half the number that would be required by a conventional representation, illustrating the compactness of the representation. The three primitives describe the following surfaces:

Primitive P1 describes the roof and back of the car.

Primitive P2 describes the windshield, bonnet, and front of the car.

Primitive P3 describes the two sides of the car.

The dimensions stored for each of the primitives are the means of the dimensions of each surface that matched with the primitive. In addition to describing the surfaces, the primitives also index the model CAR of which they are parts.

The next step in building the model is to link the primitive nodes by means of ADJACENT relation schemata. An arc is constructed between two nodes if <u>any</u> of the surfaces described by one of the nodes is adjacent to <u>any</u> of the surfaces described by the other node. Thus, the side of the car is adjacent to the back of the car, giving rise to the schema <ADJACENT P1 P3 1>. The side of the car is also adjacent to the roof of the car, but this gives rise to the same schema, because the roof and the back are described by the same primitive and one schema is used to represent both relationships. All pairs of surfaces are examined, and five relation schemata are found sufficient to describe the relationships between the surfaces in the car.

The three primitives and five relation schemata, together with the name of the car, are all the information needed to model the car (Figure 6).

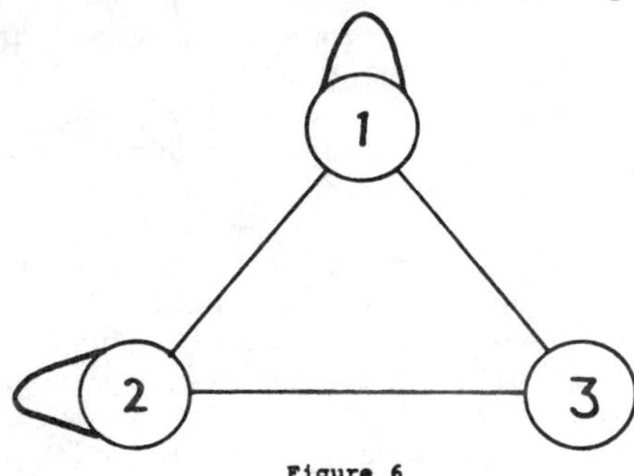

Figure 6

Note that the bottom of the car was not scanned, and so does not appear in the model. To incorporate it, two sets of scans would be necessary. The model as shown would first be constructed, and then another set of views of the car, this time on its side or its roof, would be produced. Presenting the modeller with the new set of views and the old object name would result in the model for CAR being updated to include the new surface and any new relations that were discovered.

The situation is more complex when several objects are modelled. If the descriptions of some of the surfaces of an object being modelled match with primitives already in the graph of models, the new model will share that primitive in the graph. The node is made to index the new model in addition to any others it already indexes. Similarly, relation schemata may be shared by several models, and must be indexed accordingly.

5. DISCUSSION

The advantages of the representation are as follows. The representation is compact because nodes are shared by parts of several objects. This allows the space required to store models to be reduced, and has valuable implications for recognition. Models can be constructed easily from visual data, and new models can be integrated into the network without affecting those models already in existence.

Because of the sharing in the structure, all models that are described by a part of the structure are made available simultaneously when that part of the structure is accessed. Instead of matching with each model individually, all of them are available at once and the work that is done to discriminate between models can be tailored by the context. This allows less work to be done when a scene is analyzed.

The representation is flexible. It was easy to change the domain to which the system was applied from three-dimensional vision to one-dimensional spelling correction without changing the form of the representation. It is also possible to describe objects within a domain in different terms.

The ability to compare descriptions is one of the criteria for a useful recognition. In the past, objects have each been described separately and compared by finding correspondences between two structures. In the representation presented here, a single structure is shared by all models, with parts of models that are similar being represented by the same part of the structure. Thus, instead of painfully comparing two structures and finding points of correspondence, the single structure can be examined and similarities and differences between object models can be found immediately. Similarities are indicated by shared structure, and differences are indicated by structure that is not shared.

An important requirement for a representation and recognition system, especially one that is to work with man-made objects, is an ability to deal with symmetry. Many objects have some degree of symmetry, and this has led to problems in previous systems. The difficulty arises when a symmetrical object is matched with its model description. It is not clear what parts of the object should be matched with what parts of the model because there is no unique way of matching when several parts have the same description. This problem has either been avoided by not allowing symmetric objects in the domain (Underwood and Coates (1972)), or it has been solved by resorting to finding all possible correspondences between the object and its model and choosing one of them (e.g., Barrow et al. (1972)). When there is a large amount of symmetry, as in a cube, this method can be very expensive. Using the representation in this paper, the problem of symmetry disappears. There is a single description for all the similar parts, so that there is no confusion when matching. Symmetric objects can thus be recognized with the same effort as non-symmetric objects.

The representation has been successfully applied to two domains. The first, machine vision, used surface descriptions as primitives, and relations like adjacency. The second, spelling correction, used letters as primitives and ordering relations like "precedes" and "follows". Shneier (1978) provides a full discussion of each domain. He also discusses an elegant recognition algorithm that takes advantage of the form of the representation in its analysis. The modelling and recognition systems have been fully implemented and tested. Their performance underlines the advantages of the compact representation.

6. CONCLUSIONS

This paper has presented a new representation that takes advantage of similarities in the descriptions of objects. By sharing descriptions that are common within models and across models, a compact representation was obtained that had numerous advantages over other representations. The system was implemented and applied to two domains, those of machine vision and spelling correction. In both cases, it proved possible to represent the objects in the domain in a compact manner that was especially useful for recognition. The simplification of the representation is a direct result of a generalized concept of model.

ACKNOWLEDGEMENTS

I am grateful to my colleagues in the Department of Artificial Intelligence at the University of Edinburgh for their assistance in this work, to Azriel Rosenfeld for his comments and suggestions on the form of this paper, and to the University of Witwatersrand who provided financial support.

REFERENCES

A. P. Ambler, H. G. Barrow, C. M. Brown, R. M. Burstall, and R. J. Popplestone (1975): A Versatile System for Computer-Controlled Assembly. Artificial Intelligence, Vol. 6, No. 2, pp. 129-156.

H. G. Barrow, A. P. Ambler, and R. M. Burstall (1972): Some Techniques for Recognizing

Structure in Pictures. In: Frontiers of Pattern Recognition. Ed. Watanabe. New York, Academic Press.

H. G. Barrow and R. J. Popplestone (1971): Relational Descriptions in Picture Processing. Machine Intelligence 6. Eds. B. Meltzer and D. Michie. Edinburgh University Press, pp. 377-396.

G. Falk (1972): Interpretation of Line Data as a Three-Dimensional Scene. Artificial Intelligence, Vol. 3, No. 2, pp. 101-144.

G. R. Grape (1973): Model Based (Intermediate Level) Computer Vision. Ph.D. Thesis, Department of Computer Science, Stanford University.

R. J. Popplestone, C. M. Brown, A. P. Ambler, and G. F. Crawford (1975): Forming Models of Plane- and Cylinder-Faceted Bodies from Light Stripes. Proc. 4th IJCAI, Tblisi, pp. 664-668.

M. O. Shneier (1977): Recognition Using Semantic Constraints. Proc. 5th IJCAI, Cambridge, Mass., pp. 585-589.

M. O. Shneier (1978): Object Representation and Recognition in Machine Vision. Ph.D. Thesis, Department of Artificial Intelligence, University of Edinburgh.

S. A. Underwood and C. L. Coates (1972): Visual Learning and Recognition by Computer. TR 123, Information Systems Research Laboratory, University of Texas at Austin.

D. Waltz (1975): Understanding Line-Drawings of Scenes with Shadows. In: The Psychology of Computer Vision, Ed. P. H. Winston. New York, McGraw-Hill.

P. H. Winston (1975): Learning Structural Descriptions from Examples. In: The Psychology of Computer Vision, Ed. P. H. Winston. New York, McGraw-Hill.

Overview of the Programmer's Apprentice

Charles Rich, Howard E. Shrobe, and Richard C. Waters

Artificial Intelligence Laboratory and the Laboratory for Computer Science
Massachusetts Institute of Technology
Cambridge, Mass. 02139

ABSTRACT - This note gives an overview of the Programmer's Apprentice system being developed at MIT. This system is conceived as being midway between an aid to improved programming methodology and an automatic programming system. A programmer and the apprentice work together throughout all phases of the development and maintenance of a program. The programmer does the difficult parts of design and implementation, while the apprentice acts as a junior partner and critic, keeping track of details and assisting the programmer wherever possible. A key feature of the apprentice is its ability to understand the logical structure of a program so that it can interact with the programmer in a meaningful way.

1. Introduction

The Programmer's Apprentice (PA) is an interactive system for helping programmers manage the complexity of evolutionary programming. It is being designed and implemented at MIT by Charles Rich, Howard Shrobe and Richard Waters (only some of the modules in the system are actually running at the present time). The intent is that the programmer will do the hard parts of design and implementation, while the PA will act as a junior partner and critic, keeping track of details and assisting the programmer in the documentation, debugging, and modification of his program. In order to cooperate with the programmer in this fashion, the PA must be able to "understand" what is going on. The central achievement of the Programmer's Apprentice project has been the development of a "plan" representation which facilitates the cataloging of basic programming knowledge.

The "plan" for a program is a network of operations interconnected by data flow and control flow links. This representation is a better vehicle for expressing the logical interrelationships in a program than the programming language source code. A plan is segmented into a hierarchy of subsegments, each corresponding to a conceptual unit of behavior. The plan specifies how each non-terminal segment is constructed out of the segments contained within it. Explicit dependency links are used to record the goal-subgoal and prerequisite relationships between a segment and its subsegments. Taken together, these links summarize how the behavior of a segment follows from the behavior of its subsegments and the way they are connected by control flow and data flow. A final aspect of the plan representation is that there may be more than one plan for a program or part of a program, representing different points of view.

The plan representation is also used in the PA system to construct a library of common algorithms and data structure implementations. In general, the PA attempts to understand a programmer's code in terms of these familiar plans.

This report describes research done at the Artificial Intelligence Laboratory of the Massachusetts Institute of Technology. Support for the laboratory's artificial intelligence research is provided in part by the Advanced Research Projects Agency of the Department of Defense under Office of Naval Research contract N00014-75-C-0643.

2. A Scenario of Use of the PA

The following imagined dialogue between a programmer and the PA is presented in order to illustrate the intended operation of the system. (Comments discussing the scenario are printed in italics.) The scenario illustrates the following basic areas in which the PA can assist a programmer:

1) DOCUMENTATION: The PA provides automatic, permanent, and in-depth documentation of the program. The PA remembers not only explicit commentary supplied by the programmer with the code, but also a substantial body of derived information describing the logical structure underlying the program.

2) DEBUGGING: Any discrepancy between the PA's understanding of the programmer's intent and the actual operation of the program is reported to the programmer as a potential bug.

3) MANAGING EVOLUTION: Based on its knowledge of the logical relationships between parts of a program, the PA is able to determine what parts of a program are affected by a proposed design change. It can use this information to warn the programmer of impending difficulties.

The scenario traces the design, coding, and subsequent modification of a program which deletes an entry from a hash table. The scenario picks up in the middle of a session at a point where the programmer has already made many design choices and told them to the PA. In particular, he has stated the input-output specifications for the subroutine DELETE and chosen the basic data structures to be used. The hash table is implemented as an array of linked lists called "buckets". Each of the entries in a bucket is a dotted-pair whose CAR is the key for the entry.

Programmer: The plan for the routine DELETE has three main steps: the first one hashes the input key to get an index; the second one fetches the bucket corresponding to that index from the table; and the third splices out the entry in the bucket whose key part is equal to the input key.

[The only feature of this scenario which is not a current research goal of the Programmer's Apprentice project is the use of natural English dialogue. Although the system should be able to support a sophisticated natural language "front-end", no effort has been expended in this direction to date.

The PA uses the programmer's outline of the design in order to build a plan representing the program's intended structure. References to basic programming techniques such as "splicing out" (deleting elements from a linked list) trigger the retrieval of plans from the plan library.]

PA: I think that there is a bug in this design. If the input key is equal to the key part of the first entry in a bucket then the first entry will not be spliced out.

[*After constructing a plan, the PA uses its reasoning abilities in order to check for bugs. Above, the PA finds a bug and reports it to the programmer, framing its response in terms of the "splicing" plan. In general, it is the responsibility of the programmer to supply corrections.*]

Programmer: Modify the plan as follows. Add a final step which compares the bucket after splicing with the bucket before splicing and stores the new bucket in the table under the index if the two initial cells are not identical.

PA: OK, the plan now seems correct.

[*The programmer then types in the code for* DELETE.]

Programmer:

```
(defun delete (key) ; hash table delete routine.
  (prog (bkt1 bkt2)
        (setq bkt1 (tbl (hash key))
              bkt2 (bkt-delete key bkt1))
        (cond ((not (eq bkt1 bkt2))
               ; check if first entry deleted.
               (store (tbl (hash key)) bkt1)))))
```

[*The PA analyzes the code written by the programmer in order to construct a plan for it. Comparing this plan with the plan directly described by the programmer, the PA discovers an implementation bug. The bug is so simple that the PA can suggest a correction.*]

PA: This code is not consistent with your plan. When the first entry is deleted, the code stores the bucket before splicing, rather than the bucket after splicing. Did you mean: "(STORE (TBL (HASH KEY)) BKT2)"?

Programmer: Yes, fix the code.

[*Some time later it is necessary to make a modification to the original design. The PA helps the (perhaps new) programmer maintain consistency.*]

Programmer: I want to make a change in the representation of buckets in the hashing programs. A bucket now has two parts: a count field and a list of entries as before. The count field will contain an integer equal to the length of the list of entries. Let a bucket be a dotted-pair whose CAR is the count and whose CDR is the list of entries.

[*The PA inspects the logical dependencies in the plans for the programs being worked on in order to determine the specific ways in which the programs can be affected by the proposed changes.*]

PA: The proposed change will affect DELETE as follows: After the bucket is fetched, it is passed to BKT-DELETE which does the actual deletion. However, BKT-DELETE requires a list of entries while in this new implementation, a bucket is no longer just a list of entries.

Programmer: Change the specifications of BKT-DELETE so that it expects as input a bucket of the new type, rather than a list of entries.

[*... and so the session continues with the PA looking over the programmer's shoulder.*]

3. Current Status of the PA

Rich and Shrobe [1] laid out the basic idea of a plan and the initial design of the PA. Since that time Rich, Shrobe and Waters have been working together on further aspects of the theory along with design and implementation of the PA system.

Rich's work [2] centers on the plan library. He is using the plan representation to formalize a number of common techniques in non-numerical programming involving trees, lists, and arrays. He is also studying the use of this library in the PA system for analyzing already-written programs and to provide high level abstractions for interactive program synthesis.

Shrobe [3] has implemented a deductive module, called REASON, which can reason about programs represented by plans. REASON is a dependency based system which maintains an explicit record of its control information within the same formalism as is used to represent facts. An accompanying article in these proceedings describes how REASON reasons about destructive modifications to complex and potentially shared data structures.

Waters [4] has implemented a system which can analyze the code for a program and produce a structured plan for the entire program. The basic idea behind Waters' work (which is described in detail in an accompanying article in these proceedings) is that plans for most programs are built up in a small number of stereotyped ways, and that features in the code for a program can be used to determine the structure of the plan for the program.

Our goal for the immediate future is to construct a prototype system which exhibits the kind of behavior shown in the scenario. To do this, an interactive module must be built, and the modules which have already been constructed must be connected together into an integrated system. Looking further ahead, additional modules (such as a simple program synthesis module, and one dealing with efficiency issues) will be added to the PA, and the existing ones strengthened so that the PA can take over more responsiblity from the human programmer.

REFERENCES

[1] C. Rich & H.E. Shrobe, "Initial Report on a Lisp Programmer's Apprentice", IEEE Trans. on Software Engineering, SE-4, No. 6, November, 1978.

[2] C. Rich, "A Library of Programming Plans with Applications to Automated Analysis, Synthesis and Verification of Programs", forthcoming PhD thesis, MIT AI Lab, 1979.

[3] H.E. Shrobe, "Reasoning and Logic for Complex Program Understanding", MIT/AI/TR-503, June 1979.

[4] R.C. Waters, "Automatic Analysis of the Logical Structure of Programs", MIT/AI/TR-492, April 1979.

Dependency Directed Reasoning in the Analysis of Programs Which Modify Complex Data Structures

Howard Elliot Shrobe
Artificial Intelligence Laboratory and Laboratory for Computer Science
Massachusetts Institute of Technology
545 Technology Square
Cambridge, Massachusetts 02139

Abstract

REASON is the deductive component of a larger program understanding system called the Programmer's Apprentice [1]. REASON's key features are : (1) Its use of the Truth Maintenance System [2] to record and manipulate the justifications for its deductions, (2) A discipline of explicitly recording control information in a form which may be manipulated by the reasoning system itself and (3) Its goal of producing a a "common sense" explanation of how a program functions, as opposed to the formal proofs common in verification. One particularly difficult problem which such a system must face is the analysis of program which allow destructive modifications of potentially shared data structures. Our observation is that experienced programmers tend to make simplifying assumptions when analyzing such programs; even if these assumptions are found to be false they can be useful in guiding a more accurate analysis. This paper shows how REASON mimics this behavior of expert programmers.

Introduction

REASON is the deductive component of the programmer's apprentice system, a "program understander" which is not mainly concerned with providing a rigorous proof of a program's correctness, but rather with giving a "common sense" explanation of how the intended behavior of the whole program results from the known (or assumed) behaviors of its parts. REASON is able to analyze the effect of a proposed change to a program, viewing the modification as a pertubation rather than as a whole new program requiring a new proof.

One particularly difficult problem which REASON faces is the analysis of programs which allow destructive modifications to complex and shared data structures. Apparently simple operations can produce non-trivial results; a modification of one part of a structure can change properties of the whole structure. Thus, in reasoning about the results of a particular action, a program analyzer must assess what properties besides those explicitly stated will also change. Suzuki [3] attacked the problem of verifying PASCAL programs which allow such opertions; however, the formal approach of his work is not easily adapted to the interactive, and common sense context of the programmer's apprentice.

This research was conducted at the Artificial Intelligence Laboratory of the Massachusetts Institute of Technology. Support for the Laboratory's artificial Intelligence research is provided in part by the Advanced Research Projects Agency of the Department of Defense under Office of Naval Research contract number N00014-75-C-0643, and in part by NSF grant MCS77-04828.

This general problem of knowing what changes and what remains the same has been termed the "frame problem" in [4]. In the case of common sense reasoning, one has to assume that most things don't change unless there is reason to believe otherwise. When such assumptions lead to trouble, a belief revision process is necessary. In the case of program understanding, similar techniques can also be applied. Consider the following procedure which deletes all elements of a list which are also members of a hash table.

```
(defun remove (list-1 hashtable)
    (mapc
      '(lambda (x)
                 (and (lookup x hashtable)
                      (setq list-1 (delete x list-1))))
       list-1))
```

This program has a bug which few programmers (even experts) spot when examining the code. (The reader might try to figure out what the problem is now before proceeding).
Suppose that the hashtable is implemented as an array of lists (the lists are called buckets) as is typically done in LISP. Suppose also that the parameter list-1 is bound to a list which shares some structure with one of the buckets of the table. In this case the above program will have the unintended effect of removing elements from the hashtable as well. This is because DELETE operates by side effect.

Most readers will feel cheated by this example. It doesn't seem fair to bring in the issue of structure sharing out of the blue. Quite so. This illustrates a difference between formal verification and common sense reasoning: In a verification system one must consider the most general case of a program's behavior; this is typically done by considering all input parameters of the program to be objects which *might* share structure. This forces the verifier to consider all cases of possible identity. However, the very fact that the example above seems like a trick indicates that this is not the way programmers routinely think about their code. Quite the contrary, the *tacit calculus* of expert programmers assumes that, unless otherwise stated, sharing of structure does not take place.

There is a good reason for this tacit calculus; in common sense reasoning and also in engineering disciplines we find that there is a trade off between ease of comprehension and accuracy. Simplifying assumptions are made to reduce the cognitive complexity of a problem to the point where a solution can be developed. In general the simplifying assumptions are chosen so that the solution reached is "close enough". In those rare cases where the solution is not close enough, it is debugged; however, it still plays a guiding role in the formation of the improved solution.

Our observations above indicate that programmers use more than one strategy for analyzing the effect of an action. In the more reckless strategy, one assumes that things are not changed unless there is reason to believe they do. This has the advantage of being right most of the time, requiring less effort, and allowing the programmer to form a "first order" theory of what the code does. In the more careful strategy, one does the opposite, assuming things are effected unless evidence to the contrary exists. This, has the advantage of never allowing a false conclusion to be drawn, but the disadvantage of requiring much greater effort, to the extent that it can prevent one from forming a "first order" understanding.

REASON is designed to conduct both of these forms of reasoning. More significantly, however, it is a dependency based system which can use information gathered during the "common sense" analysis to guide the "formal" analysis. Frequently, all one desires from the formal analysis is the statement that there are "screw cases" in which the behavior inferred during the informal analysis no longer obtains.

The Dependency Based Formalism

REASON is implemented in a variant of the language AMORD [5], a formalism which records both facts and the reasons for believing them. All goal states and the reasons for their existence are recorded within the same formalism. *Justifications* are a crucial form of information in REASON. When an assertion is entered into REASON's data base, it is always accompanied by a justification explaining why the new assertion is believed. To make this convenient, each assertion is assigned a unique "fact-name". For example:

```
Assertion       System-Supplied-Fact-Name

(< X Y)                   F-1
(< Y Z)                   F-2
```

The transitivity rule can be applied to F-1 and F-2 and a newly deduced fact entered into the system using the ASSERT function:

```
(Assert '(< X Z) '(Transitivity F-1 F-2))
```

ASSERT takes two arguments: the new assertion to be added to the data base and the justification for the assertion; a justification is a list whose first element is a justification name and whose remaining elements are the fact-names upon which the new assertion depends.

REASON makes deductions using *rules* which consist of two elements: a *trigger set* and a *body*. The trigger set is a list of patterns each of which has two parts: a fact-name variable and an assertion pattern. The body is a LISP expression which is evaluated in an environment in which the variables of the patterns are bound to the objects which they matched. The following is a fairly typical REASON rule:

```
(rule ((:f (Rest :list-1 :list-2))
       (:g (Member :list-2 :obj-1)))
      (assert '(member :list-1 :obj-1)
              '(List-Membership :f :g)))
```

Variables are indicated by a leading colon (:).

In these triggers, the leading single variable (:f or :g) is the fact-name variable, the remaining part of each trigger (Rest :list-1 :list-2) or (Member :list-2 :obj-1)) is the assertion pattern. A rule is applicable if all its patterns are matched by facts which have currently valid justifications (see below). The body is then executed in the environment of the match.

As each trigger is matched to an assertion, the fact-name variable of that trigger is bound to the fact-name of the matched assertion. This allows the body of the rule to refer to its triggering facts. In particular, assert statements in the body of the rule may include a justification mentioning these facts.

Assertions have one of two statuses in REASON, they are either *in* or *out*. A fact which is *in* is believed to be true. An assertion whose negation is *in* is believed to be false. If both an assertion and its negation are *in* then the data base is contradictory and corrective action is required. If neither the assertion nor its negation is *in*, then the fact is simply unknown.
The meaning of justifications such as the transitivity justification shown above is that whenever F-1 and F-2 are *in* then F-3 should also be *in*. If for some reason either F-1 or F-2 became *out*, then F-3 would lack support and would also become *out*. The *in*ing and *out*ing of facts is managed by the Truth Maintainence System [2] which ensures that no fact is in unless it has well founded support.

It is frequently necessary to *assume* that some fact holds even though no reason exists for believing it. This is often done in hypothetical reasoning as when one proves that A implies B by assuming A and deriving B. One assumes a fact because there is no apparent reason not to believe it; thus, the assumed fact is justified by making it depend on the *out*ness of its negation. This is done by the function ASSUME:

```
(Assume '(Made-of The-Moon Green-Cheese) '(Bill F-23))
```

which states that the system will believe that the moon is made of green cheese as long as it has no reason to believe that the moon is not made of green cheese and as long as it believes fact F-23. The function ASSUME builds a justifiction which has two parts: A list of assertions upon whose *in*ness the fact depends and a list of assertions upon whose *out*ness the fact depends. When the above ASSUME form is invoked it creates the assertion:

```
(Not (Made-of The-Moon Green-Cheese))        F-1001
```

and then justifies its argument assertion by stating that it depends on F-1001's being *out* and on F-23's being *in*.

```
F-1002  (Made-of The-Moon Green-Cheese) (Bill (F-23) (F-1001))
```

where the first list in the justification is the list of facts whose *in*ness supports F-2 and the second list is the *out* list. Whenever an assertion changes its status, the Truth Maintenance system propagates the change until only assertions with well-founded support remained *in*. It is, therefore, always safe to make an assumption since if this introduces an inconsistency, the TMS will cause the improperly assumed fact and all other facts which depend upon it to go *out*.

Reasoning About Simple Side-effects

A program segment is thought of as forming a *transition* between its input and output *situations*. Situations are representations of the state of affairs which obtain at a particular point of the computation. When appropriate, assertions may be situationally tagged to indicate at what points of the computation they are true. For example, to state that the first element of List-1 is Obj-22 when Segment-41 is entered we would assert:

```
(Input-Situation Segment-41 Situation-1)
((First List-1 Obj-22) Situation-1)
```

A side-effect is indicated as follows:

```
(Side-effect <object> <in-sit> <out-sit> <new-fact>)
```

Which says that the <object> has been subjected to a side-effect during the transition from the <in-sit> to the <out-sit> with the result that <new-fact> is made true in the <out-sit>. The new fact can be any relation (primitive or not). Side-effect processing consists of deducing which properties can safely be moved along the transition from <in-sit> to <out-sit> safely; I refer to this process as *transition analysis*. My general approach of explicitly recording dependencies dictates that REASON should provide a justification whenever it decides to move a fact across a transition. Similarly, if it decides not to move a fact it should justify this decision as well. These recorded dependencies allow REASON to make an initial decision based on a cursory analysis of the circumstances, while still reserving for itself the option of reconsidering in more detail at a later time. If it should reconsider, the recorded dependencies can rapidly indicate which properties depend on the simplifying assumptions of the cursory analysis.

The basic protocol is as follows: An assertion in the input situation of a transition can be moved to the output situation of the transition only if there is an explicit assertion declaring it *safe* to do so. In phase one of the analysis, simple rules are run to find reasons for not moving a fact. If such cause is found, these rules assert that it is *unsafe* to move the fact. At the end of this process each assertion is asserted to be safe to move; however, the justification for this safe assertion depends on the *out*ness of the corresponding unsafe assertion. Thus, if any reason for considering the assertion unsafe had been found, the unsafe assertion will be *in*, causing the safe assertion to be *out*. If at the end of this process a safe assertion is *in* for a particular fact, then the fact will be asserted in the output situation with its justification pointing to the safe assertion. The following rules carry out these operations:

```
The Default Assumer for the Careful Protocol
(rule ((:f (side-effect :object :in-sit :out-sit :new-fact))
       (:g (:old-fact :in-sit))
       (:h (transition :in-sit :out-sit)))
      (assume '(not (safe :g))
              '(safety-first :f :g :h)))

The Default Assumer for the Fast and Dirty Protocol
(rule ((:f (side-effect :object :in-sit :out-sit :new-fact))
       (:g (:old-fact :in-sit))
       (:h (transition :in-sit :out-sit)))
      (assume '(safe :g :in-sit :out-sit)
              '(reckless-abandon :f :g :h)))

The Safe Fact Mover
(rule ((:f (safe :old-fact :in-sit :out-sit))
       (:old-fact (:fact :in-it))
       (:g (transisiton :in-sit :out-sit)))
      (Assert '(:fact :out-sit)
              '(safe-from-side-effect :f :g)))
Make The Side-effect Appear In The New Situation
(rule ((:f (side-effect :object :in-sit :out-sit :new-fact)))
      (assert '(:new-fact :out-sit)
              '(side-effects-happen :f)))
```

where the last of these merely asserts that the relation stated in the side-effect assertion is true in the output situation; this is, of course, independent of the safe assertions.

REASON has a set of rules for determining whether a particular fact is affected by a particular side effect. If the fact is not affected then the rules assert that the fact is *safe-from* this particular side effect (and conversely). If a fact is safe-from all side effects at a particular transition then it is *safe*. The simplest such rule is the rule of direct negation which says that a fact which is explicitly negated by a side-effect is unsafe:

```
(rule ((:f (side-effect :obj :in-sit :out-sit (not :fact)))
       (:g (:fact :in-sit)))
      (Assert '(not (safe-from :f :g))
              '(direct-negation :f :g)))
```

Another simple side-effect rule concerns objects (like records) which are composite structures with several distinct fields, called *parts*. Suppose that we modify a particular record to change one of its parts to a new value. It follows, that assertions stating the old value of the affected part of the record are not safe from this side effect. However assertions mentioning other fields of the structure are safe.

```
(rule
 ((:f1 (side-effect :object-1 :s-1 :s-2
                    (:new-part-name :object-1 :new-part)))
  (:f2 ((:old-part-name :object-2 :old-part) :s-1)))
 (cond
  ((eq :old-part-name :new-part-name))
  (t
   (assert '(safe-from :f1 :f2)
           '(diff-part-side-effect :f1 :f2)))))
```

The next rule is for side-effects to objects such as arrays which have indexed-parts. Suppose we have an object with an indexed structure (for example, an ARRAY, a HASH-TABLE, or a record structure including an ARRAY) and that this object is modified to change the part indexed by INDEX-0. Also suppose that we have an assertion saying what is the part indexed by INDEX-1. Then, the side-effect should make the assertion unsafe if the two indices are identical and leave it unaffected otherwise, as expressed in the following rule:

```
(rule
 ((:f (side-effect :object :in-sit :out-sit
                   (:ip :object :new-index :new-value)))
  (:i ((:ip :object :old-index :old-value) :in-sit)))
 (assert '(if    ((equal :old-index :new-index) :input-sit)
           then  (not (safe-from :f :i))
           else  (safe-from :f :i))
         '(indexed-part-side-effect :f :i)))
```

Notice that it is altogether possible that neither the premise of the IF-THEN-ELSE, nor its negation are present in the data base and thus, that neither a safe-from assertion nor its negation will be created. In the first pass, "fast and dirty" analysis, this lack of an unsafe assertion will be taken as grounds for assuming that the assertion is safe; it will, therefore, be moved across the transistion. This will not be logically incorrect, since the justifications for the assumption are explicit and can be withdrawn; it is, however, not a very useful strategy. Even for a fast and dirty pass this strategy is a little too dirty. We would rather say that if it is *possible* that the two indices are equal, then we should not consider the assertion SAFE, but should rather do a case analysis, considering separately the two possibilities of equality and non-equality.

Since the conclusion that the assertion is not SAFE is based on the *possibility* that the indices are equal, we need a way of asserting that this possibility exists; this *possibility assertion* can then be included in the justification. I have developed some syntactic mechanisms to facilitate the use of the concept. The starting point is the observation that an assertion is possible as long as its negation is *out*; of course, if the assertion is *in* it is also possible. Thus, the following support structure captures the notion of possibility (the wavy line indicates that the dependency is on the *out*ness of the assertion, this is called non-monotonic support).

```
      F-3   (Possible ((Equal Index-0 Index-1) S-1))

F-2 (Not ((Equal Index-0 Index-1) S-1))

                 F-1 ((Equal Index-0 Index-1) S-1)
```

As a syntactic convenience, I have added an IF-POSSIBLE-THEN-ELSE construct, which is invoked as follows:

```
(If-possible (:f fact-1)
       then body-1
       else body-2)
```

This expression is interpreted in two stages. First the support structure shown above is created for an assetion which states the possibility of FACT-1. If this assertion stays *in*, then BODY-1 will be executed in a binding environment where :F is bound to the possibility assertion for F-1. If the negation of FACT-1 is *in* (i.e. FACT-1 is impossible) then BODY-2 is executed in a binding environment in which :F is bound to the negation of F-1.

Given this, the appropriate body for the rule dealing with side effects to indexed-part stuctures is:

```
(if-possible
 (:f (equal :old-index :new-index) :input-sit)
  then (assert '(not (safe-from :f :i))
               '(careful-indexed-part :f))
  else (assert '(safe-from :f :i)
               '(careful-indexed-part :f)))
```

This says that if it is at all possible that the indices are equal, the system will decide that the indexed-part assertion is not SAFE. If REASON decides that moving this assertion is important it can try backward chaining rules on the IF-THEN-ELSE assertion to create a case analysis.

More Complicated Effects

So far the analysis of side-effects has been quite simple considering only assertions about PARTS and INDEXED-PARTS. These are the most primitive notions in the system However, there are a host of more complex defined notions which have been developed to allow programs to be thought of in more high level terms.

The relations which are used in describing programs are complex in the sense that they are a logical combinaton of assertions which ultimately depend on the PART structure of the objects implementing the more abstract notion. For example, in hashing systems there is a notion of membership in the table which is defined in terms of membership in one (or more) of the INDEXED-PARTS (BUCKETS) of the table. Similarly, since we frequently implement these BUCKETS as LISTS, membership of an object in the BUCKET reduces to whether the object is the FIRST part or a MEMBER of the REST part of the list. Thus, simple side-effects to the part structure of an object can result in side-effects to derived properties of the object. For example, side-effecting a TABLE to set one BUCKET to the EMPTY-LIST will (potentially) delete several members of the table. The processes handling side-effects, therefore, must examine the way in which facts in the input situation of a transition depend on one another and use this as a guide to the transition analysis.

For example, let us define LIST membership in the standard way: an object is a MEMBER of a LIST if it is either the FIRST of the LIST or a MEMBER of the REST of the LIST.

```
(Member list object) <=>  (Or (First List Object)
                              (Member [Rest List] Object))
```

The brackets indicate a *reference expression*; they are read "the object which is ...". REASON extracts the component clauses of the right hand side of this definition, building a network of *potential dependency* assertions, which links assertions to those side-effects which might make them UNSAFE. For example, from the definition for LIST membership we can get the following potential dependency assertions:

```
(potential-dependency (member :list :object-1)
                      (first  :list :object-2))
(potential-dependency (member :list :object-1)
                      (rest :list-1 :list-2))
(potential-dependency (member :list :object)
                      (not (member :list-1 :object)))
```

Potential dependency assertions are the information used to determine that there *might* be a logical connection between a fact and a side-effect. These say that if (1) There is an assertion in the input situation which matches the first pattern and (2) There is a side-effect on the transition which matches the second pattern, then it is *possible* that the assertion is rendered UNSAFE by the side-effect. Notice that in the case of dependencies on many-to-many relations (such as MEMBER) the dependency is on the negation of the relation. If functional relationships (such as PART or INDEXED-PART) assertions are involved, a side-effect asserting a new value for the relation, such as (First List Foo), implicitly negates any previous value of the property, such as (First List Bar); for these relations the dependency pattern is not negated. The network of potential dependency assertions is completed by using a transitivity rule.

The information in the potential dependency assertions is used by a rule which monitors transitions in which facts might be made UNSAFE by a side-effect. If such situations are noticed, the rule asserts that the fact is *possibly-unsafe*. Any fact which is POSSIBLY-UNSAFE is expanded, i.e. the right-hand side of its definition is added to the data base.

```
(rule ((:f (potential-dependency :a :b))
       (:g (side-effect :object :s-in :s-out :b))
       (:h (:a :s-in)))
      (Assert '(possible (not (safe-from !:g !:h)))
              '(pd :f :g :h)))

(Rule ((:h (Possible (not (safe-from :f :g)))))
      (Assert '(Expand :g) '(pd-expand :h)))
```

Two points about these rules for determining potential dependency should be noted. First, these rules only signal the *possibility* that an assertion is affected by a side-effect; it is for other more thorough rules to explore whether or not the assertion actually is SAFE or not. This allows a many layered control structure in which one set of rules notices candidates for examination, and other sets of rules chose to examine these candidates at a level of detail deemed appropriate.

The second point to be made here, is that the potential dependency rules shown so far are actually of the "fast and dirty" variety. Remember that our earlier example showed that different local variable names might, in fact, name the identical object. Usually people rule out this possibility of "aliasing" to facilitate their analysis. However, to be completely accurate one must examine all possibilities.

The careful version of a rule for LIST membership, for example, is:

```
(rule ((:f (side-effect :obj :s-in :s-out (first :obj :new-first)))
       (:g ((member :obj-2 :old-first) :s-in)))
      (If-possible (:h (id :obj :obj-2))
             then (Assert '(possible (not (safe :g from :h)))
                          '(poss-or-se-careful :f :g :h))))
```

Once it has been determined that an assertion is possibly affected by a side-effect it remains to be determined whether the assertion is SAFE or UNSAFE. When a defined relation is possibly unsafe it is expanded into its definition; thus, the only remaining analysis is that associated with the logical connectives. Rules for these connectives are given in [6].

Once an assertion has been determined to be UNSAFE, it is then treated as a side-effect itself. This initiates a consideration of derived side-effects, propagating the side-effect through the various levels of definition.

Reducing Complexity in Side Effect Analysis

Much of the complexity in reasoning about side effects occurs in recursively defined structures which share substructure. Suppose that we know of the existence of two lists, and one of these is modified; given what we have developed so far, we must consider the possibility that this modification will also change some properties of the second list as well. However, if we knew that the two structures were *disjoint*, then this possibility would be eliminated, reducing the complexity considerably. Burstall [7], introduces some techniques for reasoning about side-effects which use this notion of disjointness to advantage. I will extend that notion in this section.

Suppose that we know that LIST-1 and LIST-2 do not share any structure and that one of these lists has an element spliced into it; since neither list can be a sub-list of the other it is not necessary to conduct a thorough investigation as outlined in the preceding sections. It is immediately obvious that the modification to the first list cannot affect the second.

The notion of list-structure can be generalized to that of recursive data structures; having made this generalization we can create a hierarchy of classification for side-effects, properties and the degree of sharing exhibited by recursive structures. It will follow that the level of sharing can limit the degree to which side-effects to one structure can effect properties of the other. Similarly, the classification of properties into levels isolates those at a higher level from less powerful side-effects.

For our purposes a recursive structure can be thought of as a labelled digraph with two distinct types of arcs: those labelled as value arcs and those labelled as structure arcs. The set of objects connected to a node by outgoing structure arcs are called the *immediate children* of the node; the set of objects reachable by outgoing value arcs are called the value set of the node. All immediate children of any node of a recursive data structure must be either terminal or non-terminals of the recursive data type. Value nodes may be objects of any type. Terminal nodes may not have outgoing structure arcs.

Actually, we are not as interested in sharing as in the lack of it: disjointness. We may identify three types of disjointness which have some utility. We have previously defined *structure sharing* as having a node in common. *Structurally disjoint* structures are those which do not share structure. For lists this means that no sublist (the transitive closure of CDR) of the two lists is shared.

Often we will have non-recursive structures such as HASH-TABLES whose parts are recursive structures. For such objects, we define structure sharing in the obvious way: namely two objects share structure if there is a part of the first and a part of the second which share structure. Thus, a HASH-TABLE and a LIST share structure if one of the table's BUCKETS shares structure with the LIST. They are structurally disjoint if there is no BUCKET of the TABLE which shares structure with the LIST.

The next type of sharing is termed *value sharing*. Recall that the nodes of a recursive structure can have parts other than those which represent the immediate children. A list is a recursive structure which has a value at each node called the FIRST. When there is an object which is a value of two recursive structures, we say that there is *value sharing*; conversely, if there is no such object we say that the structures are *value disjoint*. It follows that if two structures are value disjoint, they are also structurally disjoint.

Two objects are *totally disjoint* if (1) The objects are both structurally and value disjoint and (2) All objects pointed to by each node are totally disjoint. It follows that if two RECURSIVE-STRUCTURES are totally disjoint, then side-effects to the one can not effect the other.

Now let us classify side-effects in a manner similar to that used for structure sharing. We call side-effects *strictly structural* if they only affect the immediate children property of some node of the structure. RPLACD is the simplest such side-effect, although LIST-INSERT and LIST-DELETE, etc. are also strictly structural side-effects. Notice that a strictly structural side-effect to one structure will not affect any property of another object from which it is structurally disjoint.

We may also identify *strictly value* side-effects such as RPLACA which only change value properties. If two structures are structurally disjoint, then a strictly value side-effect to one will not affect properties of the other. A *structural side effect* is one which consists only of strictly structural and strictly value side-effects. A SORT program which works by changing both CAR and CDR pointers in a list is an example of a structural side-effect. If two objects are structurally disjoint, a structural side-effect to one will not change any property of the second.

Finally, an *indirect side effect* is one which only changes properties of VALUEs of the RECURSIVE-STRUCTURE. For example, a marking graph traversal procedure which sets the MARK property of the VALUE of each node is such an INDIRECT side-effect procedure. If two objects are VALUE DISJOINT, then INDIRECT side-effects to one will leave properties of the other unchanged.

Finally we come to a classification of properties. We can notice that some properties such as SUBLIST or LENGTH only depend on the recursive structure of the object, and not on the VALUES at each node. We call these *strictly structural properties*. More commonly, properties such as MEMQ, depend both on the recursive structure and on the identity of the various VALUES present at each node, but not on any property or sub-structure of these values; these are called *value dependent* properties. Finally, there are properties which depend both on the structure and on mutable properties of the objects present at each node. MEMBER (as opposed to MEMQ), for example, depends on the structure of the list as well as on the structure of the objects pointed to by the list.

We note that a side-effect at one level can not effect a property of a lower level. For example, a VALUE side effect cannot affect a STRICTLY STRUCTURAL property. An INDIRECT side-effect cannot affect a STRUCTURAL property.

These observations can be summarized by several simple rules of the following form:

```
(rule ((:f1 (Side-effect :obj-1 :s-in :s-out :se))
       (:f2 (Structural-Side-Effect :se))
       (:f3 (Structurally-disjoint :obj-1 :obj-2))
       (:f4 ((:fact :obj-2) :s-in)))
      (Assert (Safe-from :f1 :f4)
              (Structure-disjoint :f1 :f2 :f3 :f4)))
```

```
(rule ((:f1 (Side-effect :obj-1 :s-in :s-out:se))
       (:f2 (Structural-Side-Effect :se))
       (:f3 (Structurally-isolated :obj-2))
       (:f4 ((:fact :obj-2) :s-in)))
      (Assert (Safe-from :f1 :f4)
              (Structure-isolation :f1 :f2 :f3 :f4)))
```

Notice that since these rules assert that a particular property is SAFE, they remove the need to engage in the more complicated analysis shown earlier. A large percentage of side effects have very limited range of effect precisely because there is a strong limit on structure sharing. Thus, most of the time one of the above rules will fire and REASON's work will be done. In some rare cases, the more complex and thorough analysis will be required.

Given these ideas we can extend our fast and dirty protocol for side effect analysis even further. It appears that most programmers assume by default that the inputs to a program segment are structurally disjoint. In our first pass analysis we will assume that all recursive structures are structurally disjoint unless otherwise indicated. This is coded by making rules of the following general form:

```
(rule
 ((:f (side-effect :list-1 :sin :sout :se))
  (:g ((P :list-2) :sin)))
 (if-possible (:h (structurally-disjoint :list-1 :list-2))
        then (assert '(safe-from :f :g)
                     '(loose-living :f :g :h))
        else (assert '(possible (not (safe-from :f :g)))
                     '(careful :f :g :h))))
```

Sussman [8] argues for the importance of "almost correct theories" and debugging as a means of reducing the complexity of problem solving tasks to levels within human limits. My approach to analyzing side effects follows in this tradition. REASON's first pass analysis is not rigorous, but it is useful. Much of the time it just happens to give the right answers (for incorrect reasons). The dependencies recorded during the first pass analysis can help guide an accurate and complete investigation in a second pass analysis if the problem is considered to be worth the effort. Often, however, the first pass analysis is adequate to allow the apprentice to help analyze the consequences of proposed program modifications and to generate high level common sense explanations of the code.

References

[1] Rich, C. and Shrobe, H. [1978], "Initial Report on a LISP Programmer's Apprentice", IEEE Trans. on Soft. Eng., V4 #6, November 1978, pp. 456-467.

[2] Doyle, Jon *Truth Maintenance Systems for Problem Solving*, M.I.T. Artificial Intelligence Laboratory Technical Report 419, January 1978.

[3] Suzuki, N "Automatic Verification of Programs with Complex Data Structures", Stanford AIM-279, February 1976.

[4] McCarthy, J. and Hayes, P. "Some Philosophical Problems from the Standpoint of Artificial Intelligence", Machine Intelligence 4, American Elsevier, N.Y.

[5] deKleer, J., Doyle, J., Steele, G. & Sussman, G.J. "AMORD: Explicit Control of Reasoning", Proceedings of the Symposium on Artificial Intelligence and Programming Languages, August 1977.

[6] Shrobe, Howard *Logic and Reasoning for Complex Program Understanding*, PhD Thesis, MIT, August 1978.

[7] Burstall, R. M. "Some Techniques for Proving Properties of Programs Which Alter Data Structures", Machine Intelligence 7, Edinburgh University Press.

[8] Sussman, G.J. *A Computational Model of Skill Acquisition*, M.I.T. Department of Mathematics Ph.D. Thesis; M.I.T. Artificial Intelligence Laboratory Technical Report 297, August 1973; *A Computer Model of Skill Acquisition*, New York, American Elsiver 1975.

A FRAMEWORK FOR DISTRIBUTED PROBLEM SOLVING

Reid G. Smith

Defence Research Establishment Atlantic
Box 1012
Dartmouth, Nova Scotia, Canada, B2Y 3Z7

Abstract

The contract net framework for distributed problem solving is discussed. Task distribution is viewed as a mutual selection process, a discussion carried on between a node with a task to be executed and a group of nodes that may be able to execute the task. This leads to the use of a control formalism based on a contract metaphor, in which task distribution corresponds to contract negotiation.

The three primary components of the framework are described: communication, control, and knowledge organization. The use of the framework is illustrated for a distributed sensing system. We then discuss suitable applications and limitations of the framework.

1 Distributed Problem Solving

Distributed Problem Solving is the cooperative solution of problems by a decentralized and loosely coupled collection of knowledge-sources (KSs), each of which may reside in its own distinct processor.[1] Decentralized means that both control and data are logically, and sometimes geographically, distributed--there is neither global control nor global data storage. The KSs cooperate to solve problems by sharing tasks and/or results. Loosely coupled means that individual KSs spend the great percentage of their time in computation as opposed to communication. Such problem solvers offer advantages of speed, reliability, extensibility, the ability to handle applications with a natural spatial distribution, and the ability to tolerate errorful data and knowledge. In addition, as a result of their modularity, they offer conceptual clarity and simplicity of design.

[1] This work was supported in part by the Advanced Research Projects Agency under contract MDA 903-77-C-0322, and the National Science Foundation under contract MCS 77-02712. It was carried out on the SUMEX-AIM Computer Facility, supported by the National Institutes of Health under grant RR-00785. This paper is based on work done as part of a Ph.D. dissertation at Stanford University. The contributions of Randall Davis, Bruce Buchanan, and the rest of the staff and students of the Heuristic Programming Project are gratefully acknowledged.

2 The Contract Net Framework

The central result of the research reported here is the contract net framework for problem solving in a distributed processing environment. The framework has three major conceptual components: a control component that specifies the possible modes of interaction between processor nodes; a **knowledge organization** component that specifies how knowledge is organized in individual nodes and distributed throughout the collection of nodes; and a **communication** component that provides the basis for node interaction.

2.1 Communication And Control

2.1.1 Connection And Contract Negotiation

In the design of the communication and control components of the framework, our emphasis to date has been placed on facilitation of **task-sharing** as a means of cooperation for problem solving. The computational load for execution of subtasks of the overall problem is distributed among the nodes. To enable this distribution, there must be a means whereby nodes with tasks to be executed can find other idle nodes with KSs capable of executing those tasks. We call this the **connection problem**. (In centralized problem solvers it is called the **invocation problem**; that is, which KS to invoke at any given time for the execution of a task.) In a distributed problem solver, both sets of nodes can proceed simultaneously, engaging each other in a process of negotiation to solve the connection problem. Task distribution can thus be considered as a process of contract negotiation, or mutual selection based on a two-way transfer of information. This process gives rise to the name--the **contract net framework** [Smith, 1978b].

The collection of nodes is referred to as a contract net and the execution of a task is dealt with as a contract between two nodes. Thus, each node in the net takes on one of two roles related to the execution of an individual task: manager or contractor. A **manager** is responsible for monitoring the execution of a task and processing the results of its execution. A **contractor** is responsible for the actual execution of the task. Individual nodes are not designated a priori as managers or contractors. These are only roles, and any node can dynamically take on either role. During the course of problem solving, a particular node normally takes on both roles (perhaps even simultaneously for different contracts).

The normal method of negotiating a contract is for a node that generates a task to advertise the existence of that task to other nodes in the net with a **task-announcement** message. It then acts as the manager of that task for its duration. Many such announcements are made over the course of time as tasks are generated for execution.

Nodes in the net have been listening to the task announcements and have been evaluating their own level of interest in each task with respect to their specialized hardware and software resources. When a task of sufficient interest is found, a node submits a **bid**. A bid message indicates the capabilities of the bidder that are relevant to execution of the announced task. A manager may receive several such bids in response to a single task announcement; based on the information in the bids, it selects one (or several) node(s) for execution of the task. The selection is communicated to the successful bidder(s) through an **award** message. These selected nodes thus become contractors for that task.[1]

[1] This is a simplified version of the actual process (and does not work, for example, in the case of a task that cannot be executed due to insufficient data). We have also ignored the use of focused addressing and more specialized interactions like directed contracts. See [Smith, 1978b] for the specification of the full set of message types in the protocol and a complete discussion of the processing associated with each of the message types.

2.1.2 The Contract Net Protocol

The use of communication protocols in networks of resource-sharing computers, such as the **ARPAnet**, is by now quite familiar. The primary function of these protocols is to effect reliable and efficient communication between computers. Such low-level protocols are, however, only a start--a prerequisite for distributed problem solving. They enable bit streams to be passed between nodes but do not consider the semantics of the information being passed. We require a high-level protocol, which we call a **problem-solving protocol** (PSP), to assign problem-solving interpretations to the bit streams--to control the processes used to solve problems as opposed to the processes used to effect communication. This enables the applications programmer to focus on **what** the nodes must say to each other, as opposed to **how** to say it.

The contract net protocol is the PSP that governs all problem-solving interactions between nodes in a contract net. Task-dependent information is placed in typed slots in the messages of the protocol and is encoded in a **common internode language**. Task-independent information is encoded directly in the protocol; that is, in the specification of message types and their associated slots.

A task announcement message, for example, has four slots for task-dependent information. The **eligibility specification** is a list of criteria that a node must meet to be eligible to submit a bid. It enables a node receiving the message to decide whether or not it is able to execute the task. The **task abstraction** is a brief description of the task to be executed. It enables a node to rank the announced task relative to other announced tasks. The **bid specification** is a description of the expected form of a bid. It enables a node to include in a bid only the information about its capabilities that are relevant to the announced task. Finally, the **expiration time** is a specification of the time period during which the announcement is valid.

The common internode language provides the primitive elements for encoding task-dependent information in the task abstraction, eligibility specification, bid specification, and so on. The implemented language enables statements of the form **Respond with <value> of <attribute> of <object>** to be encoded, where some of the objects are **node, task, procedure,** and **contract**. Objects are linked together by attributes, each of which has a value (which may be another object). A **contract** object, for example, has a **manager** attribute whose value is a **node** object. The language has a grammar and a core vocabulary of terms that appear to be of use in a wide variety of applications. The vocabulary is also extensible; that is, new terms can be added for specific applications.

2.2 Example

The following is an example of the negotiation for a task that involves gathering of sensed data and extraction of signal features. It is taken from an **INTERLISP** simulation of a distributed sensing system (DSS) [**Smith, 1978a**].

The managers for this **signal** task attempt to find a set of sensor nodes such that the set has an adequate spatial distribution about the surrounding area and has an adequate distribution of sensor types. Sensor nodes, on the other hand, attempt to find managers for the signal task that are closest to them.

The eligibility specification in the signal task announcements indicates that only those nodes located in the same area as the announcer and having sensing capabilities should bid on this task. This helps to reduce extraneous message traffic and bid processing. The task abstraction indicates the type of task and the position of an individual signal group contractor. It enables a potential contractor to determine the manager to which it should respond. The bid specification indicates the information that a manager needs to select a suitable set of sensor nodes--the position of the bidder and the number of each of its sensor types.

The potential contractors listen to the task announcements from the various managers. They respond to the nearest manager with a bid that contains the information specified in the task announcement. The managers use this information to select a set of bidders and then award signal contracts. The award messages specify the sensors that each contractor is to use to provide raw data to its manager.

Sample messages that are transmitted during negotiation of the signal contracts are shown below. Terms written in upper case are included in the core common internode language, while terms written in lower case are specific to the DSS problem. The "*" indicates a broadcast message.

```
To: *                  <Managers make announcements
From: 25                               of this form.>
Type: TASK ANNOUNCEMENT
Contract: 22-3-1
Message:
  Task Abstraction:
    TASK TYPE 'signal
    NODE NAME '25 POSITION 'p
  Eligibility Specification:
    MUST-HAVE DEVICE TYPE 'sensor
    MUST-HAVE NODE NAME 'SELF POSITION area 'A
  Bid Specification:
    NODE NAME 'SELF POSITION
    EVERY DEVICE TYPE 'sensor TYPE NUMBER

To: 25                     <Sensor nodes respond to
From: 42                         the nearest manager.>
Type: BID
Contract: 22-3-1
Message:
  Node Abstraction:
    NODE NAME '42 POSITION 'q
    sensor TYPE 'S NUMBER '3
    sensor TYPE 'T NUMBER '1

To: 42                       <Several similar awards
From: 25                           are transmitted.>
Type: AWARD
Contract: 22-3-1
Message:
  Task Specification:
    sensor NAME 'S1
    sensor NAME 'S2
```

2.3 Knowledge Organization

The knowledge organization component of the framework specifies mechanisms for **retrieval** and **distribution** of knowledge in a distributed problem solver. Retrieval can be further broken down into two parts: **partitioning** and **indexing**. Partitioning indicates the ways in which the knowledge is broken up into modules; indexing indicates the handles placed on the knowledge modules so that they can be accessed.

2.3.1 Partitioning

It is common in AI problem solvers to partition expertise into domain-specific **knowledge-sources** (KSs), each of which is expert in a particular part of the overall problem. KSs are typically formed empirically, based on examination of different types of knowledge that can be brought to bear on a particular problem. In a speech-understanding problem, for example, knowledge is available from the speech signal itself, from the syntax of the utterances, and from the semantics of the task domain [Erman, 1975]. The decisions about which KSs are to be formed is often made in concert with the formation of a data hierarchy for a problem. KSs are typically chosen to handle data at one level of abstraction or to bridge two levels (see, for example [Erman, 1975] and [Nii, 1978]).

In a distributed processor there is an additional consideration: The KSs themselves will likely be distributed to different nodes, and their interactions will therefore often be more expensive than in a uniprocessor. As a result, the kernel size of the KSs must be chosen carefully, based on the characteristics of the distributed processor. KSs that are too small will result in a large amount of communication between nodes, thus reducing the speedup that can be achieved via a distributed approach. Matching of kernel size to distributed processor characteristics must at present be done via trial and error by the applications programmer.

2.3.2 Indexing

In the contract net framework, the main issue in indexing of knowledge is connecting nodes with tasks to be executed to nodes with KSs that are appropriate to execute those tasks. Two major types of knowledge are recognized for indexing: **task-centered knowledge** and **knowledge-source-centered knowledge** (KS-centered knowledge). Task-centered knowledge is useful for finding nodes capable of executing tasks and KS-centered knowledge is useful for finding tasks to be executed by a node. The contract net appears to be the first use of both kinds of knowledge at the same time.

In the DSS, for example, the task-centered knowledge used by the manager for the signal task specifies that contracts should be awarded so that the area surrounding the manager is covered with an adequate distribution of sensor types. The KS-centered knowledge used by a sensor node specifies that a signal task should be selected from the closest manager that offers such a task.

2.3.3 Distribution Of Knowledge

Distribution also has two aspects: **static distribution**, how knowledge is initially loaded into the nodes, and **dynamic distribution**, how knowledge is transferred between nodes as work on the overall problem proceeds.

The criteria for a good static distribution of knowledge are minimization of message traffic and avoidance of critical function nodes that could reduce processing speed and create reliability problems. In the DSS, for example, KSs with expertise at a particular level of the data hierarchy were placed in different nodes. This enabled nodes to carry on simultaneously with computation specific to those levels of the data hierarchy that concerned them (without the need for frequent interactions with nodes operating at different levels of the hierarchy).

In the contract net framework, dynamic distribution of knowledge can be effected in three ways. First, a node can transmit a request directly to another node for the transfer of the required knowledge. The response is the knowledge requested (e.g., the code for a procedure). Second, a node can broadcast a task announcement in which the task is a transfer of knowledge. A bid on the task indicates that another node has the knowledge and is willing to transmit it. Finally, a node can note in its bid on a task that it requires particular knowledge in order to execute the task. The manager can then send the required knowledge in the contract award if the bid is accepted. Each of these interactions is simplified by the use of a common internode language.

Dynamic distribution enables effective use of available computational resources: A node that is standing idle because it lacks information required to execute a previously announced task can acquire that information as indicated above. Dynamic knowledge distribution also facilitates the addition of a new node to an existing net; the node can dynamically acquire the procedures and data necessary to allow it to participate in the operation of the net. This is especially useful in the DSS application.

3 Discussion

There are several reasons for adopting a distributed approach to problem solving. These include speed, reliability, extensibility, and the ability to handle applications that have a natural spatial distribution. The design of the contract net framework has taken into account each of these considerations. We relate here design choices made in the framework to their underlying motivations.

In order to achieve high speed we wish to avoid bottlenecks. Such bottlenecks can arise in two primary ways: by concentrating disproportionate amounts of computation or communication at central resources, and by saturating available communications channels so that nodes must remain idle while messages are transmitted.

To avoid bottlenecks we facilitate the distribution of control and data. This is a major motivation for the use of local contract negotiation to achieve connections and task distribution and to provide a means for dynamic distribution of procedures and other data. System concurrency is also enhanced because both managers and contractors simultaneously seek each other out, finally achieving connections by mutual selection.

To avoid communications channel saturation we attempt to maintain loose-coupling. The framework is well-suited to loosely coupled systems in three respects. First, it provides a very general form of guidance in determining appropriate partitioning of problems: the notion of tasks executed under contracts is appropriate for a kernel size larger than that typically used in parallel systems. Second, the framework attempts to be efficient with respect to its use of communications channels by reducing the number and length of messages. The information in task announcements, for instance, helps minimize the amount of channel capacity consumed by communications overhead. Extraneous traffic is eliminated by the eligibility specifications of the task announcements and the bid messages are reduced in length because of the bid specifications. Finally, the framework enables dynamic distribution of procedures and other data. Thus the option exists to distribute information only when required.

Reliability is also enhanced by the distribution of control and data, together with shared responsibility for tasks (by managers and contractors). The failure of a contractor, for example, is not fatal, since its manager can re-announce the appropriate contract and recover from the failure. This strategy allows the system to recover from any node failure except that of the node that holds the original top-level problem.[1]

Extensibility is facilitated by the use of a common internode language and dynamic distribution of knowledge.

The ability to handle applications with a natural spatial distribution is facilitated by the use of local contract negotiation to achieve connection and task distribution.

4 Suitable Applications

The framework is particularly well-matched to problems that use a hierarchy of tasks and levels of data abstraction. Heuristic search problems are examples of the former, and applications that deal with sensed data (e.g., audio or video signals) are examples of the latter.

The manager-contractor structure provides a natural way to effect hierarchical control and the managers at each level in the hierarchy are an appropriate place for data integration and abstraction. The contract links between nodes assist in coordination of KSs (i.e., a manager can coordinate the actions of contractors working on related subtasks).

It also follows that the framework is primarily applicable to domains where the subtasks are large (in the loose-coupling sense) and where it is worthwhile to expend a potentially nontrivial amount of computation and communication to invoke the best KSs for each subtask. (The same basic mechanism can, however, be used simply as a means of task distribution with distributed control and shared responsibility for tasks to maintain reliability and avoid bottlenecks.)

The framework has also been designed to

[1] At the top level, contracting can distribute control almost completely, hence removing the bottlenecks that centralized controllers create. There still remains, however, the reliability problem inherent in having only a single node responsible for the top-level problem. Since this cannot be handled directly by the manager-contractor links, standard sorts of redundancy are required.

provide a more powerful mechanism for transfer of control than is available in current problem-solving systems (see **[Smith, 1978b]** for a complete discussion). The announcement-bid-award sequence of contract negotiation enables more information and more complex information to be transferred in both directions (between caller and respondent) before KS-invocation occurs. In addition, information about the complete collection of candidate KSs is available before a final selection is made. The computation devoted to the selection process, based on the information transfer noted above, is more extensive and more complex than that used in traditional approaches, and is local in the sense that selection is associated with and specific to an individual KS (rather than embodied in, say, a global evaluation function). As a result, the framework is most useful when the specific KS to be invoked at any time is not known a priori and when specific expertise is required.

5 Limitations And Extensions

We have proposed a framework that offers some ideas about what information is useful for distributed problem solving and how that information can be organized. There is still a considerable problem involved in instantiating the framework in the context of a specific task domain. The contract net protocol provides a site for embedding particular types of task-dependent information (e.g. an eligibility specification), but does not specify, for a particular problem, the content, nor how to instantiate it in a particular domain. We require more experience with the framework to better understand its utility as a mechanism for helping a user structure and understand distributed problems.

We have emphasized task-sharing as a means of internode cooperation and have attempted to provide some structured mechanisms for the communication required to effect this mode of cooperation. We have, however, not yet adequately studied **result-sharing** as a means of cooperation; that is, nodes assisting each other through sharing of partial results, based on somewhat different perspectives on the overall problem. Different perspectives arise because the nodes use different KSs (e.g., syntax vs acoustics in the case of a speech understanding system) or different data (e.g., data that is sensed at different locations in the case of a DSS). This type of cooperation appears to be of use in dealing with problems where errorful data or knowledge lead to conflicting views of the problem at individual nodes (see **[Lesser, 1978]** for a preliminary discussion). It is our intention to examine the structure of communication for this mode of cooperation with a view to extending the contract net framework so that a synthesis of the two approaches to distributed problem solving can be attempted.

References

[Erman, 1975]
L. D. Erman and V. R. Lesser, A Multi-level Organization For Problem Solving Using Many, Diverse, Cooperating Sources of Knowledge. **IJCAI4**, 1975, pp. 483-490.

[Lesser, 1978]
V. R. Lesser, **Cooperative Distributed Processing**. COINS TR 78-7, Dept. of Computer and Information Science, University of Massachusetts, May 1978.

[Nii, 1978]
H. P. Nii and E. A. Feigenbaum, Rule-Based Understanding Of Signals. In D. A. Waterman and F. Hayes-Roth (Eds.), **Pattern-Directed Inference Systems**. New York: Academic Press, 1978. Pp. 483-501.

[Smith, 1978a]
R. G. Smith and R. Davis, Applications Of The Contract Net Framework: Distributed Sensing. **Proceedings of the ARPA Distributed Sensor Net Symposium**, Pittsburgh, PA, December 1978, pp. 12-20.

[Smith, 1978b]
R. G. Smith, **A Framework For Problem Solving In A Distributed Processing Environment**. Ph.D. Dissertation, STAN-CS-78-700 (HPP-78-28) Dept. of Computer Science, Stanford University, December 1978.

THE X-O-O HEURISTIC IN GAME TREE ANALYSIS

J. Denbigh Starkey
Computer Science Department
Wahington State University
Pullman, Washington 99164

Programs for two-person games, such as chess or Go, are heavily dependent on Minimax evaluation of large game trees, which is combined with heuristics in an attempt to prune these trees as severely as possible. In particular, alpha-beta pruning, usually combined with the killer heuristic, is used in all major minimax-based programs. In this paper we shall propose a new heuristic which could be incorporated into minimax-based programs, and which should significantly increase the pruning possible during the analysis of game trees. This new heuristic, which can be combined with alpha-beta and the killer heuristic, is called the X-O-O heuristic. The development of the heuristic was prompted by the difficulty of analyzing large game trees in Go, and is based on a formalism and extension of the Go proverb "the enemy's play is my own key play".

1. Introduction.

Current programs for complex two person games such as chess or Go rely heavily on minimax-based lookahead to evaluate board positions and to select moves. In chess programs this is usually an analysis performed over good moves throughout the whole board, while in most Go situations lookahead must be restricted to local battles. In order to increase the number of nodes that can be analyzed with the computing resources available, alpha-beta tree pruning is invariably utilized, usually in conjunction with the killer heuristic [1,4].

In this paper we will introduce a new heuristic named the X-O-O heuristic. The purpose of this heuristic is to anticipate and protect against the opponent's strong moves, both offensive and defensive. In section 2 we will informally describe the heuristic, and will give examples of it in use in chess and Go. We will then define the algorithm for the heuristic precisely in section 3. We will assume that the reader knows the basic rules of chess and Go.

2. The X-O-O heuristic.

There is a Go proverb "The enemy's play is my own key play" [3]. A simple example of this is shown in Figure 1.

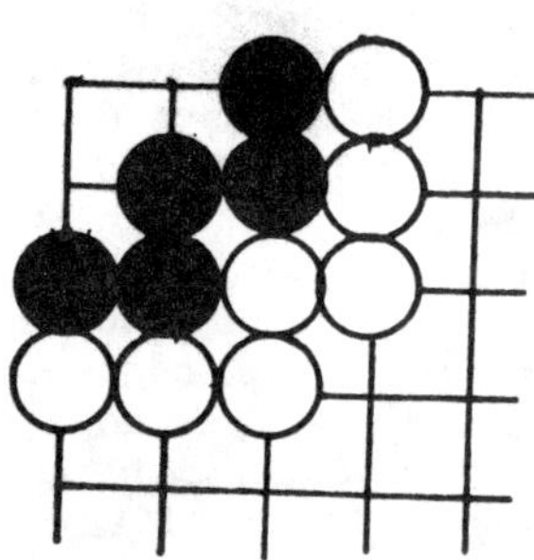

Figure 1

If it were black's move, he would play in the corner, guaranteeing the safety of his group. If it is white's move he uses the proverb to play in the corner. In its simplest form, the X-O-O heuristic is similar to the proverb in that it attempts to recognize the opponent's strongest move, and to take it away from him.

A chess example is shown in Figure 2.

BR							BK
					BP	BP	BP
			BP				
			WR		WR		
			WP	WP		WB	WB
					WP	WP	WP
							WK

Figure 2

It is White's move. In this situation current chess programs will perform extensive lookahead analysis attempting to find a mating sequence. In the same position, even a poor human player will quickly recognize the R-R8 threat, and will decide that the only way to block that move is R-R5, and so the block move is forced. No lookahead is necessary to make the move. The thought process that has occurred is:

> "If it were black's move instead of mine, does he have any obvious strong moves? Yes, he would move his rook to R8 and check me. Would I then be able to do anything about that? No, it would be checkmate. How can I stop that move? I must either capture the rook, block its path, delay him by putting him in check, guard R1, or block the path between R1 and my king. The only one of these that I can do is to block the path of the rook with R-R5, and so this is a forced move."

Figure 3 shows a similar board position.

BR							BK
					BP	BP	BP
			BP				
		BP	WR		WR		
				WB			
		WP	WP			WB	
					WP	WP	WP
							WK

Figure 3

Here the threat is the same as before, but if black plays R-R8, white needs two moves to block the threat; either P-R3 or P-R4 followed by K-R3. The X-O-O heuristic compels white to play either P-R3 or P-R4 at this move.

Figure 4 shows a Go position called the nose tesuji. It is black's turn to play, and he wants to capture the two white stones on the right. A tesuji pattern matching program decides that the probable best play is the stone marked with an X, on top of the white "nose". Black must now confirm that the white pieces cannot escape. Tackett [2,5] analyzed this position, and decided that its solution would take nearly a month on an IBM 360/67, using standard lookahead techniques. Using the X-O-O heuristic the analysis is very inexpensive. White can only escape in two directions, to the left or right. Consider an escape to the right: if it were black's move he would immediately play to the right of the two white stones, blocking all possibility of escape. Therefore the X-O-O heuristic compels white to block that move by playing there. A simple template pattern match should now show that white is trapped. A similar analysis on the left shows that white cannot escape that way either, and so black's nose tesuji is confirmed.

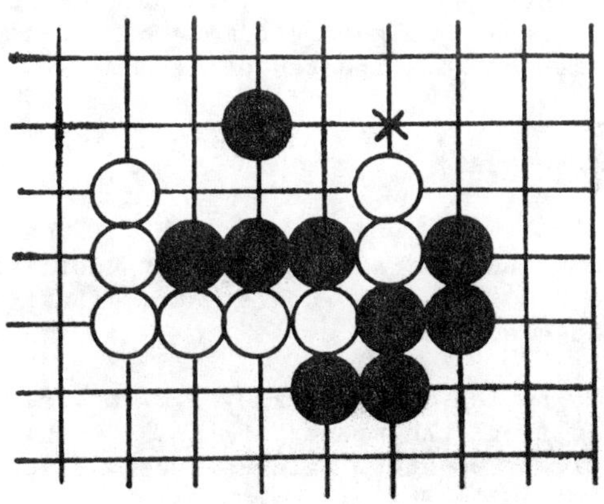

Figure 4

3. The X-O-O algorithm.

We are now ready to give the formal algorithm for the heuristic. Assume that the two players are X and O, and that it is O's turn to play.

The algorithm can then be written:

Find all very strong X moves, X1, ... , Xn.

For each Xi

(a) If there is an O move which nullifies the effect of Xi then Xi can be ignored.

(b) If Xi must be blocked now, add blocking O moves to the forced move list for Xi.

(c) If two O moves are needed to nullify the effect of Xi, say O′ and O′′, then add O′ to the forced move list for Xi.

If there are no forced move lists, then use alpha-beta lookahead as usual.

If there are forced move lists, then play a move which is in the intersection of all of the forced move lists.

4. Summary

The success of the heuristic in any given game will depend on the care with which the good X moves are selected. The list of moves should be kept as small as possible, and n should usually be much smaller than the branching factor of the minimax game tree. We are currently experimenting using the game of Go-Moku in order to obtain a good estimate of the improvements which can be expected using X-O-O.

REFERENCES

[1] Aki S.G. and Newborn M.M. "The principal continuation and the killer heuristic." Proc. of ACM National Conference, (Seattle 1977), 466-478.

[2] Benson D.B., Starkey J.D. et. al. "Computerizing the game of Go." Washington State Univ. Computer Science Dept. Tech. Report CS-76-031 (Pullman Wa 1976)

[3] Davies J. "Tesuji." Ishi Press (Tokyo 1972).

[4] Knuth D.E. and Moore R.W. "An analysis of alpha-beta pruning." Artificial Intelligence 6,4 (Winter 1975), 293-326.

[5] Tackett M.J. "A pattern recognition approach to tesuji programming in Go." Proc. of ACM/CIPS Pacific Regional Symposium (Seattle 1976).

AN EXAMINATION OF A FRAME-STRUCTURED REPRESENTATION SYSTEM

Mark Stefik
Computer Science Department
Stanford University
Stanford, California 94305

The Unit Package is an interactive knowledge representation system with representations for individuals, classes, indefinite individuals, and abstractions. Links between the nodes are structured with explicit definitional roles, types of inheritance, defaults, and various data formats. This paper presents the general ideas of the Unit Package and compares it with other current knowledge representation languages. The Unit Package was created for a hierarchical planning application, and is now in use by several AI projects.

1 INTRODUCTION

When the MOLGEN* project was started, many ideas about frame systems and semantic networks were being widely discussed, but no software was available. In collaboration** with other members of the MOLGEN project, the author developed a representation system called the "Unit Package" which became operational in July 1977. In some cases (and usually in ignorance), this work has duplicated other representation work that was happening at about the same time. The Unit Package is now being used by several other projects including two away from Stanford. It is written in INTERLISP and runs under the TENEX and TOPS20 operating systems. It is an interactive system for building knowledge-based programs. It also provides a substantial virtual memory so that knowledge bases of several thousand nodes can created without sacrificing the INTERLISP environment.

---

*MOLGEN is a joint project between the Stanford Computer Science Department, several departments of the Stanford Medical School, and the Computer Science Department at the University of New Mexico. It is active in the computer planning of molecular genetics experiments ([7], [17]). MOLGEN is supported by grant NSF MCS 78-02777 from the National Science Foundation.

**Nancy Martin and Peter Friedland made substantial contributions to the Unit Package, especially in the first year.

2 ELEMENTS OF THE REPRESENTATION

Knowledge in the Unit Package is organized as a partitioned semantic network. Following KRL [3] terminology, the nodes are alternatively called units and the links are called slots. A built-in generalization relationship provides a hierarchy with several modes of property inheritance. Conspicuous for its absence is a comprehensive inference mechanism. While the Unit Package provides some built-in inferential facilities — notably the property inheritance mechanism, the pattern matchers, and the attached procedure mechanism — most of the inference control must be provided by application-specific methods. The ideas in the Unit Package will be presented in the following order.

1) Partitions — The boundaries in the network which divide it into (possibly overlapping) explicit sets of nodes.

2) Units — The nodes in the network. The Unit Package has nodes for constant individuals and classes as well as for undetermined and abstract entities. For the latter it permits naming them, anchoring them to constants, adding details to them, and indicating whether they are the same or different (without necessarily anchoring them).

3) Slots — The links between the nodes. The fine structure of links is defined by a set of "aspects" which define their inheritance and definitional roles, datatypes, defaults, and attached procedures. These aspects provide declarative meta-knowledge which indicates how a slot is to be interpreted.

4) Attached procedures — Procedures may be attached to units, slots, or datatype units, depending on what they are used for. They are activated by messages and have explicit purposes. A small set of purposes is recognized by the Unit Package to allow automatic activation under specified circumstances. Attached procedures are the chief mechanism for making inferences in the Unit Package.

2.1 Partitions

While a knowledge base is ultimately composed of nodes and links, it is often useful to consider larger organizations of units. For this purpose the Unit Package provides a facility for partitioning a network into explicit sets. This is the same idea as the spaces in Hendrix's* partitioned semantic networks [9]. The Unit Package simply provides an efficient notation for explicit sets** and a number of functions which act on all members of sets.

2.2 Nodes

In our planning application, it is helpful to have open-ended descriptions for abstract entities and to be able to refer to individuals whose identities have not yet been determined. To represent this information the Unit Package provides four kinds of nodes as in Fig. 1 along with the computational machinery for their interpretation.

*We have not yet exploited the set notation for handling quantification.

**This could have been indicated with a member-of slot. Our implementation makes it possible to tell whether a unit is in a set without requiring that the unit be core resident.

	Constant	Variable
Individual	Instance	Indefinite
Class	Schema	Description

Figure 1. Kinds of nodes in the Unit Package

These kinds of nodes are listed here briefly and discussed in the following sections.

1) INSTANCE — Constant node that stands for a unique individual. An instance is analogous to a constant in predicate calculus.

2) SCHEMA — Constant node that stands for a class. A schema describes all of its potential progeny in the generalization hierarchy.

3) INDEFINITE NODE — Variable node that stands for an individual. Analogous to an existentially quantified variable in "predicate calculus with equality". Fundamental links for reasoning about equality are (1) "anchor" links which tie indefinite nodes to instances and (2) "co-reference" and "not-co-reference" links which tie indefinite nodes together.

4) DESCRIPTION NODE — Variable node that stands for a class. These nodes are used for matching and reasoning about abstractions, that is, incompletely described entities.

Section 3.1 compares these node types to other work on representation.

2.2.1 Nodes for Constants

An "instance" is the simplest kind of node in the Unit Package. Instances are analogous to constant terms in predicate calculus and are used to represent distinct entities, that is, "individuals" Examples of instances in the our application would be domain objects like Culture-133, a particular culture of organisms. Schemata stand for classes, that is, implicit sets and may have subclasses and instances below them in the hierarchy. Because instances do not stand for classes, they can have no nodes below them. A schema describes all of its potential progeny by expressing all of the attributes that are required for members of the class.

2.2.2 Indefinite Nodes

"Indefinite" nodes are the simplest variable nodes in the Unit Package; they stand for individuals whose identity may be unknown. They allow us to indicate that two variables are equal (or not equal) without knowing their values. This is like the augmentation of predicate calculus to predicate calculus with equality except that it is a three-valued logic permitting the logical possibility that equality may be "unknown". For example, we could have indefinite nodes for Martha's-husband or The-first-president. We may equate these indefinite nodes to each other by marking them as "co-referential". We may also "anchor" or ground them to an individual unit (e.g., George-Washington). Two indefinite nodes are said to be equal if they have the same anchor or if they are tagged as being co-referential. Two indefinite nodes are not equal if they have different anchors, if they are marked as "not co-referential", or if their scopes do not intersect*. In all other cases, equality is "unknown". Co-reference and anchor relationships are represented by slots with standard names. The need for such nodes in natural language processing (sometimes termed "intentional" nodes) has also been recognized [20]. Our experience has been that the potentially difficult parts in reasoning with these entities are (1) deciding when there is enough evidence to conclude about equality of identities and (2) combining the (possibly conflicting) attributes of the various hypothetical objects once their common identity has been concluded.

2.2.3 Description Nodes

Description nodes are variable nodes which stand for classes instead of individuals. These nodes are used in our planning application to represent open-ended goals. Whereas "anchoring" is the key to equality of indefinite nodes, matching is the key to equality of description nodes. The class defined by a schema is the set of its specializations in the hierarchy; the class defined by a description node is the set of nodes within a specified scope that match the description node. Two description nodes are said to be equal if they potentially match the same units* or if they are indicated as being co-referential. This limits the expression of match conditions to a conjunction of slots. We have found it convenient in our planning application to augment this notation with additional "constraint" units that can express arbitrary predicates involving several nodes. In our planning application, the refinement of abstract goals is accomplished by the addition of constraints to descriptions and the matching of descriptions to the knowledge base. The interpretation and manipulation of these constraints is done by our planning program and not by the Unit Package.

*Scopes, in the Unit Package, are simply a branch of the generalization hierarchy. Extending this to a more flexible form of quantification is part of the planned future work on the Unit Package.

2.3 Links

As the Unit Package has been developed, it has become necessary to provide structure for the links between the nodes. Several different "aspects" have been created to accommodate this:

1) NAME — Name of the slot.

2) VALUE — Stored value of the slot. Typically this is the name of a unit but it may be a different data-structure if the datatype aspect is other than "unit". The Unit Package distinguishes between values that are value-restrictions and those that are "terminal"**.

3) DEFINITIONAL ROLE — The role that the slot plays in the definition of the unit. The roles "PART-OF", "PROPERTY", "RELATION", "SUPER-UNIT", "EQUIVALENCE", and "DOCUMENTATION" are recognized by the Unit Package. Definitional roles are explained further in Section 2.3.1.

4) INHERITANCE ROLE — The mode of inheritance of the slot by progeny. Four distinct roles, ("S", "R", "O", and "U") are recognized in the Unit Package. Criteriality is determined from this role. Inheritance roles are discussed further in Section 2.3.2.

*The operational test for deciding whether two descriptions potentially match the same units is that the descriptions match each other.

**In an analogy with units, descriptions are like schemata and terminal values are like instances.

5) DEFAULT — Default value for the slot to be used in the absence of specific information. This aspect was much less frequently used than we originally expected.

6) DATATYPE — A link in the Unit Package need not go to another unit; it may go to an atom, integer, string, list, lambda expression, or to a value with some other "datatype". "Unit" is probably the most important datatype and is used for most of the links usually associated with semantic networks. The datatype aspect facilitates treating different kinds of values uniformly. The factoring of procedures to support this is discussed in Section 2.4.

2.3.1 Definitional Roles

A retrospective examination of how slots were being used in our genetics knowledge base made us aware that indistinguishable notations were sometimes used where distinct meanings were intended. Fig. 2 illustrates some of the slots from the representation of an organism in one of our knowledge bases. The slot chromosome is used to refer to a part of the organism; the slot gramstain refers to the visible character of the organism when a particular staining agent is applied. Without the definitional role, a general procedure to separate or remove the parts of a unit may try to "remove the gramstain" from an organism. Thus, the exosomes slot in Fig. 2 indicates (1) what exosomes the organism has (i.e. EXOSOMES (ORGANISM1) = (PMB9, PSC101)) and (2) that the exosomes are to be considered parts of the organism (i.e. PART-OF (PMB9, ORGANISM1) = T).

The idea of distinguishing between kinds of links is not new with our work. Woods [20] distinguished between "assertional" and "structural" links. We differentiate between the definitional roles "PART-OF", "PROPERTY", "RELATION", "SUPER-UNIT", "EQUIVALENCE", and "DOCUMENTATION". The role "SUPER-UNIT" has the inverse meaning of "PART-OF" and is used to annotate slots which point back from the parts of a larger concept. The role "EQUIVALENCE" is used to label the special "co-reference" and "anchor" slots used in description and indefinite units. The role "DOCUMENTATION" is used to tag slots like the modifier slot which are part of the automatic documentation of a knowledge base. More definitional roles will probably emerge as the Unit Package **is** used in additional applications.

Slot Name	Value	Definitional Role
EXOSOMES:	(PMB9, PSC101)	PART-OF
CHROMOSOME:	DNA-Structure-92	PART-OF
MORPHOLOGY:	COCCUS	PROPERTY
GRAMSTAIN:	POSITIVE	PROPERTY
CAN-EAT:	NUTRIENT-GEL	RELATION
KILLED-BY:	TETRAMYCIN	RELATION
MODIFIER:	Feitelson	DOCUMENTATION
MODIFIED:	12-MAR-79	DOCUMENTATION

Figure 2. Definitional Roles

2.3.2 Inheritance Roles

The idea of the hierarchical inheritance of properties has its roots in the inferential machinery discussed in Quillian's thesis [14]. In its simplest form, a value is defined in the most general schema to which it applies. Nodes corresponding to descendants of the schema inherit the value. As Brachman [6] points out, while a slot in an individual is intended to assert a property of the individual, a slot in a schema is often intended to restrict the legal values of corresponding slots in its potential progeny. These alternative meanings of slots (slots used to define properties versus slots used to instantiate properties) are important for the understanding of inheritance and are not always clearly differentiated in network formalisms.

In the Unit Package we have identified five standard "inheritance roles" for slots. Four roles (termed "S", "R", "O", and "U") that have been useful in the Units Package are described below. A fifth role (termed "M"), which is probably useful but which has not been implemented, is also discussed.

1) The simplest role is for direct inheritance of values by all progeny. This is termed the "S" role because the slot has the same value in the defining unit and all of its progeny.

2) The "R" role is for the inheritance of requirements; it is for slots that are criterial to the definition of a schema. The

values in schemata are interpreted as value-restrictions for the corresponding slots in progeny. The values in slots of progeny need not be the same as in the schema, but may be further restricted*. Usually the value of the slot in an instance will be "terminal", that is, an actual value instead of a description of a value. If every "R" slot in an instance has a terminal value, then the instance is fully instantiated.

3) The "O" role is similar to the "R" role except that the slot is optional (ie. not criterial). The slot in an instance need not be filled in with a terminal value. For example, in the molecular genetics domain, the organisms slot of the Culture unit has role "R" and the exosomes slot of the Bacterium unit has role "O". This is meant to indicate that every culture must have organisms, but every bacterium need not have exosomes.

4) The "U" role is for information about a node that is not inherited by its progeny. The slot value is unique at each level in the hierarchy. As with the other roles, the slot name, datatype, and role are inherited by offspring. However, the value is not inherited or used to limit the value of the slot in offspring. This role is used mainly for our bookkeeping purposes in the network such as for the creator slot in units.

The first three roles can be seen as decreasingly strict. With the "O" role, a value is optional in instances; with "R" it is required; with "S" it is directly inherited. In contrast, the "U" role ignores the nesting of values in progeny altogether. One additional role for inheritance, which we have not implemented, would allow slots in progeny to have values that override restrictions from above. (This might be termed the "M" role meaning modifications allowed). This idea was originally disallowed because it was seen as counter to the spirit of unit specialization.

Like definitional roles, inheritance roles provide meta-knowledge about the interpretation of slots. They indicate (1) transmission instructions for the information and (2) whether the value is criterial to the definition of the slot. Inheritance roles are also used by the interactive component of the Unit Package to determine what checking is performed when knowledge is entered by a user.

Before leaving the subject of inheritance, it is worth emphasizing that a generalization hierarchy should be distinguished from other hierarchical relationships from everyday life which do not indicate inheritance paths. Some common ones are "subset-of", "element-of", "part-of" and "abstraction-of". These relationships are represented in a semantic network by explicit links independent of those used for the superclass taxonomy.

2.4 Attaching Procedures

The attachment of procedures to frames is one of the representational ideas common to the new knowledge representation languages. Several older languages (such as LISP) support arbitrary attachment of procedures to data structures; the approach in frame-structured languages is more disciplined. This discipline in the Unit Package has two main elements: (1) standardized points for attachment and (2) an explicit purpose for procedures. The "purpose" of a procedure indicates when a procedure should be activated.

The Unit Package provides three standard places for attaching procedures: (1) unit attachment (2) slot attachment and (3) datatype attachment. Unit attachment is used for operations that act on a unit as a whole. Slot attachment is used for operations on a particular slot of a unit. Datatype attachment is useful for operations on slots located in units throughout the knowledge base that have values of a particular datatype. Although datatype attachment has not been reported in other frame systems, it has been used extensively in the Unit Package [17] and is similar to ideas from SIMULA.

We have adapted some terminology from SMALLTALK to describe the activation of attached procedures. A procedure is activated by "sending it a message" with a token that matches its purpose. This is an indirect form of procedure call — where the purpose of the procedure is known to the caller but the name of the procedure need not be known. The "purpose" of a procedure is usually associated with standardized activation conditions (e.g. "To-Get"); it also indicates where the

---

*The meaning of "further restricted" is determined by a function associated with the datatype of the slot. For the "number" datatype, the value-restrictions are numeric ranges or lists. For the "unit" datatype, the value-restrictions may be description nodes or ancestor specifications.

procedure's name is stored. For unit attachment, the purpose is the name of a slot containing the procedure name; for slot attachment, it is the name of an aspect; for datatype attachment, it is the name of the slot in the unit for the datatype. Functions like the matcher, which must work for all datatypes, operate by activating datatype-specific procedures using the message mechanism.

3 RELATIONSHIP TO OTHER WORK

During the period when the Unit Package was developed, many other frame-structured representation systems have also appeared. In some cases, our work has duplicated that of other groups. This section compares the Unit Package to related systems.

3.1 Other Work on Node Types

The idea of distinguishing between node types in a knowledge representation language has important implications for the design of interpreters and matchers. If node types are not distinguished, then the semantic information about abstractness and equality must be carried by some other means. Node types similar to our four categories have appeared in other contemporary representation languages. Fig. 3 summarizes what they are called in AIMDS ([15], [16]), FRL [8], KLONE ([5], [19]), KRL-Ø ([1], [3]), Levesque's System [11], and OWL ([18],[13]). This is not to say that the node types correspond exactly in these systems, but that the ideas seem to be very similar.

Several other types of nodes have appeared in representation languages. For example, KRL-Ø supported the additional node categories "relation", "proposition", and "basic". The relation category was used to represent an abstract relationship between entities and a proposition was an instantiation of a relationship specifying its truth value. (In our planning application, constraints serve some of this function although their interpretation is by the planning program instead of a general interpreter for the representation language.) "Basic" categories partition the world into simple non-overlapping categories. Categories are meant to allow quick tests (by category comparison) to decide whether an object fits a description. This partitioning is partially (but inadequately) achieved in the simple hierarchical systems by the approximate rule that two schemata are in distinct categories if neither is an ancestor of the other in the superclass hierarchy*. It is not clear that such categories can be assigned to domain objects once and for all. Further aspects of this are discussed in two recent critical examinations of KRL ([1Ø], [1]).

*One of the shortcomings of the Unit Package is illustrated by this example. There is no annotation to indicate which branches in the generalization hierarchy are mutually exclusive.

System	Instance	Schema	Indefinite	Description
AIMDS	instance	template		
FRL	instantiated frame	generic frame		
KLONE	individual nexus	generic concept	variable nexus	parametric individual
KRL-Ø	individual	specialization	manifestation	abstract
Levesque's System	instance	class	indefinite	
OWL	instance	species		

Figure 3. Node types in other representation systems

The node types in KLONE ([4], [5]) shown in Fig. 3 do not fit perfectly into the categories used in the Unit Package; KLONE distinguishes between patterns (also called descriptions or concepts) and representations of things. A generic concept in KLONE is a pattern because it does not stand directly for its potential progeny; the class is its extension in some context. Similarly, an "individual concept" in KLONE is an individualized pattern; it describes a potentially unique individual which may or may not exist (e.g. "the current king of France"). A nexus is more like the sort of individual in the Unit Package. A nexus is either constant or variable. A nexus has an "existence value" which can be "does not exist". It can have "coreference wires" to other nexuses and "description wires" to individual concepts. Thus KLONE distinguishes individualized patterns (individual concepts) from representations of individuals (nexuses). The matrix in Fig. 1 does not make this distinction. KLONE's "parametric individual" is not quite the same as a description node (i.e. variable class node) in the Unit Package. Parametric individuals are still patterns — they describe potentially many individuals — but they are not arbitrary generic descriptions; some of their values are bound by the context in which they appear, and thus they are "parameterized".

3.2 Other Work on Property Inheritance

The recognition of different forms of inheritance is not unique to the Unit Package. Goldstein and Roberts [8] distinguished two kinds of inheritance in FRL-Ø — additive and restrictive. Additive inheritance permitted a specialization to add new non-contradictory facts. This corresponds to the "R" and "O" roles above. Restrictive inheritance is used when a specialization overrides the information in a more general schema. This corresponds to the "M" role above, which we have not implemented. FRL-Ø also encouraged the use of "idiosyncratic forms" of inheritance by the use of attached procedures. These procedures effected the transmission of values from frames other than the parent. This seems to be an attempt to capture some of the "multiple-perspectives" idea of KRL using less machinery.

An elaborate proposal inheritance was proposed by Brachman [6] and then substantially elaborated by Brachman and Woods ([5], [19]). Brachman connects nodes not by a single generalization link, but rather by a complete bundle of links (called a "cable") which ties together the parts with different kinds of links. The details of these links require more explanation than is convenient here but the main insight is that inheritance of complex structures must be supported by a rich vocabulary of relationships for the parts of the inherited structure. While the scope of their developing system (KLONE) is broader than our own, the philosophy is essentially the same, namely, to develop a concise and structured representation in which the important kinds of relationships are explicit and uniformly represented for processing by general purpose network routines.

4 SUMMARY

The Unit Package is a frame-structured representation language whose main elements are partitions, nodes, links, and attached procedures. Our goal has been to develop a concise and structured representation language in which the important kinds of relationships are explicit and uniformly represented for processing by uniform network processing routines. This has led to formalisms for kinds of nodes, links, inheritance, and attached procedures. Some of these formalisms have been inspired by and instrumental for the MOLGEN planning application. Probably the most important example of this is the idea of a hierarchical variable to which one can add information and constraints. These variables provide a notation for hierarchical planning.

Some shortcomings of the Unit Package have been noted in passing. These include a need for allowing multiple generalizations, a need for explicit indication of mutual exclusion, and a more adequate use of quantification. These problems are not difficult to fix. Space does not permit discussion of more substantial representational problems beyond the current research, such as the structured representation of processes and causal relationships. The reader interested in a discussion of some unsolved problems is referred to [17].

5 ACKNOWLEDGMENTS

Many thanks to Avron Barr, Jim Bennett, Bruce Buchanan, Ed Feigenbaum, Peter Friedland, Jonathan King, and Doug Lenat who read earlier drafts of this document and whose criticisms have greatly improved its readability. Thanks also to the other members of the MOLGEN project who have helped in this work and who have shown great patience while other needs in our project have been pressing. Computing support was provided on the SUMEX-AIM facility by a grant from the Biotechnology Resources Branch of the National Institute of Health.

REFERENCES

1. Bobrow D.G., Winograd T., KRL, Another Perspective, Cognitive Science 3 29-42 (1979)

2. Bobrow D.G., Winograd T., Experience with KRL-0, One cycle of a knowledge representation language, Proc. IJCAI-77, MIT, Cambridge, Mass. August, 1977, pp. 213-222.

3. Bobrow D.G., Winograd T., An Overview of KRL, a Knowledge Representation Language, Cognitive Science 1:1. (1977) 3-46.

4. Brachman R., Personal communication, (May 1979)

5. Brachman R., Theoretical studies in natural language understanding, BBN report 3888 (September 1978)

6. Brachman R., What's in a concept: Structural foundations for Semantic Networks, BBN report 3433, (October 1976)

7. Friedland P., Knowledge-based Experiment Design in Molecular Genetics, in Proc. IJCAI-79 (this volume)

8. Goldstein I.P., Roberts R.B., NUDGE, A knowledge-based scheduling program, in Proc. IJCAI-77, MIT Cambridge, Mass., August, 1977, pp. 257-263.

9. Hendrix G.G., Expanding the Utility of Semantic Networks through Partitioning, SRI Technical Note 105 (June 1975)

10. Lehnert W., Wilks Y., A critical perspective on KRL, Cognitive Science 3:1 1-28 (1979)

11. Levesque, Mylopoulos, McCalla, Melli, and Tsotsos, A formalism for modelling, Proc. First CSCSI/SCEIO National Conference, Vancouver, 1976, pp 243-254.

12. Martin N., Friedland P., King J., Stefik M., Knowledge Base Management for Experiment Planning, in Proc. IJCAI-77, MIT, Cambridge, Mass., August, 1977, pp. 882-887

13. Martin W.A., OWL, in Proc. IJCAI-77, MIT, Cambridge, Mass., August, 1977 pp. 985.

14. Quillian R., Semantic memory, in Minsky M. (ed.) Semantic Information Processing Cambridge: MIT Press (1968)

15. Sridharan N.S., AIMDS User Manual - Version 2., Rutgers University Computer Science Technical Report CBM-TR-89. (June 1978)

16. Sridharan N.S., Knowledge representation in AIMDS and its use in BELIEVER, in Proc. IJCAI-77, Cambridge, Mass., August, 1977, pp. 990

17. Stefik M.J., Orthogonal Planning with Constraints, Report on a knowledge-based program that plans synthesis experiments in molecular genetics, (forthcoming dissertation) Computer Science Department, Stanford University (September 1979)

18. Szolovits P., Hawkinson L.B., Martin W.A., An overview of OWL, a language for knowledge representation, Technical Report MIT/LCS/TM-86 from Laboratory for Computer Science at MIT (June 1977)

19. Woods W.A., Brachman R.J., Research in Natural Language Understanding, Bolk Baranek and Newman Technical Report 3963 (August 1978)

20. Woods W.A., What's in a link: Foundations for Semantic Networks, in Bobrow D.G., Collins A. (eds.), Representation and Understanding, Academic Press (1975)

AUTOMATIC DISCOVERY OF HEURISTICS FOR NONDETERMINISTIC PROGRAMS *

Salvatore J. Stolfo
Computer Science Department
Courant Institute
New York University
251 Mercer Street
New York, New York 10012

Malcolm C. Harrison
Computer Science Department
Courant Institute
New York University
251 Mercer Street
New York, New York 10012

This paper discusses one way to limit the cost of executing declaratively specified nondeterministic programs. The approach we take is to develop control heuristics for a family of problems from traces of sample solutions generated during a training session with a human expert. Algorithms have been developed which recognize a set of patterns in the sequence of 'knowledge applications' and which compile descriptions of these patterns in a control language, called CRAPS. The CRAPS descriptions generated are then used for guidance in solving subsequent problems. We describe an implementation of this approach and give the results of several experiments.

1. INTRODUCTION

During the last few years, a number of relatively effective Artificial Intelligence programs have been written incorporating considerable amounts of knowledge, and the problem of encoding such knowledge in a useful form has emerged as one of the central problems of AI. Recently, attention has turned towards mechanisms which facilitate incorporating limited procedural or heuristic information into a primarily declarative framework (for example, Rychener's approach [4] is to build a rational "goal" structure into declarative rule-based systems, while Davis [2] favors a separate set of "meta-rules", specifying control information). The problem of acquiring, debugging and extending control information has become increasingly important. We believe that there are a number of important areas in which it might be possible to deduce control information automatically from a declarative program. These include declaratively specified problems: (1) for which there exists a relatively simple algorithmic procedure; or (2) whose performance can be improved in frequently occurring or particularly important special cases; or (3) in which particular subproblems can be solved by simple algorithmic procedures. This problem has been discussed by a number of previous workers in various forms (for example [1,3,7]); space does not permit a complete review here (see [5] for such a review and comparisons with the present work).

2. APPROACH

In our experiments, we have been working on a (slightly idealized) jigsaw puzzle, in which each piece has an average color, and four sides described by unique integers (with side i fitting side -i). A nondeterministic algorithm written in production language form for this problem can be found in [6].

The representation contains 33 productions, and is highly nondeterministic, and if executed would be hopelessly inefficient. It does not even "know" that it will find a solution (i.e. terminate) if it can repeat the production which puts a piece in the puzzle as frequently as possible, so even the crudest goal-subgoal structure is absent. (However, there is no production to remove a piece from the puzzle, which serves as a clue to an intelligent observer). It is even possible for the program to pick up a piece and then put it down immediately without doing anything with it.

However, sufficient productions are present to permit simple sequencing heuristics to reflect the usual strategies used by experi-

---

*This material is based upon work supported by the Office of Naval Research under Contract No. N00014-75-C-0571, (NR049-347).

enced puzzle-solvers:

° work on the outside edges first (build a pile of outside edges); repeat the put-piece-in-puzzle sequence until this pile is empty;

° separate the pieces in the heap into piles of the same average color, and search the appropriate pile first;

° search first for pieces which have more than one neighbor of the same average color (e.g. work on the sky first);

It may appear that automatic detection of such heuristics is a task of great difficulty. Below we outline an approach to this problem which appears to be quite successful, describe a system which has been embedded in a production system language and give some experimental results.

Our procedure is as follows: we select a 'typical' input to the program and run the program repeatedly on this input, recording the sequence of rules selected. This is repeated for other typical inputs. We then attempt to describe the better (i.e. shorter) successful sequences in a language, CRAPS, designed for this purpose and described in the next section. We then use this description to guide the program's subsequent decisions. The analysis of the solution sequences also produces a set of meta-rules which are used to dynamically alter the sequencing in the event the description does not behave properly.

Inherent in this approach is the assumption that good decision-making procedures or heuristics can be inferred from the performance of the program on only selected inputs. In general, as suggested by work on inductive inference and information theory, we give preference to short CRAPS descriptions which will generate a high proportion of short successful solutions and few long or unsuccessful solutions. We anticipate that the selection of inputs will be critical and that eventually we will want to be able to handle new inputs incrementally. Initially, however, we have concentrated on the simpler problem of getting a good solution for the non-incremental case.

As suggested by sample experiments, the execution time of a completely declarative program will usually be too long to permit a solution except in the simpler cases. Accordingly, we run the program in "training mode" in which its decisions can be observed and if necessary corrected. In initial experiments this was done by a trainer who was aware of the structure of the program; subsequently we anticipate the necessity of using techniques similar to those of Davis [2], which will enable the trainer to deal only with the external behavior of the program.

It should be noted that we have deliberately chosen to exclude information about sequences which end in failure. It is clear that, as found by Winston [8], counterexamples will be extremely valuable. However, as the reader will note below, even this simpler problem poses considerable technical difficulties, and it was our feeling that a clearer picture would emerge from the simpler approach. Furthermore, the experiments suggest that useful results can be obtained without counterexamples.

3. THE CRAPS LANGUAGE

The CRAPS language provides a semantic framework with which to specify or describe sequences of rule applications in the execution of the non-deterministic program. The operators of CRAPS are Concatenation, Repetition, Alternation and Permutation of Sequences, with enabling conditions which are DNF expressions of rule applicability. Concatenation corresponds to sequential execution of statements, and repetition corresponds to iteration statements with 'while' and 'until' termination conditions. The alternation operator specifies alternative sequences of actions much like an ALGOL-68 'case' statement or LISP 'cond' expression. The permutation primitive represents a form of concurrent execution similar to the specification of collateral expressions in ALGOL-68.

The algorithms which compile CRAPS descriptions are based on standard optimization techniques and divide and conquer pattern recognition algorithms. The input to the program consists of a sequence composed of the rules which were fired on each cycle together with the associated input/output information and the list of rules which were applicable on each cycle. The analysis also produces a set of meta-rules whose objective is to suggest productions to fire in the event the CRAPS description is inappropriate. Complete details of these algorithms can be found in [5,6].

4. EXPERIMENTS

The experiments were performed on 5 puzzles with 25-30 pieces. Over 400 productions were fired to solve a puzzle. The CRAPS description generated from a training session using one puzzle consisted of 75 concatenations and 15 repetitions. A total of 192 meta-rules were generated. The original puzzle used in the training session was easily solved using the CRAPS description; no meta-rules were needed. The second puzzle was solved in 10 1/2 minutes but required 5 meta-rule calls. The third puzzle failed to be solved because of an incorrect choice specified by the meta-rules after 193 cycles. A fourth puzzle was solved in 11 1/2 minutes with one meta-rule call. A fifth puzzle was run with the meta-rules alone and it failed to make correct decisions after 80 successful cycles were executed. Complete details of these experiments can be found in [5].

5. CONCLUSION

It is believed by many researchers that an important quality of intelligent behavior is the ability to improve performance with experience, and that generalizing a concept is a critical aspect of learning. In CRAPS, a form of generalization occurs when a repeating subsequence is collapsed into a repetition. Although quite restricted in scope, CRAPS shows how a system might learn procedures, a form of learning which we believe is very important. Although there are a number of very difficult technical problems, it seems to us that with more powerful pattern recognition techniques and more powerful generalizations of control statements, this approach could be very fruitful.

With less ambitious designs, CRAPS can be viewed as a programming aid for the designer and implementer of a large AI problem-solving knowledge base. The CRAPS approach might be useful in fine-tuning a declarative knowledge base as opposed to 'hand-compiling' control elements to effect competent performance in such a system.

The power of the descriptions produced is limited by both the expressive power of the CRAPS primitives, and the level of sophistication of the pattern recognition algorithms that have been developed. For example, during repetition detection no notion of <u>similar</u> subsequence is used; furthermore, it is not possible for alternation to appear within repetitions. Despite this, the algorithms are powerful enough to detect interesting patterns and subsequently interesting heuristics.

Our experiments suggest that this approach will have the best chance of success when the encoding of the knowledge of the problem domain is such that on any execution cycle a small number of productions and only one instantiation of each production is applicable. This suggests one way in which CRAPS should evolve: the execution traces should include not only productions but also the instantiations of productions (i.e. contextual or even goal information should be included). However, recognizing patterns in such sequences is much more difficult. We view our approach as an initial step in the understanding of this more general problem.

REFERENCES

[1] Biermann, A., "On the Inference of Turing Machines from Sample Computations, <u>Artif. Intell</u>. 3 (1972).

[2] Davis, R., "Applications of Meta-Level Knowledge to the Construction, Maintenance and Use of Large Knowledge Bases", Ph.D. Thesis, Computer Science Dept. Memo CS-76-552, Stanford University, July 1976.

[3] Fikes, R., Hart, P., and Nilsson, N., "Learning and Executing Generalized Robot Plans", <u>Artif</u>. <u>Intell</u>. 3 (1972).

[4] Rychener, M., "Control Requirements for the Design of Production System Architectures," Proc. Symp. on Artif. Intell. and Program. Lang., 1977.

[5] Stolfo, S., "Automatic Discovery of Heuristics from Sample Execution Traces for Nondeterministic Programs," Ph.D. thesis, Courant Institute, New York Univ., 1979, (in preparation).

[6] Stolfo, S., and Harrison, M., "Automatic Discovery of Heuristics for Nondeterministic Programs," (full version), Courant Institute, New York Univ., CS TR-7, 1979.

[7] Waterman, D., "Generalization Learning Techniques for Automating the Learning of Heuristics," <u>Artif</u>. <u>Intell</u>. 1 (1970).

[8] Winston, P., "Learning Structural Descriptions from Examples," MAC TR-76, Mass. Inst. of Tech., 1976.

A FACSIMILE BASED TEXT EDITOR USING HANDWRITTEN MARK RECOGNITION

Yasuhito Suenaga
Yamato Research Section
Yokosuka Electrical Communication Laboratory
Nippon Telegraph and Telephone Public Corporation
P.O.Box 8, Yokosuka, Kanagawa-ken, 238 Japan

A fundamental study on a facsimile based text editor using handwritten mark recognition is described with some experimental results. Every information for editting is given to the computer via facsimile. First, texts (handwritten, typed or printed) and five kinds of handwritten marks are input to the computer as binary pictures. Second, the marks are recognized to make the picture allocation list. Third, the fair copy of the text is constructed by rearranging the binary picture according to the list, and is output to the facsimile receiver. Manuscripts using almost any kinds of languages including English, Chinese, Japanese etc. are editted by this system. Moreover, the method described here can be combined with usual text editors or word processors, in order to reduce the keyboard based man machine interaction. Experiments based on a minicomputer controlled facsimile produced unexpectedly good results, and the report[1] was actually made using this method, with less than a half of efforts required in the usual way of Japanese manuscript writing with black ink, scissors and paste.

1. Introduction

It is usually a hard work to prepare documents, especially in Japan, where more than 2,000 kinds of kanji characters are commonly used.

Kanji text editors are available, however, the inconvenience of Kanji input operation is yet essentially unsolved.

Consequently, the greater part of documents used in Japan is still handwritten, and the development of text editors free from Kanji input operation is expected.

This paper describes a fundamental study on a text editor using only facsimiles as input and output devices. The method described here is not based on character recognition, but on mark recognition.

2. Assumption

The following conditions are assumed, in order to make the practical consideration.

(a) Characters must be handwritten, typed or printed with the color easily detected by the facsimile transmitter(e.g. black).

(b) The ruled lines of the manuscript paper should be printed with the color which is not detected by the facsimile transmitter(e.g. light blue or green).

(c) Characters must be placed according to the ruled lines.

(d) Marks are drawn by one of the following two methods:

(d-1) drawing marks directly on the manuscript paper together with characters,
(d-2) drawing marks on the other papers.

In case of (d-1), the overlapping of marks with characters or with other marks should be avoided except for the delete or space marks stated later, while the method (d-2) do not suffer from this limitation.

Fig.1 shows an example of the manuscript paper format and five kinds of marks employed here.

(1) Position mark:

The position mark is defined as a set of short lines drawn according to the ruled lines of manuscripts. The format and block size of manuscripts are estimated from this mark.

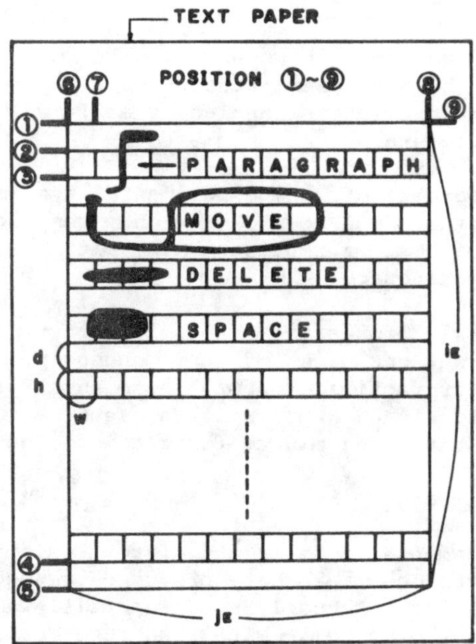

Fig.1 An example of the manuscript paper format and handwritten marks.

(2) Delete mark:

The delete mark is defined as a mass figure drawn on the character string within the blocks. The characters covered with this mark are deleted.

(3) Space mark:

The space mark is defined as a mass figure drawn on the character string, which is similar to, but wider than the delete mark. The characters covered with the space mark are replaced by the equal numbers of spaces.

(4) Paragraph mark:

The paragraph mark is defined as a hook shaped line figure which crosses the blocks vertically. This mark indicates the beginning of the new paragraph.

(5) Move mark:

The move mark is defined as a line figure which consists of an arm and a loop. The character string within the loop is extracted and inserted to the position indicated by the arm.

3. Procedure

Referring to Fig.2, the procedure of text editting is described below.

3.1 Input of texts

Original manuscripts and handwritten marks are input to the minicomputer from the facsimile transmitter. At this time, the position mark is detected, and the parameters on the text size and format are calculated.

3.2 Detection of marks for text modification

At first, the paragraph marks and the move marks are detected by searching along the center line of the space between lines.

Then the delete marks and the space marks are detected by testing the inside of blocks. In case of method (d-1) stated in 2, detected marks are completely removed from the binary picture of the manuscript.

3.3 Generation of the picture allocation list

The picture allocation list (PAL) is generated according to the detected marks. PAL consists of block numbers and addresses indicating the order. Character strings of the manuscript are virtually deleted, moved and combined in PAL.

3.4 Reconstruction of the binary image

Finally, the fair copy of the manuscript is made by rearranging the binary picture according to PAL, and output to the facsimile receiver. Put line procedures for Japanese and English are different from each other.

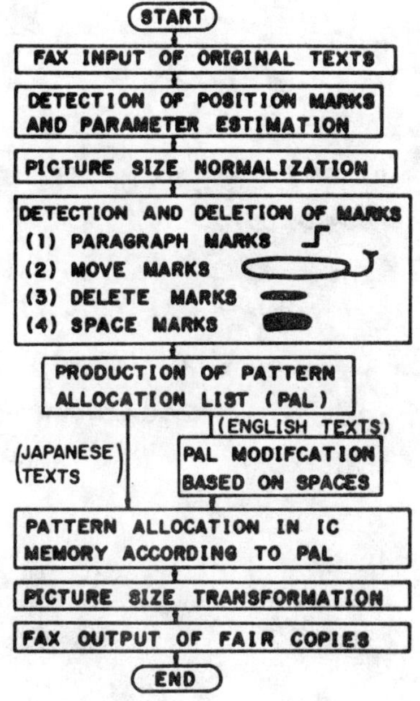

Fig.2 Flow diagram of text editting.

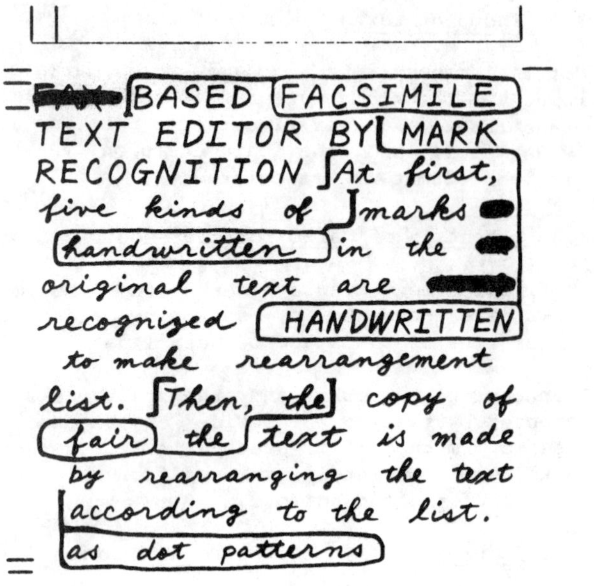

Fig.3(a) An original of a handwritten text. A common manuscript paper and an HB pencil are used.

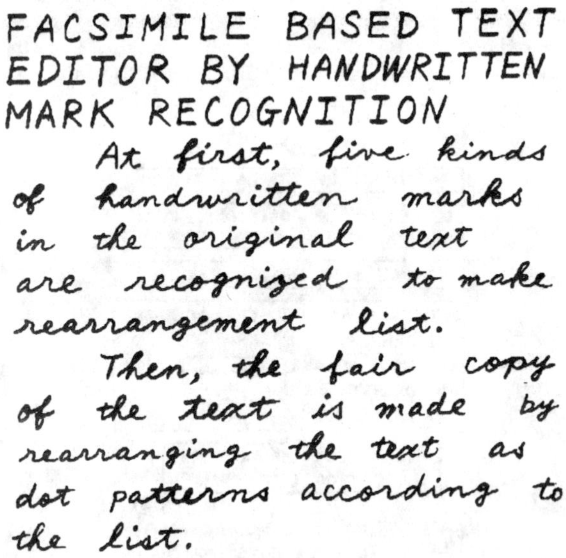

Fig.3(b) Resultant binary pattern of the manuscript made from Fig.3(a).

4. Experimental results

Fig.3(a) and (b) show an example of text editting by the system stated above. One page of the manuscript is handled as a 512 x 512 dot binary picture.

Most programs of the experimental system are made using FORTRAN-IV, and only some special input or output routines are written with an assembly language.

The total processing time is about three minutes per one page of the manuscript: one minute for facsimile input, one minute for mark recognition and the rearrangement of binary picture, and, one minute for facsimile output.

5. Conclusion

The fundamental experiments of text editting by the system described here produced unexpectedly good results. Actually, the report[1] was made by using the system, with less than a half of efforts required for ordinary way of manuscript writing with black ink, erasers, scissors and paste.

The notion and techniques stated here will be very useful for the the modification of various kinds of texts written in almost any kinds of languages.

Moreover, the method employed here can be used in combination with usual text editors, or, in future, with some Kanji OCR's, to reduce the keyboard based man machine interaction.

ACKNOWLEDGEMENTS

The author thank Dr. Junji Yamato, the chief of Yamato Research Section, Yokosuka Electrical Communication Laboratory, and the members of the same Research Section, for their invaluable advices.

REFERENCE

[1] Y.Suenaga, "Automatic text editting using handwritten mark recognition", Proc. of The 9th Conference on Image Science and Engineering, No.3-1,pp63-66, Dec.1978(in Japanese)

AUTOMATIC CONSTRUCTION OF JUNCTION DICTIONARIES AND THEIR EXPLOITATION FOR THE ANALYSIS OF RANGE DATA

Kokichi Sugihara
Information Sciences Division
Electrotechnical Laboratory
Nagata-Cho 2-6-1, Chiyoda-Ku
Tokyo, Japan 100

A knowledge-guided system is presented for the analysis of range data obtained from the three-dimensional world. A model of the world is defined by a finite set of prototypes of three-dimensional objects, from which the system establishes its own knowledge about the world in the form of a "junction dictionary". Next the system exploits the dictionary for the prediction of missing edges in the analysis of range data originated with real three-dimensional scenes, and thus constructs concise descriptions of the scenes in terms of vertices, edges, faces and spatial relationships among them. The system is flexible in the sense that the only thing an operator has to do when the world is changed is to replace the model by a new one; the system constructs its own knowledge about the new world and utilizes it for the analysis of range data.

1. INTRODUCTION

It is known that the nature of the three-dimensional objects world places great constraints on line drawings of those scenes, and these constraints are exploited for the analysis of scenes. Huffman [1] and Clowes [2] enumerated all of the permissible junctions in line drawings of a certain fundamental class of polyhedra, and used them for categorizing line-segments according to their physical types (i.e., convex edges, concave edges and contours). Walts [3], Sugihara [4] and Kanade [5] extended Huffman-Clowes method to drawings with shadows and cracks, to drawings with hidden lines and to Origami world, respectively. Those methods work well for perfect drawings. However, if drawings are imperfect, an unmanageable number of permissible junctions should be considered. Therefore, the knowledge about permissible junctions has been used for the categorization of extracted lines, but not for the extraction of missing lines.

On the contrary, the author, utilizing the advantage of range information, proposes an approach to the use of junction knowledge for the extraction of missing edges in the analysis of range data [6]. The basic idea of the approach is the following. In the analysis of range data we can distinguish convex, concave, obscuring and obscured lines from each other without using any additional information; the junction knowledge is not necessary for the line categorization. Therefore, this knowledge can be used for another purpose, that is, for the prediction of missing edges. Comparing a line drawing extracted from the range data with the list of the permissible junctions, we can tell whether the present drawing is consistent with the physical world or not, and we can, in the latter case, predict the locations and physical categories of missing edges. Thus the extraction of edges can be efficiently guided by those predictions. This approach is practical, since "noisy" raw range data can be dealt with.

One of the greatest shortcomings of the above approach (as well as other approaches to the exploitation of the junction knowledge) is the trihedral-vertex condition, that is , it is assumed that every vertex of a body in the scene has exactly three faces. If we would simply remove this assumption, there would occur an infinite number of permissible junctions, which could not be stored in a finite size of the computer memory.

The present study aims at circumventing the above shortcoming, that is, we represent the knowledge about nontrihedral junctions as well as trihedral ones. The approach we shall take is automatic compilation of the junction knowledge. A model of the world is defined by a finite set of prototypes of polyhedra, and the junction knowledge associated with this world is constructed automatically and is incorporated in the system for range-data analysis. Since the world is restricted to a finite number of polyhedra, the number of permissible junctions is also finite and the knowledge about the world does not swell out.

2. OUTLINE OF THE SYSTEM

The outline of the functions of our system is shown in Fig.1, where rectangles denote system components, circles denote information and arrows denote flow of information. It is assumed that the real world is composed of polyhedra which are taken from a finite set of prototypes. The system consists of the four subsystems:

1. Range Finder --- a subsystem which obtain range data from real scenes by triangulation,

2. Model Generator --- an interactive subsystem by which an operator can generate a model of a real world as a finite set of polyhedra,

3. Knowledge Compiler --- a subsystem whose input is a world model and whose output is a junction dictionary,

4. Range Analyzer --- a subsystem which analyzes range data and establishes concise descriptions (in terms of vertices, edges, faces and spatial relationships among them) of the scenes; in each step of the analysis the subsystem consults a junction dictionary in order to predict missing edges.

We shall go into details of those subsystem in the following sections.

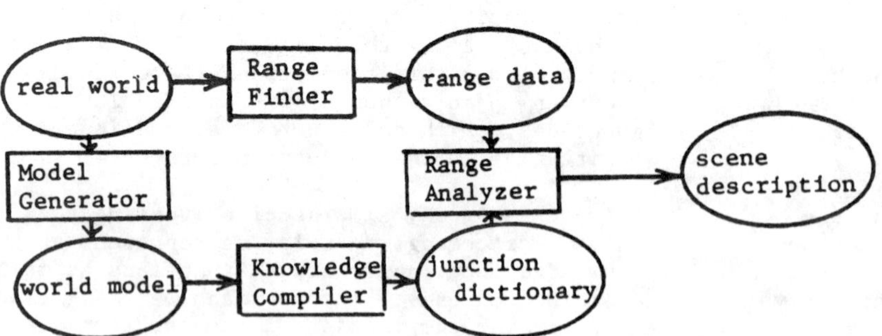

Fig.1. Outline of the system

3. RANGE OBSERVATION

Fig.2 shows a triangulation method for obtaining range information about a scene. A light beam is projected from a source O to the scene and the illuminated spot is observed from another angle by a TV camera O'. The direction of the beam is specified by the point (i,j) at which the beam intersects a fixed plane S. Let d(i,j) denote the distance of the image P'(i,j) of the illuminated spot P(i,j) from the left margin of the TV image plane, as is illustrated in Fig.2. A three-dimensional location of the point P(i,j) can be easily calculated by simple geometry, if we know d(i,j) and the spatial relation among the light source O, the TV camera O' and the plane S. We shall call the array of the data d(i,j)'s (i=1, ..., m, j=1, ..., n) a range picture (though d(i,j) is not a range itself). For practical purpose, a vertical slit light can be used instead of a spot light (see Oshima and Shirai [7]).

Note that we can not always observe the range of a given point (i,j), because the range is obtained only when the illuminated spot P(i,j) can be seen from the TV camera. The line-segment AB in Fig.2, for example, is hidden from the TV camera by another object in front of it, and thus the range data associated with this line-segment are unknown. Therefore, in the range picture (i.e., the two-dimensional array of d(i,j)'s) there are usually a few regions whose values are undefined.

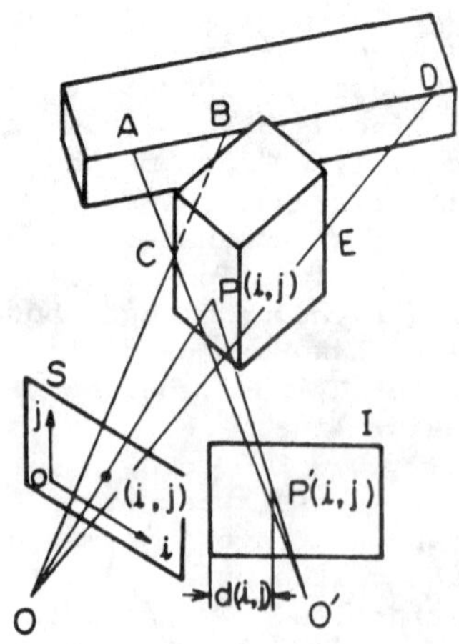

Fig.2. Range observation.

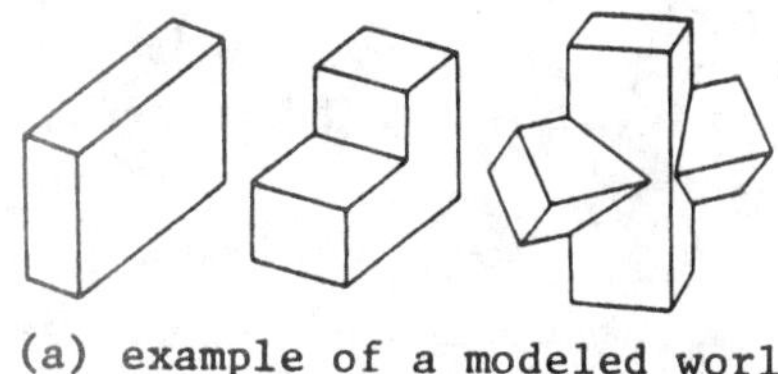

(a) example of a modeled world

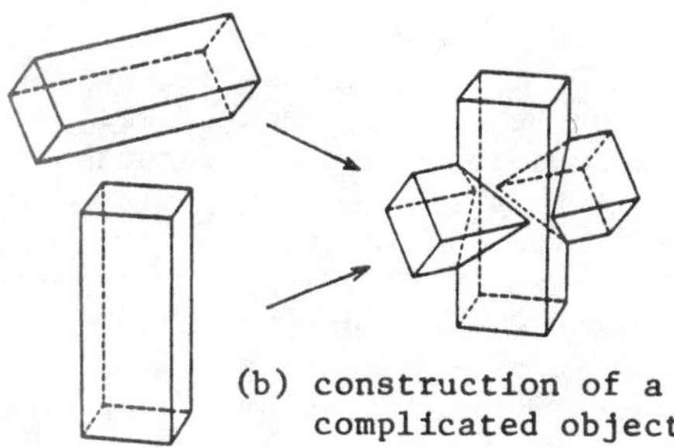

(b) construction of a complicated object

Fig.3. Modeling of the world.

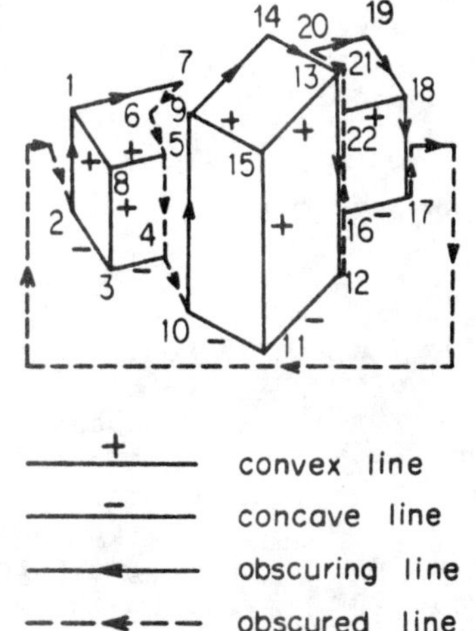

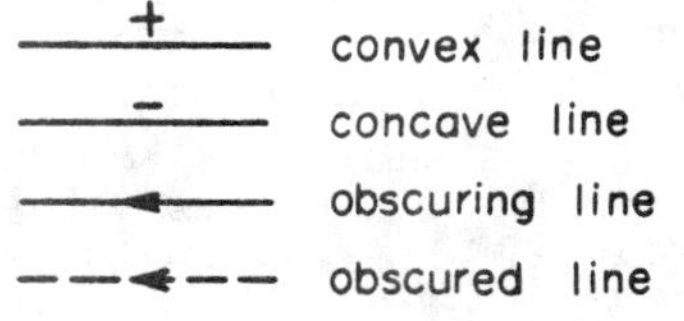

Fig.4. Line drawing representing the scene in Fig.2.

Fig.5.Spherical polygons.

4. MODELING OF A WORLD

The basic part of Model Generator is written in a high-level language named GEOMAP, which is a FORTRAN subroutine package for handling descriptions of three-dimensional solids developed by F. Kimura of Electrotechnical Laboratory [8]. This subsystem is used interactively for the construction of a world model as a set of prototypes of polyhedra. In order to construct a model of each polyhedron, an operator first (1) generates primitive polyhedra such as a rectangular brick, a wedge and a prism/cone with a polygonal base, and next (2) modifies and combines them into a required shape by set-theoretical operations such as a union, an intersection and a subtraction and/or affine transformations. An operator can also obtain two-dimensional projections of the modeled objects seen from an arbitrarily specified viewpoint.

Fig.3(a) shows an example of a modeled world. The process for the construction of the rightest object is shown in Fig.3(b), where two rectangular bricks are generated first and then they are merged into one by a set-theoretical union operation.

5. CONSTRUCTION OF JUNCTION DICTIONARIES

5.1. Line Categories

Fig.4 shows a line drawing of the scene in Fig.2, where two blocks are put on a desk surface. The lines in the drawing are classified according to their physical properties into the four categories: convex lines, concave lines, obscuring lines and obscured lines. While the first three categories occur in usual line drawings, the last category is peculiar to range pictures obtained by triangulation. For example, the right side of A in Fig.2 is obscured by C when seen from the camera O', and consequently A is on an obscured line and C is on an obscuring line, as is illustrated in Fig.4.

5.2. Enumeration of Possible Junctions

We will assume that (1) the scene is composed of polyhedra taken from a finite set of prototypes, and that (2) accidental alignments do not occur in the scene. We will call a junction possible if it can appear in a line drawing of the scene under those assumptions, and call it impossible if otherwise.

Suppose that a vertex of a polyhedron (made of solid material) is put on the center of a unit sphere. Each face around the vertex, when extended, intersect the unit sphere at a great circle, as is shown in Fig.5. These great circles divide the surface of the sphere into a finite number of spherical polygons. Then, some of the spherical polygons are in solid material and the others are in an empty space; we will call the former polygons occupied polygons and the latter ones empty polygons. A vertex of a cube, for example, generates eight spherical polygons, one of which is an occupied polygon and the other seven are empty polygons.

The light source and the camera are supposed to be put on (the same or distinct) empty polygons. Then, the subsystem classifies the area of surfaces around the vertex into the two groups: the area which is visible from both the light source and the camera (i.e., the area whose range can be observed) and the area which is invisible from either of them. And finally, the subsystem constructs a perspective view of the vertex (seen from the camera) in terms of the four categories of lines, and thus obtains a possible junction.

Special types of junctions occur when the camera or the light source is on one of the (extended) face plane. For the enumeration of such kinds of junctions, we have to consider putting the camera and/or the light source on an edge or a corner of a spherical polygon. Once the positions of the camera and the light source are fixed, the processing for the construction of a junction is the same as the above case.

The polyhedron shown in Fig.6(a) has 24 vertices (including hidden vertices which are not shown in the figure), and they are classified into three types 1, 2 and 3 as are shown in the figure: the vertex of type 1 consists of three faces which meet at three convex edges, the vertex of type 2 consists of three faces which meet at one convex edge and two concave edges, and the vertex of type 3 consists of four faces which meet at two convex edges and two concave edges. All the possible junctions associated with the vertices are listed in Figs.6(b), (c) and (d), where an arc connecting two arrowed lines denotes an obscuring/obscured relationship.

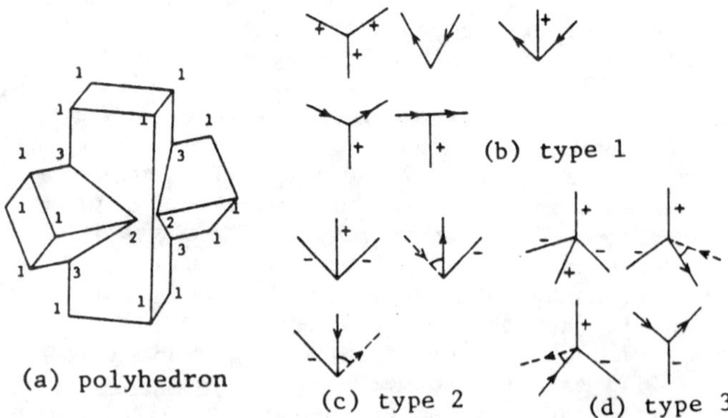

Fig.6. Construction of possible junctions.

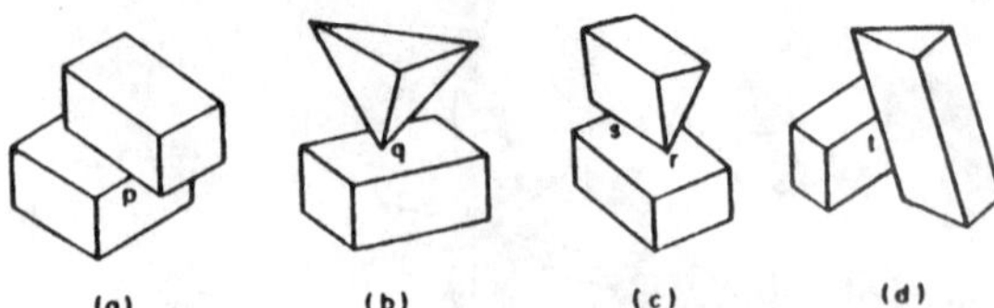

Fig.7. Possible ways of the contact of two bodies.

The above enumeration is sufficient for isolated bodies, but in real scenes several bodies contact each other. Because of the assumption (2) permissible ways of contacts of two bodies are (a) face to face, (b) point to face, (c) edge to face and (d) edge point to edge point as is shown in Fig.7. The subsystem generates the possible junctions associated with the vertices such as q and r as well as the pseudo-vertices such as p, s and t.

5.3 Junction Dictionary

A junction dictionary is constructed in a form of a directed graph whose nodes are all sub-configurations of possible junctions and whose arcs represent the relationships that the initial node can be changed into the terminal node by an addition of one line.

Part of the junction dictionary is shown in Fig.8, where seven junctions and relationships between them are illustrated. The three junctions in rectangles (t, v and y) are impossible ones and the four in circles (u, w, x and z) are possible ones. The drawings beside the possible junctions show the examples of the situations in which the junctions occur. An arrowed arc connecting two junctions denotes an addition of a line. If, for example, we add a convex line in the shaded area of the junction t in Fig.8, we get another junction u. Adding, furthermore, a concave line to u, we obtain w and thus we get the path (t, u, w) from t to w. When we exchange the order of addition of the two lines, we get another path (t, v, w). Those paths suggest the existance

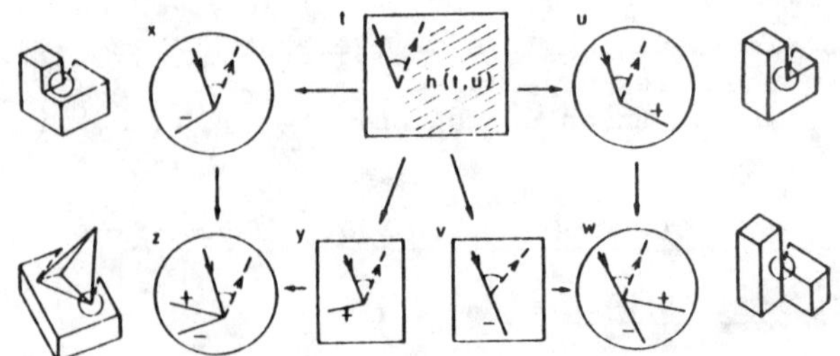

Fig.8. Part of the junction dictionary.

of new lines and guide the analysis of the range data. If a junction of the type u is found in range-data analysis, the dictionary tells us that a concave line "may" exist at that junction. If, on the other hand, a junction of the type v is found, the dictionary says that a convex line "must" exist because v is impossible and w is the only possible junction that has v as a sub-configuration.

6. RANGE DATA ANALYSIS

6.1. Experts for the Analysis

The subsystem for the range data analysis is called DARP (Dictionary-guided Analyzer for Range Picture). The input to DARP is a range picture originated with a real scene and the output is a collection of labeled line drawings of all the objects in the scene.

DARP is composed of many experts: a line predictor, when a junction is given, consults a dictionary and predicts missing lines around the given junction; a prediction tester judges whether predicted lines really exist or not; a line tracker, when a new line is found at a junction, tracks it as far as possible and extracts the whole part of the line; a straight-line adjuster finds straight lines which approximate to the strings of points extracted by the line tracker; a body partitioner, using the knowledge of what types of junctions occur when two bodies contact each other, decomposes the line drawing into smaller ones; a vertex-position corrector revises a position of a junction whenever a new line is connected to the junction.

The processing of DARP is divided into the two parts: a pre-processing and the main processing. The pre-processing consists of several routines which are executed one by one sequentially. In the main processing, on the other hand, the experts interact each other and the system chooses its next step in such a way that the information at hand is used most efficiently [6]. The control structure is based on the idea of a heterarchical program by Shirai [9]).

6.2. Example

Fig.9 shows a range picture (represented by light-stripe images) of the scene composed of two objects --- a supporting block and a complicated body consisting of two bricks; both of them are in the world model in Fig.3(a). Fig.10 shows how the system analyzes the scene.

DARP, in its preprocessing, extracts contour lines and locates junctions on them. In the main processing DARP first focuses its attention to junction J1 in Fig.10(a), where junction Ji is represented by i. J1 is a junction of type t in Fig.8. (Note that the internal lines J1J3 and J3J2 have not yet been found.) The line predictor generates predictions about new lines around J1, and the prediction tester finds a concave line. The line tracker follows it and extracts the whole line (as a string of points), and the straight-line adjuster finds a new junction, say J3, on the new line and replaces the string by two straight line-segments J1J3 and J3J2. Thus the type of J1 is changed to x in Fig.8. Since no other lines are found around J1, DARP terminates the analysis of J1.

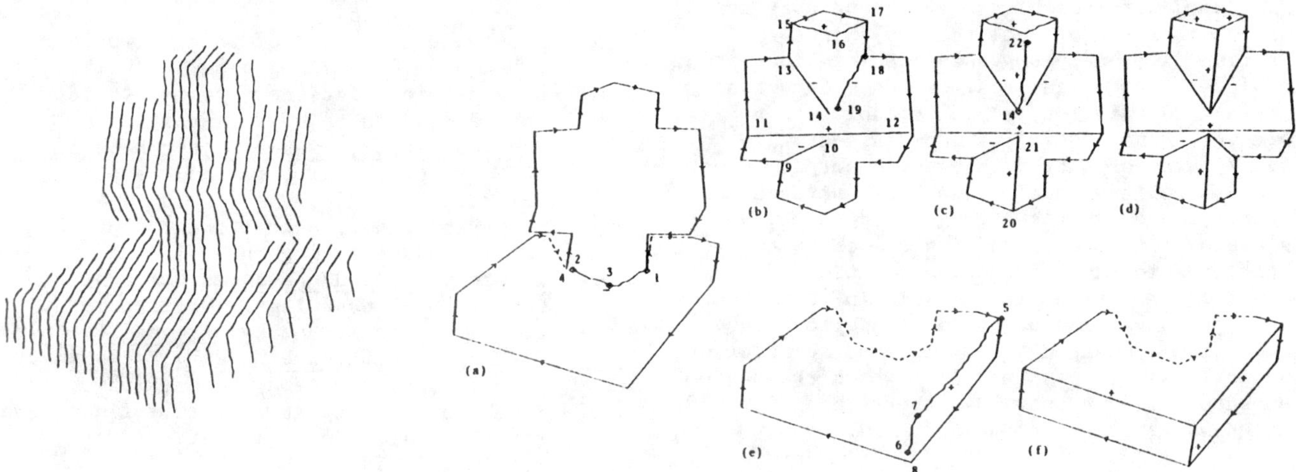

Fig.9. Example of range data.

Fig.10. Analysis of the scene shown in Fig.9.

Next DARP picks up junction J4 and the line predictor suggests a concave line in the right side of the junction. The prediction tester finds that the predicted concave line has already been extracted, and consequently the two junctions J2 and J4 are merged into one, which is renamed J2. Then, the drawing is decomposed along the concave lines J1J3 and J3J2, because J1 and J2 are the junctions that occur at the contact of two bodies (Fig.10(b) and Fig.10(e)).

When J5 is examined, a new convex line J5J6 and a new junction J7 are found (Fig.10(e)), and when J8 is examined, J8 and J6 are merged into one. By similar processing DARP establishes a concise description of the supporting block as is shown in Fig.10(f). The other body is analyzed similarly and DARP obtains the final line drawing shown in Fig.10(d). The numbers assigned to junctions show the order in which the lines and the junctions are extracted.

Though seven edges come close to each other around the central portion of the scene, DARP can construct a perfect line drawing, because the data processing is supported by appropriate predictions of missing lines based on the junction dictionary.

7. CONCLUDING REMARKS

We have studied the dictionary-guided system for the analysis of range data obtained from three-dimensional scenes. Once a world model is given as a set of polyhedra, the system enumerates all of the possible views of vertices and compiles a junction dictionary associated with the given world, and uses it for the analysis of real scenes. Since the junction dictionary suggests missing lines at each step of the analysis, the edge detection is executed efficiently and reliably. Moreover, since the dictionary suggests how to organize the extracted lines, the output is not merely a collection of lines but a structured description of vertices, edges and faces, which is useful for later processings such as the identification and/or the manipulation of objects. The system is flexible in the sense that the only thing an operator has to do when the world is changed is to replace the model of the world with a new one, from which the system generates its own knowledge about the new world and uses it for the scene analysis.

The present system has week points. First, the junction dictionary conveys only local knowledge. Therefore, the system is sometimes insensitive to global inconsistency of the drawing, and it decomposes the scene into pieces smaller than the modeled prototypes. Secondly, obscured lines can not be identified if they are caused by the edges which are out of the picture; this difficulty seems to be essential to triangulation.

ACKNOWLEDGMENTS

The author would like to express his appreciation to Dr. Noboru Sugie and Dr. Yoshiaki Shirai for valuable discussion; to Dr. Fumihiko Kimura for offering the splended software GEOMAP; to Dr. Masaki Oshima for offering a range finding device. This work has been done as part of Pattern Information Processing System Project (PIPS-Project) of Ministry of International Trade and Industry of Japan.

REFERENCES

[1] D. A. Huffman: Impossible objects as nonsense sentences, Machine Intelligence 6, B. Meltzer and D. Michie (eds.), Edinburgh Univ. Press, Edinburgh, 295-324, 1971.

[2] M. B. Clowes: On seeing things, Artif. Intell., 2 (1971), 79-116.

[3] D. Waltz: Understanding line drawings of scenes with shadows, The Psychology of Computer Vision, P. H. Winston (ed.), McGraw-Hill, New York, 19-91, 1975.

[4] K. Sugihara: Picture language for skeletal polyhedra, Comput. Gr. Image Process., 8 (1978), 382-405.

[5] T. Kanade: A theory of Origami world, CMU-CS-78-144, Carnegie-Mellon Univ., 1978.

[6] K. Sugihara: Dictionary-guided scene analysis based on depth information, Progress Report on 3-D Object Recognition (PIPS-R-No.13), Electrotech. Labo., Tokyo, 48-122, 1977.

[7] M. Oshima and Y. Shirai: Representation of curved objects using three-dimensional information, 2nd USA-Japan Computer Conference Proceedings, 108-112, 1975.

[8] F. Kimura and M. Hosaka: Program Package GEOMAP --- Reference Manual (Preliminary Version), Electrotech. Labo., Tokyo, 1977.

[9] Y. Shirai: A context sensitive line finder for recognition of polyhedra, Artif. Intell., 4 (1973), 95-119.

THE EXPERIMENTAL LISP MACHINE

Kazuo Taki,[**] Yukio Kaneda[*] and Sadao Maekawa[*]

* Dept. of Systems Engineering, Kobe University, Rokkodai, Kobe, Japan

** OMIKA Works, HITACHI Ltd., Omika cho, Hitachi shi, Ibaraki, Japan

This machine is specially designed powerful enough to implement an efficient LISP interpreter in microcodes. A LISP processor module and a main memory module are connected to the unibus of a LSI-11 system. The LISP processor module is the microcoded device with a writable control storage that interprets a LISP program in the main memory. Four microprocessor slices(Am 2903) and one microprogram sequencer(Am 2910) are used.

1. INTRODUCTION

The LISP is widely used in the artificial intelligence research community. However LISP processing systems have several nontrivial problems to be solved. One of the most important problems is that the computing time of getting solutions of the problems is much slower than the case of numerical problems. The main reason for the slow speed of computation is due to an unfitness of LISP and a conventional computer architecture at present.

An approach to this problem is to design a machine whose architecture is LISP oriented and code structure more closely reflects that of the language. The machine proposed here is an experimental microprogramable computer system for LISP. This machine is specially designed powerful enough to implement an efficient LISP interpreter in microcodes.

2. THE LISP MACHINE SYSTEM

Our LISP machine is a stand alone personel computer, and Fig.1 illustrates the structure of the machine.
The LISP processor module and the shared main memory module are connected to the UNIBUS of the LSI-11 system(DEC Co). The LSI-11 acts as the master processor of the system and plays the roles of system initialization, input and output, and controls of the LISP processor module. The LISP processor module is a microprogramed device with a writable control storage(WCS) that interprets a LISP program stored in the main memory.
The main memory module is a 64k words(32-bit words) semiconductor memory and its access time is about 75 nsec. The main memory module is also accessible from the LSI-11 using a page mode access mechanism. A data transfer unit between the LISP processor module and the main memory module is a 32-bit word.

3. THE LISP PROCESSOR MODULE

The LISP processor module is implemented with a microprogrammed architecture(Fig.2).
Its kernel consists of an arithmetic and logic unit(ALU) and a computer control unit(CCU).
The CCU has a WCS(4k of 56-bit words) to accommodate the specialized microcodes to support the LISP.

It has hardware for extracting specialized fields in a word, called field extractor, and the mapping memory which converts a main memory address into 3-bit code.

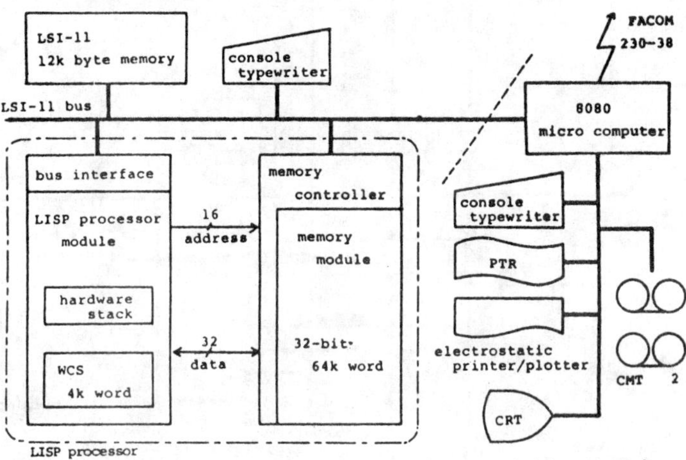

Fig.1 Hardware structure of the machine

It has not a cashe, but has a high speed stack(4k of 16-bit words) acts as a high speed main memory area for a stack, which is where most of the memory references go in LISP.
It has also three buses called A bus, Y bus and B bus. A bus is the data bus, Y bus is the destination bus and B bus is the data bus between the CCU and ALU through which a constant value is supplied to the ALU.

3.1 The ALU and CCU

The ALU is an array of four 4-bit expandable bipolar microprocessor slices(Am 2903). And the CCU is a control unit of the machine and consists of a microprogram sequencer(Am 2910), WCS and other circuits. The Am 2910 is an address sequencer intended for controlling the sequence of execution of microinstructions stored in the WCS(access time is about 150 nsec). Besides the capability of sequential access, the sequencer provides conditional branchings to any microinstructions within its 4096 microwords range. The flag register contains ALU's flags, the mapping memory flags and other flags. All these flags are available for conditional branching under the microprogram control.

3.2 The Hardware Stack, Field Extractor, Mapping Memory and Bit Addressing Unit

The hardware stack is a 4096 16-bit word memory (access time of the memory chip is about 70 nsec). Two pointer registers STP and SAR are provided for stack operations.

The field extractor locates on the A bus and all data to the ALU flow through the unit. This unit is useful to extract a fixed specified field of data.

The mapping memory is a 1k 3-bit word memory. Whenever the main memory references are made the address is gated to the unit. 1k 3-bit word memory is considered as a tag table whose entries are associated with every 64 words sections of the main memory. The supplied address is converted into three bits code which indicates the data type of the object. By using this three bits code rapid conditional jump is possible in the microcodes.

The bit addressing unit is a functional unit which tests and sets a bit on a predefined bit table in the main memory. This unit is prepared for realizing the rapid garbage collection.

3.3 Microprogram Instructions

All operations to the ALU, CCU, hardware stack,

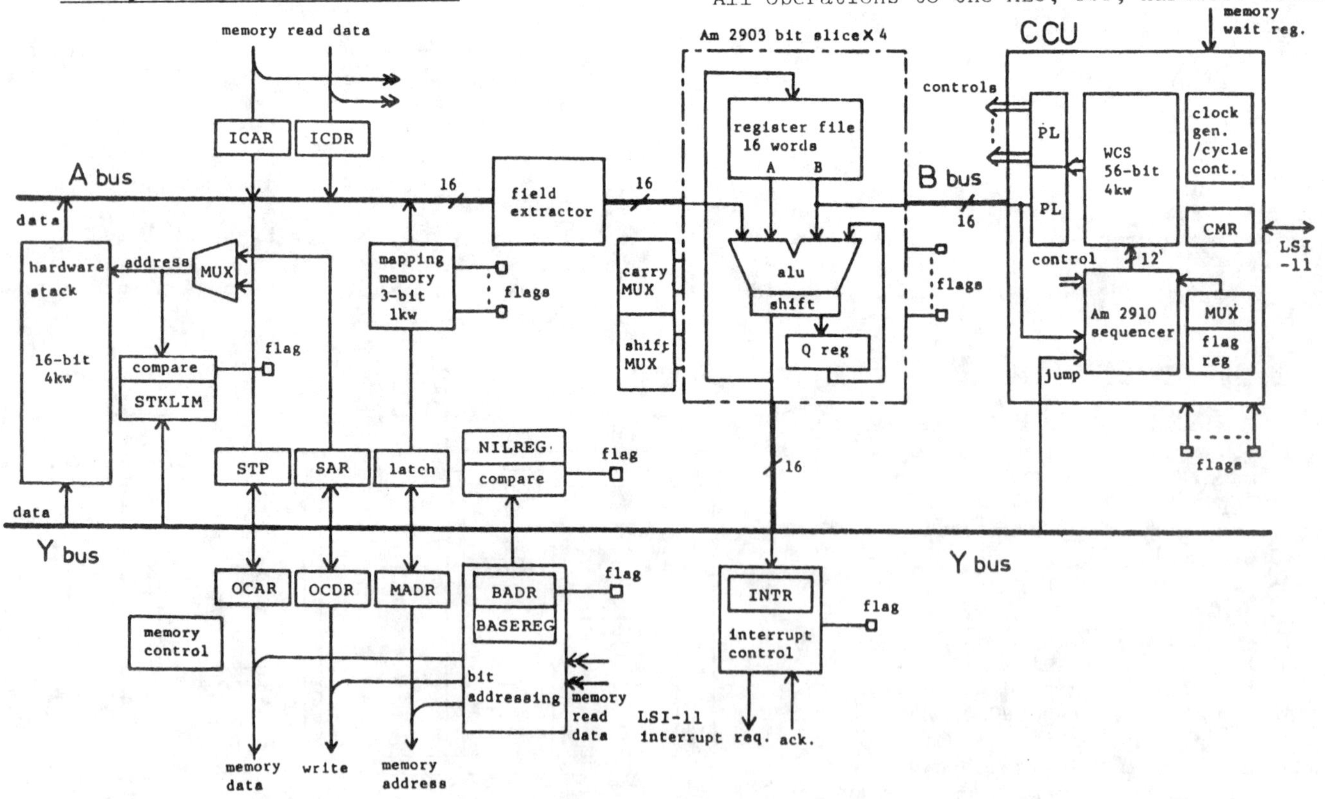

Fig. 2 LISP processor module.

mapping memory and other circuits are entirely under the control of microcode words of the WCS. The microinstruction is a 56-bit word divided into fields. Two types of microinstructions are provided. The type 1 instructions can provide a constant value to the ALU through the B bus, type 2 instructions are conditional branching instructions which can transfer controls to any microcode locations depend on condition flags.

4. DATA AND FUNCTION TYPES

There are four data types, small integer, integer, symbolic atom and list. Small integer, +8191 to -8192, doesn't occupy any memory words. Integers are represented in two's complement notation. Symbolic atom are stored as four consecutive words, each of which is divided into two 16-bit cells termed the function body cell, attribute cell, argument cell, top-value-cell, property list cell, print name cell and two unused cells.

Three types microcoded subroutine functions, MSUBR, MRSUBR and MRFSUBR are provided. MRSUBR and MRFSUBR are recursive functions and MSUBR is not.

MRSUBR: EVAL, APPLY, MAP, GET, EQUL, etc.
MRFSUBR: COND, PROG, AND, DE, SETQ, etc.
MSUBR: CAR, CDR, CONS, EQ, NULL, ATOM, etc.

5. INTERPRETER

In our system the user program is reconstructed into a binary tree structure and interpretation of the program is made by traversing the tree in the endorder fashion.

The functional calling is the basic main control structure in LISP. As mentioned above, the LISP machine function calling is made fast through the use of the hardware stack and microcodes. The stack is formatted into frames; each frame containes a header, arguments, local variable value slots, and a push down list for intermediate results. The header gives the function which owns the frame, a pointer to the function body, links this frame to previous frames, and remembers the program counter and microprogram counter.

6. SYSTEM REALIZATION AND EVALUATIONS

The hardware of the LISP processor module and the main memory module consist of about 650 IC chips and 17 universal printed circuit boards(8x7 square inches). The LISP interpreter of the machine is entirely microcoded and stored in the WCS. The program size of the first version is about 1200 microinstruction steps.

In order to evaluate our LISP machine, we executed the benchmark programs of the second LISP contest of IPSJ(Information Processing Society of Japan). Our interpreters execution times of these programs were shorter than those of any participants of the contest(almost all typical LISP systems in Japan such as HLISP installed HITAC-8800 and OLISP installed NEC system 800-2 were attended).
Examples of typical two benchmarks(e.g. TARAI and TPU) are shown in Table 1. TPU is a theorem prover based on the unit binary resolution priciple written by C.L. Chang and TARAI is a very short program which does almost recursions only except the very simple functions GREATERP and SUB1.
These measurements showed that the architecture of our machine nicely fits in the control structure of the LISP language and realizes a very rapid execution of LISP programs.

ACKNOWLEDGMENTS

The authors wish to express their thanks to Messrs. Toshio Shimada and Yoshinori Yamaguchi of Electrotecnical Laboratory for their useful suggestions and discussions.

REFERENCES

[1] Taki, K., Kaneda, Y. and Maekawa, S. "The Experimental LISP Machine." Tec. Report of the Professional Group on Computer Architecture of IPSJ, 32-3, Sept., 1978 (in Japanese).

[2] Bawden, A. et al "LISP Machine Progress Report." MIT AI Lab. Memo., No. 444, Aug., 1977.

	-----INTERPRETER-----			-----COMPILER-----	
	FAST-LISP KOBE UNIV.	HLISP	OLISP	HLISP	OLISP
TARAI-3	55	78	197	17	36
TARAI-4	1,013	1,443	3,727	330	670
TARAI-5	27,538	39,068	100,734	8,905	18,934
TARAI-6	1,011,732	---	---	322,347	---
TPU-1	904	4,790	2,262	1,029	658
TPU-2	3,426	13,411	10,262	2,871	2,064
TPU-3	1,365	5,684	3,932	1,227	850
TPU-4	1,815	8,025	5,042	1,707	1,161
TPU-5	238	866	759	181	132
TPU-6	6,728	22,849	20,241	4,893	3,617

Table 1 Execution times of the benchmark programs of the 2nd LISP contest of IPSJ (unit time is msec.)

PREDICTIVE CONTROL PARSER: EXTENDED LINGOL

Hozumi TANAKA, Taisuke SATO and Fumio MOTOYOSHI
Electrotechnical Laboratory
2-6-1 Nagata-cho, Chiyoda-ku,
100 Tokyo, Japan

We have developed a flexible parser called Extended LINGOL which is an extended version of Pratt's LINGOL. Although original LINGOL has several advantages, the results of our experiments revealed that it has some deficiencies. One of them is that each augmented context-free rule does not enable us to examine their applicability in case of some situations. Another is that the morpheme analyzer of original LINGOL is too simple to analyze aggulutinative languages such as Japanese. With respect to the former problem, we have introduced predictive control mechanism which has offered us flexible methods to implement a precise grammar with a small set of rules. Furthermore, as the mechanism avoids generating unnecessary partially parsed trees we have obtained high speed parsing. On the other hand, with respect to the latter problem, we have implemented a more powerful morpheme analyzer.

1. INTRODUCTION

The LINGOL, which was developed by V. Pratt, is a research tool for natural language processing. We implemented LINGOL on our T-5600 computer system about four years ago and used it for a while. The advantages of the LINGOL are its program size, speed, and its neat format of grammar and dictionary. It is interesting to note that the semantic interpretation method of the LINGOL is simlar to that of Montague Grammar.

The result of our experiments, however, has revealed that Pratt's LINGOL has several deficiencies mainly with respect to syntactic processing. One of them is that each augmented context-free rule does not enable us to examine their applicability. Another is that the morpheme analyzer of original LINGOL is too simple to analyze aggulutinative languages such as Japanese. In order to cope with these deficiencies, we have revised some portions of original LINGOL and added new programs to it.

2. PREDICTIVE CONTROL MECHANISM

2.1 <Advice> and <delayed-advice>

The Extended LINGOL incorporates a predictive control mechanism which enables us to examine the applicability of each rule in case of some situations. The string parser developed at New York University had implemented the same mechanism in their top-down parser [1]. However, as the LINGOL uses both top-down and bottom-up parsing algorithms, the predictive control mechanism differs from that of New York University. Descriptive format of our dictionary is,

  [<word> <syntactic-category>
    (<message-list> <cog>) <sem>]

Message-list is considered to be attached to the syntactic category of the <word> and is used later by predictive control mechanism as messages. (Fuctions of <cog> and <sem> are the same as described in [3] and [4]). The format of an augmented context-free rule in Extended LINGOL is,

  [<left> <right> (<advice> <cog>) <sem>]

The <left>-<right> pair represents a context-free rule of A ⟶ B (C). The <advice>, which is introduced in our Extended LINGOL, is an arbitrary LISP function for controlling parsing process. The evaluator of predictive control mechanism works as follows:

For each <advice> or <delayed-advice> in rules,
  if the evaluation value is true
    then do not apply the rule
    else apply it;

Suppose a Partially Parsed Tree with a root node E (PPT:E) is created at some intemediate stage of parsing. There are six possibilities to extend the tree. Four of them depend on the evaluation of <advice> in the following rules;

  (R1) A ⟶ E or
  (R2) A ⟶ E F.

(See Fig.1).

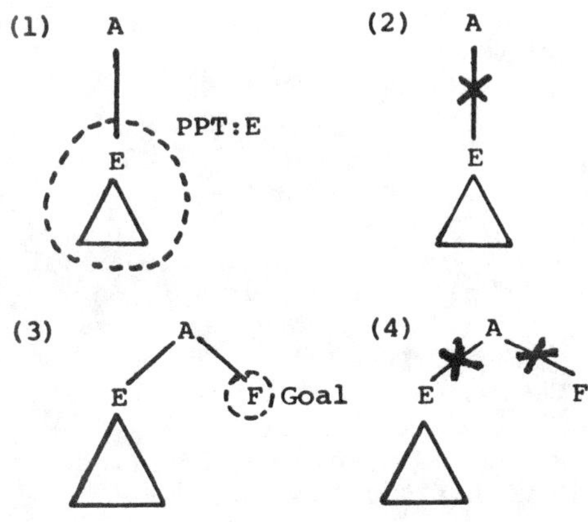

Fig.1 The result of the evaluation of advice

"X" in Fig.1 indicates that (R1) and (R2) fail to apply. Fig.1(1) indicates that (R1) applies to PPT:E. Fig.1(3) indicates that (R2) creates a new goal which predicts the next syntactic category F. In (4), a new goal is explicitly cancelled, while in (2) it is implicitly cancelled.

When a new goal is created as in Fig.1(3), we can record <delayed-advice> in the goal by using the Memo-Advice (MA) function in <advice> in the following way:

(MA <delayed-advice>)

The execution of <delayed-advice> is postponed until PPT:F will be created. (See Fig.2). With respect to <delayed-advice>, there are two more possibilities in growing PPTs depending on the evaluation value of <delayed-advice>. The <delayed-advice> acts as though it were a look-forward demon which would be activated when a goal is satisfied later.

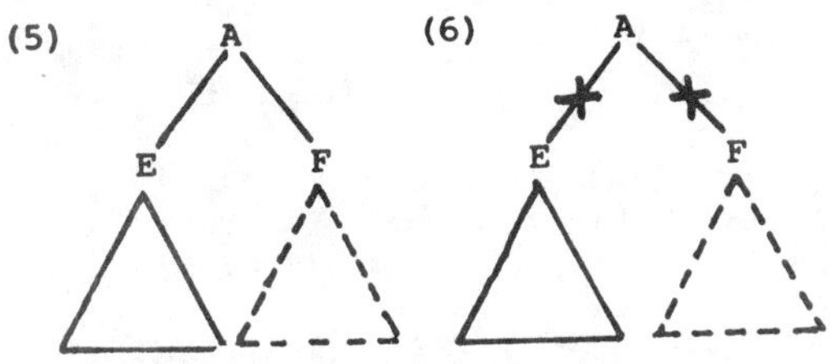

Fig.2 The result of the evaluation of <delayed-advice>

2.2 Control of Messages

In the field of advice and delayed-advice, we use messages to control parsing process. About 10 primitive functions are prepared.

A. Creating and Passing Messages: In <advice>, users can creat and pass any kind of messages from node to node upward in accordance with the growth of PPT. There are six primitive functions as shown in Fig.3. The effects of the evaluation are also stated in Fig.3.

CF rules	Primitive Functions for creating and passing messages	Message "M" sent to Node A.
A → B	(PM 'a)	(CONS 'a X)
A ← M, B ← X	(PM1 'a)	(NCONS 'a)
A → B C	(PML 'a)	(CONS 'a X)
A ← M; X → B, Y → C	(PMR 'a)	(CONS 'a Y)
	(PMRL 'a)	(CONS 'a (APPEND X Y))
	(PM2 'a)	(NCONS 'a)

Fig.3 Prmitive functions for creating and passing messages.

B. Checking Messages: When applying a context-free rule to some PPTs and goals created so far, users can ask for messages at the root node of PPTs by using the function named QM. Recall the cases of Fig.1 where (R1) and (R2) have a very simple <advice> (QM 'm).

[A E ((QM 'm)..)] ;A ⟶ E

[A (E F) ((QM 'm)..)..] ;A ⟶ E F

If a message m exist at the node E, (EVAL (QM 'm)) becomes true and two rules under consideration can not be applied ((2) and (4)), otherwise PPT:E grows in (1) or a new goal is created in (3).

C. Removing Messages: To remove a messages in the root node of PPTs, the function named RM is used.

3. EXAMPLES

In order to show how the predictive control mechanism works, we discuss two very simple examples, which inhibits the recursive application of rules of left and right recursive definitions.

Example (a)
Let us consider the following rule.

```
(R3) [NOUN (NLUN SUFFIX)
        ((OR (QM 'uncountable)
             (QM 'suffix) (PMR 'suffix))..)..]
and [estimation NOUN ((uncountable)..)..]
    [apple NOUN(()..)..]
    [s SUFFIX ((suffix)..)..]
```

Notice that the rule (R3) is left recursive, but it should not be applied recursively. The predictive control mechanism avoids the situation. The last three are from a dictionary.

The <advice> in (R3) works as follows:

```
  If NOUN is not an uncountable noun
     and Noun is not followed by a suffix
     then create a goal by applying (R3)
          and pass a message named suffix
          upward if a goal SUFFIX is satisfied;
     else do not apply (R3);(See Fig.4(a)).
```

(a)

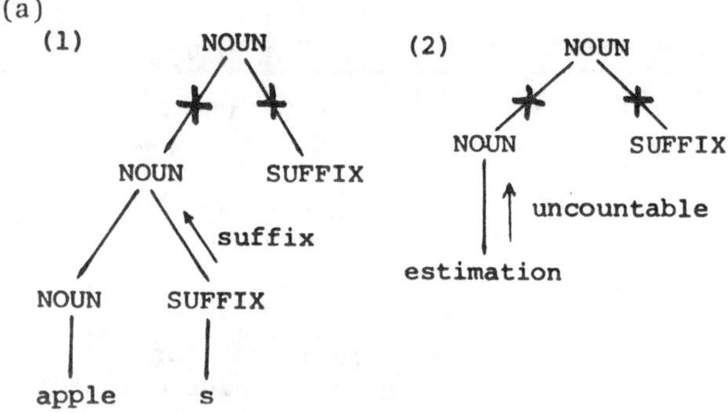

(b)

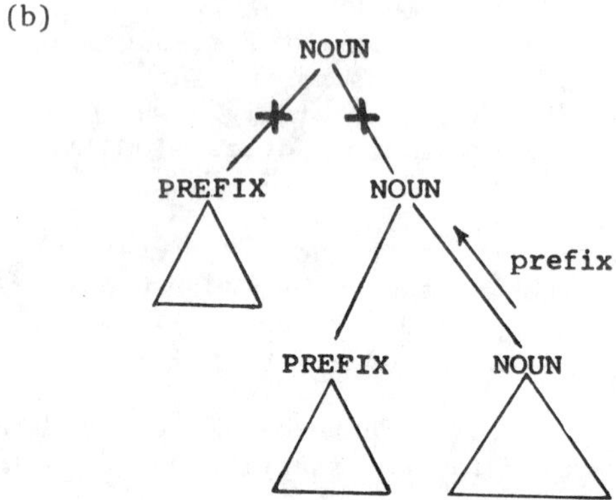

Fig.4. Example (a) and (b)

Example (b)
The following rule (R4) is right recursive.

```
  (R4) [NOUN (PREFIX NOUN)
              ((MA (OR (QM 'prefix)
                       (PM 'prefix)))..)...]
```

The <advice> creates a <delayed-advice> (OR (QM 'prefix) (PM 'prefix)). By using Fig.4(b), it is easy to follow how the <delayed-advice> prevents the right recursive application of (R4).

4. CONCLUSION

We have discussed a new parser called Extended LINGOL which has been used in our laboratory for about 3 years. Predictive control mechanism has offered us flexible methods to implement a grammar. As described in the preceding section, each context-free rule works as an active process that can pass messages to another process or creat a new process. The process can also notify the parser the applicability of the rule attached. The newly created process works as if it were a look-forward demon. The <advice> attached to each (context-free) rule expresses an action of the rule (or process). Semantic information will become available during parsing process through the message control mechanism if necessary.

Automatic segmentation algorithms in our Extended LINGOL are reported in [6]. Various experiments have been carried out in our laboratory using Extended LINGOL. Some of them are reported in [5].

REFFERENCES

[1] Grishman, R.: "Implementation of the string parser of English" in "Natural Language Processing", Algorithmic Press, 1973, 89-109.

[2] Heidorn, G. E.: "Augmented Phrase Structure Grammar", in Schank and Nash-Webber (Eds.): "Theoretical Issues in Natural Language Processing", Cambridge, Mass. 1975, 1-5.

[3] Pratt, V. R.: "A Linguistic Oriented Programming Language", IJCAI3, 1973, 372-381.

[4] Pratt, V. R.: "LINGOL - A Progress Report", IJCAI4, 1975, 422-428.

[5] Tanaka, H., Sato, T. and Motoyoshi, F.: "EXPLUS--A Semantic Parsing System for Japanese Sentences", 3rd USA-JAPAN Computer Conference, 1977, 236-240.

[6] "Manual of Extended LINGOL", Machine Inference Section, Electrotechnical Laboratory, Tokyo, 1978 (in Japanese version).

INDUCTIVE LEARNING OF CATEGORIES FROM EXAMPLES USING MINIMUM COST REPRESENTATIONS

Steven L. Tanimoto
Department of Computer Science, FR-35
University of Washington
Seattle, Washington 98195
U.S.A.

The problem of learning categories from a sequence of examples is considered in terms of maintaining a minimum-cost representation for the set of categories. Categories here are subsets of a set of natural numbers. Computational aspects of the following problems are addressed: (1) how are the category representations updated as an incremental change is made to one category, (2) how can a minimum cost representation for a new category be obtained in terms of existing ones? and (3) how does the enlargement of the known universe of objects affect representations of known categories? We then discuss extensions of our methodology to domains which include structure in the categorical descriptions.

1. INTRODUCTION

1.1 Motivation

Machine acquisition of concepts from experience is an important goal for artificial intelligence. Knowledge bases, the primary source of limitation as well as power in "expert systems" should be able to grow and thus permit the systems to improve [2]. The automation of this growth of system knowledge is then of obvious interest. In this paper we focus on a simplified learning scenario where the concepts are restricted to be categories.

1.2 Past Work

The process of learning categories from examples has been studied from several different approaches including (a) trainable pattern classifiers working with real-valued features [6] and (b) discovery of classification rules using variable-valued logic [5], and (c) formation of structural descriptions in terms of known substructures [7]. Here we discuss the learning of categories in the simple mathematical framework of countable sets as is done by Lenat [4] so as to make clear some of the computational issues involved.

1.3 Problem Formulation

The kind of learning we wish to understand is the acquisition of new "concepts" (categories of objects) and the continual refinement of the representations for known categories as new examples of old categories are encountered. For example, suppose a person Sue previously unexposed to computers is shown a personal computer and told "This computer, the ACME 1, is a home system". Sue should then know that there is a category "computer", a category "home system" and that the ACME 1 is an example of each. She may also be able to infer that the category "home system" is included in the category "computer" if the context supports that inference, e.g. if she had previously been told "Let's discuss types of computers". After being shown several more home systems she may understand "home system" to be the set {ACME 1, Apple 15, JETSETTER, ACME 2}. Suppose she is then told that the following are "cheapo's": {ACME 1, Apple 15, ACME 2}. Being unfamiliar with the computer domain, we would not expect Sue to be able to distinguish the cheapo's from the non-cheapo's except by using the information she has been told. If Sue is thinking, we would naturally expect her to infer that JETSETTER is an example of a home system that is not a cheapo. In fact, if she remembers which are the home systems, then she has an easy method for remembering the cheapo's in:

cheapo's = (home systems) - {JETSETTER}.

We would like computer programs to make similar inferences in the course of learning categories.

2. MINIMUM COST REPRESENTATIONS

2.1 Representation Scheme

Given a set S of natural numbers, a representation for S written R(S) is any one of the following forms (as applicable) and C(R(S)), the cost of R(S), is as given. (1) if S is known

to be empty, then $R(S) = \{\}$ and $C(R(S)) = 1$. (2) if S is a singleton, then $R(S) = \{a_j\}$ and $C(R(S)) = 1$. (3) if S is the extension of an initial predicate, then $R(S) = \{x|P_j(x)\}$ and $C(R(S)) = 1$.
(4) if S is a union of two other sets, then $R(S) = (R(S_1) \cup R(S_2))$ and $C(R(S)) = C(R(S_1)) + C(R(S_2)) + 1$. (5) if S is an intersection, then $R(S) = (R(S_1 \cap R(S_2))$ and $C(R(S)) = C(R(S_1)) + C(R(S_2)) + 1$. (6) if S is a complement, then $R(S) = (\sim R(S_1))$ and $C(R(S)) = C(R(S_1)) + 1$.

The cost of S is the minimum cost over all representations of S. Our cost function, while arbitrarily chosen, yields cost values that roughly reflect the amount of symbology necessary to store representations.

2.2 Updating a Single Category

The amount of the change in cost for assimilation of a new fact is bounded (when only one category is represented). The following proposition describes the cost change for updating S to S' according to $S' = S \cup \{a_i\}$ where $a_i \notin S$.

Proposition 1: $C(S') - C(S) \leq 2$
and $C(S) - C(S') \leq 3$
where $C(X)$ denotes the cost of X.

As will become clear from subsequent discussion, when several categories are simultaneously represented, an incremental change in one may affect the total cost of representation beyond the bounds of proposition 1.

3. COMPUTATIONAL CONSIDERATIONS

3.1 Computing Minimum Cost Representations

Even the problem of transforming a list representation of a category into a minimum cost representation is a nontrivial problem in combinatorial optimization. The computational complexity of this and related problems of minimum cost representation is of interest because the high cost of such processing illustrates the subtlety in learning even simple concepts.

3.2 Multiple Categories

Suppose that there are initial predicates $P_0, \ldots, P_k$ and existing categories $S_0, \ldots, S_m$. Given a new category S_{m+1} we wish to find a minimum cost representation for $\{S_0, \ldots, S_{m+1}\}$. One approach is to find a minimum cost rep. for S_{m+1} in terms of the rep's. for $S_0, \ldots, S_m$. However it is possible that the rep's. of some or all of $S_0, \ldots, S_m$ should change with the assimilation of S_{m+1}. We shall address this subsequently.

As we permit LS to handle multiple categories we need an additional representation form: $R(S) = R(S_1)$. However we now must modify our cost rules so that any given category only gets charged once.

$C(R(S))$ = the number of occurrences of all of the following in $R(S)$:

$\cap, \cup, \sim, \{a_i\}, \{\}, \{x|p_j(x)\}, R(S^1),$

where a_i is any integer, P_j is any predicate and S^1 is any category whose representation is charged separately. Note that the assimilation of new information may require changing representations for old information.

3.3 Circularity in Representation

As category representations are updated, care must be taken to avoid circular representations. If at time 1 we have S_2 represented as or in terms of $R(S_1)$, then we may not at a later time (2) change the representation of S_1 to be in terms of S_2 unless S_2 is first made independent of S_1. Prevention of circularity may be handled by maintaining a partial order on the categories, implemented as a directed acyclic graph. The algorithm below builds the representation for a collection of categories in a non-circular way by representing the simplest (least costly) categories first and building up to "inherently costly" categories (those that would be expensive if expressed independently of other categories), thus progressiving through a "topological sort" of the partial order.

3.4 Brute-force Method

The "exhaustive" computation scheme follows: FINISHEDREPS ← set of extensions of initial predicates; I ← 1; WHILE categories remain to be represented DO BEGIN ADD representations for all categories having cost at most I (in terms of representations already in FINISHEDREPS; I ← 1; END.

In order to determine whether (and how) a category S_i can be represented in terms of the members of FINISHEDREPS with a cost of I, we can simply generate all representations (finitely many when U is finite) and test to see if any represent the category under consideration. It is not hard to see that the combinatorial explosion is severe here. If the size of the universe is N, and the number of representations on FINISHEDREPS is q, then $O((N + q)^{(I + 1)/2})$ representations must be considered using this scheme.

3.5 Reducing the Computational Effort

If q, the number of complete representations is much less than n, the size of the universe, then the following approach is economical. Combinations (of the existing q categories) of successively greater cost are generated using ~, ∪, and ∩ but no singleton sets. The category S_i which is to be represented, is "matched" to each of these categories as it is generated. In matching S_i with an S_j (set represented using some combination of existing Categories), compute $S_{ij1}=S_i-S_j$, the set of numbers in S_i missing from S_j and $S_{ij2}=S_j-S_i$, the set of numbers which need to be removed from S_j in forming a representation for S_i in terms of S_j. We call $d_{ij}= | S_{ij1} |$ the deficiency of S_j (for S_i) and $e_{ij} = | S_{ij2} |$ the excess of S_j (for S_i). If $C(R(S_j)) + (2d_{ij} -1) + (2e_{ij} +1) \leq I$ then we have a representation for S_i of the form

$$((\ldots((R(S_j) \cup \{x_1\}) \cup \{x_2\}) \cup \ldots \cup \{x_{d_{ij}}\}) \cap \sim((\{y_1\} \cup \{y_2\}) \cup \ldots \cup \{y_{e_{ij}}\}) .$$

The operation of determining the deficiency set and the excess set is analogous to a process referred to as "interference matching" [3]. The above algorithm can take advantage of an additional short cut (without changing its solutions). From I and $C(R(S_j))$ the permissible deficiency plus excess is easily computed. As S_{ij1} and S_{ij2} are being computed it may be apparent that the limit will be exceeded. At such a point, further consideration of S_j can be aborted for the current value of I.

3.6 Supporting Categories

In some cases a collection of categories may have their cost reduced by introduction of a new category. If we let our system construct one, we term it a supporting category. While we have heuristics to generate supporting categories that reduce costs in specific situations, the problem of finding them in general is an open one.

3.7 Extensions

Our study has primarily been concerned with sets of natural numbers. There exist straightforward means to represent and to compute costs for structured objects such as n-tuples, labelled graphs and strings. Once again, computational complexity is a problem as one confronts the problem of subgraph isomorphism [1].

4. IMPLEMENTATION

A preliminary implementation has shown that additional heuristics and/or parallel processing are needed to make minimization of cost computationally feasible. Approximate solutions would be acceptable in most AI applications and this area is open for future work.

5. CONCLUSION

The maintainance of a minimum cost representation for a set of categories is desirable because relationships among categories are clarified and space requirements for the stored information are low. However, the complexity of computing the representations is high. Some heuristics have been given here and more are needed to simplify such computations.

REFERENCES

[1] Aho, A.V., J.E. Hopcroft, and J.D. Ullman. The Design and Analysis of Computer Algorithms, Addison-Wesley, Reading, MA. 1974.

[2] Feigenbaum, E.A. "The art of artificial intelligence: themes and case studies of knowledge engineering." Proc. IJCAI-77. MIT, Cambridge, MA, 1977, pp. 1014-1029.

[3] Hayes-Roth, F. and McDermott, J. "An interference matching technique for inducing abstractions." CACM Vol. 21, No. 5 (May 1978), pp. 401-411.

[4] Lenat, D.B. "Automated theory formation in mathematics." Proc. IJCAI-77. MIT, Cambridge, MA, 1977, pp. 833-842.

[5] Michalski, R.S. "Discovering classification rules using variable-valued logic system VL_1." Proc. Third Int. Joint Conf. on Artificial Intelligence, Stanford Univ, 1973, pp. 162-172.

[6] Nilsson, N.J. Learning Machines. NY: McGraw-Hill (1965).

[7] Winston, P. "Learning structural descriptions from examples." Ph.D. Dissertation, Dept. of Elect. Eng. TR-76, Project MAC TR-231, Sept. 1970.

Experience with the Evaluation of Natural Language Question Answerers*

Harry Tennant
Advanced Automation Group
Coordinated Science Laboratory
University of Illinois at Urbana-Champaign
Urbana, IL 61801

Research in natural language processing could be facilitated by thorough and critical evaluations of natural language systems. Two measurements, conceptual and linguistic completeness, are defined and discussed in this paper. Testing done on two natural language question answerers demonstrated that the conceptual coverage of such systems should be extended to better satisfy the needs and expectations of users.

None of the natural language papers presented at IJCAI77 reported on their programs' performance as language understanders. The reader has very little hope of thoroughly understanding the capabilities of the systems and techniques described.

The most critical dimensions of natural language performance are the range of concepts understood and the accommodation of diverse forms of expression. In this work on evaluation I have concentrated on these two aspects of performance and restricted the study to natural language question answering systems. In the paragraphs that follow, I will describe performance goals and measurement in more detail, then discuss the findings to which their use has led.

1.0 Performance Goals and Measurement

A natural language processor can be seen from two points of view: that of the designer and that of the user. The designer examines the domain of discourse of a particular application and maps out the range of concepts that are within it. The range of concepts is the CONCEPTUAL COVERAGE of the system. The designer must also accommodate the diversity with which the users will generate their statements and requests. The range of linguistic phenomena handled by the system is the LINGUISTIC COVERAGE of the system. The gauge of the success of the designers is how well the coverage has anticipated the needs of the users.

Users see a natural language question answering system and the database to which it interfaces through the perspective of their own needs and habits. They approach a database question answerer expecting it to include certain concepts, and forming utterances in their accustomed ways. The degree to which the concepts expected by a set of users can actually be found in the system's conceptual coverage is the CONCEPTUAL COMPLETENESS of the natural language processor, with respect to the set of users. Similarly, the degree to which the language of a set of users is appropriately analyzed by the system is the LINGUISTIC COMPLETENESS with respect to that set of users.

It is interesting to consider the current description techniques for natural language processors in terms of conceptual and linguistic coverage and completeness. When a paper presents twenty or so questions that are appropriately analyzed, the questions include concepts from the system's conceptual coverage, and their forms and features suggest elements of the system's linguistic coverage. Unfortunately, the conceptual and linguistic coverage of the system is not fully specified by what is found in the examples, and one cannot generalize from them. If no claim is made that the examples were in some sense typical of user inputs, nothing can be inferred about conceptual or linguistic completeness. If the paper goes on to explicitly mention handling features such as ellipsis or pronoun reference a comment is being made about the elements of linguistic coverage. Since this is not being related to the needs of a set of users, it says nothing about linguistic completeness.

*This work was supported by the Office of Naval Research under Contract N00014-75-C-0612.

2.0 Performance Testing

The ideas for testing conceptual and linguistic completeness were exercised on two natural language question answering systems, PLANES[9] and, to a lesser extent, the Automatic Advisor[7]. The performance of PLANES will be described in [8].

One tests the general competence of the natural language system by simply giving database problems to users and letting them attempt to solve them. Conceptual completeness is tested by giving database problems to subjects who are very familiar with the system, eg., the system designers. If a problem can be solved at all, the conceptual coverage must include the concepts indicated by the problem. Linguistic completeness is tested by giving users the problems that were solved in the conceptual completeness test. If a user utterance cannot be handled appropriately by the system, it is probably due to a limitation of linguistic coverage. It could, however, be due to a limitation of the conceptual coverage that was not discovered in the conceptual completeness test. For this reason, tests for conceptual completeness and linguistic completeness are not entirely independent.

3.0 Conceptual Completeness

Much work has been done and discussed in the literature on identifying the elements of linguistic coverage for improved linguistic completeness. The user testing has not led to the discovery of new elements of linguistic coverage.

The most interesting findings were in the area of conceptual completeness. Papers describing natural language processors frequently concentrate on linguistic coverage with the implicit assumption that the database determines the range of conceptual coverage. However, we found that the subjects thought in terms of the activities that the database described. The activities orientation is evidently the one that should be supported for casual users.

The activities orientation is helpful for identifying a broad class of erroneous presuppositions that may be embedded in user's queries. In the question "Which planes that flew on March 2, 1970 had maintenance on March 3?", one presupposition is that there were in fact some planes that flew on March 2. If the database lists the planes that flew on particular days, this would be a Kaplan-type presupposition [2]. However, if there was no information on flights in the database, it would be a more general form of presupposition.

Another result relating to conceptual completeness was evidence against the common assumption that users' utterances are limited to database queries. Most natural language question answerers rely on the assumption that the user will ask a question, the system will query the database to answer it, then the user will ask another and so on. This is not the way conversations work. In testing PLANES and the Automatic Advisor, users frequently made utterances that were not intended to be interpreted as database queries. Various examples follow.

1. About the database:
   1. "What do you know"?
   2. "Is that everything you know about math 195?"
2. About vocabulary:
   1. "What is a buser?"
   2. "What does howmal mean?"
3. Context setting:
   1. "Now I am talking about the year 1970".
   2. "Year is 1970".
   3. "I am interested in a7's".
4. Reference to discourse objects:
   1. "What was the last plane I talked about?"
   2. "Now combine the two"
   3. "The other ones I just mentioned"
5. Verifying or summarizing results:
   1. "Then infe 210 and infe 211 must be taken at the same time".
   2. "So all I need is junior standing and math 195".
6. Multiple query utterances:
   1. "What parts failed and what were the parts removed or installed".
7. Multiple utterance queries:
   1. "How many aircraft flew more than 10 flights in 1973? in 1972? in 1970? List aircraft by number of flights for 1970."

Each of these examples was actually typed in by users using one of the natural language processors. Many more examples in each of these categories could be imagined. A few additional examples can be found in Malhotra's work [3] on a hypothetical management information system. These examples show clearly that question answerers cannot operate on a one-database-query-per-sentence basis.

A third result was discovered while testing the Automatic Advisor. It pertains to pragmatic relationships between elements of a database domain.

One of the data domains of the Automatic Advisor is that of the topics that are covered by the engineering courses in the database. The topics covered in the lower level courses were general, those in the upper level courses were more specific. The Automatic Advisor included no pragmatic relationships among the elements of the topics domain. Consequently, when asked for the courses that dealt with computers, it returned one course, the only one which explicitly mentioned "computers" as a topic. It failed to return about ten higher level hardware and software courses and a host of others that made extensive use of computers.

The problem of misleading answers due to missing pragmatic relationships is not peculiar to the Automatic Advisor, but is common to "portable" natural language processors. Harris states that "[the portability of ROBOT] is largely possible because of the way ROBOT makes use of the database as an existing semantic structure" [1]. Indeed, ROBOT, the Automatic Advisor, and other systems are evidence that much semantic and pragmatic information does lie in the structure of the database, but the tests have illustrated the limitations of relying solely on the database for this information. This suggests that conceptual coverage should include the pragmatic relationships between data elements even though these relationships may not be expressed in the database.

4.0 Conclusion

There is a clear need for natural language processors to be evaluated. The measures and measurement techniques described in this paper suggest that meaningful testing can be performed and that its results can promote the engineering of better systems.

The findings discussed above suggest that in addition to the study of the elements of linguistic coverage, attention should be focused on conceptual coverage. Without extending conceptual coverage beyond the limits of the database contents, a natural language question answerer can do little more than a formal query language. One mainstay argument in favor of natural language processors over formal query languages is that the use of natural language processors can be learned quickly and recalled easily after a period of disuse. These claims have not been substantiated, however.

The LADDER system [6] was evaluated [4] as a query language, and users were able to use the system with some facility after "moderate training (approximately 1.5 hours) in LADDER syntax and vocabulary" [4] (they were selected to be familiar with the activities described by the database). The LADDER users were trained because, "LADDER is sufficiently demanding in its syntax and lexicon so that if no training were provided, the outcome could be predicted with certainty -- namely, the technology would be severely limited as a tool for accessing a Naval command and control database." But tests of formal query languages have shown similar performance after familiarization [5].

It seems clear that the role that natural language question answerers should play is in providing the user with more complete conceptual coverage than he can have using a formal query language. The user has gained little if he avoids the rigors of learning a formal query language only to be subjected to the rigors of learning the details of the structure of the database. If he must know the minutia of either, he will not be able to use the system effectively on an occasional basis.

References

[1] Harris, L. R. "User Oriented Data Base Query With the ROBOT Natural Language Query System." International Journal of Man-Machine Studies. Vol. 9, 1977, pp. 697-713.

[2] Kaplan, S. J. "On the Difference Between Natural anguage and High Level Query Languages." ACM78. Washington, D.C., 1978.

[3] Malhotra, A. "Design Criteria for a Knowledge-Based English Language System for Management: An Experimental Analysis." Ph.D. Thesis, MIT, MAC TR-146, 1975.

[4] Miller, H. G., R. L. Hershman, R. T. Kelly. "Performance of a Natural Language Query System in a Simulated Command Control Environment." Naval Electronics Systems Command, 1978.

[5] Reisner, P., R. F. Boyce, D. D. Chamberlin. "Human Factors Evaluation of Two Data Base Query Languages--Square and Sequel." NCC, 1975, pp.447-452.

[6] Sacerdoti, E. D. "Language Access to Distributed Data With Error Recovery." IJCAI77 1977, pp. 196-202.

[7] Tennant, H. "The Automatic Advisor." Master's Thesis, University of Illinois at Chicago Circle. 1977.

[8] Tennant, H. "The Performance of PLANES" (forthcoming).

[9] Waltz, D. L., B. A. Goodman. "Writing a Natural Language Data Base System." IJCAI77, 1977, pp. 144-150.

NETWORK TRUTH-MAINTENANCE FOR DEDUCTION AND MODELLING **

Alan M. Thompson
Information Systems Division
NASA Jet Propulsion Laboratory
4800 Oak Grove Drive
Pasadena, California 91103

Logical dependency based "Truth Maintenance" is applied to network representations of symbolic logic relations, resulting in reduced structural manipulation. Logical support is determined dynamically within existing structure by procedural specialists attached to the truth functional connectives which attempt to maintain consistency in the network. The use of context layers in addition to dependencies allows more accurate world-modelling than previous dependency-based modelling schemes. Focus of attention in deductive search and planning is accomplished by the propagation of control information through the network in addition to normal truth values.

1. The Development of Truth-Maintenance

1.1 Introduction

The problem of modelling the consequences of an action has been central to the development of automated symbolic problem solving. Selection of proper strategies for accomplishing goals may be done only when the machine has an accurate model of the state of the world at each decision point (or else has a model of its own uncertainty). Early systems required a programmer to associate with each action description a complete representation of the changes that should be made to the world model when the execution of the action was simulated. In highly coupled problem domains where single actions may alter large numbers of states,* this requirement can lead to a difficult programming problem. If an unrestricted hierarchy of definitions is allowed, the consequences of actions may become highly context dependent, and the problem of simply enumerating the affected states can easily become intractable.

In integrated problem-solving systems, in which planning and world-modelling are combined with automatic inference from logical relations, it becomes highly desirable for the modelling component to employ the same logical relationships used by the inference process. Thus, if some planned action changes a state that had been inferred from previous states, then its supporting antecedents must also be changed ("refuted support"). Similarly, if the changed state had previously been used as the justification for another state, then the dependent state may no longer be justifiably believed ("lost support"). Also, the new state may provide a justification for logically dependent states ("discovered support"). These concepts led to the notion of logical dependency as a means of maintaining the justifications of derived states and of a process of "Truth Maintenance" (TM) as a means of determining the state of belief or disbelief in expressions as a consequence of changes to the database.

1.2 Previous related work

The most complete recent systems employing TM techniques are those of Doyle [2] and London [5]. Although these systems are based on similar theoretical grounds, they differ widely in implementation and application. Doyle's system uses dependencies to determine the consequences of assumptions, to identify inconsistent sets of assumptions and to control backtracking. London's system is designed for modelling the consequences of proposed action sequences. Both of these systems allow knowledge to be expressed in localized "chunks" with the coupling to other chunks accomplished by the dependency network. Both systems depend upon a separate inference module to compute the initial justifications for states, which are then used by the TM process. In both cases, the dependencies must be explicitly declared by the inference process in clause form, i.e., as (the conjunction of) a list of the antecedents of the derived state.

A thorough background discussion on the use of logical dependencies may be found in the referenced works; this discussion is restricted to certain generalizations of the earlier methods and with the solutions to certain difficulties encountered in the use of dependencies for world-modelling. Only examples in propositional logic will be illustrated: the methods have been extended to first-order, but are not implemented as of this writing. (This is an abridged version of the original paper, which can be obtained from the author.)

1.3 Motivation and Features of the JPL System

The "ERIS"+ system being developed at JPL is designed to generalize and improve the the TM and deductive processes in several respects.

*The following definitions apply to this discussion: A statement is represented as an <u>expression</u> (normally a Predicate Calculus formula). Expressions are stored in an indexed (associative) database as <u>nodes</u>. A <u>state</u> is the truth state (represented by a <u>truth value</u> (TV), such as true, false, etc.) of a node (or its associated statement). <u>axioms</u> or <u>rules</u> are statements of known truth value whose state may not be changed. Statement <u>connectives</u> include the normal truth-functional connectives (AND, OR, etc.) plus connectives for representing causality.

**This paper presents the results of one phase of research carried out at the Jet Propulsion Laboratory, California Institute of Technology, under Contract No. NAS 7-100, sponsored by the National Aeronautics and Space Administration.

+ERIS was the Greek goddess of discord.

The propagation of logical support, one of the primary functions of truth maintenance (discovered support), is also required by deduction; as deduction pursues potential proofs, the discovery of an actual proof should result in marking the valid line of support. In addition, by removing the restriction that dependencies be explicitly declared in clause form, considerable structural manipulation could be avoided during TM processing. In ERIS, generalized TM procedures have been developed that are combined with the deductive process, resulting in a significant reduction in symbol/structure manipulation during deduction.

Rule-based systems often have the restriction that knowledge be expressed in clause form, with inference (and therefore logical support) directed only from the antecedent to the consequent of implicative rules. Since this syntax restriction can often prove burdensome, especially to non-programmers, a more general representation was desired, in which domain axioms could be expressed using any combination of relational connectives. The SRI "SNIFFER" system employed such a representation, but required "extraction" rules to place the term to be proved in the consequent of an implication [3]. In ERIS, by defining TM behavior for each statement connective the need for applying rewrite rules to reformulate domain axioms as implications during deduction has been eliminated by a graph labelling procedure that determines logical support. Also, there is no need to conduct a separate search for a proof of a statement's negation, since the TM process may result in the discovery of a line of support for either result.

Previous work has demonstrated the advantages of dependency methods over linear (chronological) context layer schemes for the control of backtracking (see [4], [5], [2]), but context switching for purposes of hypothetical reasoning or multi-world modelling requires considerable computation using dependencies alone, as compared to typical "context-list" schemes. Although ERIS uses dependencies to control backtracking (by identifying the particular assumptions responsible for conflicts), the use of context layers is available for these other activities. Furthermore, by allowing the definition of a particular subcontext for modelling purposes, the combined dependency/context scheme permits the same TM procedures to be used for both deduction and modelling, even though different behavior results. This method has resulted in greater accuracy in world-modelling than London's dependency-based technique, upon which it is based.

When the truth value of a statement is not known, the deductive process may have to examine all applicable axioms for a derivation. Focus of attention during the search is the key factor in determining the effectiveness of a deduction method when the number of domain axioms is large. In a manner analogous to the propagation of logical support for known truth values, focus of attention during deduction is propagated through the network of expressions using "meta" truth values that contain control information, such as the type of search (deduction, planning, etc.), priority, strategy advice, etc. The meta-TV's allow efficient, uniform treatment of all the propagation rules associated with statement connectives, and, by initial propagation through the domain axioms to possible antecedents of relevant nodes, they provide a way of delimiting the subdomain within which the forward (antecedent) reasoning of TM behavior is allowed. This restriction of forward inference is essential in unbounded domains to suppress the generation of irrelevant assertions. Moreover, when domain-dependent deductive strategy information is available (as a supplement to generalized syntactical strategy rules), the control information in the database can be explicitly accessed by modal operators that may be used in strategy advice expressions. Similar use of modal operators for control information was available in the MIT AMORD/TMS system [2, 1].

2. <u>The Method of Network Truth Maintenance</u>

2.1 <u>The Definition of Statement Connectives</u>

The truth-functional connectives of symbolic logic are defined by associating with the name of the connective an encoded set of rules that govern the behavior of expressions formed with the connective. The rules determine the ways in which the expression can provide logical support to the subexpressions it connects (and vice versa) and are responsible for propagating the consequences of changes in support to the affected expressions. For efficiency, the rules are embedded in a procedural specialist for the connective. When a new TV is asserted for an argument of a connective expression or an entire expression, the specialist examines the TV's of the expression and its arguments. Knowledge of the truth table for a connective is embedded in its specialist and is used to find a consistent labelling of the expression and its arguments. If the new TV was assigned to the expression, then the TV's of the arguments may have to be changed; if the new TV was assigned to one of the arguments, then the TV of the expression may change unless the expression is acting as an axiom, in which case the TV of some other argument may have to change. The specialists are also responsible for propagating control information during deduction or planning. Connectives used to represent knowledge of causality are defined to the system similarly, by providing an appropriate procedural specialist.

2.2 <u>The Notion of a "Consistency Context"</u>

Any connective expression may behave as an axiom by having "current" support for its truth value. Truth values are context sensitive; an expression may have one truth value in a given context and a different one in another context or in an earlier "layer" of the given context. A special subcontext, called the "Consistency Context" (CC), defines the subcontext within which logical support for one truth value may not be refuted by a contradictory line of support. Normal TM guarantees that TV's of true or false are well-founded, that is, that they do not depend upon a circular justification [2]. During deduction the CC is identical with the entire context, well-founded TV's may not change, and contradictions result in retracting the offending assumptions (as in [5]). During modelling, however, the CC contains only the current set of axioms and those changes made SINCE the (modelled) execution of the most recent action. Lines of support within the CC may override other support, permitting the network to change so that it reflects the world state after the execution of the action. Truth values in the global plan context are assumed not to change unless so forced by new support. Axioms behave as such by the fact that their TV is in the CC, so that even subexpressions may behave as axioms if their TV has well-founded support within the CC. For example, given the axiom (IMPLIES A (OR B C)), support for the truth of A will cause the disjunction to behave as an axiom, i.e., if B is known to be false, then C will be labelled true.

2.3 Operation During World-Modelling

There are several problems associated with the use of dependencies for world-modelling, relating to the requirement for refuting all logical support for a changed state. These problems are: local uncertainty, global uncertainty, and the need for adequate domain knowledge. Local uncertainty arises in cases where support derives from mulitple antecedents, so there is more than one possible labelling that refutes the support should the consequent be changed by an action. Suppose that C was originally proved true by the truth of A, B, and the axiom (IMPLIES (AND A B) C). If C is made false by a planned action, it is necessary to refute the conjunction. Since both A and B were true (before the action), it is indeterminate whether one or both should be changed. London outlines two approaches to the problem of local indeterminacy: the introduction of uncertainty into the network by allowing the propagation of a TV for "unknown" to refute the support for both A and B, or else by requiring domain knowledge to be sufficiently complete and, moreover, suitably expressed to determine with certainty all consequences of a state change (by forward (antecedent) inference). These alternatives are generally unacceptable, but the method discussed here offers less sensitivity to the structure of domain axioms and avoids the introduction of uncertainty in most cases.

London pointed out that, in the case of refuting conjunctive support, the spread of uncertainty can in some cases be mitigated by new lines of support emanating from the state originally changed, as would occur in the case of "exhaustive support" with complete domain knowledge [4]. Since with incomplete knowledge such new support is not guaranteed to propagate to the refuted conjunction, some uncertainty may still remain in the net. By using a multiple-level agenda mechanism, the ERIS system defers the propagation of uncertainty to a queue with lower priority than that for known truth values, so that a line of support may be found that eliminates the uncertainty without having to mark nodes as "unknown" unnecessarily.

Furthermore, unlike London's system the CC method provides a way to undo the labelling of nodes marked "unknown" in the event that uncertainty propagates to a well-founded consequence of the original state change or if uncertainty was spread to nodes in a conjunctive antecedent and subsequently one of the nodes was found to have a known refutation. This is accomplished in part by allowing well-founded TV's to override the "unknown" TV even within the CC and also by retracing the spread of uncertainty when needed to reconstruct previous support. The CC method has the additional ability to detect instances where multiple antecedents are not linked by the same connective, but in which the network is globally indeterminate following a change.

The remaining difficulty encountered in modelling is the problem of capturing all the consequences of a state change. The above discussion pertains to instantiated structure with initially known truth values, but it is often necessary to invoke deduction to determine whether nodes that could possibly have been providing support before the state change (due to unresolved uncertainty) were in fact providing support. If such nodes were supporting a state that is changed by an action, then their support must also be refuted. Failure to determine the support status of indeterminate nodes with respect to a changed state may cause some of the consequences of an action to be ignored. This is the problem of exhaustive support, as described by London [4], and is a major problem in dependency-based modelling. It is related both to the completeness of the domain knowledge and to deductive search, since the basic problem is that of proving a universal, namely the completeness of the set of consequences (or the non-existence of a line of support from the action consequent to any supposedly unaffected state). The problem of the completeness of domain knowledge is outside the scope of the system (although indeterminacy following a state change may allow it to detect incompleteness). Deducing the TV's of previously unknown states to determine their support status may place large demands on the deductive component.

3. Concluding Remarks

By allowing logical support to be determined within existing structure, the restriction that dependencies be explicitly declared in clause form is eliminated. This is accomplished by connective specialists that use graph labelling to maintain consistency in the network, greatly reducing the overhead for symbol manipulation required by the deductive process, as rewrite rules are also eliminated (except for the initial simplification of expressions). The creation of new structure is limited to the instantiation of rules during deduction. By avoiding the structural manipulation of expressions, the network becomes, in effect, a "compiled" knowledge representation, upon which the procedural specialists operate merely by the propagation of normal and "meta" truth value "signals".

REFERENCES

[1] J. DeKleer, et al., "Explicit Control of Reasoning", MIT AI Lab Memo 427, June 1977.

[2] Jon Doyle, "Truth Maintenance Systems for Problem Solving", A.I. Laboratory, MIT. AI-TR-419.

[3] Richard Fikes and Gary Hendrix, "A Network-Based Knowledge Representation and its Natural Deduction System", Proc. IJCAI-77, MIT, Cambridge, Mass., August 1977.

[4] Philip E. London, "Dependency Networks as a Representation for Modelling in General Problem Solvers", Dept. of Computer Science, U. Maryland. TR-698.

[5] Richard Stallman and Gerald Sussman, "Forward Reasoning and Dependency-Directed Backtracking in a System for Computer-Aided Circuit Analysis", MIT AI Memo 380, also in Artif. Intell., 9:2 (October 1977).

HEURISTICS FOR KNOWLEDGE ACQUISITION FROM MAPS

Perry W. Thorndyke
The Rand Corporation
Santa Monica California 90406

Acquiring knowledge from a map depends upon procedures for focusing attention, encoding information, and integrating diverse knowledge. This paper describes the heuristics people use to study and learn maps. Verbal protocols obtained from eight subjects suggested four categories of procedures that were invoked during learning: attention, encoding, evaluation, and control. The use of certain heuristics in each category was highly predictive of learning success. Good learners differed from poor learners in their ability to encode spatial information, to evaluate their learning progress, and to focus their attention in accordance with a learning plan. Many of the successful heuristics appear to be readily trainable.

1. INTRODUCTION

Any image processing system, whether human or machine, must translate the information in the sensory display into a meaningful internal description of the sensory image [1, 3]. This paper investigates how humans acquire knowledge from geographic maps. AI studies of map learning [2] have emphasized the use of cartographic knowledge to guide segmentation and interpretation of map features. The present study, in contrast, focuses on the high-level procedures that people use to select, combine, and encode map information in memory. I shall refer to these procedures as heuristics to emphasize the variety of available techniques and the lack of prescriptive learning methods. The research goal is to develop a theory of expertise in map learning by analyzing differences between good and poor learners in terms of differences in their learning heuristics.

2. THE KNOWLEDGE ACQUISITION PROCESS

Figure 1 schematizes the knowledge acquisition process. The maps used in this study contain a variety of conceptual "elements" (e.g., buildings, roads, parks). Each element has both spatial extent (shape and location relative to adjacent elements) and a linguistic label. Because map learning is an active, intentional process, it resembles a problem-solving task. The goal state corresponds to a complete memory description of the map (shown at the top of the figure), and the problem-solving operators are the heuristics the learner applies to produce the memory representation. These heuristics regulate the flow of information and determine how it will be encoded in memory.

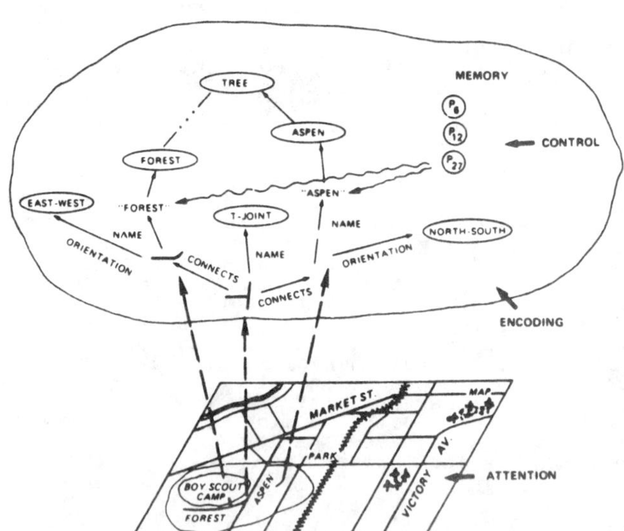

Figure 1. A schematic of the knowledge acquisition process

Attentional heuristics restrict the set of information on the map that the learner focuses on at any point in time, as illustrated in the lower portion of the figure. Encoding heuristics elaborate the information currently in focus and integrate it with other information from the map and knowledge already in memory. For example, one such procedure

(P27) might form a semantic association between the names Aspen Road and Forest Road using knowledge about their common property "trees."

Since the processing capacity (i.e., the upper bound on processing effort, size of working memory, communication channel capacity, etc.) is limited [4], only a subset of the available procedures are concurrently active. Therefore, control heuristics oversee the selection, activation, and scheduling of competing encoding and attentional procedures.

3. ANALYSIS OF LEARNING HEURISTICS

To identify the heuristics that people actually use, Cathy Stasz and I [5] collected verbal protocols from eight subjects attempting to learn real maps. On each of six trials, subjects would first study a map for two minutes and then attempt to reconstruct the map from memory. During the study period subjects thought out loud, describing their attentional focus, their study heuristics, and their evaluations of their learning progress.

Four general types of processes emerged from the protocols: attention, encoding, evaluation, and control. These processes and the heuristics subjects used to implement them are described briefly below.

Attentional processes included those by which subjects restricted eye fixations to a particular subset of the map (focus of attention) and shifted their focus of attention to a new location (attention switching). Two types of attentional heuristics were observed. The first of these, partitioning, was a procedure for focusing attention on a subset of the map information. Since a map contained too much information to be assimilated on any one trial, partitioning the map enabled a learner to attend selectively to a well-defined aspect of the map. Subjects partitioned the map either by (a) spatial region (e.g., by attending only to elements in the north of Market Street) or (b) by conceptual category (e.g., by attending only to the streets on the map).

The second type of attentional process comprised sampling heuristics. These procedures determined shifts in a subject's focus of attention among various map elements. Systematic sampling involved shifting attention according to a subject-defined algorithm (e.g., studying elements from west to east). Stochastic sampling involved shifting the focus of attention to an immediately adjacent element, but in no systematic or consistent direction. In random sampling the focus of attention jumped haphazardly around the map, with the new focus seemingly independent of the previous focus in both location and content. Memory-directed sampling occurred when a subject decided to study particular elements that had not yet been learned. For example, at the beginning of a new study trial, a subject might study the location of a river because s/he could not remember it on the previous recall trial.

When information was in a subject's focus of attention, various heuristics could be used to elaborate and encode the information in memory. These heuristics may be divided into those that operated primarily on verbal or linguistic information and those that operated primarily on shapes and location information.

Three verbal learning heuristics were observed. Counting helped subjects to cluster several elements sharing a particular property (e.g., "there are two parks on Victory Avenue"). Mnemonics were used to generate easily memorable retrieval cues for a set of names, such as "BUD," the order of the three structures on Market Street: bank, undertakers, and department store. The association heuristic involved the elaboration of the map information by association to or embellishment with some related prior knowledge. For example, one subject noted that Forest and Aspen Roads were both names for "trees."

Similarly, several heuristics for learning spatial information were observed. Visual imagery was a learning technique in which subjects constructed mental images of portions of the map. During study some subjects closed their eyes and attempted to draw shapes or name elements in a mental image and reported attempts to form a mental picture of some portion of the map. Labeling involved the generation of a verbal label for a complex spatial configuration. For example, a subject might notice that the three streets in the northwest corner of the map resembled the mathematical symbol pi. In pattern encoding a subject would notice a particular low-level shape or spatial feature of an element, such as Victory Avenue curving to the east. Finally, the relation encoding heuristic refers to the creation of a spatial relation between two or more elements. For example, one subject stated that Victory Avenue is "below the golf course" and is "parallel to Johnson."

The third type of process evident in the protocols was evaluation. Subjects would monitor their learning progress by considering what they had already learned and what they still needed to study. In particular, they would focus on an element and then determine whether or not they had learned it well enough to recall it later. This evaluation required a search and retrieval of information from memory and a comparison of that information to the representation on the map of the target element. When subjects decided they had not learned the information, they might then decide to study the element using one of the elaboration heuristics.

Finally, control or executive processes presumably directed the overall flow of processing. Since processing capacity is limited. Only a subset of the processes can be active simultaneously. The control processes include a mechanism for selecting from a set of available heuristics those to be activated (selection) and a mechanism for deciding when to deactivate a heuristic and switch to a new one (switching). For example, several subjects began to study a map with an unrestricted random sampling heuristic and then switched to a more selective partitioning heuristic.

4. ANALYSIS OF INDIVIDUAL DIFFERENCES

For each subject, the accuracy of the maps reproduced after each of the six study trials was computed as the proportion of map elements whose name and location were correctly recalled. Performance ranged widely from 94% of the map elements correct after only four trials to 39% correct after six trials.

The protocols of the successful learners (three subjects who recalled at least 90% of the elements correctly) were directly contrasted with those of the other five learners. For each subject the number of occurrences of each heuristic in the subject's six study protocols was computed. While subjects did not vary in <u>how many</u> heuristics they used, they did vary in <u>which</u> heuristics they used. The major differences between good and poor learners' use of heuristics are summarized below for each processing category.

ATTENTION. When good learners used the partitioning heuristic, it was acccompanied by either systematic or stochastic sampling. Once they had decided to focus on a defined subset of the map information, they would sample only elements in the partitioned set. In contrast, poor learners either (a) did not use the partitioning strategy, (b) used random sampling to accompany partitioning, or (c) were unable to restrict attention to elements in the partitioned set.

On later trials, when the basic framework of the map had been learned, good learners relied on memory-directed sampling to determine their focus of attention. That is, good learners knew which details were as yet unlearned and searched for and focused on that particular information. Their heuristic for selecting attentional focus was thus goal-directed. Poor learners, on the other hand, rarely used this sampling heuristic.

ENCODING. All subjects successfully learned the linguistic information; however, subjects varied in their success at learning the spatial information. Effective learners used frequent and varied spatial learning heuristics, while poor learners did not. Good learners reported constructing in memory and rehearsing a visual image of the map. They would also refine their knowledge of spatial location by noticing and encoding explicit shapes (pattern encoding) or spatial relations (relation encoding) among two or more map elements. These heuristics were used significantly more often by good learners than by poor learners. Poor learners frequently reported that they could not think of a technique for learning the spatial information in their focus of attention.

EVALUATION. All learners extensively evaluated their learning progress after each recall trial, but both the accuracy and content of subjects' evaluations differed between good and poor learners. An evaluation resulted in a decision that the subject either did or did not "know" the evaluated information. Good learners evaluated primarily unlearned elements (82% of all evaluation statements), ignoring information they had already learned. Poor learners evaluated a significantly smaller proportion (62%) of unlearned elements, and instead spent some of their study time confirming that they knew certain information. As noted above, good learners appeared to be goal-directed during studying. They would bring to each new learning trial knowledge of what information they had not yet learned, find that information on the map, and then study it using an appropriate encoding strategy. Poor learners seemed more data-driven: they would first focus on a randomly-selected map element, and then evaluate the element in memory to decide whether or not it had been learned.

When subjects assessed whether or not they knew an element, they could be either correct or incorrect in the evaluation. (Accuracy was assessed by comparing the subjects' statements about the elements with the accuracy of the reproductions on the previous trial.) Good learners were significantly more accurate in their evaluations (96% correct) than poor learners (82%). That is, good learners were superior at determining their current state of learning and "knowing what they know."

CONTROL. When good learners adopted a particular heuristic, they would continue to use it until it had achieved its purpose. For example, when good learners used partitioning, they would sample only information in the partitioned set until all elements had been considered. In contrast, poor learners frequently abandoned this heuristic abruptly and prematurely. This typically occurred when subjects could think of no heuristic for learning the sampled information.

Poor learners also failed to effectively select and use heuristics following evaluations. When a decision had been made that an element had not yet been learned, good learners immediately studied the element. However, poor learners would frequently shift their focus of attention to a new element without studying the unlearned information.

5. CONCLUSIONS

These analyses suggest that the use of powerful heuristics are principally responsible for differences in learning success. We have completed another study that demonstrates directly the utility of using these heuristics [6]. Three groups of subjects, equivalent in map learning ability, were given differential training in the use of learning heuristics. One group learned six of the effective heuristics reported here: three spatial learning strategies (imagery, relation encoding, pattern encoding), two feedback-monitoring strategies (evaluation, memory-directed sampling), and partitioning. A second group learned six heuristics that were uncorrelated with learning success. The third group received no instruction. Subjects trained to use effective heuristics improved their performance on a new map significantly more than subjects in the other two groups. Further, the magnitude of the improvement was a function of the frequency with which subjects used the trained heuristics.

These studies exemplify a growing body of research in cognitive studies of expertise and individual differences. Psychologists are beginning to view expertise as a collection well-tuned, information processes that combine to produce complex task performance. This analytic approach has, of course, been successfully applied in the contruction of knowledge-based systems in artificial intelligence. Based upon the early successes of this approach in cognitive psychology, it would appear to have a promising future in that area as well.

ACKNOWLEDGMENTS

The research reported in this paper was supported by contract N00014-78-C-0042 from the Office of Naval Research. I gratefully acknowledge the contribution of Cathleen Stasz, whose collaboration on the experimental studies made this paper possible.

REFERENCES

[1] Ballard, D.H., Brown, C.M., & Feldman, J.A. "An Approach to Knowledge-Directed Image Analysis." Proc. IJCAI-77, Cambridge, Massachusetts, 1977, 664-670.

[2] Mackworth, A.K. "On Reading Sketch Maps." Proc. IJCAI-77, Cambridge, Massachusetts, 1977, 598-606.

[3] Marr, D. "Representing Visual Information." AIM 415, Massachusetts Institute of Technology, Artificial Intelligence Laboratory, May 1977.

[4] Norman, D.A. & Bobrow, D.G. "On Data-Limited and Resource-Limited Processes." Cognitive Psychology, 1975, 7, 44-64.

[5] Thorndyke, P.W. & Stasz, C. Individual Differences in Knowledge Acquisition from Maps, R-2375-ONR, The Rand Corporation, Santa Monica, California, 1978.

[6] Thorndyke, P.W. & Stasz, C. Training Strategies for Map Learning. N-1018-ONR, The Rand Corporation, Santa Monica, California, 1979.

DESCRIPTION OF TEXTURES BY A STRUCTURAL ANALYSIS

Fumiaki Tomita*, Yoshiaki Shirai*, and Saburo Tsuji**

*Information Science Division
Electrotechnical Laboratory
Nagata-cho 2-6-1, Chiyoda-ku
Tokyo 100, Japan

**Department of Control Engineering
Osaka University
Machikaneyama-cho 1-1, Toyonaka-shi
Osaka 560, Japan

We introduce a method of a structural analysis for description of textures in natural scenes. The proposed texture analysis system automatically extracts the elements in a texture image, measures their picture properties, classifies them into some discriminable classes (one "ground" and some "figures"), and produces the description of elements in each class and also of their placement rules. This description can be used for learning and recognition of texture images. We also present a new idea for evaluating texture analyzers. In order to directly see what essential features or structurs of the given textures each analyzer extracts, we propose an analysis-by-synthesis method. That is, the synthesis program in our system reconstructs the texture image on the basis of its description. Comparing the reconstructed image with the original one, we can evaluate what information is preserved and what is lost in the description and can improve our algorithms.

1. INTRODUCTION

When we observe objects in a scene, we use the textural information as follows.
(1) identification of objects by the categories of textures,
(2) discrimination of objects by the differences of textures, and
(3) perception of a depth, a curved surface, or a inclination of a surface by the changes of textures.

Endowing machines with these recognition capabilities is not only an interesting problem in computer science but also practically important for automatic analysis of aerial photographs or medical images. Texture has been studied on at least two levels: statistical and structural [1]. On the statistical level, we regard a texture as defined by a set of statistics extracted from a large ensemble of local picture properties. On the structural level, a texture is considered to be defined by elements which occur repeatedly according to placement rules.

We have developed a structural analysis method first to segment an image into differently textured regions [2] and secondly to classify texture samples into several categories [3]. In this paper, we show what kinds of description can be given by the structural analysis and also present a new idea for evaluating texture analyzers. A conventional method for testing performance of analyzers is to evaluate their classification abilities for some texture samples whose categories are specified by a user; a better analyzer is that which gets a higher score of classification [4]. The classification ability, however, is highly dependent on both the texture samples and the categories. Since categories of natural textures are not so definite as artificially made characters, the evaluation of texture classification algorithms is dependent on their application fields. Then, in order to directly see what essential features or structures of the given textures each analyzer extracts, we propose an analysis-by-synthesis method. That is, our system first analyzes texture samples and gives their descriptions. Next, the synthesis program reconstructs the texture image on the basis of its description. Comparing the reconstructed image with the original one, we can evaluate what information is preserved and what is lost in the course of the analysis and can improve our algorithms.

2. STRUCTURAL ANALYSYS

A texture is defined as a repetitive pattern in which "elements" are arranged according to "placement rules". The proposed texture analysis system automatically extracts the elements in a texture image and measures their picture properties and their placement rules.

2.1 Preprocessing

An input image is digitized into 64x64 pixels and is quantized into 64 gray levels. Fig. 1 shows digital images of three kinds of textures. Since input conditions may change the first order statistics of brightness distributions, the input image is normalized with respect to gray scale changes so that the mean of the brightness distribution is 32 and the standard deviation is 8. Next, the normalized image is deblurred by an edge preserving averaging method to extract texture elements easily.

2.2 Extraction of Elements

A texture element is defined as a connected area with almost same gray levels. To extract such elements, pixels which are adjacent and whose gray levels are almost same are merged into regions. The merging process used here is as follows.

First, any pixels which are adjacent and whose gray level differences are less than the threshold d(=1) are merged into regions and their gray levels are averaged. Here, the total brightness change caused by averaging is examined. The total change is defined as

$$N(d) = \sum_{(x,y)} \sum |\delta_d(x,y)|$$

where $\delta_d(x,y)$ is the gray level change at a point (x,y). Next, d is increased by one (d←d+1) and the merging process is repeated until one of the following conditions is satisfied (d>4).

(1) the total change is very large, which implies that d has become large enough to merge different elements, or

(2) the total change is very small, which implies that there may be a brightness gap between different kinds of elements.

When the process stops at a threshold d* on the condition (1), the regions obtained by merging at d*-1 are used for the texture elements. When the process stops on the condition (2), the segmented region by thresholding the brightness histogram are used for the texture elements. For example, Fig. 2 shows the thus obtained elements of the images in Fig. 1.

2.3 Properties of Element

The following five kinds of properties are measured for each extracted element. They are used for global discrimination of elements.

(1) brightness

(2) area

Reptile skin (a) Straw (b) Handmade paper (c)

Fig. 1 Texture images

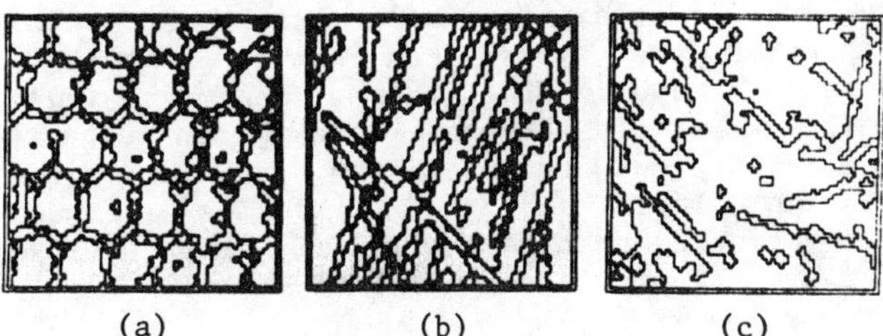

(a) (b) (c)

Fig. 2 Extracted elements

(3) size

The size of an element is defined as 2 x area/perimeter. For example, when an element is a circle of radius r, the size is r. The value of this size descriptor is not affected greatly by overlap of individuals which may be extracted as one element on the image level.

(4) directionality (direction and magnitude)

The directionality of an element is measured by the principal component analysis. The direction of the element is defined by the slope of the major axis. The magnitude D of the directionality is defined by the eigenvalues λ_1 and λ_2 ($\lambda_1 \geq \lambda_2$) of the covariance matrix for the distribution of (x,y) coordinates of points in the element, as

$$D = \frac{\lambda_1 - \lambda_2}{\lambda_1 + \lambda_2}$$

When an element is a circle, D=0. When an element is a straight line, D=1.

(5) curvatures along the contour

In the distribution of curvatures along the contour of an element is meaningful information about the complexity of the shape. We measure the k-curvature (k=5) [5] at each contour point. Next, a measured curvature ρ is classified into six zones:

i) high concave curve: $-75° \leq \rho \leq -45°$
ii) low concave curve: $-45° \leq \rho \leq -15°$
iii) straight line : $-15° \leq \rho \leq 15°$
iv) low convex curve: $15° \leq \rho \leq 45°$
v) high convex curve: $45° \leq \rho \leq 75°$
vi) zig-zag line : the other

and the occurence probabilities of curvatures in the first five zones are calculated for the element properties.

2.4 Classification of Elements

On the basis of the distributions of these properties, elements are classified into some discriminable classes. In our system, elements are classified by thresholding the histogram of each property. In computing the histogram of a property, we use the weighted value as its frequency to give large weight to dominant elements. The weighting values are shown in Table 1. For example, the frequency of brightness b is defined as the total area (not number) of elements whose brightness are b. Therefore, the system can stably analyze a texture image in which there are comparatively small number of elements. Since each property has a different domain and range, the histogram is normalized and the thresholds are set automatically at the bottoms of deep valleys between the prominent peaks, if any [3].

2.5 Description of Texture

Statistical Features

Now, the system calculates the following statistical features about elements in each class.
(1) the number of classes: Nc
(2) the mean and the deviation of each property p of elements in each class i: (μ_{ip},σ_{ip}) (i=1∿Nc and p=1∿Np, where Np is the number of properties). The weighted values in Table 1 are also used for calculating these distributions.

Table 1 Weightings in histogram computation

PROPERTY	WEIGHTING
BRIGHTNESS	AREA
SIZE	PERIMETER
AREA	AREA
DIRECTIONALITY	
.DIRECTION	AREA x MAGNITUDE
.MAGNITUDE	AREA
CURVATURES	PERIMETER

Furthermore, the following features concerning to placements of elements are easily measured.
(3) the density of elements in each class i: Ai (i=1∿Nc), which is the ratio of the total area of elements in class i to the image area.
(4) the adjacency probability between class i and class k: Pik (i,k=1∿Nc), which is defined as the probability that a boundary point of an element in class i is adjacent to that in class k. When i=k, it is especially called 'auto-adjacency probability'.

Table 2 shows the values of these textural features of the images in Fig. 1.

Figure and Ground

If there is more than one class of elements, one of them can be regarded as the "ground" of the image. The "ground" class is defined as

Table 2 Statistical features of elements and placements

TEXTURE	(a)				(b)				(c)			
No. of class	1		2		1		2		1		2	
properties	MEAN	S.D.	MEAN	S.D.	MEAN	S.D.	MEAN	S.D.	MEAN	S.D.	MEAN	S.D.
brightness	19.2	5.2	36.1	1.4	18.5	3.8	35.0	2.4	27.0	0.2	45.4	2.9
size	2.9	0.6	8.2	2.1	3.6	0.9	6.9	3.1	8.9	0.8	3.4	0.9
area	12.9	11.7	73.3	70.0	32.6	36.2	67.4	175.2	2664.5	438.3	144.1	105.2
directionality												
.magnitude (%)	56.6	26.5	34.3	24.4	78.8	28.0	71.4	22.7	7.0	6.9	28.7	29.0
.direction	16.4	4.2	17.7	2.0	17.7	2.7	17.3	1.2	17.9	0.8	23.0	3.8
curvatures												
.[-75°,-45°] (%)	4.4	6.1	5.3	4.5	1.9	3.5	4.4	3.2	9.6	2.1	8.6	5.9
.[-45°,-15°] (%)	21.0	15.2	17.9	7.7	20.8	9.8	19.8	9.9	24.7	5.1	24.3	12.8
.[-15°, 15°] (%)	13.9	13.4	16.0	8.3	32.6	17.5	32.1	16.1	28.8	5.6	22.8	13.7
.[15°, 45°] (%)	24.4	22.1	36.2	13.3	31.4	17.5	24.5	12.8	23.7	8.5	19.6	10.8
.[45°, 75°] (%)	9.1	10.5	18.9	8.5	6.1	8.6	7.0	8.0	9.2	3.1	8.3	9.9
density (%)	30		70		29		71		73		27	

adjacency-probabilities (%):

(a)	1	2
1	22	78
2	93	7

(b)	1	2
1	10	90
2	60	40

(c)	1	2
1	0	100
2	97	3

(1) a class whose average area of elements is very large (for example, class 1 of (c) in Table 2), otherwise,
(2) a class whose ratio of the deviation to the mean of areas of elements is very large (for example, class 2 of (b) in Table 2), otherwise,
(3) a class which has the largest auto-adjacency probability (for example, class 1 of (a) in Table 2).

The other classes are in turn regarded as the "figures" of the image. If the image has only one class of elements, it is regarded as both the "figure" and the "ground". For example, the "grounds" of the images in Fig. 1 are smeared with black as shown in Fig. 3.

Typical Element

The system selects one typical element from each "figure" class to give a detailed shape description of the elements in that class. The typical element in each "figure" class is the one whose shape properties are the closest to the means of those of that class. The function that evaluates the closeness of an element j in class i is defined as

$$E_{ij} = \frac{\sum_{p=1}^{N_p} \exp\left[-\frac{(x_{jp}-\mu_{jp})^2}{2\sigma_{ip}^2}\right]}{N_p}$$

where xjp is the value of a property p of an element j and the shape properties used are area, size, directionality and curvatures. For example, the dotted areas in Fig. 3 are the typical elements of the image in Fig. 1.

It is an important problem how a typical element is to be described for a detailed comparison needed in recognition phase of the system. There are many algorithms for shape analysis [6] and we should select a information preserving technique. In this paper, however, only the points in a typical element are memorized in terms of the relative coordinates from the centroid of the element for simplicity.

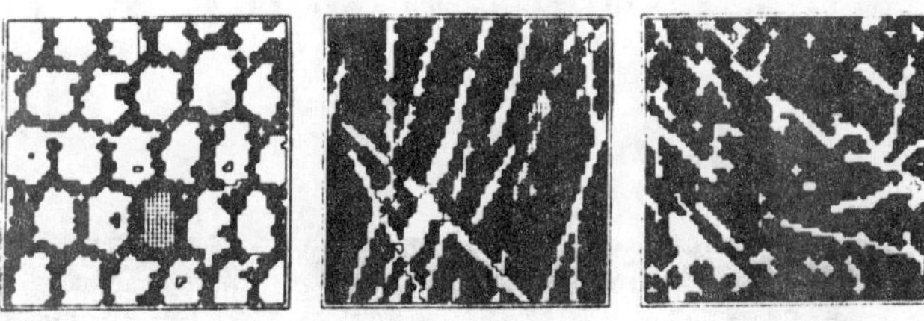

Fig. 3 "Grounds" of images (■) and typical elements (⊡) in "figure" classes (□)

Relative Position Vectors

To give a detailed description also of placements of elements, the system measures relative positions among elements in "figure" classes. A relative position between two elements is defined as the relative coordinate between their centroids. The two dimentional histogram Hik of the relative positions of every pair of elements, one in class i and the other in class k (including i=k), are computed. Here, in computing the histogram we use the weighted value as its frequency as follows. Let Eij be the closeness of an element j in class i and Ekl be that of an element l in class k. Then the weighted value is defined as min(Eij,Ekl). If the placement is regular, there are significant clusters periodically in the histogram. In such a case, the mean and deviation of each independent cluster which is nearest to the origin is measured as the placement rule Rik. They are denoted as

$$R_{ik} = [\{\mu_x^n(i,k),\mu_y^n(i,k)\},\{\sigma_x^n(i,k),\sigma_y^n(i,k)\}] \quad (n=1\sim Nik)$$

where Nik is the number of independent clusters. If there is no significant cluster, the placement rule Rik is regarded as random.

For example, Fig. 4 shows the distributions H22 of relative positions of elements in the "figure" class 2 of the image in Fig. 1(a). In this case, the placement is regarded as regular and two independent clusters (whose means are (13,-6) and (0,11)) are measured. On the other hand, those of the other images in Fig. 1 are regarded as randam.

Now, the description of texture is completed. This description can be used for learning and

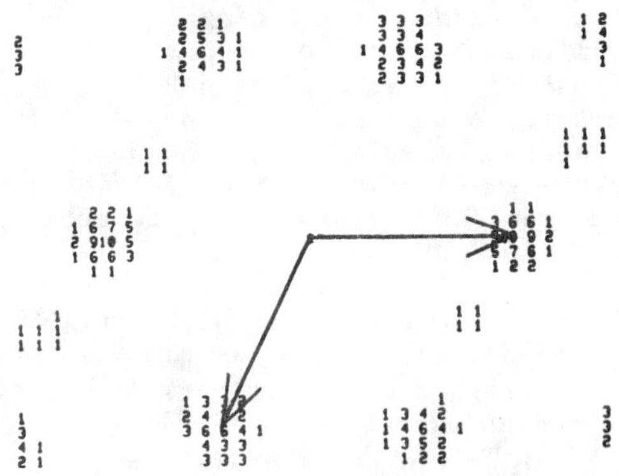

Fig. 4 2-D histogram of relative positions among elements in "figure" class

recognition (classification) of texture images. Classification experiments using only the statistical features are reported in [3].

3. RECONSTRUCTION OF TEXTURES

The synthesis program in the system generates a texture image on the basis of the description of the original texture. It reconstructs a texture image so that the statistical features may be the same as those of the original one.

3.1 Modification of Typical Element

To reconstruct the texture elements, the system uses the typical element in each "figure" class and modifies it according to the distributions of the properties of elements in its class. The properties used for modification are brightness (for light and darkness), size (for magnification and reduction), direction (for rotation), and the magnitude of directionality (for compression).

For example, let (μ_{ip},σ_{ip}) be the mean and deviation of the property p of elements in class i. The typical element is modified so that the distribution of a property p is $N[\mu_{ip},\sigma_{ip}]$ using a normal random number generater.

Modified elements in such a way are then arranged according to the placement rules as mentioned in the next section.

3.2 Placement of Modified Elements

The system determines the positions at which modified typical elements are placed as follows. If there are more than one "figure" class, one dominant "figure" class is selected. That is, the positions of elements of the dominant "figure" class (let it be now i) are at first determined according to the placement rule Rii and those of other class k are determined later according to Rik or Rkk. Our system defines a class i as the dominant one whose average deviation in the placement rule Rii is the smallest. The positions of elements in the dominant class are determined as follows.

When the placement rule Rii is regular, the distributions of relative positions in Rii is used. First, the preliminary positions are determined using the means in Rii

$$\{\mu_x^n(i,i),\mu_y^n(i,i)\}\ (n=1\sim N_{ii})$$

as shown by white points in Fig. 5 (in this case, Nii=2). Next, these preliminary positions are fluctuated according to the normal distribution

$$N[(0,0),(\sigma_x/2,\sigma_y/2)]$$

as shown by black points in Fig. 5 using a normal random generator, where σ_x and σ_y are the average deviations in Rii. These black points are the final positions at which modified elements are placed.

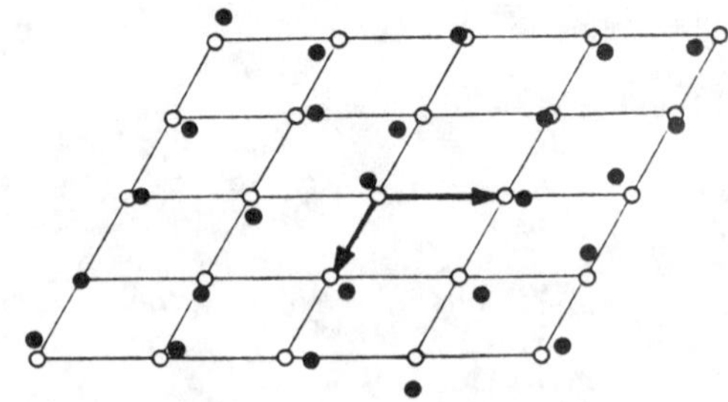

Fig. 5 Position determination in regular placement case (→: mean vector)

When the placement rule Rii is random, the system uses the density Ai of elements to determine the positions. Since the number of arranged elements is expected as

$$N_i = \frac{\text{total area of elements in class i}}{\text{average area of elements in class i}}$$

the system arranges such number of positions randomly over the image using a uniform random number generator.

Next, the position of elements in other class k(≠i) are determined in almost the same way according to the placement rule Rik or Rkk.

Refering to thus determined positions, modified elements in each "figure" class are placed. After all the "figure" elements are placed, there remains blank space which corresponds to the "ground" of the image. It is filled up with gray values on the basis of the statistical features of the "ground" class by a region growing method.

Now, the reconstruction of texture is completed. Fig. 6 shows examples of the reconstructed images from the original ones in Fig. 1.

4. DISCUSSIONS

For our experiments, we used the same texture samples from Brodatz's photographic album [7] as used in classification [3]. The structural analysis produces anthropomorphic descriptions and therefore they are easily understandable

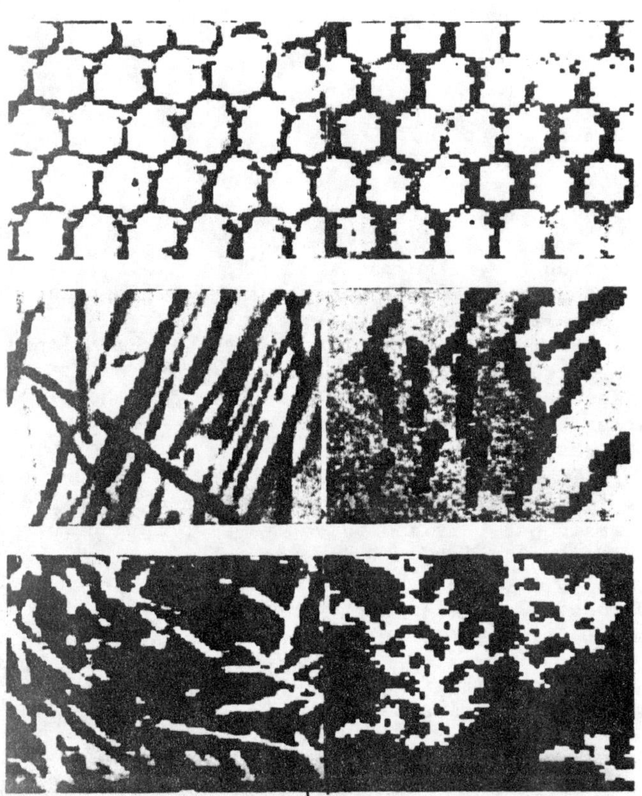

(c)

Fig. 6 Original images (left) and reconstructed images (right)

and useful. However, we found some important problems by reconstructing those texture images.

Since we only use brightness information to extract texture elements, they do not always correspond to real individuals or what human beings perceive. For example, overlapped individuals with same brightness are extracted as one element on the image level.

Also the "grounds" which the system selects do not always correspond to those which human beings select. This problem relates to the definition of elements.

The placement rules used (relative positions) is the second order statistics and may be still too simple. For example, though the position of an element is considered independently of its properties and those of surrounding elements, there are often correlations among them.

In this paper, we hardly deal with hierarchical textures. A hierarchical texture is such that a set of several elements can be regarded as a unit and many such units are arranged according to their own placement rules. Such hierarchical textures, however, are more often found in artificial textures. If we add aggregation programs [8] to our system, we would be able to describe them in the same way.

ACKNOWLEDGEMENT

The authors wish to express their thanks to members of the Computer Vision Research Section, Electrotechnical Laboratory, for their kind help.

REFERENCES

[1] Lipkin, B.C. and Rosenfeld A. (Eds.): Picture Processing and Psychopictorics, Academic Press (1970).

[2] Tomita, F., Yachida, M, and Tsuji, S.: "Detection of homogeneous regions by structural analysis," Proc. 3rd Int. Joint Conf. on Artificial Intelligence, p.564 (1973).

[3] Tomita, F., Shirai, Y., and Tsuji, S.: "Classification of textures by a structural analysis," Proc. 4th Int. Joint Conf. on Pattern Recognition, p.556 (1978).

[4] Weszka, J.S., Dyer, C.R., and Rosenfeld, A: "A comparative study of texture measures for terrain classification," IEEE Trans. SMC-6, p.269 (1976).

[5] Rosenfeld, A. and Kak, A.C.: Digital Picture Processing, New York: Academic (1976).

[6] Pavlidis, T.: "A review of algorithms for shape analysis," Computer Graphics and Image Processing, 7, p.243 (1978).

[7] Brodatz, P.: Textures, New York: Dover (1966).

[8] Marr, D.: "Early processing of visual information," MIT AI Memo, No. 340 (1975).

ALVEN: A Study on Motion Understanding by Computer*

John K. Tsotsos and John Mylopoulos
Department of Computer Science, University of Toronto
H. Dominic Covvey
Cardiovascular Unit, Toronto General Hospital, &
Computer Systems Research Group, University of Toronto
Steven W. Zucker
Department of Electrical Engineering, McGill University

Abstract

This paper presents an overview of a framework for the analysis of motion from sequences of images by computer. The framework includes:
(a) A representation of knowledge for motion concepts that is based on Minsky's frame theory and semantic networks;
(b) Associated algorithms for recognizing these motion concepts. These algorithms implement a form of feedback, by allowing competition and cooperation among local processes. They also allow a change of attention mechanism that is based on similarity links between knowledge units.

The framework is being realized with a system called ALVEN, whose structure and operation are described. The purpose behind this system is to provide an evolving research prototype for experimenting with the analysis of certain classes of biomedical imagery, and for refining and quantifying the body of relevant medical knowledge.

1.0 INTRODUCTION

The main goal of this research, from an AI viewpoint is the development of a framework for Motion Understanding by Computer. This framework is expected to provide:
(a) A representation of knowledge for motion concepts, based on frames [Minsky75] and semantic networks [Brachman79].
(b) The description of basic motion concepts such as verbs, shape transformations and temporal information in terms of the knowledge representation proposed, based on past work in motion representation [Badler75], [Tsotsos76];
(c) The development of algorithms for the analysis of pictorial data in terms of a motion knowledge base. These algorithms will be expected to generate a description of the objects and motions found in the pictorial data at different levels of abstraction, from detailed LV wall kinematics to summary statements using English-like verbs. The recognition control structure is based on the concept of competition and cooperation among local hypotheses [Zucker78] both at the low (image) level [Rosefeld,Zucker, Humel76] and at higher (conceptual) levels.

ALVEN (A Left Ventricular Wall Motion Analysis Computer Consultant), is a system for the analysis of cinecardioangiograms (films of the human left ventricle). Given such a film, the system's job is to generate a conceptual description of the shapes and motions exhibited in the film by the left ventricular wall, noting abnormalities and unusual occurrences.

From a medical point of view, ALVEN's importance is based on its ability to provide an assessment of the human left ventricle (hereinafter LV), as a functioning muscle. The aim of the research is twofold:
(a) To produce a system that can aid in the analysis of cinecardioangiograms, and which produces consistent and objective descriptions of left ventricular wall dynamics,
(b) To provide a framework for the representation of medical knowledge about the dynamics of the human left ventricle.

ALVEN is a first step towards achieving these objectives. Past descriptions of ALVEN may be found in [Tsotsos78] and [Tsotsos79].

2.0 REPRESENTATION OF KNOWLEDGE

2.1 What Needs to be Represented?

The main concern of this representational formalism is how motion concepts are to be represented and organized into a general motion concept and problem-specific concept knowledge base. There are several types of motion concepts:

a) speed of an object
b) trajectory of motion
c) descriptive motion verbs
d) qualitative trajectory descriptions - directionals
e) changes of an object's properties
f) temporal concepts: duration, start and end time, relative timing of events.

In addition, the representation must be flexible enough to handle "fuzzy" data, different levels of abstraction including linguistic levels, and to represent enough information for approximate regeneration of analyzed motions.

2.2 Representational Building Blocks

The basic entities of the representation are called frames and are used to model abstract concepts such as that of HEART or BEATing. The instantiations of the abstract concepts of the real world are modelled in the representation by frame tokens (or simply tokens). The INSTANCE-OF relationship relates tokens to the frames of which they are instances. Thus, "john's LV", an instance which represents a particular left ventricle, is related to "LV" through the INSTANCE-OF relationship.

* This paper is a summary of [Tsotsos79].

The internal structure of a frame is made up of two distinct components: information on how to instantiate the frame (fill the slots which make up the semantic components of the concept which the frame defines), and information on what concepts must be present in the description derived thus far in the analysis in order for the defined concept to apply. These two components are termed dependant and the prerequisite respectively. Both parts are made up of slots. The difference lies in the default values of the slots. The slot defaults for the dependant slots are made up of references to slots of the prerequisite part and function calls which use these values to calculate the instantiated value of the slot. Defaults in the prerequisite slots give expected values for observed data. Slots have associated with them a name, a frame type, constraints that must be satisfied by any candidate value and exceptions that are to be raised if those contraints are not satisfied.

2.3 Frame Organization

The frames which are part of a knowledge base are organized into an IS-A hierarchy in terms of the (partial order) relationship IS-A [Brachman79].

The prerequisite slots of a frame must conform to specific conditions as well. If frame A defines a motion concept for object C, the prerequisite slots must describe:

a) the motion sequences for C, including any parallel descriptions which must be added together to form the overall motion of C;

b) the motion sequences of all objects C' such that C' is a PART-OF C, thus conforming to the PART-OF hierarchy of C.

In addition to these two static organizational concepts, the representation allows the use of similarity links as an aid in transferring control between contexts and classifications during recognition.

Similarity links are associated with the frame concept defined and are based on exceptions which occur in the prerequisite components of that frame. There are three major components to the data stored along with a similarity link:

a) compatibility expression - This Boolean expression contains the necessary conditions which the two linked frames must share in order for the similarity link to be activated (i.e., the "similarities").

b) exception expression - This is a list of Boolean conditions in which the predicates are exceptions which may be raised during matching of the frame. Each of the list's elements has associated with it a time when the exception should occur. In effect, what such an expression defines is the time course of matching failures in one frame which indicate that the other frame is more relevant (i.e., the time sequence of "differences").

c) activate-support list - This is a list of generic frame names which are to be activated or supported by the similarity link.

2.4 Left Ventricular Motion Concepts

The left ventricle is standardly described by splitting up the outline into 3 segments (when viewed in the Right Anterior Oblique projection) - posterior, apical and anterior.

While the form of LV beats is not known precisely, there are some subjective data that are relevant for an initial version of the knowledge base (KB). For example, there is a separate motion frame for each of 7 phases of an LV cycle. Some phases define contraction of the LV (maximum ejection, reduced ejection), others expansion (rapid inflow, diastasis, filling by atrial contraction) and two define a state of rest (isovolumic contraction, isovolumic relaxation - isovolumic is the key here). Therefore the phase frames are IS-A linked to the frames for "contract" and "expand" as is appropriate. In each frame, all of the segments of the LV are associated with the event or sequence of events that define the segment's motions during that phase. Correspondingly, the frame for "normal LV beat" would be made up of the events which represent each phase of the LV, linked in a cycle with appropriate timing information so that together they define the cyclic beats.

Abnormalities are represented using the same structure. The segments which have abnormal motions have separate frames which describe abnormalities expected for that type of motion. Thus, for a particular abnormality, the frame would be made up of the appropriate normal and abnormal segments and phases.

3.0 A KNOWLEDGE-BASED FEEDBACK MODEL FOR ANALYSIS OF TIME-VARYING IMAGERY

There are three main components to the feedback model: (i) image analysis using system expectations; (ii) comparison of the results to the system's expectations; and (iii) adjustment of the system's state and expectations.

3.1 Image Analysis

The starting point for the system is an initial state (say, "NORMAL" LV motion is expected). Thus, the normal LV motion frame is activated along with all of its parts and generalizations (along the IS-A hierarchy). This allows generation of the first set of expectations for the next image. In our case, the first LV outline has been traced in the image. The first expectation is this same outline with a window of acceptable "normal" outlines built upon it. This is reasonable because at end-diastole (i.e., the time when the LV has completed its expansion) there is very little motion in the time spanned by the first 2 or 3 images.

The LV outline is found using an expectation guided relaxation process. Predictions enter the relaxation process in two ways: the search region and the expected edge orientation. Relaxation is only applied to the points for which a gradient operator has produced responses, i.e., in the search region. The expected orientation is included in the computation by associating with each sub-region in the region an orientation. This orientation is then used to bias the updating function to favour edge labels of the expected orientation (and those immediately compatible with that orientation). This information is coded into a "strength" function which becomes part of the relaxation updating rule.

We call the resultant outline the "essential trace" of the LV. Motion is detected for the object if the locations of any of its parts differ between the two consecutive images. Correlation of moving shape features between the two LV outlines is done in a heuristic manner. Using the correlation information, values are determined for transformation predicates. The essential kineses for an object are the changes of its physical properties and the changes in its location.

3.2 Change of Attention Mechanism

The system maintains a set of active hypotheses throughout the recognition process. This set is initially filled with the motion hypothesis the user believes is exhibited by a particular object (or objects).

Active hypotheses are organized by their "conceptual adjacency", defined in terms of the primitive relationships used to organize the knowledge base (IS-A, PART-OF and time relationships).

The system adds hypotheses to its list of active ones via activated similarity links and via the "next" temporal constraint. Similarity links are activated when one of the exceptions specified in the exception-expression is satisfied in addition to the hypothesis compatibility expression being satisfied. An active similarity link is also propagated along the motion PART-OF hierarchy in order to ensure the proper new context for the newly activated hypothesis is activated as well.

Hypotheses are deleted from the active list in two ways. If the hypothesis' expected maximum duration is exceeded, it is removed. If the values of its definitional slots can be found, it is instantiated. If the slots cannot be filled it is abandoned completely. The second way of removing hypotheses is by simple thresholding based on the leading hypothesis' certainty. Deletion of a hypothesis is propagated to all of its parts, all parent subjects, and all IS-A sons (recursively).

3.3 Focus of Attention Mechanism

The set of active hypotheses requires further organization. The prediction mechanism needs to know which are the best hypotheses at any instant in the processing, so that it can base its expectations on them. The hypotheses will be ordered by means of the certainty which the system has in them. On activation, all hypotheses are given a 50-50 chances - a certainty of 0.5. For each image afterwards, this certainty is updated using the paradigm of competition and cooperation among conceptually adjacent hypotheses.

The updating is done by a second modified relaxation labelling rule for which compatibility are defined between hypotheses depending on the type of conceptual adjacency they exhibit. For example, mutually exclusive hypotheses are those with a common direct IS-A ancestor. Hypotheses which follow or precede each other in time have large negative compatibilities to aid in their time-wise segmentation. Hypotheses which are the prerequisite slots of another hypothesis have large positive compatibilities with their parent hypothesis. A hypothesis has a compatibility dynamically set with itself for its following time interval depending on its matching progress. Finally, hypotheses linked by similarity links also have dynamically set compatibilities depending on whether one supports the other during that time interval.

4.0 PROJECT STATUS

Currently, we are in the final stage of a prototype implementation of ALVEN. The low level modules (essential trace and essential kineses) have been implemented and are being tested. The data collection module has been implemented and films are being processed. A syntax for the representation of knowledge has been defined and a compiler for entering and maintaining the KB has been implemented.

References

Badler, N., "Temporal Scene Analysis: Conceptual Descriptions of Object Movements", TR-80, Dept. of Comp. Sci., U. of Toronto, 1975.

Brachman, R., "On the Epistemological Status of Semantic Networks", in Associative Networks, N. Findler, (ed.), Academic Press, 1979.

Minsky, M., "A Framework for Representing Knowledge", in, The Psychology of Computer Vision, Winston, (ed.), McGraw-Hill, 1975.

Tsotsos, J., "A Prototype Motion Understanding System", TR-93, Dept. of Comp. Sci., U. of Toronto, 1976.

Tsotsos, J. et al., "Gross and Segmental Wall Motion Analysis in Dynamic Cardiac Imagery", Proc. Computer Applications in Medical Care, Washington, D.C., 1978.

Tsotsos, J. et al., "A Framework for Visual Motion Understanding", AI Memo 79-2, Dept. of Comp. Sci., U. of Toronto, 1979.

Zucker, S. et al., "An Application of Relaxation Labelling to Line and Curve Enhancement", IEEE Trans. on Computers, vol.C-26, 1977.

Zucker, S., "Production Systems with Feedback", in Pattern-Directed Inference Systems, Waterman and Hayes-Roth, (ed.), Academic Press,1978.

AN AUTOMOBILE WITH ARTIFICIAL INTELLIGENCE

Sadayuki Tsugawa, Teruo Yatabe, Takeshi Hirose and Shuntetsu Matsumoto
Automobile Division
Mechanical Engineering Laboratory
5-12-2 Fujimi-cho, Higashimurayama
Tokyo 189 Japan

This paper describes an automobile with artificial intelligence, which consists of a road pattern recognition unit and a problem solving unit. The vehicle is completely autonomous and can be driven without a human driver. The road pattern recognition unit involving a pair of TV cameras and a processing unit identifies obstacles in front of the vehicle and outputs data regarding to the locations of the obstacles. The problem solving unit is a microcomputer system and determines control optimal to the environment around the vehicle based on the data. The algorithm employed in it is a table-look-up method, in which the location of the optimal control is addressed in the table by key words generated from the data. The table was heuristically made by means of digital simulation. The vehicle was successfully driven under various road environments at the speed within 30 Km/h.

1. INTRODUCTION

The origins of an automobile with artificial intelligence, called an intelligent car, can be found in both the automatically driven vehicle [1] and the intelligent robot [2]. Due to the guidance system for the automatically driven vehicle, it had one serious defect that it could neither detect nor avoid obstacles on its path. Based on the performance of artificial intelligence the automatically driven vehicle was improved to the intelligent car shown in Fig. 1. It consists of a road pattern recognition unit and a problem solving unit. Then, it involves all the facilities to perform locomotion as an automobile and can move autonomously.

Fig. 1 The intelligent car.

2. ROAD PATTERN RECOGNITION

The road pattern recognition unit functions to clarify presence of obstacles in the view field in front of the vehicle. The unit consists of a pair of TV cameras and a processing unit for video signals from them. The cameras are mounted in the front part of the vehicle with a fixed interval (50 cm) along a vertical line as shown in Fig. 1.

The principle of operation of the unit is shown in Fig. 2, and processing in it is shown in Fig. 3 (a)-(c) which correspond to (a)-(c) in Fig. 2. The two images on the TV cameras, one of which is shown in Fig. 3(a), shift vertically from each other due to the camera positions, and scanning them synchronously and vertically generates two video signals. By processing the signals two pulse trains indicating brightness/darkness changing points (BDCP), one of which is shown in Fig. 3(b), are obtained. One train is delayed for a fixed time corresponding to a distance of a range where an obstacle is to be searched. The delay compensates the shift between the images. Then, the trains are checked if any part of them has same pulse sequences each other, and this results in detection of obstacles as shown in Fig. 3(c), where just real obstacles including some illusion are shown. In Fig. 3(c) the center line is rejected as it does not have any height, and the guard rail is also rejected as it is out of the present range. To cancel the illusion, height and width of obstacles are checked furthermore.

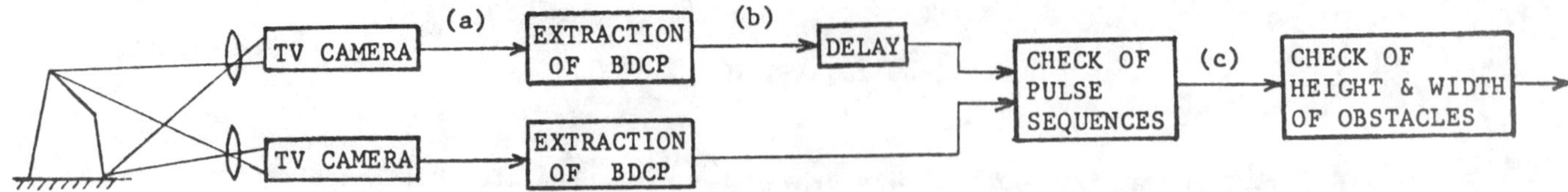

Fig. 2 Principle of operation of road pattern recognition.

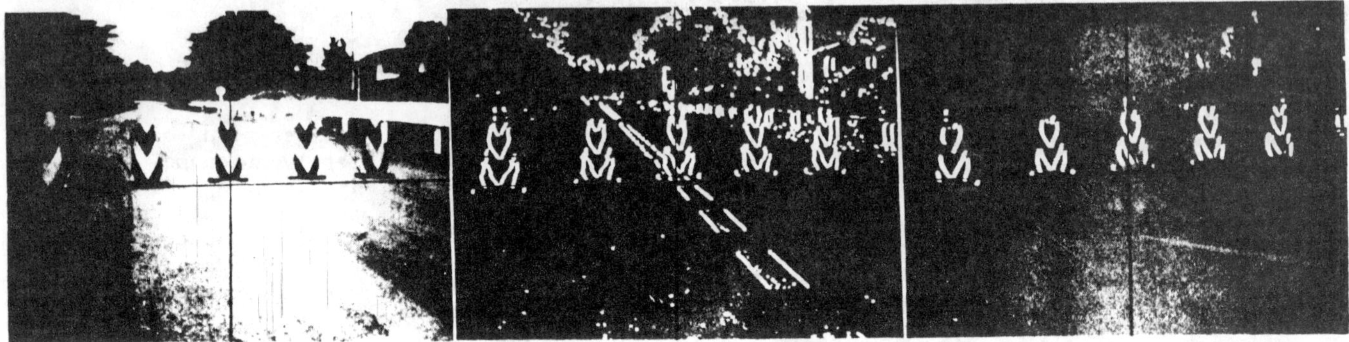

Fig. 3(a) A image on a TV camera. Fig. 3(b) Extraction of BDCP. Fig. 3(c) Detection of obstacles.

By employing different delays of more than one and the following circuits, the processing of the pulse trains is performed in parallel to identify obstacles in the whole view field. Processing the images shown in Fig. 4(a) as described above results in identification of obstacles in the view field shown in Fig. 4(b). The view field is quantized according to the ranges, in each of which obstacles are identified, and then the perspective form is converted to a plane figure form. The trapezoid in Fig.4 (b) is the view field in the plane figure and black parts in the center of it are the guard rail, i.e. obstacles.

The area of the view field is between 5 m and 20 m from the vehicle with viewing angle of 40 degree. The time required to identify obstacles is 33.3 msec for scanning one frame and 2.3 msec for processing after scanning.

3. ALGORITHM FOR DETERMINATION OF CONTROL

The problem solving unit determines control by using the data from the road pattern recognition unit. The purpose of the intelligent car is proper locomotion in road environments with safety, quickness and "keep left". Therefore the time required to determine control must be within 100 msec at most, because the vehicle running at 36 Km/h runs 1 m in 100 msec. To satisfy this requirement, a table-look-up method is employed. In the method, control is retrieved by key words from a table. The key words are generated by logical operation upon the data from

Fig. 4(a) A image on a TV camera.

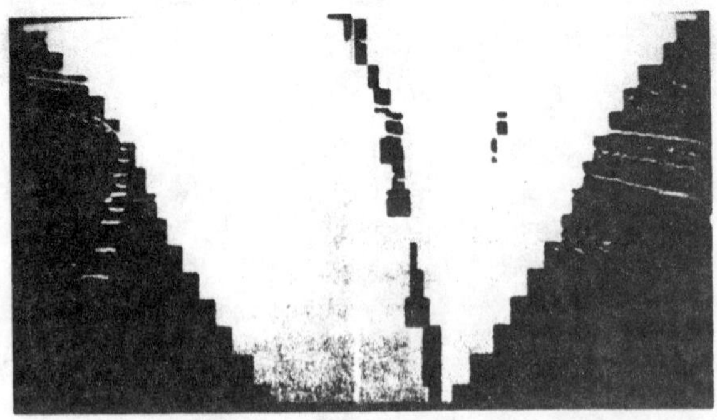

Fig. 4(b) Detection of obstacles in the image shown in Fig. 4(a).

the pattern recognition unit and have relations to the location where the control is stored. The table was made heuristically by computer simulation. Fig. 5 shows the simulation. On the display the vehicle, its view field, its trajectory and the left guard rail are drawn.

After the simulation, the following algorithm was employed in the intelligent car. By defining x_i(i=1 to 16, x_i=5 to 20) and y_i(y_i=-32 to 96) as shown in Fig. 6, the road is classified into five categories: 1) course following, 2) obstacles on the road, 3) left turning, 4) right turning and 5) dead end. In the cases of 1) or 2) a set of (x_i,y_i) maximizing y_i/x_i is the key words. In the cases of 3) or 4) a set of (x_i,y_i) indicating the corner of the turning is also the key words. To make the size of the table small, 16 kinds of x_i are decreased to 8, and 128 kinds of y_i to 32. Therefore the table has 8 x 32 elements.

The problem solving unit consists of a microcomputer system including a micro CPU, RAMs (8 KB), ROMs (3 KB), I/O interfacing LSIs, and A/D and D/A converters. The time required to get control is very short and within 33.3 msec in most cases and 100 msec at most, which include just processing in the microcomputer. A human driver usually requires more than 0.4 sec.

4. EXPERIMENTS

4.1 The Intelligent Car

The automobile is a compact car with a torque converter, some sensors and actuators. The sensors include a speed sensor for the vehicle and a angle sensor for the steering wheel. The actuators include a hydraulic actuator for the steering wheel, an electric motor for throttle valves and vacuum servo brakes.

4.2 Experimental Results

The experiments were conducted in the test truck of our laboratory. Some results are shown in Figs. 7 and 8.

5. CONCLUSION

Artificial intelligence including both pattern recognition and problem solving for locomotion has been implemented in both software and hardware to the intelligent car. The vehicle was successfully driven under various road environments at the speed within 30 Km/h.

REFERENCES

[1] Ohshima, Y. et al "Control System for Automatic Automobile Driving." In IFAC Tokyo Symposium (1965).

[2] Nilsson, N.J. et al "Preliminary Design of an Intelligent Robot." In Tou, J.T. (ed) Computer and Information Science Vol. 2, Academic Press, New York (1967).

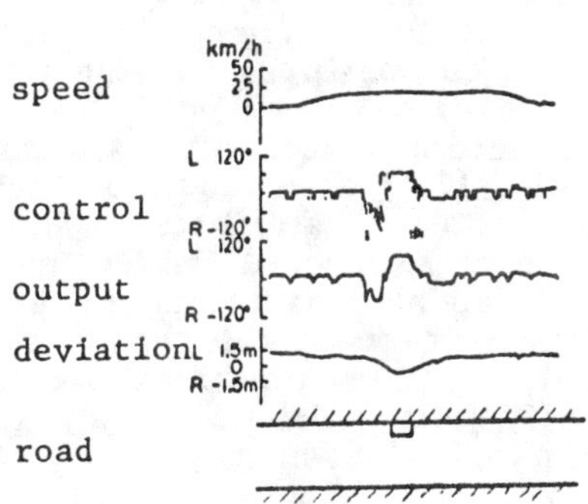

Fig. 7 Obstacle avoiding.

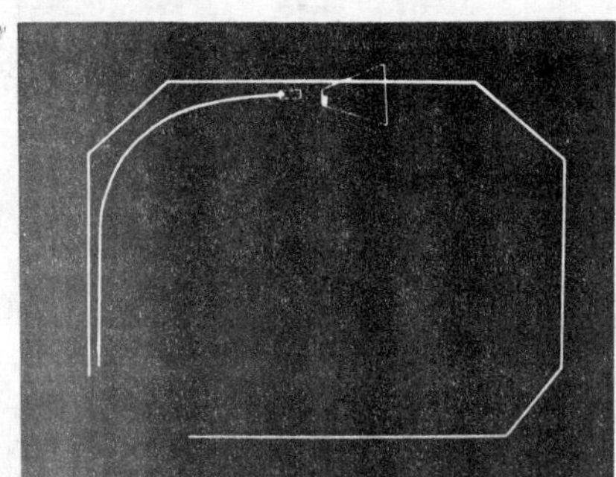

Fig. 5 Digital simulation.

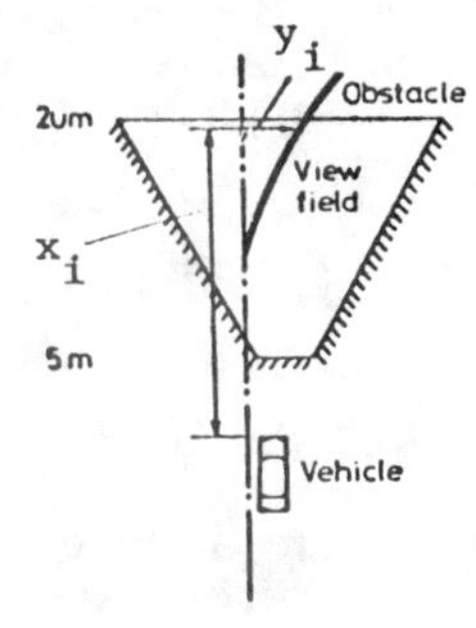

Fig. 6 Definition of x_i and y_i.

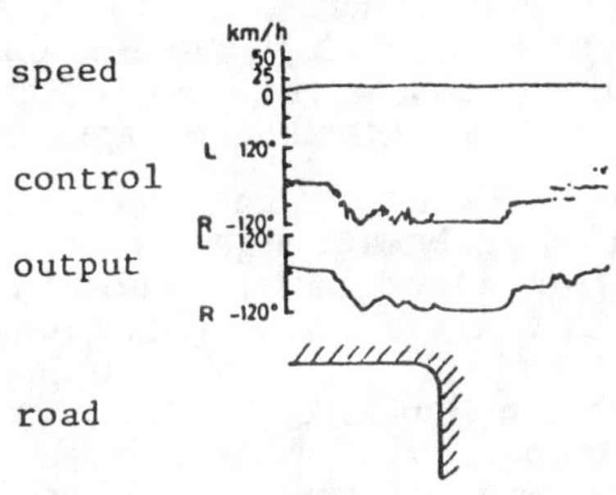

Fig. 8 Right turning.

THREE DIMENSIONAL MOVEMENT ANALYSIS OF DYNAMIC LINE IMAGES

Saburo Tsuji, Michiharu Osada, and Masahiko Yachida
Department of Control Engineering
Osaka University
Toyonaka, Osaka 560, Japan

As a part of a cine-film understanding system, this paper presents a dynamic scene analyzer which separates moving objects from the background and analyzes their motion patterns in dynamic line images such as cartoon films. Finding correspondence of regions and their segments in a sequence of input frames by a new flexible template matching method, the analyzer tracks moving regions and their segments in the dynamic images. Next, a similarity test of segment movements detects the background movement, and classifies the regions into stationary and non-stationary ones. Each in the latter group is further labeled as partly occluded, false, or moving, by examining motion patterns of its segments. Finally, the analyzer merges segments of each moving object into groups having similar motion patterns in order to obtain a meaningful partition corresponding to its components such as hands or legs.

1. INTRODUCTION

In recent years, people have studied dynamic scene analysis, which analyzes a sequence of pictures taken at a constant time interval, such as a cine film or a video record, to interpret it into meaningful descriptions on constituents of the scene and their temporal changes, as well [1,2]. Many papers have been published on detection and tracking of moving objects with [3,4] or without [5] their models in temporal records of natural scenes, interpretation of a sequence of silhouetted images into a model of static and moving constituents [6], and analysis of dynamic line images by utilizing a camera model [7] or by utilizing procedural knowledge about an actor and static objects to describe the dynamic image in terms of meaningful actions [8].

Most systems utilize a priori knowledge and models of the constituents which are very useful to efficiently analyze a large number of consecutive frames, and to solve occlusion problems. They were, however, designed to accept only limited spatio-temporal patterns as inputs; the dynamic image must satisfy both or one of strong restrictions that (1) the constituents show two dimensional movements, and (2) their shapes are almost rigid.

This paper presents a more general motion analysis system that analyzes a sequence of line images, a cartoon film, in which a personified animal moves and rotates freely in a three dimensional world. The analysis is difficult because of the following reasons:
(1) Since the line image of the object consists of curved components, it seems difficult to find strong local features which could be utilized as useful cues for motion analysis or segmentation of the moving object into meaningful parts such as its arms or legs.
(2) Since the moving object and its parts move and rotate in the three dimensional world, and since occlusion often occurs, the shape, size, and structure of each constituent change from frame to frame.
(3) The background or stationary objects may move in the image because of camera movements to track interesting objects.

An approach to overcome the above-mentioned difficulties is to develope a scene analyzer which utilizes effectively temporal patterns. The proposed system has been designed along this approach; knowledge about the shape and structure of each object in the scene, by which usual computer vision systems interpret static scenes, is not utilized, but similarities of both spatial and temporal patterns are iteratively examined with an aim of extracting useful information or cues for higher level analysis of the dynamic scene. In other words, the analyzer is a subsystem of a film-understanding system [8], and its task is to divide the scene into meaningful parts; for example, it separates moving objects from the background, and also subdivides a moving object into components showing similar movement patterns. One can arrange the results into a structural description of the detected objects on properties, spatial relations, and motion patterns.

2. SEGMENTATION OF SCENE BY MOTION ANALYSIS

2.1 INPUT IMAGE

Two animation films containing about 100 frames, in which a personified animal (Moomin) moves freely in a three dimensional world, are used to test the performance of the system. Fig.1 displays binary pictures of sampled frames in Film 1; the animal runs from the right side of the picture and then jumps over a stone. Another film, Film 2 shown in Fig.2, is one for testing the effect of the camera movement. We perceive it as if the animal moves leftwards while it moves its hands and legs but its location is almost unchanged, because objects, trees, in the background translate rightwards at an almost constant velocity.

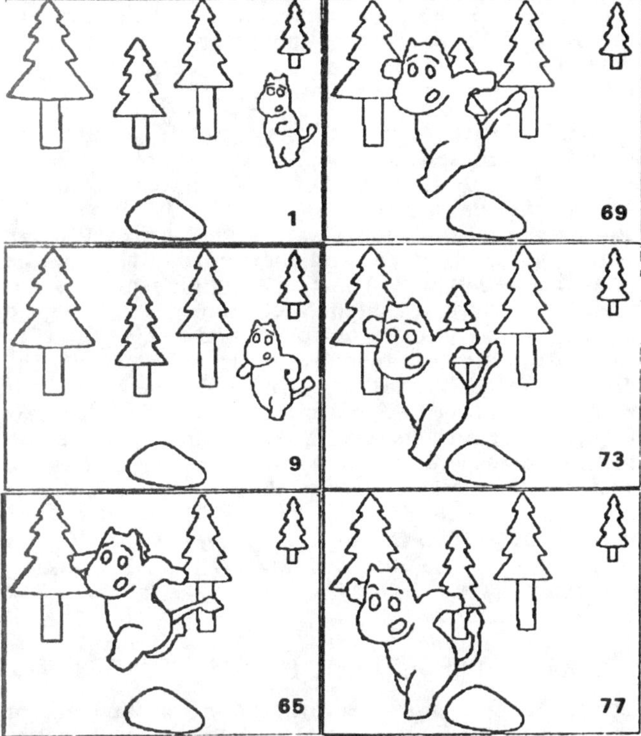

Fig.1 Sample Frames of Film 1.

An animal runs from the left side, jumps over a stone.

Fig.2 Sample Frames of Film 2.

Although the location of the animal changes little, it is perceived as it runs leftwards, because the objects in the background move to rightwards.

If a computer observes Film 1 from its first frame, where the animal is separated from the other objects, it can easily creat a model of the scene in which the segmentation of each constituent is established. Then, the successive frames will be analyzed by following moving constituents with the aid of the scene model. However, we try to analyze a more complex case; a frame in which occlusion has already occured, for example the 65th frame, is selected as the first input picture to the computer, and the successive frames are then analyzed without the already segmented model of the scene.

A TV camera is used as an input device of the system, and a digitized (200 by 200 4bit) image of each frame is converted into a binary picture by thresholding. Applying a simple thinning operator, we track every arc in the picture, and arrange the line image into lists of arcs; an arc is described in terms of end points, connected arcs, and chain coded pixels on it. Illustrated in Fig.3 is a graphical representation of the arc list of the 65th frame of Film 1.

2.2 SEGMENTATION OF SCENE BY MOTION ANALYSIS

Our system is a lower level motion analyzer which segments scenes into their constituents by examining their motion patterns, and interprets them into moving, stationary, or partly occluded objects. Movement patterns of short segments of a moving object are also analyzed in order to subdivide the object into meaningful moving parts such as hands or legs.

Most motion analyzers extract movements of the objects in consecutive frames, but they do not analyze how different parts of a moving object show different motion patterns. Our system is characterized by extraction of motion patterns of sufficiently short segments, and also by tests of similarities of the segment movements. The analysis is divided into the following phases.

(1) Interframe comparison of segments
At first, we detect regions in the scene and establish their correspondence to those of the next frame. Then, we divide all arcs into sufficiently short segments, and follow them in the line image sequence to measure how they are moving. A flexible template matching method has been developed to find correspondence between the segments in the consecutive frames. The movement patterns of the segments are examined in the next three phases.

(2) Separation of non-stationary regions from the background
The objects in the backgroud may also move in the image because of the camera movements, therefore we need to know which objects are really moving. Detecting the background movement as that of the majority of the segments in the scene, we classify the regions in the scene into stationary and non-stationary ones.

(3) Labeling non-stationary regions
The movements of the segments in the non-stationary regions are examined to classify them into partly occluded objects (for example, Region ABCD in Fig.3), moving objects, or false objects that are areas surrounded by moving objects and static objects (Region EFGHIJE in Fig.3). The results are used to creat and update a scene model. This labeling is not always correct, and the analysis is backtracked when the analysis of the later frames finds the wrong labeling in the scene model.

(4) Grouping of segments in a moving object
Finally, the similarities of the segment movements in each moving object are analyzed in order to divide the object into meaningful parts.

We have implemented the system on a mincomputer HP2108A with 256 kbyte buffer memory. The program is written in FLISP, a modified version of INTER LISP, which can control lower level programs written in FORTRAN.

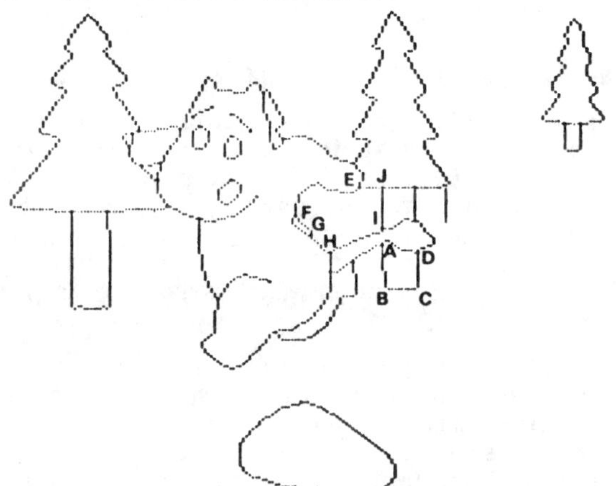

Fig.3 Graphical Representation of Arc Lists of the 65th Frame of Film 1.

3. INTERFRAME COMPARISON OF SEGMENTS

3.1 CORRESPONDENCE OF REGIONS

As mentioned in the previous section, our motion analyzer follows the movements of short segments in the sequence of line images with the aim of obtaining an interpretable goal partition of the dynamic scene. At first, the system examines correspondence of regions in the consecutive frames, and then it analyzes that of each short segment in them.

We can easily divide the input scene into regions, and obtain a list of regions for each frame, in which a region is described in terms of a location of its centroid, its size (perimeter), and a list of arcs (its boundary and internal edges). Now, we examine correspondence of regions in the sequence of frames by a simple template matching method, because changes of the line images between two consecutive frames are small.

Let R be a region in the current frame. At first, we search the region list of the next frame for a small number of regions, one of which possibly corresponds to R, such that both locations of their centroids and their perimeters are almost same as those of R. Then, the boundary of R is used as a template, and we find the best matched one of the selected regions by the following method.

At first, a distance map of the template, an array of numbers representing distance to the nearest point on the template, is created in order to easily compute a distance from the template to a region boundary by simply summing distance values in the map at every point on the boundary and then normalizing by the boundary length [9]. By a hill climbing method, we search for the best matched location of each selected region boundary to the template, and a region having the minimum distance value is selected. If the distance value is less than a threshold, we consider it as corresponding to R. Eliminating the detected pair from the region lists, we iteratively apply the method to find correspondence of all regions. The results are successful, unless changes in the structure of the line image such as appearance of a new region do not occur between two frames. The unmatched regions in this case are also recorded for higher level motion analysis.

3.2 TRACKING OF SEGMENTS IN CONSECUTIVE FRAMES

Let us consider how we can find correspondence of short segments in two regions whose correspondence has been established. Since the line image of the animal consists of curved segments, we cannot find useful singular points in it, such as true vertices in a polygonal world [6], by which we can easily establish their true correspondence between two frames. Although T joints give us useful information about segmentation between objects, two T joints in different frames not always correspond each other, because they belong to a category of *false vertices* in the polygon world.

Another difficulty for examining the correspondence of the segments is that the shape of the moving object changes from frame to frame. The body of the animal moves and rotates in the three dimensional world, and its moving parts such as its hands and legs independently rotate about different axes. Therefore, the template matching method, which assumes shape rigidness, is not adequate for examining correspondence of each portion of the object.

A flexible template matching method called as *rubber mask* technique [10] was developed for matching of a distorted pattern to its template. The method, however, is not applicable to our problem because it assumes a priori knowledge about the structures of patterns which are built in the matching program.

Therefore, we have developed a new flexible template matching method for finding correspondence of each short segment in a line pattern to that in a partly distorted one. Consider a problem to match each part of Pattern 1 shown in Fig.4 (a) to Pattern 2 in Fig.4 (b). Because of the shape distortion, we cannot establish a complete or almost complete matching of the two patterns. However, we can establish a good match of a considerable long arc of Pattern 1 to a part of Pattern 2 as shown in Fig.4 (c). Also we can match the other arcs by shifting the template (Fig.4(d),(e),(f)). Thus, we can consider points A,B,C,D, which belongs to the matched portions in the successive partial matching process, as corresponding to A′, B′, C′, and D′, respectively.

Our method utilizes this matching process. Let R and R' be two regions which consist of sets of arcs $\{a_i\}$ and $\{a_i',\}$ respectively. At first, we search $\{a_i\}$ and $\{a_i'\}$ for the best matched pair of considerably long arcs a_k and a_m' by a similar method as that for matching regions. Next, a_k is divided into segments l_1, l_2, ..., l_n shorter than a predetermined threshold value.

If one cannot match a_k precisely to a_m', we shift each segment by a small amount to obtain a better matching to a_m' and also its connected arcs as shown in Fig.5. As a result, a point which is a common terminal point of two segments in a_k, for example point 2 in Fig.5, is mapped on two different points in a_m'. Therefore, the correspondence of a segment is described with the transition of a representive point, a point located at near its center. After this type of matching process is accomplished for the selected arc, then its connected arcs are also precisely matched by the same procedure. Thus, we get a correspondence table of R to R' on the segments. We iterate the above-mentioned procedure to find correspondence of the successive frames, and representative points of segements in the first input frame are tracked by interpolation of those in the later frames. Results of tracking of segments in a moving region and a partly occluded objects from the 65th frame to the 70th frame in Film 1 are illustrated in Fig.6.

4. SEPARATION OF MOVING REGIONS FROM BACKGROUND

4.1 DETECTION OF BACKGROUND MOVEMENT

Stationary objects in the background may move in the image because of camera movements such as panning, tilting, and zooming, therefore, the system needs to detect how the background is moving in consecutive images. We consider that there are many more segments in the background than in moving objects, and they show almost a similar movement pattern; a horizontal or vertical movement by panning or tilting, and a radial movement by zooming.

Therefore, histograms of the segment movements will give us valuable information about the background movement. Fig.7 illustrates two histograms that frequencies of segment movement

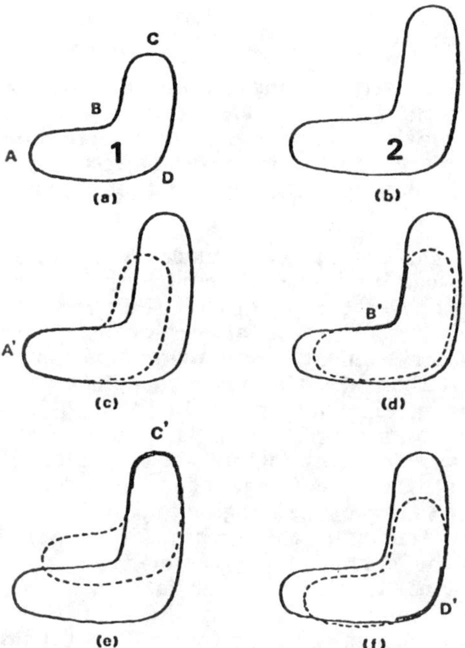

Fig.4 Flexible Template Matching.

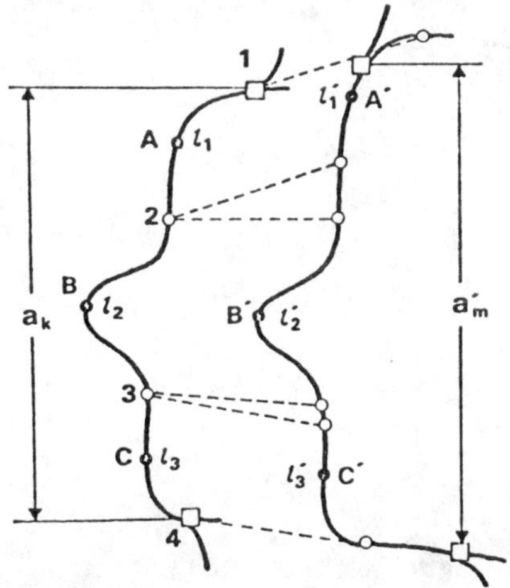

Fig.5 Correspondence of Segments.

Arc a_k is matched to Arc a_k'. a_k is divided into segments l_1, l_2 and l_3; and the best matched location of each segment to a_m' and its connected arcs is detected by a hill climbing method. As the result, correspondence of A, B, C, to A′, B′, C′ is established.

vectors in Film 1 and Film 2 are mapped on a X-Y plane. The sharp peak at (0,0) in Fig.7 (a) shows that the background of Film 1 is still, and the peaks of Fig.4 (b) suggest that Film 2 was taken while the camera was panning to track the moving object.

Subtracting the background movement from the movement vectors of all segments, we separate non-stationary regions, as those containing moving segments, from stationary ones.

4.2 LABELING OF NONSTATIONARY REGIONS

The non-stationary regions are not always parts of moving objects. Partly occluded regions of stationary objects by moving objects and regions surrounded by moving objects and stationary objects are also registered as non-stationary by the above-mentioned separation process.

Therefore, we creat a scene model after analyzing several consecutive frames. The model is a collection of descriptions of the regions on their movements, and we label a non-stationary region as moving if most of their segments are moving, and as partly occluded if a considerable long sequence of segments is not moving (a region shown in Fig.6 (b)). Next, successive frames are sequentially analyzed, and labels of corresponding regions are examined. If the structure of the line image changes between two frames, for example a new region appears, the system marks the frame in the model for higher level analysis. The system, however, manages a simple case that a partly hidden region is merged into the empty background as Region EFGHIJE in Fig.3 which disappears at the 69th frame. It is considered as a false region, and the analyzer backtracks to correct the wrong label.

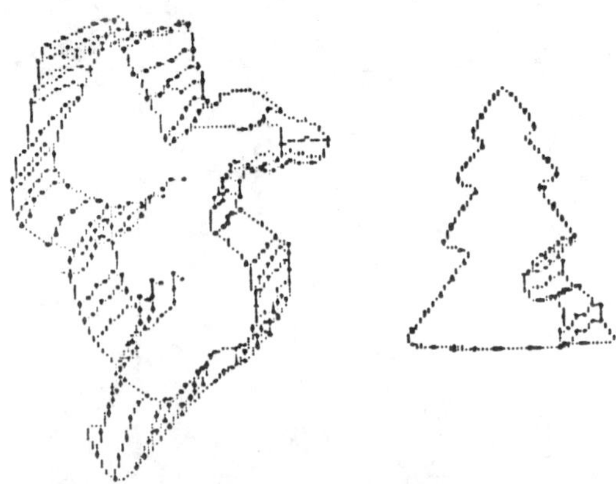

Fig.6 Tracking of Segments.

5. GROUPING OF SEGMENTS IN A MOVING OBJECT

The final process is to segment a moving region into meaningful parts showing similar movements. Since the movement vectors of all segments in each moving region have been analyzed, we can divide them into groups by a similarity test of their displacements. At first, we subtract a displacement vector of the centroid of the moving region from the movement vector of every segment in it. Fig.8 shows an example of the relative movement vectors displayed on the figure of the moving region. One can find a strong movement similarity for each group of segments such as its leg, body, and hand, therefore its segmentation is easy. We iterate comparing of each two adjacent vectors and merging them into a group

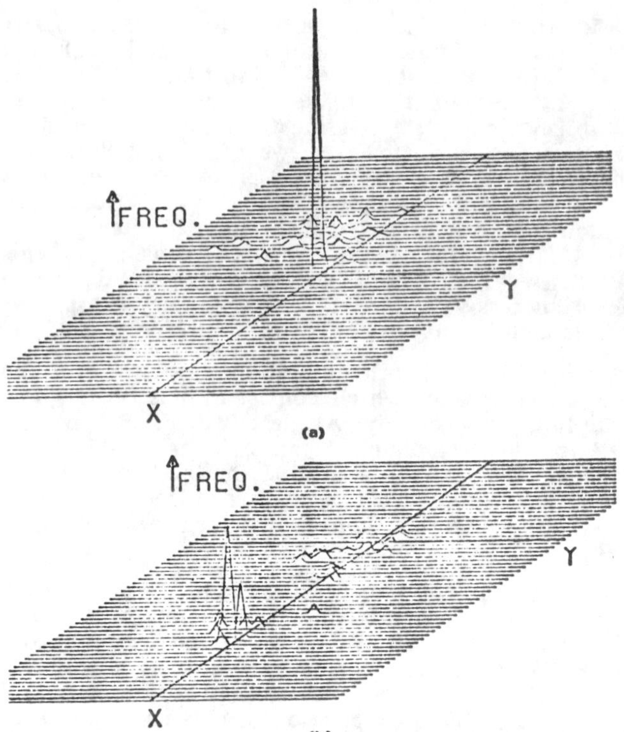

Fig.7 Detection of Background Movement.

A sharp peak in (a) shows the background is still, and peaks on X axis in (b) indicate that the camera was panning when the film was taken.

if the difference of two vectors is smaller than a threshold. Fig.8 (c) shows the result of segmentation. Next, each set of segments between two groups is divided into two parts by a test of the movement similarity. Thus, segmentation of the moving object into its hand, leg, body, and head is accomplished.

6. DISCUSSION

We have developed a motion analyzer which separates non-stationary regions from stationary ones and subdivides the moving region into meaningful components on the basis of segment movements. Usefulness of a flexible template matching method for establishing correspondence of segments in consecutive frames is shown. Similarity tests of segment movements are also useful to detect the background movement and to segment a moving region into its moving components.

However, the scene model used is very simple, and the acquired knowledge about the properties of the regions by analyzing the previous frames such that each region has been occluding (or occluded by) what regions or not, region is not used to analyze a new coming frame. We could easily implement this function, an essential function for dynamic scene analysis, to our system, and we would be able to save much computing time.

Also many important problems such as (1) analysis of the structural change of the line image, (2) semantic interpretation of moving and stationary regions, and (3) understanding meaning of the movements, are left for future research.

REFERENCE

1] W. N. Martin and J. K. Aggarwal, "Dynamic Scene Analysis" *Computer Graphics and Image Processing*, Vol.7, pp. 356-374, 1978.

2] H. H. Nagel, "Analysis for Image Sequences" *Proc. of 4th Int. Joint Conf. Pattern Recognition*, pp. 186-211, 1978.

3] M. Yachida, M. Asada and S. Tsuji, "Automatic Motion Analysis System of Moving Objects from the Records of Natural Processes" *ibid.*, pp. 7 1978.

4] Y. Ariki, T. Kanade and Y. Sakai, "An Interactive Image Modeling and Tracing System for Moving Pictures" *ibid.*, pp. 681-685, 1978.

5] R. Jain, D. Miltzer and H. H. Nagel, "Separating Non-stationary from Stationary Scene Components in a Sequence of Real World TV-Images" *Proc. 5th Int. Joint Conf. Artificial Intelligence*, pp. 612-618, 1975.

6] J. K. Aggarwal and R. O. Duda, "Computer Analysis of Moving Polygonal Images" *IEEE Trans. Comput.*, Vol. C-24, pp. 966-976, 1975.

7] N. Badler, "Three-Dimensional Motion from Two-Dimensional Picture Sequences," *Proc. of 2nd Int. Joint Conf. Pattern Recognition*, pp. 157-161, 1974.

8] S. Tsuji, A. Morizono and S. Kuroda, "Understanding a Simple Cartoon Film by a Computer Vision System" *Proc. 5th Int. Joint Conf. Artificial Intelligence*, pp. 609-610, 1977.

9] H. G. Barrow, J. M. Tennenbaum, R. C. Bolles and H. C. Wolf, "Parametric Correspondence and Chamfer Matching: Two New Techniques for Image Matching," *Proc. 5th Int. Joint Conf. Artificial Intelligence*, pp. 659-663, 1977.

10] B. Widrow, "The 'Rubber Mask' Technique - I. Pattern Measurement and Analysis" *Pattern Recognition, Vol.5*, pp. 175-198, 1973.

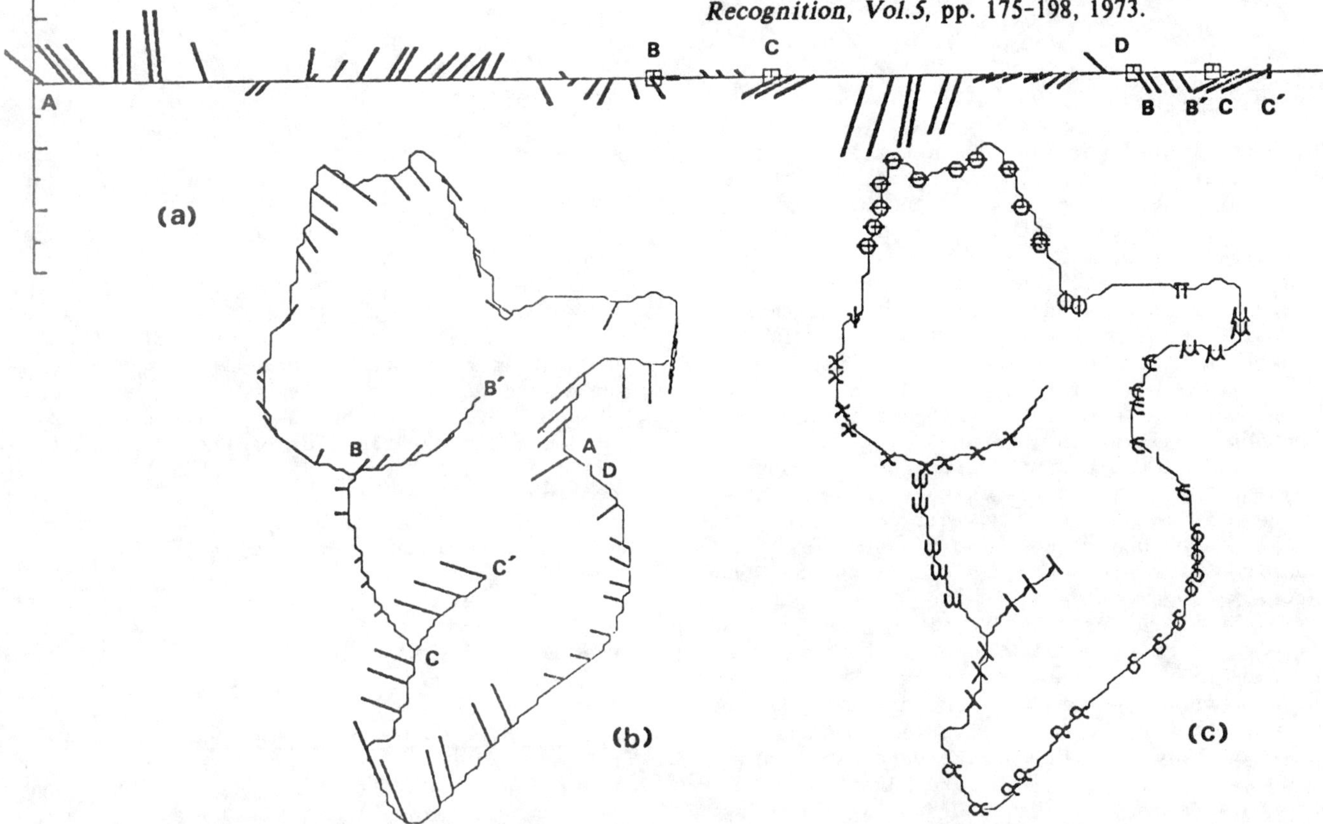

Fig.8 Grouping of Segments by Similarity of Segments Movements.
Segment movement vectors of a moving region from the 65th frame to the 70th frame relative to the centroid of the region are displayed (a) along the arcs and (b) on the image at the 65th frame. The segmentation result is shown in (c).

AN APPLICATION OF DECISION ANALYSIS TO STRATEGY-MAKING IN GAME PLAYING

Koichi Yamada
Department of Systems Science,
Tokyo Institute of Technology,
Oh-okayama, Meguro-ku, Tokyo 152,
Japan

Yahachiro Tsukamoto/ Toshiro Terano
Department of Control Engineering,
Tokyo Institute of Technology,
Oh-okayama, Meguro-ku, Tokyo 152,
Japan

This paper presents a game playing model of Score-Four that is a kind of alignment game similar to three dimensional tic-tac-toe. The present model aims at winning a game most efficiently. The pricipal proposal is an adoption of Decision Analysis, a wide-spread method of systems analysis, instead of Minimax Procedure. This paper includes a static evaluation on the state of game, a brief illustration of Decision Analysis, a method of strategy-making and an outline of a game playing machine. Based on the results from the experiments conducted with human players, we assert that Decision Analysis is a good method to make strategies which enable us to take advantage of the opponent's mistakes and it is shown that the risk caused by abandonment of the conventional assumption that the opponent selects the best move is averted by the introduction of a learning system.

1. INTRODUCTION

There are many papers as for game playing model which satisfies the following conditions.

1. Play starts from a situation which is not advantageous to either player.
2. The interest of game playing is just "to win a game" and there is no more.

If a game is played under the above conditions, it would be valid that a player adopts the assumption that the opponent selects the best of all legal moves in every situation, for he sometimes loses a game by making little of his opponent's skill. In this sense Minimax Procedure [1] on the basis of the above assumption is adequate for strategy-making when we need not dare to run a risk. However games are not always played under such conditions. For example, there are sometimes occasions when the interest of game playing is "to win a game more efficiently" rather than "to win a game". More efficient winning means winning with fewer moves in some games or with capturing more pieces of the opponent in other games, generally speaking, overwhelming one. In this case it becomes important for a player to make more efficient moves, which enable him to take advantage of his opponent's mistakes. In other words, the conventional assumption is too passive for winning a game efficiently. Similarly efficient moves should be played in occasions when a heavy handicap is imposed.

Decision Analysis [2] is effective for strategy-making in a game playing model where we are aiming at an efficient winning. In this method we can take into account the probabilities of its opponent's mistakes.

In this study, it is assumed that the opponent plays a move of the best three among all the possible moves even though he is an unskillful player. Then the key point of this method is the determination of the judgemental probabilities assigned to these three moves. We introduce an index representing the opponent's skill. It should be noted that there may be a risk caused by underestimation of the oppponent's skill or inefficiency by overestimation. This problem, however, is resolved by introducing a learning system which improves the initial value of the index step by step by evaluating the opponent's moves.

We are applying the above method to strategy-making in Score-Four game and Score-Four Playing Machine, which is a system playing with a human player, is constructed.

2. DESCRIPTION OF SCORE-FOUR GAME

Score-Four is an alignment game played by two persons; one uses black balls (simply called Blacks) and the other white balls (called Whites) as their pieces. The game is played on a board with sixteen sticks which penetrate the balls through their small hole. (See Fig.1)

Since each stick is capable of accepting four balls, the board has 64 points on which players put them. Each point is denoted by a pair of number, (m, n), where m and n mean a stick number and a horizontal plane number respectively, and $1 \leqq m \leqq 16$, $1 \leqq n \leqq 4$.

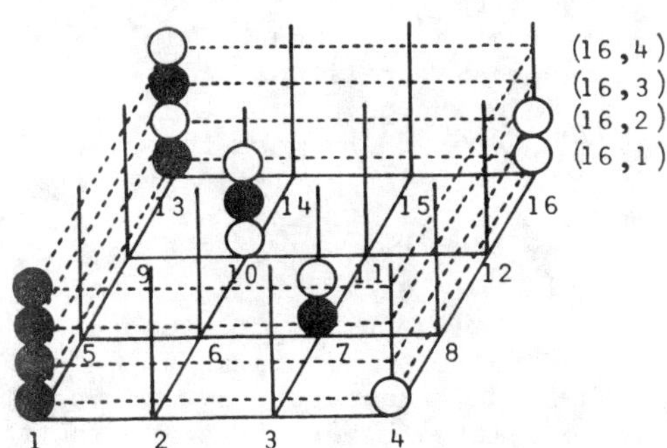

Fig.1 Board of Score-Four

Play starts with the first move of the player who has Blacks (called Player Black) and then each plays a move by turns. Players, however, can not put their balls on arbitrary points, that is, they are allowed to make a move on (m, n) only if n is eqaulto 1 or (m, n-1) is occupied. Such a point is called legal. In Fig.1, for example, (16, 3) is a legal point and (16, 4) is an illegal one. The game is won when a player forms a string of his four balls in any line, either horizontally, vertically or diagonally. If it is not won within 64 moves, it ends in a draw.

Now, we present some important properties of the game, which will help us to look for factors to evaluate a board situation.

1. The game is played on a three-dimensional board.
2. The game ends within 64 moves.
3. The number of legal moves in a board situation is equal to or smaller than 16.
4. The number of lines in which it is possible to form a string of four balls is 76.

3. METHOD OF EVALUATING BOARD SITUATIONS

A situation of the board may be determined with the consideration on all the possible states of 76 lines. Therefore we adopt them as the fundamental factors to evaluate a board situation. Each line is in one of the following eight types of states. Let α_j ($j = 1, \ldots, 8$) be an index for evaluating a line in j-th state.

STATE I (Four) : There is a string of four Blacks (Whites). We fix the index, $\alpha_1 = 150$.

STATE II (Active-Three) : Three points are occupied by Blacks (Whites) and the remainer is unoccupied and legal. If player Black (White) makes the next move and he can win a game by forming "Four", then $\alpha_2 = 70$, otherwise $\alpha_2 = 10$. (See Fig.2, a)

STATE III (Sleeping-Three) : Blacks (Whites) occupy three points in the line and the remainer is unoccupied and illegal. $\alpha_3 = 18$. (Fig.2, b)

STATE IV (Active-Two) : There are two points occupied by Blacks (Whites) and two vacant and legal points. $\alpha_4 = 4$. (Fig.2, c)

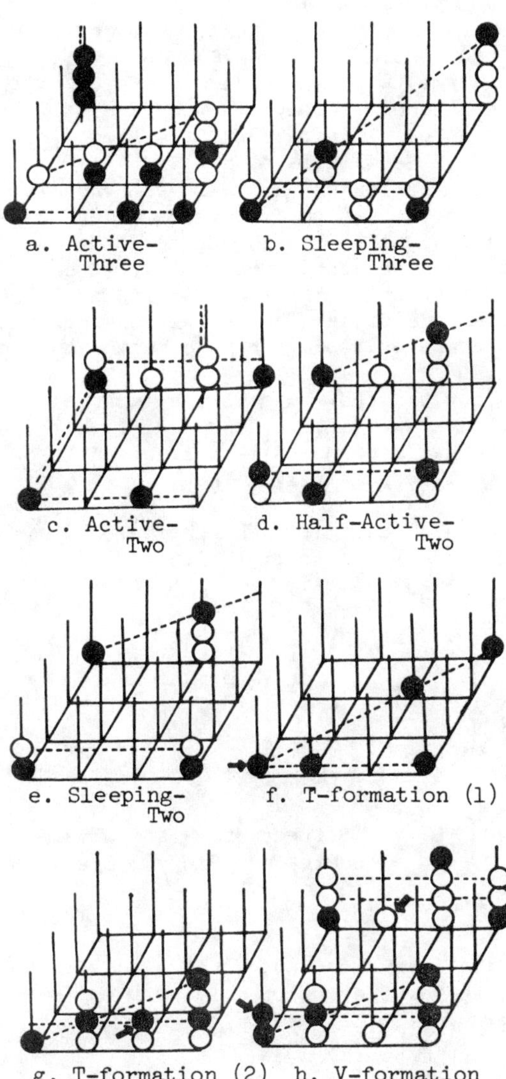

Fig.2 Factors to Evaluate a Board Situation

STATE V (Half-Active-Two) : There are two Blacks (Whites) and two vacant points; one is legal and the other is illegal. At his next turn, Player Black (White) can form "Sleeping-Three". $\alpha_5 = 5$. (Fig.2, d)
STATE VI (Sleeping-Two) : There are two Blacks (Whites) and two unoccupied and illegal points. Player Black (White) can not form "Active-Three" nor "Sleeping-Three" at his next turn. $\alpha_6 = 8$. (Fig.2, e)
STATE VII : There is only a Black (White) and the others are unoccupied. $\alpha_7 = 1$.
STATE VIII : Both Blacks and Whites exist or there is no ball in the line. $\alpha_8 = 0$.

Now we show the two important patterns on which games are won.

1. One forms two or more "Active-Three" with a move. He can surely win the game at his next move. This pattern is called "T-formation". (See Fig.2, f, g).
2. One player forms "Active-Three" where the only one vacant point is just under the vacant of his "Sleeping-Three". He can win the game at his next move. We call it "V-formation" which is shown in Fig.2, h.

So, as an additional factor, we consider whether or not there exists T- or V-formation and let $\alpha_9 = 50$.
Let us now show how to evaluate each factor as stated above. Let u_i ($i = 1, 2, \ldots, 76$) and v be the evaluations of i-th line and T- or V-formation, respectively. Then,

$$u_i = (-1)^k \alpha_j \text{ : if i-th line belongs to STATE j.} \quad (i = 1, \cdots, 76)\ (j = 1, \cdots, 8) \qquad (1)$$

$$v = \begin{cases} (-1)^k \alpha_9 & \text{: if there exists T- or V-formations of one side.} \\ 0 & \text{: otherwise.} \end{cases} \qquad (2)$$

where

$$k = \begin{cases} 0 & \text{: if the factor is evaluated for Score-Four Playing System} \\ 1 & \text{: otherwise.} \end{cases}$$

Then, static evaluation, U, of a board situation is defined as the sum of u_i ($i = 1, \cdots, 76$) and v as :

$$U(S) = \sum_{i=1}^{76} u_i + v . \qquad (3)$$

4. STRATEGY-MAKING BY DECISION ANALYSIS

First, we make a brief explanation of Decision Analysis. When one intends to make his decision about a certain problem by using Decision Analysis, he must generate the decision tree as shown in Fig.3. It represents a chronological arrangement of choices controlled by him and chance. The tree graph is composed of chance points, strategies selected by him, events dependent on chance and utilities. In the above, it is only at decision points that decision maker can decide which path he goes to. The main procedures of Decision Analysis are "folding back" at decision points and "averaging out" at chance points. In Fig.3, folding back at C_1 is the procedure to assign the maximun of u_1 and u_2 to C_1 and averaging out at C_2 means to assign the expected value of u_3 and u_4 to C_2. After he accomplishes the procedures at every points, he only has to select the strategy leading to the point where the expected utility is the largest.

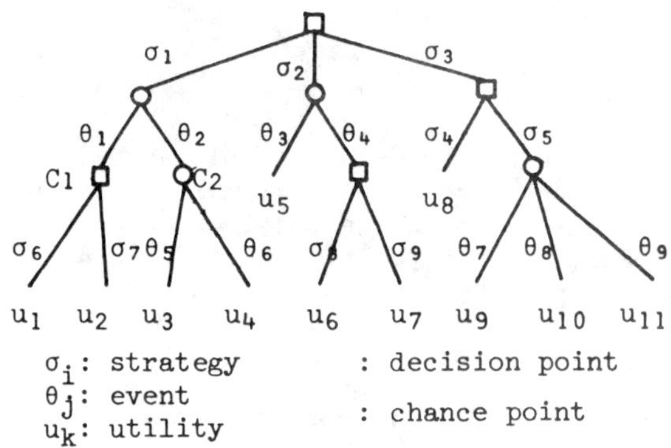

Fig.3 Decision Tree

In game playing a player can not predict the opponent's next move precisely. He can consider at best the probabilities in terms of judgemental probability. Therefore we may take the opponent's next move as an event dependent on chance.
Now let us show a way to calculate the judgemental probabilities, P_i, that the opponent plays the i-th best move, m_i. Suppose there are n legal moves at his turn. Then, first, the judgemental probabilities must satisfy the following equation :

$$\sum_{i=1}^{n} P_i = 1 . \qquad (4)$$

It is a natural assumption that the judgemental probabilities depend on the opponent's skill, because skillfil player is likely to play the best move at a high probability and on the other hand beginner frequently plays a worse move. Let by f_i be denoted an index for evaluating i-th best move where $f_1 \geqq f_2 \geqq \cdots \geqq f_n$. Then the degree of the opponent's skill may be roughly represented as follows;

$$\bar{f} = \sum_{i=1}^{n} P_i f_i \qquad (5)$$

where $\bar{f}$ means the expected value of the evaluation of the opponent's next move.
Furthermore, the concept of entropy is utilized to estimate the judgemental probabilities. Entropy in information theory [3] implies a degree of "uncertainty" or "randomness" of events. If we choose P_i $(i=1,\cdots,n)$ so as to maxmize the entropy, they are the most reasonable judgemental probabilities. It is because the maximization of uncertainty implies the safest or most temperate estimation.
Entropy, H, is defined as:

$$H = -\sum_{i=1}^{n} P_i \log_2 P_i \quad . \qquad (6)$$

By maximizing H subject to Eqs. (4) and (5), we obtain:

$$P_i/P_{i+2} = (P_i/P_{i+1})^{K_i} \quad (i=1,\cdots,n-2) \qquad (7)$$

where

$$K_i = \frac{f_i - f_{i+2}}{f_i - f_{i+1}}$$

Here, let us assume that the opponent plays only one of the best three moves m_1, m_2 and m_3. Then, from Eqs. (4), (5) and (7) we readily obtain the following equation:

$$(f_1 - \bar{f}) + (f_2 - \bar{f})x + (f_3 - \bar{f})x^K = 0 \qquad (8)$$

where $x = P_2/P_1$ and $K = (f_1 - f_3)/(f_1 - f_2)$.

If Eq.(8) has zero or positive real solution, judgemental probabilities are expressed as follows. (See APPENDIX I)

$$P_1 = \frac{1}{1 + x + x^K}$$

$$P_2 = \frac{x}{1 + x + x^K} = P_1 x \qquad (9)$$

$$P_3 = \frac{x^K}{1 + x + x^K} = P_1 x^K$$

Since it is not guaranteed that Eq.(8) has zero or a positive real solution, we show ways determine f_1, f_2, f_3 and $\bar{f}$ and examine the solvability. First, consider the case where $K=2$.
In this case one may find that f_1, f_2 and f_3 are an arithmetical progression and that P_1, P_2 and P_3 are a geometrical one. Moreover, except for the case where $\bar{f} = f_3$, Eq.(8) comes to be a quadratic one which has two real solutions - one of them is either positive or zero and the other is negative - because we are assuming that the opponent plays one of the best three moves, that is,

$$f_3 \leqq \bar{f} \leqq f_1 \quad . \qquad (10)$$

Therefore, if $\bar{f}$ takes on any value between zero and one, it is estimated that $f_1 = 1.0$, $f_2 = 0.5$ and $f_3 = 0$. Then in the case where $\bar{f} = f_3 = 0$, we obtain that $P_1 = P_2 = 0$ and $P_3 = 1$ from Eqs.(4), (5) and (7).
However it seems to be more natural than the above to consider that evaluation, f_i, for i-th move, m_i, is intimately related to the board situation, S, or to its evaluation, U(S), after m_i is played. This idea is appreciated by recalling that the facts that we sometimes find both the extreme cases where m_1 and m_2 have little differnt evaluations and where a player loses because he has played m_2 instead of m_1.
Let S_i be a board situation after a move, m_i, is played. Then, we define f_i by using $U(S_i)$-s given in Eq.(3) as follows;

$$f_i = \frac{U(S_i) - U(S_n)}{U(S_1) - U(S_n)} \qquad (11)$$

where S_1 and S_n mean the board situations after the best move and the worst one are played, respectively.
In general, it is impossible to solve Eq.(8) analytically. But if $\bar{f}$ takes any value between f_3 and 1, it is easily solved by using a computer. (See APPENDIX II) On the occasion when $\bar{f} < f_3$, Eq.(8) does not have any positive solution. It is, however, so risky to make little of the opponent's skill that we consider as if $\bar{f} = f_3$ from the view point of safety playing.
Now it is necessary to consider how to estimate $\bar{f}$. Since it is given without any reliable foundation at the beginning of games, it should be improved during the game. In this study we adopt the next equation for this purpose. Let f^k and $\bar{f}^k$ be the evaluation of the move, m^k, played by the opponent at his k-th turn and the estimation of $\bar{f}$ at the moment just after m^k is played, respectively.

$$\bar{f}^k = (1-\beta)\,\bar{f}^{k-1} + \beta f^k \quad (k=1,\ \ldots,\ 32) \qquad (12)$$

where β is a constant parameter which takes on a value between zero and one.
The above is the major algorithm to be installed by SFPM standing for Score-Four Playing Machine. In SFPM, the depth of lookahead is considered to be only two steps but it is almost enough on usual occasions, and since the static evaluation function takes into account T- and V-formations which guarantee a winning several moves ahead, the actual depth corresponds to four steps or more in the critical moment. The further details on SFPM will be presented at oral presentation.

5. EXPERIMENTS : SFPM V.S. HUMAN PLAYERS

The experiments are conducted to investigate the advantages of the method presented above. Experimental results of game playing with human players are shown in Table 1. The number of the subjects is fifteen and each plays several games under different conditions. Average nunber (A.N.) of moves required for SFPM's winning implies the index of efficiency of winning. As for conditions, $\bar{f}^0$ is the initial estimation of the opponent's skill. The conditions that $\bar{f}^0 = 1.0$ and $\bar{f}^0 = 0.5$ mean the over-estimation and underestimation respectively, because $\bar{f}^k$ of every subject took a value between 0.65 and 0.93 at the end of a game. Fig.4 shows a typical example of the fluctuations of $\bar{f}^k$ observed during a game.

Table 1. Results of Experiments.

Experiment Number	Conditions		Results of Games	A.N.
	β	$\bar{f}^0$		
I	0	1.0	7 wins and 1 defeat	43
II	0	0.8	5 wins and 3 defeats	28
III	0	0.5	4 wins and 4 defeats	35
IV	0.05	1.0	6 wins and 2 defeats	39
V	0.05	0.8	5 wins and 3 defeats	29
VI	0.05	0.5	6 wins and 2 defeats	26

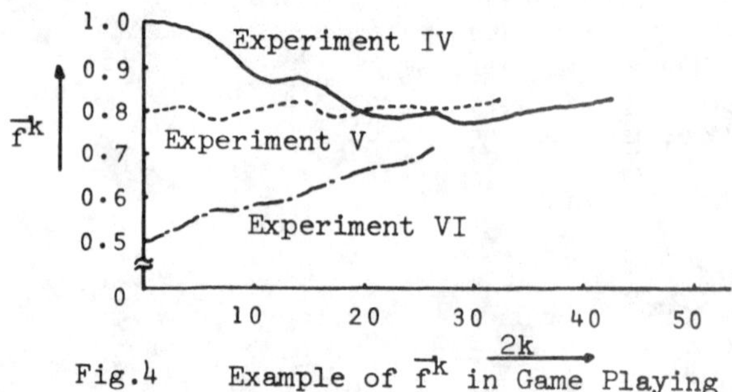

Fig.4 Example of $\bar{f}^k$ in Game Playing

Human player in this example belongs to middle class and he lost in the three experiments shown in Fig.4, but he won in Experiment III at the 34th move.
Next it is shown how SFPM plays a move in accordance with $\bar{f}^k$. When $\bar{f}^k$ is high, that is, SFPM regards its opponent as a skillful player, it inclines to form "Sleeping-Two" and "Sleeping-Three" rather than "Active-Two", "Half-Active-Two" and "Active-Three". This tendency is usually found in games played by skillful players. The tactics are adequate to game playing with skillful players for the following reasons.

1. Skillful players seldom miss blocking their opponent's "Active-Three".
2. To form "Sleepin-Two" or "Sleeping-Three" makes the opponent disadvantageous gradually because they restrict the opponent's selection of moves.
3. "Sleeping-Three" is a necessary preliminary for T- and V-formations. (Refer to Fig.2)

The tactics are, however, not efficient to defeat a beginner or an unskillful player in the sense that many moves are required to win a game, because they are the protracting tactics. On the other hand, when $\bar{f}^k$ is small, SFPM inclines to form "Active-Two", "Half-Active-Two" and "Active-Three" rather than "Sleeping-Two" and "Sleeping-Three". These tactics are effective for game playing with unskillful players who sometimes miss blocking the opponent's "Active-Three". However they are too simple to win when the opponent is skillful.
We can say from the experimental results that the figures in Experiment IV, V and VI are much improved in comparison with Experiments I, II and III. The strategy-making in Experiment I is the same as the one by Minmax Procedure.
It should be noticed that, in order that the use of Decision Analysis works well, it is necessary that the opponent's skill is known rather precisely.

6. CONCLUSIONS

In this paper we have presented a game-playing-machine which employs Decision Analysis as a substitutional method for Minmax Procedure. A game-playing-machine controlled by Minmax Procedure can not cope with the game playing in which efficiency of winning is make much of, while it works very well if it aims at only winning, in more strict words, minimizing the risk of losing. Decision Analysis is a good method to decide strategies which enable a game playing machine to take advantage of its opponent's mistakes -not playing the best move- and to win a game efficiently, while the good efficiency is obtained at the expense of increase in the risk. However, such a risk is capable of being averted to passable extent by estimating the opponent's skill correctly and assuming that he plays a move of the best three in any board situation. Learning system yields the high rate of winning and the good efficiency even though the opponent's skill is misestimsted at the beginning of a game.
Besides, we may conclude that Decision Analysis is also useful for many other games which do not satisfy the conditions stated in INTRODUCTION. Finally we suggest that the opponent's move selection is usually influenced by not only his skill but also his various biases; some players may incline to make such moves that are very offensive or very defensive [4]. If we take the bias into consideration in order to determine the judgemental probabilities, Decision Analysis must be a more useful method of strategy-making in game playing.

ACKNOWLEDGEMENTS

The authors wish to thank Dr. M. Sugeno and Mr. S. Kainuma for their perceptive comments and suggestions.

APPENDIX I

Let us transform Eq.(7), then we obtain:

$$P_3 = P_2^K P_1^{1-K} .$$

Since $x = P_2/P_1$, we can re-write it as:

$$P_3 = (P_1 x)^K P_1^{1-K} = P_1 x^K .$$

Therefore

$$P_1 + P_2 + P_3 = P_1(1 + x + x^K) = 1 ,$$

which directly leads to Eq.(9).

APPENDIX II

Let us denote Eq.(8) by $F(x) = 0$.

1. If $f_3 < \bar{f} \leqq f_1$ and $f_3 < f_2 < f_1 \equiv 1$, then

$$F(0) = f_1 - \bar{f} \geqq 0$$

and

$$\frac{d^2F(x)}{dx^2} = K(K-1)(f_3 - \bar{f})x^{K-2} < 0 \quad (x > 0).$$

Therefore Eq.(8) has only a real solution within the interval, $[0,\infty)$ and we can obtain the judgemental probabilities from Eq.(9).

2. If $\bar{f} = f_3$ and $f_3 < f_2 < f_1 \equiv 1$, then we obtain $P_1 = P_2 = 0$, and $P_3 = 1$ from Eqs.(4), (5) and (7).

3. If $f_3 \leqq \bar{f} \leqq f_1 \equiv 1$, and $f_i = f_{i+1}$ $(i = 1,2)$, then we can calculate the judgemental probabilities from Eqs.(4) and (5).

REFERENCES

[1] N.J.Nilsson, "Problem-Solving Methods in Artificial Intelligence", McGraw-Hill Book Co. 1971.

[2] H.Raiffa, "Decision Analysis, Introductory Lectures on Choices under Uncertainty", Addison-Wesley Pab. 1970.

[3] H.Sato, "Information Theory"(in Japanese), Shoka-bo, 1974.

[4] M.Eisenstadt and Y.Kareev, "Toward a Model of Human Game Playing", Department of Psychology, University of California, San Diego.

DETECTION OF THE MOVEMENTS OF MEN FOR AUTONOMOUS VEHICLES

Toshifumi Tsukiyama and Yoshiaki Shirai
Information Science Division
Electrotecnical Laboratory
Nagata-cho 2-6-1,Chiyodaku
Tokyo 100 Japan

This paper describes a method for detecting the movemens of men waking on a passage using two consecutive TV image. The method consists of three steps: (1) finding a passage region and regions of objects in a TV images, (2) locating men in the region map, and (3) detecting the movements of men using their location in tow consecutive region maps. High speed processing is to be achived by employing a special hardware for image processing.

1. INTRODUCTION

This paper describs a method for detecting the movements of men walking on a passage using two consecutive TV images. Our final goal is to develop an autonomous vehicle with a TV camera, such as the one in a hospital for guiding the blind . Here, we deal with a simplified case where a TV camera is fixed and only men are on a passage.

There have been some works for detecting moving objects using cross-correlation [1]. But they are not effective for our purpose, because the size and the orientation of moving objects may change to a great extent and the numbers of objects are not always equal between the images.

The method in this paper finds the movements of men by locating them in each image. It consists of three steps as follow: (1) finding a passage region, (2) locating men, and (3) detecting the movements of men.

In order to catch up with the movements of men the processing for finding a path should be done very fast, say every 0.7 sec. We used a special hardware for the high speed processing.

2. FINDING A PASSAGE REGION

A passage is assumed to be illuminated sufficientry by many lamps on the ceiling and color of the surface of a passage is light enough. Under these conditions, vertical surfaces are much daker than horizontal ones, up to a certain height. The mean of brightness of men is smaller than that of the passage. However, some parts of men's cloths may be a little brighter than the passage due to wrinkles. In this case, the variance of brightness of the parts is expected to be lager than that of the passage. Therefor, we use the mean and the variance of brightness of TV image to find a passage region.

Let I(i,j) denote the light intensity of the pixel at (i,j) in a image. We use the following measures for the mean M(i,j) and the variance D(i,j) at the pixel at (i,j);

$$M(i,j)=\sum_{i=1,j=1}^{3} I(i,j) \qquad 2 \leqq i,j \leqq 255$$

$$D(i,j)=\left|\sum_{k=1}^{3}[I(i,1)-I(i,3)]\right| + \left|\sum_{j=1}^{3}[I(1,j)-I(3,j)]\right|$$

Each pixel is classify into a passage region or the other region by the following procedures.

(1) If $M(i,j)>\theta 1$, then it is classified into a passage region.

(2) If $M(i,j)<\theta 2$, then it is classified into the other region.

(3) If $\theta 1 \geqq M(i,j) \geqq \theta 2$ and $D(i,j)<\theta 3$, then it is classified into a passage region.

(4) Otherwise, the pixel is classified into the other region.

θ1, θ2 and θ3 are fixed based on the first TV image.

Here, we call the other regions the object regions on the passage. The small object regions are merged with a passage region. Since the width of the passage and the direction of the TV camera are known in advance, some erroneous parts such as wall regions, can be eliminated.
Fig.1 shows an example of a TV image and a passage region.

3. LOCATING MEN

We use the shapes of men and their size in order to find men in the object regions. We define an X-Y coordinate on a plane parallel to the passage plane of which the origin is at the location of TV camera and of which the Y axis coincides with the direction of the passage. Since the range information about points on passages can be obtained from the declination of the TV camera and its height, a passage region in a TV image can be transformed to the plane as shown in Fig.2. The area surrounded with broken lines in Fig.2 represents the maximum of a passage region and we call the area a region map.
The shapes of men on a region map can be clasified into four types as shown in Fig.3 according to the position of feet. The type (d) represents the situation that one man overlaps another.

We shall explain the method for locating men on a region map using an example as shown in Fig.4. First, the region map is scanned from the bottom to the top to find the bottom point P1. Next, the curve is searched for a pair of P2 and P3 such that the width W of the curve is greater than the threshold $\theta 4$ (0.3m) for the first time. If a pair of points P2(X2,Y2) and P3(X3,Y2) satisfies the condition, the man is located at the point P4((X2+X3)/2,Y1). Third, the detected man region is deleted from the region map. The lower part of the curve is deleted from the region map. The upper part of the curve is covered with a mask like a horn as shown in Fig.5(a). If the width W of the protruded part under the mask is greater than the thresshold $\theta 5$ (0.1m), we determine that another man is also included inside the curve. Then, the shape of the mask is changed into that of Fig.(5), so that another man may be easily found later. This process repeats until no man is found.

4. DETECTING THE MOVEMENTS OF MEN

The movements of men are obtained by finding the correspondence of the positions of 'men between two consecutive region maps. Suppose that the position of the k-th man in the first and in the second region maps are (X_{1k},Y_{1k}) and (X_{2k},Y_{2k}), respectively, the distance between them is less than $V\cdot\Delta t$, where V is the maximam speed of men (assumed 1m/sec) and Δt is time interval (0.7sec). If the candidate position is only one under this condition, the correspondence is immediately determined. If there are n positions with more than one candidate, the correspondence of them is determined as follows.
Assuming that men are apt to move along the Y axis than the X axis. Now, we define a weighted distance for the k-th man as follows.

$$E_K = \sqrt{w\cdot(X_{1K} - X_{2K})^2 + (Y_{1K} - Y_{2K})^2} \qquad w>1$$

We determine the correspondence such that the following evaluation function may be minimized:

$$E = \sum_{k=1}^{n} E_K$$

Now, we consider the case where men come into or out of the region map and occlusion. A region map is divided into three zones (A,B and C zones) as shown in Fig.6. It is assumed that men always come into or go out of the region map through A or C zone.
First, the correspondence is found between men in B zone on the first map and those in the whole area on the second map. In this

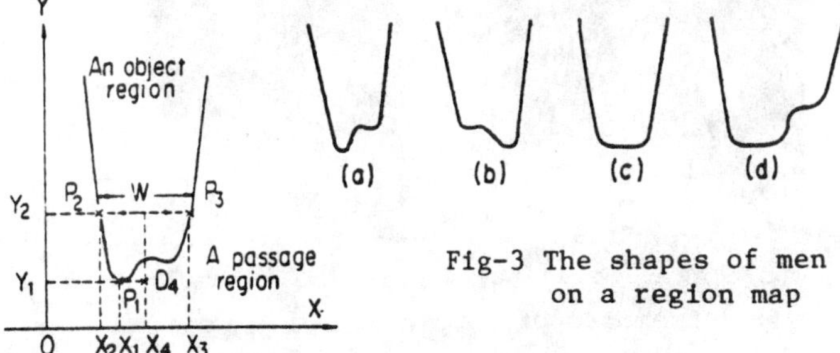

Fig-4 A simplified example of an object region

Fig-3 The shapes of men on a region map

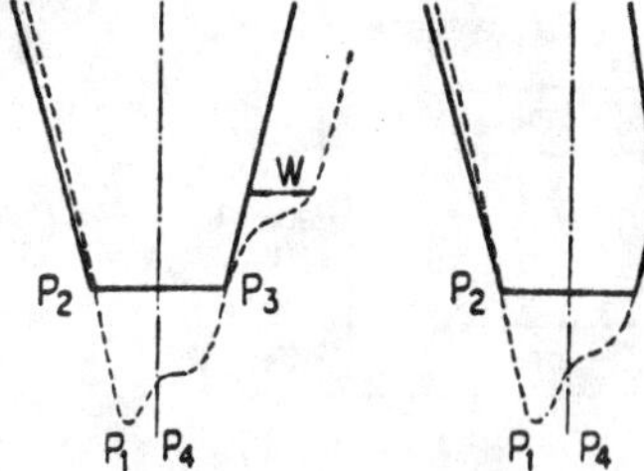

(a) An original mask (b) A modified mask

Fig-5 Example of maska on a region map

(a) An input image

(b) A passage region of the image(a)

Fig-1 An example of finding a passage region

Fig-2 The region map of the image of Fig-1

procedure some corresponding pairs are found. The remaning men in both maps are dealt with in the following way.

CASE 1 :there is no man in A and C zones on the first map.

In this case, men on the first map can not go out of the map. The remaining men on the first map are determined that they are behind some one on the second map. Conversely, the remaining men on the second map are determined to behind some one on the first map. The remaining men in A and C zones on thsecond map are determined that they have entered the map from the outside area.

CASE 2 :ther are some men in A or C zone on the first map.

The correspondence is found between men in A and C zones on the first map and the remaing men on the second map. If there still remain some men without correspondence, they are dealt with in the similar way as in CASE 1, except that the remaining men in A and c zones on the first map are determined that they have gone out of the map.

(a) The 1-st scene

(b) The 2-nd scene

(c) The 3-rd scene

(d) The 4-th scene

Fig-7 Examples of four consecutive scenes

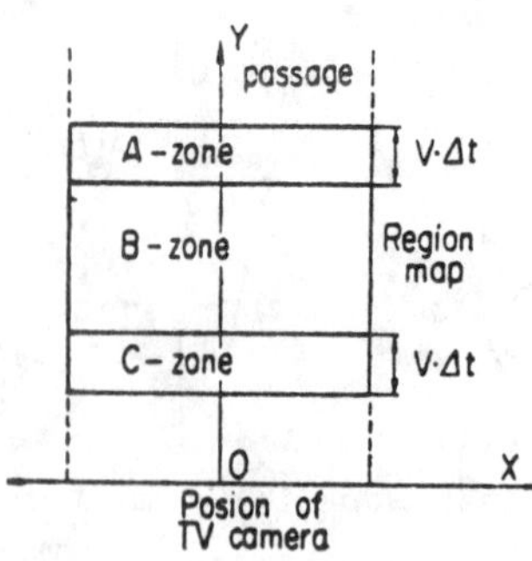

Fig-6 Three zones on a region map

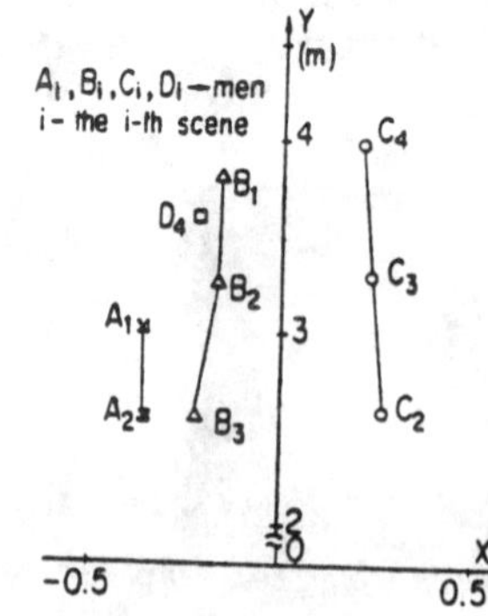

Fig-8 THe locations of men of four scenes in Fig-7

5. EXPERIMETAL RESULTS

We examine the metod in many cases. The four consecutive scenes as shown in Fig.7 are examples of input images. The men in these images are located on the map and the movements are detected as shown in Fig.8.

6. DISCUSSIONS

We used the Parallel Patten Processor (PPP) [2] for high speed processing. The PPP has several basic image procssing function in hardware, memories for pictur data and a microprogrammed processor. We estimated the time needed for finding the region of a passage. The time was 580 msec as shown in Table 1. The total time for the processings includeding the location of men and the detection of the movement is larger than the time interval (0.7sec) at present. But the improvements of the hardware and the program will make the total time less than 0.7 sec.

In order to realize autonomous vehicles, we must consider the following problems: (1) a TV camera moves on a passage, (2) a passage is hook-shaped one, and (3) there are some objects on a passage, besides men.

OPERATION	NUMBER OF INSTRUCTIONS	EXECUTION TIME	FREQUENCY IN USE	CONSUMED TIME
MASK	3 step/pixel	65 msec/image	0.4	26 msec
MEAN OF BRIGHTNESS	5 or 6	130	0.36	47
VARIANCE OF BRIGHTNESS	12	195	0.24	47
2D-CONVOLUTION	by hardware	65	3	195
REGION LABELING	by hardware	200	1	200
DATA CONVERSION	by hardware	65	1	65

An instruction of the microprogram needs 250 nsec.
The memory cycle is 1 μsec/pixel.
An image has 256x256 pixels.

Table-1 The detail of consumed time

ACKNOWLEGEMENT

The authors would like to thank the members of Computer Vision Section for their advices.

REFERENCE

[1] J.Z.butnicka, et al.,"Automatic Movement Analysis and Classification of Moving Object", the 4-th IJCPR pp.750-752 1978.

[2] K.Mori, et al.,"Design of Local Parallel Pattern Processor for Image Processing", National Computer Conference, pp.1025-1031, 1978.

PARALLEL-SERIAL PRODUCTION SYSTEMS*

Leonard M. Uhr
Computer Sciences Department
University of Wisconsin
Madison, Wisconsin 53706

This paper describes several extensions to standard Production System (PS) languages that appear to make them more conveniently usable for a wider variety of perceptual and cognitive systems. The extensions are described (giving parallel productions, multiple memories, and productions that are implied by productions), and a programming language ($(PS)^2M^n$) is presented (in Uhr, 1978) that incorporates them. Sketches are given indicating how several different kinds of cognitive and perceptual systems might be coded in this extended language, and suggestions are made as to additional extensions that might further augment the power and convenience of such a language.

1. INTRODUCTION

This paper describes a Parallel-Serial Multi-Memory Production System language, $(PS)^2M^n$, that handles 1) parallel sets of productions, 2) more than one working memory in which to look for the conditions of productions, and fire the consequences of successful productions, and 3) productions that are fired by productions. These extensions would appear to be convenient for a variety of systems, where parallel processes and dispersed memories are needed. The following such systems are briefly described:

A) Several "Knowledge Sources," all working in parallel with separate working memories, but communicating through a common single "Blackboard" memory.
B) Systems for parallel compatability relaxation, where a number of nodes are examined in parallel, for contextual information that might serve to disambiguate them.
C) Discrimination nets (e.g. for "concept formation" and "EPAM"), where a sorting tree is used to find the appropriate name.
D) Parallel-serial perceptual systems, where sensed information is successively transformed, by layers of parallel feature-detectors and characterizers, into successively more abstract memory representations.
E) Parallel search for solution paths in problem-solving.

See Uhr, 1978, for programs (in EASEy/Snobol*) for $(PS)^2M^n$ and for a traditional (serial, single-memory) Production System, along with a short Primer description of the language.

1.1 Parallel-Serial Production Systems With Many Working Memories

It is often necessary (as in systems for perception, memory search and heuristic problem-solving) to apply a whole set of transformations, or productions, to a Working Memory store in parallel. Systems with several knowledge sources frequently use parallel processes and several memories. In multi-layered or hierarchical perceptual systems, the conditions of productions must be looked for in one WM_i and the consequent acts effected on another WM_j. Therefore a whole set of WM, $WM_1, \ldots WM_N$ are needed. Each production will look at a specified WM_i (or several WM) and, if fired (because all its conditions have been satisfied by a match with elements in that WM_i), effect its consequent acts (e.g. insertions, deletions, arithmetic operations, generations of productions, deletions, arithmetic operations, generations of productions, input-output) on the specified WM_j.

---

* This research has been partially supported by National Science Foundation grant MCS76-07333.

* See Uhr, 1974a; Griswold et al., 1968.

This paper describes extensions to current Production Systems that handle such processes, without the often cumbersome code otherwise needed, but also in a well-structured and simple way.

1.2 Traditional Production Systems

A Production System (PS) (Newell and McDermott, 1975; Rychener, 1976; Waterman, 1975) consists of an ordered set of Productions (P),P1,...PM, each with a set of Conditions (C) and a set of consequent Acts (A), plus one Working Memory (WM). E.g.:

P1: RED BLUE ⇒ GREEN DELETE (RED) DELETE (BLUE)
P2: BROWN YELLOW ⇒ DIRT
P3: GREEN-DIRT = POOR-GRASS (STOP)
WM: RED BLUE YELLOW BROWN

Each Condition specifies a set of elements. An element specifies a string (or list structure) of sub-elements to be matched with strings found in WM. The match usually demands that the first sub-elements match, and that each subsequent sub-element in C_i match a subsequent (but not necessarily the next) sub-element in WM. Variables are usually bound by whatever they find in the first match where they occur (rather than have the system try all possibilities). Acts specify insertions or deletions in Working Memory, the generation of new Productions, or any of several primitive Acts, like OUTPUT, or STOP. A Production "fires" its Acts if all its Conditions are satisfied. Usually the system moves from the top Production down, until one Production fires, when it jumps back to the top, to repeat the process. Some systems use different flows, e.g. continuing on to the next production whether the prior one fired or not (note that this does not mean that Productions are applied in parallel, for each fired Production immediately effects its Acts, and therefore modifies WM). Some systems find all Productions that succeed, and then use one of a variety of criteria for choosing and firing one Production, e.g. the one that matches the most recently added element in WM (Newell and McDermott, 1975).

1.3 Parallel-Serial Multi-Memory Production Systems

Living cognitive systems effect sets of parallel transformations, and use a number of temporary buffer Working Memories. Such parallel-serial multi-layered architectures seem similarly desirable for computer-programmed systems since (once they run on the parallel-serial computers, see e.g. Duff, 1976, Lipovski, 1977, that current technology is on the verge of making feasible) they offer great economy and power.

$(PS)^2M^n$ extends traditional Production Systems so that they can conveniently handle parallel processes applied to more than one Memory. The key extensions include the following.

A) Any number of Memories can be specified and used, with sets of Productions looking at and firing into each.
B) Each Production can look at several Memories, and fire into several Memories, if desired.
C) Sets of Productions can be applied in either a Parallel or a Serial mode, as specified, and the mode can be changed during a run.
D) A Production can fire one or more Productions to be applied, as specified.
E) After a Production succeeds in firing, the system can either attempt to fire the next Production, or go back to attempt to fire the first Production, as specified.

These extensions allow for relatively convenient coding of a variety of perceptual and cognitive systems, some examples of which are described below.

1.4 Some of the Uses of Multiple Memories, and of Parallel and Dynamically Implied Productions

A single Memory can always be set up to do anything that multiple memories can do (since standard Production Systems are based on Post Productions they are universal computers, and anything can be programmed in them)-but often at a heavy price. Essentially, the system can no longer use the Memories' names and attendant pointers to directly access sub-sets of information in the relevant Memories. Rather, elements in the single Memory must be given appropriate name-like tags, and the system must use the relatively slow Production-matching routines to search for the appropriately tagged elements. All the elements in a particular Memory could be grouped together, so that only one tag was needed. But that means the system must work with and try to match a large and cumbersome list of lists - and that can be a slow and costly process. Alternately, each element can be separate, but each with the same Memory tag. But that means the search for the appropriate tag must be turned into a loop, iterating through the entire Memory.

The original development of Production Systems was directed toward work with a very small

"Working Memory" for scratch-pad-like intermediate results, one that models the human "short-term memory" that is capable of handling some small number like 7 items. For such uses there is no need to add more Memories or other structures. But for a general-purpose programming language multiple Memories serve a number of purposes.

Without a parallel capability of the sort provided in $(PS)^2M^n$, a program must make several extra passes through a set of transforms to simulate parallel processes. The first pass would not actually change the Memory; rather, it would output its set of acts each specially tagged as a temporary output. Then the program would have to keep applying a set of Productions that looked for all these tags, use the output information from the tagged elements to modify Memory, and erase all these tagged temporary elements.

The dynamic implication of transforms gives the programmer powerful control capabilities for structuring the flow of processes. Without this feature a program must use a production that adds an element to Memory that only one other Production - the one to be fired next - will succeed in matching. This means the system must make an extra cycle through its productions to find that next production, in addition to adding and deleting the identifying element. Dynamic Productions make this process direct and simple.

The present system can use dynamically implied productions, but it cannot generate them. For it can insert newly generated productions only into its main list of Productions (as is done by standard Production Systems). But it also needs the ability to insert a Production's name into the list of Consequences of another Production, and to choose that Production correctly. This needs a capability of modifying a Production, and not simply creating one, and of accessing and conveniently storing histories of the names of Productions fired. Such an extension is discussed below, as part of a more general ability to create, modify, and erase both Productions and Memories - that is, to treat productions and memories in exactly the same way.

2. EXAMPLES OF SYSTEMS THAT COULD FRUITFULLY USE $(PS)^2M^n$

2.1 Parallel Sets of "Knowledge Sources" as Parallel Communicating Production Systems

An attractive structure for cognitive and perceptual systems is one that uses a set of independent "Knowledge Sources" (e.g. Reddy, 1973, Lowerre, 1976), or "demons" (e.g. Lenat, 1977). Each works at the same time, independently of the others, and therefore could be executed in parallel by one processor in a suitable network of minicomputers, or parallel processors. All communicate with one another by passing information into and out of a common "blackboard" memory. Such systems cannot be conveniently coded in a standard Production System language like PSG or PAS-2, because the knowledge sources act in parallel, and often contain parallel processes.

Such a system can quite straightforwardly be handled by $(PS)^2M^n$, as follows: Each knowledge Source is executed in turn, since each works with its own local memory. Then, after all have completed their processes, a set of parallel production transfers their (present, intermediate) results to the common Blackboard Memory. Then a second set of parallel productions transfers selected information from the common Memory to the individual Knowledge Sources' memories.

The parallel capabilities of $(PS)^2M^n$ make the transfer of information into and out of the common Memory very convenient, since there is now no danger of unwanted interactions between Knowledge Sources. And now each Knowledge Source can itself contain a mixture of parallel and serial flows of productions. And each can contain one (or more) separate memories, whereas in a standard PS each subset of memories would have to be protected (in a very cumbersome way) from all Knowledge Sources that did not have access to it.

Most large Production-oriented programs of this sort appear to be Production Systems in spirit, but without being coded in an actual Production System language. The extensions handled by $(PS)^2M^n$ would appear to move in the direction of a language that might be suitable for convenient coding and running of such large production Production Systems.

2.2 Compatibility Pairs

A production for relaxation using pairs of compatibility labels (e.g. Zucker, 1977; Davis and Rosenfeld, 1978; Tennenbaum and Barrow, 1976) need only be a 2-tuple, designating the label to be looked at and the context label. When both are found the label is fired into an output Memory. But each label must be searched for in its designated memory, and many such productions must be applied in parallel. And to iterate to more distant contexts each must imply the next production to apply. The present system will handle deterministic constraints, if it raises a flag with each success, tests and lowers the flag after each iteration, and then stops iterating after one pass without raising the flag (meaning that nothing new has been accomplished). Extensions to be discussed below will handle probabilistic constraints and dynamic stopping rules, and also situations that mix compatibility pairs with other types of transforms.

2.3 A Production System that Uses Compatability Pairs to Choose Among Productions

Zucker, 1977, has suggested that compatibility pair relaxation techniques might fruitfully be used to choose the single judged-best Production to fire next, when a serial Production System finds that more than one Production might fire. (This is the case in those standard Production Systems that, instead of firing the first Production that succeeds, get all Productions that succeed, and then use some criterion to choose among them.)

$(PS)^2M^n$ allows such a system to be coded entirely as a parallel-serial Production System, as follows:

List all the Productions to be chosen among as a parallel set on the MASTER list (the main list of productions - see Uhr, 1978). Each Production implies all of its compatibility labels as dynamically implied Productions on its set of ACTS. Thus all Productions that succeed fire their compatibility labels onto the set of (parallel) productions that will fire next, after this parallel set has been completed. Then this parallel set of compatibility labels will be applied. This procedure continues, as in the proceeding section, until either a single production remains or no more relaxation can be done. Thus the separate relaxation phase is absorbed into and handled by the $(PS)^2M^n$ Production System.

2.4 Discrimination Nets, Concept Formation, EPAM

The program uses a tree of Productions, each making one test. The Master list starts with a Production that tests for the first node of the discrimination net (really a tree), followed by all Productions on its negative path. If it succeeds it implies the Production on its positive path to be immediately executed in the serial mode followed by all Productions on that node's negative path. Thus the fragment of a discrimination tree shown in Figure 1 needs the Productions shown in Table 1 (a number refers to the test for that node):

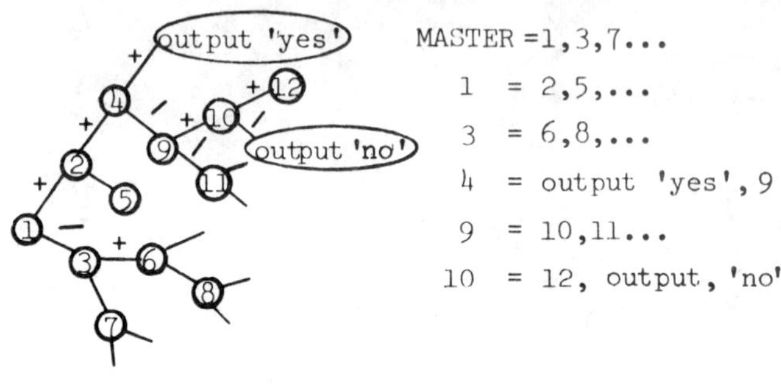

MASTER	=	1,3,7...
1	=	2,5,...
3	=	6,8,...
4	=	output 'yes', 9
9	=	10,11...
10	=	12, output, 'no'

Figure 1 Table 1

Note that the only Productions on the MASTER list are the first and the successive '-' (failure) branches from it. All other Productions are implied by Productions that fire.

This program uses a true discrimination tree, where each Production tests only the single next node. This is in sharp contrast to the EPAM program (Waterman, 1975) coded in PAS-2 (which uses a separate template for each entire path in the tree, and has no ability to dynamically imply transforms).

2.5 Layered Perceptual Systems (e.g. Cones, Pyramids, Hierarchical Relaxation)

The use of a sequence of several memories between pairs of which are sandwiched sets of parallel productions can be quite straightforwardly coded as a parallel-serial production system. Productions need only be stored as parallel sets, their INput MEMory and OUTput MEMory specified for each such set, with the OUTput MEMory for one set the INput MEMory for the corresponding subsequent set.

Dynamically implied transforms can be handled as productions that are implied as consequent acts of successful productions. Iterations through relaxation can be handled by using the same INput MEMory and OUTput MEMory for several cycles. These would be especially attractive for parallel-serial layered perceptual systems such as the cones and pyramids being developed by Hanson and Riseman, 1974; Tanimoto, 1976;

Uhr, 1972, 1974b, and others.

Such systems would benefit greatly from several extensions (that are projected for future productions systems). These include a) weights, thresholds, and probabilistic productions, b) a convenient way to iterate through a whole array of memory locations (as in the 2-dimensional retinal mosaic), applying the same set of parallel productions in parallel to each cell in the array, and c) techniques for choosing among alternative implications (as in naming and describing), and for deciding when to choose (as in deciding when to stop relaxing).

2.6 Heuristic Problem-Solving

A heuristic problem-solver could take advantages of several levels of parallel processes, given a suitable language. Typically, a whole set of heuristic evaluation functions is to be applied in parallel to a node that might be a candidate for further search. And a whole set of such candidate nodes might conveniently be evaluated in this way, in parallel.

A $(PS)^2M^n$ program with the following structure can handle such a system:

The set of heuristics is coded as a parallel set of Productions.

For a heuristically guided search for a path from a set of Givens to a Goal (or from Goal to Givens), the Givens (or the Goal) are input as elements in the first WM. The Rules of Inference (sometimes called legal moves, transformations, etc.) are coded as a parallel set of productions and put on the MASTER list. They are applied, giving the buds (which are put into a second WM) from the presently achieved expressions, deleting elements in the first WM, and firing set of heuristics (coded as a second parallel set of productions). The heuristics now look at these budded expressions, and accumulate the evaluation of each. They are followed by a serial set of productions that chooses and puts into the first WM the most highly valued expression(s), and deletes all expressions in the second WM. The Rules of Inference are again applied, and this process continues.

I have ignored a number of important details, but almost certainly several more Working Memories will be preferable - e.g. to store the pointers back from buds to their fathers for later use in getting the solution-path, and to get that path.

3. SOME ADDITIONAL EXTENSIONS THAT WOULD SEEM TO BE USEFUL

There are several further extensions that would appear to make for substantial further improvements in the ease of coding of cognitive and perceptual systems, and the resulting transparency and clarity of structure of the resulting systems. These include the following:

A) Probabilistic transforms would allow for the emerging of multiple implications, from perceptual characterizers or problem-solving heuristics. This entails rather simple extensions: 1) Associated with each element of a condition will be a number (that can be interpreted as a weight, probability, fuzzy value, or whatever the programmer desires), associated with each production will be a treshold, and associated with each implied act will be a weight. When the combined weights of successful conditions exceeds the Production's threshhold, the Production will be considered to succeed, and fire its implications with their assigned weights. 2) Several implications of the same thing will have their weights merged. 3) When this is specified in the program, then the system will choose among alternative implications from among some mutually exclusive set that the programmer has specified.

B) A set of Productions should be able to iterate conveniently through an array of memories. This would allow for very convenient and straightforward coding of perception systems, e.g. pyramids and cones, and relaxation labeling, where sets of transforms (coded as Productions) could be applied to the different cells, or regions, of the retinal image, or internal abstracted images.

C) A system should have a more general set of capabilities for creating and erasing lists (whether Productions or Memories), and adding and deleting information to and from these lists. This would allow for the convenient building, and modifying, or complex list structures and graphs of information. If done with as much generality as possible, it should also make Productions and Memories, and their manipulations, quite similar.

4. DISCUSSION

Today's production systems have a heritage much older than Post's productions, and much broader than problem-selving. For Post productions are probably the single Turing machine-equivalent formulation that most directly embodies that elusive (and possibly imaginary) entity, "intuitive thinking." The rules of inference of Euclid's geometry, and of Aristotle's syllogism, are very similar to productions. Consider the linguist's rewrite rules and transformations, the physicist's Feynam diagrams, the psychologist's S-R mappings, the "if a,b,c, then d,e,f" lines of reasoning of detective, diagnostician or trouble-shooter.

So an embodiment of thinking in terms of productions would seem especially desirable. We could use it conveniently; we could understand it; and it might well be appropriate, and powerful. But the particular production system chosen should be sufficiently flexible and powerful for convenient programming.

The three major extensions to Production Systems incorporated into $(PS)^2M^n$ - 1) the ability to apply productions in parallel, when desired, 2) the partitioning of information into several working memories, and 3) the firing of productions to be applied next by productions that are fired - often appear to go together, and to complement and enhance one another. But one might prefer to use only one, or two, of these extensions, for the following reasons:

1) If it is known that all programmers who will use the production system language will code all their programs using only serial productions, then the parallel capability is not needed. But many cognitive processes, especially in perception and associative memory search but also in heuristic deductive problem-solving, appear to have important parallel components. And although yesterday's computers are serial, today's are beginning to be parallel, and tomorrow's will become increasingly parallel.

2) From a certain esthetic perspective as to the meaning of "simplicity" the single Working Memory seems simpler than several Working Memories. But if a program uses several memory stores it seems less simple to throw them all together into one, and then do a lot of otherwise unnecessary searching and matching to find the one that is needed.

3) Productions that fire productions to be applied may well violate the simple modular structure of standard production languages, with their top-down flow through the stack of productions. But they may more closely reflect the actual operative structure and flow of the program, in the sense of the productions that actually will fire. Without this capability a program becomes cluttered up with cumbersome and time-consuming devices that make use of the addition and deletion of special data symbols to direct the program's flow.

REFERENCES

Davis, L.S. and Rosenfeld, A. Hierarchical relaxation, In: Comp. Vision Sys.(Ed. by A.R. Hanson and E.M. Riseman), New York: Academic, 1978, 101-110.

Davis, R. and King, J. An overview of production systems, CS AIM-271, Stanford, 1975.

Duff, M. J. B. CLIP 4: a large scale integrated circuit array parallel processor, Proc. IJCPR-3, 1976, 4, 728-733.

Erman, L. D. and Lesser, V. R. A multi-level organization for problem-solving, PROC. 4th IJCAI, 1975, 483-490.

Feigenbaum, E., Buchanan, B. and Lederberg, J. On generality and problem-solving, Machine Intelligence 6, Edinburgh, 1971, 165-190.

Griswold, R. E., Poage, J. F. and Polonsky, I. P., The SNOBOL4 Programming Language, Englewood-Cliffs: Prentice-Hall, 1968.

Hanson, A. R. and Riseman, E. M. Preprocessing cones: a computational structure for scene analysis, COINS TR 74C-7, U. Mass., 1974.

Lenat, D. B. Automated theory formation in mathematics, Proc. 5th IJCAI, 1977, 833-842.

Lipovski, J. On a varistructured array of processors, IEEE Trans. Comp., 1977, 26, 125-138.

Lowerre, B. T. The Harpy Speech Recognition System, Ph.D. Diss., CMU, 1976.

McDermott, J., Newell, A. and Moore, J. The efficiency of certain production system implementations, CS TR, CMU, 1976.

Newell, A. and Simon, H. A. Human Problem Solving, Prentice-Hall, 1972.

Newell, A. and McDermott, J. PSG manual, CS TR, CMU, 1975.

Reddy, D.R., et al. HEARSAY-1 speech understanding system, Proc. IJCAI-3, 1973, 185-193.

Rychener, M. D. Production Systems as a Programming Language, Ph.D. Diss., CMU, 1976.

Tanimoto, S. L. Pictorial feature distortion in a pyramid, Comp. Graphics Image Proc., 1976, 5, 333-352.

Tennenbaum, J.M. and Barrow, H.G. IGS: A paradigm for integrated image segmentation and interpretation, Proc. IJCPR 3, 1976, 504-513.

Uhr, L. Layered "recognition cone" networks that pre-process, classify and describe, IEEE Trans. Comp., 1972, 21, 758-768.

Uhr, L., EASEy: An English-like Programming language, CS TR 233, U. Wis., 1974. (a)

Uhr, L., A model of form perception and scene description, CS TR 231, U. Wis., 1974. (b)

Uhr, L., Parallel-serial production systems with several memories, CS TR 313, U. Wis., 1978.

Waterman, D. A., Adaptive production systems, Proc. 4th IJCAI, 1975, 296-303.

Zucker, S. W. Relaxation labeling and the reduction of local ambiguities, Proc. IJCPR-3, 1976, 4, 852-861.

A SYSTEM FOR FUZZY REASONING

Motohide Umano
Dept. of Applied Mathematics
Faculty of Science
Okayama University of Science
Ridai-cho, Okayama 700
JAPAN

Masaharu Mizumoto
Dept. of Management Engineering
Faculty of Engineering
Osaka Electro-Communication University
Neyagawa, Osaka 572, JAPAN

Kokichi Tanaka
Dept. of Information and Computer Sciences
Faculty of Engineering Science
Osaka University
Toyonaka, Osaka 560, JAPAN

This paper describes an implementation of a system for fuzzy reasoning which facilitates the execution of approximate reasoning from the specified propositions and gives the result in both fuzzy-set and linguistic forms. The description of the Approximate Reasoning System contains the Universe of Discourse Block which defines several universes of discourse; the Primary Term Block which defines several primary terms; the Proposition Block which states propositions using primary terms, linguistic hedges and IF ... THEN ...; and the Approximate Reasoning Block which executes approximate reasoning and linguistic approximation. The Approximate Reasoning System is implemented using the FSTDS System for fuzzy-set manipulation and is running on a FACOM 230-45S computer.

1. INTRODUCTION

Much human reasoning is fuzzy rather than precise in nature. An example of such reasoning may be "If x is *small* and x and y are *approximately equal*, then y is *more or less small*". The fuzziness in the words: *small*, *approximately equal* etc. may be defined by fuzzy sets and fuzzy relations[1]. Reasoning with fuzzy concepts has been formulated by Zadeh[2] who calls it approximate reasoning.

In this paper, we describe a system for fuzzy reasoning, called an Approximate Reasoning System, which is based on Zadeh's formulation of fuzzy reasoning. This system facilitates the definitions of universes of discourse and primary terms, the description of fuzzy propositions, and the execution of approximate reasoning using the specified fuzzy propositions. The result of approximate reasoning is given in both fuzzy-set and linguistic forms.

2. APPROXIMATE REASONING AND LINGUISTIC HEDGES

Zadeh's formulation of approximate reasoning is defined as the compositional rule of inference which is expressed in symbols[2] as

$$\begin{array}{l} P_1\text{: x is A.} \\ P_2\text{: x and y are R.} \\ \hline P_3\text{: y is A}\circ\text{R.} \end{array} \qquad (1)$$

where x and y are object names, A is a fuzzy set in U, R is a fuzzy relation in U×V, and A∘R is the composition of A and R, i.e., is a fuzzy set in V. If P_2 is a conditional proposition such as

$$P_2\text{: If x is P then y is Q.} \qquad (2)$$

where x and y are object names and P and Q are fuzzy sets in U and V, respectively, then it is translated into the fuzzy relation R of x and y using the arithmetic rule for conditional propositions[2],

$$R = (\sim P \times V) \oplus (U \times Q) \qquad (3)$$

where ×, ~ and ⊕ stand for the Cartesian product, the complement and the bounded sum, respectively.

[Example 1] Let U be a universe of discourse expressed by

$$U = \{1, 2, 3, 4\}.$$

If we have the fuzzy set *small* in U as

$$small = \{1/1, 0.6/2, 0.2/3\}$$

and the fuzzy relation *approximately equal* in U×U as

approximately equal = {1/<1,1>,
1/<2,2>, 1/<3,3>, 1/<4,4>,
0.5/<1,2>, 0.5/<2,3>, 0.5/<3,4>},

then from the premise propositions:

P_1: x is *small*.
P_2: x and y are *approximately equal*.

we can infer by approximate reasoning the consequence:

$$y = \textit{small} \circ \textit{approximately equal} = \{1/1,\ 0.6/2,\ 0.5/3,\ 0.2/4\}.$$

A linguistic hedge such as *very*, *more or less*, *much* and *slightly* can be viewed as an operator which operates on the operand fuzzy set. For example, several hedges are defined by Zadeh[3] and Lakoff[4].

The effects of some linguistic hedges are shown in Fig.1 in the case where a fuzzy set is *tall*[4].

We can obtain a fuzzy set as the consequence of approximate reasoning. If the consequence remains in fuzzy-set form, it is difficult for us to understand its meaning, as was the case in Example 1. So the consequence would be better given "*more or less small*" rather than a fuzzy set {1/1, 0.6/2, 0.5/3, 0.2/4}. Thus representing a fuzzy set approximately in a linguistic form by some appropriate hedges and fuzzy sets already defined is called linguistic approximation.

3. APPROXIMATE REASONING SYSTEM

The Approximate Reasoning System (AR System for short) facilitates the execution of approximate reasoning from the specified propositions and outputs the consequence in a linguistic form by linguistic approximation.

We shall illustrate the facilities of the Approximate Reasoning System using a simple example.

[Example 2] If we have a description in the AR System as in Fig.2, then we obtain the output as in Fig.3.

The UNIVERSE OF DISCOURSE BLOCK defines a universe of discourse U and the PRIMARY TERM BLOCK defines fuzzy sets SMALL, MIDDLE and LARGE on U. In the PROPOSITION BLOCK, we describe the propositions P1 and P2. In the AR BLOCK (APPROXIMATE REASONING BLOCK), PARA sets parameters (the threshold value of the evaluation function and the depth of nested hedges) for linguistic approximation and AR executes

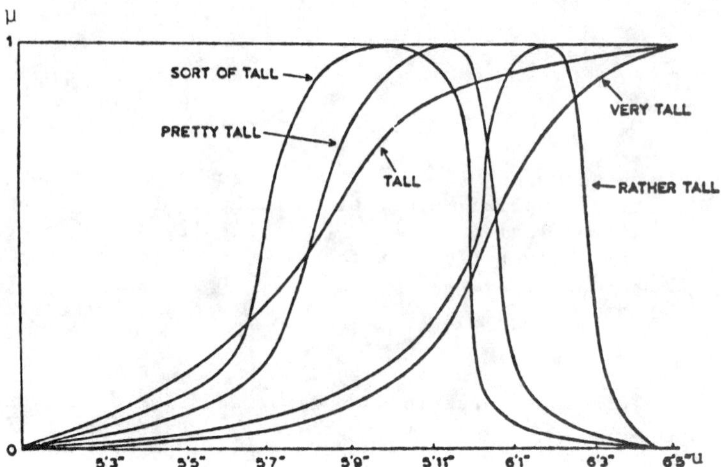

Fig.1. The effect of hedges *very*, *sort of*, *rather* and *pretty* (Lakoff[4]).

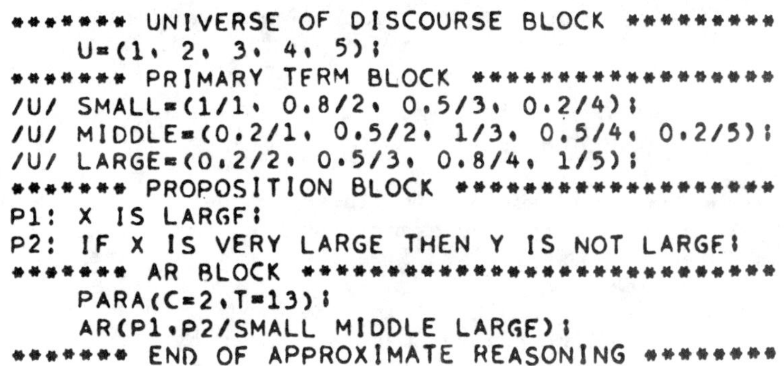

```
******* UNIVERSE OF DISCOURSE BLOCK *********
    U=(1, 2, 3, 4, 5);
******* PRIMARY TERM BLOCK *****************
/U/ SMALL=(1/1, 0.8/2, 0.5/3, 0.2/4);
/U/ MIDDLE=(0.2/1, 0.5/2, 1/3, 0.5/4, 0.2/5);
/U/ LARGE=(0.2/2, 0.5/3, 0.8/4, 1/5);
******* PROPOSITION BLOCK *******************
P1: X IS LARGE;
P2: IF X IS VERY LARGE THEN Y IS NOT LARGE;
******* AR BLOCK ****************************
    PARA(C=2,T=13);
    AR(P1,P2/SMALL MIDDLE LARGE);
******* END OF APPROXIMATE REASONING ********
```

Fig.2. A description in the Approximate Reasoning System.

```
..... OBTAINED SUFFICIENT LINGUISTIC APPROXIMATION

* LINGUISTIC APPROXIMATION...   MINUS MORE OR LESS SMALL

* PRIMARY TERM...   SMALL

* FUZZY SET WHICH IS PRIMARY TERM...
    FSFT(1/1, 0.8/2, 0.5/3, 0.2/4);

* FUZZY SET GENERATED BY COMPOSITIONAL RULE OF INFERENCE...
    FSET(1/1, 0.96/2, 0.8/3, 0.56/4, 0.5/5);

* FUZZY SET MODIFIED BY SOME HEDGES...
    FSET(1/1, 0.9197/2, 0.771/3, 0.5468/4);

* EVALUATION FUNCTION VALUE...   0.1165

* THRESHOLD VALUE...   0.130
```

Fig.3. A result of the Approximate Reasoning System.

approximate reasoning from the propositions P1 and P2, and approximates the consequence linguistically by the primary terms SMALL, MIDDLE and LARGE.

As shown in Example 2, a description in the AR System contains four blocks, namely, the Universe of Discourse Block, Primary Term Block, Proposition Block and Approximate Reasoning (AR) Block. We have no more detailed explanation of their blocks on account of limited space.

4. IMPLEMENTATION OF THE AR SYSTEM

The Approximate Reasoning System is implemented using the FSTDS System (Fuzzy-Set-Theoretic Data Structure System)[5] which enables a user to write a program in FSTDSL/FORTRAN using 52 fuzzy-set operators on fuzzy sets and fuzzy relations.

The AR System passes to the FSTDS System the sets and fuzzy sets defined in the Universe of Discourse Block and Primary Term Block. A composite term is translated into an expression in FSTDSL, that is, hedges are replaced by the corresponding operators in FSTDSL and connectives are translated into prefix operators. A conditional proposition IF ... THEN ... is translated by (3).

For the AR statement, the AR System passes the statement:

```
%CONSEQUENCE = IMAGE(P2, P1);
```

to the FSTDS System. Note that AoR in (2) reduces to the image of A under R since A is a unary fuzzy relation.

As for the linguistic approximation, we can not use the really best linguistic approximation, since it generates too many composite terms. Therefore we use the following strategy.

First, we apply each hedge to given m primary terms and compare its result with the consequence fuzzy set B. If we obtain a sufficient approximation, that is, the value of evaluation function is less than or equal to the threshold value, then it is accepted as the linguistic approximation of B. Otherwise we choose one composite term of the best approximation in the first step of linguistic approximation and apply each hedge again to it. If we cannot still obtain a good one, the same is repeated n times. If a sufficient approximation has not been obtained yet after n repetitions, the best approximation by this time would be considered as a linguistic approximation of B. There is, however, no guarantee for the really best approximation.

For the evaluation function, there might be several definitions. We have adopted the evaluation function such as

$$f(B,B') = \frac{\sum |\mu_B(u) - \mu_{B'}(u)|}{\#(U)} \qquad (4)$$

where B is the fuzzy set obtained by approximate reasoning, B' the fuzzy set modified by hedges in linguistic approximation and U a universe of discourse of B and B', and #(U) denotes the number of elements in U, $|x|$ the absolute value of real number x and Σ the ordinary sum over U.

5. CONCLUSION

We have described an Approximate Reasoning System which facilitates the definition of universes of discourse and primary terms, the description of propositions and execution of approximate reasoning and linguistic approximation. In the implementation of the AR System, the translation of the description in the AR System to FSTDSL is programmed in PL/I and the construction and manipulation of fuzzy sets and fuzzy relations are programmed in FSTDSL/FORTRAN[5], and it is currently running on a FACOM 230-45S computer. The current AR System is an interpreter version.

As a basis of question/answering system and intelligent access to database systems, fuzzy reasoning plays so important role in the interface between such systems and users that we expect the AR System will find various other applications.

REFERENCES

[1] Zadeh, L.A. "Fuzzy Sets" Information and Control 8 (1965) pp.338-353.

[2] Zadeh, L.A. "Fuzzy Logic and Approximate Reasoning" Synthese 30 (1975) pp.407-428.

[3] Zadeh, L.A. "A Fuzzy-Set-Theoretic Interpretation of Linguistic Hedges" Journal of Cybernetics 2 (1973) pp.3-34.

[4] Lakoff, G. "Hedges: A Study in Meaning Criteria and the logic of Fuzzy Concepts" Journal of Philosophical Logic 2 (1973) pp.458-508.

[5] Umano, M., Mizumoto, M. and Tanaka, K. "FSTDS System: A Fuzzy-Set Manipulation System" Inform. Sci. 14 (1978) pp.115-149.

A Knowledge-based Interactive Robot-vision System

T. Vámos
Computer and Automation Institute,
Hungarian Academy of Scs.
1111 Budapest, XI., Kende u. 13/17
Hungary

M. Báthor and L. Mérő
Computer and Automation Institute,
Hungarian Academy of Scs.
1111 Budapest, XI., Kende u. 13/17
Hungary

A robot-vision project is reported which incorporates several existing AI methods and some new results. The ambition of the project is a system which can economically complete various intelligent tasks within the scope of mini- and microcomputers. The tuned composition of the applied methods provides a new and powerful approach to RandD, engineering and workshop-operation.

1. INTRODUCTION

This paper reports on a robot-vision lab for RandD and for experimentation of specialized industrial applications. The system combines many well-known methods of recognition with some own ones /a fast template method, a quasi-parallel edge-finder etc./ but this combination provides a sophisticated goal-oriented approach for real-life problem solving.

2. PICTURE PROCESSING, RECOGNITION

The system is based on man-machine communication; the goal is the recognition of 3D industrial objects whose number is limited to 10-20 for each task. The objects are taught either by building a geometric model or by a computer-aided transformation of the real situations viewed during the learning period to create a standard model description similar to the artificial one. The camera input /Fig. 1/ is processed in overlapping pixels by a simplified version of the Hueckel-operator using only two linear templates. An estimator of the fit coordinates a weight-attribute to the stroke. These weights and some fuzzy-like parameters which are attributed to the higher picture-hierarchy are relevant elements of the heuristic search. The hairy stroke-picture /Fig. 2/ is used both by the brute-force shape estimators which provide a first guess and, by the further picture processing.Nodes

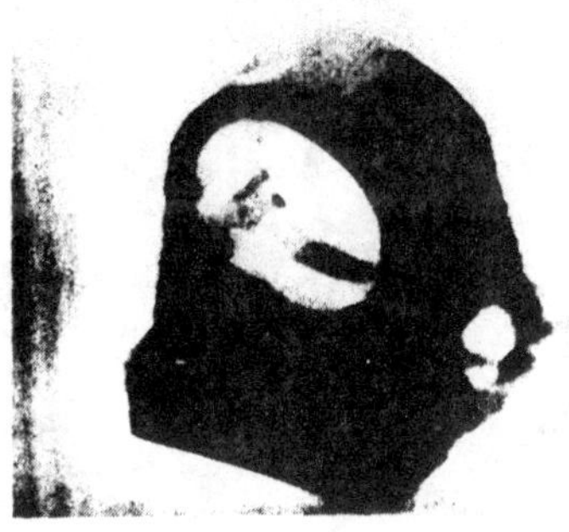

Fig.1. Digitized input /negative picture/

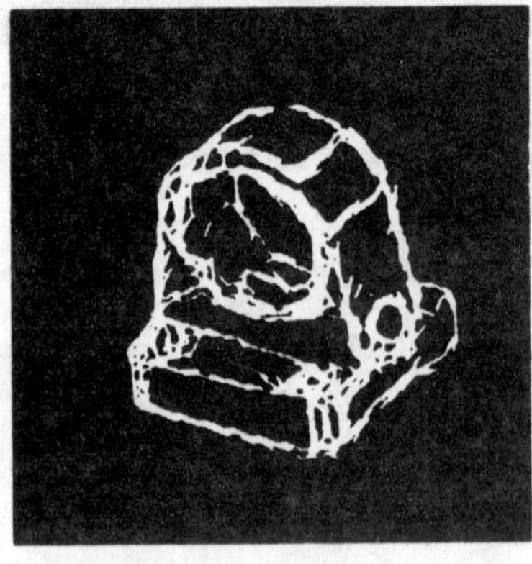

Fig.2. The strokes found in the picture

of the contour are supposed where the slope-variances of the strokes attain local maxima /Fig. 3/. Streaks along the contour lines are detected by a quasi-

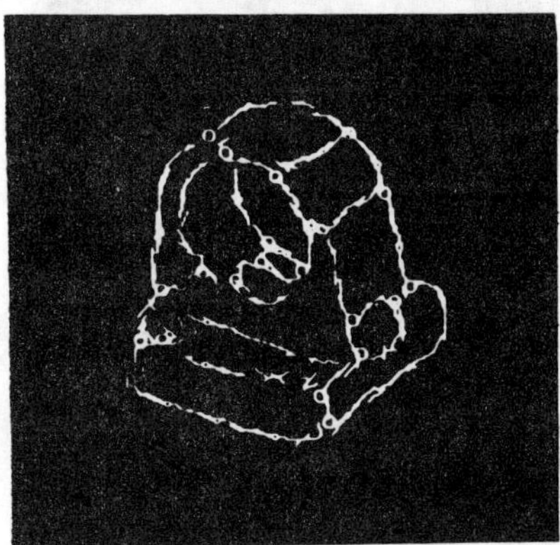

Fig.3. The streaks of strokes with the nodes found

parallel minimum-cost algorithm operating in parallel between every supposed node-pair connected by paths.

This algorithm is based on a mathematical model of the expected streaks. The requirements with the paths are expressed by four graph-theoretic criteria which mean that every contour-line should be optimally approximated by a streak and each of them by only one streak. A potential-field growing algorithm has been developed in order to find the streaks and it can be proved that the streaks provided by this algorithm satisfy the criteria of the mathematical model of the streaks. The streaks found using this algorithm are displayed on Fig. 3.

The next preprocessing algorithm merges the streaks either into line segments by uniting the approximately identically directed consecutive strokes or into arcs by comparing the slope differences. This interpretation is generally weak, due to the uncertainty of the whole process; thus a probability value is assigned to each possible interpretation, considering that each streak may have various interpretations /Fig. 4/. This value serves for the ordering of hypotheses in the linguistic recognition.

Matching the processed picture with the model and the whole knowledge base, decision on the ambiguities due to multi-

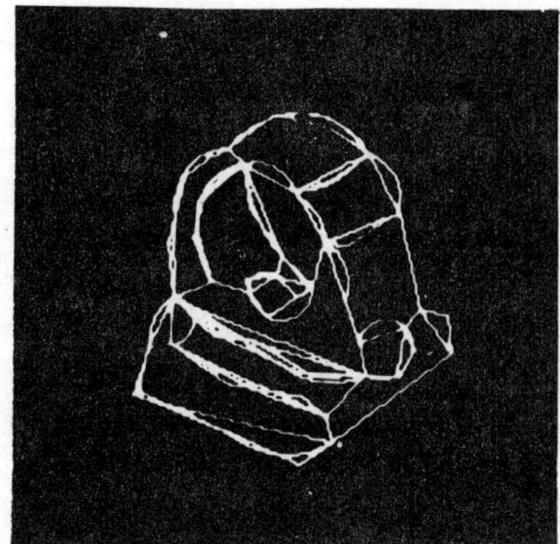

Fig. 4. All possible interpretations of the streaks

ple or failing edges and areas are solved by linguistic methods. Three accelerating heuristic tools are applied in directing the search on the problem-graph: a priori information, the weights with the calculated fuzzy-like estimation attributes of the picture hierarchy and the distance measures between pictures and models. The estimation attributes are calculated from the weights of the strokes, considering in each stage /node, streak, edge, picture part/ the reliability of the fit, decomposition and concatenation. Several distance measures are distinguished: brute-force characteristics with their special task-oriented combinations, distances similar to those used by Fu / 3 /, distances obtained from statistics of learning, special measures preprogrammed by the operator with the help of his personal experience.

The process of recognition includes the determination of orientation, namely the calculation of the transformation matrix which transforms the position of the model to the real position of the object. Modelling is used not only in the ways initiated by Roberts and later Baumgart and others but as a general tool for man-machine communication during i/ the system design, ii/ the task learning and iii/ the robot operation. Each level is different in intelligence; none of the levels can disturb its superior one but each has a systematic downward compatible interactive apparatus based on a graphic display. The graphics is 3D-2D oriented: the internal representation and manipulations refer mostly to the 3D model /Fig. 5/, the different 2D pic-

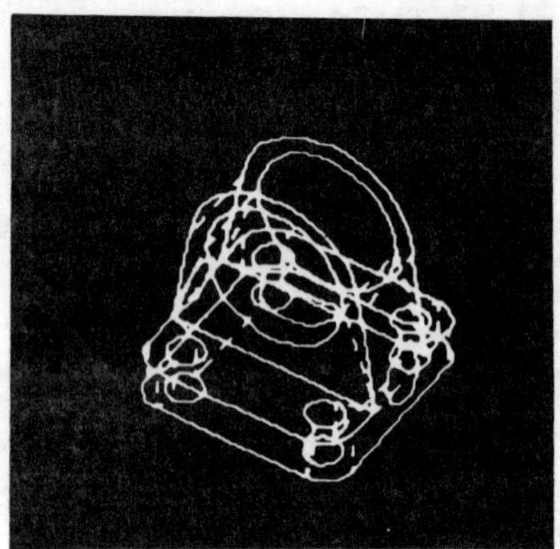

Fig. 5. 3D wire-frame model of the object

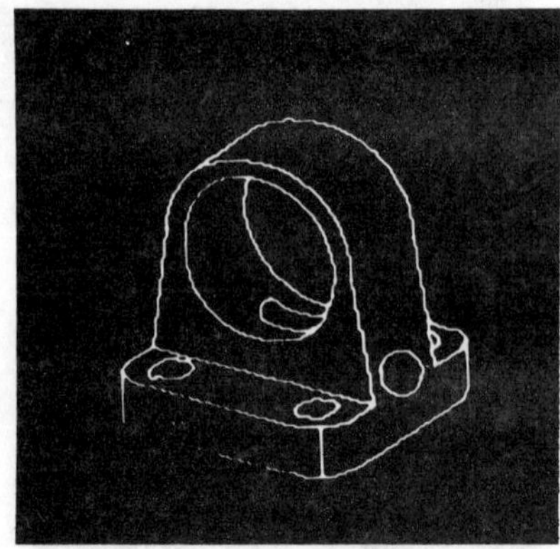

Fig. 6. A hidden line projection of the perfect model

tures to be matched with the scene are derived from that using a fast hidden line elimination algorithm. This means that all usual 3D operations are implemented /rotation, distortion, unification etc./, adapted specially to our requirements, i. e. real time, low storage capacity.

3. EXPERIMENTAL RESULTS

Robot control and hardware are usual not to be detailed here. The system uses a 16 bit 40 kB mini with a 2 μs cycle-time /VIDEOTON R-10 licence after the French CII-Mitra-15/, minidisc, magtape, graphic display.

The whole recognition procedure needs about 30-50 seconds to recognize an object shown e. g. in Fig. 1. The running times of the particular algorithms are the following. The hidden line algorithm is extremely fast, it provided e. g. Fig. 6 within 2 seconds. The edge-finding operator needs about 4 seconds for processing a TV picture input. The algorithm which assembles the strokes into streaks requires 10-15 seconds. The grammatical searching procedure of finding the possible faces and the possible object drawings in the streaks' interpretations takes 5-8 seconds. The other on-line algorithms take less than 1 or 2 seconds altogether.

Experiments have proved that the indicated heuristic search results in a time requirement depending statistically linearly on the object complexity, number of objects, number of ambiguities /edges, interpretations, shadows, partial observations/. A successful guess /e.g. a brute-force estimator/ can cut short occasionally all further trials. In unfortunate cases the interaction of the operator is also possible.

4. APPLICATIONS

The system is primarily assembly-oriented. Other applications of our results that already work are being realized recently: a recognition system in a bus-body factory identifying the metal sheets for controlling a painter robot and a man-machine system in neuro-biological research which should detect neuronal nets in microscope-sections.

REFERENCES

1/M.Báthor:Hidden-Line Algorithm for a Robot Experiment.Ph.D.Thesis,Budapest, 1977

2/B.G.Baumgart:Geometric Modelling for Computer Vision.Stanford AIM-249, 1974

3/K.S.Fu:Stochastic Tree Languages and Their Applications to Picture Processing.Int.Symp. on Multivariable Anal., Pittsburgh, 1978

4/V.Galló:A Program for Grammatical PR.4th IJCAI /Tbilisi/, 1975, pp. 628-634

5/L.Mérő:A Quasi-Parallel Contour Following Algorithm.AISB/GI Conf.on AI,Hamburg,1978, pp. 189-194

6/T.Vámos:Industrial Objects and Machine Parts Recognition,in Applications of Syntactic PR. /Ed.K.S.Fu/,Heidelberg,1977,pp. 243-267

7/T.Vámos:Automatic Control and AI/invited survey/.Prepr.of 7th IFAC World Congress /Helsinki/, 1978, 4, pp. 2355-2369

A DOMAIN-INDEPENDENT PRODUCTION-RULE SYSTEM FOR CONSULTATION PROGRAMS

William van Melle
Heuristic Programming Project
Computer Science Department
Stanford University
Stanford, California 94305

EMYCIN is a programming system for writing knowledge-based consultation programs with a production-rule representation of knowledge. The major components of the system, including an explanation program and knowledge acquisition routines, are briefly described. EMYCIN has been used to build consultation systems in several areas of medicine, as well as an engineering domain. These experiences lead to some general conclusions regarding the potential applicability of EMYCIN to new domains.

1 Introduction

The focus of much current work in artificial intelligence is the development of computer programs that aid scientists with complex reasoning tasks. Recent work has suggested that one key to the creation of intelligent systems is the incorporation of large amounts of task-specific knowledge. However, building such "knowledge-based" programs from scratch can be a very time-consuming task. We have found that the basic framework of the MYCIN program [9] could be generalized sufficiently to make possible the substitution of knowledge bases from other domains. The result of this generalization is EMYCIN*, a system for developing rule-based consultation programs. The aim of this work is to make knowledge-based systems technology more accessible to investigators in many fields.

2 Description of EMYCIN

EMYCIN is used to construct a *consultation program*, by which we mean a program which offers its user advice on some problem within its domain of expertise, much as a human consultant does. The program elicits information relevant to the case by asking the user questions during the course of the consultation. The program then applies its knowledge to the facts of the case and informs the user of its conclusions. The user is free to ask the program questions about its reasoning in order to better understand or validate the advice given.

2.1 Knowledge Organization

Knowledge in EMYCIN is represented in terms of production rules operating on associative (attribute-object-value) triples. To represent the uncertainty of data or competing hypotheses, attached to each triple is a *certainty factor* (CF), a number between -1 and 1 indicating the strength of the belief in that fact [8].

Reasoning is performed using domain knowledge encoded as *production rules*. Each rule has a *premise*, which is a conjunction of predicates over triples in the knowledge base. If the premise is true, the conclusion in the *action* part of the rule is drawn. If the premise is known with less than certainty, the strength of the conclusion is modified accordingly (see [8]). Figure 1 shows a typical rule from the domain of structural analysis (described in Section 3).

Rule 68

```
If:  1) The material composing the sub-structure
        is one of the metals,
     2) The analysis error (in percent) that is
        tolerable is less than 5,
     3) The non-dimensional stress of the sub-
        structure is greater than .5, and
     4) The number of cycles the loading is to be
        applied is greater than 10000
Then: It is definite (1.0) that fatigue is one of
  the stress behaviour phenomena in the sub-structure

PREMISE: ($AND
            (SAME CNTXT COMPOSITION (LISTOF METALS))
            (LESSP* (VAL1 CNTXT ERROR) 5)
            (GREATERP* (VAL1 CNTXT ND-STRESS) .5)
            (GREATERP* (VAL1 CNTXT CYCLES) 10000))
ACTION: (CONCLUDE CNTXT SS-STRESS FATIGUE TALLY 1.0)
```

Figure 1

English and internal Lisp forms of a SACON rule.

2.2 Application of Rules -- the Rule Interpreter

The control structure is a goal-directed backward-chaining of rules. At any given time, EMYCIN is working toward establishing the value of some attribute. To this end, the system retrieves the (precomputed) list of rules whose conclusions bear on this goal. The rule in Figure 1, for example, would be retrieved in the attempt to determine the stress of a substructure. If, in the course of evaluating the premise of one of these rules, some other piece of information is needed which is not yet known, EMYCIN sets up a subgoal to find out that information; this in turn causes other rules to be tried. Questions are asked during the consultation when the rules fail to deduce the

* "Essential MYCIN", i.e. MYCIN stripped of its domain knowledge. This work was supported in part by the NSF grant MCS 77-02712 and the Advanced Research Projects Agency, contract MDA 903-77-C-0322.

necessary information. If the user cannot supply the requested information, it remains unknown, and rules that require it will simply fail. Thus, the rules unwind to produce a succession of goals and it is the attempt to achieve each goal that drives the consultation (EMYCIN also permits a limited use of *antecedent rules*, triggered when the program receives new data or makes a conclusion).

2.3 Usefulness of the rule representation

As has been described in earlier reports of the MYCIN program [4], many of the system's important features are facilitated by the use of rules as the primary representation of knowledge. Since each rule is intended to be a single "chunk" of information, the knowledge base is inherently modular, making it relatively easy to update. Individual rules can be added, deleted or modified without drastically affecting the overall performance of the system. The rules are a convenient unit for explanation purposes. The system's ability to "read" its own rules is used extensively by the explanation program (below) and other routines which assist the user in manipulating the rule base.

2.4 Explanation Capability

EMYCIN's *explanation program* allows the user to interrogate the system's knowledge, either to find out about inferences made in the particular case at hand or to examine the static knowledge base in general. During the consultation, in response to certain user commands, EMYCIN can offer explanations of the current, past and likely future lines of reasoning (*WHY* a question was asked, or ***HOW*** a conclusion is reached). A more general form of explanation is available via the *QA Module*, which is automatically invoked after the consultation has ended, and can also be entered during the consultation to answer questions outside the scope of the special WHY/HOW commands. The QA Module accepts simple English-language questions dealing with any conclusion drawn during the consultation, or about the domain in general. The questions are parsed by pattern matching and keyword lookup, using a dictionary which is automatically constructed from the phrases used in defining the various objects and attributes of the domain. The QA module has been described in great detail elsewhere [7].

The explanation program is also a helpful high-level debugging aid for the system developer. Without having to resort to Lisp-level manipulations, she can examine any inferences that were made, find out why others failed, and thereby correct errors or omissions in the knowledge base.

2.5 Knowledge Acquisition

A substantial part of the initial effort involved in creating an EMYCIN system is spent in the acquisition phase, viz. constructing the knowledge base of the rules and the object-attribute structures upon which they operate. Thus we have devoted much effort to providing programmatic assistance for this task.

EMYCIN supplies a high-level database editor for the data structures in the system. The data must be entered in its Lisp format (understanding English rules is far too difficult, especially in a new domain where the vocabulary hasn't even been identified and organized for the program's use), but the editor handles all the bookkeeping involved in managing the rule base and performs various checks to catch a number of common user errors.

To partially bridge the gap between precise Lisp input and free-form English text, there is an intermediate "terse" rule format. This format is a simplified Algol-like language which uses the attributes and their values as operands; the operators correspond to EMYCIN predicates. E.g. SACON's Rule 68 shown in Figure 1 above could be written instead as:

```
If   Composition = (LISTOF METALS) and
     Error < 5 and
     Nd-stress > .5 and
     Cycles > 10000
Then   Ss-stress = fatigue
```

Figure 2. Stylized English format for rule input.

The terse rule format is also available on output, for users who prefer it to the more verbose English translations.

As each rule is entered, it is checked for syntactic validity, to catch spelling errors and other simple errors. Other data structures are also updated, such as the one telling the rule interpreter which rules conclude about which attributes.

2.6 Other support features

EMYCIN has facilities for maintaining a library of sample cases. These can be used for testing a complete system or for debugging a growing one. When a library consultation is rerun, the system's questions are answered by supplying the response, if any, given when the case was first run. Many such cases may be automatically rerun in background mode, with the system comparing the "results" with those of earlier runs. This makes it easy to check the performance of a new set of rules on "standard" cases.

EMYCIN's existing human-engineering features relieve the system builder of many of the tedious cosmetic concerns of producing a human-useable program. Most of these center around the consultation interaction where the system requests data from the user; they include a terminal input facility with such features as spelling correction and Tenex-style completion on altmode from a list of possible answers, and a simple help facility.

3 Applications

Several consultation systems have been written in EMYCIN. The MYCIN program (which could be viewed as the original implementation of EMYCIN) provides advice on the diagnosis of and therapy for patients with infectious diseases. There are currently some 450 rules in the MYCIN rule set, making conclusions about 85 of the 235 attributes (the remaining attributes are simply input data). Results of formal evaluations of MYCIN's competence in the domains of bacteremia (bacterial infections in the blood) and meningitis indicate that MYCIN's performance in these areas has begun to approach that of medical specialists [10].

The PUFF system [6] performs interpretation of measurements from the pulmonary function laboratory. The data from over 100 cases were used to create some 60 production rules diagnosing the presence of pulmonary disease. These rules are used to create a complete report including the input measurements, historical information, and the measurement interpretation.

The HEADMED program [5] is an application of EMYCIN

to clinical psychopharmacology. The system diagnoses a range of psychiatric disorders and can recommend drug treatment if indicated. The system contains 275 rules at present, one of which is shown in Figure 3.

```
If:  1) The diagnosis for which therapy is being
        recommended is major-depressive-disorder,
     2) The intensity of this patient's psychiatric
        disturbance is one of: moderate, mild,
     3) The current mental state of the patient is
        psychotic, and
     4) There is no recent prior episode of
        psychiatric disturbance
Then: There is strongly suggestive evidence (.8)
      that the class or category of treatments is
      antipsychotic
```

Figure 3. A sample HEADMED rule.

As a stronger test of domain independence, EMYCIN was applied to the completely non-medical domain of structural analysis. SACON (Structural Analysis Consultation) [2] provides advice to a structural engineer regarding the use of a large structural analysis program called MARC. The MARC program uses finite-element analysis techniques to simulate the mechanical behavior of objects. The goal of the SACON program is to recommend an analysis strategy to guide the MARC user in the choice of specific input data, numerical methods and material properties. The system contains some 160 rules and 50 attributes, half of which are concluded by the rules.

4 Range of Applicability -- Limitations

Although we do not have a precise characterization of domains which are most suitable for an EMYCIN application, our experience provides some general guidelines. We found that many of the simpler systems did not even make use of the inexact inference mechanism provided by CFs. It is possible that more efficient representations exist for the precise knowledge existing in such domains. However, it still seems appropriate to build a reasoning program from EMYCIN as a first test of the inference rules written by an expert. While many of the system's complicated features, such as certainty factors, may go unused in the simpler systems, those features do not substantially burden a program which does not use their extra generality.

It is not always easy to actually formulate the domain knowledge into production rules, even in the domains that have been successfully implemented so far. Our desire to keep the rule format simple is occasionally at odds with the need to encode the many aspects of scientific decision-making. For example, the process of therapy selection in MYCIN proved more amenable to a generate and test algorithm [3]. The backward-chaining of rules by the deductive system is also often a stumbling block for experts who are new to the system; however, they soon learn to structure their knowledge appropriately. In fact, some experts have felt that encoding their knowledge into rules has helped them formalize their own view of the domain, leading to greater consistency in their decisions.

The representation of facts as associative triples with CF's may not be natural or adequate for many domains. However, the triples have proved a flexible enough data structure in our investigations thus far. The specific control structure in EMYCIN, viz., goal-directed backward chaining of rules, might be considered much more restrictive.

Certainly other control structures and representations are possible. We recognize that EMYCIN is not as general as some other efforts, e.g. KRL [1], nor is it intended to be: there may well be advantages in restricting the user's options. At least during the initial formulation of the knowledge of a domain, the simple framework of a single, easily understood control structure allows the expert to focus on the knowledge in the rules themselves, and not get sidetracked by a bewildering array of control choices.

5 Conclusion

Currently the system builder still requires a fair knowledge of Lisp and the workings of EMYCIN itself. Our work aims at improving the facilities for acquiring and debugging rules, as these are the most time-consuming portion of creating a new consultation system. Our aim is to have a truly convenient "workshop" for knowledge-based system exploration, in which a knowledge engineer can relatively quickly create a functional consultation program in a new domain, try out a new set of rules, or simply discover whether a rule-based system is reasonable for the task.

Acknowledgements

The author wishes to acknowledge the contribution of Carli Scott, who programmed much of the QA Module and continues to assist in the development of new features in EMYCIN. Thanks to Carli and also to Bruce Buchanan for their helpful advice on this paper.

References

[1] Bobrow, D.G., and Winograd, T. An overview of KRL-0, a knowledge representation language. *Cognitive Science*, **1**,1, 1977.

[2] Bennett, J.S., *et al.* SACON: A Knowledge-based Consultant for Structural Analysis, Computer Science Dept, Stanford University, Memo HPP-78-23, Sept. 1978.

[3] Clancey, W.J. An antibiotic therapy selector which provides for explanations, *Proceedings of IJCAI5*, 1977.

[4] Davis, R., Buchanan, B.G., and Shortliffe, E.H. Production rules as a representation for a knowledge-based consultation system. *Artificial Intelligence*, **8**,15-45, 1977

[5] Heiser, J.F., Brooks, R.E., Ballard, J.P. Progress Report: A Computerized Psychopharmacology Advisor, *Proceedings of the 11th Collegium Internationale Neuro-Psychopharmacologicum.* Vienna, 1978.

[6] Kunz J.C., *et al.* A physiological rule based system for interpreting pulmonary function test results, HPP-78-19 (Working Paper), Heuristic Programming Project, Computer Science Dept, Stanford University, December 1978.

[7] Scott, A.C., *et al.* Explanation Capabilities Of Knowledge-Based Production Systems. *American Journal of Computational Linguistics*, Microfiche 62, 1977.

[8] Shortliffe E. H., and Buchanan B. G. A model of inexact reasoning in medicine, *Mathematical Biosciences* **23**, pp351-379, 1975.

[9] Shortliffe E. H. *Computer-based clinical therapeutics: MYCIN*, American Elsevier, 1976.

[10] Yu, V.L., *et al*, Evaluating the performance of a computer-based consultant. *Computer Programs in Biomedicine*, **9**, 95-102, 1979.

VISUAL ANALOG REPRESENTATIONS FOR NATURAL LANGUAGE UNDERSTANDING*

David L. Waltz and Lois Boggess**
Advanced Automation Group
Coordinated Science Laboratory
University of Illinois at Urbana-Champaign
Urbana, Illinois 61801

In order for a natural language system to truly "know what it is talking about," it must have a connection to the real-world correlates of language. For language describing physical objects and their relations in a scene, a visual analog representation of the scene can provide a useful target structure to be shared by a language understanding system and a computer vision system.

This paper discusses the generation of visual analog representations from input English sentences. It also describes the operation of a LISP program which generates such a representation from simple English sentences describing a scene. A sequence of sentences can result in a fairly elaborate model. The program can then answer questions about relationships between the objects, even though the relationships in question may not have been explicit in the original scene description. Results suggest that the direct testing of visual analog representations may be an important way to bypass long chains of reasoning and to thus avoid the combinational problems inherent in such reasoning methods.

1. UNDERSTANDING LANGUAGE ABOUT THE PHYSICAL WORLD

Suppose that we are given a sentence such as (1):

(1) A dog bit a mailman.

How do we understand such a sentence? What inferences do we make and what inferences can we make? To help answer these questions, suppose that we are asked:

(2) Where on his body did the dog probably bite the mailman?

We suggest that most people would answer (2) with: "on the leg," and that as a first guess, such an answer could plausibly be part of a BITING script or default slots of a frame for BITING. However, suppose that we insert one or more of the following sentences after (1) <u>before</u> asking (2):

(3a,b) The dog was a {doberman. / dachshund.}

(3c,d,e) The man was {sitting. / lying down. / 3 feet tall.}

(3f,g) The dog was {standing on its hind legs. / sitting.}

In these cases the answer to (2) could be quite different parts of the body ("arm" becomes most likely if bitten by a doberman) or one could be much more definite about the answer ("leg" becomes overwhelmingly likely if one is bitten by a dachshund while standing up).

How could we successfully model in a program the understanding process a person goes through in this example? We suggest that the simplest and most natural way to model this understanding is to build up a visual analog knowledge base (representing "person," "dog," etc. as 3-D spatial entities) and to write programs which can manipulate and integrate these visual analog representations. For the example given (1) - (3), figure 1 illustrates some of the information that would have to be included. As another example, suppose we were given the following set of sentences:

(4) A goldfish is in a goldfish bowl.
(5) The goldfish bowl is on a stand.
(6) The shelf is on a desk.
(7) The desk is in a room.

Now suppose that we are asked:

(8) Is the goldfish in the room? or
(9) Is the goldfish on the desk?

The answer to (8) should of course be "yes" and the answer to (9) should be something like "Not <u>directly</u> on, but on is still an appropriate description." How could we mechanize the answering of such questions?

---

*This work is supported by the Office of Naval Research under Contract N00014-75-C-0612

**Current address: Dr. Lois Boggess, Computer Science Dept., Mississippi State University Mississippi State, Mississippi 39762

We suggest that these questions can be easily answered if we use (4) - (7) to build an integrated visual analog structure which represents (4) - (7). Then given procedural definitions of prepositions like in and on, with the "subject" and "object"* that the prepositions relate viewed as arguments to the procedures, we can apply the procedures to the structure directly to answer the questions. Boggess [2] has written a program, described later in this paper, which works exactly in this manner. Given (4) - (7), the program constructs an analog model like that shown in figure 2.

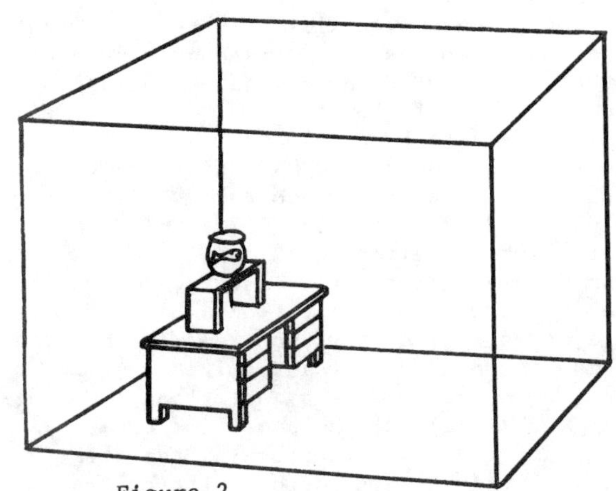

Figure 2.

In constructing the model, the program uses properties of the subject and object to decide what the preposition means in each given case. For example, on would be interpreted quite differently in "the shelf on the wall," and "the shadow on the wall." "The shelf" is assumed to touch the wall, be supported by it, and to have a preferred orientation and position (height) with respect to the wall, whereas none of these are true of "shadow." The differences in treatment are the result of noting in the lexicon that "shelf" is an ordinary physical object (requiring support) with preferred orientation--its free surface should be horizontal--whereas a "shadow" is 2-D and weightless and thus does not require support. Each object has default dimensions as well as weight, and these dimensions (actually a rectangular parallelepiped which encloses the object) can be used to construct the visual analog model.

To illustrate the interpretation of this model, consider the preposition in. If in's object is a 3-D enclosure, then all we need to do to see whether the subject is in the object is to check whether the coordinates of all the corners of the subject are within the intervals of the coordinates of the corners of the object. The answer can be found with one set of tests, regardless of how many chained statements were required to relate the subject and object in the scene description. Thus, given a model like figure 2, it is very easy to answer (8) because all the dimensions of "goldfish" are within the dimensions of "room."

---

*Given the phrase "the cat on the mat," or the sentence, "The cat is on the mat, we call cat the subject and mat the object.

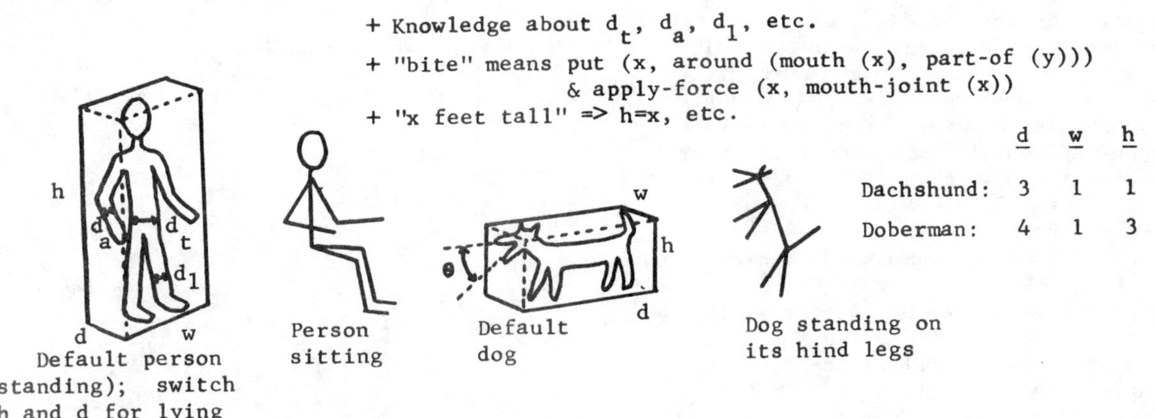

Figure 1. Some of the information needed to understand (1) - (3).

2. USING DEDUCTIVE RULES ON A DATA BASE OF ASSERTIONS.

Starting with Black [1], there have been programs which dealt with similar questions. Most of these programs have "understood" sentences like (4) - (7) by adding something equivalent to an assertion of the form (ON GOLDFISH-BOWL1 STAND1) to a data base. Answering questions about the scene described has then involved applying deductions rules such as:

(10) (ON ?A ?B) AND (ON ?B ?C) => (ON ?A ?C)

to verify that a given relationship does or does not hold between two given objects. In general, the set of assertions in the data base will define a network, i.e. any two items in the data base may be connected by an arbitrary number of deductive chains or direct assertions. For example, a chair can at the same time be at a desk, under the desk and touching the desk.

There are at least two serious difficulties with using a method like deductive chaining to understand the spatial domain, represented as a data base of assertions:

A. If there are many rules and many objects, the search for a deductive chain which can prove or disprove a given relation between two objects can involve combinational explosion. Often there will be insufficient information to decide whether a relationship holds between two objects; in such a case, all relevant paths between the objects will have to be explored before a system can decide that the problem cannot be decided.

B. Even more serious is the difficulty in formulating deduction rules properly to begin with. For example, rule (10) allows us to deduce correctly that a leaf is on a tree if the leaf is on a branch and the branch is on a tree, but it is not correct to deduce that a cow has wings if we know that a wing is on a fly and the fly is on a cow!

One obvious solution to this difficulty has been to create a number of definitions for ON--ON1, ON2, ON3, and so on, where ON1 might mean "is a part of" as in "the wing on a fly," ON2 might mean "above, touching and supported by" as in "the pencil on the desk," etc. Deduction rules can then be formulated with greater precision, but we have added an additional problem: when on is asserted to hold between two objects or used in a question a program must now decide whether ON1, ON2, ON3, or ONn is intended. More rules delimiting the classes of objects which can be related by each meaning of on must then be formulated and somehow utilized to decide which meaning(s) are appropriate.

But even a large number of such rules cannot easily substitute for the visual analog model. Suppose that (4)-(6) were followed by

(11) The desk is in a box.

In this case the goldfish may or may not be inside the box, depending on the dimensions of the box, desk, and stand (see figure 3). But how could a deduction-rule-based system give a different answer to these two cases, unless it implicitly coded metric information? And if it coded metric information, why bother with the potentially long deductive chains?

3. OPERATION OF A PROGRAM FOR UNDERSTANDING SIMPLE LANGUAGE ABOUT SPACE.

A MACLISP program has been written by Boggess [2] which can build a spatial model of sentences involving in and on relations, and answer questions about its model. Input to the program consists of normal English sentences, which are parsed with the aid of a LINGOL [9] preprocessor. LINGOL is an MIT-originated program package which accepts grammatical rules of the type S→NP+VP and produces LISP programs which can then parse input sentences according to the rules of the specified grammar. For this implementation, LINGOL was used to single out prepositions and their semantic subject and object. For example, in the sentence, "On the bed was a box," the LINGOL portion passes the preposition on, the semantic object the-bed and the semantic subject the-box to the rest of the program. Let's follow and extended example.

Input: A glass is in a box.

Resulting model: figure 4.

Figure 3.

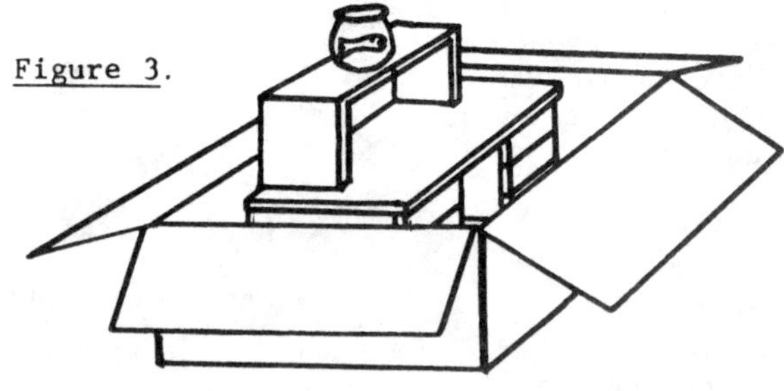

Figure 4.

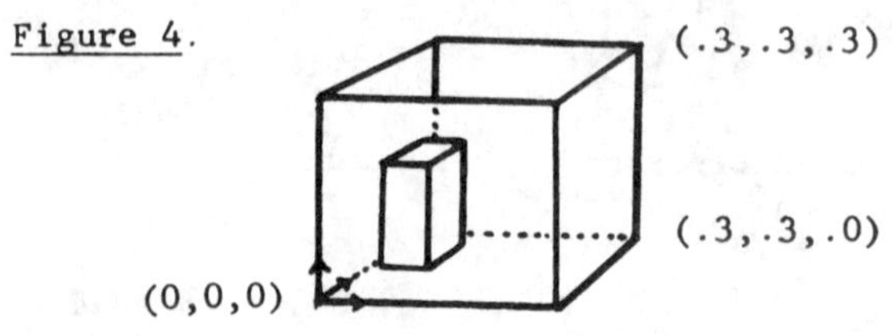

Comments: The glass has weight, so it ends up not only in the box, but at the bottom of it.

Input: The box is on a table.
Resulting model: figure 5.

Figure 5.

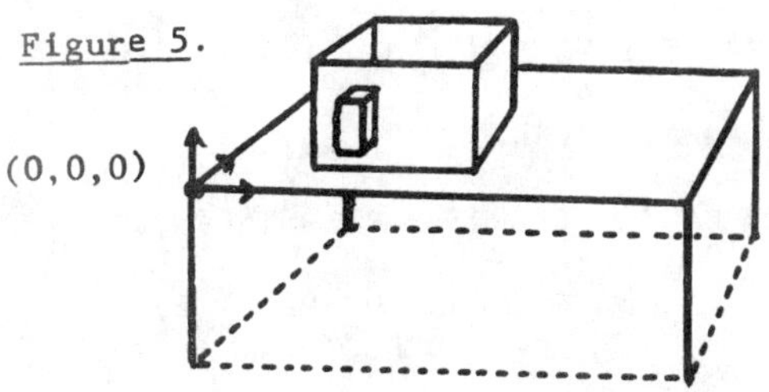

Comments: There is only one individual box known to the system, so the "the box" can be interpreted with no difficulty. Notice that the surface of the table is taken as the basic plane for the discussion so far, rather than putting the origin at, say, a point at the bottom of the table.

Inputs: The table is on a floor.
The floor is in a room.
Resulting model: figure 6.

Figure 6.

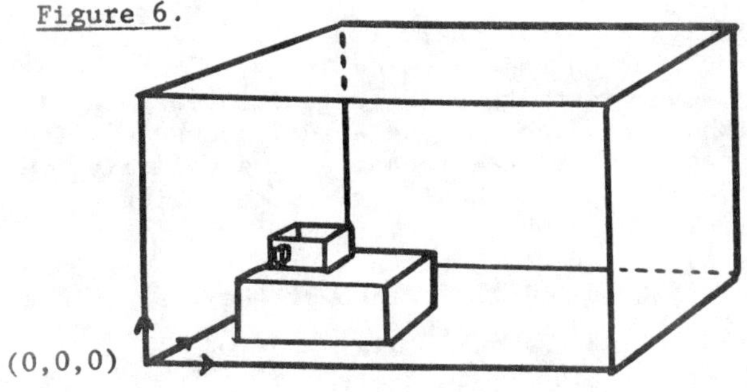

Comments: "A floor" sounds strange, but the system doesn't know for the present that tables are almost always on floors, so mentioning a particular table does not allow it to presuppose a particular floor that it could reference as the floor. As is probably becoming obvious, the model does not choose locations randomly. Rather, it tends toward a particular corner. This choice was made in hopes of avoiding the "findspace" problem [11] when several objects must be located on one surface.

The current model doesn't know that a floor is part of a room. Naturally, a default-sized floor exactly fits a default-sized room, but the model has to know that a floor belongs at "ground level" or it would try to put the floor at a more or less arbitrary level in the room. While this particular sentence sounds unusual, it is natural to speak, say, of "the floor in Jonathan's room."

Suppose after all this the user types: Is the box on the table? The response from the system is YES.
To the input: Is the box on the floor? The system responds NO.
Is the box in the room? YES
Is the glass on the table? NOT DIRECTLY, BUT ON IS STILL AN ACCEPTABLE DESCRIPTION.

The program answers these questions by directly interrogating the three-dimensional model, not by knowing that, say, if A is on B and B is in C then A is probably in C. At no time did we say that the box was in the room. But thanks to the sizes of boxes and tables and the locations of floors relative to the rest of a room, there is no question but that the box must be in the room in the most rigorous sense of the word.

It is also possible to handle situations which would be difficult for systems based on chained inference rules. For example, this program can distinguish between a glass on a tall object in a box and a glass on a small object in the box. If the tall object were large enough that the glass was exterior to the box, then this sort of model could reasonably balk at calling the glass in the box--or at least hedge, as a person might. A system built on the sort of inference rules mentioned above could have trouble distinguishing between these cases.

3.1 Use of Other Knowledge

If the preceding dialog were continued with "The room is in a house," the room would be placed within the volume of the house several feet off the ground, since rooms are weightless. While this seems odd (and could obviously be "fixed"), it is reasonable given that houses can have more than one story. In contrast, given "The house is in a field," the model puts the house on the ground, even though houses have no weight either, as far as the model is concerned. This is because a field is a 2-D object, and the in relation implies contiguity under those circumstances.

Given "A shelf is on a wall," the model uses(1) Knowledge about the free surface of a wall, (2) Knowledge that a shelf's free surface is horizontal, and (3) Knowledge about typical heights of shelves to place the shelf appropriately. The free-surface of a ceiling is downward, so after "A light is on a ceiling," the light ends up on the correct side of the ceiling surface.

4. PROGRAM IMPLEMENTATION-REPRESENTATION OF PREPOSITIONS AND OBJECTS

The examples given in the preceding section were from a session with a small program, written in MACLISP and run on the DEC-10 system at the Coordinated Science Lab. The program consists of about 45 functions, most of them fairly short. Data for the implementation consisted of twenty-two "definitions" of objects and the definitions of the prepositions themselves. Input to the program consists of English sentences--either statements or questions. Statements are expected to be either "naming" statements (Tweety is a " or "Volume-1 is a book") or locative statements ("A book is on a table," "In the room is a bed"). Output is either a set of coordinates for each object in the "mental model" or a response to the question.

4.1 Object Definitions

Some sample definitions of visually perceptible objects follow (units of measurement are meters and kilograms):

```
(TABLE PROTOTYPE
   (INSTANCE-OF FURNITURE)
   (TYPICAL-SHAPE ((HEIGHT 0.75)
                   (CROSS-SEC 1.2 0.9)))
   (FREE-SURFACE (((PLANE HORIZONTAL)
                   (FREE-DIRECTION /+Z)
                   (HEIGHT 0.75)
                   (DIMENSIONS 1/2 0.9))))
   (WEIGHT 25.0))

(BOX PROTOTYPE
   (TYPICAL-SHAPE ((HEIGHT 0.3)
                   (CROSS-SEC 0.3 0.3)))
   (FEATURES (CONTAINER OPEN-TOP))
   (WEIGHT 1.0))

(FLY PROTOTYPE
   (TYPICAL-SHAPE ((HEIGHT 3.OE-3)
                   (CROSS-SEC 3.OE-3 5.OE-3))))

(CEILING PROTOTYPE
   (TYPICAL-SHAPE ((CROSS-SEC 3.6 4.)))
   (FREE-SURFACE (((PLANE HORIZONTAL)
                   (FREE-DIRECTION /-Z)
                   (DIMENSIONS 3/6 4.0))))
   (FEATURES ((TYPICAL-HEIGHT 2.5))))

(SHELF PROTOTYPE
   (INSTANCE-OF FURNITURE)
   (FEATURES ((TYPICAL-HEIGHT 1.0)))
   (WEIGHT 1.5)
   (TYPICAL-SHAPE ((HEIGHT 0.025)
                   (CROSS-SEC 0.2 1.2)))
   (FREE-SURFACE (((PLANE HORIZONTAL)
                   (HEIGHT 0.025)
                   (DIMENSIONS 0.2 1.2)
                   (FREE-DIRECTION /+Z)))))
```

At initialization, the components of the typical-shapes are used to create a simple "mental picture" of the object, in the form of coordinates of an enclosing right parallelepiped. This permanent mental picture is kept under a "local coordinates" property, with the bottom right front taken as local origin.

The definitions specifically single out planar free surfaces on a free-surface list, since it is impossible to judge from the representation whether a planar surface is a characteristic of the object itself.
Also included in the definitions is an indication of whether the object is essentially hollow as opposed to essentially "solid" throughout. The surfaces of the latter are the boundaries of matter; the surfaces of the former enclose space. The feature CONTAINER is used to indicate an object whose interior is canonically empty. Another feature applied to CONTAINERs only and is used to indicate whether they are OPEN-TOPped or not.
TYPICAL-HEIGHT as part of a feature list indicates that an object normally would be found at a given height above the default ground-level (either the floor or the actual ground). Otherwise a clock placed randomly on a wall might end up very close to the floor. After using the program for a while, it became obvious that we needed to have such default heights for a number of items--clocks, windows, shelves, counters, cabinets, and so forth.

4.2 Preposition Definitions

Each preposition is defined as a LISP function with the subject and object as arguments. The LISP functions are based on the results of an extensive analysis of about 20 spatial locative prepositions (see [2]). In this analysis, a number of primitives were identified, such as CONTIGuous, SUPPORTed, INTERIOR (2-D and 3-D), CROSS-SECTION (of objects), PROJECTION (of CROSS-SECTIONs), TRAJECTORY, UP/DOWN, HORIZONTAL,

VERTICAL, and various coordinate systems. These primitives constitute a major result of this research. They will allow us to express neatly the meanings of the approximately 20 locative prepositions analyzed but not yet programmed, and seem on preliminary analysis to be an adequate set for the spatial use of most of the rest of the prepositions as well (prepositions form a closed set).

Each preposition seems to have a default interpretation if its subject and object are unknown, as in "the thingamajig on the whatchamacallit." The default interpretation represents a "pure" case of the prepositional relation--however the preposition can be used to describe a range of physical situations which vary from the "pure" instance by having one or more components of the default case missing or modified. For example, the pure case of above is that in which the SUBJECT is INTERIOR (3-D) but not CONTIGuous to the bottom of a volume defined by projecting the HORIZONTAL CROSS-SECTION of the OBJECT upward VERTICALly in space for a distance of on the order of 3 times the object's diameter. However, above can also be used to describe a variety of "impure" relationships in a scene, including cases where the subject is merely at a higher level than the object (as in "there are clouds above us") and cases where the 2-D projected image of the SUBJECT is INTERIOR (2-D) to the region defined by projecting the HORIZONTAL extreme of the 2-D projection of the OBJECT upward VERTICALLY (as in "the moon above Miami").

To give a better idea of what each prepositional definition is like, let us look at what the functions for on and in do. On is faced with two decisions: it must decide which surface of the object the subject is continguous to, and it must decide which side of the subject is contiguous to the object.

If the subject does not behave normally with respect to gravity (shadows, visual patterns, thin films of liquids and many insects exhibit gravity-defying behavior) then any available surface of the object will do.

If the subject is under gravitational constraints, then the routine looks for one of four possibilities: in order of preference, 1) a horizontal plane in the object, 2) if the object is three-dimensional and is not an open-topped container, then the top of the object 3) failing either of these, then any planar free-surface, and finally 4) any available surface. In any of these cases, the object requires support and by supposition the semantic object furnishes it.

Having found the surface of the object, on looks for a probable surface of the subject. A check is made to see if the subject has a marked free-surface (actually a back-handed way to see if the subject has a preferred orientation). If it has, the preferred orientation is presumed to be the canonical one, and on passes to a function called CONTIG, not a surface of the subject but the entire subject, thereby instructing CONTIG to translate the subject in whatever direction necessary to bring it into contact with the object-surface indicated. On the other hand, if the subject has no preferred orientation, on selects the canonical bottom of the subject.

The definition of the preposition in has to decide if it is dealing with a container, whether the container is open-topped, and whether the subject behaves normally with respect to gravitational constraints. It then calls one of the INTERIOR functions and, sometimes, CONTIG (when the subject is assumed to be in the bottom of a container, for instance). At present, the system has 2- and 3- dimensional interior functions, which restrict the location of their subject with respect to a plane of their object or the volume delineated by the object, respectively.

5. ASSESSMENT OF THE PROGRAM.

5.1 Inferencing Problems

One of the nice features of this "analog model" is that it holds out hope for doing inferencing and deduction by direct reference to the model, under optimum conditions, and by reference to the model plus the location restrictions under other circumstances; the construction of chains of rules can be avoided.

Two cautions are in order, however. In interpreting a description (building the model in the first place), it suffices to place objects in simplest possible relationships. If a description mentions a book on a desk, we probably visualize the book as being directly on the desk. The reverse process--judging from a mental model whether a particular preposition is an appropriate description of the relation between two objects--is not always so simple. In deciding whether "above" is an acceptable description, for instance, there is little question when one object is directly above the other, but clearly the word is acceptable even when the direct case is not applicable, and deciding these more marginal cases often leads to a lot of hedging, even from native speakers.

The second caution is best put by describing a session with the implementation: as it happened, the particular mental model produced after "a shelf is on a wall" and "a fly is on the wall" was the equivalent of figure 7.

Now suppose we were to ask if the fly is under the shelf. The program will say "yes". The correct answer, of course, if "I don't know," since on the basis of the description the fly might be under the shelf, but it might be elsewhere too. Clearly, then, the simple expedient of directly consulting the constructed model is

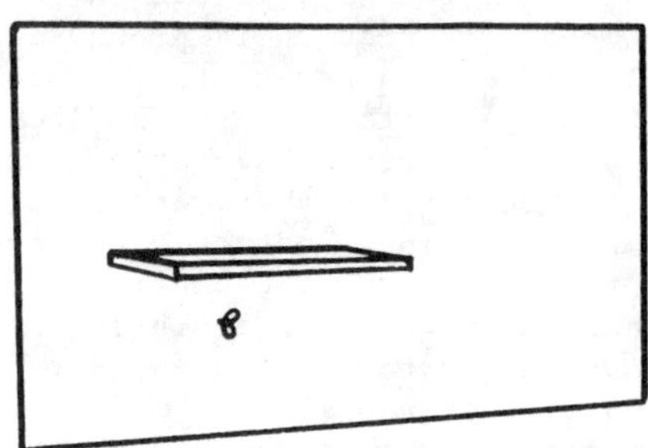

Figure 7.

a little too simple. The more freedom a model allows in choosing the location of an object, the more incidental any relations between various objects may be. In the end what we know are the location restrictions and it is based on them that we need to make judgments.

5.2 Regularities

For all the hedges and caveats of the preceding paragraphs, it was evident from the implementation that paying attention to a very small set of attributes of objects yields an astonishing amount of descriptive power. The attributes included a very rudimentary surface description, the concept of a free-surface with associated free-direction, the essential "emptiness" of containers, some notion of gravity, of contiguity, of the interior relation in two or three dimensions, of partial axes of symmetry, some awareness of scale, and a coordinate system with marked vertical direction. Clearly, these concepts do not handle all cases of descriptions using place locatives. It might even be said that they do not handle some of the most common cases (we will come back to this in a moment). But they do handle the most typical cases--the regular uses of in, on, and the other prepositions--the uses we are most likely to think of as standard. In so doing, they capture much of the descriptive power of the prepositions.

Why then could it be said that they do not handle some of the most common cases? It is well known that the most frequently occurring verbs in English are also the most irregular. Something of the same sort seems to apply to uses of the prepositions with common objects. Tables, for instance, have a tendency to be treated as if they were essentially the table top--"under the table" for most objects means under the table top but definitely not under the legs. Rugs are an exception, of course, as are floors, and there are undoubtedly other exceptions to the mini-rule of treating the table as top only.

5.3 Is on Transitive?

As another example ot the irregularity of tables, consider a scene like that in figure 8, which can be described by (12a - h):

(12a) Volume 8 is on volume 7
(12b) Volume 7 is on volume 6
⋮
(12i) Volume 2 is on volume 1.
(12j) Volume 1 is on the table.

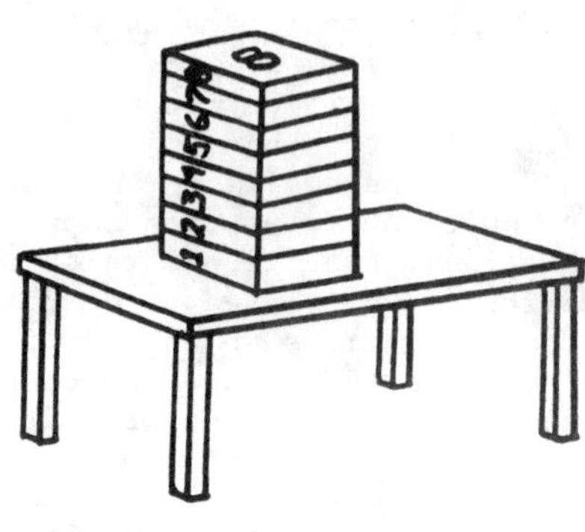

Figure 8.

Since all volumes, 1 - 8 can be said to be "on the desk" we would like some kind of transitive rule to apply, but it would not be proper (or at least it would be very odd) to say that "Volume 8 is on volume 2." The hidden regularity here is that tables (and other furniture: desks, shelves, counters, etc.) have on relations with everything they support, directly or indirectly. Most other objects do not have on relations with everything they support, so that, for example the top book on a stack of books on the ground is not normally said to be "on the ground."

Fortunately, even the most common objects (including tables) appear to be regular most of the time, with most of the prepositions. It is interesting that some of the irregularities fall into classes, like classes of irregular verbs (sing, sang, sung; drink, drank, drunk; sink, sank, sunk). For example, "the people on the bus" are actually in the bus--they aren't on the bus in the same sense that "the people on the car" would be on the car. On has the same interpretation in "on the plane," "on the subway," or "on the boat"--indeed for anything that can be boarded or alternatively that one can stand up in. So at least potentially there may be classes of irregular objects.

After all is said and done, though, it is still the case that the system seems to work, and work well, for the great majority of regular objects, and even for the irregular ones most of the time. It seems clear that basic understanding of the use of the prepositions is ours if only we pay attention to a small set of perceptually salient characteristics of the objects related.

6. PROBLEMS REMAINING

Clearly there will be surprises in programming the rest of the prepositions, and we have only begun to scratch the surface of the problems in implementing programs to deal with sentences like (1)-(3) (the "dog bites mailman" example). However, we are already aware of some problems and exceptions to the general picture presented in this paper.

One major problem was alluded to in the example in section 5 of the fly which was (arbitrarily) placed under a shelf in the mental model and could thereafter not be differentiated from a fly specifically asserted to be under the shelf. What seems to be needed is some way of keeping track of the range of possible positions available to objects described; we have debated several schemes (e.g. a probability distribution for position, a tag on objects explicitly negating accidental relationships between objects, deferring the creation of a mental model until a question is raised, etc.) but are still undecided about the best way to proceed.

Another difficulty (initially pointed out to us by Phil Johnson-Laird) is that the preposition <u>at</u> seems to have the function of specifying a canonical relation between subject and object. Thus "the chair is at the desk" describes a specific relationship--if the chair is upside down or facing away from the desk, it can no longer be naturally said to be <u>at</u> the desk. Similarly <u>at</u> picks out canonical relations in "I stood at the window," "John was at the door," "I am at my desk,"etc. <u>At</u> seems to require special scenarios for each object, and is otherwise regular only in that most scenarios require proximity of subject and object.

Many prepositions require that the positions of the speaker and/or listener with respect to the subject and object be known. For example, I could say to a listener in Japan that "Urbana is near Chicago," (it is about 130 miles away) but I would not say this to a listener 10 miles from Urbana (see [5]).

Most difficult (and most exciting) of the problems we are aware of are the transfers of meanings from the spatial domain to abstract domains. A representation of physical objects. events, and their relations should be able to be used in constructing effective representations for abstract phenomena. An important part of understanding the abstract use of prepositions involves identifying the "covert categories" [14] to which words belong. As an example, consider the phrases below:

get { into a car / into trouble / into mischief }   be { in a car / in trouble / in mischief* }

get { out of a car / out of trouble / out of mischief* }

We suggest that both <u>trouble</u> and <u>car</u> belong to a covert category which could be called "spatial enclosures," but that <u>mischief</u> does not belong to this category, even though its <u>meaning</u> is closer to <u>trouble's</u> than is <u>car</u>'s meaning. This example seems to us to be similar to the mass/count distinction in English--words like <u>house</u>, <u>person</u>, and <u>book</u> are count nouns (we can say"a house" or "two houses") whereas <u>sand</u>, <u>butter</u>, and <u>water</u> are mass nouns (we cannot say "a sand" OR "two sands," but must add a measure phrase, e.g. "a ton of sand," or "a lot of sand") Mass nouns with common measures associated with them can sometimes be used as count nouns, as in "Waiter, bring me two waters," and some nouns, like <u>paper</u>, seem to fit equally well in either category. (Such categories are extensively discussed in [12] and [14]. For those interested in this topic, Jackendoff [7] is a fascinating source of ideas; also see Waltz [13] and Pylyshyn [10].)

7. <u>RELATED WORK</u>

This research has been influenced by a number of other pieces of work; three items stand our particularly: a thesis by N. Goguen [6], a report by G. S. Cooper [4], and a paper by H.H. Clark [3]. Cooper's work developed a set of primitives and paper definitions for a number of prepositions. While the primitives proved to be inadequate when we began programming, this paper was an inspiration for the overall approach. Goguen wrote a program in many ways similar to this, but did not address the problems of multiple interpretations of prepositions. Clark's paper provided valuable insights into the coordinate systems underlying spatial language, and into the types of mental models people create from scene descriptions.

D. V. McDermott's TOPLE [8] dealt with some very interesting aspects of building a "mental model" of a scene from natural language. For example, given the sentence:

(13) The banana is under the table, by the ball.

there are two interpretations: (1) the ball can be under the table, or (2) the ball can be near the table, but not under it. If we were given

(14) The banana is under the table, by the floor lamp.

then the interpretation where the floor lamp is near but not under the table becomes more likely, based on the typical size of a floor lamp. McDermott's program is able to use size to make this type of distinction. However, the "mental model" in this work is a data base of assertions, e.g.

(UNDER TABLE1 BANANA1).

Winograd's SHRDLU [15] is probably the most closely related program, though its tasks were rather different--its "mental model" was known completely to the language understander, not constructed by descriptive natural language input.

REFERENCES

[1] Black, F., "A Deductive Question-Answering System," in Minsky (ed.) <u>Semantic Information Processing</u>, Cambridge, MA: MIT Press, 1968.

[2] Boggess, L. Computational interpretation of English spatial prepositions. Ph.D. thesis, Univ. of Illinois, Urbana, 1978.

[3] Clark, H. H "Space, Time, Semantics, and the Child," in T. E. Moore (Ed.), <u>Cognitive Development and the Acquisition of Language</u>, New York: Academic Press, 1973.

[4] Cooper, G. S. "A Semantic Analysis of English Locative Expressions." (Technical Report No.1587), Cambridge, MA: Bolt, Beranek & Newman, Inc., 1968.

[5] Denofsky, M. E. "How Near is Near? A Near Specialist." Memo No. 344, MIT AI Lab. 1976.

[6] Goguen, N. A procedural description of spatial prepositions. M.S. thesis, Moore School of Electrical Engineering, Univ.of Pennsylvania, 1973.

[7] Jackendoff, R. "A System of Semantic Primitives," in Schank and Nash-Webber (eds.), <u>Theoretical Issues in Natural Language Processing</u>, ACL, Arlington, VA, 1975.

[8] McDermott, D. Assimilation of New Information by a Natural Language-Understanding System. TR-241, MIT AI Lab, 1973.

[9] Pratt, V. R. "A Linguistics-Oriented Programming Language," Memo No.277,MIT AI Lab,1973.

[10] Pylyshyn, Z. W. "Children's Internal Description," in <u>Language, Learning, and Thought</u>. New York: Academic Press, 1977.

[11] Sussman, G. J. "The FINDSPACE Problem," Memo No. 286, MIT AI Lab, 1973.

[12] Talmy, L. "The Relation of Grammar to Cognition--A Synopsis," in <u>TINLAP-2</u>, New York: ACM, 1978, 14-24.

[13] Waltz, D. L. "On the Interdependence of Language and Perception," in <u>TINLAP-2: Theoretical Issues in Natural Language Processing-2</u>, New York: ACM, 1978, 149-156.

[14] Whorf, B. L. "A Linguistic Consideration of Thinking in Primitive Communities," in J. B. Carroll (Ed.), <u>Language, Thought</u> and <u>Reality</u>, Cambridge MA: MIT Press, 1956.

[15] Winograd, T. <u>Understanding Natural Language</u>, New York: Academic Press, 1972.

BIBLIOGRAPHY OF RELATED TOPICS

[1] Cresswell, M. J., "Prepositions and Points of View," <u>Linguistics and Philosophy</u>, 1978, 2, 1-41.

[2] Fillmore, C. J., "The Case for Case Reopened," in J. P. Kimball (Ed.), <u>Syntax and Semantics</u>, New York: Academic Press, in press.

[3] Johnson-Laird, P., "Mental Models of Meaning." Paper presented at Sloan Workshop on Computational Aspects of Linguistic Structure and Discourse Setting, University of Pennsylvania, May 1978. To appear in a book A. Joshi (Ed.) Cambridge University Press, 1980.

[4] Kosslyn, S. M. and Schwartz, S. P., "A Similation of Visual Imagery," <u>Cognitive Science</u> <u>1</u>, 3, July 1977, 265-95.

[5] Miller, G. A. and Johnson-Laird, P., <u>Language and Perception</u>, Cambridge, MA: Harvard University Press, 1976.

[6] Piaget, J. and Inhelder, B., <u>The Child's Conception of Space</u>, translated by F. J. Langdon and J. L. Lunzer, New York: W. W. Norton & Co., 1967.

[7] Sondheimer, N. K., "Spatial Reference and Semantic Nets," <u>American Journal of Computational Linguistics</u>, 1977, 71, 1-67.

[8] Wilks, Y., Grammar, <u>Meaning and the Machine Analysis of Language</u>, London: Routledge, 1972.

A Method for Automatically Analyzing Programs

Richard C. Waters

Artificial Intelligence Laboratory and Laboratory for Computer Science
Massachusetts Institute of Technology
Cambridge, Mass. 02139

ABSTRACT - This paper presents a method for automatically analyzing programs and discusses why it is a useful way to look at programs. The method is based on the idea that there are only a few basic ways in which the logical structure of programs is built up. An experiment is presented which shows that this accounts for the structure of a large class of programs. The paper discusses how the method can be used to automatically analyze the structure of a program, and how the resulting analysis can be used to guide a proof of correctness for the program. An automatic system is described which performs this type of analysis. The paper discusses the relationship between the structure building methods presented and programming language constructs.

1. Introduction

This paper presents a method (described fully in [21]) for analyzing programs. This analysis of a progarm results in a "plan" for the program which represents the underlying logical structure of the program. The analysis method is based on the observation that programs are built up in a small number of stereotyped ways referred to as plan building methods (PBMs).

An important application of PBMs is that they can be used to analyze a loop in a way which makes it easier to understand what the loop does and why. Section 2 shows why this is a more useful analysis than one based on basic structured programming constructs. Section 3 describes the PBMs in detail. Section 4 discusses how an analysis of a loop in terms of the PBMs can be used to guide a proof of correctness for the loop. It also shows why the resulting proof is more useful than a proof based on a single loop invariant.

An experiment is discussed in Section 5 which shows that the PBMs can be used to analyze a large class of programs. The experiment also shows that the pieces which result from the analysis are largely simple and easy to understand. A system (described in Section 6) has been implemented which performs PBM analysis automatically. Section 7 discusses the relationship between the PBMs and current programming language constructs.

2. Desiderata For an Analysis Method

An analysis method views a program as built up out of parts, and makes it possible to understand the relationship between the operation of the program as a whole and the operation of its parts. From the point of view of gaining an understanding of a program, the parts are subproblems. Once the parts have been understood, their understandings can be combined in order to obtain an understanding of the whole.

There are several criteria which can be used to evaluate the usefulness of an analysis method. First, given a program, it should be straightforward to identify the parts. Second, the parts should be easier to understand than the whole. Third, the process of developing an understanding of the whole based on understandings of its parts should be as easy as possible.

The development which is most similar to PBMs has been the development of structured programming constructs. Consider the loop program in Figure 1. A naive approach to looking at how this program is logically built up is based on the idea that it is constructed on a line by line basis. Given this approach, it is easy to analyze the program in order to break it up into its component parts (the six lines of the program). Further, the parts are indeed much easier to understand than the program as a whole. However, the problem with this approach is that it is not at all easy to discover what the program does once the parts are understood, because the interactions of the lines with each other are complex.

```
      I = 1;
      Z = 0;
LOOP: IF NOT(A(I)>0) THEN GOTO SKIP;
      Z = Z+A(I);
SKIP: I = I+1;
      IF I≤N THEN GOTO LOOP;
```

Figure 1: An example program.

The basic structured programming constructs (composition, if-then-else, and do-while) suggest a much better analysis method. They indicate that the program should be viewed logically as being built up hierarchically using these structured programming constructs. Figure 2 depicts the program in Figure 1 analyzed in terms of these three basic structured programming constructs. The program is analyzed as being a composition of "Z=0" with an extended form of do-while which consists of counting from 1 to N in I and a body which is an if-then-else consisting of a predicate "A(I)>0" and a then clause "Z=Z+A(I)".

This report describes research done at the Artificial Intelligence Laboratory of the Massachusetts Institute of Technology. Support for the laboratory's artificial intelligence research is provided in part by the Advanced Research Projects Agency of the Department of Defense under Office of Naval Research contract N00014-75-C-0643.

```
Z = 0;
DO I=1 TO N;
   IF A(I)>0
      THEN Z = Z+A(I);
END;
```

Figure 2: The example program in structured form.

When it is possible without transforming a program, this is an easy analysis to perform. This is true whether or not the program is written in a syntactically structured way. It is possible to write a program which cannot be analyzed in terms of the basic structured programming constructs, unless it is first transformed to change the topology of its control flow. (An example of this is a program which contains a loop with more than one entry point). However, a large number of programs can be directly analyzed in this way. In any case, the parts are easy to understand once they are isolated.

Let us now look at the structured programming oriented approach in the light of how easy it is to develop an understanding of the result based on understandings of its parts. First consider if-then-else. If the parts are understood, then it is easy to get an understanding of the whole. Namely, in a given situation an if-then-else either acts like the then clause, or like the else clause, depending on the value of the predicate. In Figure 2 the if-then-else adds A(I) to Z if A(I)>0. Composition is also an easy operation to understand. In general, these two structured programming constructs, which describe non-looping programs, meet the criteria set forth above very well.

In contrast, consider the construct do-while in the light of how easy it is to develop an understanding of the resulting program based on understandings of its parts. The body of the loop in Figure 2 can be understood as a conditional which adds A(I) to Z if A(I)>0. Unfortunately, it is not easy to go from this to an understanding that the loop adds the sum of the positive members of the first N elements of A to the initial value of Z. It is easy to conclude this if an appropriate loop invariant can be found. However, in general, it is not easy to find such an invariant.

Another problem with the analysis in the figure is that the close relationship between the statements "Z=0" and "Z=Z+A(I)" is not made clear. In order to analyze a program in such a way that things which are intimately related are closely linked together, these two statements should be put together in a single locality distinct from the rest of the loop. Having the statements spread through the loop makes it harder to understand that the program as a whole computes the sum of the positive members of the first N elements of A.

The difficulties with do-while stem from the way it looks at a loop. The body of the loop is first analyzed like any other straight-line program. This understanding of the body is then bootstrapped up to an understanding of the loop as a whole. The problem is that this bootstrapping process is far from automatic. The PBMs for loops take a different approach. They are based on the idea that the body of a loop should not be analyzed in the same way as a straight-line program. Instead, they break the loop up in order to analyze it as built up out of stereotyped loop fragments. (The lines "Z=0" and "Z=Z+A(I)" are an example of such a fragment.)

The PBMs for loops break the loop in Figure 2 up into four fragments as shown in Figure 3. The first fragment (A) counts up by one from one. It enumerates the sequence of integers {1,2, ...}. The second fragment (B) tests the sequence of integers produced by A and stops the loop when an integer greater than N is found. This has the effect of truncating the sequence of integers to the sequence {1,2, ... N}. The third fragment (C) operates on the truncated sequence of integers. It restricts the sequence by selecting only those integers which correspond to positive elements of the vector A. The last fragment (D) computes the sum of the elements of A corresponding to the integers in the restricted sequence produced by C. In the loop as a whole, the four fragments are cascaded together so that the loop computes the sum of the positive members of the first N elements of A.

```
 A           B                       C                   D
I=1;    IF I>N THEN                                  Z = 0;
I=I+1;      GOTO EXIT;   IF A(I)>0 THEN              Z = Z+A(I);
```

Figure 3: The example program analyzed by PBMs.

The key feature of the analysis above is that it breaks the loop apart along a different dimension from the one used by an analysis in terms of do-while. There are two principle advantages to looking at a loop in this new way. First, the loop is broken up into pieces which correspond to easily understood stereotyped fragments of looping behavior. Second, the way the pieces are combined is logically equivalent to composition, which makes it easy to understand.

In order to make the idea that the fragments of the loop are composed together precise, the notion of a temporal sequence of values has been developed jointly by Howard Shrobe [19] and the author [21]. Given a program, such as a loop, which is repetitively executed, it can be useful to talk about the sequence of states in which some part of the program is executed, and about the sequences of values available in those states. For example, consider the statement "Z=Z+A(I)" in the loop in Figure 2. This statement is executed in a sequence of states. There are sequences of values of I, and Z which are available in those states. These sequences are referred to as temporal sequences of values. The insight is the realization that logically, a temporal sequence of values can be treated in the same way as any aggregate data object. The concept of lazy evaluation [5, 8] uses the same insight going in the other direction. If an aggregate data object (such as a sequence of numbers) is desired, then it can be created temporally, rather than all at once, so that each piece of it is not actually created until it is needed.

Looking back at Figure 3, fragment A produces a temporal sequence of values of I. The elements of this sequence are tested by fragment C. Logically, the key relationship is that A creates data used by C. A is composed with C by passing this data from A to C. Viewed abstractly, it makes no difference whether this data is put into a vector which is passed all at once to C, or, as in the example, A and C are intermingled so that C can use each individual value created by A as soon as it is produced. Intermingling A and C is just an efficient way of implementing the data flow from A to C.

The key property of composition which makes it an easy process to understand is that the only interaction between two things which are composed together is that one passes data to the other. They have no other effect on each other. The loop fragments above have this key property. Fragment A will produce a sequence of values of I counting up from one no matter what is happening in the rest of the loop. Fragment B tests the values of I it sees no matter what else is going on in the loop. As a result, each of the fragments can be understood completely in isolation from whatever loop they are being used in. (Fragment B presents a problem because it controls the number of times the other fragments are executed. In order to maintain the independence of the fragments in the face of this interaction, the descriptions of the fragments are prohibited from making any statements about the absolute number of elements in any temporal sequence of values. As a result, from the point of view of the descriptions, the fragments do not interact because their interaction cannot affect anything in the descriptions.)

3. The Plan Building Methods

This section describes the ten PBMs which have been developed. Figure 4 shows how the PBMs are related. They are divided into two main groups. One group can be used to analyze straight-line (non-looping) programs while the other group is used to analyze recursive programs and loops.

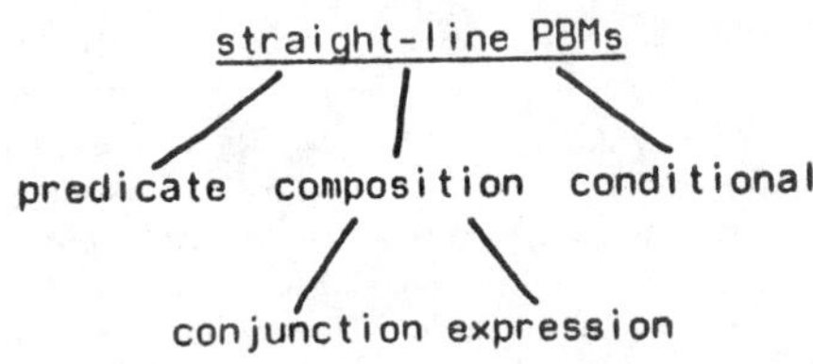

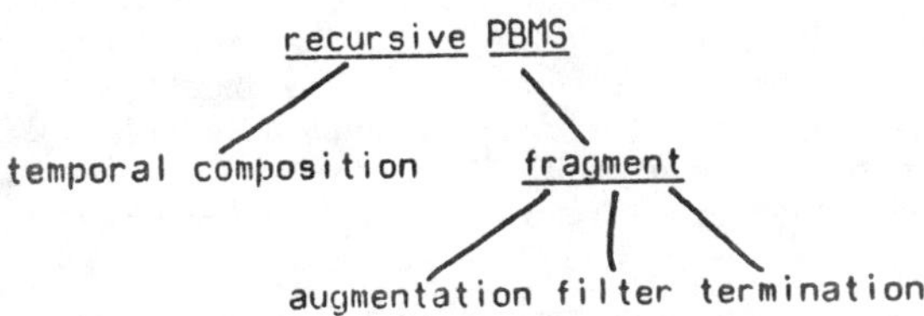

Figure 4: A taxonomy of the PBMs.

There are three basic straight-line PBMs: predicate, composition, and conditional. In addition, two special cases of composition are recognized: conjunction and expression. Figure 5 shows examples of segments of code which would be analyzed in terms of straight-line PBMs.

```
              predicate
    IF X<Y THEN GOTO L1;
       ELSE IF Z<Y THEN GOTO L2;
                ELSE GOTO L3;

     conditional          composition
  IF X<0 THEN X=-X;    Z=FIRST(SORT(A));

     conjunction            expression
  Z=COS(X); W=SIN(X);    Z=SIN(COS(X));
```

Figure 5: Examples of straight-line PBMs.

The PBM predicate is used to build up complex tests out of simpler ones. In the example, two two-way branching tests are combined into a three-way branching test. The PBM conditional combines a test with some actions in order to construct a conditional expression. It is exactly analogous to the structured programming construct if-then-else.

The PBM composition is used to construct arbitrary non-branching sections of straight-line code. Two special cases of composition are recognized because they have particularly useful logical properties. The PBM conjunction combines segments in such a way that there is no data flow between the segments. This means that the pieces are totally independent and can be understood completely in isolation from each other. It is particularly easy to understand what a conjunction does, because the specifications for the conjunction as a whole are simply the conjunction of the specifications for the segments which have been combined.

With the PBM expression, as with composition in general, there is data flow carrying the outputs of segments to the inputs of other segments. The PBM expression is more restricted than general composition in that the segments combined are required to have "substitutable" specifications. A specification is said to be substitutable if each output is described by a single assertion of the form "output=expression-involving-the-inputs". For example the segment "COS" is described by the assertion "output=cos(input)". It is easy to understand what an expression does, because substitution can be used in order to develop simple specifications for the expression as a whole.

In contrast to an expression, a general composition can combine segments with non-substitutable specifications. This makes it cumbersome to develop a description of what the result does. For example, in the composition in Figure 5, SORT might well be described as producing an output which contains the same elements as the input, and in which the elements appear in increasing order. This being the case, simple substitution will not suffice to conclude that the composition as a whole computes the minimum element in the input. Some actual deduction is required.

It is very easy to analyze a straight-line segment of a program in terms of the straight-line PBMs because it is not possible to confuse an instance of one with an instance of another. This is due to the fact that there are only three basic PBMs (predicate, composition, and conditional) and the fact that they are completely different from each other. It should be noted that it is possible to write a straight-line program which is unstructured in that it cannot be analyzed in terms of these PBMs, or in terms of structured programming constructs, without first transforming the code.

The four PBMs which build up recursive structures embody the idea that recursive structures are built up by composing together stereotyped fragments of recursive behavior in a way which is exactly analogous to the way non-branching straight-line segments of code are built up by composing simple segments together. For simplicity, the discussion below describes the recursive PBMs solely in terms of loops. The discussion in [21] shows how they apply to arbitrary singly self-recursive programs. Three of the recursive PBMs (augmentation, filter, and termination) construct loop fragments. The fourth one (temporal composition) combines fragments together.

The PBM augmentation combines an initialization which is executed once with a body which is executed repetitively in order to create a loop fragment. The resulting fragment takes in temporal sequences of values and produces temporal sequences of values. The name "augmentation" is derived from the fact that an augmentation can be added into a loop in order to augment its activities without affecting anything else the loop does.

```
          count          sum
init:     I=1;           Z=0;
body:     I=I+1;         Z=Z+X;

          max                   feedback free
init:     Z=very-small;
body:     IF X>Z THEN Z=X;      Z=2*X;
```

Figure 6: Example augmentations.

Figure 6 shows four different augmentations. Consider the second one "Z=0; Z=Z+X;" which computes a sum. The variable X is underlined in order to indicate that it stands for the place where the fragment receives a temporal sequence of values. It creates a corresponding sequence of partial sums in the variable Z. The behavior of an augmentation can be straightforwardly described in terms of a recurrence relation derived from the initialization and the body. For the summation fragment this recurrence relation is "$Z_1=0 \wedge Z_{i+1}=Z_i+X_i$". In situations where the recurrence relation has a simple solution, better specifications can be derived (such as "$Z_i=\sum_{j=1,i-1} X_j$" for the summation augmentation). A large number of the augmentations seen in programs correspond to simple actions such as counting, summing, or calculating a maximum. The count augmentation is interesting in that it does not take any temporal sequence of values as an input but rather simply generates a sequence of values. The feedback free augmentation is particularly easy to understand because is recurrence relation ("$Z_i=2*X_i$") does not refer to prior values of Z and therefore is trivially solvable.

```
IF X<0 THEN ...;
       ELSE ...;
```

Figure 7: An example filter.

The PBM filter constructs a loop fragment from a test which is repeatedly executed. The fragment takes in a temporal sequence of values and restricts the sequence by filtering out some of the values. In a loop, this action is realized by creating a restricted execution environment which is only executed on some of the iterations of the loop. The filter in the example takes in a sequence of values of X and creates two outputs: the sequence of negative values of X and the sequence of non-negative values of X.

```
IF I>N THEN GOTO EXIT;
```

Figure 8: An example termination.

Like a filter, a termination creates a fragment out of a test which is repetitively executed. Also like a filter, it takes in a temporal sequence of of values and outputs a restricted sequence of values. The restricted sequence corresponds to the initial portion of the input up to the first value which satisfies the test. However, unlike a filter, a termination has the far reaching effect that it causes the loop as whole to terminate.

The PBM temporal composition builds complex loops by combining loop fragments together. The process of combining the fragments is logically equivalent to composition. This makes it easy to understand what the resulting loop does. Figure 9 shows an example of this. The four fragments in the figure are composed together in order to yield the loop shown (which is the same as the one in Figure 1). Logically this is just a composition of D(C(B(A()))) and therefore it is clear that the

```
              Z=D(C(B(A())))     where

 A is         B is          C is             D is
I=1;     IF I>N THEN                         Z = 0;
I=I+1;     GOTO EXIT;   IF A(I)>0 THEN   Z = Z+A(I);

the loop which results from the temporal composition
         I = 1;
         Z = 0;
   LOOP: IF NOT(A(I)>0) THEN Z = Z+A(I);
         I = I+1;
         IF I≤N THEN GOTO LOOP;
```

Figure 9: An example temporal composition.

result computes the sum of the positive members of the first N elements of the array A since the augmentation A counts up by 1 from 1, the termination B truncates this sequence at N, the filter C selects the elements of the sequence which correspond to positive members of A, and the augmentation D computes a sum of these elements.

The process by which the fragments are actually combined in order to produce the resulting loop is somewhat complicated. This process is designed so that the validity of the simple logical analysis in terms of composition will be preserved. The fragments are taken apart, and their pieces are reassembled into the resulting loop. The initializations of the fragments are placed before the resulting loop. The bodies are placed inside the loop. Their arrangement in the loop is dictated by the data flow communicating temporal sequences of values between the fragments. The key idea is that if the body of one fragment uses a temporal sequence created by the body of another fragment, then the first body should be placed after the second one in the resulting loop. The action of a filter is produced by placing the bodies which receive its outputs within the scope of a conditional predicated on the filter's test.

It turns out to be straightforward to analyze a loop in order to break it apart into fragments combined by temporal composition. The analysis process is based on locating sections of the loop which do not affect any other parts of the loop. One section affects another if it either has data flow to it, or if it controls when it will be executed. Once such a section is located, it is removed as a fragment and the analysis continues. This process is sufficient to locate augmentations and filters. Consider the resulting loop in Figure 9. If it were being analyzed, the first fragment to be located would be D. This would be done by noticing that the line "Z=Z+A(I)" does not have data flow to any other part of the loop. Once this line is removed the filter C is no longer controlling the execution of anything, so it too can be isolated and removed.

Terminations are somewhat more complex because they perforce affect everything else in the loop since they determine when the loop will terminate. To allow them to be located and removed, the definition of not affect is weakened in order to allow this particular kind of effect. In order to maintain the logical structure based on composition, the descriptions of the fragments have to be prohibited from mentioning anything which a termination can affect (namely the absolute number of times anything will be executed).

4. Using PBM Analysis to Guide Verification

The most fundamental impact of the PBMs on verification is that they break up a program into a useful hierarchy of segments within segments. This structure can be used as the underlying structure of a proof of correctness, by determining specifications for each segment and then verifying these specifications. With each subproof, the method which is used to generate a proof can benefit from the fact that it only has to work on the single subproof which has been singled out by the PBMs, rather than on the program as a whole.

The impact of the PBMs on the structure of a correctness proof is greatest with regard to loops. They lead to a proof which is fundamentally different in form from the standard approach of using a single loop invariant. Consider the program in Figure 10 and how it would be verified by using a single loop invariant as originally introduced by Floyd [4] and Hoare [9]. Assertions are passed over the body of the loop in order to develop a statement of what the body does. Then an appropriate loop invariant is developed. Finally, the statement of what the body does is used to prove the invariance of the loop invariant, and the loop invariant is used to verify the specifications of the loop.

```
X = 0;
Y = 0;
L = 11;
DO K=1,10;
   IF C(K)>0 THEN DO;
      X = X+A(K);
      Y = Y+A(K)*A(L);
   END;
   L = L+1;
END;
```

the program is claimed to compute

$X=\Sigma\{1\leq i\leq 10 \mid C(i)>0\} A(i) \wedge$
$Y=\Sigma\{1\leq i\leq 10 \mid C(i)>0\} A(i)*A(i+10)$

assertion summarizing the actions of the body

$(C(K')>0 \rightarrow (X=X'+A(K') \wedge Y=Y'+A(K')*A(L'))) \wedge$
$L=L'+1 \wedge (C(K')\leq 0 \rightarrow (X=X' \wedge Y=Y')) \wedge K=K'+1$

a loop invariant

$0\leq K\leq 11 \wedge X=\Sigma\{1\leq i\leq 10 \mid C(i)>0\} A(i) \wedge$
$L=K+10 \wedge Y=\Sigma\{1\leq i\leq 10 \mid C(i)>0\} A(i)*A(i+10)$

Figure 10: Steps in a proof using a single invariant.

One of the most difficult steps in a proof of this form is the determination of an appropriate loop invariant. Considerable research has been done on ways to automatically develop invariants. Much of this work centers around heuristic methods which can be used to guide a search for an invariant [6, 12, 22]. Some of it is oriented toward directly deriving invariants for specific classes of loops [2, 3, 14]. The work of Basu and Misra is particularly interesting. They analyze the mathematical properties of a loop in order to directly derive an appropriate loop invariant for certain classes of loops.

Figure 11 shows how the program in Figure 10 would be analyzed by PBMs, and how this leads to a proof of correctness. The program is divided into six parts: an augmentation which enumerates integers in K, a termination which truncates this to the sequence of integers from 1 to 10 in K, an augmentation which enumerates the integers from 11 to 20 in L, a filter which restricts these temporal sequences of values by selecting only those elements which correspond to positive values of C(K), an augmentation which computes the sum of the indicated elements of A, and an augmentation which computes the sum of the products of the indicated elements of A. This decomposition leads to a style of proof based on composition which is very different from the proof in Figure 10. First several lemmas are proved. Each lemma summarizes the actions of one of the parts of the program. Second, the lemmas are combined by composition in order to yield the desired result.

loop fragment	values it produces
K = 1; K = K+1;	$1\leq i$ $K_i=i$
IF K>10 THEN GOTO EXIT:	$1\leq i\leq 10$ $K_i=i$
L = 11; L = L+1;	$1\leq i\leq 10$ $L_i=i+10$
IF C(K)>0 THEN	restricts K_i and L_i
X = 0; X = X+A(K);	$1\leq i\leq 10$ $X_i=\Sigma\{1\leq j\leq i \mid C(j)>0\} A(j)$
Y = 0; Y = Y+A(K)*A(L);	$1\leq i\leq 10$ $Y_i=\Sigma\{1\leq j\leq i \mid C(j)>0\} A(j)*A(j+10)$

Figure 11: Steps in a proof based on PBM analysis.

The problem of finding the loop invariant is dealt with by breaking it up into pieces. No invariant is needed in order to verify the program as a whole. Rather, each of the proofs of the lemmas requires an invariant. However, each of these proofs is so simple that it is easy to determine what the invariant should be by the methods of Basu and Misra, if not by simple recognition. It should be noted that not all programs can be decomposed by PBMs as nicely as the one in the example. There is no limit to the complexity of the pieces which result. Therefore, it may be very difficult to determine the invariant needed to prove one of the lemmas needed. Even in this situation, the PBM analysis is useful because it determines the parts of the invariant as a whole which are easy and separates them from the parts which are difficult. PBM analysis is not a uniform procedure which will determine the invariant for any loop; rather, it simplifies the problems involved with finding most of the invariant for most loops.

The fundamental difference between the form of the proof engendered by PBM analysis and the form of the proof resulting from the single invariant method becomes apparent when the proof is used for something other than giving a yes/no answer to the question of whether or not the program is correct. For example, suppose that the program were incorrect and that therefore the proof failed. The PBM proof is broken up into a sequence of steps which are directly linked to parts of the program. If the failure of the proof can be localized to one of the steps of the proof, then the bug in the program can be localized to the corresponding part of the program. The failure of a proof based on a single loop invariant does not lend itself to this kind of analysis.

5. An Experiment

The straight-line PBMs are similar to basic structured programming constructs, and can be used to analyze any straight-line program that does not have spaghetti-like control flow. The loop PBMs are more novel, and it is not immediately clear how wide their range of applicability is. An experiment was performed in order to estimate what percentage of the loops which programmers actually write can be analyzed in terms of the PBMs without anything more than trivial transformations being done. 20% of the 220 programs in the IBM FORTRAN Scientific Subroutine Package (SSP) [10] were chosen at random and analyzed in terms of the PBMs by hand. The SSP was chosen as an object of study because it is a large group of clearly written programs which is an actual commercial product.

The 44 programs chosen contained 164 loops. It was possible to analyze all of the loops with the PBMs. They were analyzed as being built up by means of the PBM temporal composition out of 442 augmentations, 6 filters, and 186 terminations. Configurations which cannot be analyzed (such as a loop with more than one entry point) did not occur in these loops. The sole difficulty was that one loop had multiple level error exits which branched outside of the loop from inside an inner loop. In order to analyze the error exits in terms of the PBMs, they had to be looked at as being explicit exits from the inner loop and the outer loop. This may or may not be a good way to look at them.

Nearly 90% of the time, the pieces which resulted from PBM analysis were very simple. Of the 442 augmentations, 374 (85%) were either easy to understand because they did not have feedback to themselves, or easy to recognize as a product, a sum, a max, a min, or a count. Only 31 (7%) were really difficult to understand. The remainder were of intermediate complexity. All 6 filters were simple comparisons with zero and therefore easily understood.

Of the 186 terminations, 165 (89%) were very simple to understand because they were simple comparisons with a fixed number, and the input which they tested was a simple sequence of numbers, most often {1,2,3, ...}. Due to the fact that their tests and inputs were so simple, it was trivial to determine the exact number of states associated with their inputs, and hence exactly when the loops they were in would terminate. Most of the 21 terminations that were more complex, were additional terminations in loops which had at least one simple termination. As a result of this, 162 (99%) of the 164 loops contained at least one simple termination, and therefore can be trivially shown to terminate.

6. An Automatic Analysis System

The author has implemented a system (described fully in [21]) which automatically analyzes programs in terms of PBMs. The system operates in two phases. A translation phase reads in a program and converts it to a language independent internal form called a "surface plan". An analysis phase then analyzes the program by looking at its surface plan.

A surface plan makes the control flow and data flow explicit independent of the syntactic constructs of any particular language. It is essentially a graph with two kinds of arcs. The nodes of the graph correspond to primitive operations such as: plus, times, and less than. One type of arc specifies the flow of a data object from one node to another. The other type of arc specifies the flow of control from one node to another. Constructs which languages use to implement data flow (such as: variables, assignment, parameters, and nesting of expressions) are not present in a plan. All information about data flow is contained in the data flow arcs. Similarly, constructs which languages use to implement control flow (such as GOTOs and sequential placement of statements) are eliminated in favor of the control flow arcs.

A translator has been written which converts FORTRAN programs, like those in the IBM SSP, into surface plans. Charles Rich [17] has written a translator which converts LISP programs into surface plans. After this conversion, the analysis phase of the system works on LISP programs just as easily as on FORTRAN programs.

The translator works by running over the program like an evaluator, creating control flow arcs, data flow arcs, and nodes which comprise a surface plan as it goes. The translator has detailed knowledge of the constructs which implement data flow and control flow. It does not have any knowledge of what the primitive functions do except how many inputs and outputs they have.

Once a program has been translated into a surface plan, it is then analyzed in terms of PBMs. This is done in two main steps. The first step looks primarily at the control flow arcs and analyzes the straight-line sections of the program while merely identifying the loops in it. This is essentially an analysis in terms of basic structured programming constructs as discussed in Section 2. The analysis is done bottom up by locating minimal configurations which can be grouped together in accordance with a PBM. Whenever such a configuration is located, it is grouped together into a single node, and the analysis continues. This process terminates when the entire program is grouped into a single node.

The first step of analysis can be compared with the system of B. Baker [1]. Her system uses graph theoretic methods in order to analyze FORTRAN programs based on their control flow in terms of basic structured programming constructs. Her system then outputs the program in a structured form. GOTOs are used in situations where an analysis in terms of the structured programming constructs is not possible.

The second analysis step analyzes the loops discovered by the earlier steps according to the four PBMs temporal composition, augmentation, filter, and termination. This analysis is based primarily on data flow connectivity and proceeds as described in Section 3. For example, augmentations are located by finding minimal subsets of the body of a loop which do not have data flow to any other part of the loop. Once an augmentation is discovered, it is removed from the loop and the remaining loop is analyzed further.

7. PBMs and Programming Language Constructs

The PBMs which are used in the first step of analysis correspond to basic structured programming constructs. If the analysis system operated on programs written in a language which required the use of these basic structured programming constructs, the first step of analysis would not be necessary. On the other hand, the loop PBMs do not correspond to any existing structured programming constructs.

However, the loop PBMs do embody natural ideas, and many

programming constructs have features in common with them. For example, there are a variety of constructs which have the feature that they separate out an augmentation and a termination, which together enumerate a sequence of values, from the rest of the loop which does something with them. The most common example of this is the DO statement. It makes a clear syntactic distinction between the enumeration of a sequence of integers and their use. However, in most languages, the DO statement does not correspond semantically to an augmentation and a termination because the programmer is not prohibited from assigning to the DO variable in the body of the loop.

The MAPC function in LISP is similar to the DO statement except that it enumerates the elements of a list instead of a sequence of integers. GENERATORS in ALPHARD [18] and ITERATORS in CLU [13], extend this concept to the enumeration of elements of arbitrary data types. The MAPCAR function in LISP is interesting because as well as enumerating the elements in a list, it contains a standard augmentation "(SETQ X NIL) (SETQ X (APPEND X result))" which forms a list of the results.

The language APL [15] has several operators which operate directly on vectors in a fashion very similar to the way PBMs operate on temporal sequences of values created by loops. For example, the reduction operator is similar to augmentation in that it applies an operator such as plus or times to the elements of a vector in order to compute the sum or product of all the elements in the vector.

The Language developed by Kahn and MacQueen [11] makes it possible to construct coroutine processes operating on sequences of values which interact in the same way as augmentations and filters. The processes can be combined together into expressions which can be evaluated either sequentially, or in parallel.

With either APL or the language of Kahn and MacQueen, in order to get the significant savings in time and space which result from implementing augmentations and filters by loops operating on temporal sequences of values the language would have to have a smart compiler. The compiler would have to know how to combine the pieces together into loops. The work which has been done on developing a compiler for APL (see for example, [7]) indicates that this is not an unreasonable goal.

8. Conclusion

The basic idea behind the analysis method presented here is that a typical loop can be looked at as a composition of stereotyped fragments of looping behavior. This point of view reflects the way many programmers analyze, understand, and reason about loops. The PBMs, and the idea of temporal sequences of values are important because they make it possible for an automatic system to analyze, understand, and reason about loops in this same straightforward way.

The PBMs were developed as part of a larger research project. The goal of this project is to develop a system (called the "Programmer's Apprentice") which can assist a person who is writing a program. Research on this system [16, 17, 19, 20, 21] is being carried out by a group consisting of Charles Rich, Howard Shrobe, and the author. The intent is that the apprentice system will cooperate with a programmer throughout all phases of work on a program and be able to communicate with him about it. The programmer will do the hard parts of design and implementation while the apprentice will act as a junior partner and critic, keeping track of details and assisting the programmer whenever possible. PBMs play an important role in the processes by which the apprentice develops an understanding of and reasons about a program.

ACKNOWLEDGMENTS

The author would like to thank Charles Rich, Gerald Roylance, Howard Shrobe, and Gerald Sussman for their assistance.

REFERENCES

[1] B. S. Baker, "An Algorithm for Structuring Flowgraphs", JACM V24 #1, pp. 98-120, January 1977.

[2] S. Basu and J. Misra, "Proving Loop Programs", IEEE Trans. on Software Eng. V1 #1, pp. 76-86, March 1975.

[3] S. Basu and J. Misra, "Some Classes of Naturally Provable Programs", Proc. 2nd Int. Conf. on Software Engineering, pp. 400-406, October 1976.

[4] R. W. Floyd, "Assigning Meaning to Programs", proc. symp. in Applied Math. V19, pp. 19-32, 1967.

[5] D.P. Friedman and D.S. Wise, "CONS Should Not Evaluate its Arguments", Indiana Technical Report 44, Nov. 1975.

[6] S. German and B. Wegbreit, "A Synthesiser of Inductive Assertions", IEEE Trans. on Software Eng. V1 #1, pp. 68-75, March 1975.

[7] L.J. Guibas and D.K. Wyatt, "Compliation and Delayed Evaluation in APL", Proc. 5th ACM POPL Conf. 1978.

[8] P. Henderson and J.H. Morris, "A Lazy Evaluator", Proc. 3rd ACM POPL Conf., 1976.

[9] C.A.R. Hoare, "An Axiomatic Basis for Computer Programming", CACM V12 #10, pp. 576-383, October 1969.

[10] IBM GH20-0205-4, "Scientific Subroutine Package Version III Programmer's Manual", IBM White Plains NY, 1970.

[11] G. Kahn and D.B. MacQueen, "Coroutines and Networks of Parallel Processes", Proceedings of IFIP Congress-77, North-Holland Publ. Co, 1977.

[12] S. Katz and Z. Manna, "Logical Analysis of Programs", CACM V19 #4, pp. 188-206, April 1976.

[13] B.H. Liskov, A. Snyder, R. Atkinson, and C. Schaffert, "Abstraction Mechanisms in CLU", CACM V20 #8, pp. 564-376, August 1977.

[14] J.H. Morris jr. and B. Wegbreit, "Subgoal Induction", CACM V20 #4, pp. 209-222, April 1977.

[15] R.P. Polivka and S. Pakin, "APL: The Language and its Usage", Prentice-Hall, Englewood cliffs NJ, 1975.

[16] C. Rich, "A Representation for Programming Knowledge and Applications to Recognition, Generation, and Cataloguing of Programs", forthcomming PhD thesis, MIT, August 1979.

[17] C. Rich and H. Shrobe, "Initial Report on a LISP Programmer's Apprentice", MIT/AI/TR-354, MIT Cambridge MA, December 1976.

[18] M. Shaw and W. A. Wulf, "Abstraction and Verification in ALPHARD: Defining and Specifying Iteration and Generators", CACM V20 #8, pp. 553-364, August 1977.

[19] H.E. Shrobe, "Reasoning and Logic for Complex Program Understanding", PhD thesis, MIT, August 1978.

[20] R.C. Waters, "A System for Understanding Mathematical FORTRAN Programs", MIT/AIM-368, MIT Cambridge MA, August 1976.

[21] R.C. Waters, "Automatic Analysis of the Logical Structure of Programs", MIT/AI/TR-492, December 1978.

[22] B. Wegbreit, "The Synthesis of Loop Predicates", CACM V17 #2, pp. 102-112, February 1974.

EXPERT: A SYSTEM FOR DEVELOPING CONSULTATION MODELS

Sholom M. Weiss and Casimir A. Kulikowski
Department of Computer Science
Rutgers University
New Brunswick, N.J. 08903

ABSTRACT

EXPERT is a system for designing and building models for consultation. An EXPERT model consists of hypotheses (which can be structured into causal and taxonomic networks); findings or observations; and decision rules for logically relating these components. A relatively simple language for describing models is employed. Logical and probabilistic rules are restricted to particular types which implicitly order the tasks performed by the control strategies: classification, question selection, and explanation. Explicit representations of decision rules are emphasized, as opposed to suboptimal scoring functions. This results in more easily predictable and correctable performance for a model. The system is currently being used to develop consultation models in domains such as rheumatology, ophthalmology, and endocrinology.

INTRODUCTION

The development of knowledge-based consultation programs that exhibit near-expert performance has progressed rapidly in recent years [1-4]. These efforts have focused on specific medical application areas and have relied on one or more experts to build a knowledge base. The hallmark of these consultation systems has been their reliance on large amounts of structured expert knowledge in the application domain [5]. In each system, the choice of knowledge representation has come first, and been a primary determinant of the type of reasoning procedures used. In contrast to traditional methods of automated diagnosis, little emphasis has been placed on the optimality of decision-making under general criteria (utility, information entropy, etc). Rather, these systems have attempted to develop representations based on simulations of the experts' conceptual structures and reasoning [6]. The various systems have been reviewed and contrasted in [7] and [8]. Szolovits and Pauker [8] point out that there is frequent and general use of categorical (explicit) decision rules in all the systems, although they all also use various kinds of heuristic scoring methods to capture the uncertainty associated with medical decisions. Unfortunately, these methods often have side effects of propagation that make the results of a consultation less clearly predictable. Despite the specific applications for which they were first developed, some of the systems, such as CASNET and MYCIN have been generalized to accept knowledge bases in other domains. After several years of developing the CASNET representation [9], enough new ideas have emerged from our own experience and that of the other AIM (Artificial Intelligence in Medicine) investigators to lead us to develop a new and more general representation of knowledge for use in consultation systems.

The new consultation scheme EXPERT, consists of a general facility for developing and testing consultation models. It was designed without being tied to a specific application. EXPERT has been used to develop models in ophthalmology, endocrinology and rheumatology. Some of the major themes in the design of EXPERT include:

1) a relatively simple language and notation to represent expert knowledge. The representation is consistent with the traditional two-level view of a diagnostic problem: selecting appropriate hypotheses or conclusions by interpreting a set of findings or observations.

2) an emphasis on categorical reasoning instead of on suboptimal scoring functions. A form of probabilistic production rules is available, which can be compatible with statistically accurate classification when appropriate data is available.

3) descriptive knowledge as a partially-ordered conceptual network, a special type of a semantic net, which, as in the CASNET system, can be pre-compiled for the interpretation of individual cases, hence leading to efficient performance.

4)an emphasis on decision methods which tend to yield predictable and correctable results. This may in some cases require that the expert provide more explicit statements of correlations among findings and a greater number of decision rules. The representation and control strategy simplify the task of correcting erroneous conclusions. Since the interaction among rules and the associated classification strategies is consistently predictable, it is not difficult to trace the changes in program behavior that will result from modification of individual rules. A novel feature of EXPERT is that it automatically detects changes in the reasoning about cases stored in its data base that will arise from modification of the decision rules. This is an important tool for incrementally generating and testing an expert model.

The process of creating and running an EXPERT decision-making model is somewhat similar to writing and running a computer program. An editor is used to create a file which will contain statements describing a model. A model is translated into an efficient internal representation by the compiler program, XP. The model may then be executed, and cases may be entered for consultation, using the program EXPERT.

MODEL DESCRIPTION

An EXPERT consultation model consists of 3 sections:

a) hypotheses,
b) findings,
c) decision rules

Findings are the facts about a patient elicited during a consultation. In a medical domain, they are the history, symptoms, signs, and laboratory test results. Findings are reported in the form of true, false, numerical, or unavailable responses to questions from EXPERT. Hypotheses are the conclusions that may be inferred by the system. They include diagnostic and prognostic decision categories, therapy recommendations, and intermediate hypotheses about pathophysiological states, expected causes of illness, or typical aggregates of findings. A measure of uncertainty is usually associated with a hypothesis.

Within the 3 sections of the model, several subsections are possible. The representation used in building a model divides the sections as follows:

```
**HYPOTHESES
*TAXONOMY
[*CAUSAL AND INTERMEDIATE HYPOTHESES]
[*TREATMENTS]
**FINDINGS
**RULES
[*FF RULES]
*FH RULES
[*HH RULES]
```

Two asterisks indicate one of the three major sections. A single asterisk indicates a subsection, and brackets indicate optional statements.

HYPOTHESES

The major hypotheses are structured into a taxonomic classification scheme. Contained within the *TAXONOMY subsection shown above are the possible diagnostic and prognostic conclusions and the useful set-subset relationships between general diagnostic categories and intermediate interpretations. As an example, we show part of a thyroid disease classification:

```
*TAXONOMY
EU     .Euthyroid (.75)
ThD    .Thyroid Dysfunction (.25)
HYPER  ..Hyperthyroidism (.05)
HYPO   ..Hypothyroidism (.20)
NOP    .No Pathology (.70)
GRAV   .Graves' Disease (.25)
```

The mnemonics for each hypothesis become a shorthand for specifying its place in the production rules. The optional weight associated with some hypotheses indicates their frequency of occurrence relative to the higher level hypotheses in which they are included. The indentation indicates the set-subset relationship among hypotheses.

The optional subsection of "*CAUSAL AND INTERMEDIATE HYPOTHESES." is used to define hypotheses that may not belong in the taxonomy because they are not explicit categories of disease. However, these intermediate hypotheses can be valuable diagnostic summaries of important combinations of events. They can stand for pathophysiological states, such as "elevated thyroid uptake," or they may abstract many findings such as "ocular symptoms of Graves' disease." It is usually much simpler to reason with a small set of such hypotheses than with the much larger set of original findings. Hypotheses which appear in the taxonomy may reappear in this section indicating a causal or superset-subset relationship with the intermediate hypotheses.

Treatments are also described within

the general notational form of hypotheses. Their interpretation is somewhat different. They may stand as a taxonomy of therapies, or they may be organized into a hierarchy of treatment plans. The top level treatment hypothesis is the general treatment plan for a particular diagnostic category and lower level nodes are subsets of possible treatments. In this case, the weights indicate the prior frequency with which it is believed that a specific treatment will be successful, given that the treatment category is indicated for the patient. An example of a treatment category is:

```
*TREATMENTS
RXTHY  Thyroid medication
RXUSP  .Thyroid USP
RXU1   ..Thyroid USP, 1 gram daily
RXU2   ..Thyroid USP, 2 grams daily
```

FINDINGS

Findings are represented as attributes that can be present, absent, or undetermined in the patient, or as a numerical variable, which when measured adopts a value within a pre-specified range. In those cases where uncertainty is associated with an observation, the uncertainty must be described explicitly in terms of additional modifying findings. For example, the accuracy of a test result can be requested, and decision rules then written to logically modify inferences about the original test. Our experience has been that uncertainty about facts tends to be circumscribed by experts to a few important situations in each medical domain. Rather than impose a generalized heuristic for handling them, the EXPERT representation encourages the model builder to pay attention to the manner in which uncertainty in each important situation affects further inferences.

For purposes of acquiring information about a patient, four question types may be employed: a) multiple choice, b) checklist, c) numerical, and d) yes-no. The checklist question differs from a multiple choice question in that the choices are not mutually exclusive, and more than one may be true. The checklist question combines many questions that could be asked individually as single questions. Although some items in a checklist may be more important than others, placing them together serves to bring up for consideration related topics at the same time. There is a higher level of control over the sequence of questioning by the system. It is possible to group several of the question types (checklist, numerical, etc.) together in the form of a questionnaire. When a member of the questionnaire is selected to be asked, all the questions must be asked in the order of the questionnaire. The questionnaire is particularly effective when used in conjunction with logical constraints among findings: the finding-to-finding, or FF, production rules.

Some questions may involve different degrees of risk or cost, which affect the general order in which they are usually sought in the course of a consultation. For example, history and symptom questions are almost always asked before a complicated laboratory test is requested. An optional cost declaration can be associated with a finding. It serves to order the acquisition of findings, since the questioning strategy seeks information about the least costly findings first. Examples of the question types are shown below:

```
**FINDINGS
*BEGIN QUESTIONNAIRE
*NUMERICAL/MIN=1/MAX=100
AGE    Age:
*MULTIPLE CHOICE
Sex:
M      Male
F      Female
*MULTIPLE CHOICE
Pregnancy test:
PREGP  positive
PREGN  negative
*CHECKLIST
Symptoms Appeared/Intensified, Past Year:
RHP    Rapid Heart, Palpitations
*END QUESTIONNAIRE
```

RULES

There are three types of rules for describing logical relationships among findings and hypotheses:

1) FF - finding to finding rules,
2) FH - finding to hypothesis rules,
3) HH - hypothesis to hypothesis rules.

The FF rules specify truth values of findings that can be directly deduced from an already established finding. They are processed in the fixed order specified by the model designer, and are crucial for establishing local control over the sequence of questions in a fashion consistent with medical practice. The format of FF rules is:

F(MNE1,TVAL) -> F(MNE2,TVAL)

where MNE1 and MNE2 are mnemonics for findings and TVAL ={T,F,U, or a number}. If the left side of the rule is satisfied, the response to the right side of the rule is known, and question MNE2 will not be asked. A simple example of an FF rule is:

F(M,T) -> F(PREGP,F)

which would rule out seeking pregnancy tests for males. The FF rules are particularly useful when used with questionnaires. They can describe conditional branchings from sections of the questionnaire. This is most advantageous when questions are consecutively ordered from the general to the specific.

FH rules are logical combinations of findings which indicate confidence in the confirmation or denial of hypotheses. The general format for these rules is:

```
 X1 & X2 & ...Xi->H(MNE,CF)  -1=< CF <=1
Where:  Xi = F(MNE,TVAL) or
    = [n:F(MNE1,TVAL), F(MNE2,TVAL)...]
```

If the logical combination of findings on the left side of the rule is satisfied, the hypothesis, MNE, is assigned a confidence value, CF. The selector argument, n in [n:F(MNE1,...], indicates that if n of the listed findings are satisfied, the bracketed condition is evaluated as true. An example of an FH rule is:

```
    F(RHP,T) & F(FFT,T) -> H(HYPER,.5)
```

which summarizes the inference:

IF: rapid heart palpitations are reported by the patient to have noticeably increased in the past year and a fine finger tremor is observed in the patient,

THEN: consider the hypothesis of hyperthyroidism with a confidence of 0.5.

Confidence measures are assigned on a scale of -1 to 1, with 1 being complete confirmation and -1 being complete denial, following the CASNET and MYCIN rationale and usage [2,9]. When in the course of a consultation several rules are applicable in inferring a hypothesis, they are compared and the single rule with the MAXIMUM absolute value of confidence in the hypothesis will prevail. The maximum is used as a fuzzy logic selector because of the disjunctive nature of the rules. Because no universal scoring function can adequately handle conjunctions of findings, we have taken the approach that requires the designer to explicitly specify separate rules for significant combinations of correlated findings. In return, the scheme guarantees predictability of weight interpretation for the model designer. This applies to the FH rules. After these rules are processed, inferences may be derived through the HH rules and the the taxonomic-causal network. These procedures are described below. The system also assigns a small bonus for hypotheses that have the greatest number of satisfied rules supporting them.

The HH rules allow the model builder to specify inferences among hypotheses and treatment selections that follow from other (diagnostic and prognostic) hypotheses. Since such higher level inferences may be sometimes modified by the presence or absence of a finding, the left hand side of HH rules may also contain assertions about findings. In addition, each HH rule must have a context defined in terms of a set of findings or hypotheses, which enables the application of efficient rule evaluation strategies over the compiled model. The context specifies a set of necessary conditions among the findings to enable evaluation of the HH rule. HH rules are evaluated in the order of specification in the model. Hypotheses are specified with a range of confidence which must be satisfied for the HH rule to be invoked. The HH rules are implemented in a table of the following form:

```
*HH RULES
*IF THERE ARE EYE AND THYROID DYSFUNCTIONS
F(EENO,F)&F(HXTH,T)
*THEN CONSIDER GRAVES' DISEASE:
F(ETHO,T)&H(EYE,.5:1.) -> H(GRAV,.9)
*END
```

CONTROL STRATEGIES

In any consultation system, the principal control strategy problem is to structure and rank conclusions. In many general situations the control of sequential questioning is also desirable, whereas in more stylized and well-defined applications, a prespecified logical control of questioning may be possible. Question selection is usually closely related to the formulation of tentative hypotheses that best explain the patient's condition.

-- Order of Evaluation --

When an assertion or result about a finding is made to the system, the rules in which this result appears are evaluated. The results are usually received in batches, as in the form of responses to a multiple choice or checklist question. The rules are evaluated in the following order to produce weights which rank the hypotheses.

1. FF rules are evaluated first. They take simple true, false, or unknown responses, and merely enlarge the set of new finding results. They are handled in the same way as results received directly in response to questions.

2. FH rules are evaluated next. Only those FH rules in which new results of findings appear need be evaluated. FH rules have the property that when the left hand side of a rule is evaluated as true or false, it remains true or false for the

remainder of the consultation session, unless an erroneous response is received.

3. HH rules are evaluated last. The IF part of each HH rule table is evaluated at the same time as the FH rules. Only HH rules found in tables which have their IF part evaluated as true are considered. All such HH rules must be reevaluated sequentially. The premises and consequents of HH rules may include hypotheses and associated intervals of confidence. Unlike findings which remain true or false, these intervals can change not only directly from finding results, but also indirectly from other rules (both FH and HH) which affect the confidence measure of a hypothesis. HH rules are evaluated in the order of their appearance in the model. There is no backwards chaining, because the order of evaluation is determined beforehand by the model builder. Self-referencing rules are therefore acceptable. Because HH rules and tables are evaluated in sequence, by their order of appearance in the model file, it is important to order the HH rules carefully. An HH rule implying a hypothesis H1, which is later needed to establish another hypothesis H2, should appear in the model file before H2 is referenced in the left side of another HH rule. The confidence ranges used in the HH rules are those which have been directly set by other FH or HH rules. They are not the adjusted weights implied by the taxonomy.

4. The above procedures result in the assignment of those confidence measures, CF(i), which can be directly determined from the rules of evidence and hypothesis weight propagation: the FH and HH rules. When more than one rule is applicable, the maximum absolute value of confidence is used. Another procedure is invoked that is helpful both in question selection and as a simple heuristic to adjust weights slightly. Each hypothesis which has some positive evidence, in the form of a satisfied rule or a partially satisfied rule (with unknown truth value) is marked. The count of such rules which apply to each hypothesis is kept. This corresponds approximately to the number of positive indicators of a hypothesis.

5. A different set of weights is derived from the taxonomy and causal network structure. Forward weights are propagated from predecessor to successor and inverse weights are propagated from successor to predecessor. A taxonomy contains implied relationships between hypotheses that can be treated similarly to causal connections. The procedures used to generate weights are similar, but not identical, to those used in CASNET [9]. After all FH and HH rules have been evaluated, the measures of confidence, CF(i), may be modified or propagated according to their the taxonomic or causal relationships. Because hypotheses which are related by causal or taxonomic connections can be topologically sorted, efficient algorithms can be used to compute the weights implied by this partially ordered network.

6. A final weight is derived from both the rule-based and taxonomic-causal net weights. It is taken as the maximum absolute value from all the indicated directions (with the appropriate sign). A small bonus (no greater than .33) may be awarded to the final weights. The bonus is given on the basis of the percentage and number of rules (derived directly from findings) that are covered by any single hypothesis. The largest bonus is given to the hypothesis which can potentially cover the most rules. The bonus effect is slight and has its greatest effect when only few results have been received, and not many high confidence rules are satisfied.

-- Sequential Test Selection --

The question selection procedures are relatively exhaustive, but straightforward and efficient. Most of the tasks performed by the selection procedure are simple and follow directly from the inference procedures. Once a single finding is selected to be asked as a question, the explicit question structure, such as a multiple choice or checklist question is invoked. Rules are examined that have been evaluated as unknown and their effect on the most likely current hypotheses is considered. Question structures temporarily override the sequential question selection procedures; the system proceeds with the pre-specified questioning order, subject to the FF rules for branching. The general sequential test selection procedure may be specified as follows:

I. Consider those rules (FH or HH) such that:

a) They set confidence measures for marked hypotheses - they are related to current evidence.

b) The confidence of the rule is greater than the current confidence in H(j) - it provides useful additional information.

II. Select an unasked finding F(i), belonging to the set of rules found in part I. such that:

a) the cost is minimum;

b) the current weight W(H) is greatest - indicating that the finding pertains to the most likely hypothesis;

c) the potential CF(H) is greatest for F(i) - so that this finding F(i) is one that can yield greater confidence in H(j) than another F(k).

THE XP AND EXPERT PROGRAMS

The system is written in FORTRAN and occupies about 70K on a DEC-20 computer. This results in relatively efficient processing and also provides the potential for implementation on a minicomputer. The program XP compiles a model for use by the EXPERT consultation program, and indicates any errors found in the model.

The consistency checking module considers the effect of modifications to a model. A data base of representative cases with known conclusions is stored, and after the model has been modified and compiled, the XP program proceeds sequentially through the cases, noting any changes in the reasoning for each stored case, as reflected in the confidence weight assignments to the major conclusions. This is a practical means of reviewing consistency in a model, short of more powerful theorem proving capabilities. It is a more empirical approach than that taken in TEIRESIAS [10], where a model of the relationships among rules and control strategy was developed to help the model builder write new rules for correcting a previously misdiagnosed case, without tracing the effect of rule changes on other cases.

The user communicates with EXPERT by responding to questions posed by the program or by using a simple command language. Commands may be issued on a sequential basis, so that the current ranking of conclusions may be determined. Explanatory information is also available, such as reasons for asking a question, or an analysis of why a hypothesis has a particular confidence weight.

RESULTS AND DISCUSSION

Several applications of the EXPERT system are in progress. Consultation models are being developed in endocrinology (thyroid diseases), ophthalmology, and rheumatology. A consultation system in rheumatic diseases appears to have strong potential for acceptance by the medical community. There is a shortage of rheumatologists in the United States, and keeping up-to-date on the interpretation of many new immunological tests can be difficult for non-specialist physicians. In collaboration with investigators at the University of Missouri we have tested the EXPERT formalism by developing a prototype consultation system for rheumatic diseases. Initially, the set of problems considered has been confined to fewer than 10 important, yet complex diagnostic categories. The model is being expanded to cover additional problem areas.

REFERENCES

1. Weiss, S., Kulikowski C., Safir A., Glaucoma Consultation by Computer, Computers in Biology and Medicine, Vol. 8, pp. 25-40 (1978).

2. Shortliffe, E., Computer-based Medical Consultation: MYCIN, Elsevier, N.Y. (1976).

3. Pople, H., Myers, J., Miller, R., The DIALOG Model of Diagnostic Logic and its use in Internal Medicine, Proceedings 4th International Joint Conference on Artificial Intelligence, pp. 848-855 (1975).

4. Duda, R., Hart, P., et al, Development of the Prospector Consultation System for Mineral Exploration, SRI Technical Report (1978).

5. Feigenbaum, E., The Art of Artificial Intelligence: I. Themes and Case Studies of Knowledge Engineering, Proceedings 5th Joint Conference on Artificial Intelligence, pp. 1014-1029 (1977).

6. Pauker, S., Gorry,G., Kassirer, J., Schwartz, W., Toward the Simulation of Clinical Cognition: Taking a Present Illness by Computer, The American Journal Of Medicine 60, pp. 981-995 (1976).

7. Pople, H., Artificial Intelligence Approaches to Computer-based Medical Consultation, IEEE Intercon Conference, (1975).

8. Szolovits, P., Pauker, S., Categorical and Probabilistic Reasoning in Medical Diagnosis, Artificial Intelligence, Vol.11, pp. 115-144 (1978).

9. Weiss, S., Kulikowski, C., Amarel, S., Safir, A., A Model-based Method for Computer-aided Medical Decision-making, Artificial Intelligence, Vol. 11, pp. 145-172 (1978).

10. Davis, R., Interactive Transfer of Expertise: Acquisition of New Inference Rules, Proceedings 5th Joint Conference on Artificial Intelligence, pp. 321-328 (1977).

ACKNOWLEDGEMENTS

This research was supported in part by grant RR-643 of the NIH Biotechnology Resources Program. The EXPERT system has been programmed by Kevin E. Kern.

LEARNING PRODUCTION RULES FOR CONSULTATION SYSTEMS

Sholom M. Weiss, Casimir A. Kulikowski, and Bernard Nudel
Department of Computer Science
Rutgers University
New Brunswick, N.J. 08903

ABSTRACT

Production rules, with associated measures of probability or confidence, play an important role in contemporary consultation systems. Procedures have been developed which learn a set of probabilistic production rules from a training sample. We have experimented with these methods, by deriving a set of production rules from a medical data base.

Production rules, with associated measures of probability or confidence, play an important role in contemporary consultation systems [1,2]. A recent AI learning system has concentrated on extracting production rules from relatively noise-free data [3], whereas more traditional pattern recognition learning methods have to a large extent dealt with statistical approaches [4]. The major advantage of production rules (and a disadvantage of most statistical methods) is the readily understandable format of the production rule for the expert who is the source of knowledge and the user of consultation systems. A theme of the present work is to show that for some applications, probabilistic productions rules can be learned from a training sample. Moreover, the form of these production rules is similar to those used in a current large-scale consultation system [8]. Some of the procedures employed appear to be analogous to those an expert would use to generate rules from experimental data. A similar goal has motivated application of variable valued logic methods [9] to rule induction in pancreatic cancer.

The problem can be stated as: given a set of h binary features and samples for class C and its logical complement C', find a relatively small set of exhaustive and mutually exclusive production rules (of the type found in decision tables) and their associated probabilities. For simplicity, and to reduce dimensionality, binary features, and a single class and its complement are considered. The task of reducing the features to this form and feature extraction, has been considered separately [5].

A somewhat analogous problem has been previously investigated in the context of learning decision trees [6,7]. Our work has some similarities to version spaces [3], but we consider a set of production rules (not a single production rule) and the data may be very noisy, i.e. the same pattern often appears in both C and its complement. In our testing, the sample data was processed so that it appeared in the following form: For six features, there are 64 possible patterns, of which 39 occurred.

	PATTERN						PROB	FREQ
1)	1	2	3	4	5	6	1.0000	4
2)	1	2	3	4	5	-6	.5000	4
3)	1	2	3	4	-5	6	.8222	45
4)	1	2	3	4	-5	-6	.7104	38
5)	1	2	3	-4	5	6	.3333	3
6)	1	2	3	-4	5	-6	.0000	10
7)	1	2	3	-4	-5	6	.6874	32
8)	1	2	3	-4	-5	-6	.4374	16
9)	1	2	-3	4	5	6	.0000	0
.								
.								
.								
64)	-1	-2	-3	-4	-5	-6	.0000	0

Table 1.

Each pattern has an associated PROB, the Probability of class C given the Pattern, and FREQ, the total frequency of the pattern (among the samples).

The solution consists of finding a smaller set of production rules (with don't care conditions on the variables in addition to yes/no) such that: the set of production rules is much smaller than the number of patterns, the frequency of occurrence for each production rule is >k, and the classification accuracy is as close as possible to that in the original data base. This is desirable because : (a) the expert can only understand and accept a limited number of rules (b) the frequency of occurrence of any rule must be large enough to produce relatively accurate estimates of probability.

What follows is an example of a set of 7 production rules which was derived for the above 64 possible patterns. The data consists of historical information taken from 341 patients with bronchial asthma. The derived classification rate for the 341 patterns, which was used to aid in predicting which patients would benefit from therapy, was competitive with other statistical methods, such as the Bayesian and the nearest neighbor methods.

	PATTERN						PROB	FREQ
1)	1	2	3	4	*	*	0.769	91.
2)	1	*	3	-4	*	6	0.606	66.
3)	1	*	3	-4	*	-6	0.315	54.
4)	*	*	-3	*	*	*	0.206	34.
5)	1	-2	3	4	*	6	0.645	31.
6)	1	-2	3	4	*	-6	0.375	32.
7)	-1	*	3	*	*	*	0.121	33.

OPTIMAL CLASSIFICATION RATE: 72.727 %
CURRENT CLASSIFICATION RATE: 71.261 %

Table 2. (* is a don't care)

In the order of increasing computation time, three procedures are described for deriving a set of production rules.

a) The features are ordered from highest to lowest in significance (this can be done in conjunction with the expert). A closeness threshold is given, for which rules with probabilities within the threshold can be combined (when logically compatible). The program proceeds to combine rules, beginning with the least significant feature (i.e. those patterns which differ only in the rightmost column). The procedure's criteria for combining patterns are similar to two important reasoning criteria used by experts: sensitivity and specificity. In this case we require a minimum frequency and a degree of closeness of probability for any pair of rules to be combined. However, the essential difference with the usual procedures for combining rules and replacing constants with variables, is that these rules have probability measures which must be taken into account. These measures change our interpretation of which rules may be combined. This is a relatively simple procedure that gives quick and often good results. For example, assume that the thresholds were set so that 2 rules could be combined either when they have probability measures within .1 of each other or when the frequency of one of them is less than .10 . In Table 1, patterns 1 and 2 could be combined because each has a small frequency. Patterns 3 and 4 could not be combined because both frequencies are above the threshold and the probability estimates differ by more than .1.

b) Without ordering the features as in (a), all possible orders (n!, where n is the number of features) are considered. This has in many instances yielded near-optimal results. Table 2 was generated using this procedure.

c) Using a search and branch and bound technique, an optimal solution can be found for a set of n production rules. AI search techniques have recently been given more attention in pattern recognition theory [7].

These procedures can result in a set of production rules which are understandable to the expert, include dependencies, and are competitive in performance with other statistical procedures. The requirement that the number of features included in a rule be no larger than eight is consistent with the maximum size that an expert is likely to provide. The number of the samples must increase if rules containing more findings are required. Rules of this form are compatible and can be incorporated in models developed with a new consultation system [8]. The examples presented correspond to a form which was suggested by a physician who felt that it would be readily understandable by other physicians. We are currently working on another application of much greater complexity in developing a consultation system in rheumatology. While this learning approach is likely to work in only small applications, it should prove interesting to see whether limited sets of rules could be learned and used in relatively de-coupled subsections of the consultation system.

ACKNOWLEDGEMENTS

This research was supported in part by grant RR-643 of the NIH Biotechnology Resources Program.

REFERENCES

1. Weiss, S., Kulikowski, C., Amarel, S., Safir, A., A Model-based Method for Computer-aided Medical Decision-making, Artificial Intelligence, Vol. 11, pp. 145-172 (1978).

2. Shortliffe, E., Computer-based Medical Consultation: MYCIN, Elsevier, N.Y. (1976).

3. Mitchell, T., Version Spaces: A Candidate elimination Approach to Rule Learning, Proceedings 5th Joint Conference on Artificial Intelligence, pp. 305-310 (1977).

4. Shimura, M., Learning Procedures in Pattern Classifiers-Introduction and Survey, Proceedings 4th International Joint Conference On Pattern Recognition, pp. 125-138 (1978).

5. Weiss, S., Kern K., Kulikowski, C., Pincus, W., An Interactive System for the Design of Classifiers in Diagnostic Applications, Proceedings 1978 International Conference on Cybernetics and Society, pp.58-62.

6. Gleser, M., Collen, M., Towards Automated Medical Decisions, Computers and Biomedical Research, Vol. 5, pp. 180-189 (1972). Vol. 11, pp. 145-172 (1978).

7. Kulkarni, A. Kanal, L., Admissible Search Strategies for Parametric and Nonparametric Hierarchical classifiers, Proceedings 4th International Joint Conference on Pattern Recognition, pp. 238-245 (1978).

8. Weiss, S., Kulikowski, C., EXPERT: A System for Developing Consultation Models, Proceedings IJCAI-1979.

9. Michalski, R., AQVAL/1--Computer Implementation of a Variable-valued Logic System VL1 and Examples of its Application to Pattern Recognition, Proceedings 1st International Joint Conference on Pattern Recognition, pp. 3-17 (1973).

AUTOMATIC PROGRAM DEBUGGING

Harald WERTZ

C.N.R.S. LA 248 L.I.T.P.
2 place Jussieu
75005 Paris
&
Département d'Informatique
Université Paris VIII - Vincennes
75571 PARIS Cédex 12

Abstract : This paper presents a system (PHENARETE) which understands and improves incompletely defined LISP programs, such as those written by students beginning to program in LISP. This system takes, as input, the program without any additional information. In order to understand the program, the system meta-evaluates it, using a library of pragmatic rules, describing the construction and correction of general program constructs, and a set of specialists, describing the syntax and semantics of the standard LISP functions. The system can use its understanding of the program to detect errors in it, to debug them and, eventually, to justify its proposed modifications. This paper gives a brief survey of the working of the system, emphasizing some commented examples.

1.0 Introduction

Much effort is spent on the development of tools to help programmers in constructing, debugging and verifying programs. From simple editors and trace-packages, the trend is towards more and more sophisticated automatic programmers [3], automatic debuggers [7] automatic assistants [6], automatic verifiers [5] or even the construction of new - semantically more firmly based - programming languages (PASCAL, ALPHARD).

Most of these tools exhibit some weaknesses such as : they impose too many constraints on the intuitions of the programmer or they work only on a very limited subset of possible programs (cf [7]) or they work only on correct programs (cf [5]).

Our aim in the design of our program understanding system was three-fold :

-1- we wanted to have a system which makes explicit the knowledge involved in constructing and debugging programs;
-2- we wanted our system not to verify the correctness of programs but their consistency and
-3- we wanted the system to provide hints for improving and correcting programs.

To this end we have built a program understanding system capable of automatically correcting and improving programs. This system, PHENARETE, assists beginning programmers during the writing and debugging of their programs.
PHENARETE anlyses the text of the program and when it detects inconsistencies or informalities, it constructs and proposes possible corrections or improvements. These propositions constitute for the beginning programmer a crucial component of his apprenticeship : basing on examples the process of improving and correcting imperfect programs, and basing on models the process of inventing future programs.

2.0 Overview of the system

The system takes as input the draft version of a LISP program and delivers as result of its treatment one or more versions of the same program, corrected and improved. PHENARETE proceeds in several steps : first it effects a preliminary analysis of the text of the program to detect and correct surface errors. Surface errors are errors detectable by local anlysis : simple syntax errors such as misspellings or parenthesis errors and errors concerning the wrong number of arguments in function calls. During this first analysis PHENARETE collects information for the following steps. Every time it meets the name of a function it automatically activates a specialist, associated with this function, by the process of data driven function invocation. These specialists represent its knowledge about the use and the effects of the associated functions.

The result of the first analysis - a syntactically correct program - is then meta-evaluated to verify the programs well-formedness. We say that a program is well-formed if it doesn't contain evident infinite loops, doesn't have statements never executed and if it doesn't contradict the set of rules incorporated in PHENARETE. Every proposition our system delivers is a well-formed program.
When PHENARETE detects some informalities or inconsistencies, it annotates the corresponding part of the program and sends the code and the annotation to the repair-man, a module designed to eliminate errors. The system stops the analysis process when it doesn't find any more possible improvements.

3.0 Organisation of PHENARETE

The system is based on four main concepts :

-1- During the analysis of a program, PHENARETE constructs an internal representation of the program in the form of cognitive atoms. These may be considered as the nodes of a network-like representation of the program. Each cognitive atom is composed of a set of facets which represent its different aspects, about which questions could be asked. The facets are filled in during the analysis process. We distinguish between three classes of cognitive atoms, those concerning variables, those concerning labels and those concerning functions.

-2- A set of specialists, i.e. a set of procedural specifications of the syntax and the operational semantics of the standard LISP functions. We distinguish between two different types of specialists :

- those describing the syntax and
- those describing the semantics

of the associated functions.

example : specialist CAR for the syntax

```
[CAR-1 (X) =>
         v (& atom (CAR X)
            & type (X) = LISTP)
         v (& S-expression (CAR X)
            & type (val (X)) = LISTP)
   else :
            modify X until CAR-1 (X) = T]
```

paraphrasing : CAR expects that its argument is - an atom and the type of the value of the argument is a list - a S-expression and the type of the value of that S-expression is a list (e.g. a function call) else CAR has to modify the argument until one of these two conditions is true

and the specialist CAR for the semantics

```
[CAR-N =>
  arg : (X (meta-eval X))
 test : (type (val (X)) = LISTP) ->
        (type (val (X)) = ?)
            -> hypothesize (X, type LISTP)
          T -> complain (X, type : LISTP)
action : if (exist (CAR X)) --> (CAR X)
      else (create (CAR, X)) --> (CAR X)]
```

or in paraphrasing : CAR-N has an argument named X, which must be evaluated. One must verify, if the type of value of the argument is a list, all is ok, else, if the type of value of the argument isn't known, one has to create a hypothetical value of type LIST for X, else, one has to call the repair-man to change the text of the program in such a way that the value of X becomes a list. The value of CAR is if there exists already a CAR of X, this CAR, else one has to create a symbolic value for X, the CAR of which will be the desired value.

Note that the internal description constructed during the analysis of each user function is used to construct two new such specialists for each user function. The specialists are the agents of the meta-evaluation and they represent the systems knowledge about the programming language used.

-3- An algorithm of meta-evaluation [2] which helps the system to understand each of the possible paths of the program. This algorithm includes modules to determine the symbolic values on which the evaluation is carried on.

-4- A set of pragmatic rules describing general program constructs and stereotyped methods to repair inconsistencies. These rules formalize and express explicitly the knowledge activated by every programmer when he is reading a program. We do not use rules concerning the task domain of the programs : our intention was to build a system which does not ask for any additional information. The system should work in any possible task domain, numeric as well as symbolic.

examples of pragmatic rules :

(1) rule of the dependence of a loop of the predicate →
if no variable of the exit-test of a loop is modified inside the loop-body, then the loop is independent of the exit-test and its execution is non-terminating or the loop will never be executed.

A slight refinement of this rule is the following rule :

(2) rule of the structural well-formedness of loops →
in a loop at least one of the variables used in the exit-test has to change its value inside the body of the loop, in such a way that its structure is simplified and converges towards the satisfaction of the exit-test.

In order to use this rule, we have implemented a small theorem prover which can prove the convergence by induction. For the proof of this rule, the theorem-prover takes the symbolic value of the variables at the entrance of the loop, and the modified symbolic values of the same variables after one meta-evaluation of the loop-body and tries to prove the convergence towards the stop test. Let us give one last example of a pragmatic rule :

(3) rule of the structure of recursive loops →

in a recursive function, the recursive calls have to be inside of selection-clauses, and at least one of the clauses must not contain a recursive call.

Actually we have about a hundred rules incorporated in the system, dealing especially with iteration and recursion. For almost every rule ther exists a dual one indicating how to modify the program in such a way that the first one is satisfied.

4.0 A Commented Example

To use PHENARETE, the user has to give to the system only the text of the draft version of the program he wants to write, without any additional information like input/output assertions, commentary, plans etc. The system will try to understand what the user wanted to do, and, if necessary, modify the text of the programm.
To give some feeling of the working of the system, let us examine some examples in detail : Our first example is a (very) erroneous version of the well known REVERSE function. Here is the actual input to the system :

```
? (P '(DE REV L1 L2 COND ULL L22 A1 T RVE A1 ONS
CRA A1 A2))
```

After having corrected the spelling errors, PHENARETE proceeds to a first analysis where she uses only her syntactic knowledge. The result of this first analysis is a syntactically correct LISP program (i.e. a program accepted by any smart LISP interpreter or compiler) :

SURFACE IMPROVEMENTS :

```
(DE REV (L1 L2)
   (COND
      ((NULL L2) L1)
      (T (REV L1 (CONS (CAR L1) L2)))))
```

These first improvements have eliminated all the syntactic errors. However, at least two semantic errors remain :

-1- in the recursive call of REV, the first argument L1 is not modified. This creates an infinit recursion (rule 1).

-2- even with a modification of L1 in the recursive call, the recursion won't stop since the stop-test has as argument L2, a list which grows longer and longer on succesive recursive calls (rule 2).

PHENARETE can not disambiguate this function - it does not know anything of the intentions of the programmer - so it gives two different propositions :

PROPOSITION 1 :

```
(DE REV (L1 L2)
   (COND
      ((NULL L2) L1)
      ((NULL L1) L2)
      (T (REV (CDR L1) (CONS (CAR L1) L2)))))

          AT LEAST YOUR FUNCTION SEEMS OK.
```

In this first proposition, PHENARETE supposed the stop-test given to be correct, but that the user omitted a second stop-test for the case where the second argument is not NULL at the initial call of REV.

PROPOSITION 2 :

```
(DE REV (L1 L2)
   (COND
      ((NULL L1) L2)
      (T (REV (CDR L1) (CONS (CAR L1) L2)))))

          AT LEAST YOUR FUNCTION SEEMS OK.
```

In this second proposition, PHENARETE supposed that the user inadvertently inverted the arguments of the stop-test, so she inverts the two arguments L1 and L2.

PHENARETE is assured that the two corrected versions of the initial draft-program (which are not identical) will stop and deliver a result when executed.

Presently we are working on some extensions to PHENARETE as to find automatically the intentions and the goals of given pieces of code. We would also like to adjoin to PHENARETE a module permitting an explanation to the user of the reasoning of the system. This would be a great help to the user.
The system is running on PDP-10, uses about 25k word memory, is implemented in VLISP [1,4], and is used by about 1000 students in our university.
A more detailed description may be found in [8].

5.0 REFERENCES

[1] CHAILLOUX J. " VLISP-10.3 manuel de référence." Dépt. Informatique, Université Paris 8, RT-17-78, 1978

[2] GOOSSENS D. "A System For Visual-Like Understanding of LISP Programs." Proc. AISB/GI Conference, Hamburg, RFA, july 17-19, 1978

[3] GREEN C. & BARSTOW D. "On Program Synthesis Knowledge." Artif. Intell. 10:3 (1978) 241-279

[4] GREUSSAY P. "Contribution à la Définition Interprétative et à l'Implémentation des Lambda-langages." Thèse, Université Paris 7, 1977

[5] IGARASHI S., LONDON R.L. & LUCKHAM D.C. "Automatic Program Verification 1 : Logical Basis and its Implementation." Acta Informatica, vol. 4, (1975) 145-182.

[6] RICH C. & SHROBE H.E. "Initial Report on a LISP Programmer's Apprentice." IEEE Transactions on Software Engineering SE-4:6 (1978) 456-467

[7] RUTH G.R. "Analysis of Algorithm Implementations." MAC-TR-130, M.I.T., Cambridge, 1974

[8] WERTZ H. "Un système de compréhension, d'amélioration et de correction de programmes incorrects." Thèse de 3ème cycle, Université Paris 6, 1978

UNDERSTANDING COMPLEX SITUATIONS*

Robert Wilensky
Division of Computer Science
University of California, Berkeley
Berkeley, California 94720

Natural language texts often refer to complex situations. Many of these situations involve relationships between people's goals. In order to build a program that understands texts, it is necessary to give the program knowledge about goal relationships and the situations to which they give rise. This knowledge constitutes a theory of planning about real world situations. We have incorporated this theory of planning into a program called PAM (Plan Applier Mechanism). As a result we now have a natural language processing system that can comprehend many complicated dramatic situations.

1. INTRODUCTION

A number of recent attempts have been made to address the problem of inference proliferation in natural language text understanding (for example, see Cullingford (1978) and Charniak (1978)). The thrust of this research has been to use knowledge to guide the inference process. By equipping an understander with knowledge of the particular situation referred to in the text, the understander makes those inferences which are the most plausible without generating many spurious or irrelevant ones.

The drawback of this approach is that a natural language understander cannot be expected to have familiarity with every situation it is going to encounter. A human reader can understand many natural language texts that contain some novel elements in them. To build a natural language understanding system that is capable of understanding such text, a more general inferential capability is needed.

1.1 PAM

PAM (Plan Applier Mechanism) is a program that uses knowledge about people's intentions to understand situations that do not necessarily conform to stereotypical sequences of events. PAM applies knowledge about plans and goals to find explanations for the events in a text. That is, PAM explains a character's actions by inferring the plan that the action is a part of, and inferring the goal that the plan is aimed at achieving. Once a character's motivation has been determined, PAM uses this inference to help interpret subsequent events.

1.2 A Problem

The intentional knowledge originally given to PAM is based on the plan representation scheme of Schank and Abelson (1977). This scheme includes a number of important goals that a character could use to achieve a goal. PAM organizes its knowledge about these entities so that it could infer a character's intentions while reading a story.

While this idea worked well for understanding simple stories, most interesting story situations do not conform to this notion of planning. Real stories tend to be about dramatic situations in which some difficulty is presented for a character. Usually, this difficulty involves a situation in which numerous goals are present at once. These goals can interact in complicated ways, and knowledge about the nature of the goal relationships is needed to understand each character's behavior.

---

*This work was supported in part by the Advanced Research Projects Agency of the Department of Defense and monitored under the Office of Naval Research under contract N00014-75-C-1111.

We have been able to formalize some of the knowledge about goal relationships needed for story understanding. By supplying PAM with this knowledge, the program is now able to understand and answer questions about many complicated stories that are beyond its former capacity, as well as the capacity of other natural language processing systems.

The goal relationships that appear to play a central role in story situations are the following:

(1) Goal subsumption - A way of planning for recurring goals.
(2) Goal conflict - An inimicable relationship between simultaneous goals of the same character.
(3) Goal competition - An inimicable relationship between simultaneous goals of different characters.
(4) Goal concord - A mutually advantageous relationship between simultaneous goals of different characters.

Goal subsumption is discussed in detail in Wilensky (1978b), and will only be touched on here. Instead, we shall be concerned with goal conflict and competition. A more detailed analysis of these relationships, as well as an analysis of goal concord, is found in Wilensky (1978a).

2. GOAL SUBSUMPTION

Goal subsumption is a form of planning in which a character plans in anticipation of having a set of goals, rather than in reaction to each individual goal. For example, consider the following story:

(1) John got a job in another town. He asked Fred if he would sell him his car.

Instead of having a single goal, here John has a goal that is likely to recur repeatedly. Since having a job gives rise to the goal of being at work each day, it is possible to plan for these recurring goals at once rather than dealing with each one as it arises. John's plan to purchase a car makes it easier to achieve each of these goals since he would no longer have to obtain possession of a vehicle on each occasion.

Goal subsumption is composed of the following components:

(1) A set of anticipated goals.
(2) Plans for each goal, each plan sharing a common precondition.
(3) A state that meets this precondition and endures over a period of time during which the goals are expected to arise (called a goal subsumption state).

2.1 Goal Subsumption Situations

Goal subsumption is a useful concept in story understanding because there are a number of frequently occurring story situations based on it. The most important of these situations occurs when a functioning goal subsumption state is abruptly terminated, and is called Goal Subsumption Termination. The following is an example of a story PAM can process that involves such a situation.

PAM Example:

INPUT: JOHN AND MARY WERE HAPPILY MARRIED. THEN ONE DAY, JOHN WAS KILLED IN A CAR ACCIDENT. MARY HAD TO FIND A JOB.

Question:

INPUT: WHY DID MARY NEED EMPLOYMENT?

RESPONSE: JOHN DIED AND SO SHE NEEDED A SOURCE OF INCOME.

PAM infers that John's death terminates a subsumption state for Mary, and that she may seek to replace it. Since traditional marriage subsumes certain ecomonic goals that can also be subsumed by having a job, PAM infers that this is the reason behind Mary's goal. This explanation is accessed and given as the answer to the question above.

3. GOAL CONFLICT

Consider the following situations:

(2) John wanted to go bowling with his friends, but he had promised Mary he would take her out to dinner that evening.
(3) John wanted to live in San Francisco, but he also wanted to live near his relatives in Kansas.
(4) John wanted to go to the football game, but it was raining outside.

In each of these stories, a character has a number of goals that interfere with one another. Such a situation is called a goal conflict. To understand a story involving a goal conflict, a story understander must be capable of detecting the presence of the conflict, and of using knowledge about the types of situations to which goal conflict may give rise. For example, suppose story (2) were continued as follows:

John decided to go bowling anyway. When he got home, Mary told John she was going to divorce him.

To understand that Mary wanted to divorce John because he had neglected her, a reader must infer that John didn't take her out to dinner. This inference is based on the fact that John's goal of taking Mary out was in conflict with another goal, and that this goal was pursued. When two goals are in conflict, and one of them is pursued, a reader can infer that the other has been abandoned. This knowledge about goal conflict is required to find an explanation for Mary's behavior.

3.1 Types of Goal Conflict

A classification of goal conflicts is needed to organize knowledge for both goal conflict detection as well as for understanding the situations to which goal conflicts give rise. We have found the following taxonomy of goal conflicts to be useful:

Goal Conflict Classification

(1) Goal conflicts based on resource limitations.
(2) Goal conflicts based on mutually exclusive states.
(3) Goal conflicts based on generating preservation goals.

Each of these classes is now described.

3.1.1 Resource Limitations

Goal conflicts based on limited resources can come about in a number of ways, depending upon the nature of the resource involved. Two important categories of resource limitations are found to exist:
(a) Shortages based on time limitations
(b) Shortages based on consumable resource limitations.
Due to a conflict based on a shortage of the consumable resource paper, we cannot afford a description of that kind of conflict here. We will discuss time limitations instead.

3.1.1.1 Time

Consider the following story:

(5) John wanted to watch the football game, but he had a paper due the next day. John watched the football game. John failed Civics.

Story (5) is an instance of a goal conflict based on a shortage of time. In order for goals to conflict due to time resources, the plans for the goals must have some time restrictions on them; the amount of time available to the planner must be less than that needed for the successful execution of the plans, and the planner must be incapable of carrying out the plans simultaneously. For example, John must synchronize his plan of watching the football game with the game's broadcast; he must initiate his plan of writing a paper sufficiently before its deadline, and he is probably incapable of executing both plans at once because they each demand his attention.

Thus a goal conflict based on a limitation of time resources really also involves a limitation of a functional object or of a person's abilities. However, the text of a story does not usually make all these limitations explicit. Instead, a reader must infer the conflict from hints in the text. Time-based goal conflicts are hinted at by one of the following occurences in the text of the story:
(1) A statement of a deadline.
(2) A statement of a limitation of a functional object.
(3) A statement of a limitation of a person's abilities.
(4) An explicit statement of a time shortage.

When one of these statements occurs in a story, the reader can infer that a time shortage exists. For example, story (5) above contains an explicit statement of a deadline. Thus the reader infers the goal conflict from the statement that John's paper was due at a certain time.

This inference can be made in PAM with the following rule:

> Rule T1:
> If
>
> a character has two or more goals,
>
> and
>
> the story specifies that the plan for one of the goals must be initiated, completed, or occurring at or before a particular point in time,
>
> then
>
> infer that a goal conflict based on a shortage of time exists among that character's goals.

Hints (2), (3) and (4) are applicable to the following stories, respectively:

(6) John wanted to simmer two dishes on his camp stove, but the stove had only one burner.

(7) John had to write a paper for a course, and read a book for an exam, but John was a very slow reader.

(8) John wanted to visit both Fred and Bill, but he didn't have enough time to see them both.

The rules needed to infer the conflict hinted at in each of these examples can be formulated similarly to rule T1 above.

When a reader sees one of these hints, the reader infers that a goal conflict is present. Of course, these are only hints, and the inference may be incorrect. For example, consider the following story:

(9) John wanted to chat with Mary, but his train left in two days.

Rule T1 says to infer that there is a goal conflict here, but this is probably not the case. Fortunately, most such situations are detectable with simple consistency checks. For example, in story (9), a consistency check would reveal that chatting usually takes much less time than is available, so that the presence of a conflict is unlikely. We shall not expand on consistency here because they are only of importance in unusual situations.

3.1.2. Mutually exclusive states

Goals often conflict because they require some states to exist that are inherently inconsistent. For example, consider the following stories:

(10) John wanted to marry Mary. He also wanted to marry Sue.

(11) John wanted to have a regular job. He also wanted to collect unemployment insurance.

Mutual exclusion is similar to Sacerdoti's "double cross" conflict (Sacerdoti, 1977). A double cross occurs whenever "each of two conjunction purposes denies a precondition of the other". Mutual exclusion is somewhat different since it applies both to double cross situations and situations in which goal states are exclusive independent of particular plans. In addition, states can be either logically or socially exclusive. For example, being unemployed and having a job are logically impossible, while being married to two different people at once is exclusive only according to the conventions of one's society.

3.1.3. Causing a preservation goal

Consider the following stories:

(12) John wanted to go to the football game, but it was raining outside.

(13) John wanted to take the night off, but he thought his boss would fire him.

In both cases, the conflict arises because execution of a plan for a goal would cause a character to have the goal of preventing something from happening. Thus a goal conflict can occur when the plan for a goal causes a character to have a preservation goal. In order to detect these conflicts, a reader must examine the plans likely to be used for each character's goals, and determine if the execution of that plan will invoke a preservation goal for that character.

3.2. Goal Conflict Situations

Goal conflicts give rise to interesting story situations. For example, consider the following situations:

(14) John wanted to watch the football game, but he had a paper due the next day.
(a) That night, John watched the football game. John failed Civics.
(b) John called his teacher and asked if he could have an extension.
(c) John decided to record the football game on his Betamax.
(d) John's teacher informed him that the deadline for the paper had been postponed.

These stories are instances of the following types of goal conflict situations:
(1) Goal abandonment - The character opts for one goal, abandoning the others. This is the case in story (14a).
(2) Goal Conflict Resolution - The character can try to resolve the conflict, as in stories (14b) and (14c).
(3) Spontaneous Goal Conflict Resolution - The conflict may be resolved by some event not initiated by the planner. Such an event occurs in story (14d).

PAM uses knowledge about the possible situations that might arise from a goal conflict to explain subsequent events. The following is an instance of a story PAM understands in this manner:

PAM Example:

INPUT: JOHN WANTED TO WATCH THE FOOTBALL GAME. HE HAD A PAPER DUE THE NEXT DAY. JOHN WATCHED THE FOOTBALL GAME. JOHN FAILED CIVICS.

Question:

INPUT: WHY DID JOHN FAIL A COURSE?

RESPONSE: BECAUSE HE FAILED TO HAND IN AN ASSIGNMENT.

PAM uses the presence of a deadline to infer a conflict. Since John pursues one of the goals, PAM infers this is a goal abandonment situation and infers the failure of John's other goal.

4. GOAL COMPETITION

Stories usually have more than one character. Goal competition arises when the fulfillment of one character's goal will interfere with the fulfillment of the goals of the other character.

Goals can compete with one another for reasons similar to those underlying goal conflict. However, the situations that can arise from goal competition are substantially different. Consider the following stories:

(15) John told Mary he wanted to watch the football game. Mary said that she wanted to watch the Bolshoi ballet.
(a) Mary put on channel 3. John got out the lawnmower.
(b) John got the old black and white TV out of the attic.
(c) Mary put on channel 3. John punched Mary in the mouth and put on the ball game.
(d) John told Mary he would take her out to the ballet if she would watch the football game with him.
(e) Mary put on channel 3. She found out that the ballet was postponed until later that day.

These stories are instances of the following types of goal competition situations:
(1) Independent goal pursuit, in which each character pursues his goals without regard to the other characters. Story (15a) contains an instance of this situation.
(2) Anti-planning, in which a character tries to interfere with another character's plan. Anti-planning occurs in examples (15c) and (15d).
(3) Easing the competition, a situation where a character tries to undo an underlying cause of the competition. An example of this is story (15b).
(4) External competition removal, in which the goal competition is removed by some action not taken by one of the competitors, as in story (15e).

4.1. Anti-planning

Anti-planning, or the process of countering one's opponent, is the most complex of these story situations. The following forms of anti-planning are distinguished:
(1) Physical Elimination
(2) Sabotage
(3) Persuasion

The plans applicable to (1) and (3) are the general plans for overpowering someone and for persuading someone, which have been discussed elsewhere (see Schank and Abelson (1977) and Wilensky (1978)). Also, Bruce and Newman (1978) point out that story situations involving several characters often involve deception. In the scheme of things used here, deception is a variation of plans of persuasion in which some of the argument used by the persuader is known to the persuader to be false. These variations are called trick options. For example, a trick option in the BARGAIN plan may be to bargain away some object one does not possess; a trick option in the THREATEN plan is to bluff, or pretend that some object is a weapon that is not (e.g., a toy gun). PAM does not currently know about the trick options of any plan, however.

4.1.1. Sabotage

Consider the following story:

(16) John and Bill both wanted to marry Mary. John began spreading nasty rumors about Bill.

John is using an anti-plan to stymie Bill's goal in order to maintain the possibility of fulfilling his own. This anti-plan is called UNDO-PRECONDITION. It involves pursuing a plan whose goal is to remove a precondition for someone else's plan. For example, in the story above, John employs the UNDO-PRECONDITION anti-plan against Bill by trying to get Mary to dislike Bill, since Bill's plan to get Mary to marry him probably requires that she be favorably disposed toward him.

The following is a computer example of PAM processing a story involving sabotage:

PAM example:

INPUT: JOHN WANTED TO WIN THE STOCKCAR RACE. BILL ALSO WANTED TO WIN THE STOCK-CAR RACE. BEFORE THE RACE, JOHN CUT BILL'S INGITION WIRE.

Question:

INPUT: WHY DID JOHN BREAK AN IGNITION WIRE?

RESPONSE: BECAUSE HE WAS TRYING TO PREVENT BILL FROM RACING.

Because John's goal and Bill's goal constitute mutually exclusive states, PAM infers the presence of goal competition. Since having a vehicle in good condition is a prerequisite for being in a race, PAM infers that John is using the UNDO-PRECONDITION plan to anti-plan against Bill.

4.1.2. Avoiding Danger

A special set of anti-planning rules is required for understanding goal competition situations based on generating a preservation goal. A particularly interesting subset of these situations occurs when a character may wish to execute a plan so as to avoid causing someone else to have a goal competitive with his. These are called <u>anticipated preservation goal</u> situations. For example, consider the following stories:

(17) John wanted to get the treasure, but it was guarded by a huge dragon.
(a) John tiptoed past the beast.
(b) John threw a rock on the other side of the beast and then got the treasure when the dragon ran over to investigate the disturbance.
(c) John poisoned the dragon's lunch.

Each of these stories demonstrates a plan that can be used to execute another plan without generating an anticipated preservation goal. These plans are given the following names:

(1) AVOID-DETECTION - executing a plan in such a way so as not to be detected by one's opponent. This is the case in story (17a).
(2) DISTRACT - turning one's opponent's attention elsewhere. In story (17b), John executes a plan to divert the dragon's attention, after which John will presumably pursue his plan to get the treasure.
(3) OVERPOWER - physically pre-empting one's opponent. John tries to reduce the dragon's physical abilities in story (17c) so that the execution of his plan for getting the treasure does not generate a preservation goal.

The following is a computer example of PAM understanding a story involving an anticipated preservation goal:

PAM example:

INPUT: JOHN WANTED TO GET THE TREASURE, BUT IT WAS GUARDED BY A DRAGON. JOHN WALKED OVER TO THE TREASURE QUIETLY.

Question:

INPUT: WHY DID JOHN SNEAK OVER TO THE TREASURE?

RESPONSE: BECAUSE HE WAS TRYING TO GET THE TREASURE AND HE WANTED TO PREVENT THE DRAGON FROM KNOWING WHERE HE WAS.

PAM infers two explanations for John's behavior. First, that he is executing a plan to get near the treasure, and second, that he was also using the AVOID-DETECTION anti-plan to prevent generating opposition from the dragon.

5. CONCLUSION

Stories are typically about interesting dramatic situations. Many such situations are based on interactions between goals. In order to build an understander that can comprehend stories about real world situations, it is necessary to have a theory of plans and goals that reflects the complexity of the real world. PAM uses such a theory to find explanations for characters' behavior. However, such knowledge should also be applicable to a broader range of AI problem areas. For example, problem solving requires a planner to consider situations in which a number of goals are present. The theory of goal relationships presented here should be useful for planning for and acting in these situations as well as for understanding them.

REFERENCES

1. Bruce, B. and Newman, D. (1978) Interacting Plans. In <u>Cognitive Science</u>, vol. 2, no. 3.
2. Charniak, E. (1978). On the use of framed knowledge in language comprehension. To appear in <u>Artificial Intelligence</u>.
3. Cullingford, R.E. (1978). Script application: Computer understanding of newspaper stories. Yale Univ. Research Report #116.
4. Sacerdoti, E. (1977). <u>A Structure for Plans and Behavior</u>, Elsevier, Amsterdam.
5. Schank, R.C. and Abelson, R.P. (1977), <u>Scripts, Plans, Goals and Understanding</u>, Lawrence Erlbaum Press, Hillsdale, N.J.
6. Wilensky, R. (1978a). Understanding goal-based stories. Yale Technical Report 140.
7. Wilensky, R. (1978b). Why John married Mary: Understanding stories involving recurring goals. In <u>Cognitive Science</u>, vol. 2, no. 3. Yale Technical Report.

Using Plans in Chess

David Wilkins
Stanford Artificial Intelligence Laboratory
Stanford University
Stanford, California

The purpose of this research is to investigate the extent to which knowledge can replace and support search in selecting a chess move and to delineate the issues involved. This has been carried out by constructing a program, PARADISE (PAttern Recognition Applied to DIrecting SEarch), which finds the best move in tactically sharp middle game positions. It encodes a large body of knowledge in the form of production rules. The program uses the knowledge base to discover plans during static analysis and to guide a small (tens of nodes) tree search. PARADISE does not place a depth limit on the search (or any other artificial effort limit), and has found combinations as deep as 19 ply. This paper describes plans, how they are produced, and how they are used to guide the search. A complete description of PARADISE appears in [12].

1. Introduction

One of the central concerns of artificial intelligence is expressing knowledge and reasoning with it. Chess has been one of the most popular domains for AI research, yet brute force searching programs with little chess knowledge play better chess than programs with more chess knowledge. There is still much to be learned about expressing and using the kind of knowledge involved in playing chess. CHESS 4.7 is probably the best chess program, and its authors make the following comments in [11]:

> *But why is the program so devoid of chess knowledge? .. Our problem is that the programming tools we are presently using are not adequate to the task. Too much work is needed to encode the sizable body of knowledge needed to significantly improve the quality of play.*

Human masters, whose play is still much better than the best programs, appear to use a knowledge intensive approach to chess (see [2]). The purpose of this research is to investigate the issues involved in expressing and using pattern-oriented knowledge to analyze a chess position, to provide direction for the search, and to communicate useful results from the search. To reduce the amount of knowledge that must be encapsulated, the domain of the program has been limited to tactically sharp middle game positions. The phrase "tactically sharp" is meant to imply that success can be judged by the gain of a material rather than a positional advantage. The complexity of the middle game requires extensive search, providing a good testing ground for attempts to replace search with knowledge and to use knowledge to guide the search and communicate discoveries from one part of the tree to another.

Since, in our chosen domain, the attacking side can generally win material with correct play, the program uses different models for the offensive and defensive players. The offensive player uses a large amount of knowledge, suggests many esoteric attacks, and invests much effort in making sure a plan is likely to work before suggesting it. The defensive player uses less knowledge and effort, tries any defense that might work, and tries only obvious counter attacks. Trying every reasonable defense enables the offense to satisfy itself that a line really does win. The size of the tree is kept small because the offensive player often finds the best move immediately.

For a knowledge based program to achieve master level performance, it seems essential that the knowledge base be amenable to modifications and additions. PARADISE provides for easy modification of and addition to its knowledge base (without adversely affecting program performance), by having the knowledge base composed of largely independent production rules which are written in a straightforward **Production-Language** (see [12]). The goal is to build an expert knowledge base and to reason with it to discover plans and verify them with a small tree search. As long as this goal is reached, the amount of execution time used is not important. When a desired level of performance is reached, the program could be speeded up considerably by switching to a more efficient representation at the cost of transparency and ease of modification.

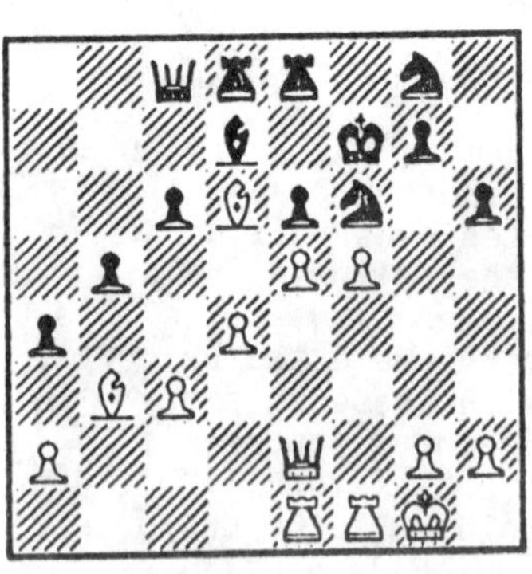

1.	Q-R5ch	NxQ
2.	PxPch	K-N3
3.	B-B2ch	K-N4
4.	R-B5ch	K-N3
5.	R-B6ch	K-N4
6.	R-N6ch	K-R5
7.	R-K4ch	N-B5
8.	RxNch	K-R4
9.	P-N3	any
10.	R-R4 mate	

Figure 0 - white to move

Because it grows small trees, PARADISE can find deeper combinations than most chess programs. Figure 0 is an example of such a combination from an actual master game. White can mate by sacrificing his queen and playing nine additional moves (against black's line of longest resistance), the next to last move not being a check. Thus the search tree must go at least 19 ply deep to find this combination. This is considerably deeper than any other current chess program could probe in a reasonable amount of time, but PARADISE solves this problem after generating a search tree of 109 nodes, in 20 minutes of CPU time on a DEC KL-10.

2. Overview of PARADISE

PARADISE uses a knowledge base consisting of about 200 production rules to find the best move in chess positions. Every production has a pattern (i.e., a complex, interrelated set of features) as its condition. Each production can be viewed as searching for all instances of its condition pattern in the position. For each instance found, the production may, as its action, post concepts (described in the next section) in the data base for use by the system in its reasoning processes. The data base can be considered as a global blackboard where productions write information. The productions are built up by levels, with more primitive patterns (e.g., a pattern which matches legal moves) being used as building blocks for more complex patterns. A search tree (the major component of most chess programs) is used to show that one move suggested by the pattern-based analysis is in fact the best.

To offset the expense of searching for patterns in the position, problems must be solved with small search trees. In fact, PARADISE can be viewed as shifting some of its search from the usual chess game tree to the problem of matching patterns. PARADISE shows that its pattern-oriented knowledge base can be used in a variety of ways to significantly reduce the part of the game tree which needs to be searched. This reduction is large enough that a high level of expertise can be obtained without placing a depth limit (or any other artificial effort limit) on the search. The various ways in which the knowledge base is used are briefly mentioned below.

Calculating primitives. PARADISE's knowledge base contains about twenty patterns (productions without actions) which are primitives used to describe a chess position. These patterns are matched once for each position. They range from matching legal moves to matching any move which can be made without immediate loss of material. The primitives are relatively complex and calculating them is expensive.

Static analysis. Given a new position, PARADISE does an expensive static analysis which uses, on the average, 12 seconds of cpu time. This analysis uses a large number of productions in the knowledge base to look for threats which may win material. It produces plans which should guide the search for several ply and should give information which can be used to stop the search at reasonable points.

Producing plans. The knowledge base is used to produce plans during static analysis and at other times. Through plans, PARADISE uses its knowledge to understand a new position created during the search on the basis of positions previously analyzed along that line of play, thus avoiding a static analysis. Plans guide the search and a static analysis is only occasionally necessary in positions created during the search. Producing a plan is not as simple as suggesting a move, it involves generating a large amount of useful information to help avoid static analyses along many different lines and to help detect success or failure of the plan as it is executed. (Examples are given later.)

Executing plans. The execution of a plan during the tree search requires using the knowledge base to solve goals specified in the plan. This use of the knowledge base could be viewed as a static analysis where the system's attention is focused on a particular goal or aspect of the position. Such a focused analysis can be done at a fraction of the cost of a full analysis which examines all aspects of the position.

Generating defensive moves. PARADISE does static analyses and executes plans only for the offense (the side for which it is trying to win material). To prove that an offensive plan succeeds, the search must show a winning line for all reasonable (i.e., any move which might be effective) defensive moves. Productions in the knowledge base are used to generate all the reasonable defenses.

Quiescence searches. When a node is a candidate for termination of the search, PARADISE uses a quiescence search to determine its value. This quiescence search may return information which will cause the termination decision to be revoked. Productions in the knowledge base provide much of the knowledge used in PARADISE's quiescence search. Quiescence searches in PARADISE investigate not only captures but forks, pins, multi-move mating sequences and other threats. Only one move is investigated at each node except when a defensive move fails.

Analysis of problem upon failure. When either the defense or offense has tried a move that failed, the search analyzes the information backed up with the refutation in an attempt to solve the problem. The knowledge base is used in this analysis to suggest plans which thwart the opponent's refutation. In this way PARADISE constructs new plans using the information gained from searching an unsuccessful plan.

Answering questions. The search often requests certain kinds of information about the current position. The knowledge base is used to provide such information. The most frequent requests ask if the position is quiescent and if there are any obviously winning moves in the position.

The above list describes eight general functions the knowledge base performs for PARADISE. This paper explains how plans are produced and executed. The productions, the static analysis, the tree search, and mechanisms for communicating information from one part of the tree to another are discussed in [12].

3. The Need for Concepts

To understand a chess position, a successful line of play must be found. Human masters understand concepts which cover many ply in order to find the best move. A knowledge based program must also have the ability to reason with concepts that are higher level than the legal moves in a chess position. The following position from [1] illustrates this.

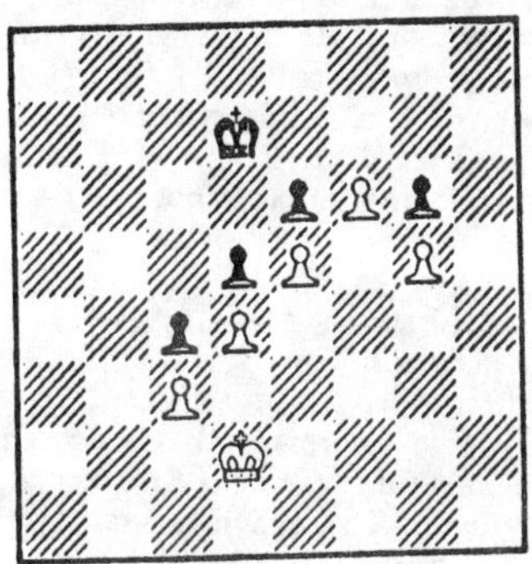

Figure 1 - white to move

In the above position, most computer chess programs would search the game tree as deep as their effort limit allowed and decide to play K-K3 which centralizes the king. They cannot search deep enough to discover that white can win since white's advantage would take more than 20 ply to show up in most evaluation functions used by computer programs. The point is that the solver of the above problem uses conceptual reasoning to solve it, and the concepts must be higher level than the legal moves in a chess position. A human master would recognize the following features (among others) in the above position: the black king must stay near his KB1 to prevent white's king bishop pawn from queening, the pawns form a blockade which the kings can't penetrate, and the kings can bypass this blockade only on the queen rook file.

For a knowledge based program to solve this problem, it must be able to express concepts at the level of conceptualization used above. The system must combine and reason with these concepts in unforseen ways. In the above example, the blockading concept would be used to develop the plan of moving the white king to the queen rook file in order to bypass the blockade, but if both black and white had pawns on their QN4 then the blockading concept would be used to decide that neither king can invade the other's territory. Expressing and using concepts is a major problem for a knowledge based chess program.

To clarify the problems involved in using concepts to reason about chess, a comparison to a well-known "expert" system such as MYCIN is helpful. The following phrase is the action part of a typical MYCIN rule (from [3]): *then there is suggestive evidence (.7) that the identity of the organism is bacteroides.* Such an action effectively adds to the plausibility score for some possible answer. This presupposes that any one writer of all the rules knows every possible solution since such rules will never create a diagnosis that has not been mentioned in the action part of some rule. Such an approach is not satisfactory for the type of reasoning needed in figure 1.

Using actions similar to those used in MYCIN rules would be similar to a chess system where the action part of each rule was to add to the plausibility score of either 1) one or more of the legal moves in the position, or 2) some prespecified object which could lead (through other rules) to recommending a legal move. Such a system would not be able to reason that a king must get past a pawn blockade to attack an opponent's pawn chain since objects cannot be prespecified (e.g., the extent of the blockade and whether or not the kings want to get around it must be determined dynamically). PARADISE must reason by linking concepts to create plans that are not implicit in the knowledge base, instead of filling in prespecified slots. To compare actual production rules, MYCIN's actions mention the names of objects while PARADISE's actions involve many variables whose instantiation is not determined until execution of the action.

4. Knowledge Sources and Concepts

When a production in PARADISE matches, it may have an action part which posts various concepts in the data base. The program is able to express and use concepts by dividing its knowledge base into various Knowledge Sources. Each Knowledge Source (KS) provides the knowledge necessary to understand and reason about a certain type of concept. In its simplest form, a KS is a group of productions which knows about some concept and a list of variables such that an instantiation of the variables represents an instance of this concept. For example, the SAFE KS in PARADISE has two variables, P1 and SQ, and contains productions which know how to make the particular square SQ safe for the piece P1. With this KS, the system can use the concept of a square being safe for a piece in its reasoning, in the expression of plans, and in the communication of discoveries from the tree search. Such concepts are a level above the patterns recognized by the productions themselves.

When a concept has a corresponding KS, PARADISE will eventually treat each instance of that concept which is present in the data base as a subgoal and use the corresponding KS to solve the subgoal in an attempt to produce a plan to realize that instance of the concept. (This may be done by creating other instances of other concepts.) There may also be concepts that have no corresponding KS and are not treated as subgoals. Such concepts are inspected by patterns attempting to match and by the searching routines. When a concept or an instance of a concept corresponds to a KS, it will sometimes be referred to as a **goal** or **subgoal**.

Concepts in the data base must contain all the information that will be needed to execute other KSes and to guide the search (see [12]). Among other things, KSes usually expect information on how likely a goal is to succeed and on how threatening a goal is (this is useful in deciding if a sacrifice is warranted). PARADISE stores information about concepts on a list of attribute-value pairs, called an **attribute list**. For reasons discussed in [12], a particular concept is expressed by giving its name, an instantiation of its arguments, and a list of attribute lists (one for each reason the concept was suggested).

When a production accesses the values of attributes in a concept, it may not care which attribute list the values come from, or it may require that the values for each attribute come from the same list, or it may want the "best" (in some sense) value for each attribute whether the different values come from the same list or not, or it may want values for one attribute to come from lists which have some particular value for another attribute. This accessing of the information in a concept is so complex that it can be looked on as pattern matching in itself. Thus the productions in a KS can be looked upon as matching patterns in the given chess position and matching patterns in different concepts.

Concepts and their accessing are quite complex. Intuitively, the productions in PARADISE are not making deductions, per se, but coming up with ideas that may or may not be right. Thus there are no "facts" that have certain deduced values that can be reasoned with. The complexity of later analysis requires that a production essentially put down "why" it thought of an idea. In this way, other productions can decide if the idea still looks right in light of what is known at that time. Most production systems avoid this complexity because the firing of a production is a deduction which adds a new piece of knowledge to the system. This piece of knowledge is assumed right and the system is not prepared to later decide that it wasn't right to make that deduction.

5. Plans

The goal of the static analysis process in PARADISE is to produce plans. Plans seem to play an important role in the problem solving process of move selection for good human chess players. Alexander Kotov in [6] writes:

. . . it is better to follow out a plan consistently even if it isn't the best one than to play without a plan at all. The worst thing is to wander about aimlessly. (p. 148)

Most computer chess programs certainly do not follow Kotov's advice. In a knowledge based program, the cost of processing the knowledge should be offset by a significantly smaller branching factor in the tree search. Plans help reduce the cost of processing knowledge by immediately focusing the program's attention on the critical part of a new position created during the search, thus avoiding a complete re-analysis of this new position. Having plans also reduces the branching factor in the search by giving direction to the search. Consider, for example, that most programs may try the same poor move at every alternate depth in the tree, always re-discovering the same refutation. PARADISE can detect when a plan has been tried earlier along a line of play and avoid searching it again if nothing has changed to make it more attractive. Most programs also suffer because they intersperse moves which are irrelevant to each other and work towards different goals. PARADISE avoids this by following a single idea (its plan) down the tree.

Plans in PARADISE can be considered as special instances of concepts since each plan has a list of attribute lists. Instead of a list of instantiations for a set of variables (as in a concept), a plan has an expression in the **Plan-Language**. The Plan-Language expresses plans of action for the side about to move, called the offense. In general, the offense wants to have a reply ready for every defensive alternative. A plan cannot therefore be a linear sequence of goals or moves but must contain conditional branches depending on the opponent's reply. When the offense is on move, a specific move or goal is provided by the plan. When the defense is on move, a list of alternative sub-plans for the offense may be given. Each alternative begins with a template for matching the move made by the defense. Only alternatives whose template matches the move just made by the defense are tried in the search. PARADISE has the following templates which adequately describe defensive moves in terms of their effects on the purpose of the plan being executed (P and SQ are variables which will be instantiated in an actual plan to particular pieces and squares, respectively): (P SQ) matches when the defense has moved the piece P to the square SQ, (NIL SQ) matches when the defense has moved any piece to SQ, (P NIL) matches when the defense has moved P (to any square), (ANYBUT P) matches when the defense has moved some piece other than P, and NIL matches any defensive move.

The plan for an offensive move can be one of two things: a particular move or a goal. A particular move is simply the name of a piece and a square. Such a plan causes PARADISE to immediately make that move with no analysis of the position other than checking that the move is legal. A goal is simply the name of a KS followed by an instantiation for each argument of the KS. When executing a goal, PARADISE will construct an instance of the KS's concept in the data base by using the given instantiations and the attribute lists of this plan as a whole. The KS will then be executed for this concept-instance (goal). Any plan produced by this execution will replace the goal in the original plan and this modified plan will be used. This process expands and elaborates plans. If executing the KS does not produce a plan then the original plan has failed.

```
(((WN N5) (((BN N4) (SAFEMOVE WR Q7)
    (((BK NIL) (SAFECAPTURE WR BR))
      ((ANYBUT BK) (SAFECAPTURE WR BK))))
  ((BN N4)(CHECKMOVE WR Q7)(BK NIL)(SAFECAPTURE WR BQ))))
((THREAT (PLUS (EXCHVAL WN N5)(FORK WR BK BR)))(LIKELY 0))
((THREAT (PLUS (EXCHVAL WN N5) (EXCH WR BQ))) (LIKELY 0)))
```

Figure 2

a plan produced by PARADISE (white to move)

Figure 2 shows a problem and one of the plans PARADISE's static analysis produces for it. ("WN" means white knight, "N5" means the square N5, etc. It should be obvious to which white rook "WR" refers.) The last two lines of the plan are attribute lists. The first five lines are the Plan-Language expression for the plan which can be read as follows:

Play N-N5. If black captures the knight with his knight, attempt to safely move the rook on Q1 to Q7. Then, if black moves his king anywhere try to safely capture the black rook on R7, and if black moves any piece other than his king, try to safely capture the king with the rook. A second alternative after black captures the knight is to attempt to safely move the rook on Q1 to Q7 with check. Then, if black moves his king anywhere try to safely capture the black queen with the rook.

SAFEMOVE, SAFECAPTURE, and CHECKMOVE are all KSes in PARADISE. After playing N-N5 and NxN for black in the tree search, PARADISE will execute either the CHECKMOVE goal or the SAFEMOVE goal. Executing the SAFEMOVE goal executes the SAFEMOVE KS which knows about safely moving a piece to a square. This KS will see that R-Q7 is safe and produce this as the continuation of the original plan, causing the system to play R-Q7 with no further analysis. If for some reason R-Q7 was not safe then the SAFEMOVE KS will try to make Q7 safe for the rook (by posting a SAFE concept). If some plan is found, the original plan will be "expanded" by replacing the SAFEMOVE goal with the newly found plan. In general, the newly found plan will contain (SAFEMOVE WR Q7) though it may come after a sacrificial decoy or some other tactic. If posting the SAFE concept does not produce a plan, then the SAFEMOVE goal has failed, and the alternative CHECKMOVE goal will be tried. If it also fails, a complete analysis of the position must be done. If black had answered N-N5 with a king move, it would not match the template (BN N4) and a complete analysis of the position would be undertaken without attempting to make Q7 safe for the rook.

A detailed description of the static analysis process in PARADISE is given in [12]. PARADISE suggests the plan in figure 2 for two different reasons. One of these two ways of suggesting this plan is briefly traced below. The system begins by posting a THREAT concept since the THREAT KS has productions which look for threats. One production recognizes the white rook could skewer the black king and rook from Q7 so it posts a MOVE concept which says the white rook would be well placed on Q7. A production in the MOVE KS, that recognizes that R-Q7 is unsafe, matches and posts a SAFE concept for making Q7 safe for the white rook. While executing the SAFE KS, one production notices that the black knight blocks the white queen's protection of Q7, and posts a DECOY goal. The DECOY KS has a production which posts a FORCE goal suggesting N-N5 as a move to decoy black's knight. The plan in figure 2 has been built up at this point, although more KSes are executed (to check for effects) before the final plan is posted.

6. Discussion of plans in PARADISE

By use of conditionals, a plan can handle a number of possible situations which may arise. The most important feature of the Plan-Language is that offensive plans are expressed in terms of the KSes. This has many advantages. Relevant productions are immediately and directly accessed when a new position is reached. The system has one set of concepts it understands (the KSes) and does not need to use a different language for plans and static analysis. The system has been designed to make the writing of productions and thus the forming of KSes reasonable to do. Thus the range of plans that can be expressed is not fixed by the Plan-Language. By forming new KSes, the range of expressible plans may be increased without any new coding (in the search routines or anywhere else) to understand the new plans. This is important since the usefulness of the knowledge base is limited by its ability to communicate what it knows (e.g., through plans).

Given a number of plans to execute, the tree search must make decisions about which plan to search first, when to forsake one plan and try another, when to be satisfied with the results of a search, and other such things. To make such decisions, it must have information about what a plan expects to gain and why. Such information was available to the productions which matched to produce the plan and must be communicated in the attribute lists of the plan so as to provide many different types of access to this knowledge. Unlike most search-based chess programs, PARADISE must use its information about a plan at other nodes in the tree since it executes a plan without analyzing the newly created positions.

To use the information about plans in an effective manner, PARADISE divides a plan's effects into four different categories which are kept separately (i.e., their values are not combined in any way). These four categories are: THREAT which describes what a plan threatens to actively win, SAVE which describes counterthreats of the opponent a plan actively prevents, LOSS which describes counterthreats of the opponent not defended against and functions the first piece to move in a plan will give up by abandoning its current location (thus providing new threats for the opponent), and LIKELY which describes the likelihood that a plan will succeed. These four categories have emerged during the development of PARADISE. Experience seems to indicate the system must have at least these four dimensions along which to evaluate plans in order to adequately guide the tree search.

Since the values for these categories must evaluate correctly at different nodes in the tree, they cannot be integers. Instead they (except LIKELY) are expressions in the Threat-Language ([12]) which can describe threats in a sophisticated manner. These expressions are evaluated in the context of the current position and may return different values for different positions. The value of LIKELY is an integer which represents the number of unforced moves the defense has before the offense can accomplish its plan. The most likely plans to succeed (e.g., the plan in figure 2) have a LIKELY of zero (every move is forcing).

The system must quickly recognize when a plan is not working and abandon it before effort is wasted investigating poor lines. On the other hand, it is expensive to completely analyze a position, so the system wants to use its plan as long as possible. To achieve a balance, plans must adequately express the purpose they intend to achieve. Productions must carefully formulate their Plan-Language expressions at the right level of detail using appropriate goals and descriptions of defensive moves. When executing a plan, the system will retrieve a goal or move from the plan to apply to a new position. Care must be taken to ensure that this move or goal is reasonable in the new position. For example, a plan which specifies that any check be played may lack detail and cause many poor checks to be investigated. On the other hand, if the plan specifies an actual move to attack the king, it may be too detailed since this move may no longer check the king in the new position (again a poor line is investigated). Plans should express their purpose by describing how the king should be attacked.

A plan should handle as many replies as possible without causing a re-analysis, but it should avoid suggesting poor moves. The templates for describing defensive moves in the Plan-Language and the various KSes have been developed to allow PARADISE's plans to accurately express their purpose. The results have been quite satisfying: the productions in PARADISE now create plans which rarely suggest poor moves but which can still be used for as many ply as a human might use his original idea.

7. Using Plans to Guide the Search

Figure 3 depicts a position from [8] and shows the plan PARADISE suggests as best after a static analysis. To show how such plans are used to guide the search, PARADISE's search for this position is sketched below.

(((WQ R7) (BK R2) (CHECKMOVE WR R5) (BK NIL) (ATTACKP BK))
((THREAT (PLUS (WIN BK) (EXCHVAL WQ R7))) (LIKELY 1)))

Figure 3 (white to move)

The search commences execution of this plan by playing QxPch and producing a new board position. The defense suggests both legal moves, KxQ and K-B1, but tries KxQ first. Since this move matches the (BK R2) template in the plan, PARADISE has ((CHECKMOVE WR R5) (BK NIL) (ATTACKP BK)) as its best plan at ply 3 of the search. Execution of the CHECKMOVE KS produces ((WR R5) (BK NIL) (ATTACKP BK)) as a plan which causes R-R5ch to be played. Black plays his only legal move at ply 4, K-N1, which matches the (BK NIL) template in the plan. Thus PARADISE arrives at ply 5 with (ATTACKP BK) as its plan. Executing the ATTACKP KS posts many concepts, including MOVE and SAFE concepts, and ((WN N6) ((NIL (SAFEMOVE WR R8)) (NIL (SAFEMOVE WN K7))) is produced as the best plan in this position. After playing N-N6, the position in figure 4 is reached.

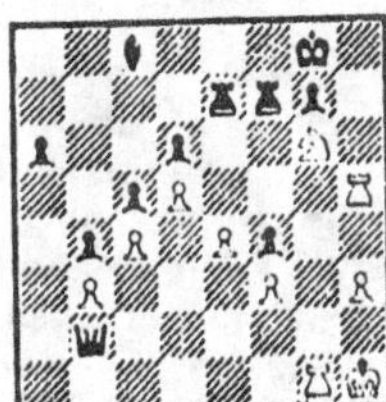

Figure 4

Productions which know about defending against R-R8 suggest (BB R6)(BB Q2)(BB N2)(BR B4)(BR B3)(BR B1). Black plays BxP first in an effort to save the bishop from the ensuing skewer. At this point the plan branches. Since both branches begin with a null template, they both match any black move at ply 6. Thus PARADISE has two plans at ply 7: (SAFEMOVE WR R8) and (SAFEMOVE WN K7). Before executing a plan for the offense, PARADISE executes the QUIESCENCE KS which looks for obviously winning moves. Here R-R8 is suggested by the QUIESCENCE KS which causes the (SAFEMOVE WR R8) plan to be executed immediately. PARADISE plays R-R8, finds that black is mated, and returns to ply 6 knowing that black's BxP leads to mate. All this has been accomplished without a static analysis; the original plan has guided the search.

At ply 6, black uses KSes to refute the mating line. No new moves are found since all reasonable defenses have already been suggested. PARADISE has a causality facility which determines the possible effects a move might have on a line of play. Using the tree generated for the mating line, the causality facility looks for effects a proposed move might have (such as blocking a square which a sliding piece moved over, vacating an escape square for the king, protecting a piece which was attacked, etc.). The causality facility recognizes that neither B-Q2 nor B-N2 can affect the mating line found for BxP so they are rejected without searching. Black plays R-B4 next, the causality facility having recognized that this move opens a flight square for the black king. Again PARADISE has both (SAFEMOVE WR R8) and (SAFEMOVE WN K7) as plans at ply 7. Both SAFEMOVE goals would succeed, but R-R8 has a higher recommendation and is played first. Black plays his only legal move at ply 8, K-B2. PARADISE no longer has a plan at ply 9. Before trying a static analysis, it executes the QUIESCENCE KS in an attempt to find an obviously winning move. R-KB8 is suggested and PARADISE immediately plays this move without doing a static analysis. This is mate so PARADISE returns to ply 6 to look for other defenses. Both R-B3 and R-B1 are tried and both are quickly refuted by playing R-R8 from the SAFEMOVE goal of the original plan, K-B2, and R-KB8 from the QUIESCENCE KS. The search then returns to ply 2 and tries K-B1 in answer to QxPch. The template in the original plan does not match K-B1 so there is no plan at ply 3. However, the QUIESCENCE KS quickly suggests Q-R8 and PARADISE returns from the search convinced that QxPch will mate.

PARADISE's plans are not always so accurate but space prevents presentation of a longer search. The above analysis uses about 130 seconds of cpu time on a DEC KL-10. It goes to a depth of 9 ply while creating only 21 nodes in the tree. Because of the guidance provided by the original plan, no static analysis was performed except on the original position. By comparison, the TECH2 program (an improved version of TECH [5]) at a depth setting of 6 discovers that it can win material with QxPch although the horizon effect hides the mate from it. For this analysis, TECH2 uses 210 seconds of cpu time and creates 439,459 nodes by making legal moves (it also makes and retracts 544,768 illegal moves).

8. Measuring PARADISE's performance

To aid in evaluating performance, PARADISE was tested on positions in [8]. This book contains tactically sharp positions from master games which are representative of tactical problems of reasonable difficulty. PARADISE's knowledge base was developed by writing productions which would enable the program to solve, in a reasonable manner, fifteen chosen positions from among the first 100 in [8]. The 85 positions not chosen were not considered during this development. This development process produced one version of the program, called PARADISE-0. Six positions were then picked at random from the remaining 85 and accurate records were kept on the work involved in getting the program to solve these reasonably. The version of the program which solves all 21 positions is called PARADISE.

PARADISE's performance on a problem is classified into one of three categories: 1) problem solved as is (possibly with a minor bug fix), 2) problem not solvable without a change to the program or a major change to the knowledge base, or 3) problem solvable with a small addition to the knowledge base. Category 3 helps measure the modifiability of the knowledge base. It is meant to include solutions which require no changes whatsoever to the program and only a small addition to the knowledge base. Small means that it takes less than 20 minutes total of human time to identify the problem and write or modify one production which will enable PARADISE, with no other changes, to solve the problem in a reasonable way (i.e., no ad hoc solutions).

Of the six positions chosen at random, two were in category 1, three were in category 3, and one was in category 2. This latter one inspired the only program changes between PARADISE-0 and PARADISE. These results speak well for the modifiability of the knowledge base, but shed little light on the generality of the program. To better test generality, PARADISE has been tested on the first 100 positions. These positions are divided into 5 groups of 20 and Reinfeld claims an increase in difficulty with increase in group number. (Eight endgame positions were eliminated, so the groups actually have 18, 19, 18, 20, and 17 positions.) PARADISE is considered to solve only the problems in category 1, while PARADISE-2 solves both category 1 and 3 problems. PARADISE would become PARADISE-2 simply by leaving in the productions written to solve problems in category 3. The following table shows what percentage of these problems can be solved by PARADISE, PARADISE-2, CAPS [1], TECH [5], CHESS 4.4 [11] running on a CDC 6400, and a human rated as class A [1]. PARADISE was limited to 45 minutes of cpu time per problem while the other programs were limited to 5 minutes.

	PARADISE	PARADISE-2	CAPS	TECH	C-4.4	HUMAN
Group I	78%	100%	67%	78%	94%	89%
Group II	68%	95%	74%	84%	95%	95%
Group III	94%	100%	61%	61%	78%	94%
Group IV	70%	95%	50%	40%	70%	80%
Group V	65%	94%	41%	47%	76%	53%
All 92	75%	97%	59%	61%	83%	83%

There were 20 problems in category 3 in the first 100, but only 13 productions were written to solve them. In two instances, an already existing production was modified. In five instances the same production solved 2 different category 3 problems. This is a strong indication that the productions being written are fairly general and not tailored to the specific problem. PARADISE already exhibits more generality in this domain than programs like TECH and CAPS. The figures for PARADISE-2 show that these problems do not push the limits of the expressibility of the production language nor the ability of the program to control the tree search. These results indicate that the generality of PARADISE is reasonable and that the modifiability of the knowledge base is excellent.

It should be noted that PARADISE uses considerably more cpu time and produces trees with considerably fewer nodes than either of the other programs. The following statistics were compiled for the 89 problems which PARADISE-2 solved in these 92. PARADISE averaged five and one-half minutes of cpu time per problem (it ranged from 19 seconds to 1958 seconds), and generated an average of 38 nodes per problem (ranging from 3 nodes to 215). On the average, PARADISE spent 53% of its time calculating primitives. There were an average of 3.7 static analyses done per problem, and less than 9% of the nodes generated had static analyses done on them. This shows that the plans do a good job of guiding the search.

9. Comparison to Plans in Robot Problem Solving

Plans are used in many domains of AI research, especially robot problem solving. ABSTRIPS [9], NOAH [10], and BUILD [4] are examples of planning systems in robot problem solving environments. Plans in these systems are very different from those in chess so a summary of these differences is more appropriate than a detailed comparison. These differences are explained in greater detail in [12]. Robot planning is frequently done in abstracted spaces which have been defined, and which omit details. Such an approach is much more difficult in chess, at least with mankind's current understanding of the game. It is not clear how to define abstracted spaces. Small details are very important in chess and cannot be readily ignored.

In the robot planning systems, the effects of an action are well defined. The program can easily and quickly determine the exact state of the world after an action. In chess, moves (actions) may subtly affect everything on the board. Chess plans cannot make many assumptions about the state of the world in the future, but must describe the expected features of new states in the plan itself and then test for these features while executing the plan.

In most robot planning systems, tests for having achieved the goal or the preconditions of an action are trivial and give well defined answers. In chess, there may be only very subtle differences between a position where a particular action is good and positions where the same action is wrong. It is also hard to know when a goal has been achieved, since there is always a chance of obtaining a larger advantage (except when the opponent has been checkmated). Thus in chess it is necessary for the plan to provide a considerable amount of information to help in the making of these decisions. This is done in PARADISE through the attribute lists in plans.

The number of things PARADISE can consider doing at any point in a plan is about an order of magnitude larger than the number of things most robot problem solvers usually contend with. There are an average of about 38 legal moves in a chess position (see [2]). When planning farther in the future than just the first action, the chess planner has many more choices than the 38 legal moves. The inability to make assumptions about future states often prevents mentioning actual moves in a plan. Instead a description of the intent is needed, and the number of such descriptions is much larger than the number of legal moves that might be made. A robot usually has a much smaller number of possible actions, so the two types of plans explode at very different rates.

The robot planners have the flavor of establishing a sequence from a small number of well-understood operations until the correct order is found, while chess planners have more a flavor of "creating" the correct plan from the many possibilities. For this reason, a system which produces good chess plans needs a large amount of knowledge and non-trivial reasoning processes to produce plans. Plans in PARADISE differ from those in robot problem solvers by specifying powerful knowledge to be applied in new situations. Plans essentially give PARADISE a perspective to use when analyzing a new position.

10. Comparison to Plans in Chess

Pitrat's program [7], which solves chess combinations, is the most important example of the use of plans in chess. The language Pitrat uses for expressing plans has four statements with the move statement and modification statement being the most important. The move statement specifies that the piece on one particular square should move to another particular square. It may also be specified that the move must be a capture. The modification statement describes a modification to be made to a particular square. This can be one of four things: removal of a friend, removal of an enemy, moving a friend to the square, or getting an enemy to move to the square.

Plans in PARADISE provide much more flexibility in expression than Pitrat's move statement. In PARADISE, types of moves other than captures can be specified (e.g., safe moves). Also, particular squares do not need to be named in PARADISE since it can use a variety of goals to express the plan. The important square to move to may change depending on the opponent's move so it is not always possible to specify such a square in advance. Pitrat's modification statement is a goal which the system tries to accomplish. These modifications are too simple to express the purposes behind their suggestion. For example, the system may want to decoy the black queen to make a square that it protects safe for white. Pitrat would express this goal as removing an enemy from the black queen's location which does not express the purpose of the plan. It will work well for the winning combination but will also allow many wrong moves since the queen may be decoyed to a square from which she can still protect the square in question. PARADISE would specify that the black queen must be decoyed to make the particular square safe, and only decoys which remove the black queen's protection would be considered. PARADISE attempts to express the purpose of each plan while Pitrat's plans express side effects that will happen if the purpose is accomplished (e.g., a square becoming vacant). Unfortunately, the same side effects may also happen when the purpose is not accomplished, causing the system to waste effort searching poor lines.

Plans in PARADISE have two more major advantages over the plans in Pitrat's system. First, PARADISE has conditionals which allow specification of different plans for different replies by the opponent. The advantages of this are obvious: the system can immediately try the correct plan instead of searching an inappropriate plan and backtracking to correct itself. Second, PARADISE's plan language is modifiable. Simply by writing new productions, new goals and concepts can be created for expressing plans and the system will automatically understand these new plans. This property is necessary for any system that wishes to extend its domain or incrementally increase its expertise. Significant additions to Pitrat's plan language would seem to require a major programming effort.

It should be noted that Pitrat's program processes nodes much faster than PARADISE and therefore can handle larger trees. It may be the case that programs will obtain better performance by using larger trees and less sophisticated plans, but the use of knowledge is only starting to be investigated by programs such as PARADISE and it is too early to draw conclusions.

11. Summary

PARADISE exhibits expert performance on positions it has the knowledge to understand, showing that a knowledge based approach can solve some problems that the best search based programs cannot solve because the solutions are too deep. The knowledge base is organized into KSes which provide concepts for PARADISE to use in its reasoning processes. These concepts are at a higher level than the ideas produced by simply matching patterns. PARADISE's knowledge base is amenable to modification. Production rules (and therefore KSes) can be quickly written and inserted in the knowledge base to improve system performance without adverse affects.

The concepts provided by the KSes are used to create plans during static analysis. The concepts communicate enough information that they can be rejected after being posted. The same concepts are used to express plans for guiding the search, and the KSes execute the plans during the search. By communicating plans down the tree, PARADISE can understand new positions on the basis of its analysis of previous positions. By having particular goals in mind when looking at a new position, the system quickly focuses on the relevant part of the data base and avoids using all its patterns. Plans in PARADISE express their purpose fairly well, without being too general or too specific. Because of the successful communication of knowledge through plans, PARADISE is able to solve a number of chess combinations with small trees and without a depth limit on its search.

One of the major issues in creating concepts is their generality. If the concepts are too general then too many details are lost, and the system does not have the necessary facts to do certain reasoning. If not general enough, the system leans toward the extreme of needing a production for every possible chess position. The concepts in PARADISE have been constructed to be as general as possible without sacrificing expert-level performance to the loss of detail. The tradeoff of generality and specificity in concepts is closely related to the tradeoff of search and knowledge. With much specific knowledge the use of knowledge becomes expensive, but fewer mistakes need to be corrected in the search. With more general knowledge, analysis is cheaper but more time must be spent correcting mistakes in the search. PARADISE uses a mix of search and knowledge which involves more knowledge and less search than previous programs which include chess middle games in their domain. This type of research should strive for generality within the confines of its commitment to knowledge-based expert performance.

REFERENCES

[1] Berliner H, "Chess as problem solving: The development of a tactics analyzer", Unpublished doctoral thesis, Carnegie-Mellon University, 1974.

[2] Charness N, "Human Chess Skill", Chapter 2, in **Chess Skill in Man and Machine**, Frey, P. (Ed), Springer-Verlag, 1977.

[3] Davis R, "Applications of meta level knowledge to the construction, maintenance and use of large knowledge bases", AIM-283, C. S. Department, Stanford University, 1976.

[4] Fahlman S E, "A planning system for robot construction tasks", **Artificial Intelligence 5**, pp. 1-49, 1974.

[5] Gillogly J, "The technology chess program", **Artificial Intelligence 3**, pp. 145-163, 1972.

[6] Kotov A, **Think Like a Grandmaster**. Dallas: Chess Digest, 1971.

[7] Pitrat J, "A chess combination program which uses plans", **Artificial Intelligence 8**, pp. 275-321, 1977.

[8] Reinfeld F, **Win At Chess**, Dover Books, 1958.

[9] Sacerdoti E D, "Planning in a hierarchy of abstraction spaces", **Artificial Intelligence 5**, pp. 115-135, 1974.

[10] Sacerdoti E D, "The nonlinear nature of plans", Stanford Research Institute Technical Note 101, January 1975.

[11] Slate D, Atkin L, "CHESS 4.5- The Northwestern University chess program", Chapter 4, in **Chess Skill in Man and Machine**, Frey, P. (Ed), Springer-Verlag, 1977.

[12] Wilkins D, "Using patterns and plans to solve problems and control search", forthcoming doctoral thesis, Computer Science Department, Stanford University.

SPEECH ACTS AND MULTIPLE ENVIRONMENTS

Yorick Wilks
Department of Language
& Linguistics
University of Essex
Colchester, England

Janusz Bien
Informatics Institute
University of Warsaw
Warsaw, Poland

This brief paper outlines joint work that implies a view of the explication of Speech Acts different from those current in AI. It is exploratory at present, but we intend that it should lead to programs as soon as possible. We propose a system that engages in dialogue with a human user so as to discuss others and in doing so, interprets the appropriate communicative force of the user's utterances. The three key features of the explication of communicative force presented are:

1. multiple environments: the ability to interpret an expression or a description relative to some particular knowledge, e.g. relative to the beliefs of one person about another. It is a generalization of the computer science approach to expression evaluation, using the notion of an environment to fix the interpretation of names occurring in the expression.
2. dual knowledge representation: an "experiential" representation is used to memorize sentences or other episodes (exemplified by pseudo-tests, or PTs), while a frame-type representation is used to memorize knowledge needed more generally for reasoning.
3. a least effort principle of understanding: considered to be a language universal, which requires (a) that the system maintain as much representation as possible in the frame-like forms, rather than in PTs, and (b) that the system maintain a highly redundant representation in the PTs, achieved by a process we call percolation of belief.

1. INTRODUCTION

Speech Acts (SAs) originated as a notion in philosophy [1] , [9] much preoccupied with the logical properties of sentences like "I promise to pay you five pounds" and, later, with access to the intentions in a speaker's head. Linguists worked with these notions subsequently but, like AI workers, they have added little that is distinctive to the original perception that utterances have a distinctive communicative force (as a threat, a promise, a warning, etc.), in addition to literal content. We believe that an AI approach to this area that is to contribute distinctively will have to make use of general principles concerning the environmental embedding of beliefs, etc., as well as a least effort maxim for their manipulation. The first of these, advocated by Bien in 1975 [2] , has been used by Cohen [5] and others of the Toronto group, but the distinctive feature we discuss here concerns the maintenance and change of such environments under a general requirement of cognitive efficiency.

2. TIRESIAS

We propose a system able to engage in a limited conversation with a human user: let us call it TIRESIAS for a reason that will appear. The topic of the conversation would be the relationships of a group of friends (see [7]) known in varying degrees to both TIRESIAS and the user. We expect sample dialogues such as:

$1 USER: Frank is coming tomorrow, I think.
$2 TIRESIAS: Perhaps I should leave.
U: Why?
T: Coming from you, $1 is a threat.
U: Does Frank hate you?
$3 T: I don't know-but you think he does, and that is what is important right now.

The important feature we require here is TIRESIAS' ability to evaluate its descriptions of persons differently in different environments Thus, at $1, TIRESIAS detects a threat (not in itself necessarily interesting) on the basis of evaluating its representation of itself, inside that of Frank, inside that of the user, which we might write (given that $\{P\}_{Q}$ is the data-structure for P inside Q, that is, Qs model of P):

{{{TIRESIAS} FRANK} USER} TIRESIAS

Note that all the data-bases are in TIRESIAS, so an outer TIRESIAS bracket exists round all evaluations, though we may sometimes omit it.

whereas at $3, when questioned, TIRESIAS is seeking to evaluate simple Frank's view of him, or {{TIRESIAS} FRANK} TIRESIAS

where he discovers that he has no specific information on what Frank thinks of him. The generation of $2, and TIRESIAS understanding of $1 as a threat, may, let us suppose, depend on a specific belief that the user believes that Frank dislikes TIRESIAS (but as $3 shows, not a belief by TIRESIAS that Frank dislikes him). Let us follow this through by examining inferences plausibly generated by TIRESIAS' construction of the two nestings of environments shown above and comparing their results.

The crucial difference here is between the evaluation of {FRANK} in {USER} and in {TIRESIAS}. Another assumption is important to what follows: the nesting of environments {FRANK} USER that the example requires will not in general exist already in the system (as it does in [5] et al). as a partition of the space of beliefs: we find it implausible and comptatationally overweight to assume that all such partitions are already marked in the system. {FRANK} USER will here be constructed by "pushing down" {FRANK} into {USER}. To put it simply, TIRESIAS will construct the user's view of Frank by inference from his views of the two participants: he will assume that user believes about Frank what he does, unless explicit information about Frank likes the user, and that Frank believes that he (Frank) hates the user, then {{FRANK} USER} TIRESIAS

will contain Frank dislikes user, since the belief of the user, that Frank likes the user, is overridden by explicit counter information. Thus, beliefs are transferred by counting in what it is reasonable for TIRESIAS to believe others believe, rather than counting out: that is to say, believing about another's beliefs only what we have explicit evidence for. To see how such structures are obtained, we must consider briefly the form of knowledge representations in the system.

3. FRAMES AND PSEUDO-TEXTS

The notion of frame is now well known [8], and here we assume in addition a variant called a pseudo-text [11] which is an information structure that is the semantic representation of a text, obtained by a semantics-driven parser such as [10]. A PT is an interconnected set of proposition representations, called templates, each of which consists of three principal nodes or terminals, that represent in right-left order, the actor, action, and object of an event. The terminals are, in fact, trees of semantic primitives, but here we shall place the English names of those trees at the terminals. In such a notation, we may write the template for "Frank is coming tomorrow", said by the user, as follows in the PT in TIRESIAS for {USER}

[* asserts □]
[Frank come □]
  tomorrow

where □ is a dummy node, and * is a pointer to the name of the PT in which we are ({USER} in this case). The same sentence would be parsed into a corresponding representation in {FRANK} with * now replacing "Frank" rather than "user". It should be emphasized that the PTs are a surface semantic representation of such sentences, and are not frames in the sense of a structure with an a priori determined list of slot and filler names to facilitate inferencing; they are essentially episodic text representations, but it is those we shall need, in addition to some frame information, to deal with the example to hand.

It will be evident that, in the description of input we have given, there is no general representation of Frank: information about him will be clustered in {FRANK}, but will also appear, as we saw, in {USER} and possibly many other PTs.

We have postulated in various publications [2] [10] the operation of a general principle of preference in language: one that asserts that the effectiveness of natural languages depends on them being constructed so that, in general, correct interpretations are those found with least effort: one could put this by saying that a system should prefer those representation that it is easiest to construct and maintain.

Now consider again the contrasting evaluations of {{{TIRESIAS} FRANK} USER} TIRESIAS and {{TIRESIAS} FRANK} TIRESIAS

If we further assume that at the privileged shallow level there is always a frame structure corresponding to the episodic PT, which contains standard slot names such as DISLIKE, then we may expect:

[ϕ DISLIKE *]

in {TIRESIAS} given that the system knows no one who dislikes it, although in {USER} may be a template (corresponding to a belief of the user)

[Frank dislikes Tiresias]

Then, on "pushing down" {TIRESIAS} into {FRANK} to get {{TIRESIAS} FRANK} TIRESIAS} in the way we sketched in the last section, no inconsistency of content is noted and no beliefs are reset. But on pushing the value of this object down into USER to get the deepest nesting shown earlier, we encounter

[Frank dislikes Tiresias]

as well as the two connected templates for $1 shown earlier in this section, and both of these items will become part of the constructed "systems view of USERs view of Frank".

4. BELIEF PERCOLATION AFTER PUSH-DOWN

Two effects may now be expected:

i) the inference from Frank dislikes Tiresias in {USER} ; together with plausible inference rules about dislike, fear, and leaving places, will generate the reply $2 even though no such consequence was derivable in {{TIRESIAS} FRANK} TIRESIAS} alone as we see at $3.

ii) on a least effort principle, the key template belief Frank dislikes Tiresias that will have been copied from {USER} into {TIRESIAS} FRANK} [*dislikes Tiresias] and into {TIRESIAS} TIRESIAS} as [Frank dislikes*] during the construction of the desired viewpoint, will now remain present when the push-down is, as it were, pulled apart: it remains in the PT copy. In this way, the beliefs of the user about Frank (about Tiresias) percolate to {TIRESIAS} FRANK} , or rather to the relevant part of {FRANK} (the privileged shallow level), and similarly to {TIRESIAS} TIRESIAS}.

This resulting, highly redundant, representation may seem a paradoxical result of a least effort principle but we maintain that this spread of beliefs from PT to PT, via push-down evaluation, leads to a structure requiring less effort when the same or similar input is encountered in the future. This is because a push-down of environments as we have described it may be considered to require considerable resources: so, for example, {FRANK} should be checked, before being evaluated in {USER} : to see if that push-down had been done lately, and, if it had, it need not be done again, since the relevant beliefs, Frank dislikes Tiresias in this case, would already have percolated into it. One may notice that such percolations, if they exist, deny the whole basis of intensional logic (the denial of p believes x $\rightarrow$ x), but seem consistent with common sense, and more technically with the sleeper effect [6] , the inference of beliefs from unreliable sources.

It should not be emphasized that we are not trespassing into possible worlds: for they require the assignment of all variables. In the recursive pushing down of PTs we envisage only relevant beliefs will be reset. It is certainly true, however, that these suggestions will impinge on the area on intensional logic (see [2] and, of course, Tiresias in the Greek myth was the seer who knew that Jocasta was the mother of Oedipus (who knew that Jocasta was the wife of Oedipus, and even that Jocasta was Jocasta, but NOT that key fact known to Tiresias). But there is no space to explore these connexions, although we do believe that even the simple considerations set out here could lead to a richer procedural explication of SAs than those current in AI.

REFERENCES

(1) J.L. Austin, "Performative utterances"(1961) Philosophical Papers, Oxford.

(2) J.S. Bien, "Towards a multiple environment model of natural language" Proc. IJCAI 4, (1975) 237-240.

(3) J.S. Bien, "Computational explication of intensionality" in A.J.C.L. Microfiche. No. 97, (1976).

(4) H. Clark & C. Marshall, "Definite Reference and Mutual Knowledge", Sloan Workshop, Pennsylvania, May 1978.

(5) P. Cohen, "Planning Speech Acts" Ph.D. Thesis, Dept. Computer Science, Univ. Toronto (1978).

(6) C. Gruder et al. "The absolute sleeper effect" Personality and Social Psychology, 36, 1978, 1061-1073.

(7) P. Hayes & M. Rosner, "Ully". Proc. AISB Conf., Edinburgh 1976, 46-49.

(8) M. Minsky, "Matter, Mind and Models" in Bobrow (ed.) Semantic Information Processing, MIT, 1968, 203-43.

(9) J. Searle, Speech Acts, Oxford, 1969.

(10) Y. Wilks, "A preferential pattern-seeking semantics, Artificial Intelligence, 6, 1975, 53-74.

(11) Y. Wilks, "Making preferences more active", Artificial Intelligence, 11 , 1978, 197-223.

RELATING PROPERTIES OF SURFACE CURVATURE TO IMAGE INTENSITY*

Robert J. Woodham
Department of Computer Science
University of British Columbia
Vancouver, B.C. V6T 1W5
Canada

Reflectance map techniques make explicit the relationship between image intensity and surface orientation. In general, however, trade-offs between image intensity and surface shape emerge which cannot be resolved in a single view. Existing methods for determining shape from a single view embody assumptions about surface curvature. The image Hessian matrix is introduced as a convenient viewer-centered representation of surface curvature. Properties of surface curvature are expressed as properties of the Hessian matrix. For several classes of surfaces, image analysis simplifies. This result has already been established for planar surfaces. Similar simplification is demonstrated for singly curved surfaces and for the subclass of doubly curved surfaces known as generalized cones. These studies help to delineate shape information that can be determined from object boundaries and shape information that can be determined from shading.

1. THE REFLECTANCE MAP

The apparent brightness of a surface element depends on the orientation of that element relative to the viewer and the light sources. Different surface elements of a nonplanar object will reflect different amounts of light towards an observer as a consequence of their differing attitude in space. A smooth opaque object will thus give rise to a shaded image (i.e., one in which brightness varies spatially) even though the object may be illuminated evenly and covered by a surface material with uniform optical properties. Shading provides essential information about the object's shape and has been exploited in machine vision [1-8].

----

* This paper describes research done at the Artificial Intelligence Laboratory of the Massachusetts Institute of Technology. Support for the laboratory's artificial intelligence research was provided in part by the Advanced Research Projects Agency of the Department of Defense under Office of Naval Research Contract N00014-75-C-0643 and in part by the Office of Naval Research under Office of Naval Research Contract N00014-77-0389.

A convenient representation for the relation between scene radiance and surface orientation is the "reflectance map", introduced by Horn [4]. A reflectance map R(p,q) gives scene radiance as a function of surface gradient (p,q) in a viewer-centered coordinate system. If z=f(x,y) is the elevation of the surface above a reference plane lying perpendicular to the optical axis of the imaging system, and if x and y are distances in this plane measured parallel to orthogonal coordinate axes in the image, then p and q are the first partial derivatives of z=f(x,y) with respect to x and y:

$$p = \frac{\partial f(x,y)}{\partial x} \qquad q = \frac{\partial f(x,y)}{\partial y}$$

The reflectance map is usually depicted as a series of contours of constant scene radiance. It can be measured directly using a photogoniometer or indirectly from the image of an object of known shape. Alternatively, a reflectance map may be derived from phenomenological models of surface reflectance or calculated from analytic models of surface microstructure. Recently, a unified approach to the specification of surface reflectance in terms of both incident and reflected beam geometry has been proposed [9]. The result has been called the bidirectional reflectance-distribution function (BRDF). The reflectance map, as defined here, can be derived in terms of the

BRDF [10].

Figure 1 shows the reflectance map corresponding to the phenomenological model of a perfectly diffuse (lambertian) surface which appears equally bright from all viewing directions. This reflectance map is given explicitly as:

$$R(p,q) = \frac{\rho(1+pp_s+qq_s)}{\sqrt{1+p_s^2+q_s^2}\ \sqrt{1+p^2+q^2}}$$

where ρ is a surface reflectance factor and (p_s,q_s) is the gradient pointing in the direction of a single distant point source of illumination. Here, $R(p,q) = \rho\cos(i)$ where i is the angle of incidence. Cos(i) has been expressed as the normalized dot product of the surface normal vector $[p,q,-1]$ and the vector $[p_s,q_s,-1]$ which points in the direction of illumination.

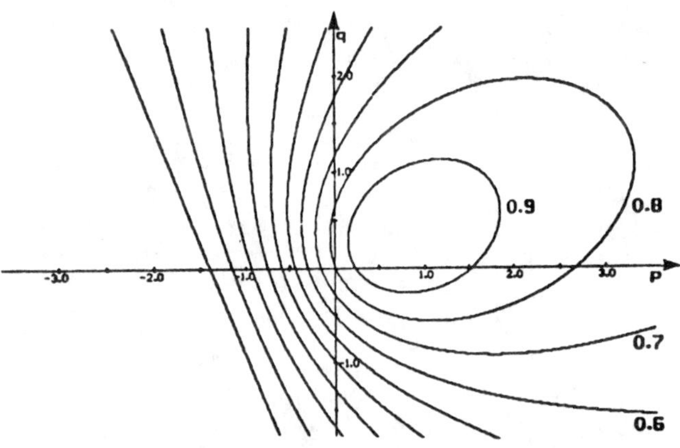

Figure 1 The reflectance map for a lambertian surface illuminated by a single distant point source with $p_s = 0.7$, $q_s = 0.3$ and $\rho = 1$. The reflectance map is plotted as a series of contours spaced 0.1 units apart.

An ideal imaging device produces image irradiance proportional to scene radiance. If I(x,y) is the image irradiance at image point (x,y), then the relevant equation is:

$$I(x,y) = R(p,q). \qquad (1)$$

Until recently, the calculation of shape from shading could be performed only by a rather tedious method involving the direct solution of the above nonlinear first-order partial differential equation, using something like the method of characteristic strip expansion [3]. Progress has been made in the development of an iterative, local method based on relaxation [5]. Both methods, however, embody assumptions about surface curvature.

One can view (1) as a single equation in the two unknowns p and q. In order to determine p and q, additional information must be provided. Knowledge of surface curvature can provide the required additional information.

2. THE IMAGE HESSIAN MATRIX H

Curvature at a point (x,y) on a surface z=f(x,y) can be specified in terms of the two principal radii of curvature r_1 and r_2 and associated directions [11]. Such a specification corresponds to an object-centered definition of surface curvature. It is convenient for image analysis to specify surface curvature in the same viewer-centered coordinate system used to define the reflectance map R(p,q).

Let H be the matrix given by:

$$H = \begin{bmatrix} \frac{\partial^2 f(x,y)}{\partial x^2} & \frac{\partial^2 f(x,y)}{\partial x \partial y} \\ \frac{\partial^2 f(x,y)}{\partial y \partial x} & \frac{\partial^2 f(x,y)}{\partial y^2} \end{bmatrix} \qquad (2)$$

H is the standard Hessian matrix of the function z=f(x,y) [12]. Here, H is called the <u>image Hessian matrix</u> of the surface z=f(x,y).

One can write the (approximate) equation:

$$[dp\ dq]' = H[dx\ dy]' \qquad (3)$$

(' denotes vector transpose) to illustrate that the matrix H relates a movement [dx,dy] in the image to the corresponding change in surface orientation [dp,dq]. If two linearly independent directions $[dx_1,dy_1]$ and $[dx_2,dy_2]$ and the corresponding $[dp_1,dq_1]$ and $[dp_2,dq_2]$ are known, then H is determined by:

$$H = \begin{bmatrix} dp_1 & dp_2 \\ dq_1 & dq_2 \end{bmatrix} \begin{bmatrix} dx_1 & dx_2 \\ dy_1 & dy_2 \end{bmatrix}^{-1} \qquad (4)$$

Image intensity determines one correspondence. By taking partial derivatives of equation (1) with respect to x and y, two equations are obtained which can be written as the single matrix equation:

$$[I_x\ I_y]' = H[R_p\ R_q]' \qquad (5)$$

(subscripts denote partial differentiation). Thus, (4) can be rewritten as:

$$H = \begin{bmatrix} I_x & dp \\ I_y & dq \end{bmatrix} \begin{bmatrix} R_p & dx \\ R_q & dy \end{bmatrix}^{-1} \quad (6)$$

Image intensity determines the change in surface orientation corresponding to a movement in the image in the direction given by $[R_p, R_q]$. This observation is the basis of Horn's original method for determining shape from shading [3]. But, equation (6) still admits an infinite number of solutions. Further constraint on the matrix H is required.

When additional properties of surface curvature are known 'a priori', they can provide the needed constraint on the matrix H. One set of constraints relates to the positive/negative definiteness of H.

> Theorem:
> An object surface $z=f(x,y)$ is convex/concave with respect to the viewer if and only if the corresponding image Hessian matrix H is positive semidefinite/negative semidefinite.

The use of convexity was explored in [5,6]. Another set of constraints relates to the eigenvalue structure of H.

> Definition:
> Let $z=f(x,y)$ be the equation of a smooth surface and let λ_1 and λ_2 be the two eigenvalues of the corresponding Hessian matrix H at image point (x_0,y_0). The surface $z=f(x,y)$ is said to be planar at (x_0,y_0) if and only if $\lambda_1 = \lambda_2 = 0$. The surface $z=f(x,y)$ is said to be singly curved at (x_0,y_0) if and only if one (but not both) of λ_1 and λ_2 is equal to zero. The surface $z=f(x,y)$ is said to be doubly curved at (x_0,y_0) if and only if λ_1 and λ_2 are not equal to zero.

3. PLANAR SURFACES

Objects whose surfaces are planar, as defined above, form the familiar blocksworld polyhedra domain. This is a degenerate case in that both I_x and I_y are everywhere zero. Horn has shown, however, that whenever at least three planes meet at a point, the orientation of each plane can be determined using the reflectance map $R(p,q)$ [4]. The technique combines the quantitative approach to interpreting line drawings developed by Mackworth [13] with the additional constraint provide by image intensity.

4. SINGLY CURVED SURFACES

An important class of surfaces are those that have the property that, through every point on the surface, there passes at least one straight line lying entirely on it. In differential geometry, such a surface is called a ruled surface. The straight line lying entirely on the surface is called a ruling. If a ruled surface has the additional property that all points on a given ruling have the same tangent plane, then the surface is called a developable surface (or a torse) [11]. Huffman charmingly refers to developable surfaces as "paper" surfaces and proposes that such surfaces possess a complexity that is midway between that of a completely general surface and that of a plane surface [14].

The notion of a singly curved surface, as defined above, is equivalent to that of a developable surface (except that planar surfaces, while certainly developable, will not be considered singly curved). It can now be shown that, from an image analysis point of view, singly curved surfaces do indeed possess a complexity that is between that of a completely general surface and that of a plane surface.

For surfaces expressed in the form $z=f(x,y)$, the equation:

$$\frac{\partial^2 f(x,y)}{\partial^2 x} \frac{\partial^2 f(x,y)}{\partial^2 y} = \left| \frac{\partial^2 f(x,y)}{\partial x \partial y} \right|^2 \quad (7)$$

is the differential equation characterizing developable surfaces. In the current notation, this equation is equivalent to the equation:

$$\det|H| = 0 \quad (8)$$

Equation (8) is satisfied at an image point (x,y) if and only if a least one of the eigenvalues of the corresponding H is zero at (x,y). For convenience, assume that at least one of λ_1 and λ_2 is nonzero at each image point (x,y). (If both eigenvalues of H are zero for all image points (x,y), then the equation $z=f(x,y)$ describes a plane). Thus, a nonplanar surface $z=f(x,y)$ is developable if and only if it is singly curved.

Let $z=f(x,y)$ be a singly curved surface. Suppose that a point (x_0,y_0) in the image is known to have gradient (p_0,q_0). Then, the Hessian matrix H at (x_0,y_0) is completely determined. H is given as the matrix product:

$$H = \begin{bmatrix} \cos(\alpha) & -\sin(\alpha) \\ \sin(\alpha) & \cos(\alpha) \end{bmatrix} \begin{bmatrix} \lambda & 0 \\ 0 & 0 \end{bmatrix} \begin{bmatrix} \cos(\alpha) & \sin(\alpha) \\ -\sin(\alpha) & \cos(\alpha) \end{bmatrix} \quad (9)$$

where

$$\lambda = \frac{\sqrt{I_x^2 + I_y^2}}{R_p\cos(\alpha) + R_q\sin(\alpha)}$$

and $$\tan(\alpha) = \frac{I_y}{I_x} .$$

As above, I_x and I_y denote the first partial derivatives of $I(x,y)$ at (x_0,y_0) and R_p and R_q denote the first partial derivatives of $R(p,q)$ at (p_0,q_0).

Given any initial image point (x_0,y_0) known to have gradient (p_0,q_0), equations (3) and (9) can be used to trace out an arbitrary family of curves on the surface $z=f(x,y)$. For singly curved surfaces, one is not confined to tracing out characteristics in the direction $[R_p,R_q]$ as required by Horn's original method for obtaining shape from shading [3].

The fact that H has one zero eigenvalue means that there is one direction of movement in the image which results in no change to surface orientation. This direction is orthogonal to the direction α determined by the vector $[I_x,I_y]$. The component of any movement $[dx,dy]$ perpendicular to $[I_x,I_y]$ is in the direction of a ruling on the surface and thus does not cause a change in gradient (p,q). The component of $[dx,dy]$ in the direction $[I_x,I_y]$ causes a change in gradient $[dp,dq]$ in the direction α where the "scale factor" for that change is given by λ.

The gradients (p,q) corresponding to points on an arbitrary singly curved surface $z=f(x,y)$ are constrained to lie on a one-parameter curve in p-q space. This illustrates that singly curved surfaces possess a complexity midway between that of a planar surface, where surface points map into a single point in p-q space, and that of a completely general surface, where surface points map into a two-parameter region in p-q space.

Figure 2 is the image of a right circular cone of base radius b and height a synthesized using the reflectance map of figure 1. (For this example, $a = 2b$.) The gradients corresponding to points on a right circular cone lie on the one-parameter curve in p-q space given parametrically by:

$$p = \tan(t) \tag{10}$$

$$q = \frac{b}{a}\frac{1}{\cos(t)}$$

where $-\pi/2 < t < \pi/2$. The parameter t has a physical interpretation. The circular cross-section of the cone can be represented, in cylindrical coordinates, by the function $r(\theta) = 1$, where θ measures angular position about the y-axis. If θ is chosen so that $\theta = 0$ points in the direction of the viewer, then the parameter t in (10) and (11) is this angle θ.

Figure 2 The synthesized image of a right circular cone, with height equal to twice the base radius and axis parallel to the image plane. The surface reflectance is lambertian with a single distant point source at $p_s = 0.7$ and $q_s = 0.3$.

Figure 3 shows the curve in p-q space determined by (10) and (11) superimposed on the reflectance map used to generate figure 2. There exists a 1-1 continuous mapping between any horizontal intensity profile from figure 2 and the curve in p-q space determined by (10) and (11). Thus, finding the point (p,q) corresponding to any image intensity point $I(x,y) = \alpha$ from figure 2 simplifies to the problem of determining reflectance map values on the curve given by (10) and (11) for which $R(p,q) = \alpha$. Since all 1-1 continuous mappings are monotonic, multiple solutions can be resolved by systematically scanning each image line from left to right. The required ratio b/a can be determined from the boundary contour in figure 2. For singly curved surfaces, image analysis using the reflectance map is straightforward.

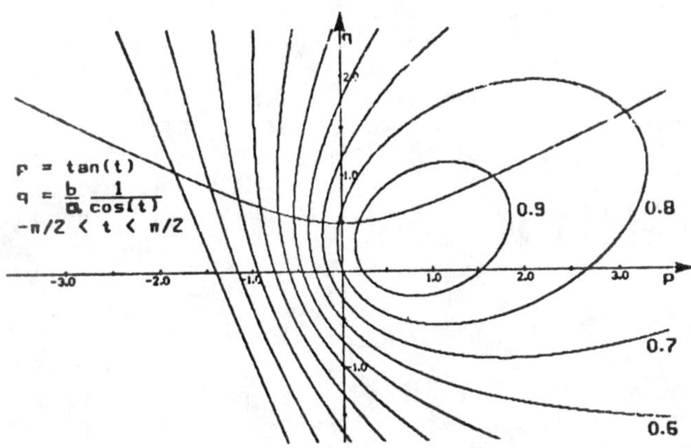

Figure 3 The one-parameter curve in p-q space corresponding to points on the cone of figure 2.

5. GENERALIZED CONES

A generalized cone is defined to be the surface swept out by moving a simple smooth cross-section $r(\theta)$ along a straight axis Λ, at the same time magnifying or contracting it in a smoothly varying way [15]. The concept of a generalized cone has its genesis in the generalized cylinder representation of Agin and Binford [16]. There, generalized cylinders were used as a convenient representation scheme for describing complex shapes. In [15], however, the generalized cone emerges not so much as a representation scheme but as an interpretation that is forced if one tries to develop a theory of how to infer the shape of objects from their silhouettes.

Some additional terminology is required. Let $h(\lambda)$ be the axial scaling function, where λ denotes distance along the Λ axis. The angle ψ between the axis Λ and a plane containing a cross-section is called the eccentricity of the cone. If $\psi=\pi/2$, then the cone called a <u>right generalized cone</u>. In addition, if the cross-section is circular, then the cone is called a <u>right generalized cone with circular cross-section</u>.

Generalized cones are, in general, doubly curved. The curvature of a generalized cone, however, conveniently decouples in its object-centered representation. For appropriate viewing conditions, this decoupling carries over to images of generalized cones. These images can be analyzed "almost" as if the surface were singly curved, as will now be shown.

Consider a right generalized cone with circular cross-section. Without loss of generality, one can assume that the axis Λ passes through the center of the circle. For the moment, one additional assumption is needed. Assume that the axis Λ is parallel to the image plane. For convenience, let the image X-Y axes be chosen so that Λ coincides with the image Y-axis. Distance along the Λ axis is then equal to distance along the Y-axis so that the axial scaling function can be denoted as $h(y)$. Further, let the circular cross-section be denoted by $r(\theta) = 1$, where $\theta = 0$ points in the direction of the viewer. The gradients corresponding to points on such a generalized cone lie in the two-parameter region in p-q space given parametrically by:

$$p = \tan(\theta) \tag{12}$$

$$q = \frac{-h'(y)}{\cos(\theta)} \tag{13}$$

where $h'(y)$ denotes the derivative of $h(y)$ with respect to y and θ varies between $-\pi/2$ and $\pi/2$.

Figure 2 was an example of a right generalized cone with circular cross-section. There, $h'(y) = -b/a$. In general, (12) and (13) define a two-parameter region in p-q space. The relevant observation, however, is that when the axis Λ is parallel to the viewing plane, the value of $h'(\lambda)$ can always be determined directly from the boundary contour. In this case, finding the (p,q) corresponding to a given image intensity point $I(x,y) = \alpha$ simplifies to a two step process. First, for the particular y, determine $h'(y)$ as the rate of change of object radius with respect to y (equivalently, as 1/2 the rate of change of object diameter with respect to y) at the object boundary along image line y. Second, as in the case of a singly curved object, scan a left to right profile to determine the correct reflectance map point on the curve given by (12) and (13).

Figure 4 illustrates. Here, the axial scaling function is a sinusoid while the cross-section remains circular. Figure 5 superimposes a collection of the curves given by (12) and (13) on the reflectance map used to generate figure 4. The surface depicted in figure 4 is everywhere doubly curved. Yet from the given viewing direction, the curvature decouples so that, from an image analysis point of view, the surface behaves as if it were single curved.

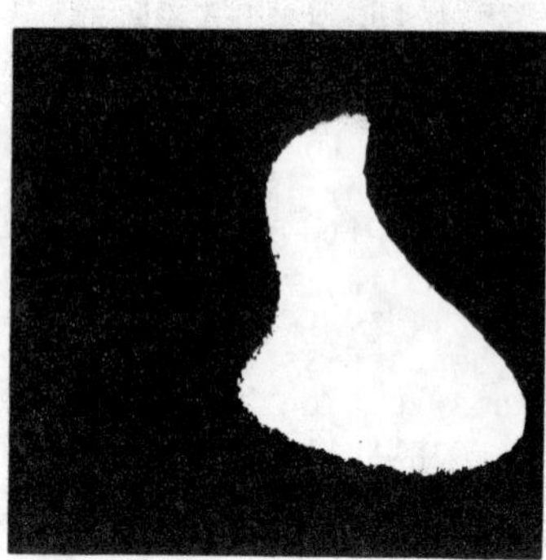

Figure 4 The synthesized image of a right generalized cone with circular cross-section and axis Λ parallel to the image plane. The axial scaling function h(y) is a sinusoid. The surface reflectance is lambertian with a single distant point source at $p_s = 0.7$ and $q_s = 0.3$.

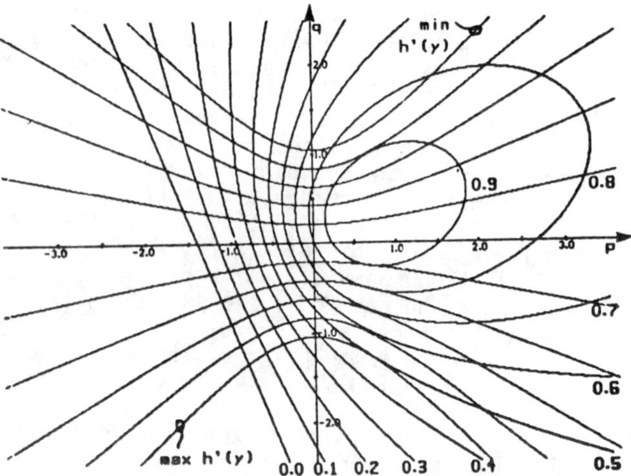

Figure 5 The region in p-q space corresponding to points on the right generalized cone of figure 4, plotted as a family of curves. The included region in p-q space lies below the curve determined by the minimum value of h'(y) and above the curve determined by the maximum value of h'(y),

Suppose now that Λ is not parallel to the image plane. Nevertheless, the image X-Y axes can still be chosen so that the projection of Λ coincides with the image Y-axis. Let the angle between the Λ axis and the viewing plane be ϕ (measured so that positive ϕ implies that Λ is tilted towards the viewer). In this case, distance along the Y-axis is the foreshortened distance along Λ given by:

$$y = \lambda\cos(\phi)$$

so that
$$h'(\lambda) = \cos(\phi)h'(y)$$

The gradients corresponding to points on such a generalized cone lie in the two-parameter region in p-q space given parametrically by:

$$p = \frac{\sin(\theta)}{\cos(\phi)[\cos(\theta) - \sin(\phi)h'(y)]} \tag{14}$$

$$q = -\tan(\phi) + \frac{-h'(y)}{\cos(\phi)[\cos(\theta)-\sin(\phi)h'(y)]} \tag{15}$$

where h'(y) and θ are as before. If ϕ is known, then one can proceed as before, with only a slight complication in the mathematical expressions required. If ϕ is unknown, two difficulties arise. First, without knowing ϕ, the curve generated by (14) and (15) cannot be determined. Second, without knowing ϕ, the image profile corresponding to a fixed value of λ cannot be determined. At best, it is possible to estimate the value of ϕ which is most consistent with the hypothesis that the image corresponds to a right generalized cone with circular cross-section.

Greater difficulty arises when the cross-section is allowed to be an arbitrary smooth convex function. Roughly speaking, it becomes impossible to resolve the trade-off between axis tilt and cross-section shape using the intensity values recorded in a single view. Let the cross-section function be given, in cylindrical coordinates, by $r = r(\theta)$. To avoid unnecessary complication, suppose once again that the axis Λ is parallel to the viewing plane. The gradients corresponding to points on such a generalized cone lie in the two-parameter region in p-q space given parametrically by

$$p = \frac{r(\theta)\sin(\theta) - r'(\theta)\cos(\theta)}{r(\theta)\cos(\theta) + r'(\theta)\sin(\theta)} \tag{16}$$

$$q = -h'(\lambda)\frac{r(\theta)}{r(\theta)\cos(\theta)+r'(\theta)\sin(\theta)} \tag{17}$$

where $h'(\lambda)$ denotes the derivative of $h(\lambda)$ with respect to λ and $r'(\theta)$ denotes the derivative of $r(\theta)$ with respect to θ.

For an arbitrary smooth convex $r(\theta)$, it is not necessarily true that the "left" boundary contour corresponds to $\theta = -\pi/2$ and the "right" boundary contour to $\theta = \pi/2$. If the left boundary contour corresponds to the value θ_L (where $-\pi < \theta_L < 0$) and the right boundary contour corresponds to the value θ_R (where $0 < \theta_R < \pi$), then $h'(\lambda)$ is given by:

$$h'(\lambda) = \frac{\text{rate of change of object diameter}}{\sin(-\theta_L) + \sin(\theta_R)}$$

The information required to determine $h'(\lambda)$ is still contained in the boundary contour but it can be used only if the values θ_L and θ_R are known. The values of θ_L and θ_R, in turn, depend on $r(\theta)$. Thus, although the decoupling between $h(\lambda)$ and $r(\theta)$ exists in the cone's object-centered representation, it is not possible to discover this decoupling from the object silhouette.

6. CONCLUSIONS

Methods for determining shape from the intensity values recorded in a single view embody assumptions about surface curvature. Such assumptions may arise from an analysis of boundary contour or from an analysis of intensity gradations across sections of smooth surface. Reflectance map techniques help make such assumptions explicit. When properties of surface curvature are known 'a priori', they can be exploited in image analysis.

7. ACKNOWLEDGEMENTS

The author would like to thank Berthold K.P. Horn for his help and intellectual guidance. Mike Brady, Anni Bruss, Mark Lavin, Tomas Lozano, Alan Mackworth, David Marr and Patrick Winston provided useful comments and criticisms.

The author would also like to thank Theresa Fong for aid in the preparation of this manuscript.

8. REFERENCES

[1] Diggelen, J. van, "A Photometric Investigation of the Slopes and Heights of the Ranges of Hills in the Maria of the Moon", Bulletin of the Astronomical Institute of the Netherlands, July, 1951.

[2] Rindfleisch, T., "Photometric method for Lunar Topography", Photogrammetric Engineering, pp. 262-276, March, 1966.

[3] Horn, B.K.P., "Obtaining Shape from Shading Information", in The Psychology of Computer Vision, P.H. Winston (ed.), McGraw-Hill, pp. 115-155, New York, 1975.

[4] Horn, B.K.P., "Understanding Image Intensities", Artificial Intelligence, Vol. 8, No. 11, pp. 201-231, 1977.

[5] Woodham, R.J., "A Cooperative Algorithm for Determining Surface Orientation from a Single View", IJCAI-77, pp. 635-641, August, 1977.

[6] Woodham, R.J., "Reflectance Map Techniques for Analyzing Surface Defects in Metal Castings", AI-TR-457, M.I.T. Artificial Intelligence Laboratory, M.I.T., Cambridge, Mass., June, 1978.

[7] Woodham, R.J., "Photometric Stereo: A Reflectance Map Technique for Determining Surface Orientation from Image Intensity", Proc. SPIE 22nd Technical Symposium, Vol. 155, San Diego, Calif., August, 1978.

[8] Horn, B.K.P., Woodham, R.J. & Silver, W.N., "Determining Shape and Reflectance Using Multiple Images", AI-Memo-490, M.I.T. Artificial Intelligence Laboratory, M.I.T., Cambridge, Mass., August, 1978.

[9] Nicodemus, F.E., Richmond, J.C. & Hisa, J.J., "Geometrical Considerations and Nomenclature for Reflectance", NBS Monograph 160, National Bureau of Standards, Washington, D.C., October, 1977.

[10] Horn, B.K.P. & Sjoberg, R.W., "Calculating the Reflectance Map", AI-Memo-498, M.I.T. Artificial Intelligence Laboratory, M.I.T., Cambridge, Mass., October, 1978.

[11] Kepr, B., "Differential Geometry", in Survey of Applicable Mathematics, K. Rectorys (ed.), M.I.T. Press, pp. 298-373, Cambridge, 1969.

[12] Luenberger, D.G., Introduction to Linear and Nonlinear Programming, Addison-Wesley, 1973.

[13] Mackworth, A.K., "Interpreting Pictures of Polyhedral Scenes", Artificial Intelligence, Vol. 4, pp. 121-137, 1973.

[14] Huffman, D.A., "Curvature and Creases: A Primer on Paper", Proc. Conf. Computer Graphics, Pattern Recognition and Data Structures, pp. 360-370, May, 1975.

[15] Marr, D. "Analysis of Occluding Contour", Proc. R. Soc. Lond. B., 197, pp. 441-475, 1977.

[16] Agin, G.J. & Binford, T.O., "Computer Description of Curved Objects", Proc. 3rd IJCAI, pp. 629-640, August, 1973.

PLAN-GUIDED ANALYSIS OF NOISY DYNAMIC IMAGES

Masahiko Yachida, Motozo Ikeda and Saburo Tsuji
Department of Control Enginering, Osaka University
Toyonaka, Osaka 560, Japan

A wide variety of processes in biology, medicine, or engineering are recorded on video tape or cine film as moving images. Computer analysis of a moving image, however, requires too much time, if whole areas of a large number of consecutive frames are examined in detail. This paper describes how a plan-guided analysis, which utilizes both a priori and acquired knowledge about the dynamic image, can efficiently and correctly extract necessary information from the video tape or cine film image. It first analyzes a coarse picture and makes a plan, which is then used in the next fine data collection and processing of the record; the plan specifies (1) frames to be sampled, (2) regions to be analyzed, covering important portions of the dynamic image, and (3) suitable operators and their parameters to be applied to the regions. The effectiveness of the method is shown by an example that analyzes a sequence of noisy radiographic images, a cine-angiogram, which needs to reliably detect curves of specified properties in a large number of frames.

1. INTRODUCTION

A wide variety of processes observed in experiments of medicine, biology, or engineering are recorded on video tape or cine film as moving images. Analysis of these images, however, have been tedious tasks of human beings; they must keep watching a large number of frames to point out feature patterns and measure their parameters. In recent years, computer analysis of moving images [1,2], such as motion analysis of hearts [3,4] or micro organisms [5,6], have been studied to reduce the human labor and extract more reliable information from the records in short time.

Because of a large amount of information content of a moving image, too much computing time is spent if whole areas of consecutive frames are examined in detail. Although a special parallel processor system could significantly reduce the computing time for preprocessing, feature extraction, or change detection, we should avoid to waste the computing power for unnecessary processing. Analysis of moving images does not require all information in the records, but only a small fractions are utilized; for example, we analyze only small subareas covering moving objects for tracking, or abruptly changing frames are more carefully examined than almost still ones for motion pattern analysis. Most motion analyzers have been designed to save the computation by utilizing models of objects in already analyzed frames to predict their locations or shapes in the current frame [1,2].

We have extended these ideas to organize a new system, a plan-guided analyzer of moving images. The plan-guided analysis is not a new idea, but has been studied to analyze complex static pictures; for example, identification of human faces [7] and analysis of chest radiographic images [8]. However, the idea is most effectively applied to analysis of a long sequence of high resolution pictures, because the computing time is of primary importance and one can significantly reduce it by utilizing the contextural information about the images in consecutive frames. The feature of our system is to fully utilize its knowledge, both a priori and acquired knowledge, about the dynamic image so as to extract correct information from the record at an extremely low computation cost. A priori knowledge contains general properties such as 'the moving objects are dark and blob-like.', which is useful to design efficient procedures. However it lacks quantitative information about a particular record, such as locations, velocities, brightness levels, and shapes of objects. The analyzer, therefore, examines a small number of low resolution pictures of the record to collect such information and make a coarse model, a sketch, of the process, by which it can estimate which frame and what regions in it are worthy examining, or what type of a feature extractor is most effective at each point in the regions. Now, the system makes a plan, specifying (1) frames to be sampled, (2) regions to be examined, and (3) effective feature extractors to be applied. Since more accurate knowledge is acquired as a result of this plan-guided analysis of a frame, the coarse model is replaced with a fine and more reliable one, describing exact properties of the objects in the current frame, which is then used to make a more effective plan of sampling and analyzing next pictures. By iterating this process, planning, analyzing and updating, the system constructs a final model of the process, containing all information required.

The purpose of utilizing the plan is not only for minimizing the computation cost, but also for increasing reliability of extracted information. Thus, the plan selects feature extractors and their parameters, considered to be most reliable, at each point. However, it is not easy to find the correct feature at every point in a noisy dynamic image such as a sequence of radiographic images. Optimization methods [9,10] are known as useful to search noisy pictures for curves or regions of specified properties. We can apply one of them to the dynamic image by embedding the properties of the object in a figure of merits. The optimization method, however, requires too much memory space and computing time, especially when a global shape property such as smoothness over a wide range is speicified, since we are forced to solve it as a high dimensional non-serial optimization problem. We, therefore, propose an improved method which utilizes an efficient search for the optimal sequence of linear segments instead of the already known inefficient search for the optimal series of pixels.

2. HARDWARE SYSTEM

Fig.1 shows a block diagram of the hardware system. The computer used is aHP-2108A, a 16bit machine with 32kw of memory, a disc (15Mbytes), a printer/plotter, a storage tube display and three terminals under a multi-user operating system. A picture memory, 256kbytes 800nsec/2bytes cycle time, is connected to the computer. We utilize this memory as a flexible buffer for video input and output from/to a VTR (video tape recorder), a TV camera, and a color display. The memory is also used as high speed random access files of dynamic images; a software subsystem swaps picture data in a segment of the memory for necessary data in disc files, on the basis of first in first out [11].

Our system is provided with a computer controlled film projector, which selects a specified frame by sending 35mm film at a rate of 15 frames/sec. At present, the TV camera is used as the transducer of the projected image, which is transformed into a 256 by 256 6bit digital picture.

3. ANALYSIS OF MOTION PATTERNS

3.1 ANALYSIS OF CINE-ANGIOGRAMS

In recent years, people have studied computer analysis of a cine-angiogram, a cine film record of a radiographic image of a beating heart in which Xray opaque dye is intermittently injected through a catheter. Their primary interest is in measuring temporal change in the volume of the heart; the computer detects the internal surface of the heart in each frame, and calculates the volume by utilizing a three dimensional model of a heart.

In this paper, a more advanced analysis is described, which detects both internal and external surfaces of the heart, and measures the spatial and temporal change in thickness of the heart wall, which gives us important measure of heart diseases.

The usual methods detect a boundary of a left ventricle by rather simple procedures; for example, an adaptive threshold method detects candidates points for the boundary, and then a simple statistical method examines their neighbors to fit line segments to the boundary [3]. A reason why such a level detecting method is applicable is that the film is taken and developed so as to show rather sharp contrast in gray values between the light ventricle and the dark background. Such a photographic noise reduction technique, however, is not applicable to a cine-angiogram for analyzing a heart wall, which has usually intermediate gray values in our radiographic images. As a result, the pictures contain much noise, masking small gray value changes on or near the surfaces. Moreover, an accurate detection of both surfaces is needed, since small errors in the locations of points on a surface cause considerable errors in the thickness measurement of the heart wall.

Another important problem, which has been already discussed, is the computation efficiency. The computer needs to examine a large number of high resolution pictures, because the heart wall occupies only a small fraction of each horizontal scan of the input pictures.

3.2 PLAN-GUIDED ANALYSIS OF WALL THICKNESS

We have developed a plan-guided analyzer for detecting both surfaces of a wall of a left ventricle and measuring temporal changes in thickness at each portion of the wall. The features of the system are as follows: (1) detection of edge points in the first frame is guided by a plan which specifies regions to be examined and promising feature extractors to be used, (2) smooth boundaries of the wall are obtained by an efficinet search method, and (3) another plan is utilized to analyze consecutive frames; it selects next frame to be sampled and guides the analyzer so as to examine it in a much more efficient manner than the first frame.

The analysis is divided into the following five phases.
(1) planning of feature extraction of first frame.
(2) search for smooth boundaries.
(3) selection of next sampling frame.
(4) analysis of consecutive frames.
(5) measurement of thickness.

3.3 INPUT PICTURES

Input of the system is a sequence of Xray images of a left ventricular chamber recorded on 35mm cine film at a rate of 60 frames/sec; thus, a record of one beating cycle contains about 50 frames. A frame is converted into a 256 by 256 6bit digital picture. Fig.2 shows an example and the result of applying a simple 3 by 3 gradient operator to it. The picture contains much noise, especially significant non-uniformity of gray values is observed in the ventricular chamber near the internal surface, where muscles and tissues attached on the surface generate much noise.

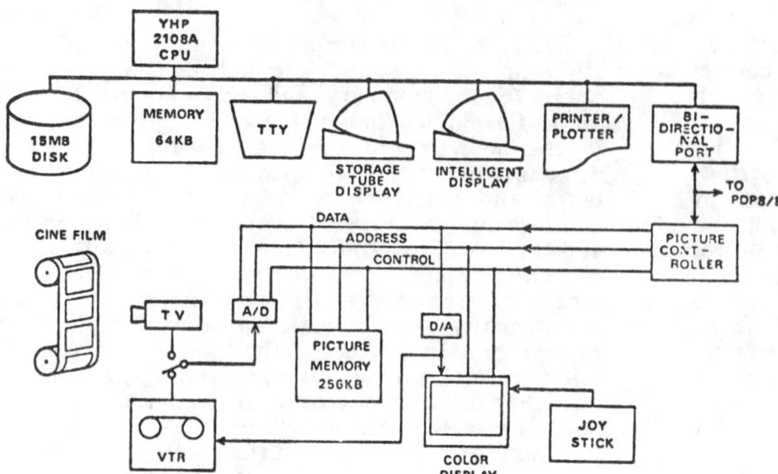

Fig. 1. Block diagram of hardware system.

Contrast of gray values between both sides of each surface is very low, since the gray values in the wall gradually increase, as the mean, with the distance from the external surface.

3.4 PLANNING OF FEATURE EXTRACTION

Because of the low picture quality of a cine-angiogram, such as low contrast and much noise, a level detecting method cannot reliably find a heart wall. If we apply a gradient operator to a small area, say a 3 by 3 window, around every point in the picture, then the enhanced noise by the operator masks the boundaries of the wall. In order to reliably detect edge points in a noisy picture, edge features should be extracted from averaged gray values in some larger local areas. Since the heart wall is a narrow region, a group of paired rectangular areas of different directions shown in Fig.3 are used as the smoothing areas. A pair of local areas, of which absolute difference of average gray values is largest in the group, are selected at every point in the picture. Each selected pair gives reliable features of the edge at that point; the edge strength and direction are decided from the already computed maximum difference and the direction of the selected areas. When this procedure is applied to a point on the boundary of the wall, it automatically selects parallelly directed areas to the boundary, therefore its output is less sensitive to the noise and is not blurred by the averaging.

This method, however, requires too much time. If differences of averaged gray values in a pair of 10 by 1 areas are computed and compared for 12 different directions at every point in a 256 by 256 picture, then a minicomputer HP-2108A spends about one hour for the computation.

We, therfore, have developed a plan-guided edge detection method to shorten the computation time. The system first compresses a 256 by 256 original

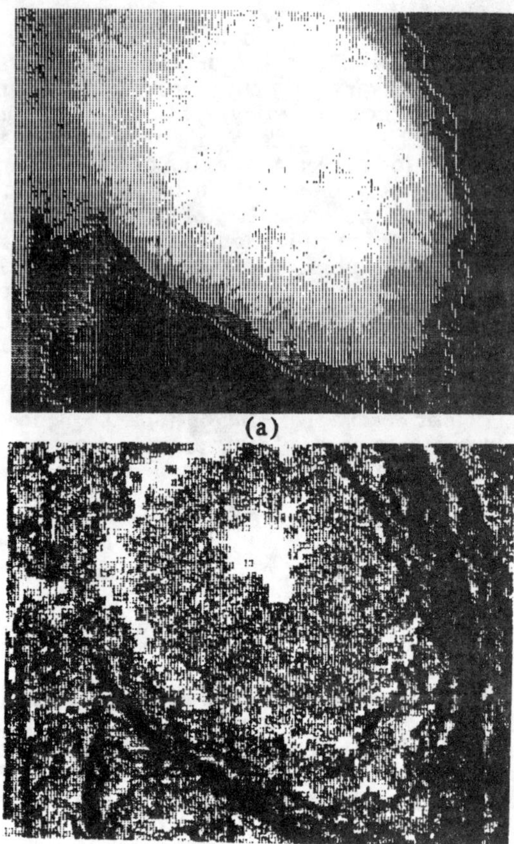

Fig. 2. (a) An input picture.
(b) The result of applying 3x3 gradient operator.

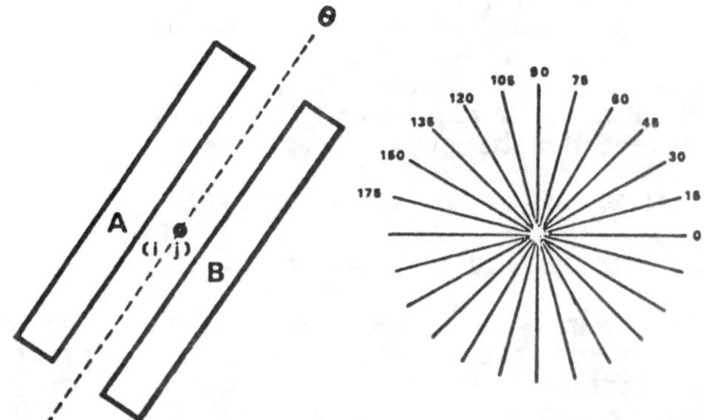

Fig. 3. Smoothing areas for edge detection and their directions.

picture into a small picture of 64 by 64 picture. Each point in the small picture is the averaged value of the 16 points in a 4x4 neighborhoods in the original picture. Applying a simple 3 by 3 gradient operator to every point in the compressed picture and thresholding it, the system decides (1) analysis regions, regions to be examined further, and (2) an approximate direction of an edge at each point in

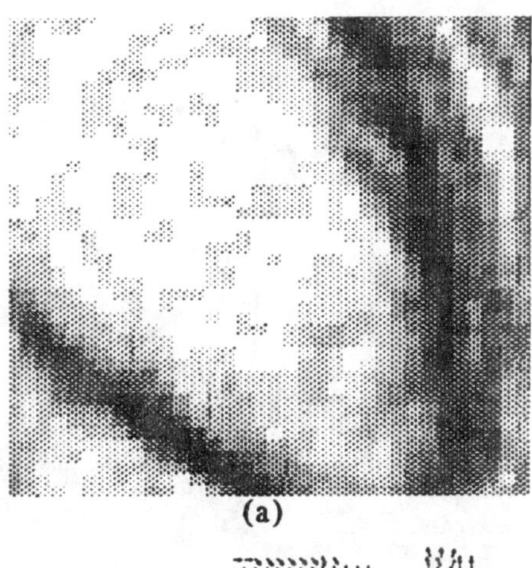

(a)

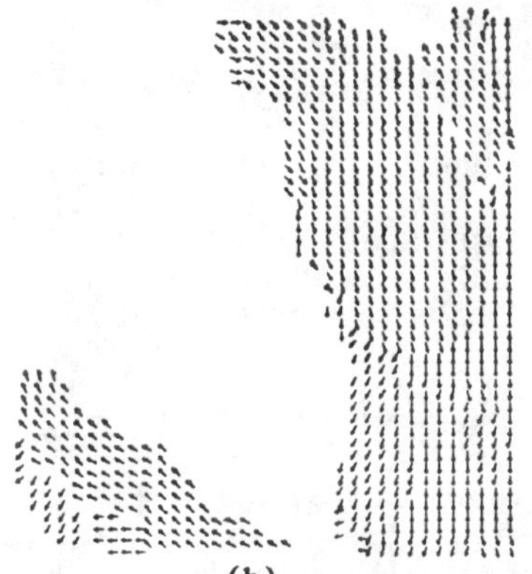

(b)

Fig. 4. (a) An edge picture of a compressed picture of Fig.2 (a). (b) Analysis regions specifying directions of edges.

them. Fig.4 (a) shows edges detected in the compressed picture by the gradient operator. This picture is less noisy than Fig.2 (b), the result of applying the same operator to the original picture, because of noise reduction by the averaging in the windows. A plan of the next edge detection is described as a map containing the analysis region and the directions of edges in them, as shown in Fig.4 (b). The analyzer utilizes this map to efficiently find features; an edge feature at each point in the analysis regions is detected by a pair of rectanglar areas perpendicular to the direction. Since the analysis regions occupy 1/3 of the input picture (we could considerably reduce them by using a higher threshold value or utilizing more heuristics) and only one selected edge direction from 12 variations is examined at each point, the computation for edge finding by this method is (1/3)x(1/12)=1/36 of that without the plan. The gradient operation to each point in the compressed image is iterated about 4000 times, 1/16 of that required for the original picture, and the operation is much simpler, therefore its computation cost is also inexpensive. The result of applying the plan-guided edge detecting method to Fig.2 (a) is shown in Fig.5, which seems much better than Fig.2 (b).

3.5 EFFICENT SEARCH FOR SMOOTH BOUNDARIES

Next phase to the edge detection is to recover the outer and inner boundaries of the heart wall in the analysis regions. Since the edge picture still contains considerable noise, and since precise detection of the boundaries is needed, usual curve followers are not applicable. Optimization methods are known as useful to find a curve of specified properties in a noisy picture. They embed the property into a figure of merit and search for the curve as a sequence of consecutive points which minimize the figure of merit, by a dynamic programming technique [9] or a heuristic method [10]. Many practical examples, and also this analysis of the heart wall, need to find smooth curves over a wide range, since small unevenness on a detected curve is considered as statistically meaningless.

In order to find a smooth curve hidden in noise, the usual methods embed a property of smoothness of a curve into a part of the figure of merit as a sum of a curvature at each point. If the smoothness over a wide range is embedded, then we are forced to sove it as a high dimensional non-serial optimization problem, which requires too much computing time and memory space.

A different approach has been studied to avoid this difficulty [12]. Since the curve to be detected is smooth, we can approximate it with a sequence of linear segments. We embed the smoothness over a wide range of a sequence of linear segments connecting points x_1 , x_2 ,..., x_n into a figure of merit $c(x_1, x_2, \ldots, x_n)$ as

$$C(x_1, x_2, \ldots, x_n) = \sum_{i=1}^{n} e(x_i) + k_1 \sum_{i=1}^{n-1} |\theta(x_{i-1}, x_i) - \theta(x_i, x_{i+1})| \quad (1)$$

Where $e(x_m, x_n)$ is a mean of edge strength along the segment connecting x_m and x_n , $\theta(x_m, x_n)$ is the inclination angle of the segment, and k_1 is a constant.

Fig. 5. Result of the plan-guided edge detection.

Now, we apply this method to detection of the wall boundaries in the edge picture. Starting points of the search are decided from a priori knowledge about the boundaries; the both boundaries have directions between 0 ° and 90 ° at the upper part of the ventricle. A sequence of 10 successive edge points on a ridge of such a direction are selected as starting points.

We apply a heuristic search to find a solution of this optimization problem, and the results are successful to many input pictures. The search, however, sometimes fails, when the outer and inner boundaries are close together at the end of the expansion period of the ventricle. Since the edge strength on the inner boundary is much larger than that of the outer one, a search for the external surface happens to cross the wall and follow the inner boundary. In order to avoid this difficulty, we utilize another knowledge that gray values on the outer boundary are darker than those on the inner one. Thus, we use a figure of merit evaluating edge strength, smoothness, and gray values, as follows.

$$C(x_1,\ldots,x_n)=\sum_{i=1}^{n}e(x_i)+k_1\sum_{i=1}^{n-1}|\theta(x_{i-1},x_i)-\theta(x_i,x_{i-1})|+k_2\sum_{i=1}^{n}|g(x_i)-G| \qquad (2)$$

Where $g(x_m, x_n)$ is the mean gray value of points on the line segment connecting x_m and x_n, G is a mean gray value of a group of candidates for starting points, and k_1, k_2 are constants. Fig.5 shows an example of results obtained by this method. The detected boundaries are arranged into a model which guides the selection and analysis of consecutive frames.

3.6 SELECTION OF FRAMES FOR ANALYSIS

In order to reduce computation for the consecutive frames, we effectively utilize the model obtained from the result of the previous analysis. First of all, narrow analysis regions are selected on the both sides of the detected boundaries, as shown in Fig.6. At present, the width of the regions is set at a length of 7 pixels. We can save the computation by examining only picture data in these regions, which are much smaller than those used for the analysis of the first frame.

As mentioned before, the system should select frames worthy examining from a great number of frames in the record. Because of intermittent movement of the heart, it is reasonable that the analyzer skips over consecutive frames in which little changes from the previously analyzed one are observed. We use a simple temporal differnce method to measure the degrees of changes. If the wall boundaries move to some extent, then there exist significant changes in the analysis regions. Sums of a gray value change at each point in the regions from that of the previously analyzed one are computed for a coming input frame, and if at least one of the sums is greater than a threshold, then the frame is analyzed, else it is skipped. Utilizing this criterion for sampling, the system analyzes about 1/3 of frames in a record as a mean, and only 1/16 at the end of the contraction or expansion period, when a wall shows very slow movement.

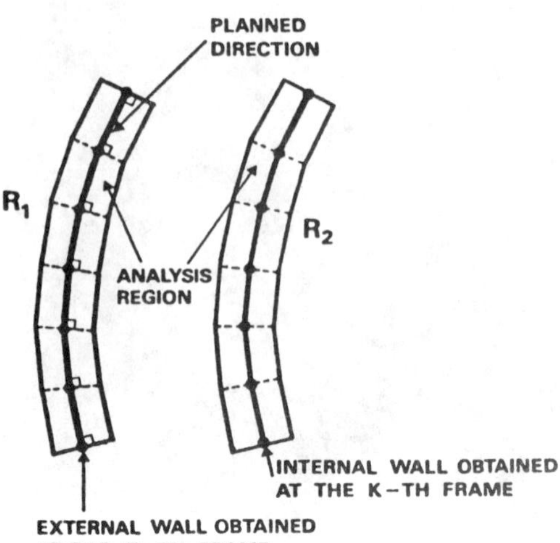

Fig. 6. Analysis regions for consecutive frames.

3.7 ANALYSIS OF CONSECUTIVE FRAMES

Edge detection and search for the boundaries in the sampled frame is guided by the model of the previously analyzed frame. The analyzer measures an edge component parallel to the nearest boundary at every point in the analysis regions. Then it searches each analysis region for a boundary using the figure of merit of (2).

3.8 MEASUREMENT OF WALL THICKNESS

In order to measure the dynamic behavior of the heart wall, we establish a correspondence between portions of the wall in successvely analyzed frames. Those areas having tissues or mustles on the internal surface of the heart are useful for finding the correspondence. Therefore, we first determine such areas having characteristic gray-level distribution along the internal boundary in the first frame. The variance of gray levels in the local area of 7x7 points is examined at every point along the internal boundary. Then, the areas where the variance of gray levels in it is the local maxima in its neighborhood and is larger than a certain threshold are selected as the areas to make correspondence.

The selected areas are then matched to those along the internal boundary in the next analyzed frame by a simple correlation method. The thickness of the heart wall is measured at these corresponded points in each frame. Fig. 7 shows the result of thickness measurement at those corresponded points of the internal boundary between the frames.

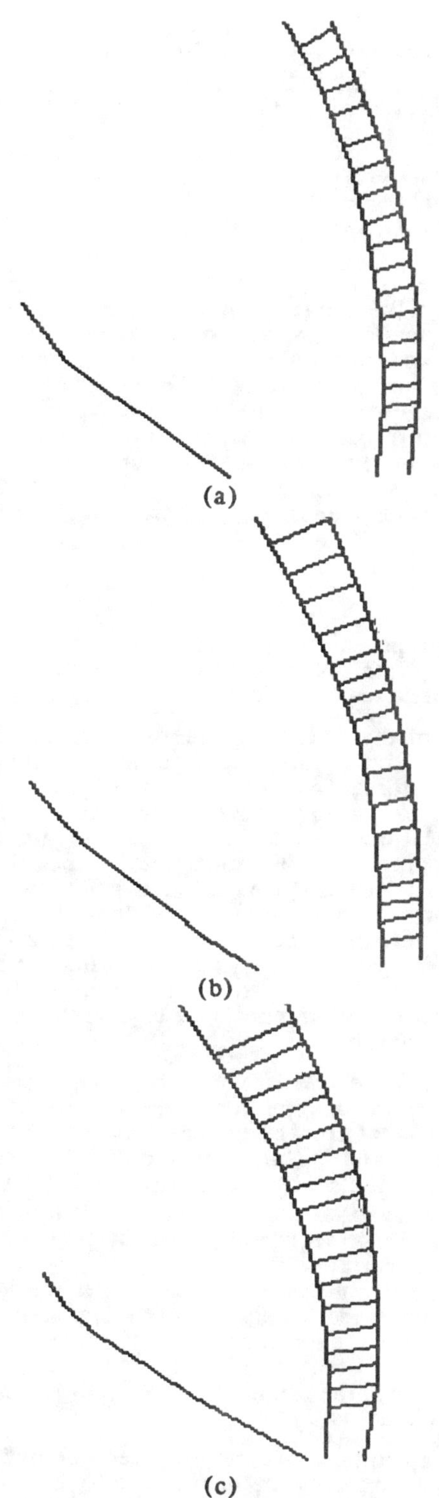

Fig. 7. Thickness of a heart wall in (a) 10th, (b) 26th and (c) 34th frames.

4. CONCLUSION

The plan-guided analysis is very effective to extract correct information from noisy dynamic images such the cine-angiogram. The system is efficient since plans select (1) frames to be sampled, (2) analysis regions of small areas, and (3) directions of edges to be detected. We have also developed a new efficient search method for a smooth curve in a noisy picture. The computation time was about 6 minutes for 1st frame, 14 seconds for analyzing a next sampled frame, and less than 1 second for deciding whether an input frame is skipped or not. We believe this approach is essential for analysis of high resolution dynamic images.

REFERENCE

[1] W. N. Martin and J. Aggarwal : *Dynamic Scene Analysis, Computer Graphics and Image Processing, 7, pp356-374, No.3, 1978.*

[2] H. H. Nagel : *Analysis for Image Sequences, Proc. 4th Intern. Joint Conf. on Pattern Recongnition, pp186-211, 1978.*

[3] T. Kaneko and P. Mancini : *Straight-line Approximation for the Boundary of the Left Venticular Chamber from a Cardiac Cineangiogram, IEEE Trans. on BME **20**,* pp413-416, Nov. 1973.

[4] L. P. Jong and C. J. Slager : *Automatic Detection of the Left Venticular Outline in Angiographs Using Television Signal Processing Technique, IEEE Trans. on BME **22**,* pp230-237, May 1975.

[5] J. O. Greaves : *The Software Structure for Reduction of Quantized Video Data of Moving Organisms, Proc. of IEEE, 63, pp1415-1425, Oct. 1975.*

[6] Y. Ariki, T. Kanade and T. Sakai : *An Interactive Image Modeling and Tracing System for Moving Pictures, Proc. 4th Intern. Joint Conf. on Pattern Recongnition, pp681-685, 1978.*

[7] M. Kelly : *Visual Identification of People by Computer, Artificial Intelligence Project Memo No. 121, Stanford Univ., July, 1970.*

[8] C. A. Harlow and S. A. Eisenbis : *The Analysis of Radiographic Images, IEEE Trans. on Comput. **22**,* pp678-689, July, 1973.

[9] U. Montanari : *On the Optimal Detection of Curves in Noisy Pictures, Commun. ACM., **14**,* pp335-345, May 1971.

[10] A. Martelli : *An Application of Heuristic Search Methods to Edge and Contour Detection, Commun. ACM., **19**,* pp73-83, Feb. 1976.

[11] M. Yachida et al. : *An Interactive System for Digital Processing of Moving Images, Trans. Inst. Elect. Commun. Engineers of Japan, **D-56**, Oct. 1978 (in Japanese).*

[12] M. Yachida, M. Ikeda and S. Tsuji : *A Knowledge Directed Line Finder for Analysis of Complex Scenes, 6th IJCAI.*

A KNOWLEDGE DIRECTED LINE FINDER FOR ANALYSIS OF COMPLEX SCENES

Masahiko Yachida, Motozo Ikeda and Saburo Tsuji
Department of Control Enginering, Osaka University
Toyonaka, Osaka 560, Japan

As a part of complex scene analysis system, this paper presents a line finder which can find a globally good line with respect to the knowledge available of the line to be sought. A variety of knowledge available of the line to be sought can be communicated to the line finding system simply in the form of descriptions so that the higher level of the program can easily use this line finding system. The optimization method is utilized to detect a globally good line with respect to the given knowledge of the line. In order to reduce the required storage space and computation time in the optimization process, we use the following techniques: 1) represent a line by a sequence of linear segments and find the good sequence of segments by the optimization method and 2) use a locus model of search to prune unpromising lines during the optimization process. Some experimental results applied to various scenes with different amount of noise and knowledge are given in the paper.

1. INTRODUCTION

Boundary detection is an important and critical stage in scene analysis to segment an input picture into meaningful regions. This process usually consists of the following two steps: (1) detection of short edge elements, and (2) connecting these edge elements into boundaries. Many methods have been proposed to detect short edge elements which apply local operations to every point of the input picture. An operator tuned up for characters of edges to be detected is usually used to enhance the edges to be sought in noisy pictures. In order to detect edge elements in noisy pictures, relatively large operators are often used to examine statistic properties of local regions. When edge elements have been found, then they are connected to form boundaries or lines. This line finding process must utilize properties about lines to be detected and must find globally good lines with regards to the properties in order to distinguish meaningful edges in noisy pictures. These properties of the lines to be sought must be separated from the line finding program and given in the form of data to the program, since minor changes of the characteristics of the sought boundary may require a major reprogramming if the properties are embedded in the program[1].

An optimization method is known to be an excellent method to find a globally good line with respect to given properties of the sought line in noisy pictures. Montanari[2] has embedded properties of lines to be detected in a merit function and utilized a dynamic programming method to determine an optimal sequence of points with respect to the given merit function from a number of possible combinations of points. Although the method is good for finding lines in noisy pictures, its drawbacks were the required computation time and storage space, and Martelli[3] has proposed an more efficient method which finds sub-optimal lines instead of optimal lines using a heuristic search method.

Both of the methods represent a line as a sequence of consecutive points, and need much computation time and storage space if they are applied for high-resolution pictures which are utilized in many applications such as medical images, aerial photographs,etc. Furthermore, shapes that the lines are expected to have, such as 'smoothness', are very important criterion to discriminate lines from noise. However, they need too much computation time and storage space if these shape information is embedded to the merit function because number of combinations of points to be searched expands to a large amount.

In this paper, we propose an efficient search method of lines in noisy pictures which represent a line as a sequence of linear segments instead of a sequence of points and find near-optimal sequence of line-segments with respect to a given figure of merit. We believe that there is little problem to approximate a line by a sequence of linear segments since (1) Small variations on a line is considered as statistically meaningless, (2) Lines we would like to find are smooth ones in many applications, and (3) Since edge elements are determined by statistical distribution of gray levels, it seems natural to determine line segments by statistical distribution of edge elements.

The advantage of the proposed method comparing with the existing methods are as follows:
(a) The required storage space and computation time is much smaller and therefore much more efficient since number of lines among which the optimum is sought is much less than the point-wise search.

(b) It can find lines in noisier pictures since shape information of the line we want to detect can be easily embedded in the figure of merit.

In order to further decrease the required storage space and computation time, we utilize the locus model of search which has been proposed by Rubin et al[4] in image interpretation task. We will utilize this search method for finding lines where only a beam of near-miss alternatives around the best line are extended to determine a near-optimal line.

For complex scenes containing many kinds of objects, analysis is usually performed in the following steps[5]: 1) detect distinct lines as the initial information that can be easily found in the scene, 2) select models of objects which contain these extracted lines and propose the lines to be examined utilizing the models of objects and their contextual relations, and 3) examine the proposed lines using the knowledge of the sought lines given by the above higher level of program (or scene analyzer) for final interpretation of the scene.

In such a scene analysis system, a line finder which can find a globally good line with respect to the knowledge given by the scene analyzer is necessary. The knowledge available on the line to be sought is not only properties of the line which can be embedded in the merit function, but also a variety of knowledge such as expected location, when to terminate the line following,etc. All of these variety of knowledge available of the line to be sought must be easily expressed by and communicated to the line finder. We will describe a line finding system which can find a good line with respect to the knowledge given in the form of descriptions by the scene analyzer.

2. FINDING SMOOTH LINES IN NOISY PICTURES

2.1 MULTISTAGE OPTIMIZATION PROCEDURE

Let us first briefly review the multistage optimization procedure. In general, an optimization problem can be formulated as follows: given a merit function $f(x_1, x_2, \ldots, x_N)$, where $0 \leq x_i \leq n_i$, $i=1,\ldots,N$, find (a) the maximal value M of the merit function f, and (b) a value $(X_1, X_2, \ldots, X_N)$ for which the maximum is achieved. If the merit function f can be expressed by a sum of terms, each of which depends on only a few variables, then a multistage optimization procedure applies. For example, if f has a simple form as

$$f(x_1,\ldots,x_N)=f_1(x_1,x_2)+f_2(x_2,x_3)+\ldots+f_{N-1}(x_{N-1},x_N) \quad (1)$$

then the following recursion formula can be used:

$$h_1(x_1)=0$$

$$h_{k+1}(x_{k+1})=\max_{0\leq x_k\leq n_k}(f_k(x_k,x_{k+1})+h_k(x_k)) \quad (2)$$

where $k=1,\ldots,N-1$ and $0 \leq x_{k+1} \leq n_{k+1}$. At each stage, the values $h_{k+1}(x_{k+1})$, $0 \leq x_{k+1} \leq n_{k+1}$, and the values $m_{k+1}(x_{k+1})$ of x_k for which the maximum is achieved must be saved in a table with n_{k+1} entries. At the end of this process, maximum value M of f can be obtained as

$$M=\max_{x_N} h_N(x_N) \quad (3)$$

The values $(X_1, \ldots, X_N)$ for which the maximum is achieved are obtained by tracing back the tables with the recursion formula:

$$X_N=m_N=\arg\max_{x_N} h_N(x_N)$$

$$X_k=m_{k+1}(X_{k+1}) \qquad k=N-1,\ldots,1 \quad (4)$$

2.2 REPRESENTATION OF A LINE BY POINTS

The existing methods to find a line in noisy pictures, represent a line as any sequence of points P_i, $k=1,\ldots,N-1$, are neighbors. The properties of the sought line are embedded in a merit function f and an optimal line is searched with respect to a given merit function using the optimization method. Let us first consider a simple problem of finding a low-curvature line having high gray values. Then, a good merit function will be the sum of gray levels along the line, minus the sum of the curvature at every point. If we denote the coordinate vectors of a point P_i by $z_i = (x_i, y_i)$ and slope of the line by $\theta(z_i, z_{i+1})$, then a curvature of a point P_i defined by three points can be given as
$\theta(z_{i-1}, z_i) - \theta(z_i - z_{i+1})$.
Then, a merit function is given as

$$f(z_1,\ldots,z_N)=\sum_{i=1}^{N} g(z_i) - k\sum_{i=2}^{N-1}|\theta(z_{i-1},z_i)-\theta(z_i,z_{i+1})| \quad (5)$$

where $g(z_i)$ are gray level of a point P_i. This is a merit function of the form

$$f(z_1,\ldots,z_N)=f_1(z_1,z_2,z_3)+\ldots+f_{N-2}(z_{N-2},z_{N-1},z_N) \quad (6)$$

and can be solved by the multistage optimization procedure.

However, this measure of curvature defined at such a small length causes serious erroneous results. Fig. 1 shows a simple example of such cases where the problem is to find a smooth line connecting A and F. In the figure, values of points marked as o are one and the others are zero. The optimization method with the merit function defined in (5) finds a path A-B-C-D-F as the optimal solution, because sum of curvatures of this path is smaller than another path. However, we perceive another path A-B-E-D-F as more meaningful or good-shaped and the path B-C-D as the line caused by noise. This error has been caused by the very local measure of curvature defined only by three consecutive points. To avoid this problem, more global properties of the line defined over a wider range should be embedded into the merit function.

If the property of the line defined by a wider range, say k points, are embedded into the merit function, it becomes the form of

$$f(z_1)=f_1(z_1,\ldots,z_k)+f_2(z_2,\ldots,z_{k+1})+\ldots$$

$$+f_i(z_i,\ldots,z_{i+k-1})+\ldots \qquad (7)$$

where all terms are functions of k variables. This is called a merit function of type k, and it is known that the required tables and computation time are exponetial with k to solve the problem with multistage optimization procedure.

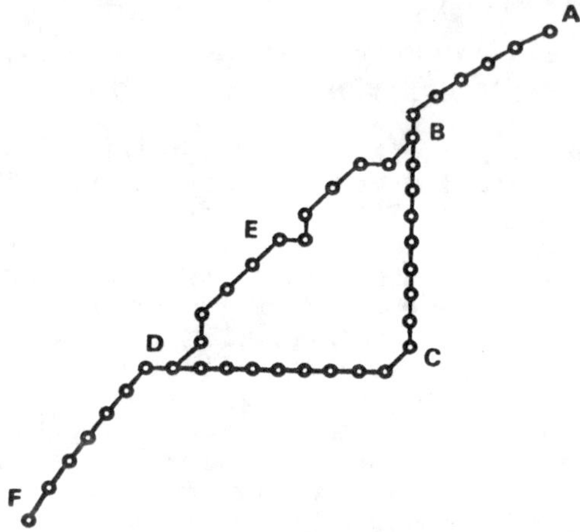

Fig. 1. An example in which curvature defined at a small length causes erroneous result.

2.3 REPRESENTATION BY LINEAR SEGMENTS

We have studied a different approach to avoid this difficulty, in which a line is represented by a sequence of connected linear segments L_1, L_2, ..., L_N of length ℓ instead of consecutive points, as shown in Fig. 2. Let us represent a linear segment L by an ordered pair of their endpoints (z_1, z_2) and call z_1 the head and z_2 the tail of the segment. Then two linear segments L and L′ are called connected if the tail of L coincides with the head of L′. If we call a connected linear segment of a segment L a successor of L, then each segment of length ℓ has $2\pi\ell$ possible successors as shown in Fig. 3. However, since the line we want to detect are smooth ones, successors having curvatures less than a certain threshold α are considered as 'legal' successors. That is, if θ (z_1, z_2) denotes the direction of the segment L (z_1, z_2), then segments L′ (z'_1, z'_2) having

$$|\theta'(z'_1,z'_2)-\theta(z_1,z_2)|\leq\alpha \qquad (8)$$

are legal successors as shown in Fig. 3.

With this representation, a merit function to find a low-curvature curve having high gray levels in which the curvature is defined by the length of 2 ℓ points can be given as

$$f(z_1,\ldots,z_N)=\sum_{i=2}^{N} g(z_{i-1},z_i)$$

$$-k\sum_{i=2}^{N-1}|\theta(z_{i-1},z_i)-\theta(z_i,z_{i+1})| \qquad (9)$$

with the constraint defined in (8), where $g(z_{i-1}, z_i)$ is a mean of gray values of the points lying on the line L_{i-1} (z_{i-1}, z_i). It will be noted that the problem of type 2 ℓ if the curve is represented by a sequence of points is reduced to the problem of type 3 with this representation. Number of stages necessary to find a curve of N points is also reduced from N stages with pointwise search to N/ℓ stages with this linewise search. Next, we will describe an algotithm to find optimal sequence of linear segments with respect to a given merit function.

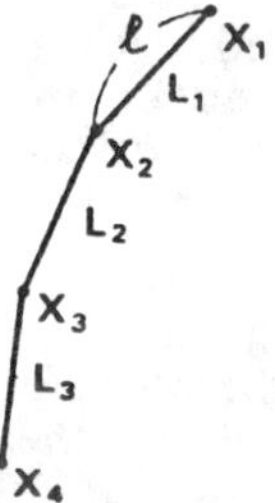

Fig. 2. Representation of a line by a sequence of linear segments L_1, L_2, ..., L_N.

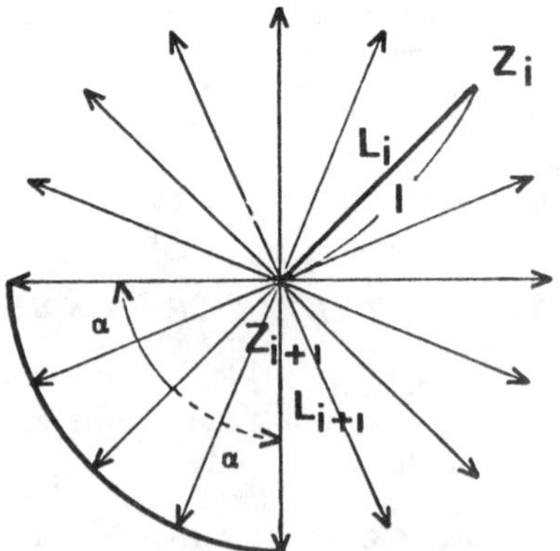

Fig. 3. Legal successors of line L.

2.4 FINDING THE OPTIMAL SEQUENCE

For the sake of simplicity, let us first consider the problem of extracting from a picture a curve which starts in the first row and ends in the last row. First of all, for each admissible z_1, successors z_2 are determined with a constraint $\pi\leq\theta$ (z_1, z_2) $\leq 2\pi$. Then, at the k-th stage, successors z_{k+1} are expanded for each admissible z_k with the constraint

$$\theta(z_{k-1}, z_k) - \theta(z_k, z_{k+1}) \lesssim \alpha$$

where k=2,..., N-1. For every value of z_k and z_{k+1}, we compute

$$h_k(z_k, z_{k+1}) = H_{k-1}(z_{k+1}, z_k) + g(z_k, z_{k+1}) + k|\theta(z_{k-1}, z_k) - \theta(z_k, z_{k+1})| \quad (10)$$

where $h_1(z_1, z_2) = g(z_1, z_2)$ and H_{k-1} is the value of the output of the previous stages for all addmissible z_{k-2}. Then we obtain the maximal value of h_k, H_k, with respect to z_{k-1} and the value of z_{k-1}, Z_{k-1}, for which the maximum is achieved. These values, H_k and Z_{k-1}, are stored in the table for every value of z_k and z_{k+1} at each stage.

This process terminates at the N-th stage when some of the segments (z_{N-1}, z_N) intersect with the last column. At this stage, the tail of each segment, z_N, which intersects with the last column is determined as the intersecting point of the segment (z_{N-1}, z_N) and the last column. For every value of z_{N-1} and z_N, we compute h_{N-1} defined in (10) and obtain the maximal value of $h_{N-1}(z_{N-1}, z_N)$, $H_{N-1}(z_{N-1}, z_N)$, and the value of z_{N-2}, Z_{N-2}, for which the maximum is achieved. Then, for all admissible z_{N-1}, we compute the maximum of $H_{N-1}(z_{N-1}, z_N)$maximum of $H_{N-1}(z_{N-1}, z_N)$ with respect to z_{N-1} and the value of z_{N-1}, Z_{N-1}, for which the maximum is achieved. Finally, we obtain the maximal value of $H_N(z_{N-1}, z_N)$, $M(H_N)$, and a value of z_N, Z_N, for which the maximum is achieved. Then, tracing back the tables with the recursion formula defined in (4), we obtain Z_N, Z_{N-1},..., Z_1 for which the maximum has been achieved.

2.5 LOCUS MODEL OF SEARCH

In order to decrease storage space and computation time, we introduce the locus model of search to this line finding system. In the multistage optimization process, all the paths generated during the optimization process are saved and evaluated until the last stage. However, it is usually not necesary to find the optimal path but it is sufficient to find good or near optimal solutions in practical applications. Therefore, we prune unpromising paths from the search tree at each stage. That is, after computing H_k at each stage, those paths having H_k less than a certain threshold are not saved in the table; and therefore, their successors are not generated at the subsequent stages. Let us denote the maximum value of H_k at the k-th stage as $M(H_k)$, then the threshold is set as $t * M(H_k)$, $0 < t < 1$. This search method suppresses exponential growth of successors and only a beam of near-miss alternatives around the best path are retained as shown in Fig. 4.

3. FINDING A LINE WITH GIVEN KNOWLEDGE

In this section, we will describe a line finding system which finds a globally good line with respect to the knowledge of the line given by the scene analyzer. A variety of knowledge is available on the line to be sought. These various knowledge of the sought line must be easily expressed by and communicated to the line finder. The line finder consists of three components; a menu, a line finding program and an interpreter as shown in Fig. 5. The menu is a list of knowledge which can be utilized by the optimization process. Then the properties of the sought line can be expressed simply by descriptions which specify which items of the menu should be used in finding the line. The descriptions given by the scene analyzer are interpreted and embedded into the line finding program by the interpreter.

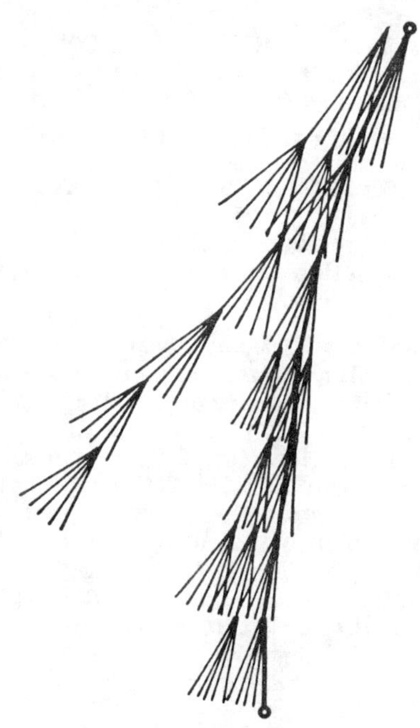

Fig. 4. A locus model of search supresses exponential growth of successors.

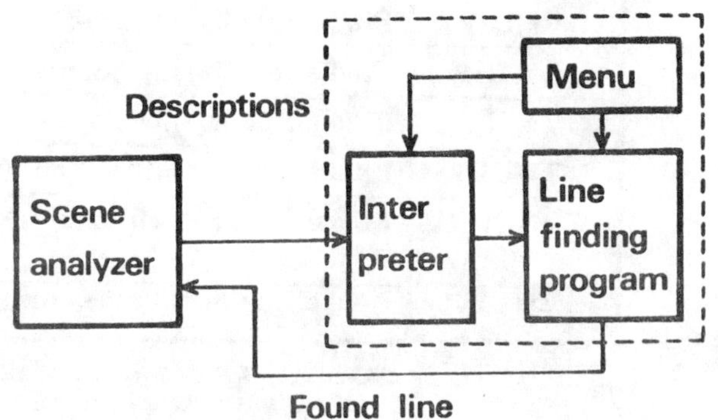

Fig. 5. Line finding system.

3.1 MENU AND INTERPRETER

The menu consists of properties of the line, some constraints on the line, constraints on the starting point, and terminating conditions, each of which is described below.

3.1.1 PROPERTIES OF THE LINE

The menu for the properties of the line is listed in table I. The properties of the sought line are specified by the format (item, weight, parameter). For example, if we would like to find the low-curvature line of homogeneous gray level showing strong edgeness, then descriptions are given to the line finder as:
(HOMGRY k_1),(EDGE k_2),(LOWCURV k_3).
Then, these properties on the line are embedded into the merit function as follows:

$$f = k_1 f_1 + k_2 f_2 + k_3 f_3$$

3.1.2 SOME CONSTRAINTS ON THE LINE

Constraints on the line which are difficult to embed in the merit function are given to the line finder as follows.

Search region: the expected location of the sought line is known using the relationship with the already found lines. This knowledge is given to the line finder as the search boundary of the line. The search boundary is given to the line finder by a sequence of representative points as (SEARCH (x_1 , y_1) ,(x_2 , y_2) ,...). If the search boundary is given, a line is sought in the region bounded by the search boundary as shown in Fig. 6. This information greatly reduces the computation time and storage space, and increases reliability of the extracted line.

Length of linear segment ℓ : we have four values for the length ℓ ; 5, 10, 20, 30, and one of them can be specified considering the maximal curvature of the line to be sought. If it is not specified, length 20 is utilized.

Constraint on the successors α : the parameter α determines number of successors generated and is given considering the maximal curvature of the line to be sought. If it is not specified, 1 radian is used for α

Threshold t : the threshold t determines the width of the beam, that is a number of lines saved in the table at each stage. If t is not given, 0.5 is used as t .

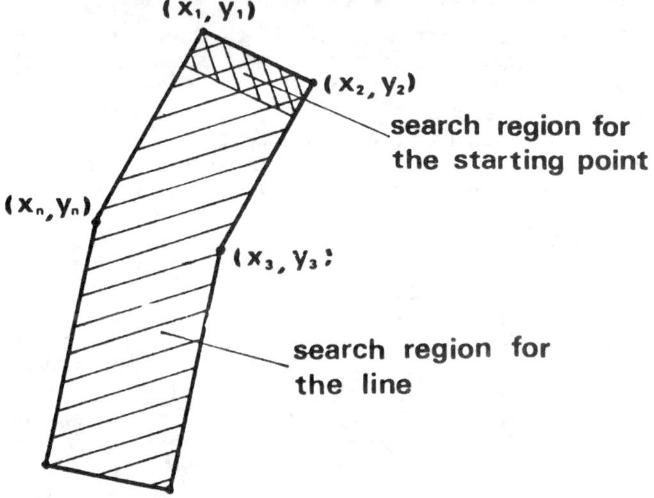

Fig. 6. Search region for the line and for the starting point.

Table I. Properties of the line

EDGE	Find a line having strong edgeness	$\sum e(z_k, z_{k+1})$
GVNGRY	Find a line having gray level G	$\sum g(z_k, z_{k+1}) - G$
HOMGRY	Find a line having homogeneous gray levels	$\sum g(z_{k-1}, z_k) - g(z_k, z_{k+1})$
GVNDIR	Find a line having edge direction D	$\sum d(z_k, z_{k-1}) - D$
HOMDIR	Find a line having homogeneous edge direction	$\sum d(z_{k-1}, z_k) - (z_k, z_{k+1})$
GVNSLP	Find a line having slope θ	$\sum \theta(z_k, z_{k+1}) - \theta$
LOWCURV	Find a low-curvature line	$\sum \theta(z_{k-1}, z_k) - \theta(z_k, z_{k+1})$
CONCURV	Find a constant-curvature line such as a circle	$\sum (\theta(z_{k-2}, z_{k-1}) - \theta(z_{k-1}, z_k)) - ((z_{k-1}, z_k) - \theta(z_k, z_{k+1}))$
GVNCURV	Find a line having the curvature C	$\sum \theta(z_{k-1}, z_k) - \theta(z_k, z_{k+1}) - C$

E (z_k, z_{k+1}); mean value of edgeness of the segment (z_k, z_{k+1})
G (z_k, z_{k-1}); mean value of gray level of the segment (z_k, z_{k+1})
D (z_k, z_{k+1}); mean value of edge direction of the segment (z_k, z_{k+1})
θ (z_k, z_{k+1}); slope of the segment (z_k, z_{k+1})

3.1.3 CONSTRAINTS ON THE STARTING POINTS

Selection of the starting points of the line is very important to reduce growth of successors in subsequent stages. We have two constraints on selecting the starting point; 1) search boundary for the starting points and 2) properties of the starting point. In many cases, more restricted search boundary is available for the starting point than for the sought line. This search boundary is given to the line finder by a sequence of representative points as

(SSERCH (x_1 , y_1) , (x_2 , y_2) ,...).

If a search boundary is given, the starting point is sought in the region bounded by the search boundary. If it is not given, the search boundary for the line is utilized.

Properties of the starting point listed on the menu are gray level, edgeness and edge direction. The properties on the starting point is given in the similar manner to the line. For example, if we would like to find the points having strong edgeness and edge direction D with weights k_1 and k_2 respectively, then the following descriptions are given:

(SEDGE k_1),(SDIREC k_2 D).

Then the following merit function is generated by the interpreter:

$$f=k_1*e(z)+k_2*|d(z)-D|$$

Then, the promising points are selected with respect to the merit function for the starting point in the search region.

3.1.4 TERMINATING CONDITIONS

There are four terminating conditions in line following as follows.

1) Line segments of the current stage intersect with line segments of the first stage. This terminating condition is used when the sought line is closed.

2) Line segments of the current stage intersect with the other lines which are already found in the picture.

3) Line segments of the current stage intersect with the line L specified as the terminating one.

4) There is no promising line segment at the current stage. That is, score of the best line segment at the current stage M_k is much smaller than the score of the best line segment of the last stage M_{k-1}, such as $M_k \leq \delta M_{k-1}$ where $\delta < 1$.

If we would like to use the terminating conditions, for example 1 and 4, then the descriptions are given to the line finder as follows;

(TERM 1), (TERM 4 δ),

where δ is a threshold.

3.2 LINE FINDING PROGRAM

When the descriptions on the sought curve are given, these are interpreted and embedded into the line finding program by the interpreter as described before. Then the line finding program seeks a globally good line with respect to the given knowledge as follows.

1) Compute the value of merit function f(z_1) for every point z_1 in the search region for the starting point, and select promising starting points. Let us denote the maximum of f(z_1) as M (f(z_1)), then those points having value of f(z_1) larger than T*M(f(z_1)) are selected as promising starting points.

2) At the first stage, determine successors z_2 for each selected points z_1 and select promising ones among z_2. For each selected point z_1 , its successors z_2 are determined with the constraint that z_2 must be in the search region for the line , and the merit function f(z_1, z_2) are computed. Then those segments having f(z_1 , z_2) larger than t*M(f(z_1 , z_2)) are selected as promising ones. If the search region for the starting point is given around the middle of the sought line, then two beams are obtained as shown in Fig. 7. In this case, one of them is followed first.

3) At the k-th stage, determine the successors z_{k+1} for each z_k and select promising ones among z_{k+1}. For each z_k , its successors are determined with constraints that z_{k+1} must be in the search region and θ (z_{k-1} , z_k)- θ (z_k , z_{k+1}) $\leq \alpha$. If the given merit function is type i ($2 \leq i \leq 4$), then we compute

$$h_k(z_k, z_{k+1}) = H_{k-1}(z_{k-1}, z_k) + f_k(z_{k-i+2}, \ldots, z_{k+1}) \qquad (11)$$

for every value of z_{k-i+2} ,... , z_{k+1}. We obtain the maximal value of h_k , H_k , with respect to z_{k-i+2} and the value of z_{k-i+2} , Z_{k-i+2} , for which the maximum is achieved , for every value of z_{k-i+3} ,... , z_{k+1}. Let us denote the maximum of H_k as M (H_k). Then, those points z_{k+1} having H_k larger than t*M (H_k) are selected as promising points. The value of H_k and Z_{k-i+2} of the promising points z_k are saved in the table.

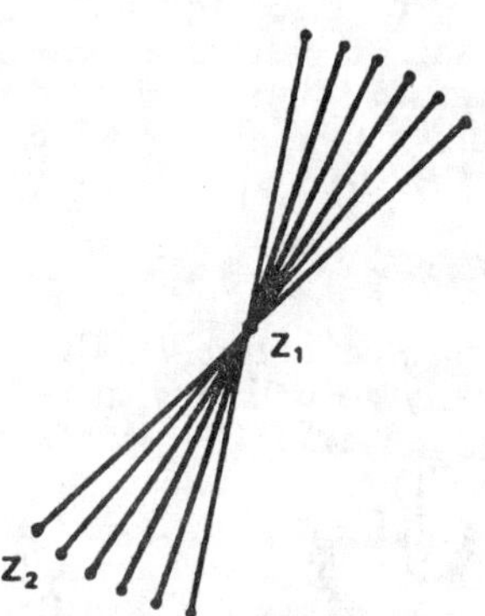

Fig. 7. Two beams are obtained if the starting point is found around the middle of the line.

4) Check the terminating conditions. If one of the terminating conditions specified by the descriptions is satisfied, then the line following is terminated. At this last stage, the tail of each segment z_N is determined as the intersecting point of the segment (z_{N-1}, z_N) and the line specified by the terminating conditions.

5) Try to follow the other end of the line using the above-mentioned procedure , with (z_2 , z_1) as the starting line segments. When both sides terminate, then obtain the maximal value of the merit function, and a sequence of line segments for which the maximum is achieved by tracing back the tables.

4. EXPERIMENTAL RESULTS

The proposed line finding system was implemented in Fortarn IV on a HP-2108 computer and was utilized for analysis of heart walls, blood vessels and complex industrial parts. We show a result on the test image shown in Fig. 8(a) by adding different amount of noise to the image. The image consists of 256 by 256 points, each point having 16 levels of gray. Our purpose is to detect smooth line 1 in the presence of noisy lines 2 and 3. In the image, the gray levels of the lines 1, 2 and 3 are 10, 11 and 12 respectively and the gray level of the background is 5. In Fig. 8 (b) and (c), independent amount of noise is added to every point. The statistical distribution of the noise at every point is normal, with mean value zero and standard deviation 4 and 6, respectively. Note that the line is recognizable in Fig. 8(b) but quite unrecognizable in Fig. 8(c).

The knowledge available of the curve is smooth, has large value of gray, starts in the first row and ends in the last row. Therefore, the descriptions given to the line finding system are as follows:
(EDGE 1), (LOWCURV 5), (SSERCH (1,1),(256,1))
(TERM 3 (1,256),(256,256))

Fig. 9(a) and (b) show the results for the images of Fig. 8(b) and (c). It will be noted that the line is detected correctly even in the presence of heavy noise. If the second description is eliminated, that is the low-curvature is not utilized, then the pass 2 is selected as shown in Fig. 9(c) which is the result for the image of Fig. 8(b).

5. CONCLUSION

We have presented a line finding system that can detect a globally good line with respect to the given knowledge of the line. The proposed method is very efficient since 1) size of tables required at each stage and number of stages is greatly reduced by representing a line by a sequence of linear segments, 2) a locus model of search is utilized to supress the exponential growth of search trees, and 3) several constraints available of the sought line are utilized to limit search space or growth of successors, such as search boundary, constraints on the starting point, etc.

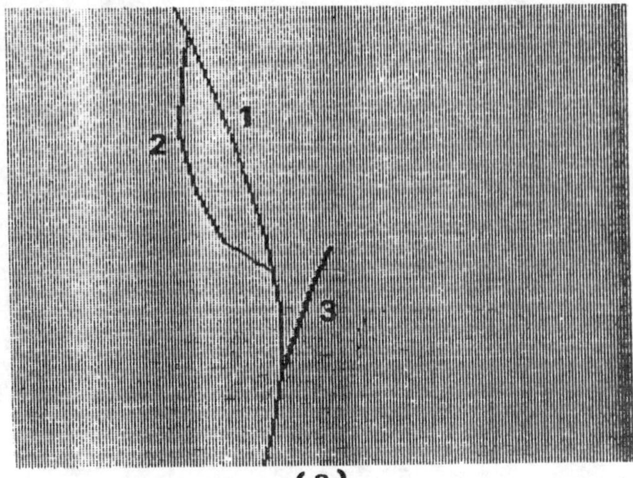

(a)

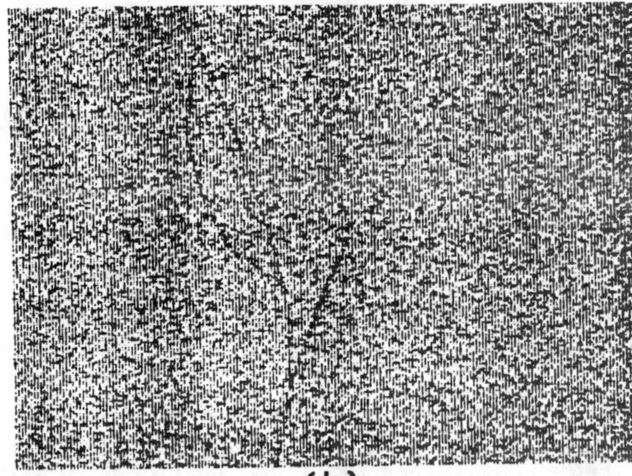
(b)

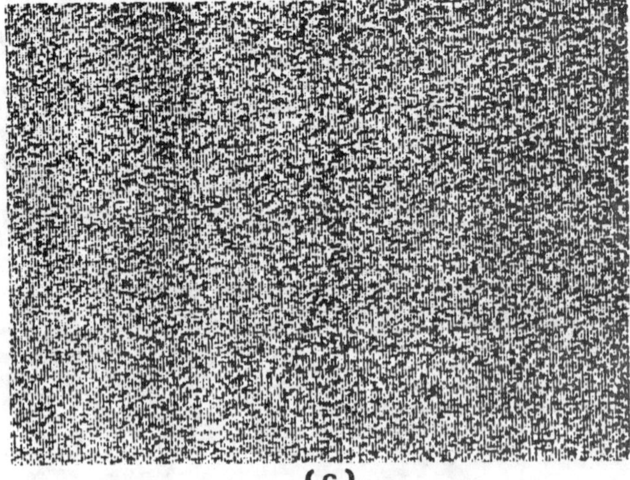
(c)

Fig. 8. Input pictures with different amount of noise.

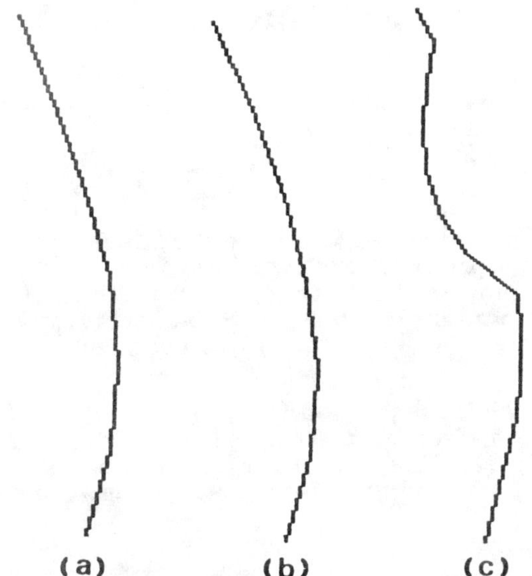

Fig. 9. Results obtained (a) for Fig. 8(b); (b) for Fig. 8(c); and (c) for Fig. 8 (b) without the knowledge of shape.

The length of linear segment ℓ seriously affects computational efficiency. Therefore, if the sought curve is smooth and can be approximated by long linear segments, then large value should be given to ℓ . On the contrary, if small variations on the line is important or the sought line has high curvature, then small value must be given to ℓ . However, it is more efficient that we first obtain an approximate line with large ℓ and then obtain more details with small ℓ in the neighborhoods of the approximated line than obtaining the line with small ℓ from the beginning.

We have used a locus model of search instead of the best first search of A* algorithm for obtaining sub-optimal solution. The reason of this selection is that its control structure is simpler than the A* algorithm and it is easier to understand the behavior of search process since the locus model does not need backtracking. Another reason which is more important is that it permits parallel computation of all the linear segments at every stage.

In this system, it is very easy to communicate the knowledge of the sought line to the line finder since a variety of knowledge can be expressed simply in the form of descriptions. The menu provided in the system is sufficient for our current tasks. However, it is easy to change the menu if it is necessary.

We have applied the proposed method for a variety of scene analysis tasks and the results have shown the effectiveness of the proposed method to find a globally good line with respect to the given knowledge. However, for complex scenes where many kinds of objects exist and a priori knowledge on the scene is not available, we must first extract distinct lines as initial information on the scene to select possible models of objects in the scene. For this purpose of extracting initial information, there exist several methods such as planning[6], detection of distinct edges[7] and extended Hough transformation[8]. The proposed line finder is then used to find subtle lines using knowledge of the objects and their contextual relations.

REFERENCE

[1] A. Martelli : *An Application of Heuristic Search Methods to Edge and Contour Detection, Commu. ACM 19, pp. 73-83, 1976.*

[2] U. Montanari : *On the Optimum Detection of Curves in Noisy Pictures, Commu. ACM 14, pp. 335-345, 1971.*

[3] A. Martelli : *Edge Detection Using Heuristic Search Methods, Comput. Grap. Image Proc. 1, pp. 169-182, 1972.*

[4] S. M. Rubin and R. Reddy : *The Locus Model of Search and Its Use in Image Interpretation, Proc. 5th IJCAI, pp. 590-595, 1977.*

[5] M. Yachida and S. Tsuji : *A Versatile Machine Vision System for Complex Industrial Parts , IEEE Trans. C-26, pp. 882-894, 1977.*

[6] M. D. Kelly : *Edge Detection in Pictures by Computer Using Planning, in Machine Intelligence, 6, pp. 379-409, 1971.*

[7] A. K. Griffith : *Edge Detection in Simple Scenes Using a Priori Information, IEEE Trans. C-22, pp. 371-381, 1973.*

[8] S. Tsuji and F. Matsumoto : *Detection of Ellipses by a Modified Hough Transformation, IEEE Trans. C-27, pp. 777-781, 1978.*

BOUNDARY DETECTION OF TEXTURED REGIONS

Masahiko Yachida, Motozo Ikeda and Saburo Tsuji
Department of Control Engineering, Osaka University
Toyonaka, Osaka 560, Japan

It is not easy to find exact locations of boundaries of textural regions since statistical properties around the boundary show mixed properties of two neighboring regions. This paper presents a method to detect exact locations of boundaries of textural regions in the scene. We first propose 'a measure of boundary' which shows large value on the boundary and very small value in other locations. Then we propose a method to find globally good boundaries with respect to the defined measure of boundary using the optimization procedure.

The initial segmentation is performed on the reduced version of the input image using multiple textural properties by the recursive thresholding method. This segmentation result on the reduced image is then utilized as a plan for detecting exact locations of textural boundaries in full size image by the proposed textural boundary detector. The proposed method has been applied to a number of textured images, and some of the results will be given in the paper.

1. INTRODUCTION

Texture is an important property for segmentation of input pictures into regions in scene analysis. Many methods have been proposed to extract meaningful textural properties of local regions such as coarseness or orientation [1]; however, few attempts have been made for detection of exact textural boundaries. Usual methods apply local operators sensitive to some statistical properties of local regions, and then the textural boundary is obtained as the boundary of regions having homogeneous textural properties.

However, such a simple method cannot find correct location of textural boundaries. The reason is that statistical properties do not change abruptly on the boundary, but gradually change from one region to another region. Therefore, there are relatively broad regions having mixed properties of two neighboring regions around the boundary. Thus, existing methods find a boundary somewhere in this broad region around the true boundary. In this paper, we propose a good measure of textural boundary and a method to find a globally good boundary with respect to the defined measure of boundary.

2. MEASURE OF TEXTURAL BOUNDARY

For the sake of simplicity, let us first consider the problem of finding the boundaries of two textural regions R_1 and R_2 that are known to have homogeneous properties P_1 and P_2 respectively. As shown in Fig. 1, the boundary exists in the region S between two homogeneous regions R_1 and R_2 and the local properties of the region S are not homogeneous and have some mixed properties of two regions. Let us define a local operator that has two regions r_1 and r_2 on both sides of a center line L as shown in Fig. 2, and denote the local properties of r_1 and r_2 as p_1 and p_2 respectively. Then, if the operator lies on the boundary, the following conditions must be satisfied:

1) p_1 is similar to P_1 and different from P_2.
2) p_2 is similar to P_2 and different from P_1.

Let us define the similarity of textural properties of p_1, p_2, P_1 and P_2 as

$$D_{11} = p_1 - P_1$$
$$D_{12} = p_1 - P_2$$
$$D_{21} = p_2 - P_1$$
$$D_{22} = p_2 - P_2$$

Then the above conditions can be stated as:

1) $D_{12} > D_{11}$, and 2) $D_{21} > D_{22}$

Therefore, we define the measure of textural

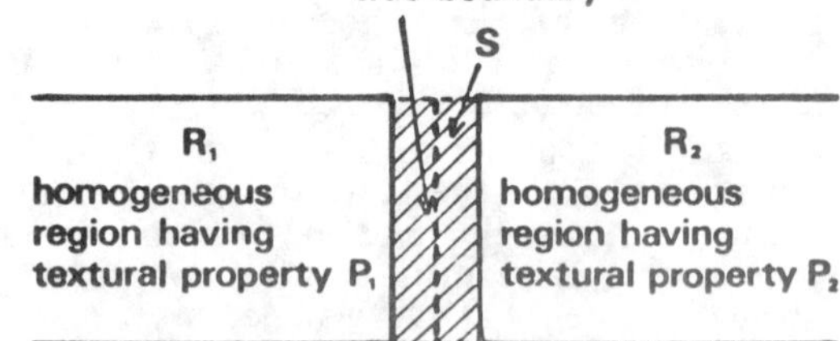

Fig. 1. Textural boundary exist somewhere between two homogeneous regions R_1 and R_2.

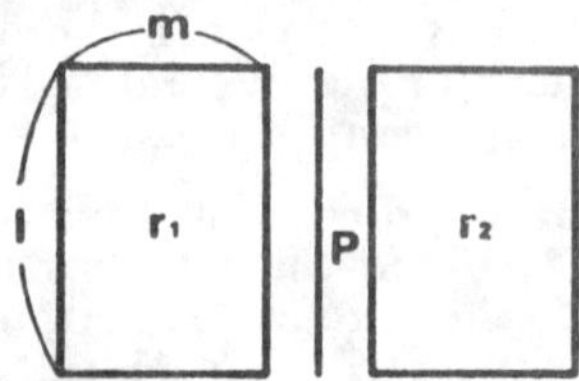

Fig. 2. A local operator.

boundary M as:

$$M = (D_{12} + D_{21}) - (D_{11} + D_{22}) \qquad (1)$$

The value of the measure M is large when the operator is on the boundary and is very small in other places. Fig. 3 shows the values of D_{11}, D_{12}, D_{21}, D_{22} and M when the operator is on the right of the boundary.

Then, the boundary can be found by searching the region S for points having large value of M. However, local decisions such as finding points having local maximum of M cannot produce a good boundary since noise causes many false boundary points and gaps on the true boundary. We utilize the optimization method to find a globally good boundary with respect to the measure M in the region S.

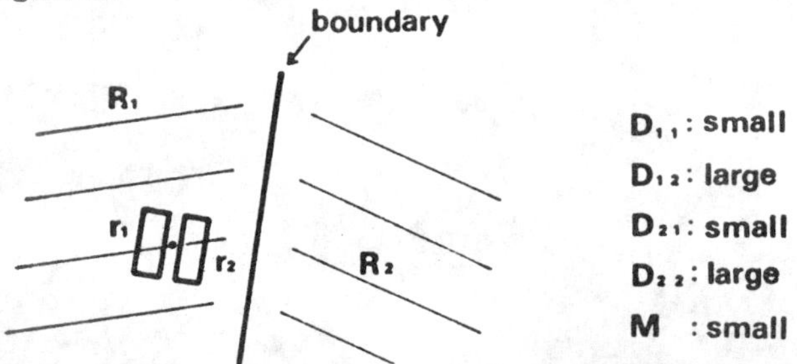

Fig. 3. The values of D_{11}, D_{12}, D_{21} and D_{22} when the operator is on the right of the boundary.

3. GLOBAL DETECTION OF BOUNDARY

Let us represent a line by any sequence of connected linear segments $L_1, L_2, \ldots, L_N$ of length ℓ, and define a merit function f of the line $(L_1, L_2, \ldots, L_N)$ as

$$f(L_1, L_2, \ldots, L_N) = M(L_1) + M(L_2) + \ldots + M(L_N) \qquad (2)$$

Where $M(L_i)$ is the measure of the boundary of the linear segment L_i computed by the local operator parallel to the linear segment L_i, as shown in Fig. 4.

Then, the sequence of linear segments $L_1, \ldots, L_N$ having the maximum value in the region S can be considered as the globally good boundary. Therefore, the problem of finding the globally good boundary becomes the problem of finding the sequence of linear segments $L_1, \ldots, L_N$ which maximizes the merit function f given in (2). This problem can be solved by the multistage optimization procedure. An efficient method for solving this problem is described by the authors[2]. We may embed shape information such as smoothness into the merit function f as

$$f(L_1, \ldots, L_N) = \sum_{i=1}^{N} M(L_i) - k \sum_{i=1}^{N-1} |\theta(L_i) - \theta(L_{i+1})| \qquad (3)$$

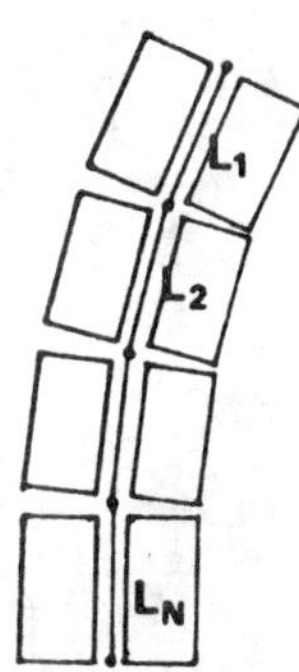

Fig. 4. Representation of a line by a sequence of linear segments $L_1, L_2, \ldots, L_N$. A local operator is set parallel to each linear segment.

Where $\theta (L_i)$ is the slope of the line L_i and k is a constant. This merit function find a boundary having large value of M and low-curvatures.

4. INITIAL SEGMENTATION OF PICTURES

We have described a global method to find exact location of boundaries in the region S. In this section, we will briefly describe a method of the initial segmentation of a picture into regions having homogeneous textural properties. Fig. 5 shows a flowchart of the initial segmentation procedure. First, the input picture is averaged to obtain the reduced version of the image. The initial segmentation is performed on this reduced image and the segmentation results are used as a plan for detecting exact locations of textural boundaries in the full size image. We use not only a single textural property but also multiple textural properties such as gray-level distribution, edges per unit area or edge direction for segmentation. After obtaining these textural properties in the image, a non-linear averaging operator proposed by Tomita and Tsuji[3] is applied to smooth textural properties of each point in the image. Then, the recursive thresholding method proposed by Tomita et al[4] is applied to segment the image using multiple textural properties.

First, the histograms of the entire image are computed for all textural properties. Then, by analyzing these histograms, the most promising property for partitioning the image is selected. That is, the property whose histogram has deep valleys between two prominent peaks is selected as the promising property for partitioning and the threshold is determined as the value of the bottom of the valley. Then, the image is segmented by the selected threshold of the selected property. For each of the segmented regions, we apply the same procedure as described above until each region has only one prominent peak in the histograms.

These segmented regions of the reduced image are utilized as the plan for detecting exact locations of the boundaries of textural regions in the full size image by the textural boundary detector described before. The plan gives the textural boundary detector the following two things: 1) search region of the boundary, and 2) textural properties of two neighboring regions to be utilized in finding the boundary.

5. EXPERIMENTAL RESULTS

To show the ability of detecting exact locations of textural boundaries, we tested the proposed method on the image shown in Fig. 6. Fig. 7 shows the initial segmentation procedure obtained for this image. Fig. 8 shows the boundaries detected by the textural boundary detector.

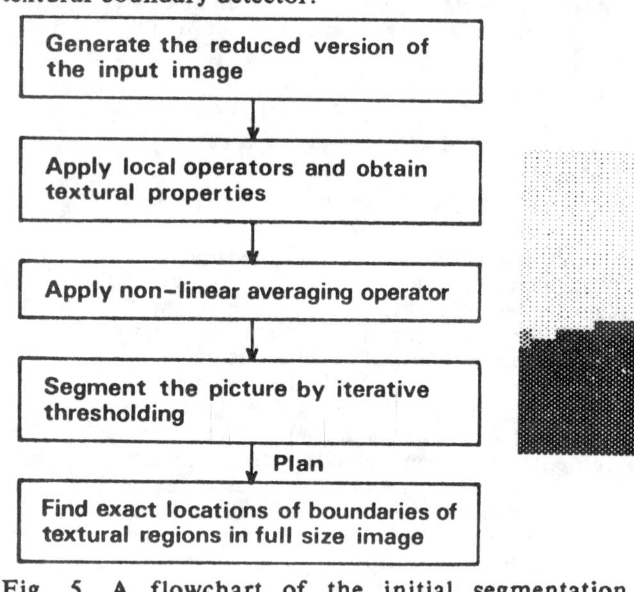

Fig. 5. A flowchart of the initial segmentation procedure.

Fig. 6. Picture containing four regions. Picture size is 256 by 256 points.

REFERENCE

[1] R. M. Haralick : *Statistical and Structural Approaches to Texture, 4th IJCPR, pp. 45-69, 1978.*

[2] M. Yachida, M. Ikeda and S. Tsuji : *A Knowledge Directed Line Finder for Analysis of Complex Scenes, 6th IJCAI.*

[3] F. Tomita and S. Tsuji : *Extraction of Multiple Regions by Smoothing in Selected Neighborhoods, IEEE Trans. SMC-7, pp. 107-109, 1977.*

[4] F. Tomita, M. Yachida and S. Tsuji : *Detection of Homogeneous Regions by Structural Analysis, 3rd IJCAI, pp. 564-571, 1973.*

Fig. 7. Initial segmentation procedure for the input picture shown in Fig. 6. (a) Result of applying the non-linear averaging operator to the reduced image of Fig. 6. Picture size is 64 by 64 points. (b) Plan region for the exact detection of boundaries.

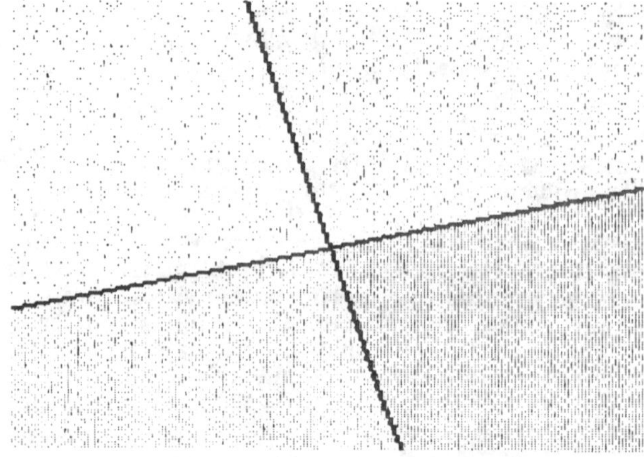

Fig. 8. Boundaries obtained by the textural boundary detector.

KNOWLEDGE-DRIVEN INTERPRETATION OF ESCA SPECTRA

Masato Yamazaki

Automatic Control Division
Electrotechnical Laboratory
Nagata-cho, Tokyo 100, Japan

Hideo Ihara

Materials Division
Electrotechnical Laboratory
Tanashi-shi, Tokyo 188, Japan

A system for automatically interpreting raw spectral data of an ESCA (Electron Spectroscopy for Chemical Analysis) is described. This system can remove background noise from the spectrum, identify each spectral peak, assign each peak to a corresponding atomic orbital and can obtain the chemical composition of a sample. A knowledge-driven method enables the system to identify very small peaks and rider peaks, and to obtain the most reliable assignment to each peak on the basis of specific chemical knowledge. Utilization of knowledge in low level processing is our main interest, while higher-level logical inference is emphasized in other knowledge-based systems, for example DENDRAL and MYCIN.

1. INTRODUCTION

An ESCA spectrometer is an important equipment which gives much information about chemical composition, bond nature and electronic structure of a sample. Considerable efforts have been done for removing large background noise[1] and for analysing bond nature from this spectrum. In this version of our system we intend to perform the composition analysis by a wide-range ESCA spectrum. It would be the first attempt to deal directly with the wide-range spectrum and to obtain a extensive result automatically.

Chemical knowledge is effectively utilized for identifying a peak and giving rational assignment to each peak. This paper briefly explains the automatic interpretation system and demonstrates an experimental result.

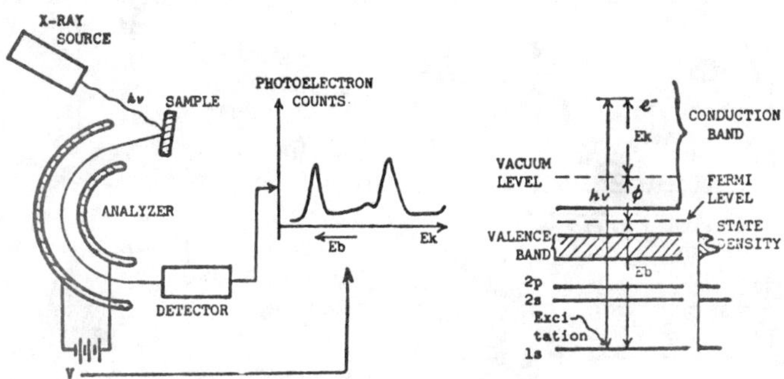

Fig.1 ESCA spectrometer and the photoelectric effect

2. ESCA SPECTROMETER

The ESCA spectrometer is illustrated in Fig.1. A monochromatic X-rays ($E_{sx} = h\nu = 1486.6$ev) is used to irradiate a sample in a vacuum. The ejected photoelectrons have a variety of kinetic energy, depending on which element and which level they come from. The binding energy E_b relative to the Fermi level is calculated by the following equation:

$$E_b = h\nu - E_K - \phi \qquad (1)$$

where E_K is the measured kinetic energy and ϕ is the work function of a sample.

Both an element and orbitals can be determined by the particular positions of a set of peaks. Relative quantity of each element can be calculated by measured peak area, or the integrated intensity, and theoretical cross section value.

3. INTERPRETATION PROCESS

3.1 Outline

Fig.2 shows in outline the identification and assignment process. Firstly, in the preprocessing stage, background noise of low frequency is removed. Secondly, in the knowledge-driven identification stage, obvious peaks and peaks related to them are identified, then peak-assignment pairs (P-A pairs) are made from these peaks and the corresponding possible assignments. This stage is carried out efficiently by making use of chemical knowledge. Thirdly, in the bottom-up identification stage, all the

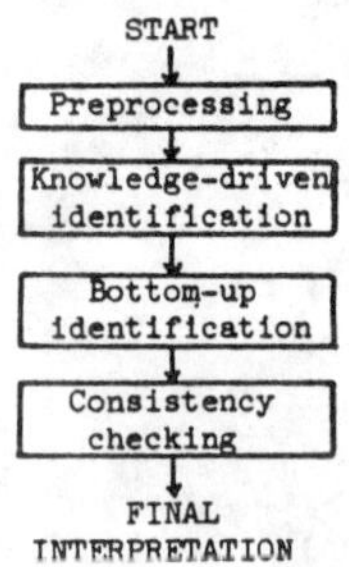

Fig. 2. Outline of the process

remaining peaks that are not relevant and are not related to other peaks are identified by a conventional statistical test. Finally, in the consistency checking stage, the Reliability and other properties of the P-A pairs are determined and the final interpretation is obtained.

3.2 Knowledge used

The chemical knowledge which will be used in the following sections consists of the expected binding energy and cross section values[2]. The former corresponds to peak position, and the latter to the peak area. These values are stored in ESCATBL as follows:

$$ESCATBL = (KNLG_1 \cdots KNLG_i \cdots KNLG_n) \quad (2)$$

$$KNLG_i = (ASS_{i1} \cdots ASS_{ij} \quad ASS_{im}) \quad (3)$$

$$ASS_{ij} = (ATOM_i \; LEVEL_{ij} \; EBE_{ij} \; CRS_{ij}) \quad (4)$$

In this formula, EBE_{ij}, the expected binding energy, and CRS_{ij}, the theoretical cross section value, are represented for each $LEVEL_{ij}$ of $ATOM_i$. Fig.3 shows part of this knowledge table.

The CRS_{ij} are normalized by setting the value of Carbon 1s to 1.000. Let S_{ai} be that of level i of the element A, and let S_{bj} be that of level j of the element B. The composition ratio is calculated as

$$A : B = S_{ai}/CRS_{ai} : S_{bj}/CRS_{bj} \quad (5)$$

```
ESCATBL (
   (H E1S 13.595 0.0002)
   (HE E1S 24.580 0.0082)
         :
   (O E2P3/2 13.614 0.0128)
   (O E2P1/2 7.0 0.0065)
   (O E2S 24.0 0.1405)
   (O E1S 532.0 2.93)
         :
   (PB E6P3/2 1 0.0291)
   (PB E6P1/2 1 0.0148)
         :
   (PB E4P1/2 764 2.12)

      )
```

Fig.3 Segment of the knowledge

3.3 Knowledge-driven identification stage

Obvious peaks and peaks related to them are identified, and possible P-A pairs are obtained as the output of this stage. The knowledge-driven mehtod used here consists of the following four steps (see Fig.4):

STEP1: The process begins by finding large peaks. A list HPEAKS of large peaks that are higher than a threshold TH is constructed by scanning through the preprocessed data DP

$$HPEAKS = (PEAK_1 \cdots PEAK_i \cdots \quad PEAK_l) \quad (6)$$

This TH is determined by an operator for terminating this stage.

STEP2: The highest peak is selected from the HPEAKS. All assignments which are consistent with the existence of this peak are chosen, and P-A pairs are made and stored in PALIST. A peak k is charactorized by a triplet as

$$PEAK_k = (HGT_k \; POS_k \; BE_k) \quad (7)$$

where HGT_k means peak height, POS_k peak position, and BE_k the binding energy value corresponding this position. From Eqs.(4) and (7), a P-A pair is represented as follows:

$$P\text{-}A = (PEAK_k \; ASS_{ij})$$

$$= ((HGT_k \; POS_k \; BE_k)(ATOM_i \; LEVEL_{ij} \; CRS_{ij})) \quad (8)$$

Comparing BEs with EBEs, matching torelance should be determined by estimated instrumental error and the possible chemical shift.

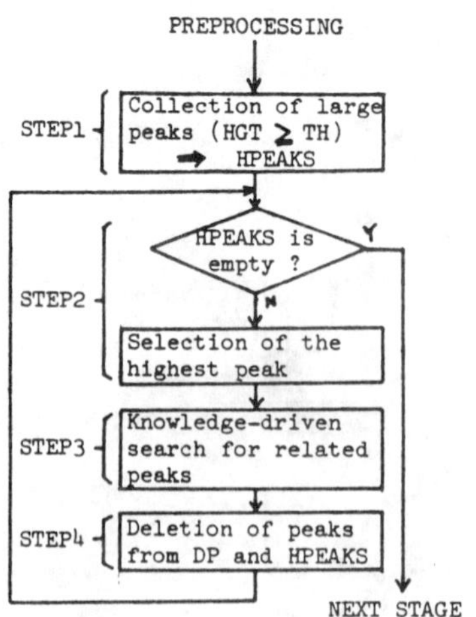

Fig. 4. Knowledge-driven identification stage

STEP3: For every candidate element the related peaks are knowledge-drivenly searched for, and all possible assignments are chosen. The P-A pairs are then made and added to the PALIST.

STEP4: The process deletes all peaks mentioned above from HPEAKS and DP. It then returns to STEP2, and repeats STEP2 through STEP4 until there remains no peak higher than the TH.

3.4 Consistency Checking stage

We explain three typical checking routines.

(1) Reliability test for P-A pairs: Let A be an element, suppose it has m levels and $CRS_1, \cdots,$ CRS_i, $,CRS_m$ be the cross section values, reliability factor RF is then defined as

$$RF = \frac{\sum_{i=1}^{m} \alpha_i \, CRS_{ai}}{\sum_{i=1}^{m} CRS_{ai}} \qquad (9)$$

where $\alpha_i = \begin{cases} 1, & \text{if such P-A pair is found} \\ -2, & \text{if such P-A pair is not found} \end{cases}$

Only reliable set of P-A pairs are selected based on this criterion.

(2) Calculation of the composition formula: Estimating peak areas on the original spectrum, calculate Eq.(5).

(3) Test of chemical shift: The chemical shift, a small deviation of a peak position, should be approximately equal for the same element and the same chemical state. So, if only a few shifts are clearly different from others under these conditions, a rational explanation of the fact would be that the identification stage has failed to find a correct peak and has found instead neighbouring one. There are two cases; 1) the correct peak is too small to identify and 2) the correct peak is a rider peak.

4. EXAMPLE

Fig.5 shows a 1024 point spectrum of a super conductive materials Pb Mo S . In the preprocessing stage step-like background noise was removed (Fig.6). Next, knowledge-driven identification began by finding the highest peak 'a'.

```
RF = 0.93
((565 857 163.1) ( S E2p3/2 165 1.11))        - g
((565 857 163.1) ( S E2p1/2 165 0.567))       - g
RF = 0.86
((158 479 532.2) ( O E1s 532.0 2.93))         - h
RF = 0.93
((88 987 36.1) ( MO E4p3/2 35 0.86))          - f
((88 987 36.1) ( MO E4p1/2 35 0.445))         - f
((1003 789 229.5) ( MO E3d5/2 227 5.62))      - a
((491 786 232.4) ( MO E3d3/2 230 3.88))       - b
((302 620 394.5) ( MO E3p3/2 392 5.94))       - c
((162 602 412.1) ( MO E3p1/2 410 3.04))       - c
((53 505 506.8) ( MO E3s 505 2.34))           - e
RF = 0.68
((61 1004 19.5) ( PB E5d5/2 19 1.58))         - i
((32 1002 21.5) ( PB E5d3/2 22 1.11))         - j
((643 882 138.6) ( PB E4f7/2 138 12.73))      - k
((432 877 143.5) ( PB E4f5/2 143 10.01))      - l
((162 602 412.1) ( PB E4d5/2 413 13.02))      - d
((98 578 435.5) ( PB E4d3/2 435 8.87))        - m
((42 363 645.5) ( PB E4p3/2 645 6.33))        - n

Pb : Mo : S = 1 : 7.4 : 9.5
```

Fig.7 Result obtained

Candidate assignments were selected as Sulfur 2s , Molybdenum 4d3/2, and Molybdenum 4d5/2. In STEP3 other peaks of Sulfur and Molybdenum were searched for, all the possible assignments were chosen for these peaks, and P-A pairs were made. Thirty-three pairs were produced on 14 peaks in this example. Reliability factor was then calculated for each element. S, Mo, Pb and O were verified and Ti, W, Ne, C and F were rejected. Final assignments and the composition ratio are shown in Fig.7. Difference of about 20% from the correct composition ratio (= 1:6:8) is thought to be due to inaccuracy of evaluated peak areas.

5. CONCLUSION

We have presented a system for interpreting ESCA spectra on the basis of chemical knowledge. Core-level peaks are identified and given rational assignments. The chemical composition of a sample is obtained. An example have shown effectiveness of our method in some difficult cases, for example, in finding a small peak, detecting a rider peak and choosing the most reasonable assignment from many alternatives.

REFERENCES

[1] J.N. Chazalviel, M. Campagna, G.K.Wertheim, and P.H. Schmidt, Physical Review B, Vol.14, No.10, 4586, Nov. 1976

[2] J.H. Scofield, J. of Elec. Spec. Rel. Phen., No.8, pp.129, 1976

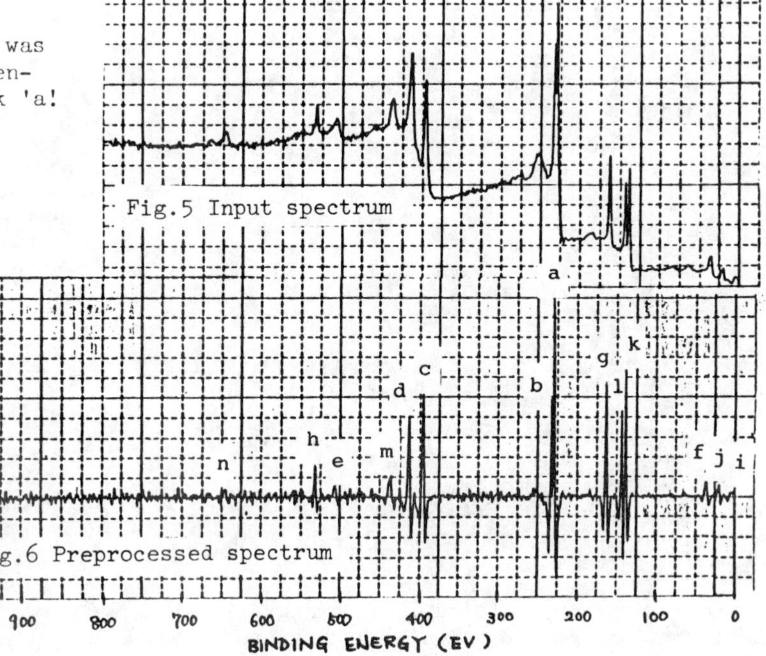

Fig.5 Input spectrum

Fig.6 Preprocessed spectrum

SYSP : A New Programming Language to the Next Generation

Toshio Yokoi, Shooichi Yokoyama, Taisuke Satoo, Fumio Motoyoshi
and Kazuhiro Fuchi

Machine Inference Section, Information Sciences Division
Electrotechnical Laboratory
2-6-1, Nagata-cho, Chiyoda-ku, Tokyo, Japan

Sysp(Structured Symbol System Processer) is a base programming language for knowledge representation, and also a non-procedural and non-von Neumman style programming language to the next generation. Logic programming, functional programming, object oriented programming etc. are integrated into a simple and transparent mechanism based on the message passing computation(QA model of computation). An overview of Sysp's framework is presented using simple examples.

1. INTRODUCTION

The research of knowledge representation demands a new type programming language for AI which is highly structured and is able to represent various aspects of knowledge naturally and uniformly. On the other hand, the one of automatic programming does new type programming(methodology and language) which is also highly structured and is able to make the process of programming more structured. These two trends aim at the same goal, for example, Sysp. It is a highly structured symbol manipulation system(in true sense, a general purpose computation system) based on Newell's physical symbol system hypothesis. Sysp consists of four co-ordinates.

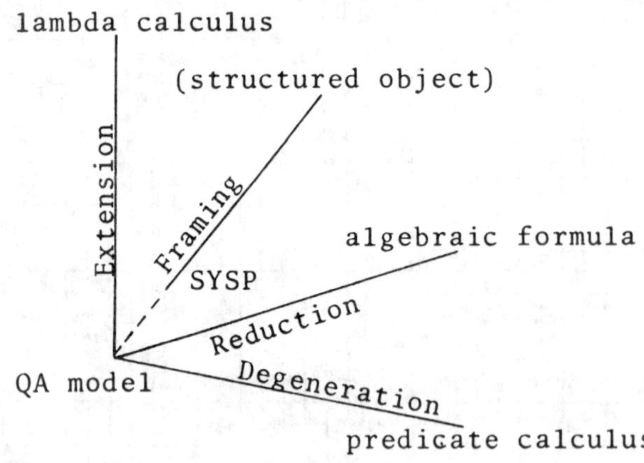

In followings, Sysp is outlined along Extension, Degeneration and Reduction co-ordinates.

2. EXTENSION to QA model

Lambda calculus is a computation model which is able to express the higher order computation naturally. So, it is available so much for the basic mechanism and semantics description of various programming languages and is extended to make its ability more powerful for this purpose. Recursion, Landin's J-operator, Reynolds's escape expression, Steele & Sussman's tail transfer mechanism and continuation function were introduced. These extensions were arranged into message passing mechanism like Actor formalism etc.[1]. The distinctive features of the mechanism are as follows.

(a) By preserving execution environment on heap instead of stack, send and receive actions are able to express coroutine and parallel computation directly.

(b) Multiple-value return and naming without side effect become possible. The composition and decomposition of data structure are expressed in non-procedural manner.

(c) The history of computation is preserved completely and easily, so that the well fitted mechanism to the evaluation of nondeterministic program is gained.

(d) In co-operation with static binding mechanism, truly necessary execution environment for a computation is clearly specified.

Moreover, QA model of computation, puts its stress on well-formed communication(question answering) mechanism for the natural and rigid representation of a problem solving process(computation). So, appropriate synchronization mechanism etc. are included inherently and the communication mechanism is made more structured.

One method of making the mechanism more structured is on message sent and received. In natural language, a sentence is classified into some types, declarative, interrogative, imperative or exclamative, so that a listener is able to understand the intention of a speaker so easily. And moreover, in interrogative sentence, it is expressed clearly what sort of answer is expected, yes-no or answer to interrogative(When... , Where... , How many... , What kinds of... etc.). Similarly, in QA model, various message types are provided. And a computation is represented as a natural "question-answering(QA) sequence".

The other method of making the communication mechanism more structured is on QA sequence. First, QA sequence is restricted to the following communication manners.

(1) When a question is sent/received, the answer must be received/sent.
(2) To send/receive the answer to the latest received/sent question.

With these restrictions, sequences starting with an action on a question and ending in an action on the corresponding answer are nested with one another. Such a sequence is called "well-structured QA sequence". The simplest well-structured QA sequence is to send/receive a question and then to receive/send the answer. These are called "atomic QA sequence".

QA sequence(computation) is reduced into some sub-QA sequence(subcomputation). Therefore, the description among sub-QA sequences gives the structure of the original QA sequence. This description is called "compound QA sequence". For example, factorial function in Lisp,

```
FACT:(LAMBDA (N) (IF (= N 0) 1
                     (* N (FACT (- N 1)))))
```

,is represented as QA sequence.

```
Fact:=>(0  ?) Then 1.=>
     =>(n  ?) Then (n  1  ?)=>-=>m.
                then (m  ?)= Fact= m.
                     then (n  m  ?)=>*=>m.
                          Then m.->
```

3. DEGENERATION to predicate calculus

It is possible to make two actions, to receive a question and to send the answer, degenerate into one action, to assert the fact. In the same manner, two actions, to send a question and to receive the answer, are made degenerate into one, to interrogate the fact. Futhermore, two actions, to assert a fact and to interrogate on the fact, are made degenerate into one object, a predicate(atomic formula).

By regarding assert and interrogate actions as atomic QA sequences, compound QA sequence is made degenerate. It is called "degenerate (compound) QA sequence". The factorial function is transformed into a partially degenerate QA sequence.

```
Fact:<=>(0 1)
     <=>(n ?m3) because (n 1 ?m1)<=>-   then
                        (m1 ?m2)<=>Fact then
                        (n m2 ?m3)<=>*
```

In this sequence, variables in the messages have some sort of indication(input or output) and the evaluation order are fixed. Next, this is transformed into a fully degenerate QA sequence.

```
<=>(Fact: 0 1)
<=>(Fact: n m3) because (-: n 1 m1)<=>   and
                        (Fact: m1 m2)<=> and
                        (*: n m2 m3)<=>
```

In this one, the variables have no indication and the fixation of the evaluation order is taken away. In order to make the meaning of Degeneration clearer, the factorial function is represented in Horn set,

```
+(Fact: 0 1)
+(Fact: n m3),-(-: n 1 m1),-(Fact: m1 m2)
             ,-(*: n m2 m3)
```

Assert action corresponds to positive clause and interrogate action does to negative clause. And further, pattern directed invocation of assert action by interrogate action corresponds to the application of Resolution rule.

In the current research on logic programming[2], it has tried to make clear the correspondence between computation structures and proof strategies without any explicit construct for control structure. By the following reasons, however, it needs to introduce appropriate procedural aspects into logic programming.

(1) Many computation sequences are condensed into one logical formula by abstracting certain aspects of the sequences, but only some of them are able to have actual meanings. That is, it is hard to say that it represents computation exactly.

(2) Proof mechanism like Resolution is powerful as basic computation mechanism, but very primitive. So, higher structures of computation can not be represented by proof strategy only.

It is so easy to introduce procedural elements for claptraps, but never desirable. Sysp makes it possible to define strict meanings of procedural elements by introducing the successive Degeneration process from QA model to predicale calculus.

4. REDUCTION to algebraic formula

Along Extension co-ordinate, lambda calculus, an applicative computation system, is extended to include imperative features preserving the advantages as it is. And again, QA model is reduced into algebraic formula, a typical applicative system. But this never means that Extension co-ordinate is traced conversely.

Send action is reduced into the composite function of receiver and message. Receive action is reduced into environment modifier function. Namely, a message is regarded as a functional form and a variable is regarded as a function which yields the value from environment as well as in GEDANKEN. Receive action is regarded as a functional form which tests whether or not the actual argument matches the message pattern and, if matched, modifies the environment by naming. Continuation(next) relation is represented as the composition of functions. In this way, a simple QA sequence is reduced mechanically into an applicative form. And further, Reduction process goes on. The factorial function is partially reduced to

```
Fact=(1•=>(0 ?);
      m:•=>m•*•(n m ?):•=>m•Fact•(m ?):•=>m•
          -•(n 1 ?):•=>(n ?))
```

Further, this is fully reduced into

```
Fact=(1•=>0•I;
      *•(I  Fact•-•(I  1):):)
```

through the transformation which simplifies environment modifier function and eliminates variables by substitution (introducing selector function). Thus, a QA sequence is reduced into an algebraic formula, its semantics is formalized as lows of algebra and it becomes possible to prove its various properties by formula manipulation, as Backus etc. point out. For comparison, the example is represented in Backus's FP[3],

```
Def !=eq•[id, 0̄] -> 1̄; *•[id, !•-•[id, 1̄]]
```

For each type of compound QA sequence, corresponding functional forms are provided. The applicative form obtained in this way is called "reduced QA sequence".

Functional programming is related to QA model through successive Reduction process. By this way, its weakpoints are covered up and its ability is extended as follows.

(1) The appropriate and natural interpretation of functional form are obtained.
(2) Advantages of other computation models, including history sensitivity, are added to in a very natural way.

5. CONCLUSION

The method for knowledge representation must be powerful, natural and formal. It must be powerful in order to represent complicated and higher order knowledge, natural in order to make it easy to use and understand, and formal in order to make possible for a computer to process represented knowledge mechanically. Sysp satisfies these three conditions sufficiently over a wide range by integrating four representative methods into one transparent mechanism. For example, factorial function is able to give natural looks in Sysp,

```
Fact:<=>(0 1)
     =>(n ?) Then (-•(n 1):  ?)=>Fact=>m.
             Then *•(m n):.=>
```

At present the main part of Sysp is implemented on EPICS-Lisp. In other papers[4], Sysp is described in more details.
AKNOWLEDGEMENTS: The authors wish to express their gratitude for the encouragement from the head of their division, Dr. H. Nishino.

REFERENCES

[1] Hewitt, C. : "Viewing Control Structures as Patterns of Passing Messages," Artificial Intelligence 8, pp.323-364 (1977)
[2] van Emden, M. H. : "Programming with Resolution Logic," in E. W. Elcock(ed.), Machine Intelligence 8, pp.266-299 (1977)
[3] Backus, J. : "Can Programming Be Liberated from the von Neumann Style? A Functional Style and Its Algebra of Programs," CACM, Vol.21, No.8, pp.613-641 (Aug. 1978)
[4] Yokoi, T. : "SYSP I.Basic Mechanism & II.Various Structures for Representation & III.Combining Various Structure," Bul. Electrotech. Lab., Vol.42, No.4 & 9 & 6 (Apr. & Sept. & June 1978) (in Japanese)

HIERARCHICAL CONCEPTS STRUCTURE FOR NATURAL LANGUAGE UNDERSTANDING SYSTEM

Sho Yoshida

Department of Electronics, Kyushu University 36

Hakozaki, Fukuoka 812, Japan

Hierarchical concepts structure is introduced to widen acceptability of input sentences of natural language understanding system.

It consists of a set of defined concepts (SDC) and scenarios each of which is a set of scenario elements. A scenario is one utilized everywhere. In our SDC concepts are defined with another concepts related through basic semantic relations. Types of these relations are presented with some examples. As compound semantic relations are composed of basic ones it is enough to construct SDC with only basic semantic relations.

1. Hierarchical concepts structure

Instead of efficiency of inference, use of scenarios[1] is in the opposite direction to afford those rich features of natural language to the system.

To overcome this situation, we introduced a set of defined concepts (SDC) and constructed a hierarchical concepts structure with scenarios.

A hierarchical concetps structure consists of a SDC and scenarios and a scenario is a set of scenario elements.

A scenario element is a partial scenario that correspond to a small part of story, and therefore can easily prepare, delete or correct.

SDC gives general (closer to natural language) definition of each concept by using basic semantic relations (and view-points) with other concepts so that it functions as to widen acceptability of input sentences of natural language understanding system.

An input sentence is analysed syntactically and the conceptual dependency representation with respect to the sentence (CDRS) is generated. CDRS is a directed, labeled graph which represents dependency relaitons among concepts expressed by words appearing in the sentence.

Figure 1 is a CDRS of a sentence "I go to school." Using this CDRS the system chooses a scenario element from a suitable scenario, say "GO TO SCHOOL" scenario and attaches this CDRS to it as an instance. We call scenario element with an instance attached in this way as semantic graph[2],[3] (with respect to a sentence ∿).

Figure 2 shows a part of "GO TO SHCOOL" scenario element with attached instance (sematic graph).

However, there may be no scenario element that fits to an input sentence "I go to school to meet my son" in any scenario. In this case, the system tries to find out general definition of "<GO>" in the SDC.

As SDC has definition for every concept, it fits to wide variety of CDRSs. Figure 3 shows "<GO>" element of SDC.

<I> —a→ <go> ←o_d— <school>

Figure 1. CDRS of " I go to school".

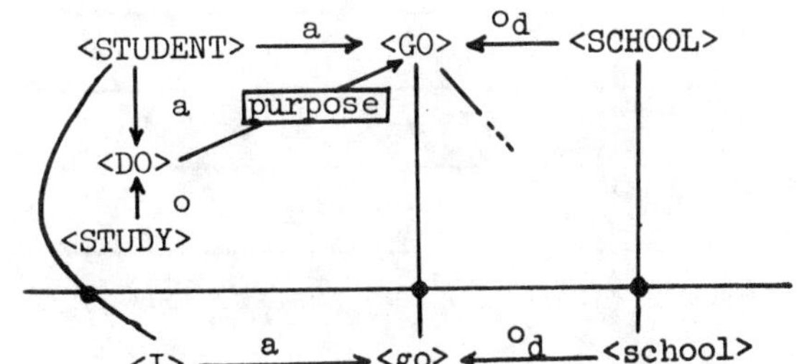

Figure 2. Semantic graph with respect to a sentence "I go to school".

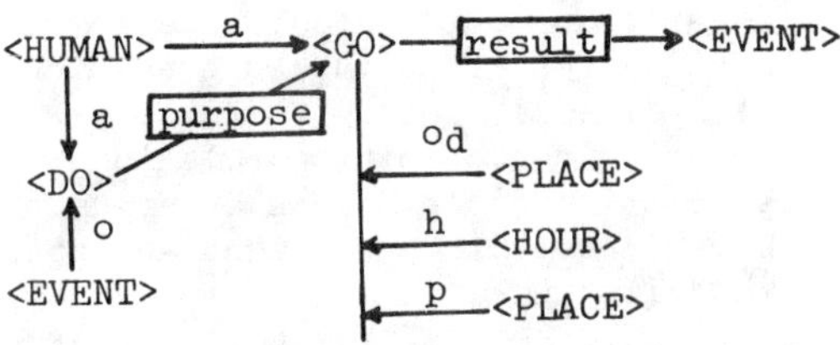

Figure 3. "<GO>" element of SDC.

2. Construction of SDC

2.1. Types of concepts

Concepts are classified into four types that roughly correspond to the concepts expressed by concrete nouns, verbs, adjectives/adverbs and abstract words as follows(see Notations).

(i) 'concrete object' concepts (ii) 'event' concepts (iii) 'modality' concepts

(iv) 'abstract thing' concepts: Abstract concepts that are designated by 'aspects (movements or modalities) of things', 'relations among things' or 'time and place'.

2.2. Semantic relations among concepts

There are following eight basic semantic relations among concepts.

(i) Super concept-subconcept relation (kind or extention relation)

(ii) Aspect relation: Relation among a 'concrete object' concept and concepts that give aspects of the concepts. This relation is given by using basic view-points such as "purpose of use", "color", "amount (thickness)". Basic view-points necessary to define <PRODUCT THING> like <PAPER> are given in Table 1.

Aspect relation	Basic view-point
Aspects about use	purpose of use, ways of use (what to use) (how to use)
Aspects about manufacturing	material, how to make
Aspects about structure	parts, arrangement,•••
Aspects about property	physical, mental,•••
Aspects about quantity	number, weight, length,•••
Aspects about aspect	color, shape, value, •••
Aspects about time	existing time
Aspects about place	existing place

Table 1. Basic view-points for <PRODUCT>.

(iii) Case relation

(iv) Cause-effect relation

(v) event-event relation other than cause-effect relation

Five relations of "logical", "accompanying", "before and after wrt. time", "condition" and "direct (indirect)" belong to this.

(vi) Descriptive definition relation

This relation describes an event using with another basic semantic relations and concepts.

(vii) Modality relation

View-points used in this relation are given by classifying "modality" concepts.

(viii) Synonym and antonym relation

2.3. Construction of SDC

i) Definition of concrete objects

Concrete objects are defined by using kind relation and aspect relation. View-points belonging to these relations are called "basic view-points" (Table 1).

a. Definition of subconcepts

Properties possessed by a super concept is inherited to its subconcepts unless otherwise stated in the definitions of them.

b. Definition of supreme concepts

It is very important that SDC contains every supreme (most general) concrete object concept that appears as a supreme concept of a given event concept in the case relation. For example, the supreme concept of the given event concept <EAT> in the (object) case relation is <things that can be objects to eat>(Figure 4). This gives judging conditions (or requirements) whether any given type of concept statisfies case relation with a given event concept. For example, if "plastic eraser" satisfies conditions "soft", "not hot", ••• then "human being" can "eat" it.

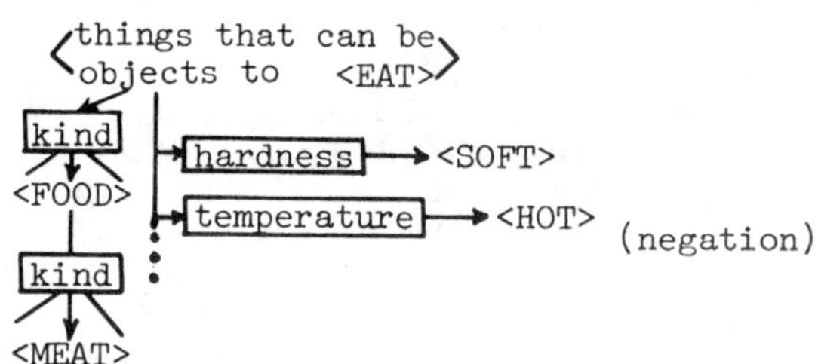

Figure 4. The supreme concept in the object case relation of <EAT>

ii) Definition of an "event" concept

This concept is defined by using case relation, cause-effect relation, event-event relation, descriptive definition relation, modality relation and synonym-antonym relation.

iii) Definition of a 'modality' concept

This concept is defined by using case relaiton, descriptive definition relation, cause-effect relation, modality relation and synonym-antonym relation.

iv) Definition of an "abstract thing" concept

This concept is defined by using case relation, cause-effect relation, modality relation, descriptive relation, kind relation and synonym-antonym relation.

3. Composition of view-points

There can be many finer view-points other than basic ones.

Is it necessary to define a concept using

all of these finer view-points?

We are getting rid of this problem by composing these finer view-points of basic semantic relations, basic view-points and other concepts.

Let $\mathbf{r}$ be an arbitrary m-ary semantic relation and $\alpha_1, \alpha_2, \cdots, \alpha_m$ be concepts for which $\mathbf{r}(\alpha_1, \alpha_2, \cdots, \alpha_m)$ can be asserted.

We obtain a relation,

$$\lambda x \mathbf{r}(\alpha_1, \alpha_2, \cdots, x, \cdots, \alpha_m)$$

from $\mathbf{r}(\alpha_1, \alpha_2, \cdots, \alpha_m)$,
where x is a concept variable and λ is an abstraction operator.

We express a concept α for which a certain semantic relation $\mathbf{r}(\alpha)$ is asserted[4] as,

$$\alpha \leftarrow\!- - \mathbf{r}(\alpha)$$

For example,

$$\alpha \leftarrow\!- - \alpha \longrightarrow\boxed{\text{kind}}\longrightarrow \beta$$

means that α is a concept for which $\alpha \longrightarrow\boxed{\text{kind}}\longrightarrow \beta$ is asserted.

Let (1) and (2) asserted.

$$\mathbf{r}(\alpha_1, \alpha_2, \cdots, \alpha_i, \cdots, \alpha_m) \quad \cdots (1)$$

$$\alpha_i \leftarrow\!- - \mathbf{r}_1(\alpha_1', \alpha_2', \cdots, \alpha_i, \cdots, \alpha_n') \quad \cdots (2)$$

Where $\mathbf{r}$, $\mathbf{r}_1$ are semantic relations and $\alpha_1, \alpha_2, \cdots, \alpha_n'$ are concepts. In this case composition of relation is defined as follows.

$$(\lambda x)\mathbf{r}(\alpha_1, \alpha_2, \cdots, x, \cdots, \alpha_m)(\alpha_i \leftarrow\!- - \mathbf{r}_1(\alpha_1', \alpha_2', \cdots, \alpha_n'))$$

By repeated application of composition and abstraction to semantic relations, we can obtain any relation from only basic semantic relations and basic view-points.

On the other hand, any sentence is expressed by CDRS briefly explained in chapter 1 by using semantic relations listed in chapter 2. For example, 'He hate him very much.' has the following CDRS.

<hate> (<he$_1$>$_a$ <him$_2$>$_o$)
└─[mod]──→ <much>
          └─[mod]──→ <very>

From this CDRS, we can define a binary hate-relation $(\lambda xy)\mathbf{r}_h(x,y)$ as follows.

$(\lambda x,y)\mathbf{r}_h(x,y) = (\lambda x,y)($<hate>$(x_a, y_o))$
└─[mod]→ <much>
     └─[mod]→ <very>

Therefore, we can define any semantic relation if we could give definition of the semantic relation by sentences (hence CDRS).

4. Concluding remarks

We discussed about general structure of SDC necessary for constructing natural language understanding system.

We proposed to introduce a hierarchal concept system in which essentially the same semantic relations are used to define concepts in each stage of hierarchy.

We could not discuss about 'mode' in this paper. For example, CDRS of a sentence, 'I should go there.' is given as follows.

<I> ──a──→ <go> ←─o_p (necessity)── <there>

Here the information given by (necessity) is a 'mode' of an event concept <go>. We singled out eighty four such modes which are used in ordinary written sentences[5]. Detailed composition rules of semantic relations including these mode will be discussed in our forth-coming paper.

Notations:

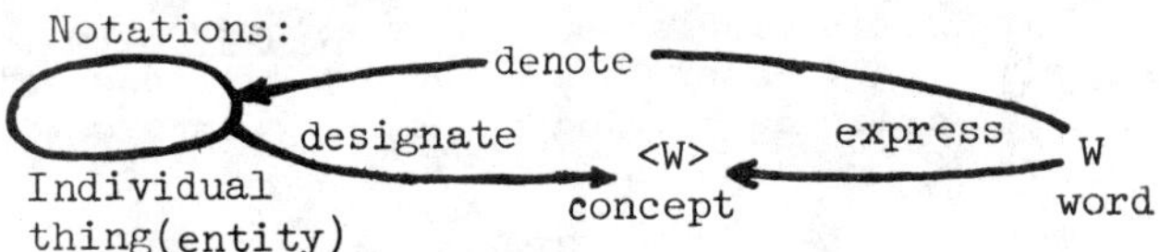

Definition of "denote", "designate" and "express"

Acknowledgements

I would like to acknowledge the contributions of H. Tsurumaru while preparing this paper. He is thankful to T. Hitaka, K. Shudo and T. Fujita for their discussions and suggestions as members of our research project. This research has been sponsord by Japanese Ministry of Education Science Foundation and Takeda Science Foundation.

References

[1] Schank,R.C. : "Conceptual Information Processing", North-holland/American elsevier, 1975.

[2] Mylopoulos,J., Cohen,P., Borgida,A. and Sugar,L. : "Semantic Networks and the Generation of Context", Proc.4-IJCAI, 1975.

[3] Hayes,P.J. : "On Semantic Nets, Frames and Associations", Proc. 5-IJCAI, 1977.

[4] Hendrix,G.G. : "Expanding the Utility of Semantic Networks through Partitioning", Proc. 5-IJCAI, 1977.

[5] Shudo,K., Tsurumaru,H. and Yoshida,S. : "A Predicative Part Processing System for Japanese English Machine Translation", Trans. IECE of Japan, E60-10, 1977.

APPROXIMATE REASONING BASED ON FUZZY LOGIC

L.A. Zadeh*
Computer Science Division
Department of Electrical Engineering and Computer Sciences
and the Electronics Research Laboratory
University of California, Berkeley
Berkeley, California 94720

During the past several years, the emergence of expert systems as a field of considerable practical as well as theoretical importance within AI has provided a strong impetus for the development of theories of approximate reasoning and credibility assessment of inference processes in knowledge-based systems.

The approach to approximate reasoning described in this paper is based on a fuzzy logic, FL, in which the truth-values and quantifiers are defined as possibility distributions which carry linguistic labels such as _true_, _quite true_, _not very true_, _many_, _not very many_, _several_, _almost all_, etc. Based on the concept of a possibility distribution, a set of translation and inference rules is developed and their application to inference from imprecise premises is illustrated by examples.

1. INTRODUCTION

It has long been recognized that much, perhaps most, of human reasoning is approximate rather than exact in nature.** And yet, logicians and cognitive scientists have devoted scant attention to the development of theories of approximate reasoning, partly because of the deeply entrenched tradition of respect for what is precise and disdain for what is fuzzy, and partly because there was no compelling need for such theories before the advent of artificial intelligence.

In recent years, however, the rapid growth of interest in natural language processing and the emergence of expert systems as an important application area within AI have made it increasingly clear that a better understanding of the processes of approximate reasoning is a prerequisite to the development of knowledge-based systems which can manipulate information that is imprecise, incomplete or not totally reliable.

In a series of papers starting in 1973 [2-7], we have advanced the view that conventional logical systems do not provide an appropriate basis for approximate reasoning and have suggested a fuzzy logic, FL, for this purpose. In contrast to two-valued and multi-valued logics, the truth-values of FL are linguistic rather than numerical, as are quantifiers exemplified by _many_, _most_, _not very many_, _few_, _several_, _almost all_, etc. Furthermore, the rules of inference in FL are approximate rather than exact. Thus, in spirit as well as in substance FL represents a sharp break with the long-standing tradition of extreme precision in logic and a move toward an accommodation with the pervasive imprecision of human thought, perception, language and decision-making.

Another important difference between FL and classical logical systems centers on the concept of truth. Thus, whereas in the latter systems [8,9] the truth of a proposition serves as a starting point for the definition

---

*Research supported by Naval Electronic Systems Command Contract N00039-78-C-0013 and National Science Foundation Grant ENG-7823143

**The terms "approximate reasoning" and "fuzzy reasoning" are frequently used interchangeably in the literature. A comprehensive exposition of the foundations of fuzzy reasoning may be found in the paper by B.R. Gaines [1].

of various basic concepts, the corresponding role in FL is played not by truth but by the concept of a possibility distribution, by which is meant a mapping associated with a variable X, π_X: U → [0,1], which assigns to each point u in the domain of X, U, the possibility that X could take u as a value. The concept of truth, then, is employed to express the compatibility of the possibility distribution induced by a proposition p with that of a reference proposition r. In this sense, the truth of a proposition is a relative concept and is a measure of its compatibility or consistency with a collection of propositions which constitute a database.

Our main concern in the present paper is with (a) the establishment of translation rules for various types of imprecise propositions; (b) inference from such propositions; and (c) the development of a conceptual framework for dealing with the issues of belief and credibility. The latter issues play a particularly important role in expert systems [10-17] as well as in the theories of evidence and decision analysis [18-24].

2. THE CONCEPT OF A POSSIBILITY DISTRIBUTION

As a preliminary to the consideration of translation rules for various types of propositions, it will be helpful to establish some of the properties of possibility distributions which will be needed in later sections.*

Informally, if X is a variable taking values in U, then a possibility distribution, Π_X, associated with X may be viewed as a fuzzy (or elastic) constraint on the values that may be assigned to X. Such a distribution is characterized by a possibility distribution function π_X: U → [0,1] which associates with each u ∈ U the "degree of ease" or the possibility that X may take u as a value.

In some cases, the constraint on the values of X is physical in origin. For example, if X is the number of students in a classroom which has, say, 50 seats, then $\pi_X(u) = 1$ for u up to 50, with $\pi_X(u)$ gradually declining to 0 at, say, u = 75. In this case, an intermediate value of π_X, say $\pi_X(65) = 0.3$, would signify that, by some explicit or implicit criterion, the degree of ease with which 65 students could be crowded into the classroom is 0.3 (on the scale from 0 to 1).

*An introductory exposition of possibility theory may be found in [29]. A historical account of the concepts of possibility and probability is contained in [30].

In most cases, however, the possibility distribution which is associated with a variable is epistemic rather than physical in origin. A basic assumption in fuzzy logic is that such epistemic possibility distributions are induced by propositions expressed in a natural language. In more concrete terms, this assumption may be stated as the

Possibility Postulate. If F is a fuzzy subset of U characterized by its membership function μ_F: U → [0,1], then the proposition "X is F" induces a possibility distribution Π_X which is equal to F. Equivalently, "X is F" translates into the possibility assignment equation $\Pi_X = F$, i.e.,

$$X \text{ is } F \longrightarrow \Pi_X = F \tag{1}$$

which signifies that the proposition "X is F" has the effect of constraining the values that may be assumed by X, with the possibility distribution Π_X identified with F.

As a simple illustration of (1), if in the proposition "X is small" small is regarded as a label of a fuzzy subset of U = {0,1,2,...} which is defined by*

$$\text{SMALL} = 1/0 + 1/1 + 0.8/2 + 0.6/3 + 0.4/4 + 0.2/5 \tag{2}$$

then

$$\begin{aligned} \text{Poss}\{X=0\} &= 1 \\ \text{Poss}\{X=1\} &= 1 \\ \text{Poss}\{X=2\} &= 0.8 \\ \text{Poss}\{X=5\} &= 0.2 \end{aligned} \tag{3}$$

where $\text{Poss}\{X=u\} = \pi_X(u)$ is the possibility that X may take u as a value.

An important aspect of the concept of a possibility distribution is that it is nonstatistical in nature. As a consequence, if P_X is a probability distribution associated with X then the only connection between Π_X and P_X is that impossibility (i.e., zero possibility) implies improbability but not vice-versa. Thus, Π_X cannot be inferred from P_X nor can P_X be inferred from Π_X.

As in the case of probabilities, one can define joint and conditional possibilities. Thus, if X and Y are variables taking values in U and V, respectively, then we can define the joint and and conditional possibility distributions

*The notation $F = \mu_1/x_1 + \cdots + \mu_n/x_n$ signifies that F is a fuzzy subset of the set $\{x_1,\ldots,x_n\}$, with μ_i, i = 1,...,n, being the grade of membership of x_i in F. Uppercase symbols (e.g., F, SMALL) are employed to denote names of sets (fuzzy or nonfuzzy).

through their respective distribution functions:

$$\pi_{(X,Y)}(u,v) = \text{Poss}\{X=u,\ Y=v\},\ u \in U,\ v \in V \qquad (4)$$

and

$$\pi_{(X|Y)}(u|v) = \text{Poss}\{X=u|Y=v\} \qquad (5)$$

where (5) represents the conditional distribution function of X given Y.

If we know the distribution function of X and the conditional distribution function of Y given X, then we can construct the joint distribution function of X and Y by forming the conjunction ($\wedge \triangleq \min$)

$$\pi_{(X,Y)}(u,v) = \pi_X(u) \wedge \pi_{(Y|X)}(v|u) \ . \qquad (6)$$

However, unlike the identity that holds in the case of probabilities, we can also obtain $\pi_{(X,Y)}(u,v)$ by forming the conjunction of $\pi_{(X|Y)}(u|v)$ and $\pi_{(Y|X)}(v|u)$:

$$\pi_{(X,Y)}(u,v) = \pi_{(X|Y)}(u|v) \wedge \pi_{(Y|X)}(v|u) \qquad (7)$$

In yet another deviation from parallelism with probabilities, the marginal possibility distribution function of X may be expressed in more than one way in terms of the joint and conditional possibility distribution functions. More specifically, we may have

(a) $$\pi_X(u) = \vee_v \pi_{(X,Y)}(u,v) \qquad (8)$$

where $\vee_v$ denotes the supremum over $v \in V$;

(b) $$\pi_X(u) = \vee_v \pi_{(X|Y)}(u|v) \qquad (9)$$

and

(c) $$\pi_X(u) = \pi_{(X|Y)}(u,\tilde{v}(u)) \qquad (10)$$

where, for a given u, $\tilde{v}(u)$ is the value of v at which $\pi_{(Y|X)}(v|u) = 1$, if $\tilde{v}(u)$ is defined for every $u \in U$.

Intuitively, (a) represents the possibility of assigning a value to X as perceived by an observer ((X,Y) observer) who observes the joint possibility distribution $\Pi_{(X,Y)}$. Similarly, (b) represents the perception of an observer ((X|Y) observer) who observes only the conditional possibility distribution $\Pi_{(X|Y)}$ and is unconcerned with or unaware of $\Pi_{(Y|X)}$. And (c) expresses the perception of an observer who assumes that v is assigned that value, if it exists, which makes $\pi_{(Y|X)}(v|u)$ equal to unity.

In relating π_X to $\pi_{(X|Y)}$ through the operator $\vee$ (supremum), we are tacitly invoking the principle of maximal restriction [4], which asserts that, in the absence of complete information about Π_X, we should equate Π_X to the maximal (i.e., least restrictive) possibility distribution which is consistent with the partial information about Π_X. In the case of (a), for example, this would be the supremum of $\pi_{(X,Y)}(u,v)$ over $v \in V$.

As will be seen in Section 3, the concept of a conditional possibility distribution plays a basic role in the formulation of a generalized form of <u>modus ponens</u> and in defining a measure of belief. What is as yet an unsettled issue revolves around the question of how to derive $\pi_{(X|Y)}$ and $\pi_{(Y|X)}$ from $\pi_{(X,Y)}$. Somewhat different answers to this question are presented in [25-27]. It may well turn out to be the case that, in contrast to probabilities, there does not exist a unique solution to the problem and that, in general, the answer depends on the perspective of the observer.

3. POSSIBILITY THEORY AND FUZZY LOGIC

As was alluded to already, the concept of a possibility distribution and the possibility theory which is based on it, play a central role in fuzzy logic by providing a means for the representation of the meaning of imprecise premises and the generation of propositions which follow logically from them.

Typically, a variable in fuzzy logic is treated as a <u>linguistic variable</u> [4], that is, a variable whose values are represented as words or sentences in a natural or synthetic language, with each such value defining a possibility distribution in the domain of the variable. In effect, what this implies is that a linguistic variable is a microlanguage with its own syntax and semantics. For example, in the case of FL, the linguistic values of the variable <u>Truth</u> may be generated by a context-free grammar and interpreted by an attributed grammar [28]. Thus, starting with (a) the primary term <u>true</u> and its antonym <u>false</u>; and (b) a finite set of modifiers and connectives such as <u>and</u>, <u>or</u>, <u>not</u>, <u>very</u>, <u>more or less</u>, <u>quite</u>, <u>extremely</u>, etc., the linguistic value of <u>Truth</u> may be represented as

true	false
not true	not false
very true	very false
not very true	not very false
more or less true	more or less false
quite true	quite false
not quite true	not quite false

not true and not false
not very true and not very false

In FL, a linguistic truth-value is regarded as a composite label of a possibility distribution in the interval [0,1], which is the set of truth-values in Lukasiewicz's L_{Aleph_1} logic. What this means is that in FL we generally deal not with numerically-valued truth-values but with their possibility distributions.

An important distinction between FL and L_{Aleph_1} is that in L_{Aleph_1}--as in all other multi-valued logics--there are only two quantifiers all and some, whereas in FL we can employ a large variety of fuzzy quantifiers exemplified by few, several, many, most, almost all, very many, not very many, etc. This feature of FL makes it possible to translate, and infer from, imprecise premises exemplified by

Most tall women are not very fat.
Among the many men who are heavy smokers, quite a few are overweight and some are heavy drinkers.
Carol has several close friends who have many children.

The meaning of a quantifier in FL is based on the concept of the cardinality of a fuzzy set. Thus, if F is a fuzzy subset of a finite set $U = \{u_1, \ldots, u_n\}$ characterized as

$$F = \mu_1/u_1 + \cdots + \mu_N/u_N$$

where μ_i is the grade of membership of u_i in F, $i = 1, \ldots, N$, then the power of F--which is roughly a measure of its cardinality--may be defined as

$$|F| = \sum_{i=1}^{n} \mu_i \ . \qquad (11)$$

Alternatively, and perhaps more appropriately, the cardinality of F may be defined as a fuzzy number, as is done in [6]. Thus, if the elements of F are sorted in descending order, so that $\mu_n \leq \mu_m$ if $n \geq m$, then the truth-value of the proposition

$$p \triangleq F \text{ has at least n elements} \qquad (12)$$

is defined to be equal to μ_n, while that of q,

$$q \triangleq F \text{ has at most n elements ,} \qquad (13)$$

is taken to be $1-\mu_{n+1}$. From this it follows that the truth-value of the proposition r,

$$r \triangleq F \text{ has exactly n elements ,} \qquad (14)$$

is given by $\mu_n \wedge (1-\mu_{n+1})$. An illustration of these alternative definitions of cardinality is provided by Example 5 in Section 4.

The translation rules for propositions expressed in a natural language form an important part of PRUF--a meaning representation language based on possibility theory [7].* In what follows, we shall present in a summarized form a subset of such rules which play a basic role in FL.

Translation Rules

1. Modifier rule. If

$$X \text{ is } F \longrightarrow \Pi_X = F \qquad (15)$$

then

$$X \text{ is mF} \longrightarrow \Pi_X = F^+$$

where m is a modifier such as not, very, more or less, etc., and F^+ is a modification of F induced by m. More specifically: If m = not, then $F^+ = F'$ = complement of F, i.e.,

$$\mu_{F^+}(u) = 1 - \mu_F(u) \ , \quad u \in U \ . \qquad (16)$$

If m = very, then $F^+ = F^2$, i.e.,

$$\mu_{F^+}(u) = \mu_F^{\ 2}(u), \quad u \in U \ . \qquad (17)$$

If m = more or less, then $F^+ = \sqrt{F}$, i.e.,

$$\mu_{F^+}(u) = \sqrt{\mu_F(u)} \ , \quad u \in U \ . \qquad (18)$$

As a simple illustration of (15), if SMALL is defined as in (2), then

$$X \text{ is very small} \longrightarrow \Pi_X = F^2 \qquad (19)$$

where

$$F^2 = 1/0 + 1/1 + 0.64/2 + 0.36/3 + 0.16/4 + 0.04/5 \ . \qquad (20)$$

It should be noted that (16)-(18) should be viewed as default rules which may be replaced by other translation rules in cases in which some alternative interpretations of the modifiers very and more or less are more appropriate.

2. Conjunctive, disjunctive and implicational rules. If

$$X \text{ is } F \longrightarrow \Pi_X = F \ \text{ and } \ Y \text{ is } G \longrightarrow \Pi_Y = G \qquad (21)$$

where F and G are fuzzy subsets of U and V,

---

*There are several implemented languages which have extensive facilities for the manipulation of fuzzy propositions and execution of fuzzy instructions. Prominent among these are FUZZY [23] and FSTDS [30].

respectively, then

(a) X is F and Y is G $\rightarrow \Pi_{(X,Y)} = F \times G$ (22)
where

$$\mu_{F\times G}(u,v) \triangleq \mu_F(u) \wedge \mu_G(v) \quad (\wedge = \min) \quad (23)$$

(b) X is F or Y is G $\rightarrow \Pi_{(X,Y)} = \bar{F} \cup \bar{G}$ (24)
where

$$\bar{F} \triangleq F \times V \;, \quad \bar{G} \triangleq U \times G \quad (25)$$

and

$$\mu_{\bar{F}\cup\bar{G}}(u,v) = \mu_F(u) \vee \mu_G(v) \;. \quad (26)$$

(c) If X is F then Y is G $\rightarrow \Pi_{(Y|X)} = \bar{F}' \oplus \bar{G}$ (27)

where $\Pi_{(Y|X)}$ denotes the conditional possibility distribution of Y given X, and the bounded sum $\oplus$ is defined by

$$\mu_{\bar{F}'\oplus\bar{G}}(u,v) = 1 \wedge (1-\mu_F(u)+\mu_G(v)) \;. \quad (28)$$

As simple illustrations of (22), (24) and (27), if

$$F \triangleq \text{SMALL} = 1/1 + 0.6/2 + 0.1/3 \quad (29)$$

$$G \triangleq \text{LARGE} = 0.1/1 + 0.6/2 + 1/3 \quad (30)$$

then

X is small and Y is large $\rightarrow \Pi_{(X,Y)}$ (31)

$$= 0.1/(1,1) + 0.6/(1,2) + 1/(1,3) + 0.1/(2,1) + 0.6/(2,2) + 0.6/(2,3) + 0.1/(3,1) + 0.1/(3,2) + 0.1/(3,3)$$

and

If X is small then Y is large $\rightarrow \Pi_{(Y|X)}$ (33)

$$= 0.1/(1,1) + 0.6/(1,2) + 1/(1,3) + 0.5/(2,1) + 1/(2,2) + 1/(2,3) + 1/(3,1) + 1/(3,2) + 1/(3,3) \;.$$

3. <u>Quantification rule</u>. If $U = \{u_1,\ldots,u_N\}$, Q is a quantifier such as <u>many</u>, <u>few</u>, <u>several</u>, <u>all</u>, <u>some</u>, <u>most</u>, etc., and

$$X \text{ is } F \rightarrow \Pi_X = F \quad (34)$$

then the proposition "QX are F" (e.g., "many X's are large") translates into

$$\Pi_{\text{Count}(F)} = Q \quad (35)$$

where Count(F) denotes the number (or the proportion) of elements of U which are in F. By definition (11), if the fuzzy set F is expressed as

$$F = \mu_1/u_1 + \mu_2/u_2 + \cdots + \mu_N/u_N \quad (36)$$

then

$$\text{Count}(F) = \sum_{i=1}^{N} \mu_i \;. \quad (37)$$

As a simple illustration of (35), if the quantifier <u>several</u> is defined as

$$\text{SEVERAL} \triangleq 0/1 + 0.4/2 + 0.6/3 + 1/4 + 1/5 + 1/6 + 0.6/7 + 0.2/8 \quad (38)$$

then

Several X's are large $\rightarrow \Pi_{\sum_{i=1}^{N} \mu_{\text{LARGE}}(u_i)}$ (39)

$$= 0/1 + 0.4/2 + 0.6/3 + 1/4 + 1/5 + 1/6 + 0.6/7 + 0.2/8$$

where $\mu_{\text{LARGE}}(u_i)$ is the grade of membership of the ith value of X in the fuzzy set LARGE.

4. <u>Truth qualification rule</u>. Let τ be a fuzzy truth-value, e.g., <u>very true</u>, <u>quite true</u>, <u>more or less true</u>, etc. Such a truth-value may be regarded as a fuzzy subset of the unit interval which is characterized by a membership function $\mu_\tau\colon [0,1] \rightarrow [0,1]$.

A truth-qualified proposition, e.g., "It is τ that X is F," is expressed as "X is F is τ." As shown in [5], the translation rule for such propositions is given by

$$X \text{ is } F \text{ is } \tau \rightarrow \Pi_X = F^+ \quad (40)$$

$$\mu_{F^+}(u) = \mu_\tau(\mu_F(u)) \;. \quad (41)$$

As an illustration, consider the truth-qualified proposition

Bob is young is very true

which by (40), (41) and (17) translates into

$$\Pi_{\text{Age(Bob)}} = \mu_{\text{TRUE}^2}(\mu_{\text{YOUNG}}(u)) \;. \quad (42)$$

Now, if we assume that

$$\mu_{\text{YOUNG}}(u) = (1 + (\tfrac{u}{25})^2)^{-1}, \quad u \in [0,100] \quad (43)$$

and

$$\mu_{\text{TRUE}}(v) = v^2, \quad v \in [0,1] \quad (44)$$

then (41) yields

$$\Pi_{\text{Age(Bob)}} = (1 + (\tfrac{u}{25})^2)^{-4} \quad (45)$$

as the possibility distribution of the age of Bob.

Used in combination, the translation rules stated above provide a system for the determination of the possibility distribution induced by a fairly complex composite proposition. For example, the proposition

If X is not very large and Y is more or less small then Z is very very large.

induces the conditional possibility distribution described by

$$\pi_{(Z|X,Y)}(w|u,v) = 1 \wedge (1 - (1-\mu^2_{\text{LARGE}}(u)) \wedge \mu_{\text{SMALL}}(v) + \mu^4_{\text{LARGE}}(w)) \;. \quad (46)$$

It should be noted that rules of this type have found practical applications in the design of fuzzy logic controllers in steel plants, cement kilns and other types of industrial process control applications in which instructions expressed in a natural language are transformed into control signals [31-33].

Rules of Inference

In our approach to approximate reasoning, the translation rules for imprecise propositions serve as a preliminary to the application of various rules of inference to the possibility distributions which are induced by such propositions, leading to other possibility distributions which upon retranslation yield the conclusions which may be drawn from the premises.

More specifically, the basic rules of inference in FL are the following.

1. Projection rule. Consider a fuzzy proposition whose translation is expressed as

$$p \longrightarrow \Pi_{(X_1,\ldots,X_n)} = F \tag{47}$$

and let $X_{(s)}$ denote a subvariable of the variable $X \triangleq (X_1,\ldots,X_n)$, i.e.,

$$X_{(s)} = (X_{i_1},\ldots,X_{i_k}) \tag{48}$$

where the index sequence $s \triangleq (i_1,\ldots,i_k)$ is a subsequence of the sequence $(1,\ldots,n)$.

Furthermore, let $\Pi_{X_{(s)}}$ denote the marginal possibility distribution of $X_{(s)}$; that is,

$$\Pi_{X_{(s)}} = \mathrm{Proj}_{U_{(s)}} F \tag{49}$$

where U_i, $i = 1,\ldots,n$, is the universe of discourse associated with X_i;

$$U_{(s)} = U_{i_1} \times \cdots \times U_{i_k} \tag{50}$$

and the projection of F on $U_{(s)}$ is defined by the possibility distribution function

$$\begin{aligned} &\pi_{X_s}(u_{i_1},\ldots,u_{i_k}) \\ &\quad = \mathrm{Sup}_{u_{j_1},\ldots,u_{j_m}} \mu_F(u_1,\ldots,u_n) \end{aligned} \tag{51}$$

where $s' \triangleq (j_1,\ldots,j_m)$ is the index subsequence which is complementary to s, and μ_F is the membership function of F.

Now let q be a retranslation of the possibility assignment equation

$$\Pi_{X_{(s)}} = \mathrm{Proj}_{U_{(s)}} F\ . \tag{52}$$

Then, the projection rule asserts that q may be inferred from p. In a schematic form, this assertion may be expressed more transparently as

$$\begin{array}{l} p \longrightarrow \Pi_{(X_1,\ldots,X_n)} = F \\ \qquad\qquad\quad \downarrow \\ q \longleftarrow \Pi_{X_{(s)}} = \mathrm{Proj}_{U_{(s)}} F \end{array} \tag{53}$$

2. Conjunction rule. Consider a proposition p which is an assertion concerning the possible values of, say, two variables X and Y which take values in U and V, respectively. Similarly, let q be an assertion concerning the possible values of the variables Y and Z, taking values in V and W. With these assumptions, the translations of p and q may be expressed as

$$\begin{array}{l} p \longrightarrow \Pi^p_{(X,Y)} = F \\ q \longrightarrow \Pi^q_{(Y,Z)} = G \end{array} \tag{59}$$

Let $\bar{F}$ and $\bar{G}$ be, respectively, the cylindrical extensions of F and G in $U \times V \times W$. Thus,

$$\bar{F} = F \times W \tag{60}$$

and

$$\bar{G} = U \times G\ . \tag{61}$$

Using the conjunction rule, we can infer from p and q a proposition which is defined by the following scheme (the reverse arrow ⟵ denotes retranslation, i.e., reverse translation):

$$r \longrightarrow \Pi^p_{(X,Y)} = F \tag{62}$$

$$q \longrightarrow \Pi^q_{(Y,Z)} = G \tag{63}$$

$$r \longleftarrow \Pi_{(X,Y,Z)} = \bar{F} \cap \bar{G} \tag{64}$$

On combining the projection and conjunction rules, we obtain the compositional rule of inference (67) which includes the classical modus ponens as a special case.

More specifically, on applying the projection rule to (64), we obtain the following inference scheme

$$\begin{array}{l} p \longrightarrow \Pi^p_{(X,Y)} = F \\ q \longrightarrow \Pi^q_{(Y,Z)} = G \\ \hline r \longleftarrow \Pi^r_{(X,Z)} = F \circ G \end{array} \tag{65}$$

where the composition of F and G is defined by

$$\mu_{F \circ G}(u,w) = \mathrm{Sup}_v(\mu_F(u,v) \wedge \mu_G(v,w)) \tag{66}$$

In particular, if p is a proposition of the form "X is F" and q is a proposition of the form "If X is G then Y is H," then (65) becomes

$$\begin{array}{l} p \longrightarrow \Pi_X = F \\ q \longrightarrow \Pi_{(Y|X)} = \bar{G}' \oplus \bar{H} \\ \hline r \longleftarrow \Pi_{(Y)} = F \circ (\bar{G}' \oplus \bar{H}) \end{array} \tag{67}$$

The rule expressed by (67) may be viewed as a generalized form of modus ponens which reduces to the classical modus ponens when F = G and F, G, H are nonfuzzy sets.

Stated in terms of possibility distributions, the generalized modus ponens places in evidence the analogy between probabilistic and possibilistic inference. Thus, in the case of probabilities, we can deduce the probability distribution of Y from the knowledge of the probability distribution of X and the conditional probability distribution of Y given X. Similarly, in the case of possibility distributions, we can infer the possibility distribution of Y from the knowledge of the possibility distribution of X and the conditional possibility distribution of Y given X.

It is important to note that the generalized modus ponens as expressed by (67) may be used to enlarge significantly the area of applicability of rule-based systems of the type employed in MYCIN and other expert systems. This is due primarily to two aspects of (67) which are not present in conventional rule-based systems: (a) in the propositions "X is F" and "If X is G then Y is H," F, G and H may be fuzzy sets; and (b) F and G need not be identical. Thus, as a result of (a) and (b), a rule-based system employing (67) may be designed to have an interpolative capability [6].

Note. Due to limitations on space, the sections dealing with credibility analysis and examples of approximate reasoning have been deleted. Full text of the paper is available on request.

REFERENCES AND BIBLIOGRAPHY

[1] B.R. Gaines, "Foundations of fuzzy reasoning," Int. J. Man-Machine Studies 6: 623-668, 1975.

[2] L.A. Zadeh, "Outline of a new approach to the analysis of complex systems and decision processes," IEEE Trans. Systems, Man & Cybernetics SMC-3: 28-44, 1973.

[3] L.A. Zadeh, "Fuzzy logic and approximate reasoning (in memory of Grigore Moisil)," Synthese 30: 407-428, 1975.

[4] L.A. Zadeh, "The concept of a linguistic variable and its application to approximate reasoning," Pt. I, Inf. Sci. 8: 119-249; Pt. II, Inf. Sci. 8: 301-357; Pt. III Inf. Sci. 9: 43-80, 1975.

[5] L.A. Zadeh, "Local and fuzzy logics" (with R.E. Bellman), in Modern Uses of Multiple-Valued Logic, J.M. Dunn & G. Epstein (eds.), D. Reidel, Dordrecht, 1977, pp. 103-165.

[6] L.A. Zadeh, "A theory of approximate reasoning," Memo M77/58, Electronics Research Laboratory, University of California, Berkeley, 1977. To appear in Machine Intelligence 9.

[7] L.A. Zadeh, "PRUF--a meaning representation language for natural languages," Int. J. Man-Machine Studies 10: 395-460, 1978.

[8] A. Tarski, Logics, Semantics, Metamathematics, Clarendon Press, Oxford, 1956.

[9] S. Haack, Philosophy of Logics, Cambridge University Press, Cambridge, 1978.

[10] E. Feigenbaum, B.G. Buchanan and J. Lederberg, "On generality and problem solving: a case study using the DENDRAL program," Machine Ingelligence 6, Edinburgh University Press, 1971.

[11] G.A. Gorry, J.P. Kassirer, A. Essig and W.B. Schwartz, "Decision analysis as the basis for computer-aided management of acute renal failure," Am. J. Medicine 55: 473-484, 1973.

[12] E.H. Shortliffe and B.G. Buchanan, "A model of inexact reasoning in medicine," Mathematical Biosciences 23: 351-379, 1975.

[13] E. Shortliffe, MYCIN: Computer-Based Medical Consultations, American Elsevier, New York, 1976.

[14] R. Duda et al., "Development of a computer based consultant for mineral exploration (PROSPECTOR)," Annual Report SRI International, Nos. 5821 and 6415, 1977.

[15] P. Szolovits, L.B. Hawkinson and W.A. Martin, "An overview of OWL, a language for knowledge representation," LCS Memo, M.I.T., 1977.

[16] J. McCarthy, "Epistomological problems of artificial intelligence," Proc. 5th IJCAI, M.I.T., 1977, pp. 1038-1044.

[17] D.G. Bobrow and T. Winograd, "An overview of KRL, a knowledge representation language," Cognitive Science 1: 3-46, 1977.

[18] R.G. Swinburne, An Introduction to Confirmation Theory, Methuen, London, 1973.

[19] P. Suppes, "The measurement of belief," J. Roy. Statist. Soc. B 36: 160-175, 1974.

[20] K.M. Colby, "Simulations of belief systems," in Computer Models of Thought and Language, R.C. Schank & K.M. Colby (eds.), W. Freeman, San Francisco, 1973.

[21] G. Shafer, A Mathematical Theory of Evidence, Princeton University Press, Princeton, 1976.

[22] B.C. Bruce, "Belief systems and language understanding," N.I.H. Report CBM-TR-41, Rutgers University, 1975.

[23] K. Noguchi, M. Umano, M. Mizumoto and K. Tanaka, "Implementation of fuzzy artificial intelligence language FLOU," IECE Tech. Report On Automation and Language, 1976.

FROM HISTORY TO COMPUTER SCIENCE : A FORMALIZATION OF THE INFERENTIAL PROCESSES OF AN HISTORIAN

Gian Piero Zarri

Centre National de la Recherche Scientifique
Laboratoire d'Informatique pour les Sciences de l'Homme
54, boulevard Raspail
75270 Paris Cedex 06 France

The object of the present paper is to discuss the results of the work carried out to define as strictly as possible the formal system of representation of the inference procedures ("hypotheses") characteristic of the RESEDA project. RESEDA is a question-answering system which operates on a data base containing biographical information concerning characters involved in the medieval history of France.

1. INTRODUCTION

1.1 The RESEDA project aims to set up an advanced question-answering system operating upon a biographical data base. The information housed within this base concerns characters involved in the medieval history of France and their socio-historical background. Strictly formulated questions are presented to the system; responses, given in the same format, are obtained by direct search through the data base or by inference procedures. The objectives of the first RESEDA/0 step of the project* were to construct a general framework for the system and to verify the adequacy of descriptive metalanguage chosen for dealing with this special sort of data. A new phase RESEDA/1 has just recently commenced. It strives towards two goals : a) making the system fully operational, in progressing beyond the phase of demonstration tests to approximate a routine practical use of the data; b) examining in theoretical and practical detail the possibility of a partially automated construction of the inductive "hypotheses" which support the system's inference operations.

1.2 In preparing for the latter, the RESEDA team has had to restudy in depth the work already accomplished on hypotheses in the first phase of the project. It was in effect necessary to establish on a more strictly defined basis, the formal conventions under which the hypotheses are drawn up, and to define these conventions down to the smallest detail. This paper relates to the results of this thorough work. With regard to the metalanguage used to represent biographical data, discussed in the IJCAI/77 report [3], I will give no more information than is strictly necessary for the full understanding of my talk; the interested reader is referred to recent papers on this subject [3,6,7].

2. AN EXAMPLE OF AN HYPOTHESIS

2.1 Fig. 1 shows the formal representation of one of the most simple hypotheses in the RESEDA system, the "hypothesis of a gift to a religious community".

2.1.1 Every hypothesis -inference procedure which can be interpreted in KRL "servant-triggers" terms, see [1]- consists of two separate parts, the "premiss" and the "condition".

2.1.1.1 The premiss provides the general framework capable of being adapted to the formal representation of any question, the answer to which can be found in the hypothesis under examination. If we use the distinction introduced by Smith [5] between "abstraction" and "generalization", we could say that the formal expression of the premiss is obtained by the abstraction of specific formulations, in RESEDA's metalanguage, of different questions which can be associated with the hypothesis.

2.1.1.2 The condition is formed of a sequence of theoretical schemata ("condition schemata") of "planes", linked by "and", "or", "not". The term "plane" [4] is reserved for expressing the representation in the data base, in terms of the metalanguage, of each elementary "episode", each "fact" -expressed in natural language- which make up the fundamental stages for a biography. For an example, refer to the episode from Pierre l'Orfèvre biography further below : "It is known

---

* RESEDA/0 was supported by a grant from the "Délégation Générale à la Recherche Scientifique et Technique" (CNRS-DGRST Contract n° 75.7.0456); the new RESEDA/1 phase is financed by the "Institut de Recherche d'Informatique et d'Automatique" (CNRS-IRIA Contract n° 78.206).

```
Hypothesis of a gift to a religious community
premiss : α
α) /-/-//k/-/-/-/
    BE-AFFECTED-BY  SUBJ   l
                    OBJ    <good>
                    MODAL  <acquisition-by-the-
                            donor's-initiative>
                    SOURCE V1
restrictions on the variables of the premiss
   schemata :
k = <geographic-localisation>
l = <religious-community>
condition :
    ( A V B V ( C Λ D ) V E V ( F Λ D ))
A) /-/-//k/-/-/-/
    BE-PRESENT      SUBJ   V1
B) /-/-//-/k/-/-/
    BE-AFFECTED-BY  SUBJ   V1
                    OBJ    q
C) /-/-//-/k/-/-/
    BE-AFFECTED-BY  SUBJ   V2
                    OBJ    r
D) (V1 COORD1 V2)   SPECIF <kinship>
E) /-/-//k/-/-/-/
   soc+BE-AFFECTED-BY SUBJ l
                      OBJ  V1 SPECIF <member-of-
                                 an-organization>
F) /-/-//k/-/-/-/
   soc+BE-AFFECTED-BY SUBJ l
                      OBJ  V2 SPECIF <member-of-
                                 an-organization>
restrictions on the variables of the condition
   schemata :
q Λ r = vault V <mark-of-identification>
```

figure 1

that around 1360 Pierre l'Orfèvre was a member of the chapter of Senlis cathedral, as their dean", which will give rise to the plane 3 in fig. 3. Translation from episode to plane is done by separating out spatio-temporal data plus bibliographic references (the "thematic") from the description proper of the episode. In the "description part" of plane 3, BE-AFFECTED-BY is the "predicate" used in the translation of the episode; SUBJ, OBJ, are the "main cases" while SPECIF simply introduces a degree of precision with respect to the argument JEAN-L'ORFEVRE which fills the slot OBJ. "soc" is a "modulator" which enables us to specify the fact that the "state" defined by the predicate is inserted into a socio-professional context; "const" carries the meaning of "verified fact".

Returning now to the condition, the information which it enables us to find in the system's data base provides a possible interpretation of the fact (episode) represented by the specific plane to which the question has been reduced. The formal expression of the condition is obtained, by abstraction, from the coding relating to the planes which are shown to be capable of fulfilling an *a priori* undefined number of specific actualizations of the premiss.

2.1.2 With regards now to the formal details of the representation of fig. 1, let me take the premiss first. The symbols k, l and V1 which appear in the "scheme of premiss", α, are "variables of the premiss schemata". In order to be bound, theses variables must satisfy the "restrictions" connected with them (the restriction on V1 is shown implicitly : variables of the type Vn can only be satisfied by the name of one of the personages recognized by the system).

Going on to the condition : the symbol "$\wedge$" which joins the two "condition schemata" C, D (F, D) has its usual meaning of "C and D" ("F and D"); "A V B" has the meaning of "A or B". The condition must therefore be interpreted in this way : an explanation of the episode represented by the premiss filled with elements drawn from the question, can be given by the planes of the data base which can be adapted to the "condition scheme" A, or to scheme B, or to two schemata C and D -which must in this case be satisfied together- or to scheme E, or to two schemata F and D.

2.2 Imagine now a question like "Why did Jean l'Orfèvre at some unspecified time, but certainly before August 1412, the time of his death, give a latin bible by legacy to the Chapter of Senlis cathedral?"; the question would be coded as in fig. 2. A reply obtained by direct-match would show that it is possible to retrace in the data base a plane -containing at least all the information distinctly specified in the question- which should already be *explicitly* connected by a "pointer-correlator" [7: 16-17] of the type CAUSE to a second plane, or a succession of planes, which would so match with the variable x.

```
/avant-août-1412/b//Senlis/b/Senlis/b/
BE-AFFECTED-BY  SUBJ    cathedral-chapter
                OBJ     bible  SPECIF  latin
                MODAL   legacy
                SOURCE  JEAN-L'ORFEVRE
                CAUSE1  ?x
```

figure 2

Let us now imagine that this explicit link does not exist; RESEDA will have to resort to the system of hypotheses to reply to the question asked.

The predicate present in the question (in our case BE-AFFECTED-BY) identifies the set of inference procedures which must be examined in order to see if there exists at least one hypothesis whose premiss can *a priori* match the type of question proposed. When this test has been passed, a real match between the question and the premiss is required. In our case, and referring back to fig. 1 and 2, the result obtained will be that from this point onwards the variables k, l and V1 will be connected to "Senlis" (the place associated with the "subject" of the attribution in the question thematic), to "cathedral-chapter", and to "Jean l'Orfèvre".

Research on the data base of planes which can satisfy the six condition schemata begins with an examination of the "volume" associated with "Jean l'Orfèvre" (volumes are permanent files -a file for each personage recognized by the system- containing "labels" identifying the planes in which the personage in question appears), in order to see if it is possible to retrace the planes of the form A, B, D and E -the condition schemata in which the (bound) variable V1 is present. In our case, it can be assumed that the search will first retrace the plane 1 in fig. 3 : "Jean l'Orfèvre lived in Senlis (location of the subject) for a period of which the starting date (code "-") is not known but which ended in August 1412".

```
1) /-/août-1412//Senlis/b/b/b//Bibl:Bozzolo/
   BE-PRESENT        SUBJ    PIERRE-L'ORFEVRE

2) (JEAN-L'ORFEVRE COORD1    PIERRE-L'ORFEVRE)
                             SPECIF  kinship

3) /vers-1360/b//Senlis/Senlis/b/b//Bibl:Bozzolo/
   const+soc+BE-AFFECTED-BY
                     SUBJ   cathedral-chapter
                     OBJ    JEAN-L'ORFEVRE
                              SPECIF  dean
```

figure 3

Secondly, we will have a series of "relation planes" (special planes without thematics) of the form D, which provide the personages V2 who are relatives of Jean l'Orfèvre. A couple of planes which satisfy (F Λ D) are planes 2 and 3 of fig. 3 : "Around 1360 Pierre l'Orfèvre, who is some non-specified relative to Jean l'Orfèvre, V1, was dean (specific term of the lexical tree <member...>) of the chapter of Senlis cathedral". The planes 1, 2 and 3 together form the reply to the question in fig. 2; the possible reasons for the gift to Senlis cathedral are therefore that Jean l'Orfèvre was an inhabitant of this town and that his family had special relations with the cathedral, given that one of his relatives had held an important position within the chapter.

3. CONCLUSION

Detailed analysis of the hypothesis "gift", proves clearly the *ad hoc* nature of RESEDA's inference corpus. However, this *ad hoc*ness does not constitute a limit on the practical utility of the system. The degree of complexity and subtlety which can be reached by the inference procedures is sufficient to cover a very large number of possible deductions. However, it cannot be denied that, at the present, RESEDA is a system containing a limited number of non-evolving structures (hypotheses), whose capacity to enrich the system by finding new relations between characters or the situations in which these characters are involved, is restricted to a closed set of pre-determined contexts.

Thus the new phase RESEDA/1 of the project intends to use a semi-automatic technique for the formation of the hypotheses. Such a mechanism should help to alleviate the handicap mentioned above, at least in the sense of facilitating a rapid and continual development of the inference corpus, if only at the quantitative level. The procedure involved should be the classical one of learning by examples, see [2] . The intended mechanism should be capable of utilizing the syntactic-semantic properties of RESEDA's formal system, in order to create the framework enabling the association of the two poles, question and answer, of the new hypothesis which is to be constructed.

REFERENCES

[1] Bobrow, D.G., Winograd, T. "An Overview of KRL, a Knowledge Representation Language." Cognitive Science. 1:1 (1977) 3-36.

[2] Hedrick, C.L. "Learning Production Systems from Examples." Artificial Intelligence. 7:1 (1976) 21-49.

[3] King, M., Ornato, M., Zarri, G.P., Zarri-Baldi, L., Zwiebel, A. "Ghosts in the Machine : An AI Treatment of Medieval History." In Proc. IJCAI-77. MIT, Cambridge, Mass., August, 1977, pp. 873-879.

[4] Quillian, M.R. "Semantic Memory." In Semantic Information Processing, Minsky, M. ed. Cambridge Mass.:The MIT Press, 1968, pp. 216-270.

[5] Smith, B. "How is a Knowledge Representation System like a Piano?" Artificial Intelligence Laboratory. AI memo 497, MIT, Cambridge, Mass., 1978.

[6] Zarri, G.P. "Sur le traitement automatique de données biographiques médiévales : le projet RESEDA." In Computing in the Humanities, Lusignan, S., North, J.S. eds. Waterloo, Ontario: University Press, 1977, pp. 151-161.

[7] Zarri, G.P., Ornato, M., King, M., Zwiebel, A., Zarri-Baldi, L. "Projet RESEDA/0 : Rapport final." Equipe Recherche Humanisme Français. CNRS, Paris, December, 1977.

CONTINUOUS RELAXATION AND LOCAL MAXIMA SELECTION

Conditions for Equivalence*+

Steven W. Zucker, Yvan G. Leclerc, John L. Mohammed
Computer Vision and Graphics Laboratory
Department of Electrical Engineering
McGill University
Montreal, Quebec, Canada

It is also a good rule not to put overmuch confidence in the observational results that are put forward until they are confirmed by theory.

Sir Arthur Eddington, 1934

1. MOTIVATION

The study of speech and image understanding systems has largely been empirical. Representations have often been designed for task domains, while algorithms were designed to make use of these representations, as well as heuristic considerations about how the algorithm should behave. Thus it has been very difficult to compare different algorithms except for the results of a few examples, to state equivalences between algorithms in anything like certain terms, or to determine the theoretical requirements for solving a particular problem.

A number of common problems facing the designers of such systems have begun to emerge, however, which suggests that it may be possible to study the power of algorithms in terms of their ability to solve these problems. One such problem is the reduction of local ambiguities, and relaxation labeling processes are a class of algorithms that have been proposed for dealing with it [1]. While many recent applications offer some insight into the relaxation computation (for a review, see [2]) a formal analysis aimed at specifying this computation more precisely is required. It is impossible, for example, to know whether two different algorithms are really equivalent (in the sense that they are implementing the same abstract computation) simply by comparing their results on a small number of experiments. Rather, the relationships between them must be expressed in an analytical fashion so that they will hold for all experiments. This paper is the beginning of such an analysis for continuous relaxation processes. It specifies the relaxation computation in terms of another, much more widely used algorithm - local maxima selection- together with a set of conditions that are sufficient for guaranteeing convergence and equivalence between the two.

The specific reasons for studying the relationships between relaxation and local maxima selection are manifold. From the relaxation point of view, maxima selection provides a model for the decision process, or part of the decision process, that relaxation is implementing. In other words, if we consider the dynamics of a relaxation process as being composed of two stages, one in which a proper ordering of the labels is obtained given the compatibility relations and the initial state, and the other in which certain of these labels are selected, then maxima selection provides a non-iterative model for the second stage. From a practical point of view, when conditions sufficient for equivalence between the two algorithms are met, they can serve as stopping criteria for the relaxation process. More generally, however, these results show that when circumstances are structured well enough, the cooperative relaxation algorithm acts the same as if it were decomposed into a purely local maxima selection process. This is exactly the kind of relationship that is desirable between two algorithms: when the stronger one is necessary, it is functional; otherwise, it reduces to the weaker one.

There is another, more abstract application of the theory that we are beginning to develop here. It derives from the decomposition result just alluded to (which is stated more formally in Sec. 3), and pertains to inferences about how local or global a given algorithm must be. In

*This research was supported by NRC grant No. A4470.

+For a much more extensive discussion for these ideas, together with references, see TR-78-15R, Dept. of Elect. Eng., McGill University.

particular, cooperation can be viewed as one way in which information can be propagated between the local parts of an algorithm, hense making it more global [3]. One surprising interpretation of our result is that circumstances exist in which this propagation is irrelevant. In other words, although a (globally) cooperative mechanism has been used in designing an algorithm for a given problem, the inherent structural complexity of the problem (in that representation) is still only local. Conditions such as those stated in the Equivalence Theorem (Sec. 3) provide a first step toward determining such requirements analytically. In turn, these computational requirements may imply certain constraints on the particular mechanisms and machinery that actually perform such functions [4].

2. BACKGROUND

The class of problems for which both relaxation and local maxima selection are applicable is one in which global labeling problems can be represented as networks of local ones. In other words, given a set of possible labels for each node in a network, the problem is to select a single label (or a smaller set of labels) to attach to each node. These labels might indicate, e.g., assertions about the presence of oriented line segments in an image [5]. The nodes in the network would then correspond to the spatial positions to be labeled, while edges would indicate which nodes were spatial neighbours. Or, the labels might indicate disparity values [6]. We shall denote such labels by the variable λ, and the full set of labels (at a node i) by Λ_i.

For continuous relaxation processes, a certainty measure is distributed over the label set at each node. We shall denote the certainty with which label λ is associated with node i by $p_i(\lambda)$. They satisfy $\sum_{\lambda\epsilon\Lambda_i} p(\lambda)=1$ and $0 \leq p_i(\lambda) \leq 1$. In the line labeling example, such a measure may be obtained from scaled feature (i.e., line) detector responses. Note that ambiguity enters the problem because feature detectors do not respond uniquely; i.e., many labels appear to be possible when looking only at the individual detector responses.

Perhaps the most common algorithm for selecting a label from among this initially ambiguous set is to perform local maxima selection (i.e., to pick the label with the maximal certainty at each node). Such an algorithm would be appropriate for our line example, if we knew that the line detector always responded most strongly at the correct orientation. This is, of course, not the case for real images, in which many different noise sources can corrupt the detectors' responses. Thus more powerful techniques seem to be necessary in general. However, as we shall show, there are instances in which such weaker techniques are appropriate.

The strength behind relaxation processes lies in their use of contextual information throughout the ambiguity reduction process. This context is based on an a priori notion of consistency or compatibility between labels on neighboring nodes, so that now some degree of cooperation takes place between nodes during the label selection process. In the line labeling example, label compatibility is an abstract way to introduce models for good continuation of orientation (i.e., orientation should vary smoothly along lines and curves) and of intensity (i.e., intensity values should vary smothly along the line and over the background); see [7]. In this paper, however, since we are discussing the relaxation mechanism in the abstract, we shall only consider compatibilities as functions over n-tuples (usually pairs) of labels on neighboring nodes into [0.1]. For example, $r_{ij}(\lambda, \lambda')$ indicates the compatibility between label λ on i and λ' on its neighbor j, where 0 corresponds to perfect incompatibility and 1 to perfect compatibility.

Given an initial labeling $p_i^0(\lambda)$, $\lambda \epsilon \Lambda_i$, $i \epsilon I$, the relaxation process iteratively updates each label's certainty factor by an amount proportional to an estimate of its consistency with the labeling over its neighborhood. If this neighbourhood consistency estimate indicates that a label is compatible with its neighbourhood labelings, then its consistency factor is increased; otherwise, it is decreased. Since many labelings may be partially consistent, the update is normalized with respect to the average neighbourhood consistency at each iteration. Thus we have updating rules of the form:

$$p_i^{k+1}(\lambda) = p_i^k(\lambda) . \frac{Q_i^k}{\sum_{\eta\epsilon\Lambda_i} p_i^k(\eta\ Q_i^k(\eta)} \qquad (2)$$

where $Q_i^k(\lambda)$ is the current consistency estimate between label λ on node i and the labeling over its neighbourhood.

The neighbourhood consistency is computed as a function of the current neighbourhood labeling and the compatibility functions. For computational reasons, this estimate has been decomposed into two parts: one in which an operation is performed to determine the pair (or n-ary) label consistency estimates; and the other in which these partial estimates are combined into a single neighbourhood estimate. The most widely used estimate is [1]:

$$Q_i^k(\lambda) = \sum_{j \epsilon J_i} C_{ij} \sum_{\lambda' \epsilon \Lambda_j} r_{ij}(\lambda,\lambda') p_j^k(\lambda') \qquad (3)$$

where J_i is the set of nodes neighbouring i and the C_{ij} terms weight the total interaction between nodes i and j. The choice of arithmetic averages in (3), however, is only heuristic. The essential point is that the neighbourhood consistency estimate is a function of the labeling over the entire neighbourhood. To emphasize this generality, we shall rewrite (3) in a more general form, and prove all of our results using this form.

The general form that we shall consider is:

$$Q_i^k(\lambda) = \underset{j \epsilon J_i}{\text{Mean}} \{ \underset{\lambda' \epsilon \Lambda_j}{\text{Norm}} \; r_{ij}(\lambda,\lambda') p_j^k(\lambda') \} \qquad (4)$$

where Mean is any standard mean (or averaging) operator; and Norm is an operator that computes the norm (or length) of a vector.

3 CONSISTENTLY ORDERED LABELINGS AND THE EQUIVALENCE THEOREM

The traditional way of viewing continuous relaxation is as numerical process for updating certainty measures. However, if we consider these certainty measures as defining a partial ordering over the labels at each node, then another way of viewing relaxation labeling is as a process that changes this partial ordering. This is the point of view that we shall adopt for the remainder of this paper, because it suggests a study of the iteration at which the partial ordering of the labels at each node becomes fixed for all further iterations. We shall say, at this iteration, that the system has become consistently ordered. The particular partial ordering that we shall concentrate on is the one specifying the relationship between the maximal and all of the non-maximal labels at each node.

There are many possible dynamical situations that can give rise to consistently-ordered labelings. Perhaps the most common situation is for the maximal labels to mutually support one another, thus driving the weaker labels to zero. It is this situation that we shall now attempt to characterize because, as we shall prove, it leads to a formal correspondence between relaxation and local maxima selection.

To define the above notions more exactly, it is necessary to introduce some notation: Let

(i) Λ_i be the full set of labels attached to node i.

(ii) M_i^k be the set of labels attached to node i that have the greatest certainty at iteration k;

(iii) N_i^k be the set of labels attached to node i with non-zero, non-maximal certainties at iteration k;

(iv) Z_i^k be the set of labels attached to node i with zero certainty at iteration k.

<u>Equivalence Theorem</u>

If, for a given relaxation process, the conditions

(i) $$\underset{m_j \epsilon M_j^{k_c}}{\text{Norm}} \; r_{ij}(m_i,m_j) p_j^{k_c}(m_j) > \underset{\lambda' \epsilon \Lambda_j}{\text{Norm}} \; r_{ij}(n_i,\lambda') p_j^{k_c}(\lambda')$$

$$\forall m_i \, \epsilon \, M_i^{k_c}, \; \forall n_i \, \epsilon \, N_i^{k_c},$$

$$\forall j \, \epsilon \, J_i$$

and

(ii) $$r_{ij}(m_i, \lambda') = r_{ij}(m_i', \lambda')$$

$$\forall m_i, m_i' \epsilon \, M_i^{k_c},$$

$$\forall \lambda' \epsilon \, M_j^{k_c} \cup N_j^{k_c},$$

$$\forall j \, \epsilon \, J_i$$

hold for every node i ε I, then

(a) the labeling $\mathcal{L}^{k_c}$ in that process is consistently ordered everywhere, and

(b) the relaxation process will converge to a final labeling with

$$\lim_{k \to \infty} p_i^k(\lambda) = \begin{cases} 1/\#M_i^{k_o} & \forall \lambda \epsilon \, M_i^{k_o} \\ 0 & \text{otherwise} \end{cases}$$

where $\#M_i^{k_o}$ denotes the number of labels in $M_i^{k_o}$. For the proof of this theorem, together with applications and interpretations, see the TR cited in the footnote on the title page.

SOLVING MECHANICS PROBLEMS USING META-LEVEL INFERENCE

Alan Bundy, Lawrence Byrd, George Luger,
Chris Mellish & Martha Palmer.
Department of Artificial Intelligence,
University of Edinburgh,
Edinburgh, Scotland.

In this paper we shall descibe a program (MECHO), written in Prolog [14], which solves a wide range of mechanics problems from statements in both predicate calculus and English. Mecho uses the technique of meta-level inference to control search in natural language understanding, common sense inference, model formation and algebraic manipulation. We argue that this is a powerful technique for controlling search while retaining the modularity of declarative knowledge representations.

Keywords : Natural Language, Mathematical Reasoning, Search Control, Meta-level Inference, Predicate Calculus, Mechanics.

1. Introduction

The work described in this paper addresses the question of how it is possible to get a formal representation of a problem from an English statement, and how it is then possible to use this representation in order to solve the problem. Our purpose in studying natural language understanding in conjunction with problem solving is to bring together the constraints of what formal representation can actually be obtained with the question of what knowledge is required in order to solve a wide range of problems in a semantically rich domain. We believe that these issues cannot sensibly be tackled in isolation. In practical terms we have had the benefits of an increased awareness of common problems in both areas and a realisation that some of our techniques are applicable to both the control of inference and the control of parsing.

Early work on solving mathematical problems stated in natural language was done by Bobrow (STUDENT - [1]) and Charniak (CARPS - [5]). However the rudimentary parsing and simple semantic structures used by Bobrow and Charniak are inadequate for any but the easiest problems. Our intention has been to build on advances in natural language processing (eg [18]) in order to study parsing and problem solving in a domain which requires sophisticated knowledge about the world. The domain we have been working in is that of mechanics problems, which deal with idealised objects such as smooth planes, light inextensible strings, frictionless pulleys etc. The idealised nature of this domain made it feasible to consider building an expert inferential system which would be able to cope with a wide range of problems. To date, our program has tackled problems in the areas of: pulley problems, statics problems, motion on smooth complex paths and motion under constant acceleration. Our intention is to continue expanding this in order to force generality into our solutions. In recent years a lot of similar work has been in progress on Physics-type domains such as ours. (eg [13], [7], [15], [11]). We have been concerned to adopt methods developed by these workers into Mecho, and to solve mechanics problems tackled by them.

This work was supported by SRC grant number B/RG 94493 and an SRC research studentship for Chris Mellish.

2. Description of the Program

The block diagram (fig 1) gives a very general overview of the structure of the MECHO program. Each block represents a closely related collection of Prolog clauses (procedures), the arrows between blocks

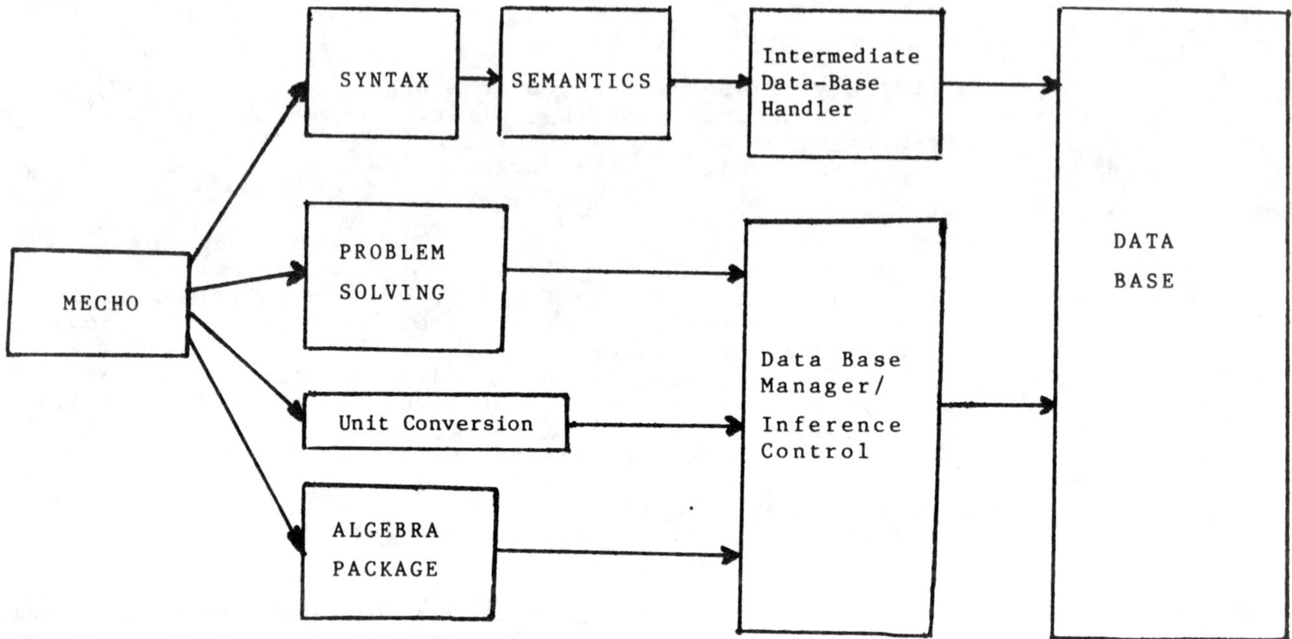

Fig 1 : Program Block Structure.

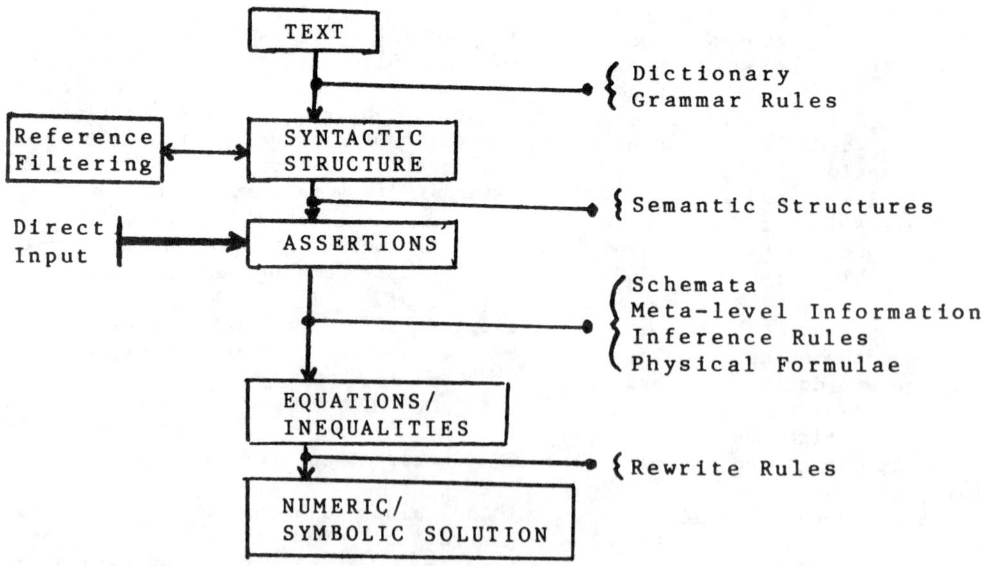

Fig 2 : Representation Structures

indicate invocation/communication links. (For practical reasons MECHO is split into three separate modules, but this is irrelevant to the overall structure). The accompanying diagram (fig 2) tries to capture the changes in representation and the various types of knowledge required during the execution of the program. The following discussion will elaborate on these.

Input to the program is in the form of English text. An example taken from the area of pulley problems would be:

> "Two particles of mass b and c are connected by a light string passing over a smooth pulley. Find the acceleration of the particle of mass b." (1)
>
> (Taken from [10])

The purpose of the natural language module is to produce a set of predicate calculus assertions which will enable the problem solver to solve the problem. This objective of producing a symbolic representation of the 'meaning' of the problem statement has been used by us as a vehicle for exploring syntax-semantics interaction. The syntactic parser calls semantic routines as soon as possible in order to interpret fragments of text and quickly reject inappropriate syntactic choices. The work of the syntax routines divides into clause syntax and phrase syntax.

The purpose of syntactic analysis at the clause level is to establish clause boundaries and, within each clause, to prepare the ground for the semantic analysis of the main verb. Clause analysis thus involves identifying the start of new phrases, assigning syntactic roles to the phrases and performing phrase analysis to interpret the internal structure of the phrases. The internal phrase analysis typically returns simply a referent (and some typing information) to the higher levels. This means that preliminary reference evaluation is carried out locally, with the information conveyed by a phrase being captured in assertions produced as 'side effects' by semantic routines called during the analysis. These semantic routines are responsible for interpreting what it means for a given object to have a certain property, and indeed for checking whether or not it can have the property. Domain specific information concerning typing, idealisation and object-property possibilities is used to answer these questions. Failure of the semantics indicates that the parse is invalid. The following (simple) example shows the kind of meta-level structures used in this process.*

```
meaning(light,Object,mass(Object,zero)).

type_constraint(light,physobj).
```

The **meaning** predicate states that the meaning of applying the property **light** to an object, is that the object has a mass of zero. **type_constraint** asserts that being a physical object is a necessary condition to having the property **light**.

It is interesting to note that the declarative assertions which give the meaning of a phrase can be specified independently of how they will be used. Meta-level information concerning the state of the analysis is used to determine whether they are used to **add** new information or to **test** neccessary constraints on previous information. (This is basically the 'given'/'new' distinction discussed in [8]).

One of the aspects of natural language understanding that has interested us especially is the way in which criteria of semantic well-formedness can be used to resolve cases of ambiguity in reference evaluation. Our program incorporates a full deductive mechanism, as opposed to semantic markers, to capture the global semantic constraints that arise during the interpretation. Reference evaluation proceeds continuously during the combined syntactic and semantic analysis with semantic information being used to filter sets of possible candidates for referents. The method used to achieve this in a general way is basically that of Waltz filtering [16]. As can be seen, the referent returned by the phrase syntax is likely to be incompletely specified and for this reason all interaction between the semantics and the data-base is handled by an intermediate data-base handler which implements

---

* The notation used here, and in following examples, follows the Prolog convention that names starting with an upper case letter are logical variables which are purely local to the structure (Prolog clause). Atoms, which are in lower case, and compound terms all stand for themselves. Rules are of the form 'P <-- Q & R' meaning 'if Q and R then P'. Most examples have undergone slight cosmetic alteration.

the inference system and reference filtering system over these referents.

The syntactic structure built by the clause syntax specifies a main verb, and positions such as 'logical subject' and 'logical object' are filled by referents. (We do not construct a complete parse tree as such). From this structure a set of assertions is generated by invoking semantic routines. The semantic analysis of the verb maps the main verb onto a base verb and establishes a mapping between the syntactic roles of the clause and the deep roles associated with the base verb. As a result the referents are fitted into conceptual slots in a way similar to conventional 'caseframe' analysis. The base verb then specifies the assertions (in terms of the referents) which follow from this mapping. Base verbs differ from case frames in that while they attempt to generalise collections of related verbs, they are not defined in terms of universal primitive roles or slots.

Given a satisfactory parse of a sentence, which produces a set of consistent assertions and disambiguates the referents, we are then able produce a set of assertions (by instantiating out the referents) about the objects in the problem. These are supplied to the problem solving module. As an example, the assertions produced for the above problem statement (1) would be:

```
isa(period,period1)
isa(particle,p1)
isa(particle,p2)
isa(string,s1)
isa(pulley,pull)
end(s1,end1,right)
end(s1,end2,left)
midpt(s1,midpt1)
fixed_contact(end1,p1,period1)
fixed_contact(end2,p2,period1)
fixed_contact(midpt1,pull,period1)
mass(p1,mass1,period1)
mass(p1,mass2,period1)
mass(s1,zero,period1)
coeff(pull,zero)
accel(p1,a1,270,period1)
accel(p2,a2,90,period1)
measure(mass1,b)
measure(mass2,c)
sought(a1)
given(mass1)
given(mass2)                                  (2)
```

In addition the following schema is cued:

```
cue pullsys_stan(sys1,pull,s1,p1,p2,period1)
```

The cueing of schemata is necessary to provide extra information, defaults etc. which are not given explicitly but are 'house rules' in this domain. (Eg That the pulley in a pulley system has negligable weight). We cue schemata, fairly simplistically, by recognising key words and certain object configurations. For example the following structure asserts that a pulley-system schema can be cued if objects can be found which satisfy the ideal-type contraints and have certain relationships between each other.

```
sysinfo( pullsys,
     [Pull,Str,P1,P2],
     [pulley,string,solid,solid],
     [ supports(Pull,Str),
       attached(Str,P1),
       attached(Str,P2)
     ]).
```

The effect of this cue would be to invoke a schema such as:

```
schema( pullsys,
     [Pull,Str,P1,P2], Time,
     [ constaccel(P1,Time),
       constaccel(P2,Time),
       cue stringsys(Str,[Lpart,Rpart]),
       (tension(Lpart,T1,Time)
            <-- coeff(Pull,zero) &
                tension(Rpart,T,Time) )
     ],
     [ coeff(Pull,zero),
       mass(Pull,zero,Time)  ]).
```

This schema asserts that in a standard pulley problem the objects undergo constant acceleration, the tension in both parts of the string are equal if there is no friction (only one rule shown), and that the friction and mass of the pulley default to zero if not otherwise given. (This example has been somewhat simplified).

The predicate calculus notation can be used to input problems directly to the problem solver - and in fact research on the problem solver has resulted in it being able to tackle a wider range of problems than the natural language module can currently handle. The representational principles behind these assertions view the objects of Newtonian Mechanics in terms of simple zero and one dimensional objects (points and lines) which are typed and have properties and relations defined over them. For example particles, pulleys, spatial points, moments of time are all types of POINT while rods, strings, paths (trajectories), and periods of time are types of LINE. Physical quantities, such as length, velocity, force etc., form the other main branch of our type hierarchy. (see [4]).

The work of the Problem Solver divides into two types of task. There is the overall strategic task of deciding what to do, how to solve the problem by producing equations which solve for unknown quantities (including intermediate unknowns introduced during the solution). On the other hand there is the tactical task of combining the input assertions with general facts and inference rules in order to prove required goals. We shall discuss each of these in turn.

Our overall strategy is a general goal directed algorithm for equation extraction developed from a study by David Marples of student engineers [12]. For instance, suppose **a1**, the acceleration of particle **p1**, is the (only) sought unknown. (Here we continue the example started above (1) (2)). Resolution of forces about **p1** will be chosen to solve for **a1** and this produces the equation:

$$-mass1.g + tension1 = mass1.a1 \quad (3)$$

All possible force contributions on **p1** are examined and since **p1** is attached to the end of the string this results in the string being considered. **tension1** was formerly unknown but the function properties of the predicate 'tension' enable it to be created (see later) to allow the equation to be formed. We have to introduce **tension1** as an unknown because it is not possible to solve for **a1** without doing so. The next step is to solve for **tension1** which is a force and involves the string **s1**. Again resolution of forces is selected - **p1**, **pull**, **p2** being objects on the string which are possible candidates for resolving about. **p1** has been previously used and only **p2** can be used without introducing unknowns. The result is the equation:

$$mass2.g - tension1 = mass2.a1 \quad (4)$$

These two equations can be solved to produce a solution for **a1**.

The input assertions provide meta-level information about whether certain quantities are **sought** or **given**. The Marples Algorithm works by traversing the list of sought unknowns in a fixed order: the (quantity) type of each unknown being used to provide a shortlist of formulae that could solve for it, and the definition of the quantity (ie the assertion which introduced it) being used to find the physical objects, times and angles involved. Notice that there is a distinction made between 'formulae', which are composed of variables over quantities (eg 'F = M * A'), and 'equations' which are instantiations of formulae (eg (3) and (4) above). In the Marples algorithm we are reasoning about the properties of formulae in order to successfully produce appropriate equations.

Before the application of a formula to produce an equation, there is a stage of qualitative analysis where general facts about the problem are used to decide applicability. Our interest here is in exploring the selective use of meta-level reasoning to guide the equation extraction process. As well as deciding applicability we have to prepare a situation within which to apply a formula. This may involve, for example, collecting together all the objects connected to a particle if we wish to resolve forces about it. General independence criteria (eg 'You can't resolve forces about the same object in linearly dependent directions') are also used to eliminate redundant equations.

The following are (simplified) examples of the meta-level structures used during the above example:

```
kind(a1,accel,
        relaccel(p1,earth,a1,270,period1)).

relates(accel,
        [resolve,constaccel-N,relaccel]).

prepare(resolve,relaccel(P,earth,A,Dir,Time),
                situation(P,Set,Dir,Time))
    <-- isa(particle,P) &
        findall(X, sameplace(X,P,Time), Set).

isform(resolve,situation(Obj,Set,Dir,Time),
               F = M * A )
    <-- mass(Obj, M ,Time) &
        accel(Obj,A,Dir,Time) &
        sumforces(Obj,Set,Dir,Time, F ).
```

The **kind** predicate asserts that a1 is a quantity of type accel defined in the given relaccel assertion. **relates** states that all the formulae whose names are given in the list, contain variables of type accel and therefore can be used to solve for acceleration. **prepare** gives the criteria for constructing the situation within which to resolve forces, and the **isform** predicate defines the equation by defining the meaning of its component variables.

The equation extraction algorithm is two pass in that it first tries to produce a solution which does not introduce new unknowns before allowing the introduction of extra (intermediate) unknowns which are added to the unknowns list and have to be eventually solved for. Notice that the quantities manipulated are purely symbolic; they can be introduced by the creation mechanism (see later) without their values being known at this stage. E.g. When the first equation (3) was formed in the above example, the quantity **tension1** was introduced without the program knowing, or trying to find, its actual value. As can be seen, it is the Marples algorithm which will eventually produce an equation which solves for **tension1**.

The data-base stores all the facts supplied by the English statement, but to bridge the gap between the explicit information derived from the problem statement and that needed to solve the problem the program requires a general knowledge of mechanics which is formalised in a set of inference rules. An example of such (object-level) inference rules would be:

```
relaccel(P1,P2,zero,Dir,Period)
     <-- constrelvel(P1,P2,Period).

constrelvel(P1,P2,Period)
     <-- fixed_contact(P1,P2,Period).
```

The first rule says that the relative acceleration between two points of reference is zero if there is a constant relative velocity between them (over a certain period), and the second rule says that two points of reference have a constant relative velocity if they are in contact (again, over a certain period). The inference rules are a set of horn clauses which have been hand ordered and contain certain typing information to guide selection. The search strategy is depth first, with pruning of semantically meaningless goals, and while this could be improved upon, current performance has not yet necessitated such a step.

An important part of our work has been the investigation of search control mechanisms which will enable effective use of this wealth of implicit knowledge. All requests to retrieve assertions from the data-base, either directly or via inference, are handled by the inference control module. This module uses information from the request along with meta-information and inference rules in an attempt to satisfy the goal. The first step involves normalisation of the goal to remove syntactic sugar or to express it in terms of a smaller set of underlying predicates. This is performed with a one pass rewrite rule set. The resulting goal is then classified according to the instantiation state of its component arguments and the possibility of using function properties and certain other mathematical properties of the predicate (such as reflexivity, symmetry and transitivity). This information is used to select appropriate proving strategies. (A basic strategy of 'unit preference' will always first check the data-base directly).

Our two most important strategies are the use of function properties to prune search and the use of equivalence class type mechanisms to direct it. The representation treats what would normally be considered functions as predicates with extra control information. Being a function means that certain arguments are uniquely determined by certain other arguments. For example, in the predicate tension(String,T,Time)' The actual tension T is determined once the String and the Time have been given.

These function properties can be used to prevent useless inference if another (different) value of a function argument is already known (uniqueness property); to create new entities to satisfy a goal if all attempts at inference have failed (existence property); and to automatically eliminate backtracking by disregarding choices made during inference (uniqueness again). Examples of the meta-level structures used by the program in performing the above are:

```
rewrite( accel(P,A,Dir,Time),
         relaccel(P,earth,A,Dir,Time),
         strategy(dbinf)  ).

meta( relaccel, 5,
      [P1,P2,A,Dir,Time],
      [pt_of_ref,pt_of_ref,accel,angle,time],
      function( [P1,P2,Time] => [A,Dir] )  ).
```

The **rewrite** rule tells us that any accel predicate can be rewritten to a relaccel predicate with the earth as the other point of reference, and that the standard inference strategy is then applicable. The **meta** predicate specifies the argument types and the function properties of the predicate relaccel.

The second major strategy, which provides an alternative to using the inference rules, is a general **similarity class** mechanism based on equivalence class ideas. Predicates which are (pseudo-) equivalence relations and would normally produce self-resolving inference rules are defined in terms of this mechanism. A tree is used to represent similarity class membership and the goal (such as 'being in the same place') is proved by establishing equivalence of roots. This can be seen as an alternative (and less explosive) axiomatisation of these predicates. Our extension over traditional uses of this method has been to allow labelled arcs and calculation during the tree traversal. Thus predicates like 'vector separation' and 'relative velocity' which have pseudo-equivalence properties can also use this strategy. Here is an example of a structure used in these cases:

```
rewrite( sameplace(P,Q,Time),
         [ sameclass(P,Q,touch(Time)),
           merge(P,Q,touch(Time))     ],
         strategy(simclass)  ).
```

This states that the predicate **sameplace** should use the general sameclass mechanism on the particular tree **touch(Time)**. Also specified is an updating mechanism for adding new **sameplace** assertions; in this case it would involve merging two separate trees.

These general strategies can be applied to a wide range of predicates and often capture important facts about the domain (eg the fact that an object cannot be in two places at once is a fact about the function properties of 'at(Object,Place,Time)'). The explicit control of new object creation coupled with the goal directed backward reasoning method of the Marples algorithm results in a create/consider-by-need type of behaviour. Restrictions, such as 'don't create' or 'don't infer', can be added to the request for a goal to be proved and this enables the Marples algorithm to be selective over its use of the Inference Control in accordance with its needs at the time.

For some mechanics problems a process of prediction is required to answer questions like "Will the particle reach the top of the slope if it starts with velocity V ?". Each question about the motion of a particle on a complex slope unpacks into a series of questions about the behaviour on simple parts of the slope. Some of these can be answered immediately on the basis of the qualitative shape of the slope, but others involve the solution of inequalities containing unknown quantities. These unknowns are declared as sought and the equation extraction algorithm is called to solve for them. The inequalities can then be solved to answer the question. Our present prediction system is special purpose and built around problems similar to those in tackled by De Kleer, ie motion problems.

Since the equations produced by the equation extraction algorithm are in terms of symbolic quantities, there is a stage of Unit Conversion where the actual values are substituted and a final unit system is selected - conversion factors being added where appropriate. (Some problems involve a combination of all sorts of different units - feet, yards, miles......). The two equations produced above ((3) & (4)) are very simple in that no particular units are involved. The only step will be the substitution of **b** and c for mass1 and **mass2** respectively giving:

$$-b.g + tension1 = b.a1 \qquad (5)$$

$$c.g - tension1 = c.a1 \qquad (6)$$

The set of simultaneous equations and/or inequalities produced by the problem solving module is passed to the algebra module (PRESS) which will solve them to produce a final answer to the problem. Let us look at how PRESS produces a solution for a1 given (5) and (6). The two equations are solved by isolating **tension1** in the second equation (which was intended to solve for **tension1**), and then using the result as a substitution into the first equation. This final result can then be simplified with **a1** being isolated on the left hand side to give the final answer:

$$a1 = g.(c-b) \;/\; (c+b) \qquad (7)$$

The extension of equation solving techniques to inequalities (there are interesting connections) has enabled us to solve the inequalities produced by the prediction problems, but in addition we have found that the information required to justify the use of certain rewrite rules is often of the form 'only if X > 0' etc. Solving and proving inequalities is therefore of direct use within the system.

However, PRESS was not developed purely as a service program for MECHO. It was intended as a vehicle to explore ideas about controlling search in mathematical reasoning using meta-level descriptions and strategies [3].

Rather than using exhaustive application over a large set of rewrite rules, it uses the meta-level stategies of isolation, collection and attraction to carefully control application of several different sets of rewrite rules. This selectivity has many advantages: principled methods for guiding search cut down useless work, identical rules may be used in different ways (eg left to right or right to left) in different circumstances without causing problems, and theoretical requirements such as proof of termination of the rewrite rules are made much easier.

When PRESS is used as an equation and inequality solver (ie as a module of MECHO), it classifies the equations (inequalities) to be solved so as to generate guidance information. An exciting area of research that we would like to expand on is that of designing inclusion and ordering criteria to classify algebraic identities which are produced by a theorem prover. This would enable the system to automatically learn new rules. The use of meta-level reasoning to place new rules into a framework where they will be selectively and correctly applied overcomes many of the obvious 'explosion' and 'looping' problems that would occur with haphazard additions to a large single rewrite rule set.

3. Discussion

Throughout the above description of the Mecho program we have constantly emphasised the importance of 'meta-information' in controlling search. This has been applied in the rejection of semantically meaningless parses, the control of inference, the extraction of equations and the guiding of algebraic manipulation.

The theme that has emerged from our work is the benefit to be gained from axiomatising the meta-level of the domain under investigation and performing inference at this level, producing object level proofs as a side effect. This is the methodology investigated by Pat Hayes in the GOLUX project [9], except that we have developed our meta-level representation for a particular domain rather than adopting general purpose representations based on resolution theorem proving systems.

In [2] we showed how GPS could be viewed in this way. At the object-level the search space can be viewed as an operator/state OR tree in which the states are nodes and the operators are arcs between them. At the meta-level the search space can viewed as a method/goal AND/OR tree in which the goals are nodes and the methods are arcs between them. A simple depth first search at the meta-level then induces a highly complex, middle-out search at the object-level.

In order to make clear the distinction we are drawing between meta-level and object-level representations in Mecho, we shall list below examples of the descriptions used at each level. When defining a notation it is usual to define the constants, variables, function symbols and predicate symbols of the language; and then to show how terms and formulae can be formed by composing them together with the logical connectives. We shall follow this type of outline in an informal fashion. (To avoid confusion with earlier terminology we shall use the words 'assertion' and 'rule' to replace 'formula').

At the object-level we have the following kinds of primitive:

constants pl, endl, mass2, al, right, 90, 270, lbs, feet etc.

variables Pl, Str, Period, Accel, F, M, etc.

function symbols +, *, cos etc.

predicate symbols accel, relaccel, mass, fixed_contact etc.

These are formed into terms such as 'M * A' and assertions such as 'F = M * A', 'accel(pl,al, 270,periodl)' etc. Finally, logical connectives are used to form these assertions into inference rules like:

```
relaccel(Pl,P2,zero,Dir,Period)
     <-- constrelvel(Pl,P2,Period).
```

The only function symbols at the object-level are for straight forward arithmetic and trigonometric functions. This is because we have recorded function properties by making meta-level assertions about object-level predicates.

At the meta-level all these object-level descriptions are meta-constants along with additional meta-constants for schema names, formula names, object types, strategy types etc. As examples of meta-level primitives we have:

constants (Any object level description). physobj, pullsys, resolve, particle, line, length, dbinf etc.

variables Type, Eqn, Goal, Strategy, Exprl etc. (see later)

function symbols Constructors for lists, sets, bags etc.

predicate symbols meaning, sysinfo, schema, kind, relates, isform, rewrite, meta etc.

Again these can be formed into meta-terms and meta-assertions and we gave several examples during the program description. What we shall now examine are the meta-rules which are formed from these assertions. (These use the same logical connectives as the object-level rules). We shall take simplified examples from each of the four main areas of our work.

The first example is a rule used by the Natural Language module, which specifies the conditions for a property to be correctly applied to a particular entity.

```
attribute(Property,Entity,State)
  <-- type_constraint(Property,Type) &
      isa(Type,Entity) &
      meaning(Property,Entity,Assertion) &
      consistent(Assertion,State).
```

This rule states that a particular Property can be attributed to an Entity in a given State (of the parse), if the Entity satisfies the type_constraint of of the Property, and if the meaning of the attribution is consistent with all the other assertions in the current State. (If, for example, the Assertion was 'mass(sl, zero)' then this would involve checking that no other **mass** was known for **sl**. It is here that we see one of the key connections with our work on Problem Solving, since this is precisely a matter of 'function properties'!).

The following is an example taken from the Marples Algorithm, and it defines the requirements for an equation to solve for a particular quantity.

```
solves_for(Q,Eqn)
  <-- kind(Q,Type,Defn) &
      relates(Type,F_list) &
      select(Formula,F_list) &
      prepare(Formula,Defn,Situation) &
      isform(Formula,Situation,Eqn).
```

This rule states that Eqn solves for Q if Q has type Type and Formula is a formula that relates Type quantities to other quantities, and if Situation is the situation within which to apply the Formula given the Defn of Q, and if Eqn is the instantiation of the formula in the given Situation. It can be seen that this rule is a direct axiomatisation of our earlier description of how the Marples algorithm extracts equations. (The select goal would specify the qualitative guidance and apply the independence criteria (given extra arguments)).

In a similar way we give the following example of rules which describe how the Inference Control uses function properties.

```
is_satisfied(Goal)
  <-- rewrite(Goal,Newgoal,Strategy) &
      decompose(Newgoal,Pred,Args) &
      meta(Pred,N,Args,Types,Func_info) &
      method(Strategy,Func_info,Newgoal).

method( strategy(dbinf),
        function(Fargs => Vals), Newgoal)
  <-- all_bound(Fargs) &
      use_function_properties(Newgoal).
```

The first rule states that Goal is satisfied if it rewrites to Newgoal whose predicate symbol has certain Func_info, and if a method is used based on the Strategy and this Func_info. (Certain arguments to meta have been ignored). The second rule states that the normal inference method will prove Newgoal given its function properties if all the function arguments, Fargs, are bound, and if object-level inferencing is performed using function property pruning.

As a final example we take a rule concerned with algebraic equation solving. This rule is interesting in that while PRESS does not currently use it, it could be derived from rules PRESS does have. Automating this procedure would be an interesting area for study.

```
solve(U,Exprl,Ans)
  <-- occ(U,Exprl,2) &
      collect(U,Exprl,Expr2) &
      isolate(U,Expr2,Ans).
```

This rule states that Ans is an equation which solves for U given Exprl if Exprl contains two occurances of U, if Expr2 is an equation derived from Exprl in which these two occurances have been collected together, and if

Ans is an equation derived from Expr2 in which U has been isolated on the left hand side.

All the above rules can be seen as classifying object-level descriptions and using this information in deciding what to do. However the effects are very different in the different areas. In the natural language processing meta-level rules monitor object-level assertions, rejecting semantically unacceptable consequences of a parse. In equation extraction the effect is to select equations using a means/ends analysis technique. In Inference Control the result is use of the most effective axiomatisation for the goal in hand, and in Algebraic manipulation multiple rewrite rules are selectively brought to bear on expressions. Thus relatively simple meta-level search strategies can induce a wide variety of complex object-level behaviours.

These meta-inference techniques were strongly suggested by our use of the programming language Prolog. The fact that Prolog procedures are also predicate calculus clauses and the fact that predicate calculus has a clear semantics, encourages the user to attach meanings to his procedures and these meanings are usually meta-theoretic. However, Prolog as a programming language only offers a single level of 'syntactic' structures (atoms, compound terms etc.), and a lack of care can lead to a blurring of theoretical distinctions. During the development of Mecho, a lack of emphasis (realisation?) of these distinctions resulted in a mixing of object and meta levels. (for example the use of Prolog variables to represent variables at both levels, the mixing of object and meta level assertions in rules such as **isform**). We plan to remove these aberrations.

Weyrauch's work on the FOL system (See [17]), is of importance in relation to this need for an adaquate theoretical formalism. The distinction between the object-level and the meta-level is fundamental within his system, and his use of 'reflection principles' is designed to capture the relation between these levels. We feel that his work is of direct value to workers in the field of expert systems, such as ourselves.

The principle of utilising 'knowledge about knowledge' is becoming increasingly important in practical AI programs. Davis and Buchanan [6] classified four different kinds of meta-level knowledge used by their TEIRESIAS system. They represent knowledge about objects and the data-structures used to describe them in **schemata** and describe the argument type characteristics of their functions in **templates**. Their program can classify and build models of the inference rules it uses and **meta-rules** are used to guide the choice of inference rules to be used and the order of using them. In MECHO, the Natural Language and Inference Control modules both use information like that stored in TEIRESIAS **templates**. MECHO meta-level inference rules are similar in spirit to TEIRESIAS **meta-rules** except that the MECHO rules are more general purpose and they generate a variety of different search strategies in different contexts.

4. Conclusion

In this paper we have discussed Mecho, a program for solving mechanics problems. We have shown how the technique of using and controlling knowledge about the domain by inference at the meta-level, can be applied to a range of different areas. Many workers in the field (eq [9], [6], [17]), have argued that controlling search by using meta-level inference is superior to built-in, smart search strategies because the search information is more modular and transparant. The argument is for systems to make explicit the full knowledge involved in their behaviour, which in turn aids the modification of their data and strategies, thus improving their robustness and generality. This leads the way to systems which could automatically modify their strategies and explain their control decisions.

We conclude that meta-level inference can be used to build sophisticated and flexible strategies, which provide powerful techniques for controlling the use of knowledge, while retaining the clarity and modularity of a declarative knowledge representation.

5. References

[1] Bobrow, D.
Natural Language input for a computer problem solving system.
PhD thesis, MIT, , 1964.

[2] Bundy, A. "Computational models for problem solving," Learning and Problem Solving (part 3), The Open Univ. Press, 1978. units 26-27 of the Open University Cognitive Psychology Course D303

[3] Bundy, A. & Welham, R.
Using meta-level descriptions for selective application of multiple rewrite rules in algebraic manipulation.
Forthcoming working paper, Dept. of Artificial Intelligence, Edinburgh., 1979.

[4] Bundy, A., Byrd, L., Luger, G., Mellish, C., Milne, R. and Palmer, M.
Mecho: A program to solve Mechanics problems.
Working Paper No. 50, Dept. of Artificial Intelligence, Edinburgh., 1979.

[5] Charniak, E.
Computer solution of calculus word problems, pages 303-316.
IJCAI, 1969.

[6] Davis, R. & Buchanan, B.G.
Meta-level knowledge: overview and applications, pages 920-927.
IJCAI, 1977.

[7] De Kleer, J.
Qualitative and quantitative knowledge in classical mechanics.
Technical Report AI-TR-352, MIT AI Lab, 1975.

[8] Haviland, S.E. & Clark, H.H.
What's new? Acquiring new information as a process in comprehension.
Journal of Verbal Learning and Verbal Behaviour 13:512-521, 1974.

[9] Hayes, P.
Computation and deduction.
Czech. Academy of Sciences, 1973.

[10] Humphrey, D.
Intermediate Mechanics, Dynamics.
Longman, Green & Co., London, 1957.

[11] Larkin, J.
Problem solving in Physics.
Technical Report, Group in Science and Mathematics Education, Berkeley, California, 1977.

[12] Marples, D.
Argument and technique in the solution of problems in Mechanics and Electricity.
Technical Report CUED/C-Educ/TRI, Dept. of Engineering, Cambridge, England, 1974.

[13] Novak, G.
Computer understanding of Physics problems stated in Natural Language.
Technical Report TR NL30, Dept. Computer Science, Univ. of Texas, Austin., 1976.

[14] Pereira, L.M., Pereira, F.C.N. and Warren, D.H.D.
User's guide to DECsystem-10 PROLOG.
Dept. of Artificial Intelligence, Edinburgh, 1978.

[15] Stallman, R.M. & Sussman, G.J.
Forward reasoning and dependency-directed backtracking in a system for computer-aided circuit analysis.
Technical Report No. 380, MIT AI Lab, 1976.

[16] Waltz, D.
Generating semantic descriptions from drawings of scenes with shadows.
Technical Report MAC AI-TR-271, MIT AI Lab, 1972.

[17] Weyhrauch, R.W.
Prolegomena to a theory of mechanized formal reasoning.
RWW Informal Note 8., Stanford University, 1979.

[18] Winograd, T.
Understanding Natural Language.
Edinburgh University Press, 1972.

What is an Image?

Harold Cohen

University of California at San Diego

B-027, UCSD, La Jolla, CA 92093

Image-making, and more particularly art-making, are considered as rule-based activities in which certain fundamental rule-sets are bound to low-level cognitive processes. AARON, a computer-program, models some aspects of image-making behavior through the action of these rules, and generates, in consequence, an extremely large set of highly evocative "freehand" drawings. The program is described, and examples of its output given. The theoretical basis for the formulation of the program is discussed in terms of cultural considerations, particularly with respect to our relationship to the images of remote cultures. An art-museum environment implementation involving a special-purpose drawing device is discussed. Some speculation is offered concerning the function of randomising in creative behavior, and an account given of the use of randomness in the program. The conclusions offered bear upon the nature of meaning as a function of an image-mediated transaction rather than as a function of intentionality. They propose also that the structure of all drawn images, derives from the nature of visual cognition.

1. INTRODUCTION

AARON is a computer program designed to model some aspects of human art-making behavior, and to produce as a result "freehand" drawings of a highly evocative kind (figs 1,2). This paper describes the program, and offers in its conclusions a number of propositions concerning the nature of evocation and the nature of the transaction -- the making and reading of images -- in which evocation occurs. Perhaps unexpectedly -- for the program has no access to visual data -- some of these conclusions bear upon the nature of visual representation. This may suggest a view of image-making as a broadly referential activity in which various differentiable modes, including what we call visual representation (note 1), share a significant body of common characteristics.

In some respects the methodology used in this work relates to the modelling of "expert systems" (note 2), and it does in fact rely heavily upon my own "expert" knowledge of image-making. But in its motivations it comes closer to research in the computer simulation of cognition. This is one area, I believe, in which the investigator has no choice but to model the human prototype. Art is valuable to human beings by virtue of being made by other human beings, and the question of finding more efficient modes than those which characterise human performance simply does not arise.

My expertise in the area of image-making rests upon many years of professional activity as an artist -- a painter, to be precise (note 3) -- and it will be clear that my activities as an artist have continued through my last ten years of work in computer-modelling. The motivation for this work has been the desire to understand more about the nature of art-making processes than the making of art itself allows, for under normal circumstances the artist provides a near-perfect example of an obviously-present, but virtually inaccessible body of knowledge. The work has been informal, and <u>qua</u> psychology lacks methodological rigor. It <u>is</u> to be hoped, however, that the body of highly specialised knowledge brought to bear on an elusive problem will be some compensation.

AARON is a knowledge-based program, in which knowledge of image-making is represented in rule form. As I have indicated I have been my own source of specialised knowledge, and I have served also as my own knowledge-engineer. Before embarking on a detailed account of the program's workings, I will describe in general terms what sort of program it is, and what it purports to do.

First, what it is <u>not</u>. It is not an "artists' tool". I mean that <u>it</u> is not interactive, it is not designed to implement key decisions made by

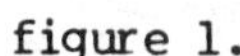

figure 1.

figure 2.

the user, and it does not do transformations upon input data. In short, it is not an instrument, in the sense that most computer applications in the arts, and in music particularly, have identified the machine in essentially instrument-like terms.

AARON is not a transformation device. There is no input, no data, upon which transformations could be done: in fact it has no data at all which it does not generate for itself in making its drawings. There is no lexicon of shapes, or parts of shapes, to be put together, assembly line fashion, into a complete drawing.

It is a complete and functionally independent entity, capable of generating autonomously an endless succession of different drawings (note 4). The program starts each drawing with a clean sheet of paper -- no data -- and generates everything it needs as it goes along, building up as it proceeds an internal representation of what it is doing, which is then used in determining subsequent developments. It is event driven, but in the special sense that the program itself generates the events which drive it.

It is not a learning program, has no archival memory, is quite simple and not particularly clever. It is able to knock off a pretty good drawing -- thousands, in fact -- but has no critical judgement that would enable it to declare that one of its drawings was "better" than another. That has never been part of the aim. Whether or not it might be possible to demonstrate that the artist moves towards higher goals, and however he might do so through his work, art-making in general lacks clear internal goal-seeking structures. There is no rational way of determining whether a "move" is good or bad the way one might judge a move in a game of chess, and thus no immediately apparent way to exercise critical judgement in a simulation.

This lack of internal goal-orientation carries with it a number of difficulties for anyone attempting to model art-making processes: for one thing, evaluation of the model must necessarily be informal. In the case of AARON, however, there has been extensive testing. Before describing the testing procedure it will be necessary to say with more care -- distinguishing here between the program's goals and my own -- what AARON is supposed to do.

Task Definition.

It is not the intent of the AARON model to turn out drawings which are, in some ill-defined and loosely-understood sense, aesthetically pleasing, though it does in practise turn out pleasing drawings. It is to permit the examination of a particular property of freehand drawing which I will call, in a deliberately general fashion, standing-for-ness.

The Photographic "Norm"

One of the aims of this paper is to give clearer definition to what may seem intuitively obvious about standing-for-ness, but even at the outset the "intuitively obvious" will need to be treated with some caution. In particular, we should recognise that unguarded assumptions about the nature of "visual" imagery are almost certain to be colored by the XXth century's deep preoccupation with photography as the "normal" image-making mode. The view that a drawn image is either:

1. representational (concerned with the appearance of things), or

2. an abstraction (i.e. fundamentally appearance-oriented, but transformed in the interest of other aims) or,

3. abstract (i.e. it doesn't stand for anything at all),

betrays just this pro-photographic filtering, and is a long way from the historical truth. There is a great wealth of imagistic material which fits none of these paradigms, and it is by no means clear even that a photograph carries its load of standing-for-ness by virtue of recording the varying light intensities of a particular view at a particular moment in time.

It is for this reason that image-making will be discussed here as the set of modes which contains visual representation as one of its members. It is also why I used the word "evocative" in the first paragraph rather than "meaningful". My domain of enquiry here is not the way in which particular meanings are transmitted through images and how they are changed in the process, but more generally the nature of image-mediated transactions. What would be the minimum condition under which a set of marks may function as an image? This question characterises economically the scope of the enquiry, and it also says a good deal about how the word "image" is to be used in this paper, though a more complete definition must wait until the end.

Art-making and Image-making.

The reader may detect some reluctance to say firmly that this research deals with art-making rather than with image-making, or vice-versa. The two are presented as continuous. Art-making is almost always a highly sophisticated activity involving the interlocking of complex patterns of belief and experience, while in the most general sense of the term image-making appears to be as "natural" as talking. All the same, art-making is a case of image-making, and part of what AARON suggests is that art-making rests upon cognitive processes which are absolutely normal and perfectly common.

figure 3.

Evaluation.

A simulation program models only a small piece of the action, and it requires a context in which to determine whether it functions as one expects that piece to function. AARON is not an artist. It simply takes over some of the functions which normally require an artist to perform them, and thus it requires the whole art-making process to be carried forward as a testing context. The program's output has to be acceptable to a sophisticated audience on the same terms as any other art, implying thereby that it must be seen as original and of high quality, not merely as a pastiche of existing work.

A valid testing procedure must therefore contain a sophisticated art-viewing audience, and the informal *in situ* evaluation of the simulation has been carried out in museum environments: the DOCUMENTA 6 international exhibition in Kassel, Germany, and the prestigeous Stedelijk Museum in Amsterdam, the two exhibits together running for almost five months and with a total audience of almost half a million museum-goers. In both of these shows drawings were produced continuously on a Tektronix 4014 display terminal and also with an unconventional hard-copy device (to be described later). A PDP 11/34 ran the program in full view of the gallery visitors (fig 3).

In addition and at other times the program's output has been exhibited in a more orthodox mode in museums and galleries in the US and in Europe.

These exhibits were not set up as scientific experiments. Nor could they have been without distorting the expectations of the audience, and thus the significance of any results. No formal records were kept of the hundreds of conversations which took place between the artist and members of the audience. This report is therefore essentially narrative, but offered with some confidence.

Audience Response.

A virtually universal first assumption of the audiences was that the drawings they were watching being made by the machine had actually been made in advance by the "real" artist, and someow "fed" to the machine. After it had been explained that this was not the case viewers would talk about the machine as if *it* were a human artist. There appeared to be a general consensus that the machine exhibited a good-natured and even witty artistic personality, and that its drawings were quite droll (fig 4). Some of the viewers, who knew my work from my pre-computing, European, days claimed that they could "recognise my hand" in the new drawings. This last is particularly interesting, since, while I certainly made use of my own body of knowledge concerning image-making in writing the program, the *appearance* of my own work never consciously served as a model for what the program was supposed to do.

More to the point, while a very small number of people insisted that the drawings were nothing but a bunch of random squiggles, the majority clearly saw them in referential terms. Many would stand for long periods watching, and describing to each other what was being drawn: always in terms of objects in the real world. The drawings seem to be viewed mostly as landscapes inhabited by "creatures", which would be "recognised" as animals, fish, birds and bugs. Occasionally a viewer would "recognise" a landscape, and once the machine's home was identified as San Francisco, since it had just drawn Twin Peaks.

It might be correctly anticipated that on those other occasions when drawings have simply been framed and exhibited without any reference to their origins, the question of their origins has never arisen, and they have met with a typical cross-section of museum-goers responses.

Even without formal evaluation, it might reasonably be claimed that the program provides a convincing simulation of human performance.

The next part of this paper is divided into five sections. In the first, a general description of the production system as a whole is given. The following three sections deal with particular parts of the production system: the MOVEMENT CONTROL part, the PLANNING part, and the part which handles the internal representation of the drawings as they proceed. The second of these, on PLANNING, also gives an account of the theoretical basis for the program. The fifth section has something to say about the function of randomness in the program, and also discusses to what extent it might be thought to parallel the use of randomness in human art-making behavior. The third and final part draws conclusions.

****

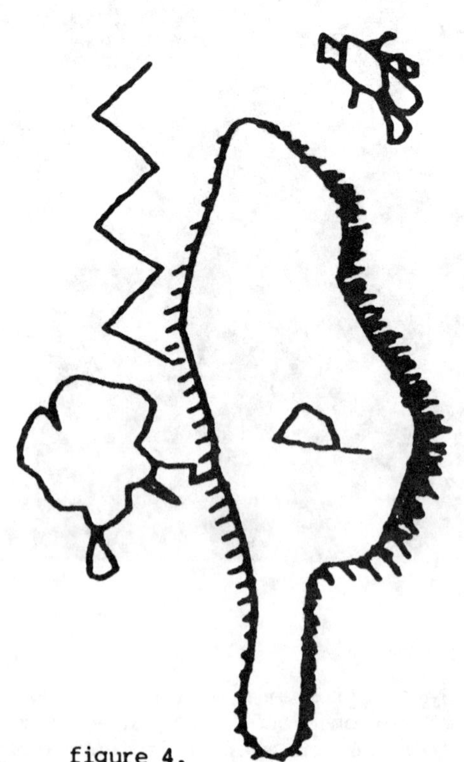

figure 4.

2. THE PROGRAM "AARON"

2.1 THE PRODUCTION SYSTEM.

The main program (note 5) has about three hundred productions. Many of these are to be regarded as micro-productions in the sense that each of them handles only a small part -- an "action-atom" -- of a larger conceptual unit of action. For example, the drawing of a single line, conceptually a single act, actually involves twenty or thirty productions on at least three levels of the system. This fine-grain control over the drawing process subscribes both to its generality -- most of these action-atoms are invoked by many different situations -- and to its flexibility, since it allows a process to be interrupted at any point for further consideration by higher-level processes.

Levels of Organisation.

The organisation of the system is heirarchical, in the sense that the higher levels are responsible for decisions which constrain the domain of action for the lower levels (fig 5). Each level of the system is responsible only for its own domain of decison-making, and there is no conceptual homunculus sitting on the top holding a blueprint and directing the whole operation. No single part knows what the drawing should turn out to be like. There is some practical advantage to this level-wise splitting up of the system, but the program was designed this way primarily for reasons of conceptual clarity, and from a desire to have the program structure itself -- as well as the material contained within it -- reflect my understanding of what the human image-making process might be like. I believe that the constant shifting of attention to different levels of detail and conceptualisation provides this human process with some of its important characteristics. Thus the left part of each production searches for combinations of up to five or six conditions, and each right part may perform an arbitrary number of actions or action-atoms, one of which may involve a jump to another level of the system.

"ARTWORK"

The topmost level of the system, the ARTWORK level, is responsible for decisions relating to the organisation of the drawing as a whole. It decides how to start, makes some preliminary decisions which may later determine when and how it is to finish, and eventually makes that determination. The program currently has no archival memory, and begins each drawing as if it has never done one before. (One can easily imagine the addition of a higher level designed to model the changes which the human artist deliberately makes in his work from one piece to the next: this level would presumably be called EXHIBITION.)

ARTWORK also handles some of the more important aspects of spatial distribution. It is my belief that the power of an image to convince us that it is a representation of some feature of the visual world rests in large part upon the image's fine-grain structure: the degree to which it seems to reflect patterns in the changes of information density across the field of vision which the cognitive processes themselves impose upon visual experience.

Put crudely, this means, for example, that a decision on the part of the reader of an image that one set of marks is a detail of another set of marks rather than standing autonomously, is largely a function of such issues as relative scale and proximity. This function is quite apart from the more obviously affective issue of shape (and hence "semantic") relationship. It is the overall control of the varying density of information in the drawing, rather than the control of inter-figural relationships, which is handled by ARTWORK.

"MAPPING" and "PLANNING"

All problems involving the finding and allocation of space for the making of individual elements in the drawing is handled by MAPPING, though its functions are not always heirarchically higher than those of PLANNING, which is responsible for the development of these individual figures. Sometimes PLANNING may decide on a figure and ask MAPPING to provide space, while at other times MAPPING may announce the existence of a space and then PLANNING will decide what to do on the basis of its availability. Sometimes, indeed, MAPPING may override a PLANNING decision by announcing that an appropriate space is not available. A good example of this occurs when PLANNING decides to do something inside an existing closed figure and MAPPING rules that there isn't enough room, or that what there is is the wrong shape.

MAPPING will be referred to again in relation to the data-structures which constitute the program's internal representation of what it is doing, and PLANNING also as one of the centrally important parts of the program.

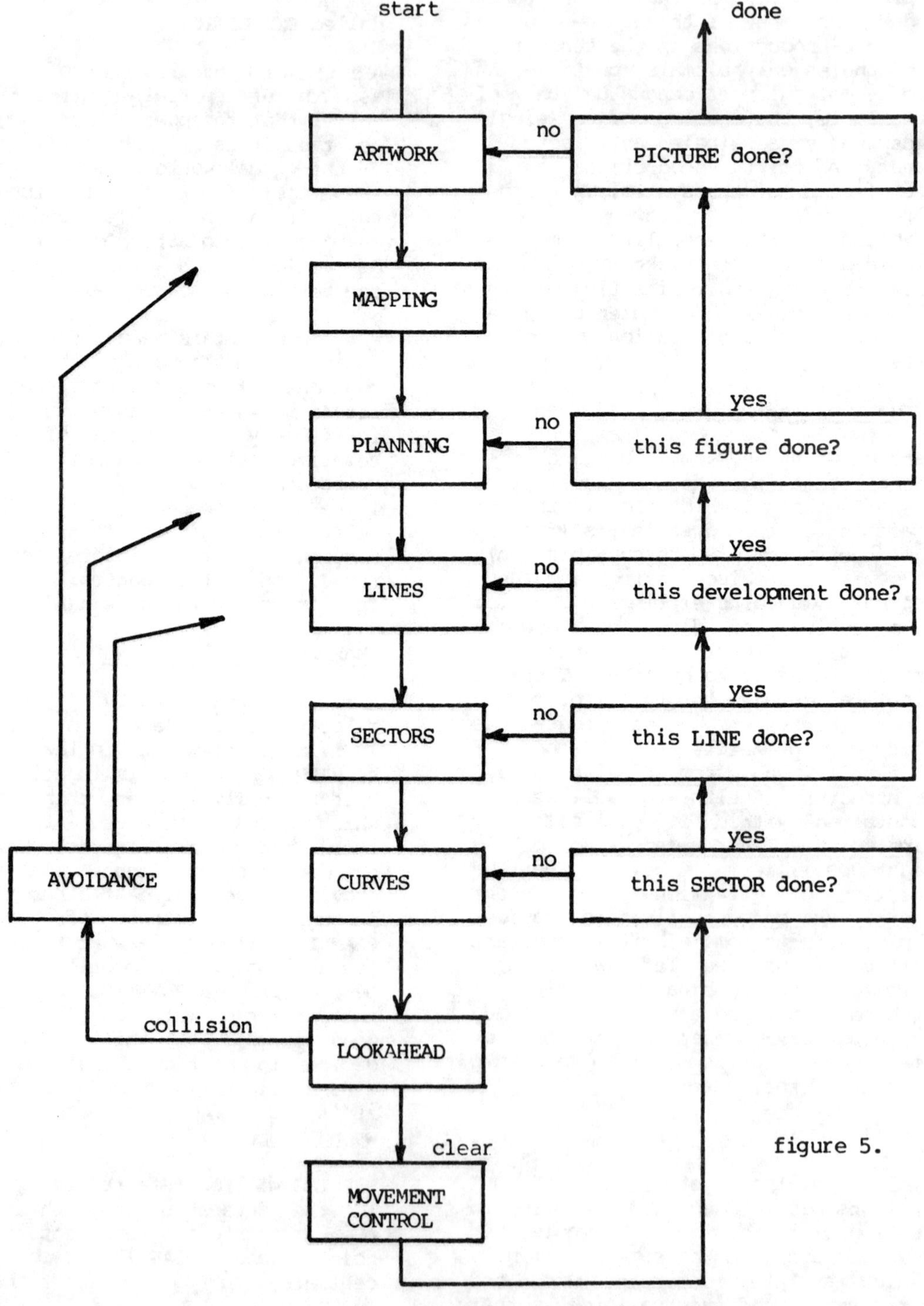
start
done
ARTWORK
no
PICTURE done?
MAPPING
PLANNING
no
yes
this figure done?
LINES
no
yes
this development done?
SECTORS
no
yes
this LINE done?
AVOIDANCE
CURVES
no
yes
this SECTOR done?
collision
LOOKAHEAD
clear
MOVEMENT
CONTROL

figure 5.

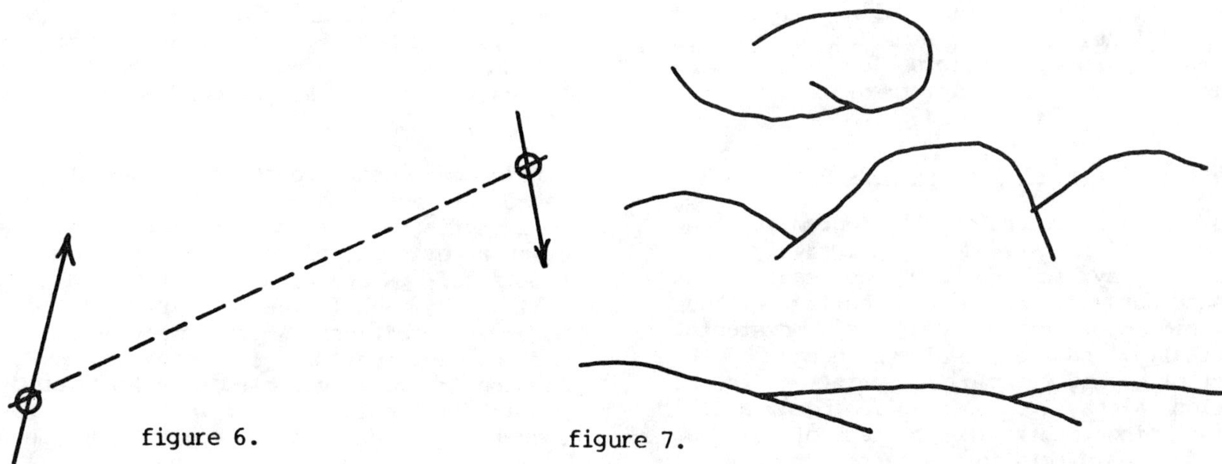

figure 6. figure 7.

LINES AND SECTORS

Below this level the heirarchical structure of the system is fairly straightforward. Each figure is the result of (potentially) several developments, each provided by a return of control to PLANNING. Each of these developments may consist of several lines, and for each of the successive lines of each development of any figure LINES must generate a starting point and an ending point, each having a direction associated with it (fig 6). It also generates a number of parameters on the basis of specifications drawn up in PLANNING which determine how the line is to be drawn: whether reasonably straight, wiggly, or strongly curved, and, if various overlapping modes are called for (fig 7), how they are to be handled.

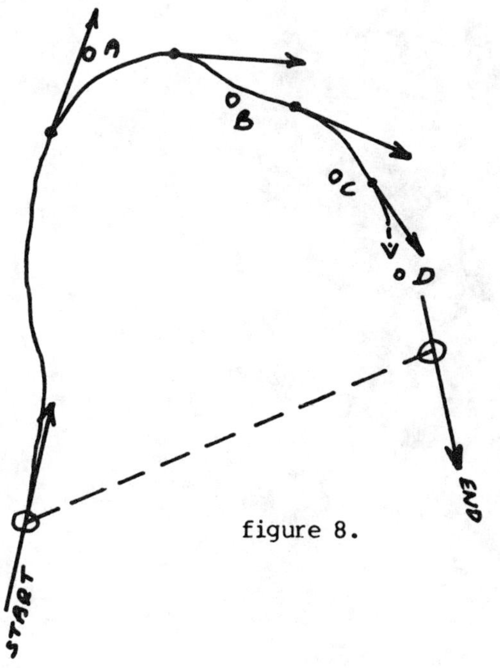

figure 8.

As I have indicated, lines are not drawn as the result of a single production. When LINES passes control to SECTORS the program does not know exactly where the line will go, since the constraint that it must start and end facing specified directions does not specify a path: there are an indeterminate number of paths which would satisfy the constraint. The program does not choose one, it generates one. SECTORS produces a series of "imagined" partial destinations -- signposts, as it were (fig 8) -- each designed to bring the line closer to its final end-state. On setting up each of these signposts it passes control to CURVES, whose function is to generate a series of movements of the pen which will make it veer towards, rather than actually to reach, the current signpost. Control is passed back to SECTORS when the pen has gone far enough towards the current signpost that it is time to look further ahead, and it is passed back to LINES when the current line has been completed and a new one is demanded by the development still in progress.

2.2 MOVEMENT CONTROL

We are now down to the lowest level of the program, and to the way in which the curves which make up the drawing are actually generated. This part is not discontinuous from the rest, of course. The flexibility of the program rests in large part upon the fact that the heirarchy of control extends downwards to the finest-grained decisions: no part of the control structure is considered to be so automatic that it should fall below the interface line. Thus, the story of how the pen gets moved around follows on from the description of how the intermediate signposts are set up.

Abstract Displays and Real Devices

In the earlier versions of the program all the development work was done exclusively on a graphic display, and the "pen" was handled as an abstract, dimensionless entity without real-world constraints upon its movements. Conceptually, however, I always thought of the problem of moving the pen from point A facing direction alpha, to point B facing direction beta, as being rather like the task of driving a car off a main road into a narrow driveway set at some known arbitrary angle to it. This is clearly not a dead-reckoning task for the human driver, but one which involves continuous feedback and a successive-approximation strategy.

It seemed quite reasonable, therefore, to be faced at some point with the problem of constructing an actual vehicle which would carry a real pen and make real drawings on real sheets of paper. That situation arose in the Fall of '76 when I was preparing to do the museum exhibitions which I mentioned earlier, and decided that if I wanted to make the drawing process visible to a large number of people simultaneously, I would need to use something a good deal bigger than the usual graphic display with its 20-inch screen.

The Turtle.

The answer turned out to be a small two-wheeled turtle (fig 9), each of its wheels independently driven by a stepping motor, so that the turtle could be steered by stepping the two motors at appropriate rates. It is thus capable of drawing arcs of circles whose radius depends upon the ratio of the two stepping rates.

Since the two wheels can be driven at the same speed in opposite directions, the turtle can be spun around on the spot and headed off in a straight line, so that this kind of device is capable of simulating a conventional x-y plotter. But it seemed entirely unreasonable to have built a device which could be driven like a car and then use it to simulate a plotter. In consequence the pen-driving procedures already in the program were re-written to generate the stepping rates for the motors directly -- to stay as close as possible to the human model's performance -- rather rather than calculating these rates as a function of decisions already made.

The advantage here was a conceptual one, with some practical bonus in the fact that the turtle does not spend a large part of its time spinning instead of drawing. It also turned out unexpectedly that the generating algorithm simplified enormously, and the quality of the freehand simulation improved noticeably.

Feedback.

The program does not now seek to any place -- in cartesian terms -- but concerns itself exclusively with steering: thus the turtle's cartesian position at the end of executing a single command is not known in advance. Nor is this calculation necessary when the turtle is operating in the real world. It was not designed as a precision drawing device, and since it cannot perform by dead-reckoning for long without accumulating errors, the principle of feedback operation was extended down into this real-world part of the program. The device makes use of a sonar navigation system (fig 10) by means of which the program keeps track of where it actually is. Instead of telling it to "go to x,y" as one would tell a conventional plotter, the program tells it "do the following and then say where you are".

A more detailed account of the turtle system, and it's effect upon the simulation of freehand drawing dynamics, is given in Appendix 1.

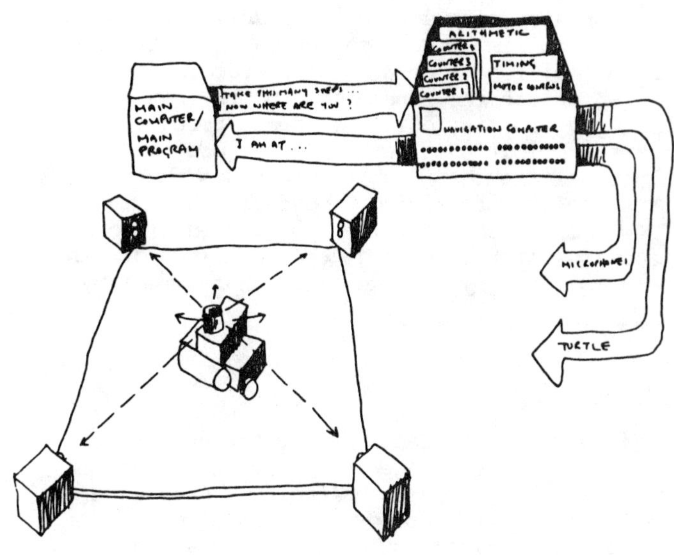

figure 10.

2.3 "PLANNING"

No single level of the program can be described adequately without reference to the other levels with which it interacts: it has already been mentioned, for example, that MAPPING may either precede PLANNING in determining what is to be done next, or it may serve PLANNING by finding a space specified there. Additionally, any development determined in PLANNING may be modified subsequently either as a result of an imminent collision with another figure or because provision exists in the program for "stacking" the current development in order to do something not originally envisaged (fig 11a,b). All the same, the drawing is conceived predominantly as an agglomeration of figures, and to that extent PLANNING, which is responsible for the development of individual figures, is of central importance.

Behavioral Protocols in Image-Making.

Of the entire program, it is also the part least obviously related to the effects which it accomplishes. While the formal results of its actions are clear enough -- an action calling for the closure of a shape will cause it to close, for example -- it is not at all clear why those actions result in the specifically evocative quality which the viewer experiences.

A rule-by rule account of this effect is not appropriate, because the individual rules do no more than implement conceptual entities -- which I will call behavioral protocols -- which are the fundamental units from which the program is built. These protocols are never explicitly stated in the program, but their existence is what authorises the rules. Thus, before describing in detail what is in PLANNING I should give an account of the thinking which preceeded the writing of the program, and try to make clear what I mean by a protocol.

Background.

It is a matter of fact that by far the greatest part of all the imagery to which we attach the name of "art" comes to us from cultures more or less remote from our own. It is also a matter of fact that within our own culture, and in relation to its recent past, our understanding of imagery rest to a great extent upon prior common understandings, prior cultural agreements, as to what is to stand for what -- prior, that is to say, to the viewing of any particular image. It is unlikely that a Renaissance depiction of the Crucifixion ("of Christ" being understood here by means of just such an agreement!) would carry any great weight of meaning if we were not already familiar both with the story of Christ and with the established conventions for dealing with the various parts of the story. Indeed, we might be quite confused to find a depiction of a beardless, curly-headed youth on the cross unless we happened to possess the now-abstruse knowledge that Christ was depicted that way -- attaching a new set of meanings to the old convention for the representation of Dionysus -- until well into the 7th century. In general, we are no longer party to the agreements which make this form acceptable and understandable. We must evidently distinguish between what is understandable without abstruse knowledge -- we can, indeed, recognise the figure on the cross as a figure -- and what is understandable only by virtue of such knowledge.

In the most general sense, all cultural conditions are remote from us, and differ only in the degree of their remoteness. We cannot really comprehend why the Egyptians made sphinxes, what Michelangelo thought the ancient world had in common with Christianity, or how the internal combustion engine was viewed by the Italian Futurists seventy years ago who wanted to tear down the museums in its honor. What abstruse knowledge we can gain by reading Michelangelo's writings, or the Futurist Manifesto, does not place us into the cultural

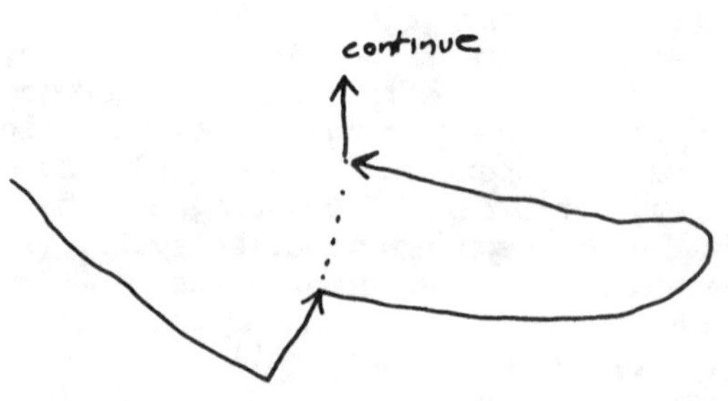

figure 11a,b.

environment in which the work is embedded. A culture is a continuum, not a static event: its understandings and meanings shift constantly, and their survival may appear without close scrutiny to be largely arbitrary. In the extreme case, we find ourselves surrounded by the work of earlier peoples so utterly remote from us that we cannot pretend to know anything about the people themselves, much less about the meanings and purposes of their surviving images.

The Paradox of Insistent Meaningfulness.

There is an implicit paradox in the fact that we persist in regarding as meaningful -- not on the basis of careful and scholarly detective work, but on a more directly confrontational basis -- images whose original meanings we cannot possibly know, including many that bear no explicitly visual resemblance to the things in the world. Presumably this state of affairs arises in part from a fundamental cultural egocentrism -- what, we ask, would _we_ have intended by this image and the act of making it? -- which is fundamentally distortive. There has also been a particular confusion in this century through the widespread acceptance of what we might call the _telecommunications model_ of our transactions through imagery, particularly since in applying that model no differentiation has been observed between the culture we live in and the cultures of the remote past. In the view of this model, original meanings have been encoded in the image, and the appearance of the image in the world effects the transmission of the meanings. Allowing for noise in the system -- the inevitability of which gives rise to the notion, in art theory, of "interpretation" -- the reception and decoding of the image makes the original meanings available.

However useful the model is as a basis for examining real telecommunication-like situations, in which the intended meanings and their transformations can be known and tracked, it provides a general account of our transactions through images which is quite inadequate. The encoding and decoding of messages requires access to the same code-book by both the image-maker and the image-reader, and that code-book is precisely what is _not_ carried across from one culture to another.

I think it is clear also that the _paradox of insistent meaningfulness_, as we might call it, constitutes the normal condition of image-mediated transactions, not an abnormal condition. It evidently extends below the level at which we can recognise the figure, but not what the figure stands for, since so much of the available imagery is not in any very obvious sense "representational" at all. The paradox is enacted every time we look at a few marks on a scrap of paper and proclaim them to be a face, when we know perfectly well that they are nothing of the sort.

Cognitive Bases for Image Structure.

In short, my tentative hypothesis in starting work on AARON was that all image-making and all image-reading is mediated by cognitive processes of a rather low-level kind, presumably processes by means of which we are able to cope also with the real world. In the absence of common cultural agreements these cognitive processes would still unite image-maker and image-viewer in a single transaction. On this level -- but not on the more complex culture-bound level of specific iconological intentionality -- the viewer's egocentricity might be justified, since he could correctly identify cognitive processes of a familiar kind in the making of the image. But let me detail this position with some care. I am not proposing that these processes make it possible for us to understand the intended meanings of some remotely-generated image: I am proposing that the intended meanings of the maker play only a relatively small part in the sense of meaningfulness. That sense of meaningfulness is generated for us by the structure of the image rather than by its content.

I hope I may be excused for dealing in so abbreviated a fashion with issues which are a good deal less than self-evident. The notion of non-enculturated behavior -- and that notion lurks behind the last few paragraphs, obviously -- is a suspect one, since all human behavior is enculturated to some degree: but my purpose was not to say what part of human behavior is dependent upon enculturating processes and what is not. It was simply to identify some of the determinants to a general image-structure which could be seen to be common to a wide range of enculturating patterns. The implication seemed strong -- and still does -- that the minimum condition for generating a sense of meaningfulness did not need to include the assumption of an intent to communicate: that the exercise of an appropriate set of these cognitive processes would itself be sufficient to generate a sense of meaningfulness.

Cognitive Skills.

The task then was to define a suitable set. I have no doubt that the options are wide, and that my own choices are not exclusive. I chose at the outset to include:

1. the ability to differentiate between figure and ground,

2. the ability to differentiate between open and closed forms, and

3. the ability to differentiate between insideness and outsideness (note 6).

AARON has developed a good deal from that starting point, and some of its current abilities clearly reflect highly enculturated patterns of behavior. For example, the program is now able to shade figures in a mode distinctly linked to Renaissance and post-Renaissance representational modes: other cultures have not concerned themselves with the fall of light on the surfaces of objects in the same way. Nevertheless, a large part of the program is involved still in demonstrating its awareness of the more primitive differentiations.

Protocols and Rules.

Against this background, I use the term protocol to mean the procedural instantiation of a formal awareness. This is clearly a definition which rests upon cognitive, rather than perceptual, modes, since it involves the awareness of relational structures. Thus, for example, the program's ability to differentiate between form and ground makes possible an awareness of the spatial relationships between forms, and generates finally a set of avoidance protocols, the function of which is to prohibit the program from ignoring the existence of one figure in drawing another one. The protocols themselves are not explicitly present in the program, and are manifested only through their enactment by the rules which describe what to do in particular circumstances where the overlapping of figures is threatened.

Figure Development

In keeping with the heirarchical structuring which informs the program as a whole, PLANNING considers a figure to be the result of a number of developments, each determined in part by what has gone before. The program enacts a number of repetition protocols, and a single development in the making of a figure can often involve the repetition of a single action (fig 12), rather than the agglomeration of different actions. The first productions to deal with the first development of any figure decide, on the basis of frequency considerations, that this figure will be closed, that it will be open, or that it will be, for the moment, "uncommitted" -- that is, a line or a complex of lines will be drawn, but only at a later stage will it be decided whether or not to close. If the primary decision is for closure,

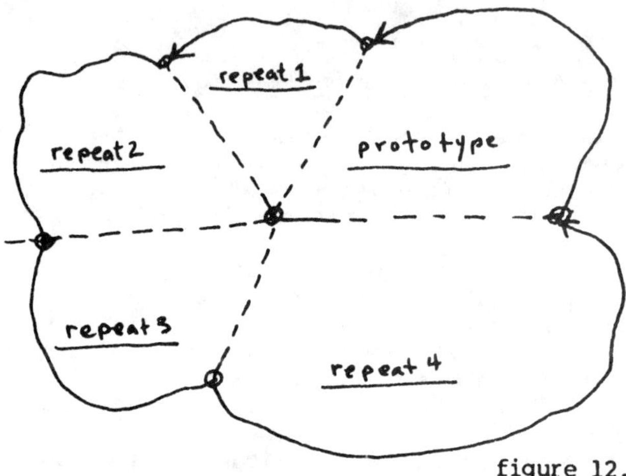

figure 12.

then PLANNING will decide between a number of options, mostly having to do with size and shape -- MAPPING permitting -- and with configuration. In some cases it will not actually draw the boundary of a closed form at all, and will leave the definition of the occupied space to await subsequent space-filling moves.

If the decision is for a non-closed form, then again a number of options are open. In both cases the available options are stated largely in terms of repetition protocols, the enactment of which determines the formal characteristics of the resulting configuration. These characteristics are not uniquely defining, however, and a number of different formal sub-groups may result from a single repetition protocol and its rules. For example, one such protocol, involving a single line in this case, requires the line to move a given distance (more-or-less) and then change direction, continuing this cycle a given number of times. All the figures marked in (fig 13) result from this: the details of implementation in the individual cases are responsive to their unique environmental conditions, and in any case may be changed at any point by the overriding avoidance protocol, which guarantees the territorial integrity of existing figures.

Thus the program will know at the beginning of each development what the current intention is, but will not know what shape will result. A closed form generated by a "go,turn, repeat" cycle may in fact turn out to be extremely long and narrow (fig 14), and a number of second developments associated with a closed-form first development will then be unavailable: there will be a limit, for example, upon what can be drawn inside it, though it may develop in other ways, as this one does.

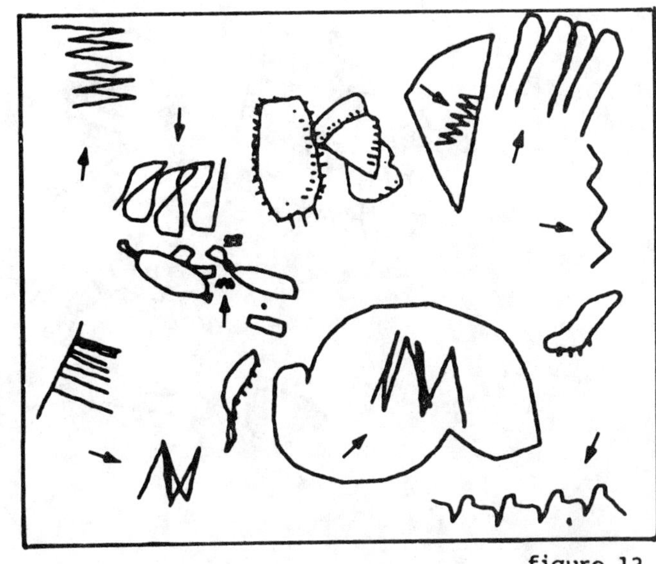

figure 13.

Proliferation.

Even with constraints of this sort there is a significant proliferation in the number of productions associated with the second development of any figure. A typical first development might be initiated by:

If (this is a first development
  and the last figure was open
  and at least n figures have been done
  and at least q of them were open
  and at least t units of space are now available)

Then
This figure will be closed
  specifications for repetition
  specifications for configuration
  to move on from this point:
  If (this is a second development
    and the first was closed
    and its properties were
      a. (size)
      b. (proportions)
      c. (complexity)
      d. (proximity to ...)

Then either
  1. divide it
  ... specifications ...
  or
  2. shade it
  ... specifications...
  or
  3. add a closed form to it
  ... specifications...
  4. do a closed form inside
  ... specifications...
  or
  5. do an open form inside
  ... specifications...

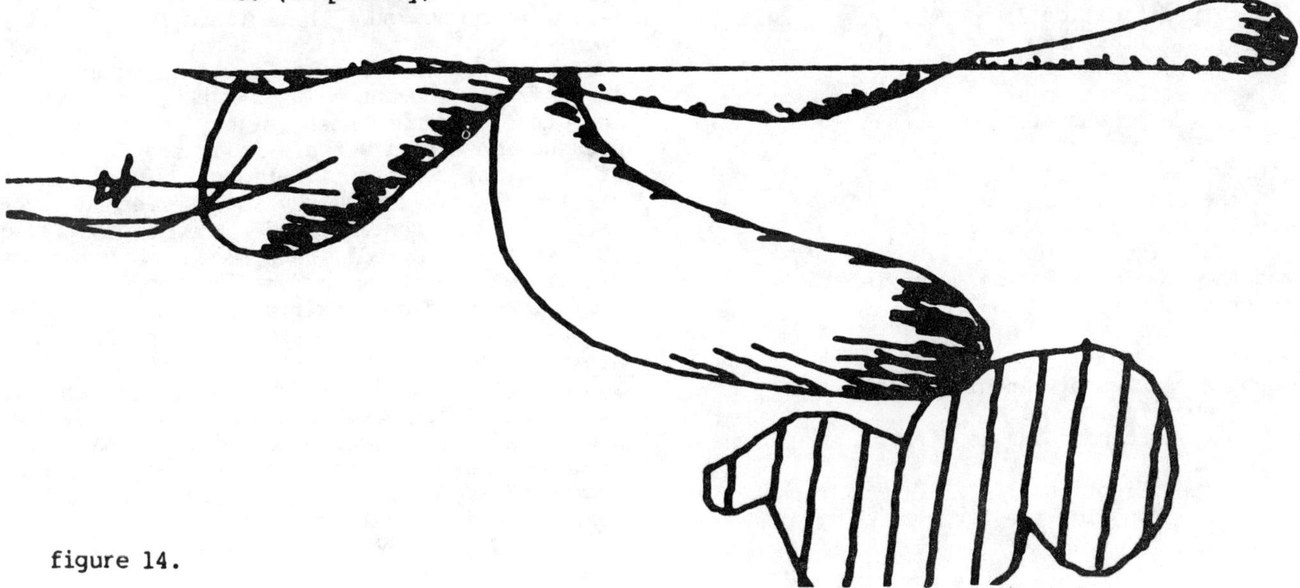

figure 14.

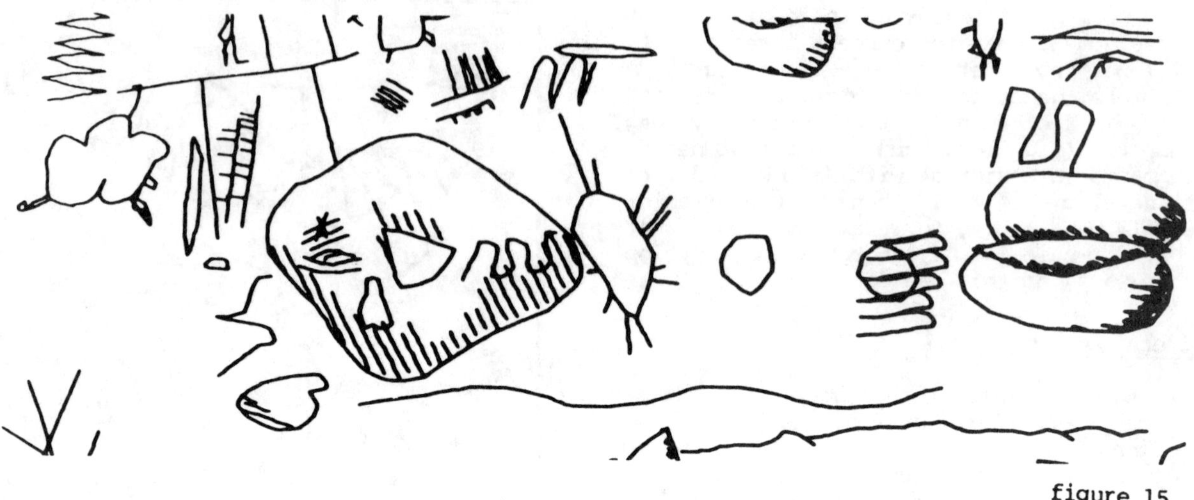

figure 15.

This is a prototype for an expanding class of productions, each responding to a different combination of properties in the first development. Similarly, continuation will require...

<u>If</u> (this is a third development
and the first was a closed form
... properties...
and the second was a closed form
... properties...)

<u>Then</u>
shade the entire figure:
specification 1:
a boulder with a hole in it
or
specification 2:
a flat shape with a hole
or
specification 3:
a penumbra.

<u>If</u> (this is a third development
and the first was closed
and the second was a series of
parallel lines inside it ...
and the remaining inside space is at
least s...)

<u>Then</u>
do another series of lines:
specification 1:
perpendicular to first...
or
specification 2:
alongside the first...
or
specification 3:
do a closed form in available
space...

(note 7).

<u>The Relationship of Closed Forms and Open Forms</u>.

The same proliferation of options occurs for open-lined structures also, but not to the same degree. One of the interesting things to come out of this program is the fact that open-line structures appear to function quite differently when they are alone in an image than when they appear in the presence of closed forms. There seems to be no doubt that closed forms exert a special authority in an image -- perhaps because they appear to refer to objects -- and in their presence open-lined structures which in other circumstances might exert similar pressure on the viewer are relegated to a sort of spatial connective-tissue function. A similar context-dependancy is manifested when material is presented inside a closed form (fig 15): it is "adopted", and becomes either a detail of the form, or markings upon it. This seems to depend upon particular configurational issues, and especially the scale relationship between the "parent" form and the newly introduced material. This manifestation is important, I believe, in understanding why we are able to recognise as "faces" so wide a range of closed forms with an equally wide range of internal markings following only a very loose distribution specification.

Limits on Development.

At the present time no figure in the program goes beyond three developments, and few go that far, for a number of reasons. In the first place, most of the (formal) behavior patterns in the program were initially intended to model a quite primitive level of cognitive performance, and for most of these a single development is actually adequate. Once a zig-zag line has been generated, repetition, for example -- as it is found in existing primitive models -- seems limited to those shown in (fig 16).

It has remained quite difficult to come up with new material general enough for the purposes of the program. It is the generality of the protocols which guarantees the generality of the whole, and new material is initiated by the introduction of new protocols. On the level of the procedures which carry out the action parts of the subsequently-developed productions, the approach has been to avoid accumulation of special routines to do special things. There is only one single procedure adapting the protocols of repetition and reversal to the generation of a range of zigzag-like forms, for example (fig 13).

But there has been another, and equally significant reason, for the limitation upon permissible developments. It is the lack of adequate, and adequately important, differentiations in the existing figures. For the primitive model represented by the earlier states of the program it was almost enough to have a set of abilities called up by the most perfunctory consideration of the current state of the drawing: the stress was on the definition of a suitable set of abilities (as represented by the right-hand parts of the productions), and as it turned out it was quite difficult to exercise those abilities without generating moderately interesting results. But for a more sophisticated model it is clearly not enough merely to extend that set of abilities, and the problem of determining why the program should do this rather than that becomes more pressing.

The limitation here can be considered in two ways. One is that I had reached the point of exhausting temporarily my own insights into the image-building process. The other is that I had not made provision in the first versions of the program for being able to recognise the kind of differentiations I would want to deal with -- since I could not know at the outset what they were going to be -- and thus lacked a structure for developing new insights. This leads to a consideration of my next topic: how the program builds its own representation of what it has done up to any point in the making of the drawing.

figure 16 .

2.4 INTERNAL REPRESENTATION

In the earlier stages of the development of the program, provision had been made for progressive access to the information stored in the data-structure, following the principal that it should not have to access more than it actually needed for the making of any particular decision. In practise, a great deal more was stored than was ever accessed. At the first level of detail the program made use of a quite coarse matrix representation, in each cell of which was stored an identifier for the figure which occupied it, and a number of codes which designated the various events which might have occurred in it: a line belonging to a closed form, a line belonging to an open form, a line junction, an unused space inside a closed figure, and so on. Obviously, it was not possible to record a great deal in this way, and data concerning the connectivity of the figure in particular required a second level of the structure.

This was an unpleasantly elaborate linked-list structure of an orthodox kind. By definition, the kind of drawing AARON makes is not merely a growing, but a continuously-changing, structure. What was a point on a line becomes a node when another line intersects it, and this change has to be recorded by updating the existing structure, which must now ideally show the four paths connecting this node to four adjacent nodes.

Both updating this structure and accessing the information contained within it proved to be quite tiresome, and the scheme was never general enough to admit of further development. As a result, it was used less and less, and decision -making has been based almost exclusively on the information contained in the matrix on the one hand, and in a third level of the structure, a simple property-list attaching to each figure, on the other. The most surprising thing about this simplistic and distinctly ad-hoc scheme is that it was actually quite adequate to the needs of the program.

Explicit Data and Implicit Data.

Human beings presumably get first-order information about a picture by looking at the picture. I have always found it quite frustrating that the program couldn't do the same thing: not because it made any difference to the program, but because it made it difficult for me to think about the kind of issues I believed to be significant. Part of the problem of using a linked-list structure to represent the connectivity of a figure, for example, derived from the fact that connectivity had to be *explicitly* recorded as it happened: it would have been much too difficult to traverse a structure of this kind post-hoc in order to *discover* facts about connectivity. If one could traverse the figure the way the eye does -- loosely speaking! -- it would not be necessary to give so much attention to recording explicitly all the data in the world without regard for whether it would ever be looked at again.

In short, the primary decision to be made was whether to accept the absolute non-similarity of picture and representation as given, devise a more sophisticated list-structure and drop the matrix representation altogether, or to drop the list-structure and develop the matrix representation to the point where it could be very easily traversed to generate information which was *implicit* within it. I opted for the latter. A description is included in Appendix 2, though at the time of writing (December '78) the implementation is not yet complete.

2.5 THE FUNCTION OF RANDOMNESS.

This section does not deal with any single part of AARON: randomness is an active decision-making principle throughout the program, and I think it is important to say why that is the case. As a preface, it might be worth recording that beyond the limits of a mathematically sophisticated community most people evidently view randomness in a thoroughly absolutist fashion, and as the opposite to an equally absolute determinism. There is a firmly-held popular belief that a machine either does exactly what it has been programmed to do, or it acts "randomly". The fact that AARON produces non-random drawings, which its programmer has never seen, has given many people a good deal of trouble.

What I mean by "randomness" is the impossibility of predicting the outcome of a choice on the basis of previously-made choices. It follows, of course, that "randomness", in this sense, can never be absolute: if the domain of choice is the set of positive integers, one must be able to predict that the outcome will be a positive integer, not a cow or a color. In AARON the domain of choice is always a great deal more constrained than that, however. The corollary to the notion of randomness as a decision-making principle is the precise delineation of the choice space: in practice, the introduction into the program of a new decision characteristically involves the setting of rather wide limits, which are then gradually brought in until the range is quite small.

Randomness by Design and by Default.

AI researchers in more demonstrably goal-oriented fields of intellectual activity must obviously spend much time and effort in trying to bring to the surface performance rules which the expert must surely have, since he performs so well. I am not in a position to know to what extent "Let's try x" would constitute a powerful rule in other activities: I am convinced that it is a very powerful rule indeed in art-making, and more generally in what we call creative behavior, provided that "x" is a member of a rigorously constrained set.

A number of artists in this century -- perhaps more in music than in the visual arts -- have deliberately and consciously employed randomising procedures: tossing coins, rolling dice, disposing the parts of a sculpture by throwing them on the floor, and so on. But this simply derives a strategy from a principle, and examples of both can be found at almost any point in history. It is almost a truism in the trade that great colorists use dirty brushes. Leonardo recommended that the difficulty of starting a new painting on a clean panel -- every painter knows how hard that first mark is to make -- could be overcome by throwing a dirty sponge at it (note 8). But one suspects that Leonardo got to be pretty good with the sponge! An artist like Rubens would himself only paint the heads and hands in his figure compositions, leaving the clothing to one assistant, the landscape to another, and so on. All the assistants were highly-qualified artists in their own right, however. The process was not unlike the workings of a modern film crew: the delegation of responsibility reduces the director's direct control, and randomises the implementation of his intentions, while the expertise and commonly-held concerns of the crew provide the limits (note 9).

Randomising in the Program: Rules and Meta-rules.

For the human artist, then, randomising is not unconstrained, and therefore cannot be characterised by the rule "If you don't know what to do, do anything". Rather, one suspects the existence of a meta-rule which says, "precisely define a space within which any choice will do exactly as well as any other choice". In AARON, the implementation of the low-order rule has the following form:

```
If
   (a and b and ...n)

      Then
      p% of the time do (x);
      q% of the time do (y);
      r% of the time do (z);
```

which fills out the description of the format discussed in PLANNING. The same frequency-controlled format is used within the action part of a production in determining specifications:

```
make a closed loop:
specification 1: number of sides
     50% of the time, 2 sides (simple loop)
     32% of the time, 3 sides
     ...
specification 2: proportion
     50% of the time, between 1:4 and 1:6
     12% of the time, between 3:4 and 7:8
     ...
specification 3.
```

AARON has only the simplest form of these meta-rules, which are used to determine the bounds of the choice space:

```
if(a) lowbound is La, highbound is Ha
if(b) lowbound is Lb, highbound is Hb
if(n) lowbound is Ln, highbound is Hn
specification taken randomly between
lowbound and higbound
```

where a,b,n are varying conditions in the state of the drawing. No consistent attempt has been made to develop more sophisticated meta-rules. In the final analysis, the existence of such rules implies a judgemental view of the task at hand, and they are consequently beyond the scope of a program like AARON, which is not a learning program and has no idea whether it is doing well or badly.

The Value of Randomness.

What does randomness do for the image-maker? Primarily, I believe its function is to produce proliferation of the decision space without requiring the artist to "invent" constantly. One result of that function is obviously the generation of a much greater number of discreet terminations than would otherwise be possible, and consequently the sense that the rule-set is a great deal more complex than is actually the case. A second result is that the artist faces himself constantly with unfamiliar situations rather than following the same path unendingly, and is obliged to pay more attention, to work harder to resolve unanticipated juxtapositions. It is a device for enforcing his own heightened participation in the generating process.

This last might seem less important in AARON: the program's attention is absolute, after all. But for the viewer the fact that AARON exercises the function is quite important. There is one level of our transactions with images on which we respond with some astuteness to what is actually there. The fact that AARON literally makes decisions every few microseconds -- not binary decisions only, but also concerning quantitative specifications -- shows clearly in the continuously changing direction of the line, in every nuance of shape, and succeeds in convincing the viewer that there is, indeed, an intelligent process at work behind the making of the drawings.

****

3. CONCLUSIONS

AARON produces drawings of an evocative kind. It does so without user intervention; without recourse to user-provided data; and without the repertoire of transformational manipulations normal to "computer graphics". It remains now, if not to propose a coherent theory of image-making, at least to pull together those fragments of explanation already given into something resembling a plausible account of why AARON works.

This will be largely a matter of putting things in the right places.

Art-making and Image-making

First: no adequate justification has yet been given for the many references to art and art-making, as opposed to images and image-making, beyond saying that the first are a special case of the second. What makes them special?

Art is a bit like truth. Every culture has, and acts out, the conviction that truth and art exist, no two cultures will necessarily agree about what they are. There is no doubt, for example, that we use the word "art" to denote activities in other cultures quite unlike what our own artists do today, for the quite inadequate reason that those earlier acts have resulted in objects which we choose to regard as art objects. If it is surprisingly difficult to say what art is, it is not only because it is never the same for very long, but also because we evidently have no choice but to say what it is for us.

All the same, no justification is possible for making reference to it without attempting to say -- once again! -- what it is, and doing so in terms general enough to cover the greatest number of examples. Also, those terms should do something to account for the extraordinary persistence of the idea of art, which transcends all of its many examples.

Briefly, my view is that this persistence stems from a persistent and fundamental aspect of the mind itself. It would be stating the obvious here to propose that the mind may be regarded as a symbol processor of power and flexibility. I will propose, rather, to regard it as devoted primarily to establishing symbolic relationships: to attaching significance to events, and asserting that this stands for that. This is, surely, a large part of what we mean by understanding.

As for art: in its specifically cultural aspects art externalises specific assertions -- the number three stands for the perfection of God, the racing car stands for the spirit of modern man, the swastika stands for the semi-mythical migrations of the Hopi people, or for a number of other things in a number of other cultures. But on a deeper level, art is an elaborate and sophisticated game played around the curious fact that within the mind things can stand for other things. It is almost always characterised by a deep preoccupation with the structures of standing-for-ness, and a fascination with the apparently endless diversity of which those structures are capable. What we see in the museums results from a complex interweaving of the highly individuated and the highly enculturated, and in consequence any single manifestation is bound firmly to the culture within which it was generated: or it is rehabilitated to serve new ends in a new culture. But ultimately, art itself, as opposed to its manifestations, is universal because it is a celebration of the human mind itself.

The Embeddedness of Knowledge

Second: much of what has come out of the writing of AARON has to be regarded simply as extensions to the body of knowledge which the program was intended to externalise. Writing it was not merely a demonstrative undertaking, and it is far from clear what has been raised to the surface and what newly discovered. I have regarded the program as an investigative tool, though for present purposes the distinction is not important.

It remains impossible to give an adequate account of this knowledge other than by reference to the program itself. There are several reasons for this. In the first place, this knowledge does not present itself initially as predominantly prescriptive. The first intuition of its existence comes in the form of an awareness that an issue -- closure, repetition, spatial distribution -- is significant: the program should be structured in terms of that issue, as well as in terms of all the other issues already contained. In this sense the left parts of the productions might eventually be taken together to represent the set of issues which AARON believes to be worth attending to in the making of an image. But this stage comes much later, and by this time an individual production functions as part of a fabric of issues, with so many threads tying it to so many knowledge sources, that a one-to-one account of how it achieves its effect is generally out of the question.

In fact, there is only a single example I can call to mind in which an effect can be ascribed with certainty to a single production: a particular class of junction in a meandering horizontal line will infallibly generate strong landscape reference, though only if the

figure 17.

branching at the junction goes off on the lower side of the line (fig 17). This degree of specificity is certainly exceptional, but less powerful as an evocator rather than more so. In general, this particular class of junction -- it is more easily characterised visually than verbally -- tends strongly to denote spatial overlap: but the specific effect is evidently quite context-dependant, and dependant also upon the precise configuration of the junction itself.

"Personality" as a Function of Complexity.

At the higher end of the scale of effects, the problem of saying what causes what becomes more difficult still. I have never been able to understand how there can be such general agreement about the "personality" which AARON's drawings project, or why that "personality" appears to be like my own in a number of respects. Personality has never been an issue on the conscious level of writing code, and I know of nothing in the program to account for it. To put the problem another way, I would not know how to go about changing the program to project a different "personality".

I assume that the personality projected by an image is simply a part of a continuous spectrum of projection, not distinguishable in type from any other part. But I am forced now to the conclusion that these more elusive elements of evocation -- personality is only one of them, presumably -- are generated out of the complexity of the program as a whole, and not from the action of program parts: that given an adequate level of complexity any program will develop a "personality". This "personality" may be more or less clear in individual cases, and may perhaps depend upon how many people have worked on the program -- AARON is almost exclusively my own work -- but it will in any case be a function of the program, and outside the willful control of the programmer. If this is the case it seems extremely unlikely that any complete causal account of the workings of a program would ever be possible.

The Continuousness of Image-making and Image-reading.

Third: I want to return to the question which lies at the root of this work. What constitutes a minimum condition under which a set of marks will function as an image?

The reader will have noted that much of what has been written here appears to bear as much upon the business of image-reading as it does upon image-making. There is no contradiction: the central issue being addressed is the image-mediated transaction itself, and image-making in particular has no meaningful, or examinable, existence outside of that transaction. Knowledge about image-making is knowledge about image-reading: both rest upon the same cognitive processes. Thus the skilled artist does not need to enquire what the viewer sees in his work: the satisfaction of his own requirements guarantees it a reading in the world, and the explicit individual readings which it will have are irrelevant to him. The trainee artist, the student, on the other hand, frequently responds to his teacher's reading of his work by objecting, "You're not supposed to see it that way", evidently unaware that the reading does not yield to conscious control. Lack of skill in image-making more often than not involves a failure to discern the difference between what is in the image-maker's mind and what he has actually put on the canvas.

It is equally true, I believe, that image-reading has no meaningful existence outside the transactional context: not because the whole event is always present -- it almost never is -- but because every act of image-reading is initiated by the unspoken assertion "What I see is the result of a willful human act". That is a part of what we mean by the word "image". However much we may amuse ourselves seeing dinosaurs in clouds or dragons in the fireplace, we have no difficulty in differentiating between marks and shapes made by man, and marks and shapes made by nature, and we do not hesitate to assign meaning in the one case where we deny it in the other: unless we belong to a culture with a more animistic attitude to nature than this one has.

In short, I believe that the first requirement of the condition in the question is the undenied assumption of human will (note 10).

The rest of the condition is given by the display of behavior which draws attention to a particular group of cognitive elements. In other words, evidence of cognitive process may be substituted for the results of an act of cognition. An actual desire to communicate -- which may include the simple desire to record the appearance of the world -- is not a necessary condition.

AARON's strength lies in the fact that it is designed to operate within, and feed into, the transactional context, not to reproduce the aesthetic qualities of existing art objects. It takes full advantage of the viewers' predispositions and does nothing to disabuse them: indeed, it might fairly be judged that some parts of the program -- the simulation of freehand dynamics, for example -- are aimed primarily at sustaining an illusion (note 11). But the illusion can only be sustained fully by satisfying the conditions given above, and once that is accomplished the transactions which its drawings generate are real, not illusory. Like its human counterpart, AARON succeeds in delineating a meaning-space for the viewer, and as in any normal transaction not totally prescribed by prior cultural agreements, the viewer provides plausible meanings.

Standing-for-ness.

Fourthly: there is a multitude of ways in which something can stand for something else, and in adopting the general term "standing-for-ness" I intended for the moment to avoid the excess meanings which cling to words like "symbol", "referrent", "metaphor", "sign", and so on: words which abound in art theory and art history. An image, I have said, is something which stands for something else, and of course it is quite plain that I have been discussing only a very small subset of such things.

What are the defining characteristics of this subset?

Before attempting to answer that question, it should be noted that, while AARON's performance is based upon vision-specific cognitive modes (note 12), there are two closely related questions which cannot be asked about AARON at all.

Images of the World and its Objects.

The first of these has to do with the fact that in the real world people make images of things.

How do people decide what marks to make in relation to those things?

It is difficult to avoid the conclusion that image-making as a whole is vision-based, even though it bears directly on the issue of appearances only occasionally. It is my belief that even when an image is not purposively referential -- as is the case with AARON -- or when the artist seeks to refer to some element of experience which has no visual counterpart, it is his ability to echo the structure of visual experience which gives the image its plausibility (note 13).

The Persistence of Motifs

The second question has to do with the fact that actual image elements, motifs, have been used over and over again throughout human history, appearing in totally disconnected cultural settings, and bearing quite different

figure 18.

meanings as they do so. What is it that makes the zigzag, the cross, the swastika, squares, triangles, spirals, mandalas, parallel lines, combs (fig 18), ubiquitous, so desirable as imagistic raw material?

My own answer to this question is that the cognitive modes and their dependant behavioral protocols are absolutely ubiquitous, and that the recurring appearance of these motifs is

figure 19.

hardly even surprising (note 14). In fact, we have only to start cataloguing the motifs to realize that most of them are simply formed through the combination of simple procedures. The swastika, for example, is both cross and zigzag, just as the mandala is cross and closed form, and the so-called diamond-backed rattlesnake motif of the Californian Indians is a symmetrically repeated zigzag (fig 19).

Taken together, these two questions point to the dualistic nature of image-making. If, as I believe to be the case, it can be shown that the representation of the world and its objects by means of images follows the same cognition-bound procedures as the simpler images I have been discussing, then it will be clear that the form of an image is a function both of what is presented to the eye and of the possession of appropriate modes.

Representation.

I said at the outset that my conclusions would bear upon the nature of visual representation, as distinct from what the AI/Cognitive Science community means by the word "representation". It is still the case that my specific concerns are with what people do when they make marks on flat surfaces to represent what they see, or think they see, in the world. All the same, some speculation is justified about possible correspondences between the two uses of the word.

It is important, for example, to note that the lines which the artist draws to represent the outline of an object do not actually correspond to its edges, in the sense that an edge-finding algorithm will replace an abrupt tonal discontinuity with a line. In fact, the edges of an object in the real world are almost never delineated by an unbroken string of abrupt tonal discontinuities. If the artist is unperturbed by the disappearance of the edge, it is likely to be because he isn't using that edge, rather than because he has some efficient algorithm for filling in the gaps. Similarly, most of the objects in the world are occluded by other objects, yet it would not normally occur to the artist that the shape of a face is the part left visible by an occluding hand (fig 20).

figure 20.

The face evidently exists for him as a cognitive unit, and will be recorded by means of whatever strategies are appropriate and available for the representation (note 15).

It is as true to your meaning of "representation" as to mine, not only that it rests upon the possession of appropriate and available strategies, but also that new strategies may be developed to fit particular concerns. Both are bound by entity-specific considerations, however: considerations, that is to say, which are independant of the particular event or object being represented and take their form from the underlying structures of the entity -- the artist's cognitive modes on the one hand and the structural integrity of a computer program on the other.

What is a Representation "Like"?

It could not be seriously maintained that a computer program is "like" a human being in a general sense, and it should not be necessary to point out that a representation in my meaning of the word is not "like" the thing represented, other than in precisely defined senses of likeness. That may not be quite obvious, however, when we consider the idea that a portrait is "like" the sitter. Even though we may be careful enough to say that the portrait LOOKS like the sitter, or that a musical passage SOUNDS like the rustling of leaves, we tend to stop short of that level of detail at which it becomes clear that the appearance of a painted portrait and the appearance of a person actually have very little in common. A representation may be _about_ appearance, but we never confuse the representation with the reality, no matter how "lifelike" it is. In fact, we might rather believe that all representations of a given class are more like each other than any of them is like the thing represented. Life follows its laws, representations follow theirs.

What is an Image?

The _purpose_ of an act of representation is to draw attention to some particular aspect of the represented object, to differentiate that aspect from its context, not to reconstitute the object itself. To that degree we might regard a visual representation as constituting a partial theory of that object and its existence, just as we might regard a computer program as constituting a theory of the process it models. But neither the artist nor the program designer has any choice but to proceed in terms of the modes which are available or which they are capable of developing. In the case of the visual representation, the making of an image, I have tried to demonstrate the cognitive bases of those modes, and also, through my own program AARON, to demonstrate their raw power in the image-mediated transaction.

That, finally, defines my use of the word "image". An image is a reference to some aspect of the world which contains _within its own structure_ and _in terms of its own structure_ a _reference_ to the act of cognition which generated it. It must say, not that the world is like this, but that it was _recognised_ to have been like this by the image-maker, who leaves behind this record: not of the world, but of the act.

APPENDIX I __ THE TURTLE SYSTEM.

When the real turtle is not running, the program simulates its path, and calculates where it would have been in an error-free world after completing each command. In this case it substitutes a chord for the arc which the real turtle would have traced out. (The straight line segments which may just be visible in the illustrations here are due to the fact that they were photographed off the Tektronix 4014 display, not from an actual turtle drawing.)

The Navigation System.

The navigation system is correct to about .2 inches: that is an absolute determined by the sonar operating frequency -- about 40KHz -- and does not change with the size of the drawing. Even with so coarse a resolution the feedback operation is efficient enough for the turtle to do everything on the floor that the program can do on the screen; indeed, if the turtle is picked up while it is drawing and put down in the wrong place it is able to find its way back to the right place and facing the correct direction.

The Dynamics of Freehand Drawing.

There are several complexities in this part of the program which are worth mentioning. One of them is that the program has to be able to accomplish dramatic shifts in scale in the drawing, to make small things which look like small examples of big things: smoothly-curved closed forms should not turn into polygons as they get smaller. This is required both on the issue of shifts in information density and also to maintain implied semantic relationships between forms.

A second complexity is that the movement of the line should convincingly reflect the dynamics of a freehand drawn line, and this should mean, roughly, that the "speed" of a line should be inversely related to the rate of change of curvature: the pen should be able to move further on a single command if it's path is not curving too radically. (The converse of this is that the amount of information needed to specify an arbitrary line should be a function of its rate of change of direction, with the straight line, specified by its two end points, as the limiting case.)

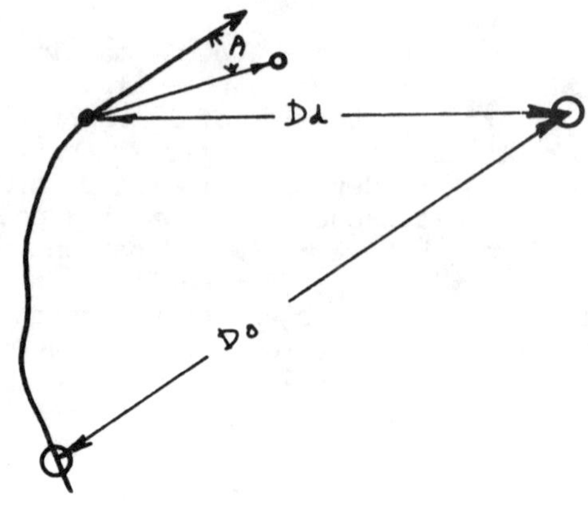

Movement Scaling.

Third, the pen should proceed more "carefully" when it is close to some final, critical position than when it has relatively far to go and plenty of time left to correct for carelessness. This, too, implies a scaling of movement in relation to the state of the local task. Finally, there is the practical problem that for any given number of cycles of a stepping pattern, the actual distance traversed by the pen will vary with the ratio of the turtle's two wheel speeds. Unfortunately, this relationship is not linear, and neither does it provide a useful simulation of freehand dynamics.

Briefly, the line-generating procedure concludes that, given the present position and direction of travel of the pen in relation to the current signpost and to the final destination, it will be appropriate to drive the two wheels at stepping rates r1 and r2, taking n steps on the faster of the two. In doing so it takes account of all of the above considerations. The ratio determined for the two speeds is a function of two variables: the angle A between the current direction and the direction to the current signpost, and a scaling factor given by the remaining distance Dd to the final destination as a proportion of the original distance Do (fig 11). This speed ratio then becomes one of the two variables in a function which yields the number of steps to be taken -- the distance to be travelled -- by the fast wheel: the other variable being the relative size of the block of space allocated to the current figure.

These functions have to be tuned with some care to be sure that each variable is correctly weighted, and to compensate for the turn-distance ratio of the turtle geometry itself. But none of this -- or any other part of the program -- involves any significant mathematical precision. There are only fifteen stepping rates available, symmetrically disposed between fast forward and fast reverse. The whole program, including extensive trigonometric operations, uses integer arithmetic -- this for historical reasons as well as limitations of available hardware -- and the geometry of the current turtle determines that it can only change direction in increments of about one sixth of a degree. (The turtle was not until recently interrupt-driven, and for design reasons this incremental direction-change factor was one degree in the earlier version.) Everything relies upon the feedback mode of operation to provide correction and to prevent error accumulation. The point is that a good car driver can drive a car with sloppy steering as well as a car with tight steering up to the point where feedback correction cannot be applied fast enough.

APPENDIX II -- MATRIX REPRESENTATION.

This description is given here primarily because it offers some insight into the kinds of considerations which the program believes to be important, and the way in which these considerations are accessed: not because there is anything particularly original from a data-structure point of view.

Much of the detail of the implementation is demanded by the word-length of the machine, and would go away in a larger machine. The intent is to make all the information relating to a particular part of the drawing effectively reside in a particular cell.

The program uses the single words representing matrix cells in different ways according to what is happening in the cells:-

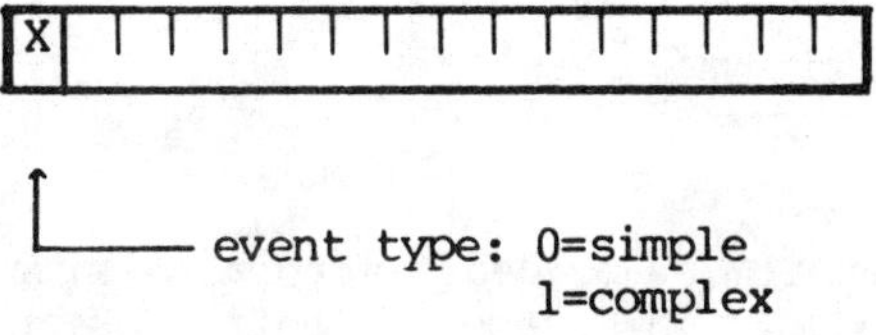

A "simple" event means, essentially, that all the data will be contained within this one word, although it will be seen that its simplicity relates to its use in a more meaningful sense:-

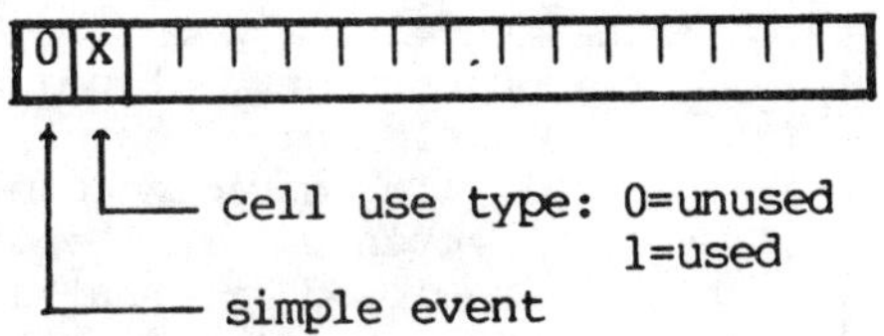

Before beginning work on the drawing, the program "roughens" the surface: that is, it declares some parts to be unuseable for the allocation of space to a new figure, although a developing figure may go into this "rough" space. This is done in order to maximise the rate of change of density across the image:-

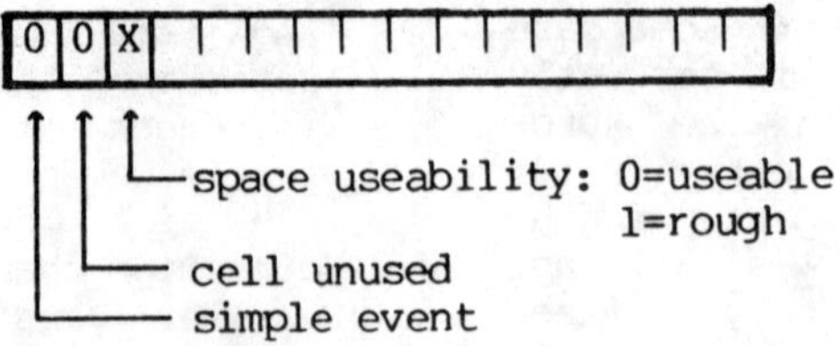

"Use" may involve either a line or some special spatial designation:=

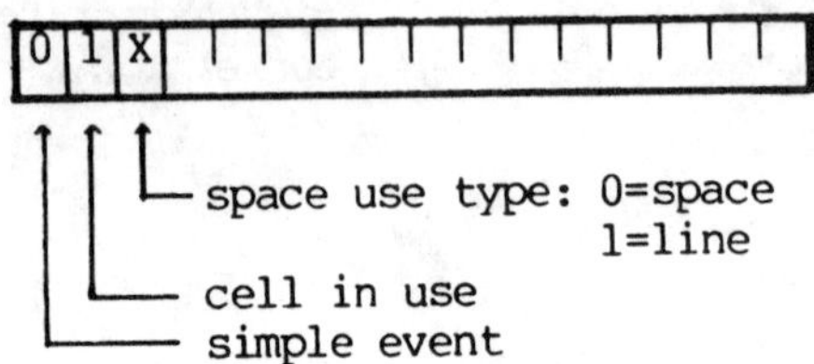

In either case, the cell will now have a figure identifier associated with it. The new version of the program uses less figures than the earlier one, and develops them further: a maximum of 32 figures is permitted:-

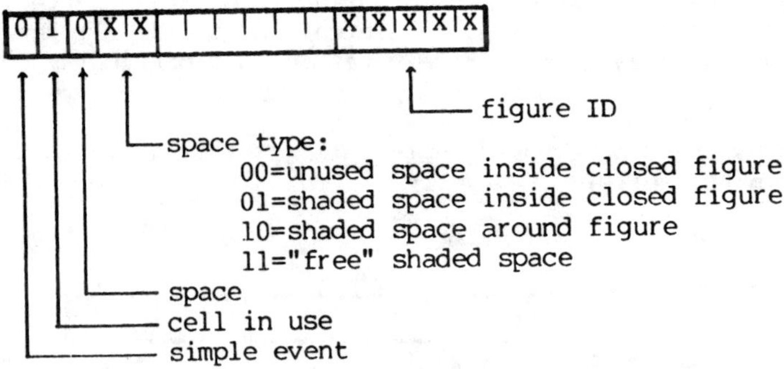

If the cell contains a line, then it can be dealt with as a simple event provided that it is not a line junction of a special kind. In this case the entry designates a line function type:-

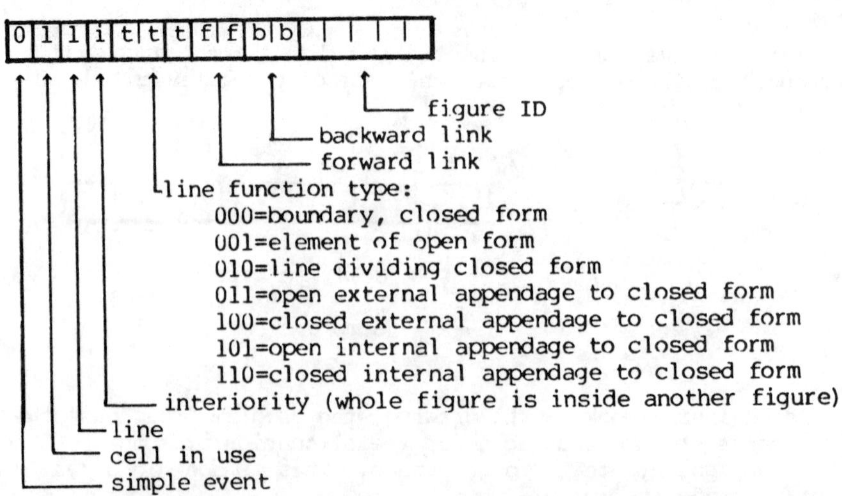

Cell Linking.

The forward and backward links are a very important device here. Lines are mapped onto the matrix as they are drawn, using an adapted form of Bresham's Algorithm to ensure that strings of cells never include corner-to-corner contiguity. This also means that for any given cell, the line it contains must have entered it from, and will subsequently leave it into, only one of four cells: thus the four-bit linking permits a complete traversal of any series of line segments not involving a complex event.

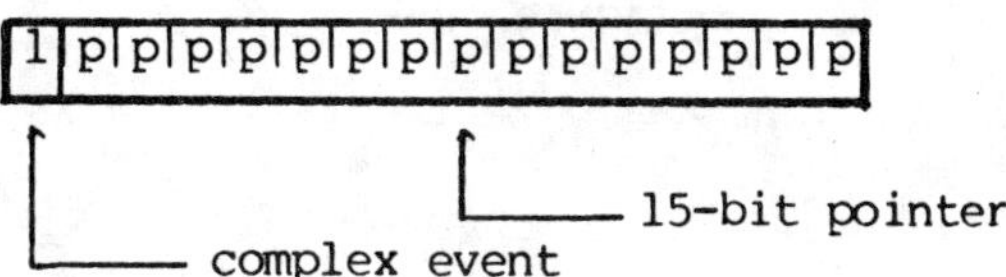

At this point, the single word is inadequate, and it is used as a pointer, words now being allocated in pairs from a freelist. Here again, one level down from the matrix, the words will be variously decoded. In particular, in the event that the cell is occupied by two figures, the two words are each used as pointers to new pairs of words, one for each figure:-

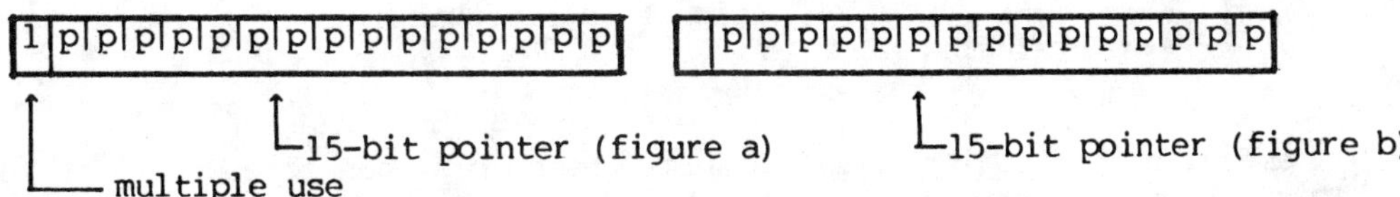

A cell at this level may contain complex events from one or both of two classes: connective and configurational. Configurational events frequently involve order-2 nodes -- nodes, that is, which fall on a continuous line -- and include sharp angles, strong curvature, and so on. In practise, the program forces complex events so that they always occur within an 8-cell displacement in x and y from another cell, and the location of the next event can then be recorded rather cheaply:-

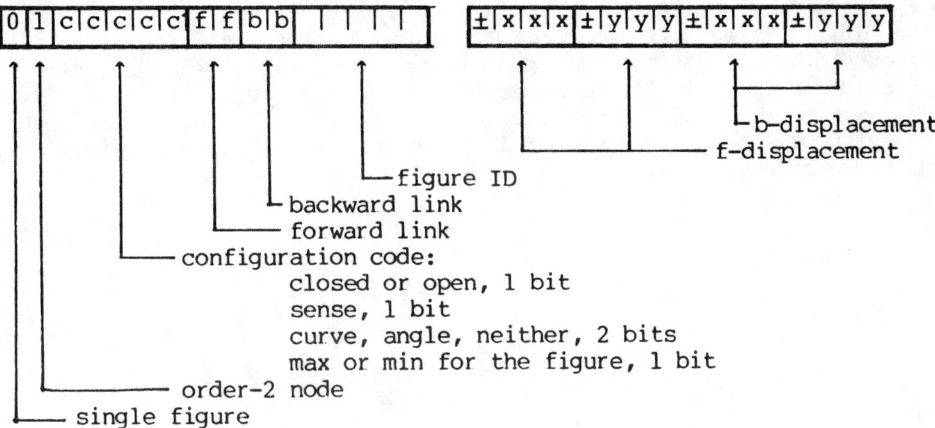

"Sense", here, means convex or concave if the line is the boundary of a closed figure, and up/right or down/left if it is not. If this is a figure node of any order other than two, one entry will be needed for each adjacent node:-

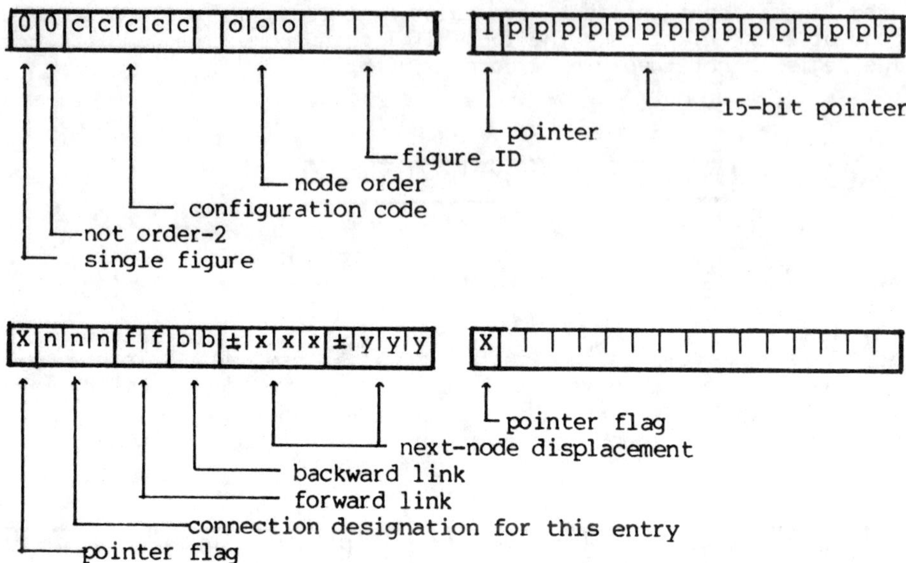

in addition to the displacements which chain this node to each of its connected nodes. This means that the traversal of the figure as it is represented by the matrix can continue from this point until the next node is reached.

Thus, the entire structure is contained essentially within the matrix, and the short lists which may be tacked onto any single cell serve merely to extend the effective capacity of that cell.

Ideally, this matrix should be as fine as possible: since the resolution of high-grade video is only 1024x1024, a matrix of this size would obviously constitute an extremely good representation. However, there are two considerations which make so fine a grain unnecessary. The first is that the program keeps a full list of all the actual coordinate pairs for each figure as it is drawing it, and can access it should some very precise intersection be required. The second is that the program is designed to simulate freehand drawing, not to do mechanical drawings, and once a figure is completed some approximation to it for purposes of avoidance or even intersection is unobjectionable. The maximum error induced by assuming a point to be at the center of a cell in a matrix of 90x160 will be about 7/8th of an inch in a sixteen-foot drawing: only three times the thickness of the line.

NOTES ON THE TEXT

note 1. The word "representation" is used here in a more general sense than it now carries within the A.I. community: the problem of formulating an internal (machine) representation of some set of knowledge differs from the more general problem primarily in its technological aspects.

note 2. "The Art of Artificial Intelligence: 1, Teams and Case Studies of Knowledge Engineering," Ed Feigenbaum, Proceedings of IJCAI5, 1977; pp.1014-1029.

note 3. In the decade before I became involved in my present concerns my work was exhibited at all of the most serious international shows, and I represented my country at many of them, including the Venice Biennale: as well as in some fifty one-man shows in London, New York and other major cities.

note 4. Different from each other, loosely speaking, in the way one might expect a human artist's drawings to differ one from another over a short period of time.

note 5. Written in "C", under the UNIX operating sustem.

note 6. I am referring here to differentiations performed in relation to the image, not in relation to the real world, with which the program has had no visual contact.

note 7. The program does not attach semantic descriptors to the things it draws: the terms "penumbra", "boulder" and so on are my own descriptions, and are used here for the sake of simplicity.

note 8. Significantly, from the point of view of my argument here, the dirty marks were intended to "suggest" the elements of a composition.

note 9. The one unconstrained randomising agent in this scenario, the final cutting of the film by the producer rather than the director, has also demonstrated itself to be devastatingly non-creative.

note 10. "Undenied" is stressed here because there exists an odd case in which the will of the artist is to produce objects which demand the contemplation of their own qualities for their own sake -- what they are rather than what they stand for -- and which thus seek to deny the viewer his normal assumptions. To the degree that this aim can actually be achieved the resulting object could not properly be called an image, and I doubt whether aesthetic contemplation could properly be called reading. Thus much of XXth Century abstract art falls outside this discussion.

note 11. It is worth noting, though, that AARON did mechanical straight-line shading for about two years -- it ran faster that way -- and in that time only two people ever remarked on the inconsistency.

note 12. I will leave aside the interesting question of whether there are not more general underlying structures which are common to all physical experience. It is presumably no accident that terms like "repetition", "closure", and others I have used in relation to visual cognition are freely used in relation to music, for example.

note 13. The control of the rate of change of information density across the surface of the image, to which I referred earlier, is the most powerful example I know in this regard. The eye is capable of handling units as small as a speck of dust and as large as the sky, but the processes which drive the eye seem always to adjust some threshold to yield a preferred distribution spanning only a few octaves.

note 14. In fact, the more theatrical explanations which range from world-wide migrations to the influence of extra-terrestrial voyagers are not even necessary.

note 15. He is unlikely to treat the boundary between face and hand as part of the face, but as part of the hand, and may very well indicate the full boundary of the face as if he could actually see it.

FLATS, A MACHINE FOR NUMERICAL, SYMBOLIC AND ASSOCIATIVE COMPUTING

Eiichi Goto[*,**], Tetsuo Ida[*], Kei Hiraki[**], Masayuki Suzuki[**] and Nobuyuki Inada[*]

* Institute of Physical and Chemical Research, 2-1, Hirosawa, Wako-shi, Saitama 351 Japan

** Department of Information Science, Faculty of Science, University of Tokyo, 7-3-1, Hongo, Bunkyo-ku, Tokyo 113 Japan

Abstract

Functional aspects of a machine called FLATS, presently (June 1979) in the design stage, are described. FLATS aims to efficiently run both numerical and algebraic programs. Overflow free and variable precision arithmetic, table look-up computation, and associative computation based on single-hit content addressed tables are introduced for advanced numerical, algebraic and symbolic computing. Hashing hardware, tag mechanism and hardware list processing are used to realize these features.

1. Introduction

Numerical computation and symbolic formula manipulation are the major practices in scientific computation. While numerical computation has a long history, computer-aided algebra or large scale formula manipulation has become practical only recently.

In this paper, we describe the architecture of FLATS, a machine which aims to efficiently run scientific computations. We consider Fortran (F) and Lisp (L) as major scientific programming languages for reasons:

(i) Scientific numerical programs are written mostly in Fortran.

(ii) Lisp is the major host language used for symbolic and algebraic systems such as REDUCE[1] and MACSYMA[2]. Moreover, Lisp has been used for writing a very large number of programs in the AI area.

Hence, high efficiency in running programs written in 'F' and 'L' is considered a minimum requirement, which is symbolized in the first two letters of 'FLATS'. 'A' in FLATS stands for associative capabilities; 'T' and 'S' stand for Table, Set and String which are the data types used in FLATS.

Many efforts have been made to increase the speed of computations by introducing parallelism[3,4,5], in which we include the pipe line architecture as a specific implementation (of parallelism). Vectorized operations on floating and fixed point numbers of fixed bit length are recognized as a class computations suited for highly parallel machines. It should be noted, however, that highly parallel algorithms are not known for or not applicable to certain computations. For example, take the Euclidian gcd algorithm. The gcd of two integers r_0 and r_1, say, is obtained by successively computing the remainder sequence $r_0, r_1, r_2, r_3 \ldots$($r_i$ is the remainder of r_{i-2} divided by r_{i-1}) until it reaches the first zero remainder $r_n = 0$ with r_{n-1} giving the gcd.

Parallel schemes faster than the Euchidian algorithm are not known. Hence, for gcd, a machine equipped with a single sophisticated high speed remainder unit would do better than parallel machines with hundreds of slower units. List processing, arbitrary precision integer arithmeter, and variable precision floating point arithmetic are other examples of operations which are not suited for contemporary highly parallel machines. The objective of FLATS is to efficiently run those operations which are not suited for highly parallel machines.

FLATS is basically a single instruction stream machine and parallelism shall be pursued only to a limited extent such as advance control, parallel hashing and parallel interpolation but it shall not incorporate parallel processor arrays.

FLATS may hence be regarded complementary to the highly parallel machine approach.

The numerical support to algebraic manipulation systems is indispensable since the process of algebraic manipulation requires exact calculation of intermediate (and final) numerical coefficients as opposed to approximations done by conventional fixed precision floating arithmetic.

Furthermore, the results of the algebraic computation must often be given to numerical computaion systems.

Functional requirement for FLATS is therefore to incorporate the different characteristics of the two languages (F and L), e.g. compile-time vs. run-time data type checks, and static vs. dynamic storage allocation, into a single architecture, without impairing the efficiency of either one.

Besides the advanced numerical features, associative capabilities have been found to be very powerful[6] in efficiently carrying out basic operations in formula manipulation.

We first give in section 2 functional specifications of FLATS from users' point of view, and in section 3 consider the implementation from architectural point of view.

2. FLATS from users' point of view

2.1 Overflow free and variable precision computing

We observe that most contemporary computer systems neither provide adequate means for handling (1) overflows, (2) precision higher than built-in standard precisions, e.g. double or quadruple, nor (3) variable precision arithmetic. The design and implementations of some important class of algorithms[7,8,9] are hampered by the lack of the systematic support of these three features.

To remedy such defects, FLATS is provided with following means:

- Integers are treated with automatic multiple-precision.
- Exponents and mantissas of floating numbers are expressed in integers as stated above, hence practically no overflow would occur.
- A variable precision scheme[10] is adopted, in which precision is specified by a status word called an ASW (Arithmetic Status Word), which is part of the PSW (Program Status Word).

These features are made available to users in an extended FORTRAN called BFORT (Bignum Fortran).

2.2 Tabulative computing

Before high speed computers came into extensive use, look-up of mathematical tables was an essential process of numerical calculation. This fact is in quite contrast to 'on-demand' computing prevalent today. To pursue further the speed-up of the present numerical computation, table look-up is becoming again a practical method, owing to the recent advances in memory fabrication technology. In FLATS, we provide following means for tabulative computing[11];

(i) Tabulative computation of numerical functions with a floating number argument such as x^{-1}, $\sqrt{x}$, e^x, sin x, log x and atan x.

(ii) Associative tabulation for (sparse) integer and/or symbolic arguments.

Linear (or quadratic) interpolation shall be used for 24 bit (single length) mantissa and cubic interpolation for 48 bit (double length) mantissa. Namely f(x) is to be computed by $f(x) = f(x_0) + f'(x_0)\Delta x + (1/2)f''(x_0)\Delta x^2 + (1/6)f'''(x_0)\Delta x^3$ where $x = x_0 + \Delta x$ and x_0 is the most significant 12 bit part of the 48 bit mantissa x and each term is assumed to be less than the previous term by a factor of 2^{-12}. The coefficients f, f', f'' and f''' are tabulated (in ROM or RAM). This cubic interpolation can be made within time of two stages of multiplications by introducing parallelism:

Stage 1. Read the coefficient table and the table of cubes of the 12 bit (in precision) Δx^3 and compute the 24 bit Δx^2 in parallel. (Table look up is assumed to be no slower than multiplication.)

Stage 2. Multiply and add in parallel.

For computing the 48 bit inverse $y = x^{-1}$, this scheme is faster than Newton iteration, which would consist of five stages of successive operations:

Stage 1. Read the 12 bit approximate inverse $y_0 = x^{-1}$ from table.

Stage 2,3. Two multiplications to get the 24 bit inverse $y_1 = (2-xy_0)y_0$.

Stage 4,5. Two multiplications to get the full 48 bit inverse $y = (2-xy_1)y_1$.

When a function, say g with (sparse) integer or symbolic arguments, is computed in tabulation mode, the value $v = g(i_1, \ldots, i_n)$ is tabulated in a content addressed table (CAT), using the tuple $(g, i_1, \ldots, i_n)$ as a search key in the CAT. In the subsequent computations of g with the same values of the arguments, the value v is fetched immediately from the CAT. Associative tabulation effectively and automatically speeds up recursions by avoiding repetitive computation. For example, the notoriously slow (exponential time) recursive computation of the Fibonacci numbers:

```
procedure Fib[n] = [n<1 -> 1;
                    T -> Fib[n-1] + Fib[n-2] ]
```

is turned into a fast algorithm (linear time for the first evaluation and O(1) time for the subsequent evaluations).

2.3 Associative capabilities and built-in data types

Starting from the pioneering associative language

LEAP[12], a variety of associative language and architectures for the associative processing have been proposed and implemented.

We consider an AMT (Address mapping table) and an *h*-op hash table (Fig. 1) as the two basic entities for building associative data structures[13]. We define an AMT as a mapping from bit patterns of fixed sizes (actually 32 bits/64 bits) into addresses (consecutive integers). An AMT may be regarded as a single-hit associative memory. A multi-hit associative scheme such as found in LEAP is to be dealt with by software, making use of arrays, linked-lists and AMT's. Table 1 gives the built-in data types in FLATS. The data types STR, INT, FLOAT, VECT (one dimensional array) are the same as in most other languages except that INT and FLOAT are of arbitrarily high precision as stated in 2.1. PAIR is the same as in Standard Lisp[14].

The data types prefixed by H denote those types obtained by hashing (*h*-op). *h*-type objects are guaranteed to be unique by virtue of hashing. The Lisp concept of 'intern' corresponds to that of *h*-op with the following differences; that *h*-op does not allow remob[15] and that *h*-op can apply to all data types in FLATS, whereas intern op in Lisp 1.5 is applicable only to atomic symbols. *h*-type objects must be read-only so as for the hashing search mechanism to work properly. Hence, HSTR objects are the same as atoms of Lisp; i.e. every different string of characters is represented as a unique pointer to a table called oblist in Lisp 1.5, or to name tables in assemblers and compilers. HINT and HPAIR objects are multi-precision integers and hashed lists, respectively. Equality check of two long integers of type HINT or two lists of type HPAIR is reduced to that of two pointers. HPAIR and HINT can be made by the shared linked list method as shown in Fig. 1.

Insertion, deletion and membership test of an AMT entry correspond to the same operations on a set. A 'set' created by *h*-op (represented by an AMT) is given[6,16] and shown in Fig. 1. In FLATS the hashed AMT (HAMT) is a synonym to 'set'.

A CAT consists of an AMT and RAM (random access memory, i.e. hardware term for VECT sharing the same addresses). A CAT can be hashed similarly to an AMT and the resultant data type is called HCAT.

These data types, especially the hashed types, have been found to be very useful in polynomial manipulation. For example, take a polynomial $P = 3AX^2 + 4BY^3$, where AX^2 and BY^3 are term identifiers; and 3 and 4 are coefficients. There are many (non-unique) ways to represent a term identifier in list forms owing to the commutative nature of multiplication. AX^2, for example, is represented in a list form ((A 1) (X 2)) and ((X 2) (A 1)) corresponding to AX^2 and X^2A respectively. The HCAT representation {A:1, X:2} is unique (AX^2 and X^2A are represented by a pointer to a unique HCAT structure). In this case, P is represented uniquely by nested HCAT's as
P = {{A:1,X:2}:3, {B:1,Y:3}:4}.

A FLATS FORTRAN program for multiplying polynomials in the HCAT normal form can be written in 9 lines:

```
      FUNCTION CATMULT (P,Q)
      C = MKCAT(0)
      SWEEP 1, P, TP=KEY, FP=VAL
      SWEEP 1, Q, TQ=KEY, FQ=VAL
      T = H(CATADD(TP, TQ))
    1 C(T) = C(T) + FP*FQ
      CATMULT = H(C)
      RETURN
      END
```

Here SWEEP is similar to DO in FORTRAN; SWEEP scans all the occurrences of keys in the specified CAT's P and Q. Function H corresponds to *h*-op above mentioned. This program would give the best known time complexity for multiplying multi-variate polynomials[6].

3. FLATS from architects' point of view

3.1 Tagged architecture

A practical solution for efficient detection of the built-in data types given in 2.3 is a tagged architecture[10,17] Table 2 gives tags to be used in FLATS.

Take numerical computation for example. Arithmetic operations on small numbers tagged as "sint" (short integer) or "sfloat" (short floating number) are to be made with standard hardware at high speed, while those on tagged "big" numbers are to be trapped and handled by microprogramming. Since "sint" or "sfloat" numbers are likely to appear with high probability in most programs, the slow down factor due to the "big" numbers is very small.

Bit-loss, a common objection against tagbit(s), can be remedied by using a specific exponent value as a 'trapping tag'. In the case of 7-bit exponent $-64 \le p \le 63$ FLOAT representation, $p = -64, \pm 63, \pm 62$ are used as the tags to denote data types other than "sfloat" with the mantissa part having different meanings given in table 2. The effective bit loss is only $\log_2(123/128) = -0.06$ bits in this scheme.

3.2 Hashing Hardware

AMT's can be implemented either by using CAM

(content addressable memory) chips or by hashing. In a previous paper[18], we presented a hardware hashing scheme which makes use of parallel read-out mechanism of memory. A parallel hashing hardward consists of multiple RAM banks, hash address sequence generators and a hashing control unit. A single comparator is attached to every RAM bank (cf. Fig. 2) in the parallel hashing hardware, whereas in CAM chip such as Intel 3104 a comparator is attached to every memory cell. Even at a chip level, a CAM requires several times more gates than a RAM chip. Hence total number of gates required for realization of CAM is greater by at least one order of magnitude than that for the hash table, with no significant speed gain over parallel hashing: The items in the hash table are searched in average O(1) memory cycle (a quantity independent of the number of items entered in the hash table), in comparison with strict O(1) used to search items entered in CAM. Since we are interested in the overall efficiency in our intended applications, it is more advantageous to invest the resource on enlargement of RAM memory than on still expensive CAM chips. Moreover, h-op of complex types such as AMT, CAT and VECT cannot be performed with CAM's.

Figure 2 shows the schematic diagram of the parallel bank hashing hardware of FLATS. Hashing is essentially the cycle (hash probe cycle) of (i) hash address generations, (ii) memory accesses, (iii) key comparisons and (iv) judgement of termination based on the comparisons. The hash tables, (i.e. AMT's and CAT's and an h-op table), are taken in main memory consisting of J banks. In a simple parallel hashing scheme with J banks, a single hash address generator and J comparators are used together with some auxiliary hash sequence control circuits. To handle key deletion, detectors of reserved words for denoting empty and deleted states are provided in each bank.

Assuming that the operations (i) - (iv) are performed in a single memory cycle, the performance of parallel hashing is given in number of memory cycles used until the completion of the probe cycles. Figure 3 shows that the average number of memory cycles in a successful search (finding a key in the table) in the worst case[19] We presume the worst average performance in the performance evaluation when key deletion and insertion are repeated alternately. It shows that the basic hash operations can be performed in a time comparable to an indirect addressing operations, e.g. for J = 16 and the load factor of a hash table α = 0.9. Note that the hashing hardware handles a fixed length key at a time. For handling variable length strings, arbitrarily long integers and lists, a shared linked list above mentioned is used with the parallel hashing hardware.

3.3 Hardware support for list processing

The hardware mechanisms essential to the speed-up of Lisp are following;

(1) run time data type checking,
(2) hardware stack,
(3) high memory bandwidth
(4) segmented memory space with automatic boundary checking for arrays etc., and
(5) instructions for Lisp primitives, such as car, cdr, cons and atom.

Note that the tagged architecture given in 3.1 is a solution to point (1).

As for point (2), we incorporate in FLATS both general (global) register and stack frame machine architecture. The basic op codes consist of four 8 bit fields as (op, r_1, r_2, r_3), where r_1, r_2, r_3 are register addresses each specifying either one of 128 global registers or one of 128 registers on the current stack frame. While the global registers are used to hold global entities, the stack registers are used for local entries and for (recursive) subroutine linkage.

In contrast to the two register address operations, r_1: = op(r_1, r_2) notably used in IBM 360/370, three register address operations r_3: = op(r_1, r_2) are used in FLATS. The three register scheme would greatly reduce the number of register to register transfer operations. For example, while no register to register transfers are needed in the three register scheme for the following codes

```
a:=add(x,y);
b:=sub(x,y);
c:=mul(x,y);
d:=div(x,y); ,
```

50% of the corresponding codes would be register to register transfers in the two register scheme as in

```
a:=x; a;=add(a,y);
b:=x; b:=sub(b,y);
c:=x; c:=mul(c,y);
d:=x; d:=div(d,y);.
```

The unit of memory banking used in hashing is actually taken to be the bit width of a single list cell (64 bits). Expansion of memory to increase the degree of parallelism (i.e. to increase J) will speed up hashing operations as shown in Fig. 3; this does not imply the requirement of higher memory bandwidth since the comparators are provided in the memory units.

Need for segmentation is clear since the main memory is conceptually divided into several segments; AMT's, CAT's, arrays, list areas, program space and so on.

Fundamental Lisp primitives given above are executed in a single memory cycle. In fact, when run-time data type check is made by hardware, car and cdr instructions are equivalent to simple load operations. Complex Lisp primitives such as member and reverse are microprogrammed.

Furthermore, by virtue of the hashing hardware, operations on property lists and the oblist which rely on linear search in most Lisp systems are performed more efficiently in FLATS.

3.4 Hardware garbage collector

Dynamic storage allocation of variable length segments of memory in FLATS requires a compactifying garbage collection scheme. The most time-consuming process in compactifying garbage collection schemes[20,21] is pointer adjustment. FLATS is to incorporate the pointer adjustment hardware given in Fig. 5.

The pointer q in Q register is to be adjusted to be $q' = q - \Delta q$, where Δq is the total number of inactive cells in the memory block between base q_0 and q. A bit table of 2^n width is set up in the memory local to the hardware. The bit table is marked by a garbage collector: '1' in the m -th bit position in column ω corresponds to the inactive cell at $q_0 + \omega 2^n + m$ in the main memory. Therefore Δq is obtained by counting 1's between the base q_0 and q. The column $(q - q_0)/2^n$ of the offset table contains the cumulative bit count Σ. The adjustment can be done in a main memory cycle when fast memory for the offset table and the bit table is used.

4. Concluding Remarks

At a users' level, FLATS is a machine both for numerical processing and for formula manipulation. Instead of devising yet another language, we provide the facilities in the framework of existing languages, Fortran and Lisp (REDUCE is to be used for the user interface language). New compilers for Fortran and Lisp are under development, which incorporate the facilities for associative processing and overflow free and variable precision arithmetic, at the same time to accept programs written in Lisp and Fortran, which have been accumulated in libraries of scientific application packages. The underlying techniques include hardware hashing, tag mechanism, and hardware list processing (including hardware garbage collection). Concurrent garbage collection is not considered, since FLATS is not intended to be used for real time applications. FLAT is to be used as a back-end processor to a conventional computer system; hence the average performance, i.e. throughput, is a more important factor than responsiveness. For the same reason, hashing is best suited for the associative processing discussed.

The associative capabilities of FLATS would also be suited for some operations for data base management.

Implementation of unified memory management of secondary and main memories using virtual tapes[22] is under consideration.

Substantial amount of software for FLATS has already been written and has been running under a FLATS simulator. Architectural design of FLATS is an outcome of the experiences with the development of the software system HLISP.[6,16] REDUCE is now running under HLISP system and are used for various applications. A version of BFORT mentioned before which translates the extended Fortran into HLISP has already been running.

References

[1] Hearn, A.C. REDUCE2 user's manual, Utah Computational Physics UCP-19 (March 1973)

[2] The MATHLAB Group, MACSYMA reference manual, Laboratory for computer science, MIT (1974)

[3] Watson, W.J. The TI ASC - A Highly Modular and Flexible Super Computer Architecture, AFIPS 1972 FJCC, AFIPS Press

[4] Russell, R.M. The CRAY-1 Computer System, CACM, Vol. 21, No. 1 (1978)

[5] Barnes, G.H., Brown, R.M., Kato, M., Kuck, D.J., Slotnick, D.L. and Stokes, R.A. The ILLIAC IV Computer, IEEE Trans. Computers, Vol. C-47, No. 8 (1968)

[6] Goto, E. and Kanada, Y. Hashing Lemmas on Time Complexity with Application to Formula Manipulation, Proc. ACM-SYMSAC, (1976)

[7] Takahasi, H. and Mori, M. "Double Exponential Formulas for Numerical Integration", Pub. Research Institute for Math. Science, Kyoto University, 9 (1974), 721-741

[8] Grau, A.A. "Algorithm 256, Modified Graeffe Method", Collected Algorithms from ACM, 256-P1-0

[9] Brent, R.P. "Fast Multiple-Precision Evaluation of Elementary Functions", JACM, Vol. 23, No. 2, (April 1976), 242-251

[10] Ida, T., and Goto, E. Overflow Free and Variable Precision Computing in FLATS, Journal of Information Processing Vol. 1, No. 3 (1978)

[11] Goto, E. and Terashima, M. MTAC - mathematical Tabulative Automatic Computing, Technical Report of Information Science, 77-03, Faculty of Science, University of Tokyo, (1977)

[12] Feldman, J.A. and Rovner, P.D. An Algol-Based Associative Languages, CACM, Vol. 12, No. 8 (1969)

[13] Goto, E., Sassa, M. and kanada, Y. Algor-

ithms and Programming with CAM's (Content Addressable Associative Memories) Technical Report of Information Science Department, 78-04, Faculty of Science, University of Tokyo, (1978) submitted for publication

[14] Marti, J.B., Hearn, A.C., Griss, M.L., and Griss, C. Standard Lisp Report, UUCS-78-101, University of Utah, 1978

[15] McCarthy, J., et. al., Lisp 1.5 Programmers Manual, MIT Press, Cambridge, Mass., 1962

[16] Sassa, M. and Goto, E. A Hashing Method for Fast Set Operations, Information Processing Letters, Vol. 5, No. 2, (1976)

[17] Feustel, E.A. On the advantage of tagged architecture, IEEE Trans. Computers, Vol. C-21, No. 9 (1972)

[18] Ida, T. and Goto, E., Performance of a Parallel Hash Hardware with Key Deletion, Proc. IFIP Congress 77, North-Holland (1977)

[19] Ida, T. and Goto, E. Analysis of Parallel Hashing Algorithms with Key Deletion, Journal of Information Processing, Vol. 1, No. 1 (1978)

[20] Wegbreit, B. A Generalized Compactifying Garbage Collector. The Computer Journal, Vol. 15, No. 3, (1972)

[21] Terashima, M. and Goto, E. Genetic Order and Compactifying Garbage Collectors, Information Processing Letters, Vol. 7, No. 1

[22] Sassa, M. and Goto, E. "V-tape", a Virtual Memory Oriented Data Type, and its Resource Requirements, Information Processing Letters, Vol. 6, No. 2, (1977)

[23] This paper is the updated version of the paper by the same authors with same title given at ACM IEEE Symposium on Computer Architecture, May 1979, Philadelphia, PA.

main types	examples	hashed types	examples
ATOM			
STRing	3STOM	HSTR	3HTOM, 'TOM', TOM (three optional representations)
INT	-0137	HINT	-137
	+137		137
FLOAT	3.1415	HFLOAT	3.1415
PAIR		HPAIR	
DLIST	(A.B)	HDLIST	(A;B)
LIST	((A 1) (B 2))	HLIST	((A,1), (B,2))
FUNC	Fib		
VECT	[3 5 6 7]	HVEC	[3,5,6,7]
AMT	{A B}	HAMT	{A,B}
CAT	{A:1 B:2}	HCAT	{A:1,B:2}

Table 1. Built-in data types in FLATS

value of exponent, p	hardware data type	meaning of a mantissa
63	address	a pointer to some data structure
62	character	upto three characters
61 ~ -61	"sfloat", exponent of short floating number	mantissa of short floating number
-62	"sint", short integer	value of short integer
-63	software use	used as a trap code which may denote software (and microprogram) identified data types, such as "big" integer and "big" floating numbers
-64	reserved bit patterns	reserved values denoting nil, empty, deleted etc.

Table 2. Hardware tags used in FLATS

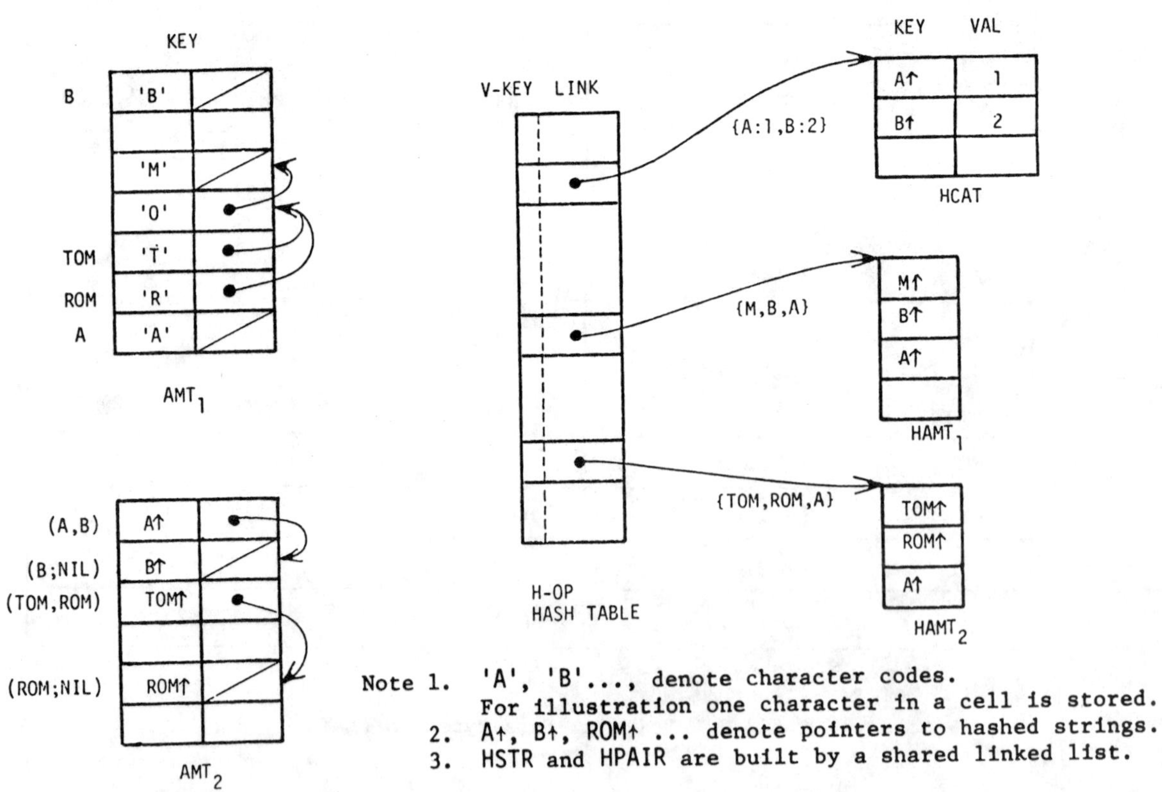

Note 1. 'A', 'B'..., denote character codes.
For illustration one character in a cell is stored.
2. A↑, B↑, ROM↑ ... denote pointers to hashed strings.
3. HSTR and HPAIR are built by a shared linked list.

Fig. 1 Realization of Built-in Data Types

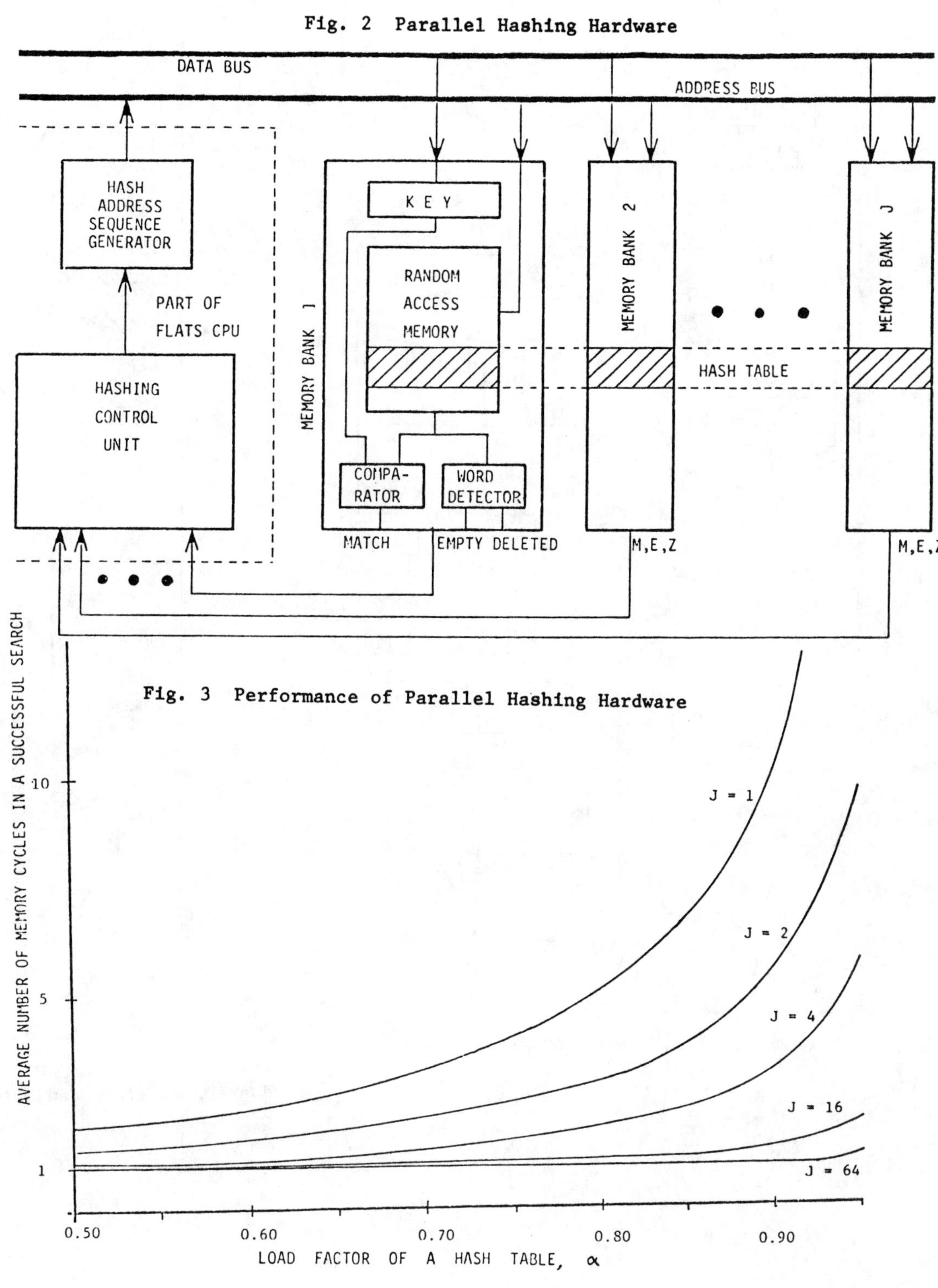

Fig. 2 Parallel Hashing Hardware

Fig. 3 Performance of Parallel Hashing Hardware

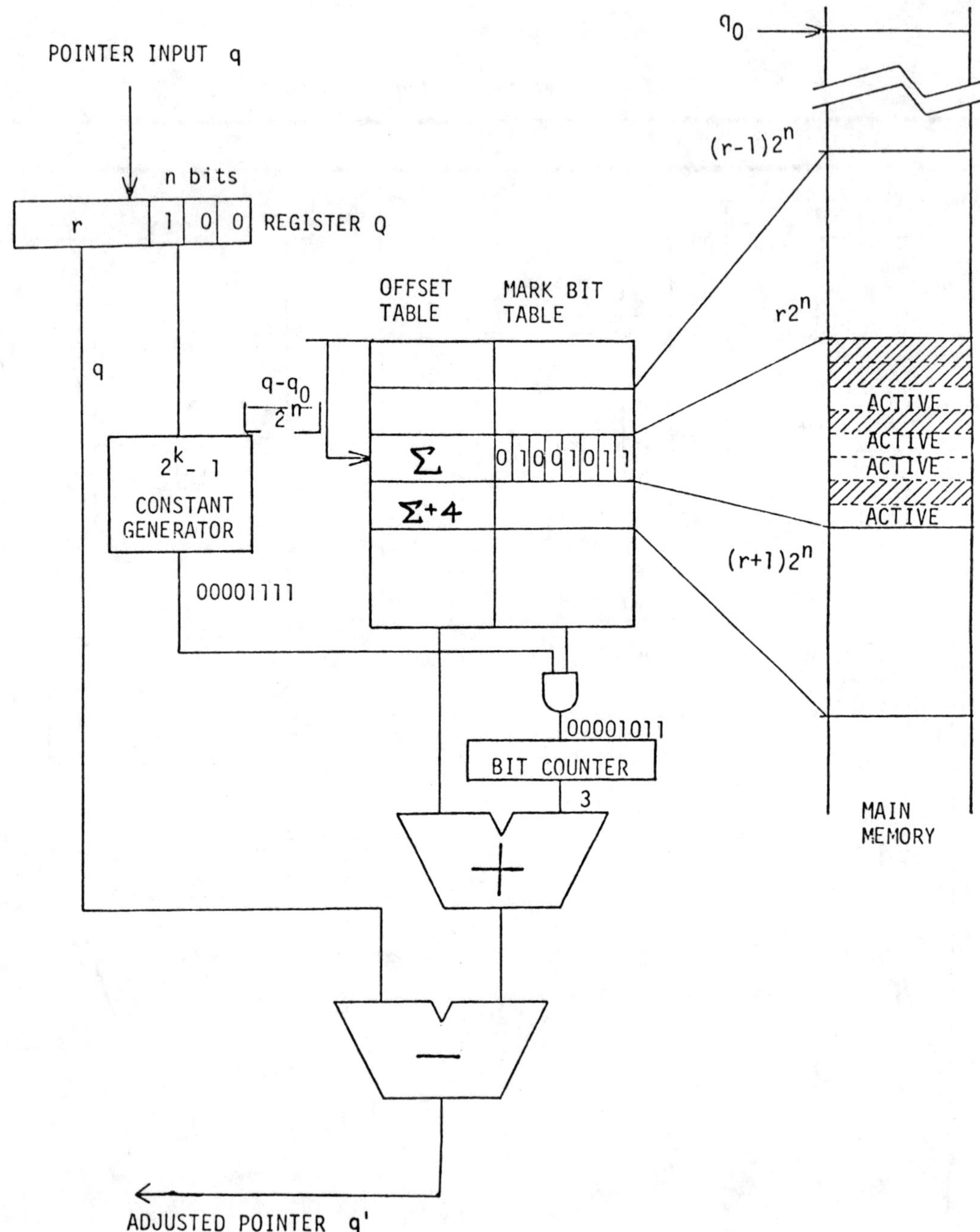

Fig. 4 Hardware for Pointer Adjustment

UTTERANCE AND OBJECTIVE: ISSUES IN NATURAL LANGUAGE COMMUNICATION

Barbara J. Grosz
Artificial Intelligence Center
SRI International
Menlo Park, California 94025 USA

Communication in natural language requires a combination of language-specific and general common-sense reasoning capabilities, the ability to represent and reason about the beliefs, goals, and plans of multiple agents, and the recognition that utterances are multifaceted. This paper evaluates the capabilities of natural language processing systems against these requirements and identifies crucial areas for future research in language processing, common-sense reasoning, and their coordination.

1 INTRODUCTION

Two premises, reflected in the title, underlie the perspective from which I will consider research in natural language processing in this paper.[1] First, progress on building computer systems that process natural languages in any meaningful sense (i.e., systems that interact reasonably with people in natural language) requires considering language as part of a larger communicative situation. In this larger situation, the participants in a conversation and their states of mind are as important to the interpretation of an utterance as the linguistic expressions from which it is formed. A central concern when language is considered as communication is its function in building and using shared models of the world.[2]

Second, as the phrase "utterance and objective" suggests, regarding language as communication requires consideration of what is said (literally), what is intended, and the relationship between the two. Recently, the emphasis in research in natural language processing has begun to shift from an analysis of utterances as isolated linguistic phenomena to a consideration of how people use utterances to achieve certain objectives. But, in considering objectives, it is important not to ignore the utterances themselves. A consideration of a speaker's[3] underlying goals and motivations is critical, but so is an analysis of the particular way in which that speaker expresses his thoughts. The choice of expression has implications for such things as what other entities may be discussed in the ensuing discourse, what the speaker's underlying beliefs (including his beliefs about the hearer) are, and what social relationship the speaker and hearer have. The reason for conjoining "utterance" and "objective" in the title of this paper is to emphasize the importance of considering both.[4]

In the remainder of this paper I want to examine three consequences of these claims for the sorts of language processing theories we develop and the kinds of language processing systems we build.

----

1 The emphasis in this paper will be on research concerned with the development of theoretical models of language use. Because of space limitations, I will not discuss a second major direction of current research in natural language processing, that concerned with the construction of natural language interfaces. The major difference between the two kinds of efforts is that research on interfaces has (to this point, though it need not) separated language processing from the rest of the system whereas one of the major concerns of research in the more theoretical direction is the interaction between language-specific and general knowledge and reasoning in the context of communication.

2 Indeed, the notion of a shared model is inherent in the word "communicate," which is derived from the Latin communicare, "to make common".

3 I will use "speaker" and "hearer" to refer respectively to the producer of an utterance and the interpreter of that utterance. Although the particular communicative environment constrains the set of linguistic and nonlinguistic devices a speaker may use (Rubin, 1977), I will ignore the differences and concentrate on those problems that are common across environments.

4 The similarity to Word and Object (Quine, 1960) is not entirely accidental. It is intended to highlight a major shift in the context in which questions about language and meaning should be considered. I believe the issues Quine raised can be addressed effectively nly in this larger context.

* Language processing requires a combination of language-specific mechanisms and general common-sense reasoning mechanisms. Specifying these mechanisms and their interactions constitutes a major research area.

* Because discourse involves multiple separate agents with differing conceptions of the world, language systems must be able to represent the beliefs and knowledge of multiple individual agents. The reasoning procedures that operate on these representations must be able to handle such separate beliefs. Furthermore, they must be able to operate on incomplete and sometimes inconsistent information.

* Utterances are multifaceted; they must be viewed as having effects along multiple dimensions. As a result, common-sense reasoning (especially planning) procedures must be able to handle situations that involve actions having multiple effects.

2 MONKEYS, BANANAS, AND COMMUNICATION

To illustrate some of the current problems in natural language processing, I want to look at a variant of the "monkey and bananas" problem (McCarthy, 1968), the original version of which is substantially as follows: There is a monkey in a room that also contains a bunch of bananas hanging from the ceiling, out of reach of the monkey. There is also a box in one corner of the room. The monkey's problem is to figure out what sequence of actions will get him the bananas. For a while at least, this problem was a favorite test case for automatic problem solvers, and there are several descriptions of how it can be solved by machine (e.g., see Nilsson, 1971). The variation I want to discuss introduces a second monkey, the need for some communication to take place, and a change of scene to a tropical forest containing banana trees. To begin, I want to leave unspecified the relationship between the two monkeys and consider a short segment of hypothetical dialogue:

(1) monkey1 (looking longingly at bananas high above him): I'm hungry.

(2) monkey2: There's a stick under the old rubber tree.

If monkey1 interprets monkey2's response as most Artificial Intelligence (AI) natural language processing systems would, he might respond with something like: "I can't eat a stick" or "I know, so what?" and, unless monkey2 helped him out, monkey1 would go hungry.[5] Although there are a few systems now that might, with suitable tweaking, be able to get far enough for a response that indicates they have figured out that monkey2 intends for the stick to be used to knock down the bananas, there are no programs yet that would be able to understand most of the nuances of this response. For example, it implies not only that monkey2 has a plan for using the stick, but also that he expects monkey1 either to have a similar plan or to be able to figure one out once he has been told about the stick.

If we complicate the scenario just slightly, then our programs would all be stuck. In particular, suppose that the tree the stick is under is not a rubber tree, but rather a different sort of tree. Monkey2 might still use the phrase "the rubber tree", either by mistake or design, if he believes the phrase will suffice to enable monkey1 to identify the tree (cf. Donnellan, 1977). No current AI natural language processing system would be able to figure out where the stick is. Their responses, at best, would be like monkey1 saying, "Whaddayamean? There aren't any rubber trees in this forest." But referring expressions that do not accurately describe the entities they are intended to identify are typical of the sort of thing that occurs all the time in conversations between humans. The question is what it will take to get computer systems closer to being able to handle these sorts of phenomena.

In the remainder of this paper I want to look at some of the research issues that need to be addressed to bring us closer to understanding why talking monkeys don't go hungry. I believe many critical language processing issues arise from our limited knowledge of how common-sense reasoning -- which includes deduction, plausible reasoning, planning, and plan recognition -- can be captured in a computational system. Consequently, research in natural language processing and common-sense reasoning must be tightly coordinated in the next few years. The root of the problem, I suspect, is the following discrepancy. Research in problem solving and deduction has focused almost exclusively on problems that a single agent could solve alone. The need for communication arises with those problems that require the resources of multiple agents, problems that a single agent has insufficient power to solve alone. As a result, language processing is typically an issue in

----

[5] There is an equal amount of sophisticated knowledge in monkey1's using the statement "I am hungry" to ask for help from monkey2 in solving his problem.

just those contexts where the aid of another agent is essential. To obtain that aid, the first agent must take into account the knowledge, capabilities, and goals of the second. In exchange for not needing quite as much knowledge or capability in the problem domain, the agent must have additional communication capabilities. For such problems, the option of proceeding without considering the independence of other agents and the need to communicate with them is not feasible.[6]

3 THE PROCESSES OF INTERPRETATION

To illustrate how language-specific processes combine with general cognitive processes (i.e., common-sense reasoning) in the interpretation of an utterance, I want to consider the monkeys and bananas example in more detail. It will be useful to view natural language interpretation as being divided into two major interacting levels. On the first, the <u>linguistic analysis level</u>, the form of an utterance is analyzed to determine its context-independent attributes. On the second, the <u>assimilation level</u>, common-sense reasoning processes operating in the context of the current cognitive state of the hearer --which includes such things as a focus of attention, a set of goals to be achieved or maintained and plans for achieving them, knowledge about the domain of discourse, knowledge about how language is used, and beliefs about the cognitive states of other agents, including other participants in the current conversation -- use these attributes to update the cognitive state and to determine what response to the utterance is required, if any.[7]

----

[6] I believe this option is becoming less feasible as well for problem solving and deduction components used for other purposes within AI. Situations in which multiple robots must cooperate introduce similar complexity even if the communication itself can be carried out in a formal language. Sacerdoti (1978) discusses the usefulness of research in natural language processing for the construction of distributed artificial intelligence systems. The issues being raised in this paper are central AI issues; they provide evidence of the interconnectedness of natural language processing research and other research in AI.

[7] This separation is useful for considering the kinds of processes involved in interpretation. The process of interpretation itself, of course, entails a great deal of interaction among the processes in the different levels. There are major research issues concerned with their coordination.

To illustrate these levels, let us return to the example and consider the interpretation of monkey2's response (2), "There's a stick under the old rubber tree," to monkey1's indirect request (1).

3.1. Linguistic Analysis

At this level, the parsing process that assigns syntactic structure to the utterance also assigns attributes to the various syntactic subphrases in the utterance and to the utterance as a whole. Many of these attributes are of a semantic nature. For example, the attributes of the phrase "the old rubber tree" might include

> The phrase is of syntactic class NP (noun phrase)
>
> The phrase is definitely determined
>
> The phrase describes a t such that TREE(t) and OLD(t), where OLD and TREE are predicate symbols[8]

Attributes of utterance (2) as a whole include its syntactic structure and such properties as:[9]

> The utterance presupposes that there exists a t such that OLD(t) and TREE(t), and that the description "OLD(t) & TREE(t)" should allow t to be determined uniquely in the current context.
>
> The utterance asserts that there exists an s such that STICK(s).
>
> The utterance asserts that UNDER(s t).

3.2. Assimilation

As attributes are extracted through the parsing process at the linguistic analysis level, common-sense reasoning processes begin to act on those attributes at the assimilation level. Two major activities are involved: completing the literal interpretation of an utterance in context, and drawing implications from that interpretation to discover the intended meaning.

----

[8] How much semantic specificity should be imposed at the linguistic level is an open research question. In particular, I have left open the question of what happens with the modifier "rubber"; suffice it to say, the question of how it modifies cannot be resolved solely at the linguistic level. Also, in a more complete analysis, the predicate OLD would indicate the set with respect to which age is evaluated.

[9] What an utterance presupposes and asserts are not necessarily components of the intended meaning, but the recognition of presuppositions and assertions is prerequisite to the assimilation level of processing.

For the example utterance (2), completing the literal interpretation in context involves the identification of the referent of the definite noun phrase, "the old rubber tree". The first attribute above indicates that a unique tree should be easily identified in context. Those objects currently in monkeyl's focus of attention are examined (perhaps requiring sophisticated common-sense reasoning) to determine whether there is such a tree among them. Assume that none is found. It may be that only two kinds of trees are present in this forest, and that one kind, say gumgum trees, resemble rubber trees, and that of all the trees near the two monkeys only one is a gumgum tree. Monekyl may tentatively assume that "rubber tree" matches "gumgum tree" closely enough to serve to identify this tree.

The sentence says there's a stick under the tree, so monkeyl might look under the tree and discover that, indeed, there is exactly one stick there. That stick must be the stick whose existence monkey2 was informing him of. The literal interpretation of the utterance is seen to be that the newly found stick is under the gumgum tree.[10]

Knowing that the sentence presupposed the existence of a rubber tree and asserted the existence of a stick, monkeyl may infer that monkey2 believes these presuppositions. Thus, monkeyl comes to believe several new things about monkey2's beliefs: in particular, that he believes these two entities exist, and that he thinks the gumgum tree is a rubber tree, or at least thinks that this description can be used to identify the tree. This fact may be important in further communications. Monkeyl may also infer that because monkey2 has just mentioned the stick and the tree, they are in his focus of attention and that he (monkey2), too, should pay special attention to these objects. The stick may be of particular importance because it was the subject of a there-insertion sentence (a syntactic position of prominence) and has been newly introduced into his focus of attention.

The second major process of assimilation is to use common-sense reasoning to determine how the utterance fits into the current set of plans and goals. In general, this is a highly complex process.[11] For the particular example of interpreting utterance (2) in the context implied by utterance (1), monkeyl must determine what, "There's a stick under the rubber tree," has to do with his problem of getting something to eat. Briefly, he must see that the sentence emphasizes the stick and must know (or infer) that such sticks are often useful tools for getting things out of trees. He must infer that monkey2 intends for him to use this stick in conjunction with a standard plan for knocking down things to acquire some bananas and accomplish his (implicitly stated) goal of not being hungry.

4 THE MULTIFACETED NATURE OF UTTERANCES

To determine what objective an utterance is intended to achieve requires determining where that utterance fits in the speaker's plans. That is, just as an agent may perform physical actions intended to alter the physical state of his environment, he may perform linguistic actions (utter sentences) intended to alter the cognitive state of the hearer. (Whatever effect an utterance eventually has on the outside world, its immediate effect is on the hearer's state.) But because a single utterance may be used to achieve multiple effects simultaneously, the problem is more complex than this analogy (or the preceding example) at first seems to suggest.[12]

The discussion so far has concentrated on a single dimension of effect: the use of an utterance to achieve what I will call a domain goal, that is, to convey information about the domain of discourse. In this section I want to discuss two other dimensions along which an utterance can have effects -- the social and the discourse -- and look at some of the problems in interpretation and generation that arise from the multifaceted nature of utterances.[13]

The social dimension includes those aspects of an utterance that concern the establishment and maintenance of interpersonal relationships. This dimension of utterance (1), "I'm hungry,"

----

[10] For more complex utterances, the process of completing the literal interpretation can involve determining the scopes of quantifiers and resolving various types of ambiguities.

[11] Cf. the analysis of a set of therapeutic interviews in Labov and Fanshel (1977).

[12] Physical actions may also have effects along multiple dimensions although they are not usually thought of as doing so. For example, a ballet dancer in leaping (rather than walking slowly) not only changes position, but also conveys a particular state of mind for the character being portrayed and a particular level of capability.

[13] These dimensions parallel the three functions of language --ideational, interpersonal, and textual -- in Halliday (1970), but the perspective I take on them is closer to that presented in Levy (1978).

is easily seen when it is compared with such choices as

(3) "How can I get some of those blasted bananas?"

(4) "Can you help me get some bananas down?"

(5) "Get me a banana."

Each of these achieves the same domain goal, informing monkey2 of monkey1's desire to obtain some bananas, but utterance (1) does not convey the same familiarity as utterance (3) or the same level of frustration. Similarly, utterance (4) makes the same request as utterance (5) but does so indirectly and, therefore, can be used with social equals. The social dimension is present in every discourse[14] and prevails in some (e.g., Hobbs, 1979). It has been largely ignored in natural language processing research to date. The assumption has been that some sort of neutral stance is possible. But not choosing is choosing not to choose (cf. Goffman, 1978), and, although there are some serious philosophical issues raised by this dimension of utterances when considering communication between people and computers, I do not think we can continue to ignore it.

The discourse dimension includes those aspects of an utterance that derive from its participation in a coherent discourse -- how the utterance relates to the utterances that preceded it and to what will follow. Typically the information a speaker wishes to convey requires several utterances. As a result the individual utterances must contain information that provides links to what went before and properly set the stage for what follows. Utterances that convey the same propositional content may differ widely in such things as the entities they indicate a speaker is focused on and hence may refer to later. As an extreme example, note that the propositional content of "Not every stick isn't under the rubber tree" is equivalent to that of utterance (2), but because it does not mention any individual stick, it does not allow whoever speaks next to make any reference to the stick that is under the gumgum tree.[15]

----

[14] Pittenger et al. (1960) point out that "no matter what else human beings may be communicating about, or may think they are communicating about, <u>they are always communicating about themselves, about one another, and about the immediate context of the communication.</u>"

[15] This example is based on one suggested by Barbara Partee for the Sloan Workshop at the University of Massachusetts, December, 1978. A discussion of her example is included in Grosz and Hendrix, 1978.

There are two characteristics of these dimensions and the multifaceted nature of utterances that introduce complications into natural language processing. First, as Halliday (1977) has pointed out, the units in which the information is conveyed along these other dimensions of meaning do not follow the constituent structure of sentences nearly so nicely as do the units conveying propositional content. In particular, the social implications of an utterance are typically reflected in choices scattered throughout it; for example, they are reflected in the choice of utterance type (a request vs. a command) and in the choice of lexical items.

Second, an utterance may relate to plans and goals along any number of these dimensions. It may be a comment on the preceding utterance itself, its social implications (or both, as is usually the case with "I shouldn't have said that"), or on some part of the domain content of the utterance. It is not simply a matter of determining where an utterance fits into a speaker's plan, but of determining which plan or plans --domain, social, or communicative -- the utterance fits into. A one dimensional analysis of an utterance is insufficient to capture the different effects (cf. Goffman, 1978).

The multifaceted nature of utterances poses problems for language generation as well. A speaker typically must coordinate goals along each of these dimensions. He must design an utterance that conveys information linking it to the preceding discourse and maintains the social relationship he has with the hearer(s) (or establishes one) as well as conveying domain-specific information.[16] The speaker's task is further complicated because he has only incomplete knowledge of the intended hearer's goals, plans, and beliefs.

5 <u>STATE OF THE ART</u>

I will use our work in natural language processing at SRI International (Robinson, 1978; Walker, 1978) as an exemplar for discussing the current state of research in this area, both because I am most familiar with it and because I think the framework it provides is a useful one for seeing not only where the field stands, but also where the next several years effort might best be expended. The system coordinates multiple sources of language-specific knowledge and combines them with certain general knowledge and common-sense reasoning strategies in

----

[16] Levy (1978) discusses how the multiple levels along which a speaker plans are reflected in what he says and the structure of his discourse.

arriving at a literal interpretation of an utterance in the context of an ongoing task-oriented dialogue.[17] A major feature of the system is the tight coupling of syntactic form and semantic interpretation. In the interpretation of an utterance, it associates collections of attributes with each phrase. For example, noun phrases are annotated with values for the attribute 'definiteness', a property that is relevant for drawing inferences about focusing (Grosz, 1977a, 1977b, 1978) and about presuppositions of existence and mutual knowledge (Clark and Marshall, 1978).

Interpretation is performed in multiple stages under control of an executive and in accordance with the specifications of a language definition that coordinates multiple "knowledge sources" for interpreting each phrase. Two sorts of processes take part in the linguistic level of analysis. First, there are processes that interpret the input "bottom up" (i.e., words -> phrases -> larger phrases -> sentences). In the analysis of utterance (2), these processes would provide attributes specifying that the phrase "a stick" is indefinite and in the subject position of a there-initial sentence and the phrase "the rubber tree" is definite and presupposes the existence of a uniquely identifiable entity. Second, there are processes that refine the interpretation of a phrase in the context of the larger phrases that contain it, doing such things as establishing a relationship between syntactic units and descriptions of (sets of propositions about) objects in the domain model. For example, the structure for "the rubber tree" would include predications of existence and treeness.

The assimilation level in the current system only goes so far as determining a literal interpretation in context. The major tasks performed here include delimiting the scope of quantifiers and associating references to objects with particular entities in the domain model, taking into account the overall dialogue and task context. In the case of our two monkeys, the system would determine whether there was a unique rubber tree in, or near, the focus of attention of the monkey (more on this shortly) and then posit, or check, the existence of a stick under it. The system does make some inferences based on the information explicitly contained in an utterance and its literal interpretation. To see the sorts of inferences it will make, consider the sequence:

(6) monkey1: I'm going out to get some bananas.
Where is the stick?
(7) monkey2: It's under the gumgum tree.

If the system (playing the role of monkey2) knows of some plan for getting bananas from a tree that involves the use of a particular stick, it would be able to make sense of monkey1's request, including identifying "the stick" as the one that is usually used to knock bananas out of trees. Furthermore, if the plan included steps prerequisite to getting a stick (e.g., getting a knapsack for carrying the relevant tools and the gathered bananas), the system would infer that they too had been performed.[18]

Initial progress has been made in overcoming the limitations of literal interpretation and including a consideration of a speaker's plans and goals in the interpretation of an utterance. Recent research on the role of planning in language processing includes that of Cohen (1978), Wilensky (1978), Carbonell (1979), and Allen (1979). Cohen (1978) views speech acts (Searle, 1969) as one kind of goal-oriented activity and describes a system that uses mechanisms previously used for planning nonlinguistic actions to plan individual speech acts (on the level of requesting and informing) intended to satisfy some goals involving the speaker's or hearer's knowledge. In Wilensky's work on story understanding (see also Schank and Abelson, 1977), the speaker's overall plans and goals, some of which are implicit, are inferred from substeps and intermediate or triggering states (e.g., inferring from "John was hungry. He got in his car." that John was going to get something to eat.) Carbonell (1979) describes a system constructed to investigate how two agents with different goals interpret an input differently; it is particularly concerned with the effect of conflicting plans on interpretation. Allen (1979) describes a system based on a model in which speech acts are

----
17 Several other systems are capable of fairly sophisticated analysis and processing at the level of coordinating different kinds of language-specific capabilities (e.g., Sager and Grishman, 1975; Landsbergen, 1976; Plath, 1976; Woods et al., 1976; Bobrow et al., 1977; Reddy et al. 1977) and of taking into account some of the ways in which context affects meaning through the application of limited action scenarios (Schank et al., 1975; Novak, 1977) or by considering (either independently or in conjunction with such scenarios) language-specific mechanisms that reference context (Hobbs, 1976; Rieger, 1975; Hayes, 1978; Mann et al., 1977; Sidner, 1979).

----
18 The system actually works on dialogues for assembling mechanical equipment. The plans it knows about are partially ordered (and not linear), and the structures it uses allow for describing plans at multiple levels of abstraction.

defined in terms of "the plan the hearer believes the speaker intended him to recognize" and has perhaps gone furthest in determining mechanisms by which a speaker's goals and plans can be taken into account in the interpretation of an utterance.

These efforts have demonstrated the feasibility of incorporating planning and plan recognition into the common-sense reasoning component of a natural language processing system, but their limitations highlight the need for more robust capabilities in order to achieve the integration of language-specific and general common-sense reasoning capabilities required for fluent communication in natural language. No system combines a consideration of multiple agents having different goals with a consideration of the problems that arise from multiple agents having separate beliefs and each having only incomplete knowledge about the others agent's plans and goals.[19] Furthermore, only simple sequences of actions have been considered, and no attempt has been made to treat hypothetical worlds.

One of the major weaknesses in current AI systems and theories (and the limitation of current systems that I find of most concern) is that they consider utterances as having a single meaning or effect. Analogously, a critical omission in work on planning and language is that it fails to consider the multiple dimensions on which an utterance can have effects. If utterances are considered operators (where "operator" is meant in the general sense of something that produces an effect), they must be viewed as <u>conglomerate</u> <u>operators</u>.

Although it does not yet go beyond literal interpretation (except by filling in unmentioned intermediate steps in the task being performed), the SRI language system does account for two kinds of effects of an utterance. In addition to determining the propositional content of an utterance (and what it literally conveys about the state of the world), the system determines whether the utterance indicates that the speaker's focus of attention has shifted (Grosz, 1977a,b, 1978; Sidner, 1979).[20]

To summarize then, one or more of the following crucial limitations is evident in every natural language processing system constructed to date (although most of these problems have been addressed to some extent in the research described above and elsewhere):

* Interpretation is literal (only propositional content is determined).
* The knowledge and beliefs of all participants in a discourse are assumed to be identical.
* The plans and goals of all participants are considered to be identical.
* The multifaceted nature of utterances is not considered.

To move beyond this state, the major problems to be faced at the level of linguistic analysis concern determining how different linguistic constructions are used to convey information about such things as the speaker's (implicit) assumptions about the hearer's beliefs, what entities the speaker is focusing on, and the speaker's attitude toward the hearer. The problems to be faced at the assimilation level are more fundamental. In particular, we need to determine common-sense reasoning mechanisms that can derive complex connections between plans and goals -- connections that are not explicit either in the dialogue or in the plans and goals themselves -- and to reason about these relationships in an environment where the problem solver's knowledge is necessarily incomplete. This is not just a matter of specifying more details of particular relationships, but of specifying new kinds of problem solving and reasoning structures and procedures that operate in the kind of environment in which natural language communication usually occurs.

6 COMMON-SENSE REASONING IN NATURAL LANGUAGE PROCESSING

The previous sections of this paper have suggested several complexities in the common-sense reasoning needs of natural language communication. A participant in a communicative situation typically has incomplete information about other participants. In particular he cannot assume that their beliefs, goals, or plans are identical. Communication is inherently interpersonal. Furthermore, the information a speaker conveys typically requires a sequence of utterances. As a result, interpretation requires recognition of different kinds of plans, and generation requires the ability to coordinate multiple kinds of actions to satisfy goals along multiple dimensions. Other complications are introduced by the

----

19 Moore (1979) discusses problems of reasoning about knowledge and belief.

20 Grosz and Hendrix (1978) discuss focusing as one of the elements of cognitive state crucial to the interpretation of both definite and indefinite referring expressions, and Grosz (1978) discusses several open problems in modeling the focusing process.

interactions among plans of different agents (Bruce and Newman, 1978; Hobbs and Robinson (1978) discuss some of the complexity of the relationship between an utterance and domain specific plans).

From this perspective, the current deduction and planning systems in AI are deficient in several areas critical for natural language processing. A review of the current state of the art in plan generation and recognition shows that the most advanced systems have one or another (but not both) of the following capabilities:[21] plans for partially ordered sequences of actions can be generated detail (Sacerdoti, 1977) and recognized (Genesereth, 1978; Schmidt and Sridharan, 1977) at multiple levels of detail in a restricted subject area. However, these programs only consider single agents, assume the system's view of the world is "the correct" one, and plan for actions that produce a state change characterized by a single primary effect.

The most important directions in which these capabilities must be extended and integrated for use in the interpretation and generation of language are the following:

* It must be possible to plan in a dynamic environment that includes other active agents, given incomplete information.
* It must be possible to coordinate different types of actions and plan to achieve multiple primary effects simultaneously.
* It must be possible to recognize previously unanticipated plans.

7 CONCLUSIONS

Common-sense reasoning, especially planning, is a central issue in language research, not only within artificial intelligence, but also in linguistics (e.g., Chafe, 1978; Morgan 1978), sociolinguistics (e.g., Goffman, 1974; Labov and Fanshel, 1977), and philosophy (e.g., Kasher, 1978). The literal content of an utterance must be interpreted within the context of the beliefs, goals, and plans of the dialogue participants, so that a hearer can move beyond literal content to the intentions that lie behind the utterance. Furthermore, it is insufficient to consider an utterance as being addressed to a single purpose. Typically, an utterance serves multiple purposes: it highlights certain objects and relationships, conveys an attitude toward them, and provides links to previous utterances in addition to communicating some propositional content.

Progress toward understanding the relationship between utterances and objectives and its effect on natural language communication will be best furthered by consideration of the fundamental linguistic, common-sense reasoning, and planning processes involved in language use and their interaction. A merger of research in common-sense reasoning and language processing is an important goal both for developing a computational theory of the communicative use of language and for constructing computer-based natural language processing systems. The next few years of research on language processing should be concerned to a large extent with issues that are at least as much issues of common-sense reasoning (especially planning issues). While common-sense reasoning research could continue without any regard for language, there is some evidence that the perspective of language processing will provide insights into fundamental issues in planning that confront AI more generally.

Finally, I want to emphasize the long-term nature of the problems that confront natural language processing research in AI. I believe we should start by adding communication capabilities to systems that have solid capabilities in solving some problem (constructing such systems first if necessary; cf. McDermott, 1976). Although it may initially take longer to create functioning systems, the systems that result will be useful, not toys. People will have a reason to communicate with such systems. Monkey2 can help monkey1 get something to eat only if he himself has a realistic conception of the complexities of monkey1's world.

----

[21] Earl Sacerdoti provided me with this characterization of the current state of affairs in AI research on problem solving as well as with much useful information about problem solving issues in general.

ACKNOWLEDGEMENTS

Preparation of this paper was supported by the National Science Foundation under Grant No. MCS76-22004, and the Defense Advanced Research Projects Agency under Contract N00039-79-C-0118 with the Naval Electronic Systems Command.

The Natural Language Research Group of the Artificial Intelligence Center at SRI International provides a stimulating environment in which to pursue research in language processing. Many of the ideas presented in this paper are the product of thought-provoking discussions, both oral and written, with members of this group, especially Douglas Appelt, Gary

Hendrix, Jerry Hobbs, Robert Moore, Nils Nilsson, Ann Robinson, Jane Robinson, Earl Sacerdoti, and Donald Walker. I would also like to thank David Levy and Mitch Marcus for many discussions about language and the insights they provided. Many of these people also provided helpful comments on this paper.

REFERENCES

Allen, J. 1979 A Plan-Based Approach to Speech Act Recognition. Technical Report No. 131/79, Department of Computer Science, University of Toronto.

Bobrow, D. G., et al. 1977. GUS, A Frame Driven Dialog System. Artificial Intelligence, 8, 155-173.

Bruce, B. and D. Newman. 1978. Interacting Plans. Cognitive Science, 2, 195-233.

Carbonell, J. G. 1979. Computer Models of Social and Political Reasoning. Ph. D. Thesis, Yale University, New Haven, Connecticut.

Chafe, W. 1978. The Flow of Thought and the Flow of Language. In T. Givon (ed.), Syntax and Semantics, Vol. 12. Academic Press, New York.

Clark, H. and C. Marshall. 1978. Definite reference and mutual knowledge. Paper presented at the Sloan Workshop on Computational Aspects of Linguistic Structure and Discourse Setting. University of Pennsylvania, Philadelphia, Pennsylvania.

Cohen, P. 1978. On Knowing What to Say: Planning Speech Acts. Technical Report No. 118, Department of Computer Science, University of Toronto, Toronto, Canada.

Collins, A. 1978. Studies of Plausible Reasoning. Volume I. BBN Report No. 3810, Bolt Beranek and Newman, Cambridge, Massachusetts.

Donnellan, K. S. 1977. "Reference and Definite Descriptions". In S. P. Schwartz (Ed.), Naming, Necessity, and Natural Kind. Ithaca, New York: Cornell University Press. Pp. 42-65.

Genesereth, M. R. 1978. Automated Consultation for Complex Computer Systems. Ph. D. Thesis, Harvard University, Cambridge, Massachusetts.

Goffman, E. 1974. Frame analysis. New York: Harper.

Goffman, E. 1978. Response Cries. Language, Vol. 54, 787-815.

Grosz, B. 1977a. The Representation and Use of Focus in Dialogue Understanding. Technical Note 151, Stanford Research Institute, Menlo Park, California.

Grosz, B. J. 1977b. The Representation and Use of Focus in a System for Understanding Dialogs. Proceedings of the Fifth International Joint Conference on Artificial Intelligence. Carnegie-Mellon University, Pittsburgh, Pennsylvania. Pp. 67-76.

Grosz, B. J. 1978. Focusing in Dialog. TINLAP-2: Theoretical Issues in Natural Language, Urbana, Illinois, 24-26 July, 1978.

Grosz, B. and G. Hendrix. 1978. A Computational Perspective on Indefinite Reference. Presented at Sloan Workshop on Indefinite Reference, University of Massachusetts, Amherst, Massachusetts, December 1978. Also Technical Note No. 181, Artificial Intelligence Center, SRI International, Menlo Park, California (in preparation).

Halliday, M.A.K. 1970. Language Structure and Language Function. In New Horizons in Linguistics, J. Lyons (ed.) (Penguin).

Halliday, M.A.K. 1977. Structure and Function in Language. Presented at Symposium on Discourse and Syntax, University of California at Los Angeles, Los Angeles, California, November 1977.

Hayes, P. J. 1978. Some Association-Based Techniques for Lexical Disambiguation by Machine. Doctoral Thesis, Ecole Polytechnique Federale de Lausanne, Lausanne, Switzerland.

Hobbs, J. 1976. A Computational Approach to Discourse Analysis. Research Report 76-2, Department of Computer Sciences, City College, City University of New York, New York, New York.

Hobbs, J. 1979. Conversation as Planned Behavior. To appear in Proceedings of the Sixth International Joint Conference on Artificial Intelligence. Stanford University, Stanford, California.

Hobbs, J. and J. Robinson 1978. Why Ask? SRI Technical Note 169, SRI International, Menlo Park, California.

Kasher, A. 1978. Indefinite Reference: Indispensability of Pragmatics. Presented at Sloan Workshop on Indefinite Reference, University of Massachusetts, Amherst, Massachusetts, December 1978.

Labov, W. and D. Fanshel. 1977. Therapeutic Discourse. New York: Academic Press.

Landsbergen, S. P. J., 1976. Syntax and Formal Semantics of English in PHLIQA1. In Coling 76, Preprints of the 6th International Conference on Computational Linguistics. Ottawa, Ontario, Canada, 28 June - 2 July 1976. No. 21.

Levy, D. 1978. Communicative goals and strategies: Between discourse and syntax. In T. Givon (ed.), Syntax and Semantics, Vol. 12. Academic Press, New York.

Mann, W., J. Moore, & J. Levin 1977. A comprehension model for human dialogue. Proceedings of the Fifth International Joint Conference on Artificial Intelligence, Carnegie-Mellon University, Pittsburgh, Pennsylvania. Pp. 77-87.

McCarthy, J. 1968. Programs with Common Sense. In M. Minsky (ed.) Semantic Information Processing, MIT Press, Cambridge, Massachusetts. Pp. 403-419.

McDermott, D. 1976. Artificial Intelligence Meets Natural Stupidity. SIGART Newsletter, no. 57, Pp. 4-9.

Moore, R. 1979. Reasoning about Knowledge and Actions. Ph.D. Thesis, Massachusetts Institute of Technology, Cambridge, Massachusetts.

Morgan, J. L. 1978. Two Types of Convention in Indirect Speech acts. In Peter Cole (ed.), Syntax and Semantics, vol. 9, Academic Press, Inc., New York, N.Y.

Nilsson, N. 1971. Problem Solving Methods in Artificial Intelligence. McGraw-Hill, New York.

Novak, G. 1977. Representations of knowledge in a program for solving physics problems. Proceedings of the Fifth International Joint Conference on Artificial Intelligence. Carnegie-Mellon University, Pittsburgh, Pennsylvania. Pp. 286-291.

Pittenger, R., Hockett, C., and Danehy J., 1960. The First Five Minutes. Paul Martineau, Ithaca, New York.

Plath, W. J. 1976. Request: A Natural Language Question-Answering System. IBM Journal of Research and Development, 20, 4, 326-335.

Quine. W. V. O. 1960. Word and Object. MIT Press, Cambridge, Massachusetts.

Reddy, D. R., et al. 1977. Speech Understanding Systems: A Summary of Results of the Five-Year Research Effort. Department of Computer Science. Carnegie-Mellon University, Pittsburgh, Pennsylvania.

Rieger, C. 1975. Conceptual Overlays: A Mechanism for the Interpretation of Sentence Meaning in Context. Technical Report TR-354. Computer Science Department, University of Maryland, College Park, Maryland.

Robinson, A. 1978. Investigating the Process of Natural-Language Communication: A Status Report. Technical Note 165. SRI International, Menlo Park, California.

Rubin, A. D. 1978. A Theoretical Taxonomy of the Differences Between Oral and Written Language. In R. Spiro et al. (eds.) Theoretical Issues in Reading Comprehension. Lawrence Erlbaum, Hillsdale, New Jersey.

Sacerdoti, E. D. 1977, A Structure for Plans and Behavior. Elsevier, New York.

Sacerdoti, E. D. 1978. What Language Understanding Research Suggests about Distributed Artificial Intelligence. Proceedings of a workshop held at Carnegie-Mellon University, December 7-8, 1978.

Sager, N. and R. Grishman. 1975. The Restriction Language for Computer Grammars. Communications of the ACM, 18, 390-400.

Schank, R. C., and Yale A.I. Project 1975. SAM -- A story understander. Research Report No. 43, Department of Computer Science, Yale University, New Haven, Connecticut.

Schank, R. and R. Abelson. 1977. Scripts, Plans, Goals, and Understanding. Laurence Erlbaum Associates, Hillsdale N.J.

Schmidt, C. F. and N. S. Sridharan. 1977. Plan Recognition Using a Hypothesis and Revise Paradigm: an Example. Proceedings of the Fifth International Joint Conference on Artificial Intelligence, Carnegie-Mellon University, Pittsburgh, Pennsylvania. Pp. 480-486.

Searle, J. 1969. Speech Acts: An Essay in the Philosophy of Language. Cambridge University Press, Cambridge, England.

Sidner, C. L. 1979. A Computational Model of Co-Reference Comprehension in English. Ph.D. Thesis, Massachusetts Institute of Technology, Cambridge, Massachusetts.

Walker, D. E. (ed.) 1978. Understanding Spoken Language. Elsevier North-Holland, New York:

Wilensky, R. 1978. Understanding Goal-Based Stories. Ph.D. Thesis. Yale University, New Haven, Connecticut.

Woods, W. A., et al. 1976. Speech Understanding Systems: Final Report. BBN Report No. 3438, Bolt Beranek and Newman, Cambridge, Massachusetts.

PROBLEM SOLVING TACTICS*

Earl D. Sacerdoti
Artificial Intelligence Center
SRI International
Menlo Park, California 94025 USA

This paper describes the basic strategies of automatic problem solving, and then focuses on a variety of tactics for improving their efficiency. An attempt is made to provide some perspective on and structure to the set of tactics. Finally, some new directions for problem-solving research are discussed, and a personal perspective is provided on where the work is headed: toward greater flexibility of control and more intimate integration of plan generation, execution, and repair.

1. AUTOMATIC PROBLEM SOLVING

For intelligent computers to be able to interact with the real world, they must be able to aggregate individual actions into sequences to achieve desired goals. This process is referred to as *automatic problem solving*, sometimes more casually called *automatic planning*. The sequences of actions that are generated are called *plans*.

Early work in automatic problem solving focused on what Newell [1] has called "weak methods." While these problem-solving strategies are quite general and are formally tractable, they are insufficient in practice for solving problems of any significant complexity. During the last decade, a number of techniques have been developed for improving the efficiency of these strategies. Since these techniques operate within the context of the general strategies, they are termed here *problem-solving tactics*. The bulk of this paper consists of a description of the problem-solving strategies and a catalogue of tactics for improving their efficiency. This is followed by an attempt to provide some perspective on and structure to the set of tactics. Finally, some new directions in problem-solving research are discussed, and a personal perspective is provided on where the work is headed: toward greater flexibility of control and more intimate integration of plan generation, execution, and repair.

Because problem solving involves exploration of alternative hypothesized sequences of actions, a symbolic model of the real world, referred to as a *world model*, is used to enable simple simulations of the critical aspects of the situation to be run as the plans are evolved. As with all models, the world models used in problem solving are abstractions or oversimplifications of the world they model.

1.1. What is Needed to Generate Plans

The general function of an automatic problem solving system, then, is to construct a sequence of actions that transforms one world model into another. There are three basic capabilities that a problem solving system must have. These are:

a. Management of State Description Models - A *state description model* is a specification of the state of the world at some time. The facts or relations that are true at any particular time can be represented as some equivalent of predicate calculus formulas. (We shall refer, somewhat loosely, to these facts and relations as *attributes* of a state.) The critical aspect of representation for problem solving is the need to represent alternative and hypothetical situations, that is, to characterize the aggregate effects of alternative sequences of actions as the problem solver searches for a solution.

----

* Preparation of this paper was supported by the Defense Advanced Research Projects Agency under contract N00039-79-C-0118 with the Naval Electronic Systems Command. Barbara Grosz, Peter Hart, Nils Nilsson, and Don Walker suggested helpful presentation tactics.

Three methods have typically been used for representing these alternatives. One method has been to include an explicit state specification in each literal or assertion (as suggested by McCarthy and Hayes [2] and implemented by Green [3]). Another alternative is to associate each literal with an implicit data context that can be explicitly referenced (as in QA4 [4]). A third choice is to have all the literals that describe the states explicitly tied up in the control structure of the problem solver (as, for example, in most problem solvers written in CONNIVER [5]).

b. Deductive Machinery - A state description model, then, contains all the information needed to characterize a particular state of the world. The information will not all be explicitly encoded, however, so a deductive engine of some sort must be provided to allow needed information to be extracted from a model. The deductions are of two types: within a particular state (this is where traditional, "monotonic" deduction systems are used), and across states (that is, reasoning about the effects of prior actions in a sequence). The deductive machinery can be viewed as a question-answering system that allows the problem solver to retrieve information about a particular state of the world from the state description model.

c. Action Models - In addition to state description models and a means of querying them, a problem solver must have a way of modelling what changes when an action is applied in an arbitrary state. Thus, an action is described by a mapping from one state description to another. Such a mapping is usually referred to as an operator. The mapping may be specified either by procedures, as in the problem solvers based on so-called AI languages [6], or by declarative data structures. In any case, they must specify at least the expressions that the action will make true in the world model and the expressions that its execution will make untrue in the world model. Usually, to help guide the heuristic search for actions that are relevant to achieve particular goals, one of the expressions to be made true by each operator is designated in some way as its "primary effect."

1.2. The Basic Control Strategy for Plan Generation

The process of generating a plan of action that achieves a desired goal state from a given initial state typically involves a extensive search among alternative sequences. A number of control strategies for tree search constitute the basic tools of all problem solving systems. Problem solving systems usually work backward from the goal state to find a sequence of actions that could lead to it from the initial state. This procedure generates a tree of action sequences, with the goal state at the root, instances of operators defining the branches, and intermediate states defining the nodes. A tree search process of some sort is used to find a path to a node that corresponds to the initial state. The path from initial state to goal then defines the plan. Two particular tree search strategies are discussed here since they are so commonly used.

The first of these is means-ends analysis, which was the central search algorithm used by GPS [7] and STRIPS [8]. This strategy works as follows. The "difference" between the initial and goal states is determined, and that instance of the particular operator that would most reduce the difference is chosen.

If this operator is applicable in the initial state, it is applied, creating a new intermediate state. If the goal is satisfied in the new state, the search is completed. Otherwise, the difference between the new state and the goal state is determined, an operator to most reduce the new difference is chosen, and the process continues.

If the chosen operator is not applicable, its preconditions are established as a new intermediate subgoal. An attempt is made, using the search strategy recursively, to find a sequence of operators to achieve the subgoal state. If this can be done, the chosen operator is now applicable and the search proceeds as described above. If the new subgoal cannot be achieved, a new instance of an operator to reduce the difference is chosen and the process continues as before.

A second important search strategy, used in simple problem solvers written in the so-called AI languages [6], is backtracking, which works in the following manner. If the goal is satisfied in the initial state, a trivial solution has been found. If not, an operator that, if applied, would achieve the goal is selected. If it is applicable in the initial state, it is applied and a solution has been found. If the chosen operator is not applicable, operators that would achieve its preconditions are found, and the search proceeds as before to find plans to render them applicable. If the search fails, a different candidate operator is chosen and the process repeats.

This strategy follows a line of action out fully before rejecting it. It thus permits the search tree to be represented elegantly; all the active parts of the search tree can be encoded by the control stack of the search procedure itself, and all the inactive parts of the search tree need not be encoded at all. Because of the full search at each cycle of the process, it is critical that the correct operator be chosen first almost always. Otherwise, the simplicity of representation offered by this strategy will be amply repaid by the inefficiency of the search.

As was discussed above, these strategies are insufficient in practice for solving problems of any significant complexity. In particular, one of the most costly behaviors of the basic problem solving strategies is their inefficiency in dealing with goal descriptions that include conjunctions. Because there is usually no good reason for the problem solver to prefer to attack one conjunct before another, an incorrect ordering will often be chosen. This can lead to an extensive search for a sequence of actions to try to achieve subgoals in an unachievable order.

2. TACTICS FOR EFFICIENT PROBLEM SOLVING

2.1. Hierarchical Planning

The general strategies described above apply a uniform procedure to the action descriptions and state descriptions that they are given. Thus, they have no inherent ability to distinguish what is important from what is a detail. However, some aspects of almost any problem are significantly more important than others. By employing additional knowledge about the ranking in importance of aspects of the problem description, a problem solver can concentrate its efforts on the decisions that are critical while spending less effort on those that are relatively unimportant.

Information about importance can be used in several ways. First, the standard strategies can be modified to deal with the most important (and most difficult to achieve) subgoals first. The solution to the most important subgoals often leaves the world model in a state from which the less important subgoals are still achievable (if not, the weaker search strategies must be employed as a last resort). The less important subgoals could presumably be solved in many ways, some of which would be incompatible with the eventual solution to the important subgoals. Thus, this approach constrains the search where the constraints are important, and avoids overconstraining it by making premature choices about how to solve less important aspects of the problem. Siklossy and Dreussi [9] used an explicit ordering of types of subgoals to guide search.

Another way to focus on the critical decisions first is to abstract the descriptions of the actions, thereby creating a simpler problem. This abstracted problem can be solved, producing a sequence of abstracted actions, and this plan can then be used as a skeleton, identifying critical subgoals along the way to a solution, around which to construct a fully detailed plan. This tactic was used in conjunction with an early version of GPS by Newell, Shaw, and Simon [7] to find proofs in symbolic logic (using abstracted operators and state descriptions that ignored the connectives and the ordering of symbols).

Finally, abstraction can be extended to involve multiple levels, leading to a hierarchy of plans, each serving as a skeleton for the problem solving process at the next level of detail. The search process at each level of detail can thus be reduced to a sequence of relatively simple subproblems of achieving the preconditions of the next step in the skeleton plan from an initial state in which the previous step in the skeleton plan has just been achieved. In this way, rather complex problems can be reduced to a sequence of much shorter, simpler subproblems. Sacerdoti applied this tactic to robot navigation tasks [10] and to more complex tasks involving assembly of machine components [11].

2.2. Hierarchical Plan Repair

A side-effect of hierarchical planning is that plans can possibly be created that appear to be workable at a high level of abstraction but whose detailed expansions turn out to be invalid. The basic idea behind the plan repair tactic is to check, as a higher level plan is being expanded, that all the intended effects of the sequence of higher-level actions are indeed being achieved by the collection of subsequences of lower-level actions. By exploiting the hierarchical structure of the plan, only a small number of effects need to be checked for. Various methods for patching up the failed plan can then be applied. This tactic was incorporated in a running system by Sacerdoti [11] and is very similar to a technique called "hierarchical debugging" articulated by Goldstein [12] for a program understanding task.

2.3. Bugging

Rather than attempt to produce perfect plans on the first attempt, it can often be more efficient to produce an initial plan that is approximately correct but contains some "bugs," and subsequently alter the plan to remove the bugs. By employing additional knowledge about bug classification and debugging, this approach allows the decisions made during the problem-solving process about which action to try next to be made with less effort, since mistaken decisions can be subsequently fixed.

Sussman, who first employed this tactic in his HACKER system [13], called it "problem-solving by debugging almost-right plans." It is often referred to in the literature as the "debugging approach" and, indeed, it has spawned interesting research in techniques for debugging programs or plans developed both by machines and by people (see, for example, Sussman [14] and Goldstein and Miller [15]). Debugging, however, is an integral part of the execution component of any problem solver. What distinguishes this approach is a tolerance for introducing bugs while generating the plan, and thus it can more accurately be called the "bugging" approach.

This tactic works by deliberately making assumptions that oversimplify the problem of integrating multiple subplans. These assumptions may cause the problem solver to produce an initial plan with bugs in it. However, if the oversimplifications are designed properly, then only bugs of a limited number of types will be introduced, and relatively simple mechanisms can be implemented to remedy each expected type of bug.

2.4. Special-Purpose Subplanners

Once a particular subgoal has been generated, it may well be the case that it is of a type for which a special purpose algorithm, a stronger method than the weak method of the general-purpose problem solver, can be brought to bear. For example, in a robot problem, the achievement of an INROOM goal can be performed by a route-finding algorithm applied to a connectivity graph representing the interconnection of rooms, rather than using more general methods applied to less direct representations of the rooms in the environment. Such a special purpose problem solver was used by Siklossy and Dreussi [9] to effect dramatic improvements in the system's performance.

Wilkins [16] employs special-purpose subplanners in a chess problem solver for subgoals such as moving safely to a given square or checking with a given piece.

Each special-purpose subplanner encodes additional knowledge about its specialty. To take advantage of it, the problem solver must incorporate information about how to recognize the special situation as well.

2.5. Constraint Satisfaction

Constraint satisfaction, the derivation of globally consistent assignments of values to variables subject to local constraints, is not usually thought of as a problem solving tactic. While it cannot be used to generate action sequences, it can play a very important role in particular subproblems, especially in determining the binding of variables when there is no clear locally computable reason to prefer one value over another. From this perspective, constraint satisfaction can be thought of as a type of special-purpose subplanner.

Stefik [17] employs constraint satisfaction to assign values to variables in generating action sequences for molecular genetics experiments.

2.6. Relevant Backtracking

As a correct plan is being searched for, a problem solver will encounter many choice points at which there are several alternative steps to be taken. Most problem solvers employ sophisticated techniques to try to make the right choices among the alternative action sequences initially. Alternatively, a problem solver could focus on sophisticated post-mortem analyses of the information gained from early attempts that fail. By analyzing the reasons for the failure of a particular sequence of actions, the problem solver can determine which action in the sequence should be modified. This is in contrast with the straightforward approach of backtracking to the most recent choice point and trying other alternatives there. Fahlman [18] developed such a system for planning the construction of complex block structures. His system associated a "gripe handler" with each choice point as it was encountered, and developed a characterization of each failure when it occurred. When a particular line of action failed, the gripe handlers would be invoked in reverse chronological order to see if they could suggest something specific to do about the failure. The effect of this mechanism is to backtrack not to the most recent choice point, but to the relevant choice point.

The tactic of relevant backtracking, which is also referred to in the literature as dependency-directed or non-chronological backtracking, was also used in a problem solver for computer-aided design developed by Latombe [19].

2.7. Disproving

Problem solvers have traditionally been automated optimists. They presume that a solution to each problem or subproblem can be found if only the right combination of primitive actions can be put together. Thus, the impossibility of achieving a given goal or subgoal state can only be discovered after an exhaustive search of all the possible combinations of potentially relevant actions.

It may well be the case that a pessimistic analysis of a particular goal, developing knowledge additional to that employed in building action sequences, would quickly show the futility of the whole endeavor. This procedure can be of particular value in evaluating a set of conjunctive subgoals to avoid working on any of them when one can be shown to be impossible. Furthermore, even if a goal cannot be shown to be impossible, the additional knowledge might suggest an action sequence that would achieve the goal. Siklossy and Roach [20] developed a system that integrated attempts to achieve goals with attempts to prove their impossibility.

2.8. Pseudo-Reduction

One of the most costly behaviors of problem solving systems is their inefficiency in dealing with goal descriptions that include conjunctions, as was noted at the end of Section 1. Ordering the conjuncts by importance, as described in the subsection on hierarchical planning above, can help, but there may still be multiple conjuncts of the same importance. One approach to the problem of selecting an order for the conjuncts is to ignore ordering them initially, finding a plan to achieve each conjunct independently. Thus, the conjunctive problem is reduced to several simpler, nonconjunctive problems. Of course, the plans to solve the reduced problems must then be integrated, using knowledge about how plan segments can be intertwined without destroying their important effects.

This tactic creates plans that are not linear orderings of actions with respect to time, but are rather partial orderings. This renders the cross-state question-answering procedure described in Section 1.1 more complicated than for other tactics.

By avoiding premature commitments to particular orderings of subgoals, this tactic eliminates much of the backtracking typical of problem solving systems. Pseudo-reduction was developed by Sacerdoti [11] and has been applied to robot problems, assembly of electromechanical equipment, and project planning [21].

2.9. Goal Regression

The problem-solving tactics we have discussed so far all work by modifying, in one way or another, the sequence of actions being developed to satisfy the goals. Goal regression modifies the goals as well. It relies on the fact that, given a particular goal and a particular action, it is possible to derive a new goal such that if the new goal is true before the action is executed, then the original goal will be true after the action is executed. The computation of the new goal, given the original goal and the action, is called <u>regressing</u> the goal over the action.

As an example, let us suppose the overall goal consists of two conjunctive subgoals. This tactic first tries to achieve the second goal in a context in which a sequence of actions has achieved the first goal (similarly to the bugging tactic).

If this fails, the second goal is regressed back across the last action that achieved the first goal. This process generates a new goal that describes a state such that if the last action were executed in it, would lead to a state in which the original second goal were true. If the regressed goal can be achieved without destroying the first goal, the tactic has succeeded. If not, the regression process continues.

This tactic requires knowledge of the inverse effects of each operator. That is, in addition to knowing how the subsequent application of an operator changes a world model, the system must know how the prior application of the operator affects a goal.

The goal regression technique was developed independently by Waldinger [22] and Warren [23].

3. WHAT'S GOING ON?

We have just finished a brief (heuristically) guided tour of some of the problem-solving tactics used recently. They constitute a diverse bag of tricks for improving the efficiency of the problem solving process. In this section we focus on the underlying reasons why these techniques seem to help.

Problem-solving is often described as state-space <u>search</u>, or as <u>exploration</u> of a tree of possible action sequences. We can find some structure for the bag of tactical tricks by remembering that search or exploration involves not only movement to new (conceptual) locations, but discovery and learning as well.

The problem solver begins its work with information about only the initial state and the goal state. It must acquire information about the intermediate states as it explores them. It must summarize this information for efficient use during the rest of the problem-solving process, and it must take advantage of all possible information that can be extracted from each intermediate state. This can require considerable computational resources. In the simplest search strategies, the information may be simply a number representing the value of the heuristic evaluation function applied at that point. It may be much more, however. It may include a detailed data base describing the situation, information about how to deal with classes of anticipated subsequent errors, and dependency relationships among the attributes describing the situation. All this information is typically stored in intermediate contexts in one of the forms discussed in the first section of this paper.

The information learned during the exploration process can be broken down into four kinds of relationships among the actions in a plan. These are:

- order relationships - the sequencing of the actions in the plan;
- hierarchical relationships - the links between each action at one level and the meta-actions above it and the more detailed actions below it;
- teleological relationships - the purposes for which each action has been placed in the plan; and
- object relationships - the dependencies among the objects that are being manipulated (which correspond to dependencies among the parameters or variables in the operators).

These relationships can be explicated and understood only by carrying out the instantiation of new points in the search space. It is thus of high value to a problem solver to instantiate and learn about new intermediate states. As a simple example of a problem-solving tactic that displays incremental learning, consider relevant backtracking. By following initial paths through the search tree, the problem solver learns which choice points are critical. Another clear example is constraint satisfaction, in which restrictions on acceptable bindings for variables are aggregated as search progresses.

The difficulty is that, as with all learning systems, the acquisition of new information is expensive. The generation of each new state is a major time consumer in many problem solving systems. Furthermore, the generation of each intermediate state represents a commitment to a particular line of action by the problem solver. Since problems of any non-toy level of complexity tend to generate very bushy search trees, a breadth-first search strategy is impossible to use. Therefore, once a line of action has begun to be investigated, a problem-solving system will tend to continue with it. It is thus of high value to a problem solver, whenever possible, to avoid generating intermediate states not on the solution path. Those states that are generated must represent a good investment for the problem solver.

Thus, there are two opposing ways to improve the efficiency of a problem solver. The first is to employ a relatively expensive evaluation function and to work hard to avoid generating states not on the eventual solution path. The second is to use a cheap evaluation function, to explore lots of paths that might not work out, but to acquire information about the interrelationships of the actions and objects in the world in the process. This information can then be used to guide (efficiently) subsequent search.

Each of the tactics described in the previous section strikes a particular balance between the value of instantiating new intermediate states and the cost of commitment to particular lines of action. While none of the tactics use one approach exclusively, each can be categorized by the one it emphasizes. Furthermore, each can be distinguished according to one of the four types of relationships they depend on or exploit. Table 1 displays a candidate categorization.

None of the tactics fit as neatly into the classification as the table suggests, because they typically have been embodied in a complete problem solving system and so must deal with at least some aspects of many of the categories.

Relationship: \ Approach:	Learn and Summarize	Choose New Move
Order	pseudo-red. generation relevant backtracking disproving	
Hierarchy	plan repair	spec.-purpose subplanners
Teleology	bugging pseudo-red. critics	regression
Object	relevant backtracking	constraint satisfaction

TABLE 1

Classification of Tactics

4. WHAT'S NEXT?

The current state of the art in plan generation allows for planning in a basically hierarchical fashion, using a severely limited (and predetermined) subset of the tactics enumerated above, by and for a single active agent satisfying a set of goals completely. The elimination of these restrictions is a challenge to workers in Artificial Intelligence. This section will discuss a number of these restrictions briefly and suggest, where possible, lines of research to ease them.

4.1. Integrating the Tactics

To date, there has been no successful attempt known to this author to integrate a significant number of the tactics we have described into a single system. What follows are some preliminary thoughts on how such an integration might be achieved.

First of all, the technique of hierarchical planning can be applied independently of any of the others. That is, all of the other techniques can be applied at each level of detail within the hierarchy. A number of interesting problems (analogous to that faced by the "hierarchical plan repair" tactic) would have to be faced in integrating their application across levels of the hierarchy.

Approaches for dealing with each of the types of relationships shown in Table 1 can probably be selected without major impact on the approaches selected for the other relationships. Thus, we can use Table 1 as a menu of possible tactics from which various collections can be constructed that make sense together in a problem solver.

Tactics that emphasize the clever selection of new paths to explore in the search space might be difficult to integrate with tactics that emphasize the learning and summarization of information derived from the portion of the search space already explored. However, the major payoff in integrating tactics might come from exactly this kind of combination. Developing a problem solver that uses both kinds of technique when appropriate will probably require the use of novel control strategies. The interesting new results from such an endeavor will derive from efforts to employ information developed by one tactic in the application of other tactics.

4.2. Flexible Control Structure

While the tactic of hierarchical planning speeds up the problem solving process greatly, it requires that a plan be fully developed to the finest detail before it is executed. In real-world environments where unexpected events occur frequently and the detailed outcome of particular actions may vary, creation of a complete plan before execution is not appropriate. Rather, the plan should be roughed out and its critical segments created in detail. The critical segments will certainly include those that must be executed first, but also may include other aspects of the plan at conceptual "choke points" where the details of a subplan may affect grosser aspects of other parts of the plan.

Hayes-Roth *et al*. [24] are developing a program based on a model of problem solving that would produce the kind of non-top-down behavior suggested here. Their model is based on a Hearsay-II architecture [25], but could probably be implemented using any methodology that allowed for explicit analysis of each of the four kinds of dependencies described in Section III above. Stefik [17] has implemented a system that, at least in principle, has the power to produce this kind of behavior. His system incorporates a flexible means of determining which planning decision to make next. His decisions are local ones; should global ones be incorporated as well, we might see a means of determining dynamically which tactic to employ in a given situation.

4.3. Planning for Parallel Execution

Problem solvers to date have been written with the idea that the plan is to be generated by a single processor and will ultimately be executed one step at a time. The development of cooperating problem solvers and algorithms for execution by multiple effectors will force a closer look at the structure of plans and the nature of the interactions between actions.

A solid start has been made in this area. Fikes, Hart, and Nilsson [26] proposed an algorithm for partitioning a plan among multiple effectors. Smith [27] developed a problem solver that distributes both the plan generation and execution tasks. The pseudo-reduction tactic creates plans that are partially ordered with respect to time, and are therefore amenable both to planning in parallel by multiple problem solvers and to execution in parallel by multiple effectors. Corkill [28] is adapting the NOAH [11] pseudo-reduction problem solver to use multiple processors in plan generation, and we at SRI are adapting it to plan for the use of multiple effectors.

4.4. Partial Goal Fulfillment

Problem solvers to date have been designed to fully satisfy their goals. As the problems we work with become more complex, and as we attempt to integrate problem solvers with execution routines to control real-world behavior, full goal satisfaction will be impossible. In particular, a system that deals with the real world may need to execute a partially satisfactory plan and see how the world reacts to it before being able to complete the next increment of planning. Thus, we must be able to plan for the partial satisfaction of a set of goals. This implies that a means must be found of prioritizing the goals and of recognizing when an adequate increment in the planning process has been achieved.

5. A PERSPECTIVE

The problems we have posed have a common theme to their solution: increased flexibility in the planning process. The metaphor of problem solving as exploration for information that was presented above suggests that the result of pursuing the problem solving process can lead to surprises as great as those encountered in plan execution. The plan execution components of problem solving systems have been forced to be quite flexible because of the surprises from the real world that they had to deal with. Therefore, especially as the tactics used in exploring for plans become more daring, the lessons that can be learned from plan execution can be extremely valuable for plan generation.

This view suggests a direction for future work in problem solving: it will become more like incremental plan repair. The means of storing and querying state description models will have to allow for efficient updating when the orders of actions are altered and when new actions are inserted in mid-plan. Planning at higher levels of abstraction will appear very similar to planning for information acquisition during plan execution.

Therefore, the best research strategy for advancing the state of the art in problem solving might well be to focus on *integrated* systems for plan generation, execution, and repair. By developing catalogues of plan execution tactics and plan repair tactics to accompany this catalogue of plan generation tactics, we can begin to deal with problems drawn from rich, interactive environments that have thus far been beyond us.

REFERENCES

1. A. Newell, "Heuristic Programming: Ill-Structured Problems," in J. Aronofsky (ed.) *Progress in Operations Research, Vol. III*, pp. 360-414 (Wiley, New York, 1969).

2. J. McCarthy and P. Hayes, "Some Philosophical Problems from the Standpoint of Artificial Intelligence," *Machine Intelligence 4*, B. Meltzer and D. Michie, eds., pp. 463-502 (American Elsevier, New York, 1969).

3. C. Green, "The Application of Theorem-Proving to Question-Answering Systems," Doctoral dissertation, Elec. Eng. Dept., Stanford Univ., Stanford, CA, June 1969. Also printed as Stanford Artificial Intelligence Project Memo AI-96 (June 1969).

4. R.F. Rulifson, J.A. Derksen and R. J. Waldinger "QA4: A Procedural Calculus for Intuitive Reasoning," Artificial Intelligence Center, Technical Note 73, Stanford Research Institute, Menlo Park, California (November 1972).

5. D.V. McDermott and G.J. Sussman, "The CONNIVER Reference Manual," MIT, Artificial Intelligence Lab., Memo No. 259, Cambridge, MA (May 1972).

6. D.G. Bobrow and B. Raphael, "New Programming Languages for Artificial

Intelligence," Computing Surveys, Vol. 6, No. 3 (Sept. 1974).

7. G.W. Ernst and A. Newell GPS: A Case Study in Generality and Problem Solving (Academic Press, New York, 1969).

8. R.E. Fikes and N.J. Nilsson, "STRIPS: A New Approach to the Application of Theorem Proving to Problem Solving," Artificial Intelligence, Vol. 2, No. 3-4, pp. 189-208 (Winter 1971).

9. L. Siklossy and J. Dreussi, "An Efficient Robot Planner Which Generates Its Own Procedures," Proc. Third International Joint Conference on Artificial Intelligence, Stanford, California, (August 1973).

10. E.D. Sacerdoti, "Planning in a Hierarchy of Abstraction Spaces," Artificial Intelligence, Vol. 5 No. 2, pp. 115-135 (Summer 1974).

11. E.D. Sacerdoti, A Structure for Plans and Behavior, (Elsevier North-Holland, New York, 1977).

12. I.P. Goldstein, "Understanding Simple Picture Programs," Tech. Note AI-TR-294, Artificial Intelligence Laboratory, MIT, Cambridge, MA (September 1974).

13. G.J. Sussman, A Computer Model of Skill Acquisition, (American Elsevier, New York, 1975).

14. G.J. Sussman, "The Virtuous Nature of Bugs," Proc. AISB Summer Conference, pp. 224-237 (July 1974).

15. M.L. Miller and I.P. Goldstein, "Structured Planning and Debugging," Proc. Fifth International Joint Conference on Artificial Intelligence, pp. 773-779, Cambridge, Massachusetts (August 1977).

16. D. Wilkins, "Using Plans in Chess," Proc. Sixth International Joint Conference on Artificial Intelligence, Tokyo, Japan (August 1979).

17. M.J. Stefik, "Orthogonal Planning with Constraints, Report on a Knowledge-Based Program that Plans Synthesis Experiments in Molecular Genetics," forthcoming dissertation, Computer Science Department, Stanford University (September 1979).

18. S.E. Fahlman, "A Planning System for Robot Construction Tasks," Artificial Intelligence, Vol. 5, No. 1, pp. 1-49 (Spring 1974).

19. J.C. Latombe, "Artificial Intelligence in Computer-Aided Design: the TROPIC System," in J.J. Allen (ed.), CAD Systems (Elsevier North-Holland, New York, 1977).

20. L. Siklossy and J. Roach, "Collaborative Problem-Solving between Optimistic and Pessimistic Problem Solvers," Proc. IFIP Congress 74, pp. 814-817 (North-Holland Publishing Company, 1974).

21. A. Tate, "Generating Project Networks," Proc. Fifth International Joint Conference on Artificial Intelligence, pp. 888-893, Cambridge, Massachusetts (August 1977).

22. R. Waldinger, "Achieving Several Goals Simultaneously," in E.W. Elcock and D. Michie (eds.) Machine Intelligence 8, pp. 94-136 (Ellis Horwood Limited, Chichester, England, 1977).

23. D.H.D. Warren, "WARPLAN: A System for Generating Plans," Department of Computational Logic, Memo No. 76, University of Edinburgh, Edinburgh (June 1974).

24. B. Hayes-Roth, F. Hayes-Roth, S. Rosenschein, and S. Cammarata, "Modeling Planning as an Incremental, Opportunistic Process," Proc. Sixth International Joint Conference on Artificial Intelligence, Tokyo, Japan (August 1979).

25. V.R. Lesser and L.D. Erman, "A Retrospective View of the Hearsay-II Architecture," Proc. Fifth International Joint Conference on Artificial Intelligence, pp. 790-800, Cambridge, Massachusetts (August 1977).

26. R.E. Fikes, P.E.Hart, and N.J. Nilsson, "Some New Directions in Robot Problem Solving," in B. Meltzer and D. Michie (eds.) Machine Intelligence 7, pp. 405-430 (Edinburgh Univ. Press, Edinburgh, 1972).

27. R.G. Smith, "A Framework for Distributed Problem Solving," Proc. Sixth International Joint Conference on Artificial Intelligence, Tokyo, Japan (August 1979).

28. D.D. Corkill, "Hierarchical Planning in a Distributed Environment," Proc. Sixth International Joint Conference on Artificial Intelligence, Tokyo, Japan (August 1979).

Artificial Intelligence Research Strategies in the Light of AI Models of Scientific Discovery

Herbert A. Simon
Department of Psychology
Carnegie-Mellon University
Pittsburgh, Pennsylvania 15213

Abstract and Introduction

Some recent artificial intelligence programs whose task is to simulate the processes of scientific discovery can be taken as models of the history and processes of discovery within the AI discipline itself. Consistently with these models, AI research relies basically on the methods of heuristic best-first search. Because of its necessarily vague and open goals, it works forward inductively (rather than backward in means-ends fashion), guided by a crude evaluation function that tests running programs to identify promising directions.

AI research is empirical and pragmatic, typically working with examples rather than theorems, and exemplifying the heuristic of learning by doing. In its essential reliance on weak methods and experiment instead of proof, it is adapted to the exploration of poorly structured task domains, showing considerable contrast in this respect to operations research or numerical analysis, which thrive best in domains possessing strong formal structure.

At scientific meetings it is customary to schedule, in addition to papers reporting specific pieces of research, "addresses," "keynote speeches," and the like, which may be described as meta-papers. The task of meta-papers is not to report research but to interpret the past and to peer into the future of the discipline. This is such a meta-paper. Presumably you expect me to say where artificial intelligence has been and where it is going.

Clearly, this is not a task for human intelligence. Human beings are notoriously incapable of reviewing history -- especially history in which they have participated -- without rationalizing outrageously to make the past conform to their picture of the present. And human forecasts of the future almost always reveal much more about the forecasters' hopes, fears, desires and dreads than they do about the shape of the world to come.

Early in the history of AI, in 1957, Allen Newell and I made some predictions that became rather notorious (Simon & Newell, 1958). Skeptics and opponents of AI used them as evidence of the recklessness and irresponsibility of the advocates of AI. (Optimistic forecasts seem to attract such charges much more often than do doomsday forecasts.)

Of course our forecasts were neither reckless nor irresponsible. As we said at the time, they represented our attempt to define in concrete terms the nature of the revolution in human affairs that was going to be produced by computers in general and artificial intelligence in particular. As scientists privileged to witness the early stages of a momentous development, we felt a responsibility to interpret that development to laymen, and the predictions were our interpretation. Nor was our forecasting seriously inaccurate, if one allows a time-stretch factor of two or three -- a not unreasonable margin of inaccuracy in such crystal-ball ventures.

I cite this little piece of history not to defend my record as either a seer or a historian, but as empirical evidence for my doubts, expressed earlier, that either foresight or hindsight are fit tasks for human intelligence. Such doubts undermine the very foundations of meta-papers, including this one.

If human intelligence is unequal to the needs of history and prophecy, perhaps we should call on artificial intelligence. Perhaps we should ask what AI has to say about the processes of discovery. After all, we do have, today, a number of artificial intelligence programs that are capable of making discoveries of one kind or another -- I have in mind particularly Doug Lenat's AM program, and Pat Langley's BACON. Perhaps these programs can tell us more about the research process than human beings can.

An AI program that makes genuine discoveries, or one that solves difficult problems, provides us with a theory of the discovery process, indeed, a theory in the most concrete and explicit form that is conceivable. Since these programs reveal to us some of the essential requisites and structure of the discovery process, we can use them to illuminate the history of discovery in the domain of artificial intelligence itself, and to provide some insight into the ways in which we can best proceed in future research and development aimed at new discoveries in that field.

This is the path I propose to pursue in this paper. First, I will summarize what seem to me some of the salient characteristics of successful artificial intelligence problem-solving systems, especially those whose basic task is to make discoveries. Next, I will ask whether this list of program characteristics suggests why the process of discovery in the AI field itself has taken the particular course that it has. Finally, I will turn to the future, and ask what lessons we might learn from this experience in our continuing efforts to extend the boundaries of AI, particularly in the directions of greater capabilities for discovery and for solving ill-structured problems. If this route seems somewhat circular -- AI illuminating itself -- I remind you that circles may be either vicious or virtuous, and I will argue that this is one of the virtuous kind.

I will not try to cover every aspect of AI, and will undoubtedly overemphasize problem-solving and heuristic search at the expense of such areas as visual pattern recognition. This lapse will be the less serious to the extent that the techniques of heuristic search are today invading the domain of pattern recognition, bringing about a greater degree of unity in outlook throughout the whole field of artificial intelligence. So I will take, as Allen Newell and I did in our Turing Lecture, heuristic search as the central paradigm for artificial intelligence (Newell & Simon, 1976).

1. AI Programs as Theories of Discovery

By a discovery program I mean a computer program whose output is not inferable in any obvious way from its input. The phrase, "in any obvious way," is essential to the definition, since we know that a program does exactly what we program it to do -- which is usually not at all the same as doing what we supposed we had programmed it to do.

2. The Nature of Discovery

Novelty, in computers as in human beings, lies in the eye of the beholder. The result is novel if it was not expected from the outset. But even this definition is ambiguous. As the numerous documented cases of independent invention attest, a discovery may be novel to the discoverer but not to the whole society, for others may already have found it. However, to produce a novelty a second time, without knowledge that it has already been discovered by others, presumably requires the same kinds of cognitive processes as were required to produce it the first time. Anything we can learn by examining the program of the original discoverer we should be able to learn also by examining the program of the reinventer.[1]

It is probably true today that within any one hour period some computer program somewhere in the world has followed a path never before traversed, to produce a novel successful result. This must occur for example, more than once in almost every game played by a hobbyist's minicomputer chess program, since chess games rarely fully repeat others that have been played in the world. However, we generally do not apply the term "discovery" to every novelty of this kind, however rational or adaptive the output may be. We require, in addition, that the novelty be in some sense remarkable or socially valuable. In particular, and borrowing language from the patent law, to be an invention, a novelty must not be "obvious to a person skilled in the art." While a minicomputer playing Class D chess discovers many novel solutions to its problems, these solutions would presumably be discovered easily by strong players, hence would not qualify as inventions in the legal sense.

Even today, after a quarter century of AI efforts, it is hard to point to fully convincing examples of discoveries by artificial intelligence programs that satisfy this stricter definition, of being neither rediscoveries nor obvious to one skilled in the art. If pressed on this point, I might want to defend certain products of chess programs, programs for musical composition and visual design, and theorem-proving programs as meeting the stricter requirements of invention, but such a defense would take me away from my main concern here.

I will draw my examples of discovery from computer programs that have mainly rediscovered what was already known, but whose discoveries are hardly trivial, and would indeed have been adjudged important if they had been genuinely new. I have in mind such examples as the discovery by Lenat's AM program of the concept of prime number and its conjecturing of the fundamental theorem of arithmetic -- that every positive integer can be represented uniquely as a product of powers of primes (Lenat, 1977). Examples of a slightly different kind are BACON's induction from empirical data of Kepler's Third Law, Ohm's Law, and the Laws of Boyle and Charles (Langley, forthcoming).

Before we take the programs that found these concepts and laws as exhibiting the essential processes for discovery, we must satisfy ourselves on one point: that the human programmers did not, in some explicit or implicit way, embed the results at the outset in the programs and their inputs. Since we have already agreed that the outputs of programs are determined by the programs (and data), what can we mean by this requirement? Simply that the derivation of the outputs from program and data be sufficiently non-obvious. This is, of course, the same criterion we apply to a mathematical theorem to determine whether it is "deep"; and it is the same as the legal requirement for invention, quoted above.

This is not to say that it is a precise criterion, statable in a formal way. The only way I know to decide whether AM or BACON, or any other program purporting to have powers of discovery (but exhibiting those powers through rediscovery) genuinely possesses such capabilities is to search the code carefully for hideaways where the conclusions may be concealed in the premises. The severity of the test will depend on how thoroughly the search is made and how strict a criterion of obviousness is applied. Since I know of no way at the present time to quantify either of these two dimensions of the test, we must still depend (as we do in evaluating the merit of scientific discoveries) on informal judgement.

From close familiarity with the AM and BACON programs, I am satisfied that these two programs pass any reasonable tests of this kind. Let me, then, comment on the structure of the programs -- on the sources of their powers of discovery. For the sake of those of you who are not acquainted with AM or BACON, I will first state briefly what each program does. As already noted, a fuller description of AM, by Doug Lenat, will be found in the Proceedings of the Fifth IJCAI (1977), and of BACON, by Pat Langley, in the Proceedings of this conference.

Lenat's AM Program AM is a system that discovers new concepts and that conjectures new relations among them. Its input consists of an initial stock of concepts (in one application, the basic notions of set theory), goals and criteria (the goal of discovering new concepts and possible relations among concepts, and criteria for evaluating the worth or interest of concepts), and heuristics for searching for new concepts. Among the criteria for judging if a concept is interesting is how closely it is related to other interesting concepts, and whether examples of it can be constructed -- not too easily, but with not too much difficulty. The search heuristics include the advice to construct examples, to

[1] This claim requires some qualifications. The reinventer may possess knowledge -- not the invention itself, but knowledge relevant to it -- that was not available to the original inventor, but which makes the job easier the second time. Later, I will have more to say on this point as it applies specifically to AI.

pay particular attention to borderline examples, to particularize when examples are found too easily, to generalize when they are hard to find. This is the kind of initial information available to AM -- initial concepts, goals and criteria, and search heuristics.

The control structure of AM guides it in a best-first search; the criteria of concept worth determine which of the concepts already attained should be the starting point for the next quantum of search. On its most celebrated run, starting with the concepts of set theory, AM discovered -- among other things -- the integers, the arithmetic operations of addition, subtraction, multiplication and division, the concept of prime number, and, as I mentioned earlier, the prime number representation theorem. When it began concerning itself with numbers possessing maximal (instead of minimal) numbers of prime factors, Lenat thought it had entered on truly new ground, only to find that this territory had earlier been explored by the self-taught Indian mathematician, Srinivasa Ramanujan. Therefore, AM must be evaluated as a rediscoverer, rather than a discoverer of new mathematical truths.

Langley's BACON Program BACON is a program that induces general laws from empirical data. Given sets of observations on two or more variables, BACON searches for functional relations among the variables. Again, it carries out a form of best-first search, in which a criterion of "simple things before complex" guides what to try next.

BACON's search is highly selective; it does not try all possibilities. It arranges the observations monotonically according to the values of one of the variables. Then it determines whether the values of some other variables follow the same (or the inverse) ordering. Picking one of these other variables, it searches for an invariant by considering the ratio (resp., product) of this variable with the original one. If the ratio (product) is not constant, it is introduced as a new variable, and the process continues. Thus, the newly defined variables in BACON correspond to the new concepts in AM, and the process is driven by a search for invariants.

It is easy to see how BACON, discovering that the product of electrical current by resistance in an electrical circuit was constant, would be led to Ohm's Law. The case of Kepler's Third Law requires BACON to generate, successively, ratios of powers of the radii of the planets orbits to powers of their periods of revolution, arriving at the invariant, D^3/P^2, after a search of a small number of possibilities.

I have mentioned only a few of the salient features of BACON. The system has at least crude means for ignoring noise as data, and a number of other interesting features, but I will leave their fuller description to the program's author. What is interesting for our purposes is that a program, equipped and organized as I have described, detects regularities in data sufficiently perceptively to rediscover important scientific laws.

AM and BACON use similar schemes of memory organization. The ability to apply the same basic processes to given information and to newly generated concepts or variables, respectively, hence to operate recursively, is guaranteed by using a homogeneous format for the storage of all data. Though the details of the data structures are different for the two programs, both use schemas -- structures of property lists -- to describe the objects with which they deal or which they generate. The main element of rigidity in their memory organizations is that the specific properties that may occur in these schemas -- the "slots" -- are specified in advance and known to the programs.

Discovery Mechanisms The theory of discovery that emerges from an examination of how these programs work contains little that should surprise us -- unless we have been seduced by the often-repeated myth that discovery processes, being "creative," somehow stand apart from the other actions of the human mind. In AM and BACON we see discoveries being produced by precisely the same kinds of symbolic processes that account for the efficacy of other AI problem-solving programs: theorem provers, chess players, puzzle solvers, diagnosis systems. A space of possible concepts and relations (AM), or of possible invariants (BACON) is searched in a highly selective, best-first manner. The search mainly works forward inductively from the given concepts or data.

The discovery programs are distinguished from most other problem-solving systems in the "vagueness" of the tasks presented to them and of the heuristic criteria that guide the search and account for its selectivity. Because the goals are very general ("find an interesting concept or relations, "find an invariant"), the use of means-ends analysis to work backward from a desired result is not very common. By and large, the programs work forward inductively from the givens of the problem and from the new concepts and variables generated from these givens.

Both programs work at a very concrete level. AM makes a major use of examples, which it is capable of generating, in searching for new concepts. BACON works with numerical data. If we observed human scientists working in the manner of these programs, we would regard them as very pragmatic. We are reminded of Faraday's notebooks, in which he recorded, day after day, the experiments that were suggested to a curious mind by the findings of the previous day's experiment. Or, we think of Mendeleev arranging and rearranging his lists of the elements until their periodic structure begins to emerge from his worksheets.

Both programs discover, they do not prove. Their task is to find regularity and pattern in nature, not to demonstrate the necessity of that pattern. Although their heuristics appear very general and weak -- they do not rely at all on semantic information about the task domain that is being explored -- they accomplish the search tasks with a remarkably small amount of trial and error. In the best tradition of heuristic schemes, they operate without any guarantees that they will succeed, but they do succeed in finding many interesting results. We would not even know how to define completeness for programs given these kinds of ill-defined tasks.

Because the tasks addresssed by these systems are poorly defined, we do not have good measures of how powerful they are. Of course, we can make our personal evaluations of the quality of their discoveries -- of how impressed we are that AM finds the prime number factorization theorem, or that BACON readily induces Ohm's Law from the data. But we do not have the precision of comparison with human performance that a chess program gives us, or a program for medical diagnosis. The difficulty of evaluating them is compounded by the absence of a yardstick for measuring the knowledge with which they are endowed at the outset, or that is embedded in the program structures. We do not know whether BACON had the same starting point as Ohm, or whether one of them was faced with an essentially simpler problem of induction than the other. Of course the same uncertainties surround all of our attempts to evaluate human discovery also. AM and BACON pose no new methodological puzzles in this respect.

How does the behavior of these programs compare with the behavior of the human scientists who have labored in the vineyards of artificial intelligence during the past 25 years? Do AM and BACON provide a true, if rough and approximate, description of that discovery effort? And what of the future of AI? Can these discovery programs help us in either prediction or strategy? Let me turn first to the history.

3. The Discovery Process in AI

Artificial intelligence has sometimes been criticized as being atheoretical, and consequently as having no solid substance. Of course, the premise might be true but the consequent false, unless we believe that all truth takes the form of rigorously proved theorems. Artificial intelligence has certainly been short of theorems, and in a field as densely populated with mathematicians and former mathematicians as is computer science, its nakedness in this respect has not gone unnoticed.

It may be objected that I am neglecting the A* algorithm, or the various interesting properties of Alpha-Beta search, or even the theorems that Kadane and I have proved about optimal evaluation functions for best-first all-or-none search (Simon & Kadance, 1975). But these isolated examples, even if we add to them all the others known to us, do not constitute a theory of artificial intelligence. At best, they provide us with some islands of theory, separated by wide expanses of an atheoretical ocean. Moreoever, the heuristics of best-first search implied by these examples were known empirically and used in running AI programs for many years before the mathematics was developed (Newell & Simon, 1956).[1].

AI as Empirical Inquiry I am afraid that we must resign ourselves to the fact (or celebrate it, depending on our taste in science) that artificial intelligence has not been a branch of mathematics, but rather a field of inductive, empirical inquiry. The main strategy of investigation has been to propose tasks requiring intelligence for their performance, to write programs for handling those tasks, and to test the efficacy and efficiency of the programs by giving them a sample of tasks drawn from the domain in question. Nearly everything we have learned about artificial intelligence over the past 25 years (and much of what we have learned about human intelligence as well), has been found by following this experimental strategy. And the body of knowledge that exists in AI today is better described as a store of experimental data and inferences drawn from them than as a collection of mathematical truths.

But the process I am describing corresponds closely to the kind of process that is carried out by AM and BACON. We have seen that both programs are inductive and experimental -- even if the product of the former's efforts are mathematical constructs and conjectures, and of the latter's, postulated functional relations among numerical variables. Neither AM nor BACON proves anything. If they produce conviction, it is the conviction of the empirical scientist, relying on some postulate of the uniformity of nature, rather than the conviction of the mathematician, relying on the certainty of the laws of logic.

Inferring Principles From Programs The problem-solving tasks that AI research has addressed during the past 25 years, like the tasks addressed by AM and BACON, seem largely fortuitous -- targets of opportunity: theorem- proving in logic and group theory, the Eights Puzzle and Missionaries & Cannibals, chess, Euclidean geometry, medical diagnosis, mass spectrogram analysis, speech recognition, parsing natural language, to mention a few. An assiduous historian could no doubt track down the reasons why each of these domains was attempted, but those reasons would not add up to a grand strategy for artificial intelligence. Probably the choice was neither much more nor much less considered than the choice of sweet peas and fruit flies as favored organisms for genetic research.

The true comparison is between these tasks, on the one hand, and the examples generated by AM or the data sets of BACON, on the other. The central inductive problem for AI has been to generalize from the performance of programs dedicated to individual tasks some principles (empirical principles, not necessarily theorems) about the mechansims required for intelligent problem-solving behavior. How successfully this problem has been solved can be judged by assessing how far new AI programs make use of the heuristics and structural principles of the programs already in existence, and by examining the extent to which AI textbooks are organized in terms of general principles.

On both scores there is evidence of steady progress in AI. In the first decade or two, one can find a number of reinventions of general principles by investigators who were exploring different task domains (or even, occasionally, the same task domain). For example, best-first search apparently appeared intially, as already noted, as a component of one version of The Logic Theory Machine, disappeared in early versions of GPS, which tended to be oriented towared depth-first search, and reappeared in the MATER chess combinations program (Baylor & Simon, 1966). As another example, schemas appear in programs as early as 1956, but were subsequently reinvented and rechristened "templates" or "frames" (Minsky, 1975; and Simon, 1972). During the past five or ten years, however, the main structural components of AI programs have been identified, and a reasonably consistent vocabulary adopted for referring to them.

This gradual progress toward awareness of general principles is reflected by the textbooks in the field. Early textbooks were little more than collections of

[1] The Logic Theory Machine, in 1956, already incorporated best-first heuristic search, while the Alpha-Beta heuristic is to be found in chess programs as early as 1958.

examples of more or less successful problem-solving programs. Beginning with Nilsson's book, Problem-solving Methods in Artificial Intelligence (Nilsson, 1971), some general threads of organization began to appear, and specific programs were not merely described, but were analyzed for their contributions to these threads. With all this progress, the contemporary books still reflect the pragmatic and empirical foundations of the field, and resemble textbooks in geology more than they resemble treatises in analytical mechanics.

Departures from the Discovery Model There is one respect in which the history of AI research departs significantly from the trace of a computer discovery program, for in the AI world, many lines of inquiry can be pursued simultaneously -- provided that the discipline is sufficiently well populated by researchers, and that the researchers are not too much driven by fads. Hence, when we try to interpret the annals as exemplifying best-first search, we must use that term loosely. To be sure, there was a period of several years during which attempts at theorem- proving nearly dominated AI research, and a more recent period when much of the inquiry was focused on problem-solving in knowledge-rich domains. When a topic like one of these seems to be progressing rapidly, it attracts much of the field's research effort, as would be true of a best-first search system. But other lines of investigation are never wholly dormant.

What has happened when the AI research strategy has departed from the discovery model? The most instructive examples are the cases where pragmatism was sacrificed to the demand for more theory and formal development. One such case is theorem-proving, where mathematical tastes have exercised greater influence than in most other AI task domains.

From the time of Hao Wang's early and successful program for proving theorems in the propositional calculus (Wang, 1960), most theorem-proving efforts have placed great emphasis on the completeness of their programs and upon employing elegant proof methods (e.g., natural deduction and resolution) from symbolic logic. Since completeness is most easily proved for breadth-first programs that do not use pragmatically constructed selective heuristics, the mainstream of research eschewed best-first search and heuristics that lacked guarantees of completeness.

When heuristics could be used that did not threaten completeness (e.g., set of support), they were adopted readily, but heuristics possessing this guarantee were not in sufficiently long supply to prevent the exponential explosion of search trees. The net result has been a general disillusionment with the progress of theorem-proving research, and a diversion of effort to other task domains within AI. Some exceptions can be found, of course. For example, in the impressive work of Bledsoe and his associates, we see exhibited a much more pragmatic attitude towards heuristics than has been characteristic of theorem-proving research in general (Bledsoe, 1977).

AI as a Residual Domain Some years ago, Allen Newell described artificial intelligence as the domain of weak methods, a description that still seems to hold (Newell, 1969). This is not because anyone prefers weak methods to strong. No one would solve a problem by heuristic search if he thought that the simplex algorithm of linear programming would do the job. But strong methods apply only in domains that have sufficiently rich and smooth structure to support them. The simplex method works only in a problem space that is convex, bounded by linear inequalities, and with a linear criterion function to be maximized. The method exploits the mathematical structure of the space to home in on solutions in a relatively direct and straightforward fashion.

AM, and to a lesser extent BACON, are designed to work in spaces that have little regular structure, or which have structure that is intiailly unknown to the program. They use the weak methods of heuristic search for the same reason that artificial intelligence has used those methods -- because not enough was known, in advance, of the shape of the problem space for stronger methods to be used.

Similarly, attempts to derive measures of computational complexity for typical AI domains have not yet yielded much of a mathematical harvest. Proofs about the dependence of amount of computation, in the worst or average cases, upon problem size depend on knowledge of structural features of the problem domain, and where such structural features are unknown or absent it becomes difficult to obtain strong mathematical results.

Necessity should not be redefined as a virtue. Yet, it makes some sense to define artificial intelligence as a residual domain -- the domain in which it has not yet been possible to substitute powerful special-purpose techniques for weak methods. At any time that such techniques are discovered for a particular subset of problems, those problems are removed from the jurisdiction of AI to that of operations research or numerical analysis. But human intelligence, applied, for instance to the discovery of new knowledge, is not limited to working in orderly domains that have strong structure, and it is the task of AI to show how intelligence works, and even to complement its working, in less well structured domains.

4. From Past to Future

If we take AM and BACON as our models of the discovery process, then we should despair of making exact forecasts of where artificial intelligence research is likely to go in the next few years. For the discovery process illustrated by those programs is myopic, its best-first search responding to intimations of opportunity. Consequently, targets will continue to shift, as they have shifted in the past, to those task domains that exhibit from time to time, most promise of movement.

Allocation of Effort One important difference has already been noted between a discovery process programmed for a serial digital computer and the social discovery process of the AI community. That community is a parallel, rather than a serial, machine. With the increase in manpower that has been attracted to the field in the past five years, the prospects are now brighter than they were earlier for maintaining sustained research activity in a number of AI domains at the same time. At the present time, for example, a more or less continuous effort of several research groups is being devoted to chess programs, to natural language understanding, to visual pattern recognition, to medical diagnosis, and to various kinds of information retrieval tasks.

The fact that a computing system has modest parallel capacity does not, however, invalidate the main features of the best-first search model. The parallel capacity is still highly limited, and does not grow exponentaillly (at least not for long), as it would have to in order to avoid decisions about what part of the tree to search next. The effort allocation problem for a parallel, but not exponentially growing, system is merely a little less poignant than the problem for a strictly serial system. At any given moment, several branches that are most promising for exploration have to be chosen, instead of a single branch. Hence, with limits of both manpower and funding in AI, increased activity in some directions means decreased activity in others.

For example, research on speech recognition appears to have receded again to a relatively low level of activity with the termination of the special ARPA funding, as has AI research on robotry. (I will have a bit more to say about robotry research later, but will simply observe now that the current boom in industrial robotry is only tenuously connected with the main stream of AI research, and makes only limited use of AI methods.) Automatic programming has never reached the level of attention that its potential importance and centrality to AI would seem to justify. Theorem- proving -- and problem-solving in general -- appear to be attracting relatively little effort currently.

Judged in terms of the contents of the Proceedings of IJCAI5 (I don't have the corresponding numbers for the current conference), natural language is attracting the most attention in AI research, followed closely by vision and the representation and acquisition of knowledge. These three areas together accounted for about 60% of all the papers.

The Evaluation function From the shifts in allocation of research effort, we can draw some conclusions about the evaluation function that is used to guide the best-first search. But we must note carefully whose evaluation function it is. To those of us who have been working in AI, it is obvious that the shifts in emphasis among speech recognition, robotry, and automatic programming (these especially, but not exclusively) have been determined to a much greater degree by the judgments of funding agencies as to what kinds of work were more likely to lead promptly to practical application, than by the judgments of the researchers as to what lines of inquiry held the greatest promise for advancing fundamental knowledge.

In part, this vulnerability of the research agenda to genuine or imagined priorities for applications is the price that AI pays for being a "big science" field, dependent for its progress on the availabity of expensive computing equipment. But some other big science fields -- for example, radio astronomy -- have attained considerable freedom in selecting their research goals, and we can only hope that AI can gradually acquire similar autonomy as the field becomes better established and the fundamental character of the phenomena it studies more widely understood.

If I were to contrast my own personal evaluation function with the function inferred from the actual present allocation of effort, I would be inclined to give considerably more attention to the domains of robotry (that is, the AI aspects of robotry) and automatic programming than these areas are now receiving. Later, I will have a few words to say about the reasons for my preferences.

Common Themes One factor that mitigates the possible damage done by the whims of funding agencies and the fads of AI research itself, is that there is a considerable overlap in the basic problems encountered, and in the basic AI mechanisms required to solve those problems in all the task domains where AI research is carried on. Best-first search, for example, is á recurring theme, regardless of whether we are concerned with theorem-proving, chess playing, or robot planning. Similar problems of data representation, organization, and access must be faced in almost all task domains. Many tasks call for natural language capabilities of wider or narrower extent. The context-dependence of knowledge acquired through search, and the extrapolation of knowledge from one context to another is a recurrent theme. Because of these commonalities, progress in our understanding of any new task is likely to contribute substantially to progress for other, temporarily dormant tasks.

But these benefits of commonality will be realized only if we pay explicit attention to the transfer problem. The existence of multiple parallel research efforts in different tasks domains increases the danger that the same principles and mechanisms will be reinvented, perhaps more than once, by specialized investigators who are unaware of work going on outside their own narrow areas. As the AI research field grows and more investigators enter it, specialization will undoubtedly grow also (it has already), and the dangers of duplication will increase correspondingly.

Perhaps the most important preventive step against reinventing wheels is to define research goals not simply in terms of constructing programs that will perform specific tasks well, but in terms of using programs as examples and test beds for generating and illuminating general principles. Computer science has its roots in both scientific and engineering traditions. For the engineer -- at least the nonacademic engineer -- the device is the thing; the proof of his pudding is in how well the system he has designed works. For the computer scientist, the device (the program) is not an end in itself, but a means for testing whether particular methods and principles, incorporated in the device, perform the functions for which they are intended. Journal referees and reviewers of funding proposals can contribute much to the development of AI by insisting on these broader goal specifications for AI research projects.

There would also appear to be room in AI research for more generalists and theorists who would devote their attention to extracting general principles by comparative analysis of programs in different task domains. Of course such activity goes on at the present time, but perhaps it would be encouraged further if we did not restrict the term "theory" to formal, mathematical developments.

It might appear that I have fallen into a contradiction. Using AM and BACON as my models of discovery programs, I pointed out the futility of trying to predict the course of discovery. Now, only a few paragraphs later, I am expressing my views about the allocation of effort. There is, in fact, no contradiction. In best-first search, choosing an evaluation function and using it to guide the allocation of effort is unavoidable. This does not mean that one can predict where the search will lead; but a well-choosen evaluation function can indicate the most productive points at which it can start. Let me offer a few illustrations.

Research on Robots One criterion of a promising task domain is that successful AI programs in the domain will rely on important components of intelligence that have not been much explored in other research. Robotry is a promising domain, because it takes us away from planning actions in simple worlds of the imagination -- where the consequences of our actions can be deduced precisely -- into planning actions in complex real worlds, where we must be prepared to readjust our estimates of the state of the world repeatedly as our actions fall short of or beside our intentions.

Methods for matching the predicted to the actual state of the world, and for correcting the former to reflect the latter, are fundamental to the success of systems that can survive in complex environments and particularly in environments where there is much uncertainty.

When I refer to robotry research, I have in mind something rather different from the development of industrial robots that is now burgeoning in a number of countries. Most industrial robots are being designed to carry out fairly restricted ranges of tasks in factory environments that are carefully tailored to the robots. Moreover, AI techniques have not played a prominent role in these developments, most of which come out of the tradition of engineering control theory.

In this application, the residual status of AI methods is again apparent. If an environment can be sufficiently smoothed and simplified, then the methods of servomechanism and control theory may provide the best means for designing flexible devices to operate in that environment. AI methods are likely to have a comparative advantage in rough and complex environments that have to be dealt with in their raw, natural form. For this reason, research on vehicles capable of locomoting autonomously on remote planets is probably more relevant to basic issues in artificial intelligence than is research on industrial robots that are to operate in factory environments. The former kinds of systems will have to be flexibly intelligent to a much higher degree than the latter.

However, I do not want to overstate the case. As the development of industrial robots goes forward, there is a need for strong capabilities in visual pattern recognition, a domain in which artificial intelligence concepts are likely to play a role of increasing prominence. The point of my example is that we don't simply want to seize on robotry as a task domain, but want to ask what aspects of robotry call especially for AI approaches, and what light is likely to be cast on general AI concerns by research focused on those aspects.

Automatic Programming A second domain I singled out as promising for AI research today is automatic programming. Here again, the general value of the research for advancing our basic understanding of artificial intelligence depends on how the problem is defined. I have especially in mind systems that would take ill-structured and incomplete descriptions of a desired program (of the sort we would give as instructions to a human programmer), and transfer them into executable code. Automatic programming, so defined, is an excellent domain in which to experiment with the automatic design of problem representations -- a problem we must address if we are to extend AI further into ill-structured domains.

An additional reason why automatic programming tasks deserve high priority on the research agenda is that they offer excellent opportunities for work on natural language and knowledge representation. Research in the latter two fields has sometimes suffered from vagueness in the specification of the task. To study natural language effectively we must study particular kinds of situations in which information and meanings have to be communicated for a definite purpose. The automatic programming task defines that purpose (as does also the closely related task of understanding problem instructions written in natural language). By the same token, we are apt to learn most effectively about the problems of knowledge representation in the context of a specific task domain like automatic programming.

If we accept necessity as the mother of invention, we must remember that another parent is needed too. Automatic programming deserves a high rating for its research potential only if there is reason to believe it can be done -- that our basic knowledge has reached the point where it is reasonable to talk about automatic design of task representation. I would argue that both the progress -- modest though it be -- that has already been made in automatic programming, and the progress in the design of representations for other domains provide favorable indications that we are ready for the next step (Hayes & Simon, 1974).

Local and Global Knowledge A problem that has plagued heuristic search systems from the beginning is that information gathered at one node in a search through a problem space is not generally usable by the system to guide its search in other parts of the space. The same information may have to be generated again and again at different nodes.

Partly, this is a problem of information organization, solvable through such devices as blackboard schemes (Lesser & Erman, 1977). In such schemes, information is not stored in association with the nodes at which it is generated, but is placed in a common space where it becomes permanently available to all parts of the program, and at all times during the exploration of the problem space.

But there is a deeper problem with making information more broadly available: the information may be true only in a local context. Then the boundaries of this context must be determined and associated with the information before it can be exported safely. There is still not much theory (or experience) in the AI literature as to how this is to be done, but some progress has been made toward solving the problem in connection with research on speech recognition programs and chess programs, both of which are promising environments in which to pursue this issue (Lesser & Erman, 1977; Perdue & Berliner, 1977).

Learning Systems In AI a great deal more progress has been made in constructing performance programs than in designing programs that learn. In the early history of artificial intelligence, the topic of self-organizing systems was pursued vigorously but, as it turned out, not particularly successfully. As the best-first search progressed, the nodes associated with this topic received low evaluations, and were gradually abandoned.

Yet the topic of learning in AI is not at all dead; rather it has been redefined. In early efforts, great importance was attached to starting systems off at or near ground level. The guarantee that they were learning was that they started off knowing almot nothing. Today, we characterize learning in a somewhat different way; we look for adaptive change, and we look for that change to be recursive and cumulative.

In the broadest sense, any program is a learning program that gradully changes over time so that on each new encounter with a particular kind of task it behaves in a more appropriate way. In neither human beings nor computers should we expect to find just a very limited number of processes called "learning processes," for there generally are a multitude of ways in which a complex system can modify itself adaptively.

Learning will generally be incremental. That is, each new step in adaptaation will itself improve the capacity for further adaptation. A problem-solving system becomes a learning system whenever it is designed so that problem solutions can be stored and used to contribute to subsequent problem-solving. Clearly, discovery programs like AM and BACON are learning programs, since their explicit task is to produce novel outputs and to use those outputs recursively.

With this broader definition of learning, a whole spectrum of AI systems qualify as learning systems. Learning can connote all degrees of pasivity or activity of the learner. Thus, at one extreme, we have interactive systems aimed at making it easier for the programmer to add new knowledge to an information structure, where the program itself is a wholly passive learner. At the other extreme, we have adaptive production systems that are able to extract information from their experiences, and use the information to improve themselves even without explicit instruction from outside. Most systems that learn from experience are aided, of course, if the experience is organized for them in a favorable way -- in a succession of carefully graded lessons. It is the skill of a good teacher to present experience in this way.

One might ask whether it is time to revive learning as a major explicit goal of AI research. Since learning pervades almost all aspects of intelligent performance, the right search strategy is probably to incorpooate learning goals in our performance systems. That seems to be a quite natural thing to do in building systems for visual pattern recognition, for example, for automatic programming, or for understanding natural language instructions.

But there are apprentices in the world as well as journeyman; and presumably the apprentice's first concern in his learning rather that his performance. So perhaps there is room, on the tree of AI research, for an active branch that works with tasks in which learning and adaptation are the central concerns. Considering the recent rapid progress that has been made in constructing adaptive production systems, good progress can be anticipated along that branch, and I would assign it a rather favorable evaluation. But the fact that some investigators specialize in learning processes should not deter the rest of us from experimenting with learning components in our performance systems.

5. Conclusion

In this paper I have reviewed the AI community as if it were a medium-size slightly parallel processor searching its way in inductive, best-first fashion through the problem space of intelligent action. I have compared it with some of the existing AI programs that best characterize the discovery process. The comparison does not yield any great surprises, but perhaps provides some reassurance.

As a typical example of a discovery program, the AI community uses weak methods uder the guidance of a somewhat imprecise evaluation function and vague ultimate goals. It tries to discover the mechanisms that enable a system like the human mind to behave purposefully, adaptively, and sometimes even effectively over a wide range of difficult and ill-structured tasks.

The search is highly pragmatic, steered and redirected by concrete empirical evidence culled from experiments with programs operating in an accidentally determined collection of task environments. The output of the research is mostly encapsulated in heuristics, not yet formalized in coherent theories of broad scope. All is confusion and mild chaos, as it should be at an exciting frontier of fundamental scientific inquiry. Although only a quarter of a century old, the search has already yielded a solid body of empirical knowledge about the nature of intelligence and the means of capturing it in programs.

6. References

Baylor, G.W., & Simon, H.A. A chess mating combinations program. AFIPS Conference Proceedings, 1966 Spring Joint Computer Conference, Boston, April 26-28, 1966, 28, 431-447. Washington, DC: Spartan Books.

Bledsoe, W.W. Non-resolution theorem proving. Artificial Intelligence, 1977, 9 (1), 1-35.

Hayes, J.R., & Simon, H.A. Understanding written problem instructions. In L.W. Gregg (Ed.), Knowledge and cognition. Potomac, MD: Lawrence Erlbaum Associates, 1974.

Langley, P. Rediscovering physics with BACON.3. Proceedings of the 6th International Joint Conference on Artificial Intelligence, forthcoming.

Lenat, D.B. The ubiwuity of discovery. Proceedings of the 5th International Joint Conference on Artificial Intelligence, 1977, 1, 1093-1105.

Lesser, V.R., & Erman, L.D. A retrospective view of the HEARSAY-II architecture. Proceedings of the 5th International Joint Conference on Artificial Intelligence, 1977, 2, 790-800.

Minsky, M. A framework for representing knowledge. In P.H. Winston (Ed.), The psychology of computer vision. NY: McGraw-Hill, 1975.

Newell, A. Heuristic programming: Ill-structured problems. In J. Aronofsky (Ed.), Progress in operations research, Vol. III. NY: Wiley, 1969.

Newell, A., & Simon, H.A. Computer science as empirical inquiry: Symbols and search. Communications of the ACM, 1976, 19, 111-126.

Newell, A., & Simon, H.A. The logic theory machine. IRE Transactions on Information Theory, Vol. IT-2, No. 3, Sept. 1956.

Nilsson, N.J. Problem-solving methods in artificial intelligence. NY: McGraw-Hill, 1971.

Simon, H.A. Artificial intelligence systems that understand. Proceedings of the 5th International Joint Conference on Artificial Intelligence, 1977, 2, 1059-1073.

Simon, H.A. The heuristic compiler. In H.A. Simon & L. Siklossy (Ed.), Representation and meaning: Experiments with information processing systems. Englewood Cliffs, NJ: Prentice-Hall, 1972.

Simon, H.A., & Kadane, J.B. Optimal problem-solving search: All-or-none solutions. Artificial Intelligence, 1975, 6, 235-248.

Simon, H.A., & Newell, A. Heuristic problem solving: The next advance in operations research. Operations Research, 1958, 6, 1-10.

Wang, H. Toward mechanical mathematics. IBM Journal of Research and Development, January 1960, 2-22.

Skill of Intelligent Robot

Kunikatsu Takase
Electrotechnical Laboratory
Tokyo, Japan

ABSTRACT

This paper reviews the development of the intelligent robot and separates skills from high level intelligence. It demonstrates that skills can be represented as virtual mechanisms programmed in software. Virtual mechanisms are defined by controlling both motion and force of a robot arm in a task related cartesian coordinate system. By adding monitoring, a skillful robot system can be built. The skill of an intelligent robot is accumulated in the form of task - particular knowledge that is a specification of the mechanism.

1. INTRODUCTION

Various intelligent robots have been developed by combining computer decision making with mechanical mechanisms, especially with robot arms. In this field the efforts have been mainly directed to developing high level intelligence system such as for solving puzzles, interpreting drawings or recognizing three-dimensional objects. There has been little study of low level intelligence relating to skill or dexterity of a robot arm. In order to make the motion of a robot arm smoother and more adaptive, a series of studies - kinematics, trajectory calculation, sensory feedback of a robot arm - were undertaken in the Artificial Intelligence Project at Stanford University. But in general we are at the dawn of the study of the skill of robot arms.

The practical study of assembly automation which started as one of the applications of intelligent robots is developing as an independent area with remarkable results. Reliable assembly systems are being released one after another. Although those are comparatively special-purpose low intelligence systems, their skills are far more dexterious than those of intelligent robots. It seems the increased skill of the intelligent robot could be obtained only through the integration of task-particular knowledge that is normally obtained, for example, during the development of special purpose systems. The "Move" command in AL, for example, and its modification are not sufficient for specifying the dexterious actions of robot arms. "Composing virtual mechanisms by software" seems to be the best control structure for the purpose.

Recently the performance of arithmetic LSI has improved remarkably enabling us to carry out the exact calculation of dynamic models of a robot arm in the servo cycle, and to compose virtual mechanisms in software.

The author has been a visiting scientist of Electrical Engineering at Purdue University, West Lafayette, IN, since August 1978 until August 1979.

2. INTELLIGENT ROBOTS

In the beginning of 1970's several Hand-Eye systems had been developed at universities and research laboratories in the world. Those robotic systems consisted of a camera and arm with 6 degrees of freedom and computer. At Stanford University a robot which could successfully solve the "instant insanity" puzzle was developed [1]. In this puzzle four cubes with different colored faces must be stacked up so that no two similar color appear on any sides. A robot made at Hitachi could understand simple drawings and build block structures as specified in the drawings [2]. At the Electrotechnical Laboratory a robot was developed, which could insert a beam into a box with small clearance using visual feedback [3]. In these robotic system intelligence had been applied to recognizing a 3-dimensional pattern, understanding a drawing, or solving puzzles.

In order to realize computer control of an arm, several elements had been studied: arm design, servo system, transformation between joint coordinates and cartesian coordinates, computer interface, and robot operating system. Although a good deal of effort was devoted to the computer control of the arm, the arm only could perform "pick and place" operations, that is, to pick up an object, to transfer it and then to place it. Some attempts were made to make the a robot arm more dexterious, for example, by adding tactile sensors in order to grasp objects more dexteriously. None of those attempts was, however, successful in developing a reliable elements to be incorporated in the robotic system.

It was in the Assembly Automation Systems developed at Stanford University (later referred to as the AL System) that an intelligent robot was first able to act in the practical world, emerging from the stage of "play" in the block world [5,6,7]. Assembly processes, such as parts mating and inserting, required adaptive object handling capabilities found only in a human workers were demonstrated. These tasks could not be performed by conventional hard automation machines.

In many cases of low volume assembly production programmability was the key factor to enhance the utility of the assembly system. In the AL system much attention paid to the design of task description language. AL offered the programming structure in which a user could describe an assembly procedure in terms of multilevel commands ranging from the simple "move" command to task-level commands [4]. High-level assembly statements would be expanded into the sequence of move-level commands in a general manner.

In an assembly system robot arms have to be skillful enough to be able to carry out parts mating and other adaptive motions. In the AL system, precise motions were controlled, based on trajectory calculation and the modification of motions based upon force feedback or touch feedback to adapt to the outer world. To integrate these functions into the system, software servoing was used, where a digital computer controlled each motor drive level directly. By using such a control scheme, the capability of the robot arm was remarkably improved.

3. PRACTICAL ASSEMBLY AUTOMATION

While general assembly automation was being studied at Stanford University, other practical research was started at several other laboratories and companies. A system, which consisted of position controlled robots and various specially designed tools was developed at Kawasaki Unimate to assemble a gasoline engine. The work demonstrated a practical approach to assembly automation. Hitachi developed a precise insertion robot which operated reliably based on active accommodation by a flexible force sensing mechanism [8]. A position controlled robot equipped with a compliance mechanism (RCC) at the wrist which could perform precise insertion quickly without force feedback was developed at Draper Laboratory [9]. At SRI a system which could carry out assembly using a passive accommodation table had been developed [10]. In these practical system, global motion was controlled by simple positioning robots and fine accommodation was accomplished by tools specially designed for the tasks.

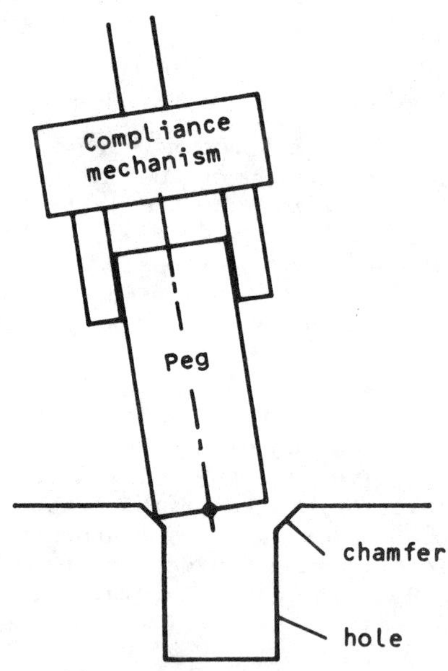

Fig. 1 Peg insertion by compliance mechanism

It would be instructive to compare the operation of a practical system with that of an intelligent robot. We will take peg insertion as an example. The robot attached with a RCC at the wrist will move a peg into a hole. As shown in Fig. 1, if there is a misalignment between the peg and the hole, the peg will be guided to the hole by the chamfer., The RCC is a compliance mechanism which provides the accommodation. If a lateral force is exerted at the tip of the peg, it will translate without rotation, and if a torque is exerted at the tip, it will rotate without translation. With the help of the chamfer any translation error

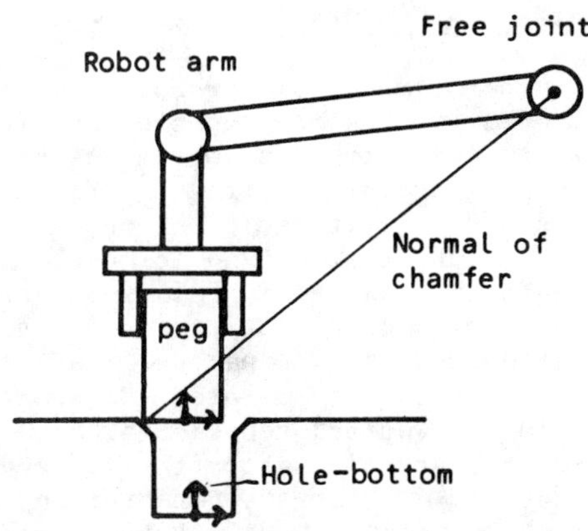

Fig. 2 Peg insertion by AL system

is corrected. During the insertion process into the hole any rotation error is corrected.

In the AL system the peg insertion could be described as:

```
MOVE peg TO hole-bottom
   WITH FORCE = 0 ALONG X,Y OF hole-bottom
```

This command means "move coordinate frame peg to hole-bottom with two proper joints free so that the x and y components of force are zero." With this method the peg insertion sometimes becomes impossible. For example, if a free joint lies close by the normal of the chamfer as shown in Fig. 2, the angle between chamfer tangent and free surface becomes less then arctangent of friction coefficient. The peg will be locked. This is indeed a probable case. This disadvantage of the AL system shows not only that the system can not perform the peg insertion in this way, but also that the system lacks the systematic representation capability of the necessary skill. It is undesirable that the operation of a robot arm is dependent on its configuration. A user would like to write machine independent programs. In general a robot arm skill consists of patterns of action to the task environment, interpretation of results, and the decision of further action. We have to represent the knowledge about an action and its result, which is task particular, so that it is robot arm independent.

4. BASIC CONTROL SCHEME FOR SKILLFUL ROBOT ARM

4.1 Control in Cartesian Coordinate Systems

If the form of assembly is defined, it is most efficient to use the special devices or tools. Not only in assembly, but in general, it is most efficient to design mechanisms suited for the task, and to control the operation of these mechanism using sensory feedback. Hitachi, Draper Laboratory, and SRI had taken this approach in developing assembly systems. Therefore it is senseless to simply compare the capabilities of special-purpose systems and intelligent robots in which generalities are most important. The skill representation capability of the intelligent robot should also be general so as to provide the skill of special-purpose tools. If we could build up virtual mechanisms by software, we would be able to utilize all task particular knowledge which is obtained from the study of special-purpose tools. And we will be able to exchange tools and skills by software.

What kind of robot arm control would be required in order to build up virtual mechanisms by software? It is motion and force control in cartesian coordinate systems. A few methods have been proposed to realize such a type of control [11,12]. We will describe here the direct servoing method in cartesian coordinates that seems to have the highest generality. As shown in Fig. 3 this system provides for the real time transformation between joint coordinates and cartesian coordinates, the transformation of acceleration and force in cartesian coordinates into joint torques. In addition, coliolis force, centrifugal force and gravity loading force are canceled in real-time.

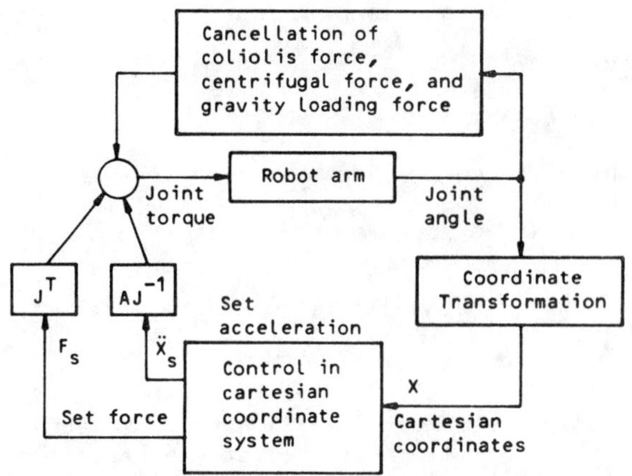

Fig. 3 Servo system for arm control in cartesian coordinate system

Each joint driving torque T is given by:

$$T = AJ^{-1}\ddot{X}_s + J^T F_s + T_n + T_g$$

where A: inertia matrix of the robot arm.

J: Jacobian matrix between joint and cartesian coordinate

$\ddot{X}_s$: set acceleration in cartesian coordinates.

F_s: set force in cartesian coordinates.

T_n: coliolis force and centrifugal torque

T_g: gravity loading torque

If the acceleration and force are given, joint driving torque is automatically computed by the system. The equation of motion becomes:

$$AJ^{-1}\ddot{X} + J^T F = AJ^{-1}\ddot{X}_s + J^T F_s$$

where $\ddot{X}$: real acceleration in cartesian coordinates.

F: real exerting force in cartesian coordinates.

Assuming that the acceleration caused by the set, force F_s is small, that $\dot{X} = \ddot{X}_s$, and that $F = F_s$. A compliance mechanism can be build up by defining F_s as:

$$F_s = \frac{1}{C} X$$

where C: compliance matrix

X: displacement from the origin

A damping mechanism is formed by setting:

$$F_s = \mu \dot{X}$$

where μ is damping coefficient. Motions are then controlled by setting the acceleration as:

$$\ddot{X}_s = \ddot{X}_r + \mu(\dot{X}_r - \dot{X}) + k(X_r - X)$$

where X_r: reference input for motion

k: stiffness or gain.

4.2 Real-time Computation

As the dynamic model of a robot arm is very complicated it has been considered impossible to compute joint torques in real-time. However, recent improvement both in calculation algorithms and in arithmetic elements has now made it realistic. Dynamic model in matrix representation, while simple, was very time consuming to compute. Bejczy developed an approximation model which was very fast to compute. The author formulated the equations of motion in a vector representation. Walker devised a recursive algorithm for evaluating the model in vector representation without redundant repetitive calculation [13]. As shown in Table, we can now calculate joint torques with this algorithm about 200 times faster than using the matrix method.

Table: List of time to compute joint forces and moment on the PDP 11/45 (Reproduced from [13])

Model	Language	Computation time
Matrix Model	Fortran	7.9 sec
Bejczy	Fortran	0.0025 sec
Walker	Fortran	0.0335 sec
Walker	Floating Point Assembler	0.0033 sec

Powerful arithmetic elements such as $16^{bit} \times 16^{bit}$ LSI multiplier with 200 nano second execution time, have also become available. It is not difficult to develop special-purpose processors with these arithmetic elements for performing fast vector calculation such as dot product or cross product. It would also be possible to make the calculation speed shown in Table ten times as fast. Above considerations show that sophisticated calculation for cartesian coordinates control could easily be carried out in less than 10 milli seconds.

4.3 Torque Controlled Robot Arm

Reliable force sensing systems have not been obtained yet, although force sensing, especially wrist force sensors have been actively studied. At the present stage it would be impossible to incorporate the force sensors into the arm control system controlling motion and force in cartesian coordinates. The author and co-workers have developed a robot arm driven by magnetic powder clutches and have demonstrated that the robot arm with open loop torque control ability could exert a force with an error of ±100 grams [14]. The author believes that it is possible to design a compact arm using torque motors, with a load capacity of 5 Kg and with a force exertion error of ±100 grams. Torque control ability of a robot arm is essential if a cartesian coordinates control system is to be successfully implemented. The use of force sensors will be necessary for the precise control of force.

4.4 Execution Monitoring

If we specify the control of the arm in task related cartesian coordinates, we can make the execution of the task independent of any specific robot arm and we can easily analyze the causality between action and its results. In usual execution monitoring, reacting forces are monitored during geometrically specified motion. The control in cartesian coordinates enables another form of execution monitoring, for example, force or compliance are specified and the resultant position or velocity are observed. In the AL system, reaction forces are tested in a threshold manner. The AL command for a peg insertion is:

```
MOVE peg TO hole-bottom

  WITH FORCE = 0 ALONG X, Y OF hole-bottom

  ON FORCE (Z WRT hole-bottom) > 18*OZ DO STOP
```

In this case, once the z component of the force exceeds 18 oz during motion, the robot arm will stop. However if the characteristics of friction between the peg and hole is as shown in Fig. 3, the peg insertion will stop half way when the velocity exceed Vc. A programmer has to have knowledge about the friction. A control scheme that specifies force and observes the resultant motion would be more suitable for this task. The peg insertion task would be more reliable if the insertion speed versus insertion depth pattern is observed in the performance of the task.

To erect a thin bar on a table is a skill which can not be realized with simple threshold tests. If the cartesian coordinates are chosen as shown in Fig. 4 and the bar is rotated about X axis, an angle versus torque graph will be obtained as shown in Fig. 5. Angle α_0, where the bottom plane of the bar comes in full touch with table surface, could be identified as the angle where the value of torque changes discontinuously in the graph.

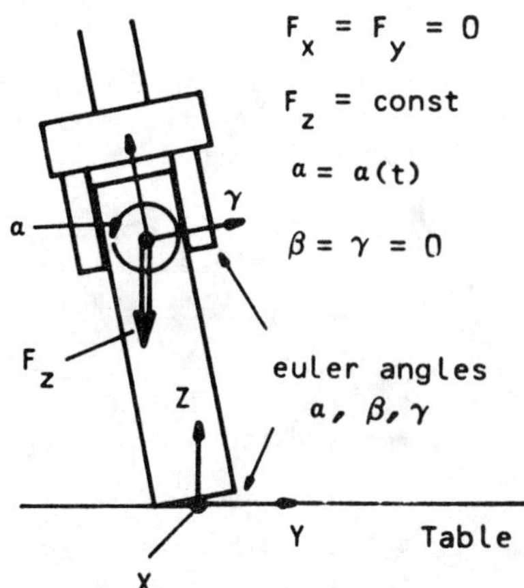

Fig. 4 Control mechanism for bar erection

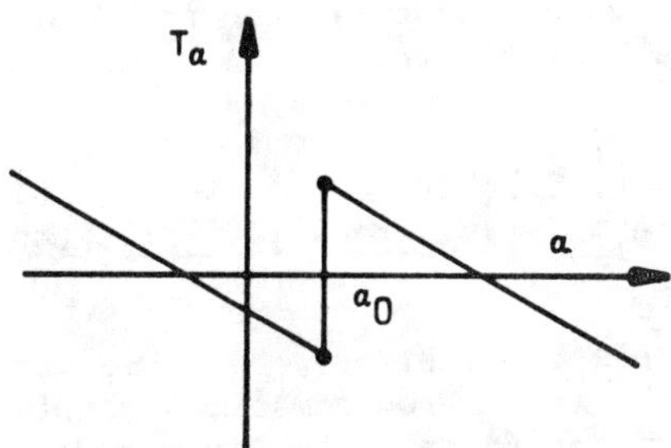

Fig. 5 Angle versus torque pattern in bar erection

CONCLUSION

The skill of a robot arm consists in the accumulation of task particular knowledge. This knowledge, that is a specification of the mechanism to perform a task, is embodied by the robot arm in the form of a virtual mechanisms in software. The realization of these virtual mechanisms is by motion and force control in cartesian coordinate systems and by monitoring the response patterns. The proposed method provides a systematic method by which to develop skills for an intelligent robot.

ACKNOWLEDGEMENTS

The author wishes to thank Prof. Richard Paul for helpful comments and for help in preparing the manuscript. He thanks Prof. King Sun Fu for encouragement and support at Purdue University. Document is prepared by Mellanie Boes and drawings by Marc Ream. He also thanks those people.

REFERENCES

[1] Feldman, J., et al., "The of Vision and Manipulation to Solve the Puzzle," In Proc. IJCAI-71, London, September 1971.

[2] Ejiri, M., et al., "A Prototype Intelligent Robot That Assembles Objects from Plane Drawings," IEEE Trans. Comp., Vol. C-21, pp. 161-170, 1972.

[3] Shirai, Y., et al., "Visual Feedback of a Robot in Assembly," ETL A.I.R. Group Memo #1, 1972.

[4] Finkel, R., et al., "AL, A Programming System for Automation," Computer Science Dept. Report CS-456, Stanford University, November 1974.

[5] Pieper, D. L., "The Kinematics of Manipulators under Computer Control," Stanford Artificial Intelligence Project Memo No. 72, October 1968.

[6] Paul, R., "Trajectory Control of a Computer Arm," In Proc. IJCAI-71, London, September, 1971.

[7] Bolles, R., et al., "The Use of Sensory Feedback in a Programmable Assembly System," Stanford Artificial Intelligence Project Memo No. 220, Stanford University, Stanford, CA, October 1973.

[8] Goto, T., et al., "Precise Insert Operation by Tactile Controlled Robot," In Proc. 4th ISIR, Tokyo, 1974.

[9] Nevins, J. L., et al., "Computer Controlled Assembly," Scientific American, Vol. 238, No. 2, pp. 62-74, February 1978.

[10] Rosen, C., et al., "Machine Intelligence Research Applied to Industrial Automation," Eighth Report, SRI International, Menlo Park, CA, August 1978.

[11] Paul, R., et al., "Compliance and Control," In Proc. JACC-76, 1976.

[12] Takase, K., "Task-Oriented Variable Control of Manipulator and its Software Servoing System," In Proc. of IFAC Symposium on Information-Control Problems in Manufacturing Technology, Tokyo, 1977.

[13] Paul, R., et al., "Advanced Industrial Robot Control Systems," First Report, Purdue University, West Lafayette, IN, May 1978.

[14] Takase, K., et al., "The Design of an Articulated Manipulator with Torque Control Ability," In Proc. 4th ISIR, Tokyo, 1974.

PANEL ON DEALING WITH UNCERTAINTY

chairman
Randall Davis
MIT
Cambridge, MA, USA

Participants

Shigetoko Kaihara
University of Tokyo Hospital
Tokyo, Japan

Edward Shortliffe
Stanford University Medical Center
Stanford, CA, USA

Lofti Zadeh
University of California
Berkeley, CA, USA

Introduction
The problem of dealing with uncertainty arises in many areas of AI research and has been attacked with a number of mechanisms. This panel is intended to bring together several of the researchers who have had direct experience with the issue, to report briefly on their efforts and discuss the relative merits of the various approaches.

The panel, originally entitled "Reasoning with Uncertainty", was renamed to encourage a broader view of the topic. "Reasoning", i.e., inference, in the face of uncertainty is only one of the manifestations of the problem and may as a result be too narrow a perspective. Part of the emphasis in the discussion will be to examine the utility of a broader view.

The problem
In the few domains where concepts and inferences can be totally formalized (e.g., pure mathematics), there is no uncertainty of the sort we are discussing here. Unfortunately, in all real problems attacked by AI, we eventually run afoul of the issue. The problem commonly has two sources. First, the basic data we have to deal with may be uncertain. This may occur due to noise (as in speech or vision), due to the fallibility of our measurement procedures (as in medical laboratory tests), or due to the inherently ill-defined nature of the concept involved (as in "block A is 'near' block B"). Second, the processing applied to that data may introduce its own uncertainty, typically because we lack a comprehensive understanding of the domain. In speech understanding, for instance, we have as yet no theory which allows us to proceed unerringly from waveforms to phonemes to words. At best we can offer plausible guesses at each stage, and must hedge our bets by making multiple such guesses.

The Questions
To provide a focus for the discussion, the participants were asked to consider each of the following questions.

Construing the issue of uncertainty in the broadest sense, what kinds of problems attacked in AI appear to have dealing with uncertainty as a truly central issue? How is uncertainty manifested in those problem areas? For example, work on deductive inference [6], modelling some aspects of common sense reasoning [9], hypothesis formation [5], and signal understanding [1] all had to deal with uncertainty of slightly different form, and all developed different mechanisms.

The psychological connection: What kind of behavior do people display when dealing with uncertainty? What can we learn from this and ought we to try to mimic it in our programs?

What are the current interesting and unsolved issues in representing and dealing with uncertainty?

What would constitute a good solution to the problem? That is, what performance characteristics would it display?

Has there been too much attention paid to the numbers? All of the schemes developed so far eventually use some numeric representation of certainty, but in some the computation and propogation of those numbers is the central concern of the scheme. As we note below, it might be argued that this is an undesirable situation.

Of these questions,the last appears to be potentially the most controversial; it might prove interesting to focus on it in more detail.

As inspiration, consider the following argument that strong emphasis on the numeric aspects of the problem is misguided. First (perhaps not surprisingly) none of the schemes developed to date has a precise notion of uncertainty, a situation which is manifested in the ill-defined nature of the numbers involved and the processing applied to them. At best, we are given rough guidelines for what the numbers are to mean and some vague assurances that they can be assigned consistently. The arithmetic then done on them is typically ad hoc and its formal properties (e.g., its relation to other models of inference) often not well understood. The overall effect -- ad hoc processing of ill-defined numbers -- does not inspire confidence in the result.

One common response is that not much attention is paid to the precise result, only the range it falls in or the overall ordering it produces. This brings up yet another problem, a by now traditional dilemma: if the systems built around these mechanisms are too sensitive to the numbers produced, that's bad because no one is ready to defend the precise numbers. Yet if the systems are relatively insensitive to the numbers, then all of that mechanism appears spurious. What is the "appropriate" level of sensitivity?

In more general terms, I suggest as a point for discussion the following claim: The numbers and numeric calculations involved in representing and dealing with uncertainty are at best artifacts. Any time the main focus of attention is on the numbers, that's a symptom of something wrong, most likely that there is too little power in the underlying approach to the problem. As a contrast, consider the HEARSAY-II [1] work on speech understanding, in which dealing with uncertainty was viewed as an issue of problem solving, and in which the system architecture and problem solving paradigm were designed to confront the issue. Various measures of uncertainty were introduced (e.g., the credibility of hypotheses, the focus of attention evaluations, etc.), but they played a far less central role because the basic approach -- which included the use of multiple cooperating knowledge sources, best-first search, etc., -- was itself capable of reasonable performance in the face of uncertainty.

As a specific example of the difference in methodology, consider HEARSAY's use of word hypothesis credibility ratings. One way to attempt to get high performance would have been to put effort into developing a finely tuned rating scheme which could be relied upon to give the best score to the correct hypothesis. But this was not done. Instead a version of best-first search was developed which first sought out multi-word hypotheses and then used these as "islands of reliability" from which to press forward the search for a good global hypothesis [2]. The power of the system came from its basic problem solving paradigm, not an elaborate arithmetic model of uncertainty.

Other mechanisms with similar abilities to deal with uncertainty have been explored in other problems:

partial matching, in which the result of the match is not just success or failure, but a symbolic indication of how closely the match was achieved and what parts failed to match;

"constraint sharing", resolving uncertainty by taking advantage of ways in which partial solutions to the problem mutually constrain each other. That is, rather than attempting to resolve every ambiguity as it arises by carefully ranking every alternative, the program continues processing and uses other results to rule out some possibilities. The technique has its roots in relaxation techniques developed for solving differential equations, but has since been applied in symbolic form to a range of AI problems (e.g., [8,3,7,4]).

The success of such mechanisms on interesting problems and their deemphasis of numeric propogation schemes is, or should be, food for thought.

References

[1] Erman L, Lesser V, A multi-level organization for problem solving using many diverse cooperating sources of knowledge, *Proc 4th IJCAI*, pp. 483-490.

[2] Lesser V, et al, Selection of word islands in the HEARSAY-II speech understanding system, *Proc 1977 IEE Conf on ASSP.*

[3] Lesser V, Corkill D, The application of AI techniques to cooperative, distributed problem solving, Technical Report, COINS Dept, UMass at Amherst.

[4] Mackworth A, Consistency in networks of relations, TR75-3, CS Dept, Univ. of British Columbia, July 1975.

[5] Pople H, The formation of composte hypotheses, *Proc 5th IJCAI*, pp 1030-1037.

[6] Shortliffe E, Buchanan B, A model of inexact reasoning in medicine, *Math Biosci*, 23,351-379(1975).

[7] Steele G, Sussman G, Constraints, AI Memo 502, Nov 1978, MIT.

[8] Waltz D, Understanding line drawings of scenes with shadows, in *Psychology of Computer Vision*, Winston, ed.

[9] Zadeh L, Fuzzy sets, *Info Control*, pp. 338-353 (1965).

PANEL: HISTORY OF ARTIFICIAL INTELLIGENCE RESEARCH, 1956-61

Edward A. Feigenbaum, Panel Chairman
Computer Science Department
Stanford University
Stanford, CA 94305

Understanding the history of the development of a body of ideas is often a precondition for a creative contribution to that body of ideas. The AI field seems to lack a sense of its own history. It is a field of practitioners rather than scholars. This is paradoxical since the field is not yet a quarter-century old, and many of the principal scientists attending its birth are still vigorously active in its development.

Realizing this, the IJCAI Program Committee organized a panel on the history of AI at IJCAI77, and the current Program Committee chose to continue this biannual educational event. As it happened, the members of the 1977 panel chose to range broadly over the "pre-history" of the field--from the Greeks through post-war cybernetics. Not discussed in detail were the critical intellectual events of the formative period, 1956-61. It is to this period that the IJCAI79 panel will devote its attention.

The formative period can be characterized by its intellectual themes, by the programs that were written to test ideas, and by the individuals who made the contributions.

The two major themes of AI work--machines that reason and perceive, and information processing models of human cognition--were much more closely intertwined then than they are now. For example, the Logic Theorist (LT, 1956), along with Samuel's Checker Player (1955-56) the first heuristic programs that ran on computers, helped to launch the "smart machines" work of our field. LT also was a major event in Psychology when its description appeared in Psychological Review as "Elements of a Theory of Human Problem Solving" (Newell and Simon). Similarly, the General Problem Solver (GPS, 1957-59) was for years a major focus of AI's problem solving research, while at the same time standing as the most complex and detailed model of a human thought process that had ever been constructed and tested.

In the formative period, the major events were clustered in a Carnegie Tech/RAND Corporation collaboration, led by Newell, Shaw, and Simon; an MIT group led by McCarthy and Minsky; and IBM projects of Samuel and Gelernter, et. al. In a remarkable burst of creativity that began in late 1955, Newell, Shaw, and Simon conceived LT; invented list processing (IPLI and II) to handle the novel programming problems of writing LT; conceived and programmed GPS and the NSS Chess Player; and made various programming innovations that were embodied in IPLIII, IV, and V (all 1957-59). Seminally related to these events were papers by Newell (1955) on an adaptive chess machine and by Simon on a behavioral theory of rational choice and the influence of the environment on problem solving and decision making. These two papers of Simon were in a sense the culmination of years of study on the bounds of individual and organizational information processing and rationality; and the processes by which people and organizations made decisions and solved problems within these bounds. It is for this work, initially addressed to economists and behavioral scientists, that Simon won the Nobel Prize in 1978. The students of Newell and Simon also produced a number of key programs of the time including: the EPAM model of human verbal learning and memory (Feigenbaum, 1959); a model of hypothesis formation in binary-choice decision making (Julian Feldman, 1959); an early natual-language understander, SAD-SAM (Lindsay); and an application to a management science problem of assembly line balancing (Tonge).

At IBM, Gelernter and his group, with support from Rochester, proceeded to program the Geometry Theorem Prover. They too created a list processing system, FLPL (Fortran List Processing Language, 1959). Samuel continued developing and experimenting with his

Checker Player, particularly the learning feature in which self-improvement of the play took place by a "hill-climbing" adjustment of the weights of an evaluation function. And Bernstein, a programmer/chess master, developed another of the early chess programs.

Other important activity had a New England locus. Two important early conferences were held there: the Dartmouth Summer Conference on Artificial Intelligence (1956) and the meeting of the IEEE Professional Group on Information Theory (1956, a conference noted as the first formal presentations of LT and of Chomsky's linguistic theory). At Lincoln Laboratory, Selfridge and Dineen wrote the first character recognition program (approximately 1955); and later Selfridge and his group wrote the influential pattern recognition system Pandemonium (1959).

McCarthy formulated a number of problems of the interaction of mathematics and mathematical logic with programming and artificial intelligence. Understanding the importance of the list structure and list processing innovations, and merging these with his thinking about formal representations and about proofs of the properties of programs, he invented the LISP notation that was the basis for the development of LISP translators at MIT in later years. Slagle, at MIT, extended ideas on heuristic search with his Symbolic Integration program, SAINT. Minsky labored to organize the cascade of early ideas and produced his important paper "Steps toward Artificial Intelligence". And McCarthy suggested the idea of time-sharing a computer, reflecting the concerns of the AI community for both economical interaction with running AI programs, and with programming efficiency.

Fortune smiled upon the editors of the collection Computers and Thought (Feigenbaum and Feldman, 1963), which turned out to contain an almost unblurred image of the intellectual activity of the formative period. Participants of this formative period have organized the IJCAI79 panel on the History of AI (1956-61). They are:

Professor Saul Amarel, Professor and Chairman, Computer Science, Rutgers University

Professor John McCarthy, Professor of Computer Science, Stanford University

Professor Herbert A. Simon, Professor of Computer Science and Psychology, Carnegie-Mellon University

Professor Edward A. Feigenbaum, Professor and Chairman of Computer Science, Stanford University.

References

Bernstein, A. and Roberts, M. deV. 1958, Computer Vs. Chess-Player, SCIENTIFIC AMERICAN, June.

Feigenbaum, E., 1961. The Simulation of Verbal Learning Behavior. PROCEEDINGS OF THE WESTERN JOINT COMPUTER CONFERENCE, 19:121-132.

Feigenbaum, E., and Feldman, J., COMPUTERS AND THOUGHT, 1963, McGraw-Hill.

Feldman, J., 1961. Simulation of Behavior in the Binary Choice Experiment, PROCEEDINGS OF THE WESTERN JOINT COMPUTER CONFERENCE, May 9-11, 1961, pp. 133-144.

Gelernter, H., 1959. Realization of a Geometry Theorem-Proving Machine,PROCEEDINGS OF THE INTERNATIONAL CONFERENCE ON INFORMATION PROCESSING, 1959, Paris:UNESCO House. pp273-282.

Gelernter, H., Hansen, J.R., and Loveland, D.W., 1960. Empirical Exploration of the Geometry Theorem Machine, PROCEEDINGS OF THE WESTERN JOINT COMPUTER CONFERENCE, May 3-5, 1960. pp143-147.

Lindsay, R.K., 1962. A Program for Parsing Sentences and Making inferences About Kinship Relations, PROCEEDINGS OF THE WESTERN MANAGEMENT SCIENCE CONFERENCE ON SIMULATION.

McCarthy, J., 1959. Programs with Common Sense, PROCEEDINGS OF THE SYMPOSIUM ON MECHANISATION OF THOUGHT PROCESSES. National Physical Laboratory, Teddington, England, London: H. M. Stationary Office.

McCarthy, J., 1960. Recursive Functions of Symbolic Expressions, COMMUNICATIONS OF THE ASSOCIATION FOR COMPUTING MACHINERY, 3(1960).

Minsky, M.L., 1961. Steps Toward Artificial Intelligence, PROCEEDINGS OF THE IRE, 1961. Special computer issue.

Newell, A., 1955. The Chess Machine, PROCEEDINGS OF THE 1955 WESTERN JOINT COMPUTER CONFERENCE, Session on Learning Machines, pp 85-111, March 1-3, 1955.

Newell, A., and Simon, H.A., 1956. The Logic Theory Machine, IRE TRANSACTIONS ON INFORMATION THEORY, IT-2(3):61-79.

Newell, A., and Shaw, J.C., 1957.Programming the Logic Theory Machine, PROCEEDINGS OF THE WESTERN JOINT COMPUTER CONFERENCE, pp230-240.

Newell, A., Shaw, J. C., and Simon, H.A., 1958a, Elements of a theory of human problem-solving, PSYCHOLOGICAL REVIEW, March, 65: 151-166.

Newell, A., Shaw, J.C., and Simon, H.A., 1958b. Chess-playing Programs and the Problem of Complexity, IBM JOURNAL OF RESEARCH AND DEVELOPMENT, 2(4):320-335.

Newell, A., Shaw, J.C., and Simon, H.A., 1959. Report on a General Problem-Solving Program, PROCEEDINGS OF THE INTERNATIONAL CONFERENCE ON INFORMATION PROCESSING,1959, Paris: UNESCO House.

Newell, A., (ed.), 1961. INFORMATION PROCESSING LANGUAGE V MANUAL, Englewood Cliffs, NJ, Prentice-Hall.

Samuel, A.L., 1959. Some Studies in Machine Learning Using the Game of Checkers, IBM JOURNAL OF RESEARCH AND DEVELOPMENT, 3(3): 210-229.

Selfridge, O.G., 1955. Pattern Recognition and Modern Computers, PROCEEDINGS OF THE 1955 WESTERN JOINT COMPUTER CONFERENCE, Session on Learning Machines, pp91-93.

Selfridge, O.G., 1959. Pandemonium: A Paradigm for Learning, PROCEEDINGS OF THE SYMPOSIUM ON MECHANISATION OF THOUGHT PROCESSES, National Physical Laboratory, Teddington, England, pp511-529.

Slagle, J., 1961. A COMPUTER PROGRAM FOR SOLVING PROBLEMS IN FRESHMAN CALCULUS (SAINT), doctoral dissertation, Massachusetts Institute of Technology, Cambridge, MA.

Tonge, F.M., 1960. An Assembly Line Balancing Procedure, MANAGEMENT SCIENCE, 7(1):21-42.

PANEL ON APPLICATION OF LANGUAGE PROCESSING SYSTEMS

Makoto Nagao (Chairman)	Kyoto University (Japan)
Hozumi Tanaka	Electrotechnical Laboratory (Japan)
Donald Walker	SRI International (USA)
Dave Waltz	Univ. of Illinois, Urbana (USA)
Yorick Wilks	University of Essex (UK)

Natural language is a powerful tool for communication among human beings. It has the flexibility for expressing information about any specifiable situation to any degree of precision required, while at the same time it also allows substantial amounts of ambiguity to be expressed. Natural language works well when the sender (speaker, writer) and the receiver (hearer, reader) are humans with similar backgrounds who are communicating in a well-defined, mutually understood context. When one of the participants is a machine, serious problems may arise.

Various attempts have been made since the early days of computing to give the machine a portion of the flexibility characteristic of the human interpretation of natural language. Procedures have been developed to provide syntactic analysis, semantic interpretation, discourse analysis, and learning, and these efforts have required representations for the different kinds of knowledge entailed and complex mechanisms to activate and control the components to yield the best interpretation possible for a given system configuration. Applications of these capabilities have been made to produce question-answering systems, natural language access to data bases, machine translation and computer aids for translators, and automated office environments. However, all of these applications are still in the experimental stage and not in actual use in a practical setting.

This panel deals with some of the problems associated with the application of language processing systems. In particular, it will address:

(1) What are the major obstacles to the realization of practical natural language processing systems in view of the accomplishments of recent research?

(2) What will be the promising areas of application in the next few years?

(3) What approaches should be taken to ensure that these predictions will be satisfied?

In addition, we want to discuss:

(4) What are the essential differences between Indo-European languages and Japanese for the construction of language processing systems: considering the characteristic forms of writing and speaking, grammatical structures, discourse, and even intrinsic patterns of thinking and knowledge representation?

(5) How can we break through the computer natural language barrier, and how will artificial intelligence contribute to that accomplishment?

A PANEL ON INDUSTRIAL APPLICATION OF ROBOTICS

Yoshiaki Shirai (Chairman)

Information Science Division
Electrotechnical Laboratory
2-6-1 Nagatacho, Chiyodaku
Tokyo 100, Japan

Objectives

This panel deals with issues of computer controlled manipulators and computer vision applied to industry. The main issues include the followings.

1. What progress has been made during these five years?
2. What are the fundamental and practical limitations of our current techniques?
3. What kinds of approach should be taken to solve the problems?
4. What are the potential applications of robotics?

Background and Some Questions

Many industrial robots are now working in factories. But they are not much different from those developed fifteen years ago except that current computer controlled manipulators have some flexibility to change jobs by choosing a program stored in computer. Most of them work only by position control. Some have tactile sensors. Few have eyes. Is there no demand for sophisticated sensors or computer vision?

Recently, much progress has been achieved in the application of computer vision. In Japan, for example, many electric companies produce and use automatic wire bonders with TV cameras for IC assembly. There are also equipments for inspection of printed circuit boards, IC chips and LSI mask patterns.

Most of the systems employ special hardwares for processing binary input images. The success of computer vision application might owe mainly to the cheap hardware cost. But few systems deal with gray images. Hardwares for processing gray images are now being developed in the PIPS project in Japan, in the ARPA project in the USA and so on. Are they going to make a contribution to industrial application?

Now the cost of computer is still considerably high. Some systems take a hierarchical organization of one computer and many image processors or actuators. The processor cost is getting less these years. Then, what will be suitable system organizations? What kind of processors are required?

Another problem is how to make computer programs efficiently. Robots usually interact with the environment which can not clearly be determined beforehand. Languages are now being developed for arm control such as AL. In computer vision, many studies have been made for learning by showing. Are they really applicable to industry?

Some researchers find importance of three-dimensional modeling for CAD/CAM and for computer vision. If such a three-dimensconal model can easily simulate the environment, it may greatly decrease programming efforts for arm control and vision.

Participants and Background

Toshiro Numakura, Hitachi Production Engineering Research Laboratory: Productivity technology

Walton A. Perkins, General Motor Research Laboratories: Industrial application of computer vision

Masahiko Yachida, Osaka University: Machine parts recognition, image sequence analysis

Yoshiaki Shirai, Electrotechnical Laboratory: 3-D computer vision

Ed Fredkin, Massachussetts Institute of Technology, Artificial Intelligence Laboratory.

VISUAL INFORMATION PROCESSING:

The structure and creation of visual representations

David Marr

M. I. T. Artificial Intelligence Laboratory and Department of Psychology
545 Technology Square, Cambridge MA 02139

For human vision to be explained by a computational theory, the first question is plain: What are the problems the brain solves when we see? It is argued that vision is the construction of efficient symbolic descriptions from images of the world. An important aspect of vision is therefore the choice of representations for the different kinds of information in a visual scene. An overall framework is suggested for extracting shape information from images, in which the analysis proceeds through three representations; (1) the primal sketch, which makes explicit the intensity changes and local two-dimensional geometry of an image, (2) the 2 1/2-D sketch, which is a viewer-centred representation of the depth, orientation and discontinuities of the visible surfaces, and (3) the 3-D model representation, which allows an object-centred description of the three-dimensional structure and organization of a viewed shape. The critical act in formulating computational theories for processes capable of constructing these representations is the discovery of valid constraints on the way the world behaves, that provide sufficient additional information to allow recovery of the desired characteristic. Finally, once a computational theory for a process has been formulated, algorithms for implementing it may be designed, and their performance compared with that of the human visual processor.

1. Introduction

Modern neurophysiology has learned much about the operation of the individual nerve cell, but unpleasantly little about the meaning of the circuits they compose in the brain. The reason for this can be attributed, at least in part, to a failure to recognize what it means to understand a complex information-processing system; for a complex system cannot be understood as a simple extrapolation from the properties of its elementary components. One does not formulate, for example, a description of thermodynamical effects using a large set of equations, one for each of the particles involved. One describes such effects at their own level, that of an enormous collection of particles, and tries to show that in principle, the microscopic and macroscopic descriptions are consistent with one another.

The core of the problem is that a system as complex as a nervous system or a developing embryo must be analyzed and understood at several different levels. Indeed, in a system that solves an information processing problem, we may distinguish four important levels of description [Marr & Poggio 1977, Marr 1977a]. At the lowest, there is basic component and circuit analysis -- how do transistors (or neurons), diodes (or synapses) work? The second level is the study of particular mechanisms: adders, multipliers, and memories, these being assemblies made from basic components. The third level is that of the algorithm, the scheme for a computation; and the top level contains the *theory* of the computation. A theory of addition, for example, would encompass the meaning of that operation, quite independent of the representation of the numbers to be added -- say Arabic versus Roman. But it would also include the realization that the first of these representations is the more suitable of the two. An algorithm, on the other hand, is a particular method by which to add numbers. It therefore applies to a particular representation, since plainly an algorithm that adds Arabic numerals would be useless for Roman. At still a further level down, one comes upon a mechanism for addition -- say a pocket calculator -- which simply implements a particular algorithm. As a second example, take the case of Fourier analysis. Here the computational theory of the Fourier transform -- the decomposition of an arbitrary mathematical curve into a sum of sine waves of differing frequencies -- is well understood, and is expressed independently of the particular way in which it might be computed. One level down, there are several algorithms for computing a Fourier transform, among them the so-called Fast Fourier Transform (FFT), which comprises a sequence of mathematical operations, and the so-called spatial algorithm, a single, global operation that is based on the mechanisms of laser optics. All such algorithms produce the same result, so the choice of which one to use depends upon the particular mechanisms that are available. If one has fast digital memory, adders, and multipliers, one will use the FFT, and if one has a laser and photographic plates, one will use an "optical" method.

Now each of the four levels of description will have its place in the eventual understanding of perceptual information processing, and of course there are logical and causal relations among them. But the important point is that the four levels of description are only loosely related. Too often in attempts to relate psychophysical problems to physiology there is confusion about the level at which a problem arises -- is it related, for instance, mainly to the physical mechanisms of vision (like the after-images such as the one you see after staring at a lightbulb) or mainly to the computational theory of vision (like the ambiguity of the Necker cube?). More disturbingly, although the top level is the most neglected, it is also the most important This is because the nature of the computations that underly perception depend more upon the computational *problems* that have to be solved than upon the particular hardware in which their solutions are implemented. To phrase the matter another way, an algorithm is likely to be understood more readily by understanding the nature of the problem that it deals with than by examining the mechanism (and the hardware) by which it is embodied. There is, after all, an analog to all of this in physics, where a thermodynamical approach represented, at least historically, the first stage in the study of matter: it succeeded in producing a theory of gross properties such as temperature. A description in terms of mechanisms or elementary components -- in this case atoms and molecules -- appeared some decades afterwards.

Our main point, therefore, is that the topmost of our four levels, that at which the necessary structure of computation is defined, is a crucial but neglected one. Its study is separate from the study of particular algorithms, mechanisms, or hardware, and the techniques needed to pursue it are new. In the rest of this article, we summarize some examples of vision theories at the uppermost level.

2. Conventional Approaches

The problems of visual perception have attracted the curiosity of scientists for many centuries. Important early contributions were made by Newton (1704), who laid the foundations for modern work on color vision, and Helmholtz (1910), whose treatise on physiological optics maintains its interest even today. Early in this century, Wertheimer (1923) noticed the apparent motion not of individual dots but instead of wholes, or "fields," in images presented sequentially, as if in a movie. In much the same way do we perceive the migration across the sky of a flock of geese, the flock somehow constituting a single entity, and not individual birds. This observation started the Gestalt school of psychology, which was concerned with describing the qualities of wholes, including solidarity and distinctness, and trying to formulate the laws that governed their creation. The attempt failed for various reasons, and the Gestalt school dissolved into the fog of subjectivism. With the death of the school, many of its early and genuine insights were unfortunately lost to the mainstream of experimental psychology.

The next developments of importance were recent and technical. The advent of electrophysiology in the 1940's and '50's made single cell recording possible, and with Kuffler's (1953) study of retinal ganglion cells -- the neurons of the eye that give rise to the optic nerve -- a new approach to the problem was born. Its most renowned practitioners are Hubel & Wiesel (1962, 1968), who since 1959 have conducted an influential series of investigations on single cell responses at various points along the visual pathway in the cat and the monkey.

This research was conducted at the Artificial Intelligence Laboratory of the Massachusetts Institute of Technology. Support for the Laboratory's artificial intelligence research is provided in part by the Advanced Research Projects Agency of the Department of Defense under Office of Naval Research contract number N00014-75-C-0643, and in part by NSF grant MCS77-07569.

Students of the psychology of perception were also affected by a technological advance, the advent of the digital computer. Most notably, it allowed Bela Julesz in 1959 to devise random-dot stereograms [see Julesz 1971], which are image pairs constructed of dot patterns that appear random when viewed monocularly, but which fuse when viewed one through each eye to give a percept of shapes and surfaces with a clear three-dimensional structure. An example is shown in figure 1. Here the image for the left eye is a matrix of black and white squares generated at random by a computer program. The image for the right is made by copying the left image and then shifting a square-shaped region at its center slightly to the left, providing a new random pattern to fill in the gap that the shift must create. If each of the eyes sees only one matrix, as if they were both in the same physical place, the result is the sensation of a square floating in space. Plainly such percepts are caused solely by the stereo disparity between matching elements in the images presented to each eye.

More recently, considerable interest has been attracted by a rather different approach. In 1971, Shepard & Metzler made line drawings of simple objects that differed from one another either by a three-dimensional rotation, or by a rotation plus a reflection (see figure 2).

1. A random-dot stereogram (the top two images) and its decoding by Marr & Poggio's (1976) cooperative algorithm. The initial state contains all possible matches within a given disparity range, and the algorithm embodies the constraints of uniqueness and continuity to eliminate false targets. Shades of grey are used to signify matches at different disparities. The figure shows the initial state, and the states after 1,2,3,4,5,6,8 and 14 iterations. The algorithm progressively reveals a nested set of tiers. This algorithm is not the one used by the human visual system.

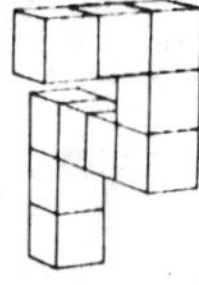

(a)

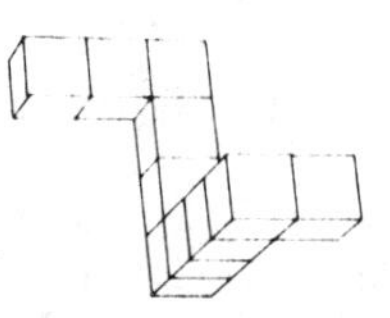

(b)

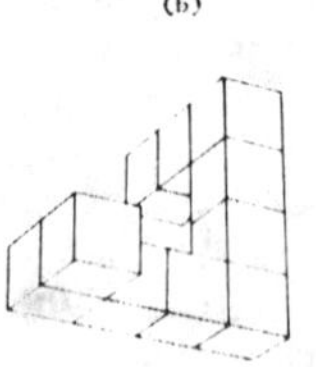

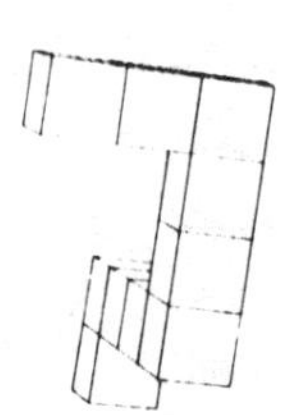

(c)

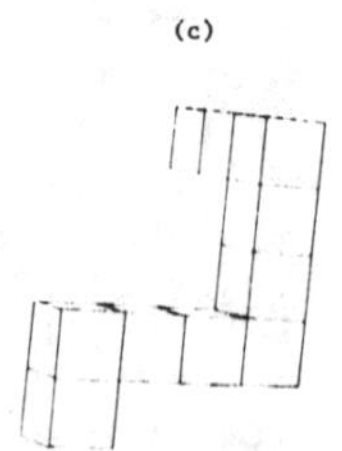

2. Some drawings similar to those used in Shepar & Meltzer's (1971) experiments on mental rotation. Those shown in (a) and (b) are identical and the relative angle between the two is 80 degrees. Those in (c) are not identical and no rotation will bring them into congruence.

They asked how long it took to decide whether two depicted objects differed by a rotation and a reflection, or merely a rotation. They found that the time taken depended on the 3-D angle of rotation necessary to bring the two objects into correspondence. Indeed, it varied linearly with this angle. One is led thereby to the notion that a mental rotation of sorts is actually being performed: that a mental description of the first shape in a pair is being adjusted incrementally in orientation until it matches the second, such adjustment requiring greater time when greater angles are involved.

Interesting and important though these findings are, one must sometimes be allowed the luxury of pausing to reflect upon the overall trends that they represent, in order to take stock of the kind of knowledge that is accessible through these techniques. For we repeat: perhaps the most striking feature of neurophysiology and psychophysics at present is that they *describe* the behavior of cells or of subjects, but do not *explain* it. What are the visual areas of the cerebral cortex actually doing? What are the problems in doing it that need explaining, and at what level of description should such explanations be sought?

3. A Computational Approach to Vision

In trying to come to grips with these problems, our group at the M.I.T. Artificial Intelligence Laboratory has adopted a point of view that regards visual perception as a problem primarily in information processing. The problem commences with a large, gray-level intensity array, which suffices to approximate an image such as the world might cast upon the retinas of the eyes, and it culminates in a *description* that depends on that array, and on the purpose that the viewer brings to it. Our particular concern in this article will be with the derivation of a description well-suited for the recognition of three-dimensional shapes.

3.1 *The Primal Sketch.* It is a commonplace that a scene and a drawing of the scene appear very similar, despite the completely different gray-level images to which they give rise. This suggests that the artist's symbols correspond in some way to natural symbols that are computed out of the image during the normal course of its interpretation. Our theory therefore asserts that the first operation on an image is to transform it into a primitive but rich description of the way its intensities change over the visual field, as opposed to a description of its particular intensity values in and of themselves. This yields a description of markedly reduced size that still captures the important aspects required for image analysis. We call it a *primal sketch* [Marr 1976]. Consider, for example, an intensity array of 1,000 by 1,000, or a million points in all. Even if the possible intensity at any one point were merely black or white -- two different brightnesses -- the number of all possible arrays would still be $2^{1,000,000}$. In a real image, however, there tend to be continuities of intensity -- areas where brightness varies uniformly -- and this tends to eliminate possibilities in which the black and white oscillate wildly. It also tends to simplify the array. Typically, therefore, a primal sketch need not include a set of values for every point in an image. As stored in a computer, it will instead constitute an array with numbers representing the directions, magnitudes, and spatial extents of intensity changes assigned to certain specific points in an image -- points that tend to be places of locally high or low intensity. The positions of these points, particularly their arrangement amongst their immediate neighbors -- that is to say, the local geometry of the image -- must also be made explicit in the primal sketch, as it would otherwise be lost. (It was implicit, of course, in the 1,000-by-1,000 array, but we are no longer retaining data for each of those million places.) One way to do this is to specify "virtual lines" -- directions and distances -- between neighboring points of interest in the sketch.

The process of computing the primal sketch involves several steps. The first is the derivation of the *raw primal sketch* [see Marr & Hildreth 1979], which involves detecting and representing the intensity changes in the image. First, the image is filtered through a set of medium bandpass second differential operators $\nabla^2 G$, (where ∇^2 is the Laplacian and G is a Gaussian distribution), and the zero-crossings in the filtered images are found (see figure 3). This representation of the intensity changes is probably complete [Marr, Poggio & Ullman 1979].

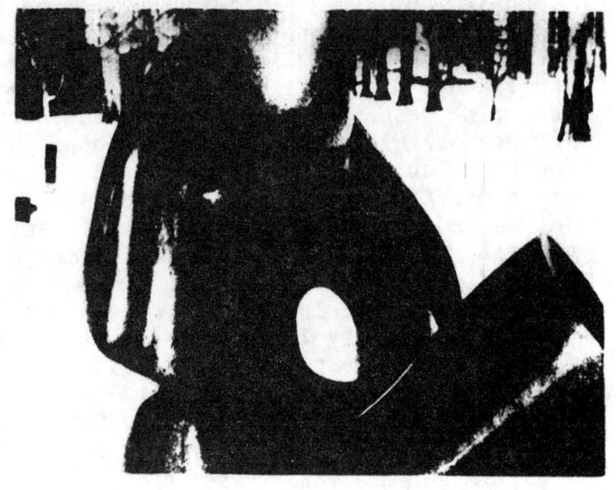

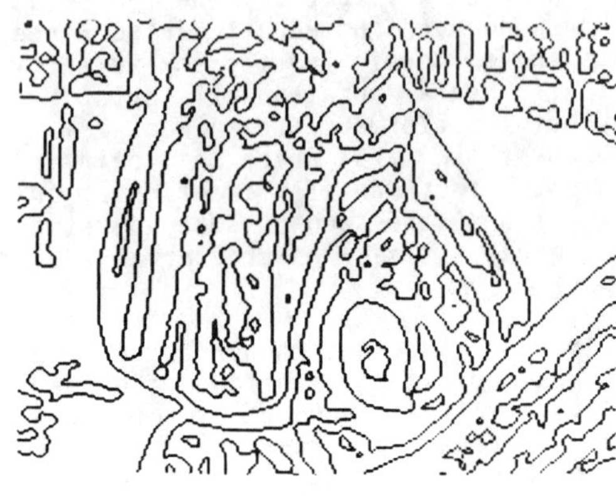

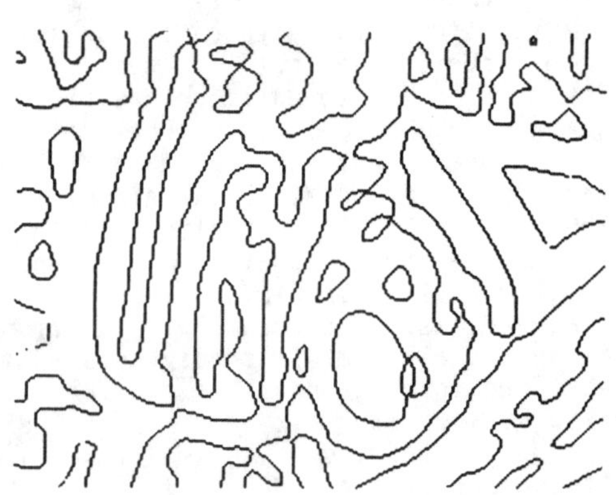

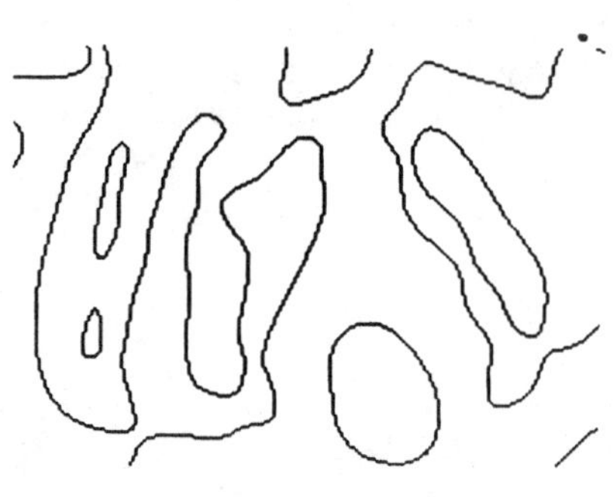

3. The image (a), which is 320 by 320 pixels, has been convolved with $\nabla^2 G$, a centre-surround operator with central excitatory region of width 2σ = 6, 12 and 24 pixels. These filters span approximately the range of filters that operate in the human fovea. (b), (c), and (d) show the zero-crossings of the filtered images. These are the precursors of the raw primal sketch (from Marr & Hildreth 1979 figure 6).

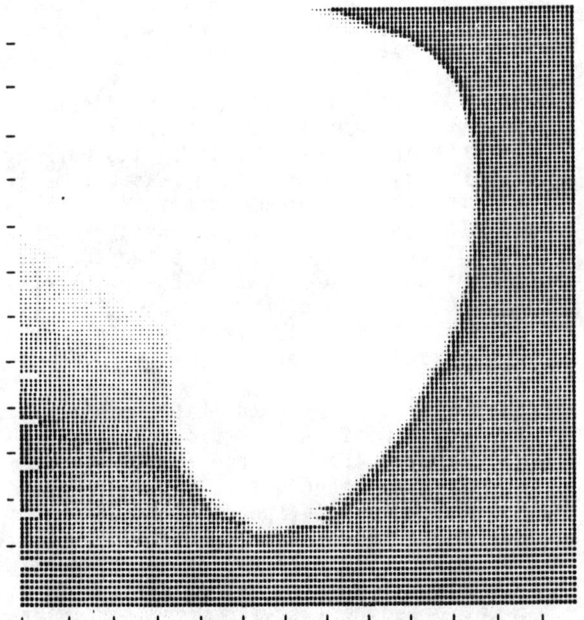

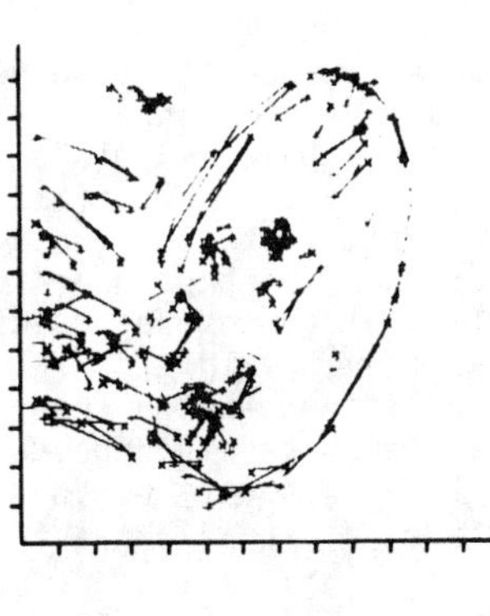

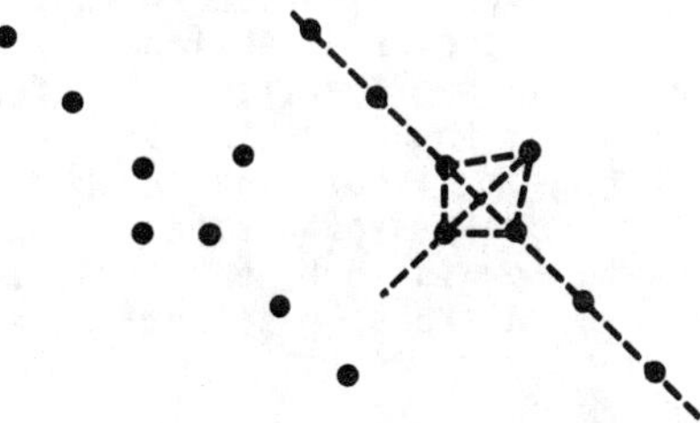

4. The primal sketch makes explicit information held in an intensity array (a). There are two kinds of information: (b) one concerns changes in intensity, represented by oriented edge, bar and blob primitives, together with associated parameters that measure the contrast and spatial extent of the intensity change; and the other (c) is the local geometry of significant places in the image. Such places are marked by place-tokens, which can be defined in a variety of ways, and the geometric relations between them are represented by virtual lines (Marr 1976 figures 7 and 12a).

Although in general there is no reason why the zero-crossings found by the different channels should be related, in practise they will be. The reason is that most intensity changes in an image arise from physical phenomena that are spatially localized. This constraint allowed Marr & Hildreth to formulate the ***spatial coincidence assumption*** which states: If a zero-crossing is present in a set of independent $\nabla^2 G$ channels over a contiguous range of sizes, and it has the same position and orientation in each channel, then the set of such zero-crossings may be taken to indicate the presence of an intensity change in the image that is due to a single physical phenomenon (a change in reflectance, illumination, depth or surface orientation).

This assumption allows one to combine the zero-crossings from different channels into edge-segment descriptors, bars and blobs (see figure 4b), which constitute the raw primal sketch. To obtain the full primal sketch, these primitive elements are grouped, perhaps hierarchically, into units called place-tokens, which associate properties like length, width, brightness and so forth with positions in the image [Marr 1976]. Virtual lines may then be used to represent the local geometry of these place tokens (see figure 4c and Stevens 1978).

Recently, Marr & Ullman (1979) have extended the work of Marr & Hildreth to include the detection and use of directional selectivity. They have proposed specific roles for the X- and Y-channels found originally by Enroth-Cugell & Robson (1966), and in an explicit model for one class of cortical simple cell, they showed how to combine X and Y information to form a directionally selective unit.

3.2 ***Modules of Early Visual Processing.*** The primal sketch of an image is typically a large and unwieldy collection of data, even despite its simplification relative to a gray-level array; for this is the unavoidable consequence of the irregularity and complexity of natural images. The next computational problem is thus its decoding. Now the traditional approach to machine vision assumes that the essence of such a decoding is a process called ***segmentation***, whose purpose is to divide a primal sketch, or more generally an image, into regions that are meaningful, perhaps as physical objects. Tenenbaum & Barrow (1976), for example, applied knowledge about several different types of scene to the segmentation of images of landscapes, an office, a room, and a compressor. Freuder (1974) used a similar approach to identify a hammer in a simple scene. Upon finding a blob, his computer program would tentatively label it as the head of a hammer, and begin a search for confirmation in the form of an appended shaft. If this approach were correct, it would mean that a central problem for vision is arranging for the right piece of specialized knowledge to be made available at the appropriate time in the segmentation of an image. Freuder's work, for example, was almost entirely devoted to the design of a system that made this possible. But despite considerable efforts over a long period, the theory and practice of segmentation remain rather primitive, and here again we believe that the main reason lies in the failure to formulate precisely the goals of this stage of the processing -- a failure, in other words, to work at the topmost level of visual theory. What, for example, is an object? Is a head an object? Is it still an object if it is attached to a body? What about a man on horseback?

Marr (1978) argued that the early stages of visual information processing ought instead to squeeze the last possible ounce of information from an image before taking recourse to the descending influence of "high-level" knowledge about objects in the world. Let us turn, then, to a brief examination of the physics of the situation. As we noted earlier, the visual process begins with arrays of intensities projected upon the retinas of the eyes. The principal factors that determine these intensities are (1) the illuminant, (2) the surface reflectance properties of the objects viewed, (3) the shapes of the visible surfaces of these objects, and (4) the vantage point of the viewer. Thus if the analysis of the input intensity arrays is to operate autonomously, at least in its early stages, it can only be expected to extract information about these four factors. In short, early visual processing must be limited to the recovery of localized physical properties of the visible ***surfaces*** of a viewed object -- particularly local surface dispositions (orientation and depth) and surface material properties (color, texture, shininess, and so on). More abstract matters such as a description of overall three-dimensional shape must come after this more basic analysis is complete.

An example of early processing is stereopsis. Imagine that images of a scene are available from two nearby points at the same horizontal level --- the analog of the images that play upon the retinas of your left and right eyes. The images are somewhat different, of course, in consequence of the slight difference in vantage. Imagine further that a particular location on a surface in the scene is chosen from one image; that the corresponding location is identified in the other image; and that the relative positions of the two versions of that location are measured. This information will suffice for the calculation of depth -- the distance of that location from the viewer. Notice that methods based on gray-level correlation between the pair of images fail to be suitable because a mere grey-level measurement does not reliably define a point on a physical surface. To put the matter plainly, numerous points in a surface might fortuitously be the same shade of gray, and differences in the vantage points of the observer's eyes could change the shade as well. The matching must evidently be based instead on objective markings that lie upon the surface, and so one has to use changes in reflectance. One way of doing this is to obtain a primitive description of the intensity changes that exist in each image (such as a primal sketch), and then to match these descriptions. After all, the line segments, edge segments, blobs, and edge termination points included in such a description correspond quite closely to boundaries and reflectance changes on physical surfaces. The stereo problem -- the determination of depth given a stereo pair of images -- may thus be reduced to that of matching two primitive descriptions, one from each eye; and to help in this task there are physical constraints that translate into two rules for how the left and right descriptions are combined:

Uniqueness. Each item from each image may be assigned at most one disparity value -- that is to say, a unique position relative to its counterpart in the stereo pair. This condition rests on the premise that the items to be matched have a physical existence, and can be in only one place at a time.

Continuity. Disparity varies smoothly almost everywhere. This condition is a consequence of the cohesiveness of matter, and it states that only a relatively small fraction of the area of an image is composed of discontinuities in depth.

In the case of random-dot stereograms, the computational problem is rather well-defined, essentially because of Julesz's demonstration that random-dot stereograms, containing no monocular information, still yield stereopsis. In 1976, Marr & Poggio developed a method for computing local disparities in a pair of random-dot stereograms by an iterative, parallel procedure known technically as a cooperative algorithm (see figure 1, and Marr, Poggio & Palm 1977). This sort of algorithm has the property that it can be defined completely in terms of simple local interactions because at each of its iterations, each point is affected only by a calculation performed on its immediate neighborhood. Yet all points are so affected during each successive iteration, so the transformations take on a complex global nature. Subsequent comparison of the algorithm's performance with psychophysical data showed that it did not hold up well as a model for human stereopsis. To be sure, it performed better than people do on the standard stereograms like that shown in figure 1; but it did not explain people's ability to see stereograms in which one of the two images is defocused slightly or enlarged slightly relative to the other. These observations led Marr & Poggio (1979) to devise another algorithm, this one based on the human use of spatial-frequency-tuned channels and vergence eye movements. This algorithm is consistent with all of the currently known psychophysical data.

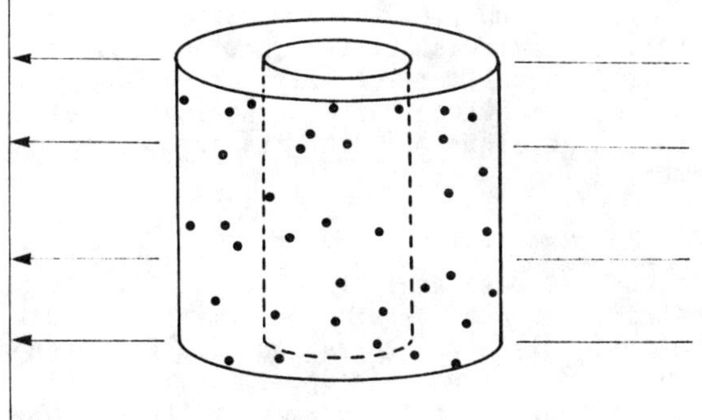

5. The motion analogue of the random-dot stereogram. Two transparent, concentric cylinders are rotated in opposite directions. Each has dots scattered on its surface. A movie camera photographs the scene from the side, and each frame contains only a pattern of random dots. When a human watches the movie, however, he immediately perceives the two counter-rotating cylinders (from Ullman 1979).

A second example of early visual processing concerns the derivation of structure from motion. It has long been known that as an object moves relative to the viewer, the way its appearance changes provides information that we can use to determine its shape (Wallach & O'Connell 1953). The motion analog of a random-dot stereogram is illustrated in figure 5, and as expected, humans can easily perceive shape from a succession of frames, each of which on its own is merely a set of random-dots. In various papers and a forthcoming book on the subject, Ullman (1979a & b) decomposed the problem into two parts: matching the elements that occur in consecutive images; and deriving shape information from measurements of their changes in position. Ullman then showed that these problems can be solved mathematically. His basic idea is that in general, nothing can be inferred about the shape of an object given only a set of sequential views of it; for some extra assumptions have to be made. Accordingly, he formulates an assumption of rigidity, which states that if a set of moving points has a *unique* interpretation as a rigid body in motion, that interpretation is correct. (The assumption is based on a theorem which he proves, stating that three distinct views of four noncoplanar points on a rigid body are sufficient to determine uniquely their three-dimensional arrangement in space.) From this he derives a method for computing structure from motion. The method gives results that are quantitatively superior to the ability of humans to determine shape from motion, and which fail in qualitatively similar circumstances. Ullman has also devised a set of simple algorithms by which the method may be implemented.

3.3 *The $2\frac{1}{2}$-Dimensional Sketch.* Both of the techniques of image analysis discussed in the preceding paragraphs provide information about the relative distances to various places in an image. In the case of stereopsis, it is the matching of points in a stereo pair that leads to such information. In the case of structure from motion, it is the matching of points in successive images. More generally, however, we know that vision provides several sources of information about shapes in the visual world. The most direct, perhaps, are the aforementioned stereo and motion, but texture gradients in a single image are nearly as effective. Furthermore, the theatrical techniques of facial make-up reveal the sensitivity of perceived shapes to shading (see Horn 1975), and color sometimes suggests the manner in which a surface reflects light. It often happens that some parts of a scene are open to inspection by some of these techniques, and other parts to inspection by others. Yet different as the techniques are, they all have two important characteristics in common: they rely on information from the image rather than *a priori* knowledge about the shapes of the viewed objects; and the information they specify concerns the depth or surface orientation at arbitrary points in an image, rather than the depth or orientation associated with particular objects (see Table 1).

<u>Table 1</u>

The form in which various early visual processes deliver information about the changes in a scene.

r = depth

δr = small, local changes in depth

Δr = large changes in depth

$\underset{\sim}{s}$ = local surface orientation

Information source	Natural parameter
Stereo	Disparity, hence especially δr and Δr
Motion	r, hence δr, Δr
Shading	$\underset{\sim}{s}$
Texture gradients	$\underset{\sim}{s}$
Perspective cues	$\underset{\sim}{s}$
Occlusion	Δr
Contour	$\underset{\sim}{s}$

In order to make the most efficient use of different and often complementary channels of information deriving from stereopsis, from motion, from contours, from texture, from color, from shading, they need to be combined in some way. The computational question that now arises is thus how best to do this, and the natural answer is to seek some representation of the visual scene that makes explicit just the information these processes can deliver. We seek, in other words, a representation of surfaces in an image that makes explicit their shapes and orientations, much as the Arabic representation of a number makes explicit its composition by powers of ten. It might be contrasted with the representation of a surface as a mathematical expression, in which the orientation is only implicit, and not at all apparent. We call such a representation the $2\frac{1}{2}$-dimensional sketch (Marr & Nishihara 1978; Marr 1978), and in the particular candidate for it shown in figure 6, surface orientation is represented by covering an image with needles. The length of each needle defines the dip of the surface at that point; so that zero length corresponds to a surface that is perpendicular to the vector from the viewer to the point, and increasing lengths denote surfaces that tilt increasingly away from the viewer. The orientation of each needle defines the local direction of dip.

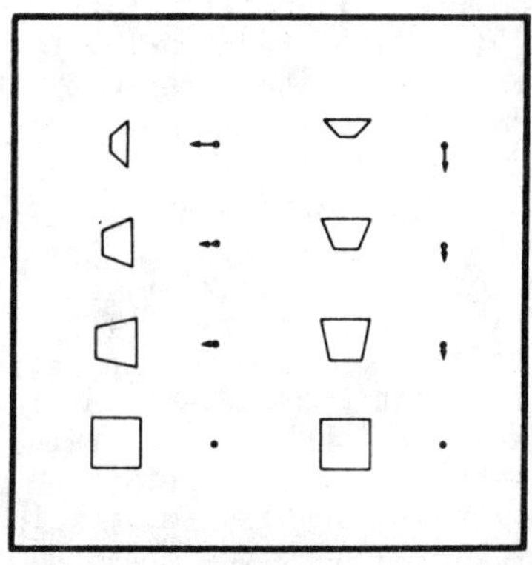

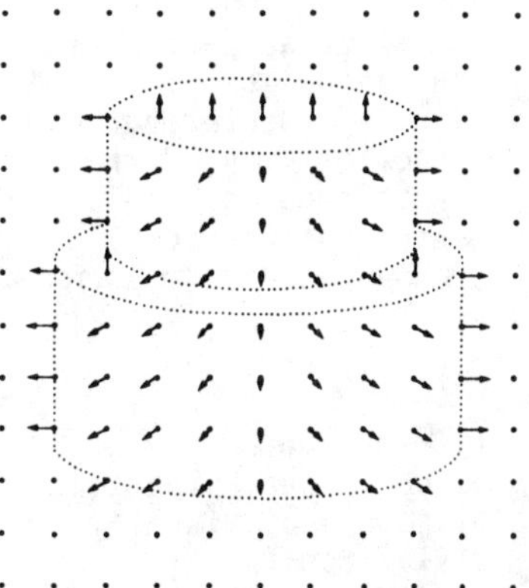

6. Illustration of the $2\frac{1}{2}$-dimensional sketch. In (a) the perspective views of small squares placed at various orientations to the viewer are shown. The dots with arrows show a way of representing the orientations of such surfaces symbolically. In (b), this representation is used to show the surface orientations of two cylindrical surfaces in front of a background orthogonal to the viewer. The full $2\frac{1}{2}$-dimensional sketch would include rough distances to the surfaces as well as their orientations, contours where surface orientation changes sharply, and contours where depth is discontinuous (subjective contours). A considerable amount of computation is required to maintain these quantities in states that are consistent with one another and with the structure of the outside world (see Marr 1978 section 3). (From Marr & Nishihara 1978 figure 2).

Our argument is that the $2\frac{1}{2}$-D sketch is useful because it makes explicit information about the image in a form that is closely matched to what image analysis can deliver. To put it another way, we can formulate the goals of this stage of visual processing as being primarily the construction of this representation, discovering, for example, what are the surface orientations in a scene, which of the contours in the primal sketch correspond to surface discontinuities and should therefore be represented in the $2\frac{1}{2}$-D sketch, and which contours are missing in the primal sketch and need to be inserted into the $2\frac{1}{2}$-D sketch in order to bring it into a state that is consistent with the nature of three-dimensional space. This formulation avoids the difficulties associated with the terms "region" and "object" -- the difficulties inherent in the image segmentation approach; for the gray level intensity array, the primal sketch, the various modules of early visual processing, and finally the $2\frac{1}{2}$-dimensional sketch itself deal only with discovering the properties of *surfaces* in an image. One is pleased about that, for we know of ourselves as perceivers that surface orientation can be associated with unfamiliar shapes, so its representation probably precedes the decomposition of the scene into objects. One is thus free to ask precise questions about the computational structure of the $2\frac{1}{2}$-D sketch and of processes to create and maintain it. We are currently much occupied with these matters.

4. Later Processing Problems.

The final components of our visual processing theory concern the application of visually derived surface information for the representation of three-dimensional shapes in a way that is suitable specifically for recognition (Marr & Nishihara 1978). By this we mean the ability to recognize a shape as being the same as a shape seen earlier, and this in essence depends on being able to describe shapes consistently each time they are seen, whatever the circumstances of their positions relative to the viewer. The problem with local surface representations such as the $2\frac{1}{2}$-D sketch is that the description depends as much on the viewpoint of the observer as it does on the structure of the shape. In order to factor out a description of a shape that depends on its structure alone, the representation must be based on readily identifiable geometric features of the overall shape, and the dispositions of these features must be specified relative to the shape in itself. In brief, the coordinate system must be "object-centered," not "viewer-centered." One aspect of this deals with the nature of the representation scheme that is to be used, and another with how to obtain it from the $2\frac{1}{2}$-D sketch. We begin by discussing the first, and will then move on to the second.

4.1 *The 3-D Model Representation.* The most basic geometric properties of the volume occupied by a shape are (1) its average location (or center of mass); (2) its overall size, as exemplified, for example, by its mean diameter or volume; and (3) its principal axis of elongation or symmetry, if one exists. A description based on these qualities would certainly be inadequate for an application such as shape recognition; after all, one can tell little about the three-dimensional structure of a shape given only its position, size, and orientation. But if a shape itself has a natural decomposition into components that can be so described, this volumetric scheme is an effective means for describing the relative spatial arrangement of those components. The illustration of figure 7 shows a familiar version of this type of description, the stick figure (see Blum 1973). The recognizability of the animal shapes depicted in the illustration is surprising considering the simplicity of representation used to describe them.

The reason such a description works so well lies, we think, in (1) the volumetric (as opposed to surface-based) definition of the primitive elements -- the sticks -- used by the representation; (2) the relatively small number of elements used; and (3) the relation of elements to each other rather than to the viewer. In short, this type of shape representation is volumetric, modular, and can be based on object-centered coordinates. The figure 8 illustrates the scheme of representation that was developed from these ideas. Here the description of a shape is composed of a hierarchy of stick-figure specifications we call 3-D models. In the simplest, a single axis element is used to specify the location, size, and orientation of the entire shape; the human body displayed in the illustration will serve as an instance. This element is also used to define a coordinate system that will specify the dispositions of subsidiary axes, each of these specifying in turn a coordinate system for 3-D models of "arm," "hand," and so on. This hierarchical structure makes it possible to treat any component of a shape as a shape in itself. It also provides flexibility in the detail of a description.

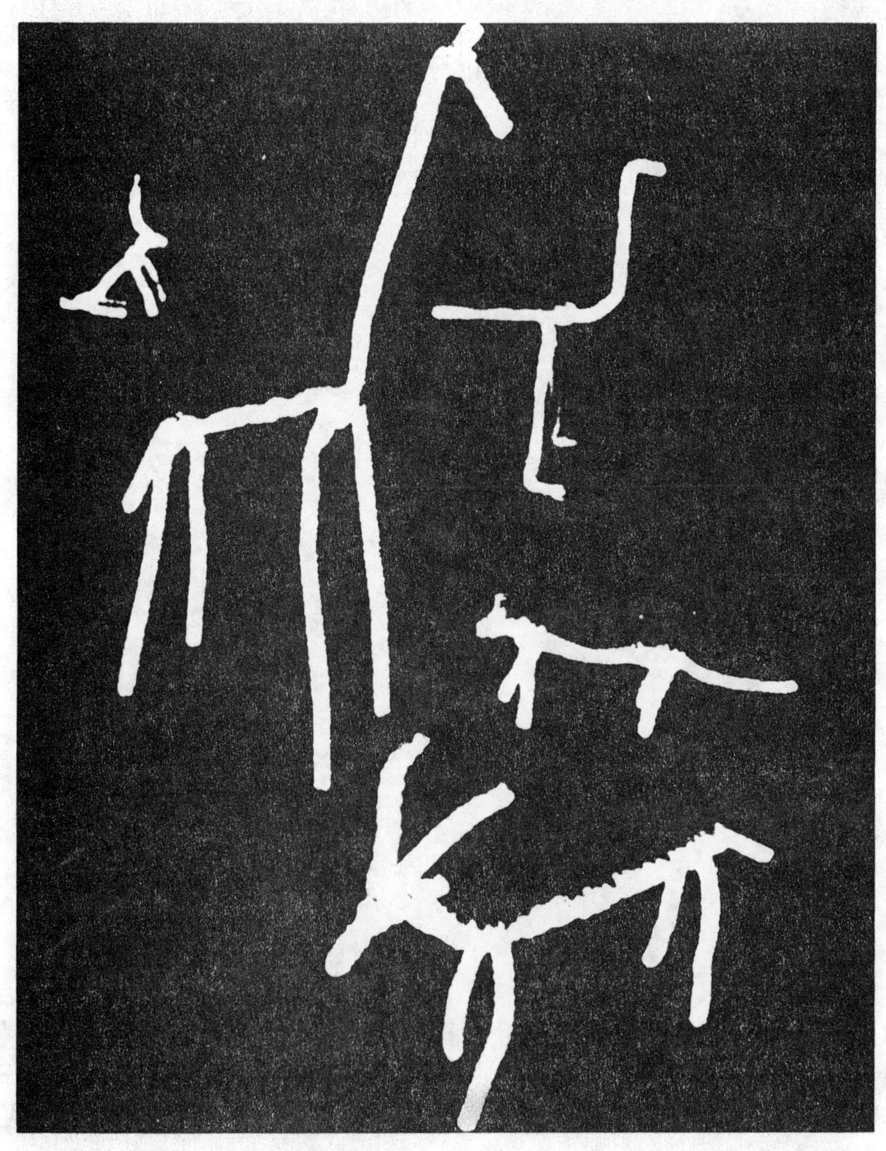

7. The portrayal of animals by a small number of pipecleaners serves to show that the representation of a three-dimensional shape need not make explicit its surface in order to describe it so well that it can easily be recognised. The success of the representation is due, one suspects, in large measure to the correspondence between the pipecleaners and the axes of the volumes they stand for. (From Marr & Nishihara 1978 figure 1).

8. The arrangement of 3-D models into the representation of a human shape. First the overall form -- the "body"-- is given an axis. This yields an object-centred coordinate system which can then be be used to specify the arrangement of the "arms," "legs," "torso," and "head." The position of each of these is specified by an axis of its own, which in turn serves to define a coordinate system for specifying the arrangement of further subsidiary parts. This gives a hierarchy of 3-D models, shown here extending downwards as if they were cylindrical, but that is purely for illustrative convenience. (From Marr & Nishihara, 1978 figure 3).

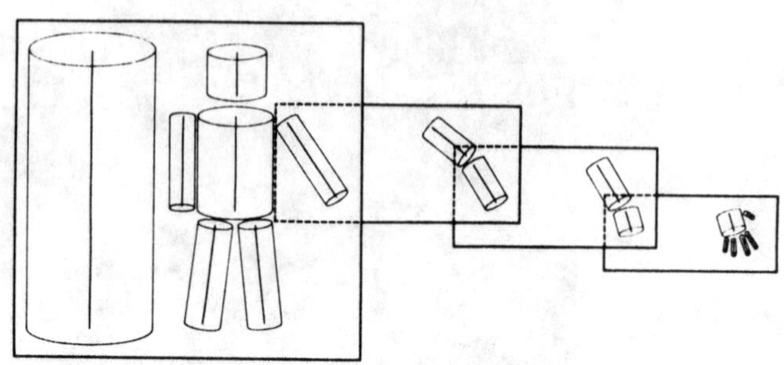

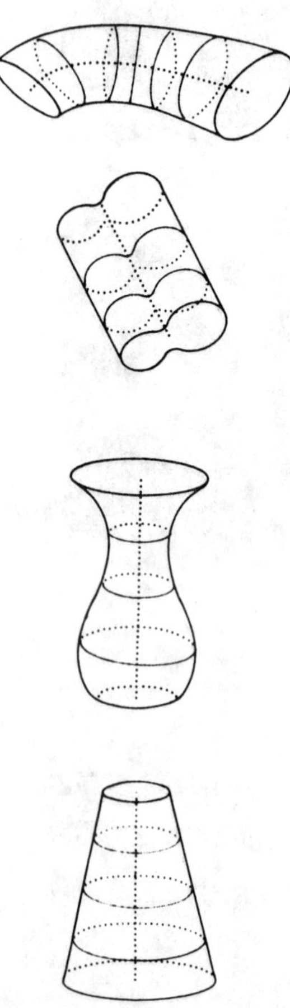

9. The definition of a generalized cone. It is the surface created by moving a cross-section along a given straight axis. The cross-section may vary smoothly in size, but its shape remains constant. Several examples are shown here. In each, the cross-section is shown at several positions along the trajectory that spins out the construction.

4.1.1 *Shapes Admitting 3-D Model Descriptions.* If the scheme for a given shape is to be uniquely defined and stable over unimportant variations such as viewpoint -- if, in a word it is to be canonical -- its definition must take advantage of any salient geometrical characteristics that the shape inherently possesses. If a shape has natural axes, then those should be used. The coordinate system for a sausage should take advantage of its major axis, and for a face, of its axis of symmetry.

Highly symmetrical objects, like a sphere, a square, or a circular disc, will inevitably lead to ambiguities in the choice of coordinate systems. For a shape as regular as a sphere this poses no great problem, because its description in all reasonable systems is the same. One can even allow other factors, like the direction of motion or spin, to influence the choice of coordinate frame. For other shapes, the existence of more than one possible choice probably means that one has to represent the object in several ways, but this is acceptable provided that their number is small. For example, there are four possible axes on which one might wish to base the coordinate system for representing a door, namely the midlines along its length, its width, and its thickness, and also the axis of its hinges. (This last would be especially useful to represent how the door opens.) For a typewriter, there are two reasonable choices, an axis parallel to its width, because that is usually its largest dimension, and the axis about which a typewriter is roughly symmetrical.

In general, if an axis can be distinguished in a shape, it can be used as the basis for a local coordinate system. One approach to the problem of defining object-centered coordinates is therefore to examine the class of shapes having an axis as an integral part of their structure. Consider, accordingly, the class of so-called *generalized cones*, each of these being the surface swept out by moving a cross-section of constant shape but smoothly varying size along an axis, as shown in figure 9. Binford (1971) has drawn attention to this class of constructions, suggesting that it might provide a convenient way of describing three-dimensional surfaces for the purposes of computer vision [see also Agin 1972, Nevatia 1974]. We regard it as an important class not because the shapes themselves are easily describable, but because the presence of an axis allows one to define a canonical local coordinate system. Fortunately, many objects, especially those whose shape was achieved by growth, are described quite naturally in terms of one or more generalized cones. The animal shapes of figure 7 provide some examples; the individual sticks are simply the axes of generalized cones that approximate the shapes of parts of these creatures. Many artifacts can also be described in this way -- say a car (a small box sitting atop a longer one) or a building (a box with a vertical axis).

It is important to remember, however, that there exist surfaces that cannot conveniently be approximated by generalized cones, for example a cake that has been transected at some arbitrary plane, or the surface formed by a crumpled newspaper. Cases like the cake could be dealt with by introducing a suitable surface primitive for describing the plane of the cut, in much the same way as an axis in the 3-D model representation is a primitive that describes a volumetric element. But the crumpled newspaper poses apparently intractable problems.

4.2 *Finding the Natural Coordinate System.* Even if a shape possesses a canonical coordinate frame, one still is faced with the problem of finding it from an image. Our own interest in this problem grew from the question of how to interpret the *outlines* of objects as seen in a two-dimensional image [Marr 1977b], and our starting point was the observation that when one looks at the silhouettes in Picasso's "Rites of Spring" (reproduced here in figure 10), one perceives them in terms of very particular three-dimensional shapes, some familiar, some less so. This is quite remarkable, because the silhouettes could in theory have been generated by an infinite variety of three-dimensional shapes which, from other viewpoints, would have no discernible similarities to the shapes we perceive. One can perhaps attribute part of the phenomenon to a familiarity with the depicted shapes, but not all of it, because one can use the medium of a silhouette to convey a new shape, and because even with considerable effort it is difficult to imagine the more bizarre three-dimensional surfaces that could have given rise to the same silhouettes. The paradox, then, is that the bounding contours in Picasso's "Rites" apparently tell us more than they should about the shape of the figures. For example, neighboring points on such a contour could in general arise from widely separated points on the original surface, but our perceptual interpretation usually ignores this possibility.

The first observation to be made is that the contours that bound these silhouettes are contours of surface discontinuity, which are precisely the contours with which the $2\frac{1}{2}$-D sketch is concerned. Secondly, because we can interpret the silhouettes as three-dimensional shapes, then implicit in the way we interpret them must lie some *a priori* assumptions that allow us to infer a shape from an outline. If a surface violates these assumptions, our analysis will be wrong, in the sense that the shape we assign to the contours will differ from the shape that actually caused them. An everyday example is the shadowgraph, where the appropriate arrangement of one's hands can, to the surprise and delight of a child, produce the shadow of a duck or a rabbit.

What assumptions is it reasonable to suppose that we make? In order to explain them, we need to define the four constructions that appear in figure 11. These are (1) a three-dimensional surface Σ; (2) its image or silhouette S_V as seen from a viewpoint V; (3) the bounding contour C_V of S_V; and (4) the set of points on the surface Σ that project onto the contour C_V. We shall call this last the ***contour generator*** of C_V, and we shall denote it by Γ_V.

Observe that the contour C_V, like the contours in the work of Picasso, imparts very little information about the three-dimensional surface that caused it. Indeed, the only obvious feature available in the contour is the distinction between convex and concave places -- that is to say, the presence of inflection points. In order that these inflections be "reliable," one needs to make some assumptions about the way the contour was generated, and we choose the following restrictions [Marr 1977]:

1. Each point on the contour generator Γ_V projects to a different point on the contour C_V.
2. Nearby points on the contour C_V arise from nearby points on the contour generator Γ_V.
3. The contour generator Γ_V lies wholly in a single plane.

The first and second restrictions say that each point on the contour of the image comes from one point on the surface (which is an assumption that facilitates the analysis but is not of fundamental importance), and that where the surface looks continuous in the image, it really is continuous in three dimensions. The third restriction is simply the demand that the difference between convex and concave contour segments reflects properties of the surface, rather than of the imaging process.

It turns out to be a theorem that if the surface is smooth (for our purposes, if it is twice differentiable with continuous second derivative) and if restrictions 1 through 3 hold for all distant viewing positions in any one plane (as illustrated in figure 11), then the viewed surface is a generalized cone. (The converse is also true: if the surface is a generalized cone, then conditions 1 through 3 will be found to be true).

This means that if the convexities and concavities of a bounding contour in an image are actual properties of a surface, then that surface is a generalized cone or is composed of several such cones. In brief, the theorem says that a natural link exists between generalized cones and the imaging process itself. The combination of these two must mean, we think, that generalized cones will play an intimate role in the development of vision theory.

10. "Rites of Spring" by Pablo Picasso. We immediately interpret such silhouettes in terms of particular three-dimensional surfaces -- this despite the paucity of information in the image itself. In order to do this, we plainly must invoke certain a priori assumptions and constrainsts about the nature of shapes.

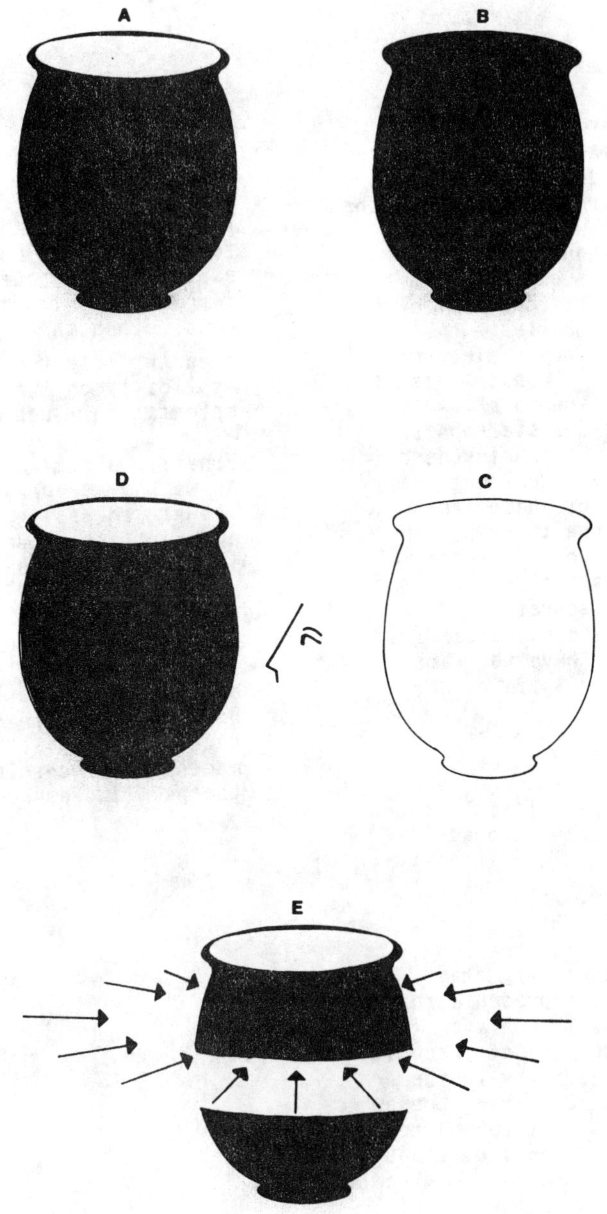

11. Four structures of importance in studying the *a priori* conditions mentioned in figure 10. (a) shows a three-dimensional surface Σ. (b) shows its silhouette S_V as seen from viewpoint V. (c) shows the contour C_V of S_V, and (d) shows the set of points Γ_V on Σ that project onto the contour. Finally, (e) illustrates schematically the meaning of the phrase "all distant viewing directions that lie in a plane."

5. Discussion.

We have tried in this survey of visual information processing to make two principal points. The first is methodological: namely that it is important to be very clear about the nature of the understanding we seek. The results we try to achieve should be precise ones, at the level of what we call a computational theory. The critical act in formulating computational theories turns out to be the discovery of valid constraints on the way the world is structured -- constraints that provide sufficient information to allow the processing to succeed. Consider stereopsis, which presupposes continuity and uniqueness in the world, or structure from visual motion, which presupposes rigidity, or shape from contour, which presupposes the three restrictions just discussed, or even edge detection, which presupposes the assumption of spatial coincidence. The discovery of constraints that are valid and universal leads to results about vision that have the same quality of permanence as results in other branches of science.

The second point is that the critical issues for vision seem to us to revolve around the nature of the representations and the nature of the processes that create, maintain, and eventually interpret them. We have suggested an overall framework for visual information processing (summarized in table 2), that includes three categories of representation upon which the processing is to operate. The first encompasses representations of intensity variations and their local geometry in the input to the visual system. One among these, the primal sketch, is expressly intended to be an efficient description of these variations which captures just that information required by the image analysis to follow. The second category encompasses the representations of visible surfaces -- the descriptions, in other words, of the physical properties of the surfaces that caused the images in the first place. The nature of these representations -- the $2\frac{1}{2}$-dimensional sketch in particular -- is determined primarily by what information can be extracted by modules of image analysis such as stereopsis and structure from motion. Like the primal sketch of the previous category, the $2\frac{1}{2}$-dimensional sketch is intended to be a final or output representation: this is where the separate contributions from the various image-analysis modules can be combined into a unified description. The third category encompasses all representations which are subsequently constructed from information contained in the $2\frac{1}{2}$-D sketch. The designs of these tertiary representations are determined largely by the use to which they are to be put, as was the case for the 3-D model representation, to be used for shape recognition. If one had wanted instead, for example, to represent a shape simply for later *reproduction*, say by the milling of a block of metal, then the $2\frac{1}{2}$-D sketch would itself have been sufficient, as the milling process depends explicitly on information about local depth and orientation, such as that sketch can provide.

Finally, a remark of a rather different nature. As we have seen, some aspects of human early visual processing, like stereopsis, have apparently been understood well enough to implement them in machines [Marr & Poggio 1979, Marr & Grimson 1979]. The computational power required by these early proceses is prohibitive, and until recently the prospects for real-time implementation of human-like early vision were remote. It now appears, however, that the emerging VLSI and CCD technologies will be able to supply the necessary processing power. This could make the next two decades very interesting.

Table 2

A framework for the derivation of shape information from images.

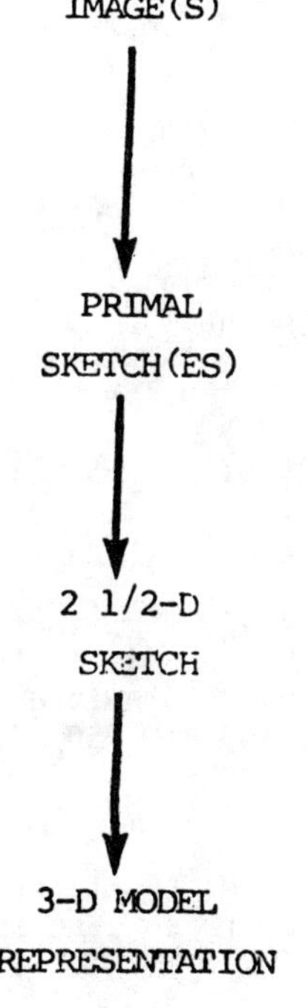

Describes the intensity changes present in an image, labels distinguished locations like termination points, and makes explicit local two-dimensional geometrical relations.

Represents contours of surface discontinuity, and depth and orientation of visible surface elements, in a coordinate frame that is centered on the viewer.

Shape description that include volumetric shape primitives of a variety of sizes, whose positions are defined using an object-centered coordinate system. This representation imposes considerable modular organization on its descriptions.

ACKNOWLEDGEMENTS: I thank Keith Nishihara and Michael Feiertag for help in assembling this survey. I thank the Royal Society for permission to reproduce figures 3, 4, 6, 7, and 8, and the M.I.T. press for figure 5.

References

Agin, G. J. 1972 Representation and description of curved objects. Stanford Artificial Intelligence Project, Memo AIM-173, Stanford University.

Binford, T. O. 1971 Visual perception by computer. Presented to the IEEE Conference on Systems and Control, Miami, December.

Blum, H. 1973 Biological shape and visual science, (part 1). *J. theor. Biol.*, *38*, 205-287.

Freuder, E. C. 1975 A computer vision system for visual recognition using active knowledge. *M. I. T. A. I. Lab. Technical Report 345.*

Helmholtz, H. L. F. von 1910 Treatise on physiological optics. Translated by J. P. Southall, 1925, N.Y. Dover Publications.

Horn, B. K. P. 1975 Obtaining shape from shading information. In *The Psychology of Computer Vision*, Ed. P. H. Winston. McGraw-Hill, New York, pp115-155.

Hubel, D. H. & Wiesel, T. N. 1962 Receptive fields, binocular interaction and functional architecture in the cat's visual cortex. *J. Physiol., Lond. 160* 106-154.

Hubel, D. H. & Wiesel, T. N. 1968 Receptive fields and functional architecture of monkey striate cortex. *J. Physiol. (Lond.) 195*, 215-243.

Julesz, B. 1971 *Foundations of Cyclopean perception.* Chicago: The University of Chicago Press.

Kuffler, S. W. 1953 Discharge patterns and functional organization of mammalian retina. J. Neurophysiol. 16, 37-68.

Marr, D. 1976 Early processing of visual information. *Phil. Trans. Roy. Soc. B. 275*, 483-524.

Marr, D. 1977a Artificial Intelligence - a personal view. *Artificial Intelligence 9*, 37-48.

Marr, D. 1977b Analysis of occluding contour. *Proc. Roy. Soc. B. 197*, 441-475.

Marr, D. 1978 Representing visual information. *Lectures on mathematics in the life sciences, volume 10, Some Mathematical Questions in Biology*, 101-180.

Marr, D. & Nishihara, H. K. 1978 Representation and recognition of the spatial organization of three-dimensional shapes. *Proc. Roy. Soc. B. 200*, 269-294.

Marr, D. & Poggio, T. 1976 Cooperative computation of stereo disparity. *Science 194*, 283-287.

Marr, D. & Poggio, T. 1977 From understanding computation to understanding neural circuitry. *Neurosciences Res. Prog. Bull. 15*, 470-488.

Marr, D. & Poggio, T. 1979 A theory of human stereo vision. *Proc. Roy. Soc. Lond.* (in the press).

Marr, D., Poggio, T. & Palm, G. 1977 Analysis of a cooperative stereo algorithm. *Biol. Cybernetics 28*, 223-239.

Marr, D., Poggio, T. & Ullman, S. 1979 Bandpass channels, zero-crossings and early visual information processing. *J. opt. Soc. Am.*, (in the press).

Marr, D. & Ullman, S. 1979 Directional selectivity and its use in early visual processing. (In preparation).

Nevatia, R. 1974 Structured descriptions of complex curved objects for recognition and visual memory. Stanford Artificial Intelligence Project, Memo AIM-250, Stanford University.

Newton, I. 1704 *Optics*. London.

Shepard, R. N. & Metzler, J. 1971 Mental rotation of three-dimensional objects. *Science, 171*, 701-703.

Stevens, K. A. 1978 Computation of locally parallel structure. *Biol. Cybernetics 29*, 19-28.

Tenenbaum, J. M. & Barrow, H. G. 1976 Experiments in interpretation-guided segmentation. *Stanford Research Institute Technical Note 123.*

Ullman, S. 1979a The interpretation of structure from motion. *Proc. Roy. Soc. Lond.* (in the press).

Ullman, S. 1979b *The interpretation of visual motion.* M.I.T. press, March.

SOME SPECULATIONS ON LANGUAGE

Bernard Meltzer
Casa Uzzarini
Rosola di Zocca
Modena, Italy

ABSTRACT

Artificial intelligence as well as neurophysiological studies of recent decades suggest a unitary view of language, in which natural language constitutes only part of the total language of the organism; the latter is a single but complex structure containing also the symbol-systems and their transformations responsible for mental processes. Following Sloman, the dogma that communication is the main function of language is opposed, and implications of the unitary thesis in respect of a number of linguistic and psychological questions are briefly discussed.

1. INTRODUCTION

In his "Computers and Thought" lecture David Marr has dealt with the language of visual processing. He has presented hypotheses, a theory, of what at least parts of it may be and of transformations which take place in it in the process of vision. The language is not English or Japanese or French or whatever - when we see we are not speaking or even conscious of primal sketches or of stick figures, but a language nevertheless it is. And the existence and nature of such a language is not only theoretical, for physiologists have started to discover experimentally the alphabet of languages at work in the visual processes of animals. Not being a biologist myself, I shall rely for my remarks on such matters on a fascinating article published in 1977 by Horace B. Barlow [1].

According to Barlow, work on recording the responses of single nerve-cells in the visual pathway of animals like fish or monkeys when the visual input is manipulated, has shown that the eye is using an alphabet of only one or two dozen different symbols. The referents of these symbols are so-called "trigger features," such as the appearance of a small dark spot, or the movement of an object upwards in a particular region, in the visual field.

Of course it is not only in vision that a processing language is at work - examples abound in all other areas of artificial intelligence. Thus for example, the English-paraphrase programs of Schank and his collaborators employ outlandish words like MTRANS and PTRANS, which by no stretch of the imagination could be considered to be English or any other natural language, but nevertheless are an essential part of the working system.

Now, in their narrow man-centered way, people have generally considered natural languages as <u>the</u> languages "par excellence," and thought of other symbol-systems that may be employed as rather secondary to these. It is true that in electronic digital computer systems we have become familiar with other "languages" such as Algol or an assembly language or a machine code, but in biological organisms little recognition has been given to the existence or importance of a wider dimension to language. This is because, in Barlow's words, "human consciousness resides at the interface between internal and external language," and since we seem to be clearly conscious only of the external one - the one we talk in - we have assigned a pecking order to languages. Very distinguished scholars, for example, have denied any kind of language whatsoever to other species of animals. And distinguished philosophers have even claimed that thought is synonymous with language (natural language, that is to say), ignoring - for example - dreams and daydreams, obviously intelligent behaviour of animals, the way music "speaks" to us, etc.

2. A PROPOSAL

The work of the last few decades in artificial intelligence, as well as the work of neurophysiologists of the kind described by Barlow, and - especially - some recent philosophical analysis of Aaron Sloman, of the University of Sussex [2], lead me to make the suggestion that a new view of language is emerging, one that is essentially biology-based. Namely, language is not to be thought of as being primarily natural language, nor even is it to be thought of essentially as being of two different kinds, viz. external (i.e. natural) and internal (i.e. processing), but in any biological or computer system, whether a man or a rat or David Marr's program it is <u>one thing</u>, which we in our anthropocentric way arbitrarily and misleadingly divide into external and internal.

Though it is one thing it is not a simple thing. This is obvious in a computer program, where the language might, for instance, be hierarchically organised into many parts:

first, say, a so-called top-level part, e.g. Algol, which is the only part the writer of the program uses and is usually aware of, then an interpreter which converts to the assembly code of the machine, then a translator which converts the result into its machine code. However, even in computer systems the organisation of the language need not be quite so neat as this. For example, in the days long ago when I wrote programs and did not merely talk about them, I remember the beautiful language of Lisp, which I used, having a facility whereby one could (usually for efficiency's sake) interpolate in one's top-level Lisp program slabs of machine code.

But in biological systems it is quite certain that the structure and transformations of the language are more complicated than a stratified hierarchical scheme with neat transformations level by level.

Let me give a rather simple example of the close association and continuity between external and internal languages. (I shall continue for convenience, in our present state of knowledge of these things, to use the terms "external" and "internal," although my present thesis is that epistemologically this distinction is misleading.) Consider the change that occurs in our learning of elementary arithmetic as children. When we are first taught how to add, we do it in terms of the teacher's instructions, consciously using natural language words and phrases such as "carries" or "two threes are six," but when we become proficient and do such sums in the usual almost automatic, "unthinking" way, there are practically no remnants left in our consciousness of these instructions and expressions. But nobody can doubt that, though we are not conscious of it, symbolic processing is taking place: the activity has very largely passed from the external to the internal language. But note how easy and "natural" the transitions between the two are: if, after attaining proficiency, we are faced with a specially hard or long sum, we will sometimes make the opposite transition and revert to the external part of the language, perhaps saying to ourselves "I must remember to carry 2 when I've finished adding this column."

The claim, the hypothesis, I want to make then is the following:

<u>All mental processes in any biological system are merely transformations that take place in its single language, and this language may be activated at any "level."</u>

(I put "level" in inverted commas, since - as I explained before - I do not wish to imply that the language has a strictly hierarchical structure.)

I make the further claim that this view will throw new light on a number of interesting issues and puzzles, such as:

The semantics of natural language.

The interaction of our different modalities of cognition, such as vision and understanding of language.

The origin and development of human language.

How the arts, such as poetry and music, act on us.

The nature of hypnotism, dreams and so-called "inspiration."

Elucidation of theories of the unconscious of the Freudian type.

The understanding and modelling of purposiveness.

Later in this talk I shall say a little about some of these applications of my thesis - a little only, I'm afraid, partly because of the limitations of time allowed me here, but mainly because my ideas on these matters are still embryonic, or even sub-embryonic, whatever that might mean! But first I want to consider briefly why the view I am presenting may appear a very strange one to many in the field of linguistic studies.

3. IS COMMUNICATION THE MAIN FUNCTION OF LANGUAGE?

Perhaps the reason the view of language I am expounding has taken so long to reveal itself is that linguists, philosophers and others have assumed as a dogma that the main or sole purpose of language is communication. I would say, on the contrary, its main purpose is for enabling effective and meaningful action to occur, whether overtly, e.g. in commands, or not overtly, e.g. in the stimulation of a muscle fibre in an organism. To demonstrate this convincingly and in detail is beyond the scope of this lecture and involves some careful philosophical analysis, on which a very notable start has been made by Aaron Sloman in the paper I referred to earlier. He there discusses the two opposed views, the usual one which insists on the primacy of <u>communication</u>, and the new one which insists on the primacy of representation. The former, of which Wittgenstein was the most distinguished and extreme exponent, holds that language is essentially a social phenomenon and meanings are essentially things to be communicated, so that it is impossible for anything to use a language solely for private purposes. The second view holds that the essence of language is storage of information for use and manipulation by an individual, and communicative potential is only an evolutionary side-effect of this function.

Even Barlow, in the otherwise so lucid a paper which I cited earlier, seems to have allowed himself to get quite confused by clinging to the communication dogma. For instance, in discussing Winograd's famous program for the understanding of English, he expresses the hope that - as is not the case in that program - an isomorphism would be found to exist between the internal and external languages in the case of our brains. There seems to me to be absolutely no reason to expect this, and I would think Barlow, at the time he wrote the paper, must still have thought that natural language by itself is so fundamental that the internal languages must in some sense merely mirror it.

4. THE BASE AND SEMANTICS OF LANGUAGE

I said earlier that language is for enabling effective and meaningful acts to occur. Now, as Sloman writes, "The most basic and primitive type of symbol-use is the execution of instructions." By the base of a unitary language I shall signify that part of the language which consists of instructions for some act to occur. The following are three examples which spring to mind: (a) In ordinary computer programs the machine-code would be part of the base. (b) In Winograd's language program I referred to earlier, which dealt with the manipulation of toy blocks of various shapes and colours, the base would include instructions like CLEARTOP, used for clearing off anything lying on top of a particular block to enable it to be used for some construction or other purpose. (c) In animals the base would include, for example, instructions to muscle fibre to twitch.

Now the claim is, and it is a very large one, that all the functioning and meaning of language ("external" and "internal") is dependent on this base. It is a very large claim, and to substantiate it one must show how descriptive meaning can evolve out of so-called "procedural" meaning (the kind of meaning representation that was characteristic of Winograd's program). This is the main theme of Sloman's paper - in fact, he appears to consider this the central problem of the semantics of language.

I think the study of mental processes in general could benefit from a mathematical study of the properties of the class of languages possible with a given base. To some extent it might be modelled on the Turing theory of a universal computing machine, in which the base typically consisted of only four instructions, say, "move to the left," "move to the right," "print 1," and "stop." But the theory would differ considerably from Turing's, because - firstly - much larger and more interesting bases would need to be considered, and - secondly - the languages to be considered would have complex structures and transformations like compiling, interpreting and others.

So much, or rather so little as far as this lecture is concerned, for the semantics and base of language. I now wish to say a little too about other consequences and aspects of the unitary view of language.

5. SOME ASPECTS OF THE UNITARY VIEW OF LANGUAGE

5.1 Interaction of Modalities

It is inconceivable that the functioning of different modalities do not share a common language, for otherwise how could we envisage a cow when we hear a moo? Poets who compose sentences like, "the morning light creaks down the stairs," which make perfectly good sense to us are trying to re-create this common language. By the way, I am slightly inclined to think that poets and musicians may be readier to accept the views I am espousing than many biologists and computer scientists!

5.2 Origin of Natural Language

It has been notoriously difficult for linguists and other scholars to make progress on explaining how human language came into being, and the fact that in spite of the large number of different languages all over our globe, there is much structural similarity in their grammars.

on the present view, language existed in man and animals long before so-called human language, and the question takes on a new form: how and when did our ancestors hit on the marvelous technical devices for bringing out their language "into the open," both by visual means (cave paintings and signs) and by aural ones (spoken words)? If this is indeed what happened, then of course there would be o mystery about the similarity of our languages since presumably evolution would have generated substantially the same "internal" language in all members of our species.

5.3 Functioning of Art

Poetry is particularly interesting to consider since while it uses natural language exclusively, it seems - in so far as it is poetry and not prose - to be attempting to evoke "deeper levels" of the internal language. It sets up resonances which are quite indescribable in natural language and at best can only be conveyed by analogy. Some of the most effective, the most moving poetry is notorious for having no discernible "meaning" in the ordinary discursive sense, and yet clearly a very great deal of meaning in terms of mental process. It seems that, as in the example of "creaking light" I mentioned earlier, poetry tries to re-create, to mirror, to represent in natural language very significant parts of our "internal" language.

Music (i.e. pure music) eschews discursive language altogether, and so - not having to act through that pathway - appears able to make a more direct and often more powerful evocation of our "internal" language.

I shall say no more about the other arts, apart from remarking that the study of dance and the "language" of gestures generally, from the present point of view, might be particularly rewarding, because comparative studies of other animal species would be more feasible than for the aural, graphic and plastic arts.

5.4 Hypnotism, Dreams and "Inspiration"

The basic phenomenon in hypnotism must be the transfer of commands from the "external" to the "internal" language. It would therefore be a promising subject of investigation for getting to know more about the relationships between different parts of the organism's language.

Dreams and the phenomena of "inspiration" are to be interpreted as relatively autonomous activities of the internal language and should therefore be able to throw light on its nature.

5.5 Psychology of the Unconscious

Freud of course initiated the study of the internal language of human beings, in a bold, broadly categorical but crude way. In the field of artificial intelligence a start has already been made in the work of Colby and others to tease out, in much more detail than that of Freud, the internal languages at work in different kinds of mental disorder. But, from the present point of view, psychopathology becomes only part of the wider issue of the study of human language (especially its "internal" part), and is likely to make more solid progress when the latter is better understood.

6. CONCLUDING REMARKS

Nobody could be more aware than I am myself of how sketchy this discussion has been. I have given little solid guidance on how one is to unravel the details of the structures and transformations of the unitary languages. But of course that is precisely one of the main objectives of the more basic types of research in artificial intelligence, and I may perhaps have succeeded in clarifying a little that objective and its import for understanding ourselves. Nor have I indicated that the paradigm I have been expounding is a fairly natural sequel to the work of the last decades on transformational grammar, with its emphases on "deep structure" and transformational schemata - in fact a view not so very different from the present one has been developed by a distinguished member of the "Chomsky" school, namely J.A. Fodor [3]. But perhaps the best way to end this talk and suggest where it is pointing is by an anecdote.

Some years ago, at the University of Edinburgh, before I pensioned myself out of it, the late Jacques Monod - the very distinguished French scientist - was invited to open officially the first university department of molecular biology in Britain. At a sherry party I was introduced to him, and by way of making conversation, and with my tongue largely in my cheek, I remarked, "I think that in fifteen or twenty year's time biology and artificial intelligence will have conflated into one subject." I thought such a controversial suggestion was good for a reasonably extended discussion. But Monod immediately flashed back, "Of course!" End of conversation, while I recovered my breath. Tonight's talk can appropriately end there, with my tongue now only half-way up my cheek.

REFERENCES

[1] Barlow, Horace B., "The languages of the brain." In The Encyclopaedia of Ignorance, Vol. 2, edited by Ronald Duncan, Miranda Weston-Smith, Pergamon Press, 1977, pp. 259-272.

[2] Sloman, Aaron. "The primacy of non-communicative language." To appear in Proceedings of the 5th Informatics ASLIB Conference, The Queen's College, Oxford, England, 26-28 March, 1979.

[3] Fodor, J.A. The Language of Thought, Hassocks, Sussex, 1976.

SUPPLEMENT*

Table of Contents

* Includes those papers not received in time to appear alphabetically in the Proceedings.

CONTROLLING KNOWLEDGE DEDUCTION IN A DECLARATIVE APPROACH

Hervé Gallaire
ENSAE - CERT
2, Avenue Edouard Belin
31055 Toulouse Cedex
France

Claudine Lasserre
ENSAE
10, Avenue Edouard Belin
31055 Toulouse Cedex
France

This paper* is concerned with the problem of introducing user-defined heuristic control over the deduction process in a knowledge based system. Control information is seen as being just another piece of data, separated from the knowledge base the use of which it controls and from the theorem prover. A declarative approach to control expression was retained. Control information is embedded in user's metarules taken from the metalanguage presented in this paper. This metalanguage and a theorem prover interpreting it have been implemented. Examples of its use are given and discussed.

1. INTRODUCTION

The process of deducing information from a knowledge base and from deduction rules is central to many fields : proof theory, problem solvers, expert systems in many areas. Whatever the approach followed, be it more declarative or more procedural, the major problem encountered is that of guiding the deduction process, namely the control problem.

Expressing control over the deduction process is but one aspect of metaknowledge, as shown in [3] ; we give here an application-independent formalism for expressing application-dependent control, which is a way of heuristically guiding a general process. The metarules presented here for that purpose have been developed in a declarative context and as such come close to ideas from [2] ; we were influenced by [5] and [8] too.

The paper is organized as follows. Section 2 presents the framework of this study and the PROLOG system we use for knowledge and metaknowledge expression. Section 3 gives an overview of the possible levels and means for metaknowledge expression while section 4 presents the metalanguage we have defined and examples of its use.

---

* Study sponsored in part by CNRS and DGRST.

2. THE DERIVATION PROCESS

2.1. A point of view for deduction control

Reasoning strategies have been of main concern in many fields of A.I investigated at CERT [9], [12]. For instance Data Base systems need to be enhanced with deduction of implicit information from the explicit one or with checking of integrity constraints to be satisfied by the stored data ; CAD systems need problem solving techniques for exhibiting some kind of intelligence in the design process [10], etc.

Most of the systems built at CERT rely on a declarative approach [15]. But we do not deny the practical interest of more procedural approaches [15]. In these studies the choice was guided by the interest in separating knowledge expression from the expression of algorithmic information on how to use it, and in studying this relationship ; a declarative approach, together with the use of logic as a formalism, proved to provide a very interesting basis for that. Its benefits in knowledge representation - ease of specification, clarity, adaptability, ease of modification of the knowledge base, power of the deductive or proof mechanism - are well known. Besides, we don't believe the proof mechanism to be more complex, although it is more powerful, than dynamic pattern-directed invocation ; it is reasonably efficient when improvements are made in specific areas such as clause indexing and retrieval.

As the declarative approach makes it necessary

to express "how to use what we know" ie metaknowledge, it gives a good framework for experimenting not only the different possible levels of metaknowledge expression but its different effects on the same data too. Here stands the basic point of this paper, namely that metarules - ie rules on how to use the knowledge base [2]- can actually be expressed in a declarative manner separately from the knowledge the use of which they control. It is important to note that the necessity of expressing control is not an additional work which could be viewed as a default of the declarative approach : as argued in [5], the possibility for the user to mix control to his program in the procedural approach will raise a problem of interpreter control instead of a program control problem.

This study on control of the deduction mechanism rests upon the logical system PROLOG as a formalism and inference mechanism both for rules and metarules. Ideas developed here could as well be carried over to other systems, such as rule-based systems, production systems, provided they offer features similar to the second-order logic ones that PROLOG gives.

2.2. Notations and interpretations

We shall use the First order predicate calculus (FOPC) under clausal form, restricted to Horn clauses [8] and assume the reader to be familiar with theorem proving [1]. We use the following notation :

(1) +A -B1.. -Bn stands for (B1∧..∧Bn) ⟶ A
(2) +A stands for A
(3) -B1.. -Bn stands for ¬(B1∧..∧Bn)

Literals are either positive (eg + A) or negative (eg - Bi). A is the head of the clause, the rest of it is its body.

These Horn clauses can be interpreted in many different ways. Their standard interpretation is : if x,y.. are all variables in the clause, then (1) asserts that for all x,y.. A if B1 and ... and Bn ; (2) asserts that for all x,y.. A ; and (3) asserts that for no x,y.. B1 and ... Bn (i.e. ¬∃x∃y.. B1∧..∧Bn). Other interpretations are possible, in terms of problem solving ((1) being an operator, (2) an assertion, (3) a problem), or of programming languages, ((1) and (2) being procedures, (3) a procedure call). We shall stick to the logic language as much as possible in the sequel.

As for the proof procedure we shall only consider derivation or refutation procedures, based on resolution, restricted to linear strategies starting from purely negative clauses. At each step i of the derivation we are given the first (negative) parent clause Ci (FPCL) ; we have to choose the literal -Cij in Ci as the literal to be resolved upon at this step (Cij is called SEL) ; we also have to choose among all clauses those whose head unifies with Cij (making the UNIFCLSET) ; finally we have to choose in UNIFCLSET the second parent clause (SELCL) ; resolution yields resolvent C'i ; Cij is said to be the parent of the literals in the body of SELCL. All the above choices will be guided by a strategy.

2.3. Background on PROLOG

PROLOG [13] is a theorem prover which takes as input a set of Horn clauses of type (1) and (2) above and a theorem to be proved, or actually its negation of type (3). It uses a static strategy complete for Horn clauses, namely LUSH resolution [6]; it is "top-down", starting from the purely negative clause it is given ; it chooses as SEL the leftmost literal in FPCL, working "depth-first", and chooses clauses from UNIFCLSET in the exact order they were input to the theorem prover by the user. Further, the process is controlled by an automatic backtracking mechanism activated in case of incorrect clause choice and in order to find all proofs of the alleged theorem. Very important to our work is that, due to LUSH resolution results, any other SEL selection strategy would preserve completeness.

We must note that PROLOG implementation is not complete, due to the unbound depth-first mechanism and to the lack of loop checks. But PROLOG exhibits great advantages for metaknowledge expression : it allows using clauses and predicates as terms, i.e as arguments of other predicates ; through built-in predicates it offers access to input-output, to the proof tree (ETAT predicate) and to the various parts of clauses and terms (VAR, UNIV predicates) ; one can also alter the set of axioms (ADD and SUPP predicates) ; it is also possible to alter the standard backtrack step by eliminating return points : any selection of the '/' predicate in a SELCL will suppress all remaining choices for all the already solved literals in SELCL and for their parent.

Example : the following is a set of axioms for proving that Z is an element of list L satisfying predicate P. The '.' is the concatenation symbol and NIL is the empty list.

(1) +ELEM(X.Y,X) -P(X)
(2) +ELEM(X.Y,Z) -ELEM(Y,Z)

When used to prove $\exists$Z ELEM(L,Z) axiom (1) will unify Z and the first element of the given list L ; then if Z satisfies P, the theorem will have been proved (the value of Z being the answer of PROLOG). Due to PROLOG strategy for choosing SELCL, axiom (2) is used in case axiom (1) does not yield the empty clause, i.e when P(X) cannot be proved ; in that case a new theorem is to be proved, namely $\exists$Z ELEM(Y,Z), where Y is the rest of the list. If +P(b), +P(c) are axioms and the theorem to prove is $\exists$Z ELEM(a.b.c.NIL,Z), the derivation tree will be :

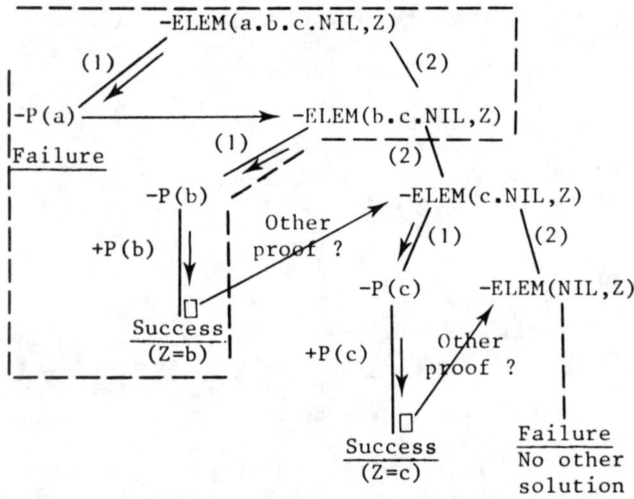

Recall that PROLOG gives all possible proofs ; hence when success is recorded an alternative is looked for. In this tree the arrows indicate the order in which the nodes of the tree are built. If one wanted only one proof of that theorem, it would be simple to modify (1) and to write it +ELEM(X.Y,X) - P(X) -/ . In that case we would get a tree limited to the one enclosed in the box above.

3. PARAMETERS OF THE DERIVATION PROCESS

A choice strategy rests upon a selection function. Such a function may or may not depend on the object on which it bears ; for instance it may depend on the specific clause from which to extract SEL, or it may not depend on the specific UNIFCLSET from which to extract SELCL. Similarly it may or may not depend on the context of the object on which it bears ; by context we mean the derivation tree or part of it.

The information needed by the selection function may be either implicit or explicitly specified by the user. Autonomous selection functions use implicit information (which may even be void, eg the leftmost-literal-first rule seen in PROLOG) as in the literal-with-the-least-number-of-instantiated-variables-first rule, or in the shortest-clause-first rule, etc. Such functions will not be discussed in this paper, although an interactive choice of such strategies is offered to the user in some systems.

This paper is precisely concerned with the expression of information to be used by selection functions ; we shall only deal with the means of expression, not with designing specific criteria. Important to this work is the notion of context ; to express context information, the user must choose between a local context (part of the proof tree, eg the parent of a literal, its parameters, its descendants) and a more global one (ancestors of a literal, the whole proof tree itself). Although the declarative approach that we follow, especially the logic one, seems to be well suited to that latter choice through the notion of proof, we have not investigated it, thus restricting ourselves to local context expression. Neither shall we discuss the pragmatic control expression that clause writing always conveys [7].

There are two basic ways for expressing control of the deduction process.

a. As is typical of the procedural approach, control information can be mixed with the knowledge base, ie with the application data (clauses) used in the derivation process. For instance the user can modify his set of clauses so that the order of his original clauses in the UNIFCLSET they belong to becomes dependent on SEL. We do not reject such an approach ; its systematic use is reported in [9].

b. More coherently with the declarative approach, one can separate control information from the knowledge base ; at the user level this becomes another piece of data, ie a set of clauses expressing a heuristic control. This is the choice that was made here.

We shall now present our metalanguage for stating the metarules expressing this heuristic control. It uses content-directed invocation [2] heavily - and we feel we have the correct tools for it. Our metalanguage is coherent with the base language [5].

4. A PROPOSAL FOR A METALANGUAGE

There are two types of metarules in this language, expressing control either over the choice of SEL or over the choice of SELCL ; for the user writing them, such metarules are true assertions, in the logical sense, about priorities and orderings as explained below ; they will be used as axioms by the theorem prover.

4.1. Ordering of UNIFCLSET

The METAL metarules to be described here have as primary purpose the expression of assertions on priorities of individual clauses in UNIFCLSET, SELCL being the clause of higher priority. Then let P, R be terms or variables, let L be a term L1.L2...Lr.NIL or a variable (see 2.3 for the '.' notation and for NIL) ; let C1,...Cn be positive literals ; then Metarule

+ METAL(P,L,R,K) -C1 ... -Cn

asserts that any user's clause matching (unifying) with clause +P-L1-..-Lr has priority K in the UNIFCLSET it belongs to, provided R matches the parent of SEL and the existential closure of C1∧...∧Cn can be proved ; in the sequel we talk more simply of the proof of C1∧...∧Cn. We must remark that :

- Li,R,P are terms in METAL but literals in user's clauses (second order feature).

- when any of P, L is a variable, the process of matching will instantiate it ; similarly when R is a variable it is instantiated to the value of SEL ; this feature allows to have metarules applying to many user's clauses, the target clauses, thus avoiding much redundancy, and making it easier to write metarules by specifying just what is necessary to match the target clause(s).

- the matching process is constrained not to instantiate any uninstantiated variable of the target clauses or of the parent of SEL at the time matching takes place ; this restriction, enforced by the theorem prover means that a metarule shouldn't be used when it aims at a special case of a target clause. This restriction implies that during the proof of C1∧...∧Cn no variable in P, L,R is instantiated.

- there is a default metarule asserting a MEAN priority value for clauses which aren't target of any metarule : +METAL(P,L,R,MEAN) where P, L,R are variables.

- the set of metarules may be conflicting ie a clause might be the target of two metarules ; as no meta-metarule has been introduced yet, we cannot handle it differently from PROLOG, ie the first metarule that is proved is retained.

- the Ci predicates can be defined by any valid PROLOG set of axioms.

Example : +METAL(P(X,a),L,R(X,Y),0)
-PRED1(X,a) -PRED2(Y)
-PRED3(L,F)

This metarule asserts that priority 0 is the priority of any rule the head of which unifies with P(X,a), the parent of SEL unifying with R(X,Y), provided the conditions PRED are provable. The matching process must comply with the above restrictions - eg as 'a' is constant, X variable, this is not allowed to match P(T,U) where T,U are variables, but P(b,a) would pass the test ; during a proof of PRED1(X,a) it is not allowed to instantiate X more than it is already.

4.2. Choice of SEL

We are to introduce local context evaluation for SEL selection ; there are two selection factors :

- backtracking blocking corresponding to a dynamic '/' introduction

- literal freezing preventing the theorem prover from choosing as SEL a frozen literal ; this feature, the most interesting of all features we present, allows for very dynamic control regimes.

Let P,L,C1,..,Cn be as described for METAL metarules ; let I and F be terms to be described below ; then

+METAX(P,L,I,F) -C1... -Cn

asserts that if +P -L1-..-Lr matches the candidate SELCL, and if C1∧...∧Cn is provable, then :

- if I is the term INH(I1....Im.NIL) where each Ij matches some Lh, any backtracking on Lh and on its parent will be blocked ; INH (NIL) blocks P only ; if I is NIL no blocking occurs.

- if F is the term FRZ(F1,V1).....FRZ(Fs,Vs).NIL where each Fj matches some Lh, then Lh will be frozen as long as none of its arguments appearing in list Vj is instantiated (ie anything but a pure variable) ; if F is NIL no literal is to be frozen.

We must remark that much of what was noted for METAL metarules applies to METAX ones and is not repeated here, especially for instantiation. Also, there might be cases where all literals are frozen ; we unblock the situation by choosing the leftmost one (default rule). We are now to see examples and to examine more deeply the freezing capability, already investigated but solved differently by Colmerauer [16].

Examples on freezing literals

The following set of PROLOG clauses can be used to prove that two trees X,Y have identical lists of leaves when traversed from left to right :

```
+IDLF(X,Y)-LF(X,S)-LF(Y,S)
+LF(X,X.NIL) - ATOM(X)
+LF(U.V,Z) -LF(U,X) -LF(V,Y) - CONC(X,Y,Z)
+CONC(NIL,Y,Y)
+CONC(A.Z,Y,A.V) -CONC(Z,Y,V)
```

If it has been given clauses ATOM(a), ATOM(b), ATOM(c) and if IDLF((a.b).c, a.(b.c)) is a theorem to be proved, PROLOG will succeed ; however the control regime of this proof is quite unsatisfactory for, if it were to fail, much useless work might have been carried out before checking anything. This is a classical example for coroutine need, as a coroutine would allow checking each leaf as soon as it is uncovered in Xor Y. The following metarules, together with the default rule, will do :

```
+METAX(P,L,NIL,FRZ(LF(X,S),S.NIL).NIL)
+METAX(P,L,NIL,FRZ(CONC(U,V,Z),U.Z.NIL).NIL)
```

The first metarule will prevent the theorem prover from choosing LF(X,S) as SEL as long as S is not instantiated ; the second one will do similarly for CONC(U,V,Z) whenever both U and Z are uninstantiated.

A different and even more interesting example is the classical Sieve of Eratosthenes problem. The following is the list of PROLOG clauses that might be necessary to prove Primes(X) where X is the list of prime numbers

```
+Primes(2.X) -Integers(2.Y) -Sieve(2.Y,X)
+Integers(P.(Q.R)) -Succ(P,Q) -Integers(Q.R)
+Sieve(P.IN,P.PR)-Filter(P,IN,NEW)-Sieve(NEW,PR)
+Filter(P,Q.IN,OUT)-Mult(P,Q)-Filter(P,IN,OUT)
+Filter(P,Q.IN,Q.OUT)-Filter(P,IN,OUT)
```

The Succ(P,Q) predicate is satisfied iff the value of Q is the value of P plus 1 ; the Mult(P,Q) predicate is satisfied iff Q is a multiple of P (definitions not given here for lack of space). As argued in [11] where it is presented, due to PROLOG selection rule this neat example will not work as it is. However it is quite easy to fix with the following :

```
+METAX(X,L,NIL,FRZ(Integers(S.T),T.NIL).NIL)
+METAX(X,L,NIL,FRZ(Sieve(U,V),U.NIL).NIL)
+METAX(X,L,NIL,FRZ(Filter(M,N,K),N.NIL).NIL)
```

Snapshots will explain how the proof proceeds :

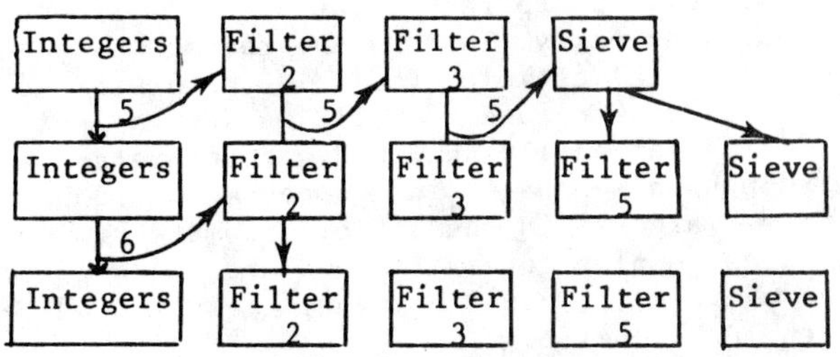

4.3 - Implementation principles

There is no major problem in such an implementation, although particular attention is to be paid to allow correct backtracking, fair selection of frozen literals. The theorem prover has been coded in PROLOG mainly for ease of modification and for its unification algorithm. As we piled up levels of interpretation the result is rather inefficient, but our goal is attained. We emphasize how useful both the non first-order features of PROLOG and the possibility to examine its own data structures, i.e. terms and clauses, are. Due to the very simple access to those structures (UNIV, VAR, ...) it is possible to build powerful mechanisms.

Of course this theorem prover is not a major innovation in the field ; one can argue that it behaves with respect to PROLOG in a manner quite similar to CONNIVER's behaviour with respect to MICROPLANNER. This is basically true from the viewpoint of the theorem prover ; what we gave back to the user is some control over lists of possibilities, over backtrack, over the context mechanism [14]. This similarity is only superficial. We give more to the user because what he can examine in our case is not just a list of possibilities, but it is a list of methods in the CONNIVER sense ; the method body can be scrutinized, modified, reordered whereas it cannot happen with CONNIVER ; this is due to the content-directed invocation feature that we mentioned earlier and of which we saw some important effects in 4.2. We recognize that out context handling mechanisms, which are roughly the SUPP and ADD predicates of PROLOG, are not as powerful as CONNIVER's. Our goal was different and this remains a possible extension for this work.

5. DISCUSSION

The points we want to stress are the following :

a. User responsibility - Metarules give the user much freedom ; a correct use of metarules goes through an understanding of how the derivation process should go ; then the user will be tempted to use this knowledge and modify his own algorithm so as to take advantage of this understanding directly. This is the reason why we did not give real examples for METAL metarules nor for backtracking use of METAX metarules ; simple examples can easily be fixed without metarules, although this usually introduces much redundancy and awkwardness in the set of axioms. From our studies in plan generation, we are aware of cases where a '/' could be dynamically introduced with much benefit.

b. Extensions - Any time a language is defined, one may propose extensions to it. Among all the extensions we have been thinking of, one is to allow user-defined FRZ predicates ; such a need has been found in another plan generation program where redundant tests could be avoided by properly defined freezing conditions ; such an extension is quite simple to incorporate to our theorem prover.

c. Related topics - Much of the interest of metarules comes from the dynamic ordering of literals (4.2) ; clearly this is related to the many producer-consumer discussions, to the call by opportunity or call by necessity choice ; the Primes problem is discussed in [11] and in a different framework in [4] ; we believe the simple tools given here compare favorably with those given there. We use a data flow mechanism (instantiation) ; more explicit control mechanisms such as message passing have not been looked for. Note that it is possible to define and implement a theorem prover which could take advantage of the connections between variables to select literals ; for instance, in the Prime example the instantiation of a variable unfreezes just one literal, and usually a theorem prover can watch such instantiations. Expressing specific properties of predicates, e.g. that they are true functions, is not covered here although it is an important domain to be investigated. We believe "intelligent" backtracking to be an important topic deserving more attention ; we only note that to be intelligent it must be prepared during the derivation process ; the tools we give are but one step in that direction. Finally interactive control expression has not been covered at all.

ACKNOWLEDGMENTS

We would like to thank A. FAHMY for the many discussions we had with him on this topic and on PROLOG use. P. HAYES comments on this paper are gratefully acknowledged.

REFERENCES

[1] Chang, C.L. and Lee, R. "Symbolic Logic and Mechanical Theorem Proving" Academic Press, 1973

[2] Davis, R. "Generalized Procedure Calling and Content Directed Invocation." In Proc. Symposium on AI and Programming Languages, Rochester, August 1977, p 45-54

[3] Davis, R. and Buchanan, B.G. "Metalevel knowledge Overview and Applications." In Proc. IJCAI-77, MIT, Mass., August 1977, pp 920-927.

[4] Friedman, D. and Wise, D. "Unbounded Computational Structures." Software, Practice and Experience. Vol. 8, pp 407-416 (1978).

[5] Hayes, P. "In Defence of Logic." In Proc. IJCAI-77, pp 559-565.

[6] Hill, R. "Lush Resolution and its Completeness." DCL-Memo 78, University of Edinburgh, Aug. 1974.

[7] Kowalski, R. "Algorithm = Logic + Control." Depart. of Computing and Control. Imperial College, London, 1976.

[8] Kowalski, R. "Logic for Problem Solving" DCL-memo 75, University of Edinburgh, 1974.

[9] Lasserre, C. "Apport de la logique mathématique dans les systèmes de décision en robotique." Thèse Université Paul Sabatier, Toulouse, 1978.

[10] Latombe, J.C. (Ed.) "Artificial Intelligence and Pattern Recognition in Computer Aided Design." North Holland, 1978.

[11] Mc Cabe, F.G. "Programmer's Guide to IC-PROLOG 0.7." Department of Computing and Control. Imperial College, London, 1979.

[12] Nicolas, J.M. and Gallaire, H. "Data Base-Theory vs Interpretation." In Logic and Data Bases, Plenum Pub. Co, 1978.

[13] Roussel, Ph. "PROLOG : Manuel de Référence et d'utilisation." Groupe d'Intelligence Artificielle. UER de Marseille-Luminy.

[14] Sussman, G. and Mc Dermott, D. "From Planner to Conniver." In Proc. FJCC 1972, pp 1171-1179.

[15] Winograd, T. "Frame Representations and the declarative procedural controversy" In Representation and Understanding. Academic Press, 1975.

[16] Colmerauer, A. Personal Communication.

META-INTERPRETATION OF RECURSIVE LIST-PROCESSING PROGRAMS

Daniel GOOSSENS
Université PARIS VIII
Route de la Tourelle
75012 PARIS

Presented is an implemented program understanding system called CAN. CAN relies on a meta-interpretation process which brings to light two new concepts concerning meta-interpretation of recursive programs: vicious circles and constructive induction. These notions express CAN's ability to extract from program code classes of data for which interpretation of the code would not stop, and in general, to relate classes of data with abstract values and environments.

keywords: Meta-interpretation, unification, conceptual representations, program understanding, propagation, vicious circle, constructive induction.

1. INTRODUCTION

Works on program verification [10] [13] have brought many useful techniques for proving properties of programs, but all the implemented systems which derived from them were to be used by expert mathematicians rather than expert programmers. That is, those systems may do nothing with a program on its own. They are intended to be interactively used by programmers who are acquainted with formal specifications manipulations and who understand their programs.
Recent works on program understanding have demonstrated the need of domain dependent knowledge [7] [15] and other types of pragmatic knowledge [19] [20]. However, systems in these areas are not equally efficient. More precisely, the systems which support these works may fail on simple tasks which are beyond the scope of their effective specificity. That is, their domain of application is far from fitting with what an expert programmer would consider as "simple", or "visually understandable".
CAN is a powerful tool for such systems since:

- It understands programs independently of traditionnal applications for understanding (verification, correction, improvement)

- It is particularly well suited for extracting on its own only what is "visually understandable" in a program. This prevents CAN from getting stuck on intricate problems. This is a necessity if CAN is expected to be a tool for problem solvers. A part of CAN has been especially developed for the visual understanding of programs which manipulate flat lists.

CAN meta-interprets program bodies in abstract environments [1] [2] [4] [5] [9] [14] [19] [21]. We use conceptual representations [21] in order to represent abstract values of program variables and relations among them. Our conceptual representations are either patterns, or predicate-style assertions which may not be translated into patterns. Our patterns involve element-type and segment-type variables. segment-type variables include index mathematical notations for flat lists. They also involve auto-references.
Conceptual representation of meanings is our bypass of the traditionnal "set of properties". Conceptual representations may be confronted and compared more easily than assertions, most often with unification procedures, which yield valuable and non-trivial information [6].
CAN involves a sophisticated unification process of conceptual representations.

2. META-INTERPRETATION

When confronted with LISP code, the meta-interpreter most often faces the case where a function is applied on its arguments.
The meta-interpretation of (F A1 A2 ... An) involves the following steps:

first, CAN meta-interprets each of the Ais which should be evaluated on a simple interpretation. this yields a set of possible abstract values and environments for each Ai.
Second, CAN confronts each combination of these values and environments with F's CAN definition. After this confrontation, CAN knows:

- What conditions must hold on the Ais and the environment so that F may apply

- which features of the abstract values and the environment are relevant for the contruction of F's abstract value and side-effects.

Third, CAN propagates this information over the current environment and on the "prototype" abstract value which is part of F's CAN definition.

LISP functions are conceptually defined [21] within CAN. Here are the conceptual definitions of the CAR, CDR and MEMBER functions:

("!" denotes an element variable and "?" a segment variable)

(CAR ()) = ()
(CAR (!a ?b)) = !a
(CDR ()) = ()
(CDR (!a ?b)) = (?b)

(MEMBER !x ($!a_1$ ... $!a_n$!x ?b)) = (!x ?b)

(MEMBER !x ($!a_1$ ... $!a_n$)) = ()

(where: $!a_i \neq !x$; i[1,n])

That is, the CAR function returns the first element of a list, the CDR function returns the list without its first element. (MEMBER X Y) tests wether the element X is contained in the list Y, at the top-level. If it is the case, MEMBER returns the part of the list which starts from the first occurence of X.

CAN also handles the cases where F is a control structure, a functional variable, an escape label, or an unknown atom. The meta-interpretation of a LISP program is expected to yield a conceptual representation of its meaning.

Example:

Suppose that F is MEMBER, and that the meta-interpretation of its two arguments gave the two abstract values: (on !1 !2) and (?3 !1).The application of MEMBER on "(on !1 !2)" and "(?3 !1)" amounts to checking whether the list (?3 !1) contains the structure (on !1 !2). The confrontation of these values with MEMBER's prototype values is performed by a unification process of conceptual representations [6].

The unification of

[!x ($!a_1$ ... $!a_n$!x ?b)]

with [(on !1 !2) (?3 !1)]
(where $!a_i \neq !x$) gives only one case:

!x = (on !1 !2)
?3 = $!a_1$ ... $!a_n$ (on !1 !2) ?b1
?b = ?b1 !1

since !1 in (?3 !1) may not contain (on !1 !2).

The propagation of this information on the prototype value (!x ?b) of MEMBER gives the returned abstract value: ((on !1 !2) ?b1 !1). This value is still functionally related to the environment since ?3 is also replaced in the environment by what it is associated to.
The reader is invited to perform the same task for the second rule of MEMBER's definition.

3. UNIFICATION OF CONCEPTUAL REPRESENTATIONS

The problem is, given two conceptual representations, to find the complete set of its unifiers (it's most general unifier [16] [17] [18]).

For theorem proving purposes, The task of unification may be limited to checking wether two structures can fit or not [11]. In that case, it suffices to find one unifier or show that there is none. Rather, CAN needs a conceptual representation of the complete set of unifiers of two conceptual representations, since it needs to know not only if they fit together, but under what exact constraints [5].

In the case where segment variables are restricted to ?-type variables (that is, when index notations are excluded), the problem amounts to solve an equation in a free monoid with a neutral element (the empty sequence). Our implemented unifier exhibits about the same performances as [16] and [17] (the neutral element makes very few differences). It involves too the algorithm for A-C Unification [12] [18] and a splitting algorithm [17] extended for index mathematical notations.

What is new within CAN's unification procedure concerns the unification of patterns which include index notations, auto-references, element-type variables with restricted domain, and negation.
A detailed description of its actual performances is given in [6].

4. META-INTERPRETATION OF ITERATIVE AND RECURSIVE PROGRAMS

At some stage of the process, the following program:

```
(DE MEMBER (X L)
    (COND ((NULL L) NIL)
          ((EQUAL X (CAR L)) L)
          (T (MEMBER X (CDR L)))))
```

is transformed into:

```
1  (MEMBER !x ()) = ()
2  (MEMBER !x (!x ?b)) = (!x ?b)
3  (MEMBER !x (!y ?b)) = (MEMBER !x (?b))
        (where !x ≠ !y)
```

This says among other things that if MEMBER's first argument is different from the CAR of its second argument, then the value is the recursive call: (MEMBER !x (?b)). If CAN were to go on like previously, it would confront the arguments !x and (?b) with each of the three cases. In fact, this is exactly what CAN will do, but more carefully, so as to avoid looping forever.
Application of rule 3 on !x and (?b) needs the following preconditions:

```
!x = !x'
?b = !y ?b'        (A)
```

in which case the value is (MEMBER !x' (?b')). But this is what CAN was meta-interpreting (modulo a change of the variables'name). We consider (A) as a "vicious circle". The meta-interpretation process stops at each vicious circle, and CAN "multiplies" it by a fictive number n of recursions. From (A), CAN is able to obtain abstract representations of flat lists:

$$!x = !x$$
$$?b = !y_1 \; ... \; !y_n \; ?b$$

(where $!y_i \neq !x$ and $n \neq 0$)

This says that if the second argument of MEMBER is a list whose n first elements are different from its first argument, then they will be deleted after the nth recursive call. The meta-interpreter will then go on with the two first rules of MEMBER, and obtain the final conceptual representation of MEMBER which we used in the second paragraph.
The concept of vicious circle is important since it does not coincide with the first recursive call in a program.
For the following example:

```
(DE FOO (L)
   (IF (CAR L) (FOO (CONS (CDR L)))
       (CDR L)))
```

the meta-interpreter will never reach a vicious circle, and yield the final conceptual representation:

(FOO ()) = ()
(FOO (() ?b) = (?b)
(FOO (<u>!a</u>)) = ()
(FOO (<u>!a</u> <u>?b</u>)) = ()

(underlined variables may not be assigned the NIL value)

5. VICIOUS CIRCLES

A vicious circle is encountered when the meta-interpretation of some form f in an environment E1 leads to the meta-interpretation of f in an environment E2 such that E1 and E2 "may be identified".
Formally, the two environments will be identifiable if their unification gives a unifier which contains no "transmitter". A transmitter is a couple of variables bindings of the form:

$$v1 = f(v2)$$
$$v2 = H$$

With the restriction that if f(v2) contains v1 and H contains v2, the couple is considered as a vicious circle.

Here are some examples of LISP programs where the first recursive call does not coincide with a vicious circle:

```
(DE FOO (X Y) (FOO Y X))

(DE FOO (L M)
   (IF (NULL L) NIL
      (FOO (CDR M) (CONS (CAR M) L))))

(DE FOO (L M P Q)
   (COND ((NULL L) T)
         ((EQUAL (CAR L) M)
          (FOO (CDDR L) P Q (CADR L)))))
```

6. CONSTRUCTIVE INDUCTION (multiplication by "n")

The notion of vicious circle is motivated by the fact that if a substitution (unifier) is a vicious circle, it may be "multiplied by n" by a simple algorithm (i.e its general form after "n" recursive calls may be constructed).
From a variable binding of the form: v = f(v) the algorithm will obtain: (* v n f(v)) which may be seen as a complex variable whose name is v and f(v) is a conceptual representation with auto-references (everywhere v is). In other words, f(v) restricts v's domain. "n" names the fictive number of successive recursive calls. It relates different complex variables to each other.
In some cases, the induction algorithm may generate mathematical index notations such as those involved in MEMBER's CAN definition, instead of conceptual representations with auto-references. i.e in the case:

$$v = \text{-A- } v \text{ -B-}$$

the algorithm will obtain:

$$v = \text{-A-}_1 \; ... \; \text{-A-}_n \;\; v \;\; \text{-B-}_n \; ... \; \text{-B-}_1$$

(where $n \neq 0$)

(where -A- and -B- are any sequence of conceptual representations. They may involve indexed elements and even sequences whose length depend on the index)

The advantage is that the unification process of conceptual representations is particularly well suited for the unification of such forms.

7. RECURSIVITY

From the program:

```
(DE VECMAT (L M)
   (IF (NULL L) M
       (DCONS (CAR L) (VECMAT (CDR L)
                              (CONS NIL M)))))
```

where

(DCONS !x ((?a_1)...(?a_n)))

= ((!x ?a_1)...(!x ?a_n))

The meta-interpreter will get:

1 (VECMAT () !m) = !m
2 (VECMAT (!1 ?2) (?3)) = ((!1 ?a_1)...(!1 ?a_k))

and ((?a_1)...(?a_k)) = (VECMAT (?2) (() ?3))

Recursivity will be handled by the same processes.
as the unification of ((?a_1)...(?a_k))

and ((!1 ?a'_1)...(!1 ?$a'_{k'}$))

yields a vicious circle, the induction algorithm is applied. here, from:

?a_i = !1 ?a_i

CAN gets:

?a_i = !1_1 ... !1_n ?a_i

By propagation and with the initialisation:

((?a_1)...(?a_k)) = (()$_1$...()$_n$?3)

(the right conceptual representation is the abstract value of M when case 1 is encoutered. The initialisation is performed via the unification of the two conceptual representations and propagation of the results.)
CAN finally obtains the conceptual representation of vecmat:

(VECMAT (!1_1 ... !1_n) ((?b_1)...(?b_m)))

= ((!1_1 ... !1_n)$_1$ ... (!1_1 ... !1_n)$_n$

(!1_1 ... !1_n ?b_1)...(!1_1 ... !1_n ?b_m))

8. TERMINATION

The meta-interpretation of a program yields a set of rules which contain recursive calls, as a first approximation. As was shown, the same meta-interpretation process may be pursued. So, CAN may find which rules data can "go" to, when "coming out" of a recursive rule. That is, find which rules refer to which rules.
If a recursive rule refers only to itself, or if a group of rules which refer to one another refers to no rule "outside", then a class of data is determined for which simple interpretation of the program never ends. Here are some simple examples:

example 1:

```
(DE FOO (X Y)
   (IF (ATOM X) (FOO Y X) X))
```

CAN yields:

(FOO !list !b) = !list
(FOO !atom !list) = !list
(FOO !atom1 !atom2) = infinite-loop

example 2:

```
(DE FOO (L M)
   (IF (NULL L) M
       (FOO (CDR M) (CONS (CAR M) L))))
```

CAN yields:

(FOO () !m) = !m
(FOO ($\underline{?1}$) ()) = (() $\underline{?1}$)
(FOO ($\underline{?1}$) (!2)) = (!2 $\underline{?1}$)
(FOO ($\underline{?1}$) (!2 ?3)) = infinite-loop

example 3:

```
(DE FOO (X L)
  (IF (EQUAL X (CAR L))
      L
      (FOO X (CDR L))))
```

CAN yields:

(FOO () (!a_1 ... !a_n)) = ()

with !a_i ≠()

(FOO $\underline{!b}$ (!a_1 ... !a_n)) = infinite-loop

with !a_i ≠ $\underline{!b}$

(foo !c (!a_1 ... !a_n !c ?d)) = (!c ?d)

with !a_i ≠!c

(underlined variables may not be replaced by the NIL value)

Here is an example of a different kind:

```
(DE FOO (L M)
    (IF (EQUAL L M) T
         (FOO (CDR L) (CONS (CAR L) M))))
```

CAN yields:

```
(FOO !1 !1) = T
(FOO () (?2)) = infinite-computation
(FOO (!1  ... !1  !1  ... !1  ?2) (?2)) = T
        1       n   n       1
```

and

$(!1_{i+1} \ldots !1_n\ !1_n \ldots !1_1\ ?2) \neq (!1_i \ldots !1_1\ ?2)$

$i \in [1,n]$

For this last example, CAN is not able to explicitly describe the class of data for which there is infinite computation. It is implicitly defined by the set of cases which do not fit the rules above, plus those which fit the second rule.

9. USING CAN: THE INTERACTIVE PROGRAMMER ASSISTANT.

CAN is an interactive program understanding system. When CAN is run, the user may type in LISP functions, or LISP expressions. When an expression is typed in, CAN gives its abstract value. There may be several cases. If the expression is (ATOM X) for instance, CAN will respond:

CASE 1: X=!atom1 VALUE: t

CASE 2: X=!¬atom1 VALUE: nil

The user can focus on any of the cases or keep them all.
A practical use of the CAN system, then, is the following: the user first types in a program he has just written. Once the program is understood by CAN, the user may type in any LISP expression involving calls to the program. He will get the corresponding abstract values. Note that CAN is a simplifier. That is, if it is not able to understand an expression E, E's abstract value is E itself (with an implicit meta-evaluation request). In other words, E may not be simplified further.
If the expression is an assertion about the program, it may meta-evaluate to T or NIL, but CAN's performances in this domain still raise the need for a theorem prover.
One common use is to type a call to the program on restricted classes of data. i.e if the program has name FOO and argument X, the user may define a unary LISP predicate P which is true for a restricted class of X's, then focus on the cases where (P X) may evaluate to T, and call (FOO X).

For instance, if FOO is in fact a pattern-matching function MATCH with back-referencing (two occurences of the same variable must be assigned the same value) and the user wants to test wether back-referencing works fine, he may first build several kinds of abstract values for MATCH's arguments by the "focus on" technique described above, and then call MATCH on them

One future work will be to develop a system for proving theorems about list structures by structural induction, which uses CAN as a simplification sub-system.
We expect that CAN will greatly help the task of proving theorems by structural induction since, for instance, many of the LISP theorems proved in [22] already meta-evaluate to the LISP truth-value T when given to CAN.

10. CONCLUSION

We have designed a system whose job is to understand what an expert programmer could consider as "visually understandable". CAN does no problem solving. CAN's meta-interpretation process is straightforward, and simple interpretation is a simple case of meta-interpretation [5]. We then think that CAN should be put in the service of expert programmers, or program understanding systems which would be specialised in narrow areas, since conceptual representations are much more easily manipulated than LISP code, for instance. It may effectively be expected that the size of program understanding systems is directly related to the number of ways of representing a relation within a programming language.
The CAN system is written in VLISP-10 [3] [8] and occupies about 20K words.

REFERENCES

[1] BALZER, GOLDMAN & WILE (1977) "Meta-evaluation as a tool for program understanding" 5th IJCAI, MIT Cambridge, August 1977

[2] BOYER, ELSPASS & LEVITT (1975) "SELECT--A formal system for testing and debugging programs by symbolic execution" Int. Conf. on Reliable Software, April 1975, pp. 234-245.

[3] CHAILLOUX (1976) "VLISP-10 manuel de référence" Dept. d'informatique, Univ. PARIS 8, RT 17-76.

[4] GOOSSENS (1978) "A system for visual-like understanding of LISP programs" A.I.S.B. Conf. Hamburg, July 1978.

[5] GOOSSENS (1978) "Compréhension visuelle de programmes controlée par méta-filtrage" Groplan: Bulletin de l'AFCET, Groupe Programmation et langages, 1978

[6] GOOSSENS (1978) "L'unification au service de la compréhension" RT-14. Dept. d'informatique, Université de Vincennes.

[7] GREEN & BARSTOW (1975) "A hypothetical dialogue exhibiting a knowledge base for a program understanding system" Stanford A.I. Lab. MA 258, Cpt Science Dept. Report n. Stancs-75-476.

[8] GREUSSAY (1977) "Contribution a la définition interprétative et à l'implémentation des λ-langages" Thèse, Université PARIS 8.

[9] HEWITT & SMITH (1975) "Towards a programming apprentice" IEEE Trans. on soft. engineering, Vol. SE-1. pp. 26-45.

[10] HOARE & LAUER (1973) "Consistent and complementary formal theories of the semantics of programming languages" Ibid 3, pp. 145-182.

[11] HUET (1975) "A unification algorithm for typed lambda-calculus" Theoritical computer science 1. pp 27-57

[12] HULLOT J.M. (1979) "Associative-commutative pattern-matching" 6th IJCAI. Aug 1979. Tokyo.

[13] IGARASHI, LONDON, LUCKHAM (1975) "Automatic program verification I: A logical basis and its implementation" Acta Informatica, Vol. 4, pp. 145-182.

[14] KING (1975) "A new approach to program testing" Int. Conf. on reliable software, April 1975, pp. 228-233.

[15] RICH & SCHROBE (1975) "Understanding LISP programs: Towards a programming apprentice" Master's Thesis, EECS M.I.T.

[16] SIEKMANN (1975) "String unification" Essex university, Memo CSM-7.

[17] SIEKMANN LIVESEY (1975) "Termination and decidability results for string unification" Essex university, CSM-12.

[18] STICKEL (1975) "A complete unification algorithm for associative-commutative functions" 4th Ijcai, Tbilisi Georgia USSR. sept. 1975.

[19] WERTZ (1978) "Un système de compréhension, de programmes incorrects" Proc. 3ème colloque sur la programmation, Paris B. Robinet éd. pp 31-49.

[20] WERTZ (1978) "Un système de compréhension, d'amélioration, et de correction de programmes incorrects" Thèse de 3ème cycle, Univ. P. et M. CURIE.

[21] YONEZAWA & HEWITT (1976) "Symbolic evaluation using conceptual representations for programs with side-effects" M.I.T., A.I. Lab., AI-Memo 399.

[22] BOYER & MOORE (1973) "Proving theorems about LISP functions", Stanford University, Stanford CA. 486-493.

IMAGE PROCESSING BY EXPERIMENTAL ARRAYED PROCESSOR

Hitoshi Matsushima Takeshi Uno Masakazu Ejiri

Central Research Laboratory
Hitachi Ltd.,
Higashi-koigakubo 1-280,
Kokubunji, Tokyo 185, Japan

An image processor based on an arrayed structure was implemented. It has five design features: (1) memory unit separation into a picture memory for images and a control data memory for programs, (2) processing unit separation into a parallel processing part and a serial processing part, (3) parallel processing by an arrayed structure, (4) use of a special micro-processor for an array's processing element, and (5) direct control of parallel processing by programming. It deals with images consisting of 256 x 256 pixels and processes them by sixteen processing elements. The original images are given by a TV camera. The processed images are outputted to CRT display equipments. The basic operations in the array are data conversions, local operations, sequential processings, manipulations between two images and so on. By using those operations, many kinds of image processing can be done in this processor.

1. INTRODUCTION

Many proposals for pattern processing have been made to date, and some have been practically implemented, especially for certain industrial and medical applications, in which special processors such as image analyzers are in practical use. However, most image processors can only deal with binary images.[1]

On the otherhand, recently large-scale pattern processors have been studies in some research laboratories.[2] However there are still problems in developing image processors for multi-leveled images. For example, processors tend to become too big and expensive.

However, recent developments in commercially available IC's have had a profound effect on the size, speed, and cost of hardware. In addition, the need for general purpose image processors is getting stronger. Thus, the image processor presented here was experimentally developed. The outstanding feature in our image processor IP is parallel processing ability.

This paper described the principles and basic operation in this IP.

This work was contracted with the Agency of Industrial Science and Technology, Ministry of International Trade and Industry, as a part of the National Research and Development Program "Pattern Information Processing System."

2. DESIGN PLINCIPLES

The main points considered in establishing our IP are discussed below.

Information included in images depends on the two-dimensional arrangement of pixel's values. So two-dimensional memory access is employed for data utilization. Therefore, the memory was separated into two distinct parts, one for images and the other for control data. The former has useful functions for parallel processing of images.

In image processing, the same operations are repeated many times. In these cases, increasing processing speed by ordinary computer architectures is not efficient. Therefore, the execution unit in our IP was separated into a conventional mini-computer's central processing unit and a parallel processing part. The former mainly deals with control data and sometimes processes pixels one by one, while the latter usually processes pixels by the parallel processing.

In the parallel processing part, an arrayed structure was adopted, mainly to increase processing speed. In pre-processing of feature-extraction of images the same operator is executed at every sampling point. For such position-invariant processes, an arrayed structure is very useful. Many sampling data are inputted to many processing elements at a time. Then all processing elements execute the same operation simultaniously. Increasing the mumber of processing elements by a certain factor should cause the processing time to decrease by the same factor.

One cause reducing the effect of an arrayed structure is the occurrance of irregular flow such as conditional jump. In such cases, all processing elements can not be controlled by one sequence. Some PEs will have to be in a halt state. To avoid this problem and increase efficiency of parallel processing, a special micro-processor was developed which can absorb irregularities and do such special calculations as summing products, table look up and getting hamming-distance at high speed.

It is difficult to control the array. Therefore a usage of micro-instructions was planned to control executions in a processing element and data's flows between the array and a picture memory.

3. SYSTEM OUTLINE

A block diagram of our IP is shown in Fig. 1. It consists of a parallel processing part and the other part. The former comprises a processing element array(PE Array), a picture memory(PM), local registers(LR), a micro-instruction control(MC) and input/output control(IOC).

Image data are inputted through the IOC and stored in the PM. They are originally obtained 6 bits in the IOC. The image data are then transmitted to the PE Array through the LR. The LR can store a 4 x 4 local-image or an 8 x 8 one. The PE Array processes it parallelly, and the results are stored again in the PM.

The PM is a memory for images consisting of three banks of 256 x 256 pixels. The access to the PM is controlled by micro-instructions in a program. The accessing unit is a 4 x 4 square with the upper-left corner address (4n,4m), or one pixel. The letters n and m stand for integer from 0 to 63.

The PE Array consists of sixteen processing element(PE). Each PE is a special micro-processor comprising a controller, which interprets commands and controls calculations in synchronization with an external clock. The commands comprise addition, subtraction, multiplication, summing products, logical operation,

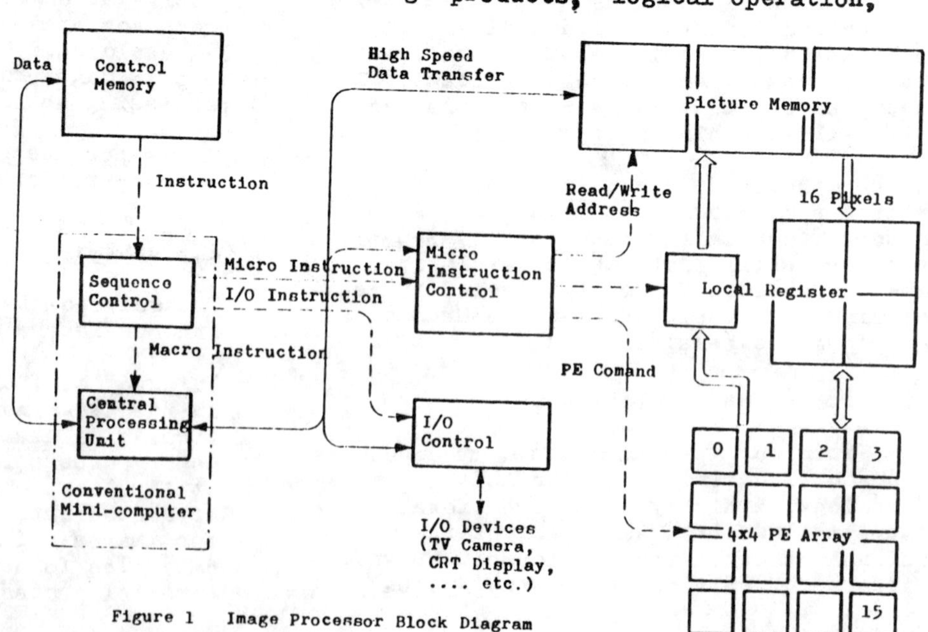

Figure 1 Image Processor Block Diagram

table look up and so on. Each PE has a 256 words 16 bits scratch pad memory. The scratch pad memory can store a sequence of PE commands. Therefore each PE can execute its own program. The depth of calculations is twelve bits long. The execution time is 0.35 μS and the cycle time of the PM is 0.7 μS.

The LR has shift functions in an 8 x 8 local image. The PE Array can obtain the free 4 x 4 square pixels from the PM by these functions. Also, PEs can comunicate each other through the LR.

4. BASIC OPERATIONS

In order to describe functions in the PE Array, several notational definitions are given as follows;

D(x,y); a value of pixel(x,y) in the original image.

$$\mathbb{D}(x,y)=\begin{bmatrix} D(x,y), & \cdots & ,D(x+4,y) \\ \vdots & \vdots & \vdots \\ D(x,y+4), & \cdots & ,D(x+4,y+4) \end{bmatrix}$$

R(x,y); a result by a certain operation in a PE of the PE Array.

F(),G(); functions executed by a combination of PE's commands.

In the PE Array, sixteen PEs process local images in the LR simultaneously. Therefore sixteen results $\mathbb{R}(x,y)$;

$$\mathbb{R}(x,y)=\begin{bmatrix} R(x,y), & \cdots & ,R(x+3,y) \\ \vdots & \vdots & \vdots \\ R(x,y+3), & \cdots & ,R(x+3,y+3) \end{bmatrix}$$

are obtained simultaneously.

The representative basic operations in the PE Array are as follows.

(a) Data conversion.
R(x,y)=F(D(x,y))
This is used for thresholding, contrast stretching and so on. In a thresholding of a 256 x 256 image, it takes about 11.5 mS.

(b) Local operation.
$R(x,y)=F(\mathbb{D}(x,y))$
For example, in a case of two-dimentional filterings the results are as follows.

$$R(x+m,y+n)=\sum_{i=0}^{4}\sum_{j=0}^{4} f(i,j)\times D(x+i+m,y+j+m)$$

$0\leq m\leq 3;\quad 0\leq n\leq 3$
where f(i,j)s are weight coefficients.

In all PEs, twenty-five times' executions of the PE command "SUM OF PRODUCT" are done. It takes 34.4 mS in a 256 x 256 image. By this local operation, spacial differentiation, noise elimination. template matching, and so on are available.

(c) Sequential processing.
$R(x,y)=F(\mathbb{D}(x,y),\mathbb{Q}(x-s,y-t))$
$\mathbb{Q}(x,y)=G(\mathbb{D}(x,y),\mathbb{Q}(x-s,y-t))$
Where $\mathbb{Q}$ is PE's internal states specified by several flags and contents of the scratch pad memory. The point (x-s,y-t) shows a preceding processing point to point (x,y). Values of letter s and t depend on a scanning in the PM.
This calculation is used for histogram's calculation, area counting and so on. For example, the processing speed of obtaining pixel value's distributions is 28 mS.

(d) Manipulation between two images.
$R(x,y)=F(\mathbb{D}_1(x,y),\mathbb{D}_2(x,y))$
where $\mathbb{D}_1(x,y)$ and $\mathbb{D}_2(x,y)$ show values of different images' pixels.
For example, it takes about 18 mS to get an add-image or exclusive OR-image from two images.

5. CONCLUSION

An image processor based on an arrayed structure was implemented. It deals with images consisting of 256 x 256 pixels and processes them by a 4 x 4 processing elements' array. It was constructed in 1977 and used to study processor's architecture for the object recognition. By these studies, it has been established that the array of our IP is useful for high speed processing.

The basic operations in the array are data conversions, local operations, sequential processings, manipulations between two images.and so on. By them, many kinds of image processing can be done in this array.

REFERENCES

[1] M. J. E. Golay, "Hexagonal Parallel Pattern Transformations", IEEE Trans. Comput., Vol. C-18, pp. 733-740, Aug. 1969.

[2] K. S. Fu, "Special Computer Architectures for Pattern Recognition and Image Processing An Overview", Proc. AFIPS, Vol. 57,pp.1003-1013, June 1978.

AUTHOR/CO-AUTHOR INDEX

Note: Volume II begins with page 610.
Papers are arranged alphabetically by first author - A-M, Vol. I; N-Z, Vol. II.
A supplement containing papers received late is found at the back of Vol. II.

AUTHOR/CO-AUTHOR INDEX (Cont'd.)

TOPIC INDEX FOR TECHNICAL PAPERS

NOTE: Papers are listed by first authors only.

TOPIC INDEX FOR TECHNICAL PAPERS

TOPIC INDEX FOR TECHNICAL PAPERS

TOPIC INDEX FOR TECHNICAL PAPERS

TOPIC INDEX FOR TECHNICAL PAPERS